LE NORD AND PICARDY
Pages 192–205

CHAMPAGNE
Pages 206–217

ALSACE AND LORRAINE
Pages 218–233

Reims

NORTHEAST FRANCE

Strasbourg

Troyes

Dijon

BURGUNDY AND FRANCHE-COMTÉ
Pages 326–351

THE MASSIF CENTRAL
Pages 352–371

CENTRAL FRANCE AND THE ALPS

Lyon

Grenoble

THE RHÔNE VALLEY AND FRENCH ALPS
Pages 372–391

THE SOUTH OF FRANCE

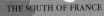

LANGUEDOC-ROUSSILLON
Pages 476–497

PROVENCE AND THE CÔTE D'AZUR
Pages 498–531

Ajaccio

CORSICA
Pages 532–543

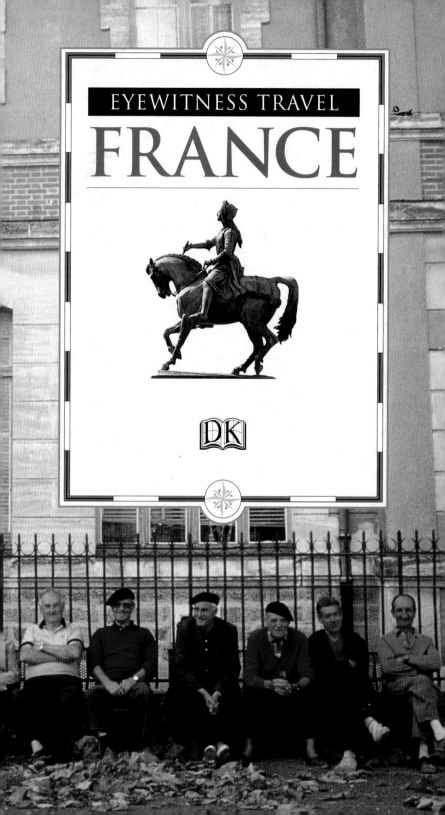

LONDON, NEW YORK,
MELBOURNE, MUNICH AND DELHI
www.dk.com

PROJECT EDITOR Rosemary Bailey
ART EDITOR Janis Utton
EDITORS Tanya Colbourne, Fiona Morgan,
Anna Streiffert, Celia Woolfrey
DESIGNERS Joy FitzSimmons, Erika Lang, Clare Sullivan
MAP CO-ORDINATORS Simon Farbrother, David Pugh
RESEARCHER Philippa Richmond

MAIN CONTRIBUTORS
John Ardagh, Rosemary Bailey, Judith Fayard, Lisa Gerard-Sharp,
Colin Jones, Alister Kershaw, Alec Lobrano, Anthony Roberts,
Alan Tillier, Nigel Tisdall

PHOTOGRAPHERS
Max Alexander, Neil Lukas, John Parker, Kim Sayer

ILLUSTRATORS
Stephen Conlin, John Lawrence, Maltings Partnership,
John Woodcock

Reproduced by Colourscan (Singapore)
Printed and bound by South China Printing Co. Ltd., China

First published in Great Britain in 1994
by Dorling Kindersley Limited
80 Strand, London WC2R 0RL

**Reprinted with revisions 1994, 1995, 1996, 1997, 1998, 1999,
2000, 2001, 2002, 2003, 2004, 2005, 2006, 2007, 2008**

Copyright 1994, 2008 © Dorling Kindersley Limited, London
A Penguin Company

A CIP CATALOGUE RECORD IS AVAILABLE FROM THE BRITISH LIBRARY.

ISBN: 978 1 40532 095 5

FLOORS ARE REFERRED TO THROUGHOUT IN ACCORDANCE WITH FRENCH
USAGE; IE THE "FIRST FLOOR" IS THE FLOOR ABOVE GROUND LEVEL.

Front cover main image: Aloxe-Corton, Burgundy

**The information in this
DK Eyewitness Travel Guide is checked annually.**
Even though every effort has been made to ensure that this book
is as up-to-date as possible at the time of going to press. Some
details, however, such as telephone numbers, opening hours,
prices, gallery hanging arrangements and travel information
are liable to change. The publishers cannot accept responsibility
for any consequences arising from the use of this book, nor
for any material on third-party websites, and cannot guarantee
that any website address in this book will be a suitable
source of travel information.
We value the views and suggestions of our readers very highly.
Please write to: Publisher, DK Eyewitness Travel Guides, Dorling
Kindersley, 80 Strand, London WC2R 0RL.

CONTENTS

Bust of Charlemagne

INTRODUCING
FRANCE

PARIS AND ÎLE DE
FRANCE

◁ **Men sitting outside boys' school, Montlaur village, Corbières, Languedoc-Roussillon**

Grape harvest in Alsace

The fishing village of St-Jean-de-Luz in the Pyrenees

Palais des Papes, Avignon

HOW TO USE THIS GUIDE

This guide helps you to get the most from your visit to France. It provides both expert recommendations and detailed practical information. *Introducing France* maps the country and sets it in its historical and cultural context. The 15 regional chapters, plus *Paris and Ile de France*, describe important sights, with maps, pictures and illustrations. Throughout, features cover topics from food and wine to culture and beaches. Restaurant and hotel recommendations can be found in *Travellers' Needs*. The *Survival Guide* has tips on everything from the French telephone system to transport.

PARIS AND ILE DE FRANCE

The centre of Paris has been divided into five sightseeing areas. Each has its own chapter, which opens with a list of the sights described. A further section covers Ile de France. All sights are numbered and plotted on an area map. The detailed information for each sight follows the map's numerical order, making sights easy to locate within the chapter.

Sights at a Glance lists the chapter's sights by category: Churches, Museums and Galleries; Historic Buildings, Squares and Gardens.

All pages relating to Paris and Ile de France have green thumb tabs.

A locator map shows where you are in relation to other areas of the city centre.

1 Area Map
For easy reference, the sights are numbered and located on a map. Sights in the city centre are also shown on the Paris Street Finder *on pages 156–69.*

2 Street-by-Street Map
This gives a bird's eye view of the key areas in each chapter.

A suggested route for a walk is shown in red.

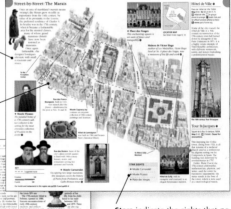

Stars indicate the sights that no visitor should miss.

3 Detailed information
The sights in Paris and Ile de France are described individually. Addresses, telephone numbers, opening hours and information on admission charges and wheelchair access are also provided for each entry.

1 Introduction
The landscape, history and character of each region is described here, showing how the area has developed over the centuries and what it offers to the visitor today.

Each area of France can be quickly identified by its colour coding, shown on the inside front cover.

2 Regional Map
This shows the road network and gives an illustrated overview of the whole region. All interesting places to visit are numbered and there are also useful tips on getting around the region by car and train.

3 Detailed information
All the important towns and other places to visit are described individually. They are listed in order, following the numbering on the Regional Map. Within each town or city, there is detailed information on important buildings and other sights.

Story boxes highlight noteworthy features of the top sights.

FRANCE AREA BY AREA
Apart from Paris and Ile de France, France has been divided into 15 regions, each of which has a separate chapter. The most interesting towns and places to visit have been numbered on a *Regional Map*.

For all the top sights, a Visitor's Checklist provides the practical information you will need to plan your visit.

4 France's top sights
These are given two or more full pages. Historic buildings are dissected to reveal their interiors. The most interesting towns or city centres are shown in a bird's eye view, with sights picked out and described.

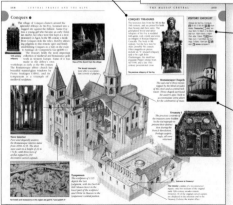

INTRODUCING FRANCE

DISCOVERING FRANCE

The chapters of this book have been divided into 16 colour-coded regions that reflect the diversity of France. These are based on the country's historical regions that were often defined by their geography and landscape as much as by

Gothic detail from Le Nord region

their influence and power.

Each has developed its own special flavour: its own architecture, cuisine, customs, music, dress, dialect and even language. The following pages give a taste of these areas and show you what there is to see and do.

Pyramide du Louvre in Paris, from across the fountain pools

PARIS AND THE ILE DE FRANCE

- Fantastic art at the Louvre
- Café life *par excellence*
- Captivating Versailles

The pleasures of Paris can be picked off at leisure any time of the year. The **Louvre** (see pp100–3), **Picasso Museum** (see pp90–1), and **Pompidou Centre** (see pp92–3) may be on some people's ideal itinerary, while others may want to scale the **Eiffel Tower** (see p113) and shop

Les Deux Magots, one of Paris's most famous cafés

in the *grands boulevards*, or follow in the steps of the famous from **Montmartre** (see pp132–3) to the **Père Lachaise Cemetery** (see p135). Whatever your fancy, there are cafés and brasseries to soak up the atmosphere, particularly on the **Left Bank** (see pp116–127) and in the **Marais** (see pp80–93). For a day excursion, there are plenty of châteaux to visit, none more exalted than Louis XIV's fabulous palace at **Versailles** (see pp168–71).

LE NORD AND PICARDY

- Bustling Channel ports
- Lofty Gothic cathedrals
- Lille art collection

The countryside north of Paris undulates towards Flanders and to the cliffs and sandy beaches around the Channel ports of **Dunkerque** (see p197), **Calais** (see pp196–7) and **Boulogne-sur-**

Mer (see p196). You can try your luck at the races, at **Chantilly** (see pp204–5) and **Le Touquet** (see p196), or go to the lakes and woodland of the **Valley of the Somme** (see p199), a name synonymous with the fatal trench warfare of World War I. High spots are the great Gothic cathedrals, such as **Amiens** (see p200), the largest in France, and the city of **Lille** (see p198), which has one of the best art galleries in the country.

CHAMPAGNE

- Sparkling Champagne houses
- Royal Reims
- Gothic churches in Troyes

Champagne means only one thing: fizzy white wine. Visit the producers' chalk caves in **Épernay** (see p211) and the premises of the *grandes marques* in **Reims** (see pp210–1), where you will also find a great slice of French history in **Reims Cathedral** (see p212). **Troyes** (see pp216–7), the region's former capital, is a delightful town of many Gothic churches, while the castle keep at **Chaumont** (see p217) has echoes of its former residents, the Counts of Champagne. On the wild side is the **Vallée de la Meuse** (see p214) in the rocky Ardennes, while the region around **Lac du Der-Chantecoq** (see p215) is known for its half-timbered churches.

Heidsieck Champagne label

ALSACE AND LORRAINE

- **Alsace Wine Route**
- **Picturesque half-timbered towns**
- **Strasbourg, crossroads of Europe**

Abutting Germany and Switzerland, this is a delightful, gentle rural area of vineyards and orchards, and pretty, half-timbered villages and towns such as **Colmar** *(see p227)*, best seen along the 180-km (110-mile) **Route du Vin** *(see p232–3)*. In the north the **Vosges** mountains *(see p225)* attract skiers, and nearby is the **Gérardmer lake** *(see p225)* for summer water sports. The region is full of forts and castles, including the romantic **Château du Haut-Koenigsbourg** *(see pp228–9)*. The main town is **Strasbourg** *(see pp230–1)*.

The old town of Strasbourg, best explored on its pretty waterways

NORMANDY

- **D-Day beaches**
- **Cider and Calvados**
- **Magnificent Mont-St-Michel**

Visit Claude Monet's garden at **Giverny** *(see p266)* and see the lily pond and bridge just as he painted them. Normandy's blustery skies and billowing seas inspired the Impressionists who visited **Dieppe** *(see p263)*, **Le Havre** *(see p262)* and pretty **Honfleur** *(see p262)*, while *tout* Paris used to decamp to

Normandy's Mont-St-Michel, one of the most enchanting sights in France

the resorts of **Cabourg** *(see p255)*, **Deauville** *(see p255)* and **Trouville** *(see p255)*. Their beaches are known for the World War II D-Day landings. Normandy's farmlands are renowned for their cider, Calvados, butter and cheese. Don't miss the **Abbaye de Mont-St-Michel** *(see pp256–61)* or **Rouen Cathedral** *(see pp264–5)*.

BRITTANY

- **Sandy beaches**
- **Mysterious Carnac**
- **Delightful fishing ports**

In the far northwest, this Celtic corner of France is a land with a language and culture of its own. Buffeted by the Atlantic, its rocky shores and sandy beaches, peppered with picturesque fishing ports, make it a prime spot for family beach vacations. Prehistory sighs in the wind here, and megalithic sites abound, especially in the mysterious rock formations at **Carnac** *(see p278)*.

To steep yourself in Breton culture, visit **Quimper** *(see p274)*, eat crêpes, drink cider and try to attend a *pardon*, a feast of a local saint, when traditional costumes are worn. They take place between March and October. Find out about them at the **Musée de Bretagne** *(see p285)* in the region's capital, Rennes.

THE LOIRE VALLEY

- **Fairytale Renaissance châteaux**
- **Chartres Cathedral**
- **Le Mans, motor racing**

The fabulous châteaux of the Loire capture all the elegance and culture of France. Here the French nobles lived out the Renaissance in style. Wines have made towns such as **Saumur** *(see p292)* famous. Historic centres include **Tours** *(see pp296–7)* and **Chartres** *(see pp307–311)*, which has stunning stained glass in its magnificent cathedral windows, and **Orléans** *(see pp312–3)*, saved from the English by Joan of Arc, who is celebrated in a 10-day festival leading up to the anniversary of the city's liberation on 8 May. To the north is **Le Mans** *(see p291)*, another lovely old town, best known for its motor racing circuit. The 24-hour race is held in June.

Château de Chenonceau in the Loire Valley, across the River Cher

Côte de Nuits vineyard in Burgundy, part of the Côte d'Or region

BURGUNDY AND FRANCHE-COMTE

- **Gastronomic paradise**
- **Impressive abbeys**
- **Fine trekking and skiing**

Burgundy is corpulent France, conjuring up *boeuf bourguignon* and delicious wines that are among the most expensive in the world. The Dukes of Burgundy's legacy is splendid **Dijon** *(see pp340–2)*, but the true architectural gem is the **Hôtel-Dieu** in Beaune *(see pp346–7)*. The wealth of the Church is evident in harmonious Romanesque churches and abbeys, especially **Vézelay** *(see pp336–7)*. **The Franche-Comté's** *(see pp349–51)* lakes, mountains, woods and waterfalls are perfect for trekking, canoeing and skiing.

MASSIF CENTRAL

- **Wild, beautiful landscapes**
- **Dramatic Gorges du Tarn**
- **Treasures of Ste-Foy**

This is the place to go to enjoy the great outdoors. A plateau of extinct volcanoes, spas and lakes, the landscape reaches dramatic heights in the **Gorges du Tarn** *(see pp370–1)*. The **Cévennes** *(see p353)*, one of the least populated parts of the country, is known for its wild flowers and birds of prey. Remote villages and ancient churches top hills and are tucked in valleys. The Abbaye de Ste-Foy in **Conques** *(see pp368–9)* has one of the most celebrated reliquaries in Christendom.

THE RHONE VALLEY AND FRENCH ALPS

- **Lyon's enticing *bouchons***
- **Grenoble and the ski slopes**
- **Elegant Evian-les-Bains**

The south of France begins at **Lyon** *(see pp380–1)*, France's second largest city, where the River Saône joins the River Rhône and the Mediterranean starts to scent the air. The commercial and military capital of Roman Gaul is now a gastronomic capital known for its *bouchons* (bistros) and local wines from **Beaujolais** *(see p377)* as well as the Rhône. Natural attractions in the region include the dramatic, cave-pocked **Ardèche** *(see pp384–5)* and, to the east, **Grenoble** *(see pp388–9)* and the Alps where you'll find the elegant spa town of **Evian-les-Bains** *(see p391)* beside Lac Léman.

Wine from the Rhône Valley

POITOU AND AQUITAINE

- **Marais Poitevin's canals**
- **Historic Poitiers**
- **Bordeaux wine châteaux**

Set against a long coast of sandy beaches, this largely flat region runs from the port of **La Rochelle** *(see p416)* and the popular holiday island of **Île d'Oléron** *(see p417)* to the Basque country. When La Rochelle is busy in summer, escape to the **Marais Poitevin** *(see pp408–9)*, a network of lily-blanketed canals teeming with wildlife. There are two historic centres – **Poitiers** *(see pp412–3)*, whose cathedral has the oldest carved choir stalls in France, and **Bordeaux** *(see pp420–3)*, beside the River Garonne. The latter has been long known as a wine port serving the magnificent surrounding châteaux estates.

PERIGORD, QUERCY AND GASCONY

- **Sarlat Market**
- **Lascaux's famous caves**
- **Toulouse Space Park**

Cut by the majestic Dordogne, Lot and Tarn rivers, this is bucolic, green France, where water activities help to beat the summer sun. Every town has a weekly market brimming with local produce, such as *foie gras* and **Agen** *(see p440)* prunes. Best known is the Wednesday market in **Sarlat-la-Caneda** *(see pp432–3)*, though stunning architecture makes it worth a visit any day of the week.

Rocamadour *(see pp436–7)* and **Moissac** *(see pp442–3)* are other architectural high points, while prehistoric man has left his mark in the famous **Lascaux caves** *(see pp402–3)*. **Toulouse** *(see pp446–7)* is the major town. Try its sausages and visit the hi-tech Space Park.

Sarlat Market, famous for *foie gras* and walnuts

THE PYRENEES

- Biarritz beaches
- Parc National des Pyrénées wildlife
- The shrine at Lourdes

The Pyrenees mountain range stretches from the Atlantic to the Mediterranean, forming a natural border with Spain. On the Atlantic coast is the **Basque country** *(see p449)* where **Bayonne** *(see p452)* is known for its ham and **Biarritz** *(see p452)*, a surfers' town, is renowned for its by-gone glories as the resort choice of kings. The **Parc National des Pyrénées** *(see pp460–1)* is at the heart of the mountains which are spectacular for walking and trekking. Skiers come in winter. **Lourdes** *(see pp458–9)* brings pilgrims all year round.

Flowers, butterflies, animals and birds brighten the Pyrenees trails

LANGUEDOC-ROUSSILLON

- Collioure, the artists' resort
- Carcassonne, fairytale walled town
- Pont du Gard, a Roman triumph

These are sunny, rolling lands of olives, vines, cypress trees and sunflowers, where old farm buildings have been baked by the sun. The Pyrenees reach the Mediterranean here, on the **Côte Vermeille** *(see p482)*, where the prettiest resort is **Collioure** *(see p483)*, long familiar to artists. To the

The fairytale sight of Carcassonne, restored in the 19th century

north is **Carcassonne** *(see pp488–9)*, a dreamy fortified town that has been perfectly restored. Romantics might also want to seek it out as the last stronghold of the persecuted Cathars. **Nîmes** *(see pp496–7)* was a major Roman city with a well-preserved amphitheatre and an astonishing aqueduct, the **Pont du Gard** *(see p495)*. It was the highest bridge the Romans ever built.

PROVENCE AND THE CÔTE D'AZUR

- The French Riviera
- Cannes' ritzy Film Festival
- Monte-Carlo Casino

St-Tropez *(see p516)*, **Nice** *(see pp526–7)*, **Menton** *(see p529)* – the French Riviera is the most fabulous waterfront

in the world. Admire top yachts in **Antibes** *(see p521)*, catch the rising stars at **Cannes' film festival** *(see p520)* and break the bank in **Monte-Carlo** *(see pp530–1)*. There is plenty to do all year round so it's best to avoid August when it can be incredibly busy. Away from the coast there are glorious ancient towns, from **Avignon** *(see p503)*, where popes built a palace, and **Aix** *(see p511)*, where good King Renée ruled, to Roman **Arles** *(see pp508–9)* and the cowboy country of the **Camargue** *(see pp510–1)*.

CORSICA

- Myrtle-scented maquis
- Beautiful sandy beaches
- Fortified towns

A mountainous island with coves and sandy beaches, Corsica is the place to hike, especially in spring, when the aromatic maquis puts on its best show. On the coast there are fortified towns such as **Bonifacio** *(see p543)* and **Porto** *(see p541)*, set in a magical bay. Napoleon Bonaparte was born in **Ajaccio** *(see p543)*. Find out about the island's history and customs in the Musée de la Corse in **Corte** *(see p540)*, which is a good base for exploring enchanting, remote Castagmiccia.

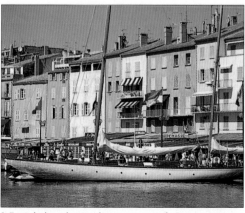

St-Tropez harbour, the most glamorous resort on the Provence coast

Putting France on the Map

France, one of the largest countries in Europe, has airline connections with most cities in the world. Paris is the major transport hub with two international airports; others include Bordeaux, Lille, Lyon, Nice and Toulouse. There are good, high-speed rail links with the rest of Europe, and a network of efficient motorways. A number of ferry routes cross the Mediterranean to Corsica and beyond. Cross-Channel ferries serve several ports, with the Channel Tunnel providing an alternative link by rail.

France, known as the "Hexagon" due to its six-sided shape, is bordered by six countries: Spain across the Pyrenees to the south; Italy and Switzerland beyond the Alps; Luxembourg and Belgium to the north; and Germany on the other side of the Rhine. The United Kingdom lies across the English Channel (La Manche).

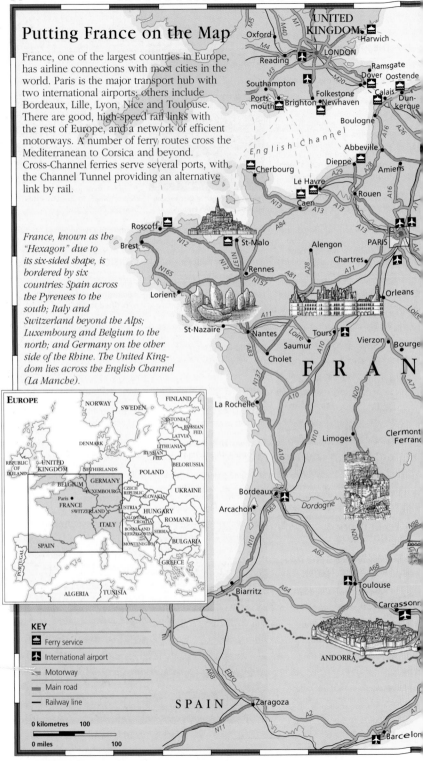

KEY

🚢	Ferry service
✈	International airport
▬	Motorway
▬	Main road
▬	Railway line

0 kilometres   100

0 miles   100

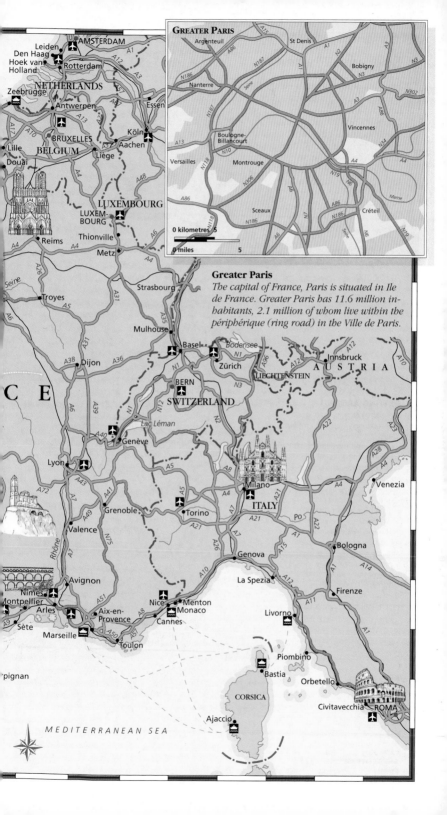

GREATER PARIS

Argenteuil
St Denis
Bobigny
Nanterre
Boulogne-
Billancourt
Versailles
Montrouge
Vincennes
Sceaux
Créteil

0 kilometres 5
0 miles 5

Seine
Marne

A15 A86 N187 N2 A3 N3 N302 A3 A86 N34 A4 A4 N19 N6 A86 N186 N19
N186 N186 N206 A6 N7 A6 Seine N6
N186 N118 N118 N10 A13 N118 N186

Greater Paris
The capital of France, Paris is situated in Ile de France. Greater Paris has 11.6 million inhabitants, 2.1 million of whom live within the périphérique (ring road) in the Ville de Paris.

AMSTERDAM
Leiden
Den Haag
Hoek van
Holland
Rotterdam
NETHERLANDS
Zeebrugge
Antwerpen
Essen
Köln
BRUXELLES
BELGIUM
Aachen
Lille
Liège
Douai
LUXEMBOURG
LUXEM-
BOURG
Reims
Thionville
Metz
Strasbourg
Troyes
Mulhouse
Basel
Bodensee
Innsbruck
AUSTRIA
Dijon
Zürich
LIECHTENSTEIN
BERN
SWITZERLAND
Lac Léman
Genève
Lyon
Milano
ITALY
Venezia
Grenoble
Torino
Po
Bologna
Valence
Genova
La Spezia
Firenze
Avignon
Nîmes
Nice
Menton
Monaco
Montpellier
Arles
Aix-en-
Provence
Cannes
Livorno
Sète
Marseille
Toulon
Piombino
pignan
Bastia
Orbetello
CORSICA
Civitavecchia
ROMA
Ajaccio

MEDITERRANEAN SEA

Seine
Rhône

A1 A12 A17 A67 A13 A4 A48 A26 A5 A6 A31 A36 A38 A39 A40 A43 A41 A49 A72 A7 A26 A10 A8 A5 A5 A21 A4 A21 A22 A23 A28 A4 A14 A1 A11 A12 A15 A22 A10
N1 N2 N3 N4 N5 N7 N75 N1 N2

Regional France

France has a population of around 61 million, and receives over 75 million visitors a year. It covers an area of 543,965 sq km (210,025 sq miles). Paris is the largest city, followed by Lyon, Marseille and the conurbation of Lille-Lens-Valenciennes. The Loire, Seine, Garonne and Rhône are the longest of France's many rivers. This book divides the country into 15 regions, plus a separate section for Paris and Ile de France, although officially France comprises 22 *régions*.

GETTING AROUND

In spite of its size, France is relatively easy to travel around. There is a well-organized rail network, and travelling times are considerably shortened between towns with a high-speed TGV link *(see p683)*. Most motorways have expensive tolls but are fast and efficient for longer distances. City by-passes are usually free and some longer sections of motorway may also be free. Smaller roads are usually a more interesting way to discover the country's varied landscape *(pp686–8)* and they are almost invariably well-maintained and signposted.

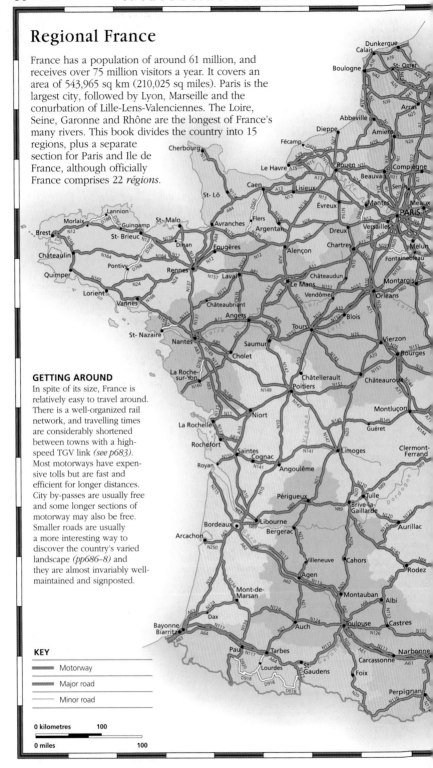

KEY

━━━ Motorway

━━━ Major road

─── Minor road

0 kilometres   100

0 miles   100

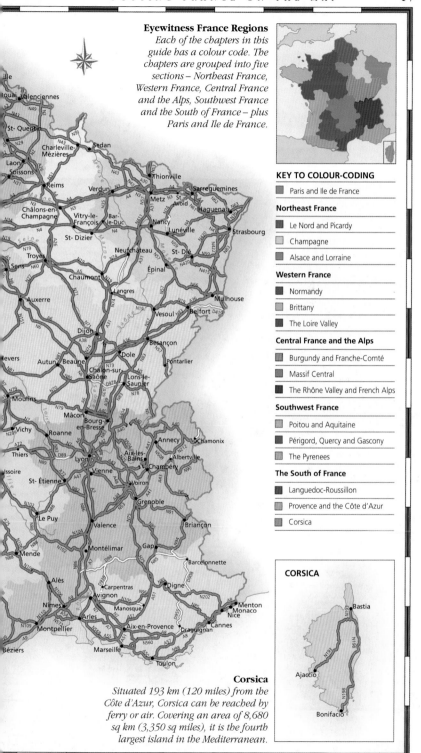

Eyewitness France Regions
*Each of the chapters in this
guide has a colour code. The
chapters are grouped into five
sections – Northeast France,
Western France, Central France
and the Alps, Southwest France
and the South of France – plus
Paris and Ile de France.*

KEY TO COLOUR-CODING

    Paris and Ile de France

Northeast France

    Le Nord and Picardy

    Champagne

    Alsace and Lorraine

Western France

    Normandy

    Brittany

    The Loire Valley

Central France and the Alps

    Burgundy and Franche-Comté

    Massif Central

    The Rhône Valley and French Alps

Southwest France

    Poitou and Aquitaine

    Périgord, Quercy and Gascony

    The Pyrenees

The South of France

    Languedoc-Roussillon

    Provence and the Côte d'Azur

    Corsica

CORSICA

Corsica
*Situated 193 km (120 miles) from the
Côte d'Azur, Corsica can be reached by
ferry or air. Covering an area of 8,680
sq km (3,350 sq miles), it is the fourth
largest island in the Mediterranean.*

A PORTRAIT OF FRANCE

The French are convinced that their way of life is best, and that their country is the most civilized on earth. Many millions of visitors agree with them. The food and wine are justly celebrated. French culture, literature, art, cinema, and architecture can be both profound and provocative. Whether cerebral, sensual, or sportive, France is a country where anyone might feel at home.

France's landscape ranges from high mountain plateaux to lush farmland, traditional villages to chic boulevards. Its regional identities are equally diverse. The country belongs to both northern and southern Europe, and encompasses Brittany with its Celtic maritime heritage, the Mediterranean sunbelt, Germanic Alsace-Lorraine, and the hardy mountain regions of the Auvergne and the Pyrenees. Paris remains the linchpin, with its famously brusque citizens and intense tempo. Other cities range from the huge industrial conglomeration of Lille in the north, to Marseille, the biggest port on the Mediterranean. The differences between north and south, country and

Marianne, symbol of France

city are well-entrenched, indeed cherished. Advances such as the TGV (high-speed train), internet and mobile phone technology have helped reduce distance (both physical and emotional) yet have simultaneously provoked an opposite reaction: as life in France becomes more city-based and industrialized, so the desire grows to safeguard the old, traditional ways and to value rural life.

The idea of life in the country – *douceur de vivre* (the Good Life), long tables set in the sun for the wine and anecdotes to flow – is as seductive as ever for residents and visitors alike. Nevertheless, the rural way of life has been changing. Whereas in 1945 one

Château de Saumur, one of the Loire's most romantic and complete castles

◁ Café life in St-Tropez, one of the country's many pleasures person in three worked in farming, today it is only one in 16. France's main exports used to be luxury goods like perfumes and Cognac; today, such exports have been overtaken by cars, telecommunications equipment, nuclear power stations and fighter aircraft.

People remain firmly committed to their roots, however, and often retain a place in the country where they go back for holidays or retirement. On average, there are more French people

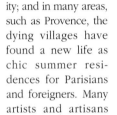

The popular *moto* (scooter)

Chanel chic

who have second homes than any other nationality; and in many areas, such as Provence, the dying villages have found a new life as chic summer residences for Parisians and foreigners. Many artists and artisans from the towns now live and work in the country; and entrepreneurs have set up factory workshops there, more feasible in the age of the fax, the computer and the Internet.

Social changes have come about since the decline in the influence of the Catholic Church. Today only 14 percent of people attend mass regularly. Many couples live together before marriage, and are allowed the same tax status as married couples. Abortion is now legal.

Feminism in France has quite a different look than in Anglo-Saxon countries. It seems that in France, even feminists are unwill-

ing to condemn frivolous feminity and sex-appeal. As EU citizens, women in France have full legal equality with men, but French attitudes remain traditional. A flirtatious gallantry is the norm between the sexes, even in public life. The election of Edith Cresson in 1991 as France's first woman prime minister may have appeared a milestone, but her crushing unpopularity in that role, followed by the 1999 corruption case against her as an EU Commissioner (leading to the resignation of the entire Commission), arguably held back the cause of women's equality in French politics.

SOCIAL CUSTOMS AND POLITICS

French social life, except between close friends, has always been marked by formality – handshaking, the use of titles *("Monsieur le President")*, the infrequent use of first names, the preference for the formal *vous* rather than the intimate *tu*. However, this is changing among the younger generation,

The May 1968 uprising, a catalyst for profound change in France

Farming in Alsace-Lorraine

who now call you by your first name, and use *tu* even in an office context. Standards of dress have become much more informal too, though the French are still very concerned to dress well, and they judge others by their clothes: they prefer an elegantly casual Cardin pullover to an ill-fitting formal suit.

Formality lingers on, however, and France remains very legalistic – whether you are buying a house, exporting an antique or getting divorced. But the French are insouciant about their famous red tape. Rules and laws are there to be ingeniously evaded, twisted, or made more human. This sport of avoiding cumbersome bureaucracy has a name of its own, *le système D*, to be accompanied with a shrug and a smile.

The old sharp Left/Right ideological divide which used to dominate French politics, had recently given way to a more centre-focused consensus fostered by the influential François Mitterrand, President from 1981 to 1995. It reappeared however in a dramatic manner in May 2002, with the re-election of the Conservative Jacques Chirac

Charles de Gaulle

as President, after an uncomfortable five-year "cohabitation" with the Socialist Lionel Jospin as Prime Minister, followed shortly by a huge swing to the far right in the general elections. The real power, though, remains in the hands of the upper bourgeoisie through both state and business appointments, notwithstanding the occasional flash of Republican spirit in the form of strikes and mass demonstrations. Unemployment and insecurity fuel support for the far right and growing racism against Jews, Arabs and black immigrants, many of whom are from former French colonies. French political independence on the international stage asserted itself in 2003 when President Chirac refused to agree to a UN Security Council Resolution to authorize military action against Iraq. The French also voted against adopting the new European Constitution in 2005.

CULTURE AND THE ARTS

Culture is taken seriously in France, and writers, intellectuals, artists and fashion designers are held in high social esteem. As a result, the state finances a

Designer Thierry Mugler at the Paris collections

large network of provincial arts centres, and has traditionally given subsidies which have allowed experimentation in art and design. The French remain justly proud of their own serious cinematic tradition, and are determined to defend it against pressures from Hollywood. Other activities – from the music industry to the French language itself – are subject to the same protectionist attitudes.

Traditional Breton costumes, worn for festivals and *pardons*

Avant-garde art and literature and modern architecture all enjoy strong patronage in France. Some of the more exciting architectural projects range from the striking modern buildings in Paris – the Louvre pyramid and La Grande Arche at La

Défense – to the post-modern housing developments of Nîmes, Montpellier, and Marseille in the south.

MODERN LIFE

While one half of the French were heralding in the new millennium in true Gallic style, the other half were plunged into darkness caused by the worst storms to hit Europe since records began. This is an extreme illustration of French ambivalence towards modernism. France's agro-business is one of the most modern in the world, but the peasant farmer is deeply revered. France hankers after a leading role in the world, yet the country effectively closes down for the whole of August, when the French take to the roads and coastal resorts ... of France! However, two recent changes have somewhat forced the pace: the Internet, which France has embraced keenly, despite the obvious threat to its previously revolutionary communications network, Minitel; and the Euro, which, in one fell swoop, has swept away Europe's oldest decimalized currency, the Franc.

A view through the base of La Grande Arche, part of the huge business complex on the edge of Paris

The traditional game of *boules or pétanque,* still extremely popular – especially in the south

The French are enthusiastic, discerning consumers. Even small towns have excellent, stylish clothes shops. Street markets bring in the best of local produce. In addition, France has Europe's largest hypermarkets, which have

been steadily ousting the local grocery or corner shop. These are remarkably French in what they sell: a long delicatessen counter may have a wonderful display of 100 or so French cheeses and

Southern produce: melons, peaches, and apricots

charcuterie, while the huge range of fresh vegetables and fruit is a tribute to their role in French cuisine.

However, under modern pressures, eating habits have been polarizing in a curious way. The French used to eat well every day as a matter of course. Today they are in a hurry, and for most meals of the week they will eat simply – either a quick fried steak or pasta dish at home, or a snack in town (hence the wave of fast-food places that have sprung up, in defiance of

French tradition). But meals still remain an important part of French culture – not just for the food and wines, but also for the pleasure of lengthy, unhurried meals and good conversation around a table, among family or friends. They will reserve their gastronomy for the once-or-twice-a-week special occasion, or the big family Sunday lunch which remains an important French ritual. It is at these times that the French zest for life really comes into its own.

Remote farm – a nostalgic reminder of rural life

The Classic French Menu

The traditional French meal consists of at least three courses. *Les entrées* or *hors d'oeuvre* (starters or appetizers) include soups, egg dishes, salads or *charcuterie*, such as sliced sausage or hams. There may be a separate fish course before the main course. Otherwise, *les plats* (main courses) will be a choice of meat and fish dishes, often served with a sauce and accompanied by potatoes, rice or pasta and vegetables. The cheese course comes before the dessert. Desserts may include sorbets, fruit tarts and creamy or chocolate concoctions. A fixed-price menu is the cheapest option. For more information on French restaurants, see pp596–9.

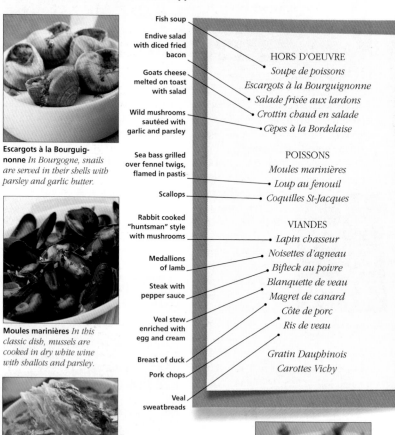

Fish soup

Endive salad with diced fried bacon

Goats cheese melted on toast with salad

Wild mushrooms sautéed with garlic and parsley

HORS D'OEUVRE
Soupe de poissons
Escargots à la Bourguignonne
Salade frisée aux lardons
Crottin chaud en salade
Cèpes à la Bordelaise

Escargots à la Bourguignonne *In Bourgogne, snails are served in their shells with parsley and garlic butter.*

Sea bass grilled over fennel twigs, flamed in pastis

Scallops

POISSONS
Moules marinières
Loup au fenouil
Coquilles St-Jacques

Rabbit cooked "huntsman" style with mushrooms

Medallions of lamb

Steak with pepper sauce

Veal stew enriched with egg and cream

Breast of duck

Pork chops

Veal sweatbreads

VIANDES
Lapin chasseur
Noisettes d'agneau
Bifteck au poivre
Blanquette de veau
Magret de canard
Côte de porc
Ris de veau

Gratin Dauphinois
Carottes Vichy

Moules marinières *In this classic dish, mussels are cooked in dry white wine with shallots and parsley.*

Gratin Dauphinois *Layers of potato are covered in cream, topped with Gruyère cheese and slowly baked.*

Carottes Vichy *Cooked in Vichy water with sugar, carrots take on a delicious, sweet glaze. They are served garnished with parsley.*

BREAKFAST

The French rarely eat cereal, eggs or meat for breakfast; assorted breads, spread with butter and jams, are their morning choice. These include *croissants* (flaky, buttery crescent-shaped pastries); a piece of *baguette* (the classic long thin loaf); *pain au chocolat* (an oblong of croissant dough rolled round a tablet of chocolate, then baked); and *brioche* (an airy, egg-enriched yeast bread or roll). They are washed down with coffee or tea, or hot chocolate for children. Hotels will usually offer fresh fruit juice, too. The most common form of coffee at breakfast is *café au lait*, espresso served with warm milk.

Typical French breakfast selection

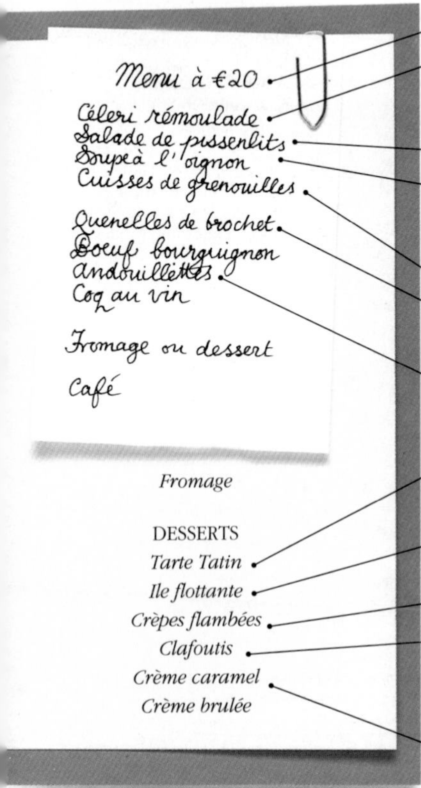

Menu à €20 — Fixed-price menu of the day

Céleri rémoulade — Grated celeriac in a piquant mayonnaise

Salade de pissenlits — Dandelion-leaf salad

Soupe à l'oignon — Dark, rich onion soup topped with bread and grilled cheese

Cuisses de grenouilles — Frogs' legs

Quenelles de brochet — Light, fluffy poached pike dumplings

Boeuf bourguignon

Andouillettes — Small tripe sausages, usually grilled

Coq au vin

Fromage ou dessert

Café

Boeuf Bourguignon *Beef is cooked in red Burgundy wine with bacon, baby onions and button mushrooms.*

Fromage

DESSERTS

Tarte Tatin — Upside-down baked apple tart

Ile flottante — Meringues floating in a creamy sauce

Crêpes flambées — Sugared crêpes flamed in liqueur

Clafoutis — Baked fruit and batter dessert, often made with cherries

Crème caramel — Egg custard with a caramel sauce

Crème brulée

Coq au vin *A male chicken is flamed in brandy, then stewed in wine with button mushrooms and onions.*

Fromage *Any good French restaurant will take pride in offering a good range of perfectly matured regional cheeses, including, as available, cows', ewes' and goats' milk, blue, soft and hard varieties.*

Crème Brulée *This rich, creamy custard is covered with brown sugar, grilled to form a crisp topping.*

The Wine of France

Picker's hod

Winemaking in France dates back to pre-Roman times, although it was the Romans who disseminated the culture of the vine and the practice of winemaking throughout the country. The range, quality and reputation of the fine wines of Bordeaux, Burgundy, the Rhône and Champagne in particular have made them rôle models the world over. France's everyday wines can be highly enjoyable too, with plenty of good value wines now emerging from the southern regions.

Traditional vineyard cultivation

WINE REGIONS

Each of the 10 principal wine-producing regions has its own identity, based on grape varieties, climate and *terroir* (soil). *Appellation contrôlée* laws guarantee a wine's origins and production methods.

KEY

- ☐ Bordeaux
- ☐ Burgundy
- ☐ Champagne
- ☐ Alsace
- ☐ Loire
- ☐ Provence
- ☐ Jura and Savoie
- ☐ The Southwest
- ☐ Languedoc-Roussillon
- ☐ Rhône

(Map of France with labelled cities: Paris, Reims, Strasbourg, Nantes, Tours, Dijon, Clermont-Ferrand, Lyon, Bordeaux, Pau, Toulouse, Marseille, Perpignan; rivers Marne, Loire, Dordogne, Garonne, Rhône)

0 kilometres 150
0 miles 150

HOW TO READ A WINE LABEL

Even the simplest label will identify the wine and provide a key to its quality. It will bear the name of the wine and its producer, its vintage if there is one, and whether it comes from a strictly defined area (*appellation contrôlée* or VDQS) or is a more general *vin de pays* or *vin de table*. It may also have a regional grading, as with the *crus classés* in Bordeaux. The shape and colour of the bottle is also a guide to the kind of wine it contains. Green glass is often used since this helps to protect the wine from light.

The property or producer

Château-bottled, rather than a wine from a merchant or grower's co-operative

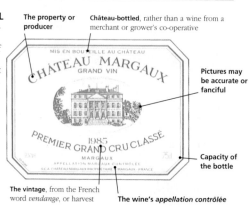

MIS EN BOUTEILLE AU CHÂTEAU

CHÂTEAU MARGAUX
GRAND VIN

PREMIER GRAND CRU CLASSÉ
1985

APPELLATION MARGAUX CONTRÔLÉE
SCA CHÂTEAU MARGAUX PROPRIÉTAIRE À MARGAUX - FRANCE

Pictures may be accurate or fanciful

Capacity of the bottle

The vintage, from the French word *vendange*, or harvest

The wine's *appellation contrôlée*

HOW WINE IS MADE

Wine is the product of the juice of freshly picked grapes, after natural or cultured yeasts have converted the grape sugars into alcohol during the fermentation process. The yeasts, or lees, are normally filtered out before bottling.

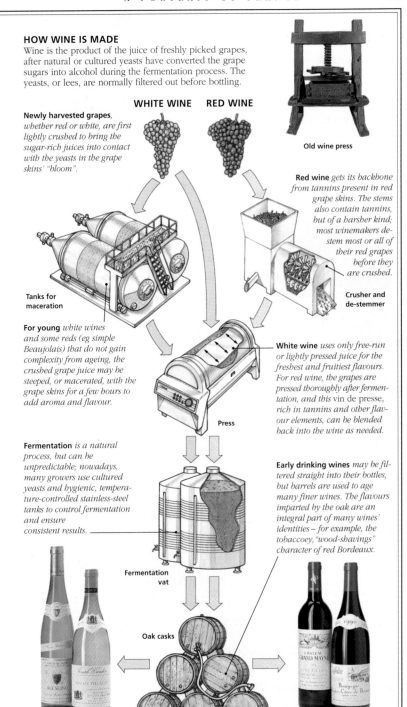

Old wine press

WHITE WINE **RED WINE**

Newly harvested grapes, *whether red or white, are first lightly crushed to bring the sugar-rich juices into contact with the yeasts in the grape skins' "bloom".*

Red wine *gets its backbone from tannins present in red grape skins. The stems also contain tannins, but of a harsher kind; most winemakers de-stem most or all of their red grapes before they are crushed.*

Tanks for maceration

Crusher and de-stemmer

For young *white wines and some reds (eg simple Beaujolais) that do not gain complexity from ageing, the crushed grape juice may be steeped, or macerated, with the grape skins for a few hours to add aroma and flavour.*

White wine *uses only free-run or lightly pressed juice for the freshest and fruitiest flavours. For red wine, the grapes are pressed thoroughly after fermen- tation, and this* vin de presse, *rich in tannins and other flav- our elements, can be blended back into the wine as needed.*

Press

Fermentation *is a natural process, but can be unpredictable; nowadays, many growers use cultured yeasts and hygienic, tempera- ture-controlled stainless-steel tanks to control fermentation and ensure consistent results.*

Early drinking wines *may be fil- tered straight into their bottles, but barrels are used to age many finer wines. The flavours imparted by the oak are an integral part of many wines' identities – for example, the tobaccoey, "wood-shavings" character of red Bordeaux.*

Fermentation vat

Oak casks

Different shades of glass identify the wine regions

Bottle shapes typical of red Bordeaux (left) and Burgundy

Artists in France

Artists have always been inspired by France, especially since landscape became a legitimate subject for art in the 19th century. Art and tourism have been closely linked for over a century, when the establishment of artists' colonies in the forest of Fontainebleau, Brittany, and the south of France did much to make these areas attractive to visitors. Today, one of the pleasures of touring the countryside is the recognition of landscapes made famous in paintings.

Follower of *the French Classical tradition of landscape painting, Jean-Baptiste-Camille Corot recorded* The Belfry of Douai *(1871).*

Le Nord and Picardy

Gustave Courbet, *socialist and leader of the Realist School of painting, captured this famous coastal town in* The Cliffs at Etretat after a Storm *(1869).*

Normandy

Paris and Ile d France

Brittany

Loire Valley

Emile Bernard *was fascinated by the wild, almost primitive character of the Breton landscape and the individuality of its inhabitants. He was one of the community of artists based in Pont Aven. His* La Ronde Bretonne *(1892) portrays local Celtic customs.*

Poitou and Aquitaine

Neo-Impressionist *artist and exponent of Pointillism, Paul Signac indulged his love of maritime subjects on the coasts of France.* Entrance to the Port at La Rochelle *(1921) shows his use of myriad dots of colour to represent nature.*

Périgord, Quercy and Gascony

Pyrenees

Languedoc-Roussillon

Théodore Rousseau, *the leading light of the Barbizon School (see p181) of landscape painters, visited the Auvergne in 1830. It was here that he began to paint "en plein air" (in the open air). The results are seen in this sensitively observed scene,* Sunset, Auvergne *(c.1830).*

A few months *before his tragic death in July 1890, Vincent Van Gogh painted the* Church at Auvers. *He noted that the building "appears to have a violet-hued blue colour; pure cobalt".*

In his Eiffel Tower *(1926) Robert Delaunay investigated the abstract qualities of colour. His wife, artist Sonia Delaunay, said, "The Eiffel Tower and the Universe were one and the same to him".*

Alsace and Lorraine

Champagne

Scenes from *everyday life were realistically rendered by Gustave Courbet, as here in* Young Ladies of the Village Giving Alms to a Cow Girl in a Valley near Ornans *(1851–2).*

Burgundy and Franche-Comté

Maurice Utrillo *painted this village scene,* The Church of Saint Bernard in Summer *(1924), while staying at his mother's home. The sombre tone and emptiness reflect his unhappy life.*

The Massif Central

The Rhône Valley and French Alps

Provence and the Côte d'Azur

Landscape at Collioure *(1905) depicts the vivid colours of this little Catalan fishing village. It was here that Henri Matisse founded the art movement of the Fauves, or "Wild Beasts", who used exceptionally bright, expressive colours.*

The French Riviera *attracted many artists (see pp472–3). Raoul Dufy particularly appreciated its pleasures, seen in this typical scene of blue skies and palm trees,* La Jetée Promenade à Nice *(1928).*

| 0 kilometres | 100 |
| 0 miles | 100 |

Writers in France

Colette's house in Burgundy

Writers and intellectuals traditionally enjoy high prestige in France. One of the most august of French institutions is the Academie Française, whose 40 members, most of them writers, have pronounced on national events and, on occasion, held public office.

Monument to Baudelaire

The work of many French novelists is deeply rooted in their native area, ranging from the Normandy of Gustave Flaubert to Jean Giono's Provence. In addition to their literary merit, these novels provide a unique guide to France's regional identities.

THE NOVEL

The farmland of the Beauce, where Zola based his novel, *La Terre*

Marcel Proust, author of *Remembrance of Things Past*

The first great French writer was Rabelais, in the 16th century, a boisterous, life-affirming satirist *(see p295)*. Many writers in the Age of Enlightenment which followed emphasized the classic tradition of reason,

clarity and objectivity in their work. The 19th century was the golden age of the French humanist novel, producing Balzac, with his vast fresco of contemporary society; Stendhal, a fierce critic of the frailties of ambition in *Scarlet and Black*; and Victor Hugo, known for epics such as *Les Misérables*. George Sand broke ground with her novels such as *The Devil's Pool* which depicted peasant life, albeit in an idealized way. In the same century, Flaubert produced his masterwork *Madame Bovary*, a study of provincialism and misplaced romanticism. In contrast, Zola wrote *Germinal*, *La Terre*, and other studies of lower-class life.

Marcel Proust combined a poetic evocation of his boyhood with a portrait of high society in his long novel,

Remembrance of Things Past. Others have also written poetically about their childhood, such as Alain-Fournier in *Le Grand Meaulnes* and Colette in *My Mother's House*.

A new kind of novel emerged after World War I. Jean Giono's *Joy of Man's Desiring*, and François Mauriac's masterly *Thérèse Desqueyroux*, explored the impact of landscape upon human character. Mauriac, and also George Bernanos in his *Diary of a Country Priest*, used lone spiritual struggle as a theme. The free-thinker André Gide was another leading writer of the inter-war years with his *Strait is the Gate* and the autobiographical *If it Die*.

In the 1960s Alain Robbe-Grillet and others experimented with the Nouveau Roman which subordinated character and plot to detailed physical description. Critics held it in part responsible for the recent decline of the novel. Despite this decline, new, avant-garde works continue to see the light of day.

Hugo's novel *Les Misérables*, made into a musical in the 1980s

THEATRE

The three classic playwrights of French literature, Racine, Molière, and Corneille, lived in the 17th century. Molière's comedies satirized the vanities and foibles of human nature. Corneille and Racine wrote noble verse tragedies. They were followed in the 18th century by Marivaux, writer of romantic comedies, and Beaumarchais whose *Barber of Seville* and *Marriage of Figaro* later became operas.

Molière, the 17th-century dramatist

Victor Hugo's dramas were the most vigorous product of the 19th century. The exceptional dramatists of the 20th century range from Jean Anouilh, author of urbane philosophical comedies, to Jean Genet, ex-convict critic of the establishment. In the 1960s, Eugene Ionesco from Romania and Samuel Beckett from Ireland were among the pioneers of a new genre, the "theatre of the absurd". Since then, no major playwrights have emerged but experimental work flourishes in state-subsidized theatre companies.

POETRY

The greatest of early French poets was Ronsard, who wrote sonnets about nature and love in the 16th century. Lamartine, a major poet of the early 19th century, also took nature as one of his themes (his poem *Le Lac* laments a lost love). Later the same century, Baudelaire *(Les Fleurs du mal)* and Rimbaud *(Le Bateau Ivre)* were judged to be provocative in their day. Nobel prizewinner in 1904, Frédéric Mistral wrote in his native Provençal tongue. The greatest poet of the 20th century is considered to be Paul Valéry, whose work is profoundly philosophical.

PHILOSOPHY

France has produced a large number of leading philosophers in the European humanist tradition. One of

Sartre and de Beauvoir in La Coupole restaurant in Paris, 1969

the first was Montaigne, in the 16th century, an inspired moralist who established the essay as an art form. Then came Descartes, the master of logic, and the philosopher Pascal. The 18th century produced two great figures – Voltaire, the supreme liberal, and Rousseau, who preached the harmonizing influence of living close to nature.

In the 20th century, Sartre, de Beauvoir and Camus used the novel as a philosophical vehicle. Sartre led the existentialist movement in Paris in the early 1940s with his novel *Nausea* and his treatise *Being and Nothingness*. Camus' novel, *The Outsider,* was equally influential.

Throughout the '70s and '80s the radical ideas of the structuralists seized Paris (Barthes, Foucault etc). Post-structuralism relayed this rationalist approach into the '90s, with Derrida, Kristeva, Deleuze and Lyotard.

Novels by Albert Camus, who won the Nobel Prize in 1957

FOREIGN WRITERS

Many foreign writers have visited and been inspired by France, from Petrarch in 14th-century Avignon to Goethe in Alsace in 1770–71. In the 20th century the Riviera attracted novelists Somerset Maugham, Katherine Mansfield, Ernest Hemingway and Graham Greene. In 1919 the American Sylvia Beach opened the first Shakespeare and Company bookshop in Paris, which became a cultural centre for expatriate writers. In 1922 she was the first to publish James Joyce's masterwork, *Ulysses.*

Hemingway with Sylvia Beach and friends, Paris 1923

Romanesque and Gothic Architecture in France

France is rich in medieval architecture, ranging from small Romanesque churches to great Gothic cathedrals. As the country emerged from the Dark Ages in the 11th century, there was a surge in Romanesque building, based on the Roman model of thick walls, round arches and heavy vaults. French architects improved this basic structure, leading to the flowering of Gothic in the 13th century. Pointed arches and flying buttresses were the key inventions that allowed for much taller buildings with larger windows.

LOCATOR MAP

① *Romanesque abbeys & churches*

⑬ *Gothic cathedrals*

ROMANESQUE FEATURES

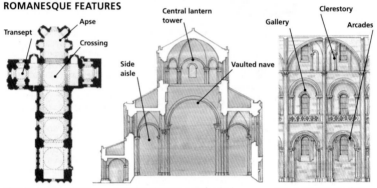

The plan of Angoulême — Transept, Apse, Crossing

A section of Le Puy — Central lantern tower, Side aisle, Vaulted nave

The massive walls — Gallery, Clerestory, Arcades

The plan of Angoulême *shows the cross-shape and the rounded eastern apse typical of Romanesque architecture.*

A section of Le Puy *reveals a high barrel-vaulted nave with round arches and low side aisles. Light could enter through windows in the side aisles and the central lantern tower.*

The massive walls *of the nave bays of St-Etienne support a three-storey structure of arcades, a gallery and clerestory.*

GOTHIC FEATURES

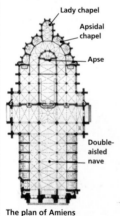

The plan of Amiens — Lady chapel, Apsidal chapel, Apse, Double-aisled nave

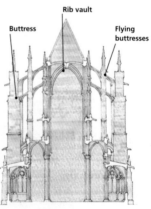

A section of Beauvais — Rib vault, Buttress, Flying buttresses

Pointed arches — Triforium, Tracery, Pointed arch

The plan of Amiens *shows the nave and apse flanked by a continuous row of chapels.*

A section of Beauvais *shows how the nave could be raised to staggering heights thanks to exterior support from flying buttresses.*

Pointed arches *withstood greater stress, permitting larger windows as in the nave at Reims.*

WHERE TO FIND ROMANESQUE ARCHITECTURE

WHERE TO FIND GOTHIC ARCHITECTURE

TERMS USED IN THIS GUIDE

Basilica: Early church with two aisles and nave lit from above by clerestory windows.

Clerestory: A row of windows illuminating the nave from above the aisle roof.

Rose: Circular window, often stained glass.

Buttress: Mass of masonry built to support a wall.

Flying buttress: An arched support transmitting thrust of the weight downwards.

Portal: Monumental entrance to a building, often decorated.

Tympanum: Decorated space, often carved, over a door or window lintel.

Vault: Arched stone ceiling.

Transept: Two wings of a cruciform church at right angles to the nave.

Crossing: Centre of cruciform where transept crosses nave.

Lantern: Turret with windows to illuminate interior, often with cupola (domed ceiling).

Triforium: Middle storey between arcades and clerestory.

Apse: Termination of the church, often rounded.

Ambulatory: Aisle running round east end, passing behind the sanctuary.

Arcade: Set of arches and supporting columns.

Rib vault: Vault supported by projecting ribs of stone.

Gargoyle: Carved grotesque figure, often a water spout.

Tracery: Ornamental carved stone pattern within Gothic window.

Flamboyant Gothic: Carved stone tracery resembling flames.

Capital: Top of a column, usually carved.

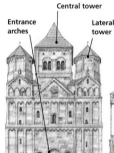

Central tower
Entrance arches
Lateral tower

The west façade of Marmoutier Abbey *with its towers, narrow windows and small portal give it a fortified appearance.*

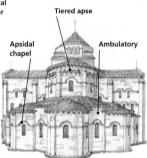

Tiered apse
Apsidal chapel
Ambulatory

The east end of Nevers *has a rounded apse surrounded by a semi-circular ambulatory and radiating chapels. The chapels were added to provide space for altars.*

Stepped tower
Sculpted portal
Rose
Apse
Chapel
Buttress

The west façade of Laon *has decorative, sculpted portals and a rose window characteristic of Gothic style.*

The east end of Beauvais, *with its delicate buttresses topped by pinnacles, is the culmination of High Gothic.*

Rural Architecture

French farmhouses are entirely products of the soil, built of stone, clay or wood, depending on what materials are found locally. As the topography changes so does the architecture, from the steeply-sloped roofs covered in flat tiles in the north to the broad canal-tiled roofs of the south.

Despite this rich regional diversity, French farmhouses fall into three basic categories: the *maison bloc*, where house and outbuildings share the same roof; the high house, with living quarters upstairs and livestock or wine cellar below; and courtyard farmsteads, their buildings set around a central court.

Shuttered window in Alsace

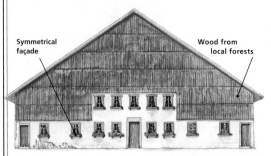

Symmetrical façade

Wood from local forests

The chalet *is typical of the Jura, Alps and Vosges mountains. The* maison bloc *housed both family and livestock throughout the winter. Gaps between the gable planks allowed air to circulate around crops stored in the loft, and an earth ramp behind gave wagons access. Many lofts also had a threshing floor.*

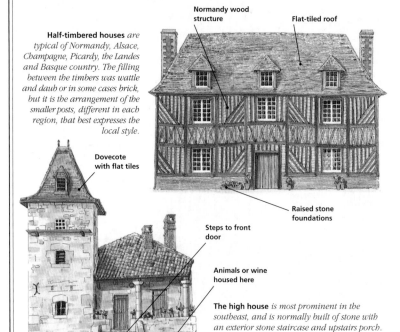

Normandy wood structure

Flat-tiled roof

Half-timbered houses *are typical of Normandy, Alsace, Champagne, Picardy, the Landes and Basque country. The filling between the timbers was wattle and daub or in some cases brick, but it is the arrangement of the smaller posts, different in each region, that best expresses the local style.*

Dovecote with flat tiles

Raised stone foundations

Steps to front door

Animals or wine housed here

The high house *is most prominent in the southeast, and is normally built of stone with an exterior stone staircase and upstairs porch. Wine growers' barrels could be stored on the ground floor without hoisting, or livestock stabled there. High houses in the Lot Valley often boast a dovecote.*

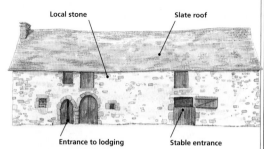

The long house *is the oldest form of* maison bloc, *with family and livestock at opposite ends of the building – originally one room. In this Breton version, separate doorways lead to house and stable. A dividing wall only became common in the 19th century.*

Local stone

Slate roof

Entrance to lodging

Stable entrance

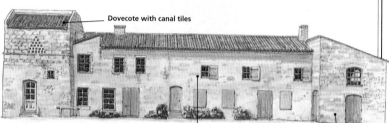

Dovecote with canal tiles

The word "mas" *generally refers to any Provençal farmhouse. In the Camargue and the Crau, it is a farmstead for large-scale sheep farming built in an "agglomerated" style: the outbuildings, although attached to one another, are of different heights. Often, a dovecote is included.*

Ochre and beige colours of the south

Rendered façade

Pebble and brick wall

Half-timber and brick

Compressed cob: *pisé*

Sun-dried adobe bricks

Pebbles in lime mortar

Brick, flint and chalk

WALLS

Limestone, granite, sandstone and pebbles were all used for building walls. But if no stone was available, clay was dug for infilling half-timbered houses, as wattle and daub. The alternative was to use a cob mixture *(pisé)*, pressed into blocks in a process called *banchage*. Adobe (sundried brick) was also used but fired brick was fairly rare as it was expensive to bake. However, brick was sometimes used as trim or combined with chalk or pebbles in a "composite" walling. Walls were generally rendered with mortar.

Flat terracotta tiles in colours of local sand

Pantiles, used in Flanders and Picardy

Canal clay tiles typical of the south

ROOFING

Two roof styles distinguish the north and south. Northern roofs are steeply pitched, so that any rainwater runs off easily. In the south, roofs are covered with canal clay tiles, and more gently sloped to prevent the tiles sliding off.

FRANCE THROUGH THE YEAR

The French, with their farming roots, are deeply aware of the changing seasons, and the mild climate means they can celebrate outdoors most of the year. History and tradition are honoured with *fêtes*, such as Bastille Day (14 July). For culture lovers, thousands of arts festivals are held throughout France, ranging from the huge Avignon Theatre Festival down to small village events. Large national sports events, such as the Tour de France cycle race, are a key feature in the calendar. Throughout the year, festivals take place celebrating every kind of food and wine. In high summer, the cities empty and French and foreign visitors flock to the beaches and countryside.

SPRING

France's outdoor life resumes in spring, terrace-cafés filling up in the sunshine. Easter is a time of Catholic processions, and concerts of sacred music. The Cannes Film Festival in May is the best known of the season's many conventions and trade fairs.

MARCH

International Half Marathon beginning and ending at Château de Vincennes.
Tinta' Mars *(fortnight)*, Langres. Cabaret and musical evenings at various venues.
Grenoble Jazz Festival *(fortnight Mar)*. Jazz concerts.
Banlieues Blues Jazz Festival *(Mar)*, Saint-Denis. Jazz music.
Six Nations Rugby Tournament, Stade de France, Paris.

La Bravade procession honoring Saint Torpes in St-Tropez

Rugby ball

Formula One racing at the Monaco Grand Prix

Festival d'Amiens *(mid-Mar/early Apr)*. Celebrated jazz festival at various venues.

APRIL

Festival de Pâques *(Easter week)*, chamber music festival, Deauville *(see p255)*.
Feria Pascale *(Easter week)*. The whole town parties as the bull-fighting season begins, Arles *(see pp508–9)*.
Lourdes Pilgrimage *(Palm Sun to Oct, see p459)*.
Floréal Musical d'Epinal *(early Apr–mid-May)*. Multi-genre music festival, Epinal.
Bourges Spring Festival *(end Apr/early May, see p313)*,

Spring asparagus

modern music.
Europa Jazz Festival, Le Mans. Jazz musicians from all over the world perform.
Joan of Arc Festival *(end Apr–early May)*, pageant and cathedral service, Orléans *(see p312)*.
Paris International Marathon from Place de la Concorde to Avenue Foch.

MAY

Asparagus harvest, notably in the Loire.
International Grand Prix de Monaco *(Ascension weekend, see p530)*.
La Bravade *(16–18 May)*, St-Tropez *(see p516)*.

Cannes Film Festival *(second and third week).*
Gypsy Pilgrimage *(late May),* Stes-Maries-de-la-Mer *(see p510).*
Fête de la Transhumance *(end May).* Herds are taken up to summer pastures.
International Garden Festival *(mid-May–mid-Oct),* Chaumont sur Loire.
Nîmes Feria *(Pentecost),* bull-fights and street music festival *(see p496).*
Grandes Eaux Musicales *(Apr –Oct: Sun; Jul –Sep: Sat –Sun),* Versailles. Classical music in

Traditional transhumance of animals to summer pastures

the grounds of the château.
Puy-du-Fou Pageant *(May–Sep).* Audio-guides and horse stunts evoke local life through the ages *(see p290).*

Football Cup Final *(second week),* Stade de France, Paris.
Le Printemps des Arts *(mid-May–Jun),* Nantes area. Baroque dance and music.

SUMMER

The French holiday season begins in mid-July, with the return to work and school *(la rentrée)* in early September. Beaches, marinas and camp sites are all full to bursting. Every village has its *fête* and there are countless festivals and sporting events.

JUNE

French Tennis Open *(last wk May –first wk Jun),* Stade Roland Garros, Paris.
Strasbourg International Music Festival *(Jun– Jul).*
International Sailing Week *(early Jun),* La Rochelle.

The rose season in full bloom

Le Mans 24-Hour Automobile Race *(second or third w/e, see p291).*
Fête de la Musique *(21 Jun),* music events all over France.
Fête de St-Jean *(24 Jun),* music, bonfires and fire-works all over France.
Gay Pride March *(23 Jun),* The march engulfs Paris.
Tarasque Festival *(last w/e),* Tarascon *(see p507).*

JULY

Festival d'Art Lyrique *(Jun–Jul),* Aix-en-Provence *(see p511).*
Avignon Theatre Festival *(all month, see p503).*
Paris-Plage *(mid-Jul–mid-Aug).* Paris gets an annual

Cyclists in the final stage of the Tour de France cycle race

Bullfighting in Mont-de-Marsan

temporary beach.
Tombées de la Nuit *(first week),* Rennes. Arts festival.
Troménie *(2nd Sun Jul),* Locronan. Procession of pen-itents *(see p273).*
Comminges Music Festival *(Jul–end Aug, see p462).*
Nice Jazz Festival *(late-Jul).*
Mont-de-Marsan Feria *(third w/e).* Bullfights and music *(see p425).*
International Jazz Festival *(second half),* Antibes and Juan-les-Pins *(see p521).*
Jazz Vienne *(first two weeks),* Vienne *(see p382).*
Fête de St-Louis *(around 25 Aug),* Sète *(see p492).*
Tour de France cycle race *(1st three weeks).* The grand finale takes place on the Champs-Elysées, Paris.
Francofolies *(mid-Jul),* Music festival at La Rochelle.

Holiday-makers on a crowded beach in Cannes on the Côte d'Azur

AUGUST

Pablo Casals Festival
(end Jul–mid-Aug),
Prades *(see p480)*.
**Les Rendezvous de
l'Erdre** *(last w/e)*,
Nantes. Jazz and river-
boats *(see p290)*.
Mimos *(1st week)*,
Périgueux. World famous
international mime
festival.

**Avignon Theatre
Festival performer**

Fête du Jasmin *(first w/e)*,
Grasse *(see p517)*. Floats,
music, dancing in town.
Foire aux Sorciers
(first Sun), Bué (nr
Bourges). Costumed
witch and wizard festi-
val and folk groups.
**Parade of Lavender
Floats** *(first or
second weekends)*,
Digne
(see p517).

Fête de la Véraison
(first or second w/e), medieval
celebration of thanksgiving
for the bounty of the fruit
harvest, Châteauneuf-du-
Pape *(see p502)*.
Interceltic Festival *(second
week)*, Celtic arts and music,
Lorient.
Feria – Bullfight *(mid-Aug)*,
Dax *(see p425)*.
**St-Jean-Pied-de-Port-Basque
Fête** *(mid-Aug, see p454)*.

AUTUMN

In wine regions, the grape
harvest is the occasion for
much gregarious jollity, and
every wine village has its
wine festival. When the new
wine is ready in November
there are more festivities. The
hunting season begins –
everywhere there is game
shooting. In the southwest,
migrating birds are trapped.

SEPTEMBER

**Deauville American film
Festival** *(first fortnight)*.
Picardy Cathedral Festival
(mid-Sep), classical concerts
in the region's cathedrals.
"Musicades" *(first fortnight)*,
Lyon. Classical concerts.
Le Puy "Roi de l'Oiseau",
(second week), Renaissance-
style festival *(see p365)*.
Grape harvest, wine regions
throughout France.
Journées du Patrimoine,
(3rd w/e). Over 14,000 historical buildings can be visited,
many not normally open.

Ceremony for the Induction of new Chevaliers at the Hospice de Beaune

OCTOBER

Dinard British film Festival
(first week, see p281).
Nuit Blanche *(first Sat)*,
Paris. Museums stay
open all night.
Prix de l'Arc de Triomphe
(first Sun), Horse racing
at Longchamp, Paris.
**Espelette Red Pepper
Festival** *(last w/e, see
p453)*, Basque region.
**Abbey de Fontevraud
Music** *(to spring, p294)*.

Classical cello

NOVEMBER

**Dijon International Food
and Wine Festival** *(first two
weeks)*. Traditional gas-
tronomic fair.
Apple Festival *(mid-
Nov)*, Le Havre.
**Wine Auctions and Les
Trois Glorieuses** *(third
w/e)*, Beaune *(see
p346)*.
Truffle season *(until
Mar)*, Périgord, Quercy
and Provence.

WINTER

Christmas wreath

At Christmas, traditional nativity plays are held in churches and there are fairs and markets throughout France. In the Alps and the Pyrenees, and even the Vosges and Massif Central, the ski-slopes are crowded. In Flanders and Nice, carnivals take place before Lent.

DECEMBER

Critérium International de la Première Neige *(early Dec)*, Val d'Isère. First competition of the season.

JANUARY

Monte-Carlo Rally *(usually mid-Jan, see p530)*.
Limoux Carnival *(until Mar)*. Street festival held since the Middle Ages.
Fashion shows. Summer

Downhill skier on the slopes in the French Alps

The Taj Mahal re-created at the Lemon Festival in Menton

collections, Paris.
Festival du Cirque *(end)*, Monaco. International event.
Festival de la Bande Dessinée *(last w/e)*. International strip cartoon festival, Angoulême.

FEBRUARY

Lemon Festival *(mid-Feb–Mar)*, Menton *(see p529)*.
Nice Carnival and the Battle of Flowers *(late Feb–early Mar, see p526)*.
Paris Carnaval, *(date varies, check)*, Quartier St-Fargeau.
Fête de Mimosa, *(3rd Sun)*, Bormes-les-Mimosas.

Celebrating the Nice Carnival and the Battle of Flowers

Bastille Day parade past the Arc de Triomphe

PUBLIC HOLIDAYS

New Year's Day (1 Jan)
Easter Sunday and Monday
Ascension Day (sixth Thursday after Easter)
Whit Monday (second Monday after Ascension)
Labour Day (1 May)
VE Day (8 May)
Bastille Day (14 Jul)
Assumption Day (15 Aug)
All Saints' Day (1 Nov)
Remembrance Day (11 Nov)
Christmas Day (25 Dec)

The Climate of France

Set on Europe's western edge, France has a varied, temperate climate. An Atlantic influence prevails in the north-west, with westerly sea winds bringing humidity and warm winters. The east experiences Continental temperature extremes with frosty, clear winters and often stormy summers. The south enjoys a Mediterranean climate with hot, dry summers and mild winters, punctuated by violent winds.

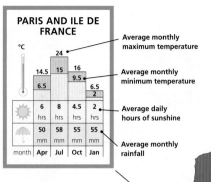

PARIS AND ILE DE FRANCE

°C

	Apr	Jul	Oct	Jan
max °C	14.5	24	16	6.5
min °C	6.5	15	9.5	2
sun	6 hrs	8 hrs	4.5 hrs	2 hrs
rain	50 mm	58 mm	55 mm	55 mm
month	Apr	Jul	Oct	Jan

- Average monthly maximum temperature
- Average monthly minimum temperature
- Average daily hours of sunshine
- Average monthly rainfall

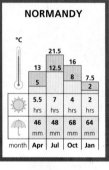

NORMANDY

°C

	Apr	Jul	Oct	Jan
max °C	13	21.5	16	7.5
min °C	5	12.5	8	2
sun	5.5 hrs	7 hrs	4 hrs	2 hrs
rain	46 mm	48 mm	68 mm	64 mm
month	Apr	Jul	Oct	Jan

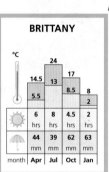

BRITTANY

°C

	Apr	Jul	Oct	Jan
max °C	14.5	24	17	8
min °C	5.5	13	8.5	2
sun	6 hrs	8 hrs	4.5 hrs	2 hrs
rain	44 mm	39 mm	62 mm	63 mm
month	Apr	Jul	Oct	Jan

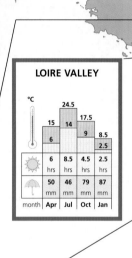

LOIRE VALLEY

°C

	Apr	Jul	Oct	Jan
max °C	15	24.5	17.5	8.5
min °C	6	14	9	2.5
sun	6 hrs	8.5 hrs	4.5 hrs	2.5 hrs
rain	50 mm	46 mm	79 mm	87 mm
month	Apr	Jul	Oct	Jan

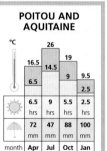

POITOU AND AQUITAINE

°C

	Apr	Jul	Oct	Jan
max °C	16.5	26	19	9.5
min °C	6.5	14.5	9	2.5
sun	6.5 hrs	9 hrs	5.5 hrs	2.5 hrs
rain	72 mm	47 mm	88 mm	100 mm
month	Apr	Jul	Oct	Jan

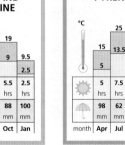

PYRENEES

°C

	Apr	Jul	Oct	Jan
max °C	15	25	19	10
min °C	5	13.5	7.5	0.5
sun	5 hrs	7.5 hrs	5.5 hrs	3.5 hrs
rain	98 mm	62 mm	78 mm	93 mm
month	Apr	Jul	Oct	Jan

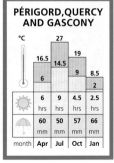

PÉRIGORD, QUERCY AND GASCONY

°C

	Apr	Jul	Oct	Jan
max °C	16.5	27	19	8.5
min °C	6	14.5	9	2
sun	6 hrs	9 hrs	4.5 hrs	2.5 hrs
rain	60 mm	50 mm	57 mm	66 mm
month	Apr	Jul	Oct	Jan

Le Havre

PARIS

Rennes

Tours

Nantes

Bordeaux

Montauban

Biarritz

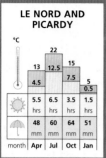

LE NORD AND PICARDY

°C

	22		
13	12.5	15	
4.5		7.5	5
			0.5

☀	5.5 hrs	6.5 hrs	3.5 hrs	1.5 hrs
☂	48 mm	60 mm	64 mm	51 mm
month	Apr	Jul	Oct	Jan

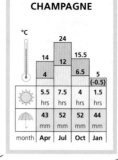

CHAMPAGNE

°C

	24		
14	12	15.5	
4		6.5	5
			(-0.5)

☀	5.5 hrs	7.5 hrs	4 hrs	1.5 hrs
☂	43 mm	52 mm	52 mm	44 mm
month	Apr	Jul	Oct	Jan

ALSACE AND LORRAINE

°C

	25		
14.5	13.5	15	
4.5		6.5	3.5
			(-1.5)

☀	5.5 hrs	7.5 hrs	3 hrs	1.5 hrs
☂	48 mm	57 mm	43 mm	33 mm
month	Apr	Jul	Oct	Jan

BURGUNDY AND FRANCHE-COMTE

°C

	25.5		
14.5	14	15.5	
5		9	4
			(-1)

☀	6 hrs	8.5 hrs	4 hrs	1.5 hrs
☂	52 mm	51 mm	58 mm	59 mm
month	Apr	Jul	Oct	Jan

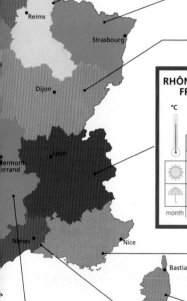

RHÔNE VALLEY AND FRENCH ALPS

°C

	26.5		
15	15	17	
6		8	6
			(-0.5)

☀	6 hrs	9.5 hrs	4.5 hrs	2 hrs
☂	68 mm	61 mm	80 mm	54 mm
month	Apr	Jul	Oct	Jan

PROVENCE AND CÔTE D'AZUR

°C

	26.5		
17	19.5	21	
10		13	12.5
			5

☀	7.5 hrs	11 hrs	6.5 hrs	5 hrs
☂	62 mm	16 mm	108 mm	83 mm
month	Apr	Jul	Oct	Jan

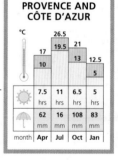

MASSIF CENTRAL

°C

	25.5		
15		17.5	
	13		7
4		7	(-0.5)

☀	5.5 hrs	8.5 hrs	4.5 hrs	2.5 hrs
☂	45 mm	48 mm	51 mm	29 mm
month	Apr	Jul	Oct	Jan

LANGUEDOC-ROUSSILLON

°C

	28.5		
17.5	17	20	
8		10.5	11
			2

☀	7.5 hrs	11 hrs	6 hrs	4.5 hrs
☂	55 mm	20 mm	110 mm	72 mm
month	Apr	Jul	Oct	Jan

CORSICA

°C

	28.5		
17.5	18	21.5	
8.5		12.5	13.5
			5

☀	7 hrs	11 hrs	6.5 hrs	4.5 hrs
☂	66 mm	15 mm	107 mm	62 mm
month	Apr	Jul	Oct	Jan

Map labels: Reims, Strasbourg, Dijon, Lyon, Clermont-Ferrand, Nîmes, Nice, Bastia

THE HISTORY OF FRANCE

The only European country facing both the North Sea and the Mediterranean, France has been subject to a particularly rich variety of cultural influences. Though famous for the rootedness of its peasant population, it has also been a European melting pot, even before the arrival of the Celtic Gauls in the centuries before Christ, through to the Mediterranean immigrations of the 20th century.

Fleur-de-lys, the royal emblem

Roman conquest by Julius Caesar had an enduring impact, but from the 4th and 5th centuries AD, waves of Barbarian invaders destroyed much of the Roman legacy. The Germanic Franks provided political leadership in the following centuries, but when their line died out in the late 10th century, France was socially and politically fragmented.

THE FORMATION OF FRANCE

The Capetian dynasty gradually pieced France together over the Middle Ages, a period of great economic prosperity and cultural vitality. The Black Death and the Hundred Years' War brought setbacks, and the dynasty's power was seriously threatened by the rival Burgundian dukes. France recovered, however, and flourished during the Renaissance, followed by the grandeur of Louis XIV's reign. During the Enlightenment, in the 18th century, French culture and institutions were the envy of Europe.

The Revolution of 1789 ended the absolute monarchy and introduced major social and institutional reforms, many of which were endorsed and consolidated by Napoleon. Yet the Revolution also inaugurated the instability which has remained a hallmark of French politics: since 1789, France has known five republics, two empires and three brands of royal power, plus the Vichy government during World War II.

Modernization in the 19th and 20th centuries proved a slow process. Railways, the military service and radical educational reforms were crucial in forming a sense of French identity among the citizens.

Rivalry with Germany dominated French politics for most of the late 19th and early 20th century. The population losses in World War I were traumatic for France, while during 1940–44 the country was occupied by Germany. Yet since 1945, the two countries have proved the backbone of the developing European Union.

Inlaid marble table top showing the map of France in 1684

◁ *La République*, painted by Charles Landelle in 1848

Prehistoric France

The earliest traces of human life in France date back to around 2 million BC. From around 40,000 BC, *Homo sapiens* lived an itinerant existence as hunters and gatherers. Around 6000 BC, following the end of the Ice Age, a major shift in lifestyle occurred, as people settled down to herd animals and cultivate crops. The advent of metal-working allowed more effective tools and weapons to be developed. The Iron Age is associated particularly with the Celts, who arrived from the east during the first millennium BC. A more complex social hierarchy developed, consisting of warriors, farmers, artisans and druids (Celtic priests).

Bronze Age vase, Brittany

FRANCE IN 8000 BC

☐ *Former coastline*

☐ *Present-day land mass*

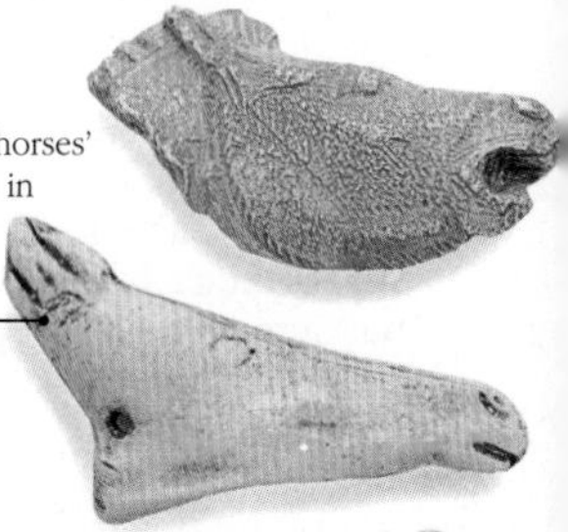

These carvings of horses' heads were found in the Pyrenees and date from around 9000 BC.

Carnac Stone Alignments *(4500–4000 BC)*
The purpose of the extensive networks of megaliths around Carnac (see p278) remains obscure. They possibly served in pagan rituals or as an astronomical calendar.

The mammoth, here carved from animal bone, was a thick-coated giant who died out after the end of the Ice Age.

Cro-Magnon Man
This skull, dating to c.25,000 BC, was discovered at Cro-Magnon in the Dordogne in 1868. In comparison with most of his predecessors, Cro-Magnon Man was tall, robust, and had a large head. He differed only marginally from us.

PREHISTORIC ART

The rich deposits of cave art in France have only been recognized as authentic for just over a century. They include wall paintings and daubings but also various engraved objects. Venus figurines, carved with flint tools, probably had ritual and religious rather than erotic purposes.

TIMELINE

2,000,000 BC Early hominid societies	**30,000** Cro-Magnon Man	*Painting of bulls in Lascaux*	
2,000,000 BC	**30,000**	**25,000**	**20,000**
	400,000 Discovery of fire by *Homo erectus*	**28,000** The first Venus sculptures, possibly representing fertility goddesses	*Primitive stone tool*

Doorway, Roquepertuse
Religion was an important part of Celtic life. The Celts made a cult of severed heads – presumably of their enemies – as seen in this sanctuary doorway dating from the 3rd century BC.

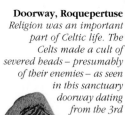

The prehistoric hunter's quarry is here represented by a flock of chamois carved on a piece of bone.

This carved bone, found in Laugerie Basse in the Dordogne, shows a bison chased by a man with a spear.

This highly stylized female figure, a Venus figurine found in southwest France, was carved from mammoth tusk in around 20,000 BC.

WHERE TO SEE PREHISTORIC FRANCE

The Lascaux cave paintings in Périgord *(see p434)* are among the best in the world. Further cave decoration is found around Les Eyzies *(pp434–5)*, at the Vallée des Merveilles near Tendes in the Alpes-Maritimes *(p529)* and in the Grotte du Pech Merle in the Lot Valley *(p438)*. The intriguing menhirs at Filitosa in Corsica *(pp542–3)* are about 4,000 years old.

The Lascaux *cave paintings, dating from 16,000–14,000 BC, include images of bulls and mammoths.*

Copper Axe *(c.2000 BC)*
Copper tools preceded the arrival of the stronger and more malleable bronze alloy. Iron was to prove the toughest and most useful metal of all.

Bronze Armor
Bronze and Iron Age people were highly warlike. The Celtic Gauls were feared even by Romans. Their protective armour, such as this breastplate dating from 750–475 BC, was light but reasonably effective.

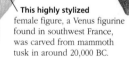

15,000 Hunters live on wandering herds of mammoth, rhinoceros, and reindeer. Art includes the Lascaux caves and Val Camonica/Mont Bego engravings

7000–4500 Neolithic revolution: farming, megaliths, and menhir stone sculptures

600 Greek colony at Marseille. Mediterranean luxury goods exchanged for tin, copper, iron, and slaves. Early urban development

15,000	10,000	5,000

10,000 End of Ice Age. More regions become inhabitable

10,000–6000 Mammoth herds disappear and hunters must rely on animals of the forest, including wild boar and aurochs

1200–700 Arrival of the Celts during the Bronze and Iron Ages

500 Celtic nobles bury their dead with riches such as the Vix treasure *(see p334)*

Celtic helmet

Roman Gaul

The Romans had annexed the southern fringe of France by 125–121 BC. Julius Caesar brought the rest of Gaul under Roman control in the Gallic Wars (58–51 BC). The province of Gaul prospered: it developed good communications, a network of cities crammed with public buildings and leisure facilities such as baths and amphitheatres, while in the countryside large villas were established. By the 3rd century AD, however, barbarian raids from Germany were causing increasing havoc. From the 5th century barbarians began to settle throughout Gaul.

Roman mosaic from Vienne

FRANCE IN 58 BC

☐ *Roman Gaul*

Emperor Augustus, who was considered a living God, was worshipped at this altar.

Roman Dolce Vita

The Romans brought material comfort and luxury, and wine-growing became widespread. This 19th-century painting by Couture conveys a contemporary view of Roman decadence.

Vercingetorix

The Celtic chieftain Vercingetorix was Julius Caesar's greatest military opponent. This bronze statue is at Alise-Sainte-Reine (see p334),the Gauls' final stand in 51 BC.

LA TURBIE

This impressive monument near Monaco was erected in 6 BC by the Roman Senate. It celebrates Augustus's victory over the Alpine tribes in 14–13 BC. Badly pillaged for its stone, restoration only began in the 1920's.

TIMELINE

125–121 BC Roman colonization of Southern Gaul

31 BC Frontiers of the Three Gauls (*Gallia Celtica, Gallia Aquitania* and *Gallia Belgica*) established by Augustus

Augustus

200 BC	100	0	AD 100

58–51 BC Julius Caesar's Gallic Wars result in establishment of Roman Gaul

Julius Caesar

16 BC Maison Carrée built in Nîmes (*see pp496–7*)

52–51 BC Vercingetorix revolt

AD 43 Lugdunum (Lyon) established as capital of the Three Gauls

THE HISTORY OF FRANCE

Dancing Girl
Celtic art continued uninfluenced by Roman naturalistic ideals. This bronze statuette of a young woman dates from the 1st–2nd century AD.

A statue of Augustus was placed at the top of the original monument.

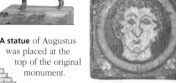

Enamelled Brooch
This decorative Gallo-Roman brooch dates from the second half of the 1st century BC.

WHERE TO SEE GALLO-ROMAN FRANCE

Gallo-Roman remains are to be found all over France, many of them in Provence. In addition to La Turbie *(see p529)* there is the Roman amphitheatre in Arles *(p485)* and the theatre and triumphal arch in Orange *(p502)*. Elsewhere, there are ruins at Autun in Burgundy *(p339)*, the Temple d'Auguste et Livie in Vienne *(p382)*, Les Arènes at Nîmes *(pp496–7)* and fragments of Vesunna in Périgueux *(p434)*.

Les Arènes in Nîmes, *built at the end of the 1st century AD, is still in use today.*

The Claudian Tables
In AD 48, Emperor Claudius persuaded the Senate to allow Gauls full Roman citizenship. The grateful Gauls recorded the event on stone tables found at Lyon.

The 44 tribes subjugated by Augustus are listed on an inscription, with a dedication to the emperor.

Emperor Augustus
Augustus, the first Roman Emperor (27 BC–AD 14), upheld the Pax Romana, an enforced peace which allowed the Gauls to concentrate on culture rather than war.

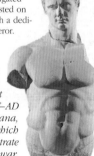

AD 177 First execution of Christian martyrs, Lyon. Sainte Blandine is thrown to the lions, who refuse to harm her

Sainte Blandine

360 Julian, prefect of Gaul, proclaimed Roman Emperor. Lutetia changes name to Paris

200	300	400

275 First Barbarian raids

313 Christianity officially recognized as religion under the rule of Constantine, the first Christian emperor

406 Barbarian invasion from the east. Settlement of the Franks and Germanic tribes

476 Overthrow of the last Roman emperor leads to end of the western Roman Empire

The Monastic Realm

The collapse of the Roman Empire led to a period of instability and invasions. Both the Frankish Merovingian dynasty (486–751) and the Carolingians (751–987) were unable to bring more than spasmodic periods of political calm. Throughout this turbulent period, the Church provided an element of continuity. As centres for Christian scholars and artists, the monasteries helped to restore the values of the ancient world. They also developed farming and viticulture and some became extremely powerful, dominating the country economically as well as spiritually.

9th-century gold chalice

FRANCE IN 751

☐ Carolingian Empire

Charlemagne (742–814)
The greatest of Carolingian rulers, Charlemagne created an empire based on strictly autocratic rule. Powerful and charismatic, he could neither read nor write.

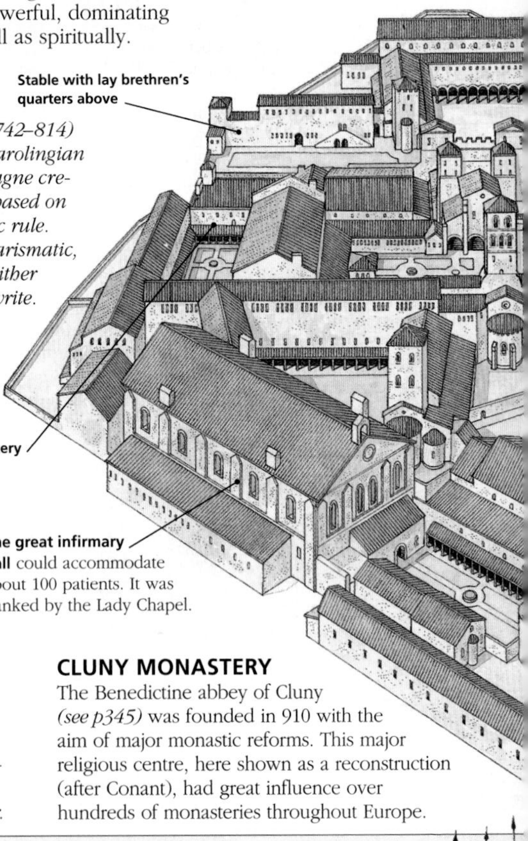

Stable with lay brethren's quarters above

Bakery

The great infirmary hall could accommodate about 100 patients. It was flanked by the Lady Chapel.

Saint Benedict
Saint Benedict established the Benedictine rule: monks were to divide their time between work and prayer.

CLUNY MONASTERY

The Benedictine abbey of Cluny *(see p345)* was founded in 910 with the aim of major monastic reforms. This major religious centre, here shown as a reconstruction (after Conant), had great influence over hundreds of monasteries throughout Europe.

TIMELINE

481 Clovis the Frank becomes first Merovingian king

508 Paris made capital of the Frankish kingdom

c.590 Saint Colombanus introduces Irish monasticism to France

732 Battle of Poitiers: Charles Martel repulses Arab invasion

500	600	700

496 Conversion of Clovis, king of the Franks, to Christianity

629–37 Dagobert I, the last effective ruler of the Merovingian dynasty, brings temporary unity to the Frankish kingdom

Dagobert I

751 Pepin becomes first king of the Carolingian dynasty

Baptism of Clovis
The Frankish chieftain Clovis was the first barbarian ruler to convert to Christianity. He was baptized in Reims in 496.

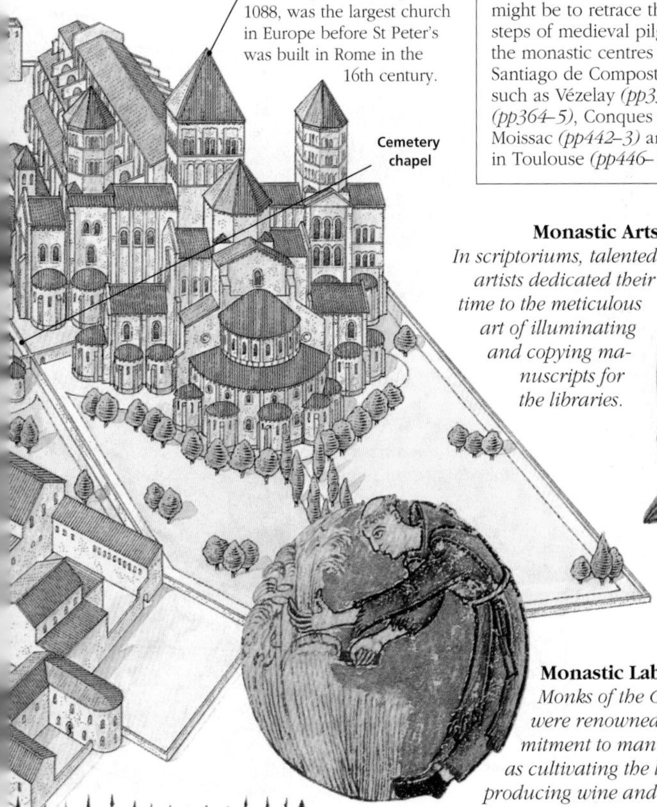

The abbey church, begun in 1088, was the largest church in Europe before St Peter's was built in Rome in the 16th century.

Cemetery chapel

WHERE TO SEE MONASTIC FRANCE

The monastic realm has survived in austere Cistercian abbeys in Burgundy, such as Fontenay (*see pp332–3*). Little remains of Cluny, but some of the superb capitals can still be admired (*p345*). The best way to experience monastic France might be to retrace the steps of medieval pilgrims and visit the monastic centres on the route to Santiago de Compostela (*pp400–01*), such as Vézelay (*pp336–7*), Le Puy (*pp364–5*), Conques (*pp368–9*), Moissac (*pp442–3*) and St-Sernin in Toulouse (*pp446–7*).

Cluny capitals

Monastic Arts
In scriptoriums, talented artists dedicated their time to the meticulous art of illuminating and copying manuscripts for the libraries.

Monastic Labour
Monks of the Cistercian rule were renowned for their commitment to manual labour such as cultivating the land and producing wine and liqueurs.

Carolingian soldiers

1096 First Crusade

1066 Conquest of England by the Normans

987 Hugh Capet, first Capetian ruler

800   **900**   **1000**

843 Treaty of Verdun: division of the Carolingian Empire into three parts including West Francia

1077 Bayeux tapestry

910 Foundation of the Benedictine monastery of Cluny

800 Coronation of Charlemagne as Holy Roman Emperor

William the Conqueror's teering his ship on the Bayeux tapestry

Gothic France

The Gothic style, epitomized by soaring cathedrals *(see pp32–3)*, emerged in the 12th century at a time of growing prosperity and scholarship, crusades and an increasingly dominant monarchy. The rival French and Burgundian courts *(see p343)* became models of fashion and etiquette for all of Europe. *Chansons de gestes* (epic poems) performed by troubadours celebrated the code of chivalry.

Medieval knights in combat

FRANCE IN 1270

☐ *Royal territory*

☐ *Other fiefs*

Ciborium of Alpais

Alpais, a renowned 12th-century goldsmith in Limoges, made this superb ciborium used to hold wafers for the Holy Communion.

Winch to lift up stone sections

Courtly Love

According to the code of chivalry, knights dedicated their service to an ideal but unapproachable lady. Courtesy and romance were introduced in art and music.

The king supervised the building of the cathedral, accompanied by the architect.

Draper's Window
The textile trade benefited from the era of urban prosperity. This stained-glass window in a church in Semur-en-Auxois (see p335) shows wool washers at work.

TIMELINE

c.1100 First edition of the epic poem *Chanson de Roland*

1117 Secret marriage of the scholar Abelard and his student Héloise. Her uncle, canon Filibert, does not approve and forces him to become a monk while she retires as a nun

1154 Angevin Empire created by Anglo-Norman dynasty starting with Henry Plantagenet, count of Anjou and king of England (as Henry II)

1100	1125	1150	1175

1115 Saint Bernard founds the Cistercian abbey at Clairvaux

1120 Rebuilding of the abbey of St-Denis; birth of the Gothic style

King Philip Augustus, who adopted the fleur-de-lys emblem

1180–1223 Reign of Philip Augustus

The Crusades
In an attempt to win back the Holy Land from the Turks, Philip Augustus set out on the Third Crusade (1189) alongside England's Richard the Lion-Heart and Holy Roman Emperor Frederick Barbarossa.

Lacelike sculpture adorned the façades of the Gothic cathedrals.

Stone masons cut stones on site.

ELEANOR OF AQUITAINE
Strong-willed and vivacious Eleanor, duchess of independent Aquitaine, contributed to the conflict between France and England. In 1137 she married the pious Louis VII of France. Returning from a Crusade, Louis found that their marriage had broken down. After the annulment in 1152, Eleanor married Henry of Anjou, taking her duchy with her. Two years later Henry successfully claimed the throne of England. Aquitaine came under English rule and thus the Angevin Empire began.

Eleanor of Aquitaine *and Henry II are buried in Fontevraud (p294).*

Holy Relic
Throughout the Middle Ages most churches could boast at least one saint's relic. The cult of relics brought pilgrims and more riches.

St Bernard *(1090–1153) Key figure of the Cistercian rule and counsellor to the pope, St Bernard preached rigorous simplicity of life.*

THE BUILDING OF A CATHEDRAL
In affluent, mercantile towns, skilled masons constructed towering Gothic cathedrals of revolutionary design, such as Chartres (*see pp308–11*) and Amiens (*pp202–3*). With their improbable height and lightness they were a testimony to both faith and prosperity.

Louis IX on his death bed

1226 Louis IX crowned king

1270 Death of Louis IX at Tunis in the Eighth Crusade

1305 Papacy established in Avignon

1200	1225	1250	1275	1300

1214 Battle of Bouvines. Philip Augustus begins to drive the English out of France

1259 Normandy, Maine, Anjou, and Poitou acquired from England

1285 Philip the Fair crowned

1297 Louis IX is canonized, becoming Saint Louis

The Hundred Years' War

The Hundred Years' War (1337–1453), pitting England against France for control of French land, had devastating effects. The damage of warfare was amplified by frequent famines and the ravages of bubonic plague in the wake of the Black Death in 1348. France came close to being permanently partitioned by the king of England and the duke of Burgundy. In 1429–30 the young Joan of Arc helped rally France's fortunes and within a generation the English had been driven out of France.

Public execution, in Froissart's 14th-century chronicle

FRANCE IN 1429

☐ France

▨ Anglo-Burgundy

Angels with trumpets announce the Last Judgment.

Men of War

One of the reasons men enlisted as soldiers was hope for plunder. Both the French and English armies lived off the land, at the expense of the peasantry.

The elect, springing resurrected from their graves, are ushered into heaven.

The Black Death

The plague of 1348–52 caused 4–5 million deaths, about 25 per cent of the French population. For want of medicines people had to put their faith in prayers and holy processions.

14th-century flame-thrower

TIMELINE

1346 Battle of Crécy: French defeated by English

1328 Philip VI, first Valois monarch

1356 French defeat at Battle of Poitiers

1325	1350	1375

1337 Start of the Hundred Years' War

Plague victims

1348–52 The Black Death

1358 Bourgeois uprising in Paris led by Etienne Marcel. The Jacquerie peasant uprising in Northern France

Medieval Medicine

The state of the heavens was widely held to influence earthly conditions, such as health, and a diagnosis based on the zodiac was considered reliable. The standby cure for all sorts of ailments was blood letting.

English Longbow

The king's troops fought against England, but the individual French duchies supported whichever side seemed more favourable. In the confused battles, English bowmen excelled. Their longbows caused chaos among the hordes of mounted French cavalry.

Christ as Supreme Judge is flanked by angels bearing the instruments of the Passion.

Archangel Michael, resplendent with peacock wings, holds the judgment scales. The weight of sinners outbalances the elect.

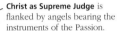

John the Baptist is accompanied by the 12 apostles and the Virgin Mary, dressed in blue.

The damned, with hideously twisted faces, fall into Hell.

THE LAST JUDGMENT

With war, plague and famine as constant visitors, many people feared that the end of the world was nigh. Religious paintings, such as the great 15th-century altarscreen by Rogier van der Weyden in the Hôtel-Dieu in Beaune *(see pp346–7)*, reflected the moral fervour of the time.

Attack on Heresy

The general anxiety spilled over into anti-Semitic pogroms and attacks on alleged heretics, who were burned at the stake.

1415 Battle of Agincourt. French defeat by Henry V of England

1429 Intervention of Joan of Arc: Charles VII crowned king

1453 End of the Hundred Years' War. Only Calais remains in English hands

1400

1425

1450

1411 *Les Très Riches Heures du Duc du Berry* prayer book, by Paul and Jean de Limbourg *(see p204)*

1419 Charles VI of France makes Henry V of England his heir

1431 Joan of Arc burned at stake as witch by the English

Joan of Arc

Renaissance France

As a result of the French invasion of Italy in 1494, the ideals and aesthetic of the Italian Renaissance spread to France, reaching their height during the reign of François I. Known as a true Renaissance prince, he was skilled in letters and art as well as sports and war. He invited Italian artists, such as Leonardo and Cellini, to his court and enjoyed Rabelais' bawdy stories. Another highly influential Italian was Catherine de' Medici (1519–89). Widow of Henri II, she virtually ruled France through her sons, François II, Charles IX and Henri III. She was also one of the major players in the Wars of Religion (1562–93) between Catholics and Protestants, which divided the nobility and tore the country to pieces.

Masked lute-player

FRANCE IN 1527

☐ *Royal territory*
☐ *Other fiefs*

The corner towers are a Gothic feature transformed by Italian lightness of touch into pure decoration.

Galerie François I, Fontainebleau
The artists of the School of Fontaine-bleau blended late Italian Renaissance style with French elements.

Power Behind the Throne
Catherine de' Medici dominated French politics from 1559–89.

AZAY-LE-RIDEAU

One of the loveliest of the Loire châteaux, Azay was begun in 1518 *(see p296)*. Italian influences are visible and it is clear that this is a dwelling meant for pleasure rather than defence.

TIMELINE

1470 First printing presses established in France

Prototype tank by Leonardo da Vinci

1519 Leonardo da Vinci dies in the arms of François I at the French court in Amboise

1536 Calvin's *Institutes of the Christian Religion* leads to a new form of Protestantism

1470	1480	1490	1500	1510	1520	1530

1477 Final defeat of the Dukes of Burgundy, who sought to establish a middle kingdom between France and Germany

1494–1559 France and Austria fight over Italian territories in the Italian Wars

1515 Reign of François I begins

Golden coin showing the fleur-de-lys and the salamander of François I

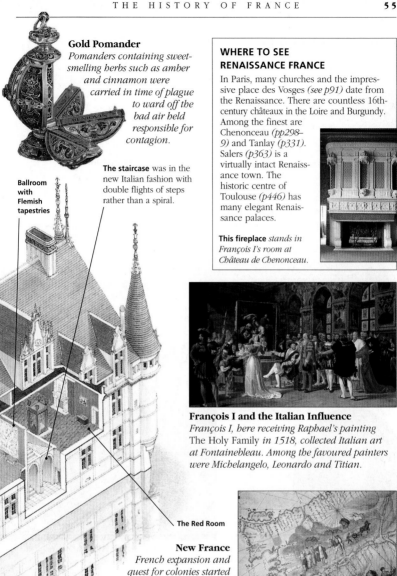

Gold Pomander
Pomanders containing sweet-smelling herbs such as amber and cinnamon were carried in time of plague to ward off the bad air held responsible for contagion.

Ballroom with Flemish tapestries

The staircase was in the new Italian fashion with double flights of steps rather than a spiral.

The Red Room

WHERE TO SEE RENAISSANCE FRANCE

In Paris, many churches and the impressive place des Vosges *(see p91)* date from the Renaissance. There are countless 16th-century châteaux in the Loire and Burgundy. Among the finest are Chenonceau *(pp298–9)* and Tanlay *(p331)*. Salers *(p363)* is a virtually intact Renaissance town. The historic centre of Toulouse *(p446)* has many elegant Renaissance palaces.

This fireplace *stands in François I's room at Château de Chenonceau.*

François I and the Italian Influence
François I, here receiving Raphael's painting The Holy Family *in 1518, collected Italian art at Fontainebleau. Among the favoured painters were Michelangelo, Leonardo and Titian.*

New France
French expansion and quest for colonies started with Cartier's expedition to Canada in 1534 (see p282).

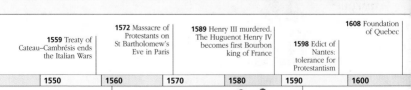

1540	1550	1560	1570	1580	1590	1600

1559 Treaty of Cateau–Cambrésis ends the Italian Wars

1572 Massacre of Protestants on St Bartholomew's Eve in Paris

1589 Henry III murdered. The Huguenot Henry IV becomes first Bourbon king of France

1598 Edict of Nantes: tolerance for Protestantism

1608 Foundation of Quebec

1539 Edict of Villers Cotterets makes French the official language of state

1562 Wars of Religion between Catholics and Protestants start

St Bartholomew's Eve Massacre

1593 Henry IV converts to Catholicism and ends the Wars of Religion

The Grand Siècle

The end of the Religious Wars heralded a period of exceptional French influence and power. The cardinal ministers Richelieu and Mazarin paved the way for Louis XIV's absolute monarchy. Political development was matched by artistic styles of unprecedented brilliance: enormous Baroque edifices, the drama of Molière and Racine, and the music of Lully. Versailles *(see pp174–7)*, built under the supervision of Louis' capable finance minister Colbert, was the glory of Europe, but its cost and Louis XIV's endless wars proved expensive for the French state and led to widespread misery by the end of his reign.

Emblem of the Sun King

FRANCE IN 1661

☐ *Royal territory*

▨ *Avignon (papal enclave)*

Molière *(1622–73)*
Actor-playwright Molière performed many plays for Louis XIV and his court, though some of his satires were banned. After his death, his company became the basis of the French state theatre, the Comédie Française.

Madame (married to Monsieur) as Flora

Monsieur, the king's brother

Madame de Maintenon
In 1684, following the death of his first wife Marie-Thérèse, Louis secretly married his mistress Mme de Maintenon, then aged 49.

THE SUN KING AND HIS FAMILY
Claiming to be monarch by divine right, Louis XIV commanded court painter Jean Nocret to devise this allegorical scene in 1665. Surrounded by his family, the king appears as the sun god Apollo.

TIMELINE

1610–17 Marie de' Medici acts as Regent for Louis XIII

Cardinal Richelieu

1624 Cardinal Richelieu becomes principal minister

1634 Foundation of the literary society Académie Française

1642–3 Death of Louis XIII and Cardinal Richelieu. Accession of Louis XIV with Mazarin as principal minister

1610	1620	1630	1640	1650

1617 Louis XIII accedes at the age of 17

1631 Foundation of *La Gazette*, France's first newspaper

1637 Descartes' *Discourse on Method*

1635 Richelieu actively involves France in the Thirty Years' War

1648–52 The Fronde: French civil wars

Louis XIV's Book of Hours
After a lively and libertine youth, Louis became increasingly religious. His Book of Hours *(1688–93) is in Musée Condé (see p205).*

Royal Wedding
Louis XIII and Anne of Austria were married in 1615. After his death, Anne became regent for the young Louis XIV with Cardinal Mazarin as minister.

Louis XIV as Apollo

Anne of Austria as Cybele

Baroque Figurine
The royal glory was reflected in the arts. This objet d'art *features a Christ in jasper on a pedestal decorated with gilded cherubs and rich enamelling.*

The dauphin (the king's son)

Grande Mademoiselle, the king's cousin, as Diana

Queen Marie-Thérèse as Juno

WHERE TO SEE ARCHITECTURE OF THE GRAND SIÈCLE

Paris boasts many imposing Grand Siècle buildings, such as the Hôtel des Invalides *(see p114)*, the Dôme church *(p115)* and the Palais du Luxembourg *(pp126–7)*, but the Château de Versailles *(pp174–7)* is the ultimate example of the flamboyance of the period. Reminders of this glory include the sumptuous Palais Lascaris in Nice *(p528)* and the Corderie Royale in Rochefort *(p417)*. At the same time, military architect Vauban constructed mighty citadels, such as Neuf-Brisach *(see p226)*.

Versailles' *interior is a typical example of the gilded Baroque style.*

Playwright Jean Racine (1639–99)

1661 Death of Mazarin: Louis XIV becomes his own principal minister

1680 Creation of the theatre Comédie Française

1685 Revocation of the Edict of Nantes of 1598: Protestantism banned

1709 Last great famine in French history

1660	1670	1680	1690	1700

1662 Colbert, finance minister, reforms finances and the economy

1682 Royal court moves to Versailles

1686 Opening of the Café Procope (first coffee house in Paris)

1689 Major wars of Louis XIV begin

17th-century cannon

Enlightenment and Revolution

Plate of Louis XVI's execution

In the 18th century, Enlightenment philosophers such as Voltaire and Rousseau redefined man's place within a framework of natural principles, thus challenging the old aristocratic order. Their essays were read across Europe and even in the American colonies. But although France exported worldly items as well as ideas, the state's increasing debts brought social turmoil, triggering the 1789 Revolution. Under the motto "Liberty, Equality, Fraternity", the new Republic and its reforms had a far-reaching impact on the rest of Europe.

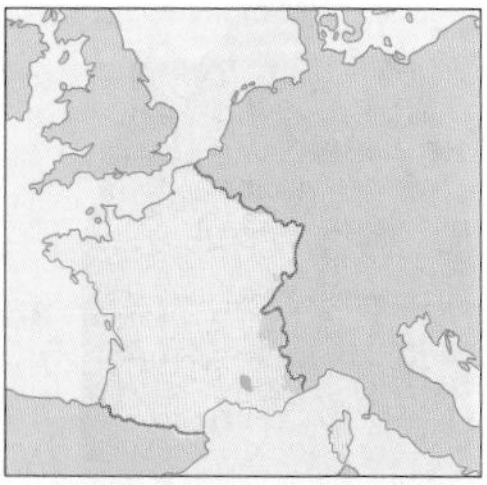

FRANCE IN 1789

☐ *Royal France*

▨ *Avignon (papal enclave)*

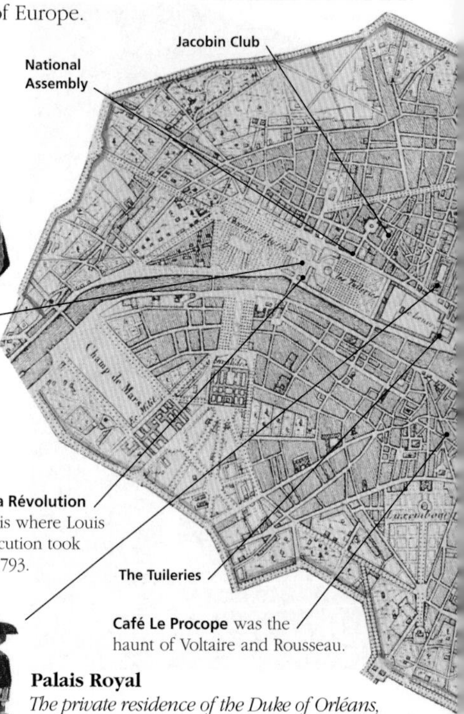

Jacobin Club

National Assembly

Voltaire *(1694–1778)*
Voltaire, master of satire, wrote numerous essays and the novel Candide. *His fierce critiques sometimes forced him into exile abroad.*

The Guillotine
This infamous invention was introduced in 1792 as a humane alternative to other forms of capital punishment, which had usually involved torture.

Place de la Révolution
(see p98) is where Louis XVI's execution took place in 1793.

The Tuileries

Café Le Procope was the haunt of Voltaire and Rousseau.

Palais Royal
The private residence of the Duke of Orléans, the Palais Royal (see p99) became a centre of revolutionary agitation from 1789. It was also the site of several printing presses.

TIMELINE

1715 Death of Louis XIV, accession of Louis XV

1743–64 Mme de Pompadour, Louis XV's favourite, uses her influence to support artists and philosophers during her time at court

1715	1725	1735	1745	1755

Physician's protective costume worn during the plague

1720 Last outbreak of plague in France: population of Marseille decimated

1751 Publication of the first volume of Diderot's *Encyclopaedia*

1756–63 Seven Years' War: France loses Canada and other colonial possessions

Revolutionary Symbols
The motifs of the Revolution such as the blue, white and red of the tricolor even appeared on wallpaper in the 1790s.

WHERE TO SEE 18TH-CENTURY FRANCE

The Palais de l'Elysée, built in 1718 *(see p108)*, is an outstanding example of 18th-century Parisian architecture. Examples across France include the curious Saline Royale in Arc-et-Senans *(p350)*, the Grand Théâtre in Bordeaux *(p422)* the elegant mansions in Condom *(p440)* and the merchants' houses in Ciboure *(p453)*. The Château de Laàs in Sauveterre de Béarn is a feast of 18th-century art and furniture *(p458)*.

The Grand Théâtre *in Bordeaux is an excellent example of elegant 18th-century architecture.*

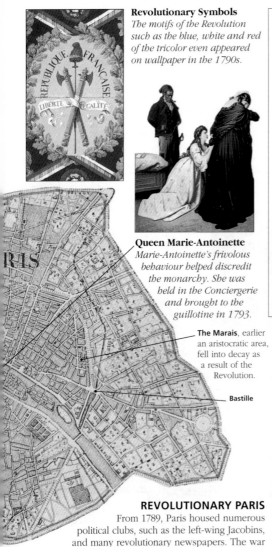

Queen Marie-Antoinette
Marie-Antoinette's frivolous behaviour helped discredit the monarchy. She was held in the Conciergerie and brought to the guillotine in 1793.

The Marais, earlier an aristocratic area, fell into decay as a result of the Revolution.

Bastille

REVOLUTIONARY PARIS
From 1789, Paris housed numerous political clubs, such as the left-wing Jacobins, and many revolutionary newspapers. The war tune *La Marseillaise,* introduced by volunteers from the south, was soon heard everywhere.

Revolutionary Calendar
A new calendar was introduced, the months named after seasonal events. This engraving shows Messidor, the month of harvest.

1768 Annexation of Corsica

1789 Storming of the Bastille, and establishment of constitutional monarchy: abolition of feudalism

1783 First balloon ascent, by the Montgolfier brothers

Model of the Bastille

1765	1775	1785	1795

1774 Accession of Louis XVI

Electors' card for the Convention of 1792

1794 Overthrow of Robespierre and end of the Terror

1762 Rousseau's *Emile* and the *Social Contract*

1778–83 France aids the 13 colonies in the War of American Independence

1792 Overthrow of Louis XVI: establishment of First Republic

Napoleonic France

Two generations of Napoleons dominated France from 1800 to 1870. Napoleon Bonaparte took the title of Emperor Napoleon I. He extended his empire throughout most of western Europe, placing his brothers and sisters on the thrones of conquered countries. Defeated in 1814 and replaced by the restored Bourbon dynasty, followed by the 1830 Revolution and the so-called July Monarchy, the Napoleonic clan made a comeback after 1848. Napoleon I's nephew, Louis Napoleon, became President of the Second Republic, then made himself emperor as Napoleon III. During his reign Paris was modernized and the industrial transformation of France began.

Légion d'Honneur

EUROPE IN 1812

☐ *Napoleonic rule*

◼ *Dependent states*

Musée du Louvre
The museum had opened in 1792, but it flourished during Napoleon's reign. He took a personal interest in both acquisitions and organization.

Napoleon, as First Consul, is crowned by Chronos, the God of Time.

The Laurel, crown of the Roman emperors

The revolutionary tricolor flag was kept throughout the empire.

Imperial Insignia
Napoleon I created a new titled aristocracy, who were allowed coats of arms. Only his, however, was permitted a crown. The eagle symbol was adopted in 1800, an evocation of Imperial Rome.

Légion d'Honneur medal

TIMELINE

1800 Establishment of the Bank of France

1804 Napoleon crowned as Emperor. Napoleonic Civil Code established

Josephine's bed at Malmaison

1809 Josephine and Napoleon divorce. She retains Château Malmaison *(see p173)*

1814 Defeat of Napoleon by the Allies (England, Russia, Austria and Prussia). Napoleon exiled to Elba

1800	1810	1820

1802 Treaty of Amiens brings temporary peace to Europe

1802 Establishment of the Légion d'Honneur

1803 Resumption of wars to create the Napoleonic Empire

1806 Arc de Triomphe commissioned

1815 The "Hundred Days": Napoleon returns from Elba, is defeated at Waterloo and exiled to St Helena

July Revolution
Three days of street-fighting in July 1830 ended unpopular Bourbon rule.

The Napoleons
This imaginary group portrait depicts Napoleon I (seated), his son "Napoleon II" – who never ruled (right) – Napoleon's nephew Louis Napoleon (Napoleon III) and the latter's infant son.

The Civil Code, created by Napoleon, is here shown as a tablet.

Napoleon on Campaign
A dashing general in the late 1790s, Napoleon remained a remarkable military commander throughout his reign.

EMPIRE FASHION

Greek and Roman ideals were evident in architecture, furniture, design, and fashion. Women wore light, Classical tunics, the most daring with one shoulder or more bare. David and Gérard were the fashionable portraitists, while Delacroix and Géricault created many Romantic masterpieces.

Madame Récamier *held a popular salon and was renowned for her beauty and wit. David painted her in 1800.*

NAPOLEONIC GLORY

Though professing himself a true revolutionary, Napoleon developed a taste for imperial pomp. However, he also achieved some long-lasting reforms such as the Civil Code, the new school system and the Bank of France.

1832 Cholera epidemics begin	**1851** Coup d'état by Louis Napoleon	**1852** Louis Napoleon crowned as Emperor Napoleon III	
1838 Daguerre experiments with photography	**1848** Revolution of 1848: end of July Monarchy and establishment of the Second Republic		
1830	**1840**	**1850**	**1860**
1830 Revolution of 1830: Bourbon Charles X replaced by the July Monarchy of King Louis-Philippe	**1840** Large-scale railway building	**1853** Modernization of Paris by Haussmann	**1859–60** Annexation of Nice and Savoy
	Train on the Paris – St-Germain line	**1857** Baudelaire (*Les Fleurs du Mal*) and Flaubert (*Mme Bovary*) prosecuted for public immorality	

The Belle Epoque

The decades before World War I became the *Belle Epoque* for the French, remembered as a golden era forever past. Nevertheless this was a politically turbulent time, with working-class militancy, organized socialist movements, and the Dreyfus Affair polarizing the country between Left and anti-semitic Right. New inventions such as electricity and vaccination against disease made life easier at all social levels. The cultural scene thrived and took new forms with Impressionism and Art Nouveau, the realist novels of Gustave Flaubert and Emile Zola, cabaret and cancan and, in 1895, the birth of the cinema.

Art Nouveau vase by Lalique

FRANCE IN 1871

☐ *Under Third Republic*

▨ *Alsace and Lorraine*

Universal Exhibition
The 1889 Paris exhibition was attended by 3.2 million people. Engineer Eiffel's breathtaking iron structure dominated the exhibition and caused great controversy at the time.

Statue of Apollo by Aimé Millet

Stage

Copper-green roofed cupola

Backstage area

Peugeot Car *(1899)*
The car and bicycle brought new freedom, becoming a part of people's leisure time. Peugeot, Renault and Citroën were all founded before World War I.

The auditorium in gold and purple seated over 2,000 guests.

TIMELINE

Woman on the barricades in 1871

1869 Opening of the Suez Canal, built by Ferdinand de Lesseps

1871 The Paris Commune leads to the Third Republic

1880s Scramble for colonies in Africa and Asia begins

1889 Universal Exhibition in Paris; Eiffel Tower built

1865	1870	1875	1880	1885	1890

1870–71 Franco-Prussian War: defeat and overthrow of Napoleon III; France cedes Alsace and Lorraine to Germany

1874 Impressionist movement begins

1881–6 Reforms in education by Jules Ferry

1885 Pasteur produces vaccine for rabies, the first tested on a human

1890 Peugeot constructs one of the earliest automobiles

Poster Art
The poster was revolutionized by Art Nouveau, with designs by Alphonse Mucha particularly popular. This one from 1897 is for beer, the beverage of the lost Alsace and Lorraine, which became a "patriotic" drink.

WHERE TO SEE THE BELLE EPOQUE
Belle Epoque buildings include the Negresco Hotel, Nice *(see p526)*, the Grand Casino in Monte-Carlo *(p530)* and the Palais Hotel in Biarritz *(p452)*. The Musée d'Orsay in Paris *(pp120–21)* exhibits Art Nouveau objects and furniture.

Staircase at the Opera
The grand staircase had coloured marble columns and a frescoed ceiling. As this painting by Beroud from 1887 shows, it soon became a showcase for high society.

Guimard's *Metro entrance is a typical example of the elegant, swirling lines of Art Nouveau.*

Emperor's pavilion

Grand Foyer with balconies and lavishly decorated ceiling

Grand staircase

OPERA NATIONAL GARNIER
Founded by Napoleon III in 1862, the new opera was opened to great public acclaim in 1875 and became a focus of Belle Epoque social life. Designed by Charles Garnier, its extravagant exterior was matched by its sumptuous interior decor.

The Divine Sarah
Actress Sarah Bernhardt (1844–1923) worked in all theatrical genres, dominating the Paris stage.

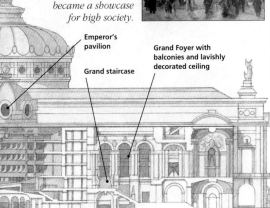

1895 First public cinema by the Lumière brothers

Caricature of Zola

1894–1906 The alleged treason of Dreyfus sparks the Dreyfus Affair, involving the author Zola among others

1909 Blériot flies the Channel

1918 Armistice ends the war

1917 Mutinies in the army suppressed by Pétain

1916 Battle of Verdun

1895	1900	1905	1910	1915

1905 Official separation of church and state

1913 Publication of Proust's first volume of *Remembrance of Things Past*

1898 Marie and Pierre Curie discover radium

1914 World War I breaks out

French recruit, 1916

1919 Treaty of Versailles

Avant-Garde France

Despite the devastation wrought by two world wars, France retained its international renown as a centre for the avant garde. Paris in particular was a magnet for experimental writers, artists and musicians. The cafés were full of American authors and jazz musicians, French surrealists and film makers. The French Riviera also attracted colonies of artists and writers, from Matisse and Picasso to Hemingway and Scott Fitzgerald, along with the wealthy industrialists and aristocrats arriving in automobiles or the famous Train Bleu. And from 1936 paid holidays meant that the working classes could also enjoy the new fashion for sunbathing.

FRANCE IN 1919

☐ *French territory*

African Gods of Creation

Art Deco 1925
The International Exhibition in Paris in 1925 launched the Art Deco style: geometrical shapes and utilitarian designs, adapted for mass-production.

Dancers in heavy cardboard costumes

The Jazz Age
Paris welcomed American jazz musicians, such as Sidney Bechet in 1925 and Dizzy Gillespie (left), co-founder of Bebop in the 1940s.

Citroën Goddess *(1956)*
This elegant model became an icon of the new French consumerism evident in the 1950s and '60s.

The costumes and scenery by the Cubist Léger were striking and made to look partly mechanical.

TIMELINE

Air France aircraft, 1937

1920 French Communist Party founded. Publication of Tristan Tzara's Dadaist Manifesto

1928 Premiere of *Un Chien Andalou* by Luis Buñuel and Salvador Dalí

1933 Air France begins operation

1937 Premiere of *La Grande Illusion* by Jean Renoir

1920	1930

1924 Olympic Games in Paris. André Breton publishes the *Surrealist Manifesto*

Detail of poster for the 1924 Olympics

1929–39 The Depression

1936–38 The "Popular Front": radical social programme introduced, including paid holidays

1938 Munich Conference: height of appeasement

Coco Chanel (1883–1971)
Chanel, here photographed by Man Ray, revolutionized fashion in the 1920s with her elegant but comfortable clothes.

Par Avion
France pioneered the use of airmail, starting in 1927.

First Man and Woman

WORLD WAR II

Following the collapse of the Third Republic in 1940, Paris and the north and west parts of France were occupied by the Germans until the Liberation in 1944. Southeast France formed the collaborationist Vichy state, led by Marshal Pétain and Pierre Laval. Meanwhile, the Free French movement was led by Charles de Gaulle, with Jean Moulin coordinating the operations of the many different Resistance factions.

German soldiers *liked to pose in front of the Eiffel Tower during the occupation of Paris.*

LA CREATION DU MONDE (1923)
Artistic experimentation thrived in the early 20th century. *La Création du Monde* by Les Ballets Suédois had costumes by Léger and music by Milhaud. Diaghilev's Ballets Russes also competed for avant-garde artists like Picabia, Cocteau, Satie and Sonia Delaunay.

The African theme was based on text by Blaise Cendrars.

Josephine Baker (1906–75)
The music hall flourished in the 1920s with Mistinguett and Josephine Baker as its undisputed queens.

1940		1950	
1940 German offensive: the Fall of France. Vichy government led by Pétain	**1949** Establishment of NATO. Founding of the Council of Europe		**1958** 5th Republic begins under President de Gaulle
1942 The whole of France controlled by Germany		**1956** Late in her career, Edith Piaf crowns her success at Carnegie Hall, New York	
1944 D-Day: Allied landings in Normandy (June). Liberation of Paris (August)	**1946** Sartre establishes *Les Temps Modernes.* First Cannes Film Festival	**1954** France withdraws from Indo-China after Battle of Dien Bien Phu. Start of Algerian insurrection	
1939 Declaration of World War II	**1945** End of the war. Votes for women		

Modern France

After the 1950s, the traditional foundations of French society changed: the number of peasant farmers plummeted, old industries decayed, jobs in the service sector and high-technology industries grew dramatically, and the French came to enjoy the benefits of mass culture and widespread consumerism. High prestige projects, such as Concorde, TGV, La Défense and the Pompidou Centre, brought international acclaim. Efforts for European integration and the inauguration of the Channel Tunnel aim towards closer relations with France's neighbours.

Lemon squeezer by Philippe Starck

FRANCE TODAY

☐ *France*

▨ *European Union*

Pompidou Centre *(1977)*
The Pompidou Centre's controversial building changed the aspect of the historic quarter of Beaubourg. A major arts centre, it has revitalized the formerly rundown area (see pp92–3).

New Wave Film
Directors like Godard and Truffaut launched a refreshing, personal style of films, such as Jules et Jim *(1961).*

La Grande Arche was opened in 1989 to commemorate the bicentenary of the Revolution.

Shopping centre

LA DÉFENSE
The huge modernist business centre at La Défense *(see p130)*, on the edge of Paris, was developed in the 1960s and has become a prime site for the headquarters of major multinational companies.

TIMELINE

1960 First French atomic bomb. Decolonization of black Africa	**1963** First French nuclear power station	**1968** May demonstrations	**1973** Extension of the Common Market (EU) from six to nine states	**1980** Giverny, Monet's garden, opens to the public *(see p266)*
	1966 France leaves NATO	**1969** Pompidou replaces de Gaulle as president	**1974** Giscard d'Estaing elected president	
1960		**1970**		**1980**
1962 Evian agreements lead to Algerian independence	**1965** First French satellite	**1970** Charles de Gaulle dies	**1976** Concorde's first commercial flight	**1981** Mitterrand becomes president and heads Socialist governments 1981–6
	1967 Common Agricultural Policy, subsidizing Europe's farmers			

1977 Jacques Chirac first mayor of Paris since 1871. Opening of the Pompidou Centre

EU Flag
France has been one of the leading forces in the European Union ever since the move toward closer European collaboration began in the 1950s.

TGV
The TGV (Train à Grande Vitesse) is one of the world's fastest trains (see pp682–3). It typifies the French government's commitment to high technology and improved communications.

The Fiat Tower is one of Europe's tallest towers, at a height of 178 m (584 ft).

Fashion by Lacroix
Despite less demand for haute couture, Paris is still a major fashion centre. The designs shown on the catwalk, here by Christian Lacroix, remain proof of the world-renowned skills of French designers.

MAY 1968

The events of May 1968 began as a political revolt by left-wing students against the Establishment and had a profound influence on French society. Around 9 million workers, and leading intellectuals like Jean-Paul Sartre, joined the rebellion, demanding better pay, better study conditions and the overhaul of traditional values and institutions.

Student riots *starting in Nanterre, just outside Paris, sparked widespread rioting and industrial unrest in France.*

Palais de la Défense was built first and houses the centre for industry.

François Mitterrand

1987 Mitterrand and Thatcher sign agreement for Channel Tunnel. Trial in Lyon of ex-SS Officer Klaus Barbie

1994 Channel Tunnel opens

2002 National Front defeat Socialists in 1st round of presidential campaign. France rallies to re-elect Jacques Chirac to save the day

1990 | **2000** | **2010**

1991 Edith Cresson is first woman prime minister

1989 Bicentennial celebration of the French Revolution

2002 Euro replaces franc as legal tender

1996 France mourns Mitterrand, who dies after a long illness

2007 Centre-right Nicolas Sarkozy elected president

2005 Prince Rainier III of Monaco dies and is succeeded by his only son, Prince Albert II

Kings and Emperors of France

Following the break-up of the Roman Empire, the Frankish king Clovis consolidated the Merovingian dynasty. It was followed by the Carolingians, and from the 10th century by Capetian rulers. The Capetians established royal power, which passed to the Valois branch in the 14th century, and then to the Bourbons in the late 16th century, following the Wars of Religion. The Revolution of 1789 seemed to end the Bourbon dynasty, but it made a brief come-back in 1814–30. The 19th century was dominated by the Bonapartes, Napoleon I and Napoleon III. Since the overthrow of Napoleon III in 1870, France has been a republic.

768–814 Charlemagne

743–751 Childéric III

716–721 Chilpéric II

695–711 Childebert II

566–584 Chilpéric I

558–562 Clothaire I

447–458 Merovich

458–482 Childéric I

674–691 Thierri III

655–668 Clothaire III

628–637 Dagobert I

954–986 Lothaire

898–929 Charles III, the Simple

884–888 Charles II, the Fat

879–882 Louis III

840–877 Charles I, the Bald

1137–80 Louis VII

987–996 Hugh Capet

1031–60 Henri I

1060–1108 Philippe I

400	500	600	700	800	900	1000	110
MEROVINGIAN DYNASTY				CAROLINGIAN DYNASTY		CAPETIAN DYNAST	
400	500	600	700	800	900	1000	110

751–768 Pépin the Short

721–737 Thierri IV

711–716 Dagobert III

691–695 Clovis III

668–674 Childéric II

637–655 Clovis II

584–628 Clothaire II

562–566 Caribert

511–558 Childebert I

996–1031 Robert II, the Pious

986–987 Louis V

936–954 Louis IV, the Foreigner

888–898 Odo, Count of Paris

882–884 Carloman

877–879 Louis II, the Stammerer

814–840 Louis I, the Pious

482–511 Clovis I

1108–37 Louis VI, the Fat

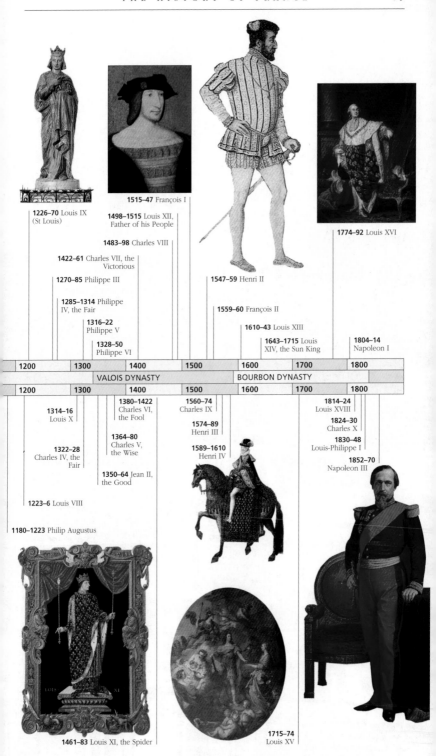

1226–70 Louis IX (St Louis)

1515–47 François I

1498–1515 Louis XII, Father of his People

1483–98 Charles VIII

1422–61 Charles VII, the Victorious

1270–85 Philippe III

1285–1314 Philippe IV, the Fair

1316–22 Philippe V

1328–50 Philippe VI

1547–59 Henri II

1559–60 François II

1610–43 Louis XIII

1643–1715 Louis XIV, the Sun King

1774–92 Louis XVI

1804–14 Napoleon I

| 1200 | 1300 | 1400 | 1500 | 1600 | 1700 | 1800 |

VALOIS DYNASTY   BOURBON DYNASTY

| 1200 | 1300 | 1400 | 1500 | 1600 | 1700 | 1800 |

1314–16 Louis X

1380–1422 Charles VI, the Fool

1560–74 Charles IX

1574–89 Henri III

1589–1610 Henri IV

1364–80 Charles V, the Wise

1322–28 Charles IV, the Fair

1350–64 Jean II, the Good

1223–6 Louis VIII

1180–1223 Philip Augustus

1814–24 Louis XVIII

1824–30 Charles X

1830–48 Louis-Philippe I

1852–70 Napoleon III

1461–83 Louis XI, the Spider

1715–74 Louis XV

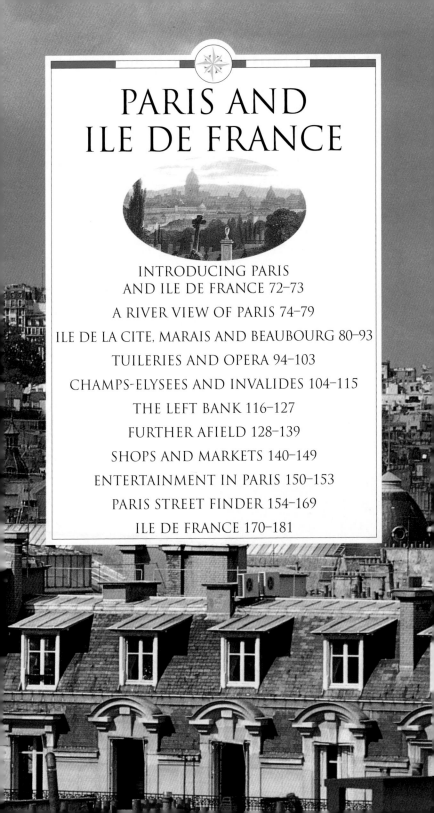

PARIS AND
ILE DE FRANCE

Introducing Paris and Ile de France

The French capital is rich in museums, art galleries and monuments. The Louvre, Eiffel Tower and Pompidou Centre are among the most popular sights. Surrounding Paris, the Ile de France takes in 12,000 sq km (4,600 sq miles) of busy suburbs and commuter towns punctuated by châteaux, the most celebrated being Versailles. Further out, suburbia gives way to farmland, forests and the magnificent palace of Fontainebleau.

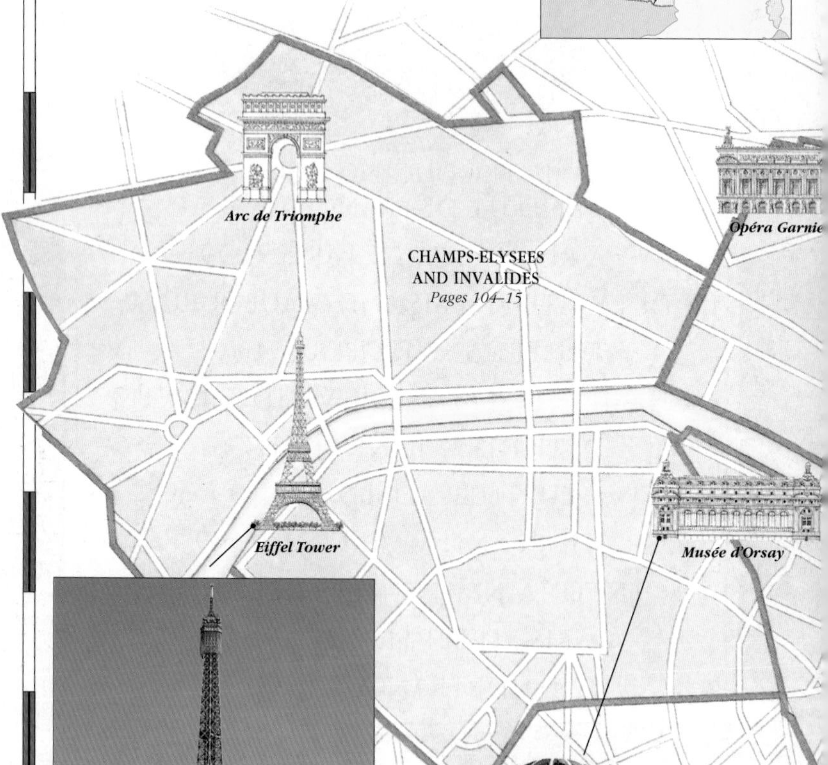

Arc de Triomphe

Opéra Garnier

CHAMPS-ELYSEES AND INVALIDES
Pages 104–15

Eiffel Tower

Musée d'Orsay

The Eiffel Tower, *designed for the Universal Exhibition of 1889, scandalized contemporary critics but is now the capital's most famous landmark (see p113).*

The Musée d'Orsay, *opened in 1986, was created from a late 19th-century railway terminus (see pp120–1). Its magnificent collection of 19th- and early 20th-century art (notably Impressionist art) includes Jean-Baptiste Carpeaux's Four Quarters of the World (1867–72).*

◁ **Rooftop view of Sacré-Coeur and the Butte Montmartre**

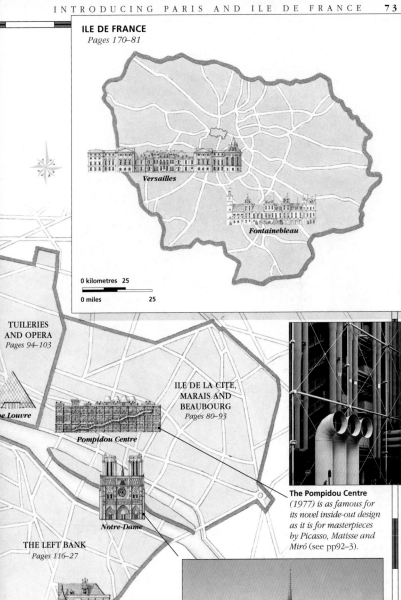

ILE DE FRANCE
Pages 170–81

Versailles

Fontainebleau

0 kilometres   25

0 miles   25

TUILERIES
AND OPERA
Pages 94–103

e Louvre

Pompidou Centre

ILE DE LA CITÉ,
MARAIS AND
BEAUBOURG
Pages 80–93

Notre-Dame

THE LEFT BANK
Pages 116–27

Musée de Cluny

0 kilometres   1

0 miles   0.5

The Pompidou Centre
*(1977) is as famous for
its novel inside-out design
as it is for masterpieces
by Picasso, Matisse and
Miró (see pp92–3).*

Notre-Dame, *a stunning example of Gothic architecture begun in 1163, took two centuries and armies
of medieval workers to complete (see pp86–7). Architect
Viollet-le-Duc designed the spire in the 19th century.*

A RIVER VIEW
OF PARIS

**Sculpture on the
Pont Alexandre III**

The remarkable French music-hall star Mistinguett described the Seine as a "pretty blonde with laughing eyes". The river most certainly has a beguiling quality, but the relationship that exists between it and the city of Paris is far more than one of flirtation.

No other European city defines itself by its river in the same way as Paris. The Seine is the essential point of reference to the city: distances are measured from it, street numbers determined by it, and it divides the capital into two distinct areas, the Right Bank on the north side of the river and the Left Bank on the south side. These are as well-defined as any of the official boundaries. The city is also divided historically: the east is linked to the city's ancient roots and the west to the 19th–20th centuries.

Practically every building of note in Paris is either along the river bank or within a stone's throw of it. The quays are lined by fine bourgeois apartments, magnificent townhouses, world-renowned museums and striking monuments.

Above all, the river is very much alive. For centuries fleets of small boats used it, but motorized land traffic stifled this once-bustling scene. Today, the river is busy with commercial barges and massive *bâteaux mouches* pleasure boats carrying sightseers up and down the river.

The Latin Quarter Quayside is on the left bank of the Seine. Associated with institutes of learning since the Middle Ages, it acquired its name from the early Latin-speaking students.

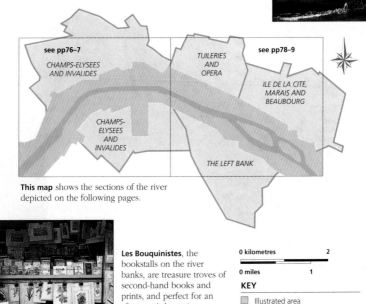

see pp76–7

CHAMPS-ELYSEES
AND INVALIDES

TUILERIES
AND
OPERA

see pp78–9

ILE DE LA CITE,
MARAIS AND
BEAUBOURG

CHAMPS-
ELYSEES
AND
INVALIDES

THE LEFT BANK

This map shows the sections of the river depicted on the following pages.

Les Bouquinistes, the bookstalls on the river banks, are treasure troves of second-hand books and prints, and perfect for an afternoon's browsing.

0 kilometres   2

0 miles   1

KEY

☐ Illustrated area

◁ **Point Alexandre III, encrusted with exuberant statuary**

From Pont de Grenelle to Pont de la Concorde

The grand monuments along this stretch of the river are remnants of the Napoleonic era and the Industrial Revolution. The elegance of the Eiffel Tower, the Petit Palais and the Grand Palais is matched by more recent buildings, such as the Palais de Chaillot and the skyscrapers on the Left Bank.

Palais de Chaillot
Built for the 1937 Exhibition, the spectacular colonnaded wings house several museums, a theatre and a cinema (p110).

The Palais de Tokyo
Bourdelle's statues adorn the façades *(p110)*.

**Bateaux Parisiens
Tour Eiffel
Vedettes de Paris
Ile de France**

Trocadéro Ⓜ

**Passerelle
Debilly**

**The Pont
Bir-Hakeim** has a dynamic statue by Wederkinch rising at its north end.

**Pont
d'Iéna**

Maison de Radio France
is an imposing circular building, designed in 1960, which houses studios as well as a radio museum.

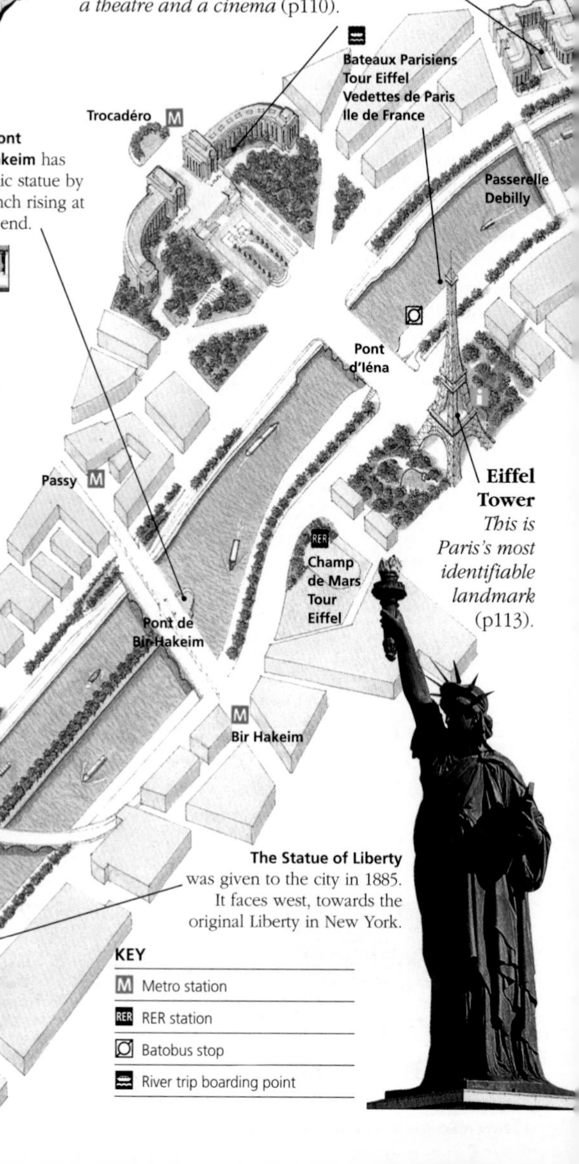

Passy Ⓜ

**Eiffel
Tower**
This is Paris's most identifiable landmark (p113).

RER **Champ
de Mars
Tour
Eiffel**

**Pont de
Bir-Hakeim**

Ⓜ
Bir Hakeim

RER **Prés. Kennedy
Radio France**

The Statue of Liberty
was given to the city in 1885. It faces west, towards the original Liberty in New York.

Pont de Grenelle

KEY

Ⓜ	Metro station
RER	RER station
Ⓞ	Batobus stop
☰	River trip boarding point

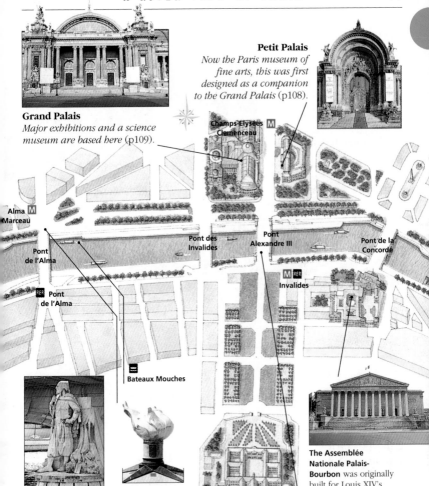

Grand Palais
Major exhibitions and a science museum are based here (p109).

Petit Palais
Now the Paris museum of fine arts, this was first designed as a companion to the Grand Palais (p108).

Champs-Élysées Clemenceau Ⓜ

Alma Ⓜ
Marceau

Pont de l'Alma

Pont des Invalides

Pont Alexandre III

Pont de la Concorde

Invalides Ⓜ RER

RER Pont de l'Alma

Bateaux Mouches

The Zouave, a statue on the central pier, is a useful gauge for checking flood levels.

The Liberty Flame is a memorial to the fighters of the French Resistance during World War II.

The Assemblée Nationale Palais-Bourbon was originally built for Louis XIV's daughter. It has accommodated the lower house of the French Parliament since 1830.

Dôme Church
The majestic gilded dome (p115) is here seen from Pont Alexandre III. Napoleon's tomb is installed in the crypt.

Pont Alexandre III
Flamboyant statuary decorates Paris's most ornate bridge (p109).

From Pont de la Concorde to Pont de Sully

The historic heart of Paris lies on the banks and islands of the east river. At its centre is the Ile de la Cité, a natural stepping stone across the Seine and the cultural core of medieval Paris. Today it is still vital to Parisian life.

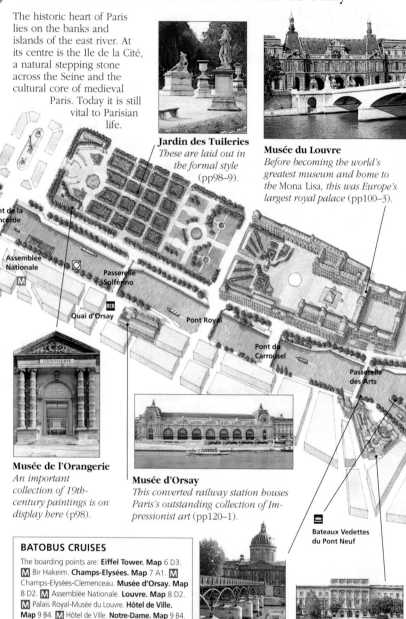

Jardin des Tuileries
These are laid out in the formal style (pp98–9).

Musée du Louvre
Before becoming the world's greatest museum and home to the Mona Lisa, *this was Europe's largest royal palace* (pp100–3).

Pont de la Concorde

Assemblée Nationale M

Passerelle Solférino

Quai d'Orsay RER

Pont Royal

Pont du Carrousel

Passerelle des Arts

Musée de l'Orangerie
An important collection of 19th-century paintings is on display here (p98).

Musée d'Orsay
This converted railway station houses Paris's outstanding collection of Impressionist art (pp120–1).

Bateaux Vedettes du Pont Neuf

BATOBUS CRUISES

The boarding points are: **Eiffel Tower. Map** 6 D3. M Bir Hakeim. **Champs-Elysées. Map** 7 A1. M Champs-Elysées-Clemenceau. **Musée d'Orsay. Map** 8 D2. M Assemblée Nationale. **Louvre. Map** 8 D2. M Palais Royal-Musée du Louvre. **Hôtel de Ville. Map** 9 B4. M Hôtel de Ville. **Notre-Dame. Map** 9 B4. M St-Michel. **St-Germain-des-Prés. Map** 8 E3. M St-Germain des Prés. **Jardin des Plantes. Map** 13 C1. M Jussieu. *Departures mid-Nov–mid-Mar: 10:30am–4:30pm daily (5pm mid-Dec–early Jan); mid-Mar–mid-Nov: 10am–7pm (9:30pm Jun–Aug); every 20 min.* www.batobus.com

Passerelle des Arts This steel reconstruction of Paris's first cast-iron bridge (1804) was inaugurated in 1984.

Hôtel des Monnaies, the Mint, was built in 1778, and has an extensive coin and medallion collection in its old milling halls.

For hotels and restaurants in this region see pp550–5 and pp600–6

HOW TO TAKE A SEINE CRUISE

Bateaux Vedettes Pont Neuf Seine Cruise
The boarding point is:
Square du Vert-Galant (Pont Neuf). **Map** 8 F3.
Tel 01 46 33 98 38.
Ⓜ *Pont Neuf.* RER *Châtelet/St-Michel.* 🚌 27, 58, 67, 70, 72, 74, 75. **Departures** Mar–Oct: 10am, 11:15am, noon, 1:30–10:30pm (every 30 min) daily; Nov–Feb: 10:30am, 11:15am, noon, 2–6:30pm (every 45 min), 8pm, 10pm Mon–Thu; 10:30am, 11:15am, noon, 2–6:30pm, 8pm, 9–10:30pm (every 30 min) Fri–Sun. **Duration** 1 hr. Snacks available on board. **www.vedettesdupontneuf.fr**

Bateaux Mouches Seine Cruise
The boarding point is:
Pont de l'Alma. Map 6 F1.
Tel 01 42 25 96 10.
Ⓜ *Alma-Marceau.* RER *Pont de l'Alma.* 🚌 28, 42, 63, 72, 80, 92. **Departures** Apr–Sep: 10am–11pm daily (every 30 min); Oct–Mar: 11am–9pm daily (every 45 min). **Duration** 1hr 15 min. **Lunch cruise** 1pm daily (boarding 12:15pm). **Dinner cruise** Mar–Nov: boarding 7:30–8:30pm daily. **Duration** 2hr 15 min. Jacket and tie. The largest cruise boats, with a capacity of between 600 and 1,400 passengers.

Vedettes de Paris Ile de France Seine Cruise
Main boarding point is:
Pont d'Iéna. Map 6 D2.
Tel 01 44 18 19 50.
Ⓜ *Trocadéro, Bir Hakeim.* RER *Champ-de-Mars– Tour Eiffel.* 🚌 22, 30, 32, 42, 44, 63, 69, 72, 82, 87. **Departures** 10am–10pm daily (11am–6pm Nov–Feb, until 9pm Sat) (every 30 min). **Duration** 1hr. **Port cruise** 3pm. An industrial view of the river; depart Port de la Rapée (rive droite). **Duration** 1hr 30 min. Relatively small, glass-walled boats. **www.vedettesdeparis.com**

Bateaux Parisiens Tour Eiffel Seine Cruise
The boarding point is:
Pont d'Iéna. Map 6 D2.
Tel 08 25 01 01 01.
Ⓜ *Trocadéro, Bir Hakeim.* RER *Champ-de-Mars–Tour Eiffel.* 🚌 42, 82. **Departures** Apr–Sep: 10am–11pm daily (every 30 min). **Lunch cruise** 12:15pm daily. **Duration** 2hr 15 min. **Dinner cruise** boarding 7–8:15pm daily. **Duration** 3hr. Jacket and tie. Bateaux Parisiens are luxurious Bateaux Mouches. **www.bateauxparisiens.com**

Ile de la Cité
This tiny island on the Seine was first inhabited around 200 BC by a Celtic tribe known as the Parisii (pp82–3).

Conciergerie
During the Revolution this building, with its distinctive towers, became notorious as a prison (p83).

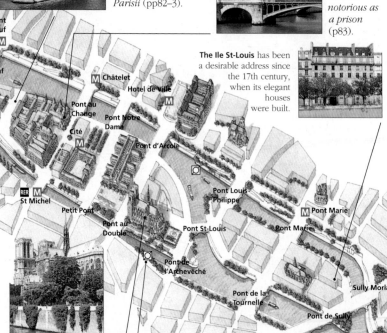

The Ile St-Louis has been a desirable address since the 17th century, when its elegant houses were built.

Pont Neuf Ⓜ

t Neuf

Châtelet Ⓜ

Hotel de Ville Ⓜ

Pont au Change

Pont Notre Dame

Cité Ⓜ

Pont d'Arcole

RER Ⓜ St Michel

Petit Pont

Pont au Double

Pont St-Louis

Pont de l'Archevêché

Pont Louis-Philippe

Pont Marie Ⓜ

Pont Marie

Sully Morland Ⓜ

Pont de la Tournelle

Pont de Sully

Notre-Dame
This towering cathedral surveys the river (pp86–7).

🚢 Bateaux Parisiens

ILE DE LA CITÉ, MARAIS AND BEAUBOURG

The Right Bank is dominated by the modernistic Forum des Halles and Pompidou Centre in the Beaubourg. These are Paris's most thriving public areas, with millions of tourists, shoppers and students flowing between them. Young people flock to Les Halles, shopping for the latest street fashions, but you should avoid the area at night. Renovations to improve Les Halles are taking place from 2008. All roads from here appear to lead to the Pompidou Centre, an avant-garde assembly of pipes, ducts and cables housing the Musée National d'Art Moderne. The smaller streets around the centre are full of art galleries housed in crooked, gabled

The motto of the city of Paris

buildings. The neighbouring Marais was abandoned by its royal residents during the 1789 Revolution, and it descended into architectural wasteland before being rescued in the 1960s. It has since become a very fashionable address, though small cafés, bakeries and artisans still survive in its streets.

Notre-Dame cathedral, the Palais de Justice, and Sainte-Chapelle continue to draw tourists to the Ile de la Cité, despite extensive redevelopment of the island in the last century. At the eastern end a bridge connects with the Ile St-Louis, a former swampy pastureland transformed into a residential area with pretty, tree-lined quays and mansions.

SIGHTS AT A GLANCE

Islands & Squares
Ile St-Louis ❼
Forum des Halles ❽❸
Place des Vosges ❶❾
Place de la Bastille ㉑

Churches
Sainte-Chapelle ❹
Notre-Dame pp86–7 ❻
St-Gervais–St-Protais ❾
St-Eustache ❶❷

Historic Buildings
Conciergerie ❷
Palais de Justice ❸
Hôtel de Ville ❶⓪
Tour St-Jacques ❶❶

GETTING THERE
Metro stations include Châtelet, Hôtel-de-Ville and Cité. Buses 47 and 29 serve Beaubourg and the Marais respectively. Several bus routes cross Ile de la Cité and Ile St-Louis.

Museums and Galleries
Crypte Archéologique ❺
Hôtel de Sens ❽
Pompidou Centre pp92–3 ❶❹
Musée d'Art et d'Histoire du Judaisme ❶❺
Hôtel de Soubise ❶❻
Musée Picasso ❶❼
Musée Carnavalet ❶❽
Maison de Victor Hugo ❷⓪

Bridges
Pont Neuf ❶

KEY
▨ Street by Street map *pp82–3*
▨ Street by Street map *pp88–9*
Ⓜ Metro station
Ⓞ Batobus boarding point
Ⓡ RER station

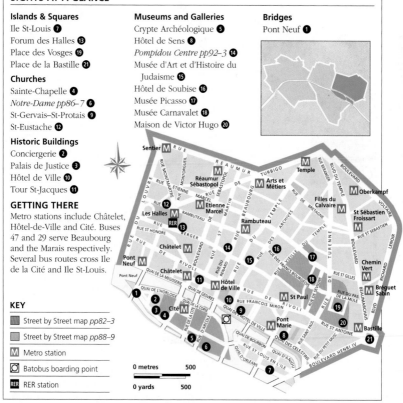

0 metres   500
0 yards   500

◁ **View of the Conciergerie and the Pont au Change**

Street-by-Street: Ile de la Cité

The origins of Paris are on the Ile de la Cité, the boat-shaped island on the Seine first inhabited by Celtic tribes in the 3rd century BC. One tribe, the Parisii, eventually gave its name to the city. The island offered a convenient river crossing on the route between northern and southern Gaul and was easily defended. In later centuries the settlement was expanded by the Romans, the Franks and the Capetian kings to form the nucleus of today's city.

Remains of the first buildings can still be seen today in the archaeological crypt of the great medieval cathedral of Notre-Dame. At the other end of the island is Sainte-Chapelle, another Gothic masterpiece.

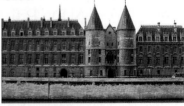

★ Conciergerie
This sinister-looking building was the country's chief prison during the Revolution ❷

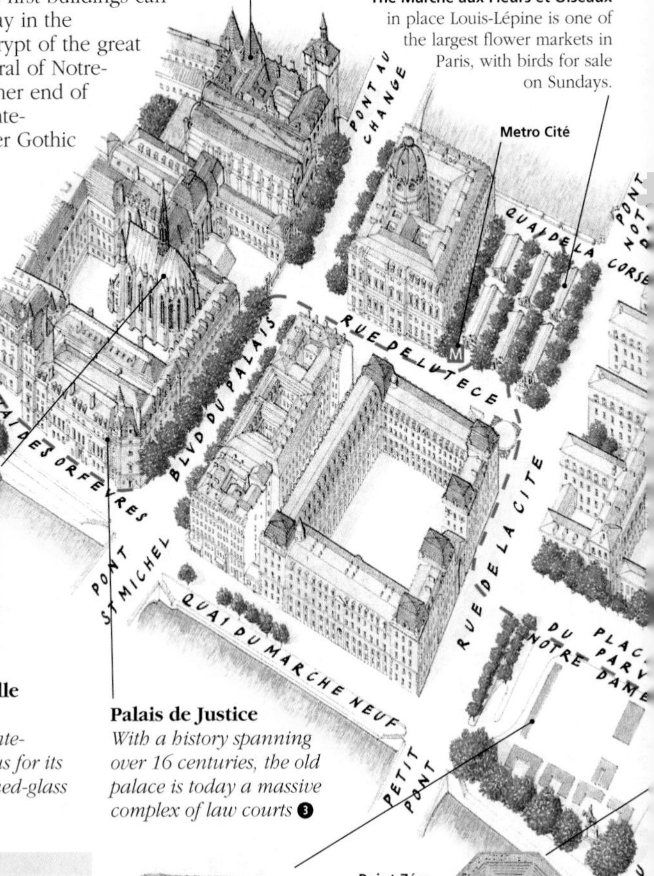

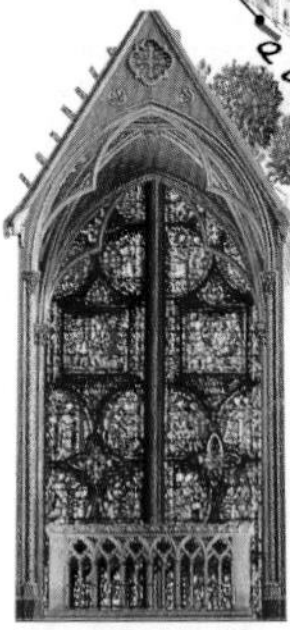

The Marché aux Fleurs et Oiseaux in place Louis-Lépine is one of the largest flower markets in Paris, with birds for sale on Sundays.
Metro Cité
To Pont Neuf
PONT AU CHANGE
QUAI DE LA CORSE
RUE DE LUTECE
M
BLVD DU PALAIS
QUAI DES ORFEVRES
PONT ST MICHEL
QUAI DU MARCHE NEUF
RUE DE LA CITE
DU NOTRE DAME
PETIT PONT
To Latin Quarter

★ Sainte-Chapelle
A jewel of Gothic architecture, Sainte-Chapelle is famous for its magnificent stained-glass windows ❹

Palais de Justice
With a history spanning over 16 centuries, the old palace is today a massive complex of law courts ❸

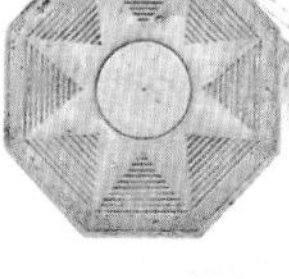

Point Zéro marks the spot from which all road distances are measured in France.

CRYPTE
DU
PARVIS

Crypte Archéologique
Deep under the square lie remnants of houses dating back 2,000 years ❺

STAR SIGHTS

- ★ Notre-Dame
- ★ Sainte-Chapelle
- ★ Conciergerie

KEY

— — — Suggested route

Hôtel Dieu, a large hospital serving central Paris, was founded in AD 651 by St Landry, Bishop of Paris.

LOCATOR MAP
See Street Finder maps 8, 9

★ **Notre-Dame**
This cathedral is a superb example of French medieval architecture **6**

Musée Notre-Dame, founded in 1951, contains exhibits and documents commemorating the great events in Notre-Dame's history.

Square Jean XXIII, a formal garden with a Neo-Gothic fountain opened in 1844, is an ideal spot from which to view the east end of the cathedral.

RUE D'ARCOLE
PONT D'ARCOLE
RUE CHANOINESSE
RUE DU CLOITRE NOTRE DAME
SQUARE JEAN XXIII

| 0 metres | 100 |
| 0 yards | 100 |

Pont Neuf, the city's oldest bridge

Pont Neuf **1**

75001. **Map** 8 F3. **M** *Pont Neuf, Cité.*

Despite its name (New Bridge), this bridge is the oldest in Paris and has been immortalized by major literary and artistic figures. The first stone was laid by Henri III in 1578, but it was Henri IV (whose statue stands at the centre) who inaugurated it and gave it its name in 1607.

Conciergerie **2**

1 quai de l'Horloge 75001. **Map** 9 A3. **Tel** *01 53 40 60 93.* **M** *Cité.* ⏰ *9:30am–6pm daily (9am–5pm Nov–Feb; last adm 30 min before closing).* ⚫ *1 Jan, 1 May, 25 Dec.* 🎫 *Combined ticket with Sainte-Chapelle (see p84) available.* 📷 📹 *phone to check.* 🖥 **www**.monum.fr

Forming part of the huge Palais de Justice, the historic Conciergerie served as a prison from 1391–1914. Henri IV's assassin, François Ravaillac, was imprisoned and tortured here in 1610.

During the Revolution the building was packed with over 4,000 prisoners. Its most celebrated inmate was Marie-Antoinette, who was held in a tiny cell until her execution in 1793. Others included Charlotte Corday, who stabbed Revolutionary leader Marat.

The Conciergerie has a superb four-aisled Gothic hall, where guards of the royal household once lived. Renovated during the 19th century, the building retains its 11th-century torture chamber and 14th-century clock tower.

A sculptured relief on the Palais de Justice

Palais de Justice ❸

4 bd du Palais (entrance by the Cour de Mai) 75001. **Map** 9 A3. **Tel** 01 44 32 50 00. Ⓜ Cité. ◯ 9am–6:30pm Mon–Fri. ● public hols & Aug recess.

This huge block of buildings making up the law courts of Paris stretches the entire width of the Ile de la Cité. It is a splendid sight with its Gothic towers lining the quays. The site has been occupied since Roman times when it was the governors' residence. It was the seat of royal power until Charles V moved the court to the Marais following a bloody revolt in 1358. In April 1793 the notorious Revolutionary Tribunal began dispensing justice from the Première Chambre Civile, or first civil chamber. Today the site embodies Napoleon's great legacy – the French judicial system.

Crypte Archéologique ❺

Pl du Parvis Notre-Dame 75004. **Map** 9 A4. **Tel** 01 55 42 50 10. Ⓜ Cité. ◯ 10am–6pm Tue–Sun (last adm 30 mins before closing). ● 1 Jan, 1 & 8 May, 1 & 11 Nov, 25 Dec. 🖾 ◎ ⬚

Situated beneath the *parvis* (main square) of Notre-Dame and stretching 120 m (393 ft) underground, the crypt was opened in 1980.

There are Gallo-Roman streets and houses with an underground heating system, sections of Lutetia's 3rd-century BC wall, and remains of the cathedral. Models explain the development of Paris from a settlement of the Parisii, the Celtic tribe who inhabited the island 2000 years ago, giving their name to the present city.

Notre-Dame ❻

See pp86–7.

Sainte-Chapelle ❹

2 bd du Palais 75001. **Map** 9 A3. 🛈 01 53 40 60 80. Ⓜ Cité. ◯ Mar–Oct: 9:30am–6pm daily; Nov–Feb: 9am–5pm daily. ● 1 Jan, 1 May, 1 & 11 Nov, 25 Dec. 🖾 Combined ticket with Conciergerie (see p83) available. ◎ 🖾 ⬚ www.monum.fr

Ethereal and magical, Sainte-Chapelle has been hailed as one of the greatest architectural masterpieces of the Western world. In the Middle Ages the devout likened this church to "a gateway to heaven". Today no visitor can fail to be transported by the blaze of light created by the 15 magnificent stained-glass windows, separated by pencil-like columns soaring 15 m (50 ft) to the star-studded roof. The windows portray more than 1,000 biblical scenes in a kaleidoscope of red, gold, green and blue. Starting from the left near the entrance and proceeding clockwise, you can trace the scriptures from Genesis through to the Crucifixion and the Apocalypse.

The chapel was completed in 1248 by Louis IX to house what was believed to be Christ's Crown of Thorns and fragments of the True Cross (now in the treasury at Notre-Dame). The king, who was canonized for his good works, purchased the relics from the Emperor of Constantinople, paying three times more for them than for the entire construction of Sainte-Chapelle.

The building actually consists of two separate chapels. The sombre lower chapel was used by servants and lower court officials, while the exquisite upper chapel, reached by means of a narrow spiral staircase, was reserved for the royal family and its courtiers. A discreetly placed window enabled the king to take part in the celebrations unobserved.

During the Revolution the building was badly damaged and became a warehouse. It was renovated a century later by architect Viollet-le-Duc.

Today, evening concerts of classical music are held regularly in the chapel, taking advantage of its superb acoustics.

The magnificent interior of Sainte-Chapelle

Ile St-Louis **❼**

75004. **Map** 9 B-C4-5. **M** *Pont Marie, Sully Morland.* **St-Louis-en-l'Ile Tel** *01 46 34 11 60.* ☐ *9am–noon, 3pm–7pm Tue–Sun.* ● *public hols.* **Concerts**

Across Pont St-Louis from Ile de la Cité, smaller Ile St-Louis is a little haven of quiet streets and riverside quays. There are luxurious restaurants and shops, including the famous ice-cream maker Berthillon. Almost everything on the Ile was built in classical style in the 17th century. The church of **St-Louis-en-l'Ile**, with its marble and gilt Baroque interior, was completed in 1726 from plans by royal architect Louis de Vau. Note the 1741 iron clock at the church entrance, the pierced iron spire, and a plaque given in 1926 by St-Louis, Missouri. The church is also twinned with Carthage cathedral in Tunisia, where St-Louis is buried.

The interior of St-Louis-en-l'Ile

Hôtel de Sens **❽**

1 rue du Figuier 75004. **Map** 9 C4. **Tel** *01 42 78 14 60.* **M** *Pont-Marie.* ☐ *1:30–7pm Tue–Sat.* ● *public hols.* 📷

One of only a handful of medieval buildings still standing in Paris, the Hôtel de Sens is home to the Forney arts library. During the period of the Catholic League in the 16th century, it was turned into a fortified mansion and occupied by the Bourbons, the Guises and Cardinal de Pellevé.

St-Gervais–St-Protais **❾**

Pl St-Gervais 75004. **Map** 9 B3. **Tel** *01 48 87 32 02.* **M** *Hôtel de Ville.* ☐ *5:30am –10pm daily.* **Organ concerts**

Named after Gervase and Protase, two Roman soldiers martyred by the Emperor Nero, the origins of this magnificent church go back to the 6th century. It boasts the earliest Classical façade in Paris, dating from 1621, with a triple-tiered arrangement of Doric, Ionic and Corinthian columns.

Behind the façade lies a late Gothic church renowned for its association with religious music. François Couperin (1668–1733) composed his two masses for this church's organ.

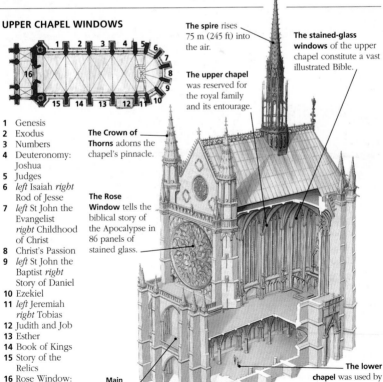

UPPER CHAPEL WINDOWS

1. Genesis
2. Exodus
3. Numbers
4. Deuteronomy: Joshua
5. Judges
6. *left* Isaiah *right* Rod of Jesse
7. *left* St John the Evangelist *right* Childhood of Christ
8. Christ's Passion
9. *left* St John the Baptist *right* Story of Daniel
10. Ezekiel
11. *left* Jeremiah *right* Tobias
12. Judith and Job
13. Esther
14. Book of Kings
15. Story of the Relics
16. Rose Window: The Apocalypse

The spire rises 75 m (245 ft) into the air.

The stained-glass windows of the upper chapel constitute a vast illustrated Bible.

The upper chapel was reserved for the royal family and its entourage.

The Crown of Thorns adorns the chapel's pinnacle.

The Rose Window tells the biblical story of the Apocalypse in 86 panels of stained glass.

The lower chapel was used by servants and commoners.

Main portals

Notre-Dame ⑥

No other building epitomizes the history of Paris more than Notre-Dame. Built on the site of a Roman temple, the cathedral was commissioned by Bishop de Sully in 1159. The first stone was laid in 1163, marking the start of two centuries of toil by armies of Gothic architects and medieval craftsmen. It has been witness to great events of French history ever since, including the coronations of Henry VI in 1422 and Napoleon Bonaparte in 1804. During the Revolution the building was desecrated and rechristened the Temple of Reason. Extensive renovations (including the addition of the spire and gargoyles) were carried out in the 19th century by architect Viollet-le-Duc.

★ West Façade
The beautifully proportioned west façade is a masterpiece of French Gothic architecture.

387 steps lead to the top of the south tower, where the famous Emmanuel bell is housed.

★ Galerie des Chimères
The cathedral's legendary gargoyles (chimères) gaze menacingly from the cathedral's ledge.

★ West Rose Window
This window depicts the Virgin in a medallion of rich reds and blues.

STAR FEATURES

★ West Façade and Portals

★ Flying Buttress

★ Rose Windows

★ Galerie des Chimères

The Kings' Gallery features 28 stone images of the kings of Judah.

Portal of the Virgin
The Virgin surrounded by saints and kings is a fine composition of 13th-century statues.

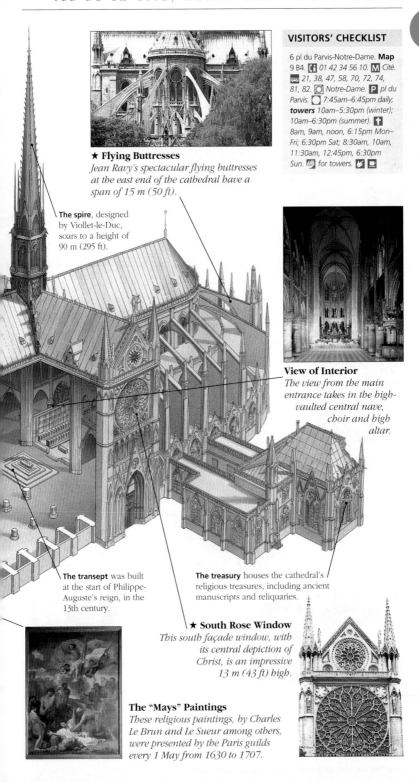

★ **Flying Buttresses**
*Jean Ravy's spectacular flying buttresses
at the east end of the cathedral have a
span of 15 m (50 ft).*

The spire, designed
by Viollet-le-Duc,
soars to a height of
90 m (295 ft).

View of Interior
*The view from the main
entrance takes in the high-
vaulted central nave,
choir and high
altar.*

The transept was built
at the start of Philippe-
Auguste's reign, in the
13th century.

The treasury houses the cathedral's
religious treasures, including ancient
manuscripts and reliquaries.

★ **South Rose Window**
*This south façade window, with
its central depiction of
Christ, is an impressive
13 m (43 ft) high.*

The "Mays" Paintings
*These religious paintings, by Charles
Le Brun and Le Sueur among others,
were presented by the Paris guilds
every 1 May from 1630 to 1707.*

Street-by-Street: The Marais

Once an area of marshland (*marais* means swamp), the Marais grew steadily in importance from the 14th century, by virtue of its proximity to the Louvre, the preferred residence of Charles V. Its heyday was in the 17th century, when it became a fashionable area for the monied classes, many of whose grand mansions (*hôtels*) have now been restored as museums. Once again fashionable, chic designer boutiques alternate with small restaurants and stores.

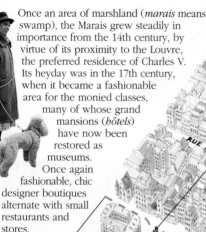

To the Pompidou Centre

★ **Musée Picasso**
The palatial home of a 17th-century salt-tax collector is the setting for the most extensive collection of Picassos in the world ⓱

Rue des Francs-Bourgeois, built in 1334, was named after the *francs* – almshouses for the poor at Nos. 34 and 36.

Musée Cognacq-Jay contains an exquisite collection of 18th-century paintings and furniture.

Hôtel de Lamoignon was built in 1584 and houses Paris's historical library.

Rue des Rosiers, heart of the city's oldest Jewish quarter, is lined with 18th-century houses, stores and restaurants serving hot pastrami and borscht.

KEY

– – – Suggested route

| 0 metres | 100 |
| 0 yards | 100 |

★ **Musée Carnavalet**
Occupying two large mansions, this museum covers the history of Paris from Prehistoric and Gallo-Roman times ⓲

For hotels and restaurants in this region see pp550–5 and pp600–6

★ Place des Vosges
*This enchanting square is
an oasis of peace and
tranquillity* ⑲

LOCATOR MAP
See Street Finder maps 9, 10

Maison de Victor Hugo
Author of Les Misérables, *Victor Hugo
lived at No. 6 place des Vosges, now
a museum of his life and work* ⑳

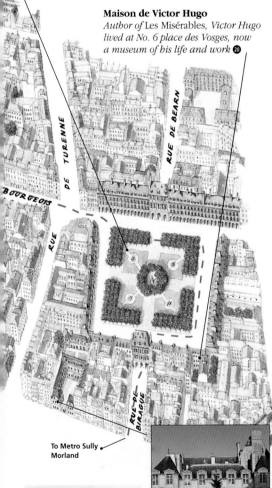

**To Metro Sully
Morland**

STAR SIGHTS

★ Musée Picasso

★ Musée Carnavalet

★ Place des Vosges

Hôtel de Sully, with its
orangerie and courtyard, is an
elegant Renaissance mansion.

Hôtel de Ville ⑩

Pl de l'Hôtel de Ville 75004.
Map 9 B3. *Tel* 01 42 76 40 40.
Ⓜ *Hôtel-de-Ville.* ◯ to groups:
phone to arrange (01 42 76 54 04).
◐ public hols, and for official
functions (phone to check). ♿

Home of the city council, the
Hôtel de Ville is a 19th-
century reconstruction of the
17th-century town hall burned
down by insurgents of the
Paris Commune in 1871. It is
a highly ornate example of
Third Republic architecture,
with elaborate stonework,
turrets and statues overlooking
a pedestrianized square.

The 16th-century Tour St-Jacques

Tour St-Jacques ⑪

Square de la Tour St-Jacques 75004.
Map 9 A3. Ⓜ *Châtelet.* ◐ for
renovations.

This imposing late Gothic
tower, dating from 1523, is all
that remains of a medieval
church used as a rendezvous
by pilgrims setting out for
Compostela in Spain. The
building was destroyed by
revolutionaries in 1797.
  Earlier, Blaise Pascal, the
17th-century philosopher,
mathematician, physicist and
writer, used the tower for
barometric experiments. His
statue stands at the base of
the tower, which is now used
as a meteorological station.

St-Eustache ⓬

Pl du Jour 75001. **Map** 9 A1. *Tel 01 42 36 31 05.* Ⓜ *Les Halles.* RER *Châtelet-Les-Halles.* ✝ *12:30pm Mon–Fri, 6pm Mon–Sat, 9:30am, 11am, 6pm Sun.* **Concerts**

With its Gothic plan and Renaissance decoration, St-Eustache is one of Paris's most beautiful churches. Its massive interior is modelled on Notre-Dame, with five naves and side and radial chapels. The 105 years (1532–1637) it took to complete the church saw the flowering of the Renaissance style, which is evident in the magnificent arches, pillars and columns.

St-Eustache has hosted many ceremonial events including the baptisms of Cardinal Richelieu and Madame de Pompadour, and the funerals of fabulist La Fontaine, Colbert (prime minister of Louis XIV), 17th-century dramatist Molière, composer Rameau and the revolutionary orator Mirabeau. It was here that Berlioz first performed his *Te Deum* in 1855 and Liszt his *Messe Solenelle* in 1866. Today talented choir groups perform here regularly and organ recitals are held on Sundays at 5:30pm.

Forum des Halles ⓭

75001. **Map** 13 A2. Ⓜ *Les Halles.* RER *Châtelet-Les-Halles.*

Known simply as Les Halles and built amid much controversy on the site of the famous old fruit and vegetable market, the complex occupies 7 ha (750,000 sq ft), partly above and partly below ground, and has a reputation for being unsafe, particularly at night. The underground levels 2 and 3 are occupied by a varied array of shops, from clothes boutiques to megastores. Above ground there are well-tended gardens, pergolas and mini-pavillions. Also outside are the palm-shaped buildings of metal and glass which house two cultural centres for art and poetry. Extensive renovations to improve the area, beginning in 2008, will take several years to complete.

St-Eustache and sculptured head, *l'Ecoute,* **by Henri de Miller**

Pompidou Centre ⓮

See pp92–3.

Musée d'Art et d'Histoire du Judaïsme ⓯

Hôtel de St-Aignan, 71 rue du Temple 75003. **Map** 13 B2. *Tel 01 53 01 86 60.* Ⓜ *Rambuteau.* ☐ *11am–6pm Mon–Fri, 10am–6pm Sun.* ● *Jewish hols.* 🖼 🔊 🖥 🛍 www.mahj.org

This museum in a Marais mansion, the elegant Hôtel de St-Aignan, brings together collections formerly scattered around the city, and commemorates the culture of French Jewry from medieval times to the present. Visitors learn that there has been a sizeable Jewish community in France since Roman times, and some of the world's greatest Jewish scholars – Rashi, Rabenu Tam, the Tosafists – were French. Much exquisite craftsmanship is displayed, with elaborate silverware, Torah covers, fabrics, and items of fine Judaica and religious objects for use both in the synagogue and in the home. There are also photographs, paintings, and cartoons and historical documents, including some on the antisemitic Dreyfus Affair more than a century ago.

Hôtel de Soubise ⓰

60 rue des Francs-Bourgeois 75003. **Map** 9 C2. *Tel 01 40 27 60 96.* Ⓜ *Rambuteau.* ● *to the public.*

This imposing mansion, built from 1705 to 1709 for the Princesse de Rohan, is one of two main buildings housing the national archives (the other one being the Hôtel de Rohan). It boasts a majestic courtyard and 18th-century interior decoration by some of the best-known artists of the time.

Notable items held here include Natoire's *rocaille* work in the Princess's bedchamber and Napoleon's will, in which he asks for his remains to be returned to France. Unfortunately the interior is only accessible by appointment to historical researchers.

Musée Picasso ⓱

Hôtel Salé, 5 rue de Thorigny, 75003. **Map** 10 D2. 🆔 *01 42 71 25 21.* Ⓜ *St-Sébastien Froissart.* ☐ *9:30am–5:30pm Wed–Mon (6pm Apr–Sep).* ● *for renovations from Jul 2008–10.* 🖼 📷 🔊 🛍 *groups by appointment only.* 🛍 🛍 www.musee-picasso.fr

On the death of the Spanish-born artist Pablo Picasso (1881–1973), who lived most of his life in France, the French State inherited one quarter of his works in lieu of death duties. In 1986, it used them to create the Musée

Woman Reading **(1932) by Pablo Picasso**

Picasso in the beautifully restored Hôtel Salé, one of the loveliest buildings in the Marais. It was built in 1656 for Aubert de Fontenay, collector of the dreaded salt tax (*salé* means "salty").

Comprising over 200 paintings, 158 sculptures, 88 ceramic works and some 3,000 sketches and engravings, this unique collection shows the enormous range and variety of Picasso's work, including examples from his Blue, Pink and Cubist periods.

Highlights to look out for are his Blue period *Self-portrait*, painted at age 20; *Still Life with Caned Chair*, which introduced collage to Cubism; the Neo-Classical *Pipes of Pan*; and *The Crucifixion*.

The museum works closely with other galleries throughout the world, frequently loaning canvases for special exhibitions elsewhere, so specific works by Picasso may not always be visible.

A magnificent 17th-century ceiling painting by Charles Le Brun

Musée Carnavalet ®

23 rue de Sevigné 75003. **Map** 10 D3. **Tel** 01 44 59 58 58. Ⓜ St-Paul. ◷ 10am–6pm Tue–Sun (rooms open in rotas: phone to check). ⬤ public hols. ◉ 🖪 ring for times. 🖪 **www**.carnavalet.paris.fr

Devoted to the history of Paris since Prehistoric times, this vast museum is in two adjoining mansions. They include entire decorated rooms with gilded panelling, furniture and *objets d'art*; many works of art, such as paintings and sculptures of prominent

personalities; and engravings showing Paris being built.

The main building is the Hôtel Carnavalet, built as a town house in 1548 by Nicolas Dupuis. The literary hostess Madame de Sévigné lived here between 1677 and 1696, entertaining the intelligentsia of the day and writing her celebrated *Lettres*. Many of her possessions are in the first-floor exhibit covering the Louis XIV era.

The 17th-century Hôtel le Peletier, opened in 1989, features reconstructions of early 20th-century interiors and artifacts from the Revolution and Napoleonic era. The Orangery houses a new department devoted to Prehistory and Gallo-Roman Paris. The collection includes pirogues discovered in 1992, during an archaeological dig in the Parc de Bercy, which unearthed a neolithic village.

Place des Vosges ®

75003, 75004. **Map** 10 D3. Ⓜ Bastille, St-Paul.

This perfectly symmetrical square, laid out in 1605 by Henri IV, is considered among the most beautiful in the world. Thirty-six houses, nine on each side, are built over arcades which today accommodate antiques shops and fashionable cafés. The square has been the scene of many historical events over the centuries, including a three-day tournament in celebration of the marriage of Louis XIII to Anne of Austria in 1615.

Maison de Victor Hugo ®

6 pl des Vosges 75004. **Map** 10 D4. **Tel** 01 42 72 10 16. Ⓜ Bastille. ◷ 10am–6pm Tue–Sun. ⬤ public hols. 🖾 🖪 **Library** **www**.musee-hugo.paris.fr

The French poet, dramatist and novelist lived on the second floor of the former Hôtel Rohan-Guéménée, the

largest house on the square, from 1832 to 1848. It was here that he wrote most of *Les Misérables*. On display are reconstructions of some of the rooms in which he lived, complete with his desk, the furniture he made, his pen-and-ink drawings, and mementos from the important periods of his life, from his childhood to his exile between 1852 and 1870. There are also regular temporary exhibitions.

Marble bust of Victor Hugo by Auguste Rodin

Place de la Bastille ㉑

75004. **Map** 10 E4. Ⓜ Bastille.

Nothing remains of the infamous prison stormed by the revolutionary mob on 14 July 1789, the event that sparked the French Revolution.

The 52-m (170-ft) Colonne de Juillet stands in the middle of the traffic-clogged square to honour the victims of the July Revolution of 1830. On the south side of the square (at 120 rue de Lyon) is the 2,700-seat **Opéra National Bastille**, completed in 1989, the bicentennial of the French Revolution.

The "genius of liberty" statue on top of the Colonne de Juillet

Pompidou Centre ⓮

The Pompidou is like a building turned inside out: escalators, lifts, air and water ducts and even the massive steel struts that make up the building's skeleton are all on the outside. This allowed the architects, Richard Rogers, Renzo Piano and Gianfranco Franchini, to create a flexible exhibition space. Among the artists featured in the museum are Matisse, Picasso, Miró and Pollock, representing such schools as Fauvism, Cubism and Surrealism. The Pompidou also keeps abreast of the Paris art scene with frequently changing temporary exhibitions. Outside in the Piazza, crowds gather to watch street performers.

KEY

☐ Exhibition space

☐ Non-exhibition space

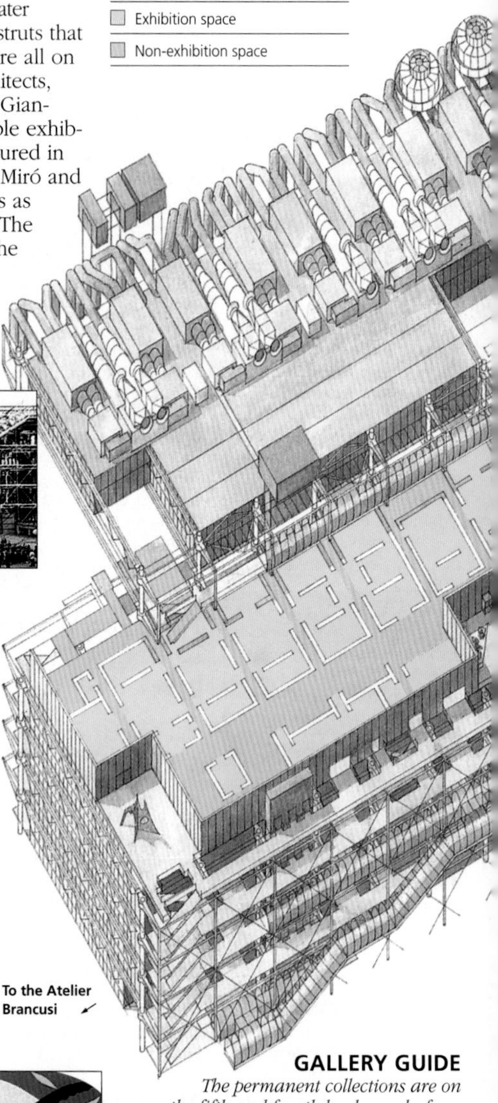

This riotous jumble of glass and steel, known as Beaubourg, is Paris's top tourist attraction, built in 1977 and drawing over seven million visitors a year.

Mobile on Two Planes *(1955)*
20th-century American artist Alexander Calder introduced the mobile as an art form.

To the Atelier Brancusi ↙

GALLERY GUIDE

The permanent collections are on the fifth and fourth levels: works from 1905–60 are on the former, contemporary art on the latter. The first and sixth levels are for temporary exhibitions; the first, second and third house a library. The lower levels make up "The Forum", the focal public area, with a performance centre, cinema and children's workshop.

Sorrow of the King *(1952)*
This collage was created by Matisse using gouache-painted paper cut-outs.

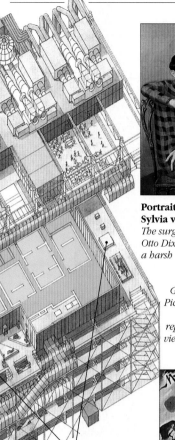

Basin and Sculpture Terrace

Portrait of the Journalist Sylvia von Harden *(1926)*
The surgical precision of Otto Dix's style makes this a harsh caricature.

VISITORS' CHECKLIST

Centre d'Art et de Culture Georges Pompidou, pl G Pompidou, 75004. **Map** 9 B2. *Tel* 01 44 78 12 33. M Rambuteau, Châtelet, Hôtel de Ville. 21, 29, 38, 47, 58, 69, 70, 72, 74, 75, 76, 81, 85, 96. RER Châtelet-Les-Halles. P Centre G Pompidou. MNAM & temp exhibs: 11am–9pm Wed–Mon; Atelier Brancusi: 2–6pm Wed–Mon; Library: noon–10pm Mon, Wed–Fri, 11am–10pm w/e.
www.centrepompidou.fr

Le Duo *(1937)*
Georges Braque, like Picasso, developed the Cubist technique of representing different views of a subject in a single picture.

With the Black Arc
(1912) The transition to Abstraction, one of the major art forms of the 20th century, can be seen in the works of Wassily Kandinsky.

Stravinsky Fountain
This fountain, which was inaugurated in 1983, is in the place Igor Stravinsky near the Pompidou Centre. It was designed by sculptors Jean Tinguely and Niki de Saint Phalle, both of whom are represented in the Pompidou Centre.

BRANCUSI WORKSHOP

The Atelier Brancusi, on the rue Rambuteau side of the piazza, is a reconstruction of the workshop of the Romanian-born artist Constantin Brancusi (1876–1957), who lived and worked in Paris. He bequeathed his entire collection of works to the French state on condition that his workshop be rebuilt as it was. The collection includes over 200 sculptures and plinths, 1600 photographs, exhibited in rotation, and tools Brancusi used to create his works. Also featured are some of his more personal items such as documents, pieces of furniture and his book collection.

Interior of the Brancusi workshop, designed by Renzo Piano

TUILERIES AND OPÉRA

The 19th-century grandeur of Baron Haussmann's *grands boulevards* offsets the bustle of bankers, theatre-goers, sightseers and shoppers who frequent the area around the Opéra. A profusion of shops and department stores, ranging from the exclusively expensive to the popular, draws the crowds. Much of the area's older character is found in the early 19th-century shopping arcades, with elaborate steel and glass roofs. They are known as *galeries* or *passages*, and were restored to their former glory in the 1970s. Galerie Vivienne, which is the smartest, has an elaborate, patterned mosaic floor. The passage des Panoramas, passage Verdeau and the tiny passage des Princes are more old-style Parisian. These streets abound with food stores of all kinds,

Lamppost of vestal virgin outside the Opéra

noted for their mouthwatering displays of expensive jams, spices, pâtés, mustards and sauces.

The Tuileries area lies between the Opéra and the river, bounded by the vast place de la Concorde in the west and the Louvre to the east. The Louvre palace combines one of the world's greatest art collections with IM Pei's avant-garde glass pyramid. Elegant squares and formal gardens give the area its special character. Monuments to monarchy and the arts coexist with modern luxury at its most ostentatious. Place Vendôme, home to exquisite jewellery shops and the luxurious Ritz Hotel, is a heady mix of the wealthy and the chic. Parallel to the Jardin des Tuileries are two of Paris's foremost shopping streets, the rue de Rivoli and rue St-Honoré, full of expensive boutiques, bookshops and deluxe hotels.

SIGHTS AT A GLANCE

Museums and Galleries
Galerie Nationale du Jeu de Paume **6**
Musée des Arts Décoratifs **11**
Grévin **3**
Musée du Louvre pp100–3 **14**
Musée de l'Orangerie **8**

Squares, Parks and Gardens
Jardin des Tuileries **9**
Place de la Concorde **7**
Place Vendôme **5**

Monuments
Arc de Triomphe du Carrousel **12**

Historic Buildings
Opéra de Paris Garnier **2**
Palais Royal **13**

Churches
La Madeleine **1**
St-Roch **10**

Shops
Les Passages **4**

GETTING THERE
This area is well served by the metro system, with stations at Tuileries, Pyramides, Palais Royal, Madeleine and Opéra, among others. Bus routes 24 and 72 pass along quai des Tuileries and quai du Louvre, while routes 21, 27 and 29 serve avenue de l'Opéra.

KEY
▢ Street-by-Street map pp96–7
Ⓜ Metro station
ℹ Tourist information

0 metres   500
0 yards   500

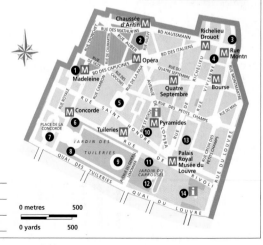

◁ **View of the place de la Concorde and the Obelisk**

Street-by-Street: Opéra Quarter

It has been said that the whole world will pass you by if you sit for long enough at the Café de la Paix (opposite the Opéra National Garnier). During the day, the area is a centre of commerce, tourism and shopping, with mammoth department stores lining the *grands boulevards*. In the evening, the clubs and theatres attract a totally different crowd, and the cafés along boulevard des Capucines throb with life.

Statue by Gumery on the Opéra

★ **Opéra National de Paris Garnier**
Dating from 1875, the grandiose opera house has come to symbolize the opulence of the Second Empire ❷

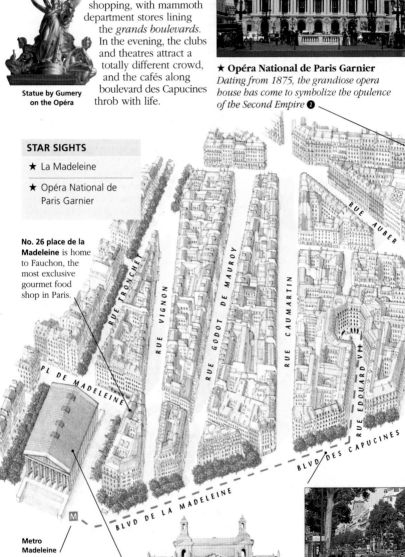

STAR SIGHTS

★ La Madeleine

★ Opéra National de Paris Garnier

No. 26 place de la Madeleine is home to Fauchon, the most exclusive gourmet food shop in Paris.

RUE AUBER

RUE TRONCHET

RUE VIGNON

RUE GODOT DE MAUROY

RUE CAUMARTIN

RUE EDOUARD VII

PL DE MADELEINE

BLVD DES CAPUCINES

BLVD DE LA MADELEINE

Ⓜ **Metro Madeleine**

★ **La Madeleine**
The original model of the Madeleine can be seen at the Musée Carnavalet (see p91) ❶

Boulevard des Capucines (No. 14) is where the Lumière brothers staged the first public screening of a movie on 28 December 1895.

LOCATOR MAP
*See Street Finder
maps 4, 7, 8*

Musée de l'Opéra
contains the
scores of every
ballet and opera
performed at the
Opéra, and memor-
abilia ranging
from Nijinsky's
dancing shoes to
Pavlova's tiara.

PL DIAGHILEV

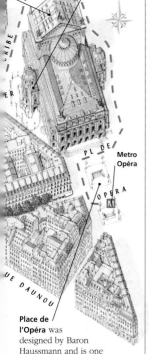

**Metro
Opéra**

**Place de
l'Opéra** was
designed by Baron
Haussmann and is one
of Paris's busiest intersections.

KEY

— — — Suggested route

0 metres	100
0 yards	100

Marochetti's *Mary Magdalene Ascending to Heaven* in La Madeleine

La Madeleine ❶

Pl de la Madeleine 75008. **Map** 3 C5.
Tel 01 44 51 69 00. Ⓜ *Madeleine.*
◯ 9am–7pm daily. ✝ 12:25pm,
6:30pm Mon–Fri, 11am Sat, 11am,
6pm Sun. 📷 🎵 *Concerts*

Modelled after a Greek
temple, La Madeleine was
begun in 1764 but not consecrated as a church until
1845. Before that, there
were proposals to turn
it into a stock exchange,
a bank, or a theatre.

A colonnade of Corin-
thian columns encircles
the building and sup-
ports a sculptured frieze.
The inside is crowned
by three ceiling domes
and lavishly decorated
with fine sculptures,
rose marble and gilt.

Opéra National de Paris Garnier ❷

Pl de l'Opéra 75009. **Map** 4 DF. 📠
01 40 01 22 63. Ⓜ *Opéra.* ◯
10am–4:30pm daily. ● *public hols.*
📷 📸 www.operadeparis.fr

Sometimes compared to a
giant wedding cake, this
extravagant building was
designed by Charles Garnier
for Napoleon III in 1862. The
Prussian War and the 1871
uprising delayed the opening
of the building till 1875.

The interior is famous for its
Grand Staircase made of
white Carrara marble, topped
by a huge chandelier, as well
as for its auditorium bedecked
in red velvet and gold, with a
false ceiling painted by Chagall
in 1964. Restored to its full

glory, it is primarily used for
dance (it is home to Ballet de
l'Opéra de Paris), but shares
operatic productions with the
Opéra Bastille (see p153).

Grévin ❸

10 bd Montmartre 75009. **Map** 4
F4. **Tel** 01 47 70 85 05. Ⓜ *Grands
Boulevards.* ◯ 10am–6:30pm Mon–
Fri (7pm Sat, Sun & school hols).
📸 📷 www.grevin.fr

Founded in 1882, this
is a Paris landmark,
on a par with Madame
Tussauds. The histori-
cal scenes include
Louis XIV at Versailles
and the arrest of
Louis XVI. Notable
figures from the
worlds of art, politics,
film and sport are
also on display. On

**Sign outside
the Grévin**

the first floor is a holography
museum devoted to optical
tricks. The museum also
houses a 320-seat theatre.

Les Passages ❹

75002. **Map** 4 F5. Ⓜ *Bourse.*

The early 19th-century glass-
roofed shopping arcades
(known as *galeries* or *passages*)
are concentrated between
boulevard Montmartre and
rue St-Marc. They house an
eclectic mixture of small stores
selling anything from designer
jewellery to rare books and art
supplies. One of the most
charming is the Galerie
Vivienne (off the rue Vivienne
or the rue des Petits Champs)
with its mosaic floor and
excellent tearoom.

Place Vendôme ❺

75001. **Map** 8 D1. Ⓜ *Tuileries.*

Perhaps the best example of 18th-century elegance in the city, the architect Jules Hardouin-Mansart's royal square was begun in 1698. The original plan was to house academies and embassies behind its arcaded façades, but instead bankers moved in and created sumptuous mansions for themselves. The square's most famous residents include Frédéric Chopin, who died here in 1849 at No. 12, and César Ritz, who established his famous hotel at No. 15 in 1898.

Monet's *Waterlilies (Nymphéas)* on display in the Musée de l'Orangerie

Galerie Nationale du Jeu de Paume ❻

Jardin des Tuileries, place de la Concorde 75008. **Map** 7 C1. *Tel 01 47 03 12 50.* Ⓜ *Concorde.* ◯ noon–9pm Tue, noon–7pm Wed–Fri, 10am–7pm Sat. ⬤ 1 Jan, 1 May, 25 Dec. 🎦 ♿ 🎟 🅿 ▣ www.jeudepaume.org

The Jeu de Paume – literally "game of the palm" – was built as two royal tennis courts by Napoleon III in 1851 on the north side of the Tuileries gardens. The courts were later converted into an art gallery and exhibition space. The Jeu de Paume has rotating exhibitions of contemporary art and houses the Centre National de la Photographie. Its sister site is the Hôtel de Sully *(see p89).*

Place de la Concorde ❼

75008. **Map** 7 C1. Ⓜ *Concorde.*

One of Europe's most magnificent and historic squares, covering over 8 ha (20 acres), the place de la Concorde was a swamp

The 3,200-year-old obelisk from Luxor

until the mid-18th century. It became the place Louis XV in 1775 when royal architect Jacques-Ange Gabriel was asked by the king to design a suitable setting for an equestrian statue of himself.

The monument, which lasted here less than 20 years, was replaced by the guillotine (the Black Widow, as it came to be known), and the square was renamed place de la Révolution. On 21 January 1793 Louis XVI was beheaded, followed by over 1,300 other victims including Marie Antoinette, Madame du Barry, Charlotte Corday (Marat's assassin) and revolutionary leaders Danton and Robespierre.

The blood-soaked square was optimistically renamed place de la Concorde after the Reign of Terror finally came to an end in 1794. A few decades later the 3,200-year-old Luxor obelisk was presented to King Louis-Philippe as a gift from the viceroy of Egypt (who also donated Cleopatra's Needle in London).

Flanking the rue Royale on the north side of the square are two of Gabriel's Neo-classical mansions, the Hôtel de la Marine and the exclusive Hôtel Crillon.

Musée de l'Orangerie ❽

Jardin des Tuileries, place de la Concorde 75008. **Map** 7 C1. *Tel 01 44 77 80 07.* Ⓜ *Concorde.* ◯ 9am–12:30pm Wed–Mon (groups), 12:30–7pm (individuals). ⬤ 1 May, 25 Dec. 🎦 🅾 ♿ 🎟 by appt. ▣ www.musee-orangerie.fr

Paintings from Claude Monet's crowning work, representing part of his waterlily series, fill the two oval ground floor rooms. Known as the *Nymphéas*, most of the canvases were painted between 1899 and 1921.

This superb work is complemented by the Walter-Guillaume collection, including 27 Renoirs, notably *Young Girls at the Piano,* works by Soutine and 14 Cézannes, including *The Red Rock.* Picasso is represented by works including *The Female Bathers,* and Rousseau by 9 paintings, notably *The Wedding.* Other works are by Sisley and Modigliani.

Jardin des Tuileries ❾

75001. **Map** 8 D1. Ⓜ *Tuileries, Concorde.* ◯ 7am–9pm Apr–Sep; 7:30am–7:30pm Oct–Mar.

These Neoclassical gardens once belonged to the Palais des Tuileries, which the Communards razed to the ground in 1871. They were laid out in the 17th century by André Le Nôtre, who created the broad central avenue and topiary arranged in geometric designs. Ongoing restoration has created a new garden with lime and chestnut trees, and striking modern sculptures.

St-Roch ⑩

296 rue St-Honoré 75001. **Map** 8 E1. **Tel** 01 42 44 13 20. Ⓜ Tuileries. ◯ 8:30am–7pm daily. ◯ non-religious public hols. ◉ **Concerts**

This huge church was designed by Jacques Lemercier, architect of the Louvre, and its foundation stone was laid by Louis XIV in 1653. It is a treasure house of religious art, much of it from now-vanished churches and monasteries, and contains the tombs of the playwright Pierre Corneille, the royal gardener André Le Nôtre and the philosopher Denis Diderot.

Vien's *St Denis Preaching to the Gauls* (1767) in St-Roch

Musée des Arts Décoratifs ⑪

Palais du Louvre, 107 rue de Rivoli 75001. **Map** 8 E2. **Tel** 01 44 55 57 50. Ⓜ Palais Royal, Tuileries. ◯ 11am–6pm Tue–Fri (until 9pm Thu); 10am–6pm Sat & Sun. **Library** ◉ public hols. 🖾 **www**.lesartsdecoratifs.fr

Occupying the northwest wing of the Palais du Louvre (along with the Musée de la Publicité and the Musée de la Mode et du Textile), this

The Buren Columns in the main courtyard of the Palais Royal

museum offers an eclectic mix of decorative art and domestic design from the Middle Ages to the present day. The Art Nouveau and Art Deco rooms include a reconstruction of the home of couturier Jeanne Lanvin. Other floors show Louis XIV, XV and XVI styles of decoration and furniture. Contemporary designers are also represented. The restaurant has breathtaking views over the Tuileries gardens.

Arc de Triomphe du Carrousel ⑫

Pl du Carrousel 75001. **Map** 8 E2. Ⓜ Palais Royal.

This rose-marble arch was built by Napoleon to celebrate various military triumphs, notably the Battle of Austerlitz in 1805. The crowning statues, added in 1828, are copies of the famous Horses of St Mark's which Napoleon stole from Venice, which he was subsequently forced to return after his defeat at Waterloo in 1815.

Palais Royal ⑬

Pl du Palais Royal 75001. **Map** 8 E1. Ⓜ Palais Royal. **Buildings** ◉ to the public.

This former royal palace has had a turbulent history. It was built by Cardinal Richelieu in the early 17th century, passing to the Crown on his death and becoming the childhood home of Louis XIV. Under the 18th-century royal dukes of Orléans, it became the epicentre of brilliant gatherings, interspersed with periods of gambling and debauchery. It was from here that the clarion call to revolution roused the mobs to storm the Bastille on 14 July 1789.

Today the southern section of the building houses the Councils of State and the Ministry of Culture. Just west of the palace at 2 rue de Richelieu is the Comédie Française, established by Louis XIV in 1680. Luxury shops occupy the rear section of the palace, where artists such as Colette and Cocteau once lived.

The Arc de Triomphe du Carrousel crowned by Victory riding a chariot

Musée du Louvre ⓮

The Musée du Louvre, containing one of the most important art collections in the world, has a history dating back to medieval times. First built as a fortress in 1190 by King Philippe-Auguste to protect Paris against Viking raids, it lost its keep in the reign of François I, who replaced it with a Renaissance-style building. Thereafter, four centuries of kings and emperors improved and enlarged it. The latest addition is the collection of Arts from Africa, Asia, Oceania and the Americas, in the Pavillon des Sessions.

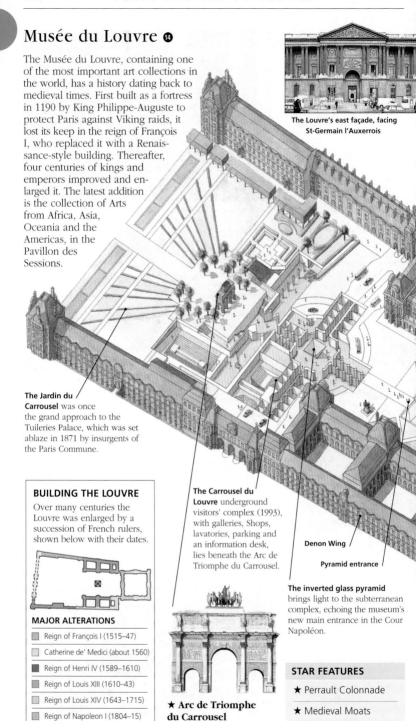

The Louvre's east façade, facing St-Germain l'Auxerrois

The Jardin du Carrousel was once the grand approach to the Tuileries Palace, which was set ablaze in 1871 by insurgents of the Paris Commune.

BUILDING THE LOUVRE

Over many centuries the Louvre was enlarged by a succession of French rulers, shown below with their dates.

MAJOR ALTERATIONS

- ◻ Reign of François I (1515–47)
- ◻ Catherine de' Medici (about 1560)
- ◼ Reign of Henri IV (1589–1610)
- ◻ Reign of Louis XIII (1610–43)
- ◻ Reign of Louis XIV (1643–1715)
- ◻ Reign of Napoleon I (1804–15)
- ◻ Reign of Napoleon III (1852–70)
- ◻ IM Pei (1989) (architect)

The Carrousel du Louvre underground visitors' complex (1993), with galleries, Shops, lavatories, parking and an information desk, lies beneath the Arc de Triomphe du Carrousel.

Denon Wing

Pyramid entrance

The inverted glass pyramid brings light to the subterranean complex, echoing the museum's new main entrance in the Cour Napoléon.

★ **Arc de Triomphe du Carrousel**
This triumphal arch was built to celebrate Napoleon's military victories in 1805.

STAR FEATURES

★ Perrault Colonnade

★ Medieval Moats

★ Arc de Triomphe du Carrousel

For hotels and restaurants in this region see pp550–5 and pp600–6

THE GLASS PYRAMID

Plans for the modernization and expansion of the Louvre were first conceived in 1981. They included the transfer of the Ministry of Finance from the Richelieu wing of the Louvre to new offices elsewhere, as well as a

new main entrance designed by architect IM Pei in 1989. Made of metal and glass, the pyramid enables the visitor to see the buildings around the palace, while allowing light down into the underground visitors' reception area.

VISITORS' CHECKLIST

Map 12 E2. Automatic ticket booths at Carrousel du Louvre, 99 rue de Rivoli, 75001. Ⓜ Palais Royal, Musée du Louvre. 🚌 21, 27, 39, 48, 68, 69, 72, 95. 🚇 Châtelet-Les-Halles. 🚊 Louvre. 🅿 Carrousel du Louvre (entrance via av du Général Lemonnier); pl du Louvre, rue St-Honoré. ⬤ 9am–6pm Mon, Thu, Sat, & Sun, 9am–10pm Wed & Fri. History of the Louvre rooms open Sat, Sun only. ⬤ 1 Jan, 1 May, 25 Dec. 🎫 (free 1st Sun of each month and for under 18; reduced price for Nocturnals after 6pm). 🚻 partial 01 40 20 59 90. 📞 phone 01 40 20 53 17. 🎬 **Lectures, films, concerts** 01 40 20 55 55. 🔲 🔲 🔲 🔲 www.louvre.fr **Advance bookings:** www.ticketweb.com

Cour Marly is the glass-roofed courtyard that now houses the *Marly Horses (see p103).*

Richelieu Wing

Cour Puget

Hall Napoléon is situated under the pyramid.

Cour Khorsabad

Sully Wing

Cour Carrée

Cour Napoléon

★ **Perrault's Colonnade**
The east façade, with its majestic rows of columns, was built by Claude Perrault, who worked on the Louvre with Louis Le Vau in the mid-17th century.

The Salle des Caryatides is named after the four monumental statues created by Jean Goujon in 1550 to support the upper gallery. Built for Henri II, it is the oldest room in the palace.

The Louvre of Charles V
In about 1360, Charles V transformed Philippe-Auguste's old fortress, with its distinctive tower and keep, into a royal residence.

★ **Medieval Moats**
The base of the twin towers and the drawbridge support of Philippe-Auguste's fortress can be seen in the excavated area.

Exploring the Louvre's Collection

Owing to the vast size of the Louvre's collection, it is useful to set a few viewing priorities before starting. The collection of European paintings (1400–1848) is comprehensive, with over half the works by French artists. The extensively renovated departments of Oriental, Egyptian, Greek, Etruscan, and Roman antiquities feature numerous new acquisitions and rare treasures. The varied display of *objets d'art* includes furniture and jewellery.

The Raft of the Medusa (1819)
by Théodore Géricault

EUROPEAN PAINTING:
1200 TO 1848

Painting from northern Europe (Flemish, Dutch, German and English) is well covered. One of the earliest Flemish works is Jan van Eyck's *Madonna of the Chancellor Rolin* (about 1435), showing the Chancellor of Burgundy kneeling in prayer before the Virgin and Child. Hieronymus Bosch's *Ship of Fools* (1500) is a satirical account of the futility of human existence.

Mona Lisa (about 1504) by
Leonardo da Vinci

In the fine Dutch collection, Rembrandt's *Self-portrait*, his *Disciples at Emmaus* (1648) and *Bathsheba* (1654) are examples of the artist's genius.

The three major German painters of the 15th and 16th centuries are represented by important works. There is a youthful *Self-portrait* (1493) by Albrecht Dürer, a *Venus* (1529) by Lucas Cranach and a portrait of the great humanist scholar Erasmus by Hans Holbein.

The impressive collection of Italian paintings is arranged in chronological order from 1200 to 1800. The father figures of the early Renaissance, Cimabue and Giotto, are here, as is Fra Angelico, with his *Coronation of the Virgin* (1435), and Pisanello, with his delightful *Portrait of Ginevra d'Este* (about 1435). Several paintings by Leonardo da Vinci are on display, for instance the *Virgin with the Infant Jesus and St Anne*, which is as enchanting as his *Mona Lisa*.

The Louvre's fine collection of French painting ranges from the 14th century to 1848.

Paintings after this date are housed in the Musée d'Orsay *(see pp120–21)*. Outstanding is Enguerrand Quarton's *Villeneuve-les-Avignon Pietà* (1455). The great 18th-century painter of melancholy, JA Watteau, is represented, as is JH Fragonard, master of the Rococo, whose delightfully frivolous subjects are evident in *The Bathers* from 1770.

EUROPEAN SCULPTURE:
1100 TO 1848

Early Flemish and German sculpture in the collection has many masterpieces such as Tilman Riemenschneider's *Virgin of the Annunciation* from the end of the 15th century and a life-size nude figure of the penitent Mary Magdalen by Gregor Erhart (early 16th century). An important work of Flemish sculpture is Adrian de Vries's long-limbed *Mercury and Psyche* from 1593, which was originally made for the court of Rudolph II in Prague.

The French section opens with early Romanesque works, such as the figure of Christ by a 12th-century Burgundian sculptor, and a head of St. Peter. With its eight black-hooded mourners, the late 15th-century tomb of Philippe Pot (a high-ranking official in Burgundy) is one of the more unusual pieces. Diane de Poitiers, Henri II's mistress, had a large figure of her namesake Diana, goddess of the hunt, installed in the courtyard of her castle west of Paris. It is now in the Louvre.

The tomb of Philippe Pot (late 15th century) by
Antoine le Moiturier

The celebrated *Marly Horses* (1745) by Guillaume Coustou

The works of French sculptor Pierre Puget (1620–94) have been assembled in the Cour Puget. They include a figure of Milo of Crotona, the Greek athlete who got his hands caught in the cleft of a tree stump and was eaten by a lion. The wild horses of Marly now stand in the Cour Marly, surrounded by other masterpieces of French sculpture, including Jean-Antoine Houdon's early 19th-century busts of famous men such as Diderot and Voltaire.

The collection of Italian sculpture includes such splendid exhibits as Michelangelo's *Slaves* and Benvenuto Cellini's Fontainebleau *Nymph*.

ORIENTAL, EGYPTIAN, GREEK, ETRUSCAN, AND ROMAN ANTIQUITIES

A substantial overhaul of the Louvre has boosted its collection of antiquities, which range from the Neolithic period to the fall of the Roman Empire. Among the new exhibits are Greek and Roman glassware dating from the 6th century BC. Important works of Mesopotamian art include one of the world's oldest legal documents, a basalt block bearing the code of the Babylonian King Hammurabi, dating from about 1700 BC.

The warlike Assyrians are represented by delicate carvings and a spectacular reconstruction of part of Sargon II's (722–705 BC) palace with its winged bulls. A fine example of Persian art is the enamelled brickwork depicting the king of Persia's personal guard of archers (5th century BC).

Most Egyptian art was made for the dead, who were provided with the things they needed for the after life. Examples include the life-like funeral portraits such as the *Squatting Scribe*, and several sculptures of married couples.

The departments of Greek, Roman and Etruscan antiquities contain a vast array of fragments, among them some exceptional pieces. There is a geometric head from the Cyclades (2700 BC) and an elegant swan-necked bowl hammered out of a gold sheet (2500 BC). The two most famous Greek marble statues, the *Winged Victory of Samothrace* and the *Venus de Milo*, both belong to the Hellenistic period (late 3rd to 2nd century BC), when more natural-looking human forms were produced.

The undisputed star of the Etruscan collection is the terracotta sarcophagus of a married couple who look as though they are attending an eternal banquet, while the highlight of the Roman section is a 2nd-century bronze head of the Emperor Hadrian.

Venus de Milo (Greece, late 3rd–early 2nd century BC)

OBJETS D'ART

The catch-all term *objets d'art* (art objects) covers a vast range of items: jewellery, furniture, clocks, watches, sundials, tapestries, miniatures, silver and glassware, cutlery, Byzantine and Parisian carved ivory, Limoges enamels, porcelain, French and Italian stoneware, rugs, snuffboxes, scientific instruments, and armour. The Louvre has well over 8,000 pieces, from many ages and regions.

Many of these precious objects came from the Abbey of St-Denis, where the kings of France were crowned. The treasures include a serpentine stone plate from the 1st century AD with a 9th-century border of gold and precious stones, a porphyry vase which Suger, Abbot of St-Denis, had mounted in gold in the shape of an eagle, and the golden sceptre made for King Charles V in about 1380.

The French crown jewels include the coronation crowns of Louis XV and Napoleon, scepters, swords, and other accessories of the coronation ceremonies. On view also is the Regent, one of the purest diamonds in the world, which Louis XV wore at his coronation in 1722.

One whole room is taken up with a series of tapestries called the *Hunts of Maximilian*, originally executed for Emperor Charles V in 1530. The large collection of French furniture ranges from the 16th to the 19th centuries and is assembled by period, or in rooms devoted to donations by distinguished collectors. On display are pieces by exceptionally prominent furniture-makers such as André-Charles Boulle, cabinet-maker to Louis XIV, who worked at the Louvre in the late 17th to mid-18th centuries.

Squatting Scribe (about 2500 BC), a life-like Egyptian funeral sculpture

Gilded bronze statues by a number of sculptors, decorating the central square of the Palais de Chaillot

CHAMPS-ELYSÉES
AND INVALIDES

The River Seine bisects this area, much of which is built on a monumental scale, from the imposing 18th-century buildings of Les Invalides to the Art Nouveau avenues surrounding the Eiffel Tower. Two of Paris's grandest avenues dominate the neighbourhood to the north of the Seine: the Champs-Elysées has many smart hotels and shops but today is more downmar-

Ornate lamppost on Pont Alexandre III

ket; while the more chic rue du Faubourg St-Honoré has the heavily guarded Palais de l'Elysée. The village of Chaillot was absorbed into the city in the 19th century, and many of its opulent Second Empire mansions are now embassies or company headquarters. Streets around the place du Trocadéro and Palais de Chaillot are packed full of museums and elegant cafés.

SIGHTS AT A GLANCE

Historic Buildings and Streets
Avenue des Champs-Elysées ❷
Palais de l'Elysée ❸
Les Egouts ⓮
No. 29 Avenue Rapp ⓱
Champ-de-Mars ⓲
Ecole Militaire ⓳
Hôtel des Invalides ㉑

Museums and Galleries
Petit Palais ❹
Grand Palais ❺
Musée d'Art Moderne de la Ville de Paris ❼
Musée Galliera ❽

Musée National des Arts Asiatiques Guimet ❾
Cité de l'Architecture et du Patrimoine ❿
Musée Dapper ⓫
Palais de Chaillot ⓭
Musée du Quai Branly ⓯
Musée de l'Armée ㉒
Musée Rodin ㉕
Musée Maillol ㉗

Churches
St-Louis-des-Invalides ㉓
Dôme Church ㉔
Sainte-Clotilde ㉖

Monuments and Fountains
Arc de Triomphe ❶
Eiffel Tower p113 ⓰

Modern Architecture
UNESCO ⓴

Gardens
Jardins du Trocadéro ⓬

Bridges
Pont Alexandre III ❻

GETTING THERE

Metro stations in this area include Etoile, Trocadéro and Champs-Elysées. Bus routes 42 and 73 serve the Champs-Elysées; routes 82 and 69 serve avenue de Suffren and rue St-Dominique respectively.

KEY

▦	Street-by-Street map *pp106–7*
Ⓜ	Metro station
RER	RER station
⬜	Batobus boarding point
ℹ	Tourist information

0 metres   500
0 yards   500

Street by Street: Champs-Elysées

The formal gardens that line the Champs-Elysées from the place de la Concorde to the Rond-Point have changed little since they were laid out by the architect Jacques Hittorff in 1838. The gardens were used as the setting for the World Fair of 1855, which included the Palais de l'Industrie, Paris's response to London's Crystal Palace. The Palais was later replaced by the Grand Palais and the Petit Palais, which was created as a showpiece of the Third Republic for the Universal Exhibition of 1900. They sit on either side of an impressive vista that stretches from the place Clémenceau across the elegant curve of the Pont Alexandre III, with its four strong anchoring columns, to the Invalides.

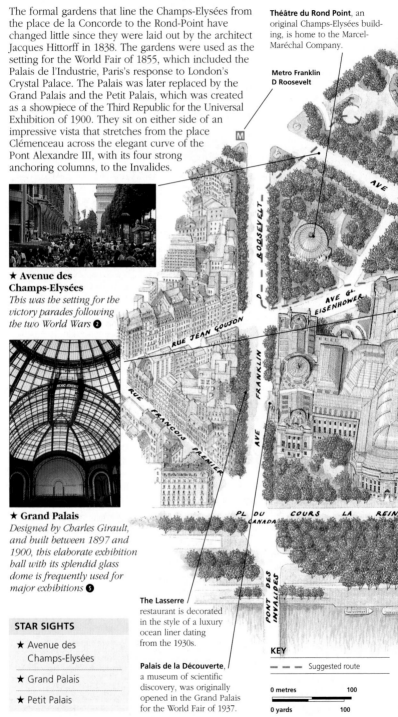

Théâtre du Rond Point, an original Champs-Elysées building, is home to the Marcel-Maréchal Company.

Metro Franklin D Roosevelt

★ **Avenue des Champs-Elysées**
This was the setting for the victory parades following the two World Wars ❷

★ **Grand Palais**
Designed by Charles Girault, and built between 1897 and 1900, this elaborate exhibition hall with its splendid glass dome is frequently used for major exhibitions ❺

The Lasserre restaurant is decorated in the style of a luxury ocean liner dating from the 1930s.

Palais de la Découverte, a museum of scientific discovery, was originally opened in the Grand Palais for the World Fair of 1937.

STAR SIGHTS

★ Avenue des Champs-Elysées

★ Grand Palais

★ Petit Palais

KEY

– – – Suggested route

0 metres   100

0 yards   100

For hotels and restaurants in this region see pp550–5 and pp600–6

The Jardins des Champs-Elysées, with their fountains, flowerbeds and pleasure pavilions, have been a popular spot since the 19th century.

LOCATOR MAP
See Street Finder maps
2, 3, 6, 7

Metro
Champs-
Elysées-
Clémenceau

To place
de la
Concorde

★ **Petit Palais**
The art collections of the city of Paris are housed here. They contain artifacts ranging from antique sculptures to landscape paintings by the Barbizon School ❹

Pont Alexandre III
This ornate, single-span structure symbolizes the optimism of the Belle Epoque at the turn of the 20th century.

To the Invalides

The east façade of the Arc de Triomphe

Arc de Triomphe ❶

Place Charles de Gaulle, 75008.
Map 2 D4. Ⓜ *Charles de Gaulle-Etoile.* ***Tel*** *01 55 37 73 77.* ***Museum*** ◯ *Apr–Sep: 10am–11pm daily; Oct–Mar: 10am–10.30pm daily (last adm 30 mins earlier).* ◉ *Jan 1, May 1, 8 May, Jul 14, Nov 11, 25 Dec.* ♿ ⓞ
♺ ⓞ www.monum.fr

After his greatest victory, the Battle of Austerlitz in 1805, Napoleon promised his men they would "go home beneath triumphal arches." The first stone of what was to become the world's most famous triumphal arch was laid the following year. But disruptions to architect Jean Chalgrin's plans and the demise of Napoleonic power delayed completion. Standing 50 m (164 ft) high, the Arc is encrusted with reliefs, shields, and sculptures. The viewing platform offers spendid views.

On 11 November 1920 the body of the Unknown Soldier was placed beneath the arch to commemorate the dead of World War I. The tomb's eternal flame is lit every evening.

High relief by JP Corot, celebrating the Triumph of Napoleon

BARON HAUSSMANN

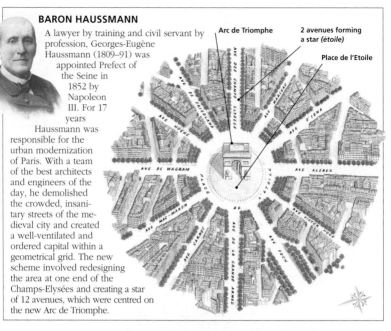

A lawyer by training and civil servant by profession, Georges-Eugène Haussmann (1809–91) was appointed Prefect of the Seine in 1852 by Napoleon III. For 17 years Haussmann was responsible for the urban modernization of Paris. With a team of the best architects and engineers of the day, he demolished the crowded, insanitary streets of the medieval city and created a well-ventilated and ordered capital within a geometrical grid. The new scheme involved redesigning the area at one end of the Champs-Elysées and creating a star of 12 avenues, which were centred on the new Arc de Triomphe.

Arc de Triomphe

2 avenues forming a star *(étoile)*

Place de l'Etoile

Avenue des Champs-Elysées ❷

75008. **Map** 3 A5. Ⓜ *Charles de Gaulle-Etoile, George V, Franklin D Roosevelt, Champs-Elysées - Clemenceau, Concorde.*

The majestic avenue "of the Elysian Fields" (the name refers to a mythical Greek heaven for heroes), first laid out in the 1660s by the landscape designer André Le Nôtre, forms a 3 km (2 mile) straight line from the huge place de la Concorde to the Arc de Triomphe. The 19th century saw it transformed from horseride into elegant boulevard. Today it's a crowded tourist trap with notorious traffic, but the Champs-Elysées keeps its style, its memories – and a special place in the French heart. National parades are held here, the finish of the annual Tour de France cycle race is always in the Champs-Elysées, and, above all, it is where Parisians instinctively go at times of great national celebration.

Palais de l'Elysée ❸

55 rue du Faubourg-St-Honoré 75008. **Map** 3 B5. Ⓜ *St-Philippe-du-Roule.* 🔲 *to the public.*

Amid splendid gardens, the Elysée Palace was built in 1718 and has been the official residence of the President of the Republic since 1873. Several occupants left their mark. Louis XV's mistress, Madame de Pompadour, had the whole site enlarged. After the Revolution, it became a dance hall. In the 19th century, it was home to Napoleon's sister Caroline

Elysée guard

Murat, and his wife Empress Josephine. The President's Apartments are today on the first floor.

Petit Palais ❹

Av Winston Churchill 75008. **Map** 7 B1. **Tel** 01 53 43 40 00. Ⓜ *Champs-Elysées-Clemenceau.* 🔲 *10am–6pm Tue–Sun.* 🔲 *public hols.* 🏷️ 🎫 *for exhibitions.* 📷 🔲 ♿ 🔲

Built for the Universal Exhibition in 1900 to stage a major display of French art, this jewel of a building was renovated in 2005 and houses the Musée des Beaux-Arts de la Ville de Paris. The architect, Charles Girault, arranged the palace around a semi-circular

GRAND PALAIS

Exhibition space   Iron supports

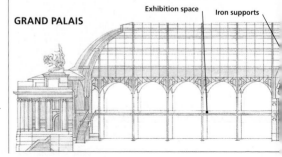

Pont Alexandre III, built 1896–1900 for the Universal Exhibition

courtyard and garden, similar in style to the Grand Palais. Permanent exhibits, housed on the Champs-Elysées side, include the Dutuit Collection of medieval and Renaissance *objets d'art*, paintings and drawings; the Tuck Collection of 18th-century furniture and *objets d'art*; and the City of Paris collection, with work by Ingres, Delacroix and Courbet,

Entrance to the Petit Palais

and the landscape painters of the Barbizon School. Temporary exhibitions are housed in the Cours de la Reine wing.

Grand Palais ❺

Porte A, av Général Eisenhower 75008. **Map** 7 A1. **Tel** 01 44 13 17 17. Ⓜ *Champs-Elysées-Clemenceau.* ⃝ *for temporary exhibitions only; 10am–8pm Wed–Mon.* ⬤ *1 May, 25 Dec.* 🚫 ⬤ ♿ 🏛 📷 🛒 **www**.rmn.fr *Palais de la Decouverte:* av Franklin D. Roosevelt 75008. **Tel** 01 56 43 20 21. Ⓜ *Franklin D. Roosevelt.* ⃝ *9:30am–6pm Tue–Sat, 10am–7pm Sun & public hols.* 🎫 ⬤ 📷 **www**.palais-decouverte.fr

Built at the same time as the Petit Palais opposite, this huge, glass-roofed palace has a fine Classical façade adorned with statuary and Art Nouveau ironwork. Bronze flying horses and chariots stand at the four corners. The Great Hall and the recently restored glass cupola can be admired during exhibitions. On the west side of the building, with a separate entrance, the **Palais de la Découverte** is an imaginative child-oriented science museum.

Pont Alexandre III ❻

75008. **Map** 7 A1. Ⓜ *Champs-Elysées-Clemenceau.*

This is Paris's prettiest bridge, with exuberant Art Nouveau decoration of gilt and bronze lamps, cupids and cherubs, nymphs and winged horses at either end. It was built between 1896 and 1900 to commemorate the 1892 French-Russian alliance, and in time for the Universal Exhibition in 1900. Pont Alexandre III was named after Tsar Alexander III (father of Nicholas II), who laid the foundation stone in October 1896.

The style of the bridge reflects that of the Grand Palais, to which it leads on the Right Bank. The construction of the bridge is a marvel of 19th-century engineering. It consists of a 6-m (18-ft) high single-span steel arch across the Seine. The design was subject to strict controls that prevented the bridge from obscuring the view of the Champs-Elysées or the Invalides, so today you can still enjoy the magnificent views from here.

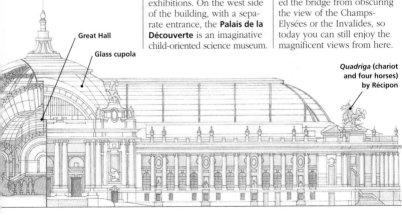

Great Hall

Glass cupola

Quadriga (chariot and four horses) by Récipon

Musée d'Art Moderne de la Ville de Paris ❼

Palais du Tokyo, 11 av du Président-Wilson 75016. **Map** 6 E1. **Tel** 01 53 67 40 00. Ⓜ Iéna, Alma-Marceau. ⬤ 10am–6pm Tue–Sun (until 10pm Wed). ⬤ 1 Jan. 🖼 for temporary exhibitions 🚻 🔧 📷 📱 www.mam.paris.fr

This museum covers trends in 20th-century art and is located in the east wing of the Palais de Tokyo. The Fauves and Cubists are well represented here. Highlights include Raoul Dufy's gigantic mural, *The Spirit of Electricity* (created for the 1937 World Fair), and Matisse's *The Dance* (1932). There is also a collection of Art Deco furniture.

Musée Galliera ❽

10 ave Pierre 1er de Serbie 75116. **Map** 6 D1. **Tel** 01 56 52 86 00. Ⓜ Iéna, Alma-Marceau. ⬤ 10am–6pm Tue–Sun & 2–6pm some public hols, but check as only open for exhibitions. 🖼 **Children's room.** www.galliera.paris.fr

Devoted to the evolution of fashion, this museum, also known as the Musée de la Mode et du Costume, is housed in the Renaissance-style palace built for the Duchesse Maria de Ferrari Galliera in 1892. The collection includes more than 100,000 outfits and fashion accessories, from the 18th century to the present day. Donations have been made by such fashionable women as Baronne Hélène de Rothschild and Princess Grace of Monaco. Eminent couturiers such as Balmain and Balenciaga have donated their designs to the museum.

Often extremely fragile, the fashion exhibits are displayed in rotation, usually in two major exhibitions each year. These shows can highlight a particular couturier's career or explore a single theme.

Trocadéro fountains in front of the Palais de Chaillot

Musée Dapper ⓫

35bis rue Paul-Valéry, 75016. **Map** 2 D5. **Tel** 01 45 00 01 50. Ⓜ Victor-Hugo. ⬤ 11am– 7pm Wed–Mon. 🖼 www.dapper.com/fr

A world-class ethnographic research centre, this is one of France's premier showcases of African art and culture. Located in an attractive building with an "African" garden, it is a treasure house of colour and powerful, evocative work from the black nations. The focus is on pre-colonial folk arts, with sculpture, carvings and tribal work, but there is later art, too. The highlight is tribal masks, with a dazzling, extra-ordinary array of richly carved religious, ritual and funerary masks, as well as theatrical ones used for comic, magical or symbolic performances.

Jardins du Trocadéro ⓬

75016. **Map** 6 D2. Ⓜ Trocadéro.

These beautiful gardens cover 10 ha (25 acres). Their centrepiece is a long rectangular ornamental pool, bordered by stone and bronze-gilt statues, which looks spectacular at night when the fountains are illuminated. The statues include *Woman* by Georges Braque and *Horse* by Georges Lucien Guyot. On either side of the pool, the slopes of the Chaillot hill lead gently down to the Seine and the Pont d'Iéna. There is a freshwater aquarium in the northeast corner of the gardens, which are richly laid out with trees, walkways, small streams and bridges.

Palais de Chaillot ⓭

Pl du Trocadéro 75016. **Map** 5 C2. Ⓜ Trocadéro. **Théâtre National de Chaillot Tel** 01 53 65 30 00. **Musée de l'Homme Tel** 01 44 05 72 72. ⬤ Wed–Mon. **Musée de la Marine Tel** 01 53 65 69 69. ⬤ Wed–Mon. ⬤ 1 Jan, 1 May, 25 Dec.

The Palais, with its huge, curved colonnaded wings each culminating in a vast pavillion, has three museums and a theatre. Designed in Neo-Classical style for the 1937 Paris Exhibition by Azéma, Louis-Auguste Boileau and Jacques Carlu, it is adorned with sculptures and bas-reliefs. On the walls of the pavillions are gold inscriptions which were written by the poet and essayist, Paul Valéry. The square *(parvis)* between the two pavillions

Musée National des Arts Asiatiques Guimet ⑨

6 pl d'Iéna 75016. **Map** 6 D1. **Tel** 01 56 52 53 00. Ⓜ Iéna. ◯ 10am–6pm Wed–Mon. 📷 📖 ♿ 🖥
Panthéon Bouddhique, 19 av d'Iéna. **Tel** 01 40 73 88 11.
www.museeguimet.fr

One of the world's leading museums of Asian art, the Guimet has a fine collection of Cambodian (Khmer) art. It was set up in Lyon in 1879 by Emile Guimet, and then moved to Paris in 1884. It includes a comprehensive Asian research centre.

Buddha head from Musée Guimet

Cité de l'Architecture et du Patrimoine ⑩

Palais de Chaillot, pl du Trocadéro 75016. **Map** 5 C2. **Tel** 01 58 51 52 00. Ⓜ Trocadéro. ◯ noon–8pm Mon, Wed–Fri, 11am–7pm Sat & Sun. 📷 📖 🍴 🖥

This museum charts the development of French architecture through the ages and includes three-dimensional models of great French cathedrals, such as Chartres (*see pp308–11*). There is also a reconstruction of a Le Corbusier-designed apartment.

PALAIS DE CHAILLOT

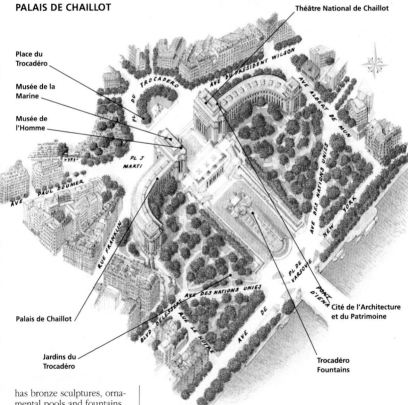

Place du Trocadéro

Musée de la Marine

Musée de l'Homme

Théâtre National de Chaillot

Palais de Chaillot

Jardins du Trocadéro

Cité de l'Architecture et du Patrimoine

Trocadéro Fountains

has bronze sculptures, ornamental pools and fountains. Steps lead down from the terrace to the **Théâtre National de Chaillot**, which has productions covering all eras and genres of theatre.

The **Musée de l'Homme**, in the west wing, stages temporary exhibitions tracing human evolution through a series of anthropological exhibits. The museum is undergoing extensive renovation. Next door is the **Musée de la Marine**, devoted to French naval history and aspects of the modern-day navy. The east wing contains the Cité de l'Architecture et du Patrimoine (*see above*).

Les Egouts ⑭

Opposite 93 quai d'Orsay 75007.
Map 6 F2. 📞 *01 53 68 27 81 (in English).* Ⓜ *Alma-Marceau.* ○ *11am–4pm (5pm in summer) Sat–Wed.* ● *last 3 wks Jan.* 🎫 🎞 🚻

One of Baron Haussmann's finest achievements, the majority of Paris's sewers (*égouts*) date from the Second Empire. If laid end to end the 2,100 km (1,300 miles) of sewers would stretch from Paris to Istanbul. They are a popular tourist attraction. All tours have been limited to a small area around the quai d'Orsay entrance and are now on foot. A sewer museum has been established here where visitors can discover the mysteries of underground Paris. There are also displays showing how the machinery used in the sewers has changed over the years.

Musée du Quai Branly ⑮

37 quai Branly. **Map** 6 E2. **Tel** *01 56 61 70 00.* Ⓜ *Alma-Marceau.* ▣ *Pont-de-l'Alma.* ○ *10am–6:30pm Tue–Sun (until 9:30pm Thu).* 🎫 🚻
🚻 **Exhibitions, theatre, film, library.** www.quaibranly.fr

Built to give the arts of Africa, Asia, Oceania and the Americas a platform as shining as that for Western art in the city, this museum has a massive collection of more than 300,000 objects. It is particularly strong on Africa, with stone, wooden and ivory masks, as well as ceremonial tools. The Jean Nouvel-designed building, which is raised on stilts, is a worthwhile sight in itself, while the ingenious use of glass in its construction allows the surrounding greenery to act as a natural backdrop for the collection.

Aztec mask, Musée du Quai Branly

Eiffel Tower ⑯

See p113.

Original Art Nouveau doorway at No. 29 avenue Rapp

No. 29 Avenue Rapp ⑰

75005. **Map** 6 E2. Ⓜ *Pont-de-l'Alma.*

A prime example of Art Nouveau architecture, No. 29 avenue Rapp won its designer, Jules Lavirotte, first prize at the Concours des Façades de la Ville de Paris in 1901. Its ceramics and brickwork are decorated with animal and flower motifs intermingling with female figures. These are super-imposed on a multi-coloured sandstone base to produce a façade that is deliberately erotic, and was certainly subversive in its day. Also worth visiting nearby is Lavirotte's building, complete with watch-tower, which can be found in the square Rapp.

Champ-de-Mars ⑱

75007. **Map** 6 E3. Ⓜ *Ecole-Militaire.* ▣ *Champ-de-Mars–Tour-Eiffel.*

The vast gardens stretching from the Eiffel Tower to the Ecole Militaire (Military School) were originally a parade ground for young officer cadets. The area has since been used for horse-racing, balloon ascents and mass ceremonies to celebrate the anniversary of the Revolution on July 14th. The first ceremony was held in 1790, in the presence of a glum, captive, Louis XVI.

Mammoth exhibitions were held here in the late 19th century, among them the 1889 World Fair for which the Eiffel Tower was erected.

Ecole Militaire ⑲

1 pl Joffre 75007. **Map** 6 F4.
Ⓜ *Ecole-Militaire.* **Visits** *by special permission only – contact the Commandant in writing.*

The Royal Military Academy of Louis XV was founded in 1751 to educate 500 sons of impoverished officers. Louis XV and Madame de Pompadour commissioned architect Jacques-Ange Gabriel to design a building that would rival Louis XIV's Hôtel des Invalides. Financing the building became a problem so a lottery was authorized and a tax was raised on playing-cards. One of the main features is the central pavilion – a magnificent example of the French Classical style, with ten Corinthian columns and a quadrangular dome. Four figures adorn the entablature frieze, symbolizing France, Victory, Force and Peace.

An early cadet at the academy was Napoleon, whose passing-out report stated that "he could go far if the circumstances are right".

A 1751 engraving showing the planning of the Ecole Militaire

Eiffel Tower ⑯

Built for the Universal Exhibition of 1889, and to commemorate the centennial of the Revolution, the 324 m (1,063 ft) Eiffel Tower (Tour Eiffel) was meant to be a temporary addition to Paris's skyline. Designed by Gustave Eiffel, it was fiercely decried by 19th-century aesthetes. It stood as the world's tallest building until 1931, when New York's Empire State Building was completed.

Eiffel Tower seen from the Trocadéro

VISITORS' CHECKLIST

Champ-de-Mars–Tour Eiffel, 75007
Map 6 D3. *Tel* 01 44 11 23 23.
Ⓜ *Bir Hakeim.* 🚌 42, 69, 72, 82, 87 to Champ-de-Mars. 🚇 *Champ-de-Mars.* 🅿 *Tour Eiffel.* 🕐 Sep–mid-Jun: 9:30am–11pm daily; mid-Jun–Aug: 9am–midnight. 🎫 📷 🍴 ♿ www.tour-eiffel.fr

DARING FEATS

The tower has always inspired crazy stunts. In 1912, Reichelt, a Parisian tailor, attempted to fly from the parapet with only a cape for wings. He plunged to his death in front of a large crowd.

Stuntman Reichelt

The third level, 276 m (905 ft) above the ground, can hold 800 people at a time.

★ **Viewing Gallery**
On a clear day it is possible to see for 72 km (45 miles), including a distant view of Chartres Cathedral.

STAR FEATURES

★ Eiffel Bust

★ Viewing Gallery

The double-decker lifts have a limited capacity, and during the tourist season there can be long waits. Queuing for the lifts requires patience and a good head for heights.

Cineiffel
This small audio-visual museum shows historical film footage of the tower.

The second level is at 115 m (376 ft), separated from the first level by 359 steps or a few minutes in the lift.

Jules Verne restaurant is rated highly in Paris, offering not only superb food, but a breathtaking panoramic view.

★ **Eiffel Bust**
The achievement of Eiffel (1832–1923) was honoured by Antoine Bourdelle, who placed this bust under the tower in 1929.

The first level, 57 m (187 ft) high, can be reached by lift or by 360 steps. There is a post office here.

LES INVALIDES

Musée de l'Armée   Hôtel des Invalides   Cour d'Honneur

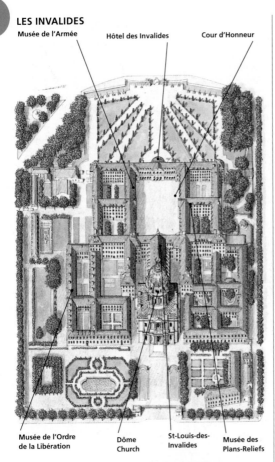

Musée de l'Ordre
de la Libération   Dôme
Church   St-Louis-des-
Invalides   Musée des
Plans-Reliefs

was completed in 1676 by
Jules Hardouin-Mansart. He
later incorporated the Dôme
Church, with its glittering
golden roof, which was built
as Louis XIV's private chapel.
Nearly 6,000 soldiers once
resided here. Today there are
fewer than 100.

The harmonious Classical
façade is one of the most
impressive sights in Paris. The
building houses the Musée de
l'Armée and the Musée de
l'Ordre de la Libération. This
was set up to honour feats of
heroism during World War II
under the leadership of Charles
de Gaulle. The story is told
using documents, photographs
and mementos. The Musée
des Plans-Reliefs also houses a
large collection of military
models of French forts.

Musée de l'Armée ㉒

Hôtel des Invalides 75007. **Map** 7 A3.
Tel 01 44 42 38 77. **M** Varenne,
Latour-Maubourg, Invalides. ◯ 10am–
6pm (5pm winter) daily; some sections may be closed during
renovations in 2008. ● 1st Mon of
month, 1 Jan, 1 May, 1 Nov, 25 Dec.
📸 ◯ ♿ 🎧 🛒 🎁

This is one of the most
comprehensive museums of
military history in the world.
It is housed in two galleries,
situated on either side of the
magnificent courtyard of the
Hôtel des Invalides and in the
newly opened "Priests' Wing"
with the World War II galleries.

A major exhibit recalls the
victories and defeats of France
through history, dedicated
mainly to the Napoleonic
era. The emperor's death mask
and stuffed horse, Vizier, are
on display. Other exhibits include François I's ivory hunting
horns, Oriental arms from
Japan, and a model of the
1944 Normandy landing.

UNESCO ⑳

7 pl de Fontenoy 75007. **Map** 6 F5.
📞 01 45 68 10 60 (in English).
M Ségur, Cambronne. ◯ for guided
tours only: 3pm Tue (English), 3pm
Wed (French). ● public hols. ♿ 🎧
🍴 🎁 www.unesco.org

This is the headquarters of
the United Nations
Educational, Scientific and
Cultural Organization
(UNESCO). Its aim is to
contribute to international
peace through education,
science and culture.

UNESCO is a treasure-trove
of modern art, including an
enormous mural by Picasso,
ceramics by Joan Miró and
sculptures by Henry Moore,
and the calm Japanese garden
by Nogushi. Exhibitions and
films are also held here.

Hôtel des Invalides ㉑

75007. **Map** 7 A3. **Tel** 01 44 42 37
72. **M** Latour-Maubourg, Invalides,
Varenne. ◯ 10am–6pm (5pm winter)
daily. ● 1 Jan, 1 May, 1 Nov, 25 Dec.
www.invalides.org

This imposing building, from
which the area takes its name,
was commissioned by Louis
XIV in 1670 for his wounded
and homeless veterans. Designed by Libéral Bruand, it

The façade of the Musée de l'Armée

Altar of St-Louis-des-Invalides with banners seized in battle

St-Louis-des-Invalides ㉓

Hôtel des Invalides 75007. **Map** 7 A3. Ⓜ Invalides, Latour-Maubourg, Varenne. **Tel** 01 44 42 37 72. ◯ 10am–5:30pm (4:30pm winter) daily.

Also known as the "soldiers' church", this is the chapel of the Hôtel des Invalides. It was built from 1679 to 1708 by Jules Hardouin-Mansart, according to Bruand's design. The stark, Classical interior is well-proportioned, designed in the shape of a Greek cross.

There is a fine 17th-century organ, built by Alexandre Thierry, on which the first performance of Berlioz's *Requiem* was given on 5 December 1837, with more than 200 musicians and choristers participating.

Dôme Church ㉔

Hôtel des Invalides, 129 rue de Grenelle, 75007. **Map** 7 A3. **Tel** 01 44 42 38 77. Ⓜ Latour-Maubourg, Varenne, Invalides. ▤ 28, 49, 63, 69, 80, 82, 83, 87, 92, 93 to Les Invalides. 𝖱𝖤𝖱 Invalides. ◯ Tour Eiffel. ◯ Oct–Mar: 10am–5pm; Apr–Sep: 10am–6pm daily. ◯ 1st Mon of month, 1 Jan, 1 May, 17 Jun, 1 Nov, 25 Dec. 🎦 ⬛ 🚻 restr. 🚫 🖳 🅰

Jules Hardouin-Mansart was asked in 1676 by the Sun King, Louis XIV, to build the Dôme Church to complement the existing buildings of the

Invalides military refuge, designed by Libéral Bruand. The Dôme was to be reserved for the exclusive use of the Sun King and as the location of royal tombs.

The resulting masterpiece is one of the greatest examples of 17th-century French architecture, the period known as the *grand siècle*. After Louis XIV's death, plans to bury the royal family in the church were abandoned.

The main attraction is the tomb of Napoleon; 20 years after his death on the island of St Helena, his body was returned to France and installed in this magnificent crypt, encased in six coffins in an enormous red porphyry sarcophagus.

Dôme Church with cupola, first gilded in 1715

Musée Rodin ㉕

79 rue de Varenne 75007. **Map** 7 B3. **Tel** 01 44 18 61 10. Ⓜ Varenne. ◯ 9:30am–5:45pm (4:45pm winter) Tue–Sun; garden 1 hr later (5pm winter). ◯ 1 Jan, 1 May, 25 Dec. 🎦 🚻 restricted. 🖳 🅰 www.musee-rodin.fr

Auguste Rodin (1840–1917), regarded as one of the greatest French sculptors, lived and worked in the Hôtel Biron, an elegant 18th-century mansion, from 1908 until his death. In return for a state-owned flat and studio, Rodin left his work to the nation, and it is now exhibited here.

Some of his most celebrated sculptures are on display in the garden: *The Burghers of Calais, The Thinker, The Gates of Hell (see p120)* and *Balzac*.

The indoor exhibits are arranged in chronological order, spanning the whole of Rodin's career. Highlights include *The Kiss* and *Eve*.

Sainte-Clotilde ㉖

12 rue de Martignac 75007. **Map** 7 B3. 🛈 01 44 18 62 60. Ⓜ Solférino, Varenne, Invalides. ◯ 9am–7:30pm daily. ◯ non-religious public hols. **Concerts**

Designed by the German-born architect Franz Christian Gau and built in 1846–56, this Neo-Gothic church was inspired by the 19th-century enthusiasm for the Middle Ages, popularized by such writers as Victor Hugo.

The interior decoration includes wall paintings by James Pradier and stained-glass windows with scenes relating to the patron saint of the church. The composer César Franck was organist here from 1858 to 1890.

Musée Maillol ㉗

61 rue de Grenelle 75007. **Map** 7 C4. **Tel** 01 42 22 59 58. Ⓜ Rue du Bac, Sèvres-Babylone. ◯ 11am–6pm Wed–Mon (last entry 5:15pm). ◯ publ hols. 🅰 🖳 🅰 www.museemaillol.com

This museum was created by Dina Vierny, muse to Aristide Maillol. His work is here in all its forms: drawings, engravings, paintings, sculpture and decorative objects. Also displayed is Dina Vierny's private collection of naïve art, works by Matisse, Dufy, Picasso and Rodin, and top temporary exhibitions. Allegorical figures of the city of Paris and the four seasons adorn Bouchardon's fountain outside.

Rodin's *The Thinker* in museum garden

THE LEFT BANK

The Left Bank has long been associated with poets, philosophers, artists and radical thinkers of all kinds. It still has its share of bohemian street life and pavement cafés, but the smart set has moved in, patronizing Yves St-Laurent and the exclusive interior design shops in rue Jacob.

The Latin Quarter is the ancient area lying between the Seine and Luxembourg Gardens, and is today filled with bookshops, art galleries and cafés. The boulevard St-Michel, bordering the Latin quarter and St-Germain-des-Prés, has slowly given way to commerce, and is full of

Clock in the Musée d'Orsay

fast-food outlets and cheap shops. The surrounding maze of narrow, cobbled streets has retained its character, with ethnic shop and avant-garde theatres dominated by the façade of the Sorbonne, France's first university, built in 1253. Many Parisians dream of living near the Luxembourg Gardens, a quiet area with charming old streets, gateways, and elaborate gardens full of paths, lawns and tree-lined avenues. Students come here to chat, and on warm days, old men still meet underneath the chestnut trees to play chess or the traditional French game of *boules*.

SIGHTS AT A GLANCE

Churches
Panthéon ⓭
St-Etienne-du-Mont ⓬
St-Germain-des-Prés ❺
St-Julien-le-Pauvre ❿
St-Séverin ❾

St-Sulpice ⓯
Val-de-Grâce ⓱

Museums and Galleries
Musée de Cluny ❽
Musée Eugène Delacroix ❻
Musée d'Orsay pp120–1 ❶

Fountains
Fontaine de l'Observatoire ⓰

Historic Buildings and Streets
Boulevard St-Germain ❷
Ecole Nationale Supérieure des Beaux Arts ❹
Palais du Luxembourg ⓮
Quai Voltaire ❸
Rue de l'Odéon ❼
La Sorbonne ⓫

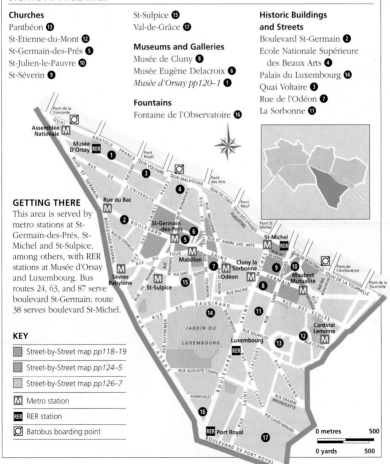

GETTING THERE
This area is served by metro stations at St-Germain-des-Prés, St-Michel and St-Sulpice, among others, with RER stations at Musée d'Orsay and Luxembourg. Bus routes 24, 63, and 87 serve boulevard St-Germain; route 38 serves boulevard St-Michel.

KEY
▮	Street-by-Street map *pp118–19*
▮	Street-by-Street map *pp124–5*
▮	Street-by-Street map *pp126–7*
Ⓜ	Metro station
RER	RER station
Ⓞ	Batobus boarding point

| 0 metres | 500 |
| 0 yards | 500 |

◁ **Jardin du Luxembourg with Panthéon**

Street-by-Street: St-Germain-des-Prés

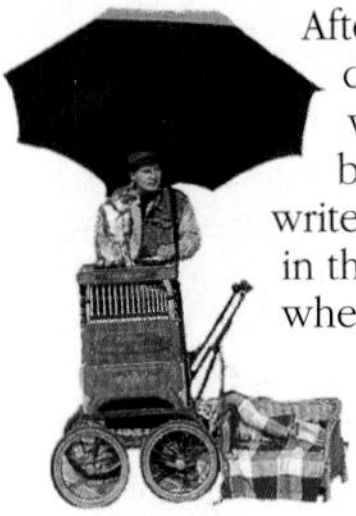

After World War II, St-Germain-des-Prés became synonymous with intellectual life centred on bars and cafés. Philosophers, writers, actors and musicians mingled in the cellar nightspots and brasseries, where existentialist philosophy co-existed with American jazz.

Organ grinder in St-Germain

The area is now smarter than in the heyday of Jean-Paul Sartre and Simone de Beauvoir, the enigmatic singer Juliette Greco and the New Wave film-makers.

However, the writers are still around, enjoying the pleasures of sitting in Les Deux Magots, Café de Flore and other haunts. The 17th-century buildings have survived, but signs of change are evident in the affluent shops dealing in antiques, books and fashion.

Les Deux Magots became a focus of bohemian and literary activity in the 1920s.

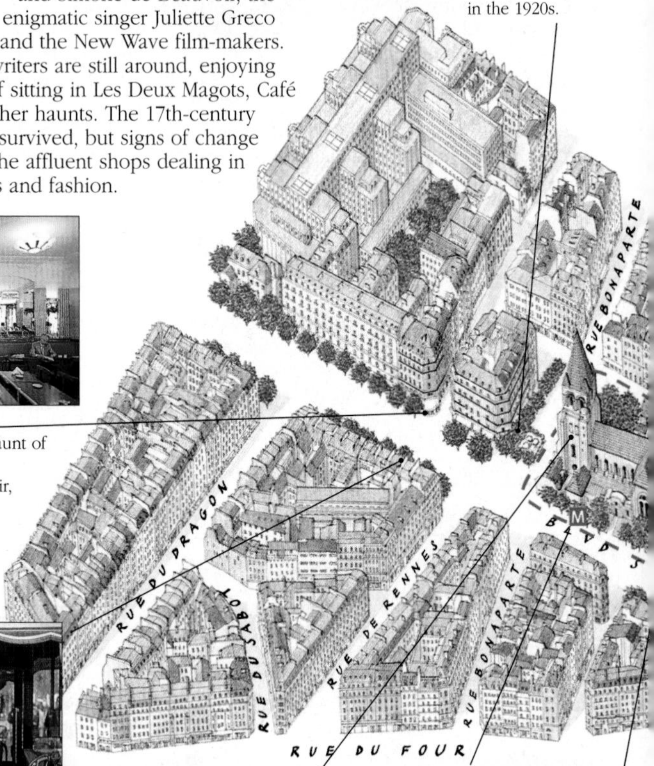

Café de Flore, the former favourite haunt of Jean-Paul Sartre, Simone de Beauvoir, and other French intellectuals, still has a classic Art Deco interior.

RUE DU DRAGON

RUE DU SABOT

RUE DE RENNES

RUE BONAPARTE

RUE DU FOUR

Metro St-Germain-des-Prés

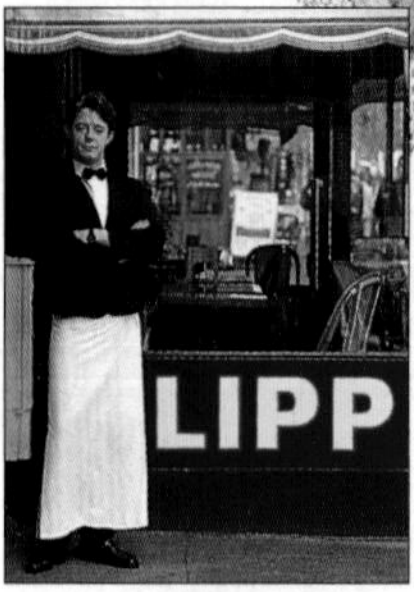

Brasserie Lipp, decorated with colourful ceramics, is a renowned brasserie frequented by politicians.

★ **St-Germain-des-Prés**
The philosopher René Descartes is among the notables buried here in Paris's oldest church ❺

★ **Boulevard St-Germain**
Café terraces, boutiques, cinemas, restaurants and bookshops characterize the central section of the Left Bank's main street ❷

STAR SIGHTS

* ★ St-Germain-des-Prés
* ★ Boulevard St-Germain
* ★ Musée Delacroix

KEY

– – – Suggested route

LOCATOR MAP
See Street Finder maps 7, 8

★ Musée Delacroix
The home of the Romantic painter Eugène Delacroix (1798–1863) is now a museum devoted to his art ❻

Palais Abbatial was the residence of abbots from 1586 till the 1789 Revolution.

Rue de Buci was for centuries an important street and the site of some Real Tennis courts. It now holds a lively market.

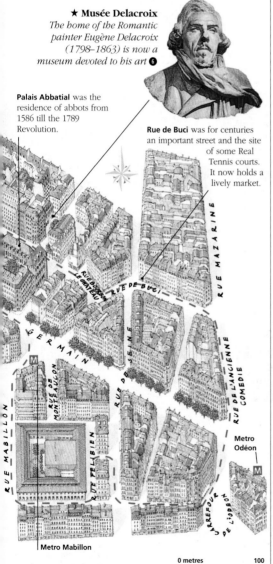

Metro Odéon

Metro Mabillon

| 0 metres | 100 |
| 0 yards | 100 |

Musée d'Orsay ❶

See pp120–1.

Boulevard St-Germain ❷

75006, 75007. **Map** 8 D4. Ⓜ
Solférino, Rue du Bac, St-Germain-des-Prés, Mabillon, Odéon.

The Left Bank's most celebrated thoroughfare curves across three districts from the Ile St-Louis to the Pont de la Concorde. The architecture is homogeneous because the boulevard was another of Baron Hauss-mann's bold strokes of 19th-century urban planning, but it encompasses a wide range of different lifestyles from bohemian to bourgeois.

Starting from the east, it passes Musée de Cluny and the Sorbonne. It is most lively from boulevard St-Michel to St-Germain-des-Prés, with its café culture.

Quai Voltaire ❸

75006, 75007. **Map** 8 D3.
Ⓜ *Rue du Bac.*

The quai Voltaire is now home to some of the most important antiques dealers in Paris. Many famous people have lived in the attractive 18th-century houses, among others Voltaire at No. 27 and Richard Wagner, Jean Sibelius and Oscar Wilde at No. 19.

Plaque marking the house in quai Voltaire where Voltaire died in 1778

Musée d'Orsay **❶**

In 1986, 47 years after it had closed as a mainline railroad station, Victor Laloux's turn-of-the-century building reopened as the Musée d'Orsay. Built as the Orléans railway terminus in the heart of Paris, it narrowly avoided demolition in the 1970s. In the conversion to a museum much of the original architecture was retained.

The museum presents the rich diversity of visual arts from 1848 to 1914 and explains the social and technological context in which they were created. The displays are currently being reorganized. Although the majority of the exhibits are paintings and sculptures, furniture, the decorative arts, cinema and the newspaper industry are also represented.

Young Dancer of Fourteen **(1881)** by Edgar Degas

The Gates of Hell *(1880–1917)*
Rodin included figures that he had already created, such as The Thinker *and* The Kiss, *in this famous gateway.*

Dancing at the Moulin de la Galette *(1876)*
Renoir painted this picture outside to capture the light as it filtered through the trees.

The Dance *(1867–8)*
Carpeaux's dynamic sculpture caused a scandal when it was first unveiled in 1869.

KEY TO FLOORPLAN

- Architecture & Decorative Arts
- Sculpture
- Painting before 1870
- Impressionism
- Neo-Impressionism
- Naturalism and Symbolism
- Art Nouveau
- Temporary exhibitions
- Non-exhibition space

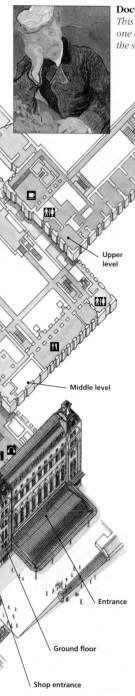

Doctor Paul Gachet *(1890)*
*This portrait by Van Gogh is
one of three and was painted
the same year the artist died.*

GALLERY GUIDE

*The ground floor has works
from the mid- to late 19th
century. The middle level
features Art Nouveau
decorative art and late
19th- to early 20th-
century paintings
and sculptures.
The upper level has
Impressionist and
Neo-Impressionist art.*

VISITORS' CHECKLIST

Quai Anatole France, 75007.
Map 8 D2. *Tel* 01 40 49 48 14.
Ⓜ *Solférino.* 🚌 24, 68, 69, 84 to
quai A. France; 73 to rue de la
Légion d'Honneur; 63, 83, 84, 94
to bd St-Germain. 🚆 💺 🅾️
Musée d'Orsay. 🅿️ Quai A. France.
⭘ 9:30am–6pm Tue–Sun (9:45pm
Thu; last entry 1 hr before closing).
⬤ 1 Jan, 1 May, 25 Dec.
🖼 🅾️ ♿ 🛒 🍴 📷 *Concerts*
phone 01 40 49 47 50.
www.musée-orsay.fr

Upper level
Middle level
Entrance
Ground floor
Shop entrance

EXPLORING THE MUSÉE D'ORSAY

Many of the paintings in
the Musée d'Orsay came
from the Louvre and the
Impressionist collection
once in the Jeu de Paume.
Paintings from before 1870
are on the ground floor,
presided over by Thomas
Couture's massive *Romans
of the Decadence*. Neo-
Classical masterpieces, like
Ingres's *La Source*, hang
near Romantic works like
Delacroix's turbulent *Tiger
Hunt*. These exotic visions
contrast with Realist works
by artists like Courbet and
early canvases by Degas and
Manet, including the latter's
famous *Olympia*.

The museum's central
aisle overflows with sculpture,
from Daumier's satirical busts
of members of parliament to
Carpeaux's exuberant *The
Dance* and Rodin's *The
Gates of Hell*. Decorative
arts and architecture are on
the middle level, where
there is also a display of Art
Nouveau – sinuous lines

Blue Waterlilies (1919)
by Claude Monet

characterize Lalique's
jewellery and glassware and
the designs of Hector
Guimard, who produced the
characteristic curvy entrances
of the Paris metro.

Among the many high-
lights of the Impressionist
rooms on the upper level
are Monet's *Rouen Cathedral*
series (*see p267*) and Renoir's
joyful *Moulin de la Galette*.
The Post-Impressionist
collection includes the *Église
d'Auvers* by Van Gogh and
works by Cézanne, Seurat's
pointillist compositions such
as *Le Cirque*, Gauguin's
highly coloured Symbolist
works, Toulouse-Lautrec's
depictions of
Parisian
women and
nightlife, and
Rousseau's
charmingly
naive dream
world. Among
the highlights
of the post-
1900 display
is Matisse's
*Luxe, Calme
et Volupté.*

Le Déjeuner sur l'Herbe (1863) by Edouard Manet

The façade of the Ecole Nationale Supérieure des Beaux Arts

Ecole Nationale Supérieure des Beaux Arts ❹

14 rue Bonaparte 75006. **Map** 8 E3. *Tel* 01 47 03 50 00. Ⓜ St-Germain-des-Prés. ◯ groups by appt only on Mon pm (01 47 03 50 00 to book). 🖼 ▭ *Library* www.ensba.fr

The main French school of fine arts has an enviable position at the corner of the rue Bonaparte and the river-side quai Malaquais. It is housed in several buildings, the most imposing being the 19th-century Palais des Etudes. A host of budding French and foreign painters and architects have crossed the courtyard, which contains a 17th-century chapel, to learn in the ateliers of the school. Many American architects have studied here over the past century.

St-Germain-des-Prés ❺

3 pl St-Germain-des-Prés 75006. **Map** 8 E4. *Tel* 01 55 42 81 33. Ⓜ St-Germain-des-Prés. ◯ 8am–7pm daily. *Concerts* 8pm Tue, Thu.

This is the oldest church in Paris, originating in 542 as a basilica to house holy relics. It became an immensely powerful Benedictine abbey, rebuilt in the 11th century, but most of it was destroyed by fire in 1794. Major restoration took place in the 19th century. One of the three original towers survives, housing one of the oldest belfries in France. The interior of the church is an interesting mix of architec-tural styles, with 6th-century marble columns, Gothic vaulting and Romanesque arches. Famous tombs include that of 17th-century philoso-pher René Descartes.

Musée Eugène Delacroix ❻

6 rue de Fürstenberg 75006. **Map** 8 E4. *Tel* 01 44 41 86 50. Ⓜ St-Germain-des-Prés. ◯ 9.30am–5pm Wed–Mon. ● 1 Jan, 1 May, 25 Dec. 🖼 📷 ▯ www.musee-delacroix.fr

The leading non-conformist Romantic painter Eugène Delacroix lived and worked here from 1857 till his death in 1863. Here he painted *The Entombment of Christ* and *The Way to Calvary* (which now hang in the museum). He also created superb murals for the Chapel of the Holy Angels in the nearby St-Sulpice church.

The apartment and garden studio has a portrait of George Sand, Delacroix self-portraits and sketches.

Jacob Wrestling with the Angel by Delacroix, in St-Sulpice (see p127)

Rue de l'Odéon ❼

75006. **Map** 8 F5. Ⓜ Odéon.

Opened in 1779 to improve access to the Odéon theatre, this was the first street in Paris to have pavements with gutters and it still has many 18th-century houses.

Sylvia Beach's bookshop, the original Shakespeare & Company, stood at No. 12 from 1921 to 1940. It was a magnet for writers like James Joyce, Ezra Pound and Hemingway.

Musée de Cluny ❽

6 pl Paul-Painlevé. **Map** 9 A5. *Tel* 01 53 73 78 16. Ⓜ St-Michel, Odéon, Cluny. 🅁🅴🆁 St-Michel. ◯ 9:15am–5:45pm Wed–Mon. ● 1 Jan, 1 May, 25 Dec. 🖼 📷 ▯ *Concerts*. www.musee-moyenage.fr

The museum (officially the Musée National du Moyen Age) is a unique combination

Stone heads of the Kings of Judah carved around 1220

St-Séverin ❾

1 rue-des-Prêtres-St-Séverin 75005. **Map** 9 A4. *Tel* 01 42 34 93 50. Ⓜ St-Michel. ◯ 11am–7:30pm daily.

St-Séverin, one of the most beautiful churches in Paris, is named after a 6th-century hermit who lived in the area. It is a perfect example of the Flamboyant Gothic style. Construction finished in the early 16th century and included a remarkable double aisle encircling the chancel. In the garden stands the church's medieval gable-roofed charnel house.

Gargoyles adorning the gables of the Flamboyant Gothic St-Séverin

The School woodcarving (English, early 16th century)

LADY WITH THE UNICORN TAPESTRIES

These six outstanding tapestries are fine examples of the millefleurs style. Developed in the 15th and early 16th centuries the style is noted for its graceful depiction of animals and people and its fresh and harmonious colours.

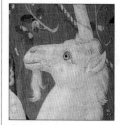

The poetic elegance of a unicorn on the sixth tapestry

of Gallo-Roman ruins, incorporated into a medieval mansion (in newly created medieval gardens), and one of the world's finest collections of medieval art and crafts. Its name comes from Pierre de Chalus, Abbot of Cluny, who bought the ruins in 1330. The present building dates from 1485–98. Among the star exhibits are the tapestries, remarkable for their quality, age and state of preservation. The highlight of the sculpture section is the Gallery of the Kings, while one of Cluny's most precious items, the Golden Rose of Basel from 1330, is found in the collection of jewellery and metalwork. Other treasures include stained glass, woodcarvings and books of hours.

St-Julien-le-Pauvre ⑩

1 rue St-Julien-le-Pauvre 75005. **Map** 9 A4. *Tel* 01 43 54 52 16. Ⓜ St-Michel. ◯ 9:30am–1:30pm, 3–6pm daily. ✝ 12:15pm Tue–Sat. **Concerts**

The church is one of the oldest in Paris, dating from between 1165 and 1220. The university held its official meetings in the church until 1524, when a student protest created so much damage that university meetings were barred from the church by parliament. It has belonged to the Melchite sect of the Greek Orthodox Church since 1889, and is now the setting for classical and religious concerts.

La Sorbonne ⑪

47 rue des Ecoles 75005. **Map** 9 A5. *Tel* 01 40 46 22 11. Ⓜ Cluny-La Sorbonne, Maubert-Mutualité. 📷 only by appt. Write to Service des Visites.

The Sorbonne, seat of the University of Paris until 1969, was established in 1253 by Robert de Sorbon, confessor to Louis IX, for 16 poor scholars to study theology. From these modest origins,

the college became the centre of scholastic theology. In 1469, three printing machines were brought from Mainz, and the first printing house in France was founded. The college's opposition to liberal 18th-century philosophical ideas led to its suppression during the Revolution. It was re-established by Napoleon in 1806, and the 17th-century buildings replaced. In 1969 the Sorbonne split into 13 separate universities, but the building still holds some lectures.

St-Etienne-du-Mont ⑫

Pl Ste-Geneviève 75005. **Map** 13 A1. *Tel* 01 43 54 11 79. Ⓜ Cardinal Lemoine. ◯ noon–7:30pm Mon, 8:45am–7:30pm Tue–Sun (closed lunchtime Sat & Sun). ● Mon in Jul–Aug. 📷 ✝

This remarkable church houses the shrine of Saint Geneviève, the legendary patron saint of Paris, and the remains of the great literary figures Racine and Pascal. Some parts of the building are Gothic, others Renaissance, including the eye-catching rood screen.

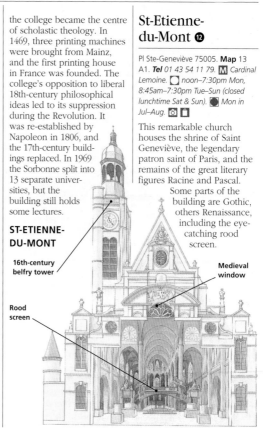

ST-ETIENNE-DU-MONT

16th-century belfry tower

Rood screen

Medieval window

Street by Street: Latin Quarter

Since the Middle Ages this riverside quarter has been dominated by the Sorbonne, and acquired its name from the early Latin-speaking students. It dates back to the Roman town across from the Ile de la Cité; at that time the rue St-Jacques was one of the main roads out of Paris. The area is generally associated with artists, intellectuals and a bohemian way of life; it also has a history of political unrest. In 1871, the place St-Michel became the centre of the Paris Commune, and in May 1968 it was a site of student uprisings. Today the eastern half has become sufficiently chic, however, to house members of the Establishment.

Latin jazz

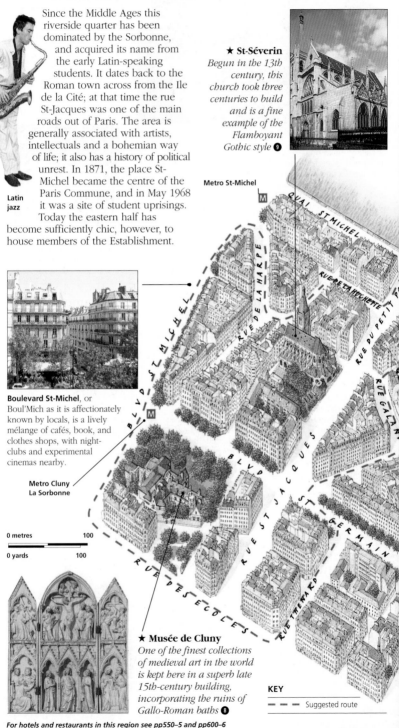

★ St-Séverin
Begun in the 13th century, this church took three centuries to build and is a fine example of the Flamboyant Gothic style ❾

Metro St-Michel

Boulevard St-Michel, or Boul'Mich as it is affectionately known by locals, is a lively mélange of cafés, book, and clothes shops, with night-clubs and experimental cinemas nearby.

Metro Cluny La Sorbonne

| 0 metres | 100 |
| 0 yards | 100 |

★ Musée de Cluny
One of the finest collections of medieval art in the world is kept here in a superb late 15th-century building, incorporating the ruins of Gallo-Roman baths ❽

KEY

- - - Suggested route

For hotels and restaurants in this region see pp550–5 and pp600–6

LOCATOR MAP
See Street Finder maps 8, 9, 12, 13

★ **St-Julien-le-Pauvre**
Rebuilt in the 17th century, this church was used to store animal feed in the Revolution ❿

Metro
Maubert
Mutualité

STAR SIGHTS

★ Musée de Cluny

★ St-Séverin

★ St-Julien-le-Pauvre

Panthéon ⓭

Pl du Panthéon 75005. **Map** 13 A1.
Tel 01 44 32 18 00. Ⓜ Maubert-
Mutualité, Cardinal-Lemoine.
RER Luxembourg. ◯ Apr–Sep:
10am–6:30pm daily; Oct–Mar:
10am–6pm daily. ● 1 Jan, 1 May, 25
Dec. 🎫 📷 ✎ www.monum.fr

When Louis XV recovered from illness in 1744, he was so grateful that he conceived a magnificent church to honour Saint Geneviève, the patron saint of Paris. The French architect Jacques-Germain Soufflot planned the church in Neo-Classical style. Work began in 1764 and was completed in 1790 under the control of

The Panthéon Interior
The interior has four aisles arranged in the shape of a Greek cross, from the centre of which the great dome rises.

Guillaume Rondelet. But with the Revolution underway, the church was soon turned into a pantheon – a monument housing the tombs of France's great heroes. Napoleon returned it to the Church in 1806, but it was secularized and then desecularized once more before finally being made a civic building in 1885.

The façade, inspired by the Rome Pantheon, has a pediment relief by David d'Angers depicting the mother country granting laurels to her great men. Those resting here include Voltaire, Rousseau and Zola, and the ashes of Pierre and Marie Curie, Alexandre Dumas and André Malraux.

**Iron-
Framed
Dome**
The fresco in the dome's stone cupola represents the Glorification of Sainte Geneviève, *commissioned by Napoleon in 1811.*

The dome lantern

The dome galleries

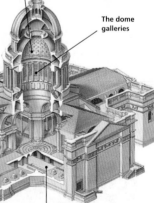

Entrance

Crypt
Under the building, the vast crypt divides into galleries flanked by Doric columns. Many French notables rest here, including Voltaire and Emile Zola.

Street-by-Street: Luxembourg Quarter

Situated only a few steps from the bustle of St-Germain-des-Prés, this graceful and historic area offers a peaceful haven in the heart of a modern city. The Jardin du Luxembourg and Palais du Luxembourg dominate the surroundings. The gardens became fully open to the public in the 19th century under the ownership of the Comte de Provence (later to become Louis XVIII), when for a small fee visitors could come in and feast on fruit from the orchard. Today the gardens, palace and old houses on the streets to the north remain unspoilt and attract many visitors.

STAR SIGHTS

★ St-Sulpice

★ Palais du Luxembourg

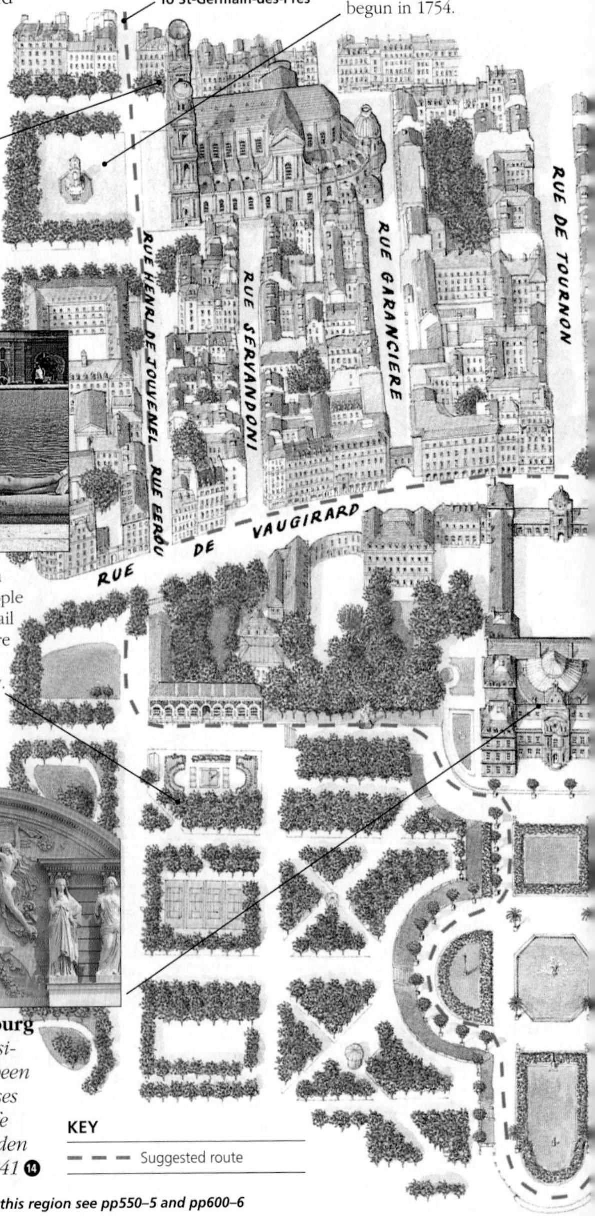
To St-Germain-des-Prés
RUE HENRI DE JOUVENEL
RUE SERVANDONI
RUE GARANCIERE
RUE DE TOURNON
RUE FEROU
RUE DE VAUGIRARD

Place St-Sulpice, ringed by flowering chestnut trees, was begun in 1754.

★ St-Sulpice
This huge Classical church, by six different architects, took more than a century to build ⓯

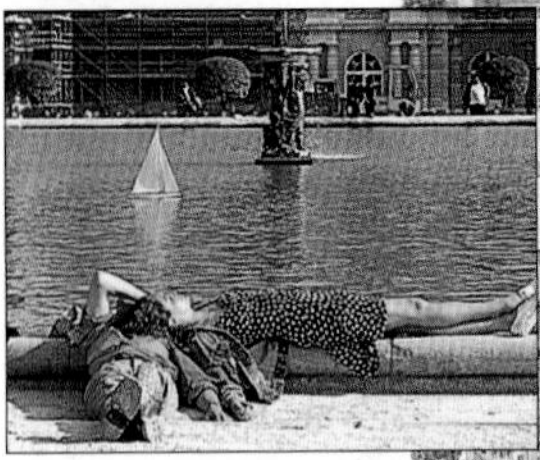

Jardins du Luxembourg is a popular garden where people come to relax, sunbathe, sail boats in the pond or admire the many beautiful statues erected in the 19th century.

0 metres 100
0 yards 100

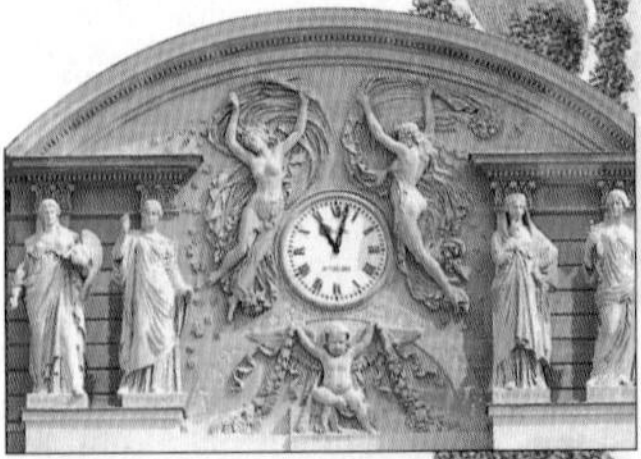

★ Palais du Luxembourg
First built as a royal residence, the palace has been used for various purposes from prison to Luftwaffe headquarters. This garden façade was added in 1841 ⓮

KEY

– – – Suggested route

For hotels and restaurants in this region see pp550–5 and pp600–6

LOCATOR MAP
See Street Finder maps 8, 12, 13

Fontaine de Médicis is a 17th-century fountain in the style of an Italian grotto. It is thought to have been designed by Salomon de Brosse.

Saint Geneviève, patron saint of Paris, whose prayers saved Paris from the Huns in AD 451, is honoured by this statue by Michel-Louis Victor in 1845.

Palais du Luxembourg ⑭

15 rue de Vaugirard 75006. **Map** 8 E5. **Tel** *01 44 54 19 49.* Ⓜ *Odéon.* RER *Luxembourg.* 🗓 *groups only, by appt one Sat per month, 10:30am & 2:30pm. Apply 3 months in advance.* **Tel** *01 42 34 20 60.* 📷 *www.senat.fr*

Now the home of the French Senate, this palace was built to remind Marie de' Médici, widow of Henri IV, of her native Florence. It was designed by Salomon de Brosse in the style of the Pitti Palace in Florence. By the time it was finished (1631) she had been banished from Paris, but it remained a royal palace until the Revolution. In World War II it served as headquarters for the Luftwaffe. The Musée du Luxembourg in the east gallery often hosts art exhibitions organized by the Senate.

St-Sulpice ⑮

Pl St-Sulpice 75006. **Map** 8 E5. **Tel** *01 42 34 59 98.* Ⓜ *St-Sulpice.* 🕖 *7:30am–7:30pm daily.* 📷 **Concerts**

This huge and imposing church was started in 1646 and took more than a century to finish. The result is a simple façade with two tiers of elegant columns and two mismatched towers at the ends. Large arched windows fill the vast interior with light.

In the side chapel to the right are murals by Eugène Delacroix, including *Jacob Wrestling with the Angel (see p122)* and *Heliodorus Driven from the Temple.*

Carpeaux's fountain sculpture

Fontaine de l'Observatoire ⑯

Pl Ernest Denis, av de l'Observatoire 7500. **Map** 12 E2. RER *Port Royal.*

Situated at the southern tip of the Jardin du Luxembourg, this is one of the finest fountains in Paris. The central sculpture, by Jean-Baptiste Carpeaux, was erected in 1873. Made of bronze, it has four women holding aloft a globe representing four continents – the fifth, Oceania, was left out for reasons of symmetry. There are some subsidiary figures, including dolphins, horses and a turtle.

Val-de-Grâce ⑰

1 pl Alphonse-Laveran 75005. **Map** 12 F2. **Tel** *01 40 51 51 92.* Ⓜ *Gobelins.* RER *Port Royal.* 🕛 *noon–6pm Tue, Wed, Sat, Sun.* ● *Aug.* 🗓 🎫 *except for nave.* ♿

This is one of the most beautiful churches in France, and forms part of a military hospital complex. Built for Anne of Austria (wife of Louis XIII) in gratitude for the birth of her son, young Louis XIV himself laid the first stone in 1645.

The church is noted for its dome. In the cupola is Pierre Mignard's enormous fresco, with over 200 triple-life-size figures. The six huge marble columns framing the altar are similar to St Peter's in Rome.

The Classical two-storey west front of St-Sulpice with its two towers

FURTHER AFIELD

Many of Paris's famous sights are slightly out of the city centre. Montmartre, long a mecca for artists and writers, still retains much of its bohemian atmosphere, and Montparnasse is full of bustling cafés and theatre crowds. The famous Cimetière du Père Lachaise numbers Chopin, Oscar Wilde and Jim Morrison among its dead, and, along with the parks and gardens, provides a tranquil escape from sightseeing. Modern architecture can be seen at Fondation Le Corbusier and La Défense, and there is a huge selection of museums to visit. To the northeast, the science museum at La Villette provides an educational family day out.

SIGHTS AT A GLANCE

Museums and Galleries
Musée Marmottan
    Claude Monet **5**
Musée du Cristal de
    Baccarat **6**
Musée Gustave Moreau **9**
Palais de la Porte Dorée **20**
Musée National d'Histoire
    Naturelle **24**

Churches and Mosques
St-Alexandre-Nevsky **7**
Sacré-Coeur **11**
Mosquée de Paris **27**

Parks and Gardens
Bois de Boulogne **2**
Parc Monceau **8**
Parc des Buttes-Chaumont **17**
Parc Montsouris **23**
Jardin des Plantes **25**
Parc André Citroën **28**

Cemeteries
Cimetière de Montmartre **13**
Cimetière du Père Lachaise **18**
Cimetière du Montparnasse **30**

Historic Districts
Montmartre pp132–3 **10**
Canal St-Martin **16**
Montparnasse **29**

**Historic Buildings and
    Streets**
Rue La Fontaine **4**
Moulin Rouge **12**
Château de Vincennes **21**
Catacombs **31**

Modern Architecture
La Défense **1**
Fondation Le Corbusier **3**
Bercy **19**
Bibliothèque Nationale
    de France **22**
Institut du Monde
    Arabe **26**

Markets
Marché aux Puces
    de St-Ouen **14**

Theme Parks
*Cité des Sciences et
    de l'Industrie pp136–7* **15**

KEY

	Main sightseeing area
=	Major roads

0 kilometres   4
0 miles   2

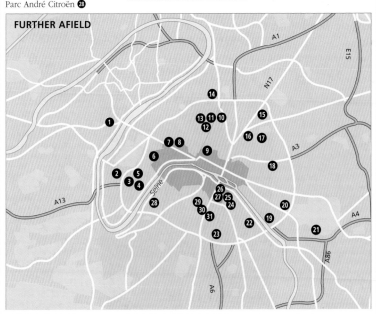

FURTHER AFIELD

West of the City

La Défense ❶

La Grande Arche. **Tel** 01 49 07 27
27. 🚉 La Défense. ◯ 10am–7pm
daily (8am Apr–Sep). 🖼 ♿ 🍴 📷
See **The History of France** pp66–7.
www.grandearche.com

This skyscraper business city
on the western edge of Paris
is the largest office development in Europe. La Grande
Arche is an enormous hollow
cube large enough to contain
Notre-Dame cathedral.
Designed by Danish architect
Otto von Spreckelsen in the
late 1980s, the arch houses a
gallery and a conference
centre, and has superb views.

La Grande Arche in La Défense

Bois de Boulogne ❷

75016. Ⓜ Porte Maillot, Porte
Dauphine, Porte d'Auteuil, Sablons.
◯ 24 hrs daily. 🖼 to specialist
gardens and museum. ♿

Located between the
western edges of Paris
and the River Seine, this
865-ha (2,137-acre) park
offers a vast belt of
greenery for strolling,
cycling, riding, boating,
picnicking, or spending
a day at the races. The
Bois de Boulogne was
once part of the im-
mense Forêt du Rouvre.
In the mid-19th century
Napoleon III had the
Bois designed and
landscaped by Baron
Haussmann along the
lines of Hyde Park in
London. Several self-
contained parks within
the forest include the

Pré Catalan and the Bagatelle
gardens, with architectural
follies and an 18th-century
villa famous for its rose
garden. The villa was built in
just 64 days as the result of a
bet between the Comte
d'Artois and Marie-Antoinette.
    By day the Bois is busy
with families, joggers and
walkers, but after dark it is
notoriously seedy – and
best avoided.

Fondation Le Corbusier ❸

8–10 square du Docteur-Blanche
75016. **Tel** 01 42 88 41 53. Ⓜ
Jasmin. ◯ 1:30pm–6pm Mon, 10am–
12:30pm & 1:30pm–6pm (5pm Fri)
Tue–Fri, 10am–5pm Sat. ● pub hols,
Aug, 24 Dec–2 Jan. 🎞 **Films, videos**.
www.fondationlecorbusier.asso.fr

In a quiet corner of Auteuil
stand the villas La Roche and
Jeanneret, the first two
Parisian houses built by the
brilliant and influential 20th-
century architect Charles-
Edouard Jeanneret, better
known as Le Corbusier. Built
at the start of the 1920s, they
demonstrate his revolutionary
use of white concrete in Cubist
forms. Rooms flow into each
other allowing maximum light
and volume, and the houses
stand on stilts with windows
along their entire length.
    Villa La Roche was owned by
the art patron Raoul La Roche.
Today, the villas hold lectures
on Le Corbusier and his work.

A landscaped island in the Bois de Boulogne

**An Art Nouveau window in the
rue la Fontaine**

Rue la Fontaine ❹

75016. **Map** 5 A4. Ⓜ Michel-Ange
Auteuil, Jasmin. 🚉 Radio-France.

The rue la Fontaine
and surrounding streets act
as a showcase for some of
the most exciting early
20th-century, low-cost architecture, featuring sinuous
decorative detail. At No. 14
stands the Castel Béranger,
which firmly established the
reputation of architect Hector
Guimard. He went on to
design the city's Art Nouveau
metro entrances.

Musée Marmottan-Claude Monet ❺

2 rue Louis Boilly 75016. **Tel** 01 44 96
50 33. Ⓜ Muette. ◯ 10am–6pm
Tue–Sun. ● 1 Jan, 1 May, 25 Dec.
🖼 ♿ 📷
www.marmottan.com

The museum was
created in the 19th-
century mansion of the
famous art historian,
Paul Marmottan, in
1932. He bequeathed
his house, plus his
Renaissance, Consular
and First Empire paint-
ings and furniture, to
the Institut de France.
    In 1971 the museum
acquired a fabulous
collection of work by
Impressionist painter
Claude Monet, the
bequest of his son,
Michel. Some of Monet's
most famous paintings

are here, including
Impression – Sunrise (hence
the term "Impressionist"), a
painting of Rouen Cathedral
(see p267), and the *Waterlilies*
series *(see p98)*. Also here is
the work painted at Giverny
during the last years of Monet's
life. This includes *The
Japanese Bridge* and *The
Weeping Willow*. The
iridescent colours and daring
brush-strokes make these
some of the museum's most
powerful works.

Part of Monet's personal
art collection was passed
on to the museum, including
work by fellow Impressionists
Camille Pissarro, Pierre-
Auguste Renoir and Alfred
Sisley. The museum also displays medieval illuminated
manuscripts and 16th-century
Burgundian tapestries.

Musée du Cristal de Baccarat ⑥

11 pl des Etats Unis 75016. *Tel 01
40 22 11 00.* Ⓜ *Boissière.*
◯ *10am–7pm Mon, Wed–Sat.*
● *public hols.* ⚑ 📷 📹 *by appt.*
www.baccarat.fr

The Musée du Cristal, also
known as the Musée Baccarat,
displays over 1,200 items
made by the Baccarat company, which was founded in
1764 in Lorraine in eastern
France. These include dinner
services created for the royal
and imperial courts of Europe
and many of the best contemporary pieces produced in the
workshops, such as fine
vases, candelabras, decanters
and perfume bottles, as well as
watches and jewellery.

In the glassworks itself
you can see some
of the technical
skills used to
shape and
decorate the
crystal ware,
such as fine
cutting,
wheel-
engraving,
gilding and
enamelling.

**Le Vase d'Abyssinie,
made of Baccarat
crystal and bronze**

Colonnade beside the *naumachia* basin in Parc Monceau

North of the City

St-Alexandre-Nevsky Cathedral

St-Alexandre-Nevsky ⑦

12 rue Daru 75008. **Map** 2 F3.
Tel 01 42 27 37 34. Ⓜ *Courcelles,
Ternes.* ◯ *3–5pm Tue, Fri, Sun.* ⚑
✝ *6pm Sat, 10:30am Sun.*

This imposing Russian
Orthodox cathedral with its
five golden-copper domes
signals the presence of a large
Russian community in Paris.
Designed by members of the
St Petersburg Fine Arts Acad-
emy and financed jointly by
Tsar Alexander II and the local
Russian community, it was
completed in 1861.

Inside, a wall of icons
divides the church in two.
The Greek-cross plan and the
rich mosaics and frescoes
decorating the interior walls
are Neo-Byzantine in style,
while the exterior and gilt
domes are traditional Russian
Orthodox in design.

Parc Monceau ⑧

Bd de Courcelles 75017. **Map** 3 A3.
Tel 01 42 27 08 64. Ⓜ *Monceau.*
◯ *7am–8pm daily (10pm summer).*

This green haven dates back
to 1778 when the Duc de
Chartres commissioned the
painter-writer and amateur
landscape designer Louis
Carmontelle to create a magnificent garden. The result
was an exotic landscape full
of architectural follies in the
English and German style.

In 1852 the land was
acquired by the state and
made into a chic public park.
A few of the original features
remain, among them the *naumachia* basin – an ornamental
version of a Roman pool used
for simulating naval battles.

Musée Gustave Moreau ⑨

14 rue de la Rochefoucauld 75009.
Map 4 E3. *Tel 01 48 74 38 50.*
Ⓜ *Trinité.* ◯ *10am–12:45pm, 2–
5:15pm Wed–Mon.* ● *some public
hols.* ⚑ 📷 📹
www.musee-moreau.fr

The Symbolist painter
Gustave Moreau (1826– 98),
known for his symbolic
works depicting biblical and
mythological fantasies, lived
and worked in this handsome
town house. *Jupiter and
Semele,* one of the artist's outstanding works, is displayed
here, along with other major
paintings, and some of the
collection's 7,000 drawings and
1,000 oils and watercolours.

Montmartre ⑩

The steep *butte* (hill) of Montmartre has been associated with artists for 200 years.

Théodore Géricault and Camille Corot came here at the start of the 19th century, and in the 20th century Maurice Utrillo immortalized the streets in his works. Today, street artists thrive predominantly on the tourist trade, but much of the area still preserves its rather louche, villagey pre-war atmosphere. The name of the area is ascribed to martyrs who were tortured and killed in the area around AD 250, hence *mons martyrium*.

Streetside painter

Montmartre Vineyard
This is the last Parisian vineyard. The harvest is celebrated on the first Saturday in October.

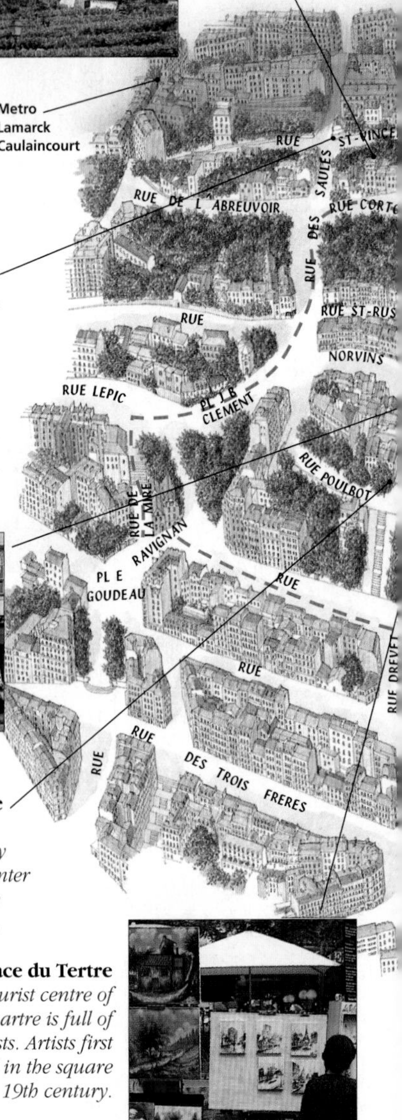

Metro
Lamarck
Caulaincourt

RUE DE L ABREUVOIR

RUE DES SAULES

RUE ST-VINCE

RUE CORTO

RUE ST-RUS

NORVINS

RUE LEPIC

PL T B CLEMENT

RUE POULBOT

RUE DE LA VARE

RAVIGNAN

PL E GOUDEAU

RUE

RUE

RUE

RUE DREVET

RUE DES TROIS FRERES

Au Lapin Agile
"The Agile Rabbit", once a literary haunt, is now a nightclub.

A la Mère Catherine
This was a favourite restaurant of Russian cossacks. They would shout "Bistro!" (meaning "quick") – which gave the bistro its name.

MAISON CATHERINE

A LA MERE CATHERINE

Espace Montmartre Salvador Dalí
Some 330 works by the Surrealist painter and sculptor are on display here.

Place du Tertre
The tourist centre of Montmartre is full of portraitists. Artists first exhibited in the square in the 19th century.

KEY

– – – Suggested route

0 metres	100
0 yards	100

For hotels and restaurants in this region see pp550–5 and pp600–6

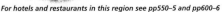

Musée de Montmartre
*Changing, Montmarte-related
exhibitions usually include
works by artists who lived
here, such as this* Portrait
of a Woman *(1918) by
Amedeo Modigliani.*

LOCATOR MAP
See Street Finder maps 3, 4

Sacré-Coeur
*This Neo-
Romanesque
church, started in
the 1870s and
completed in
1914, contains
many treasures,
such as this figure
of the* Virgin Mary
and Child *(1896)
by P Brunet* ⓫

St-Pierre de Montmartre
*This is an early Parisian
church with origins dating
back to the 6th century.*

The funiculaire, or cable
railway, at the end of the rue
Foyatier takes you to the foot
of the basilica of the Sacré-Coeur.
Metro tickets are valid for it.

To metro Anvers

Square Willette lies below
the forecourt of the Sacré-
Coeur. It is laid out on the
side of the hill in a series of
descending terraces with
lawns, shrubs, trees and
flowerbeds.

Musée de la Halle Saint Pierre
*Exhibitions here showcase
Outsider Art and Art Brut, such
as this piece by S Feleggakis.*

Sacré-Coeur ⓫

Parvis de Notre Dame 75018. **Map** 4
F1. *Tel 01 53 41 89 00.* Ⓜ *Abbesses
(then funiculaire to steps of Sacré-
Coeur), Anvers.* 🚌 *30, 54, 80, 85.*
Basilica ◯ *6am–11pm daily.* **Dome
& crypt** ◯ *9am–6pm daily.* 📷 🚻
*11:15am, 6:30pm, 10pm Mon–Thu;
3pm Fri;. 10pm Sat; 11am, 6pm,
10pm Sun (Vespers 4pm).*
www.sacre-coeur-montmartre.com

The Sacré-Coeur basilica,
dedicated to the Sacred Heart
of Christ and consecrated in
1919, was built as a result of a
private religious vow made at
the outbreak of the Franco-
Prussian war. Two Catholic
businessmen, Alexandre
Legentil and Hubert Rohault
de Fleury, promised to finance
the basilica should France be
spared from assault. Despite
the war and the Siege of
Paris, invasion was averted
and work began in 1875 to
Paul Abadie's designs. Never
considered very graceful, the
basilica is vast and impressive, and one of France's
most important Roman
Catholic buildings.

**The stained glass
gallery** affords a view
of the whole interior.

The ovoid dome is
the second-highest
point in Paris, after
the Eiffel Tower.

**The Great Mosaic of
Christ** (1912–22), by
Luc Olivier Merson,
dominates the
chancel vault.

Bronze doors
in the portico
show the Last
Supper and
other biblical
scenes.

The crypt vaults house a
chapel containing Alexandre
Legentil's heart in a stone urn.

Moulin Rouge ⓬

82 bd de Clichy 75018. **Map** 4 E1.
Tel 01 53 09 82 82. Ⓜ *Blanche.*
Shows *at 9pm & 11pm daily.* 📷
See p145. **www**.moulinrouge.com

Built in 1885, the Moulin
Rouge was turned into
a dance hall as early as 1900.
Henri de Toulouse-Lautrec
immortalized the wild and
colourful cancan shows here
in his posters and drawings of
famous dancers such as Jane
Avril. The high-kicking routines
continue today in glittering,
Las Vegas-style revues.

Cimetière de
Montmartre ⓭

20 av Rachel 75018. **Map** 4 D1.
Tel 01 53 42 36 30. Ⓜ *Place de
Clichy.* ◯ *8:30am–5:30pm Mon–Sat,
9am–5:30pm Sun (6pm summer).* ♿

This has been the resting
place for many luminaries of
the creative arts since the
beginning of the 19th century.

The composers Hector Berlioz
and Jacques Offenbach (who
wrote the famous cancan
tune), Russian dancer Waslaw
Nijinsky, and film director
François Truffaut are just a
few of the famous people
who have been buried here
over the years.

There is also a Montmartre
cemetery near square Roland-
Dorgelès, known as the St-
Vincent cemetery. This is
where the French painter
Maurice Utrillo is buried.

**African stall in the Marché aux
Puces de St-Ouen**

Marché aux Puces
de St-Ouen ⓮

Rue des Rosiers, St-Ouen 75018. Ⓜ
Porte-de-Clignancourt. ◯ *9am–6pm
Sat–Mon. See* **Shops and Markets**
p142. **www**.les-puces.com

This is the oldest and largest
of the Paris flea markets,
covering 6 ha (15 acres)
near the Porte de Clignancourt.
In the 19th century, rag merchants and tramps would
gather outside the fortifications that marked the city
limits and offer their wares
for sale. Today the area is
divided into separate markets,
and is well-known for its
heavy Second Empire furniture and ornaments. Although
there are few bargains to be
had, this does not deter the
huge weekend crowds.

Cité des Sciences et
de l'Industrie ⓯

See pp136–7.

Canal St-Martin

M Jaurès, J Bonsergent, Goncourt.

A walk along the quays on either side of the Canal St-Martin gives a glimpse of how this thriving, industrial, working-class area of the city looked at the end of the 19th century. The 5-km (3-mile) canal, opened in 1825, provided a shortcut for river traffic between loops of the Seine. A smattering of brick-and-iron factories and warehouses survive from this time along the quai de Jemmapes. Here, too, is the legendary Hôtel du Nord, from Marcel Carné's 1930s film of the same name. The canal itself is quietly busy with barges and anglers; around it the tree-lined quays with quirky shops and cafés, iron footbridges and public gardens are ideal for a leisurely stroll.

Parc des Buttes-Chaumont

Rue Manin 75019 (access from rue Armand Carrel). No phone. M Botzaris, Buttes-Chaumont. ◯ 7am–8:15pm (10:15pm Jun–15 Aug; 9:15pm May & 16 Aug–30 Sep) daily.

For many this is the most pleasant and unexpected park in Paris. Urban planner Baron Haussmann converted the hilly site from a rubbish dump and quarry with gallows at the foot, to English-style gardens in the 1860s. His partner on the project was landscape architect Adolphe Alphand, who was also responsible for a vast 1860s programme to provide Haussmann's elegant new pavement-lined Parisian avenues with benches, street-lights, newspaper kiosks and urinals (see p108).

Others involved in the creation of this highly praised park were the engineer Darcel and the landscape gardener Barillet-Deschamps. They created a lake, made an island with real and artificial rocks, gave it a Roman-style temple, and added a waterfall, streams and footbridges

Boats moored at Port de l'Arsenal

leading to the island. Today, in summer, visitors will also find boating facilities, donkey rides and beautiful lawns.

East of the City

Cimetière du Père Lachaise

16 rue du Repos,75020. **Tel** 01 55 25 82 10. M Père Lachaise, A Dumas. ▤ 26, 62, 69 to Pl Gambetta P Pl Gambetta ◯ 8am–5:30pm (6pm Apr–Nov; from 9am Sun & hols) daily.

Paris's most prestigious cemetery is set on a wooded hill overlooking the city. The land was once owned by Père de la Chaise, Louis XIV's confessor, but it was bought by order of Napoleon in 1803. The cemetery became so popular that the boundaries were extended six times during the 19th century. Here are buried celebrities such as writer Honoré de Balzac and composer Frédéric Chopin, and more recently, singer Jim Morrison and actors Simone Signoret and Yves Montand.

Bercy

75012. M Bercy, Cour St-Emilion.

This former wine-trading quarter just east of the city centre, with its once-grim riverside warehouses and pavilions and slum housing, has been transformed into an ultra-modern district beside the Seine. A new automatic metro line (Line 14) links it to the heart of the city.

Centrepiece of this new district is the Palais d'Omni-sports de Paris-Bercy (POPB), now the city centre's principal venue for major concerts, as well as its premier sports stadium. The vast pyramidal structure, its steep sides clad with real lawns, has become a contemporary landmark for the eastern part of central Paris.

Other architecturally adventurous administrative and commercial buildings dominate the skyline, notably Chemetov's Ministry of Finance building, and Frank Gehry's American Center (which opened in 2005 as the Museum of Cinema and Cinémathèque Française).

At the foot of these structures, the imaginative 70-ha (173-acre) Parc de Bercy provides a welcome green space. Former wine stores and cellars along Cours St Emilion have been restored as restaurants, bars and shops. Some of the warehouses have been restructured as the Pavillons de Bercy, one of which contains the Musée des Arts Forains (Fairground Museum).

Rivertrips for eight people can be reserved from the Marina de Bercy (tel 01 53 59 60 00; www.navicite.com).

Bercy's striking American Center, designed by Frank Gehry

Cité des Sciences et de l'Industrie ⓯

This hugely popular science and technology museum occupies the largest of the old Villette slaughterhouses, which now form part of a massive urban park. Architect Adrien Fainsilber has created an imaginative interplay of light, vegetation and water in the high-tech, five-storey building, which soars 40 m (133 ft) high, stretching over 3 ha (7 acres). At the museum's heart is the Explora exhibit, a fascinating guide to the worlds of science and technology. Visitors can take part in computerized games on space, the earth and ocean, computers and sound. On other levels there are a children's science city, cinemas, a science newsroom, a library and shops.

Modern folly in the Parc de la Villette

Planetarium
In this 260-seat auditorium you can watch eclipses and fly over Martian landscapes, thanks to their "Allsky" video system.

Le Nautile
This full-scale model of the Nautile, France's technologically advanced exploration submarine, represents one of the most sophisticated machines in the world.

★ Ariane
Rocket displays explain how astronauts are sent into space, and include an example of the European rocket Ariane.

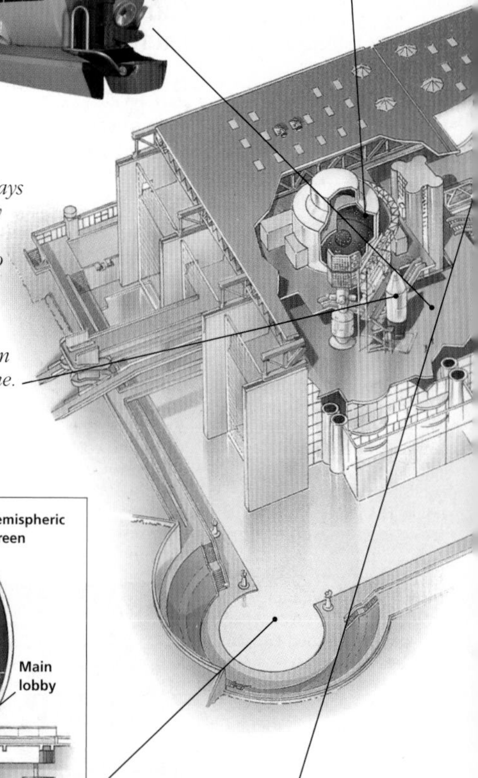

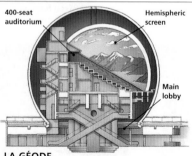

400-seat auditorium

Hemispheric screen

Main lobby

LA GÉODE

This giant entertainment sphere houses a huge hemispherical cinema screen, 1,000 sq m (11,000 sq ft), showing IMAX films on nature, travel and space.

The moat was designed by Fainsilber so that natural light could penetrate into the lower levels of the building.

The main hall is vast, with a soaring network of shafts, bridges, escalators, and has a cathedral-like atmosphere.

STAR EXHIBITS

★ Children's City

★ Ariane

★ La Géode

VISITORS' CHECKLIST

30 av Corentin-Cariou 75019.
🎫 01 40 05 80 00. Ⓜ Porte
de la Villette. 🚌 75, 151, PC2,
PC3. ⬜ 10am–6pm Tue–Sat
(7pm Sun). 📷 🐕 🍴 🛍 🏪
📽 Shows, films, videos,
library, conference centre.
www.cite-sciences.fr

Cupolas
*The two glazed domes,
17 m (56 ft) in diameter,
filter the flow of natural
light into the main hall.*

The greenhouse is a
square hothouse, 32 m
(105 ft) high and wide,
linking the park to the
building.

To La Géode

Mirage Aircraft
*A full-size model of the
French-built jet fighter is one
of the exhibits illustrating
advances in technology.*

Walkways
*The walkways cross the
encircling moat to link the
various floors of the museum
to the Géode and the park.*

★ Children's City
*In this lively, extensive
area children can
experiment and play
with machines that
show how scientific
principles work.*

Bibliothèque Nationale de France

Bibliothèque Nationale de France ㉒

Quai François-Mauriac 75013. **Tel** 01 53 79 59 59. Ⓜ Bibliothèque François-Mitterrand. ◯ 10am–7pm Mon–Sat, 1–7pm Sun. ● public hols, 2 wks mid-Sep. 📷 ♿ 🍴 🔲 www.bnf.fr

These four great book-shaped towers house 10 million volumes. The libraries offer over 400,000 titles. Other resources include digitized illustrations, sound archives and CD-ROMs. There are also frequent temporary exhibitions.

Palais de la Porte Dorée ⑳

293 av Daumesnil 75012. **Tel** 01 44 74 84 80. Ⓜ Porte Dorée. ◯ 10am–5:15pm Wed–Mon. ● 1 May. 📷 ♿ restricted. 🔲

The Cité Nationale de l'Histoire et de l'Immigration, housed in the Palais de la Porte Dorée, is a museum devoted to immigration in France. The palace itself is an Art Deco building designed by architects Albert Laprade and Léon Jaussely for the city's grand colonial exhibition in 1931.

The cellar also contains tropical fish collections, along with tortoises and crocodiles.

Château de Vincennes ㉑

Av de Paris 94300 Vincennes. **Tel** 01 48 08 31 20. Ⓜ Château de Vincennes. 🚆 Vincennes. ◯ 10am–noon, 1:15–5pm daily (6pm May–Aug). ● 1 Jan, 1 May, 1 & 11 Nov, 25 Dec. **Chapel & donjon** 📷 🎫 only. 🔲

The Château de Vincennes was the permanent royal residence until the 17th century, before the court moved to Versailles. The donjon, the tallest fortified medieval building in Europe, the Gothic chapel, 17th-century pavillions and moat are all worth seeing.

Beyond lies the Bois de Vincennes. Once a royal hunting ground, it is now a landscaped forest with ornamental lakes and a racecourse.

South of the City

Parc Montsouris ㉓

Bd Jourdan 75014. **Tel** 01 45 88 28 60. Ⓜ Pte d'Orléans. 🚆 Cité Universitaire. ◯ 8am–8:30pm (5:30pm winter) daily.

This English-style park, the second largest in Paris, was laid out by the landscape architect Adolphe Alphand from 1865–1878. With its restaurant, lawns, and lake – home to a variety of birds – it is popular with students and children.

Skull of the reptile dimetrodon

Musée National d'Histoire Naturelle ㉔

2 rue Buffon 75005. **Map** 14 D1. **Tel** 01 40 79 54 79. Ⓜ Jussieu, Austerlitz. ◯ 10am–6pm Wed–Mon. ● 1 May. 📷 ♿ restr. 🔲 🔲 📚 **Library** www.mnhn.fr

The highlight of the museum is the Grande Galerie de l'Evolution. There are also four other departments: palaeontology, featuring skeletons, casts of various animals and an exhibition showing the evolution of the vertebrate skeleton; palaeobotany, devoted to plant fossils; mineralogy, including gemstones; and entomology, with some of the oldest fossilized insects on earth. The bookstore is in the house that was occupied by the naturalist Buffon, from 1772 until his death in 1788.

Jardin des Plantes ㉕

57 rue Cuvier 75005. **Map** 13 C1. **Tel** 01 40 79 56 01. Ⓜ Jussieu, Austerlitz. ◯ 8am–5:30pm (5pm winter) daily.

The botanical gardens were established in 1626 when Jean Hérouard and Guy de la Brosse, Louis XIII's physicians, obtained permission to found a royal medicinal herb garden. A school of botany, natural history, and pharmacy followed and the garden opened to the public in 1640. One of the city's great parks, it contains a natural history museum, botanical school and zoo.

As well as beautiful vistas and walkways flanked by ancient statues, the park has an alpine garden with plants from Corsica, Morocco, the Alps and the Himalayas, and an unrivalled display of herbaceous and wild plants. The Cedar of Lebanon here, originally from Britain's Kew Gardens, was the first to be planted in France.

Rue Mouffetard, one of several markets near Jardin des Plantes

For hotels and restaurants in this region see pp550–5 and pp600–6

Institut du Monde Arabe ㉖

1 rue des Fossés St-Bernard 75005.
Map 9 C5. *Tel 01 40 51 38 38.* M
Jussieu, Cardinal-Lemoine. **Museum
& temp exhibs** ☐ *10am–6pm Tue–
Sun.* **Library** ☐ *1–8pm Tue–Sat.* 🈺
📷 ♿ 🖥 🍴 www.imarabe.org

This magnificent modern
building was designed by
French architect Jean Nouvel,
and cleverly combines high-
tech details with the spirit of
traditional Arab architecture.
From the fourth to seventh
floors there is a comprehensive
display of Islamic works of art
from the 9th to the 19th
centuries including glassware,
ceramics and sculpture. The
museum's highlight is the fine
collection of *astrolabes*, the
much-prized tool used by the
ancient Arabic astronomers.

Institut du Monde Arabe, covered with photosensitive lightscreens

Mosquée de Paris ㉗

Pl du Puits de l'Ermite 75005. *Tel 01
45 35 97 33.* M *Place Monge.* ☐
9am–noon, 2–6pm Sat–Thu. ●
Muslim hols. 🈺 📷 🖥 🍴 **Library**
www.mosquee-de-paris.org

Built in the 1920s in the
Hispano-Moorish style, these
buildings are the centre for
Paris's Muslim community.
Once used solely by scholars,
the mosque has expanded
over the years and now
houses some salubrious
but fun Turkish baths, a
fine restaurant, and beautiful
salon de thé.

Parc André Citroën ㉘

Rue Balard 75015. *Tel 01 40 71 74
03.* M *Javel, Balard.* ☐ *7:30am–
dusk Mon–Fri (9am w/e, public hols).*

Designed by both landscapers
and architects, this park is a
fascinating blend of styles,
ranging from wildflower
meadow in the north to sophisticated monochrome mineral and sculpture gardens in
the southern section. Modern
water sculptures dot the park.

Tour Montparnasse

Montparnasse ㉙

75014 & 75015. **Map** 11 & 12.
M *Vavin, Raspail, Edgar Quinet.*

The name Montparnasse was
first used ironically
in the 17th century, when
arts students performed their
work on a "mount" of rubble
left over from quarrying.
In ancient Greece, Mount
Parnassus was dedicated to
poetry, music and beauty.
By the 19th century, crowds
were drawn to the local
cabarets and bars by duty-
free prices. The mixture of
art and high living was particularly potent in the 1920s and
1930s when Hemingway,
Picasso, Cocteau, Giacometti,
Matisse and Modigliani were
"Montparnos," as the residents
were called. This epoch ended
with World War II. The modern *quartier* is dominated
by the much-hated Tour
Montparnasse, although the
view from the top (the 56th
floor) is spectacular.

Cimetière du Montparnasse ㉚

3 bd Edgar Quinet 75014. **Map** 12 D3.
Tel 01 44 10 86 50. M *Edgar Quinet.*
☐ *mid-Mar–Nov: 8am–6pm Mon– Fri,
8:30am–6pm Sat, 9am–6pm Sun;
Dec–mid-Mar: closes 5:30pm.*

Montparnasse cemetery
opened in 1824. Among those
buried here are Serge
Gainsbourg, Charles
Baudelaire, Jean-Paul Sartre
and Simone de Beauvoir,
and Guy de Maupassant.

Catacombs ㉛

1 av du Colonel Henri Rol-Tanguy
75014. **Map** 12 E3. *Tel 01 43 22 47
63.* M *Denfert-Rochereau.* ☐
10am– 4pm Tue–Sun. ● *public hols.*
🈺 📷 www.catacombes.paris.fr

A long series of quarry
tunnels built in Roman times,
the catacombs are now lined
with ancient bones and
skulls. Thousands of rotting
corpses were transported
here in the 1780s to absorb
the excess from the insanitary
Les Halles cemetery.

**Skulls and bones stored in the
catacombs**

SHOPS AND MARKETS

For many people, Paris epitomizes luxury and good living. Exquisitely dressed men and women sip wine by the banks of the Seine against the backdrop of splendid French architecture, or shop from small specialist shops. The least expensive way of joining the chic set is to create French style with accessories or costume jewellery. Alternatively, try shopping in the January or July sales. If your budget allows, take the opportunity to buy world-famous Paris fashions, or feast on the wonderful gourmet delicacies, displayed with consummate artistry. Parisian shopping streets and markets are the ideal place to indulge in the French custom of strolling for the express purpose of seeing and being seen. For up-to-the-minute high fashion, the rue du Faubourg-St-Honoré is hard to beat, with its exquisite couture window displays. Browsing around the bookstalls along the Seine is another favourite French pastime. A survey of some of the best and most famous places to shop follows.

Shopping in avenue Montaigne

OPENING HOURS

Shops are usually open from 10am–7pm, Monday to Saturday, but hours can vary. Many department stores stay open late on Thursday, while boutiques may shut for an hour or two at midday. Markets and local neighbourhood shops close on Mondays. Some places shut for the summer, usually in August, but they may leave a note on the door suggesting an open equivalent nearby.

PAYMENT AND VAT

Cash is readily available from the ATMs in most banks, which accept both credit and bank debit cards. Visa and MasterCard are the most widely accepted credit cards.

A sales tax (TVA) from 5.5–19.6 per cent is imposed on most goods and services in EU countries. Non-EU residents shopping in France are entitled to a refund of this if they spend a minimum of 175€ in one shop in one day. You must have been resident in France for less than six months and either carry the goods with you out of the country within three months of purchase, or get the shop to forward them to you. Larger shops will generally supply a form (*bordereau de détaxe* or *bordereau de vente*) and help you to fill it in. When you leave France or the EU you present the form to Customs, who either permit you to be reimbursed straightaway, or forward

The Chanel logo, recognized worldwide

your claim to the place where you bought the merchandise; the shop eventually sends you a refund.

SALES

The best sales (*soldes*) are held in January and July, although you can sometimes find sale items before Christmas. If you see goods labelled *Stock*, it means that they are stock items, reduced for clearance. *Dégriffé* means designer labels, (with the label cut out) marked down, frequently from the previous year's collections. *Fripes* indicates that the clothes are second-hand.

THE CENTRE OF PARIS COUTURE

The couture houses are concentrated on the Right Bank, around rue du Faubourg-St-Honoré and avenue Montaigne.

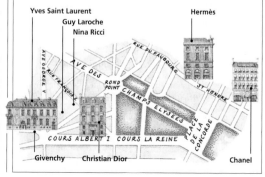

DEPARTMENT STORES

Much of the pleasure of shopping in Paris is derived from going to the small specialist shops. But if time is short, try the *grands magasins* (department stores). Some still operate a ticket system for selling goods. The shop assistant writes up a ticket for goods from their own boutique which you take to one of the cashiers. You then return with your validated ticket to pick up your purchase. This can be time-consuming, so go early in the morning and don't shop on

The 1865 façade of Au Printemps department store

Kenzo designerwear in the place des Victoires

Saturdays, unless you enjoy a crush. The French do not pay much attention to queues so be assertive! One peculiarity of a visit is that the security guards may ask to inspect your bags as you leave. These are random checks and should not be taken as an implication of theft.

All department stores have places to eat, although the stores themselves tend to have different emphases. **Au Printemps** is noted for its exciting and innovative household goods section, vast cosmetic range and large menswear store. The clothes departments for women and children are well stocked. Fashion shows are held at 10am on Tuesdays (and each Friday from April to October: by invitation only). The lovely domed restaurant in the cupola often hosts chic after-hours parties, which are

private, but a visit to the restaurant during shopping hours is worthwhile.

BHV (Le Bazar de l'Hôtel de Ville) is a DIY enthusiast's paradise, and sells a host of other items, such as fashion decor. The Left Bank's **Le Bon Marché** was Paris's first department store and today is its chicest. The designer clothing sections are well-sourced, the high-end accessories are excellent and the own-brand linen has a good quality to price ratio. The prepared food sections serve restaurant-quality fare to take away.

Galeries Lafayette is perhaps the best-known department store and has a wide range of clothes available at all price levels. Its first-floor trends section plays host to lots of innovative designers.

La Samaritaine is one of the city's oldest and most iconic stores. In June 2005 it closed for extensive renovation

Cartier, one of the world's most exclusive stores

which is expected to last five to six years.

Virgin Megastore is open until late and has an excellent record selection and an impressive book section. **FNAC** specializes in records, books (foreign editions can be found at Les Halles), and electronic equipment, while **FNAC Digitale** sells a wide range of the latest technological equipment.

ADDRESSES

Au Printemps
64 bd Haussmann 75009.
Map 4 D4. **Tel** 01 42 82 50 00.
www.printemps.com

BHV
52–64 rue de Rivoli 75004.
Map 9 B3. **Tel** 01 42 74 90 00.

Le Bon Marché
24 rue de Sèvres 75007.
Map 7 C5. **Tel** 01 44 39 80 00.

FNAC
Forum des Halles, 1 rue Pierre
Lescot 75001. **Map** 9 A2.
Tel 01 40 41 40 00.

FNAC Digitale
77–81 bd St-Germain 75006. **Map** 9
A5. **Tel** 0825 020 020.

Galeries Lafayette
40 bd Haussmann 75009. **Map** 4 E4.
Tel 01 42 82 34 56.

La Samaritaine
19 rue de la Monnaie 75001.
Map 8 F2.

Virgin Megastore
52–60 av des Champs-Elysées
75008. **Map** 2 F5. **Tel** 01 49 53 50
00. **www**.virginmegastore.fr

Clothes and Accessories

For many people Paris is synonymous with fashion, and Parisian style is the ultimate in chic. More than anywhere else in the world, women in Paris seem to be in tune with current trends and when a new season arrives appear, as one, to don the look. Though less trend-conscious generally, Parisian men are aware of style, and mix and match patterns and colours with *élan*. Finding the right clothes at the right price means knowing where to shop. For every luxury boutique on the avenue Montaigne, there are ten young designers' shops waiting to become the next Jean-Paul Gaultier – and hundreds more selling imitations.

HAUTE COUTURE

Paris is the home of *haute couture*. The original *couture* garments, as opposed to the imitations and adaptations, are one-off creations, designed by one of the nine *haute couture* houses listed with the Fédération Française de la Couture. The rules for being classified are fairly strict, and many of the top designers are not included. Astronomical prices put *haute couture* beyond the reach of all but a few immensely deep pockets, but it is still the lifeblood of the fashion industry providing inspiration for the mass market.

WOMEN'S CLOTHES

Most *couture* houses are found on or near the rue du Faubourg-St-Honoré and avenue Montaigne: **Christian Dior**, **Pierre Cardin**, **Chanel**, **Christian Lacroix**, **Versace**, **Givenchy**, **Nina Ricci** and **Yves Saint Laurent**.

Hermès has classic country chic. **MaxMara's** Italian elegance is popular in France and no one can resist a **Giorgio Armani** suit. The legendary **Prada** store has stuck to the Right Bank but many fashion houses prefer the Left Bank.

Many designers have a Left Bank branch in addition to their Right Bank bastions, and they all have ready-to-wear shops here. For sheer quality there's **Georges Rech**, and **Jil Sander** for exquisite tailoring. Try **Sonia Rykiel** for knitwear, and **Barbara Bui** for soft, feminine clothes. In the Saint-Germain-des-Près district, the **Comptoir des Cotonniers** stocks excellent basics, and **Vanessa Bruno** is extremely popular for feminine flair.

For ready-to-wear head to place des Victoires. **Kenzo** is here (although there is a new flagship store near the Pont Neuf), along with fellow Japanese designers **Comme des Garçons**, with its quirky fashion for both sexes. In nearby rue du Jour find the timeless elegance of **Agnès B**.

The Marais is a haven for up-and-coming designers. One of the best streets is the rue des Rosiers, which includes Issey Miyake's **Pleats Please**. **Nina Jacob** is on the neighbouring rue des Francs-Bourgeois, and daring designer **Azzedine Alaïa's** is just around the corner.

The Bastille area has trendy boutiques, as well as some more established names, including **Jean-Paul Gaultier**. **Isabel Marant's** boutique is renowned for its originality.

Young designers' clothes are found at **Colette**, **Stella Cadente**, and **Zadig and Voltaire**.

CHILDREN'S CLOTHES

Lots of options for children exist in various styles and many price ranges. Many top designers of adult clothes also have boutiques for children. These include **Kenzo**, **Baby Dior**, **Agnès B**. Ready-to-wear shops such as **Jacadi** and **Du Pareil au Même** are serviceable and wide-ranging; and **Tartine et Chocolat's** best-selling garments are overalls.

Bonpoint stocks adorably chic clothing for mini-Parisians. **Petit Bateau** is coveted as much by grown-ups as it is by children. The inevitable has finally happened – children now have their own concept store in **Bonton**.

For little feet, **Froment-Leroyer** probably offers the best all-round classics.

MEN'S CLOTHES

Men don't have the luxury of *haute couture* dressing and their choice is limited to ready-to-wear. On the Right Bank, there's **Giorgio Armani**, **Pierre Cardin**, **Lanvin** (also good for accessories) and **Yves Saint Laurent**. On the Left Bank, **Michel Axael** and **Jean-Charles de Castelbajac** are known for their ties and **Francesco Smalto's** elegant creations are worn by some of the world's leading movie stars. **Yohji Yamamoto's** clothes are for those who are intent on making a serious fashion statement, while **Gianni Versace** is classic, suave, and Italian in style.

The ultimate in Parisian elegance for men, however, is a suit, custom-made shirt or silk tie from **Charvet**.

VINTAGE AND SECOND-HAND STORES

The vintage craze hit Paris some time back and there are some wonderful shops to plunder for a retro look. The best of the bunch is **Didier Ludot**, where an Aladdin's Cave of chic *haute couture* is elegantly displayed. The **Depôt-Vente de Buci-Bourbon** is another good place to bargain hunt. A cheaper option is to head for one of the second-hand consignment stores. Chic Parisians discard their outfits with the seasons so it is very easy to pick up some quality items, often in top condition, from places such as **Réciproque** in Passy or **Alternatives** in the Marais.

A cheaper option for sample pieces and sale stock can be found at **Le Mouton à Cinq Pattes**.

JEWELLERY

The *couture* houses probably stock some of the best jewellery and scarves. **Chanel's** jewels are classics and **Christian Lacroix's** are fun. **Boutique YSL** is a great place for accessories.

Among the main expensive Paris jewellery outlets are **Boucheron**, **Mauboussin** and **Poiray**. They are for the serious jewellery buyer. Other top retailers include **Harry Winston** and **Cartier**. **Dinh Van** has some quirky pieces, whilst **Mikimoto** is a must for pearls and **H Stern** has some innovative designs using semi-precious and precious stones. For a range of more unusual jewellery and accessories, try the **Daniel Swarovski Boutique**, which is owned by the Swarovksi crystal family.

SHOES AND BAGS

For both classic and wild footwear designs, you can't beat **Miu Miu**. **Rodolphe Ménudier** and **Christian Louboutin** are mainstays for sexy stilettos. **Carel** stocks smart basics and **Jonak** is a must for good imitations of designer footwear.

For ladies handbags, nothing beats **Chanel** or **Dior** at the top end of the scale, although **Goyard** comes close. Mid-range bags from **Furla** are a great compromise. Fabric bags from **Jamin Puech** or **Vanessa Bruno** are a feature in every chic Parisian closet. For those with tighter purse strings, cheap, cheerful and stylish bags can be found at **Lollipops**.

LINGERIE

For modern lingerie go to **Fifi Chachnil**, whose shop is filled with colourful underwear. **La Boîte à Bas** sells fine French stockings, whereas **Princesse Tam Tam** offers quality items at reasonable prices, while divine designer underwear can be found at cult store **Sabbia Rosa**. The ultimate in Parisian lingerie can be bought off the peg or made to order at **Cadolle**, the store which invented the bra.

DIRECTORY

WOMEN'S CLOTHES

Agnès B
2–3–6–10–19 rue du Jour. 75001. **Map** 9 A1.
Tel 01 45 08 56 56.
One of several branches.

Azzedine Alaïa
7 rue de Moussy 75004.
Map 9 C3.
Tel 01 42 72 19 19.

Barbara Bui
23 rue Etienne-Marcel 75001. **Map** 9 A1.
Tel 01 40 26 43 65.
www.barbarabui.com
One of four branches.

Chanel
42 av Montaigne 75008.
Map 3 A5. *Tel 01 47 23 74 12. One of several branches.* **www**.chanel.com

Christian Dior
30 av Montaigne 75008.
Map 6 F1.
Tel 01 40 73 73 73.
www.dior.com

Christian Lacroix
73 rue du Faubourg-St-Honoré 75008. **Map** 3 B5.
Tel 01 42 68 79 00.
www.christian-lacroix.com

Colette
213 rue St-Honoré 75001.
Map 8 D1.
Tel 01 55 35 33 90.
www.colette.fr

Comme des Garçons
54 rue du Faubourg St-Honoré 75008. **Map** 2 E3.
Tel 01 53 30 27 27.

Comptoir des Cotonniers
59 rue Bonaparte 75006.
Map 8 E3.
Tel 01 43 26 07 56.
One of several branches.

Georges Rech
54 rue Bonaparte 75006.
Map 8 E3.
Tel 01 43 26 84 11.
www.georges-rech.fr
One of several branches.

Giorgio Armani
50 rue du Faubourg St-Honoré 75008. **Map** 2 E3. *Tel 01 42 61 55 09*
www.giorgioarmani.com

Givenchy
3 av Georges V 75008.
Map 2 E5.
Tel 01 44 31 50 00.
www.givenchy.com

Hermès
24 rue du Faubourg-St-Honoré 75008. **Map** 3 C5.
Tel 01 40 17 46 00.
www.hermes.com
One of several branches.

Isabel Marant
16 rue de Charonne 75011. **Map** 10 F4.
Tel 01 49 29 71 55.

Jean-Paul Gaultier
6 rue Vivienne 75002.
Map 8 F1.
Tel 01 42 86 05 05.
One of several branches.

Jil Sander
52 av Montaigne 75008.
Map 6 F1.
Tel 01 44 95 06 70.

Kenzo
3 pl des Victoires 75001.
Map 8 F1.
Tel 01 40 39 72 00.
One of several branches.

MaxMara
31 av Montaigne 75008.
Map 6 F1.
Tel 01 47 20 61 13.
One of several branches.

Nina Jacob
23 rue des Francs-Bourgeois 75004.
Map 10 D3.
Tel 01 42 77 41 20.

Nina Ricci
39 av Montaigne 75008.
Map 6 F1.
Tel 01 40 88 67 60
www.ninaricci.fr

Pierre Cardin
27 av de Marigny 75008.
Map 3 B5.
Tel 01 42 66 68 98.
www.pierrecardin.com
One of two branches.

Pleats Please
3 bis rue des Rosiers

75004. **Map** 9 C3.
Tel 01 40 29 99 66.
One of two branches.

Prada
10 av Montaigne
75008. **Map** 6 F1.
Tel 01 53 23 99 40.

Sonia Rykiel
175 bd St-Germain
75006. **Map** 8 D4.
Tel 01 49 54 60 60.
www.soniarykiel.com
One of several branches.

Stella Cadente
4 quai des Célestins
75004. **Map** 9 C4.
Tel 01 44 78 05 95.
www.stella-cadente.com

Vanessa Bruno
25 rue St-Sulpice 75006.
Map 8 E5.
Tel 01 43 54 41 04.

Versace
41 rue François 1er 75008.
Map 2 F5.
Tel 01 47 42 88 02.
www.versace.com

Yves Saint Laurent
38 rue du Faubourg-St-Honoré 75008. **Map** 3 C5.
Tel 01 42 65 74 59.
One of several branches.

Zadig & Voltaire
9 rue du 29 Juillet 75001.
Map 8 D1.
Tel 01 42 92 00 80.

DIRECTORY

CHILDREN'S CLOTHES

Bonpoint
320 rue St-Honoré 75001.
Map 9 A2.
Tel 01 49 27 94 82.
www.bonpoint.com
One of several branches.

Bonton
82 rue de Grenelle 75007.
Map 6F3.
Tel 01 44 39 09 20.

Du Pareil au Même
1 rue St-Denis 75001.
Map 9 B3
Tel 01 42 36 07 57
One of several branches.

Froment-Leroyer
7 rue Vavin 75006.
Map 12 E1.
Tel 01 43 54 33 15.
www.froment-leroyer.fr
One of several branches.

Jacadi
17 rue Tronchet 75008.
Map 3 C5.
Tel 01 42 65 84 98.
www.jacadi.fr

Petit Bateau
116 av des Champs
Elysées 75008. **Map** 2 E4.
Tel 01 40 74 02 03.

Tartine et Chocolat
105 rue du Faubourg-St-
Honoré 75008. **Map** 3 B5.
Tel 01 45 62 44 04.

MEN'S CLOTHES

Charvet
28 pl Vendôme
75001. **Map** 4 D5.
Tel 01 42 60 30 70.

Francesco Smalto
44 rue François 75008.
Map 2 F5.
Tel 01 47 20 96 04.
www.smalto.com

**Jean-Charles de
Castelbajac**
10 rue de Vauvilliers
75001.
Tel 01 55 34 10 10
www.jedecastelbajac.com

Gianni Versace
41 rue François 1er
75008. **Map** 2 F5.
Tel 01 47 42 88 02.
www.versace.com

Giorgio Armani
(see p143).

Kenzo
(see p143).

Lanvin
15 rue du Faubourg St-
Honoré 75008.
Map 10 F4.
Tel 01 44 71 31 33.
www.lanvin.com
One of several branches.

Michel Axael
121 bd St-Germain
75006.
Map 8 E4.
Tel 01 43 26 01 96.

Pierre Cardin
(see p143).

Yohji Yamamoto
47 rue Etienne
Marcel 75001.
Map 9 A1.
Tel 01 45 08 82 45.

Yves Saint Laurent
12 pl St-Sulpice 75006.
Map 8 D4.
Tel 01 43 26 84 40.

VINTAGE AND SECOND-HAND STORES

Alternatives
18 rue du Roi-de-Sicile
75004.
Map 9 C3.
Tel 01 42 78 31 50

**Depôt-Vente de
Buci-Bourbon**
6 rue de Bourbon-le-
Château 75006.
Map 8 E4.
Tel 01 46 34 45 05.

Didier Ludot
19-24 Galerie Mont-
pensier 75001.
Map 8 E1.
Tel 01 42 96 06 56.
www.didierludot.com

**Le Mouton à
Cinq Pattes**
8 rue St-Placide 75006.
Map 8 D5.
Tel 01 45 48 86 26.
One of several branches.

Réciproque
95 rue de la Pompe
75016. **Map** 5 A1.
Tel 01 47 04 30 28.

JEWELLERY

Boucheron
26 pl Vendôme 75001.
Map 4 D5.
Tel 01 42 61 58 16.
www.boucheron.com

Cartier
13 rue de la Paix 75002.
Map 4 D5.
Tel 01 58 18 23 00.
One of several branches.

**Daniel Swarovski
Boutique**
7 rue Royale 75008.
Map 3 C5.
Tel 01 40 17 07 40.
www.daniel-
swarovski.com

Dinh Van
15 rue de la Paix
75002.
Map 4 D5.
Tel 01 42 86 02 66.
One of several branches.

H Stern
3 rue Castiglione 75001.
Map 8 D1.
Tel 01 42 60 22 27.
www.hstern.net
One of several branches.

Harry Winston
29 av Montaigne 75008
Map 6 F1.
Tel 01 47 20 03 09
www.harrywinston.com

Mauboussin
20 pl Vendôme 75001.
Map 4 D5.
Tel 01 44 55 10 00.
www.mauboussin.com

Mikimoto
8 pl Vendôme 75001.
Map 4 D5.
Tel 01 42 60 33 55.

Poiray
1 rue de la Paix 75002.
Map 4 D5.
Tel 01 42 61 70 58.

SHOES AND BAGS

Carel
4 rue Tronchet 75008.
Map 4 D4.
Tel 01 43 12 37 00.
One of several branches.

Christian Louboutin
38-40 rue de Grenelle
75007. **Map** 6 F3.
Tel 01 42 22 33 07.

Furla
8 rue de Sèvres 75006.
Map 7 C5.
Tel 01 40 49 06 44.
One of several branches.

Goyard
233 rue St-Honoré 75001.
Map 3 C5.
Tel 01 42 60 57 04.

Jamin Puech
61 rue de Hauteville
75010.
Tel 01 40 22 08 32.

Jonak
70 rue de Rennes 75006.
Map 12 D1.
Tel 01 45 48 27 11.

Lollipops
60 rue Tiquetonne 75002.
Map 9 A1.
Tel 01 42 33 15 72.
www.lollipops.fr

Miu Miu
219 rue St-Honoré
75001. **Map** 8 D1.
Tel 01 58 62 53 20.
www.miumiu.com

Rodolphe Ménudier
14 rue de Castiglione
75001. **Map** 8 D1.
Tel 01 42 60 86 27.

Vanessa Bruno
25 rue St-Sulpice 75006.
Map 8 E5.
Tel 01 43 54 41 04.

LINGERIE

La Boîte à Bas
27 rue Boissy-d'Anglas
75008. **Map** 3 C5.
Tel 01 42 66 26 85.

Cadolle
4 rue Cambon 75001.
Map 4 D5.
Tel 01 42 60 94 20.

Fifi Chachnil
231 rue St-Honoré
75001. **Map** 8 D1.
Tel 01 42 61 21 83.
www.fifichachnil.com
One of several branches.

Princesse Tam Tam
52 bd St-Michel 75006.
Map 8 F5.
Tel 01 42 34 99 31.
One of several branches.

Sabbia Rosa
73 rue des Sts-Pères
75006.**Map** 8 D4.
Tel 01 45 48 88 37.

Gifts and Souvenirs

Paris has a wealth of stylish gift options, from designer accessories to Eiffel Tower paperweights. Shops on the rue de Rivoli and around major tourist attractions offer a range of cheap holiday paraphernalia, or go to one of the souvenir stores such as **Les Drapeaux de France.**

PERFUME

Many shops advertise discounted perfume. They include **Eiffel Shopping** near the Eiffel Tower. The **Sephora** chain has a big selection, or try the department stores for a range of beauty brands which are hard to find elsewhere.

Parfums Caron has many scents created at the turn-of-the-19th century, which are unavailable elsewhere. Beautifully packaged perfumes made from natural essences are available from **Annick Goutal. Guerlain** has the ultimate in beauty care, while the elegant shops of **L'Artisan Parfumeur** specialize in exquisitely packaged scents evoking specific memories.

HOUSEHOLD GOODS

It is difficult to ignore some of the world's most elegant tableware. Luxury homeware stores line the rue Royale. **Lalique's** Art Nouveau and Art Deco glass sculptures are collected all over the world. Impeccable silverware comes from **Christofle.**

For significant savings on porcelain and crystal, try **Lumicristal**, which stocks Baccarat, Daum and Limoges crystal, or why not go to **Baccarat** itself.

La Chaise Longue has a selection of fun gift ideas to suit most tastes and **Bô** has a wide range of contemporary goods to add a new lease of life to any home.

BOOKS

Some large department stores have a books section, and there are several English-language bookshops such as **W H Smith** and **Brentano's**. The cosy **Shakespeare & Co** and **Red Wheelbarrow Bookstore** are good for convivial browsing among expats. French-language bookshops include **La Hune** specializing in art, cinema, fashion and photography and **Gilbert Joseph** for educational books.

SPECIALIST SHOPS

A La Civette is perhaps Paris's most beautiful tobacconists, stocking a vast range of cigars behind specially humidified store windows.

One of the world's most famous and delightful toy-stores is **Au Nain Bleu** while the name **Cassegrain** is synonymous with high-quality stationery and paper products.

DIRECTORY

SOUVENIR SHOPS

Les Drapeaux de France
1 pl Colette 75001.
Map 8 E1.
Tel 01 40 20 00 11.

PERFUME

Annick Goutal
16 rue de Bellechasse 75007.
Map 7 C3.
Tel 01 45 51 36 13.
One of several branches.

L'Artisan Parfumeur
24 bd Raspail 75007.
Map 12 D1.
Tel 01 42 22 23 32.
One of several branches.

Eiffel Shopping
9 av de Suffren 75007.
Map 6 D3.
Tel 01 45 66 55 30.

Guerlain
68 av des Champs-Elysées 75008. **Map** 2 F5. *Tel 01 45 62 52 57.* www.guerlain.com

Parfums Caron
34 av Montaigne 75008.
Map 6 F1.
Tel 01 47 23 40 82.

Sephora
70 av des Champs-Elysées 75008. **Map** 7 B1.
Tel 01 53 93 22 50.
www.sephora.fr
One of several branches.

HOUSEHOLD GOODS

Baccarat
11 pl de la Madeleine 75008. **Map** 3 C5.
Tel 01 42 65 36 26.

Bô
8 rue St-Mérri 75004.
Map 9B2.
Tel 01 42 74 55 10.

La Chaise Longue
30 rue Croix-des-Petits-Champs 75001. **Map** 8 F1.
Tel 01 42 96 32 14.

Christofle
24 rue de la Paix 75002.
Map 4 D5.
Tel 01 42 65 62 43.

www.christofle.com
Lalique
11 rue Royale 75008.
Map 3 C5.
Tel 01 53 05 12 12.

Lumicristal
29 rue de Paradis 75010.
Tel 01 45 23 23 73.

BOOKS

Brentano's
37 av de l'Opéra 75002.
Map 4 E5.
Tel 01 42 61 52 50.
www.brentanos.fr

Gibert Joseph
26 bd St-Michel 75006.
Map 8 F5.
Tel 01 44 41 88 88.

La Hune
170 bd St-Germain
75006. **Map** 8 D4.
Tel 01 45 48 35 85.

Red Wheelbarrow Bookstore
22 rue St-Paul 75004.
Map 10 D4.
Tel 01 48 04 75 08.
www.theredwheel

barrow.com

Shakespeare & Co
37 rue de la Bûcherie 75005.
Map 9 A4.
Tel 01 43 25 40 93.

W H Smith
248 rue de Rivoli 75001.
Map 7 C1.
Tel 01 44 77 88 99.

SPECIALIST SHOPS

A La Civette
157 rue St-Honoré 75001.
Map 8 F2.
Tel 01 42 96 04 99.

Au Nain Bleu
5 bd Malesherbes 75008.
Map 3 C5.
Tel 01 42 65 20 20.
www.aunainbleu.com
One of several branches.

Cassegrain
422 rue St-Honoré 75008. **Map** 3 C5.
Tel 01 42 60 20 08.
www.cassegrain.fr.

Food and Drink

Paris is as famous for food as it is for fashion. Gastronomic treats include *foie gras*, cold meats from the *charcuterie*, cheese and wine. Certain streets are so overflowing with food shops that you can put together a picnic for 20 in no time: try the rue Montorgueil (*see Map 9 A1*). The rue Rambuteau, running on either side of the Pompidou Centre, has a marvellous row of fishmongers and delicatessens.

BREAD AND CAKES

There is a vast range of breads and pastries in France's capital. The *baguette* is often translated as "French bread"; a *bâtard* is similar but thicker, while a *ficelle* is thinner. A *fougasse* is a crusty, flat loaf often filled with onions, cheese, herbs or spices.

Croissants can be bought *ordinaire* or *au beurre* – the latter is flakier and more buttery. *Pain au chocolat* is a chocolate-filled pastry eaten for breakfast, and *chausson aux pommes* is filled with apples. There are also pear, plum and rhubarb variations. A *pain aux raisins* is a bread-like wheel filled with custard and raisins.

Poilâne sells perhaps the only bread in Paris known by the name of its baker (the late Lionel, brother of Max) and his hearty wholewheat loaves are tremendously popular.

Many think **Ganachaud** bakes the best bread in Paris. Thirty different kinds, including ingredients such as walnuts and fruit, are made in the old-fashioned ovens.

Les Panetons is a good chain bakery. Favourites here include five-grain bread, sesame rolls, and *mouchoir aux pommes*, a variation on the traditional *chausson*.

Many of the Jewish delicatessens have the best ryes and the only pumper-nickels in town. One of the best is **Sacha Finkelsztajn**.

Le Moulin de la Vierge uses a wood fire to bake organic breads and rich pound cakes. **J L Poujauran** is known for his black-olive bread and nut-and-raisin wholegrain breads.

Pierre Hermé is to cakes what Chanel is to fashion, while **Ladurée**'s macaroons are legendary.

CHOCOLATE

Like all food in France, chocolate is to be savoured. **Christian Constant's** low-sugar creations are made with pure cocoa and are known to connoisseurs. **Dalloyau** makes all types of chocolate and is not too expensive (it is also known for its pâtisserie and cold meats). **Fauchon** is world famous for its luxury food products. Its chocolates are excellent, as is the pâtisserie. Robert Linxe at **La Maison du Chocolat** is constantly inventing fresh, rich chocolates with mouth-watering exotic ingredients. **Richart** boasts beautifully presented and hugely expensive chocolates, which are usually coated with dark chocolate or liqueur-filled.

CHARCUTERIE AND FOIE GRAS

Charcuteries often sell cheese, snails, truffles, smoked salmon, caviar and wine as well as cold meats. **Fauchon** has a good grocery, as does the department store **Le Bon Marché**. **Hédiard** is a luxury shop similar to Fauchon, and **Maison de la Truffe** sells *foie gras* and sausages as well as truffles. For Beluga caviar, Georgian tea and Russian vodka, go to **Petrossian**.

The Lyon and Auvergne regions of France are the best known for their *charcuterie*, and **Chrétienne Jean-Jacques** sells excellent examples. **Pou** is a sparklingly clean and popular store selling *pâté en croute* (pâté baked in pastry), *boudins* (black and white puddings), Lyonnais sausages, ham and *foie gras*. Just off the Champs-Elysées, **Vignon** has superb *foie gras* and Lyonnais

sausages as well as popular prepared food.

Together with truffles and caviar, *foie gras* is the ultimate in gourmet food. Though most specialist food shops sell *foie gras*, you can be sure of quality at **Comtesse du Barry**, which has six outlets in Paris. **Divay** is relatively inexpensive and will ship overseas. **Labeyrie** has a range of beautifully packaged *foie gras* suitable for giving as presents.

CHEESE

Although camembert is undoubtedly a favourite, there is an overwhelming range of cheeses available and a friendly *fromager* will always help you choose. **Marie-Anne Cantin** is one of the leading figures in the fight to protect traditional production methods, and her fine cheeses are available from the store that she inherited from her father. Some say that **Alléosse** is the best cheese delicatessen in Paris – all the cheeses are made according to traditional methods. **Fromagerie Quatrehomme** sells farm-made cheeses, many of which are in danger of becoming extinct, these include a rare and delicious truffle Brie (when in season). **Boursault** is one of the best shops in Paris for all types of cheese – the *chèvre* (goat's cheese) is particularly good, and outside on the pavement the daily specials are offered at remarkably reasonable prices. **Barthélemy** in the rue de Grenelle has a truly excep-tional Roquefort. **Androuët** is a Parisian institution with several branches across the city. Try a pungent Munster or a really ripe Brie. A charming cheese shop, **La Fermette**, offers a dazzling array of dairy products, which the staff will encase in plastic for the journey home, imperative when bringing cheese through customs.

Well-heeled locals queue in the street to buy oozing *livarot* and sharp *chèvre* from **La Fromagerie d'Auteuil**.

WINE

The chain store which has practically cornered the everyday tippling market is **Nicolas** – there is a branch in every neighbourhood with a range of wines to suit all pockets. As a rule, the sales-people are knowledgeable and helpful. Try the charming **Legrand Filles et Fils** for a carefully chosen selection of high-end champagnes. **Caves Taillevent** on the rue du Faubourg-St-Honoré is worth a sightseeing tour. It is an enormous, overwhelming cellar with some of the most expensive wine.

Cave Péret on the rue Daguerre has a vast selection of wines and can offer personal advice to help you with your purchase. The beautiful **Ryst-Dupeyron**, in the St-Germain quarter, displays whiskies, wines, ports and Monsieur Ryst's own Armagnac. He will even personalize a bottle for that special occasion.

Other great wine stores include **Lavinia**, which is the largest in Europe, and, by contrast, **Renaud Michel** at Place de la Nation, whose small boutique is very well stocked and well connected. The staff in **Les Caves Augé** are also very knowledgeable and friendly.

DIRECTORY

BREAD AND CAKES

Ganachaud
226 rue des Pyrénées 75020.
Tel 01 43 49 30 93.

J L Poujauran
20 rue Jean-Nicot 75007.
Map 6 F2.
Tel 01 43 17 35 20.

Ladurée
75 av des Champs-Elysées 75008. **Map** 2 F5. *Tel 01 40 75 08 75.*

Le Moulin de la Vierge
105 rue Vercingétorix 75014. **Map** 11 A4.
Tel 01 45 43 15 16.

Les Panetons
113 rue Mouffetard 75005. **Map** 13 B2.
Tel 01 47 07 12 08.

Pierre Hermé
72 rue Bonaparte 75006.
Map 8 E4.
Tel 01 43 54 47 77.

Poilâne
8 rue du Cherche-Midi 75006. **Map** 8 D4.
Tel 01 45 48 42 59.
www.poilane.fr

Sacha Finkelsztajn
27 rue des Rosiers 75004.
Map 9 C3.
Tel 01 42 72 78 91

CHOCOLATE

Christian Constant
37 rue d'Assas 75006.
Map 12 E1.
Tel 01 53 63 15 15.

Dalloyau
101rue du Faubourg-St-Honoré 75008. **Map** 3 B5.

Tel 01 42 99 90 00.

Fauchon
26 pl de la Madeleine 75008. **Map** 3 C5.
Tel 01 70 39 38 00.

La Maison du Chocolat
225 rue du Faubourg-St-Honoré 75008. **Map** 2 E3.
Tel 01 42 27 39 44.

Richart
258 bd St-Germain 75007. **Map** 7 C2.
Tel 01 45 55 66 00.

CHARCUTERIE AND FOIE GRAS

Chrétienne Jean-Jacques
58 rue des Martyrs 75009.
Map 4 F2.
Tel 01 48 78 96 45.

Comtesse du Barry
1 rue de Sèvres 75006.
Map 8 D4.
Tel 01 45 48 32 04.

Divay
4 rue Bayen 75017.
Map 2 D2.
Tel 01 43 80 16 97.

Hédiard
21 pl de la Madeleine 75008. **Map** C5.
Tel 01 43 12 88 88.

Labeyrie
11 rue d'Auteuil 75016.
Map 5 A5.
Tel 01 42 24 17 62.

Le Bon Marché
24 rue de Sèvres 75007.
Map 7 C5.
Tel 01 44 39 80 00.

Maison de la Truffe
19 pl de la Madeleine 75008. **Map** 3 C5.

Tel 01 42 65 53 22.

Petrossian
18 bd Latour-Maubourg 75007. **Map** 7 A2.
Tel 01 44 11 32 22.

Pou
16 av des Ternes 75017.
Map 2 D3.
Tel 01 43 80 19 24.

Vignon
14 rue Marbeuf 75008.
Map 2 F5.
Tel 01 47 20 24 26.

CHEESE

Alléosse
13 rue Poncelet 75017.
Map 2 E3.
Tel 01 46 22 50 45.

Androuët
134 rue Mouffetard 75005.
Map 13 B1.
Tel 01 45 87 85 05.

Barthélémy
51 rue de Grenelle 75007.
Map 8 D4.
Tel 01 45 48 56 75.

Boursault
71 av du Général-Leclerc 75014. **Map** 12 D5.
Tel 01 43 27 93 30.

La Fermette
86 rue Montorgueil 75002.
Map 9 A1.
Tel 01 42 36 70 96.

La Fromagerie d'Auteuil
58 rue d'Auteuil 75016.
Map 5 A5.
Tel 01 45 25 07 10.

Fromagerie Quatrehomme
62 rue de Sèvres 75007.
Map 7 C5.

Tel 01 47 34 33 45.

Marie-Anne Cantin
12 rue du Champ-de-Mars 75007.
Map 6 F3.
Tel 01 45 50 43 94.

WINE

Les Caves Augé
116 bd Haussman 75008.
Map 3 C4.
Tel 01 45 22 16 97.

Cave Péret
6 rue Daguerre 75014.
Map 12 D4.
Tel 01 43 22 08 64.

Caves Taillevent
199 rue du Faubourg-St-Honoré 75008.
Map 2 F3.
Tel 01 45 61 14 09.

Lavinia
3–5 bd de la Madeleine 75008.
Map 4 D5.
Tel 01 42 97 20 20

Legrand Filles et Fils
1 rue de la Banque 75002.
Map 8 F1.
Tel 01 42 60 07 12.

Nicolas
35 bd Malesherbes 75008.
Map 3 C5.
Tel 01 42 65 00 85.

Renaud Michel
12 pl de la Nation 75012.
Tel 01 43 07 98 93.

Ryst-Dupeyron
79 rue du Bac 75007.
Map 8 D3.
Tel 01 45 48 80 93.

Arts and Antiques

In Paris you can either buy art and antiques from shops and galleries with established reputations, or from flea markets and avant-garde galleries. Many of the prestigious antiques shops and galleries are located around the rue du Faubourg-St-Honoré and are worth a visit even if you can't afford to buy. On the Left Bank is Le Carré Rive Gauche, an organization of 30 antiques dealers.

EXPORTING

Objets d'art over 50 years old, worth more than a given amount, will require a *Certificat pour un bien culturel* to be exported (provided by the vendor), plus a *licence d'exportation* for non-EU countries. Seek professional advice from the large antique shops. The **Centre des Renseignements des Douanes** has a booklet, *Bulletin Officiel des Douanes*, with all the details.

ANTIQUES

If you wish to buy antiques, you might like to stroll around the areas that boast the most galleries – in Le Carré Rive Gauche around quai Malaquais, try **L'Arc en Seine** and **Anne-Sophie Duval** for Art Nouveau and Art Deco. Rue Jacob is still one of the best places to seek beautiful objects, antique or modern. Close to the Louvre, the

Louvre des Antiquaires comprises 250 shops selling mainly expensive, quality furniture. Many of the prestigious antiques stores are are near rue du Faubourg-St-Honoré including **Didier Aaron**, expert on furniture from the 17th and 18th centuries. **Village St-Paul** is the most charming group of antiques shops and is also open on Sundays. In the south of the city, **La Village Suisse** also groups many art and antiques dealers.

ART GALLERIES

Established art galleries are located on or around the avenue Montaigne. The **Louise Leiris** gallery was founded by D.H. Kahnweiler, the dealer who "discovered" both Georges Braque and Pablo Picasso. The gallery still shows Cubist masterpieces.

On the Left Bank **Galerie Maeght** has a tremendous stock of paintings at prices to

suit most budgets; he also publishes fine art books.

Rue Louise-Weiss, known as Scène Est, has become the area for cutting-edge creativity and innovation. The **Air de Paris** gallery is popular.

In the Marais try **Yvon Lambert** and **Galerie du Jour Agnès B**, in the Bastille, **Levignes-Bastille** and **L et M Durand-Dessert**, also a fashionable place to buy catalogues on new artists, if not their works.

AUCTION HOUSES

The great Paris auction centre, in operation since 1858, is **Drouot-Richelieu**. Bidding can be intimidating since most of it is done by dealers. Beware of the auctioneer's high-speed patter. *La Gazette de L'Hôtel Drouot* tells you what auctions are coming up when. Drouot-Richelieu also has its own auction catalogue. The house only accepts cash and French cheques, but there is an exchange desk in-house. A 10–15 per cent commission to the house is charged, so remember to add it on to any price you hear. You may view from 11am–6pm on the day before the sale, and from 11am to noon on the morning of the sale.

DIRECTORY

EXPORTING

Centre des Renseignements des Douanes
84 rue d'Hauteville 75010. **Tel** 08 20 02 44 44. www.douane.gouv.fr

ANTIQUES

Anne-Sophie Duval
5 quai Malaquais 75006. **Map** 8 E3. **Tel** 01 43 54 51 16. www.annesophieduval.com

L'Arc en Seine
31 rue de Seine 75006. **Map** 8 E3. **Tel** 01 43 29 11 02.

Didier Aaron
118 rue du Faubourg-St-Honoré 75008. **Map** 3 C5. **Tel** 01 47 42 47 34. www.didieraaron-cie.com

Louvre des Antiquaires
2 pl du Palais Royal 75001. **Map** 8 E2. **Tel** 01 42 97 27 27.

Village St-Paul
Between the quai des Célestins, the rue St-Paul and the rue Charlemagne 75004. **Map** 9 C4.

La Village Suisse
78 av de Suffren 75015. **Map** 6 E4. www.levillagesuisseparis.com

ART GALLERIES

Air de Paris
32 rue Louise-Weiss 75013. **Map** 14 E4. **Tel** 01 44 23 02 77.

Galerie du Jour Agnès B
44 rue Quincampoix 75004. **Map** 9 B2. **Tel** 01 44 54 55 90.

Galerie Maeght
42 rue du Bac 75007. **Map** 8 D3. **Tel** 01 45 48 45 15.

L et M Durand-Dessert
28 rue de Lappe 75011. **Map** 10 F4. **Tel** 01 48 06 92 23.

Levignes-Bastille
27 rue de Charonne 75011. **Map** 10 F4. **Tel** 01 47 00 88 18.

Louise Leiris
47 rue de Monceau 75008. **Map** 3 A3. **Tel** 01 45 63 28 85.

Yvon Lambert
108 rue Vieille-du-Temple 75003. **Map** 10 D2. **Tel** 01 42 71 09 33.

AUCTION HOUSES

Drouot-Richelieu
9 rue Drouot 75009. **Map** 4 F4. **Tel** 01 48 00 20 20. www.drouot.fr

Markets

For eye-catching displays of wonderful food or a lively shopping atmosphere, there is no better place than a Paris market. There are large covered food markets; markets where stalls change regularly; and permanent street markets. Some of the more famous markets, with approximate opening times, follows. While you are enjoying browsing round the stalls, remember to keep an eye on your money and be prepared to bargain.

FOOD MARKETS

The French still shop daily, hence food markets are always packed. Most fruit and vegetable markets are open from around 8am–1pm and from 4–7pm Tuesday to Saturday, and from 9am–1pm Sunday. Watch out for rotten produce – buy product loose, not in boxes. A little language is useful for specifying *pas trop mûr* (not too ripe), or *pour manger ce soir* (to be eaten tonight).

FLEA MARKETS

It is often said that you can no longer find bargains at the Paris flea markets. Though this may be true, it is still worth going to one for the sheer fun of browsing. Whether you pick up any real bargains has as much to do with luck as with judgement. Often the sellers themselves have little or no idea of the true value of their goods – which can work either for or against you. The biggest and most famous market, incorporating several smaller ones, is the Marché aux Puces de St-Ouen. Keep an eye on your wallet, as pickpockets frequent these markets.

Marché d'Aligre

Pl d'Aligre 75012. **Map** 10 F5. Ⓜ Ledru-Rollin. ◯ 9am–1pm & 4–7:30pm Tue–Sat, 9am–1:30pm Sun.

Reminiscent of a Moroccan bazaar, this must be the cheapest and liveliest market in the city. Here traders hawk ingredients such as North African olives, groundnuts and hot peppers, and there are even a few halal butchers. Stalls on the square sell mostly second-hand clothes and bric-à-brac. This is a less affluent area of town with few tourists and many Parisians.

Marché Enfant Rouges

39 rue de Bretagne 75003. **Map** 10 D2. Ⓜ Temple, Filles-du-Calvaire. ◯ 8:30am–1pm, 4–7pm Tue–Sat (until 8pm Fri, Sat), 8:30am–2pm Sun.

This part-covered fruit and vegetable market dates from 1620. Famous for the freshness of its produce, on Sunday mornings street singers and accordionists help enliven the proceedings.

Marché St-Germain

4–8 rue Lobineau 75006. **Map** 8 E4. Ⓜ Mabillon. ◯ 8am–1pm, 4–8pm Tue–Sat, 8am–1:30pm Sun.

St-Germain is one of the few covered markets left in Paris and it has been further enhanced by renovation. Here you can buy Italian, Mexican, Greek, Asian and organic produce.

Rue Lepic

75018. **Map** 4 F1. Ⓜ Blanche, Lamarck-Caulaincourt. ◯ 9am–7pm daily.

The rue Lepic fruit and vegetable street market is situated conveniently close to the sights of Montmartre in this refreshingly unspoilt winding old quarry road.

Rue Montorgueil

75001 & 75002. **Map** 9 A1. Ⓜ Les Halles. ◯ 9am–7pm daily (subject to change).

The paved rue Montorgueil is what remains of the old Les Halles market. Here you can buy exotic fruit and vegetables like green bananas and yams, or sample offerings from the delicatessens.

Rue Mouffetard

75005. **Map** 13 B2. Ⓜ Pl Monge. ◯ 8am–1pm Tue–Sun.

This is one of the oldest market streets in Paris, and although it has become touristy it is still a charming winding street full of quality food. There is also a lively African market down the nearby side street of rue Daubenton.

Rue Poncelet

75017. **Map** 2 E3. Ⓜ Ternes. ◯ 8am–noon, 4–7:30pm Tue–Sat, 8am–12:30pm Sun.

Situated away from the main tourist areas, this market street is worth visiting for its authentic French atmosphere. Choose from many bakeries, pâtisseries and *charcuteries*.

Marché de la Porte de Vanves

Av Georges-Lafenestre & av Marc-Sangnier 75014. Ⓜ Porte-de-Vanves. ◯ 7am–3 or 5pm, & 7am–5pm Sat & Sun respectively.

Porte de Vanves is a small market selling good-quality bric-à-brac and junk as well as some second-hand furniture. It's best to get to the market early on Saturday morning for the best choice of wares. Artists exhibit nearby.

Marché aux Puces de Montreuil

Porte de Montreuil, 93 Montreuil 75020. Ⓜ Porte-de-Montreuil. ◯ 8am–6pm Sat, Sun & Mon.

Go early to the Porte de Montreuil flea market, where you'll have a better chance of picking up a bargain. The substantial second-hand clothes section attracts many young people. Stalls sell everything from used bicycles to bric-à-brac and exotic spices.

Marché aux Puces de St-Ouen

(see p134.)

This is the most well known, the most crowded and the most expensive of all the flea markets. Here you'll find a range of markets, locals dealing from their car boots, and a number of large buildings packed with stalls. Some of them are very upmarket; others sell junk. A *Guide des Puces* (guide to the flea markets) can be obtained from the information kiosk in the Marché Biron on the rue des Rosiers.

Rue de Seine and Rue de Buci

75006. **Map** 8 E4. Ⓜ Odéon. ◯ 8am–1pm, 4–7pm Tue–Sat, 9am–1pm Sun.

The stalls here are expensive and crowded but sell quality fruit and vegetables. There is also a large florist's and two excellent pâtisseries.

ENTERTAINMENT IN PARIS

Whether your preference is for classical drama, avant-garde theatre, ballet, opera or jazz, cinema or dancing the night away, Paris has it all. There is plenty of free entertainment too, from the street performers outside the Pompidou Centre to musicians busking all over town and in the metros.

Parisians themselves like nothing better than strolling along the boulevards or sitting at a pavement café

nursing a drink as they watch the world go by. If, however, you're looking for the ultimate "Oh la-la!" experience, you can take in any of the celebrated nightclubs.

For fans of spectator sports there is tennis, the Tour de France or horse racing. Recreation centres and gyms cater to the more active. And for those disposed to more leisurely pursuits, there is always a quiet game of boules to be played in the park.

The glass façade of the Bastille Opéra

BOOKING TICKETS

Depending on the event, tickets can often be bought at the door, but for popular events it is wiser to purchase tickets in advance at the **FNAC** chains or **Virgin Megastore**. Theatre box offices open daily from about 11am–7pm. Most accept credit card bookings by telephone.

THEATRE

From the grandeur of the **Comédie Française** to slapstick farce and avant-garde drama, theatre is flourishing, both in Paris and in its suburbs. Founded in 1680 by royal decree, the Comédie Française is the bastion of French theatre, aiming to keep classical drama in the public eye and to perform works by the best modern playwrights. Formerly the second theatre of the Comédie Française, the **Odéon Théâtre de l'Europe** now specializes in plays from other countries, performed in their original language. In an

underground auditorium in the Art Deco Palais de Chaillot, the **Théâtre National de Chaillot** is famed for staging some very lively productions of European classics. The **Théâtre National de la Colline** specializes in contemporary drama.

Among the most important of the serious independents is the **Comédie des Champs-Elysées**, while for over 100 years the **Palais Royal** has been known as the temple of risqué farce. The café theatres such as **Théâtre d'Edgar** and **Au Bec Fin** are always good venues for seeing the best of the emerging new talent.

In the summer, street theatre thrives in tourist areas such as the Pompidou Centre, Les Halles and St-Germain-des-Prés. Open-air performances of Shakespeare and classic French plays are given at the Shakespeare Garden in the Bois de Boulogne.

CLASSICAL MUSIC

Paris has many first-class venues with an excellent range of opera, classical and contemporary music productions. Opened in 1989, the ultra-modern 2,700-seat **Opéra National de Paris Bastille** stages classic and modern operas. The beautifully renovated **Opéra National Garnier** also puts on operas.

The **Salle Pleyel** is Paris's principal concert hall, housing the Orchestre de Paris and Radio France's Philharmonic Orchestra. Both the **Théâtre des Champs-Elysées** and the **Théâtre du Châtelet** are recommended for their varied high-quality programmes. Venues for chamber music include the **Salle Gaveau**, the **Théâtre de la Ville** and the

LISTINGS MAGAZINES

Pariscope, Zurban and *L'Officiel des Spectacles* are the best listings magazines in Paris. Published every Wednesday, you can pick them up at any news-stand. *Le Figaro* also has a good listings section on Wednesdays. *The City* is published quarterly in English, and is available at news-stands or W H Smith (*see p145*).

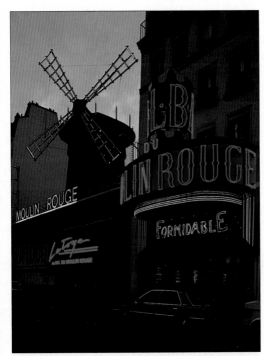

The famous silhouette of the Moulin Rouge nightclub

charming Rococo Théâtre du Grévin (see p97). Paris's newest venue is the **Cité de la Musique** in the Parc de la Villette. It is home to the renowned contemporary music group, the Ensemble InterContemporain, directed by Jonathan Nott.

DANCE

The French are very vocal in their appreciation or dislike of dance, and those who fail to please are subjected to boos, hisses and mass walkouts in mid-performance.

The opulent **Opéra National Garnier** has space for 450 artists and is home to the Ballet de l'Opéra de Paris, which has earned a reputation as one of the best classical ballet companies in the world. Government support has helped the **Théâtre de la Ville** to become Paris's most important venue for modern dance, with subsidies keeping ticket costs relatively low.

The **Maison des Arts de Créteil** stages famous overseas companies, as well as its own much praised productions.

CLUBS AND CABARET

Music in Paris clubs tends to follow the trends set in the US and Britain. Only a few clubs such as **Balajo**, once frequented by Edith Piaf, and the ultra-hip **Showcase**, under the Alexandre III bridge, are genuinely up-to-the-minute with their music.

La Locomotive attracts a mixed crowd to its three-level mainstream house nights. **Les Bains** is the old standby nightspot attracting fashion and show business people.

For comedy in English, try **La Java**. The stage of this club, where Edith Piaf once performed, now showcases British and American comedians.

When it comes to picking a cabaret, the rule of thumb is simple: the better known places are best. The **Folies-Bergère** is the oldest music hall in Paris and probably the most famous in the world. It is closely rivalled by the **Lido** and the **Moulin Rouge**, birthplace of the cancan. **Paradis Latin** is the most "French" cabaret in the city. It shows variety acts whose sketches are enlivened by remarkable special effects and scenery.

ROCK, JAZZ AND WORLD MUSIC

The top international acts are usually to be found at the enormous arenas such as **Palais Omnisports Paris-Bercy** or the **Zénith**. For a more intimate atmosphere, the legendary **Olympia** has assigned seating and good acoustics. To hear indigenous rock groups like Les Negresses Vertes and Mano Negra go to **La Cigale** or **Elysée-Montmartre** in the Pigalle area.

Jazz-crazy Paris has innumerable packed clubs where the best talent in the world can be heard on any evening. All the great jazz musicians have performed at **New Morning**, which also hosts African, Brazilian and other sounds. For Dixieland go to **Le Petit Journal St-Michel**.

World music and jazz lovers alike can see top acts and dance until dawn at the excellent **Chapelle des Lombards**.

La Locomotive, a huge disco on three levels

CINEMA

Paris is the world's capital of film appreciation. It was the cradle of the cinematograph nearly 100 years ago. Then in the late 1950s and early 1960s the city nurtured that very Parisian vanguard movement, the New Wave, when film directors such as François Truffaut and Jean-Luc Godard revolutionized the way films were made and perceived.

There are now more than 370 screens within the city limits, distributed among over 100 cinemas. Most are concentrated in cinema belts, which enjoy the added appeal of nearby restaurants and shops. The Champs-Elysées has the densest cinema strip in town, where you can see the latest Hollywood smash or French *auteur* triumph, as well as some classic re-issues.

In the vicinity of the Opéra de Paris Garnier, the cinemas in the Grands Boulevards include two notable landmarks: the 2,800-seat **Le Grand Rex**, with its Baroque decor, and the **Max Linder Panorama**, which was completely refurbished in the 1980s. The place de Clichy is the last Parisian stronghold of Pathé, while the hub of Right Bank cinema is in the Forum des Halles mall. France's largest screen is at **La Géode**.

On the Left Bank, Odéon-St-Germain-des-Prés has taken over from the Latin Quarter as the city's heartland for art and repertory cinemas. The new, and huge, **MK2 Bibliothèque** points to the future with its collection of 14 screens, a bar, shops and exhibition space.

The dome of the 2,800-seat Le Grand Rex cinema

SPORT

Paris is host to some of the foremost sporting events in the world. City-wide frenzy sweeps Paris when the Tour de France bicycle race finishes there in July. From late May to mid-June Parisians live and breathe tennis during the **Roland Garros** national tennis championship. The Prix de l'Arc de Triomphe, held at the **Hippodrome de Longchamp** on the first Sunday in October, provides the opportunity to see the rich in all their finery as well as first-class flat racing.

The **Palais Omnisports Paris-Bercy** is the venue for a vast range of events, including the Paris tennis open, and rock concerts, as is the new **Stade de France** at St-Denis. **Parc des Princes** is home to Paris's top football team, Paris St-Germain.

THE CELEBRATED CAFES OF PARIS

One of the most enduring images of Paris is the Left Bank café scene where great artists, writers and eminent intellectuals consorted. Before World War I, hordes of Russian revolutionaries, including Lenin and Trotsky, whiled away their days in the Rotonde and the Dôme in Montparnasse. In the 1920s, Surrealists dominated café life. Later came the American writers led by Ernest Hemingway and Scott Fitzgerald, whose haunts included La Coupole. After World War II, Jean-Paul Sartre and other Existentialists shifted the cultural scene northwards to St-Germain.

Newspaper reading remains a typical café pastime

DIRECTORY

BOOKING TICKETS

FNAC
26 av des Ternes 75017.
Map 2 D3.
Tel 01 44 09 18 00.
Forum Les Halles, 1 rue
Pierre Lescot 75001.
Map 9 A2.
Tel 08 25 02 02 02.
www.fnac.com

Virgin Megastore
52–60 av des Champs-
Elysées 75008.
Map 2 F5.
Tel 01 49 53 50 00.
www.virginmegastore.fr

THEATRE

Au Bec Fin
6 bis rue Thérèse 75001.
Map 8 E1.
Tel 01 42 96 29 35.

**Comédie des
Champs-Elysées**
15 av Montaigne 75008.
Map 6 F1.
Tel 01 53 23 99 19.

Comédie Française
1 pl Colette 75001. **Map**
8 E1. *Tel* 08 25 10 16 80.
www.comedie-
francaise.fr

**Odéon Théâtre de
l'Europe**
Ateliers Berthier, 8 bd
Berthier 75017. **Map** 4 D1.
Tel 01 44 85 40 40.
www.theatre-odeon.fr

Palais Royal
38 rue Montpensier
75001. **Map** 8 E1.
Tel 01 42 97 40 00.

Théâtre d'Edgar
58 bd Edgar-Quinet
75014. **Map** 12 D2.
Tel 01 42 79 97 97.

**Théâtre National de
Chaillot**
Pl du Trocadéro
75016. **Map** 5 C2.
Tel 01 53 65 30 00.

**Théâtre National de
la Colline**
15 rue Malte-Brun 75020.
Tel 01 44 62 52 52.

CLASSICAL MUSIC

Cité de la Musique
221 av Jean-Jaurès
75019.
Tel 01 44 84 44 84.
www.cite-musique.fr

**Opéra National de
Paris Bastille**
120 rue de Lyon 75012.
Map 10 E4.
Tel 08 92 89 90 90.
www.operadeparis.fr

**Opéra National de
Paris Garnier**
Pl de l'Opera 75009. **Map**
4 E5. *Tel* 08 92 89 90 90.

Salle Gaveau
45 rue la Boétie 75008.
Map 3 B4.
Tel 01 49 53 05 08.
www.sallegaveau.com

Salle Pleyel
252 rue du Faubourg St-
Honoré 75008. **Map** 2 E3.
Tel 01 42 56 13 13
www.sallepleyel.fr

**Théâtre des
Champs-Elysées**
15 av Montaigne 75008.
Map 6 F1.
Tel 01 49 52 50 00.
www.theatredeschamps
elysees.fr

Théâtre du Châtelet
Pl du Châtelet 75001.
Map 9 A3.
Tel 01 40 28 28 40.
www.chatelet-theatre.
com

Théâtre de la Ville
2 pl du Châtelet 75004.
Map 9 A3.
Tel 01 42 74 22 77.
www.theatredelaville-
paris.com

DANCE

**Maison des Arts de
Créteil**
Pl Salvador Allende 94000
Créteil.
Tel 01 45 13 19 19.
www.maccreteil.com

Opéra Garnier
(See Classical Music.)

Théâtre de la Ville
(See Classical Music.)

CLUBS AND
CABARET

Les Bains
7 rue du Bourg-L'Abbé
75003. **Map** 9 B1.
Tel 01 48 87 01 80.

Balajo
9 rue de Lappe 75011.
Map 10 E4.
Tel 01 47 00 07 87.
www.balajo.fr

Folies-Bergère
32 rue Richer 75009.
Tel 01 44 79 98 90.
www.foliesbergere.com

La Java
105 rue du Faubourg-du-
Temple 75010.
Tel 01 42 02 20 52.

La Locomotive
90 bd de Clichy 75018.
Map 4 D1.
Tel 01 53 41 18 88.

Lido
116 bis av des Champs-
Elysées 75008. **Map** 2 E4.
Tel 01 40 76 56 10.
www.lido.fr

Moulin Rouge
82 bd de Clichy 75018.
Map 4 E1.
Tel 01 53 09 82 82.
www.moulinrouge.fr

Paradis Latin
28 rue du Cardinal-Lemoine
75005. **Map** 9 B5.
Tel 01 43 25 28 28.

Showcase
Porte des Champs-Elysées
75007. **Map** 7 A1.
www.showcase.fr

ROCK, JAZZ AND
WORLD MUSIC

**Chapelle des
Lombards**
19 rue de Lappe 75011.
Map 10 F4.
Tel 01 43 57 24 26.

La Cigale
120 bd Rochechouart
75018. **Map** 4 F2.
Tel 01 49 25 89 99.

Elysée-Montmartre
72 bd Rochechouart
75018. **Map** 4 F2.
Tel 01 44 92 45 36.

New Morning
7–9 rue des Petites-Ecuries
75010.
Tel 01 45 23 51 41.

Olympia
28 bd des Capucines
75009. **Map** 4 D5.
Tel 08 92 68 33 68.
www.olympiahall.com

**Palais Omnisports
Paris-Bercy**
8 bd de Bercy 75012.
Map 14 F2.
Tel 08 92 39 04 90.
www.ticketnet.fr

**Le Petit Journal
St-Michel**
71 bd St-Michel 75005.
Map 12 F1.
Tel 01 43 26 28 59.

Zénith
211 av de Jean-Jaurès
75019.
Tel 01 42 08 60 00.
www.le-zenith.com

CINEMA

La Géode
26 av Corentin-Cariou
75019.
📞 08 92 68 45 40.

Le Grand Rex
1 bd Poissonnière 75002.
📞 08 92 68 05 96.
www.legrandrex.com

**Max Linder
Panorama**
24 bd Poissonnière 75009.
📞 08 92 68 00 31.

MK2 Bibliothèque
128–162 av de France
75013.
📞 08 92 69 84 84.
www.mk2.com

SPORT

**Hippodrome de
Longchamp**
Bois de Boulogne 75016.
Tel 01 44 30 75 00.

**Palais Omnisports
Paris-Bercy**
(see Rock section)

Stade de France
93210 La Plaine St-Denis
Tel 08 92 70 09 00.
www.stadedefrance.fr

Parc des Princes
24 rue du Commandant-
Guilbaud 75016.
Tel 0825 075 077.

**Stade Roland
Garros**
2 av Gordon-Bennett
75016.
Tel 01 47 43 49 56.
www.fft.fr

PARIS STREET FINDER

The map references given with sights, shops and entertainment venues described in the Paris section of the guide refer to the maps on the following pages. Map references are also given for Paris hotels *(see pp550–5)* and restaurants *(pp600–6)*, and for useful addresses in the *Travellers' Needs* and *Survival Guide* sections at the back of the book. The maps include not only the main sightseeing areas but also the most important districts for hotels, restaurants, shopping and entertainment venues. The key map below shows the area of Paris covered by the *Street Finder*, with the *arrondissement* numbers for the various districts. The symbols used for sights and other features on the *Street Finder* maps are listed opposite.

Paris is divided into 20 *arrondissements*, outlined in orange and numbered on this map.

0 kilometres   1

0 miles   0.5

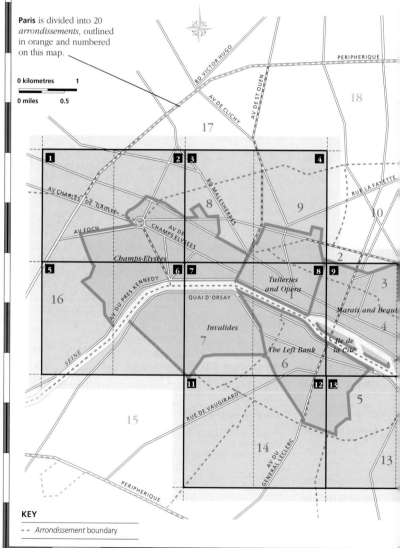

KEY

- - *Arrondissement* boundary

HOW THE MAP REFERENCES WORK

The first figure tells you which *Street Finder* map to turn to.

Hôtel de Ville ⓾

Pl de l'Hôtel-de-Ville 75004.
Map 9 B3. *Tel* 01 42 76 40 40.
Ⓜ *Hôtel-de-Ville.* ⬭ to groups:
phone to arrange (01 42 76 54 04).
⬤ public hols and for official
functions (phone to check). ♿

The letter and number give the grid reference. Letters go across the map's top and bottom; figures on its sides.

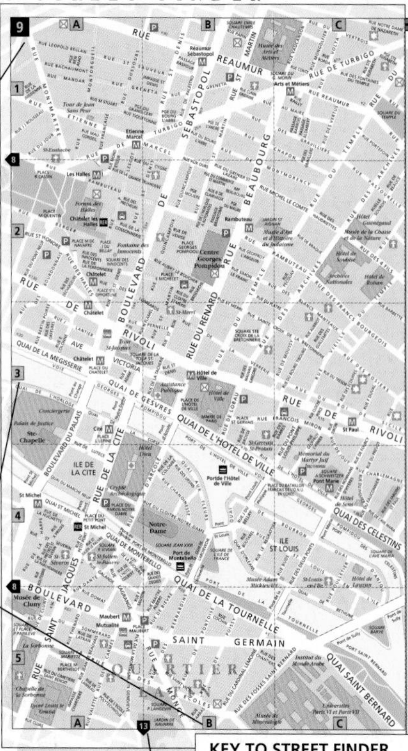

The map continues on page 13 of the Street Finder.

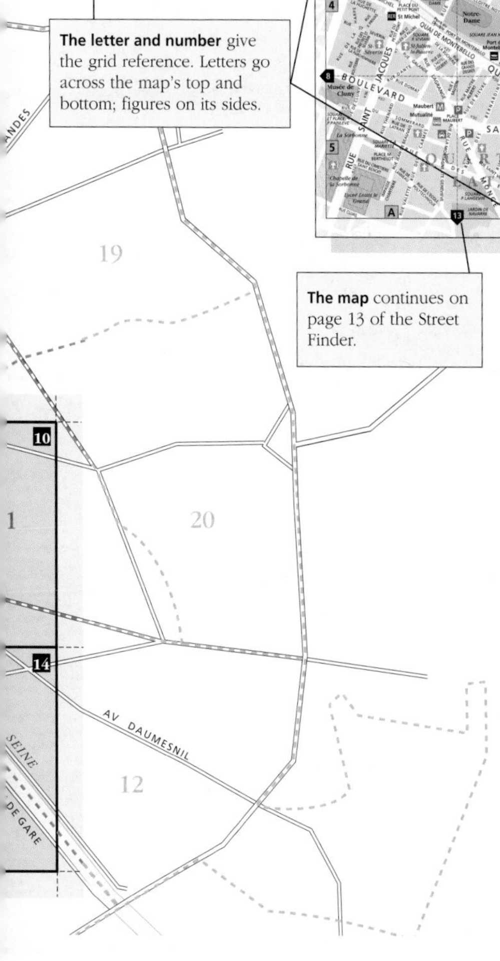

KEY TO STREET FINDER

▨	Major sight
▨	Other sight
▨	Other building
Ⓜ	Metro station
RER	RER station
⬛	Main bus stop
⬛	River boat boarding point
P	Main car park
ⓘ	Tourist information
✚	Hospital with casualty unit
▣	Police station
✝	Church
✡	Synagogue
⊠	Post office
═	Railway line
▬	Autoroute
▬	Pedestrian street
◄130	House number (main street)

SCALE OF MAP PAGES

0 metres   200
0 yards   200

1:12,000

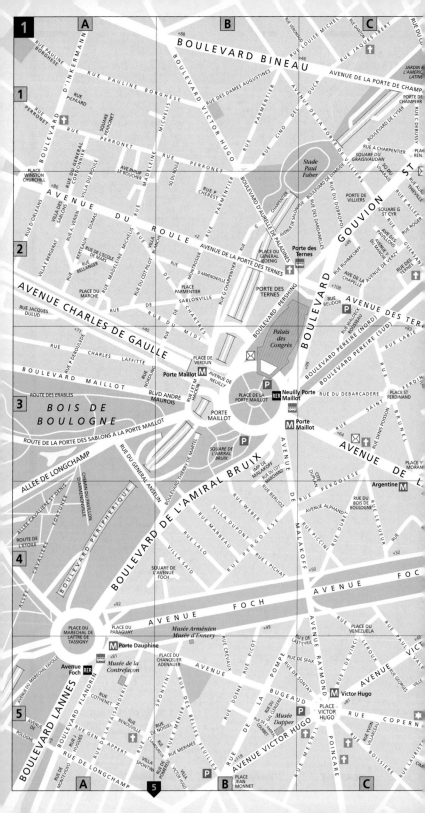

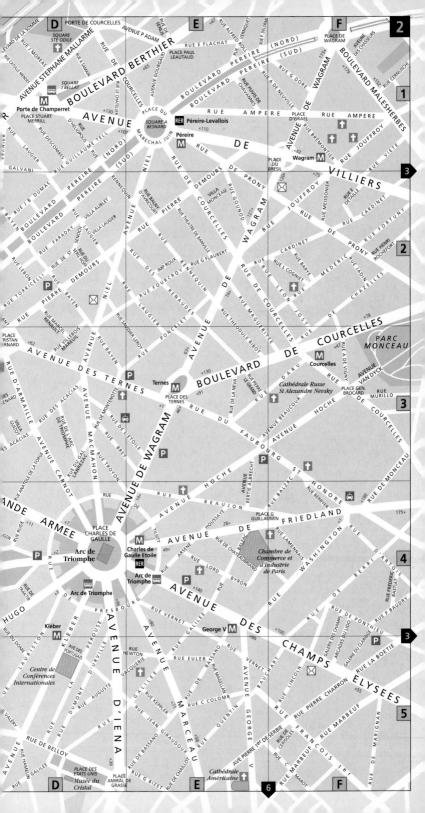

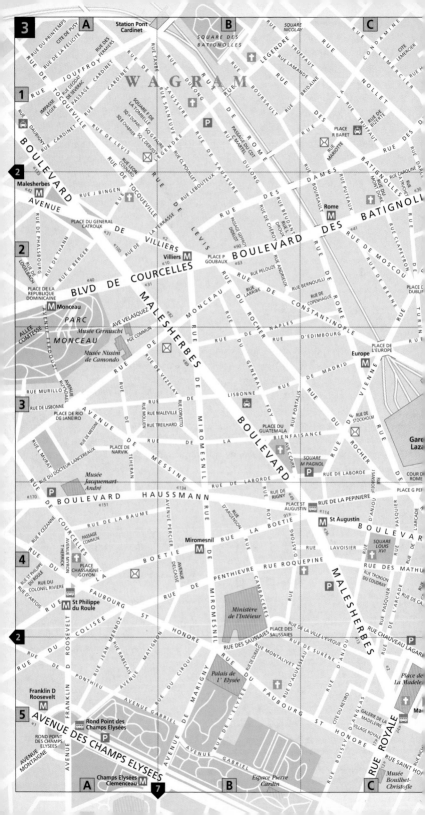

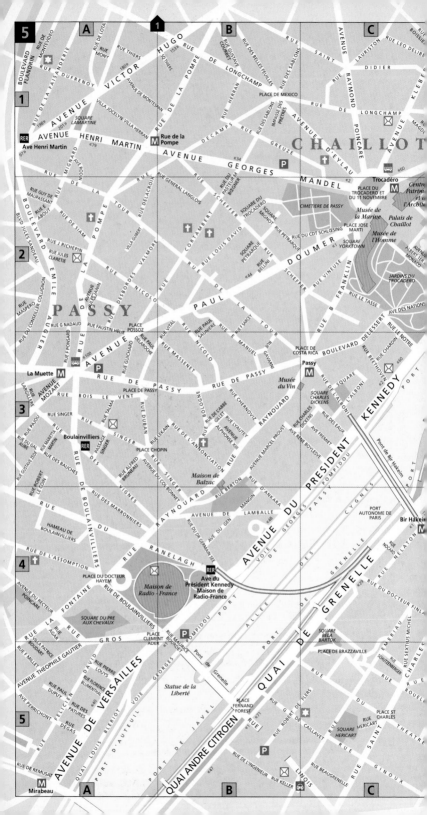

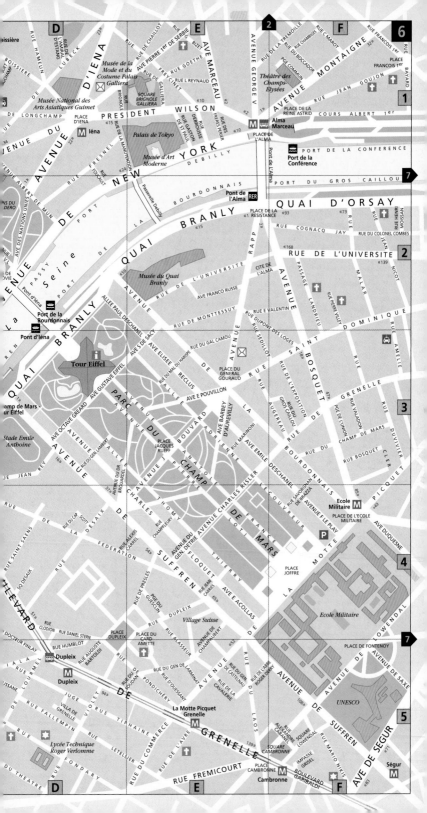

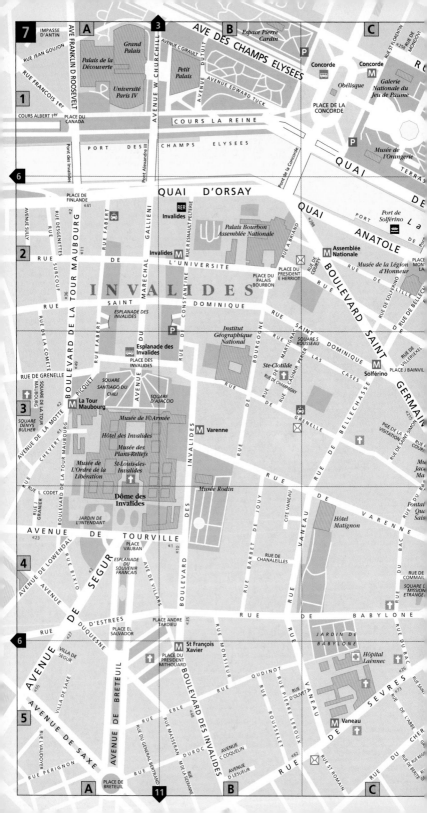

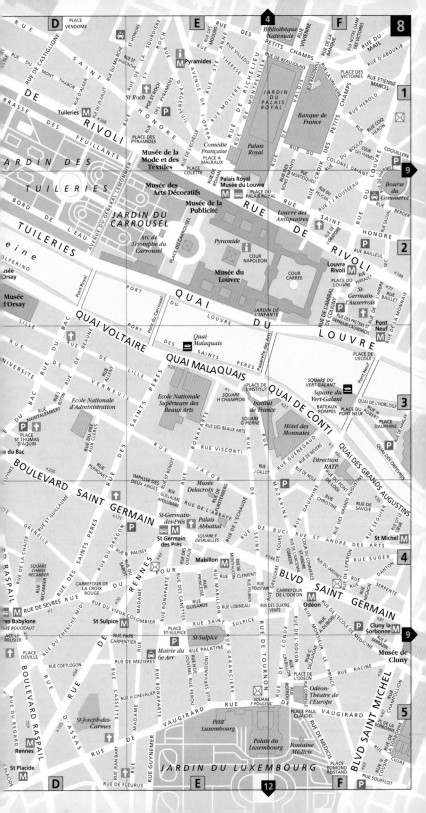

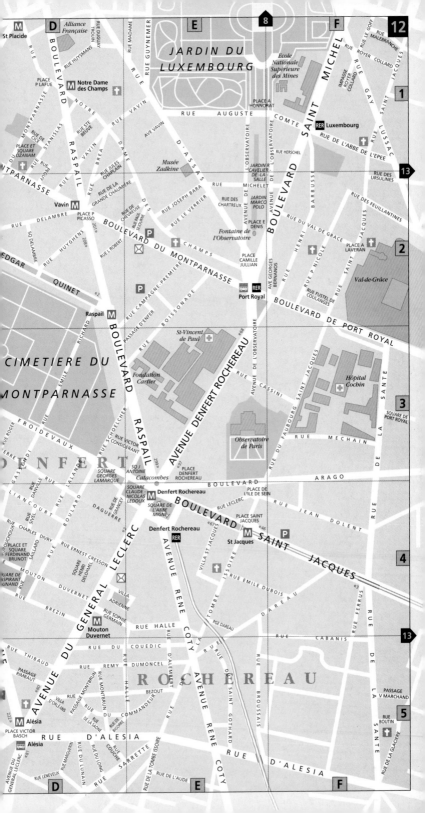

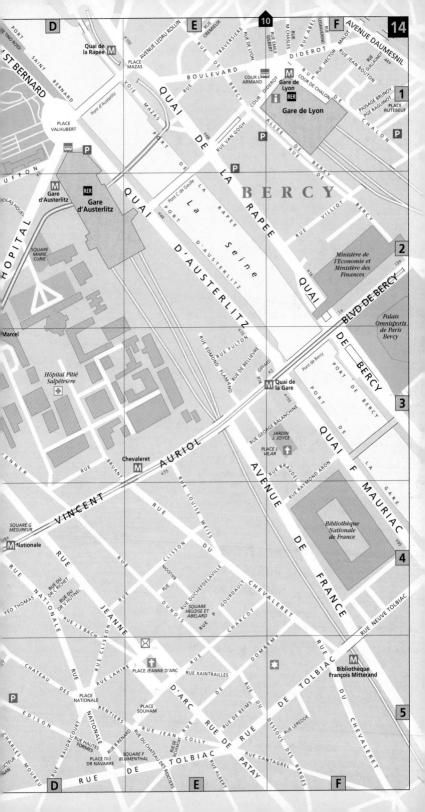

ILE DE FRANCE

Set at the heart of France, with Paris as its hub, Ile de France extends well beyond the densely populated suburbs of the city. Its rich countryside incorporates a historic royal region of monumental splendour central to *"la gloire de la France"*.

The region became a favourite with French royalty after François I transformed Fontainebleau into a Renaissance palace in 1528. Louis XIV kept the Ile de France as the political axis of the country when he started building Versailles in 1661. This Classical château created by the combined genius of Le Nôtre, Le Vau, Le Brun and Jules Hardouin-Mansart is France's most visited sight. It stands as a monument to the power of the Sun King and is still used for state occasions. Rambouillet, closely linked with Louis XVI, is now the summer residence of the French president, while Malmaison was the favourite home of Empress Josephine. To the north, the Château d'Ecouen offers a showcase of Renaissance life and to the south Vaux-le-Vicomte boasts some of the loveliest formal gardens in France.

Nourished by the Seine and Marne rivers, the Ile de France is a patchwork of chalky plains, wheatfields and forests. The serene, poplar-lined avenues and rustic charm of the region have been an inspiration to painters such as Corot, Rousseau, Pissarro and Cézanne.

SIGHTS AT A GLANCE

Châteaux and Museums
Château de Dampierre **8**
Château de Fontainebleau **13**
Château de Malmaison **5**
Château de Rambouillet **9**
Château de Sceaux **7**
Château de Vaux-le-Vicomte **11**
Château de Versailles **6**
Musée National de la Renaissance **2**

Towns
Provins **12**
St-Germain-en-Laye **4**

Abbeys and Churches
Abbaye de Royaumont **1**
Basilique St-Denis **3**

Theme Parks
Disneyland Resort Paris **10**

KEY
	Greater Paris
	Central Paris
✈	International airport
═	Motorway
═	Major road
═	Minor road

0 kilometres   20
0 miles   10

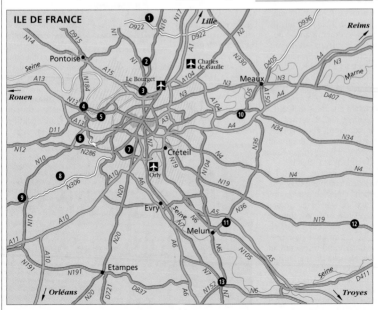

ILE DE FRANCE

◁ **Magnificent formal gardens at the Château Vaux-le-Vicomte**

The vaulted Gothic refectory of Abbaye de Royaumont

Abbaye de Royaumont ❶

Fondation Royaumont, Asnières-sur-Oise, Val-d'Oise. *Tel* 01 30 35 59 70. ☐ *daily.* 🖼 ♿ ✂ *phone* 01 30 35 59 91. 🎵 *Concerts.*
www.royaumont.com

Set among woods "near water and far from mankind," 30 km (20 miles) north of Paris, Royaumont is the finest Cistercian abbey in the Ile de France. Chosen for its remoteness, the abbey's stark stonework and simplicity of line reflect the austere teachings of St Bernard. However, unlike his Burgundian abbeys, Royaumont was founded in 1228 by Louis IX and his mother, Blanche de Castille. "St Louis" showered the abbey with riches and chose it as a royal burial site.

The abbey retained its royal links until the Revolution, when much of it was destroyed. It was then a textiles mill and orphanage until its revival as a cultural centre. The original pillars still remain, along with a gravity-defying corner tower and the largest Cistercian cloisters in France, which enclose a charming Classical garden. The monastic quarters border one side of the cloisters.

The Château de Royaumont, erected as the abbot's palace on the eve of the Revolution, is set apart and resembles an Italianate villa. In the grounds are monks' workshops, woods, ponds, and Cistercian canals.

In summer, concerts are held in the abbey on weekends (01 34 68 05 50 for details).

Musée National de la Renaissance ❷

Château d'Ecouen, Val-d'Oise. *Tel* 01 34 38 38 50. ☐ *Wed–Mon.* ● *1, Jan 1, May, 25 Dec.* **Park** ☐ *daily; no animals* 🖼 ♿ ✂ 🍴
www.musee-renaissance.fr

This imposing moated château is curiously adrift, halfway between St-Denis and Royaumont. Now a Renaissance museum, Ecouen's magnificent quadrilateral exterior provides an authentic setting for an impressive collection of paintings, tapestries, coffers, carved doors and staircases salvaged from other 16th-century châteaux.

Ecouen was built in 1538 for Anne de Montmorency, adviser to François I and Commander-in-Chief of his armies. As the second most powerful person in the kingdom, he employed Ecole de Fontainebleau artists and craftsmen to adorn his palace. Their influence is apparent in the ravishing painted fireplaces, depicting biblical and Classical themes in mysterious landscapes. The most striking room is the chapel, containing a gallery and vaulted ceilings painted with the Montmorency coat of arms.

Upstairs is one of the finest series of 16th-century tapestries in France. Equally compelling are the princely apartments, the library of illuminated manuscripts, a collection of vivid ceramics from Lyon, Nevers, Venice and Faenza, and Iznik, and a display of early mathematical instruments and watches. Recent acquisitions include 153 16th- and 17th-century engravings from France, Italy, Germany and Holland.

Basilique St-Denis ❸

2 rue de Strasbourg, St-Denis, Seine-St-Denis. *Tel* 01 48 09 83 54. Ⓜ *Line 13 Basilique de St-Denis* ☐ *daily.* ● *1 Jan, 1 May, 25 Dec.* 🖼 ♿ ✝ 8:30am, 10am Sun. www.monum.fr

According to legend, the decapitated St-Denis struggled here clutching his head, and an abbey was erected to commemorate the martyred bishop. Following the burial of Dagobert I in the basilica in 638, a royal link with St-Denis began, which was to span 12 centuries. Most French kings were entombed in St-Denis, and all the queens of France were crowned here. The elegant, early Gothic basilica rests on Carolin-

Statue of Louis XVI at St-Denis

gian and Romanesque crypts. Of the medieval effigies, the most impressive are of Charles V (1364) and a 12th-century likeness in enamelled copper of Blanche de France with her dog. The mask-like

The west wing of Musée National de la Renaissance

The Renaissance tomb of Louis XII and Anne de Bretagne in St-Denis

serenity of these effigies is in sharp contrast with the graphically realistic Renaissance portrayal of agony present in the grotesque mausoleum of Louis XII and Anne de Bretagne. Both are represented as naked figures, their faces eerily captured at the moment of death. Above the mausoleum, effigies of the finely dressed royal couple contemplate their own nakedness. As a reflection of humanity in the face of death, the tombs have few rivals.

St-Germain-en-Laye ❹

Yvelines. 42,200. Maison Claude Debussy, 38 rue au Pain. **Tel** 01 34 51 05 12. Tue–Wed, Fri–Sun. **www**.saintgermainenlaye.fr

Dominating the Place Général de Gaulle in this chic suburb is the legendary Château de St-Germain, birthplace of Louis XIV. Louis VI built the original stronghold in 1122 but only the keep and St-Louis chapel remain. Under François I and Henri II, the medieval upper tiers were demolished, leaving a moated pentagon. Henri IV built the pavillion and terraces that run down to the Seine, and Louis XIV had Le Nôtre landscape the gardens before leaving for Versailles in 1682.

Today the château houses the **Musée d'Archéologie Nationale**, which exhibits archaeological finds from prehistory to the Middle Ages. Created by Napoleon III, the collection includes a 22,000-year-old carved female, a megalithic tomb, a bronze helmet from the 3rd century BC, and Celtic jewellery. The finest treasure is the Gallo-Roman mosaic pavement.

Musée d'Archéologie Nationale
Château de St-Germain-en-Laye. **Tel** 01 39 10 13 00. Wed–Mon. **www**.musee-antiquitesnationales.fr

Château de Malmaison ❺

Rueil-Malmaison, Hauts-de-Seine. **Tel** 01 41 96 20 49. Wed–Mon; times vary according to season; phone for details. 1 Jan, 25 Dec. restr. **www**.chateau-malmaison.fr

Situated 15 km (9 miles) west of Paris, this 17th-century estate is now best known for its Napoleonic associations. Bought by Josephine as a retreat from the formality of the Emperor's residences at the Tuileries and Fontainebleau, it has charming rural grounds. While Josephine loved this country manor, Napoleon scorned its entrance as fit only for servants. Instead, he had a curious drawbridge built at the back of the château.

The finest rooms are the frescoed and vaulted library, the canopied campaign room, and the sunny Salon de Musique, hung with paintings from Josephine's private collection. Napoleon's restrained yellow canopied bedroom contrasts the bedchamber Josephine died in, a magnificent indulgence bedecked in red. Many of the rooms overlook the romantic "English" gardens and the famous rose garden which was cultivated by Josephine after her divorce.

Memorabilia abound, from imperial eagles to David's moody portrait of Napoleon, or Gérard's painting of the languid Josephine reclining on a chaise-longue.

Château Bois Préau, set in the wooded grounds, houses a museum dedicated to Napoleon's exile and death.

Empress Josephine's bed at Château de Malmaison

Château de Versailles ❻

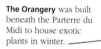

The present palace, started by Louis XIV in 1668, grew around Louis XIII's original hunting lodge. Architect Louis Le Vau built the first section, which expanded into an enlarged courtyard. From 1678, Jules Hardouin-Mansart added north and south wings and the Hall of Mirrors. He also designed the chapel, completed in 1710. The Opera House (L'Opéra) was added by Louis XV in 1770. André Le Nôtre enlarged the gardens and broke the monotony of the symmetrical layout with expanses of water and creative use of uneven ground. Opposite the château is the Musée des Carrosses, housing a collection of royal carriages.

Garden statue of a flautist

★ Formal Gardens
Geometric paths and shrubberies are features of the gardens.

The Orangery was built beneath the Parterre du Midi to house exotic plants in winter.

Fountain of Latona
Four marble basins rise to Balthazar Marsy's statue of the goddess Latona.

Water Parterre

★ Château
Under Louis XIV, Versailles became the centre of political power in France.

Dragon Fountain
The fountain's centrepiece is a winged monster.

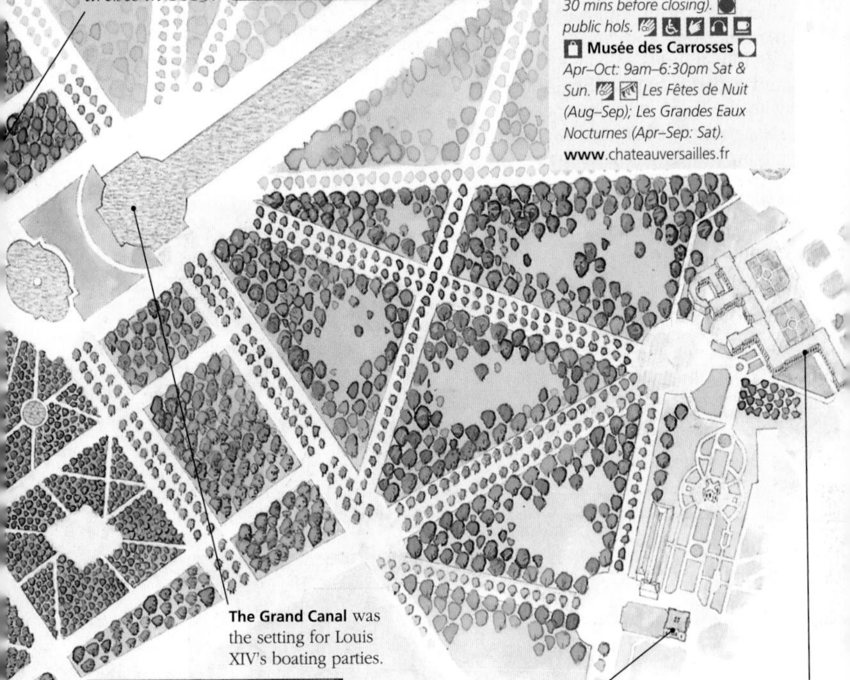

The King's garden
features a mirror pool
in the 19th-century
garden created by
Louis XVIII.

Colonnade
*Mansart designed
this circle of marble
arches in 1685.*

VISITORS' CHECKLIST

Versailles, Yvelines. *Tel 01 30 83
78 00.* 🚌 *171 from Paris.* RER
Versailles Rive Gauche. 🚊 *Versailles Chantiers, Versailles Rive
Droite.* **Château** ⬭ 9am–6:30pm
(5:30pm winter) Tue–Sun. ⬤
some public hols; phone to check.
📷 **Grand Trianon & Petit
Trianon** ⬭ noon–6:30pm
(5:30pm winter) daily (last adm:
30 mins before closing). ⬤
public hols. 📷 ♿ 🅿 🎁 🖼
📷 **Musée des Carrosses** ⬭
Apr–Oct: 9am–6:30pm Sat &
Sun. 📷 🎵 *Les Fêtes de Nuit
(Aug–Sep); Les Grandes Eaux
Nocturnes (Apr–Sep: Sat).*
www.chateauversailles.fr

The Grand Canal was
the setting for Louis
XIV's boating parties.

Fountain of Neptune
*Groups of sculptures spray
spectacular jets of water in Le
Nôtre's 17th-century garden.*

Petit Trianon
*Built in 1762 as a
retreat for Louis XV,
this small château
became a favourite
with Marie-Antoinette.*

★ Grand Trianon
*Louis XIV built this
small palace of
stone and pink
marble in 1687 to
escape the rigours
of court life, and
to enjoy the
company of
Madame de
Maintenon.*

STAR FEATURES

★ Château

★ Formal Gardens

★ Grand Trianon

Inside the Château de Versailles

The sumptuous main apartments are on the first floor of this vast château complex. Around the Marble Courtyard are the private apartments of the king and queen. On the garden side are the state apartments where official court life took place. These were richly decorated by Charles Le Brun with coloured marble, stone and wood carvings, murals, velvet, silver and gilded furniture. Beginning with the Salon d'Hercule, each state room is dedicated to an Olympian deity. The climax is the Hall of Mirrors (renovated in 2007), where 17 great mirrors face tall arched windows.

KEY TO FLOORPLAN

- ☐ South wing
- ☐ Coronation room
- ☐ Madame de Maintenon's apartments
- ☐ Queen's apartments and private suite
- ☐ State apartments
- ☐ King's apartments and private suite
- ☐ North wing
- ☐ Non-exhibition space

★ **Queen's Bedroom**
In this room the queens of France gave birth to the royal children in public view.

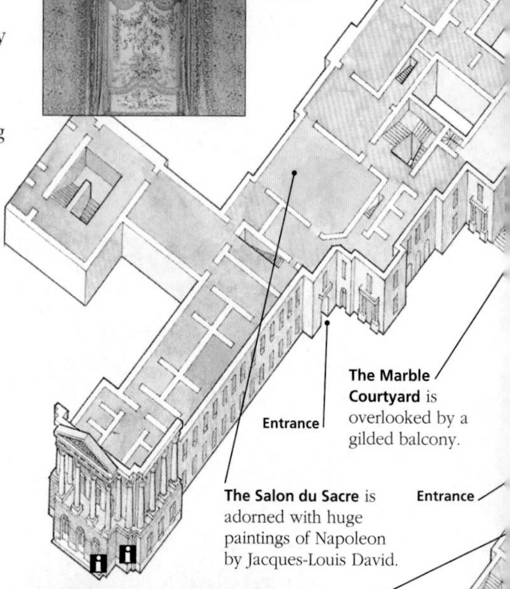

The Marble Courtyard is overlooked by a gilded balcony.

Entrance

The Salon du Sacre is adorned with huge paintings of Napoleon by Jacques-Louis David.

Entrance

★ **Salon de Vénus**
A statue of Louis XIV stands amid the rich marble decor of this room.

Stairs to ground floor reception area

★ **Chapelle Royale**
The chapel's first floor was reserved for the royal family and the ground floor for the court. The beautiful interior is decorated with Corinthian columns and white marble, gilding and Baroque murals.

STAR FEATURES

- ★ Chapelle
- ★ Salon de Vénus
- ★ Hall of Mirrors
- ★ Queen's Bedroom

★ Hall of Mirrors
Great state occasions were held in this room stretching 70 m (233 ft) along the west façade. Here in 1919 the Treaty of Versailles was ratified, ending World War I.

Oeil-de-Boeuf

The King's Bedroom is where Louis XIV died in 1715.

The Cabinet du Conseil was used by the king to receive his ministers and family.

Salon de la Guerre
The room's theme of war is reinforced by Antoine Coysevox's stuccoed relief of Louis XIV riding to victory.

Louis XVI's library features Neo-Classical panelling and the king's terrestrial globe.

Salon d'Apollon
Designed by Le Brun and dedicated to the god Apollo, this was Louis XIV's throne room. A copy of Hyacinthe Rigaud's famous portrait of the king (1701) hangs here.

Salon d'Hercule

TIMELINE

Louis XV

1667 Grand Canal begun			**1793** Louis XVI and Marie-Antoinette executed	**1833** Louis-Philippe turns the château into a museum
1668 Construction of new château by Le Vau		**1722** 12-year-old Louis XV occupies Versailles		

1650	1700	1750	1800	1850

	1671 Interior decoration by Le Brun begun	**1715** Death of Louis XIV. Versailles abandoned by court	**1789** King and Queen forced to leave Versailles for Paris	**1919** Treaty of Versailles signed on 28 June
1661 Louis XIV enlarges château		**1682** Louis XIV and Marie-Thérèse move to Versailles	**1774** Louis XVI and Marie-Antoinette live at Versailles	

Château de Sceaux ❼

Sceaux, Hauts-de-Seine. *Tel* 01 41 87 29 50. ◯ Wed–Mon. ● public hols. ⟐ ◪ www.tourisme-hautsdeseine.com

The Parc de Sceaux, bounded by elegant villas, is an appealing mixture of formal gardens, woods and water containing Classical gardens designed by Le Nôtre. The gardens use water to great effect, with tiered waterfalls and fountains presenting a moving staircase that cascades into an octagonal basin. This feeds into the Grand Canal and offers a poplar-lined view to the Pavillon de Hanovre. This elegant pavillion is one of several that adorn the park, which also contains Mansart's Classical Orangerie. Today this is the setting for exhibitions and, in summer, classical music concerts.

Built for Colbert in 1670, the original château was demolished and rebuilt in Louis XIII style in 1856. The stylish fake contains the Musée de l'Ile de France, which celebrates the landscapes and châteaux of the region with paintings, furniture and sculpture.

Château de Dampierre ❽

Dampierre-en-Yvelines, Yvelines. *Tel* 01 30 52 53 24. ◯ Apr–mid-Oct: daily pm. ◪ ⟐ restricted. ◪ ⊞ www.chateau-de-dampierre.fr

After Versailles and Rambouillet, Dampierre is the most celebrated château

southwest of Paris. Built in 1675 for the Duc de Chevreuse, the exterior of the château is a harmonious composition of rose-coloured brick and cool stone, designed by Hardouin-Mansart.

By contrast, the interior sumptuously evokes Versailles, particularly in the royal apartments and the Louis XIV dining room. The grandest room is the frescoed Salle des Fêtes, remodelled in the 19th century in triumphal Roman style. The rooms overlook gardens landscaped by Le Nôtre.

Château de Rambouillet

Château de Rambouillet ❾

Rambouillet, Yvelines. *Tel* 01 34 83 00 25. ◯ Wed–Mon. ● 1 Jan, 1 May,1 & 11 Nov, 25 Dec, and when president in residence. ◪ ⟐ www.monum.fr

The château borders the deep Forêt de Rambouillet, once the favourite royal hunting ground. This ivy-covered redbrick château, flanked by five stone towers, is curious rather

than beautiful. Adopted as a feudal castle, country estate, royal palace and Imperial residence, it reflects a composite of French royal history. Since 1897, it has been the president's official summer residence.

Inside, oak-panelled rooms are adorned with Empire-style furnishings and Aubusson tapestries. The main façade overlooks Classical parterres. Nearby is the Queen's Dairy, given by Louis XVI to Marie-Antoinette so that she could play milkmaid.

Environs About 28 km (17 miles) north on the D11 is the **Château de Thoiry**, which has a large zoo of around 800 animals and an innovative play area for children.

Disneyland Resort Paris ❿

Marne-la-Vallée, Seine-et-Marne. *Tel* 08 25 30 60 30. ◯ daily. ▧ Marne-la-Vallée-Chessy. ▣ TGV from Lille or Lyon. ▭ from both airports. ◪ ⟐ www.disneylandparis.com

Disneyland Resort Paris covers 200 ha (500 acres), with two theme parks; seven hotels; facilities for shopping, dining and convention centres. Most interesting are the Parks – the first with its five themed Lands, offering magic dominated by Sleeping Beauty Castle, and Walt Disney Studios, paying homage to the movies.

Minnie Mouse

Château de Vaux-le-Vicomte ⓫

Maincy, Seine-et-Marne. *Tel* 01 64 14 41 90. ◯ end-Mar–mid-Oct: daily. ◪ ⊞ www.vaux-le-vicomte.com

Set north of Melun, not far from Fontainebleau, the château enjoys a peaceful rural location. Nicolas Fouquet, a

---

SÈVRES PORCELAIN

In 1756 Madame de Pompadour and Louis XV opened a porcelain factory near Versailles at Sèvres to supply the royal residences with tableware and *objets d'art*. Thus began the production of exquisite dinner services, statuettes, Etruscan-style vases, romantic cameos and porcelain paintings, depicting grand châteaux or mythological scenes. Sèvres porcelain is typified by its translucence, durability and narrow palette of colours.

Le Pugilat (1832), one of a pair of vases from Sèvres

ANDRE LE NÔTRE

As the greatest French landscape gardener, Le Nôtre (1613–1700) created masterpieces in château gardens all over France. His Classical vision shaped many in the Ile de France, such as those at Dampierre, Sceaux and Vaux-le-Vicomte. At Vaux he perfected the concept of the *jardin à la française*: avenues framed by statues and box hedges; water gardens with fountains and ornate pools; graceful terraces and geometrical parterres "embroidered" with motifs. His genius lay in architectural orchestration and a sense of symmetry, typified by the sweeping vistas of Versailles, his greatest triumph.

Provins ⑫

Seine-et-Marne. 🕍 *12,000.* 🚊 🚌
🛈 *Chemin de Villecran (01 64 60 26 26).* 🚍 *Sat.* **www**.*provins.net*

As a Roman outpost, Provins commanded the border of Ile de France and Champagne. Today, it offers a coherent vision of the medieval world. Ville Haute, the upper town, is clustered within high 12th-century ramparts, complete with crenellations and defensive ditches. The ramparts to the west are the best preserved. Here, between the fortified gateways of Porte de Jouy and Porte St-Jean, the fortifications are dotted with square, round and rectangular towers.

The town is dominated by Tour César, a keep with four corner turrets and a pyramid shaped roof. The moat and fortifications were added by the English during the Hundred Years' War. A guard-room leads to a gallery and views over the place du Chatel, a busy square of medieval gabled houses, and over the wheatfields beyond.

Provins is proud of its crimson roses. Every June, a floral celebration is held in the riverside rose garden, marked by a medieval festival with falconry and jousting.

powerful court financier to Louis XIV, challenged the architect Le Vau and the decorator Le Brun to create the most sumptuous palace of the day. The result is one of the greatest 17th-century French châteaux. However, it also led to his downfall. Louis and his ministers were so enraged – because its luxury cast the royal palaces into the shade – that they arrested Fouquet.

The interior is a gilded banquet of frescoes, stucco, caryatids and giant busts. The Salon des Muses boasts Le Brun's magnificent frescoed ceiling of dancing nymphs and poetic sphinxes. La Grande Chambre Carrée is decorated in Louis XIII style with panelled walls and an impressive triumphal frieze, evoking Rome. However, its many rooms feel touchingly intimate and the scale is not overwhelming.

Yet Vaux-le-Vicomte's continuing fame is due to André Le Nôtre's stunning gardens. The landscape designer's early training as a painter is evident in the magnificent succession of terraces, ornamental lakes and fountains, which descend to a formal canal. On Friday and Saturday evenings in summer, the castle is lit with over 2,000 candles and classical music is played in the gardens.

Château de Vaux-le-Vicomte seen across the gardens designed by Le Nôtre

Château de Fontainebleau ⑬

Ceiling detail from the Salle de Bal

Fontainebleau is not the product of a single vision but is a bewildering cluster of styles from different periods. Louis VII built an abbey here which was consecrated by Thomas Becket in 1169. A medieval tower survives but the present château harks back to François I. Originally drawn by the local hunting, the Renaissance king created a decorative château modelled on Florentine and Roman styles. Fontainebleau's abiding charm comes from its relative informality and spectacular forest setting. While impossible to cover in a day, the *grands appartements* provide a sumptuous introduction to this royal palace.

Ground floor

Jardin de Diane
Now more romantic than Classical, the garden features a bronze fountain of Diana as huntress.

★ **Escalier du Fer-à-Cheval**
This imposing horseshoe-shaped staircase by Jean Androuet du Cerceau, built in 1634, lies at the end of Cour du Cheval Blanc. Its ingenious design allowed carriages to pass beneath the two arches.

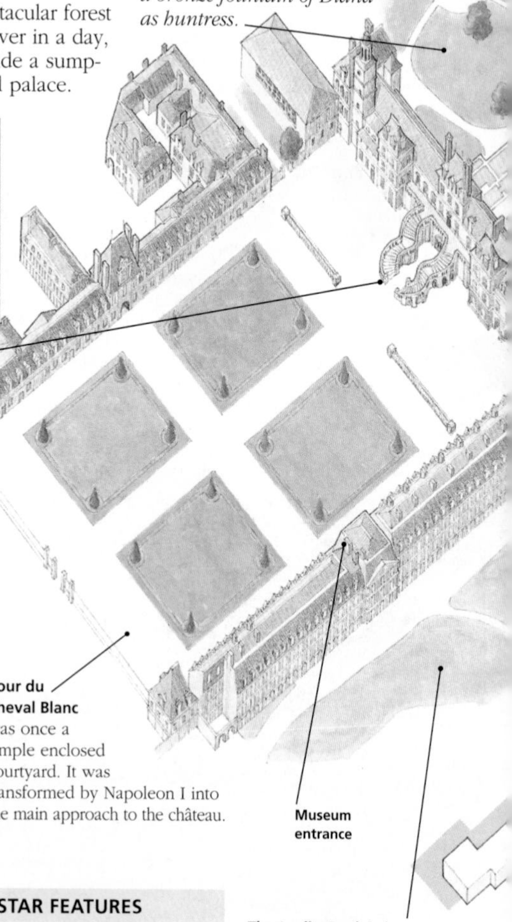

KEY TO FLOORPLAN

☐	Petits Appartements
☐	Galerie des Cerfs
☐	Musée Chinois
☐	Musée Napoléon
☐	Grands Appartements
☐	Salle Renaissance
☐	Appartements de Madame de Maintenon
☐	Grands Appartements des Souverains
☐	Escalier de la Reine/ Appartements des Chasses
☐	Chapelle de la Trinité
☐	Appartement Intérieur de l'Empereur

Cour du Cheval Blanc
was once a simple enclosed courtyard. It was transformed by Napoleon I into the main approach to the château.

Museum entrance

The Jardin Anglais is a romantic "English" garden, planted with cypress and plantain trees. It was redesigned in the 19th century by Maximilien-Joseph Hurtault.

STAR FEATURES

★ Escalier du Fer-à-Cheval

★ Salle de Bal

★ Galerie François I

For hotels and restaurants in this region see pp555–6 and pp606–7

Porte Dorée
Originally a feudal gate-house, this was transformed into the entrance pavillion to the forest by Gilles Le Breton for François I.

Cour Oval

VISITORS' CHECKLIST

Seine-et-Marne. *Tel 01 60 71 50 70.* ☐ 9:30am–5pm (6pm Jun–Sep) Wed–Mon. 🎨 ♿ 📷 🚻 *Gardens* ☐ 9am–5pm (6pm Mar–Apr & Oct, 7pm May–Sep). ● *1 Jan, 1 May, 25 Dec.* **www.musee-chateau-fontainebleau.fr**

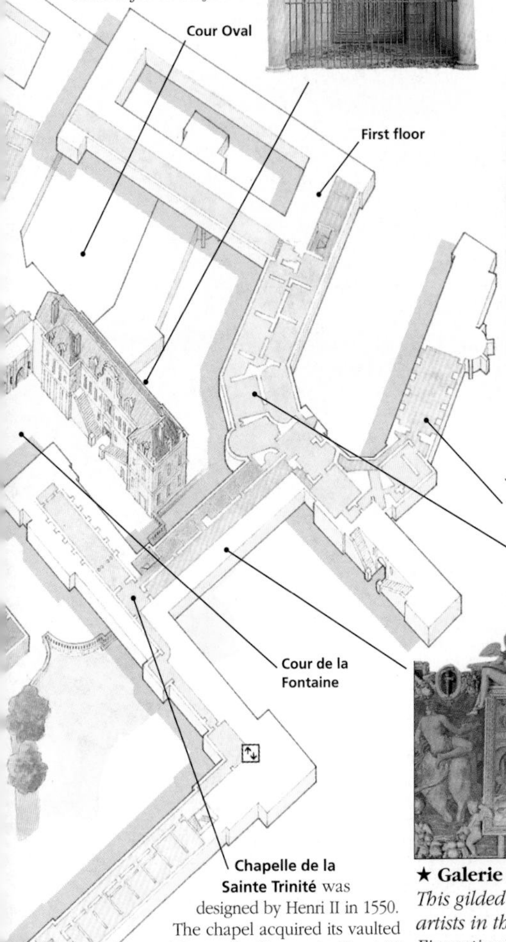

First floor

★ **Salle de Bal**
The Renaissance ballroom, designed by Primaticcio (1552), was finished under Henri II. His emblems adorn the walnut coffered ceiling, forming a pattern reflected in the parquet floor.

The Appartements de Napoléon I
house his grandiose throne in the Emperor's Salle du Trône, formerly the Chambre du Roi.

Cour de la Fontaine

Chapelle de la Sainte Trinité was designed by Henri II in 1550. The chapel acquired its vaulted and frescoed ceiling under Henri IV and was completed by Louis XIII.

★ **Galerie François I**
This gilded gallery is a tribute to the Italian artists in the Ecole de Fontainebleau. *Rosso Fiorentino's allegorical frescoes pay homage to the king's wish to create "a second Rome".*

THE BARBIZON SCHOOL

Artists have been drawn to the glades of Fontainebleau since the 1840s, when a group of landscape painters, determined to paint only from nature, formed around Théodore Rousseau and Millet. They settled in the nearby hamlet of Barbizon where the Auberge Ganne, a museum dedicated to the *Ecole de Barbizon*, is located.

***Spring at Barbizon*, painted by Jean-François Millet (1814–75)**

NORTHEAST
FRANCE

Introducing Northeast France

The rolling plains of Northern France run from the English Channel to the wooded Ardennes hills and the Vosges mountains of Alsace. Apart from sombre battle memorials, the area has France's finest gothic cathedrals – and a long tradition of brewing good quality beers. There is fine wine, too, in Champagne and Alsace. The old heavy industry has gone, while Lille's growth as a transport hub has brought new prosperity. This map shows some of the most interesting sights.

LE NORD AND PICARDY
(See pp192–205)

Amiens Cathedral

Amiens cathedral *is renowned for its fine wood carvings and its nave, the highest in France* (see pp202–3).

Beauvais Cathedral

Château de Compiègne

Reims Cathedral

The pride of Beauvais *is its Gothic cathedral and astronomical clock* (see p200) *which escaped heavy bombing during World War II.*

Half-timbered houses *and Renaissance mansions line the streets and alleys of Troyes' Old Town* (see p216), *rebuilt after the great fire in 1524. Its cathedral has remarkable stained-glass windows.*

Troyes Cathedral

The legacy of World War I *is strong in this area of former battlefields. The Douaumont Memorial outside Verdun (see pp190–91), with its 15,000 graves, is only one of many memorials and cemeteries here.*

Haut-Koenigsbourg, *a castle painstakingly rebuilt by Kaiser Wilhelm II when Alsace-Lorraine was under German rule, is one of Alsace's most popular attractions (see p228).*

Strasbourg, *seat of the Council of Europe, has a fine Gothic cathedral (see pp230–31) surrounded by delightful historic buildings.*

Douaumont Memorial

Porte Chaussée Verdun

Place Stanislas, Nancy

CHAMPAGNE
(See pp206–217)

ALSACE AND LORRAINE
(See pp218–33)

Strasbourg Cathedral

Haut-Koenigsbourg

0 kilometres	50
0 miles	50

The Flavours of Northeast France

The cuisine of northeast France is robust and warming, with rich beef stews, suckling pig, sausages and hams, dumplings and sauerkraut dishes, many of them closely related to German or Flemish staples. There is good fish from the Atlantic and from freshwater lakes and rivers. Vegetables and fruit are produced in abundance, and often served in a variety of savoury and sweet tarts, of which *quiche lorraine*, with bacon, eggs and cream, is the best known. Rich cakes are popular, especially *Kougelhopf*, a ring-shaped cake of raisins and almonds soaked in kirsch, and madeleine sponge cakes.

Leeks from a local market

Golden mirabelle plums alongside the more usual variety

LE NORD AND PICARDY

The northern coast offers a wide variety of fish dishes, the most popular being steamed mussels served with chips (fries). Herrings are pickled, soused, grilled or smoked and North Sea shrimps fried and eaten whole. Chicken may be cooked in beer, duck is made into pies and terrines, and eel served smoked as a starter.

The market gardens (*hortillons*) of Picardy are famous for their vegetables, often made into delicious soups. Leeks or chicory, braised or in gratins, accompany many dishes. Strong, washed-rind cheeses, such as Maroilles, are typical of the region.

Beer is often drunk with meals in the northeast, where traditional methods and small breweries thrive.

CHAMPAGNE

Champagne encompasses arable plains, wooded uplands as well as vineyards, and produces game, *charcuterie* and delicious freshwater fish. Nothing, however, can compete with its main claim to fame, Champagne itself, which is often used as a luxury cooking ingredient as well as, of course, being enjoyed in its own right.

Brioche | Ancienne | Madeleines | Boule de campagne
Siegle (rye) | | | Poîlane

Tarte d'abricot

Selection of typical regional breads and patisserie

REGIONAL DISHES AND SPECIALITIES

The classic dish of the region is *choucroute garni*, a platter of pickled cabbage, flavoured with juniper berries, and cooked with white wine, ham hock and smoked pork belly. Smoked Montbeliard and Strasbourg sausages are added towards the end of cooking. Sausages come in many variations, from *saucisses de Strasbourg* to *bratwurst*, made from **Beetroot** veal and pork, *lewerzurscht* (liver sausage), *andouillettes* (spicy chitterling sausages), *boudin noir* (black pudding of pork and pig's blood) and *boudin blanc* (white meat without blood). There are are also smoked hams, cooked hams and many different terrines, such as *presskopf* (pig's brawn in jelly) and the jellied white meat terrine, *potjevleesch*. *Langue lucullus* is smoked ox tongue studded with *foie gras*, a speciality of Valenciennes.

Ficelle picardie *Pancakes are filled with mushrooms and ham in creme fraîche sauce, and baked with grated cheese.*

Display of traditional northern French charcuterie

Wild boar, deer, rabbit, hare, quail, partridge and woodcock are all found in the Ardennes, made into game pâtés and terrines as well as roasts and stews. The Ardennes is also noted for its fine quality smoked ham, while *jambon de Reims* is cooked ham with mustard, champagne and Reims vinegar. Troyes is famous for its *andouillettes*, usually served with onions or baked in a creamy mustard sauce. Fish come from the small lakes east of Troyes and trout are abundant in the clear streams of the Ardennes. The two best cheeses of Champagne are Chaource and Langres.

ALSACE AND LORRAINE

Rolling pastures, orchards, pine forests and rivers produce the ingredients of

Alsatian cooking. Meat is important, particularly pork, roasted or made into hams and sausages. In winter, game stews abound. There is a strong tradition of raising geese; after all, *foie gras* production originated in

Shopping at the fish market in the port of Boulogne

Strasbourg. The rivers are a good source of pike, trout, crayfish and carp, often cooked in beer and served on festive occasions. Locally grown vegetables include cabbage, potatoes and turnips, and fruit includes bilberries, quince, redcurrants and the golden mirabelle plums of Lorraine, the latter prized for both jam and *eau de vie* (fruit brandy). The best-known cheese is Munster, a soft cow's milk cheese.

The white wines of Alsace range from steely, bone-dry Riesling (the region's finest variety) to aromatic Muscat and Gewurztraminer. For more on the wines of Alsace, see pp232–3.

ON THE MENU

Anguille au vert Eel baked with green herbs and potatoes.

Cassolette de petits gris Snails in champagne sauce.

Flamiche aux poireaux Leek tart.

Flammekueche Pizza-style tart topped with bacon, creme fraîche and onions.

Marcassin à l'Ardennaise Wild boar with celeriac.

Potée champenoise Pork, ham, sausage, beans and vegetable stew.

Potée Lorraine Casserole of salt pork with vegetables.

Zewelwai A rich onion tart.

Truite à l'Ardennaise *Trout is stuffed with breadcrumbs and finely chopped Ardennes ham, then baked.*

Carbonnade de boeuf *Steak and caramelized onions are covered with beer and cooked for three hours.*

Babas au rhum *These are dry yeast cakes of raisins, eggs and butter, doused in rum and served with cream.*

France's Wine Regions: Champagne

Since its fabled "invention" by the monk Dom Pérignon in the 17th century, no other wine has rivalled champagne as the symbol of luxury and celebration. Only wines made in this region by the *Méthode Champenoise* can be called champagne *(see p210)*. Most champagne is non-vintage: the skill of the blenders, using reserves of older wines, creates consistency and excellence year on year. The "big names" *(grandes marques)*, command the prestige and prices, but many small growers and cooperatives also produce excellent-value wines well worth seeking out.

Giant carved barrel, Épernay

LOCATOR MAP

☐ *Champagne wine region*

Grapes going for pressing, Montagne de Reims

WINE REGIONS

Champagne is a compact wine region, largely in the French *département* of the Marne. Certain areas within it are particularly identified with certain styles of wine. The Aube is famous not only for champagne but also for an eccentric and pricy still wine, Rosé des Riceys.

Soissons

La Ferté-sous-Jouarre

Châte
Thier

Petit Morin

Grand Morin

Nogent
sur-Sein

KEY FACTS ABOUT CHAMPAGNE

Location and Climate
The cool, marginal climate creates the finesse that other sparkling wines strive for, but seldom achieve. Chalky soils and east- and north-facing aspects help produce the relatively high acidity champagne needs.

Grape Varieties
Three varieties are grown, red **Pinot Noir** and **Pinot Meunier**, and white **Chardonnay**. Most champagne is a blend of all three, though Blanc de Blancs is 100 per cent Chardonnay and Blanc de Noirs, although white, is made only from red grapes.

Good Producers
Grandes Marques: Bollinger, Gosset, Krug, Möet et Chandon, Joseph Perrier, Louis Roederer, Pol Roger, Billecart-Salmon, Veuve Clicquot, Taittinger, Ruinart, Laurent Perrier, Salon.
Négociants, cooperatives & growers: Boizel, M Arnould, Cattier, Bricout, Drappier, Ployez-Jacquemart, H Blin, Gimmonet, Andre Jacquart, Chartogne-Taillet, Vilmart, Alfred Gratien, Emile Hamm, B Paillard, P Gerbais.

Good Vintages
2005, 2003, 2000, 1998, 1996, 1990.

BOLLINGER
Special Cuvée
Champagne   *Ay-France*
BRUT

From a name *famous even to non-wine lovers, this is in the classic* brut *(dry) style; only* brut non dosage *or* brut sauvage *is drier.*

KEY

■	Champagne *appellation* area
☐	Vallée de la Marne district
☐	Montagne de Reims district
☐	Côte de Sézanne district
☐	Côte des Blancs district
☐	Aube district

0 kilometres   15

0 miles   15

Champagne Charlie *was immortalized in a British music-hall song as a high-living, devil-may-care figure.*

Meticulously laid out vineyards of a maison de champagne

Pink champagne, *often with hints of soft fruit flavours, makes perfect summer drinking; it normally gains its colour from the blending of red and white wines.*

From the respected *house of Deutz, this vintage Blanc de Blancs is champagne in a lighter style, made entirely from Chardonnay grapes.*

Champagne blender

For those who *prefer a less dry champagne, a demi-sec, like this wine from Canard-Duchêne, makes the ideal choice.*

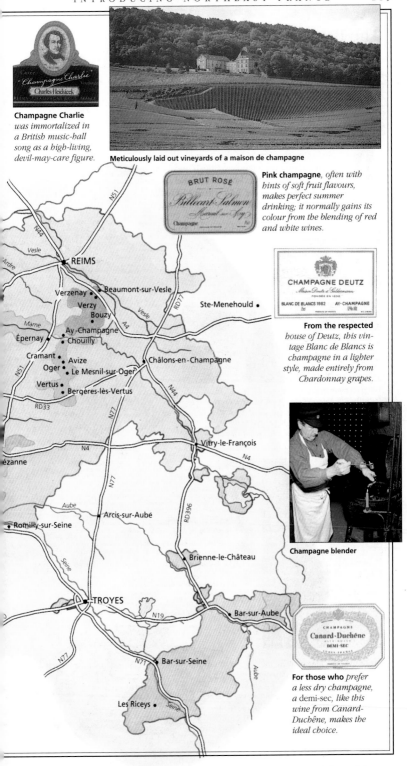

The Battle of the Somme

The many cemeteries that cover the Somme region serve as a poignant reminder of the mass slaughter that took place on the Western Front in World War I (which ended with the Armistice on 11 November 1918). Between 1 July and 21 November 1916, the Allied forces lost more than 600,000 men and the Germans at least 465,000. The Battle of the Somme, a series of campaigns conducted by British and French armies against fortified positions held by the Germans, relieved the hard-pressed French at Verdun; but hopes of a breakthrough never materialized, and the Allies only managed to advance 16 km (10 miles).

British World War I soldier

LOCATOR MAP

☐ *Somme battlefield*

Beaumont Hamel Memorial Park, a tribute to the Royal Newfoundland Regiment, has a huge bronze caribou.

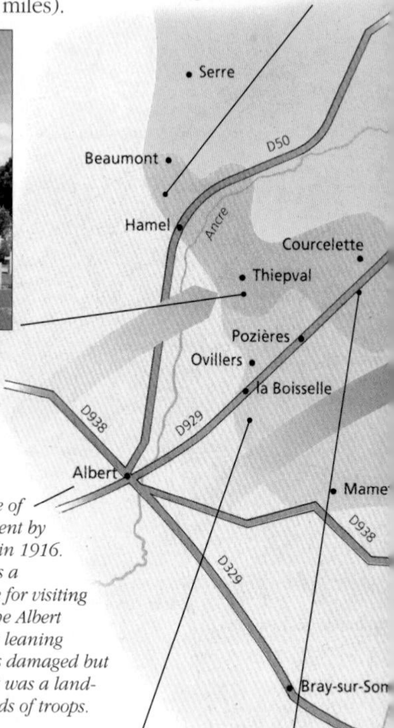

Thiepval Memorial *was designed by Sir Edwin Lutyens. It dominates the landscape of Thiepval, one of the most hard-fought areas of the battle, appropriately chosen as a memorial to the 73,367 British soldiers with no known grave.*

Albert *was the site of heavy bombardment by German artillery in 1916. Today, the town is a convenient centre for visiting the battlefields. The Albert Basilique, with its leaning Virgin statue, was damaged but is now restored. It was a landmark for thousands of troops.*

Lochnager Mine Crater, formed by the largest of the British mines exploded on 1 July, 1916, lies on the ridge by La Boiselle.

The British Tank Memorial, *on the main road from Albert to Bapaume, commemorates the first use of tanks in warfare on 15 September, 1916. The attack was a limited success; the tanks of World War I were too slow and unreliable to transform warfare dominated by artillery, machine guns and barbed wire.*

Propaganda in World War I *was employed by both sides to maintain support at home. This French postcard has a popular image for civilian consumption. It shows a dying soldier kissing the flag, under the tender gaze of a ministering nurse, affirming his faith in the cause with his last breath.*

Delville Wood South African Memorial and Museum show the importance of Commonwealth forces in the Somme.

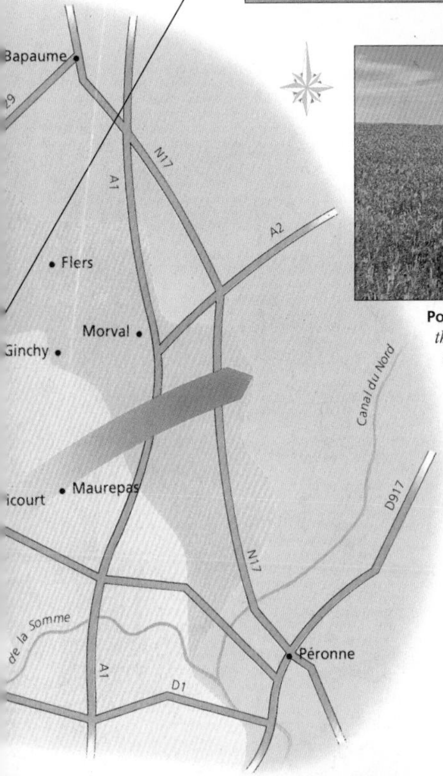

VISITORS' CHECKLIST

D929, D938 from Albert.
🛈 30 pl de la République, 80800 Corbie. **Tel** 03 22 96 95 76.
www.tourisme-albert.net **Albert Basilique, Beaumont Hamel Memorial Park, Delville Wood, La Boiselle, Thiepval & Pozières memorials** ◯ daily.
Ulster Tower ◯ Feb–Mar: Tue–Sun; Apr–Nov: daily. **South African Memorial,** Delville Wood, Longueval. **Tel** 03 22 85 02 17.
◯ Feb–Nov: Tue–Sun. ◯ hols.
Historial de Péronne
Tel 03 22 83 14 18. ◯ May–Sep: daily; Oct– Apr: Tue–Sun. ◯ mid-Dec–mid-Jan. 🔲 ♿ 🖊 📷 🔲
www.historial.org

Bapaume

Flers

Morval

Ginchy

Maurepas

Péronne

Canal du Nord

de la Somme

Poppies *were one of the few plants to grow on the battlefield. Ghengis Khan brought the first white poppy from China and, according to legend, it turned red after battle. Today poppies are a symbol of remembrance.*

KEY

- ▦ Allied forces
- ▦ German forces
- ▢ Front Line before 1 July, 1916
- ▦ Front Line progress July–September 1916
- ▦ Front Line progress September–November 1916

0 kilometres   5
0 miles   5

The Front Line trenches *stretched from the North Sea to the Swiss frontier; only by keeping underground could men survive the terrible conditions. Trenches remain in a few areas, including the Beaumont Hamel Park.*

LE NORD AND PICARDY

PAS DE CALAIS · NORD · SOMME · OISE · AISNE

*B*eneath the modern skin of France's northernmost region, the sights and monuments bear witness to the triumphs and turbulence of its past: soaring Gothic cathedrals, stately châteaux along the river Oise, and the battlefields and memorials of World War I.

The Channel ports of Dunkerque, Calais and Boulogne, and the refined resort of Le Touquet, are the focal points along a busy coastline that stretches from the Somme estuary to the Belgian frontier. Boulogne has a genuine maritime flavour, and the white cliffs running from here to Calais provide the most dramatic scenery along the Côte d'Opale.

Flemish culture holds sway along the border with Belgium: an unfamiliar France of windmills and canals where the local taste is for beer, hotpots and festivals with gallivanting giants. Lille is the dominant city here, a sprawling modern metropolis with a lively historic heart and an excellent art museum. To the southwest, the grace of Flemish architecture is handsomely displayed in the central squares of Arras, the capital of Artois.

From here to the Somme valley the legacy of World War I, with its memorial cemeteries and poppy-strewn battlefields, makes compelling viewing.

Cathedrals are the main appeal of Picardy. In Amiens, its capital, Cathédrale Notre-Dame is a pinnacle of the Gothic style – its magnificence echoed by the dizzying achievements at Beauvais further south. Splendid cathedrals at Noyon, Senlis and the delightful hilltop town of Laon chart the evolution of the Gothic. Closer to Paris, two châteaux command attention. Chantilly, the epicentre of French equestrianism, boasts gardens by Le Nôtre and a 19th-century château housing copious art treasures. Compiègne, bordered by a large and inviting forest, plays host to a lavish royal palace favoured by French rulers from Louis XV to Napoleon III.

Memorial cemetery in Vallée de la Somme, an area still haunted by the memory of World War I

◁ Catamarans on the busy beach of Le Touquet Paris-Plage

Exploring Le Nord and Picardy

As the gateway to England and Belgium, this northern corner of France is buzzing with business and industries, with the large, Euro-oriented city of Lille offering great culture as well as a new high-tech district. Yet peace and quiet is never far away. The coast between the historic port of Boulogne-sur-Mer and the Vallée de la Somme has a rich birdlife and is perfect for a relaxing seaside visit. Inland, the many Gothic cathedrals such as Amiens and Beauvais make an impressive tour, and the World War I battlefields and memorials provide an important insight into 20th-century history. Further south, the grand châteaux at Compiègne and Chantilly – which has the fascinating Musée Condé – are easily visited en route to or from Paris.

KEY

▬	Motorway
▬	Major road
▬	Secondary road
▬	Minor road
▬	Scenic route
▬	Main railway
▬	Minor railway
▬	International border
▬	Regional border

Lively outdoor café in the historic Grand' place in the heart of Arras

DUNKERQUE ❹   Malo-les-B
Ost
Gravelines
Channel Tunnel
❸ CALAIS
A16   Canal de la Basse Colme
Bergues
Cap Blanc-Nez
❻
Cap Griz Nez   A16
A25
FLANDRE MARITIM
D940   Guînes
Cassel
Wimereux
SAINT-OMER ❺   Arques
N42   La Coupole   Hazebr
BOULOGNE-   ❷
SUR-MER   Desvres   A26   N43
Samer   D341   Aire-sur-la
Fauquembergues
N1   D928   Béthur
LE TOUQUET ❶   Étaples
Montreuil-sur-Mer   Bruay-la-Buissière
Canche
Berck-sur-Mer   N39   Hesdin   N41
Saint-Pol   Tincqu
-sur-Ternoise
Fort-Mahon-Plage   Authie   Frévent   NOR
Vron
D940   Crécy-en-
Ponthieu
Le Crotoy   Nouvion   Douliens   La Pomr
Saint-Valéry-   A16
sur-Somme   Bernaville
Ault   Abbeville
D925   Fressenneville   VALLÉE   N25
A28   Flixecourt   DE   Albe
Dieppe   Gamaches   Airaines   Samara   LA   Cort
Rouen   Picquigny   SOMME
D901   AMIENS ❿
Hornoy
Saint-Saulflieu
Aumale   N29   Poix-de-   D935
Picardie   Essertaux   Bouc
Grandvilliers   N1
A16   Breteuil
Marseille-   D916
en-Beauvaisis   Crèvecoeur   Montd
Songeons   -le-Grand   Wavignies
D901   Saint-Just-
Gournay-en-Bray   en-Chaussée
BEAUVAIS ⓫   N31   Bresles   Clermo
D981   Noailles
Mouy
Gisors   A16   Creil
N1   SEN
Méru   CHANTILLY ⓰   1
PARC ASTERIX
Paris   A1

0 kilometres   25
0 miles   25

For additional map symbols see back flap

SIGHTS AT A GLANCE

The meandering waters in the Vallée de la Somme

GETTING AROUND

The main entry point into the region is Calais (and the Channel Tunnel terminal 3 km/2 miles south). From here, autoroutes A16 and A26/A1, several major N roads, and mainline rail services run directly to Paris. In addition, TGVs serve Calais-Frethun, Lille and Paris. There is a dense road network throughout the region. With their many local bus and train connections, Lille and Amiens make good bases. The A26 (or *Autoroute des Anglais*) crosses the whole region from Calais to Troyes, via Arras and Laon, giving easy access to eastern Picardy. It's also a useful route if you're heading south and want to avoid Paris.

Poppies, the symbol of World War I battlefields, in the Vallée de la Somme

Le Touquet beach at low tide

Le Touquet ❶

Pas de Calais. 6,500. 🚉 🚌
ℹ Palais de l'Europe (03 21 06 72 00).
🗓 Thu & Sat (Jun–mid-Sep: also Mon).
www.letouquet.com

Properly known as Le Touquet Paris-Plage, this resort was created in the 19th century and became fashionable with the rich and famous between the two World Wars.

A vast pine forest, planted in 1855, spreads around the town sheltering stately villas. To the west, a grid of smart hotels, holiday residences and sophisticated shops and restaurants borders a long, sandy beach. A racecourse and casino are complemented by seaside amusements and sports facilities, including two excellent golf courses, horse-riding and land yachting.

Further inland, the hilltop town of **Montreuil** has lime-washed 17th-century houses, abundant restaurants and a tree-shaded rampart walk.

Boulogne-sur-Mer ❷

Pas de Calais. 45,000. 🚉 🚌
ℹ Parvis de Nausicaa (03 21 10 88 10). 🗓 Wed & Sat (pl Dalton), Sun (pl Vignon). **www**.tourisme-boulognesurmer.com

An important fishing port and busy marina, Boulogne rewards its visitors well. Its attractions come neatly boxed in a walled Haute Ville, with the Porte des Dunes opening on to a 17th–19th-century

ensemble of Palais de Justice, Bibliothèque and Hôtel de Ville in **place de la Résistance**.

The 19th-century **Basilique Notre-Dame** is capped by a dome visible for miles. Inside, a bejewelled wooden statue represents Boulogne's patroness, Notre-Dame de Boulogne. She is wearing a *soleil*, a head-dress also worn by women during the *Grande Procession* held annually in her honour. Nearby, the powerful moated 13th-century **Château**, built for the Counts of Boulogne, is now a well-organized historical museum.

In the centre of town, shops, hotels and fish restaurants line the quai Gambetta on the east bank of the river Liane. To the north lie Boulogne's beach and **Nausicaa**, a vast, spectacular and innovative aquarium and Sea Centre.

North of the town, the **Colonne de la Grande Armée** was erected in 1841 as a monument to Napoleon I's planned invasion of England in 1803–5. From the top there is a panoramic view along the coast towards Calais. This is the most scenic stretch of the Côte d'Opale (Opal Coast),

with the windblown headlands of **Cap Gris-Nez** and **Cap Blanc-Nez** offering breathtakingly extensive views across the Channel.

🏛 **Château**
Rue de Bernet. **Tel** 03 21 10 02 20.
⊙ Wed–Mon. ⬤ 1 Jan, 1 May, 25 Dec.

🐟 **Nausicaa**
Bd Sainte-Beuve. **Tel** 03 21 30 99 99. ⊙ daily. ⬤ 3 wks Jan, 25 Dec.
🖼 ♿ www.nausicaa.fr

Calais ❸

Pas de Calais. 80,000. 🚉 🚌
⛴ ℹ 12 bd Clémenceau (03 21 96 62 40). 🗓 Wed, Thu & Sat.
www.calais-cotedopale.com

Calais is a busy cross-Channel port with a sandy beach to the west. Clumsily rebuilt after World War II, it seems to have little to offer at first sight. Many visitors never get closer than the huge Cité Europe shopping mall by the Eurotunnel exit.

The **Musée des Beaux Arts et de la Dentelle**, however, has works by the Dutch and Flemish Schools, and recalls the town's lace-making industry. Also on show are studies for

The windswept Cap Blanc-Nez on the Côte d'Opale

For hotels and restaurants in this region see pp556–8 and pp607–10

The Burghers of Calais by Auguste Rodin (1895)

Auguste Rodin's famous statue *The Burghers of Calais* (1895). The statue stands outside the Flemish Renaissance-style Hôtel de Ville, and celebrates an event during Edward III's siege of Calais in 1347, when six burghers offered their lives to save the rest of the town.

Musée de la Guerre, housed in a battle-scarred German blockhouse, offers a detailed account of local events during World War II.

🏛 **Musée des Beaux Arts et de la Dentelle**
25 rue Richelieu. **Tel** 03 21 46 48 40. ⭘ Wed–Mon (Sun pm). ⬤ public hols. 📷 ♿

🏛 **Musée de la Guerre**
Parc Saint Pierre. **Tel** 03 21 34 21 57. ⭘ May–Sep: daily; mid-Feb–Apr & Oct– mid-Nov: Wed–Mon. 📷 ♿

Dunkerque ❹

Nord. 🏠 200,000. 🚉 🚌 🛳
ℹ Rue Amiral Ronarc'h (03 28 66 79 21). 🛍 Wed, Sat.
www.ot-dunkerque.fr

Though a major industrial port, Dunkerque has much Flemish character. Start a tour from place du Minck, with its fresh fish stalls. Nearby **Musée Portuaire** celebrates the town's maritime history. In the old centre, a statue commemorates local hero Jean Bart, a 17th-century corsair, who lies in **Eglise St-Eloi**. Its belfry (1440) offers fine views.

Musée des Beaux Arts has an exhibition of the dramatic evacuation of 350,000 British

and French troops in 1940, and works by artists Vasarely and César. The **Musée d'Art Contemporain** features ceramics and glassware.

🏛 **Musée Portuaire**
9 quai de la Citadelle. **Tel** 03 28 63 33 39. ⭘ Wed–Mon. ⬤ 1 Jan, 1 May, 25 Dec. 📷 ♿

The port at Dunkerque

🏛 **Musée des Beaux Arts**
Pl du Général de Gaulle. **Tel** 03 28 59 21 65. ⭘ Wed–Mon. ⬤ 1 Jan, 1 Nov, 25 Dec. 📷 🎫 ♿ gr.fl.only.

🏛 **Musée d'Art Contemporain**
Av des Bains. **Tel** 03 28 29 56 00. ⭘ Wed–Mon. ⬤ pub hols. 📷 ♿

St-Omer ❺

Pas de Calais. 🏠 15,000. 🚉 🚌 ℹ 4 rue Lion d'Or (03 21 98 08 51). 🛍 Sat. **www**.tourisme-saintomer.com

Refined St-Omer seems untouched. Pilasters adorn the 17th- and 18th-century houses lining the cobbled streets, one of which, **Hôtel Sandelin**, is now a museum of fine and decorative arts. The cathedral has original 13th-century tiles and a huge organ. The **Bibliothèque Municipale** contains rare manuscripts from the Abbaye St-Bertin, a ruined 15th-century abbey east of town.

5 km (3 miles) from St-Omer, **La Coupole** is an informative WW2 museum inside a converted bunker.

🏛 **Hôtel Sandelin**
14 rue Carnot. **Tel** 03 21 38 00 94. ⭘ Wed–Sun. 📷 ♿ gr. fl.

🏛 **Bibliothèque Municipale**
40 rue Gambetta. **Tel** 03 21 38 35 08. ⭘ Tue–Sat. ⬤ public hols.

🏛 **La Coupole**
Tel 03 21 93 07 07. ⭘ daily. ⬤ last week Dec–1st week Jan.

CHANNEL CROSSINGS

Calais is only 36 km (22 miles) southeast of the English coast, and crossing the waters of the Channel – which the French know as La Manche (the Sleeve) – has inspired many intrepid exploits. The first crossing by balloon was in 1785 by Jean Pierre Blanchard; Captain M Webb made the first swim in 1875; and Louis Blériot's pioneering flight followed in 1909. Plans for an undersea tunnel, first laid as early as 1751, were finally achieved in 1994 with the opening of a railway link between Fréthun and Folkestone.

Children watching Louis Blériot taking off, 1909

Flandre Maritime ❻

Nord. 🏘 5,000. 🚆 Lille. 🚌 Bergues.
🚌 Dunkerque. 🛈 Bergues, Le Beffroi,
pl Henri Billiaert (03 28 68 71 06).

South of Dunkerque lies a
flat, agricultural plain with
narrow waterways and expansive skies – an archetypal
Flemish landscape with
canals, cyclists and ancient
windmills. The **Noordmeulen**,
built just north of
Hondschoote in 1127, is
thought to be the oldest
windmill in Europe.

From Hondschoote the D3
follows the Canal de la Basse
Colme west to Bergues, a fortified wool town with fine
16th–17th-century Flemish
works in its **Musée Municipal**.
Further south, the hilltop
town of **Cassel** has a cobbled
Grande place with 16th–18th-
century buildings, and views
across Flanders and Belgium
from its Jardin Public.

🏛 Musée Municipal
1 rue du Mont de Piété, Bergues.
Tel 03 28 68 13 30. 🕐 Wed–Mon.
⬤ Nov–Mar. 🎴

Lille ❼

Nord. 🏘 220,000. ✈ 🚆 🚌 🛈
Palais Rihour (03 59 57 94 00). 🛍
daily. **www**.lilletourism.com

Transformed in recent years,
not least by the advent of
Eurostar and its election as
European City of Culture 2004,

**Flower stalls in the arcades of the
Vieille Bourse in Lille**

Musicians in place du Général de Gaulle, in the heart of Vieux Lille

Lille has excellent shops and
markets and a powerful sense
of its historic Flemish identity
– the Flemish name, Rijssel, is
still used and some of the
area's one million residents
speak a Franco-Flemish patois.
With heavy industry declining,
the city has turned to high-
tech. A modern commercial
quarter, including the Euralille
shopping complex, adjoins
Lille Europe station, the TGV/
Eurostar/ Thalys rail interchange. The city's "metro" VAL,
is a driverless automatic train.

The city's charm lies in its
historic centre, Vieux Lille – a
mass of cobbled squares and
narrow streets that are packed
with stylish shops, cafés and
restaurants. Place du Général
de Gaulle forms its hub, with
façades including the 17th-
century **Vieille Bourse** (Old
Exchange). Adjacent stand the
Nouvelle Bourse and the
Opéra, both built in the early
20th century. The moated

five-point brick Citadel by
Vauban is also worth a look.

🏛 Musée de l'Hospice Comtesse
32 rue de la Monnaie. **Tel** 03 28 36 84
00. 🕐 Wed–Sun, Mon pm. 🎴
A hospital was founded here
in 1237. Now its 15th- and
17th- century buildings house
exhibitions. The Sick Room
has a barrel-vaulted ceiling,
the Community Wing a Delft
kitchen. There is a collection
of ancient instruments.

🏛 Palais des Beaux-Arts
Pl de la République. **Tel** 03 20 06 78 00.
🕐 Wed–Sun, Mon pm. 🎴 🎫 ♿
One of the best art collections
outside Paris, the museum is
strong on Flemish works, including Rubens and Van Dyck.
Other highlights are *Paradise
and Hell* by Dirk Bouts, Van
Goyen's *The Skaters*, Goya's
The Letter, Delacroix's *Médée*
as well as works by Courbet
and Impressionist paintings.

Arras ❽

Pas de Calais. 👥 45,000. 🚉 🚌 ℹ️ Hôtel de Ville, pl des Héros (03 21 51 26 95). 🛒 Wed, Sat. www.ot-arras.fr

The centre of Arras, capital of the Artois region, is graced by two picturesque cobbled squares enclosed by 155 houses with 17th-century Flemish-style façades. A triumph of postwar reconstruction, each residence in the **Grand' place** and the smaller place des Héros has a slightly varying design, with some original shop signs still visible.

A monumental **Hôtel de Ville** rebuilt in the Flamboyant Gothic style stands at the west end of place des Héros – in the foyer are two giants, Colas Dédé and Jacqueline, who swagger round the town during local festivals. From the basement you can take a lift up to the belfry for superb views, or take a guided tour into the labyrinth of underground passages below Arras. These were cut in the limestone in the 10th century. They have often served as shelter; during World War I as a subterranean army camp.

The huge Abbaye St-Vaast includes an 18th–19th-century Neo-Classical cathedral and the **Musée des Beaux-Arts**. The museum contains some fine examples of medieval sculpture including a pair of beautiful 13th-century angels. Among other exhibits are a local *arras* (hanging tapestry) and 19th-century works by the School of Arras, a group of realist landscape painters.

🏛 **Hôtel de Ville**
Pl des Héros. *Tel* 03 21 51 26 95. ◯ daily. 🎫 oblig for les boves. 📷

🏛 **Musée des Beaux Arts**
22 rue Paul Doumer. *Tel* 03 21 71 26 43. ◯ Wed–Mon. ● public hols. 📷

Vallée de la Somme ❾

Somme. ✈️ 🚉 🚌 Amiens. ℹ️ Rue Louis XI, Péronne (03 22 84 42 38). www.somme-tourisme.com

The name of the Somme is synonymous with the slaughter and horror of trench warfare during World War I (*see pp190–91*). Yet the Somme valley also means pretty countryside, a vast estuary wetland, and abundant wildlife. Lakes and woods alongside provide enjoyable camping, walking and fishing.

Battlefields lie along the river and its tributaries north and northeast of Amiens, and extend north to Arras. Neat World War I Commonwealth cemeteries cover the area. The **Historial de la Grande Guerre** at Péronne gives a thoughtful introduction. Parc Mémorial Beaumont-

Roadside shrine, Somme Valley

Hamel, near Albert, is a real battlefield being allowed to disappear in its own time. Travel to Vimy Ridge Canadian Memorial, near Arras, to see a bloodbath battle site preserved as it was, and to Notre-Dame de Lorette, the landmark French National Cemetery.

West of Amiens, **Samara** – Amiens' Gallo-Roman name – is France's largest archaeological park, with reconstructions of prehistoric dwellings, and exhibitions explaining early crafts like flint-cutting and corn-grinding. Further downstream, Eglise St-Vulfran at Abbeville is noted for its Flamboyant Gothic west front with beautifully carved 16th-century door panels.

St-Valéry-sur-Somme is a charming harbour resort with a historic upper town and a tree-lined promenade looking across the estuary. William departed for England from here in 1066. Birdwatchers should visit the Maison de l'Oiseau on the D3 nearby, or the Parc Ornithologique de Marquenterre on the far shore near delightful Le Crotoy. In summer, a little train links the two sides, passing through dunes and marshes.

🏛 **Historial de la Grande Guerre**
Château de Péronne. *Tel* 03 22 83 14 18. ◯ Oct–Mar: Tue–Sun; Apr–Sep: daily. ● mid-Dec–mid-Jan. 📷 ♿ 📁 www.historial.org

🏛 **Samara**
La Chaussée-Tirancourt. *Tel* 03 22 51 82 83. ◯ mid-Mar–mid-Nov: daily. 📷 ♿

Boating on the river Somme

16th-century carvings on Eglise St-Vulfran in Abbeville, Somme Valley

Amiens ⑩

Somme. 🗺 130,000. 🚃 🚌
ℹ 6 bis rue Dusevel (03 22 71 60 50).
🛒 Wed & Sat.
www.amiens.com/tourisme

There is more to Amiens, the capital of Picardy, than its **Cathédrale Notre-Dame** *(see pp202–3)*. The picturesque quarter of St-Leu is a pedestrianized area of low houses and flower-lined canals with waterside restaurants, bars and artisans' shops. Further east are **Les Hortillonnages**, a colourful patchwork of marshland market gardens, once tended by farmers using punts which now ferry visitors around the protected natural site.

The **Musée de Picardie** has many fine medieval and 19th-century sculptures and 16th–20th-century paintings, including a remarkable set of 16th-century group portraits, commissioned as offerings to the cathedral. To the south is the Cirque d'Hiver which Jules Verne (1828–1905) inaugurated in 1889. **Maison à la Tour**, his newly renovated home, has over 700 objects spread over four floors relating to the famous author, who lived here from 1882 until 1900.

🏛 **Musée de Picardie**
48 rue de la République. *Tel 03 22 97 14 00.* ◯ Tue–Sun. ● 1 Jan, 1 May, 1 Nov, 11 Nov, 25 Dec. 🎫 &

🏛 **Maison à la Tour**
2 rue Charles Dubois. *Tel 03 22 45 45 75.* ◯ Easter–mid-Oct: daily; mid-Oct– Easter: Wed–Mon. 🎫

The clock depicts Christ surrounded by the 12 apostles.

Mechanical figures perform scenes from the Last Judgment.

Solstice indicator

Clock showing age of the world

Astronomical clock in Beauvais cathedral

Beauvais ⑪

Oise. 🗺 58,000. ✈ 🚃 🚌 ℹ 1 rue Beauregard (03 44 15 30 30). 🛒 Wed, Sat. www.beauvaistourisme.fr

Heavily bombed in World War II, Beauvais is now a modern town with one outstanding jewel. Though never completed, **Cathédrale St-Pierre** is a poignant, neck-cricking finale to the vaulting ambition that created the great Gothic cathedrals. In 1227 work began on a building designed to soar above all predecessors, but the roof of the chancel caved in twice from lack of support before its completion in the early 14th century. Delayed by wars and inadequate funds, the transept was not completed until 1550. In 1573 its crossing collapsed after a tower and spire were added. What remains today is nevertheless a masterpiece, rising 48 m (157 ft) high. In the transept much of the original 16th-century stained glass survives, while near the north door is a 90,000-part astronomical clock assembled in the 1860s. What would have been the nave is still occupied by the remnants of a 10th-century church known as the Basse-Oeuvre.

The former Bishop's Palace is now home to the **Musée Départemental de l'Oise**. The collection includes archaeological finds, medieval sculpture, tapestries and local ceramics. Beauvais has a long tradition of tapestry manufacture, and examples from

VIOLLET-LE-DUC

The renowned architectural theorist Viollet-le-Duc (1814–79) was the first to fully appreciate Gothic architecture. His 1854 dictionary of architecture celebrated medieval building techniques, showing that the arches and tracery of Gothic cathedrals were solutions to architectural problems, not mere decoration. His restoration work included Château de Pierrefonds, Notre-Dame in Paris *(see pp86–7)* and Carcassonne *(see pp488–9)*.

Medieval architects, as drawn by Viollet-le-Duc

the French national collection are shown in the **Galerie Nationale de la Tapisserie.**

🏛 **Musée Départemental de l'Oise**
Ancien Palais Episcopal, 1 rue du Musée. *Tel 03 44 11 43 83.*
⬜ Wed–Mon. ⬤ 1 Jan, Easter, 1 May, 9 Jun, 25 Dec. 🈺

🏛 **Galerie Nationale de la Tapisserie**
22 rue St-Pierre. *Tel 03 44 15 39 10.*
⬜ Tue–Sun. 🈺 ⬤ 1 Jan, 25 Dec.

Noyon ⓬

Oise. 🏘 15,200. 🚉 ℹ pl de l'Hôtel de Ville (03 44 44 21 88). ⬤ Wed & Sat, first Tue of each month. **www**.noyon.com/tourisme

Noyon has long been a religious centre. The **Cathédrale de Notre-Dame**, dating from 1150, is the fifth to be built on this site and was completed by 1290. It provides a harmonious example of the transition from Romanesque to Gothic style.

A local history museum, the **Musée du Noyonnais**, occupies part of the former Bishop's Palace, and at the cathedral's east end is a rare half-timbered chapter library built in 1506.

Jean Calvin, the Protestant theologian and one of the leaders of the Reformation, was born here in 1509 and is commemorated in the small **Musée Jean Calvin.**

🏛 **Musée du Noyonnais**
Ancien Palais Episcopal, 7 rue de l'Evêché. *Tel 03 44 09 43 41.*
⬜ Wed-Mon. ⬤ 1 Jan, 11 Nov, 25 Dec. 🈺

The rib-vaulted nave of Cathédrale de Notre-Dame, Noyon

Path through Forêt de Compiègne

Compiègne ⓭

Oise. 🏘 50,000. 🚉 🚌 ℹ pl de l'Hôtel de Ville (03 44 40 01 00). ⬤ Wed & Sat. **www**.compiegne.fr

Compiègne is where Joan of Arc was captured by the Burgundians in 1430. A 16th-century Hôtel de Ville with a towering belfry rules over the centre, but the town is most famous for its royal **Château.**

Designed as a summer residence for Louis XV, the château was completed by Louis XVI, restored by Napoleon and later became a residence of Napoleon III and Empress Eugénie. Tours of the Imperial Apartments progress through private chambers, such as the sumptuous bedrooms of Napoleon I and Marie-Louise.

Within the château, the Musée du Second Empire and Musée de l'Impératrice display furniture, memorabilia and portraits, while the Musée de la Voiture is an entertaining assembly of historic carriages, bicycles and early motor cars.

South and east of the town the old hunting grounds of **Forêt de Compiègne** spread as far as Pierrefonds, with ample space for walks and picnics beneath its oaks and beeches. East of the D130 Les Beaux Monts provide majestic views back to the château.

The Clairière de l'Armistice, north of the N31, marks the spot where the armistice of World War I was signed on 11 November 1918. The small **Musée Wagon de l'Armistice** has a replica of the railway

carriage where the ceremony took place, which was used again in World War II by Hitler as a humiliating venue for the signing of the French surrender on 22 June 1940.

🏰 **Château de Compiègne**
Pl du Général de Gaulle. *Tel 03 44 38 47 00.* ⬜ Wed–Mon. ⬤ 1 Jan, 1 May, 1 Nov, 25 Dec. 🈺 **www**.musee-chateau-compiegne.fr

🏛 **Musée Wagon de l'Armistice**
Clairière de l'Armistice (direc. Soissons). *Tel 03 44 85 14 18.*
⬜ Wed–Mon. ⬤ Jan: Mon ams, 1 Jan, 25 Dec. 🈺

Château de Pierrefonds

Château de Pierrefonds ⓮

Oise. *Tel 03 44 42 72 72.*
⬜ daily. ⬤ 1 Jan, 1 May, 1 & 11 Nov, 25 Dec. 🈺 🎵 **Concerts**

The immense Château de Pierrefonds dominates the small village below. A mighty castle was constructed here by Louis d'Orléans in the 14th century, but by 1813 it had become a picturesque ruin which Napoleon I purchased for less than 3,000 francs.

In 1857, Napoleon III commissioned the architect Viollet-le-Duc to restore it, and in 1884 Pierrefonds was reborn as an imperial residence. The exterior, with its moat, drawbridge, towers and double sentry walks, is a diligent reconstruction of medieval military architecture. The interior, by contrast, is enlivened by the romantic fancies of Viollet-le-Duc and his patron. There are guided tours and a historical exhibition.

Amiens Cathedral

Work on the largest cathedral in France started around 1220, financed by profits from the cultivation of woad, a plant valued for its blue dye. It was built to house the head of St John the Baptist, brought back from the Crusades in 1206 and a magnet for pilgrims, which is still displayed here. Within 50 years Notre-Dame was complete, a masterpiece of engineering – Gothic architecture carried to a bold extreme. Restored in the 1850s by Viollet-le-Duc *(see p200)*, and having miraculously survived two World Wars, the cathedral is famous for its rich array of statues and reliefs, which inspired John Ruskin's *The Bible of Amiens* in 1884.

★ **West Front**
The King's Gallery, a row of 22 colossal statues representing the kings of France, spans the west front. The statues are also thought to symbolize the Kings of Judah.

St Firmin Portal is decorated with figures and scenes from the life of St Firmin, the martyr who brought Christianity to Picardy and became the first bishop of Amiens.

The Calendar shows signs from the Zodiac, with the corresponding monthly labours below. It depicts everyday life in the 13th century.

Weeping Angel
Sculpted by Nicolas Blasset in 1628, this sentimental statue in the ambulatory became a popular image during World War I.

STAR FEATURES

★ West Front

★ Nave

★ Choir Stalls

★ Choir Screens

Central Portal
Scenes from the Last Judgment adorn the tympanum, with the Beau Dieu, *a statue of Christ, between the doors.*

Towers
Two towers of unequal
height frame the west
front. The south tower
was completed in
1366; the north in
1402. The spire was
replaced twice, in
1627 and 1887.

VISITORS' CHECKLIST

Cathédrale Notre-Dame, pl
Notre-Dame. *Tel 03 22 80 03 41.*
◻ Apr–Sep: 8:30am–6:30pm;
Oct–Mar: 8:30am–5:30pm. ◻ 1
Jan, last Sun Sep. ✝ 9am daily
(Wed: noon); Sun: 9am,
10.15am, 11.30am, 6pm. ◯ ☐

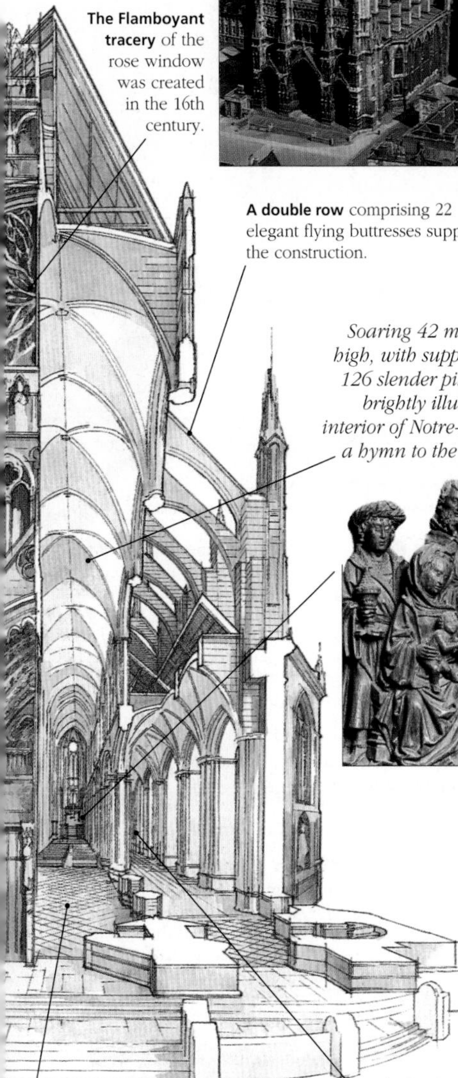

The Flamboyant
tracery of the
rose window
was created
in the 16th
century.

A double row comprising 22
elegant flying buttresses supports
the construction.

★ **Nave**
Soaring 42 m (138 ft)
high, with support from
126 slender pillars, the
brightly illuminated
interior of Notre-Dame is
a hymn to the vertical.

★ **Choir Stalls**
The 110 oak choir
stalls (1508–19)
are delicately
carved with over
4,000 biblical,
mythical and real
life figures.

The flooring was laid down in
1288 and reassembled in the
late 19th century. The faithful
followed its labyrinthine shape
on their knees.

★ **Choir Screens**
Vivid scenes from the
lives of St Firmin and St
John, carved in the
15th–16th centuries,
adorn the ambulatory.

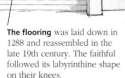

Senlis ⑮

Oise. 🏠 *17,000*. 🚃 🛈 *pl du Parvis Notre-Dame (03 44 53 06 40).* 🏛
Tue & Fri. **www**.senlis-tourisme.fr

Senlis, 10 km (6 miles) east of Chantilly, is worth visiting for its Gothic cathedral and the well-preserved historic streets in the old town that surround it. **Cathédrale Notre-Dame** was constructed during the second half of the 12th century and the sculpted central doorway of its west front, depicting the Assumption of the Virgin, influenced later cathedrals such as Amiens *(see pp202–3)*. The spire of the south tower dates from the 13th century, while the Flamboyant south transept, built in the mid-16th century, makes an ornate contrast with the austerity of earlier years. Opposite the west front, a gateway leads to the ruins of the Château Royal and its gardens. Here the **Musée de la Vé001nerie**, housed in a former priory, celebrates hunting through paintings, old weapons and trophies.

The **Musée d'Art** recalls the town's Gallo-Roman past, and also has an excellent collection of early Gothic sculpture.

🏛 **Musée de la Vénerie**
Château Royal, pl du Parvis Notre-Dame. **Tel** *03 44 32 00 83.* ◻ *Wed pm–Mon.* ● *1 Jan, 1 May, 25 Dec.* 🎦 📷 *oblig.*

🏛 **Musée d'Art et d'Archéologie**
Ancien Evêché, 2 pl Notre-Dame. **Tel** *03 44 32 00 81.* ◻ *Wed pm–Mon.* ● *1 Jan, 1 May, 25 Dec.* 🎦

Les Très Riches Heures du Duc de Berry, on show in Chantilly

Chantilly ⑯

Oise. 🏠 *12,500*. 🚃 🛈 *60 av du Maréchal Joffre (03 44 67 37 37).* 🏛 *Wed & Sat.*
www.chantilly-tourisme.com

The horse-racing capital of France, Chantilly offers a classy combination of château, park and forest that has long made it a popular excursion. With origins in Gallo-Roman times, the château of today started to take shape in 1528, when the famous Anne de Montmorency, Constable of France, had the old fortress replaced and added the Petit Château. During the time of the Great Prince of Condé (1621–86), renovation work continued and Le Nôtre created a park and fountains which made even Louis XIV jealous. Destroyed in the Revolution,

CHANTILLY HORSE RACING

Chantilly is the capital of thoroughbred racing in France, a shrine to the long-standing love affair between the French upper classes and the world of horses. It was the firm belief of Prince Louis-Henri de Bourbon, creator of Chantilly's monumental Grandes Ecuries, that he would one day be reincarnated as a horse. Horse racing was introduced from England around 1830 and soon became very popular. The first official race meeting was held here in 1834 and today around 3,000 horses are trained in the surrounding forests and countryside. Every June, Chantilly becomes the focus of the social and flat racing season when top riders and their thoroughbreds compete for its two historic trophies, the Prix du Jockey-Club and Prix de Diane-Hermès.

Prix Equipage de Hermès, one of many prestigious races at Chantilly

the Grand Château was again rebuilt and its receptions and hunting parties became crowded by the fashionable high society of the 1820s–30s. It was finally replaced by a Renaissance-style château in the late 19th century.

Today the Grand Château and the Petit Château form the **Musée Condé**, displaying art treasures collected by its last private owner, the Duke of Aumale. These include work by Raphael, Botticelli, Poussin and Ingres, and an entertaining gallery of 16th-century portraits by the Clouet brothers. Among the most precious items is the famous 15th-century illuminated manuscript *Les Très Riches Heures du Duc de Berry*, reproductions of which are on view. You can also tour the stately apartments, with decorative conceits ranging from frolicking monkeys to triumphant battles.

Asterix with friends, Parc Astérix

Both châteaux are somewhat upstaged by the magnificent stables (Grandes Ecuries), an equestrian palace designed by Jean Aubert in 1719 which could accommodate 240 horses and 500 dogs. It is occupied by the **Musée Vivant du Cheval**, presenting various breeds of horses and ponies, and riding displays.

🏛 **Musée Condé**
Château de Chantilly. *Tel* 03 44 62 62 62. ◯ Wed–Mon. 🎫 📷

🐎 **Musée Vivant du Cheval**
Grandes Ecuries du Prince de Condé, Chantilly. *Tel* 03 44 57 13 13. ◯ Wed–Mon (winter pms only). 🎫 ♿
www.museeducheval.fr

Parc Astérix ⑰

Plailly. 📞 03 44 62 34 34. ◯ Apr–Aug: daily; Sep–early Oct: Wed & w/e. ◯ some Mon & Fri in May–Jun (check). 🎫 ♿ www.parcasterix.fr

Near Charles de Gaulle Airport a small fortified Gaulish village has its own customs controls, currency and radio station (Menhir FM).

One of the most popular theme parks in France, it is dedicated to Asterix the Gaul and all the other characters in Goscinny and Uderzo's famous cartoon strip: Getafix, Obelix, Cacofonix *et al.* The Romans are driven crazy as they try to subdue these larger than life Gauls, who dodge patrolling Roman centurions. Hilarious battles take place.

The Parc is as much about French history as about the cartoons. Via Antiqua and the Roman City are lighthearted but genuinely educational. Rue de Paris shows Paris through the centuries, including the construction of Notre-Dame cathedral. There are non-historical attractions too, like a dolphinarium and Zeus' Thunder high-speed rollercoaster. Check out the latest rides – there's usually something new every year.

Laon ⑱

Aisne. 🏠 26,000. 🚉 🚌 *Hôtel-Dieu, pl du Parvis Gauthier de Montagne (03 23 20 28 62).* 🗓 Wed–Thu & Sat.
www.paysdelaon.com

The capital of the Aisne *département*, Laon occupies a dramatic site on top of a

The pedestrianized rue Châtelaine, a main shopping street in Laon

Rose window in the 13th-century Cathédrale de Notre-Dame, Laon

long, narrow ridge surrounded by wide plains. The old town, on top of the mount, is best approached by Poma, an automated cable car that swings up from the railway station to the place du Général Leclerc.

The pedestrianized rue Châtelaine leads to Laon's splendid **Cathédrale de Notre-Dame**. Completed in 1235, the cathedral lost two of its original seven towers in the Revolution but remains an impressive monument to the early Gothic style.

Details include the deep porches of the west façade, the four-storey nave, and the carved Renaissance screens enclosing its side chapels. The immense 13th-century rose window in the apse represents the Glorification of the Church. Protruding from the cathedral's western towers are statues paying tribute to the oxen used to haul up stone for its construction.

The rest of medieval Laon rewards casual strolling: a promenade rings the 16th-century **Citadelle** further east, while to the south you can follow the ramparts past the Porte d'Ardon and Porte des Chenizelles to **Eglise St-Martin**, with views of the cathedral from rue Thibesard.

South of Laon is Chemin des Dames, named after Louis XV's daughters who used to take this route, but more often remembered as a World War I battlefield and lined with cemeteries and memorials.

CHAMPAGNE

MARNE · ARDENNES · AUBE · HAUTE-MARNE

*C*hampagne is a name of great resonance, conjuring up images
of celebration and the world-famous cathedral at Reims. Yet
beyond the glamour lies an unspoilt rural idyll of two
strikingly contrasting landscapes: the rolling plains of Champagne,
giving way to lakes and water meadows to the south, and the dense
forests and hills of the Ardennes in the north.

The so-called "sacred triangle of Champagne", linking Épernay, Reims and Châlons-en-Champagne, is like a magnet for wine lovers. Here, the experience of drinking fine champagne is enhanced by gourmet meals of stuffed trout, Ardennes ham and the famous sausages called *andouillettes*.

The sign-posted *route touristique du champagne* wends its way through vineyards towards endless cereal plains stretching southwards to the "lake district", an area of oak forests, water meadows and streams.

On the border between France and Belgium lies the Ardennes, named after the Celtic word for deep forest. This wild border land of dramatic valleys, deciduous forests and hills is cut by the meanderings of the river Meuse. Border fortifications include the vast citadel of Sedan and the star-shaped bastion of Rocroi, as well as the Maginot Line outposts built before World War II. The Ardennes may offer appealing countryside but Champagne is culturally superior, with impressive towns that have painstakingly restored historic centres. It has some striking churches, from the Gothic majesty of Reims cathedral to the rustic charm of its typical wooden *champenoises* churches. These feature vivid stained-glass windows by the famous School of Troyes, whose subtle craftsmanship seems to typify the appeal of this quiet region.

Timber-framed *champenoise* church at Lac du Der-Chantecoq

◁ Cathédrale St-Etienne at Châlons-en-Champagne

Exploring Champagne

Champagne's fizz draws wine lovers to the sacred triangle between Reims, Épernay and Châlons-en-Champagne, but the region also attracts culture lovers to its great churches, notably Reims Cathedral. Reims abounds in gastronomic restaurants but Troyes, the former capital of Champagne, makes the most delightful base. Much of Champagne is flat or gently undulating, and the wild and wooded Ardennes to the north attracts walkers and nature-lovers. North of Reims, the Ardennes canal can be explored by barge or pleasure boat from Rethel; to the south, water sports are popular on the lakes to the east of Troyes.

Fishing by a canal in Montier-en-Der near Lac du Der-Chantecoq

GETTING AROUND

The region's main autoroute is the A26, which reaches Reims in under 3 hours from Calais, and also provides easy access to most of the region all the way down to Troyes and Langres (via the A5). The A4 motorway also links Reims to Paris and Alsace. Paris-Reims by the new TGV high-speed train takes 45 minutes. Rail transport within the region is reasonably good, and so are the roads. To explore the wine-growing region, follow the signposted roads marked "Route de Champagne".

Windmill at Verzenay, Parc Naturel de la Montagne de Reims

A *grande marque* champagne from Reims

SIGHTS AT A GLANCE

Argonne ❼
Châlons-en-Champagne ❾
Charleville-Mézières ❺
Chaumont ⓫
Épernay ❷
L'Épine ❽
Langres ⓬
Reims ❶
Rocroi ❹
Sedan ❻
Troyes ❿
Vallée de la Meuse ❸

Givet

VALLÉE DE LA MEUSE

❸

ROI

❺ CHARLEVILLE-MÉZIÈRES

A203

❻ SEDAN

Poix-Terron

Raucourt-et-Flaba
Carignan
Mouzon
N43

D977
D964

Le Chesne

D947

Vouziers
Buzancy

Aisne

D982

A R G O N N E
❼

le-sur-Tourbe
Les Islettes

A4
Sainte-Menehould

Metz

PINE

Givry-en-Argonne

E -

Sermaize-les-Bains

try-le-François
Thiéblemont-Farémont

Marne
N4

Saint-Dizier

Nancy

D57

Lac du Der-Chantecoq

ontier-en-Der
Wassy
Chevillon

D384

Joinville

Poissons

ne-le-Château

Soulaines-Dhuys

D427

Doulaincourt

Colombey-les-deux-Églises
N19

Vignory
N74

Bologne
Andelot

Juzennecourt

Bourmont

Nancy

A5

A31

CHAUMONT ⓫

D396

D65

Clefmont

Châteauvillain

D417

ntigny-r-Aube

Arc-en-Barrois

Nogent-en-Bassigny

Bourbonne-les-Bains

D417

LANGRES ⓬

N19

Laferté-sur-Amance

Chalindrey

Fayl-Billot

Auberive

D428

Longeau

Vesoul

A31

Dijon

The Old Town in Monthermé in Vallée de la Meuse, encircled by the river

KEY

— Motorway
— Major road
— Secondary road
— Minor road
— Scenic route
— Main railway
— Minor railway
— International border
— Regional border

0 kilometres   25

0 miles   25

Gilded reliquary (1896), with body of St Remi, in Basilique St-Remi, Reims

Reims ❶

Marne. 🏛 *200,000.* ✈ 🚌 🚪 ℹ *2 rue Guillaume de Machault (03 26 77 45 25).* 🗓 *daily.*
www.reims-tourisme.com

Pronounced like the French word "prince" without the "p", Reims is home to some of the best known *grandes marques* in Champagne, mostly grouped around the Basilique St-Remi. But the city has another, much earlier, claim to fame: since the 11th century, all the kings of France have come to this "city of coronations" to be crowned in its remarkable Gothic **Cathédrale Notre-Dame** *(see pp212–13).*

Although World War II bombing destroyed much of Reims' architectural coherence, there are some remarkable monuments here. The **Crypto-portique**, part of the forum, and Porte Mars, a triumphal Augustan arch, recall the Roman past. In 1945, the German surrender was taken in the **Musée de la Reddition** in Eisenhower's French HQ during World War II.
Musée des Beaux Arts houses a fine collection of 15th- and 16th-century canvases depicting biblical scenes, portraits by the Cranachs, *The Death of Marat* by David, and more than 20 landscapes by Corot. Also here are the Barbizons, Impressionists and modern masters.

In 1996 Reims celebrated the 1,500-year anniversary of the baptism of Clovis, first King of the Franks, in its cathedral.

🏛 Ancien Collège des Jésuites & Planetarium

1 pl Museux. *Tel 03 26 85 51 50.* **Collège** 🔵 *for renovation until 2009.* Founded in 1606, this college was a hospice until 1976. Nowadays its 300-year-old vines, Romanesque wine cellars and Baroque interior play their part as atmospheric film sets, notably for the film of Zola's *Germinal* (1992) and *Queen Margot* (1993). Highlights include the refectory's ceiling and the kitchen, the only room where fireplaces were permitted in an austere Jesuit establishment. A double spiral staircase leads to a Baroque library with yet another magnificent ceiling. Housed in the same building since 1979 is the **Planetarium**, with views of the sky from everywhere in the world. The site is undergoing renovation and will be closed until 2008.

🏠 Basilique St-Remi

Pl St-Rémi. ⚪ *daily.* ♿
Now marooned in a modern quarter, this Benedictine abbey church, the oldest church in Reims, began as a Carolingian

Porte Mars, a reminder of Reims in Roman times

METHODE CHAMPENOISE

To produce its characteristic bubbles, champagne has to undergo a process of double fermentation.
First fermentation: The base wine, made from rather acidic grapes, is fermented at 20°–22°C in either stainless steel tanks or, occasionally, in oak barrels. It is then siphoned off from the sediment and kept at colder temperatures to clear completely, before being drawn off and blended with wines from other areas and years (except in the case of vintage champagne). The wine is bottled and the *liqueur de tirage* (sugar, wine and yeast) is added.
Second fermentation: The bottles are stored for a year or more in cool, chalky cellars. The yeast converts the sugar to alcohol and carbon dioxide, which produces the sparkle, and the yeast cells die leaving a deposit. To remove this, the inverted bottles are turned and tapped daily *(remuage)* to shift the deposits into the neck of the bottle. Finally, the deposits are expelled by the process known as *dégorgement*, and a bit of sugar syrup *(liqueur d'expédition)* is added to adjust the sweetness before the final cork is inserted.

Champagne Mumm of Reims

basilica dedicated to Saint Rémi (440–533). Inside, an Early Gothic choir and radiating chapels can be seen, as well as sculpted Romanesque capitals in the north transept.

🏛 Musée St-Remi

53 rue Simon. *Tel* 03 26 85 23 36. ⬜ *daily pm only.* ⬤ *1 Jan, 1 May, 14 Jul, 1 & 11 Nov, 25 Dec.* 🎫

Set in the former abbey, the adjoining museum encloses the original Gothic chapter-house within its cloistered 17th-century shell. On display in the museum are archeological artifacts, 15th-century tapestries depicting the life of Saint Rémi, and a varied collection of weapons dating from the 16th–19th centuries.

Épernay ②

Marne. 🚹 *28,000.* 🚉 🛈 *7 av de Champagne (03 26 53 33 00).* 🔺 *Wed, Sat & Sun.* **www**.ot-epernay.fr

The sole reason for visiting Épernay is to burrow into the chalky *caves* and taste the champagne. This rather undistinguished town lives off the fruits of its profitable champagne industry. As proof, the avenue de Champagne quarter abounds in mock-Renaissance mansions. **Moët & Chandon,**

Statue of Dom Perignon at Moët

dating back to 1743, is the largest and slickest *maison,* the star of the Moët-Hennessy stable. Its cellars stretch some 28 km (18 miles) underground.

The group also owns other champagne houses, such as Mercier, Krug, Pommery, Veuve Clicquot and Canard Duchêne. When the recession took the fizz out of Champagne in 1993, Moët made a number of people redundant, and provoked the first ever strike in the industry.

There is little to choose between a visit to the cellars of Moët & Chandon or **Mercier** – both are in Avenue de Champagne. Mercier has the distinction of displaying a giant tun (cask) created for the 1889 Paris Exhibition, and takes you through the *caves* in an electric train.

De Castellane offers a more personalized tour, accompanied by a heady *dégustation.*

🏛 Moët & Chandon

20 av de Champagne. *Tel* 03 26 51 20 20. ⬜ *Apr–mid-Nov: daily; mid-Nov–Mar: Mon–Fri.* 🎫 🎫 *only.* **www**.moet.com

🏛 Mercier

70 av de Champagne. *Tel* 03 26 51 22 22. ⬜ *mid-Mar–Nov: daily; Dec–mid-Mar: Thu–Mon.* 🎫 ♿ 🎫 *oblig.* **www**.champagnemercier.com

🏛 De Castellane

57 rue de Verdun. *Tel* 03 26 51 19 11. ⬜ *daily (Jan–Mar: Sat & Sun only).* 🎫 ♿ *restr.* 🎫 *oblig.* **www**.castellane.com

Dégorgement *is the final removal of the yeast deposits from the bottle. The neck of the bottle is plunged in freezing brine and the frozen block of sediment is then removed.*

Seductive marketing *of champagne since the 19th century has ensured its continuing success.*

The bubbles in champagne *are produced during the second fermentation. Champagnes, especially vintage ones, improve with ageing.*

Reims Cathedral

The magnificent Gothic Cathédrale Notre-Dame at
Reims is noted for its harmony and monumentality.
A cathedral has stood on this site since 401, but the
present building was begun in 1211. Reims has been
the backdrop for coronations from medieval times till
1825, when Charles X was crowned. The coronation of
Charles VII here in 1429 was attended by Joan of Arc.
  During the Revolution, the rood screen and windows
were destroyed but the stonework survived. World War I
damage was finally fully restored in 1996, to coincide
with the 1,500th anniversary of the baptism of Clovis,
King of the Franks, at Reims, which was considered the
first coronation of a French king.

★ Great Rose Window
*Best seen at sunset, the
13th-century window
shows the Virgin sur-
rounded by the apostles
and angel musicians. It is
set within a larger window,
a feature common in
13th-century architecture.*

The Nave
*Compared with the nave at
Chartres (see pp308–11),
Reims is taller. Its elegant
capitals are decorated with
naturalistic floral motifs
such as ivy and berries.*

WEST FAÇADE

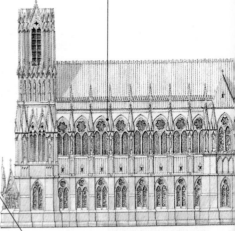

SOUTH FAÇADE

★ Smiling Angel
*Rich in statuary,
Reims is often called
"the cathedral of
angels." Situated
above the left (north)
portal, this enigmatic
angel with unfurled
wings is the most cele-
brated of the many
that grace the building.*

★ Gallery of the Kings
*The harmonious west façade, decorated
with over 2,300 statues, is the most notable
feature at Reims. Fifty-six stone effigies of
French kings form the Gallery of the Kings.*

PALAIS DU TAU

The archbishop's palace adjoining the cathedral is named after its T-shaped design, based on early episcopal crosses. (Tau is Greek for T.) The palace, built in 1690 by Mansart and Robert de Cotte, encloses a Gothic Chapel and the 15th-century Salle du Tau, rooms associated with French coronations. On the eve of a coronation, the future king would spend the night in the palace. After being crowned in the cathedral, he held a magnificent banquet in the palace. The Salle du Tau, or banqueting hall, is the finest room in the palace, with a magnificent barrel-vaulted ceiling and walls hung with 15th-century

Arras tapestries. The palace now houses a museum of statuary and tapestries from the cathedral, including a 15th-century tapestry of the baptism of Clovis, the first Christian king.

Salle du Tau – the banqueting hall

VISITORS' CHECKLIST

Cathédrale Notre-Dame, pl du Cardinal Luçon. **Tel** 03 26 47 55 34. ◯ 7:30am–7:30pm daily. ✝ 8am & 7pm Mon–Fri; 8am Sat; 9:30am & 11am Sun. 📷 ♿ 🎥 by appt only. **www**.cathedrale-reims.com **Palais du Tau Tel** 03 26 47 81 79. ◯ Tue–Sun. ● 1 Jan, 1 May, 1 & 11 Nov, 25 Dec. 🎫

Apse Gallery
The restored claire-voie *(open work) gallery on the apse is crowned by statues of mythological beasts.*

The radiating chapels of the apse are supported by flying buttresses and adorned with octagonal pinnacles.

South transept

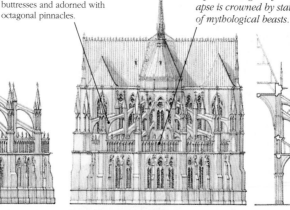

APSE

The clerestory windows pioneered Gothic tracery by dividing the lights with slender bars of stone, creating a decorative, intersecting pattern.

Pinnacles on the flying buttresses shelter guardian angels, symbolic protectors of the cathedral.

STAR FEATURES

★ Gallery of the Kings

★ Smiling Angel

★ Great Rose Window

Chagall Window
The windows in the axial chapel were designed by the 20th-century artist Marc Chagall and made by local craftsmen. This one depicts the Crucifixion and the Sacrifice of Isaac.

The *sentier touristique*, a walk along the ramparts of Rocroi

Vallée de la Meuse ❸

Ardennes. 🏠 8,900. 🚊 Revin.
🛈 2 rue Victor Hugo, Revin (03 24 40 19 59).

The Meuse meanders through the Ardennes among spectacular scenery of wild gorges, woods and warped rock formations of granite or schist.

Dramatically situated on a double meander of the Meuse, **Revin** is an unremarkable town in an exceptional site, with the Vieille Ville enfolded in the north bend. From the quay, you can see wooded **Mont Malgré Tout** and a route dotted with observation points and steep trails. Just south is **Dames de la Meuse**, a rocky outcrop over the river gorge.

Monthermé lies on two banks, with the Vieille Ville clustered on the charming left bank. The rocky gorges around **Roche à Sept Heures** on the far bank entice climbers and ramblers. The jagged crest of **Rocher des Quatre Fils d'Aymon** suggests the silhouette of four legendary local horsemen.

Rocroi ❹

Ardennes. 🏠 2,600. 🚊 🚊 Revin
🛈 14 pl d'Armes (03 24 54 20 06).
🛒 Tue & 1st Mon of month. **www.** otrocroi.com

Set on the Ardennes plateau, the unique star-shaped citadel of Rocroi was originally built under Henri II in 1555, and later made impregnable by Vauban in 1675 *(see p226)*.

The main attraction is the walk along the ramparts from the southern gateway. The nature reserve at Rièzes is home to orchids and carnivorous plants.

Charleville-Mézières ❺

Ardennes. 🏠 58,000. 🚊 🚊
🛈 4 pl Ducale (03 24 55 69 90). 🛒 Tue, Thu & Sat.
www.charleville-tourisme.com

This riverside ford was originally two towns. The sombre medieval citadel of Mézières only merged with the neat Classical town of Charleville in 1966. Mézières has irregular slate-covered houses curving around a bend in the Meuse. Battered fortifications and gateways are visible from avenue de St-Julien. Tucked into the ramparts is the much remodelled Gothic **Notre-Dame de l'Espérance**.

The centrepiece of Charleville is **place Ducale**, a model of Louis XIII urban planning,

echoing place des Vosges in Paris *(see p91)*. The poet Arthur Rimbaud was born nearby in 1854. His modest birthplace at No. 12 rue Bérégovoy is still there, along with his childhood home on the Meuse at 7 quai Arthur Rimbaud.

Just along the quayside is the Vieux Moulin, the town house whose view inspired *Le Bateau Ivre*, Rimbaud's greatest poem. Inside is the small **Musée Rimbaud**, with manuscripts and photographs by the poet.

🏛 **Musée Rimbaud**
Quai Arthur Rimbaud. **Tel** 03 24 32 44 65. 🕐 Tue–Sun. ● 1 Jan, 1 May, 25 Dec. 🆓 (free first Sun of month).

Sedan ❻

Ardennes. 🏠 23,000. 🚊 🚌 🛈
Château Fort, pl du Château (03 24 27 73 73). 🛒 Wed & Sat.

Just to the east of Charleville is the **Château de Sedan**, the largest fortified castle in the whole of Europe. There has been a bastion on these slopes since the 11th century, but each Ardennes conflict has spelt a new tier of defences for Sedan.

In 1870, during the Franco-Prussian War, with 700 Prussian cannons turned on Sedan, Napoleon III surrendered and 83,000 French prisoners were deported to Prussia. In May 1940 after capturing Sedan, German forces reached the French coast a week later.

The seven-storeyed bastion contains sections dating from medieval times to the 16th

The 19th-century poet Rimbaud, whose birthplace was Charleville

century. Highlights of any visit are the ramparts, the 16th-century fortifications and the magnificent 15th-century eaves in one tower. The **Musée du Château**, in the south wing, is rather jumbled, with a section on military campaigns.

The bastion is surrounded by 17th-century slate-roofed houses which hug the banks of the Meuse. These reflect the city's earlier prosperity as a Huguenot stronghold.

🏛 **Musée du Château**
1 pl du Château. *Tel 03 24 27 73 73.*
⬛ *mid-Mar–mid-Sep: daily; mid-Sep–mid-Mar: w/e* 🈲 *Tue–Fri pms.*

Environs
Further south is **Fort de Vitry-la-Ferté**, one of the few forts on the Maginot line to have come into direct and devastating combat with the enemy in 1940.

Courtyard inside the heavily fortified Château de Sedan

Gargoyle on Basilique de Notre-Dame de l'Epine

Argonne ❼

Ardennes & Meuse. 🚉 *Châlons.* 🚌 *Ste-Menehould.* 🛈 *5 pl du Général Leclerc, Ste-Menehould (03 26 60 85 83).* **www**.argonne.fr

East of Reims, the Argonne is a compact region of pictur-esque valleys and forests, dotted with priories, trenches and war cemeteries.

As a wooded border between the rival bishoprics of Champagne and Lorraine, the Argonne was home to abbeys and priories. Now ruined, the Benedictine abbey of **Beaulieu-en-Argonne** boasts a 13th-century wine press and has forest views.

Just north is **Les Islettes**, known for its faïence pottery and tiles. The hilly terrain here was a battleground during the Franco-Prussian War and World War I. The disputed territory of **Butte de Vauquois**, north of Les Islettes, bears a war memorial.

L'Épine ❽

Marne. 🏠 *600.* 🚉 *Châlons.* 🚌 🛈 *Mairie (03 26 66 96 99).*

L'Épine is worth visiting if only for a glimpse of the **Basilique de Notre-Dame de l'Épine** surrounded by wheat-fields. Designed on the scale of a cathedral, this 15th-century Flamboyant Gothic church has been a pilgrimage site since medieval times. Even French kings have come here to venerate a "miraculous" statue of the Virgin.

On the façade, three gabled portals are offset by floating tracery, a gauzy effect remini-scent of Reims cathedral. All around are gruesome gar-goyles, symbolizing evil spirits and deadly sins, chased out by the holy presence within. Unfortunately, the most risqué sculptures were destroyed, judged obscene by 19th-century puritans. The subdued Gothic interior contains a 15th-century rood-screen and the venerated statue of the Virgin.

CHAMPAGNE TIMBER CHURCHES

Skirting Lac du Der-Chantecoq lies a region of woodland and water meadows, containing twelve Romanesque and Renaissance half-timbered churches with curious pointed gables and *caquetoirs*, rickety wooden porches. They have intimate and often beautifully carved interiors with stained-glass windows designed in the vivid colours of the School of Troyes. Rural roads link churches at Bailly-le-Franc, Chatillon-sur-Broué, Lentilles, Vignory, Outines, Chavanges and Montier-en-Der.

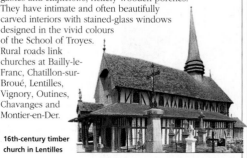

16th-century timber church in Lentilles

Châlons-en-Champagne ❾

Marne. 🏠 48,000. 🚇 🚌 🚏
3 quai des Arts (03 26 65 17 89).
🛒 Wed, Fri am, Sat, Sun am.
www.chalons-tourisme.com

Encircled by the river Marne and minor canals, Châlons' sleepy bourgeois charm is made up of half-timbered houses and gardens mirrored in canals. Nearby are vineyards producing Blanc de Blancs.

From quai de Notre-Dame there are views of old bridges and the Romanesque towers of **Notre-Dame-en-Vaux**, a masterpiece of Romanesque-Gothic. Behind the church is a well-restored medieval quarter and the **Musée du Cloître**, containing the original Romanesque cloisters.

Cathédrale St-Etienne, by the canal, is a cool Gothic affair with a Baroque portal, Romanesque crypt and vivid medieval windows. Beyond is **Le Petit Jard**, riverside gardens overlooking the Château du Marché, and a turreted toll gate built by Henri IV. The neighbouring place de la République has lively bars and restaurants.

🏛 Musée du Cloître de Notre-Dame-en-Vaux
Rue Nicolas Durand. **Tel** 03 26 64 03 87. ⬜ Wed–Mon. ⬤ 1 Jan, 1 May, 1 & 11 Nov, 25 Dec. 🈁 🈂

Troyes ❿

Aube. 🏠 62,000. 🚇 🚌 🚏 16 bd Carnot (03 25 82 62 70). 🛒 daily.
www.tourisme-troyes.com

Troyes is a delight, a city of magnificent Gothic churches and charming 16th-century courtyards, in a historical centre shaped like a champagne cork. The city is famous for its heritage of stained glass and sausages (andouillettes), its knitwear industry and factory shops.

The battered Flamboyant Gothic west front of the **Cathédrale St-Pierre-et-St-Paul** opens on to a splendid vaulted interior. The nave is bathed in mauvish-red rays

Statuary in Troyes' Cathédrale St-Pierre-et-St-Paul

from the 16th-century rose window, complemented by the discreet turquoise of the Tree of Jesse window and the intense blue of the medieval windows of the apse.

Nearby, **Eglise St-Nizier** glitters in the faded quarter behind the cathedral with its shimmering tiled Burgundian roof. Inside, it is lit by windows in a range of warm mauves and soothing blues.

The Gothic **Basilique St-Urbain** boasts grand flying buttresses and particularly fine windows which have recently been restored. **Eglise Ste-Madeleine** is noted for its elaborate 16th-century rood screen resembling lacey foli-

Rue Larivey, a typical street with half-timbered houses, in Troyes

age, grapes and figs. Beyond is a wall of windows in browns, reds and blues. The ruelle des Chats, which is a quaint covered passageway, connects rue Charbonnet and rue Champeaux.

Set in one of the best-preserved quarters, **Eglise St-Pantaléon** faces a Renaissance mansion. A Gothic and Renaissance interior houses an imposing collection of 16th-century statuary and severe grisaille windows.

🏛 Musée d'Art Moderne
14 pl St-Pierre.
Tel 03 25 76 26 80. ⬜ Tue–Sun.
⬤ public hols. 🈁 🈂
Beside the cathedral, the former episcopal palace is now a museum of modern art, with a sculpture by Rodin, and an especially fine collection of Fauvist paintings, as well as other modern art.

🏛 Hôtel du Petit Louvre
Rue de la Montée St-Pierre.
Courtyard only ⬜ daily.
Set off quai Dampierre, this newly restored hôtel particulier boasts a fish-scale roof, medieval tower, Renaissance courtyard, staircase and well. The highlight is a façade adorned with quizzical multi-coloured faces.

Environs

The city's green playground, **Lac et Forêt d'Orient**, is 25 km (15 miles) east of Troyes. The forest is dotted with marshes, nature reserves and smaller lakes. Lac d'Orient, the largest artificial lake in Europe, is popular for sailing, with water-skiing on Lac Amance, and fishing at Lac du Temple.

Chaumont ⑪

Haute-Marne. 🏠 26,000. 🚉 🚌 pl du Général de Gaulle (03 25 03 80 80). 🗓 Wed & Sat. **www**.ville-chau-mont.fr

As the former residence of the Counts of Champagne, this feudal town enjoyed great prestige in the 13th century. On the far side of a ravine, the old town is on a rocky spur, with the Palais de Justice and the medieval castle keep dominating.

The keep is a reminder that this quiet administrative centre had a formidable past. This impression is confirmed by the Renaissance town houses which are bulging with *tourelles d'escaliers*, turreted staircases.

Basilique St-Jean-Baptiste, a grey-stone Champenois church, is the most remarkable monument in Chaumont. The interior is enlivened by a spider's web of vaulting, a striking turreted staircase and Renaissance galleries. Near the entrance is a tiny chapel containing an unsettling *Mise au Tombeau* (1471), an intense multi-coloured stone group of 10 mourners gathered around Christ laid out on a shroud in his tomb. In the left transept is a bizarre but beguiling *Tree of Jesse*. On this ill-lit Renaissance stone relief, a family tree sprouts from the sleeping Jesus, who slumbers unawares – much like Chaumont itself.

Environs

Twenty-three kilometres (14 miles) to the northwest of Chaumont, **Colombey-les-Deux-Eglises** will forever be associated with General Charles de Gaulle (1890–1970). The de Gaulles bought

Cathédrale St-Mammès in Langres

their home, **La Boisserie**, in 1933, but had to abandon it during the war, when it was badly damaged. After its restoration, de Gaulle would return to La Boisserie from Paris at weekends to write his memoirs and plan his comeback. He eventually died here on 9 November 1970. The house is now a museum.

In the village churchyard, the General and President of France (1958–69) lies in a simple tomb. However, a giant granite cross of Lorraine, erected in 1972, dominates the skyline – a grandiose memorial more in keeping with de Gaulle's notion of *la gloire*.

🏛 La Boisserie
Colombey-les-Deux-Eglises. **Tel** 03 25 01 52 52. 🕐 Feb–Nov: Wed–Mon. 🎟 ♿

Langres ⑫

Haute-Marne. 🏠 10,000. 🚉 🚌 🛈 square Olivier Lahalle (03 25 87 67 67). 🗓 Fri. **www**.tourisme-langres.com

Set on a rocky spur, Langres lies beyond Chaumont, in the backwaters of southern Champagne. This ancient bishopric was one of the gateways to Burgundy and the birthplace of the encyclopedist, Denis Diderot (1713–84). Langres promotes itself as a land of springs, claiming that its proximity to the sources of the Seine and Marne grant it mystical powers.

Virtually the whole town is enclosed by medieval ramparts, Langres' undoubted attraction. A succession of towers and parapets provide glimpses of romantic town gates and sculpted Renaissance mansions, with panoramic views of the Marne valley, the Langres plateau, the Vosges and, on a clear day, even Mont Blanc.

Near Porte Henri IV is the much-remodelled **Cathédrale St-Mammès**. The gloomy vaulted interior, in Burgundian Romanesque style, is redeemed by the sculpted capitals in the apse, reputedly taken from a temple of Jupiter. The town's Musée d'Art et d'Histoire has some interesting collections.

Langres' lively summer season includes historical re-enactments, theatre and fireworks.

Memorial to General de Gaulle at Colombey-les-Deux-Eglises

ALSACE AND LORRAINE

MEURTHE-ET-MOSELLE · MEUSE · MOSELLE · BAS-RHIN
HAUT-RHIN · VOSGES

*A*s border regions, Alsace and Lorraine have been fought over
for centuries by France and Germany, their beleaguered
past recalled by many a military stronghold and cemetery.
Today, the region presents only a peaceful aspect with pastel-painted
villages, fortified towns and sleepy vineyards.

At the northeast frontier of France, bordered by the Rhine, Alsace forms a fertile watershed between the mountains of the Vosges and the Black Forest in Germany. Lorraine, with its gentle rolling landscape on the other side of the mountains, is the poorer cousin but is more overtly French in character.

EMBATTLED TERRITORY

Caught in the wars between France and Germany, Alsace and part of Lorraine have changed nationality four times since 1871. Centuries of strife have made border citadels of Metz, Toul and Verdun in Lorraine, while Alsace abounds with castles, from the pastiche folly of Haut-Koenigsbourg to Saverne's ruined fortress, built to guard a strategic pass in the Vosges. However, the area has a strong identity of its own, taking pride in local costumes, traditions and dialects. In Alsace, Route des Vins vineyards nudge pretty villages in the Vosges foothills. Strasbourg, the capital, is a cosmopolitan city with a 16th-century centre, while Nancy, Lorraine's historical capital, represents elegant 18th-century architecture and town planning.

Much of the attraction of this region lies in its cuisine. Lorraine offers beer and quiche lorraine. In Alsace, cosy *winstubs*, or wine cellars, serve sauerkraut and flowery white wines, such as Riesling and Gewürztraminer.

Villagers enjoying the view from their window in Hunspach, north of Strasbourg in the northern Vosges

◁ Half-timbered houses with flower-clad balconies along the Route du Vin in Alsace

Exploring Alsace and Lorraine

Visitors seeking art and architecture will be amply rewarded by the charming medieval towns and excellent city museums of the region. Undiscovered Lorraine is the place to clamber over military citadels, walk in unspoiled countryside and unwind at relaxing spas. By contrast, Alsace offers magnificent forests and rugged mountain drives in the Vosges, quaint villages and rich wines. The Route des Vins *(see pp232–3)* is one of the region's many scenic routes. It is particularly popular during the wine harvest festivities but is worth visiting in any season.

SIGHTS AT A GLANCE

Betschdorf ⑱
Château du Haut-
  Koenigsbourg ⑬
Colmar ⑩
Eguisheim ⑨
Gérardmer ⑤
Guebwiller ⑦
Metz ③
Mulhouse ⑥
Nancy ④
Neuf-Brisach ⑧
Obernai ⑮
Ribeauvillé ⑫
Riquewihr ⑪
Saverne ⑰
Sélestat ⑭
Strasbourg ⑯
Toul ②
Verdun ①

Field of sunflowers just outside the village of Turckheim

0 kilometres   20

0 miles   10

The picturesque village of Riquewihr on the Route du Vin

GETTING AROUND

There are good road and
rail links between Strasbourg,
Colmar and Nancy, and on
to Switzerland and Germany.
The main roads to and
through the regions are the
N3, N4, A31, and A35, the
A4 to Paris, and the N59
and the tunnel under the
Vosges. The spectacular
journey over the Vosges and
along the Route des Vins is
best made by car or on
organized trips from Colmar
or Strasbourg. The TGV link
to the region from Paris
takes 2 hours 20 minutes.

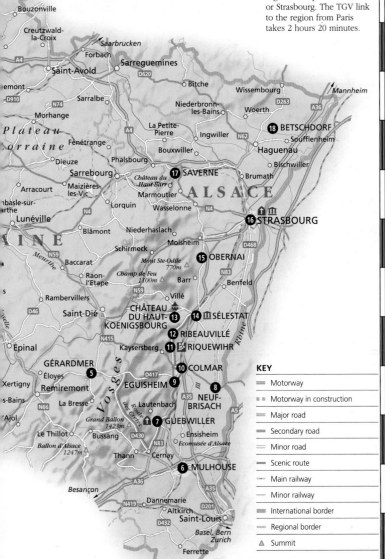

KEY

▬	Motorway
▬ ▬	Motorway in construction
▬	Major road
▬	Secondary road
▭	Minor road
▬	Scenic route
▭▭	Main railway
─	Minor railway
▬	International border
▬	Regional border
△	Summit

The Ossuaire de Douaumont, a sentinel for the regiments of crosses on the battlefields of Verdun

Verdun ❶

Meuse. 👥 21,000. 🚌 🚗 ℹ️ pl de la Nation (03 29 86 14 18). 🗓 Fri. www.verdun-tourisme.com

Verdun will be forever remembered for the horrors of the 1916–1917 Battle of Verdun, when about a million men died in almost a whole year of continuous bloodshed that is considered the worst single battle of the Great War. The Germans intended to strike a blow at French morale by destroying the forts of Douaumont and Vaux (which had been built to prevent a repeat of the humiliating French defeat of the Franco-Prussian war of 1870) and capture Verdun, France's northeastern stronghold. The French fought simply to prevent the town being taken. The stalemate and the killing continued here right up to the end of the war, and not until 1918 did the Germans draw back from their positions just 5km from the town.

Several poignant museums, memorials, battle sites and cemeteries can be visited in the hills just outside Verdun on the north side. In this devastated region, nine villages were obliterated without trace. The **Musée-Memorial de Fleury** tells their story. Nearby, the **Ossuaire de Douaumont** contains the unidentified bones of over 130,000 French and German dead. One of the most striking monuments to the Battle of Verdun is Rodin's memorial in Verdun itself. It depicts the winged figure of Victory unable to soar

triumphant because she has become caught in the remains of a dead soldier.

The town of Verdun was heavily fortified over the centuries. The crenellated **Porte Chaussée**, a medieval river gateway, still guards the eastern entrance to the town and is the most impressive of the remaining fortifications.

Although battered by war damage, the **Citadelle de Verdun** retains its 12th-century tower, the only relic from the original abbey that Vauban incorporated into his new military design. Now a war museum, the **Citadelle Souterraine**, it recreates Verdun's role in WWI. The citadel casemates come to life as grim trenches, and the presentation ends by showing how the "Unknown Soldier" was chosen for the symbolic tomb under the Arc de Triomphe in Paris *(see p107)*.

The town centre is dominated by the cathedral, where Romanesque elements were rediscovered after the 1916 bombardments.

The 16th-century cloisters of Eglise St-Gengoult in Toul

🏛 **Citadelle Souterraine**
Ave du 5ième R.A.P. **Tel** 03 29 86 14 18. ⬜ daily. ⬤ Jan. 📷 ♿

Toul ❷

Meurthe-et-Moselle. 👥 17,000. 🚌 🚗 ℹ️ parvis de la Cathédrale (03 83 64 11 69). 🗓 Wed & Fri. www.ot-toul.fr

Lying within dark forests west of Nancy, the octagonal fortress city of Toul is encircled by the Moselle and the Canal de la Marne. Along with Verdun and Metz, Toul was one of the 4th-century bishoprics. In the early 18th century, Vauban built the citadel, from which the ring of defensive waterways, the octagonal city ramparts and the **Porte de Metz** remain.

The **Cathédrale St-Etienne**, begun in the 13th century, took over 300 years to build. It suffered damage in World War II but the purity of the Champenois style has survived, notably in the arched, high-galleried interior. The imposing Flamboyant Gothic façade is flanked by octagonal towers. Rue du Général-Gengoult, behind the Gothic **Eglise St-Gengoult**, contains a clutch of sculpted Renaissance houses. North of the city the local "grey" Côtes de Toul wines are produced.

Environs South of Toul, near the town of Neufchâteau, is the birthplace of Joan of Arc at **Domrémy-La-Pucelle**. Next door to the house where she was born is an interpretation centre with an exhibition about her remarkable life.

The vast **Parc Régional de Lorraine** takes in red-tiled cottages, vineyards, forests, cropland, *chaumes* (high pastureland), marshes and lakes. Inns in the area are especially noted for their quiche lorraine and *potée lorraine*, a bacon casserole.

Jupiter Slaying a Monster on the Column of Merten in La Cour d'Or

Metz ❸

Moselle. 130,000. *pl d'Armes (03 87 55 53 76).* Sat. www.mairie-metz.fr

An austere yet appealing city, Metz sits at the confluence of the Moselle and the Seille. Twenty bridges criss-cross the rivers and canals, and there are pleasant walks along the banks. This Gallo-Roman city, now the capital of Lorraine, has always been a pawn in the game of border chess – annexed by Germany in 1870, regained by France in 1918.

Set on a hill above the Moselle, the **Cathédrale St-Etienne** overlooks the historic centre. The Gothic exterior flaunts impressive flying buttresses and long-necked gargoyles. Inside, stained-glass windows, from Gothic to modern, including some by Chagall, present walls of shimmering light.

To the northwest of the cathedral, a narrow wooden bridge leads across to the island of Petit Saulcy, site of the oldest French theatre still in use. Located on the other side of the cathedral, the **Porte des Allemands**, span-

ning a river, more resembles a medieval castle because of its bridge, defensive towers and 13th-century gate with pepper-pot towers.

In the Vieille Ville, place St-Louis is a delightful square bordered by lofty, arcaded 14th-century mansions. **Eglise St-Pierre-aux-Nonnains** claims to be one of the oldest churches in France. The external walls and the ruined façade date from Roman times, while much of the rest belongs to the 7th-century convent that occupied the site. Nearby is the frescoed 13th-century **Chapelle des Templiers**, built by the Knights Templar.

🏛 Musée de la Cour d'Or

2 rue du Haut-Poirier. *Tel 03 87 68 25 00.* Wed–Mon. publ hols. Also known as the Musée d'Art et d'Histoire, this fascinating collection is set in the Petits-Carmes, a deconsecrated 17th-century monastery incorporating Gallo-Roman thermal baths and a medieval tithe barn. On display are Merovingian stone carvings, Gothic painted ceilings and a variety of German, Flemish and French paintings.

WHITE STORKS

Until recently, the white stork, traditionally a symbol of good fortune, was a frequent sight in northeast France. White storks spend the winter in Africa, but migrate north to breed. However, the gradual draining of marshy ground, pesticides and electric cables have threatened their survival here. A programme to reintroduce them to the area has set up breeding centres, as at Molsheim and Turckheim, which means these striking birds can once again be seen in Alsace-Lorraine.

The 13th-century Chapelle des Templiers, with restored frescoes, in Metz

Place Stanislas in Nancy, with statue of Stanislas Leczinski, Duke of Lorraine and father-in-law of Louis XV

Nancy ❹

Meurthe-et-Moselle. 🏙 105,000.
🚆 🚍 🚌 🛈 14 pl Stanislas (03 83 35 22 41). 🅿 Tue–Sat. www.ot-nancy.fr

Lorraine's historic capital backs on to the Canal du Marne and the river Meurthe. In the 18th century, Stanislas Leczinski, Duke of Lorraine (see p302), transformed the city, making it a model of 18th-century town planning.

Nancy's second golden age was the turn of this century, when glassmaker Emile Gallé founded the Ecole de Nancy, a forerunner of the Art Nouveau movement in France.

Nancy's principal and most renowned landmark is **place Stanislas**. Laid out in the 1750s, this elegantly proportioned square is enclosed by highly ornate gilded wrought-iron gates and railings, beautifully restored in 2005. Lining the square are fine *hôtels particuliers* (town houses), and chic restaurants.

An Arc de Triomphe leads to Place de la Carrière, a gracious, tree-lined square. At the far end, flanked by semicircular arcades, is the Gothic **Palais du Gouvernement**. Next door in the Parc de la

Pépinière is Rodin's statue of Claude Lorrain, the landscape painter, born near Nancy.

The Grande Rue provides a glimpse of medieval Nancy. Of the original fortifications only the Porte de la Craffe remains, which was used as a prison after the Revolution.

🏠 Eglise et Couvent des Cordeliers et Musée Régional des Arts et Traditions Populaires
64 & 66 grande rue. **Tel** 03 83 32 18 74. ⬜ Wed–Mon. ⬛ 1 Jan, Easter Sun, 1 May, 14 Jul, 25 Dec. 🖼
The Dukes of Lorraine are buried in the crypt and the adjoining converted monastery contains the Musée Régional des Arts et Traditions Populaires, covering folklore, furniture, costumes and crafts.

🏛 Musée des Beaux Arts
3 pl Stanislas. **Tel** 03 83 85 30 72. ⬜ Wed–Mon. ⬛ some public hols. 🖼 ♿ 🎥
Recent renovation and a modern extension have enabled 40 per cent more of the museum's remarkable collection of 14th- to 20th-century European art to be seen, including works by Delacroix, Manet, Monet, Utrillo and Modigliani. The Daum glassware is stunning.

🏛 Musée Historique Lorraine
Palais Ducal, 64 grande rue.
Tel 03 83 32 18 74. ⬜ Wed–Mon. ⬛ 1 Jan, 1 May, 14 Jul, 1 Nov, 25 Dec. 🖼
The Museum of the History of Lorraine has a rich collection of archaeological finds, sculptures and paintings, including two by Georges de la Tour.

🏛 Musée de l'Ecole de Nancy
36–38 rue de Sergent Blandan.
Tel 03 83 40 14 86. ⬜ Wed–Sun. ⬛ 1 Jan, 1 May, 14 July, 1 Nov, 25 Dec. 🖼 🎥
Exhibits in reconstructed Art Nouveau settings include furniture, fabrics and jewellery, as well as the fanciful glassware of Emile Gallé, founder of the Ecole de Nancy.

Arc de Triomphe in place Stanislas, leading to place de la Carrière

Vosges landscape seen from the Route des Crêtes

THE ROUTE DES CRÊTES

This strategic mountain road, 83 km (50 miles) long, connects the Vosges valleys from Col du Bonhomme to Cernay, east of Thann, often through woodland. Hugging the western side of the Vosges, the Route des Crêtes was created during World War I to prevent the Germans from observing French troop movements. When not shrouded in mist, there are breathtaking views over Lorraine from its many "crests" (*crêtes*).

Gérardmer **❺**

Vosges. 👥 *10,000.* 🚌 🚲
ℹ️ *4 pl des Déportés (03 29 27 27
27).* 🛒 *Thu & Sat.* **www**.gerardmer.
net

Nestling on the Lorraine
side of the Vosges, on the
shore of a magnificent lake
stretching out before it,
Gérardmer is a setting rather
than a city. In November
1944, just before its liberation,
Gérardmer was razed by the
Nazi scorched-earth policy,
but has since been recon-
structed. Saw mills and woodcarving remain local trades,
though tourism is fast replacing the textile industry.

Gérardmer is now a popu-
lar holiday resort. In winter,
the steep slopes of the Vosges
Cristallines around the town
turn it into a ski resort, while
the lake is used for watersports in summer. The town's
attractions also include lakeside walks and boat trips, as
well as Géromée cheese, similar to the more famous
Munster, from just over the
Alsatian border. Gérardmer
also boasts the oldest tourist
information office in the
country, dating from 1875.

The scenic drives and
mountain hikes in the Vosges
attract adventurous visitors.
Most leave the lakeside bowl
to head for the Alsatian
border via the magnificent
Route des Crêtes, which can
be joined at the mountain
pass of Col de la Schlucht.

Recreating village crafts in Ecomusée d'Alsace in Ungersheim

Mulhouse **❻**

Haut Rhin. 👥 *125,000.* ✈️ 🚉 🚌
ℹ️ *9 av du Maréchal Foch (03 89 35
48 48).* 🛒 *Tue, Thu & Sat.*
www.tourisme-mulhouse.com

Close to the Swiss border,
Mulhouse is an industrial city,
badly damaged in World War
II. However, there are
technical museums and
shopping galleries, as well as
Alsatian taverns and Swiss
wine bars. Most visitors use
the city as a base for exploring the rolling hills of the
Sundgau on the Swiss border.

Of the museums, **Musée de
l'Impression sur Etoffes**, at 14
rue Jean-Jacques Henner,
is devoted to textiles and
fabric painting, while **Musée
Français du Chemin de Fer**, at
2 rue Alfred Glehn, has a

collection of steam and elec-
tric locomotives A revamped
**Musée National de l'Auto-
mobile**, at 192 avenue de
Colmar, boasts over 100
Bugattis, a clutch of Mercedes
and Ferraris and Charlie
Chaplin's Rolls Royce. In
Place de la République is the
Musée Historique, in the
Renaissance former town hall.

Alsatian black pig in Ecomusée
d'Alsace in Ungersheim

Environs
At Ungersheim, north of
Mulhouse, the **Ecomusée
d'Alsace** consists of rural
settings transplanted here to
preserve and display the
region's heritage. The 12th-
century fortified house from
Mulhouse is a dramatic building, complete with Gothic
garden. Farms are run along
traditional lines, with livestock
such as the Alsatian black pig.
Rural crafts can be seen in their
original settings.

🏛 **Ecomusée d'Alsace**
Chemin du Grosswald. **Tel** *03 89 74
44 74.* ⏰ *Apr–Nov: daily.* 📷 ♿ ▢

The lake at Gérardmer, offering sporting and leisure activities

Guebwiller ❼

Haut Rhin. 🏠 *11,800.* 🚌 ℹ️ *73
rue de la République (03 89 76 10 63).*
🏛️ *Tue & Fri.* **www.**florival.net

Surrounded by vineyards and
flower-filled valleys, Guebwiller is known as "the gateway to the valley of flowers".
However, as an industrial
town producing textiles and
machine tools, it feels cut off
from this rural setting. The
houses are dignified, but the
caves and churches make it
worth a visit.

Set on a pretty square, **Eglise
Notre-Dame** combines
Baroque theatricality with Neo-
Classical elegance, while
Eglise des Dominicains boasts
Gothic frescoes and a fine
rood screen. **Eglise St-Léger**,
the richly ornamented
Romanesque church, is the
most rewarding, especially the
façade, triple porch and portal.

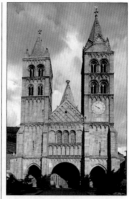

Eglise St-Léger in Guebwiller

Environs
The scenic Lauch valley, northwest of Guebwiller, is known
as "Le Florival" because of its
floral aspect. **Lautenbach** is
used as a starting point for
hikes through this recognized
zone de tranquillité. The

village has a pink Roman-
esque church, whose portal
depicts human passion and
the battle between Good and
Evil. The square leads to the
river, a small weir, *lavoir*
(public washing place) and
houses overhanging the water.

Neuf-Brisach ❽

Haut Rhin. 🏠 *2,100.* 🚌 ℹ️ *Palais
du Gouverneur, 6 pl d'Armes (03 89
72 56 66).* 🏛️ *1st & 3rd Mon of each
month.* **www.**tourisme-rhin.com

Situated near the German
border, this octagonal citadel
is the military strategist
Vauban's masterpiece. Built
between 1698 and 1707, the
citadel forms a typical star-
shaped pattern, with
symmetrical towers enclosing
48 equal squares. In the centre,
from where straight streets
radiate for ease of defence,

THE CITADEL OF NEUF-BRISACH

The outer ring of defences
was built around two moats.

Porte de Bâle

Place d'Armes,
once the parade
ground, provided the
innermost refuge.

**Porte de
Strasbourg**
was originally
protected
by a draw-
bridge.

Bastion

The fortress
is divided
into 48 îlôts
or squares.

The fortress walls
are 9 m (30 ft) high
and 4.5 m (14.5 ft)
wide at their base.

The Porte de Belfort
houses the Musée
Vauban. A walk links
Porte de Belfort with
Porte de Colmar.

Porte de Colmar

The celebrated Issenheim altarpiece by Matthias Grünewald in Colmar

is the place d'Armes and the Eglise St-Louis, which was added in 1731–6. This is the usual homage to Louis XV, implying that the church was dedicated to the King, rather than the saint.

The Porte de Belfort houses the **Musée Vauban**, which includes a model of the town, showing the outlying defences, now concealed by woodland. They represent Vauban's barrier to the fortress and it is to his credit that the citadel was never taken.

🏛 **Musée Vauban**
Pl Porte de Belfort. *Tel 03 89 72 03 93.* ⏱ May–Oct: Wed–Mon; Nov–Apr: groups only, by appt. 🎫 ♿

Eguisheim ⑨

Haut Rhin. 🏘 1,500. 🚃 ℹ 22a grand'rue (03 89 23 40 33). www.ot-eguisheim.fr

Eguisheim is a most exquisite small town, laid out within three concentric rings of 13th-century ramparts. The ensemble of austere fortifications and domestic elegance within makes for a surprisingly harmonious whole.

In the centre of town is the octagonal feudal **castle** of the Counts of Eguisheim. A Renaissance fountain in front has the statue of Bruno Eguisheim, born here in 1002. He became Pope Léon IX and was later canonized.

The grand'rue is lined with half-timbered houses, many showing their construction

date. Close to the castle is the **Marbacherhof**, a monastic tithe barn and cornhall. On a neighbouring square, the modern parish church retains the original Romanesque sculpted tympanum.

The rest of the town has its share of Hansel-and-Gretel atmosphere, while inviting courtyards offer tastings of *grands crus*. From rue de Hautvilliers, outside the ramparts, a marked path leads through scenic vineyards.

Colmar ⑩

Haut Rhin. 🏘 68,000. 🚃 🚌 ℹ 4 rue d'Unterlinden (03 89 20 68 92). 🗓 Mon, Wed, Thu & Sat. www.ot-colmar.fr

Colmar is the best preserved city in Alsace. As a trading post and river port, Colmar had its heyday in the 16th century, when wine merchants shipped their wine along the waterways running through

the picturesque canal quarter, now known as **Petite Venise**. "Little Venice" is best seen on a leisurely boat trip that takes you from the tanners' quarter to the Rue des Tanneurs. The adjoining Place de l'Alsacienne Douane is dominated by the **Koifhüs**, a galleried customs house with a Burgundian tiled roof, overlooking half-timbered pastel houses which sport sculpted pillars.

Nearby, the place de la Cathédrale quarter is full of 16th-century houses. **Eglise St-Martin**, essentially Gothic, has a noted south portal. To the west, the place des Dominicains, with cafés, is dwarfed by the Gothic **Eglise Dominicaine**. Inside is *La Vierge au Buisson de Roses* (1473), the red and gold "Virgin of the Rosebush" by Martin Schongauer, a renowned painter and native son of Colmar.

Place d'Unterlinden, the adjoining square, has the **Musée d'Unterlinden**. Set in a Dominican monastery, it displays early Rhenish paintings. The highlight is the Issenheim altarpiece. A masterpiece of emotional intensity, it is part of an early 16th-century Alsatian panel painting by Matthias Grünewald.

In the historic centre, the quaint rue des Têtes has the former wine exchange, a Renaissance town house known as the Maison des Têtes because of the grimacing heads on the gabled façade. And in rue Mercière, **Maison Pfister**, with its slender stair turret and galleried flower-decked façade, has come to typify the city.

Along the Quai de la Poissonerie in the Petite Venise area of Colmar

For hotels and restaurants in this region see pp561–2 and pp612–14

Riquewihr ⓫

Haut Rhin. 🏘 *1,100.* 🖃
🛈 *2 rue de 1ère Armée (03 89 49
08 40).* 🖃 *Fri.*
www.ribeauville-riquewihr.com

Vineyards run right up to the
ramparts of Riquewihr, the
prettiest village on the Route
du Vin *(see pp232–3)*. Deeply
pragmatic, Riquewihr
winemakers plant roses at the
end of each row of vines –
both for their pretty effect
and as early detectors of
parasites. The village belonged
to the Counts of Wurtemberg
until the Revolution and has
grown rich on wine, from
Tokay and Pinot Gris to
Gewürztraminer and Riesling.
Virtually an open-air museum,
Riquewihr abounds in
cobbled alleys, geranium-clad
balconies, galleried courtyards,
romantic double ramparts and
watchtowers.

From the Hôtel de Ville, the
rue du Général de Gaulle
climbs gently past medieval
and Renaissance houses, half-
timbered, stone-clad or
corbelled. Oriel windows vie
with sculpted portals and
medieval sign boards. On the

right lies the idyllic **place des
Trois Eglises**. A passageway
leads through the ramparts
to the vineyards on the hill.
Further up lies the **Dolder**, a
13th-century belfry, followed
by the **Tour des Voleurs** (both
are museums, the latter with a
medieval torture chamber),
marking the second tier of
ramparts. Beyond the gateway
is the **Cour des Bergers**,
gardens laid out around the
16th-century ramparts.
Visitors outnumber the locals,
in summer or during the
superb Christmas market.

The pretty – and popular – village
of Riquewihr, set among vineyards

Ribeauvillé ⓬

Haut Rhin. 🏘 *4,800.* 🚉 🖃
🛈 *1 grand'rue (03 89 49 08 40).* 🖃
Sat. **www**.ribeauville-
riquewihr.com

Overlooked by three ruined
castles, Ribeauvillé is stiflingly
prettified, as may be expected
from a favoured town on the
Route du Vin. This status is
partly due to healthy sales of
the celebrated *grands crus*
of Alsace, especially Riesling.
There are ample
opportunities for tastings,
particularly near the park, in
the lower part of town *(see
pp232–3)*.

On the grand'rue (No. 14)
is the **Pfifferhüs**, the minstrels'
house. As locals declare,
Ribeauvillé is the capital of the
kougelhopf, the almond-
flavoured Alsatian cake.

Tortuous alleys wind past
steep-roofed artisans' and
vignerons' houses in the upper
part of the town. Beyond are
Renaissance fountains, painted
façades and **St Grégoire-le-
Grand**, the Gothic parish
church. A marked path, which
begins in this part of town,
leads into the vineyards.

Château du Haut-Koenigsbourg ⓭

Orschwiller. **Tel** *03 88 82 50 60.*
⭕ *daily.* ⬤ *1 Jan, 1 May, 25 Dec.*
📷 ♿ 🏠 🍴
www.haut-koenigsbourg.fr

Looming above the pretty
village of St-Hippolyte, this
castle is the most popular
attraction in Alsace. In 1114,
the Swabian Emperor,
Frederick of Hohenstaufen,
built the first Teutonic castle
here, which was destroyed in
1462. Rebuilt and added to
under the Habsburgs, it
burned down in 1633. At the
end of the 19th century, Kaiser
Wilhelm II commissioned
Berlin architect Bodo Ebhardt
to restore the castle. The
result of his painstaking work
was a precise reconstruction
of the original building.

Despite a drawbridge, fierce
keep and rings of fortifications,
this warm sandstone hybrid is

too sophisticated for a feudal
château. The Cour d'Honneur
is a breathtaking re-creation,
with a pointed corner turret
and creaky arcaded galleries.
Inside are gloomy "Gothic"
chambers and "Renaissance"
rooms. La Grande Salle is the
most far-fetched, with a Neo-
Gothic gallery and ornate
panelling. From the

battlements, almost 750 m
(2,500 ft) above the Alsace
plain, stretches a Rhineland
panorama, bordered by the
Black Forest and the Alps. On
the other side are views,
from the high Vosges to
villages and vineyards
below.

Upper garden

West bastion

West wing

Outer walls

Chapelle St-Sébastien outside Dambach-la-Ville, along the Route du Vin

Sélestat ⑭

Bas Rhin. 🏘 17,000. 🚉 🚌 👔 *Commanderie Saint Jean, bd du Général Leclerc (03 88 58 87 20).* 🏪 *Tue, Sat.* www.selestat-tourisme.com

During the Renaissance, Sélestat was the intellectual centre of Alsace, with a tradition of humanism fostered by Beatus Rhenanus, a friend of Erasmus. The **Bibliothèque Humaniste** has a collection of editions of some of the earliest printed books, including the first book to name America, in 1507. Nearby are the Cour des Prélats, a turreted ivy-covered mansion, and the Tour de l'Horloge, a clocktower. **Eglise Ste-Foy** is 12th-century, with an octagonal belltower. Opposite is **Eglise St-Georges**, glittering with green and red "Burgundian tiles".

🏛 **Bibliothèque Humaniste**
1 rue de la Bibliothèque.
Tel 03 88 58 07 20.
⬜ *Mon, Wed–Sat am; (Jul–Aug: Wed–Mon exc. Sun am).* ⬤ *public hols.* 📷
www.ville-selestat.fr/bhselestat

Environs

Medieval **Dambach-la-Ville**, another pretty town, is linked to Andlau and red-tiled Itterswiller by a delightful rural road through vineyards.

Ebersmunster, a picturesque hamlet, has an onion-domed abbey church, whose Baroque interior is a sumptuous display of gilded stucco.

Obernai ⑮

Bas Rhin. 🏘 11,000. 🚉 🚌 👔 *pl du Beffroi (03 88 95 64 13).* 🏪 *Thu.* www.obernai.fr

At the north end of the Route du Vin, Obernai retains a flavour of authentic Alsace: residents speak Alsatian, at festivities women wear traditional costume, and church services are well-attended in the cavernous Neo-Gothic **Eglise St-Pierre-et-St-Paul**. The place du Marché is well-preserved, and features the gabled **Halle aux Blés**, a 16th-century corn hall (now a restaurant) above a former butcher's shop, with a façade adorned with cows' and dragons' heads. Place de la Chapelle, the adjoining square, has a Renaissance fountain and the 16th-century **Hôtel de Ville** and the **Kapellturm**, the galleried Gothic belfry. Side streets have Renaissance and medieval timber-framed houses. A stroll past the cafés on rue du Marché ends in a pleasant park by the ramparts.

Young *Alsaciens* in traditional costume

Environs

Odile, Alsace's seventh-century patron saint, was born in Obernai but she is venerated on **Mont Sainte-Odile**, to the west.

Molsheim, a former bishopric and fortified market town 10 km (6 miles) north, is noted for its Metzig, a Renaissance-style butchers' guildhall.

Le Mémorial de l'Alsace-Moselle at Schirmeck commemorates the 10,000 who died at the Struthof concentration camp across the valley.

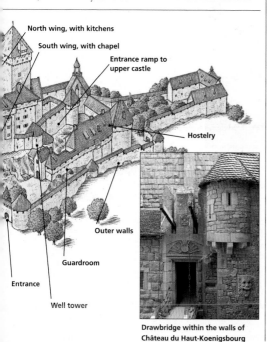

North wing, with kitchens
South wing, with chapel
Entrance ramp to upper castle
Hostelry
Outer walls
Guardroom
Entrance
Well tower

Drawbridge within the walls of Château du Haut-Koenigsbourg

For hotels and restaurants in this region see pp561–2 and pp612–14

Strasbourg ❻

Halfway between Paris and Prague, Strasbourg is not surprisingly often known as "the crossroads of Europe". The city wears its European cosmopolitanism with ease – after all, its famous cathedral has catered to both Catholic and Protestant congregations – and as one of the capitals of the European Union has sensibly located the futuristic European Parliament building some way from the historic centre. One of the ways to see this, along with the more traditional city sights, is to take a boat trip along the waterways encircling the Old Town. On the way you will take in the Ponts-Couverts, covered bridges linked by medieval watchtowers that provide an observation point for the four Ill canals, and the scenic Petite France, once the tanners' district, dotted with mills and criss-crossed by bridges.

Cathedral statue

Barge on the canal

The central portal of the west façade of the cathedral

🏛 Cathédrale Notre-Dame

A masterpiece of stone lacework, the sandstone cathedral "rises like a most sublime, wide-arching tree of God", as Goethe marvelled. Though construction began in the late 11th century (the choir is Romanesque, the nave is Gothic), it ended only in 1439, with the completion of the west façade, begun in 1277. The three portals are ornamented with statues. But the crowning glory is the rose window. The south portal leads to the Gothic Pillar of Angels (c. 1230), set beside the Astronomical Clock: mechanical figures appear accompanied by chimes at 12:31pm. There are wonderful views over the city from the viewing platform, and on some summer evenings there are organ concerts.

In place de la Cathédrale, Maison Kammerzell, now a popular restaurant, was once a rich merchant's mansion, its highly elaborate, carved façade dating from mid-15th–late-16th centuries.

🏛 Palais Rohan

2 pl du Château. **Tel** 03 88 52 50 00. ◻ Wed–Mon. ⬤ 1 Jan, Good Fri, 1 May, 1 & 11 Nov, 25 Dec. ⬚ ₺ www.musee-strasbourg.org

Designed by the king's architect, Robert de Cotte, in 1730, this grand Classical palace was intended for the Prince-Bishops of Strasbourg. It houses three museums: the Musée des Beaux Arts; the Musée Archéologique; and the Musée des Arts Décoratifs, which contains the sumptuous State Apartments and one of the finest collections of ceramics in France.

The Musée d'Art Moderne et Contemporain on Strasbourg's waterfront

VISITORS' CHECKLIST

Bas Rhin. 🏘 400,000.
✈ 12 km (7.5 miles) SW
Strasbourg. 🚃 pl de la Gare
(08 92 35 35 35). 🚌 pl des
Halles (03 88 23 43 23).
🛈 17 pl de la Cathédrale (03
88 52 28 28). 🛍 Wed, Fri.
🎻 International Music Festival
(Jun–Jul). www.ot-strasbourg.fr

has fascinating exhibits on local traditions and popular arts and crafts.

🏛 Musée de l'Oeuvre Notre-Dame

3 pl du Château. *Tel* 03 88 52 50 00. ⬜ Tue–Sun. 🌑 1 Jan, Good Fri, 1 May, 1 Nov, 25 Dec. 🎫 ♿ ground fl.

The cathedral's impressive museum contains much of its original sculpture, as well as magnificent 11th-century stained glass. This sombre gabled house also displays a collection of Medieval and Renaissance Alsatian art.

🏛 Musée d'Art Moderne et Contemporain

1 pl Hans-Jean Arp. *Tel* 03 88 23 31 31. ⬜ Tue–Sun. 🌑 1 Jan, Good Fri, 1 May, 1 & 11 Nov, 25 Dec. 🎫 ♿ 🍴 🎬 Concerts, cinema.

Adrien Fainsilber's cultural flagship for the 21st century is a marvel of glass and light (particularly at night when it appears to float on the river). Its superb collections run from 1860–1950 and from 1950 onwards. The Art Café is welcome respite for art-weary feet.

STRASBOURG CITY CENTRE

Ponts-Couverts ①
Petite France ②
Maison Kammerzell ③
Cathédrale Notre-Dame ④
Musée de l'Oeuvre
   Notre-Dame ⑤
Palais Rohan ⑥
Musée Alsacien ⑦

0 metres	250
0 yards	250

Key to Symbols see back flap

🏛 Musée Historique

3 pl de la Grande Boucherie. *Tel* 03 88 52 50 00. ⬜ Tue–Sun. 🌑 1 Jan, Good Fri, 1 May, 1 & 11 Nov, 25 Dec. 🎫 ♿

The museum occupies the 16th-century city abattoir and focuses on Strasbourg's political and military history.

🏛 Musée Alsacien

23 quai St-Nicolas. *Tel* 03 88 52 50 00. ⬜ Wed–Mon. 🌑 1 Jan, Good Fri, 1 May, 1 Nov, 25 Dec. 🎫

Housed in a series of interconnecting Renaissance buildings, the museum

Ponts-Couverts with medieval watchtowers over the canals

The Alsace Route des Vins

Meandering over 180 km (110 miles) from Marlenheim to Thann, the picturesque wine route takes in historic towns with cobbled streets, medieval timber-framed houses and Renaissance fountains. Romantically appointed *winstubs,* or cellars, offer traditional *choucroute garnie* and flowery white Alsatian wines.

Alsatian wine master

Dedicated wine lovers could spend two or three days covering the route at leisure, or may want to make shorter trips in either direction to or from Colmar. For a refreshing contrast from the unremitting charm of the towns and villages, escape occasionally into *sentiers viticoles* – lovely paths through the vineyards themselves.

Harvesting grapes in Alsace

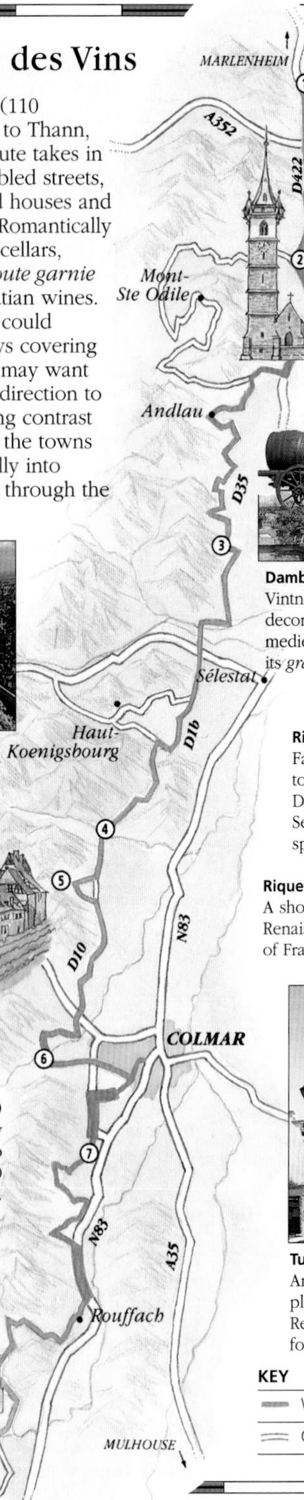

Molsheim ①
Renaissance building and Riesling vineyard vie for attention with Bugatti motor museum

Obernai ②
The galleried Kapellturm in the place du Marché dates from the 13th–16th centuries

Dambach-la-Ville ③
Vintner's carts now serve as decoration in this pretty medieval town renowned for its *grand cru* Frankstein.

Ribeauvillé ④
Famed for its Riesling, the town celebrates Pipers' Day, the first Sunday in September, with a fountain spouting free wine.

Riquewihr ⑤
A showcase of medieval and Renaissance houses, this is one of France's most visited towns

Turckheim ⑥
Ancient buildings encircle place Turenne in this Renaissance town famous for its Brand wine.

Eguisheim ⑦
This ancient town ringed by medieval houses produces two *grands crus*, Eichberg (Oak Hill) and Pfersigberg (Peach Hill).

Guebwiller ⑧
Eglise St-Léger dates from the Middle Ages, when Guebwiller grew rich on wine. Today it is a busy textile town.

MARLENHEIM

STRASBOURG →

Mont-Ste Odile

Andlau

Sélestat

Haut-Koenigsbourg

COLMAR

Rouffach

MULHOUSE

THANN

0 kilometres   5

0 miles   5

KEY

━━━ Wine route

═══ Other roads

The 12th-century chapel of the Château du Haut-Barr, near Saverne

Saverne ⑰

Bas Rhin. 🏘 *10,500.* 🚉 🚌
🛈 *37 grand rue (03 88 91 80 47).*
🗓 *Tue & Thu.* **www**.ot-saverne.fr

Framed by hills, and situated on the river Zorn and the Marne-Rhine canal, Saverne is a pretty sight. The town was a fief of the prince-bishops of Strasbourg and its sandstone Château des Rohan was a favourite summer residence. Today, it houses the **Musée du Château des Rohan**, whose collection traces Saverne's past. On the far side of the château, the grand'rue is studded with restaurants and timber-framed Renaissance houses.

🏛 **Musée du Château des Rohan**
Château des Rohan. *Tel 03 88 91 06 28.* ☐ *Mar–Nov: Wed–Mon pms (mid-Jun–mid-Sep: all day); Dec–Feb: Sun pm.* 🎫 🚫 restricted.

Environs
To the southwest, perched on a rocky spur, the ruined **Château du Haut-Barr** – once commanded the vital pass of Col de Saverne. In **Marmoutier**, 6 km (3.5 miles) further south, is a renowned abbey church with a Romanesque-Lombard façade and octagonal towers.

Betschdorf ⑱

Bas Rhin. 🏘 *3,600.* 🛈 *La Mairie (03 88 54 44 92).* **www**.betschdorf.com

The vibrant village of Betschdorf borders the Forêt de Haguenau, 45 km (27 miles) north of Strasbourg. Many residents occupy timber-framed houses dating from the 18th century, when pottery made the village prosperous. Generations of potters have passed down the knowledge of the characteristic blue-grey glaze to their sons, while the women have been entrusted with decorating it in cobalt blue. A pottery museum, with a workshop attached, displays rural ceramics.

Betschdorf pottery

Betschdorf is a good place to try *tartes flambées* – hot, crispy bases topped with cheese or fruit.

Environs
Another pottery village, **Soufflenheim**, lies 10 km (6 miles) southeast. Its earth-coloured pottery is usually painted with bold flowers. To the north, close to the German border, the picturesque town of **Wissembourg** has many half-timbered houses and the second-largest church in Alsace after Strasbourg Cathedral, Eglise St-Pierre et St-Paul.

WESTERN FRANCE

Introducing Western France

The western regions of France have played very different historical roles, from the royal heartland of the Loire Valley to separatist Celtic Brittany. These are mainly rich farming regions, with fishing important along the coasts. Heavy industry and oil refineries are concentrated around Rouen and Le Havre. Visitors come for the wonderful beaches, quiet rural byways and the sumptuous Loire châteaux. This map shows some of the region's most celebrated sights.

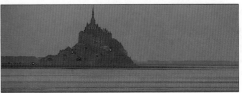

The evocative silhouette of Mont-St-Michel *has welcomed pilgrims since the 11th century. Today nearly one million visitors a year walk across the causeway to the island abbey* (see pp256–61).

Guimiliau Parish Close

Mont-St-Michel

BRITTANY
(See pp268–85)

Carnac Megaliths

The megaliths of Carnac *are evidence of early settlers in Brittany. These ancient granite blocks, arranged in intriguing patterns, date back to 4000 BC and are thought to have had a religious or astronomical purpose* (see p279).

The Bayeux Tapestry (see pp252–3) *shows William the Conqueror's invasion of England from the French point of view. Among its 58 scenes, key events such as the Battle of Hastings in 1066 are depicted with great vigour and finesse. Here, two of William's messengers are shown hurrying to meet him.*

Bayeux Tapestry

Rouen Cathedral

Château de Chambord *is the largest and most extravagant of the Loire châteaux* (see pp302–3). *François I transformed the original hunting lodge to a luxurious moated castle in 1519. Its splendour was completed by Louis XIV in 1685. Inside the 440 rooms are François' salamander emblem and 365 fireplaces, one for every day of the year.*

NORMANDY
(See pp246–67)

Chartres Cathedral

Le Mans Cathedral

Château de Chambord

Château de Villandry

Château de Chenonceau

THE LOIRE VALLEY
(See pp286–313)

| 0 kilometres | 50 |
| 0 miles | 50 |

The Flavours of Western France

The Atlantic coast, the rich agricultural hinterland of dairy farms, orchards and vegetable fields, and the rivers of the Loire Valley combine to produce some of France's best loved food. Vegetables are grown in abundance in Brittany and the alluvial soils of the Loire, and the orchards of Normandy are bountiful. Fish from the windswept coast of Brittany or the channel ports of Normandy play a key role in the cuisine. Hearty meat dishes range from the celebrated duck of Rouen to the rabbit and game of the Sologne in the Loire. Fine cheeses are made here, and butter is the favoured cooking medium.

Normandy apples

Norman cheese-producer displaying his wares

NORMANDY

Normandy's lush green pastures, dotted with brown and white cows, and orchards heavy with apples, make it a great source of veal, milk, cheese, cream, butter, apples and pears. Duck is a speciality, as is *pre-salé* lamb from the salt-rich marshes around Mont-St-Michel. Many vegetables are grown and wild mushrooms thrive in the damp meadows and woodlands in autumn. Fish is important, with catches of sole, plaice and mackerel, skate and herrings, and 80 per cent of France's scallops, plus a great variety of shellfish.

Camembert is Normandy's most famous cheese; others include Pont l'Evêque, the pungent-smelling Livarot, rich Brillat-Savarin and Petit-Suisse, a small, fresh white cheese eaten with sugar.

Apples symbolize Normandy above all, and cider is traditionally drunk with food while Calvados, the powerful apple brandy, is served with meals as *le trou normand*.

BRITTANY

Thousands of kilometres of coastline yield an abundance of fish and seafood. Oysters are highly prized, as are mussels, harvested both wild and cultivated. Other fish

Artichokes   **Asparagus**   **Watercress**

Shallots   **Broccoli**

Radishes

Some of the favourite vegetables of western France

REGIONAL DISHES AND SPECIALITIES

Fish dominates the menus here, most spectacularly in the *plateau de fruits de mer*, featuring oysters, crabs, langoustines, prawns, shrimps, cockles and clams, piled on a bed of ice. Oysters are served simply with lemon or shallot vinegar, but can also come stuffed, gratinéed or wrapped in pastry. Fresh fish may be grilled, baked in sea salt (*sel de Guérande* is the best) braised in cider or served with *beurre blanc* ("white butter" sauce with shallots, wine vinegar and cream). Lobster is often served *à l'Armoricaine*. *Cotriade*, the Breton fish stew, combines a selection of the catch of the day with onions and potatoes. *Moules marinières* (mussels steamed in white wine with shallots and butter) is the popular classic. As a change from fish, look for *gigot de sept heures* – lamb slowly pot-roasted for seven hours.

Pears

Homard à l'armoricaine
Lobster, served in a herby tomato and onion sauce, enriched with brandy.

Superb Breton oysters for sale at a regional fish market

caught include monkfish, tuna, sardines, scallops and lobster. Pig-rearing is important, so expect roast pork, smoked sausages, hams and *boudin noir* (black/blood pudding), delicious served with apples. A great delicacy is the *pre-salé* lamb from Ile de Ouessant, served with haricot beans. Artichokes are the symbol of Brittany, an indication of the importance of vegetables, especially winter produce like cauliflower, onions and potatoes.

Crêpes (pancakes), both sweet and savoury, are a key element of the Breton diet. They come as buckwheat *galettes* with savoury fillings such as ham, cheese, spinach or mushrooms, or as lacy light dessert versions with sweet fillings and known as *crêpes dentelles* (*dentelle* meaning "lace").

THE LOIRE VALLEY

This huge region takes pride in a truly diverse range of specialities. Grass-fed cattle are raised in Anjou, and sheep in the Berry region. Excellent free-range chick-

Cheese and charcuterie at Loches market in the Loire Valley

ens, *poulet fermier Loué*, are raised in Touraine and the Orléanais. The forests and lakes of the Sologne yield deer, wild boar, pheasant, partridge, hare and duck. Charcuterie includes *rillettes*, (shredded and potted pork), and ham from the Vendée. The Atlantic coast produces a variety of fish and the Loire itself is a source of pike, shad, tench, salmon, eels and lampreys. Mushrooms are cultivated in the limestone caves around Saumur, but of the many vegetables grown, best of all is Sologne asparagus. Superb goats' cheeses include St Maure de Touraine, ash-coated Valençay and the little Crottins de Chavignol.

ON THE MENU

Alose à l'oseille Shad in a sorrel sauce.

Côte de veau vallée d'Auge Veal in mushrooms, cream and cider or Calvados.

Far aux pruneaux Egg batter pudding baked with prunes.

Kig ha farz Meat and vegetable hotpot with buckwheat dumpling.

Marmite Dieppoise Assorted fish stewed in cider or white wine with cream.

Tergeule Creamy baked rice pudding with cinnamon.

Tripes à la Mode de Caen Tripe with calves' feet, onions or leeks, herbs and cider.

Sole Normande *Baked sole in sauce of egg and cream, garnished with mussels, oysters, mushrooms and prawns.*

Canard Rouennais *Duclair duck, part-roasted then finished in a rich sauce of duck liver and shallots.*

Tarte tatin *Caramelized upside-down apple tart, originally made at the Hotel Tatin in the Loire Valley.*

France's Wine Regions: the Loire

With a few exceptions, the Loire is a region of good rather than great wines. The fertile agricultural soils of the meandering flatlands of the "Garden of France" are fine for fruit and vegetables, less so for the production of great wines. The cool, northern, Atlantic-influenced climate nonetheless produces refreshing reds and summer rosés, both dry and lusciously sweet white wines and attractively bracing sparkling wines. Dry white wines are very much in the majority here, and are usually intended for early consumption, so vintages in the Loire tend to matter less than in the classic red wine regions.

Cabernet Franc, red grape of the Loire

LOCATOR MAP

☐ *Loire wine region*

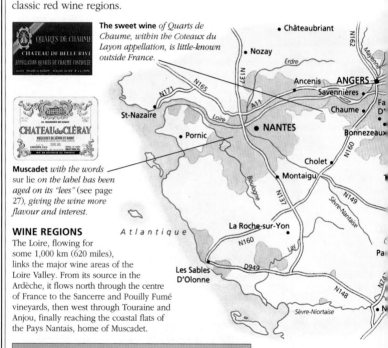

The sweet wine *of Quarts de Chaume, within the Coteaux du Layon appellation, is little-known outside France.*

Muscadet *with the words* sur lie *on the label has been aged on its "lees" (see page 27), giving the wine more flavour and interest.*

WINE REGIONS

The Loire, flowing for some 1,000 km (620 miles), links the major wine areas of the Loire Valley. From its source in the Ardèche, it flows north through the centre of France to the Sancerre and Pouilly Fumé vineyards, then west through Touraine and Anjou, finally reaching the coastal flats of the Pays Nantais, home of Muscadet.

Clos de l'Echo, Chinon, producer of fine, herbaceous red wine

KEY

☐ Pays Nantais

☐ Anjou-Saumur

☐ Haut-Poitou

☐ Touraine

☐ Central Vineyards

0 kilometres   15

0 miles   15

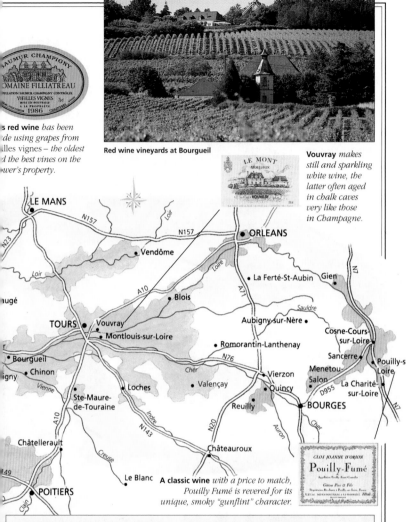

s red wine *has been
de using grapes from
lles vignes – the oldest
I the best vines on the
wer's property.*

Red wine vineyards at Bourgueil

Vouvray *makes
still and sparkling
white wine, the
latter often aged
in chalk caves
very like those
in Champagne.*

LE MANS

Vendôme

ORLEANS

La Ferté-St-Aubin   Gien

augé

Blois

TOURS   Vouvray

Montlouis-sur-Loire

Aubigny-sur-Nère

Cosne-Cours-
sur-Loire

Romorantin-Lanthenay

Bourgueil

Sancerre   Pouilly-s
Loire

igny   Chinon

Vierzon

Menetou-
Salon

La Charité-
sur-Loire

Loches   Valençay

Quincy

Ste-Maure-
de-Touraine

Reuilly   BOURGES

Châtellerault

Châteauroux

Le Blanc   **A classic wine** *with a price to match,
Pouilly Fumé is revered for its
unique, smoky "gunflint" character.*

POITIERS

KEY FACTS ABOUT LOIRE WINES

Location and Climate
Fertile agricultural soils support
fruit, vegetables and cereals; the
poorer soils support grapes. The
climate is cool, influenced by the Atlantic,
giving the wines a refreshing acidity.

Grape Varieties
The **Melan de Bourgogne** makes
simple, dry white wines. The
Sauvignon makes gooseberryish,
flinty dry whites, finest in Sancerre and
Pouilly Fumé but also good in Touraine.
The **Chenin Blanc** makes dry and medium
Anjou, Savennières, Vouvray, Montlouis
and Saumur, sparkling Vouvray and Saumur,
and the famous sweet whites, Bonnezeaux,

Vouvray and Quarts de Chaume.
Summery reds are made from the
Gamay and the fruity,
herbaceous **Cabernet Franc.**

Good Producers
Muscadet: Sauvion, Guy Bossard,
Luneau-Papin. *Anjou, Savennières,
Vouvray:* Richou, Ogereau, Nicolas
Joly, Huet, Domaine des
Aubuissières, Bourillon-Dorléans, Jacky Blot,
Domaine Gessey. *Touraine* (white): Château
de Chenonceaux. *Saumur-Champigny* (red):
Filliatreau, Chateâu du Hureau. *Chinon,
Bourgueil:* Couly-Dutheil, Yves Loiseau. *San-
cerre, Pouilly Fumé, Ménétou-Salon:* Francis
Cotat, Vacheron, Mellot, Vincent Pinard.

From Defence to Decoration

The great châteaux of the Loire Valley gradually evolved from purely defensive structures to decorative palaces. With the introduction of firearms, castles lost their defensive function and comfort and taste predominated. Defensive elements like towers, battlements, moats and gatehouses were retained largely as symbols of rank and ancestry. Renaissance additions, like galleries and dormer windows, added elegance.

Salamander emblem of François 1

Slate and stone walls

Fortifications with pepper-pot towers removed

Circular tower, formerly defensive

Corbelled walkways, once useful in battle

Angers (see p291), *a fortress built from 1230–40 by Louis IX, stands on a rocky hill in the town centre. In 1585, Henri III removed the pepper-pot shaped towers from 17 fortifications which were formerly 30 m (98 ft) high.*

Chaumont (see p306) *was rebuilt in 1445–1510 in Renaissance style by the Amboise family. Although it has a defensive appearance, with circular towers, corbelled walkways and a gatehouse, these features are mainly decorative. It was restored after c.1833.*

Decorated turret

Azay-le-Rideau (see p296), *regarded as one of the most elegant and well-designed Renaissance châteaux, was built by finance minister Gilles Berthelot (1518–1527) and his wife Philippa Lesbahy. It is a mixture of traditional turrets with Renaissance pilasters and pinnacles. Most dramatic is the interior staircase with its three storeys of twin bays and an intricately decorated pediment.*

Renaissance carved windows

Pilasters (columns)

Cylindrical tower

Dormer windows

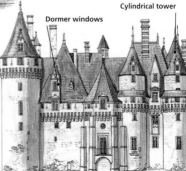

Ussé (see p295) *was built in 1462 by Jean de Bueil as a fortress with parapets containing openings for missiles, battlements and gunloops. The Espinay family, chamberlains to both Louis XI and Charles VIII, bought the château and changed the walls overlooking the main court-yard to Renaissance style with dormer windows and pilasters. In the 17th century the north wing was demolished to create palatial terraces.*

Breton Traditions

Brittany was christened Breiz Izel (Little Britain) by the Welsh and Cornish migrants who fled here in the 5th and 6th centuries AD and imposed their customs, language and religion on the local Gauls. Brittany resisted Charlemagne, the Vikings, the Normans, English alliances and even French rule until 1532. Today, Breton is taught in some schools, and a busy calendar keeps Brittany in touch with its past and with other Celtic regions.

Breton music *has strong Celtic links. Instruments like the* biniou, *similar to the bagpipes, and the oboe-like* bombarde *are often heard at local festivals.*

Bigouden lace headdresses

A pardon *is an annual religious festival honouring a local saint. The name derives from the granting of indulgences to pardon the sins of the past year. Some* pardons, *like those at Ste-Anne d'Auray and Ste-Anne-la-Palud, still attract thousands of pilgrims who carry banners and holy relics through the streets. Most* pardons *take place between April and September.*

Lace *coiffe*   Felt hat   Linen *coiffe*   Small headdress

Wooden clogs

Embroidered apron

Baggy Breton trousers

Breton costumes, *still seen at pardons and weddings, varied as each area had distinctive headdresses or* coiffes. *Artists like Gauguin often painted the costumes. There are good museum collections in Quimper (see p274) and Pont l'Abbé in Pays Bigouden (see p273).*

Brittany's Coastal Wildlife

With its granite cliffs, sweeping bays, rias and deep estuaries, the Brittany coastline contains a wealth of varied wildlife habitats. Parts of the coast have a tidal range of more than 50 m (150 ft), the highest in France, and this great variation in sea level divides marine life into several distinct zones. Most of the

Starfish region's famous shellfish, including mussels, clams, and oysters, live on the lower shore, either on rocks or in muddy sand where they are submerged for most of the day. Higher zones are the preserve of limpets and barnacles and several kinds of seaweed which can survive out of the water for long periods. Above the sea, towering cliffs offer a nursery for seabirds and a foothold for many kinds of wild flowers.

Cliffs at the Pointe du Raz, Brittany

The Ile de Bréhat at low tide

FEATURES OF THE COAST
This scene shows some of the wildlife habitats found on the Brittany coastline. When exploring the shore, make a note of the tide times, particularly if you plan to walk along the foot of the cliffs.

Salt-marsh flowers are their best in late summe

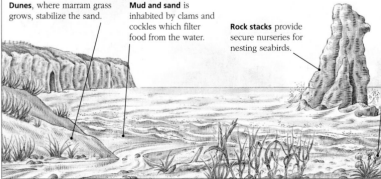

Dunes, where marram grass grows, stabilize the sand.

Mud and sand is inhabited by clams and cockles which filter food from the water.

Rock stacks provide secure nurseries for nesting seabirds.

OYSTER BEDS

Like most marine molluscs, oysters begin their lives as tiny floating larvae. The first step in *ostréiculture*, or oyster cultivation, consists of providing the larvae with somewhere to settle, which is usually a stack of submerged tiles. The developing oysters are later transferred to beds and left to mature before being collected for the market.

Oyster beds at Cancale

Clifftop turf often contains a narrow band of wild flowers sandwiched between fields and the sea.

Rockpools are flooded twice daily by the tide. They are inhabited by fish, molluscs, sea anemones, and sponges.

COASTAL WILDLIFE

The structure of this shore determines the wildlife that lives on it. In a world beset by wind and waves, rocks provide solid anchorage for plants and a secure habitat for many small animals. Muddy sand is rich in nutrients, and has a greater abundance of life – although most of this is concealed beneath the surface.

Cliffs

The rock dove *is a cliff-dwelling ancestor of the well-known city pigeon.*

Thrift *is a common spring flower, found on exposed ledges near the sea.*

Rocks and Rockpools

Seaweed *of many different varieties is exposed each day by the falling tide.*

The limpet, *a slow-moving creature, scrapes tiny plants from the rock surface.*

The goby, *with its sharp eyesight, dashes for cover at the first sign of movement above.*

Crabs *live at many different water depths. Some species are extremely good swimmers.*

Mud and Sand

Cockles *live in large numbers just beneath the surface of muddy sand.*

The curlew *has a forceps-like curved beak for extracting shellfish from mud and sand.*

NORMANDY

EURE · SEINE-MARITIME · MANCHE · CALVADOS · ORNE

The quintessential image of Normandy is of a lush, pastoral region of apple orchards and contented cows, cider and pungent cheeses – but the region also spans the windswept beaches of the Cotentin and the wooded banks of the Seine valley. Highlights include the great abbey churches of Caen, the mighty island of Mont-St-Michel and Monet's garden at Giverny.

Normandy gets its name from the Viking Norsemen who sailed up the river Seine in the 9th century. Pillagers turned settlers, they made their capital at Rouen – today a cultured cathedral city that commands the east of the region. Here the Seine meanders seaward past the ancient abbeys at Jumièges and St-Wandrille to a coast that became an open-air studio for Impressionist painters during the mid- and late 19th century.

North of Rouen are the chalky cliffs of the Côte d'Albâtre. The mood softens at the port of Honfleur and the elegant resorts of the Côte Fleurie to the west. Inland lies the Pays d'Auge, with its half-timbered manor houses and patch-eyed cows. The western half of Normandy is predominantly rural, a *bocage* countryside of small, high-hedged fields with windbreaks composed of beech trees.

The modern city of Caen is worth visiting for its two great 11th-century abbey churches built by William the Conqueror and his queen, Matilda. Close by in Bayeux, the story of William's invasion of England is told in detail by the town's famous tapestry. Memories of another invasion, the D-Day Landings of 1944, still linger along the Côte de Nacre and the Cotentin Peninsula. Thousands of Allied troops poured ashore on to these magnificent beaches in the closing stages of World War II. The Cotentin Peninsula is capped by the port of Cherbourg, still a strategic naval base. At its western foot stands one of France's greatest attractions: the monastery island of Mont-St-Michel.

Half-timbered manor house in the village of Beuvron-en-Auge, near Lisieux

◁ Rich pastures and brown and white Norman cattle, the traditional wealth of the province

Exploring Normandy

Normandy's rich historical sights and diverse landscape make it ideal for touring by car or bicycle.
Rewarding coastal drives and good beaches can be
found along the windswept Côte d'Albâtre and the
Cotentin Peninsula. Further south is one of France's
most celebrated sights, Mont-St-Michel. Inland,
follow the meanders of the Seine valley, passing cider
orchards and half-timbered houses along the way, to
visit historic Rouen and Monet's garden at Giverny.

Apple trees in blossom in the Pays d'Auge

KEY

Motorway
Major road
Secondary road
Minor road
Scenic route
Main railway
Minor railway
Regional border

Cap de la Hague
Beaumont-Hague
Barfleur
CHERBOURG
COTENTIN
Les Pieux
Saint-Vaast-la-Hougue
Valognes
D902
N13
D650
Sainte-Mère-Église
D2
D14
CÔTE DE NACRE
Arromanches-les-Bains
Grandcamp-les-Bains
Carentan
BAYEUX
Luc-sur-Mer
D514
Saint-Jean-de-Daye
Lessay
Vire
D572
N13
Saint-Lô
Balleroy
Marigny
D971
Caumont-l'Éventé
Évrecy
Agon-Coutainville
COUTANCES
N174
D13
A84
D577
Bréhal
Percy
BASSE-NORM
D971
Gavray
Vire
Clécy
GRANVILLE
Saint-Pair-sur-Mer
Villedieu-les-Poêles
Vassy
Flers
Sartilly
La Haye-Pesnel
Tinchebray
D924
Brécey
Collines de Normandie
PARC RÉGIONA
MONT-ST-MICHEL
AVRANCHES
D977
Mortain
Dinan
Ducey
Saint-Hilaire-du-Harcouët
Domfront
A84
Saint-James
Le Teilleul
Juvigny-sous-Andaine
N176

SIGHTS AT A GLANCE

Rennes

The Côte d'Albâtre coastline

GETTING AROUND

Access to and through the region from Calais is quick and direct on the A28–A29, which links up with the A13 motorway to Paris, and runs west to Caen, and beyond on the A84. There are also main road and rail links to the cross-Channel ports of Dieppe, Le Havre, Caen (Ouistreham) and Cherbourg. Travel by public transport beyond these arteries is limited. The region is threaded with minor roads, particularly delightful in the Pays d'Auge and Cotentin Peninsula. The main airports are Rouen, Le Havre and Caen.

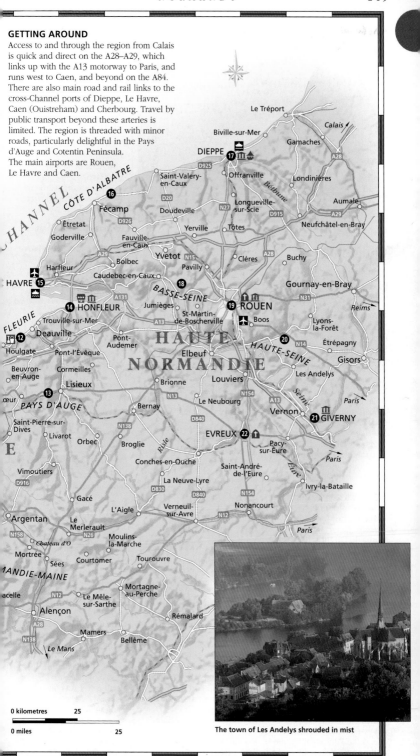

The town of Les Andelys shrouded in mist

0 kilometres 25

0 miles 25

Rugged cliffs on the Cotentin Peninsula

Cotentin ❶

Manche. 🚶 🚌 🚉 ⛴ *Cherbourg.*
ℹ *2 quai Alexandre III (02 33 93 52 02).* **www.**manchetourisme.com

Thrusting into the English Channel, the Cotentin Peninsula has a landscape similar to Brittany's. Its long sandy beaches have wild and windblown headlands around Cap de la Hague and Nez de Jobourg. The latter is a worthwhile goal for bird-watchers – gannets and shearwaters fly by in large numbers. Along the east coast stretch the expansive sands of Utah Beach, where American troops landed as part of the Allied invasion on 6 June 1944. Inland, Ste-Mère-Eglise commemorates these events with its poignant **Musée Airborne** (Airborne Troops Museum). Just outside Ste-Mère-Eglise, the **Ferme Musée du Cotentin** has farm animals and activities which give an insight into rural life in the early 1900s, while further north in the market town of Valognes the **Musée Régional du Cidre et du Calvados** celebrates the thriving local talent for making cider and Calvados.

Two fishing ports command the Peninsula's northeast corner: Barfleur and St-Vaast-la-Hougue, the latter famous for oysters and a base for boat trips to the Ile de Tatihou. The Val de Saire is ideal for a scenic drive, with a view point at La Pernelle the best place to survey the coast. On the west side of the Peninsula, warmed by the Gulf Stream, the resort of Barneville-Carteret offers sandy beaches and summer boat trips to the Channel Islands. The low-lying, marshy landscape east of Carentan forms the heart of the Parc Régional des Marais du Cotentin et du Bessin.

🏛 Musée Airborne
14 rue Eisenhower, Ste-Mère-Eglise. **Tel** 02 33 41 41 35. ◯ Feb–Nov: daily. ● Dec–Jan. 🎟 ♿
www.airborne-museum.org

🏛 Ferme Musée du Cotentin
Rte de Beauvais, Ste-Mère-Eglise. **Tel** 02 33 95 40 20. ◯ Jun–Sep: daily; Feb sch hols–May & Oct sch hols: daily pms. 🎟

🏛 Musée Régional du Cidre et du Calvados
Rue du Petit-Versailles, Valognes. **Tel** 02 33 40 22 73. ◯ Apr–Sep: Wed–Mon (Jul & Aug: daily). ● Sun am. 🎟

Cherbourg ❷

Manche. 🏘 *44,100.* 🚶 🚌 🚉 ⛴ ℹ *2 quai Alexandre III (02 33 93 52 02).* 🛒 Tue, Thu & Sat.
www.ot-cherbourg-cotentin.fr

Cherbourg has been a strategic port and naval base since the mid-19th century. The French Navy still uses its harbours, as do transatlantic ships and cross-Channel ferries from England and Ireland. For a good view of the port, drive to the hilltop **Fort du Roule**, which houses the **Musée de la Libération**, recalling the D-Day invasion and the subsequent liberation of Cherbourg. Most activity is centred on the flower-filled market square, place Général de Gaulle, and along shopping streets such as rue Tour-Carrée and rue de la Paix. The fine art in the **Musée Thomas-Henry** includes 17th-century Flemish works, and portraits by Jean François Millet, born in Gréville-Hague. **Parc Emmanuel Liais** has small botanical gardens and a densely packed **Musée d'Histoire Naturelle**.

The **Cité de la Mer**, opened in 2002, has a cylindrical deep-sea aquarium, the world's largest visitable submarine and many other wonders.

🏛 Musée de la Libération
Fort du Roule. **Tel** 02 33 20 14 12. ◯ May–Sep: Mon pm–Sat & Sun pm; Oct– Apr: Wed–Sun pms & pub hols 🎟 ♿

🏛 Musée Thomas-Henry
Rue Vastel. **Tel** 02 33 23 39 30. ◯ May–Sep: daily; Oct–Apr: Wed–Sun pms. ● public hols. 🎟 ♿

🏛 La Cité de la Mer
Gare Maritime Transatlantique. **Tel** 02 33 20 26 26. ◯ daily. ● 25 Dec, 1 Jan, 3 wks Jan. 🎟 🍴 📷 🛒 www.citedelamer.com

Cherbourg town centre

Coutances ❸

Manche. 🏘 *11,500.* 🚌 🚉 ℹ *pl Georges Leclerc (02 33 19 08 10).* 🛒 Thu. **www.**coutances.fr

From Roman times until the Revolution, the hill-top town of Coutances was the capital of the Cotentin. The slender **Cathédrale Notre-Dame**, a fine example of Norman Gothic architecture, has a soaring 66 m (217 ft) lantern tower. Founded in the 1040s by Bishop Geoffroi de Montbray, it was financed by the local de Hauteville family using monies gained in Sicily where they had founded a kingdom a few years earlier. The town was badly damaged during World War II but the cathedral, the churches of St Nicholas and St Peter, and the beautiful public gardens with their rare plants, all survived.

The back of Coutances cathedral with its squat lantern tower

Granville ❹

Manche. 🏠 *13,500.* 🚊 🚌 🚢
ℹ️ *4 cours Jonville (02 33 91 30 03).*
📅 *Wed, Sat.* **www**.ville-granville.fr

Ramparts enclose the upper town of Granville, which sits on a spur overlooking the Baie du Mont-St-Michel. The walled town was developed from fortifications built by the English in 1439.

The **Musée de Vieux Granville**, in the town gate-house, recounts Granville's long-seafaring tradition. The chapel walls of the **Eglise de Notre-Dame** are lined with tributes from local fishermen to their patroness, Notre-Dame du Cap Lihou.

The lower town is an old-fashioned seaside resort with a casino, promenades and public gardens. From the port there are boat trips to the Iles Chausey, a scattering of low-lying granite islands.

Le Musée Christian Dior is housed in Les Rhumbs, the fashion designer's childhood home, surrounded by a beautiful cliff garden.

🏛 **Musée de Vieux Granville**
2 rue Lecarpentier.
***Tel** 02 33 50 44 10.* ◯ *Apr–Sep; Wed–Mon; Oct– Mar: Wed, Sat & Sun pms.* ● *1 Nov, 22 Dec–Jan.* 🎟

🏛 **Musée Christian Dior**
Villa les Rhumbs. ***Tel** 02 33 61 48 21.* ◯ *mid-May–Sep:daily; gardens open all year.* 🎟

D-DAY LANDINGS

In the early hours of 6 June 1944, Allied forces began landing on the shores of Normandy, the first step in a long-planned invasion of German-occupied France, known as Operation Overlord. Parachutists were dropped near Ste-Mère-Eglise and Pegasus Bridge, and sea-borne assaults were made along a string of code-named beaches. US troops landed on Utah and Omaha in the west, while British and Canadian troops, which included a contingent of Free French commandos, landed at Gold, Juno and Sword. Over sixty years on, the beaches are still referred to by their code names.

American troops coming ashore during the Allied invasion of France

Pegasus Bridge, where the first French house was liberated, is a natural starting point for a tour around the sights and memorials. Further west, evocative ruins of the artificial harbour towed across from England survive at Arromanches-les-Bains.

There are British, German and American war cemeteries at La Cambe, Ranville and St-Laurent-sur-Mer. War museums at Bayeux, Caen, St-Mère-Eglise and Cherbourg provide background on D-Day and the ensuing Battle for Normandy.

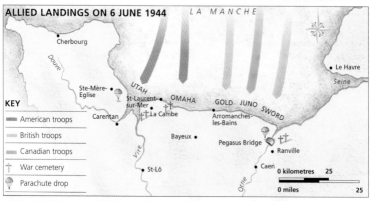

ALLIED LANDINGS ON 6 JUNE 1944   LA MANCHE

Cherbourg

Douve

Ste-Mère-Eglise

St-Laurent-sur-Mer   UTAH   OMAHA   GOLD   JUNO   SWORD

Le Havre

Seine

Carentan   La Cambe   Arromanches-les-Bains

Bayeux

Pegasus Bridge

Ranville

KEY
▬ American troops
▬ British troops
▬ Canadian troops
✝ War cemetery
⚑ Parachute drop

Vire

St-Lô

Caen

Orne

0 kilometres   25
0 miles   25

By the end of D-Day, over 135,000 men had been brought ashore, with losses totalling around 10,000.

Avranches ⑤

Manche. 🏛 *9,500.* 🚌 🚉 ℹ️ *2 rue
Général-de-Gaulle (02 33 58 00 22).*
📧 *Sat.* **www.**ot-avranches.com

Avranches has been a re-
ligious centre since the 6th
century and is the final staging-
post for visitors to the abbey on
Mont-St-Michel. The origins of
the famous abbey lie in a vision
experienced by Aubert, the
Bishop of Avranches. One night
in 708 the Archangel Michael
instructed him to build a church
on the nearby island. Aubert's
skull, with the finger-hole made
in it by the angel, can be seen
in the treasury of **St-Gervais**
in Avranches. The best views
of Mont-St-Michel are from
the **Jardin des Plantes**. After
the Revolution, 203 illuminated manuscripts were rescued
from Mont-St-Michel's abbey.
These and some 14,000 others
are held in the **Musée des
Manuscrits du Mont-St-Michel.**
The **Musée Municipal** illustrates life in the Cotentin over
the centuries, with a model of
Avranches cathedral, which
was pulled down in 1794. Just
outside town is the **Musée de
la Seconde Guerre Mondiale.**

🏛 **Musée des Manuscrits du
Mont-St-Michel**
Pl d'Estouteville. **Tel** 02 33 79 57 00.
⬤ *Tue–Sun.* ⬤ *Jan, 1 May, 1 Nov,
25 Dec.* 📷

🏛 **Musée Municipal**
Place Jean de Saint-Avit. **Tel** 02 33
68 35 83. ⬤ *Jun–Sep: daily.* 📷

Remains of Mulberry Harbour from World War II off the Côte de Nacre

Mont-St-Michel ⑥

See pp256–9.

Côte de Nacre ⑦

Calvados. ✈️ *Caen.* 🚌 🚉 *Caen,
Bayeux.* ⛴️ *Caen-Ouistreham.*
ℹ️ *pl St-Pierre, Caen (02 31 27 14
14).* 📧 *Sun.* **www.**tourisme-caen.fr

The stretch of coast between
the mouths of the rivers Orne
and Vire was dubbed the
Côte de Nacre (Mother of
Pearl Coast) in the 19th
century. More recently it has
become known as the site of
the D-Day Landings when
Allied troops poured ashore
at the start of Operation
Overlord *(see p251).* The
associated cemeteries,
memorials and museums, and
the remnants of the Mulberry

Harbour at Arromanches-les-
Bains, provide focal points
for a visit. However, the
coastline is equally popular as
a summer holiday destination,
offering long, sandy beaches
backed by seaside resorts
such as Courseulles-sur-Mer
and Luc-sur-Mer, which are
more relaxed than the resorts
of the Côte Fleurie further east.

Bayeux ⑧

Calvados. 🏛 *15,500.* 🚌 🚉 ℹ️
Pont-St-Jean (02 31 51 28 28). 📧 *Sat,
Wed.* **www.**bayeux-bessin-
tourism.com

Bayeux was the first town to
be liberated by the Allies in
1944 and fortunate to escape
war damage. Today, an
attractive nucleus of 15th–
19th-century buildings remains

BAYEUX TAPESTRY

A lively comic strip justifying William the Conqueror's
invasion of England, this 70-m (230-ft) long embroidered hanging was commissioned by Bishop
Odo of Bayeux. Offering insights into 11th-century
life, and an action-packed account of Harold, King of
England's defeat at the Battle of Hastings, the tapestry
is valued as a work of art, an historical document,
an early example of spin and an entertaining read.

Harold's retinue sets off for France
to inform William that he will
succeed to the English throne.

Trees with interlacing branches
are sometimes used to divide
the tapestry's 58 scenes.

around its central high streets, rue St-Martin and rue St-Jean. The latter is lined with shops and cafés.

Above the town rise the spires and domed lantern tower of the Gothic **Cathédrale Notre-Dame**. Beneath its interior is an 11th-century crypt decorated with restored 15th-century frescoes of angels playing musical instruments. The original Romanesque church that stood here was consecrated in 1077, and it is likely that Bayeux's famous tapestry was commissioned for this occasion by one of its key characters, Bishop Odo.

The tapestry is displayed in a renovated seminary, **Centre Guillaume-le-Conquérant-Tapisserie de Bayeux**, which gives a detailed audio-visual explanation of events leading up to the Norman conquest. On the southwest side of the town, the restored **Musée Mémorial de la Bataille de Normandie** traces the events of the Battle of Normandy in World War II, with an excellent film compilation made from contemporary newsreels.

🏛 **Centre Guillaume-le-Conquérant-Tapisserie**
Rue de Nesmond. **Tel** 02 31 51 25 50. ☐ daily. ● 1–2 Jan, 25–26 Dec. 🎧 ♿

🏛 **Musée Mémorial de la Bataille de Normandie**
Bd Fabian-Ware. **Tel** 02 31 51 46 90. ☐ daily. ● 1 Jan, 25–26 Dec, last 2 wks Jan. 🎧 ♿

The Abbaye aux Hommes in Caen

Caen ❾

Calvados. 🏠 117,200. ✈ 🚆 🚌 🚢
ℹ pl St-Pierre (02 31 27 14 14). 🛒
Fri & Sun. **www**.ville-caen.fr

In the mid-11th century Caen became the favoured residence of William the Conqueror and Queen Matilda, and despite the destruction of three-quarters of the city during World War II, much remains of their creation. The monarchs built two great abbeys and a castle on the north bank of the river Orne, bequeathing Caen a core of historic interest that justifies penetrating its industrial estates and postwar housing.

Much-loved by the citizens of Caen, the **Eglise St-Pierre** was built on the south side of the castle in the 13th–14th centuries, with an impressively ornate Renaissance east end added in the early 16th century. The frequently copied 14th-century belltower was destroyed in 1944 but has now been restored. To the east, rue du Vaugueux is the central street in Caen's small Vieux Quartier (Old Quarter). Now pedestrianized, the street still has some lovely half-timbered buildings. A walk west, along rue St-Pierre or boulevard du Maréchal Leclerc, leads to the city's main shopping district.

The English have a last meal on land before boarding with hunting dogs and falcons.

Wide moustaches distinguish the English characters from the clean-shaven Normans.

The coloured wool used to embroider the linen has faded little since the 11th century.

Latin inscriptions caption each main scene in the work and embody the heroic ideals shared by all the participants.

Borders provide wry comment through fables and asides.

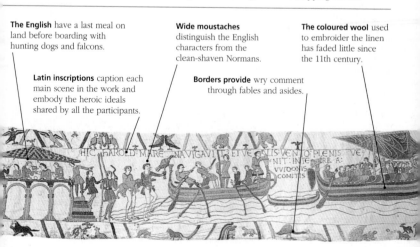

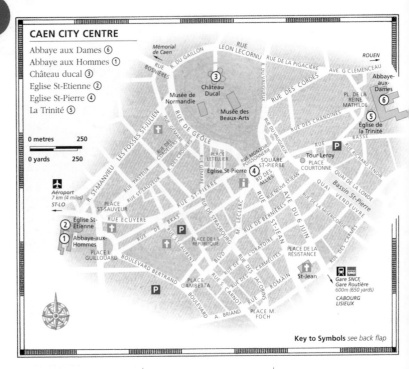

CAEN CITY CENTRE

Abbaye aux Dames ⑥
Abbaye aux Hommes ①
Château ducal ③
Eglise St-Etienne ②
Eglise St-Pierre ④
La Trinité ⑤

0 metres 250
0 yards 250

Abbaye-aux-Hommes

Esplanade Jean-Marie Louvel. **Tel** 02 31 30 42 81. ☐ daily. ● 1 Jan, 1 May, 25 Dec. 🔗 & restr. 📷 oblig.
Work began on William's Abbey for Men in 1063 and was almost complete by his death 20 years later. The abbey church, **Eglise St-Etienne**, is a masterpiece of Norman Romanesque, with a severe, unadorned west front crowned with 13th-century spires. The sparingly decorated nave was roofed in the early 12th century with stone vaulting that anticipates the Gothic style.

Abbaye-aux-Dames

Pl de la Reine Mathilde. **Tel** 02 31 06 98 98. ☐ daily. ● 1 Jan, 1 May, 25 Dec. 📷 oblig. &
Like William's Abbaye-aux-Hommes, Matilda's Abbey for Women also has a Norman Romanesque church, **La Trinité**, flanked by 18th-century buildings. Begun in 1060, it was consecrated six years later. Queen Matilda lies buried in the choir under a slab of black marble, and her beautifully restored abbey, with its creamy Caen stone, makes a serene, dignified mausoleum.

Château ducal

Esplanade du Château. **Musée des Beaux Arts Tel** 02 31 30 47 70. **Musée de Normandie Tel** 02 31 30 47 50. **Museums** ☐ Wed–Mon. ● 1 Jan, Easter, 1 May, Ascension, 1 Nov, 25 Dec. 🔗 &
The ruins of Caen's castle, one of the largest fortified enclosures in Europe, offer spacious lawns, museums and rampart views. A wide-ranging fine art collection, strong on 17th-century French and Italian painting, is exhibited in the **Musée des Beaux Arts**. The **Musée de Normandie** recalls traditional life in the region with utensils and displays on farming and lace.

Mémorial de Caen

Esplanade Dwight-Eisenhower. **Tel** 02 31 06 06 44. ☐ mid-Jan–Dec: daily. ● 25 Dec, 2 weeks in Jan. 🔗 & **www**.memorial-caen.fr
In the northwest of Caen, close to the N13 ring-road (exit 7), Mémorial is a museum dedicated to peace, placing the events of D-Day into the context of World War II using a host of interactive and audio-visual techniques, including stunning compilations of archive and fictional film.

A recent extension gives a wider perspective on cultural, religious, border and ecological conflicts in the second half of the 20th century.

Lush Orne valley in the Suisse Normande

For hotels and restaurants in this region see pp563–6 and pp614–18

Suisse Normande ⑩

Calvados & Orne. ✈ Caen. 🚂 🚌
Caen, Argentan. 🛈 2 pl St-Sauveur,
Thury-Harcourt (02 31 79 70 45).
www.ot-suisse-normande.com

Though hardly like the mountains of Switzerland, the cliffs and valleys carved out by the river Orne as it winds north to Caen have become popular for walking, climbing, camping and river sports. The area is also ideal for a rural drive. Its highest and most impressive point is the Oëtre Rock, off the D329, where you can look down over the dramatic gorges created by the river Rouvre.

Parc Naturel Régional de Normandie-Maine ⑪

Orne & Manche. ✈ Alençon. 🚂
🚌 Argentan. 🛈 Carrouges (02 33
27 40 62). www.parc-naturel-nor-mandie-maine.fr

The southern fringes of central Normandy have been incorporated into France's largest regional park. Among the farmland and forests of oak and beech are several small towns. **Domfront** rests on a spur overlooking the river Varenne. The spa town **Bagnoles-de-l'Orne** offers a casino and sports facilities, while **Sées** has a Gothic cathedral. The **Maison du Parc** at Carrouges

Poster of Deauville, about 1930

has information on walks, cycling, and canoeing.

🎣 Maison du Parc
Carrouges. **Tel** 02 33 81 75 75.
☐ Mon–Fri. ⬤ public hols.

Environs
Just north of the park is the **Chateau d'O**, a Renaissance château with fine 17th-century frescoes. The **Haras du Pin** is France's national stud, called "a horses' Versailles" for its 17th-century architecture. Horse shows, dressage events and various tours take place throughout the year.

Côte Fleurie ⑫

Calvados. ✈ 🚂 🚌 Deauville.
🛈 pl de la Mairie, Deauville (02 31
14 40 00). www.deauville.org

The Côte Fleurie (Flowery Coast) between Villerville and Cabourg has been planted with chic resorts which burst

into bloom every summer. **Trouville** was once a humble fishing village, but in the mid-19th century caught the attention of writers Gustave Flaubert and Alexandre Dumas. By the 1870s Trouville had acquired grand hotels, a railway station and pseudo-Swiss villas along the beachfront. It has, however, long been outclassed by its neighbour, **Deauville**, created by the Duc de Morny in the 1860s. This resort boasts a casino, racecourses, marinas and the famous beachside catwalk, Les Planches.

For something quieter, head west to smaller resorts such as Villers-sur-Mer or Houlgate. **Cabourg** further west is dominated by the turn-of-the-century Grand Hôtel (see p551) where novelist Marcel Proust spent many summers. Proust used the resort as a model for the fictional Balbec in his novel *Remembrance of Things Past*.

Pays d'Auge ⑬

Calvados. ✈ Deauville. 🚂 🚌
Lisieux. 🛈 11 rue d'Alençon, Lisieux
(02 31 48 18 10). www.lisieux-tourisme.com

Inland from the Côte Fleurie, the Pays d'Auge is classic Normandy countryside, lushly woven with fields, wooded valleys, cider orchards, dairy farms and manor houses. Its capital is **Lisieux**, a cathedral town devoted to Ste Thérèse of Lisieux, canonized in 1925, who attracts hundreds of thousands of pilgrims each year. Lisieux is an obvious base for exploring the region, but nearby market towns, such as St-Pierre-sur-Dives and Orbec, are smaller and more attractive.

The best way to enjoy the Pays d'Auge is to potter around its minor roads. Two tourist routes are devoted to cider and cheese, while picturesque manor houses, farmhouses and châteaux testify to the wealth of this fertile land. **St-Germain-de-Livet** can be visited, as can **Crèvecoeur-en-Auge**, and the half-timbered village of **Beuvron-en-Auge** is charming.

APPLES AND CIDER

Apple orchards are a familiar feature of the Normandy countryside, and their fruit a fundamental ingredient in the region's gastronomic repertoire. No self-respecting pâtisserie would be without its *tarte normande* (apple tart), and every country lane seems to sport an *Ici Vente Cidre* (cider sold here) sign. Much of the harvest forms the raw material for cider and Calvados, an apple brandy aged in oak barrels for at least two years. A local brew is also made from pears, and known as *poiré* (perry).

A crop ranging from sour cider apples to sweet eating varieties

Mont-St-Michel 6

The 10th-century abbey

Shrouded by mist, encircled by sea, soaring proud above glistening sands – the silhouette of Mont-St-Michel is one of the most enchanting sights in France. Now linked to the mainland by a causeway, the island of Mont-Tombe (Tomb on the Hill) stands at the mouth of the river Couesnon, crowned by a fortified abbey that almost doubles its height. Lying strategically on the frontier between Normandy and Brittany,

St Michael

The 11th-century abbey

Mont-St-Michel grew from a humble 8th-century oratory to become a Benedictine monastery that had its greatest influence in the 12th and 13th centuries. Pilgrims known as *miquelots* journeyed from afar to honour the cult of St Michael, and the monastery was a renowned centre of medieval learning. Major engineering works are now in place to begin reversing the silting up of the sea around the island.

The mid-18th-century abbey

St Aubert's Chapel
A small 15th-century chapel built on an outcrop of rock is dedicated to Aubert, the founder of Mont-St-Michel.

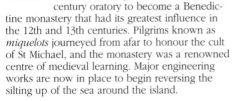

Gabriel Tower

Entrance

★ Ramparts
English attacks during the Hundred Years' War led to the construction of fortified walls with imposing towers.

TIMELINE

700	1000	1300	1600	1900
966 Benedictine abbey founded by Duke Richard I	**1211–28** Construction of La Merveille	**1434** Last assault by English forces. Ramparts surround the town	**1789** French Revolution: abbey becomes a political prison	**1874** Abbey declared a national monument **1922** Services again held in abbey church
1017 Work on abbey church starts		**1516** Abbey falls into decline	**1877–9** Causeway built	**1895–7** Belfry, spire and statue of St Michael added
708 St Aubert builds an oratory on Mont-Tombe		**1067–70** Mont-St-Michel depicted in Bayeux Tapestry *Bayeux Tapestry detail*		**1969** Benedictine monks return

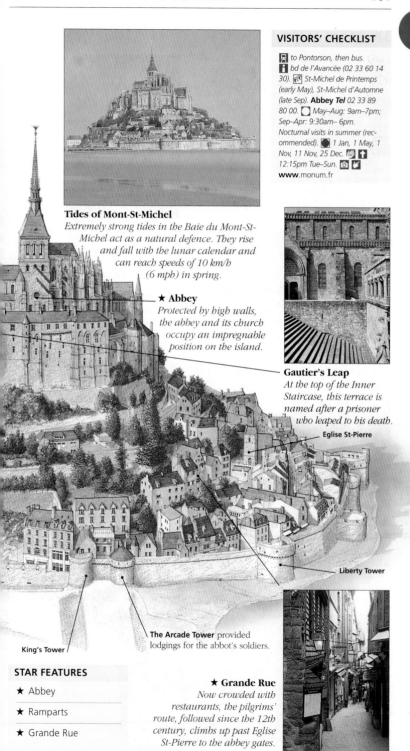

VISITORS' CHECKLIST

🚊 to Pontorson, then bus. 🛈 bd de l'Avancée (02 33 60 14 30). 🎭 St-Michel de Printemps (early May), St-Michel d'Automne (late Sep). **Abbey Tel** 02 33 89 80 00. ◯ May–Aug: 9am–7pm; Sep–Apr: 9:30am– 6pm. Nocturnal visits in summer (recommended). ● 1 Jan, 1 May, 1 Nov, 11 Nov, 25 Dec. 🏷 🚻 12:15pm Tue–Sun. 📷 🎦 **www.**monum.fr

Tides of Mont-St-Michel
Extremely strong tides in the Baie du Mont-St-Michel act as a natural defence. They rise and fall with the lunar calendar and can reach speeds of 10 km/h (6 mph) in spring.

★ Abbey
Protected by high walls, the abbey and its church occupy an impregnable position on the island.

Gautier's Leap
At the top of the Inner Staircase, this terrace is named after a prisoner who leaped to his death.

Eglise St-Pierre

Liberty Tower

King's Tower

The Arcade Tower provided lodgings for the abbot's soldiers.

STAR FEATURES

★ Abbey

★ Ramparts

★ Grande Rue

★ Grande Rue
Now crowded with restaurants, the pilgrims' route, followed since the 12th century, climbs up past Eglise St-Pierre to the abbey gates.

The Abbey of Mont-St-Michel

The present buildings bear witness to the time when the abbey served both as a Benedictine monastery and, for 73 years after the Revolution, as a political prison. In 1017 work began on a Romanesque church at the island's highest point, building over its 10th-century predecessor, now the Chapel of Our Lady Underground. A monastery built on three levels, La Merveille (The Miracle) was added to the church's north side in the early 13th century.

Cross in the choir

★ Church
Four bays of the Romanesque nave survive. Three were pulled down in 1776, creating the West Terrace.

★ La Merveille
The Miracle is a Gothic masterpiece – a three-storey monastic complex built in only 16 years.

Refectory
The monks took their meals in this long, narrow room, which is flooded with light through tall windows.

Knights' Room
The rib vaults and finely decorated capitals are typically Gothic.

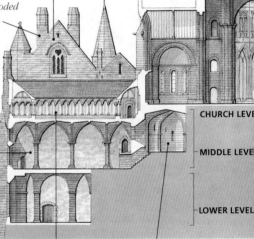

CHURCH LEVEL

MIDDLE LEVEL

LOWER LEVEL

Crypt of the Thirty Candles is one of two 11th-century crypts built to support the transepts of the main church.

★ Cloisters
The cloisters with their elegant columns in staggered rows are a beautiful example of early 13th-century Anglo-Norman style.

VISITING THE ABBEY

The three levels of the abbey reflect the monastic hierarchy. The monks lived at the highest level, in an enclosed world of church, cloister and refectory. The abbot entertained his noble guests on the middle level. Soldiers and pilgrims further down on the social scale were received at the lowest level. Guided tours begin at the West Terrace at the church level and end in the almonry, where alms were dispensed to the poor. The almonry is now a bookshop and souvenir hall.

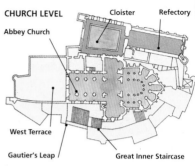

CHURCH LEVEL
Cloister • Refectory • Abbey Church • West Terrace • Gautier's Leap • Great Inner Staircase

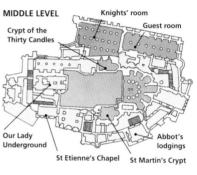

MIDDLE LEVEL
Knights' room • Guest room • Crypt of the Thirty Candles • Our Lady Underground • St Etienne's Chapel • St Martin's Crypt • Abbot's lodgings

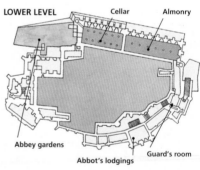

LOWER LEVEL
Cellar • Almonry • Abbey gardens • Abbot's lodgings • Guard's room

Church Interior
A Flamboyant Gothic choir was built in 1446–1521, held up by crypts with massive supporting pillars.

St Martin's Crypt is an 11th-century barrel-vaulted chapel that preserves the austere forms of the original Romanesque abbey.

The abbot's lodgings were close to the abbey entrance, and he received prestigious visitors in the guest room. Poorer pilgrims were received in the almonry.

Benedictine Monks
Today a small monastic community lives in the abbey, continuing the religious traditions introduced by the Benedictines in 966.

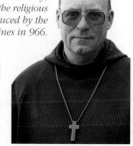

STAR FEATURES

★ Church

★ La Merveille

★ Cloisters

Mont-St-Michel by night ▷

Honfleur ⑭

Calvados. 🏛 8,500. 🚉 Deauville.
ℹ quai Lepaulmier (02 31 89 23 30).
🛒 Wed, Thu, Sat, Sun. www.ot-honfleur.fr

A major defensive port in the 15th century, Honfleur has blossomed into one of Normandy's most appealing harbours. At its heart is the 17th-century **Vieux Bassin** (Old Dock), with its picturesque tall houses (6-7 storeys).

Honfleur became a centre of artistic activity in the 19th century. Eugène Boudin, the seascape painter, was born here in 1824, as was the composer Erik Satie in 1866. Courbet, Sisley, Pissarro, Renoir and Cézanne all visited Honfleur, often meeting at the Ferme St-Siméon, now a luxury hotel. Painters still work from Honfleur's quayside, and exhibit in the **Greniers à Sel**, two salt warehouses built in 1670. These lie to the east of the Vieux Bassin in an area known as l'Enclos, which made up the fortified heart of the town in the 13th-century.

The **Musée de la Marine** displays mementos of Honfleur's nautical past, with a warren of Norman interiors next door in the former prison. Place Ste-Catherine has an unusual 15th-century church built by ship's carpenters. The **Musée Eugène-Boudin** documents the artistic appeal of Honfleur and the Seine estuary, with works ranging from Eugène Boudin to Raoul Dufy. **Les Maisons Satie** use extracts from Satie's music to guide you round imaginative reconstructions of the rooms.

🏛 **Greniers à Sel**
Rue de la Ville. ℹ 02 31 89 23 30.
◯ for guided tours & exhibitions.
🎫 obligatory, except during summer exhibs. 🖼 ♿

🏛 **Musée de la Marine**
Quai St Etienne. **Tel** 02 31 89 14 12.
◯ Apr–Jun & Sep: Tue–Sun; Jul & Aug: daily; Oct–mid-Nov & mid-Feb–Nov: pm Tue–Sun. ◯ 1 May. 🖼 ♿

🏛 **Musée Eugène-Boudin**
Pl Erik Satie, rue de l'Homme de Bois. **Tel** 02 31 89 54 00. ◯ mid-Mar–Sep: Wed–Mon; Oct–Dec & mid-Feb–mid-Mar: Wed–Mon pm, Sat, Sun. ◯ Jan–mid-Feb. 🖼 ♿

🏛 **Les Maisons Satie**
67 bd Charles V. **Tel** 02 31 89 11 11.
◯ Wed–Mon. ◯ Jan–mid-Feb. 🖼

Quai St-Etienne in Honfleur

Le Havre ⑮

Seine-Maritime. 🏛 194,000. ✈ 🚉
🚢 🚏 ℹ 186 bd Clemenceau (02 32 74 04 04). 🛒 daily.
www.lehavretourisme.com

Strategically positioned on the Seine estuary, Le Havre (The Harbour) was created in 1517 by François I after the nearby port of Harfleur silted up.

During World War II it was virtually obliterated by Allied bombing, but despite a vast industrial zone which stands beside the port, it still has appeal. It is an important yachting centre, and its beach has two blue flags (very clean!).

Much of the city centre was rebuilt in the 1950s–1960s by August Perret, whose towering **Eglise St-Joseph** (a UNESCO World Heritage site) pierces the skyline. On the seafront, the **Musée Malraux** has works by, amongst others, local artist Raoul Dufy. France's biggest skateboard park is also on the seafront.

🏛 **Musée Malraux**
2 bd Clemenceau. **Tel** 02 35 19 62 62. ◯ Wed–Mon. ◯ public hols.

Côte d'Albâtre ⑯

Seine-Maritime. 🚉 🚏 🚢 ℹ quai du Carénage, Dieppe (02 32 14 40 60). www.dieppetourisme.com

The Alabaster Coast gets its name from the chalky cliffs and milky waters that characterize the Normandy coastline between Le Havre and Le Tréport. It is best known for the **Falaise d'Aval** west of Etretat, eroded into an arch. The author Guy de Maupassant, born near Dieppe in 1850, compared these cliffs to an elephant dipping its trunk into the sea. From Etretat, a chain of coastal roads runs east across a switchback of breezy headlands and wooded valleys to Dieppe.

Fécamp is the only major town along this route. Its Benedictine abbey was once an important pilgrimage centre after a tree trunk said to contain drops of Christ's Blood was washed ashore here in the 7th century. This is enshrined in a reliquary at the entrance to the Lady Chapel of the abbey church, La Trinité.

The vast **Palais Bénédictine** is a Neo-Gothic-and-Renaissance homage to the ego of Alexander Le Grand, a local wine and spirits merchant who rediscovered the monks' recipe for Bénédictine, the famous herbal liqueur. Built

Woman with Parasol (1880) by Boudin in the Musée Eugène-Boudin

The cliffs at Falaise d'Aval, famously likened to an elephant dipping its trunk into the sea

in 1882, it incorporates a distillery and an eccentric museum packed with curios. The adjacent halls provide an aromatic account and tastings of the 27 herbs and spices which make up the elixir.

🏛 Palais Bénédictine
110 rue Alexandre Le Grand, Fécamp.
Tel 02 35 10 26 10. 🔲 daily. 🔴
Jan. 🔲 www.benedictine.fr

View of Dieppe from the château and museum above the town

Dieppe 🟠

Seine-Maritime. 🏠 36,000. 🔲 🔲
🔲 🔲 quai du Carénage (02 32 14
40 60). 🔲 Tue, Thu & esp. Sat.
www.dieppetourisme.com

Dieppe exploits a break in the chalky cliffs bordering the Pays de Caux, and has won historical prestige as a Channel fort, port and resort. Prosperity came during the 16th and 17th centuries, when local privateer Jehan Ango raided the Portuguese and English fleets, and a trading post called Petit Dieppe was founded on the West African coast. At that time, Dieppe's population was already 30,000, and included a 300-strong

community of craftsmen carving imported ivory. This maritime past is celebrated in **Le Château-Musée**, the 15th-century castle crowning the headland to the west of the seafront. Here you can see historical maps and model ships, a collection of Dieppe ivories, and paintings that evoke the town's development as a fashionable seaside resort during the 19th century. Dieppe had the nearest beach to Paris and it quickly responded to the developing passion for promenading, seawater cures and bathing.

Today Dieppe's broad seafront is given over to lawns, seaside amusements and car parks, and its liveliest streets surround the battle-scarred **Eglise St-Jacques** to the south. If the weather is poor, visit **L'Estran-La Cité de la Mer**, an exhibition centre with models on maritime themes.

🏛 Le Château-Musée
Tel 02 35 06 61 99. 🔲 Jun–Sep:
daily; Oct–May: Wed–Mon.
🔲 1 Jan, 1 May, 1 Nov, 25 Dec. 🔲
www.mairie-dieppe.fr

🏛 L'Estran La Cité de la Mer
37 rue de l'Asile Thomas. **Tel** 02 35
06 93 20. 🔲 daily. 🔴 1 Jan, 25
Dec. 🔲 🔲

Basse-Seine 🟠

Seine-Maritime & Eure. 🔲 Le Havre,
Rouen. 🔲 🔲 Yvetot. 🔲 Le Havre.
🔲 Yvetot (02 35 95 08 40).

Meandering seaward from Rouen to Le Havre, the river Seine is crossed by three spectacular road bridges: the Pont de Brotonne, the Pont de Tancarville and the Pont de

Normandie (completed in 1995, it links Le Havre and Honfleur). The grace and daring of these modern bridges echo the soaring aspirations of the abbeys founded on the river's banks in the 7th and 8th centuries. The abbeys now provide good stepping stones for a tour of the Lower Seine valley.

West of Rouen is the harmonious Eglise de St-Georges at **St-Martin-de-Boscherville** which until the Revolution was the church of a small walled abbey. Its 12th-century chapter house has remarkable biblical statues and carved capitals. From here the D67 runs south to the riverside village of La Bouille.

As you head northwest, an hourly car ferry at Mesnil-sous-Jumièges takes you over to the colossal ruins of the **Abbaye de Jumièges**. The abbey was founded in 654 and once housed 900 monks and 1,500 servants. The main abbey church dates from the 11th century; its consecration in 1067 was a major event, with William the Conqueror in attendance.

The D913 strikes through oak and beech woods in the Parc Régional de Brotonne to the 7th-century **Abbaye de St-Wandrille**. The Musée de la Marine de Seine at **Caudebec-en-Caux** gives an engrossing account of many aspects of life on this great river over the past 130 years or so.

Monk from Abbaye de St-Wandrille

Rouen ⑲

Founded at the lowest point where the Seine could be bridged, Rouen has prospered through maritime trade and industrialization to become a rich and cultured city. Despite the severe damage of World War II, the city boasts a wealth of historic sights on its right bank, all within walking distance of the central Cathédrale Notre-Dame, frequently painted by Monet. In turn a Celtic trading post, Roman garrison and Viking colony, Rouen became the capital of the Norman Duchy in 911. It was captured by Henry V in 1419 after a siege during the Hundred Years' War. In 1431 Joan of Arc was burned at the stake here in place du Vieux-Marché.

Rouen, a thriving port on the river Seine

Exploring Rouen

From the cathedral, the rue du Gros Horloge runs west under the city's Great Clock, to the place du Vieux Marché and its post-war Eglise Ste-Jeanne-d'Arc. Rue aux Juifs leads past the 15th-century Gothic **Palais de Justice**, once Normandy's parliament, to the smart shops and cafés around rue des Carmes. Further east, between the St-Maclou and St-Ouen churches, are half-timbered houses in the rue Damiette and rue Eau de Robec. North, in place Général de Gaulle, is the 18th-century **Hôtel de Ville**.

🏛 Cathédrale Notre-Dame

This Gothic masterpiece is dominated by the famous west façade (see p267), painted

Cathédrale Notre-Dame, Rouen

by Monet, which is framed by two unequal towers – the northern Tour St-Romain, and the later Tour du Beurre, supposedly paid for by a tax on butter consumption in Lent. Above the central lantern tower rises a Neo-Gothic spire, made from cast iron and erected in 1876. Recently restored, both the 14th-century northern Portail des Libraires and the 14th-century southern Portail de la Calende are worth seeing for their precise sculpting and delicate tracery. Many of the cathedral's riches are access-

ible by guided tour only, including the tomb of Richard the Lionheart, whose heart was buried here, and the rare 11th-century semi-circular hall crypt, rediscovered in 1934. The choir/chancel was badly hit by the 1999 storm.

🏛 Eglise St-Maclou

This Flamboyant Gothic church has an intensively

SIGHTS AT A GLANCE

Aître St-Maclou ⑨
Cathédrale Notre-Dame ⑦
Eglise St-Maclou ⑧
Eglise St-Ouen ⑩
Gros-Horloge ②
Hôtel de Ville ⑪
Musée des Beaux Arts ⑤
Musée de la Céramique ④
Musée d'Histoire Naturelle ⑫
Musée le Secq des Tournelles ⑥
Palais de Justice ③
Place du Vieux-Marché ①

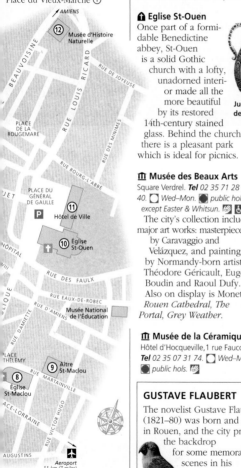

timbers of its buildings, set around the quadrangle, are carved with a macabre array of grinning skulls, crossed bones, coffins and grave-diggers' implements.

⛪ Musée d'Histoire Naturelle

198 rue Beauvoisine. **Tel** 02 35 71 41 50. ◯ Tue–Sun. 🖼
This newly refurbished museum is the second largest of its kind in France, holding more than 800,000 objects.

🔒 Eglise St-Ouen

Once part of a formidable Benedictine abbey, St-Ouen is a solid Gothic church with a lofty, unadorned interior made all the more beautiful by its restored

Jug from Musée de la Céramique

14th-century stained glass. Behind the church there is a pleasant park which is ideal for picnics.

⛪ Musée des Beaux Arts

Square Verdrel. **Tel** 02 35 71 28 40. ◯ Wed–Mon. ● public hols except Easter & Whitsun. 🖼 ♿
The city's collection includes major art works: masterpieces by Caravaggio and Velázquez, and paintings by Normandy-born artists Théodore Géricault, Eugène Boudin and Raoul Dufy. Also on display is Monet's *Rouen Cathedral, The Portal, Grey Weather.*

⛪ Musée de la Céramique

Hôtel d'Hocqueville, 1 rue Faucon. **Tel** 02 35 07 31 74. ◯ Wed–Mon. ● public hols. 🖼

VISITORS' CHECKLIST

Seine Maritime. 🗺 108,800.
✈ 11 km (7 miles) SE Rouen.
🚆 gare rive droite, pl Bernard Tissot (08 92 35 35 35). 🚌 25 rue des Charrettes (0825 076 027). 🛈 25 pl de la Cathédrale (02 32 08 32 40). 🚋 Tue–Sun. 🎉 Feast of Joan of Arc (late May). **www.**rouentourisme.com

Exhibits of 1,000 pieces of Rouen faïence – colourful glazed earthenware – together with other pieces of French and foreign china are displayed in a 17th-century town house. The works trace the history of Rouen faïence to its zenith in the 18th century.

⛪ Musée Le Secq des Tournelles

Rue Jacques-Villon. **Tel** 02 35 88 42 92. ◯ Wed–Mon. ● public hols. 🖼 ♿ ground floor only.
Located in a 15th-century church, this wrought ironwork museum exhibits antique ironmongery ranging from keys to corkscrews and Gallo-Roman spoons to mighty tavern signs.

⛪ Musée Flaubert

51 rue de Lecat. **Tel** 02 35 15 59 95. ◯ Tue–Sat. ● public hols. 🖼
Flaubert's father was a surgeon at Rouen Hospital, and his family home combines memorabilia with an awesome – and occasionally gruesome – display of 17th–19th-century medical equipment.

GUSTAVE FLAUBERT

The novelist Gustave Flaubert (1821–80) was born and raised in Rouen, and the city provides the backdrop for some memorable scenes in his masterpiece, *Madame Bovary.* Published in 1857, this realistic study of a country doctor's wife driven to despair by her love affairs provoked a scandal that made Flaubert's name. His famous stuffed green parrot, which can be seen in the Musée Flaubert, was always perched on his writing desk.

Flaubert's stuffed parrot

decorated west façade with a five-bay porch and carved wooden doors depicting biblical scenes. Behind the church, its *aître*, or ossuary, is a rare surviving example of a medieval cemetery for the burial of plague victims. The

Château Gaillard and the village of Les Andelys, in a loop of the river Seine

Haute-Seine ⑳

Eure. 🛩 Rouen. 🚊 Vernon, Val de
Reuil. 🚌 Gisors, Les Andelys.
ℹ️ Les Andelys (02 32 54 41 93).
http://office-tourisme-ville-andelys.fr

Southeast of Rouen, the river
Seine follows a convoluted
course, with most points of
interest on its north bank.
At the centre of the Forêt de
Lyons, once the hunting
ground for the Dukes of
Normandy, is the country
town of **Lyons-la-Forêt**, with
half-timbered houses and an
18th-century covered market.
     To the south the D313
follows the gracefully curving
Seine to the town of **Les
Andelys**. Above it tower the
ruins of Château Gaillard
which Richard the Lionheart,
as King of England and Duke
of Normandy, built in 1197 to
defend Rouen from the
French. They eventually took
the castle in 1204.

Giverny ㉑

Eure. 🏘 600. ℹ️ 36 rue Carnot,
Vernon (02 32 51 39 60).
www.cape-tourisme.fr

In 1883 the Impressionist
painter Claude Monet rented
a house in the small village of

Giverny, and worked here
until his death. The house,
known as the **Fondation
Claude Monet**, and its garden
are open to the public. The
house is decorated in the
colour schemes that Monet
admired; the gardens are
famous as the subject of
some of the artist's studies.
Only copies are on show, but
there are outstanding original
19th- and 20th-century art
works in the **Musée d'Art
Américain** nearby.

🏛 **Fondation Claude Monet**
Giverny, Gasny. **Tel** 02 32 51 28 21.
🕐 Apr–Oct: Tue–Sun. 🈂️
www.fondation-monet.com

🏛 **Musée d'Art Américain**
99 rue Claude Monet, Giverny.
Tel 02 32 51 94 65. 🕐 Apr–Oct:
Tue–Sun; Nov: Thu–Sun. 🈂️ ♿
www.maag.org

Évreux ㉒

1 Eure. 🏘 55,000. 🚊 🚌 ℹ️ 1ter pl
du Général de Gaulle (02 32 24 04
43). 🛒 Wed & Sat. **www.**ot-pays-
evreux.fr

Though considerably dam-
aged in the war, Évreux is a
pleasant cathedral town set in
wide, agricultural plains. At
its heart, the **Cathédrale Notre-
Dame** is renowned for its
14th–15th century stained
glass. The building is predominantly Gothic, though
Romanesque arches survive
in the nave and Renaissance
screens adorn its chapels.
Next door, the former Bishop's
Palace houses the **Musée
Municipal**, with Roman
bronze statues of Jupiter and
Apollo and fine 18th-century
furniture and decorative art.

Monet's garden at Giverny, restored to its original profuse glory

Monet's Cathedral Series

In the 1890s Claude Monet made almost 30 paintings of Rouen's cathedral, several of which are now in the Musée d'Orsay in Paris (see pp120–21). He studied the effects of changing light on its façades, and described both the surface detail and huge bulk, putting colour before contour. The archetypal Impressionist, Monet said he conceived this series when he watched the effects of light on a country church, "as the sun's rays slowly dissolved the mists ... that wrapped the golden stone in an ideally vaporous envelope".

HARMONY IN BLUE AND GOLD (1894)

Monet selected a close vantage point for the series and was keen on this southwest view. The sun would cast afternoon shadows across the carved west front, accentuating the cavernous portals and the large rose window.

Monet's sketch, one of many of Rouen, parallels the shimmering effect of the paintings.

Harmony in Brown (1894) is the only finished version of a frontal view of the west façade. Analysis has shown that it was begun as a southwest view like the others.

Harmony in Blue (1894), compared with Harmony in Blue and Gold, shows the stone of the west façade further softened by the diffuse light of a misty morning.

The Portal, Grey Weather (1894) was one of several canvases in the grey colour group which showed the cathedral façade in the soft light of an overcast day.

BRITTANY

FINISTÈRE · CÔTES D'ARMOR · MORBIHAN · ILLE-ET-VILAINE

Jutting defiantly into the Atlantic, France's northwest corner has long been culturally and geographically distinct from the main bulk of the country. Known to the Celts as Armorica, the land of the sea, Brittany's past swirls with the legends of drowned cities and Arthurian forests. Prehistoric megaliths arise mysteriously from land and sea, and the medieval is never far from the modern.

A long, jagged coastline is the region's great attraction. Magnificent beaches line its northern shore, swept clean by huge tides and interspersed with well-established seaside resorts, seasoned fishing ports and abundant oysterbeds. The south coast is gentler, with wooded river valleys and a milder climate, while the west, being exposed to the Atlantic winds, has a drama that justifies the name Finistère – the End of the Earth.

Inland lies the Argoat – once the Land of the Forest, now a patchwork of undulating fields, woods, and rolling moorland. Parc Régional d'Armorique occupies much of central Finistère, and it is in western Brittany that Breton culture remains most evident. In Quimper, and in the Pays Bigouden, crêpes and cider, traditional costumes, and Celtic music are still a genuine part of the Breton lifestyle. Eastern Brittany has a more conventional appeal. Vannes, Dinan and Rennes, the Breton capital, have well-preserved medieval quarters where half-timbered buildings shelter inviting markets, shops, crêperies, and restaurants. The walled port of St-Malo on the Côte d'Emeraude recalls the region's maritime prowess, while the remarkably intact castles at Fougères and Vitré are reminders of the mighty border-fortresses that protected Brittany's eastern frontier before its final union with France in 1532.

Women dressed in traditional costume and *coiffe*, the typical Breton lace head-dress

◁ Characteristic pink granite cliffs on the Côte de Granit Rose, northern Brittany

Exploring Brittany

Ideal for a seaside holiday, Brittany offers enjoyable drives along the headlands and beaches of the northern Côte d'Emeraude and Côte de Granit Rose, while the south coast boasts wooded valleys and the prehistoric sites of Carnac and the Golfe du Morbihan. The parish closes *(see pp276–7)* provide an intriguing insight into Breton culture, as does the cathedral town of Quimper. Be sure to visit the regional capital, Rennes, and the great castle at Fougères, and in summer take a boat trip to one of Brittany's islands.

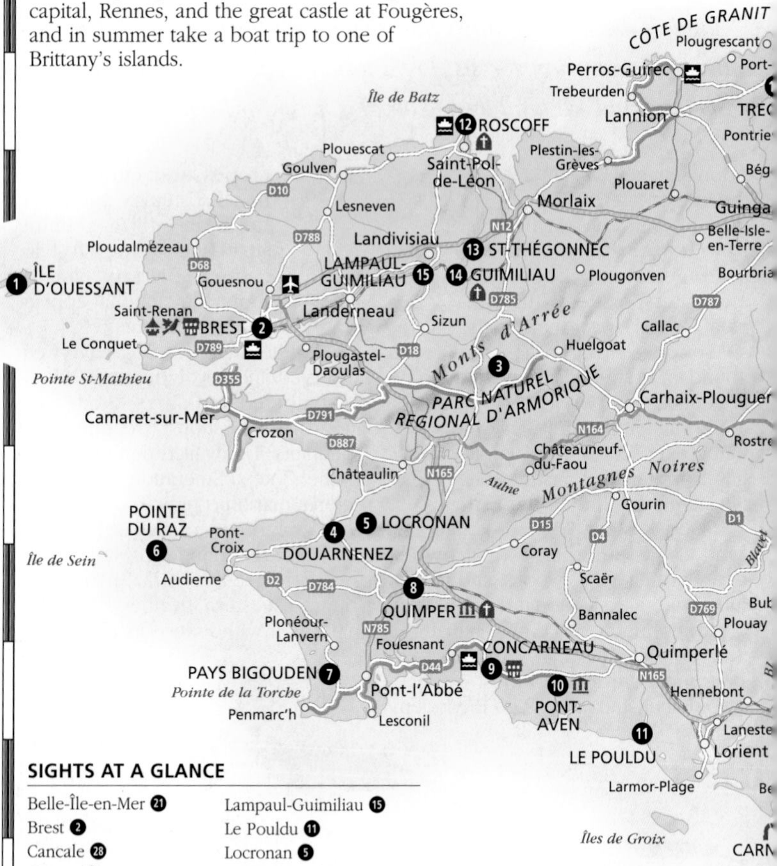

CÔTE DE GRANIT
Plougrescant
Port-
Perros-Guirec
Trebeurden
Lannion
TRE
Pontrie
Île de Batz
12 ROSCOFF
Plouescat
Goulven
Saint-Pol-de-Léon
Plestin-les-Grèves
Plouaret
Bég
Morlaix
Guinga
Lesneven
D10
N12
Belle-Isle-en-Terre
Landivisiau
13 ST-THÉGONNEC
Ploudalmézeau
D788
LAMPAUL-GUIMILIAU 15
14 GUIMILIAU
Plougonven
Bourbria
1 ÎLE D'OUESSANT
D68
Gouesnou
D785
D787
Saint-Renan
Landerneau
Sizun
Monts d'Arrée
Callac
BREST 2
Le Conquet
D789
Plougastel-Daoulas
D18
Huelgoat
3
Pointe St-Mathieu
D355
PARC NATUREL REGIONAL D'ARMORIQUE
Carhaix-Plouguer
Camaret-sur-Mer
D791
Crozon
N164
Rostre
D887
Châteauneuf-du-Faou
Châteaulin
N165
Aulne
Montagnes Noires
Gourin
POINTE DU RAZ
6
Pont-Croix
4
5 LOCRONAN
D15
D1
DOUARNENEZ
Coray
D4
Île de Sein
Audierne
D2
D784
Scaër
Blavet
8
QUIMPER
Bannalec
D769
Bub
Plonéour-Lanvern
N785
Plouay
Fouesnant
CONCARNEAU
Quimperlé
PAYS BIGOUDEN 7
D44
9
N165
Pointe de la Torche
Pont-l'Abbé
10
Hennebont
Penmarc'h
Lesconil
PONT-AVEN
11
Laneste
LE POULDU
Lorient
Larmor-Plage
Be
Îles de Groix
CARN
PRESQU'ÎLE DE QUIBERO
Quibe
Le Pa
BELLE ÎLE

SIGHTS AT A GLANCE

Belle-Île-en-Mer 21
Brest 2
Cancale 28
Carnac 19
Combourg 30
Concarneau 9
Côte d'Emeraude 26
Côte de Granit Rose 16
Dinan 29
Douarnenez 4
Forêt de Paimpont 25
Fougères 32
Golfe du Morbihan 23
Guimiliau 14
Île de Bréhat 18
Île d'Ouessant 1
Josselin 24
Lampaul-Guimiliau 15
Le Pouldu 11
Locronan 5
Parc Régional d'Armorique 3
Pays Bigouden 7
Pointe du Raz 6
Pont-Aven 10
Presqu'île de Quiberon 20
Quimper 8
Rennes 31
Roscoff 12
St-Malo 27
St-Thégonnec 13
Tréguier 17
Vannes 22
Vitré 33

KEY

- Motorway
- Major road
- Secondary road
- Minor road
- Scenic route
- Main railway
- Minor railway
- Regional border

Lighthouse on the Île de Bréhat, Côte de Granit Rose

GETTING AROUND

Expressways N12/N165 en-circle Brittany, giving easy access to coastal areas and to Rennes, Brittany's capital. Travel across the less popul-ous interior can be slower. Brittany can be reached by air to Brest, Nantes and Rennes airports, by Channel ferries to St Malo and Roscoff, by autoroutes from Normandy, the Loire, and A11 from Paris, or by TGV direct from Paris and Lille.

Half-timbered houses in the medieval part of Rennes

Île d'Ouessant ①

Finistère. ⚑ 930. ✈ Ouessant (via Brest). 🚢 Brest, then boat. 🚌 Le Conquet, then boat. 🛈 pl de l'Eglise, Lampaul (02 98 48 85 83). www.ot-ouessant.fr

A well-known Breton proverb declares "He who sees Ouessant sees his own blood". Also known as Ushant, the island is notorious among sailors for its fierce storms and strong currents. However, this westerly point of France has a pleasant climate in summer and, though often bleak and stormy, can be surprisingly mild in winter. Part of the Parc Naturel Régional d'Armorique, the windswept island supports migrating birds and a small seal population, which may be observed from the Pern and Pen-ar-Roc'h headlands.

Two museums shed light on the island's defiant history, dogged by shipwreck and tragedy. At Niou Uhella, the **Ecomusée d'Ouessant** has furniture made from driftwood and wrecks, often painted blue and white in honour of the Virgin Mary. Nearby at Phare du Créac'h, the **Musée des Phares et Balises** explains the history of Brittany's many lighthouses and their keepers.

🏛 **Ecomusée d'Ouessant**
Maison du Niou. **Tel** 02 98 48 86 37. ⬜ daily. &

🏛 **Musée des Phares et Balises**
Pointe de Créac'h. **Tel** 02 98 48 80 70. ⬜ daily. 📷 &

Brest ②

Finistère. ⚑ 153,000. ✈ 🚉 🚌 🚢 to islands only. 🛈 8 av Georges-Clemenceau (02 98 44 24 96). ⬜ daily. www.brest-metropole-tourisme.fr

A natural harbour protected by the Presqu'île de Crozon, Brest is France's premier Atlantic naval port with a rich maritime history. Heavily bombed during World War II, it is now a modern commercial city where cargo vessels, yachts and fishing boats ply the waters. The Cours Dajot

Windswept moorlands near Ménez-Meur, Parc Régional d'Armorique

promenade has good views of the Rade de Brest. The **Château** houses a naval museum with historic maps, maritime paintings, model ships, carved wooden figureheads and nautical instruments.

Across the Penfeld river – reached by Europe's largest lifting bridge, the Pont de Recouvrance – is the 14th-century **Tour de la Motte Tanguy**. By the Port de Plaisance, **Océanopolis** "sea centre" has three vast pavilions simulating temperate, tropical and polar ecosystems.

🏰 **Château de Brest**
Tel 02 98 22 12 39. ⬜ Apr–mid-Sep: daily; mid-Sep–mid-Dec & Feb–Mar: Wed pm–Mon. 📷

🗼 **Tour de la Motte Tanguy**
Sq Pierre Peron. **Tel** 02 98 00 88 60. ⬜ Jun–Sep: daily; Oct–May: Wed–Thu, Sat–Sun pms. ⬛ 1 Jan, 1 May, 25 Dec.

🐠 **Océanopolis**
Port de Plaisance du Moulin Blanc. **Tel** 02 98 34 40 40. ⬜ Apr–early Sep: daily; early Sep–Mar: Tue–Sun. ⬛ 1 Jan, 25 Dec. 📷 &
www.oceanopolis.com

Traditional boatbuilding at Le Port Musée, Douarnenez

Parc Naturel Régional d'Armorique ③

Finistère. 🚉 Brest. 🚌 Chateaulin, Landernau. 🚌 Le Faou, Huelgoat, Carhaix. 🛈 Le Faou (02 98 81 79 30).

The Armorican Regional Nature Park stretches west from the moorlands of the Monts d'Arrée to the Presqu'île de Crozon and Ile d'Ouessant. Within this protected area lies a mixture of farmland, heaths, remains of ancient oak forest and wild, open spaces. The park and its scenic coastline is ideal for walking, riding and touring by bicycle or car.

Huelgoat is a good starting point for inland walks, while **Ménez-Hom** (330 m, 1,082 ft) at the beginning of the Crozon Peninsula, has excellent views.

The main information centre for the park is at **Le Faou**. Nearby at **Ménez-Meur** is a wooded estate with wild and farm animals, and a Breton horse museum. Scattered around the park are 16 small, specialist museums, some paying tribute to country traditions like hunting, fishing and tanning. The **Musée de l'Ecole Rurale** at Trégarvan recreates an early 20th-century rural school, while other museums cover subjects as diverse as medieval monastic life, rag-and-bone men and the lifestyle of a Breton country priest. Contemporary crafts and art can be seen at the **Maison des Artisans** in Brasparts.

For hotels and restaurants in this region see pp566–8 and pp618–20

Douarnenez ❹

Finistère. 🚗 16,700. 🚐
🛈 1 rue du Docteur Mével (02 98
92 13 35). 🅿 Mon–Wed.
www.douarnenez-tourisme.com

At the start of this century
Douarnenez used to be
France's leading sardine port;
today it is still devoted to
fishing, but is also a tourist
resort with beaches on both
sides of the Pouldavid estuary.

Nearby lies the tiny **Île
Tristan**, linked with the tragic
love story of Tristan and Iseult.
In the 16th century it was the
stronghold of a notorious
brigand, La Fontenelle.

The picturesque **Port du
Rosmeur** offers cafés, fish
restaurants and boat trips
around the bay, with a lively
early morning *criée* (fish
auction) held in the nearby
Nouveau Port. The Port-Rhu
has been turned into a floating
museum, **Le Port Musée**, with
over 100 boats and several
shipyards. Some of the larger
vessels can be visited.

🏛 **Le Port Musée**
Pl de l'Enfer. **Tel** 02 98 92 65 20. 🔲
Apr–Oct: daily. 🌐 ♿ www.port-
musee.org

Locronan's 15th-century Eglise St-
Ronan, seen from the churchyard

Locronan ❺

Finistère. 🚗 1,000. 🛈 pl de la
Mairie (02 98 91 70 14). www.
locronan.org

During the 15th–17th
centuries Locronan grew
wealthy from the manufacture
of sail-cloth. After Louis XIV
ended the Breton monopoly
on this trade, the town
declined – leaving an elegant

ensemble of Renaissance
buildings that attract many
visitors. In the town's central
cobbled square stands a late
15th-century church dedicated
to the Irish missionary St
Ronan. Down Rue Moal is the
delightful **Chapelle Notre-
Dame-de-Bonne-Nouvelle**
with a cavalry and a fountain.
Every July Locronan is the
scene of a *Troménie*, a
hilltop pilgrimage held in
honour of St Ronan. The more
elaborate *Grande Troménie*
takes place every six years.

Pointe du Raz ❻

Finistère. 🚉 Quimper. 🚌 Quimper,
then bus. 🛈 Audierne (02 98 70 12
20); Maison du Site (02 98 70 67 18).
www.pointeduraz.com

The dramatic Pointe du Raz,
almost 80 m (262 ft) high, is a
headland jutting into the
Atlantic at the tip of Cap
Sizun. The views of jagged
rocks and pounding seas are
breathtaking. Further west is
the flat Ile de Sein and
beyond that the lighthouse of
Ar Men. Despite being only
1.5 m (5 ft) above sea level,

The awe-inspiring cliffs of Pointe du Raz

Ile de Sein is nevertheless
home to 260 inhabitants, and
can be reached by boat from
Audierne in an hour.

Pays Bigouden ❼

Finistère. 🚌 Pont l'Abbé. 🛈 Pont
l'Abbé (02 98 82 37 99).

Brittany's southwest tip
is known as the Pays
Bigouden, a windy peninsula
with proud and ancient traditions. The region is famous
for the women's tall *coiffes* still
worn at festivals and *pardons*
(see p243), which can also be
seen at the **Musée Bigouden**.

Along the Baie d'Audierne
is a brooding landscape of
weather-beaten hamlets and
isolated chapels – the 15th-
century calvary at **Notre-
Dame-de-Tronoën** is the
oldest in Brittany. There are
invigorating sea views from
Pointe de la Torche (a good
surfing spot) and from the
Eckmühl lighthouse.

🏛 **Musée Bigouden**
Le Château, Pont l'Abbé. **Tel** 02 98
66 09 09. 🔲 Easter hols–May: Mon–
Sat; Jun–Sep: daily. 🌑 1 May. 🌐

Quimper

Finistère. 🏠 67,250. ✈ 🚆 🚍
ℹ️ *pl de la Résistance (02 98 53 04
05)*. 🖼 *Wed, Sat.* **www**.quimper-
tourisme.com

The ancient capital of
Cornouaille, Quimper has a
distinctly Breton character.
Here you can find Breton
language books and music
on sale, buy a traditional
costume and tuck into some
of the best crêpes and cider
in Brittany. Quimper gets its
name from *kemper*, a Breton
word meaning the confluence
of two rivers, and the Steir
and Odet still flow through
this relaxed cathedral city.

West of the cathedral lies a
pedestrianized area known
as **Vieux Quimper**, full of
shops, crêperies and half-
timbered houses. Rue Kéréon
is the main thoroughfare, with
the place au Beurre and the
picturesque *hôtels particuliers*
(mansions) of rue des
Gentilshommes to the north.

Quimper has been pro-
ducing faïence, elegant hand-
painted pottery, since 1690.
The design often features
decorative flowers and
animals framed by blue and
yellow borders. Now mainly
decorative, faïence
is today exported to
collectors all over
the world. In the
southwest of the
city lies the
oldest factory,
**Faïenceries
HB-Henriot**,
which is open
to visitors from
March to October.

**Typical faïence plate
from Quimper**

🏛 **Cathédrale
St-Corentin**
Quimper's cathedral
is dedicated to the city's
founder-bishop St Corentin.
Begun in 1240 – its colourfully painted interior now
restored – it is the earliest
Gothic building in Lower
Brittany, and was bizarrely
constructed with its choir at a
slight angle to the nave, perhaps to fit in with some since-
disappeared buildings. The
two spires of the west façade
were added in 1856. Between
them rides a statue of King

The Martyrdom of St Triphine (1910) by Sérusier, Pont-Aven School

Gradlon, the mythical founder
of the drowned city of Ys. After
this deluge he chose Quimper
as his new capital and St
Corentin as his spiritual guide.

🏛 **Musée des Beaux-Arts**
40 pl St-Corentin. **Tel** *02 98 95 45
20*. ⬤ *Jul–Aug: daily; Sep–Jun:
Wed–Mon.* ⬤ *most public hols;
Nov–Mar: Sun am.* 🎟 ♿
www.musee-beauxarts.quimper.fr
Quimper's art museum is one
of the best in the region. The
collection is strong on late
19th- and early 20th-century
artists, and their work – such
as Jean-Eugène Buland's *Visite
à Ste-Marie de Bénodet*
– offers a valuable
insight into the
way visiting
painters
perpetuated a
romantic view
of Brittany.
Also on show
are works by
members of the
Pont-Aven School
and local artists
like J-J Lemordant
and Max Jacob.

🏛 **Musée Départemental
Breton**
1 rue de Roi-Gradlon. **Tel** *02 98 95
21 60*. ⬤ *Jun–Sep: daily; Oct–May:
Tue– Sat; Sun pm.* 🎟 ♿
The 16th-century Bishop's
Palace has collections of
Breton costumes, furniture
and faïence, including
Cornouaille *coiffes*, ornately
carved box-beds and ward-
robes, and turn-of-the-century
tourist posters for Brittany.

Concarneau 9

Finistère. 🏠 20,000. 🚍 ⛴ *only
for islands*. ℹ️ *quai d'Aiguillon (02
98 97 01 44)*. 🖼 *Mon & Fri.*
www.tourismeconcarneau.fr

An important fishing port,
Concarneau's principal
attraction is its 14th-century
Ville Close (walled town),
built on an island in the harbour and encircled by massive
lichen-covered granite
ramparts. Access is by bridge
from place Jean Jaurès. Parts
of the ramparts can be toured,
and the narrow streets are full
of shops and restaurants. The
Musée de la Pêche, housed in
the port's ancient barracks,
explains the local techniques
and history of sea-fishing.

🏛 **Musée de la Pêche**
3 rue Vauban. **Tel** *02 98 97 10
20*. ⬤ *May–Sep: daily.* ⬤ *public
hols.* 🎟 ♿

**Fishing boats in Concarneau's busy
harbour**

For hotels and restaurants in this region see pp566–8 and pp618–20

Pont-Aven ❿

Finistère. 🏠 3,000. 🚌
🚶 5 pl de l'Hôtel de Ville (02 98 06 04 70). 🚉 Tue, Sat.
www.pontaven.com

Once a market town of "14 mills and 15 houses", Pont-Aven's picturesque location in the wooded Aven estuary made it attractive to many late 19th-century artists.

In 1888 Paul Gauguin, along with like-minded painters Emile Bernard and Paul Sérusier, developed a crude, colourful style of painting known as Synthetism. Drawing inspiration from the Breton landscape and its people, the Ecole de Pont-Aven (Pont-Aven School) worked here and in nearby Le Pouldu until 1896.

The town is devoted to art and has 50 private galleries, along with the informative **Musée Municipal** which documents the achievements of the Pont-Aven School. The surrounding woods proved inspirational to many artists, and offer pleasant walks – one leads through the Bois d'Amour to the **Chapelle de Trémalo**, where the wooden Christ in Gauguin's *Le Christ Jaune* still hangs.

🏛 **Musée Municipal**
Pl de l'Hôtel de Ville. **Tel** 02 98 06 14 43. ◻ daily. ● early Jan–mid-Feb; between exhibitions. 📷 ♿

Notre-Dame-de-Kroaz-Baz, Roscoff

Le Pouldu ⓫

Finistère. 🏠 4,000. 🚌 🚶 Pouldu Plage, rue C. Filiger (02 98 39 93 42).

A quiet port at the mouth of the river Laïta, Le Pouldu has a small beach and good walks. Its main attraction is **Maison de Marie Henry**, a reconstruction of the inn where Paul Gauguin and other artists stayed between 1889 and 1893. They covered every inch of the dining room, including the window-panes, with self-portraits, caricatures and still-lifes. These were discovered in 1924 beneath layers of wallpaper.

🏛 **Maison de Marie Henry**
10 rue des Grands Sables. **Tel** 02 98 39 98 51. ◻ Apr–May: Sat–Sun & public hols pms; Jun–Sep: Wed pm–Mon pm; Jul–Aug: daily. 📷

Roscoff ⓬

Finistère. 🏠 3,690. 🚇 🚌 ⛴ 🚶 46 rue Gambetta (02 98 61 12 13). 🚉 Wed.
www.roscoff-tourisme.com

Once a Corsairs' haunt, Roscoff is now a thriving Channel port and seaside resort. Signs of its wealthy seafaring past can be found in the old port, particularly along rue Amiral Réveillère and in place Lacaze-Duthiers. Here the granite façades of the 16th- and 17th-century ship-owners' mansions, and the weather-beaten caravels and cannon decorating the 16th-century **Eglise Notre-Dame-de-Kroaz-Baz**, testify to the days when the privateers of Roscoff were as notorious as those of St-Malo *(see p282)*.

The famous French onion sellers (Johnnies) first crossed the Channel in 1828, selling their plaited onions door to door as far as Scotland. The **Maison des Johnnies** tells their colourful history. The **Thalado** is an informative sea-weed exhibition centre. From the harbour you can take a boat trip to the peaceful **Ile de Batz**. Near Pointe de Bloscon are tropical gardens.

🏛 **Maison des Johnnies**
48 rue Brizeux. **Tel** 02 98 61 25 48. ◻ daily. ● Jan. 📷

🏛 **Thalado**
5 rue Victor Hugo. **Tel** 02 98 69 77 05. ◻ Apr–Oct: daily. 📷

PAUL GAUGUIN IN BRITTANY

Carving, Chapelle de Trémalo

Paul Gauguin's (1848–1903) story reads like a romantic novel. At the age of 35 he left his career as a stockbroker to become a full-time painter. From 1886 to 1894 he lived and worked in Brittany, at Pont-Aven and Le Pouldu, where he painted the landscape and its people. He chose to concentrate on the intense, almost "primitive" quality of the Breton Catholic faith, attempting to convey it in his work. This is evident in *Le Christ Jaune* (Yellow Christ), inspired by a woodcarving in the Trémalo chapel. In Gauguin's painting, the Crucifixion is a reality in the midst of the contemporary Breton landscape, rather than a remote or symbolic event. This theme recurs in many of his paintings from the period, including *Jacob Wrestling with the Angel* (1888).

Le Christ Jaune (1889) by Paul Gauguin

St-Thégonnec ⑬

Finistère. 🚉 🔾 *daily.* ♿

This is one of the most complete parish closes in Brittany. Passing through its triumphal archway, the ossuary is to the left. The calvary, directly ahead, was built in 1610 and perfectly illustrates the extraordinary skills Breton sculptors developed as they worked with the local granite. Among the many animated figures surrounding the central cross, a small niche contains a statue of St Thégonnec with a cart pulled by wolves.

Guimiliau ⑭

Finistère. 🔾 *daily.* ♿

Almost 200 figures adorn Guimiliau's intensely decorated calvary (1581–88), many wearing 16th-century dress. Among them you can contemplate the legendary torment of Katell Gollet, a servant girl tortured by demons for stealing a consecrated wafer to please her lover. The church is dedicated to St Miliau and has a richly decorated south porch. The baptistry's elaborate carved oak canopy dates from 1675.

Font canopy from 1675, Guimiliau

Lampaul-Guimiliau ⑮

Finistère. 🔾 *daily.* ♿

Entering through the monumental gate, the chapel and ossuary lie to the left, while the calvary is to the right. Here, however, it is the church that demands most attention. The interior is zealously painted and carved, including some naive scenes from the Passion depicted along the 16th-century rood-beam dividing the nave and choir.

Parish Closes

Reflecting the religious fervour of the Bretons, the Enclos Paroissiaux (parish closes) were built during the 15th–18th centuries. At that time Brittany had few urban centres but many wealthy rural settlements that profited from maritime trading and the manufacture of cloth. Grand religious monuments, some taking over 200 years to complete, were built by small villages inspired by spiritual zeal and the more earthly desire to rival their neighbours. Some of the finest parish closes lie in the Elorn valley, linked by a well-signposted Circuit des Enclos Paroissiaux.

The enclosure, *surrounded by a stone wall, is the hallowed area. By following the wall, visitors are drawn towards the triumphal arch, shown here in Pleyben.*

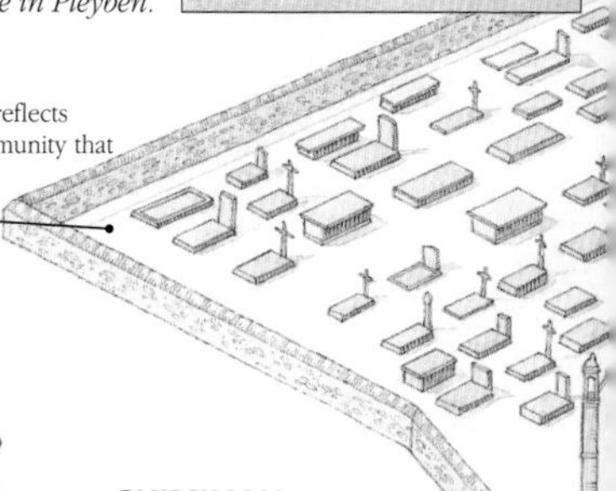

The small cemetery reflects the size of the community that built these great churches.

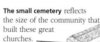

GUIMILIAU PARISH CLOSE

The three essential features of a parish close are a triumphal gateway marking the entry into the hallowed enclosure, a calvary depicting scenes from the Passion and Crucifixion, and an ossuary beside the church porch.

The calvary *is unique to Brittany, and may have been inspired by the crosses set on top of menhirs (see p279) by the early Christians. They provide a walk-around Bible lesson, often with the characters in 17th-century costumes as in this example from St-Thégonnec.*

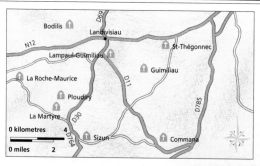

Brittany's parish closes *are mostly in the Elorn Valley. As well as St-Thégonnec, Lampaul-Guimiliau and Guimiliau, other parish closes to visit include Bodilis, La Martyre, La Roche-Maurice, Ploudiry, Sizun and Commana. Further afield lie Plougastel-Daoulas and Pleyben, while Guéhenno is in the Morbihan region.*
ℹ 14 av Maréchal Foch, Landivisiau (02 98 68 33 33).

Church interiors *are usually adorned with depictions of local saints and scenes from their lives, along with ornately carved beams and furniture. This is the altarpiece in Guimiliau.*

In the ossuary bones exhumed from the cemetery would be stored. Built close to the church entrance, the ossuary was considered a bridge between the living and the dead.

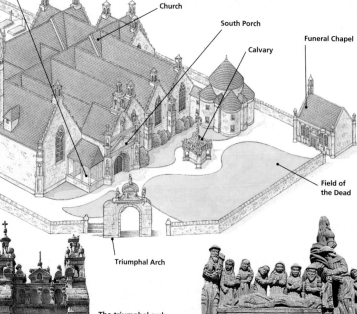

Church

South Porch

Calvary

Funeral Chapel

Field of the Dead

Triumphal Arch

The triumphal arch *at St-Thégonnec, a monumental entrance, heralds the worshipper's arrival on sacred ground, like the righteous entering heaven.*

Carvings in stone *were created as biblical cartoons to instruct and inspire visitors. Their clear message is now often obscured by weather and lichen, but this one in St-Thégonnec is well preserved.*

The chapel of Notre-Dame, perched on the cliffs above the beach of Port-Blanc, Côte de Granit Rose

Côte de Granit Rose 16

Côtes d'Armor. ☒ ⊟ ⊟ *Lannion.*
🛈 *Lannion (02 96 46 41 00).* ⊟
Thu. **www.**ot-lannion.fr

The coast between Paimpol
and Trébeurden is known as
the Côte de Granit Rose due
to its pink cliffs. These are
best between Trégastel and
Trébeurden; their granite is
also used in neighbouring
towns. The coast between
Trébeurden and Perros-Guirec
is one of Brittany's most
popular family holiday areas.
    Further east there are
quieter beaches and coves,
as at **Trévou-Tréguignec** and
Port-Blanc. Beyond Tréguier,
Paimpol is a working fishing
port that once sent huge cod
and whaling fleets to fish off
Iceland and Newfoundland.

Tréguier 17

Côtes d'Armor. 🏠 *2,950.*
🛈 *67 rue Ernest-Renan (02 96 92 22
33).* ⊟ *Wed.*

Overlooking the estuary of
the Jaundy and Guindy rivers,
Tréguier stands apart from the
seaside resorts of the Côte de
Granit Rose. It is a typically
Breton market town, with
one main attraction, the
14th–15th century **Cathédrale
St-Tugdual**. It has three towers,
one Romanesque, one Gothic,
and one 18th-century. The last,
financed by Louis XVI with
winnings from the Paris Lottery, has holes pierced in the
shapes of playing card suits.

Environs
Chapelle St-Gonery in
Plougrescant has a leaning
lead spire and a 15th-century
painted wooden ceiling.

Ile de Bréhat 18

Côtes d'Armor. 🏠 *420.* ⊟ ⊟
*Paimpol, then bus to Pointe de l'Arc-
ouest (Mon–Sat winter; daily summer), then boat.* 🛈 *Paimpol (02 96
20 83 16).* **www.**paimpol-goelo.com

A 15-minute crossing from
the Pointe de l'Arcouest, the
Ile de Bréhat is actually two
islands, joined by a bridge,
which together are only 3.5
km (2.2 miles) long. With
motorized traffic banned, and
a climate mild enough
for mimosa and a variety of
fruit trees to flourish, it has a
relaxing atmosphere. Bicycle
hire and boat tours are
available in the main town,
Port-Clos, and you can walk
to the island's highest point,
the **Chapelle St-Michel**.

Chapelle St-Michel, a landmark on
Ile de Bréhat

Carnac 19

Morbihan. 🏠 *4,600.* ⊟ 🛈 *74
avenue des Druides (02 97 52 13 52)*
www.ot-carnac.fr

Carnac is one of the world's
great prehistoric sites, with
almost 3,000 menhirs in
parallel rows, and an excellent
Musée de Préhistoire.
    The 17th-century **Eglise St-
Cornély** is dedicated to St
Cornelius, patron saint of
horned animals, scenes from
whose life are painted on its
wooden ceiling. The town is
a popular seaside resort.

⌂ Accueil Le Menec
Tel *02 97 52 29 81.* ◯ *daily.* 📷
summer only. 📷 *obligatory Apr–Sep.*

🏛 Musée de Préhistoire
10 pl de la Chapelle. **Tel** *02 97 52 22
04.* ◯ *daily.* ● *Wed am, Jan, 1 May,
25 Sep, 25 Dec.* 📷 🛈
www.museedecarnac.com

Presqu'île de Quiberon 20

Morbihan. 🏠 *5,200.* ☒ *Quiberon
(via Lorient).* ⊟ *Jul–Aug.* ⊟ ⊟
Quiberon. 🛈 *Quiberon (08 25 13
56 00).* ⊟ *Sat, Wed (summer).*
www.quiberon.com

Once an Island, the slender
Quiberon peninsula has a
bleak west coast with sea-
punished cliffs, known as the
Côte Sauvage. The east is
more benign. At the peninsula's southern tip is the fishing
port and resort of **Quiberon**,
with a car ferry to Belle-Ile. In
1795 10,000 Royalist troops
were massacred here in an ill-
fated attempt to reverse the
French Revolution.

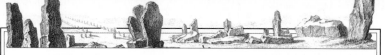

Brittany's Prehistoric Monuments

At Carnac, thousands of ancient granite rocks were arranged in mysterious lines and patterns by Megalithic tribes as early as 4000 BC. Their original purpose remains obscure: the significance was probably religious, but the precise patterns also suggest an early astronomical calendar. Celts, Romans and Christians have since adapted them to their own beliefs.

The Gavrinis Tumulus, Golfe du Morbihan

MEGALITHS

There are many different formations of megaliths, all with a particular purpose. Words from the Breton language, such as *men* (stone), *dole* (table) and *hir* (long), are still used to describe them.

Menhirs, *the most common megaliths, are upright stones, standing alone or arranged in lines. Those in circles are known as cromlechs.*

Dolmen, *two upright stones roofed by a third, were used as a burial chamber, such as the Merchant's Table at Locmariaquer.*

Allée couverte, *upright stones placed in a row and roofed to form a covered alley, can be seen at Carnac.*

A tumulus *is a dolmen covered with stones and soil to form a burial mound.*

KEY

| | Megalithic sites |
| | Alignments |

0 kilometres 10
0 miles 5

Brittany's major megalithic sites

Alignment at Carnac

Menhirs of all shapes in a field near Carnac

Belle-Île-en-Mer ㉑

Morbihan. 🏠 5,200. ✈ Quiberon
(via Lorient). ⛴ from Quiberon.
ℹ quai Bonnelle (02 97 31 81 93).
📅 Sat, Sun. www.belle-ile.com

Brittany's largest island lies
14 km (9 miles) south of
Quiberon and can be reached
in 45 minutes by car ferry
from Quiberon. The coast has
cliffs and good beaches;
inland lie exposed highlands
intersected by sheltered
valleys. In the main town, Le
Palais, stands the **Citadelle
Vauban**, a 16th-century star-
shaped fortress, and there are
fine walks and views along
the southern Côte Sauvage.

Breton seafarer, off Belle-Ile's coast

Cloisters of St-Pierre in Vannes

Vannes ㉒

Morbihan. 🏠 58,000. 🚆 🚌 ℹ 1
rue Thiers (08 25 13 56 10). 📅 Wed &
Sat. www.tourisme-vannes.com

Standing at the head of the
Golfe du Morbihan, Vannes
was the capital of the Veneti,
a seafaring Armorican tribe
defeated by Caesar in 56 BC.
In the 9th century Nominoë,
the first Duke of Brittany,
made it his power base. The
city remained influential up
until the signing of the union
with France in 1532, when
Rennes became the Breton
capital. Today it is a busy
commercial city with a well-
preserved medieval quarter,
and a good base for exploring
the Golfe du Morbihan.

The impressive eastern
walls of old Vannes can be
viewed from the promenade
de la Garenne. Two of the
city's old gates survive at
either end: Porte-Prison in the

north, and the southern Porte-
Poterne with a row of 17th-
century wash houses close by.

Walking up from Porte St-
Vincent, you find the city's
old market squares, still in
use today. The **place des Lices**
was once the scene of
medieval tournaments and the
streets around the rue de la
Monnaie are full of well-
preserved 16th-century houses.

Begun in the 13th century,
Cathédrale St-Pierre has since
been drastically remodelled
and restored. The Chapel of
the Holy Sacrament houses
the revered tomb of Vincent
Ferrier, a Spanish saint who
died in Vannes in 1419.

Opposite the west front
of the cathedral, the old
covered market **La Cohue**
(meaning throng or hubbub)
was once the city's central
meeting place. Parts of the
building date from the 13th
century, and a small museum
inside displays art and
artifacts relevant to the history
of the area.

Housed in the 15th-century
Château Gaillard, the **Musée**

d'**Archéologique** is a rich
assembly of finds from
Morbihan's many prehistoric
sites, including jewellery,
pottery and weapons. There
is also a gallery of medieval
and Renaissance *objets d'art*.

🏛 **Musée d'Archéologique**
Château Gaillard, 2 rue Noé.
Tel 02 97 01 63 00. 🕐 daily (Oct–
mid-Jun: pms only). 🔴 public hols. 🖾

Environs
To the south of the city the
Parc du Golfe is a beautiful
leisure park with many
amusements, a butterfly
conservatory, an automaton
museum and an aquarium
that boasts over 400 species
of fish. Northeast of Vannes,
off the N166, lie the romantic
ruins of the 15th-century
Tours d'Elven.

Golfe du Morbihan ㉓

Morbihan. ✈ Lorient. 🚆 🚌 ⛴
Vannes. ℹ Vannes (08 25 13 56 10).
www.tourisme-vannes.com

Morbihan means "little sea"
in Breton, an apt description
for this landlocked expanse
of tidal water. Only
connected to the Atlantic by a
small channel between the
Locmariaquer and Rhuys
peninsulas, the gulf is dotted
with islands. Around 40 are
inhabited, with the **Ile d'Arz**
and the **Ile aux Moines** the
largest. These are served by
regular ferries from Conleau
and Port-Blanc respectively.

Around the gulf several small
harbours earn a living from
fishing, oyster cultivation and

The picturesque fishing port of Le Bono in Golfe du Morbihan

Young holidaymakers on the beach at Dinard, a classic seaside resort on the Emerald Coast

tourism. There is a wealth of megalithic sites, notably the island of **Gavrinis** where stone carvings have been excavated (*see p279*). There are boat trips to Gavrinis from Larmor-Baden and around the gulf from Locmariaquer, Auray, Vannes and Port-Navalo.

The medieval Château de Josselin on the banks of the river Oust

Josselin ❷

Morbihan. 🌇 2,500. 🚊 🚹 *pl de la Congrégation (02 97 22 36 43)*. 🚢 Sat. www.paysdejosselin-tourisme.com

Overlooking the river Oust, Josselin is dominated by a medieval **Château** owned by the de Rohan family since the end of the 15th century. Only four of its nine towers survive. The elaborate inner granite façade incorporates the letter "A" – a tribute to the much-loved Duchess Anne of Brittany (1477–1514), who presided over Brittany's "Golden Age". Tours are given of the 19th-century interior, and in the former stables there is a Musée des Poupées with 600 dolls. In the town, **Basilique Notre-**

Dame-du-Roncier contains the mausoleum of the castle's most famous owner and constable of France, Olivier de Clisson (1336–1407). West of Josselin at Kerguéhennec, the grounds of an 18th-century château have become a modern sculpture park.

⚜ **Château de Josselin**
Tel 02 97 22 36 45. 🕐 *Apr–May, Oct & sch hols: Sat–Sun & public hols, pms only; Jun–Sep: daily.*
🈸 &

Forêt de Paimpont ❷

Ille-et-Vilaine. 🚊 Rennes. 🚍 Monfort-sur-Meu. 🚍 Rennes. 🚹 Plélan (02 99 06 86 07).

Also known as the Forêt de Brocéliande, this forest is a last remnant of the dense primeval woods that once covered much of Armorica. It has long been associated with the legends of King Arthur, and visitors still come to search for the magical

Legendary sorcerer Merlin and Viviane, the Lady of the Lake

spring where the sorcerer Merlin first met Viviane, the Lady of the Lake. The small village of **Paimpont** provides a good base for exploring both the forest and its myths.

Côte d'Emeraude ❷

Ille et Vilaine & Côtes d'Armor. 🚹
🚫 Dinard–St-Malo. 🚊 🚢 🚢
🚹 Dinard (02 99 46 94 12). www.ot-dinard.com

Between Le Val-André and the Pointe du Grouin, near Cancale, sandy beaches, rocky headlands and classic seaside resorts stretch along Brittany's northern shore. Known as the Emerald Coast, its self-proclaimed Queen is the aristocratic resort of **Dinard**, "discovered" in the 1850s and still playing host to the international rich.

To its west are resorts like St-Jacut-de-la-Mer, St-Cast-le-Guildo, Sables d'Or-les-Pins and Erquy, all with tempting beaches. In the Baie de la Frênaye, the medieval **Fort La Latte** provides good views from its ancient watchtower, while the lighthouse that dominates **Cap Fréhel** nearby offers even more extensive panoramas.

East of Dinard, the D186 runs across the **Barrage de la Rance** to St-Malo. Built in 1966 it was the world's first dam to generate electricity by using tidal power. Beyond St-Malo, coves and beaches surround La Guimorais, while around the Pointe du Grouin the seas are often truly emerald.

SEAFARERS OF ST-MALO

St-Malo owes its wealth and reputation to the exploits of its mariners. In 1534 Jacques Cartier, born in nearby Rothéneuf, discovered the mouth of the St Lawrence river in Canada and claimed the territory for France. It was Breton sailors who voyaged to South America in 1698 to colonize the Iles Malouines, known today as Las Malvinas or the Falklands. By the 17th century St-Malo was the largest port in France and famous for its corsairs – privateers licensed by the king to prey on foreign ships. The most illustrious were the swashbuckling René Duguay-Trouin (1673–1736), who captured Rio de Janeiro from the Portuguese in 1711, and the intrepid Robert Surcouf (1773–1827), whose ships hounded vessels of the British East India Company. The riches won by trade and piracy enabled St-Malo's ship-owners to build great mansions known as *malouinières*.

Explorer Jacques Cartier (1491–1557)

St-Malo ㉗

Ille-et-Vilaine. 🏠 53,000. ✈ 🚉 🚌 ⛴ 🚪 esplanade St-Vincent *(08 25 13 52 00).* 🛒 *Mon–Sat.* **www**.saint-malo.fr

Once a fortified island, St-Malo stands in a commanding position at the mouth of the river Rance.

The city is named after Maclou, a Welsh monk who came here in the 6th century to spread the Christian message. During the 16th–19th centuries the port won prosperity and power through the exploits of its seafarers. St-Malo was heavily bombed in 1944 but has since been scrupulously restored and is now a major port and ferry terminal as well as a resort.

The old city is encircled by ramparts that provide fine views of St-Malo and its islands. Take the steps up by the **Porte St-Vincent** and walk clockwise, passing the 15th-century **Grande Porte**.

Within the city is a web of cobbled streets with tall 18th-century buildings housing shops, fish restaurants and crêperies. Rue Porcon-de-la-Barbinais leads to **Cathédrale St-Vincent**, with its sombre 12th-century nave contrasting with the stained glass of the chancel. On cour La Houssaye, the 15th-century Maison de la Duchesse Anne has been carefully restored.

St-Malo seen at low tide through the gate of Fort National

♜ Château de St-Malo

Pl Châteaubriand, near the Marina. **Tel** *02 99 40 71 57.* ☐ *Apr–Sep: daily; Oct–Mar: Tue–Sun.* ● *1 Jan, 1 May, 1 & 11 Nov, 25 Dec.* 🖼

St-Malo's castle dates from the 14th–15th centuries. The great keep contains a museum of the city's history, including the adventures of its state-sponsored corsairs. From its watch towers there is an impressive view. Nearby, in the place Vauban, a tropical aquarium has been built into the ramparts, while on the edge of town, the Grand Aquarium has a shark tank and simulated submarine rides.

🏰 Fort National

☐ *Jun–Sep: daily at low tide.* 🖼

Constructed in 1689 by Louis XIV's famous military architect, Vauban, this fort can be reached on foot at low tide and offers good views of St-Malo and its ramparts. At low tide you can also walk out to **Petit Bé Fort** (open Easter–mid-Nov) and **Grand Bé**, where St-Malo-born writer François-René de Chateaubriand lies buried. From the top there are great views along the whole of Côte d'Emeraude *(see p281)*.

🏰 Tour Solidor

St-Servan. **Tel** *02 99 40 71 58.* ☐ *Apr–Sep: daily; Oct–Mar: Tue–Sun.* ● *1 Jan, 1 May, 1 & 11 Nov, 25 Dec.* 🖼

To the west of St-Malo in St-Servan, the three-towered Tour Solidor was built in 1382. Formerly a toll house, it was also a prison under the Revolution, and now houses an intriguing museum devoted to the ships and sailors that rounded Cape Horn, with ship models, logs and various nautical instruments.

Environs

When the tide is out, good beaches are revealed around St-Malo and in the nearby suburbs of St-Servan and Paramé. A passenger ferry runs to Dinard in summer *(see p281)* and the Channel Islands and there are boat trips up the Rance to Dinan, and out to the Iles Chausey, Ile de Cézembre and Cap Fréhel.

At Rothéneuf you can visit the **Manoir Limoëlou**, home of the navigator Jacques Cartier. Nearby, on the coast, Les Rochers Sculptés is a

Cancale oysters, prized for their taste since Roman times

beguiling array of granite faces and figures carved into the cliffs by a local priest, Abbé Fouré, at the end of the 19th century.

🏚 **Manoir Limoëlou**
Rue D Macdonald-Stuart, Limoëlou-Rothéneuf. *Tel* 02 99 40 97 73. ◯ Jul–Aug: daily; Sep–Jun: Mon–Sat. ● public hols. 🎫 ⭑

Cancale ㉘

Ille-et-Vilaine. 🏘 5,350. 🚉 🛈 44 rue du Port (02 99 89 63 72). 🖹 Sun. **www**.cancale-tourisme.fr

A small port with views across the Baie du Mont-St-Michel, Cancale is entirely devoted to the cultivation and consumption of oysters. Prized by the Romans, the acclaimed flavour of Cancale's oysters is said to derive from the strong tides that wash over them daily. You can survey the beds from a *sentier des douaniers* (coastguards' footpath, the GR34) running along the cliffs.

There are plenty of opportunities for sampling the local speciality provided by a multitude of bars and restaurants along the busy quays of the Port de la Houle, where the fishing boats arrive at high tide. Devotees should pay a visit to the **Musée de l'Huître, du Coquillage et de la Mer.**

🏛 **Musée de l'Huître, du Coquillage et de la Mer – La Ferme Marine**
Aurore. *Tel* 02 99 89 69 99. ◯ mid-Jun–mid-Sep: daily; mid-Feb–mid-Jun & mid-Sep–Oct: Mon–Fri pm. 🎫 in English 2pm daily. 🎫

Dinan ㉙

Côtes d'Armor. 🏘 10,000. 🚉 🚍
🛈 9 rue du Château (02 96 87 69 76). 🖹 Thu. **www**.dinan-tourisme.com

Set on a hill overlooking the wooded Rance valley, Dinan is a modern market town with a medieval heart. Surrounded by ramparts, the well-kept, half-timbered houses and cobbled streets of its Vieille Ville have an impressive, unforced unity best appreciated by climbing to the top of its 15th-century **Tour d'Horloge**, in rue de l'Horloge. Nearby, **Basilique St-Sauveur** contains the heart of Dinan's most famous son, the 14th-century warrior Bertrand du Guesclin.

Behind the church, Les Jardins Anglais offer good views of the river Rance and the viaduct spanning it. A couple of streets further north, the steep, geranium-decorated rue du Jerzual winds down through the 14th-century town gate to the port. Once a busy harbour from which cloth was shipped, it is now a

quiet backwater where you can take a pleasure cruise, or walk along a towpath to the restored 17th-century **Abbaye St-Magloire** at Léhon.

The **Musée du Château** houses a small museum of local history. Next to it is the 15th-century **Tour de Coëtquen**. From here are walks beside the ramparts along the promenade des Petits Fossés and the promenade des Grands Fossés.

⛪ **Musée du Château**
Château de la Duchesse Anne, rue du Château. *Tel* 02 96 39 45 20. ◯ daily. ● Jan, 1 week Feb, public hols. 🎫

Author and diplomat François-René de Chateaubriand (1768–1848)

Combourg ㉚

Ille-et-Vilaine. 🏘 5,000. 🚉 🚍
🛈 23 pl Albert Parent (02 99 73 13 93). 🖹 Mon. **www**.combourg.org

A small, sleepy town beside a lake, Combourg is completely overshadowed by the great, haunting **Château de Combourg**. The buildings seen today date from the 14th and 15th centuries. In 1761 the château was bought by the Comte de Chateaubriand, and the melancholic childhood spent there by his son, the author and diplomat François-René de Chateaubriand (1768–1848), is candidly described in his entertaining chronicle, *Mémoires d'Outre-Tombe*.

Empty after the Revolution, the château was restored in the 19th century and is open for tours. One room has the belongings of François-René de Chateaubriand.

⛪ **Château de Combourg**
23 rue des Princes. *Tel* 02 99 73 22 95, 02 99 73 29 81. ◯ Jul–Aug: daily; Apr–Jun & Sep–Oct: Sun–Fri. 🎫 **www**.combourg.net

View over Dinan and the Gothic bridge crossing the river Rance

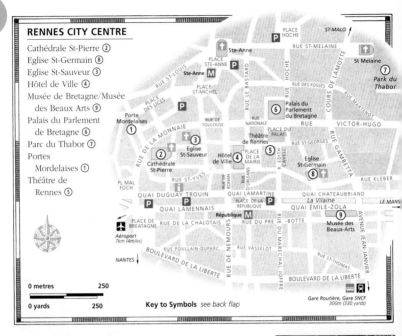

RENNES CITY CENTRE

Cathédrale St-Pierre ②
Eglise St-Germain ⑧
Eglise St-Sauveur ③
Hôtel de Ville ④
Musée de Bretagne/Musée
  des Beaux Arts ⑨
Palais du Parlement
  de Bretagne ⑥
Parc du Thabor ⑦
Portes
  Mordelaises ①
Théâtre de
  Rennes ⑤

0 metres   250
0 yards   250

Key to Symbols see back flap

Rennes ③

Ille-et-Vilaine. 212,500.
11 rue St-Yves (02 99 6711 11).
Tue–Sat. www.tourisme-rennes.com

Founded by the Gauls and
colonized by the Romans,
Rennes is strategically located
where the Vilaine and Ille
rivers meet. After Brittany's
union with France in 1532, the
town became regional capital.
In 1720 a fire lasting for six
days devastated the city. Today
a small part of the medieval
city survives, together with
the neat grid of 18th-century

The lively market at place des Lices
in the heart of Rennes

buildings that arose from the
ashes. Around this historic
core are the tower blocks and
hi-tech factories of modern
Rennes – a confident provincial
capital with two universities
and a thriving cultural life.
　Wandering through the
streets that radiate from the
place des Lices and the place
Ste-Anne, it is easy to imagine
what Rennes was like before
the Great Fire. Now mostly
pedestrianized, this area has
become the city's youthful
heart with plenty of bars,
crêperies and designer shops.
At the western end of rue de
la Monnaie stands the 15th-
century **Portes Mordelaises**,
once part of the city's ramparts.
　Close by, **Cathédrale St-
Pierre** was completed in 1844,
the third on this site. Note the
carved 16th-century Flemish
altarpiece. Nearby is the 18th-
century **Eglise St-Sauveur**. Just
south of the attractive rue St-
George, **Eglise St-Germain**
has a typically Breton belfry
and wooden vaulting. In the
place de la Mairie stands the
early 18th-century **Hôtel de
Ville** and the Neo-Classical
Théâtre de Rennes. The **Parc
du Thabor**, once part of a
Benedictine monastery,
is ideal for walks and picnics.

**Half-timbered houses lining the
narrow streets of old Rennes**

🏛 Palais du Parlement
de Bretagne

Pl du Parlement. ⬜ Tourist Office
for guided tours (02 99 67 11 66).
www.parlement-bretagne.com
Rennes' Law Courts, built in
1618–55, were the seat of
the region's governing body
until the Revolution. Severely
damaged by fire during riots
over fish prices in 1994, the
major restoration work is
all but complete, including the
unique coffered ceiling and
gilded woodwork of the
Grande Chambre. Today,
only the Salle des Pas Perdus,
with its vaulted ceilings, sadly
remains closed.

⌂ Musée de Bretagne, Musée des Beaux Arts

46 bd Magenta. **Tel** 02 23 40 66 70 *(Musée de Bretagne).* **Tel** 02 23 62 17 45 *(Musée des Beaux Arts).* ◯ *Tue–Sun.* ◉ *public hols.* **www.mbar.org**

The permanent collection of the Musée de Bretagne includes examples of traditional Breton furniture and costume, and displays on Brittany's prehistoric megaliths, the growth of Rennes, rural crafts and the fishing industry. Since 2005, the museum has changed its focus, with more emphasis on exhibits from outside the city.

In the same building, the **Musée des Beaux Arts** has a wide-ranging collection of art from the 14th century to the present, including a room of art on Breton themes. There are paintings by Gauguin, Bernard and other members of the Pont-Aven School *(see p275),* and three works by Picasso, including the lively *Baigneuse* painted at Dinard in 1928.

Environs

Just south of Rennes, the **Eco-musée du Pays de Rennes** traces the history of a local farm since the 17th century.

Some 16 km (10 miles) to the southeast of Rennes is **Châteaugiron**, a charming medieval village, with an imposing castle and houses preserving their wooden eaves.

⌂ Ecomusée du Pays de Rennes

Ferme de la Bintinais, rte de Châtillon-sur-Seiche. **Tel** 02 99 51 38 15. ◯ *Feb–mid-Jan: Tue–Sun.* ◉ *w/e ams, public hols.*

♣ Château de Châteaugiron

Tel 02 99 37 89 02. ◯ *Jul–mid-Sep: daily; Jun: Sun; by appt rest of year.*

Fougères ❷

Ille-et-Vilaine. 🚶 *23,000.* 🚌 **ℹ** *2 rue Nationale (02 99 94 12 20).* 📅 *Sat.* **www.ot-fougeres.fr**

A fortress town close to the Breton border, Fougères rests on a hill overlooking the Nançon river. In the valley below, and still linked to the Haute Ville by a curtain of ancient ramparts, stands the mighty 11th–15th century

The mighty fortifications of Château de Fougères

Château de Fougères. To get a good overview of the château, go to the gardens of place aux Arbres behind the 16th-century **Eglise St-Léonard**. From here you can descend to the river and the medieval houses around place du Marchix. The Flamboyant Gothic **Eglise St-Sulpice**, with its 18th-century wood-panelled interior and granite retables, is well worth visiting.

A walk around the castle's massive outer fortifications reveals the ambitious scale of its construction, with 13 towers and walls over 3 m (10 ft) thick. You can still climb the castle's ramparts and towers to get a feel of what it was like to live and fight within its staggered defences. Much of the action in Balzac's novel *Les Chouans* (1829) takes place in and around Fougères and its castle.

♣ Château de Fougères

Pl Pierre-Simon. **Tel** 02 99 99 79 59. ◯ *Feb–Dec: daily.*

Overhanging timber-frame houses on rue Beaudrairie, Vitré

Vitré ❸

Ille-et-Vilaine. 🚶 *16,000.* 🚌 🚆 **ℹ** *pl Général de Gaulle (02 99 75 04 46).* 📅 *Mon & Sat.* **www.ot-vitre.fr**

The fortified town of Vitré is set high on a hill overlooking the Vilaine valley. Its medieval **Château** is complete with pencil-point turrets and picturesque 15th–16th century buildings in attendance. The castle was rebuilt in the 14th–15th centuries and follows a triangular plan, with some of its ramparts walkable. There is a museum of local treasures in the Tour St-Laurent.

To the east, rue Beaudrairie and rue d'Embas have overhanging timber-frame houses with remarkable patterning.

The 15th–16th century **Cathédrale Notre-Dame**, built in Flamboyant Gothic style, has a south façade with an exterior stone pulpit. Further along rue Notre-Dame, the promenade du Val skirts around the town's ramparts.

To the southeast of Vitré on the D88, the **Château des Rochers-Sévigné** was once the home of Mme de Sévigné (1626–96), famous letter-writer and chronicler of life at the court of Louis XIV. The park, chapel and some of her rooms are open to the public.

♣ Château de Vitré

Tel 02 99 75 04 54. ◯ *Apr–Sep: daily; Oct–Mar: Wed–Mon (Sat pms only).* ◉ *1 Jan, Easter, 1 Nov, 25 Dec.*

♣ Château des Rochers-Sévigné

Tel 02 99 96 76 51. ◯ ◉ *same as above.* ⬛ restricted.

THE LOIRE VALLEY

INDRE · INDRE-ET-LOIRE · LOIR-ET-CHER · LOIRET · EURE-ET-LOIR
CHER · VENDEE · MAINE-ET-LOIRE · LOIRE-ATLANTIQUE · SARTHE

Renowned for its sumptuous chateaux, the glorious valley of the Loire, now classified a UNESCO World Heritage Site, is rich both in history and architecture. Like the river Loire, this vast region runs through the heart of French life. Its sophisticated cities, luxuriant landscape and magnificent food and wine add up to a bourgeois paradise.

The lush Loire Valley is supremely regal. Orléans was France's intellectual capital in the 13th century, attracting artists, poets and troubadours to the royal court. But the medieval court never stayed in one place for long, which led to the building of magnificent châteaux all along the Loire. Chambord and Chenonceau, the two greatest Renaissance châteaux, remain prestigious symbols of royal rule, resplendent amid vast hunting forests and waterways.

Due to its central location, culture and fine cuisine, Tours is the natural visitors' capital. Angers is a close second but more authentic are the historic towns of Saumur, Amboise, Blois and Beaugency, strung out like jewels along the river. This is the classic Loire Valley, a château trail which embraces the Renaissance gardens of Villandry and the fairytale turrets of Ussé. Venture northwards and the cathedral cities of Le Mans and Chartres reign supreme, their medieval centres bordered by Gallo-Roman walls. Nantes in the west is a breezy, forward-looking port and gateway to the Atlantic.

Southwards, the windswept Vendée is edged by a wild, sandy coastline that is perfect for windsurfers and nature lovers alike. Inland, the Loire's more peaceful tributaries and the watery Sologne beg to be explored. Also ripe for discovery are troglodyte caves, sleepy hamlets, and small Romanesque churches decorated with frescoes. Inviting inns offer game, fish and abundant fresh vegetables to be lingered over with a light white Vouvray wine or a full-bodied Bourgeuil. Over-indulgence is no sin in this rich region.

The river Loire at Montsoreau, southeast of Saumur

◁ The fairytale Château de Saumur towering above the town and the river Loire

Exploring the Loire Valley

The lush valley landscape, studded with France's greatest châteaux, is the main attraction. Numerous river cruises are available, while the sandy Atlantic coast offers beach holidays. Peaceful country holidays can be had in the Vendée, and in the Loir and Indre valleys. Wine tours focus on Bourgueil, Chinon, Muscadet, Saumur and Vouvray vintages. The most charming bases are Amboise, Blois, Beaugency and Saumur, but culture-lovers are well-provided for throughout the region.

Countryside around Vouvray

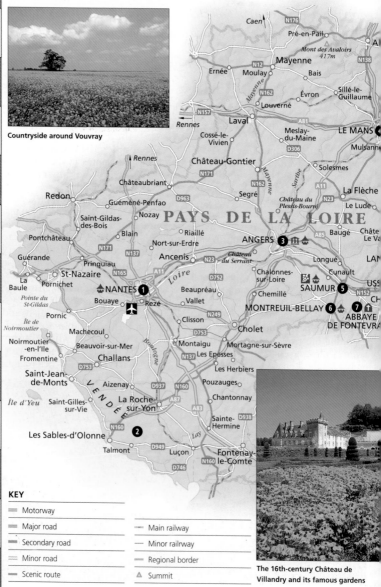

PAYS DE LA LOIRE

VENDÉE

Caen   N176
Pré-en-Pail
Mont des Avaloirs
417m   N138
Ernée   Moulay   Mayenne   Bais   Évron   Sillé-le-Guillaume
N12   N162   Louverné   Meslay-du-Maine   LE MANS
Rennes   N157   Laval   A81   Mulsanne
Cossé-le-Vivien   D306
Château-Gontier   Solesmes   La Flèche
Rennes   N171   Segré   N162   A11   N23   Le Lude
Châteaubriant   Château du Plessis-Bourré
Redon   Guémené-Penfao   D963   Baugé   Châte Le Va
Saint-Gildas-des-Bois   Nozay   Riaillé   ANGERS ③ 🏛 ⛪   A85
Pontchâteau   Blain   Nort-sur-Erdre   N23   Château du Serrant   Longué   LAN
Guérande   N171   Ancenis   Chalonnes-sur-Loire   Cunault   USS
Prinquiau   N137   Loire   D752   SAUMUR ⑤   N152   CH
La Baule   St-Nazaire   N165   A11   NANTES ①   Beaupréau   Chemillé   MONTREUIL-BELLAY ⑥ ⑦ ABBAYE DE FONTEVRA
Pornichet   Bouaye   Rezé   Vallet
Pointe du St-Gildas   Pornic   Clisson   N249   Cholet
Île de Noirmoutier   Machecoul   D753   Montaigu   Mortagne-sur-Sèvre
Noirmoutier-en-l'Île   Beauvoir-sur-Mer   Challans   N137   Les Epesses
Fromentine   D753   Les Herbiers
Saint-Jean-de-Monts   Aizenay   D937   N160   Pouzauges
Île d'Yeu   Saint-Gilles-sur-Vie   La Roche-sur-Yon   A87   Chantonnay
A83   Sainte-Hermine   D938
Les Sables-d'Olonne ②   N160   Lay   Luçon   Fontenay-le-Comte
Talmont   D949   N160
D746

KEY

═══ Motorway

━━━ Major road

─── Secondary road

═══ Minor road

─── Scenic route

┉┉┉ Main railway

─ ─ ─ Minor railway

▬▬▬ Regional border

△ Summit

The 16th-century Château de Villandry and its famous gardens

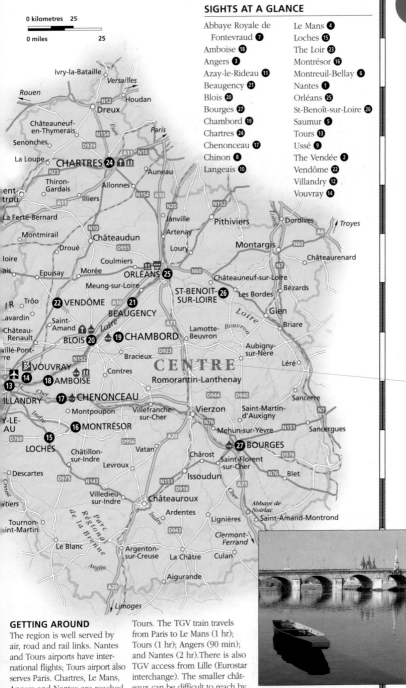

0 kilometres   25

0 miles   25

Ivry-la-Bataille

Versailles

Rouen

N12

Houdan

Dreux

Châteauneuf-
en-Thymerais

N154

Paris

Senonches

D939

La Loupe

N23

CHARTRES **24**

Auneau

ent-
trou

Thiron-
Gardais

Illiers

Allonnes

N154

N10

La Ferté-Bernard

A11

N20

N152

Montmirail

N10

Janville

Pithiviers

Dordives

Troyes

loire

Droué

Châteaudun

D955

Artenay

Montargis

N60

A6

ais

Epuisay

Morée

Coulmiers

Loury

Châteaurenard

Trôo

Meung-sur-Loire

ORLÉANS **25**

N60

Châteauneuf-sur-Loire

N7

Bézards

Lavardin

22 **VENDÔME**

A10

21

**ST-BENOIT-
SUR-LOIRE** **26**

Les Bordes

Gien

Château-
Renault

Saint-
Amand

BEAUGENCY

Loire

Beuvron

Briare

Aubigny-
sur-Nère

illé-Pont-
re

BLOIS **20**

19 **CHAMBORD**

Lamotte-
Beuvron

Léré

N152

Bracieux

D923

VOUVRAY

14

18 **AMBOISE**

Contres

CENTRE

Romorantin-Lanthenay

Sancerre

13

ILLANDRY

17 **CHENONCEAU**

Cher

Villefranche-
sur-Cher

Vierzon

Saint-Martin-
d'Auxigny

N7

Y-LE-
AU

Montpoupon

D944

D940

N151

Sancergues

16 **MONTRÉSOR**

A20

Mehun-sur-Yèvre

15

LOCHES

D956

Châtillon-
sur-Indre

Vatan

N76

27 **BOURGES**

D976

Descartes

D975

N143

Levroux

Chârost

Saint-Florent-
sur-Cher

Blet

N76

itiers

D918

N151

Issoudun

A71

Tournon-
int-Martin

Villedieu-
sur-Indre

Indre

Châteauroux

Ardentes

Lignières

Abbaye de
Noirlac

Saint-Amand-Montrond

Le Blanc

Parc
Régional
de la Brenne

D943

Clermont-
Ferrand

Argenton-
sur-Creuse

La Châtre

Culan

Anglin

Aigurande

A20

Limoges

GETTING AROUND

The region is well served by air, road and rail links. Nantes and Tours airports have international flights; Tours airport also serves Paris. Chartres, Le Mans, Angers and Nantes are reached from Paris by the A11, and the A10 links Orléans, Blois and Tours. The TGV train travels from Paris to Le Mans (1 hr); Tours (1 hr); Angers (90 min); and Nantes (2 hr). There is also TGV access from Lille (Eurostar interchange). The smaller châteaux can be difficult to reach by public transport, but there are tours from major tourist centres.

A bridge over the Loire river pictured at dawn

Tomb of François II and his wife, Marguerite de Foix, in Cathédrale St-Pierre

Nantes ❶

Loire-Atlantique. 🏛 270,000. ✈
🚌 🚆 ℹ 3 cours Olivier-de-Clisson
(08 92 46 40 44). 🗓 Tue–Sun.
www.nantes-tourisme.com

For centuries, Nantes disputed with Rennes the title of capital of Brittany. Yet links with the Plantagenets and Henri IV also bound it to the "royal" river Loire. Since the 1790s it has officially ceased to be part of Brittany, and, though still Breton at heart, it is today capital of the Pays de la Loire.

Visually, Nantes is a city of variety, with high-tech towers overlooking the port, canals and Art Nouveau squares. Chic bars and restaurants cram the medieval nucleus, bounded by place St-Croix and the château.

The **Cathédrale St-Pierre et St-Paul**, completed in 1893, is notable both for its sculpted Gothic portals and Renaissance tomb of François II, the last duke of Brittany.

More impressive is the **Château des Ducs de Bretagne**, where Anne of Brittany was born in 1477 and where the Edict of Nantes was signed by Henri IV in 1598, granting Protestants religious freedom. The château underwent major restoration work in 2005 and now houses a new museum charting the history of Nantes, including the city's colonial links and slave-trading activities in the 18th and 19th centuries.

⛪ Château des Ducs de Bretagne
Pl Marc Elder. **Tel** 02 51 17 49 00. 🕐 phone to check schedule. 🏛

Environs
From Nantes, boats cruise the Erdre and Sèvre Nantaise rivers, passing minor châteaux, Muscadet vineyards and gentle countryside. Some 30 km (20 miles) southeast of Nantes is **Clisson**, a town razed to the ground during the Vendée Uprising of 1793, and later rebuilt along Italian lines, with Neo-Classical villas, brick belltowers and red-tiled roofs. On a rocky spur overlooking the Sèvre Nantaise river is the ruined 13th-century **Château de Clisson**, which is undergoing restoration.

⛪ Château de Clisson
Tel 02 40 54 02 22.
🕐 Wed–Mon. 🔴 1 May,
Christmas hols. 🏛 📷

The Vendée ❷

Vendée and Maine-et-Loire.
✈ Nantes. 🚌 🚆 La Roche-sur-Yon.
ℹ La Roche-sur-Yon (02 51 36 00 85)
www.vendee-tourisme.com

The counter-revolutionary movement which swept western France between 1793 and 1799 began as a series of uprisings in the Vendée, still an evocative name to the French. As a bastion of the *Ancien Régime*, the region rebelled against urban Republican values. But a violent massacre in 1793 left 80,000 royalists dead in one day as they tried to cross the Loire at St-Florent-le-Vieil. The Vendée farmers were staunch royalists, and, although they ultimately lost, the region remains coloured by conservatism and religious fervour to this day.

This local history is dramatically retraced at **Le Puy du Fou** in Les Epesses, south of Cholet, with its spectacular summer evening live show, 'Cinéscenie'. More sober accounts are given at Logis de La Chabotterie near St-Sulpice-de-Verdon, and the Musée du Textile in Cholet, whose flax and hemp textiles provided the royalist heroes with their kerchiefs: originally white, then blood-red.

The tranquil Vendée offers green tourism inland, in the *bocage vendéen*, a wooded backwater with paths and nature trails. The Atlantic coast between the Loire and La Rochelle has beaches, yet the only sizeable resort here is **Les Sables d'Olonne**, with boat trips to the salt-marshes, out to sea or to the nearby **Ile**

The harbour at Ile de Noirmoutier in the Vendée

d'Yeu. To the north, the marshy **Ile de Noirmoutier** is connected to the mainland at low tide via the Gois causeway.

Inland lies the remote **Marais Poitevin** (*see p408*), its marshes home to bird sanctuaries and fine churches (Maillezais, Vix, Maillé) in hamlets bordered by canals. It is France's largest complex of man-made waterways, largely reclaimed for farming in the west, whilst further east is a nature lover's paradise. Coulon is the main centre for hiring punts.

The Apocalypse Tapestry in Angers

Angers ❸

Maine-et-Loire. 🏠 156,300. ☒ 🚌 🚆 ℹ 7 *pl Kennedy* (02 41 23 50 00). 🅿 Tue–Sun. **www**.angersloiretourisme.com

Angers is the historic capital of Anjou, home of the Plantagenets and gateway to the Loire Valley. The town has a formidable 13th-century **Château** (*see p242*). Inside is the longest (103m) and one of the finest medieval tapestries in the world. It tells the story of the Apocalypse, with battles between hydras and angels.

A short walk from the castle is the **Cathédrale St-Maurice**, noted for its façade and 13th-century stained-glass windows. Close by is Maison d'Adam, with carvings showing the tree of life. The nearby **Galerie David d'Angers**, housed in the glass-covered ruins of a 13th-century church, celebrates the sculptor born in Angers. Across the river Maine, the Hôpital St-Jean, a hospital for the poor from 1174 to 1854, houses the **Musée Jean Lurçat**. Its prize exhibit is the exquisite *Chant du Monde* tapestry, which was created by Lurçat in 1957. In the same building is **Le Musée de la Tapisserie Contemporaine**, with displays of ceramics and paintings.

⛫ **Château d'Angers**
Tel 02 41 86 48 77. ⬜ daily. ⬤ 1 Jan, 1 May, 1 & 11 Nov, 25 Dec. 🎫

🏛 **Galerie David d'Angers**
33 bis rue Toussaint. **Tel** 02 41 05 38 90. ⬜ Oct–Jun: daily; Jul–Sep: Tue–Sun. ⬤ most public hols. 🎫

🏛 **Musée Jean Lurçat / Le Musée de la Tapisserie Contemporaine**
4 bd Arago. **Tel** 02 41 24 18 45. ⬜ Jun–Sep: daily; Oct–May: Tue–Sun. ⬤ most public hols. 🎫 ♿

Environs
Within a 20-km (13-mile) radius of Angers lie the Classical **Château de Serrant** and the moated **Château du Plessis-Bourré**, a decorative pleasure dome encased in a feudal shell. Follow the Loire east along the sandbanks and dykes, enjoying the rustic fish restaurants en route.

⛫ **Château de Serrant**
St-Georges-sur-Loire. **Tel** 02 41 39 13 01. ⬜ Jul–Aug: daily; Apr–Jun & Sep –mid-Nov: Wed–Mon. 🎫 ⬤ oblig. **www**.chateau-serrant.net

⛫ **Château du Plessis-Bourré**
Ecuillé. **Tel** 02 41 32 06 01. ⬜ Jul–Aug: daily; Apr–Jun & Sep: Thu pm–Tue (Feb, Mar, Oct, Nov: Thu–Tue pm only). 🎫 ⬤ oblig. **www**.plessis-bourre.com

Le Mans ❹

Sarthe. 🏠 150,000. ☒ 🚌 🚆 ℹ rue de l'Etoile (02 43 28 17 22). 🅿 Tue–Sun. **www**.lemanstourisme.com

Ever since Monsieur Bollée became the first designer to place an engine under a car bonnet, Le Mans has been synonymous with the motor trade. Bollée's son created an embryonic Grand Prix, since when the event (*see p37*) and associated **Musée Automobile** have

---

Stained-glass Ascension window in the Cathédrale St-Julien, Le Mans

remained star attractions. Cité Plantagenêt, the ancient fortified centre, is surrounded by the greatest Roman walls in France, best seen from the quai Louis Blanc. Once insalubrious and abandoned, the area has been extensively restored, and is now used for filming epics such as Cyrano de Bergerac, set amongst its Renaissance mansions, half-timbered houses, arcaded alleys and tiny courtyards. The crowning point is the Gothic **Cathédrale St-Julien**, borne aloft on flying buttresses, with its Romanesque portal rivalling that of Chartres. Inside, the Angevin nave opens into a Gothic choir, complemented by sculpted capitals and a 12th-century Ascension window.

🏛 **Musée Automobile**
Circuit des 24 Heures du Mans. **Tel** 02 43 72 72 24. ⬜ Feb–Nov: daily; Dec–Jan: weekends. 🎫 ♿

Le Mans racetrack: a 1933 print from the French magazine *Illustration*

Saumur ❺

Maine-et-Loire. 🏛 *32,000.* 🚃 🚌 🛈
pl de la Bilange (02 41 40 20 60). 🔄 *Thu,
Sat.* **www**.saumur-tourisme.com

Saumur is celebrated for its
fairytale château, cavalry
school, mushrooms and
sparkling wines. Its stone
mansions recall the city's
17th-century heyday, when it
was a bastion of Protestantism
and vied with Angers as the
intellectual capital of Anjou.

High above both town and
river is the turreted **Château
de Saumur**. The present
structure was
started in the 14th-
century by Louis I
of Anjou and
remodelled later by
his grandson, King
René. Collections
include medieval
sculpture, and
equestrian exhibits.

The Military
Cavalry School,
established in
Saumur in 1814, led
to the creation of the **Musée
des Blindés**, which exhibits
150 different armoured vehicles,
and of the prestigious Cadre
Noir horse-riding formation.

The Château de Saumur and spire of St-Pierre seen from the Loire

King René's
coat of arms

Morning training sessions and
stable visits, along with
occasional evening performances, can be seen at the
Ecole Nationale d'Equitation.
The nearby subterranean
**Parc Pierre et
Lumière** (sculptures
in the tufa cave walls
of prominent local
tourist sites), is well
worth a visit; as is
Europe's largest
dolmen, with its
collection of pre-
historic implements,
in Bagneux.

Before you leave
the area, be sure to
sample the local
méthode champenoise sparkling
wine – the best in France outside Champagne – in one of
the many wine cellars or at the
Maison des Vins in town.

⛴ **Château de Saumur**
Tel 02 41 40 24 40. 🔴 for
renovation until 2008.

Ecole Nationale d'Equitation
St-Hilaire-St-Florent. *Tel 02 41 53 50
60.* 🔲 *Apr–mid-Oct: Mon pm–Sat.*
*(Phone for details of performance
times).* 🔴 *public hols.* 🈹 🈺 🈴
oblig. 🖳 **www**.cadrenoir.com

Environs
The lovely **Eglise Notre-Dame**
at Cunault, an 11th-century
Romanesque priory church,
has a fine west door and
carved capitals, while an
amazing subterranean fort and
myriad caves and tunnels can
be seen at **Château de Brézé**.

Montreuil-Bellay ❻

Maine-et-Loire. 🏛 *4,500.* 🚃 🚌
🛈 *pl du Concorde (02 41 52 32 39).*
🔄 *Tue (& Sun, mid-Jun–mid-Sep).*

Set on the river Thouet 17 km
(11 miles) south of Saumur,
Montreuil-Bellay is one of the
region's most gracious small
towns and is an ideal base for
touring Anjou. The towering
roofline of the Gothic collegiate
church overlooks walled mansions and surrounding vineyards
(wine-tasting recommended).
The **Chapelle St-Jean** was an
ancient hospice and pilgrimage centre.

The imposing **Château de
Montreuil-Bellay**, established
in 1025, is a veritable fortress
with its 13 interlocking towers,
barbican and ramparts.

A gracious 15th-century
house lies beyond the fortified
gateway, complete with vaulted
medieval kitchen and an oratory decorated with 15th-cen-
tury frescoes.

⛴ **Château de Montreuil-
Bellay**
Tel 02 41 52 33 06. 🔲 *Apr–Nov:
daily.* 🈹 🈺 *oblig.*

TROGLODYTE DWELLINGS

Some of the best troglodyte settlements in France have been
carved out of the soft limestone (tufa) of the Loire Valley, especially around Saumur, Vouvray and along the river Loir. The
caves, cut out of cliff-faces or dug underground, have been a
source of cheap, secure accommodation for centuries. Today
they are popular as *résidences secondaires*, or used for wine
storage and mushroom growing. Some are now restaurants or
hotels, and old quarries at Doué-la-Fontaine accommodate a
zoo and a 15th-century amphitheatre. At Rochemenier, near
Saumur, is a well-preserved troglodyte village museum. A
central pit is surrounded by a warren of caves, barns, wine
cellars, dwellings and even a simple underground chapel.

Heralded by chimney pots, the underground hamlet of
nearby La Fosse was inhabited until 20 years ago by three
families, and is now a museum of family life underground.

A typical troglodyte dwelling

Court Life in the Renaissance

François I's reign, from 1515 to 1547, witnessed the apogee of the French Renaissance, characterized by an intense period of château-building and an interest in humanism and the arts. The itinerant court travelled between the pleasure palaces of Amboise, Blois and Chambord in the Loire. Days were devoted to hunting, falconry, *fêtes champêtres* (country festivals) or *jeu de paume*, a forerunner of tennis. Nights were given over to feasting, balls, poetry and romantic assignations.

Lute and mandolin *music were much in vogue, as were Italian recitals and masquerades. Musicians played at the twice-weekly balls, where the pavane and galliard were danced.*

The antics *of François I's fools, Triboulet and Caillette, amused the court. Yet they were often mistreated: courtiers regularly nailed Caillette's ears to a post for fun, daring him to remain silent.*

RENAISSANCE FEASTS

Dinner usually took place before 7pm to the accompaniment of Italian music. Humanist texts were read aloud and the king's fools amused the courtiers.

Courtiers used their own knives at dinner. Forks were still rare, although their use was spreading from Italy.

A typical royal dinner comprised smoked eel, salted ham, veal pâté, egg and saffron soups, roast game and boiled meats, as well as fish dishes in lemon or gooseberry sauce.

The cost of lavish damask, satin and silk costumes often sent courtiers into debt.

Diane de Poitiers *(1499–1566) became the mistress of the future Henri II when he was 12 years old. Two years later he married Catherine de' Medici, but Diane remained his favourite until his death.*

Artists symbolized love *in different ways during the Renaissance. Winged hearts charmingly perform the function here.*

The Grand Moûtier cloisters

Abbaye Royale de Fontevraud ❼

Maine-et-Loire. 🚌 *from Saumur.*
Tel *02 41 51 71 41.* ⭘ *daily.* ⬤ *1 Jan, 1 May, 1 & 11 Nov, 25 Dec.* 📷
www.abbaye-fontevraud.com

The Abbaye Royale de Fontevraud is the largest and most remarkably intact medieval abbey in Europe. It was founded in the early 12th century by Robert d'Arbrissel, a visionary itinerant preacher who set up a Benedictine community of monks, nuns, nobles,

THE PLANTAGENETS

The legendary counts of Anjou were named after the *genêt*, the sprig of broom Geoffrey Plantagenet wore in his cap. He married Matilda, daughter of England's Henry I. In 1154, when their son Henry – who had married Eleanor of Aquitaine *(see p51)* – acceded to the English throne, the Plantagenet dynasty of English kings was founded, fusing French and English destinies for 300 years.

Effigies of Henry II, Plantagenet king of England, and Eleanor of Aquitaine

lepers and vagabonds. The radical founder entrusted the running of the abbey to an abbess, usually from a noble family, and the abbey became a favourite sanctuary for the female aristocracy, including Eleanor of Aquitaine.

From 1804 to 1963 the abbey was used as a prison, since when the buildings have been undergoing painstaking restoration by the French State. Wandering around the abbey buildings and gardens gives a fascinating insight into monastic life. The focal point

was the Romanesque abbey church, consecrated in 1119. It boasts beautifully carved capitals and an immense single nave with four domes, one of the finest examples of a cupola nave in France. Inside are the painted effigies of the Plantagenets dating from the early 13th century: Henry II of England, his redoubtable wife Queen Eleanor of Aquitaine, their crusading, non-English-speaking son Richard the Lion-Heart and Isabelle d'Angoulême, widow of his infamous brother, King John of England.

The abbey's nuns lived around the Renaissance **Grand Moûtier cloisters**, forming one of the largest nunneries in France, and the leper colony was housed in the **St-Lazare priory**, now the atmospheric abbey hotel *(see p555)*. Of the monastic quarters, only the **St-Benoît chapel and cloisters** survive. Most impressive is the octagonal kitchen with its fireplaces and chimneys in the **Tour Evraud**, a rare example of secular Romanesque architecture.

The abbey, now an important arts centre, regularly hosts concerts and exhibitions.

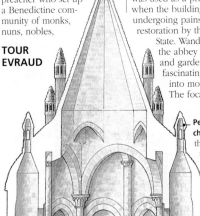

TOUR EVRAUD

Pepperpot chimneys top the towers of the kitchen, restored in the 20th century.

Fireplace alcoves that look like side chapels housed the ovens.

Chinon ❽

Indre-et-Loire. 🏠 *9,000.* 🚉 🚌
ℹ *pl Hofheim (02 47 93 17 85).*
🗓 *Sun.* **www**.chinon.com

The Château de Chinon is an important shrine in Joan of Arc country and, as such, wheedles money from all passing pilgrims. It was here in 1429 that the saint first recognized the disguised dauphin (later Charles VII),

and persuaded him to give her an army to drive the English out of France. Before that, Chinon was the Plantagenet kings' favourite castle. Although the **château** is now mostly in ruins, the ramparts are an impressive sight from the opposite bank of the Vienne river. The town's bijou centre is like a

Stallholder at Chinon's market

medieval film set. **Rue Voltaire**, lined with 15th- and 16th-century houses and once enclosed by the castle walls, represents a cross-section of Chinonais history. At No. 12 is the **Musée Animé du Vin**, where animated figures tell the story of wine-making. **No. 44** which houses the Musée d'Art et d'Histoire, is a

Vineyard in the Chinon wine region

stone mansion where, in 1199, Richard the Lion-Heart is said to have died. The grandest mansion is the **Palais du Gouverneur,** with its double staircase and loggia. More charming is the **Maison Rouge** in the Grand Carroi, studded with a red-brick herringbone pattern.

The 15th-century **Hostellerie Gargantua,** where Rabelais' lawyer father once practised, is now an agreeable inn *(see p555).* The great Renaissance writer lived nearby in the Rue de la Lamproie.

The 1900s market, with stallholders in period costume, folk dancing and music is a must (3rd Sat Aug).

Musée Animé du Vin
12 rue Voltaire. *Tel 02 47 93 25 63.* mid-Mar–mid-Oct: daily.

Environs
5 km (3 miles) southwest of Chinon is **La Devinière,** birthplace of François Rabelais, the 16th-century writer, priest, doctor and humanist scholar.

La Devinière
Seuilly. *Tel 02 47 95 91 18.* daily. 1 Jan, 25 Dec.

Château d'Ussé **9**

Indre-et-Loire. Langeais, then taxi. *Tel 02 47 95 54 05.* mid-Feb–mid-Nov: daily.

The fairytale Château d'Ussé enjoys a bucolic setting overlooking watery meadows and the river Indre. Its romantic white turrets, pointed towers and chimneys inspired Charles Perrault's *Sleeping Beauty.*

Constructed in the 15th century, the castle was gradually transformed into an aristocratic château, which is still privately owned *(see p242).* However, the sunless and musty interior is rather disappointing and the *Sleeping Beauty* tableaux are clumsily presented.

The château's delightful Renaissance chapel, framed by the oak forest of Chinon, has lost its Aubusson tapestries, but retains a lovely della Robbia terracotta *Virgin.*

Château de Langeais **10**

Indre-et-Loire. Langeais. *Tel 02 47 96 72 60.* daily. 25 Dec.

Compared with neighbouring towns, Langeais is distinctly untouristy and has a welcoming, unpretentious feel. Its château is fiercely feudal, built strictly for defence with a drawbridge, portcullis and no concessions to the Renaissance. It was constructed by Louis XI in just four years, from 1465–9, with hardly an alteration since then. The ruins of an impressive keep, built by Foulques Nerra in AD 994, stand in the small château courtyard.

A *son et lumière* in the Salle de la Chapelle represents the marriage of Charles VIII and his child-bride Anne of Brittany in 1491. Many of the well-furnished rooms have intricate designs on the tiled floors, and all are hung with fine 15th- and 16th-century Flemish and Aubusson tapestries.

FRANÇOIS RABELAIS

Rabelais, born in 1494, was a priest, doctor, diplomat and humanist scholar noted for his wisdom and tolerance. He is best remembered for his many ribald satires (written as "medicine" for his patients), such as *Pantagruel* and *Gargantua,* set around his native Chinon.

Infant Pantagruel, depicted by Doré in 1854, was fed on the milk of 17,913 cows

Château d'Azay-le-Rideau ⓫

Indre-et-Loire. 🚇 🚌 *Azay-le-Rideau.* **Tel** *02 47 45 42 04.*
⬜ *daily.* ⬤ *1 Jan, 1 May, 25 Dec.* 🎫
🎦 **Son et Lumière**: *Jul–mid-Sep.*

Balzac called Azay-le-Rideau
"A multi-faceted diamond set
in the Indre". It is the most
beguiling and feminine of Loire
châteaux, created in the early
16th century by Philippa Lesbahy, wife of François I's cor-
rupt finance minister. Although
Azay is superficially Gothic
(*see pp54–55, 242*), it clearly
shows the transition to the
Renaissance: the turrets are
purely decorative and the
moats are picturesque pools.
Azay was a pleasure palace,
lived in during fine weather
and deserted in winter.

The interior is equally
delightful, an airy, creaking
mansion smelling faintly of
cedarwood and full of lovingly
re-created domestic detail. The
first floor is furnished in the
Renaissance style, with a fine
example of a portable Spanish
cabinet and exquisite tapestries. The ground floor has
19th-century furniture, dating
from the period of the
château's restoration. The
four-storey grand staircase is
unusual for its time, being
straight as opposed to spiral.

Wine-tasting opportunities
in the village are a welcome
reminder that vineyards are
all around. Unlike most Loire
villages, Azay is lively at night,
thanks to the château's poetic
son et lumière.

The Château de Villandry's *jardin d'ornement*

Château de Villandry ⓬

Indre-et-Loire. 🚇 *Tours, then taxi.*
Tel *02 47 50 02 09.* ⬜ **Château:**
mid-Feb–mid-Nov: daily. **Gardens:**
daily. 🎫 🎦 🚻 *Mar–Oct.*
www.chateauvillandry.com

Villandry was the last great
Renaissance château built in
the Loire Valley, a perfect
example of 16th-century
architecture. Its gardens were
restored to their Renaissance
splendour early in the last
century by Dr Joachim
Carvallo, whose grandson
now continues his work.

The result is a patchwork of
sculpted shrubs and flowers on
three levels: the kitchen garden
(*jardin potager*), the ornamental garden (*jardin d'ornement*)
and, on the highest level, the
water garden (*jardin d'eau*).
There are signs to explain the
history and meaning behind
each plant: the marrow, for instance, symbolized fertility; the
cabbage, sexual and spiritual
corruption. Plants were also
prized for their medicinal prop-

erties: cabbage helped to cure
hangovers, while pimento
aided digestion.

The delicate roots of the 52
kms (32 miles) of box hedge
that outline and highlight
each section mean that the
whole 10 acres of gardens
must be hand-weeded.

A *chocolatier* in Tours

Tours ⓭

Indre-et-Loire. 🏯 *140,000.* ✈ 🚇
🚌 🛈 *78 rue Bernard Palissy
(02 47 70 37 37).* 🛍 *Tue–Sun.*
www.ligeris.com

Tours is the most appealing
of the major Loire cities,
thanks to bourgeois prosperity,
an intelligent restoration programme and its university
population. It is built on the
site of a Roman town, and
was a centre of Christianity
in the 4th century under St
Martin, bishop of Tours. In
1461 Louis XI made the city
the French capital and it
prospered. During Henri IV's
reign the city lost favour with
the monarchy and the capital
left Tours for Paris.

Bombarded by the Prussians
in 1870, and bombed in
World War II, Tours suffered
extensive damage. By 1960,
the middle classes had abandoned the historic centre and

Château d'Azay-le-Rideau reflected in the river Indre

For hotels and restaurants in this region see pp568–72 and pp620–5

it became a slum, full of crumbling medieval masonry. Regeneration of the city has succeeded due to the popular policies of Jean Royer, mayor of Tours from 1958 to 1996.

The pedestrianized **place Plumereau** is Tours' most atmospheric quarter, set in the medieval heart of the city and full of cafés, boutiques and galleries. Streets such as rue Briçonnet reveal half-timbered façades, hidden courtyards and crooked towers. A gateway leads to place St-Pierre-le-Puellier, a square with sunken Gallo-Roman remains and a Romanesque church converted into a café. A few streets away in place de Châteauneuf lies the Romanesque **Tour Charlemagne**, all that remains of St Martin's first church. West of here is the highly yuppified artisans' quarter, centred on the rue du Petit St-Martin.

The **Cathédrale St-Gatien**, in the eastern sector of the city, was begun in the early 13th century and completed in the 16th. Its Flamboyant Gothic façade is blackened and crumbling but still truly impressive, as are the medieval stained-glass windows.

The **Musée des Beaux Arts**, set in the former archbishop's

Cathédrale St-Gatien in Tours

palace nearby, overlooks Classical gardens and a giant cedar of Lebanon. Its star exhibits are *Christ in the Garden of Olives* and *The Resurrection* by Mantegna, and a room devoted to the modern artist Olivier Debré.

Further west, is the **Eglise St-Julien**, whose Gothic monastic cells and chapter-house contain a small wine museum. Next door, the **Musée du Compagnonnage** displays hundreds of finely-created works by master craftsmen of the guilds.

Across the rue Nationale lies the town's finest Renaissance building, the **Hôtel Goüin**. A former silk merchant's house, it is now the Touraine Archae-ological history museum.

🏛 **Musée des Beaux Arts**
18 pl François Sicard. **Tel** 02 47 05 68 73. ◯ Wed–Mon. ● 1 Jan, 1 May, 1 & 11 Nov, 25 Dec. 🖼

🏛 **Hôtel Goüin**
25 rue du Commerce. **Tel** 02 47 66 22 32. ◯ Tue–Sun. ● 1 Jan, 25 Dec. 🖼 ♿

Environs
Just outside Céré la Ronde, on the D764 from Montrichard to Loches, lies the 15th-century **Château de Montpoupon** and its excellent Musée du Ven-eur, which looks at the impor-tant role of horses in hunting.

Backgammon players in Tours' place Plumereau

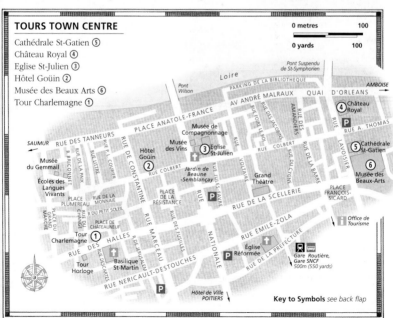

TOURS TOWN CENTRE

Cathédrale St-Gatien ⑤
Château Royal ④
Eglise St-Julien ③
Hôtel Goüin ②
Musée des Beaux Arts ⑥
Tour Charlemagne ①

0 metres 100
0 yards 100

Key to Symbols see back flap

Château de Chenonceau ⑰

A romantic pleasure palace, Chenonceau was
created from the Renaissance onwards by a series
of aristocratic women. A magnificent avenue
bordered by plane trees leads to symmetrical
gardens and the serene vision that Flaubert praised
as "floating on air and water". The château
stretches across the river Cher with a 60-m (197-ft) gallery
built over a series of arches, its elegant beauty
reflected in the languid waters. The grandeur
continues inside with splendidly furnished rooms,
airy bedchambers and fine
paintings and tapestries.

Turreted Pavilion
*This was built between
1513 and 1521 by Catherine
Briçonnet and her husband,
Thomas Bohier, over the foun-
dations of an old water mill.*

Chapelle
*The chapel has a
vaulted ceiling
and pilasters sculp-
ted with acanthus
leaves and cockle-
shells. The stained
glass, destroyed by a
bomb in 1944, was
replaced in 1953.*

Catherine de' Medici's Garden
*Lavish court receptions and transvestite balls
were held under Catherine's auspices.*

TIMELINE

1533 Marriage of Catherine de' Medici (1519–89) to Henri II
(1519–59). Chenonceau becomes a Loire royal palace

1559 On Henri's death, Catherine forces the
disgraced Diane to accept the Château de
Chaumont in exchange for Chenonceau

Catherine de' Medici

1789 Chenonceau
is spared in the
French Revolution
thanks to
Madame Dupin

1500	1600	1700	1800

1575 Louise de Lorraine (1554–1601) marries
Henri III, Catherine's third and favourite son

1547 Henri II offers Chenonceau to
Diane de Poitiers, his lifelong mistress

1863 Madame Pelo
restores the châtea
its original

1730–99 Madame Dupin, a "farmer-
general's" wife, makes Chenonceau
a salon for writers and philosophers

1513 Thomas Bohier acquires medieval Chenonceau. His
wife, Catherine Briçonnet, rebuilds it in Renaissance style

VISITORS' CHECKLIST

Chenonceaux. from Tours. **Tel** 02 47 23 90 07. 08 20 20 90 90. daily. gr. fl. only. www.chenonceau.com

Grande Galerie
The elegant gallery crowning the bridge is Florentine in style, created by Catherine de' Medici from 1570–76.

The Creation of Chenonceau

The women responsible for Chenonceau each left their mark. Catherine Briçonnet, wife of the first owner, built the turreted pavilion and one of the first straight staircases in France; Henri II's mistress, Diane de Poitiers, added the formal gardens and arched bridge over the river; Catherine de' Medici transformed the bridge into an Italian-style gallery (having evicted Diane following her husband's death in 1559); Louise de Lorraine, bereaved wife of Henri III, inherited the château in 1590 and painted the ceiling of her bedchamber black and white (the colour of royal mourning); Madame Dupin, a cultured 18th-century châtelaine, saved the château from destruction in the Revolution; and Madame Pelouze undertook a complete restoration in 1863.

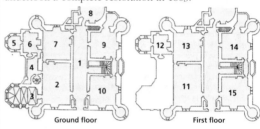

Ground floor **First floor**

CHÂTEAU GUIDE

The main living area was in the square-shaped turreted pavilion in the middle of the river Cher. Four principal rooms open off the Vestibule on the ground floor: the Salle des Gardes and the Chambre de Diane de Poitiers, both hung with 16th-century Flemish tapestries; the Chambre de François I, with a Van Loo painting; and the Salon Louis XIV. On the first floor, reached via the Italianate staircase, are other sumptuous apartments including the Chambre de Catherine de' Médicis and the Chambre de Vendôme.

1 Vestibule
2 Salle des Gardes
3 Chapelle
4 Terrasse
5 Librairie de Catherine de' Médicis
6 Cabinet Vert
7 Chambre de Diane de Poitiers
8 Grande Galerie
9 Chambre de François I
10 Salon Louis XIV
11 Chambre des Cinq Reines
12 Cabinet des Estampes
13 Chambre de Catherine de' Médicis
14 Chambre de Vendôme
15 Chambre de Gabrielle d'Estrées

1913 The château is bought by the Menier family, the *chocolatiers* who still own it today

1941 Chenonceau chapel is damaged in a bombing raid

Diane de Poitiers

Chambre de Catherine de' Médicis

Vouvray ⑭

Indre-et-Loire. 🏠 *3,500.*
ℹ *12 rue Rabelais (02 47 52 68 73).*
🔶 *Tue & Fri.*

Just east of Tours is the village of Vouvray, home of the delicious white wine that Renaissance author Rabelais likened to taffeta.

Nothing has changed in the quality of Vouvray's wines. The star vineyard is **Huet** where, since 1990, grapes have been grown according to bio-dynamic methods: manual weeding, natural fertilisers and no chemicals. In the preface to his novel *Quentin Durward*, Sir Walter Scott sang the praises of its dry white wines which are still to this day matured in chestnut barrels. Gaston Huet also hit the headlines in 1990 with his protests against the building of tracks for the TGV train over Vouvray vineyards. A French compromise was eventually reached and tunnels were built under the hilly vineyards.

The **Chateau de Montcontour**, where monks first planted vines in the 4th century, has its own wine-making museum in the impressive 10th-century cellars hewn out of the tufa rock.

The medieval town of Loches

Huet
11–13 rue de la Croix-Buisée.
Tel *02 47 52 78 87.* 🔲 *Jul–Aug: Mon–Sat for wine tastings; cellar visits by reservation only.*
⬤ *public hols.*

⛴ **Château de Moncontour**
Route de Rochecorbon. **Tel** *02 47 52 60 77.* 🔲 *Jun–Sep: daily; Oct–May: Mon–Fri.* 🏷 🔲 *Visits can be followed by wine tastings.*
www.moncontour.com

Loches ⑮

Indre-et-Loire. 🏠 *7,000.* 🚉 🚌
ℹ *pl de la Marne (02 47 91 82 82).*
🔶 *Wed & Sat.* **www**.loches-tourainecotesud.com

This unspoilt medieval town is removed from the château trail in the Indre valley. It is a backwater of late Gothic gateways and sculpted façades. Its keep boasts the deepest dungeons in the Loire. The Logis Royal is associated with Charles VII and his mistress Agnès Sorel. It is also where Joan of Arc pleaded with Charles to go to Reims and be crowned. Anne of Brittany's chapel is decorated with ermines, and contains an effigy of Agnès Sorel.

⛴ **Logis Royal de Loches**
Tel *02 47 59 01 32.* 🔲 *daily.*
⬤ *25 Dec, 1 Jan.* 🏷

THE HEROINE OF FRANCE

Joan of Arc is the quintessential French national heroine, a virginal warrior, a woman martyr, a French figurehead. Her divinely led campaign to "drive the English out of France" during the Hundred Years' War has inspired plays, poetry and films from Voltaire to Cecil B de Mille. Responding to heavenly voices, she appeared on the scene as champion of the dauphin, the uncrowned Charles VII. He faced an Anglo-Burgundian alliance which held most of northern France, and had escaped to the royal châteaux on the Loire. Joan con-

vinced him of her mission, mustered the French troops and in May 1429 led them to victory over the English at Orléans. She then urged the dithering Charles to go to Reims to be crowned. However, in 1430 she was captured and handed over to the English. Accused of witchcraft, she was burnt at the stake in Rouen in 1431 at the age of 19. Her legendary bravery and tragic martyrdom led to her canonization in 1920.

Earliest known drawing of Joan of Arc (1429)

Portrait of Joan of Arc *in the Maison Jeanne d'Arc in Orléans (see p312). She saved the city from the English on 8 May 1429, a date the Orléannais still celebrate annually.*

Montrésor ⑯

Indre-et-Loire. 🏠 400. 🛈 43 grande rue (02 47 92 70 71). www.tourisme-valdindrois-montresor.com

Classed as one of "the most beautiful villages in France", Montrésor does not disappoint. It is set on the river Indrois, in the loveliest valley in Touraine. The village became a Polish enclave in the 1840s. In 1849 a Polish nobleman, Count Branicki, bought the 15th-century **Château**, built on the site of

Farm building and poppy fields near the village of Montrésor

one of Foulques Nerra's 11th-century fortifications. It has remained in the family ever since, its interior unchanged.

🏰 **Château de Montrésor**
Tel 02 47 92 60 04. ◻ Apr–11 Nov: daily; Dec–Mar: Sat & Sun pms. 🎫
🖺 🛆 restricted.

Château de Chenonceau ⑰

See pp288–9.

Amboise ⑱

Indre-et-Loire. 🏠 12,000. 🚉 🚌
🛈 quai du Général de Gaulle (02 47 57 09 28). 🛒 Fri & Sun am. www.amboise-valdeloire.com

Few buildings are more historically important than the **Château d'Amboise**. Louis XI lived here; Charles VIII was born here and died here; François I was brought up here, as were Catherine de' Medici's 10 children. The château was also the setting for the 1560 Amboise Conspiracy, an ill-fated Huguenot plot against François II. Visitors are shown the metal lace-work balcony which served as a gibbet for 12 of the 1,200 conspirators who were put to death. The **Tour des Minimes**, the château's original entrance, is

Amboise seen from the Loire

famous for its huge spiral ramp up which horsemen could ride to deliver provisions.

On the ramparts is the beautifully restored Gothic **Chapelle St-Hubert**, Leonardo da Vinci's burial place. Under the patronage of François I, the artist lived in the nearby manor house of **Clos-Lucé**, whose gardens exhibit models of Leonardo's inventions constructed from his sketches.

🏰 **Château d'Amboise**
Tel 08 20 20 50 50. ◻ daily.
⬤ 1 Jan, 25 Dec. 🎫 🖺
www.chateau-amboise.com

🏛 **Clos-Lucé**
2 rue de Clos-Lucé. **Tel** 02 47 57 00 73.
◻ daily ⬤ 1 Jan, 25 Dec 🎫 🛆 restricted. www.vinci-closluce.com

A romantic heroine, *Joan of Arc was a popular subject for artists. This painting of her is by François Léon Benouville (1821–59).*

Burnt at the stake – *a scene from* St Joan, *Otto Preminger's 1957 epic film, which starred Jean Seberg.*

Château de Chambord ⑲

Henry James once said, "Chambord is truly royal – royal in its great scale, its grand air, and its indifference to common considerations." The Loire's largest residence, brainchild of the extravagant François I, began as a hunting lodge in the Forêt de Boulogne. In 1519 this was razed and the creation of present-day Chambord began, to a design probably initiated by Leonardo da Vinci. By 1537 the towers, keep and terraces had been completed by 1,800 men and three master masons. At one point, François suggested diverting the Loire to flow in front of his château, but he settled for redirecting the nearby Cosson instead. His son Henry II continued his work, and Louis XIV completed the 440-roomed edifice in 1685.

The Château de Chambord with the river Cosson, a tributary of the Loire, in the foreground

The Salamander
François I chose the salamander as his enigmatic emblem. It appears over 800 times throughout the château.

★ Roof Terraces
This skyline of delicate cupolas has been likened to a miniature Oriental town. The roof terraces include a forest of elongated chimney pots, miniature spires, shell-shaped domes and richly sculpted gables.

The chapel was begun by François I shortly before his death in 1547. Henri II added the second storey and Louis XIV the roof.

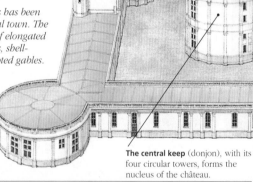

The central keep (donjon), with its four circular towers, forms the nucleus of the château.

STAR FEATURES

★ Roof Terraces

★ Vaulted Guardrooms

★ Grand Staircase

TIMELINE

1519–47 The Count of Blois' hunting lodge demolished by François I and the château created

1547–59 Henri II adds the west wing and second storey of the chapel

1725–33 Inhabited by Stanislas Leczinski, exiled king of Poland who was made duke of Lorraine

1748 The Maréchal de Saxe acquires Chambord. On his death two years later, the château yet again falls into decline

1500	1600	1700	1800	1900

1547 Death of François I

1669–85 Louis XIV completes the building, then abandons it

1670 Molière's *Le Bourgeois Gentilhomme* staged at Chambord

1840 Chambord declared a *Monument Historique*

1970s Chambord is restored and refurnished and the moats re-dug.

Molière

★ Vaulted Guardrooms
*Arranged in the form of
a Greek cross around
the Grand Staircase,
the vaulted guard-
rooms were once
the setting for royal
balls and plays. Their
ceilings are decorated
with François I's initials
and salamander motif.*

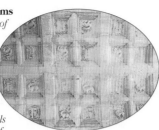

VISITORS' CHECKLIST

Blois, then taxi or bus. *Tel 02
54 50 40 00*. ☐ Apr–mid-Jul &
mid-Aug–Sep: 9am–6:15pm
daily; mid-Jul–mid-Aug: 9am–
7:30pm; Oct–Mar: 9am–5:15pm.
☐ 1 Jan, 1 May, 25 Dec.
Les Clairs de Lune (illuminations;
Jul–mid-Sep). 📷 ⬛ ✔
www.chambord.org

The lantern tower is 32 m
(105 ft) high. Surmounting
the terrace, it is supported
by arched buttresses and
crowned by a fleur-de-lys.

François I's Bedchamber is
where the king, hurt by a failed
romance, scratched a message
on a pane of glass: " *Souvent
femme varie, bien fol est qui s'y
fie.*" (Every woman is fickle,
he who trusts one is a fool.)

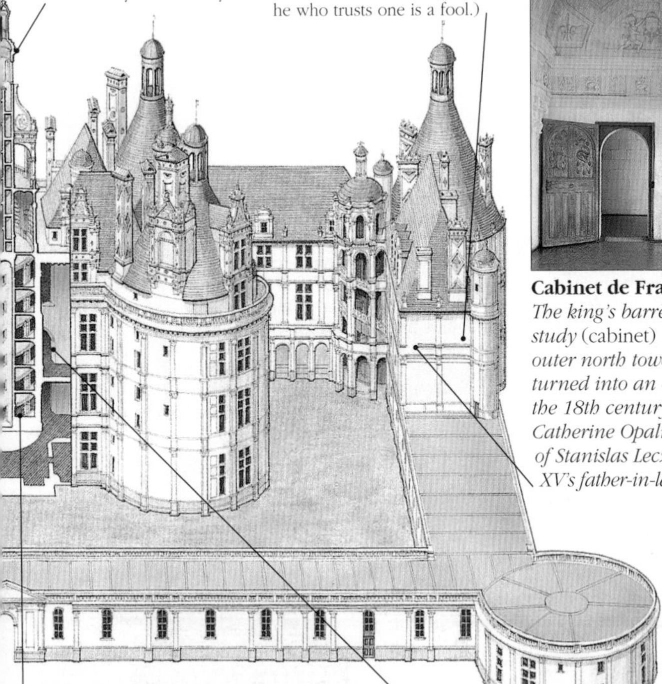

Cabinet de François I
*The king's barrel-vaulted
study (cabinet) in the
outer north tower was
turned into an oratory in
the 18th century by Queen
Catherine Opalinska, wife
of Stanislas Leczinski (Louis
XV's father-in-law).*

★ Grand Staircase
*This innovative double-helix staircase was
supposedly designed by Leonardo da Vinci.
It ensures that the person going up and the
person going down cannot meet.*

Louis XIV's Bedchamber
*Louis XIV's bedchamber lies within the
Sun King's state apartments, the grandest
quarters in the château.*

Blois's Cathédrale St-Louis and Hôtel de Ville seen from across the Loire

Blois ⑳

Loir-et-Cher. 🏠 60,000. 🚇 🚌
ℹ️ 23 pl du château (02 54 90 41
41). 🏛️ Tue, Thu & Sat.
www.ville-de-blois.com

Once a fief of the counts of
Blois, the town rose to
prominence as a royal domain
in the 15th century, retaining
its historic façades and refined
atmosphere to this day. Architectural interest abounds in
Vieux Blois, the hilly, partially
pedestrianized quarter enclosed
by the château, cathedral and
river. Four well-signposted
walking tours act as a gentle
introduction to the noble
mansions and romantic courtyards that grace the Loire's
most beguiling town.

Set back from the north
bank of the river, the **Château
de Blois** was the principal
royal residence until Henri IV
moved the court to Paris in
1598 – Louis XIV's creation
of Versailles (see pp174–7)
was to mark the final eclipse
of Blois. The château's four
contrasting wings make a

harmonious whole. The Salle
des Etats Generaux, the only
part of the building surviving
from the 13th century, housed
the council and court, and is
the largest and best-preserved
Gothic hall in France. The
adjoining late 15th-century
Louis XII wing infuses Gothic
design with Renaissance spirit,
sealed with the king's porcupine symbol and motto.

The 16th-century François I
wing is a masterpiece of the
French Renaissance containing
a monumental spiral staircase
in an octagonal tower. By
contrast, the 17th-century
Gaston d'Orléans wing is a
model of Classical sobriety.

Blois is authentically furnished and hung with paintings portraying its troubled
and bloody past. These
include a graphic
portrayal of the
murder of the Duc
de Guise in 1588.
Suspected of heading
a Catholic plot
against Henri III,
he was stabbed to
death by guards in

King Louis XII's porcupine symbol

the king's chamber. The most
intriguing room is Catherine
de' Medici's study where, of
the 237 carved wooden wall
panels, four are secret cabinets
said to have stored her poisons.

François I Staircase

*Built between 1515 and
1524, this octagonal
staircase is a master-
piece of the
early French
Renaissance.*

The gallery
provided an
ideal setting
for viewing
jousts and re-
ceptions held
in the inner
courtyard.

**François I's
salamander
motif** adorns
the openwork
balustrades.

The staircase
within the
tower slopes
appreciably
more steeply
than the bal-
ustrades.

Louis XII wing of the Château de Blois

Dominating the eastern sector of the city, the **Cathédrale St-Louis** is a 17th-century reconstruction of a Gothic church that was almost completely destroyed by a hurricane in 1678. Behind the cathedral the former bishop's palace, built in 1700, is the **Hôtel de Ville** (town hall). The surrounding terraced gardens have lovely views over the city and river. Opposite the cathedral is the **Maison des Acrobates**, carved with characters from medieval farces including acrobats and jugglers.

Place Louis-XII, the marketplace, is overlooked by splendid 17th-century façades, balconies and half-timbered houses. Rue Pierre de Blois, a quaint alley straddled by a Gothic passageway, winds downhill to the medieval Jewish ghetto. The rue des Juifs boasts several distinguished *hôtels particuliers* (mansions), including the galleried **Hôtel de Condé**, with its Renaissance archway and courtyard, and the **Hôtel Jassaud**, with magnificent 16th-century bas-reliefs above the main doorway. On the rue du Puits-Châtel, also rich in Renaissance mansions, is the galleried **Hôtel Sardini**, once owned by Renaissance bankers.

Place Vauvert is the most charming square in Vieux Blois, with a fine example of a half-timbered house.

♟ Château de Blois
Tel 02 54 90 33 33. ☐ 9am–12:30pm, 1:30–5:30pm daily (9am–6:30pm Apr–Sep). ● 1 Jan, 25 Dec. ✎ ✐ **Son et Lumière** Apr–Sep.

Covered Gothic passageway in Rue Pierre de Blois

The nave of the abbey church of Notre-Dame in Beaugency

Beaugency ㉑

Loiret. 🏠 7,500. 🚆 🚌 🚻 3 pl de Docteur-Hyvernaud (02 38 44 54 42). ☐ Sat. **www**.beaugency.fr

Beaugency has long been the eastern gateway to the Loire. This compact medieval town makes a peaceful base for exploring the Orléanais region. Exceptionally for the Loire, it is possible to walk along the river banks and stone *levées*. At quai de l'Abbaye there is a good view of the 11th-century bridge which, until modern times, was the only crossing point between Blois and Orléans. An obvious target for enemy attack, it was captured four times by the English during the Hundred Years' War before being retaken by Joan of Arc in 1429.

The town centre is dominated by a ruined 11th-century watchtower. It stands on **place St-Firmin**, along with a 16th-century belltower (the church was destroyed in the Revolution) and a statue of Joan of Arc. Period houses line the square. Further down is the **Château Dunois**, built on the site of the feudal castle by one of Joan of Arc's *compagnon d'armes*. Its regional museum features an array of costumes, furniture and antique toys. Facing the Château Dunois is **Notre-Dame**, a Romanesque abbey church that witnessed the annulment of the marriage between Eleanor of Aquitaine and Louis VII in 1152, leaving Eleanor free to marry the future Henry II of England.

Nearby is the medieval clocktower in rue du Change and the Renaissance **Hôtel de Ville**, with its façade adorned with the town's arms. Equally charming is the nearby ancient mill district, around the rue du Pont and the rue du Rü, with its streams and riot of flowers.

♟ Château Dunois (Musée Daniel Vannier)
3 pl Dunois. **Tel** 02 38 44 54 42. ● until 2008. ✎ ✐ oblig.

Châteaux Tour of the Sologne

The mysterious Sologne is a secretive landscape of woods and marshes edged by vineyards. Wine-lovers can indulge in tastings of Loire Valley wines accompanied, in season, by a dinner of succulent wild game from the region's forests, popular hunting grounds for centuries. The Sologne is a hunter's paradise and devotees of the sport can see today's hounds, as well as hunting trophies of the past.

This ambling rural route takes in some of the Loire's most varied châteaux. The five on this tour – for which a couple of days is required – represent a delightful encapsulation of regional architecture. All styles are here, from feudal might to Renaissance grace and Classical elegance. Several are inhabited but can still be visited.

Château de Beauregard ②
Beauregard was built around 1520 as a hunting lodge for François I. It contains a gallery with 327 portraits of royalty.

Château de Chaumont ①
Chaumont is a feudal castle with Renaissance embellishments and lofty views over the river Loire *(see p242)*.

N152

← AMBOISE

① D751

Pontlevoy

0 kilometres 5

0 miles 5

KEY

▬▬▬ Tour route

═══ Other roads

Vendôme ㉒

Loir-et-Cher. 🏠 18,500. 🚌 🚊
ℹ 47 rue Poterie (02 54 77 05 07).
🅿 Fri & Sun.

Once an important stop for pilgrims en route to Compostela in Spain, Vendôme is still popular with modern pilgrims, thanks to the TGV rail service. Though a desirable address with Parisian commuters, the town still manages to retain its provincial charm. Vendôme's old stone buildings are encircled by the river Loir, its lush gardens and chic restaurants reflected in the water.

The town's greatest monument is the abbey church of **La Trinité**, founded in 1034. Its Romanesque belltower (all that remains of the original structure) is overshadowed by the church portal, a masterpiece of Flamboyant Gothic tracery. The interior is embellished with Romanesque capitals and 15th-century choir stalls.

Commanding a rocky spur high above the Loir is the ruined **château**, built by the counts of Vendôme in the 13th –14th centuries. Down below, rowing boats may be rented for gently exploring the meandering backwaters of the Loir, past a medieval *lavoir*, elegant buildings and a plane tree planted in 1759.

Vendôme's native son Rochambeau, hero of the American Revolution

The Loir ㉓

Loir-et-Cher. 🚊 Tours. 🚌 Vendôme.
🚌 Montoire-sur-le-Loir. ℹ 16 pl Clémenceau, Montoire-sur-le-Loir (02 54 85 23 30).

Compared with the royal river Loire, the tranquil Loir to the north has a more rural charm. The stretch between Vendôme and Trôo is the most rewarding, offering troglodyte caves *(see p292)*, walking trails, wine-tasting, fishing and boat trips.

Les Roches-l'Evêque is a fortified village with cave dwellings visible in the cliff-face. Just downstream is **Lavardin**, with its Romanesque church, half-timbered houses, Gothic bridge and ruined château ringed by ramparts. In **Montoire-sur-le-Loir**, the Chapelle St-Gilles, a former leper colony, has Romanesque frescoes. **Trôo**, the next major village, is known for its Romanesque Eglise de St-Martin and a laby-

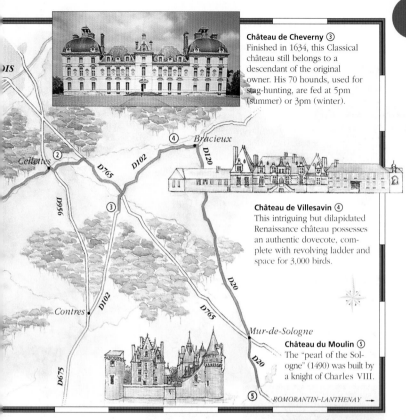

Château de Cheverny ③
Finished in 1634, this Classical
château still belongs to a
descendant of the original
owner. His 70 hounds, used for
stag-hunting, are fed at 5pm
(summer) or 3pm (winter).

Château de Villesavin ④
This intriguing but dilapidated
Renaissance château possesses
an authentic dovecote, complete with revolving ladder and
space for 3,000 birds.

Château du Moulin ⑤
The "pearl of the Sol-
ogne" (1490) was built by
a knight of Charles VIII.

ROMORANTIN-LANTHENAY →

---

rinth of troglodyte dwellings.
St-Jacques-des-Guérets, facing
the village of Trôo, has a frescoed Romanesque chapel, as
does **Poncé-sur-le-Loir**, farther
downstream. On the slopes are
vineyards producing Jasnières
and Côteaux du Vendômois.
Wine-tastings enliven sleepy
Poncé and **La Chartre-sur-le-
Loir**. The cliffs on the opposite
bank are studded with caves,
commonly used as wine cellars.
   Northward, the **Forêt de
Bercé** abounds with paths and
streams, while to the west the
small town of **Le Lude** sits on
the south bank of the Loir,
dominated by its romantic
15th-century château.
   Some 20 km (12 miles)
west of Le Lude lies the town
of **La Flèche**, whose main
attraction is the Prytanée
Nationale Militaire, originally
a Jesuit college founded by
Henri IV in 1603. Philosopher
René Descartes was one of
the college's earliest and most
illustrious pupils.

Chartres ㉔

Eure-et-Loir. 🏠 42,400. 🚌 🚆
ℹ pl de la Cathédrale (02 37 18 26
26). 🗓 Tue, Wed, Thu, Sat, Sun.
www.chartres-tourisme.com

Chartres has the greatest
Gothic cathedral in Europe
(*see pp308–11*), and its
churches should not be
ignored. The Benedictine
abbey church of **St-Pierre** has
lovely medieval stained-glass
windows, while **St-Aignan**
abuts 9th-century ramparts. By
the river is the Romanesque
Eglise de St-André, a deconsecrated church used for art
exhibitions and concerts. The
Musée des Beaux Arts, in the
former episcopal palace,
offers a fine collection of 17th
and 18th-century furniture,
Renaissance enamels and
paintings by Vlaminck.
   As one of the first urban
conservation sites in France,
Chartres is a success story.
Quirky half-timbered houses

**One of the many washhouses
along the Eure river**

abound along such cobbled
streets as the rue des Ecuyers.
Steep staircases known as
tertres lead down to the river
Eure providing views of mills,
humpback stone bridges,
washhouses and the cathedral.
   In the Grenier de Loens, next
to the cathedral, is the Centre
International du Vitraux. The
building's 13th-century vaulted
storerooms are also used for
temporary exhibitions.

🏛 **Musée des Beaux Arts**
29 cloître Notre-Dame. **Tel** 02 37 90
45 80. ◻ Wed–Mon. ◼ Sun am,
and 1 Jan, 1 & 8 May, 1 & 11 Nov,
25 Dec. 🈵 🎫

Chartres Cathedral

According to art historian Emile Male, "Chartres is the mind of the Middle Ages manifest." Begun in 1020, the Romanesque cathedral was destroyed by fire in 1194. Only the north and south towers, south steeple, west portal and crypt remained; the sacred *Veil of the Virgin* relic was the sole treasure to survive. Peasant and lord alike helped to rebuild the church in just 25 years. Few alterations were made after 1250 and, fortunately, Chartres was unscathed by the Wars of Religion and the French Revolution. The result is a Gothic cathedral with a true "Bible in stone" reputation.

Part of the Vendôme Window

Elongated Statues
These statues on the Royal Portal represent Old Testament figures.

STAR FEATURES

★ Stained-Glass Windows

★ South Porch

★ Royal Portal

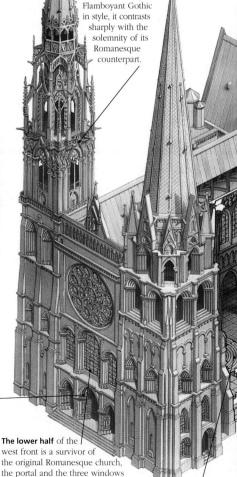

The taller of the two spires dates from the start of the 16th century. Flamboyant Gothic in style, it contrasts sharply with the solemnity of its Romanesque counterpart.

Gothic Nave
As wide as the Romanesque crypt below it, the nave reaches a lofty height of 37 m (121 ft).

★ Royal Portal
The central tympanum of the Royal Portal (1145–55) shows Christ in Majesty.

The lower half of the west front is a survivor of the original Romanesque church, the portal and the three windows dating from the mid-12th century.

Labyrinth

THE LABYRINTH

The 13th-century labyrinth, inlaid in the nave floor, was a feature of most medieval cathedrals. Pilgrims followed the tortuous route on their knees, echoing the way to Jerusalem and the complexity of life, in order to reach Christ. The journey – 262 m (851 ft) of broken concentric circles – took at least one hour.

VISITORS' CHECKLIST

Pl de la Cathédrale. **Tel** 02 37 21 75 02. ☐ 8:30am–7:30pm daily. 9am Tue & Fri; 11:45am & 6:15pm Mon –Sat (6pm Sat); 9:15am (in Latin), 11am & 6pm (crypt) Sun. ◎ ⬇ ✉ ⚑
www.cathedrale-chartres.com

Our Lady of the Pillar
Carved from dark pear wood, this 16th-century replica of a 13th-century statue is a striking shrine which is often surrounded by candles.

Vaulted Ceiling
A network of ribs supports the vaulted ceiling.

★ **Stained-Glass Windows**
The windows cover a surface area of over 2,600 sq m (28,000 sq ft).

★ **South Porch**
Sculpture on the South Porch (1197–1209) reflects New Testament teaching.

The Crypt
This is the largest crypt in France, most of it dating from the early 11th century. It houses the Veil of the Virgin *relic and comprises two galleries, a series of chapels and the 9th-century St Lubin's vault.*

The Stained Glass of Chartres

Donated by royalty, aristocracy, priests and the merchant brotherhoods between 1210 and 1240, this glorious collection of stained glass is world-renowned. Around 176 windows illustrate biblical stories and daily life in the 13th century. During both World Wars the windows were dismantled piece by piece and removed for safety. There is an on-going programme, begun in the 1970s, to restore the windows in the cathedral.

Stained glass above the apse

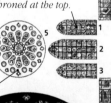

Redemption Window
Six scenes illustrate Christ's Passion *and death on the Cross (c.1210).*

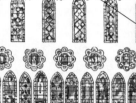

★ Tree of Jesse
This 12th-century stained glass shows Christ's genealogy. The tree rises up from Jesse, father of David, at the bottom, to Christ enthroned at the top.

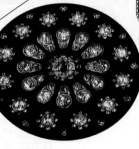

★ West Rose Window
This window (1215), with Christ seated in the center, shows the Last Judgment.

KEY

1 Tree of Jesse	**12** Noah	**22** St Anthony and St Paul	**33** St Theodore and St Vincent
2 Incarnation	**13** St John the Evangelist	**23** Blue Virgin	**34** St Stephen
3 Passion and Resurrection	**14** Mary Magdalene	**24** Life of the Virgin	**35** St Cheron
4 North Rose Window	**15** Good Samaritan and Adam and Eve	**25** Zodiac Window	**36** St Thomas
5 West Rose Window	**16** Assumption	**26** St Martin	**37** Peace Window
6 South Rose Window	**17** Vendôme Chapel Windows	**27** St Thomas à Becket	**38** Modern Window
7 Redemption Window	**18** Miracles of Mary	**28** St Margaret and St Catherine	**39** Prodigal Son
8 St. Nicholas	**19** St Apollinaris	**29** St Nicholas	**40** Ezekiel and David
9 Joseph	**20** Modern Window	**30** St Remy	**41** Aaron
10 St Eustache	**21** St Fulbert	**31** St James the Greater	**42** Annunciation
11 St Lubin		**32** Charlemagne	**43** Isaiah and Moses
			44 Daniel and Jeremiah

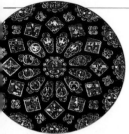

North Rose Window
This depicts the Glorification of the Virgin, *surrounded by the kings of Judah and the prophets (c.1230).*

4

GUIDE TO READING THE WINDOWS

Each window is divided into panels, usually read from left to right, bottom to top (earth to heaven). The number of figures or abstract shapes used is thought to be symbolic: three stands for divinity, while the number four symbolizes the material world or the four elements.

Mary and Child in the sacred mandorla (c.1150)

Two angels doing homage before the celestial throne

Christ's triumphal entry into Jerusalem on Palm Sunday

Upper panels of the Incarnation Window

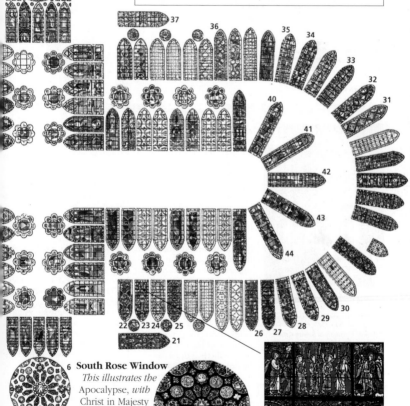

37 36 35 34 33 32 31
40 41 42 43 44
30 29 28 27 26
22 23 24 25 21

6 South Rose Window
This illustrates the Apocalypse, *with* Christ in Majesty *(c.1225).*

STAR WINDOWS

★ West Rose Window

★ Tree of Jesse

★ Blue Virgin Window

★ **Blue Virgin Window**
The window's bottom panel depicts the conversion of water into wine by Christ at The Marriage at Cana.

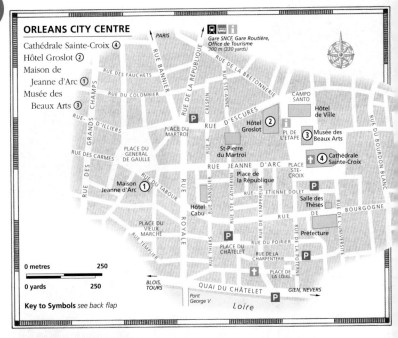

ORLEANS CITY CENTRE

Cathédrale Sainte-Croix ④
Hôtel Groslot ②
Maison de
  Jeanne d'Arc ①
Musée des
  Beaux Arts ③

Key to Symbols *see back flap*

0 metres 250
0 yards 250

Orléans' Cathédrale Sainte-Croix

Orléans ㉕

Loiret. 112,500.
2 pl Etape (02 38 24 05 05).
Tue–Sun. www.tourisme-orleans.com

Orléans' dazzling new bridge symbolizes the city's increasing importance at the geographic heart of both France and Europe. As a tourist, however, one is struck by the city's continued attachment to its past, most particularly to Joan of Arc. It

was from here that the Maid of Orléans saved France from the English in 1429 *(see p300)*. Since her martyrdom at Rouen in 1431, Joan remains a presence in Orléans. Every 29 April and 1, 7–8 May her liberation of the city is re-enacted in a pageant and a blessing in the cathedral.

Orléans' historic centre was badly damaged in World War II, but much has been reconstructed, and a faded grandeur lingers in Vieil Orléans, the quarter bounded by the cathedral, the river Loire and the **place du Martroi**. The latter, a Classical but rather windswept square, has an equestrian statue of the city's heroine. Nearby the half-timbered **Maison de Jeanne d'Arc** was rebuilt from period dwellings in 1961 on the site where Joan had lodgings in 1429.

From place du Martroi, the rue d'Escures leads past Renaissance mansions to the cathedral. **Hôtel Groslot** is the grandest, a 16th-century red-brick mansion where kings Charles IX, Henri III and Henri IV all stayed. The 17-year-old François II died here in 1560 after attending a meeting of the Etats Généraux

with his child-bride, Mary, later Queen of Scots. The building served as Orléans' town hall from 1790 to 1982, and the sumptuously decorated interior, with its Joan memorabilia, is still used for marriages and official ceremonies.

Virtually opposite the Hôtel Groslot and alongside the new town hall is the **Musée des Beaux Arts**, displaying European works of art from the 16th to the 20th centuries.

The **Cathédrale Sainte-Croix** nearby is an imposing edifice begun in the late 13th century, destroyed by the Huguenots (Protestants) in 1568, and then rebuilt in supposedly Gothic style between the 17th and 19th centuries.

Hôtel Groslot
Pl de l'Etape. *Tel* 02 38 79 22 30.
daily. sporadically.

Musée des Beaux Arts
Pl Ste-Croix. *Tel* 02 38 79 21 55. Tue–Sat & Sun pm. 1 Jan, 1 May, 1 Nov, 25 Dec. free 1st Sun of month.

Maison de Jeanne d'Arc
3 pl du Général de Gaulle. *Tel* 02 38 52 99 89. Tue–Sun. 1 Jan, 1 & 8 May, 1 Nov, 25 Dec; Nov–Apr: ams. free 2nd Sun of month.

Joan of Arc stained-glass window in
Orléans' Cathédrale Sainte-Croix

St-Benoît-sur-Loire ㉖

Loiret. 🏠 2,000. 🚌 🚉 **ℹ** 44 rue
Orléanaise (02 38 35 79 00).
www.saint-benoit-sur-loire.fr

Situated along the river
Loire between Orléans and
Gien, St-Benoît-sur-Loire
boasts one of the finest
Romanesque abbey churches
in France (1067–1108). It
is all that survives of an
important monastery founded
in AD 650 and named
after St Benedict, patron
saint of Europe. His relics
were brought from Italy at
the end of the 7th century.

The church's belfry porch
is graced with carved capitals
depicting biblical scenes.
The nave is tall and light,
and the choir floor is an
amazing patchwork of Italian
marble. Daily services with
Gregorian chant are open to
the public.

Bourges ㉗

Cher. 🏠 80,000. 🚉 🚌
ℹ 21 rue Victor Hugo (02 48 23 02
60). 🏠 Tue–Sun.
www.ville-bourges.fr

This Gallo-Roman city retains
its original walls but is best
known as the city of Jacques
Coeur, financier and foreign
minister to Charles VII. The
greatest merchant of the
Middle Ages and a self-made
man *par excellence*, it was in
his capacity as an arms dealer
that he established a tradition
maintained for four centuries,
as Napoléon III had cannons
manufactured here in 1862.

Built over part of the walls,
the **Palais Jacques Coeur** is a
Gothic gem and a lasting memorial to its first master. It
was finished in 1453,
and incorporates
Coeur's two
emblems, scallop
shells and
hearts, as
well as his
motto: *"A
vaillan coeur, rien
impossible"* – to the
valiant heart, nothing
is impossible. The
obligatory tour
reveals a barrel-
vaulted gallery, a
painted chapel and a chamber that had Turkish baths.

Bourges also flourishes as a
university town and cultural
mecca, renowned for its spring
festival of music.

Rue Bourbonnoux leads to
St-Etienne, the widest Gothic
cathedral in France and the
one most similar to Paris's
Notre-Dame. The west façade
has five sculpted portals, the

Stained-glass window in
the Cathédrale St-Etienne

central one
depicting an
enthralling *Last
Judgment*. In the
choir are vivid
13th-century
stained-glass
windows pre-
sented by the
guilds. The
crypt holds the
marble tomb
of the 14th-
century Duc de
Berry, best
known for commissioning the
illuminated manuscript the
*Très Riches Heures (see
pp204–5).* From the top of the
north tower stretch views of
the beautifully restored
medieval quarter and the
marshes beyond. Beside the
cathedral is a tithe barn and
the remains of the Gallo-
Roman ramparts.

The **Jardin des
Prés Fichaux**,
set along the
river Yèvre,
contains
pools, and an
open-air theatre.
To the north lie the
Marais de Bourges,
where gardeners
transport their
produce by boat.

Statue of
Jacques Coeur

🏛 **Palais Jacques Coeur**
Rue Jacques Coeur. **Tel** 02 48 24 79
42. 🗓 daily. ● 1 Jan, 1 May,
1 & 11 Nov, 25 Dec. 🎫 🎥

Environs
About 35 km (22 miles) south
of Bourges in the Berry region
is the **Abbaye de Noirlac**.
Founded in 1136, it is one of
the best-preserved Cistercian
abbeys in France.

Statue in the Jardin des Prés Fichaux

CENTRAL FRANCE AND THE ALPS

Introducing Central France and the Alps

The geological contrasts of this region reflect its enormous variety, from the industrial and gastronomic metropolis of Lyon to the largely agricultural landscape of Burgundy. The mountains of the Massif Central and the Alps attract visitors for winter sports, superb walking and other outdoor activities. The major sights of this richly rewarding area, both natural and architectural, are shown here.

Basilique Ste-Madeleine, *the famous pilgrimage church crowning the hill-top village of Vézelay, is a masterpiece of Burgundian Romanesque. It is renowned for its vividly decorated tympanum and capitals (see pp336–7).*

The Abbaye de Ste-Foy *in the village of Conques (see pp366–7) is one of the great pilgrimage churches of France, with a fabulous treasury of medieval and Renaissance gold reliquaries.*

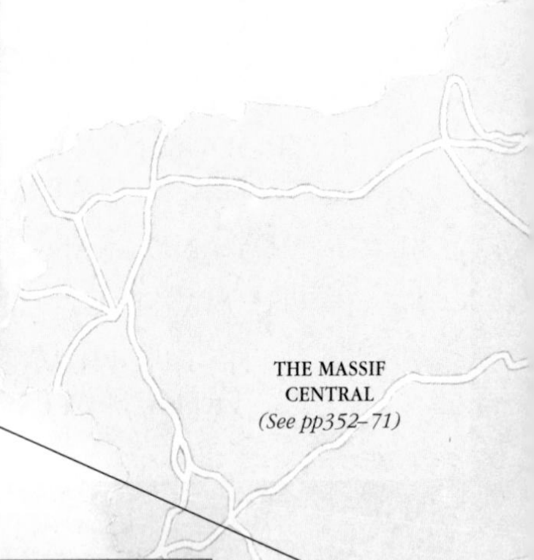

THE MASSIF CENTRAL
(See pp352–71)

Abbaye de Ste-Foy, Conques

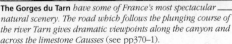

The Gorges du Tarn *have some of France's most spectacular natural scenery. The road which follows the plunging course of the river Tarn gives dramatic viewpoints along the canyon and across the limestone Causses (see pp370–1).*

The Abbaye de Fontenay, *founded by Saint Bernard in the early 12th century, is the oldest Cistercian monastery in France (see pp332–3). This well-preserved Romanesque abbey is a perfect testimony to the severe ideal of the Cistercian life.*

Abbaye de Fontenay

...deleine, ...elay

Palais des Ducs, Dijon

Théâtre Romain, Autun

BURGUNDY AND FRANCHE-COMTE
(See pp326–51)

Brou Abbey Church, Bourg-en-Bresse

Mont Blanc

Temple d'Auguste et Livie, Vienne

THE RHONE VALLEY AND FRENCH ALPS
(See pp372–91)

Palais Idéal du Facteur Cheval, Hauterives

Le Puy

Gorges du Tarn

| 0 kilometres | 50 |
| 0 miles | 50 |

The Flavours of Central France

The renowned gastronomic tradition of Lyon and the rich wine and food of Burgundy combine to make central France a gourmet paradise. The great chefs of the region have a wide choice of excellent local produce: fine Bresse chicken, Charolais beef and Morvan ham; wildfowl and frogs from the marshes of the Dombe; fish from the Saône and the Rhône; and fat snails called "oysters of Burgundy". Franche-Comté and the Jura contribute smoked sausages, farmhouse cheeses, walnut oil and fish from glacier-fed lakes. In the Massif Central, sturdy regional fare features salted hams, pork, Cantal cheese, the celebrated green lentils of Le Puy and wild mushrooms.

Chanterelle mushrooms

A mountain farmer shows off his fine salt-cured ham

BURGUNDY AND FRANCHE-COMTE

Burgundy is one of France's top wine regions so, not surprisingly, wine plays a major role in the cuisine, such as in the signature dish, *boeuf bourguignon*, made from Charolais beef marinated and then stewed in good red wine, with baby onions, bacon and mush-

rooms added. Other specialities include *coq au vin* and *oeufs en meurette*. Dijon's famous mustard appears most classically with steak and in *moutarde au lapin*, rabbit in a creamy mustard sauce. Burgundy and Franche-Comté produce some of the most celebrated French cheeses: Epoisses, a cow's milk cheese washed with *marc de Bourgogne*, Cîteaux, made by monks, and the magnificent Vacherin-Mont d'Or, a winter

treat to be scooped straight from its wooden box. Blackcurrants are widely grown and contribute to many desserts as well as the famous Kir: white wine with cassis (blackcurrant liqueur).

THE MASSIF CENTRAL

The peasant cuisine of the Auvergne is well known in France due to the many cafés run by Auvergnats in Paris, where they serve local

Tomme de Savoie   Fourme d'Ambert   Raclette   Roquefort

St-Nectaire   Emmenthal   Reblochon

Mouthwatering array of classic French cheeses

REGIONAL DISHES AND SPECIALITIES

The cuisine of central France is rich with sauces using wine, butter and cream, which enhance almost every dish: snails in butter and garlic; potatoes cooked with cheese and cream; and beef, lamb and chicken stewed slowly in reduced wine sauces, often with cream or butter added at the end of cooking. Mushrooms are cooked in cream sauces, and fish is often baked in a creamy gratin. Most indulgent of all is the Alpine fondue, where cheeses are melted, together with Kirsch and wine, in a special earthenware fondue pot. This is placed on a burner on the table, and cubes of bread are speared onto special long forks and dipped into the cheese. Traditionally, anyone who loses their bread in the pot must kiss everyone else at the table.

String of onions

Oeufs en meurette *This Burgundian dish is eggs poached in red wine with onions, mushrooms and bacon.*

Traditional charcuterie on sale in a Lyon market

dishes like pork stuffed with cabbage, or *aligot*. Le Puy lentils, grown in the fertile volcanic soils of the Puy-en-Velay basin, combine well with sausages or *petit salé*, or are served cold as a salad. Good beef comes from the Salers cattle of the Auvergne or from the Limousin, where there is also plentiful game. Wild mushrooms are eagerly sought in season. Cheeses include Cantal, one of the country's oldest, and similar in flavour to Cheddar, and the famous blue Roquefort, ripened in the limestone caves of the Lozère.

THE RHONE VALLEY AND THE FRENCH ALPS

Lyon is famous for its traditional bistros, *bouchons*, where the cooks are often women, known as *mères*, who dish up substantial fare like onion soup, lyonnais sausages and *charcuterie*. The markets of Lyon are equally famous, stocked with the region's wide range of fruit, particularly apricots, peaches and juicy berries.

Redcurrants and blackberries for sale by the punnet

Vegetables include onions, chard and cardoons, and the most northerly outpost of the olive is at Nyons. The Bresse region is famous for its high-quality chickens.

The Dombes lakes and the Alps are good sources of fish, such as perch, trout and lake salmon. Bony perch is most delicious eaten as *quenelles de brochet*, filleted fish blended, made into dumplings and baked in a creamy sauce. From the Alps comes a wide range of cheeses. As well as being delicious to eat fresh, they will often be found melted in *raclettes* or fondues, or layered with sliced potato to make an unctuous *gratin dauphinois*.

ON THE MENU

Chou farci Cabbage stuffed with pork and herbs.

Gigot Brayaude Leg of lamb baked over sliced potatoes and *lardons* of bacon.

Gougère Cheesy *choux* pastry baked in a ring-shape.

Jambon persillé Ham and parsley in aspic jelly.

Pochouse Freshwater fish (carp, pike, eel and trout) stewed in white wine.

Potée savoyarde Hotpot made with vegetables, chicken, ham and sausage.

Salade auvergnate Cubes of Auvergne ham, Cantal cheese and walnuts.

Petit salé *A speciality of the Auvergne region, salt pork is cooked in wine with tiny green Puy lentils.*

Aligot *Slivers of Cantal cheese are beaten into buttery, garlicky mashed potato until the mixture forms long strands.*

Clafoutis *This is usually made with black cherries, baked in batter and laced with Kirsch, a cherry liqueur.*

France's Wine Regions: Burgundy

Grape-picker's basket

Burgundy and its fine wines have inspired awe for centuries. The fame of the region's wines spread throughout Europe in the 14th century, under the Valois Dukes of Burgundy. The system of dividing wine areas into designated *appellations*, of which there are a bewildering number, came into effect in 1935. Even today, the classification system remains dauntingly complex. But despite its impenetrable image, this is unmissable territory for the "serious" wine lover, with its rich vinous history and tradition and dazzling *grands crus*.

LOCATOR MAP

☐ Burgundy wine region

Clos de Vougeot on the Côte de Nuits

WINE REGIONS

Between Chablis in the north and the Côte Chalonnaise and Mâconnais in the south is the Côte d'Or, incorporating Côte de Nuits and Côte de Beaune. The Beaujolais region *(see pp376–7)* lies below Mâcon.

PRINCIPAL WINE AREAS

Chablis
Auxerre •

DIJON

KEY

☐ Chablis

☐ Côte de Nuits

☐ Côte de Beaune

☐ Côte Chalonnaise

☐ Mâconnais

☐ Beaujolais

Beaune •

Chalons-sur-Saône

Mâcon

0 kilometres   50

0 miles   50

Villefranche-sur-Saône

LYON

KEY FACTS ABOUT BURGUNDY

Location and Climate
The continental climate (bleak winters and hot summers) can be very variable, making vintages a crucial quality factor. The best vineyards have chalky soil and face south or east.

Grape Varieties
Burgundy is at least relatively simple in its grape varieties. Red Burgundy is made from **Pinot Noir**, with its sweet flavours of raspberries, cherries and strawberries, while the **Gamay** makes red Mâcon and Beaujolais. **Chardonnay** is the principal white variety for Chablis and white Burgundy, though small amounts of **Aligoté** and **Pinot Blanc** are grown and the **Sauvignon** is a speciality of St Bris.

Good Producers
White Burgundy: Jean-Marie Raveneau, René Dauvissat, La Chablisienne, Comtes Lafon, Guy Roulot, Etienne Sauzet, Pierre Morey, Louis Carillon, Jean-Marc Boillot, André Ramonet, Hubert Lamy, Jean-Marie Guffens-Heynen, Olivier Merlin, Louis Latour, Louis Jadot, Olivier Leflaive.
Red Burgundy: Denis Bachelet, Daniel Rion, Domaine Dujac, Armand Rousseau, Joseph Roty, De Montille, Domaine de la Pousse d'Or, Domaine de l'Arlot, Jean-Jacques Confuron, Robert Chevillon, Georges Roumier, Leroy, Drouhin.

Good Vintages
(Reds) 2005, 2002, 1999, 1996.
(Whites) 2005, 2001, 1996, 1995.

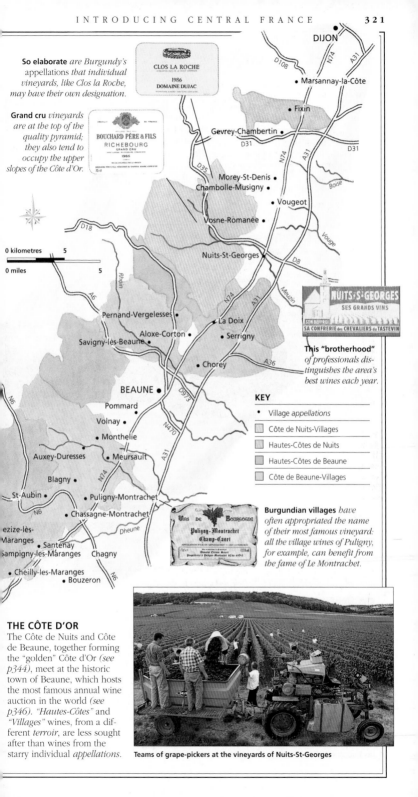

DIJON

So elaborate are Burgundy's appellations *that individual vineyards, like Clos la Roche, may have their own designation.*

CLOS LA ROCHE
1986
DOMAINE DUJAC

Grand cru *vineyards are at the top of the quality pyramid; they also tend to occupy the upper slopes of the Côte d'Or.*

BOUCHARD PÈRE & FILS
RICHEBOURG
GRAND CRU
1986

• Marsannay-la-Côte

• Fixin

Gevrey-Chambertin •

Morey-St-Denis •
Chambolle-Musigny •

• Vougeot

Vosne-Romanée •

Nuits-St-Georges •

0 kilometres   5
0 miles   5

Pernand-Vergelesses •

Aloxe-Corton •   • La Doix

Savigny-lès-Beaune •   • Serrigny

• Chorey

NUITS·S·GEORGES
SES GRANDS VINS
SA CONFRÉRIE des CHEVALIERS du TASTEVIN

This "brotherhood" *of professionals distinguishes the area's best wines each year.*

BEAUNE •

Pommard

Volnay •

• Monthelie

Auxey-Duresses •   • Meursault

Blagny •

St-Aubin •

• Puligny-Montrachet

• Chassagne-Montrachet

ezize-lès-
Maranges   • Santenay
Sampigny-lès-Maranges   Chagny

• Cheilly-les-Maranges
• Bouzeron

KEY

•	Village *appellations*
☐	Côte de Nuits-Villages
☐	Hautes-Côtes de Nuits
☐	Hautes-Côtes de Beaune
☐	Côte de Beaune-Villages

Vins de BOURGOGNE
Puligny-Montrachet
Champ-Canet

Burgundian villages *have often appropriated the name of their most famous vineyard: all the village wines of Puligny, for example, can benefit from the fame of Le Montrachet.*

THE CÔTE D'OR
The Côte de Nuits and Côte de Beaune, together forming the "golden" Côte d'Or *(see p344)*, meet at the historic town of Beaune, which hosts the most famous annual wine auction in the world *(see p346)*. "Hautes-Côtes" and "Villages" wines, from a different *terroir*, are less sought after than wines from the starry individual *appellations*.

Teams of grape-pickers at the vineyards of Nuits-St-Georges

The French Alps

In any season, the Alps are one of the most spectacular regions of France – a majestic mountain range stretching south from Lake Geneva almost to the Mediterranean, and climaxing in Europe's loftiest peak, the 4,800-m (15,770-ft) Mont Blanc. The area encompasses the old regions of Dauphiné and Savoie, once remote and independent (Savoie only became part of France in 1860). They have prospered since alpine holidays and skiing became popular over the last century, but are still very conscious of their distinct identity.

Children in traditional Savoie costumes

The Alpine landscape in winter: chalets and skiers on the slopes at Courchevel

WINTER

The ski season usually starts just before Christmas, and finishes at the end of April. Most resorts offer both cross-country and downhill skiing,

A cable car at Courchevel, part of Les Trois Vallées complex

with many pistes linking two or more ski stations. The less energetic can still enjoy the landscape from some of the highest cable cars *(téléphériques)* in the world.

Of the 100 or more French Alpine resorts, the most popular include **Chamonix-Mont Blanc**, the historic capital of Alpine skiing and site of the first Winter Olympics in 1924; **Megève**, which boasts one of the best ski schools in Europe; **Morzine**, a year-round resort on the Swiss border, overlooked by the modern, car-free resort of **Avoriaz**; modern **Albertville**, site of the 1992 Winter Olympics; **Les Trois Vallées**, which include glamorous

A downhill skier at Val d'Isère

Courchevel and **Méribel**, and the lesser-known **Val Thorens/Les Ménuires**; **Tignes**, a year-round resort; **Les Arcs** and **La Plagne**, both purpose-built; and **Val d'Isère**, a favourite among the rich and famous.

ALPINE FLOWERS

In spring and early summer the pastures of the French Alps are ablaze with flowers. These include blue and yellow gentians, bellflowers, lilies, saxifrages and a variety of orchids. Steep mountain meadows cannot be farmed intensively, and the absence of fertilizers and weed killers enables wild flowers to flourish.

Spring gentian (*Gentiana verna*)

Martagon lily (*Lilium martagon*)

The French Alps in spring: flower-filled meadows overlooked by brilliant white peaks

SPRING AND SUMMER

The Alpine summer season starts in late June, extending to early September – most resorts close in October and November

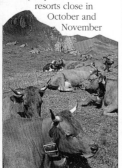

Bell-ringing dairy cows in an Alpine pasture

between the hiking and skiing seasons. After the spring thaw, flower-filled pastures, snow-fed mountain lakes and a huge number of marked trails make this area a hiker's paradise. In the Chamonix area alone there are over 310 km (195 miles) of hiking trails. The best known long-distance route is the **Tour du Mont Blanc**, a 10-day hike via France, Italy and Switzerland. The **GR5** traverses the entire Alps, passing through the **Parc National de la Vanoise** and **Parc Régional du Queyras** (*see p387*) to the south. *Téléphériques* give access to the higher trails, where the views are even more awesome. Be sure to bring plenty of warm, waterproof clothing: the weather can change very quickly.

Many resorts are now concentrating on broadening their summer appeal – golf, tennis, mountain biking, horse-riding, paragliding, canoeing, white water rafting, glacier skiing and mountain climbing are all widely available.

Mountain climbers scaling the heights around Mont Blanc

Geology of the Massif Central

The Massif Central covers almost one-fifth of France and is over 250 million years old. Most of its peaks have been eroded to form a vast plateau split into deep valleys. The heart of the Massif consists of hard, igneous rocks like granite, with softer rocks such as limestone at its margins. Different rock types are reflected in the landscape and buildings; in the eroded Gorges du Tarn, the houses are built of russet-coloured limestone. Massive granite farmhouses are a feature of Limousin and Le Puy-en-Velay is distinguished by its giant basalt pillars.

LOCATOR MAP
Extent of the Massif Central

Basalt *is a dark, fine-grained rock formed by volcanic lava. A common building stone in the Auvergne, it is often cut into blocks and bonded with lighter-coloured mortar. In the medieval town of Salers (see p363), basalt was used for most of the buildings, including this one in the Grande Place.*

This granite portal *is found in the Romanesque church at Moutier d'Ahun (see p356). Granite underlies much of the Massif Central.*

Schist tiling *is featured on these roofs at Argentat. Schist is a crystalline rock which splits readily into layers. It is particularly common on the edge of the Massif, and provides an effective roofing material.*

Limestone walls *can be seen on houses in Espalion (see p366). Of all the rocks in the Massif Central, it is among the most easily worked. It splits readily and is soft enough to be cut into blocks with a hand saw. As with granite, its colour and consistency vary from area to area.*

Montluçc

Moutier d'Ahun •

Limoges •

Clermor Ferran

Dordogne

• Saler

• Argentat

Cère

Lot

Mi

Tarn

0 kilometres   50

0 miles   50

Crystallized lava, *like this dramatic curtain of columns at Prades, formed when liquid basalt seeped through the surrounding rock and solidified to form giant crystals.*

KEY

■	Sedimentary rock
■	Surface volcanic rock
■	Granite
■	Metamorphic rock

vers

Loire

Saône

Lyon ●

● St-Etienne

● Le-Puy-en-Velay

Rhône

Limestone plateaux (causes) *are typical of this region. Gorges, where rivers have cut through layers of this slightly soluble rock, run deep into the Massif Central.*

This mature landscape *at Mont Aigoual is the highest point in the Cévennes (see p367), dividing rivers flowing into the Atlantic and the Mediterranean. Its granite and schist rocks show erosion.*

RECOGNIZING ROCKS

Geologists divide rocks into three groups. Igneous rocks, like granite, are formed by volcanic activity and either extruded on to the surface or intrude into other rocks below ground. Sedimentary rocks are produced by sediment build-up. Metamorphic rocks have been transformed by heat or pressure.

SEDIMENTARY ROCK

Oolitic limestone *often contains fossils and small amounts of quartz.*

SURFACE VOLCANIC ROCK

Basalt, *which can form very thick sheets, is the most common lava rock.*

GRANITE

Pink granite, *a coarse-grained rock, is formed deep in the earth's crust.*

METAMORPHIC ROCK

Muscovite schist *is a medium-grained mud or clay-based rock.*

BURGUNDY AND FRANCHE-COMTÉ

YONNE · NIÈVRE · CÔTE D'OR · SAÔNE-ET-LOIRE
HAUTE-SAÔNE · DOUBS · JURA

Burgundy considers itself the heart of France, a prosperous region with world-renowned wine, earthy but excellent cuisine and magnificent architecture. Franche-Comté to the east combines gentle farmland with lofty Alpine forests.

Under the dukes of Valois, Burgundy was France's most powerful rival, with territory extending well beyond its present boundaries. By the 16th century, however, the duchy was ruled by governors appointed by the French king, but it still managed to keep its privileges and traditions. Once a part of Burgundy, Franche-Comté – the Free County – struggled to remain independent of the French crown, and was a province of the Holy Roman Empire until annexed by Louis XIV in 1674.

Burgundy, now as in the past, is a wealthy region, a centre of medieval religious faith which produced Romanesque masterpieces at Vézelay, Fontenay, and Cluny. Dijon is a splendid city, filled with the great palaces of the old Burgundian nobility and a collection of great paintings and sculptures in the Musée des Beaux Arts. The vineyards of the Côte d'Or, the Côte de Beaune and Chablis yield some of the world's most venerated wines. Other richly varied landscapes – from the wild forests of the Morvan to the lush farmland of the Brionnais – produce snails, Bresse chickens and Charolais beef.

Franche-Comté has none of this opulence, though its capital, Besançon, is an elegant 17th-century city with a tradition of clockmaking. Topographically the Franche-Comté is divided into two, with gently-rolling farmland in the Saône valley and high Alpine scenery to the east. This forest country of Alpine torrents filled with trout is also the home of great cheeses, notably Vacherin and Comté, and of the characteristic yellow wine of Arbois.

The prehistoric site of the Roche de Solutré near Mâcon

◁ Vineyards at Santenay in the world-renowned Côte de Beaune district

Exploring Burgundy and Franche-Comté

Burgundy is arguably France's richest province – historically, culturally, gastronomically and economically. This lush kernel of a once great power possesses a concentration of unique Romanesque architecture in Fontenay and Vézelay, along with some of the world's most venerated wines. Dijon is a must for lovers of art, architecture, and food. Franche-Comté is better suited for outdoor holidays, such as trekking and canoeing in wild scenery and crystal-clear rivers.

Burgundian riverscape near Fonten

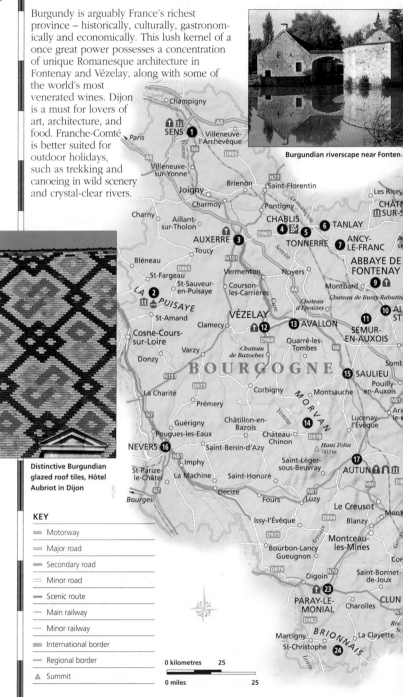

Distinctive Burgundian glazed roof tiles, Hôtel Aubriot in Dijon

KEY

▬	Motorway
▬	Major road
▬	Secondary road
▭	Minor road
▬	Scenic route
▬	Main railway
---	Minor railway
▬	International border
▬	Regional border
△	Summit

0 kilometres   25

0 miles   25

SIGHTS AT A GLANCE

Abbaye de Fontenay ❾
Alise-Ste-Reine ❿
Arbois ㉗
Arc-et-Senans ㉙
Autun ⓱
Auxerre ❸
Avallon ⓭
Beaune ⓴
Belfort ㉝
Besançon ㉛
Brionnais ㉔
Cascades du Hérisson ㉖
Chablis ❹
Champlitte ㉚
Château d'Ancy-le-Franc ❼
Château de Tanlay ❻
Châtillon-sur-Seine ❽
Cluny ㉒
Côte d'Or ⓳
Dijon ⓲
Dole ㉘
La Puisaye-Forterre ❷
Mâcon ㉕
Morvan ⓮
Nevers ⓰
Ornans ㉜
Paray-le-Monial ㉓
Ronchamp ㉞
Saulieu ⓯
Semur-en-Auxois ⓫
Sens ❶
Tonnerre ❺
Tournus ㉑
Vézelay ⓬

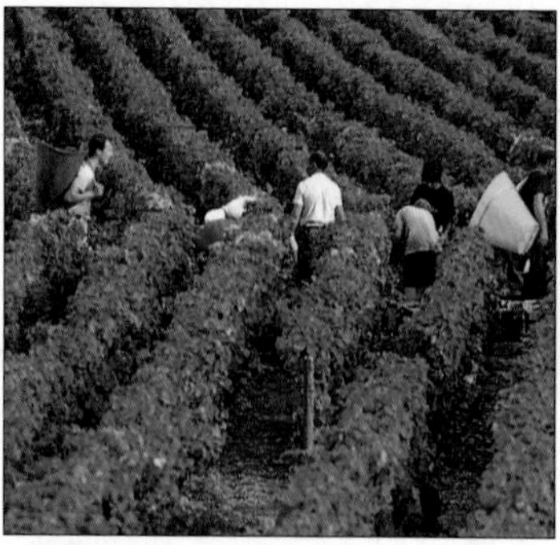

Wine harvest in Nuits-St-Georges, Côte d'Or

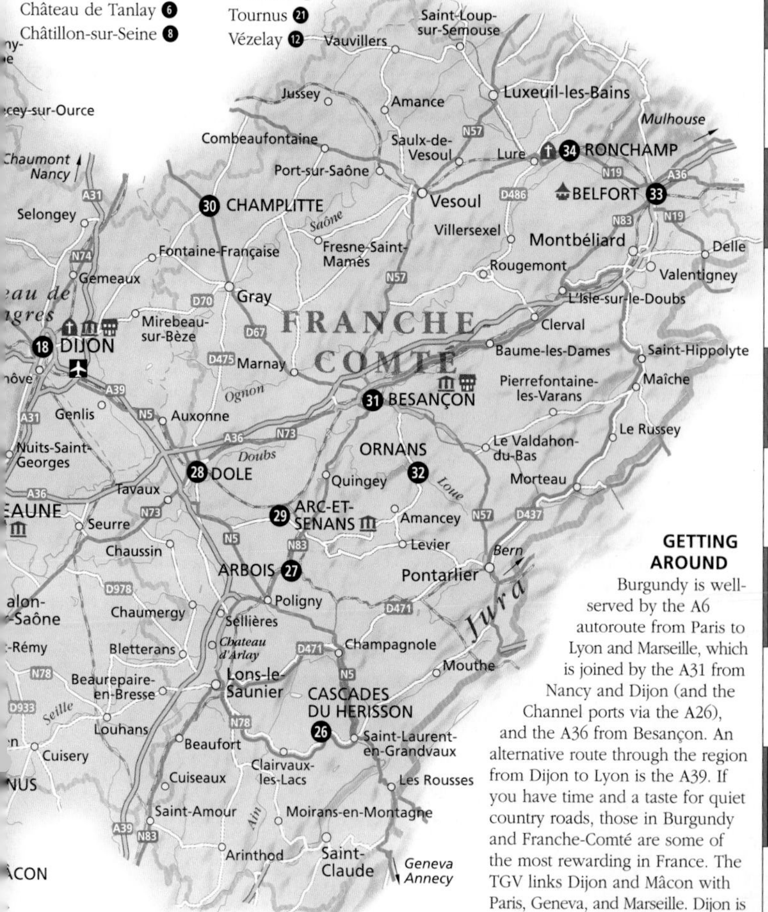

GETTING AROUND

Burgundy is well-served by the A6 autoroute from Paris to Lyon and Marseille, which is joined by the A31 from Nancy and Dijon (and the Channel ports via the A26), and the A36 from Besançon. An alternative route through the region from Dijon to Lyon is the A39. If you have time and a taste for quiet country roads, those in Burgundy and Franche-Comté are some of the most rewarding in France. The TGV links Dijon and Mâcon with Paris, Geneva, and Marseille. Dijon is a major rail hub and connects other towns in the region; its international airport serves most European destinations.

La Sainte Châsse, 11th-century reliquary in the Treasury in Sens

Sens ●

Yonne. 🏘 30,000. 🚉 🚌 ℹ pl Jean-Jaurès (03 86 65 19 49). 🛒 Mon & Fri. www.office-de-tourisme-sens.com

The little town of Sens, at the confluence of the rivers Yonne and Vanne, was important before Caesar came to Gaul. It was the Senones whose attempt to sack the Roman Capitol in 390 BC was thwarted by a flock of geese.

The **Cathédrale St-Etienne** is Sens' outstanding glory. Begun before 1140 it is the oldest of the great Gothic cathedrals and its noble simplicity influenced many other churches. Louis IX *(see p51)* did the town the honour of getting married here in 1234.

The exquisite stained-glass windows from the 12th–16th centuries show biblical scenes, including the Tree of Jesse, and a tribute to Thomas Becket who was exiled here. His liturgical robes are in the Treasury (part of the **Musées de Sens**), which has one of the finest collections in France, including a beautiful Byzantine reliquary.

🏛 **Les Musées de Sens** Pl de la Cathédrale. **Tel** 03 86 64 46 22. 🕐 Wed–Mon (phone to check times). 📷 ♿ 🎧

La Puisaye-Forterre ●

Yonne, Nièvre. 🚉 Auxerre, Clamecy, Bonny-sur-Loire, Cosne-Cours-sur-Loire. 🚌 St-Fargeau, St-Sauveur-en-Puisaye. ℹ Charny (03 86 63 65 51).

The strange, secret forest country of La Puisaye-Forterre was immortalized by Colette (1873–1954), who was born at **St-Sauveur** in "a house that smiled only on its garden side…". The town's 17th-century château now houses the **Musée Colette**.

The best way to explore the region is on foot or by bike around its watery woodlands, orchards and meadows. Alternatively, take a ride on the *Transpoyaudin*, a 27 km (17 mile) train ride from St-Sauveur to Villiers St-Benoît.

An unusual, hands-on visit can be made to **Château de Guédelon**, a 25-year project exactly recreating a medieval castle, using only original building methods and materials found locally. Nearby is the genuine 13th-century **Château de Ratilly**, with a pottery workshop and art exhibitions. More of this can be seen in **St-Amand**, the centre of Puisaye stoneware production, much of which was traditionally fired in the 18th-century horizontal kiln at Moutiers. Both the pottery and local frescoes (see the

Colette in the 1880s at St-Sauveur

churches at **Moutiers** and **La Ferté-Loupière**) made use of locally mined ochre, a major export in the 19th century. The pink brick **Château de St-Fargeau** housed the exiled Grande Mademoiselle *(p57)*.

🏛 **Musée Colette** Château St-Sauveur-en-Puisaye. **Tel** 03 86 45 61 95. 🕐 Apr–Oct: Wed–Mon; Nov, Feb–Mar: w/e & sch hols pms. 📷

Auxerre ●

Yonne. 🏘 40,000. 🚉 ℹ 1–2 quai de la République (03 86 52 06 19). 🛒 Tue & Fri. www.ot-auxerre.fr

Beautifully sited overlooking the Yonne river, Auxerre justly prides itself on a fine collection of churches along with a charming pedestrianized main square, the place Charles-Surugue.

The Gothic **Cathédrale St-Etienne** took over three centuries to build and was completed in about 1560. It is famous for its intricate 13th-century stained glass. The choir with its slender columns and colonettes is the epitome of Gothic elegance, while the western portals are decorated with beautiful flamboyant sculpture which has been sadly mutilated by war and weather. The Romanesque crypt is adorned by unique 11th–13th-century frescoes, including one depicting Christ on a white horse. The badly pillaged treasury is less impressive, but still has an interesting collection of illuminated manuscripts.

Château de St-Fargeau in the Puisaye-Forterre region

For hotels and restaurants in this region see pp572–5 and pp625–9

St Germanus, mentor of St Patrick and bishop of Auxerre in the 5th century, was buried at the former abbey church of **St-Germain**. The abbey was founded by Queen Clothilde, wife of Clovis *(see pp48–9)*, the first Christian king of France, and hence is an important shrine. The crypt is partly Carolingian, with tombs and 11th–13th century frescoes. The former abbey houses the **Musée St-Germain** with local Gallo-Roman finds.

🏛 **Musée St-Germain**
2 pl St-Germain. **Tel** 03 86 18 05 50 ◯ Wed–Mon. ⬤ some public hols. 📷 🚫

Medieval fresco in Cathédrale St-Etienne at Auxerre

Chablis ➍

Yonne. 👥 2,700. 🚉 🚌 ⓘ 1 rue du Maréchal de Lattre de Tassigny (03 86 42 80 80). ⬤ Sun.

There can be no question that Chablis tastes best in Chablis. Although this is one of the

The intriguing spring of Fosse Dionne in Tonnerre

most famous wine villages on earth, its narrow stone streets still have an air of sleepy prosperity. February processions in nearby Fyé, attended by the wine brotherhood of Piliers Chablisiens, honour St Vincent, patron saint of wine-growers.

Tonnerre ➎

Yonne. 👥 6,200. 🚉 🚌 ⓘ pl Marguerite de Bourgogne (03 86 55 14 48). ⬤ Sat & Wed. **www**.tonnerre.fr

The mystical cloudy-green spring of **Fosse Dionne** is a good reason to visit the small town of Tonnerre. An astonishing volume of water bursts up from the ground into an 18th-century washing-place. Due to its depth and strong currents it has never been thoroughly explored and local legend has it that a serpent lives on undisturbed.

The **Hôtel-Dieu** is 150 years older than the Hôtel-Dieu in Beaune *(see p346–7)*.

It was founded by Margaret of Burgundy in 1293 to care for the poor. In the Revolution it lost its tiling but the barrel-vaulted oak ceiling survived.

🏥 **Hôtel-Dieu & Musée**
Rue du Prieuré. **Tel** 03 86 55 14 48 ◯ Apr–Oct: Wed–Mon; Nov–Mar: Mon & Wed–Sat. 📷 ♿ 🚫

Château de Tanlay ➏

Tanlay. **Tel** 03 86 75 70 61. ◯ Apr–mid-Nov: Wed–Mon. 📷 🚫 oblig. ♿

The moated Château de Tanlay is a beautiful example of French Renaissance, built in the mid-16th century. There is a *trompe l'oeil* in the Grande Galerie and, in the corner tower, an intriguing School of Fontainebleau painted ceiling. Its antique divinities represent famous Protestants and Catholics in the 16th century, such as Diane de Poitiers as Venus.

The Renaissance façade and *cour d'honneur* of Château de Tanlay

Abbaye de Fontenay ❾

The tranquil Abbey of Fontenay is the oldest surviving Cistercian foundation in France and offers a rare insight into the Cistercian way of life. It represents the spirit of the order in the sublime gravity of its Romanesque church and its plain but elegant chapterhouse, in early Gothic style. The abbey was founded in 1118 by St Bernard. Situated deep in the forest, it offered the peace and seclusion the Cistercians sought. Supported by the local aristocracy, the abbey began to thrive and remained in use until the Revolution when it was sold and converted into a paper mill. In 1906 the abbey came under new ownership and was restored to its original appearance.

Dovecote
A magnificent circular dovecote, built in the 13th century, is situated next to the kennel where the precious hunting dogs of the dukes of Burgundy were guarded by servants.

The 17th-century abbot's lodgings were built when the abbots were appointed by royal favour.

The bakehouse is no longer intact but the 13th-century oven and chimney have survived.

The visitors' hostel is where weary wanderers and pilgrims were offered board and lodging by the monks.

★ Cloisters
For a 12th-century monk a walk through the cloisters was an opportunity for meditation and provided shelter from the weather.

Warming Room

In the forge monks produced their own tools and hardware.

Fontenay "Prison"
It may be that this 15th-century building was actually used to lock up not local miscreants but important abbey archives, in order to protect them against damage by rats.

Scriptorium
Manuscripts were copied here. The adjacent Warming Room was used to warm chilled hands

★ Abbey Church
Rich decoration has no place in this church from the 1140s. But the severe architectural forms, the warm colour of the stone and the diffused light convey a grandeur of their own.

VISITORS' CHECKLIST

Marmagne. **Tel** 03 80 92 15 00.
🚉 Montbard. 🕐 10am–5pm daily (11 Nov–Mar: 10am–noon, 2–5pm daily). 🈳 ♿ 🎦 📷
www.abbayedefontenay.com

Dormitory
Monks slept in long rows on straw mattresses in this large, unheated room. The timberwork roof is from the late 15th century.

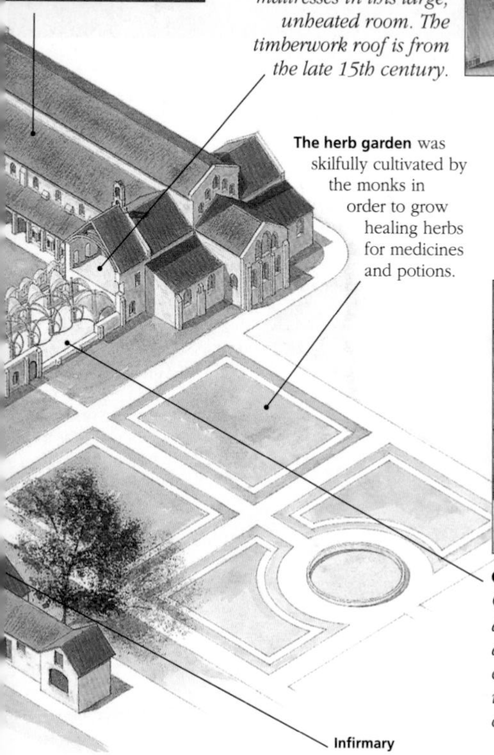

The herb garden was skilfully cultivated by the monks in order to grow healing herbs for medicines and potions.

STAR FEATURES

★ Abbey Church

★ Cloisters

Chapterhouse
Once a day, monks and abbot assembled in this room to discuss matters concerning the community. It derives much of its charm from the elegant 12th-century piers and the rib-vaults.

Infirmary

ST BERNARD AND THE CISTERCIANS

In 1112 Bernard, a young Burgundian nobleman, joined the Cistercians. At the time the order was still obscure, founded 14 years earlier by a group of monks who wanted to turn their back on the elaborate lifestyle of Cluny *(see pp48–9)*, renounce the world, and espouse poverty and simplicity of life. During Bernard's lifetime the Cistercians became one of the largest and most famous orders of its time. Part of this success was clearly due to Bernard's powerful personality and his skills as a writer, theologian and statesman. He reinforced the poverty rule, rejecting all forms of embellishment. In 1174, only 21 years after his death, he was canonized.

The Virgin Protecting the Cistercian Order, by Jean Bellegambe

Château d'Ancy-le-Franc ❼

Ancy-le-Franc. **Tel** 03 86 75 00 25.
⬤ Apr–mid-Nov: Tue–Sat. 🔲 📷
obligatory. **www**.chateau-ancy.com

The classical Renaissance façade of Château d'Ancy-le-Franc gives an austere impression. Its inner courtyard, however, has rich ornamentation. The château was built in the 1540s by the Italian Sebastiano Serlio, for the Duke of Clermont-Tonnerre. Most of the interior decorations were carried out by Primaticcio and other members of the Fontainebleau School (see pp180–81). Diane de Poitiers, the duke's sister-in-law and mistress of Henry II, is portrayed in the *Chambre de Judith et Holophernes*.

In the outbuildings a vintage car and carriage museum displays over 80 vehicles.

The staid façade of Château d'Ancy-le-Franc

The vase of Vix in the Musée du Châtillonnais, Châtillon-sur-Seine

Châtillon-sur-Seine ❽

Côte d'Or. 👥 5,837. 🚌 🚉 ℹ️ pl
Marmont (03 80 91 13 19). 🏪 Sat.

World War II left Châtillon a smoking ruin, hence the town's resolutely modern aspect. But the past is still present in the **Musée du Châtillonnais**, where the magnificent Vix treasure is displayed. In 1953, the tomb of a Gaulish princess, dating from the 6th century BC, was discovered near Vix at Mont Lassois. The trove of jewellery and artifacts of Greek origin includes a stunning bronze vase, 164 cm (66 in) high and weighing 208 kg (459 lb).

Another point of interest is the Romanesque **Eglise St-Vorles** containing an *Entombment* with Christ and mourners splendidly sculpted (1527).

At the nearby source of the river Douix, which runs into the Seine, is a beautiful grotto.

🏛 **Musée du Châtillonnais**
Rue du Bourg. **Tel** 03 80 91 24 67.
⬤ Jul–Aug: daily; Sep–Jun: Wed–Mon.
● 1 Jan, 1 May, 25 Dec. 🔲 📷

Abbaye de Fontenay ❾

See pp332–3.

Alise-Ste-Reine ❿

Côte d'Or. 👥 3,275. ℹ️ pl
Bingerbruck (03 80 96 89 13).

Mont Auxois, above the little village of Alise-Ste-Reine, was the site of Caesar's final victory over the heroic Gaulish chieftain Vercingétorix

in 52 BC after a six-week siege (see p46). The first excavations here were undertaken in the mid-19th century, and they uncovered the vestiges of a thriving Gallo-Roman town, with theatre, forum and well-laid-out street plan. The **Musée Alésia** has a collection of artifacts, jewellery and bronze figures from the site.

Alise is dominated by Aimé Millet's gigantic moustachioed statue of Vercingétorix, which was placed here in 1865 to commemorate the first excavations. Cynics feel that it bears a more than passing resemblance to Napoleon III, who sponsored the dig.

🏛 **Musée Alésia**
Rue de l'Hôpital. **Tel** 03 80 96 10 95.
● for renovation until 2010. 🔲

Environs

In the vicinity lies **Château de Bussy-Rabutin**. The spiteful 17th-century soldier and wit Roger de Bussy-Rabutin created its highly individualistic

Excavations at the Roman site near Alise-Ste-Reine

decor, while exiled from Louis XIV's court. One room is dedicated to portraits of his many mistresses, as well as a couple of imaginary ones.

⚜ **Château de Bussy-Rabutin**
Bussy-le-Grand. *Tel* 03 80 96 00 03.
◯ Tue–Sun. ⬤ 1 Jan, 1 & 11 Nov, 25 Dec.

Semur-en-Auxois ⓫

Côte d'Or. ⬛ 5,000. ◼ ◼ 2 place Gaveau (03 80 97 05 96). ◼ Sun. www.ville-semur-en-auxois.fr

Approached from the west, Semur-en-Auxois comes as a surprise on an otherwise uneventful road. Its massive round bastions built in the 14th century (one of them with an unnerving gash in it) suddenly appear, towering over the Pont Joly and the peaceful river Armançon.

The **Eglise Notre-Dame** dates from the 13th and 14th centuries, and was modelled on the cathedral of Auxerre. The fragile high walls had to be restored in the 15th and 19th centuries. The church houses significant artworks, from the tympanum showing the legend of Doubting Thomas on the north doorway, to the 15th-century *Entombment* by Antoine le Moiturier. The stained glass presents the legend of Saint Barbara, and the work of different guilds such as butchers and drapers.

Environs
The village of Epoisses is the site of the moated **Château d'Epoisses**, its 11th–18th-century construction blending medieval towers with fine Renaissance details, and a huge 15th-century dovecote. Epoisses is also the home of one of Burgundy's most re-

Semur-en-Auxois by the river Armançon

Stained-glass window in Eglise Notre-Dame at Semur-en-Auxois

vered cheeses, to be sampled at the local café or *fromagerie*.

⚜ **Château d'Epoisses**
Epoisses. *Tel* 03 80 96 40 56.
◯ Jul–Aug: Wed–Mon (grounds: all year). ◼ ◼ ◼ ground floor only.

Vézelay ⓬

See pp336–7.

Avallon ⓭

Yonne. ⬛ 9,000. ◼ ◼ ◼ 6 rue Bocquillot (03 86 34 14 19). ◼ Sat & Thu. www.avallonnais-tourisme.com

A fine old fortified town, Avallon is situated on a granite spur between two ravines by the river Cousin.

Avallon suffered in the wars of Saracens, Normans, English and French, which accounts for its defensive aspect. The town is quiet and rather beautiful, full of charming details. The main monument is the 12th-century Romanesque **Eglise St-Lazare**, with two carved doorways. The larger illustrates the signs of the zodiac, the labours of the month, and the musicians of the Apocalypse. The nave is decorated with sophisticated acanthus capitals and polychrome statuary.

The **Musée de l'Avallonnais** features an intricate Venus mosaic from the 2nd century AD, and Georges Rouault's (1871–1958) series of Expressionist etchings, the *Miserere*.

🏛 **Musée de l'Avallonnais**
4 rue du College. *Tel* 03 86 34 03 19.
◯ May–Oct: Wed–Mon pms; Nov–Apr: Sat–Sun pms. ◼

Environs
To the southwest of Avallon is the 12th-century Château de Bazoches, given to Maréchal de Vauban by Louis XIV in 1675, and transformed by him into a military garrison.

Miserere by Georges Rouault in the Musée d'Avallonnais, Avallon

Vézelay ⑫

Decorated capital

The golden glow of the Basilique Ste-Madeleine crowning Vézelay's hill is visible from afar. Tourists follow in the footsteps of medieval pilgrims, ascending the narrow street up to the former abbey church. In the 12th century, at the height of its glory, the abbey claimed to house relics of Mary Magdalene and was also an important meeting point for pilgrims en route to Santiago de Compostela in Spain (see pp400–1). Today its attraction lies in the Romanesque church with its magnificent sculpture and Gothic choir.

View of Vézelay
The abbey dominates Vézelay's surroundings as it once dominated the religious and worldly affairs of the area.

Nave of Ste-Madeleine
The nave was rebuilt between 1120–35, using alternate dark and light stone in the transverse arches.

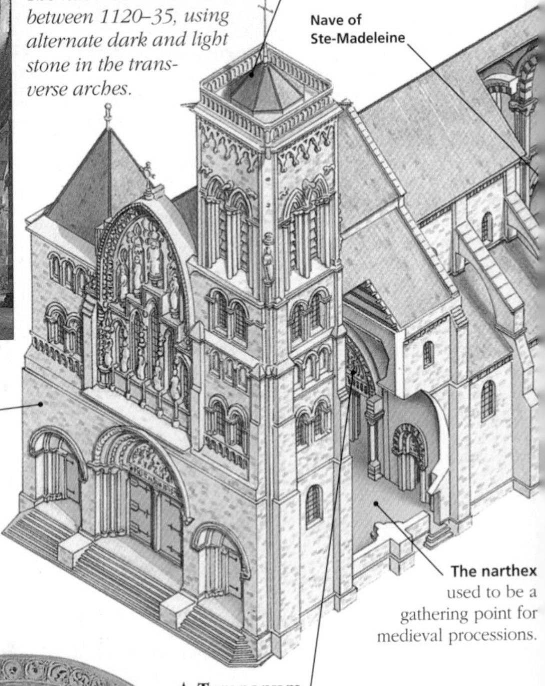

Tour St-Michel was built in 1230–40. It derives its name from the statue of the archangel in the tower's southwest corner.

Nave of Ste-Madeleine

The façade dates from 1150 and has a large 13th-century window. It was about to collapse when Viollet-le-Duc was commissioned to restore it according to old plans in 1840.

The narthex used to be a gathering point for medieval processions.

★ **Tympanum**
This masterpiece of sculpture (1120–35) shows Christ on His throne, stretching out His hands from which rays of light descend on to the apostles.

STAR FEATURES

★ Tympanum

★ Capitals

Tour St-Antoine was built at the same time as the choir, in the late 12th century. Its counterpart on the north side was never finished.

VISITORS' CHECKLIST

Basilique Ste-Madeleine, Vézelay.
Tel *03 86 33 39 50.* 🚉 *Sermizelles.*
🕐 *6am–8pm daily (7am–dusk winter).* ✝ *7am, 12:30pm, 6pm Tue–Fri; 8am, 11am, 12:30pm, 6pm Sat; 8am, 11am, 6pm Sun.*
📷 **www**.vezelay.cef.fr

The chapterhouse and cloister are the only parts remaining from the 12th-century monastic buildings. Viollet-le-Duc rebuilt the cloister and restored the rib-vaulted chapterhouse, once a graceful background for the monks' daily assemblies.

Crypt of Ste-Madeleine
The Romanesque crypt houses relics once thought to be Mary Magdalene's. The vault was rebuilt in 1165.

★ Capitals
The capitals in the nave and narthex are exquisitely carved, and give a vivid rendering of the stories of Classical antiquity and the Bible. The master who created them remains unknown.

Choir of Ste-Madeleine
The choir was rebuilt in the last quarter of the 12th century in the then modern Gothic style of the Ile de France.

Morvan, a region of rivers and forests, well-suited to fishing and other outdoor pursuits

Morvan ⑭

Yonne, Côte d'Or, Nièvre, Saône et Loire. ✈ Dijon. 🚉 Autun, Mombard. 🚌 Château-Chinon, Saulieu, Avallon. 🛈 2 pl St Christophe, Château-Chinon (03 86 85 06 58); Maison du Parc, St-Brisson (03 86 78 79 00). www.morvan-tourisme.org

Morvan is a Celtic word meaning Black Mountain, which is a good description of this area seen from afar. The immense, sparsely inhabited plateau of granite and woodland appears suddenly in the centre of the rich Burgundy hills and farmland. Stretching roughly north to south, it gains altitude as it proceeds southwards, reaching a culminating point of 901 m (2,928 ft) at **Haut-Folin**.

The Morvan's two sources of natural wealth are abundant water and dense forests of oak, beech and conifer. In the old days lumber used to be floated out of the area to Paris via a network of lakes and rivers. Today it travels by truck, and the Yonne, Cousin and Cure rivers are instead used for recreation and the production of electricity.

The Morvan has always been a poor, remote area. Each of its largest towns, Château-Chinon in the centre and Saulieu on the outskirts, has barely 3,000 inhabitants.

During World War II, the Morvan was a bastion of the French Resistance. Today a Regional Nature Park, its attraction is its wildness. Information on a wide variety of outdoor activities, inclu-

ding cycling, canoeing, skiing, and horse trekking, is available at the **Maison du Parc** at St-Brisson where there is also the very moving **Musée de la Resistance**. There are plenty of short walking trails, and two well-signed long-distance paths: the GR13 (Vézelay to Autun) and the Tour du Morvan par les Grands Lacs.

🏛 **Musée de la Résistance**
Maison du Parc, St-Brisson. **Tel** 03 86 78 79 06. ◯ Easter–mid-Nov: Wed–Mon (Jul & Aug: daily). 🌐 🗎 🔒 ♿

Saulieu ⑮

Côte d'Or. 🚾 3,000. 🚉 🚌 🛈 24 rue d'Argentine (03 80 64 00 21). 🛒 Thu & Sat. www.saulieu.fr

On the edge of the Morvan, Saulieu has been a shrine of Burgundian cooking ever since the 17th century. The town was then a staging post on the Paris to Lyon coach road. Today the tradition is maintained by the famous chef Bernard Loiseau at the **Côte d'Or** restaurant (see p598). Yet there is more to Saulieu than ris de veau de lait braisé or poularde truffée à la vapeur. The Romanesque **Basilique St-Andoche**, built in the early 12th century, has decorated capitals with representations of the Flight into Egypt and a

Nevers faïence vase

comical version of the story of Balaam and his donkey waylaid by the Angel.

Nevers ⑯

Nièvre. 🚾 41,000. 🚉 🚌 🛈 Palais Ducal, rue Sabatier. (03 86 68 46 00). 🛒 Sat. www.nevers-tourisme.com

Like all Burgundian towns fronting the Loire, Nevers should be approached from the west side of the river for a full appreciation of its noble site. Though lacking historical importance, the town has much to show. Considered to be the earliest of the Loire châteaux, the **Palais Ducal** has a long Renaissance façade framed by polygonal towers and a broad esplanade. The Romanesque 11th-century **Eglise St-Etienne** has graceful monolithic columns and a wreath of radiating chapels. In the crypt of the Gothic **Cathédrale St-Cyr** is a 16th-century sculpted Entombment, and the foundations of a 6th-century baptistry, discovered in 1944, after heavy bombing. The contemporary stained-glass windows are also noteworthy. The overlordship of Nevers passed to the Gonzaga family in the 16th century. They brought with them an Italian school of artists skilled in faïence making and glass-blowing.

The industry has remained and the modern pottery is still traditionally decorated in blue, white, yellow and green, with its curious trademark, the little green arabesque knot, or *noeud vert*. The best place to view it is at the **Musée Municipal** and the best place to buy it is the 17th-century **Faïencerie Montagnon**.

🏛 Musée Municipal Frédéric Blandin
16 rue Saint-Geneste. *Tel 03 86 71 67 91.* ● *for renovation until further notice.*

Environs

Just south of Nevers, the 19th-century **Pont du Guetin** carries the Loire Canal majestically across the Allier river. The church at **St-Parize-le-Châtel** has a jolly Burgundian menagerie sculpted on the capitals of the crypt.

The *Temptation of Eve* in Autun

Autun ⑰

Saône-et-Loire. 🏘 18,000. 🚉 🚌 ℹ 2 av Charles de Gaulle (03 85 86 80 38). 🛒 Wed & Fri. **www**.autun-tourisme.com

Augustodunum, the town of Augustus, was founded in the late 1st century BC. It was a

The imposing Porte St-André in Autun, once part of the Roman wall

great centre of learning, with a population four times what it is today. Its theatre, built in the 1st century AD, could seat 20,000 people.

Today Autun is still a delight, deserving gastronomic as well as cultural investigation. The magical **Cathédrale St-Lazare** was built in the 12th century. It is special because of its sculptures, most of them by the mysterious 12th-century artist Gislebertus. He sculpted both the capitals inside and the glorious Last Judgment tympanum over the main portal. This masterpiece, called a "Romanesque Cézanne" by André Malraux, escaped notice and was saved from destruction during the Revolution because it had been plastered over in the 18th century. Inside, some of the capitals can be seen close-up in a room in the tower. Look also for the

sculpture of Pierre Jeannin and his wife. Jeannin was the president of the Dijon parliament who prevented the Massacre of St Bartholomew (*see pp54–5*) spreading with the perceptive remark, "the commands of very angry monarchs should be obeyed very slowly".

The brilliant collection of medieval art at the **Musée Rolin** includes the bas relief *Temptation of Eve*, by Gislebertus. There is also the 15th-century painted stone Virgin of Autun, and the *Nativity of Cardinal Rolin* by the Master of Moulins, from about 1480.

The monumental **Porte St-André** and **Porte d'Arroux**, and the ruins of the **Théâtre Romain** and the **Temple de Janus**, are reminders of Autun's glorious Roman past.

🏛 Musée Rolin
3 rue des Bancs. *Tel 03 85 52 09 76.* ◯ Wed–Mon. ● public hols.
📷 📹

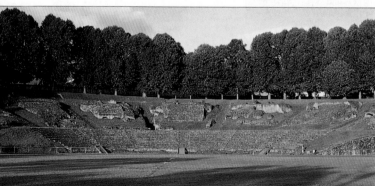
Remains of the Roman theatre at Autun, dating from the 1st century AD

Street by Street: Dijon ⑱

The centre of Dijon is noted for its architectural splendour – a legacy from the Dukes of Burgundy *(see p343)*. Wealthy parliament members also had elegant *hôtels particuliers* built in the 17th–18th centuries. The capital of Burgundy, Dijon today has a rich cultural life and a renowned university. The city's great art treasures are housed in the Palais des Ducs. Dijon is also famous for its mustard *(see p318)* and *pain d'épice* (gingerbread), a reminder of the town's position on the spice route. It became a major rail hub during the 19th century and now has a TGV link to Paris.

Hôtel de Vogüé
This elegant 17th-century mansion is decorated with Burgundian cabbages and fruit garlands by Hugues Sambin.

★ Notre-Dame
This magnificent 13th-century Gothic church has a façade with gargoyles, columns and the popular Jacquemart clock. The chouette *(owl)* is reputed to bring good luck when touched.

Musée des Beaux Arts
The collection of Flemish masters here includes this 14th-century triptych by Jacques de Baerze and Melchior Broederlam.

Place de la Libération was created by Mansart in the 17th century.

★ Palais des Ducs
The dukes of Burgundy held court here, but the building seen today was mainly built in the 17th century for the parliament. It now houses the Musée des Beaux Arts.

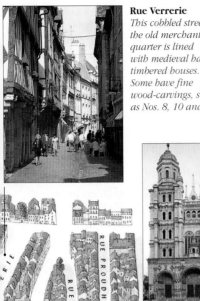

Rue Verrerie
This cobbled street in the old merchants' quarter is lined with medieval half-timbered houses. Some have fine wood-carvings, such as Nos. 8, 10 and 12.

VISITORS' CHECKLIST

Côte d'Or. 🏠 153,000. ✈ 5 km (3 miles) SSE Dijon. 🚉 🚌 Cours de la Gare ⓘ Pavillon, place Darcy & 11 rue des Forges (08 92 70 05 58). 🛒 Tue, Thu–Sat. 🎭 Florissimo (2010 next); Festival de Musique (Jun); Fêtes de la Vigne (Sep). **Hôtel de Vogüé** only inner courtyard open. **Musée Magnin** (03 80 67 11 10) ⬤ Tue–Sun. ⬤ 1 Jan, 25 Dec. 🖥 www.dijon-tourism.com

★ St-Michel
Begun in the 15th century and completed in the 17th century, St-Michel's façade combines Flamboyant Gothic with Renaissance details. On the richly carved porch, angels and biblical motifs mingle with mythological themes.

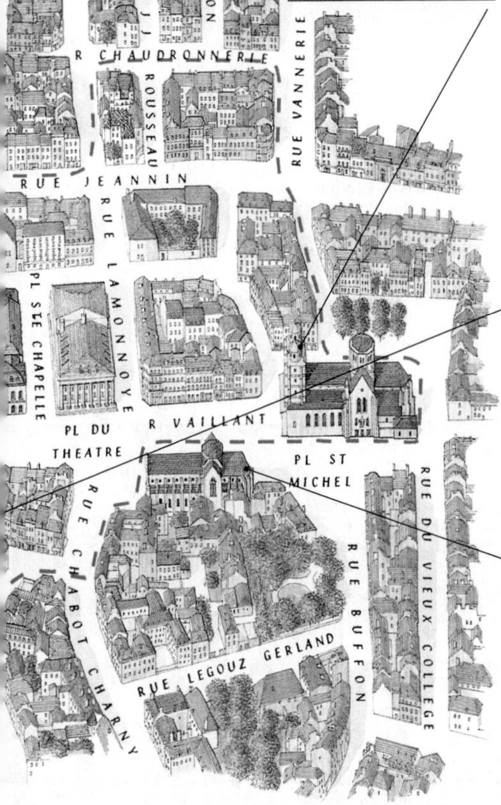

Musée Magnin
A collection of French and foreign 16th–19th-century paintings are displayed among period furniture in this 17th-century mansion.

Eglise St-Etienne dates back to the 11th century but has been rebuilt many times. Its characteristic lantern was added in 1686.

STAR SIGHTS

★ Palais des Ducs

★ Notre-Dame

★ St-Michel

KEY

- - - Suggested route

0 metres   100

0 yards   100

Well of Moses by Claus Sluter, in the Chartreuse de Champmol

Exploring Dijon

The centre of Dijon is a warren of little streets that reward exploration. The rue des Forges, behind the Palais de Ducs, was the main street until the 18th century and is named after the jewellers and goldsmiths who had workshops there. The tourist office, housed in Hôtel Chambellan at No. 34, is Flamboyant Gothic with a stone spiral staircase and wooden galleries. At No. 38 the Maison Maillard, built in 1560, has a stone façade decorated by Hugues Sambin.

Rue Chaudronnerie has a number of houses of note, especially the Maison des Cariatides at No. 28, with ten fine stone carved caryatids framing the windows. Place Darcy is lined with hotels and restaurants; the Jardin Darcy is delightful.

🏛 Musée des Beaux Arts

Palais des Etats de Bourgogne, Cour de Bar. **Tel** 03 80 74 52 70. ◯ Wed–Mon. ⬤ 1 Jan, 1 May, 8 May, 14 Jul, 1 & 11 Nov, 25 Dec. ♿ limited. 📷

Dijon's prestigious art collection is housed in the former Palais des Ducs *(see p340)*. The Salle des Gardes on the first floor is dominated by the giant mausoleums of the dukes, with tombs sculpted by Claus Sluter (c.1345–1405). Other exhibits include two gilded Flemish retables and a portrait of Philip the Good by Rogier van der Weyden.

The art collection has Dutch and Flemish masters and sculpture by Sluter and Rude. There are also Swiss and German primitives, 16th–18th century French paintings, and the Donation Granville of 19th- and 20th-century French art. Also note the ducal kitchens with six fireplaces, and the Tour Philippe le Bon, 46 m (150 ft) tall with a fine view of Burgundian tiled roof tops.

🔒 Cathédrale St-Bénigne

Pl Ste-Bénigne. **Tel** 03 80 30 39 33. ◯ daily. 📷 ♿

Little remains of the 11th-century Benedictine abbey first founded in honour of St Bénigne. Beneath the church is a Romanesque crypt with a fine rotunda ringed by three circles of columns.

🏛 Musée Archéologique

5 rue du Docteur Maret. **Tel** 03 80 30 88 54. ◯ Wed–Mon. ⬤ most public hols.

The museum is housed in the old dormitory of the Benedictine abbey of St-Bénigne. The 11th-century chapterhouse, its stocky columns supporting a barrel-vaulted roof, houses a fine collection of Gallo-Roman sculpture. The ground floor, with its lovely fan vaulting, houses the famous head of Christ by Claus Sluter, originally from the *Well of Moses*.

🏯 Chartreuse de Champmol

1 bd Chanoine Kir. ⬤ for renovation.

This was originally the site of a family necropolis built by Philip the Bold, destroyed during the Revolution. All that remains is a chapel doorway and the famous *Well of Moses* by Claus Sluter. It is now in the grounds of a psychiatric hospital east of Dijon railway station, not very easy to find but definitely worth the effort. Despite its name, it is not a well, but a monument, its lower part probably originally surrounded by water. Sluter is renowned for his deeply cut carving and here his work, depicting six prophets, is exquisitely lifelike.

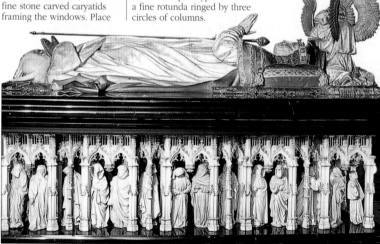

The tomb of Philip the Bold by Claus Sluter, now in the Salle des Gardes of the Musée des Beaux Arts

For hotels and restaurants in this region see pp572–5 and pp625–9

The Golden Age of Burgundy

While the French Capetian dynasty fought in the Hundred Years' War (see pp52–3), the dukes of Burgundy built up one of the most powerful states in Europe, which included Flanders and parts of Holland. From the time of Philip the Bold (1342–1404), the ducal court became a cultural force, supporting many of Europe's finest artists, such as painters Rogier Van der Weyden and the Van Eyck brothers and sculptor Claus Sluter. The duchy's dominions were, however, broken up after the death of Duke Charles the Bold in 1477.

The tomb of Philip the Bold *in Dijon was made by the Flemish sculptor Claus Sluter, who was among the most brilliant artists of the Burgundian golden age. The dramatic realism of the mourners is one of the most striking features of this spectacular tomb, begun while the duke was still alive.*

BURGUNDY IN 1477

☐ *Extent of the duchy at its peak*

THE MARRIAGE OF PHILIP THE GOOD

Philip the Good, duke from 1419–67, married Isabella of Portugal in 1430. This 17th-century copy of a painting by Van Eyck shows the sumptuous wedding feast, when Philip also inaugurated the chivalric Order of the Golden Fleece.

The dukes surrounded themselves with luxury, including fine gold and silverware.

Isabella of Portugal

The Duchess of Bedford, Philip's sister

Greyhounds were popular hunting animals at the Burgundian court.

Philip the Good is dressed in white ceremonial finery.

Burgundian art, *such as this Franco-Flemish Book of Hours, reflected the Flemish origins of many of the dukes' favourite artists.*

Dijon's Palais des Ducs *was rebuilt in 1450 by Philip the Good to reflect the glory of the Burgundian court, a centre of art, chivalry and glorious feasts. Empty after Charles the Bold's death, it was reconstructed in the 17th century.*

Wine harvest in the vineyards of Nuits-St-Georges, part of the Côte d'Or district

Côte d'Or ⑲

Côte d'Or. ✈ Dijon. 🚃 🚌 Dijon, Nuits-St-Georges, Beaune, Santenay. ℹ Dijon (03 80 63 69 49).

In winemaking terms, the Côte d'Or includes the Côte de Beaune and the Côte de Nuits in a nearly unbroken line of vines from Dijon to Santenay. Squeezed in between the flat plain of the Saône to the southeast and a plateau of rough woodland to the north-west, this narrow escarpment is about 50 km (30 miles) long. The grapes of the great Burgundy vineyards grow in the golden reddish soil of the slope (hence the name of the area).

The classification of the characteristics of the land is fabulously technical and elaborate, but for the layman a rough rule of thumb might be that 95 per cent of the best

Narrow street in Beaune's historic centre

vines are on the uphill side of the N74 thoroughfare (see pp320–21). The names on the signposts haunt the dreams of wine lovers the world over: Gevrey-Chambertin, Vougeot, Chambolle-Musigny, Vosne-Romanée, Nuits-St-Georges, Aloxe-Corton, Meursault, and Chassagne Montrachet.

Typical grape basket in the Musée du Vin de Bourgogne at Beaune

Beaune ⑳

Côte d'Or. 🏠 23,000. 🚃 🚌 ℹ 6 bd Perpeuil (03 80 26 21 30). 🛒 Sat, Wed. 🎵 Baroque Music (Jul).

The old centre of Beaune, snug within its ramparts and encircling boulevards, is easy to explore on foot. Its indisputable treasure is the **Hôtel-Dieu** (see pp346–7). The Hôtel des Ducs de Bourgogne, built in the 14th–16th centuries, houses the **Musée du Vin de Bourgogne**. The building, with its flamboyant façade, is as interesting as its display of traditional winemaking equipment.

Farther to the north lies the **Collégiale Notre-Dame**, begun in the early 12th century. Inside this mainly Romanesque church hang five very fine 15th-century woollen and silk tapestries. With hints

of early Renaissance style, they delicately illustrate the life of the Virgin Mary in 19 scenes.

🏛 **Musée du Vin de Bourgogne**
Rue d'Enfer. **Tel** 03 80 22 08 19.
◯ Apr–Nov: daily; Dec–Mar: Wed–Mon. 🎟

Tournus ㉑

Saône-et-Loire. 🏠 6,500. 🚃 🚌 ℹ pl de l'Abbaye (03 85 27 00 20). 🛒 Sat. **www**.tournugeois.fr

The Abbaye de St-Philibert is one of Burgundy's oldest and greatest Romanesque buildings. It was founded by a group of monks from Noirmoutier who had been driven from their island by invading Normans in the 9th century, who brought with them relics of their patron saint, Philibert (still in the choir). Rebuilt in the 10th–12th centuries, the well-fortified abbey church is

Dovecote in Cormatin château gardens, Mâconnais

Nave of St-Philibert in Tournus

made from lovely pale pink stone, with black and white vaulting inside.

The 17th-century Hôtel-Dieu has its original rooms intact with the furniture, equipment and pharmacy on display. It also houses the **Musée Greuze** dedicated to Tournus' most famous son, the artist Jean-Baptiste Greuze (1725–1805).

Environs
Southwest of Tournus lies the Mâconnais landscape of hills, vineyards, orchards, red-tiled farmhouses and Romanesque churches. **Brancion** is a pretty hill village, **Chapaize** has an 11th-century church and there is a sumptuous Renaissance château at **Cormatin**. The village of **Taizé** is the centre of a world-famous ecumenical community. To the north, **Chalon-sur-Saône** features the Musée Niepce, dedicated to the inventor of photography.

Cluny ㉒

Saône-et-Loire. 🟍 4,800. 🚆 🛈 6 rue Mercière (03 85 59 05 34). 🏪 Sat. **www**.cluny-tourisme.com

The little town of Cluny is overshadowed by the ruins of its great abbey. The **Ancienne Abbaye de Cluny** was once the most powerful monastic foundation in Europe *(see pp48–9)*. The abbey was founded by William the Pious, Duke of Aquitaine in 910. Within 200 years, Cluny had become the head of a major reforming order with monasteries all over Europe. Its

abbots were considered as powerful as monarchs or popes, and four of them are venerated as saints. By the 14th century, however, the system was in decline. The abbey was closed in 1790 and the church was later dismantled.

The guided tour presents the abbey remains, notably the Clocher de l'Eau Bénite (Holy Water Belltower), **Musée d'Art**, housed in the former abbot's palace, and its figured capitals displayed in the 13th-century flour-store. In the town, don't miss the 12th-century **Eglise St-Marcel**.

Southwest of the town, the chapel in **Berzé-la-Ville** is decorated with superb 12th-century frescoes, similar to those once seen at Cluny.

🄰 Ancienne Abbaye de Cluny
Tel 03 85 59 15 93. ⬜ *daily.* 🏠 🄳

🏛 Musée d'Art
Palais Jean de Bourbon. **Tel** 03 85 59 15 93. ⬜ *daily.* ⬤ *1 Jan, 1 May, 1 & 11 Nov, 25 Dec.* 🏠 🄳

Paray-le-Monial ㉓

Saône-et-Loire. 🟍 10,000. 🚆 🛈 25 av Jean-Paul II (03 85 81 10 92). 🏪 Fri. **www**.paraylemonial.fr

Dedicated to the cult of the Sacred Heart of Jesus, the **Basilique du Sacré-Coeur** has made Paray-le-Monial one of the most important sites of pilgrimage in modern France. Marguerite-Marie Alacoque, who was born here in 1647, had rather gory visions from which the cult later developed, sweeping across France in the 19th century. The church is a small version of the now lost abbey church of Cluny, with particularly harmonious and pure Romanesque architecture.

A visit to the **Musée de Paul Charnoz** provides an interesting insight into industrial artistic tile production from the 19th-century to the present.

Situated on place Guignaud is the ornate **Maison Jayet**, dating from the 16th century, which houses the town hall.

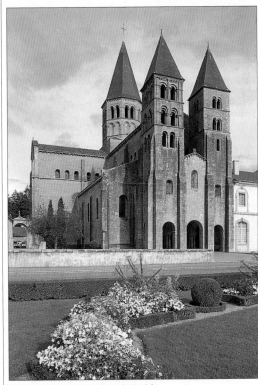

Basilique du Sacré-Coeur at Paray-le-Monial

Hôtel-Dieu

Christ-de-Pitié

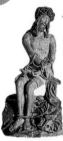

After the Hundred Years' War, many of Beaune's inhabitants suffered the effects of poverty and famine. To remedy this, the chancellor, Nicolas Rolin, and his wife founded a hospice here in 1443, which was inspired by the architecture of Northern French hospitals. The Rolins provided an annual grant, and vines and salt-works for income. Today the hospice is considered a medieval jewel, with its superb geometric multi-coloured Burgundian roof tiles. It houses two religious masterpieces: the *Christ-de-Pitié* statue, carved from wood, and Rogier van der Weyden's polyptych.

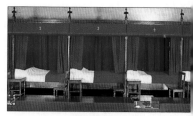

★ Great Hall of the Poor
The hall, with its carved, painted roof, has 28 four-poster beds, each one often used by several patients at a time. Meals were served from central tables.

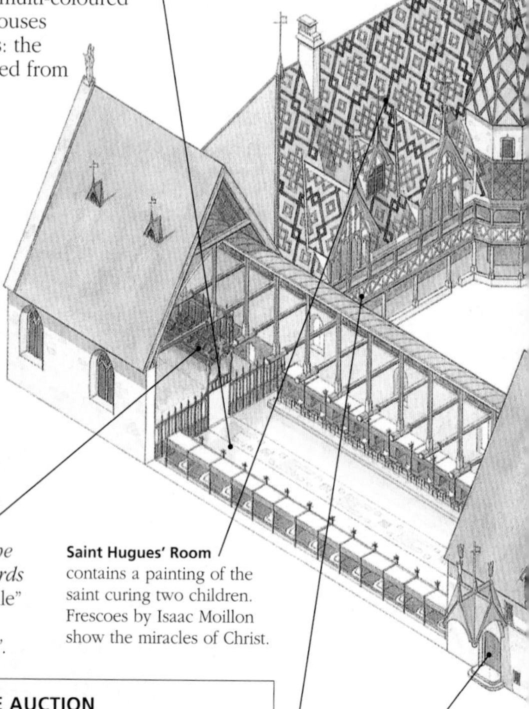

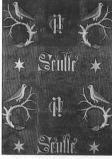

Tribute to Rolin's Wife
A recurring motif features the entwined letters N and G, birds and stars, and the word "Seulle" *referring to Rolin's wife Guigone, his "one and only".*

Saint Hugues' Room contains a painting of the saint curing two children. Frescoes by Isaac Moillon show the miracles of Christ.

Entrance

Saint Anne's Room has a tableau of nuns working in what was once the linen room, and a colourful feast-day tapestry.

ANNUAL CHARITY WINE AUCTION

On the third Sunday in November, an annual charity auction in Beaune is the centrepiece of three days of festivities known as *Les Trois Glorieuses*. Saturday sees the banquet of the Confrérie des Chevaliers du Tastevin at the Château Clos de Vougeot. On Sunday the auction of wine from the 61 ha (151 acres) of vineyards, owned by nearby hospitals, takes place. Its prices are the benchmark for the entire vintage. On Monday at La Paulée de Meursault there is a party where growers bring along bottles of their best vintages to enjoy.

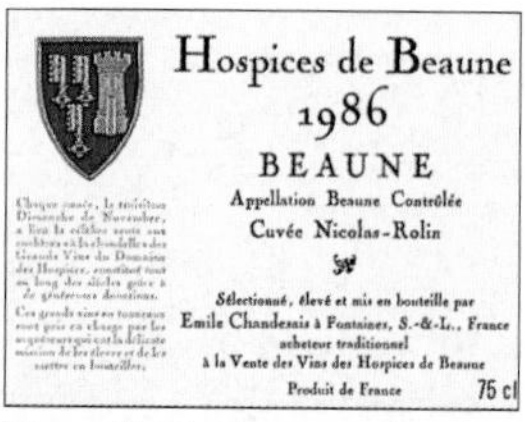

Wine sold at the famous auction

STAR FEATURES

- ★ Great Hall
- ★ Last Judgment Polyptych by Rogier van der Weyden

For hotels and restaurants in this region see pp572–5 and pp625–9

Kitchen

The centrepiece of the kitchen is a Gothic fireplace with a dual hearth and a mechanical spit, made in 1698, which is turned by a wooden "robot".

VISITORS' CHECKLIST

Rue de L'Hôtel-Dieu, Beaune. **Tel** 03 80 24 45 00. ⬤ *Apr–mid Nov: 9–6:30pm daily; mid-Nov–Mar: 9–11:30am, 2–5:30pm daily.* 🖼 📷 ☑ **Wine Auction** 3rd Sun Nov: Les Halles de Beaune *(03 80 24 45 00).* www.hospices-de-beaune.tm.fr

Cour d'Honneur

The buildings of Hôtel-Dieu are arranged around a splendid central courtyard. This is flanked by a wooden gallery, above which rise high dormer windows topped by weather vanes. The courtyard well is a fine example of Gothic wrought-iron work.

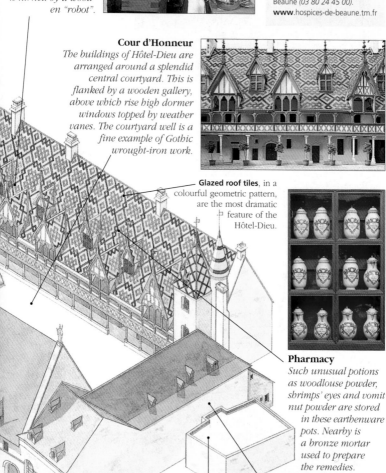

Glazed roof tiles, in a colourful geometric pattern, are the most dramatic feature of the Hôtel-Dieu.

Pharmacy

Such unusual potions as woodlouse powder, shrimps' eyes and vomit nut powder are stored in these earthenware pots. Nearby is a bronze mortar used to prepare the remedies.

St Louis' Room

★ Last Judgment Polyptych

The naked figures shown in Rogier van der Weyden's 15th-century polyptych were briefly given clothing in the 19th century. At the same time, the altarpiece was cut in half so that the outer and inner panels could be seen together.

Château de Pierreclos in the Mâconnais region

Brionnais ㉔

Saône-et-Loire. ✈ Mâcon.
🚊 Paray-le-Monial, Roanne.
🚌 Paray-le-Monial.
ℹ Marcigny (03 85 25 39 06).

The Brionnais is a
small and peaceful
rural district,
squeezed between
the river Loire and
the Beaujolais foot-
hills in the far south
of Burgundy.

Its agricultural staple
is the white Charolais
cow, which can be seen
grazing everywhere. For
a closer look at this
regional symbol, visit
the lively cattle-market
in **St-Christophe** on
Thursday afternoons.

Capital in St-
Julien-de-Jonzy

The area has an abundance
of Romanesque churches,
most of which are built of the
local ochre-coloured stone.
The 11th-century church of
Anzy-le-Duc has a majestic
three-tiered polygonal tower
and exquisitely carved capitals.
Semur-en-Brionnais was the
birthplace of Cluny's famous
abbot St Hugues. Its church
is inspired by his great
monastery. The church at **St-
Julien-de-Jonzy** has
a very finely carved
tympanum.

A small town by
the river Genette, **La
Clayette** is graced
by a château set in
a lake. It is not open
to the public, but has
a vintage car museum
and in summer is the
setting for a *son et
lumière* show.

Southeast of La
Clayette the lonely
Montagne de Dun
rises just over 700 m
(2,300 ft) and offers a panorama over the gentle, green
Brionnais hills. This is some of
the best picnic country in
Burgundy, full of sleepy
corners and quiet byways.

Mâcon ㉕

Saône-et-Loire. 🏠 36,000. ✈ 🚊
🚌 ℹ 1 pl Saint Pierre (03 85 21 07
07). 🛒 Sat.
www.macon-tourism.com

At the frontier between
Burgundy and the south,
Mâcon is an industrial town
and wine centre on the Saône.

The lack of churches is due
to fervent anti-clericalism
during the Revolution, when
14 were destroyed. A 17th-
century convent has been
turned into the **Musée des
Ursulines**. Its collections
include French and Flemish
painting and an exhibition on
the prehistoric site of Solutré.
On the charming place aux
Herbes, where the market is
held, the **Maison de Bois** is a
15th-century wooden house
covered with bizarre carvings.

🏛 Musée des Ursulines
Allée de Matisco. **Tel** 03 85 39 90
38. ◯ Tue–Sat & Sun pm. ⬤ some
public hols. 🎫

Environs
The great **Roche de Solutré**
rises dramatically above the
Pouilly-Fuissé vineyards in the
Mâconnais district *(see p345)*.
Below the rock, finds from the
Stone Ages have established it
as a major archaeological site.

Mâconnais is also the land of
the Romantic poet Lamartine
(1790–1869). Born in Mâcon,
he spent his childhood at Milly
Lamartine and later lived at
Château de St-Point. **Château
de Pierreclos** is associated
with his epic poem *Jocelyn*.

Charolais cattle grazing on the gentle hills of the Brionnais

Franche-Comté

A region of woods and water, the Franche-Comté offers exceptional natural beauty combined with opportunities for canoeing, trekking and skiing. Apart from towns well worth visiting, this is a region to explore in the wild. Glorious scenery with grottoes and cascading waterfalls can be found all along the Vallée du Doubs. Further south are the spectacular sources of the rivers Lison and Loue. The Reculées is an area of extraordinary formations of ridges and waterfalls such as Baume-les-Messieurs. In Région des Lacs, the silent, peaceful lakes are surrounded by mountain peaks and virgin forests.

Nature at its purest at Source du Lison in the Franche-Comté

Cascades du Hérisson 26

Pays-des-Lacs. **i** *Clairvaux-les-Lacs (03 84 25 27 47).* 🗓 *Wed.*

The village of Doucier, at the foot of the Pic de l'Aigle, is the starting point for the valley of the river Hérisson, one of the finest natural settings in the Jura. Leave the car at the park by the Moulin Jacquand and walk up the trail through the woods to a spectacular waterfall, the 65-m (213-ft) Cascade de L'Eventail, and beyond to the equally impressive Cascade du Grand Saut. The walk, which takes about two hours there and back, is steep at times and can be slippery, so proper shoes are essential.

Arbois 27

Jura. 🏘 *3,600.* 🚉 **i** *10 rue de l'Hôtel de Ville (03 84 66 55 50).* 🗓 *Fri.* **www**.arbois.com

The jolly wine town of Arbois lies on the vine-covered banks of the river Cuisance. It is famous for the sherry-like *vin jaune* (yellow wine) of the district. On the north side of the town is **Maison de Pasteur**, the preserved house and laboratory of the great scientist Louis Pasteur (1822–95), the first to test vaccines on humans.

Environs
Southeast of Dole is the 18th-century **Château d'Arlay**, with immaculately kept gardens.

Dole 28

Jura. 🏘 *28,000.* 🚉 🚌 **i** *6 pl Grevy (03 84 72 11 22).* 🗓 *Tue, Thu & Sat.* **www**.dole.org

The busy town of Dole lies where the Doubs meets the Rhine-Rhône canal. The former capital of the Comté was always a symbol of the region's resistance to the French. The region had become used to relative independence, first under the Counts of Burgundy and then as part of the Holy Roman Empire. Though always French-speaking, its people did not appreciate the idea of the French absolute monarchy and in 1636 endured a very long siege. The town finally submitted to Louis XIV, first in 1668, and again in 1674.

There is a charming historic quarter in the centre of town, full of winding alleys, houses dating back to the 15th century, and quiet inner courtyards. Place aux Fleurs offers an excellent view of this part of town and the mossy-roofed, 16th-century **Eglise Notre-Dame**.

Virgin and Child on the north portal of Eglise Notre-Dame, Dole

The Saline Royale at Arc-et-Senans

Arc-et-Senans ㉙

Doubs. 🏛 1,400. 🚇 🛈 Ancienne
Saline Royale (03 81 57 43 21).
www.ot-arcetsenans.fr

Designated a World Heritage
Site since 1982, the Saline
Royale (royal salt works) at
Arc-et-Senans were designed
by the great French architect
Claude-Nicolas Ledoux (1736–
1806). He envisaged a development built in concentric
circles around the main buildings. However, the only ones
to be completed (in 1775)
were the buildings used for
salt production. Nevertheless,
these show the staggering
scale of Ledoux's idea: salt
water was to be piped from
Salins-les-Bains nearby, and
fuel to reduce it was to come
from the Chaux forest. The
enterprise, which was never a
success, was closed down in
1895, but the buildings remain.
The **Musée Ledoux Lieu du
Sel** displays intriguing models
of the grand projects imagined
by the visionary architect.

🏛 **Musée Ledoux Lieu du Sel**
Saline Royale.
Tel 03 81 54 45 45. ◯ daily. ◯
Jan, 25 Dec. 🎫 🗎 🔲 🕭 gr.floor.

Champlitte ㉚

Haute Saône. 🏛 1,900. 🚇 🛈 33B
rue de la République (03 84 67 64 10).

In the small town of Champlitte, the **Musée des Arts et
Traditions Populaires** was
created by a local shepherd
who collected artifacts connected with disappearing local
customs. One of the poignant
displays housed in this Renais-

sance château recalls the emigration of 400 citizens to Mex-
ico in the mid-19th century.

🏛 **Musée des Arts et
Traditions Populaires**
Pl de l'Eglise. **Tel** 03 84 67 82
00. ◯ Jun–Aug: daily; Sep–May:
Wed–Mon. ◯ Sun ams, 1 Jan, 1
Nov, 25 Dec. 🎫 🗎 🔲

Besançon ㉛

Doubs. 🏛 120,000. 🚇 🚇
🛈 2 pl de la Première Armée Française
(03 81 80 92 55). ◯ Tue–Sat & Sun
am. www.besancon-tourisme.com

Besançon supplanted Dole as
the capital of the Franche-
Comté in the 17th century.
It began as an ecclesiastical
centre and is now an
industrial one, specializing in
precision engineering. The
stately architecture of the old
town, often enriched with
elegant wrought-iron work,
is a 17th-century legacy.
Behind the fine Renaissance
façade of the Palais Granvelle,
in the grande rue, lies the
new **Musée du Temps**, a
staggering collection of millions of 'time-pieces' of all
ages, shapes and sizes – a
timely tribute to Besançon's
renown as a clock and watch-
making centre. An interactive
exhibition on the third floor
invites reflection on the rela-
tivity of the notion of time.
Further along the same
street are the birthplaces of
novelist Victor Hugo (1802–85)
at No. 140 and the Lumière
brothers (see p63) at place
Victor Hugo. Behind **Porte
Noire**, a Roman arch, is the
12th-century Cathédrale St-
Jean. In its belltower is the

extraordinary **Horloge
Astronomique** – try to be
there on the hour, when the
automatons pop out.
The stunning **Musée des
Beaux Arts et d'Archéologie**
occupies the old corn market.
Its collection includes works
by Bellini, Cranach, Rubens,
Fragonard, Boucher, Ingres,
Goya, Matisse and Picasso.
Vauban's citadel overlooking
the river Doubs has magnificent views and houses the
intriguing **Musée Comtois** with
a collection of local artifacts.

🏛 **Musée du Temps**
Palais Granvelle, 96 grande rue. **Tel**
03 81 87 81 50. ◯ Tue–Sun pms.
◯ 1 Jan, 1 May, 1 Nov, 25 Dec. 🎫
🗎 🕭

🕭 **Horloge Astronomique**
Rue de la Convention. **Tel** 03 81 81
12 76. ◯ Apr–Sep: Wed–Mon;
(Thu–Mon winter). ◯ Jan. 🎫 🗎

🏛 **Musée des Beaux Arts et
d'Archéologie**
1 pl de la Révolution. **Tel** 03 81 87 80
49. ◯ Wed–Mon. 🎫 free Sun.
🗎 🔲

🏛 **Musée Comtois**
La Citadelle, rue des Fusillés de la
Résistance. **Tel** 03 81 87 83 83. ◯
daily. ◯ Tue in winter, 1 Jan, 25 Dec.
🎫 🗎 🔲 🔲

**The fantastic astronomical clock in
Besançon, made in 1857–60**

Ornans ㉜

Doubs. 🏛 4,300. 🚇 🛈 7 rue
Pierre Vernier (03 81 62 21 50).
🗎 3rd Tue of month

The great Realist painter
Gustave Courbet was born at
Ornans in 1819. He painted
the town in every possible
light. His *Enterrement à*

The striking Chapelle Notre-Dame-du-Haut by Le Corbusier at Ronchamp

Ornans proved to be one of the most influential paintings of the 19th century. This delightful riverside town shows Courbet's paintings in his childhood home, now turned into the **Musée Courbet**.

🏛 Musée Courbet
Pl Robert Fernier. *Tel 03 81 62 23 30.* ☐ Apr–Oct: daily; Nov–Mar: Wed–Mon. ● 1 Jan, 1 May, 1 Nov, 25 Dec. 📷 📷 www.musee-courbet.com

Environs
A canoeist's paradise, the **Vallée de la Loue** is the loveliest in the Jura. The D67 follows the river from Ornans eastwards to Ouhans, from where it is only a 15-minute walk to its magnificent source. Various belvederes offer splendid views over the area.

Southwest of Ornans, the spectacular **Source du Lison** *(see p349)* is a 20-minute walk from Nans-sous-Ste-Anne.

Belfort 🔢

Territoire de Belfort. 🏘 52,000. 🚉
🚌 🛈 2 bis rue Clemenceau (03 84 55 90 90). 🛒 Wed–Sun.
www.ot-belfort.fr

The symbol of Belfort is an enormous pink sandstone lion. It was built (rather than carved) by Frédéric Bartholdi (1834–1904), whose other major undertaking was the Statue of Liberty.

Belfort's immensely strong **citadel**, designed by Vauban under Louis XIV, withstood three sieges, in 1814, 1815 and 1870. Today this remarkable array of fortifications provides an interesting walk and extensive views of the surroundings. The **Musée d'Art et d'Histoire**, housed in some of the billets, displays models of the original fortifications as well as regional art and artifacts (closed Tuesdays).

Ronchamp 🔢

Haute Saône. 🏘 3,000. 🚉
🛈 14 pl du 14 juillet (03 84 63 50 82). 🛒 Sat.
www.tourisme-ronchamp.com

Le Corbusier's **Chapelle Notre-Dame-du-Haut** dominates this former miners' town. A sculpture rather than a building, its swelling concrete form was finalized in 1955. Inside, light, shape and space form a unity.

There is also a **Musée de la Mine** evoking the industry and the life of local miners.

Le Miroir d'Ornans in the Musée Courbet, Ornans

THE MASSIF CENTRAL

ALLIER · AVEYRON · CANTAL · CORRÈZE · CREUSE · HÂUTE-LOIRE
HAUTE-VIENNE · LOZÈRE · PUY DE DOME

The Massif Central is a region of strange, wild beauty – one of France's best-kept secrets. It is surprisingly little known beyond its sprinkling of spas and the major cities of Clermont-Ferrand, Vichy and Limoges. However, the new autoroutes through the heart of its uplands have started to open up this previously remote region.

The huge central plateau of ancient granite and crystalline rock that makes up the Massif Central embraces the dramatic landscapes of the Auvergne, Limousin, Aveyron and Lozère. Once a testing crossroads for pilgrims, and strung with giant volcanoes, it is a region of unsuspected richness, from the spectacular town of Le Puy-en-Velay, to the unique treasures at Conques.

With its crater lakes and hot springs, the Auvergne is the Massif Central's lush volcanic core, an outdoor paradise offering activities from hiking in summer to skiing in winter. It also has some of France's most beautiful Romanesque churches, medieval castles and Renaissance palaces. To the east are the mountain ranges of Forez, Livardois and Velay; to the west are the giant chains of extinct volcanoes, the Monts Dômes, Monts Dore and the Monts du Cantal. The Limousin, on the northwestern edge of the Massif Central, is gentler country with green pastures and blissfully empty roads.

The Aveyron spreads into the southwest from the Aubrac mountains, carrying with it the rivers Lot, Aveyron and Tarn through gorges and valleys with their cliff-hanging villages. To the east in the Lozère are the Grands Causses, the vast, isolated uplands of the Cévennes. These barren plateaux give farmers a poor living, but have been a favourite route with adventurous travellers across the centuries.

La Bourboule, a spa town in the Monts Dore

◁ The summit of Puy Mary, 1,787 m (5,863 ft), offering a superb view to walkers who attempt the ascent

Exploring the Massif Central

Nature is at its most magnificent in the volcanic mountain ranges and wild river gorges of the Massif Central. This is a vast and unspoiled territory which offers spectacular sightseeing and every imaginable outdoor activity, with rafting, paragliding, canoeing and hiking among the many choices. There are hundreds of churches, châteaux and museums to nourish lovers of history, architecture and art; and good, hearty regional cooking and wonderful local wines for lovers of good living.

| 0 kilometres | 25 |
| 0 miles | 25 |

KEY

═══	Motorway
═ ═	Motorway under construction
═══	Major road
───	Secondary road
┅┅┅	Minor road
───	Scenic route
┈┈┈	Main railway
┄┄┄	Minor railway
═══	Regional border
△	Summit

Limestone cliffs of the Gorges du Tarn

GETTING AROUND

There is a good air and rail service connecting Paris with the major towns of Limoges, Clermont-Ferrand (direct flights from UK) and Vichy. Many of the most interesting towns and sights are easily accessible only by car, and motorail from Calais to Brive is an effortless way of getting to the region with a car. Most minor roads are well kept, but slow going in the mountains. A few roads are vertiginous, especially the road to the summit of Puy Mary, which is utterly breathtaking. The A71/A75 through the Auvergne is a magnificent road (and toll-free).

SIGHTS AT A GLANCE

Aubusson ②
Château de Lapalisse ⑤
Clermont-Ferrand ⑩
Collonges-la-Rouge ⑯
Conques ㉒
Corniche des Cévennes ㉔
Gorges du Tarn ㉖
Grands Causses ㉕
Issoire ⑧
La Chaise-Dieu ⑲
Le Puy-en-Velay ⑳
Limoges ①
Montluçon ③
Monts Dômes ⑫
Monts Dore ⑬
Monts du Cantal ⑱
Moulins ④
Orcival ⑪
Rodez ㉓
St-Nectaire ⑨
Salers ⑰
Thiers ⑦
Turenne ⑮
Uzerche ⑭
Vallée du Lot ㉑
Vichy ⑥

Autumn view of the foothills of
Puy Mary in the Monts du Cantal

IE NY SCAY CVEL REMEDDE METT
RE AVX OVELLES PVSSAYGE
COVRIR TOVES NE LES PVIS SE
COVRIS MIEVX MEVLT VALVT
DEVX ME DEMETRE
1577

A Limoges enamel plaque, *The Bad Shepherd*

Limoges ❶

Haute-Vienne. 🏛 *200,000.* ✈ 🚄
🚍 ℹ *12 bd de Fleurus (05 55 34
46 87).* 🚏 *daily.*
www.tourismelimoges.com

The capital of the Limousin
has two hearts: the old Cité
and the rival château
on an adjacent rise, now the
commercial centre of the
modern city. The Cité was
ravaged by the Black Prince
during the Hundred Years'
War and today it is a quiet
place of half-timbered houses
and narrow streets.

It was not until the 1770s
that Limoges became
synonymous with porcelain.
The legendary local ware is on
display at the superb **Musée
National Adrien-Dubouché**.
More than 10,000 exhibits
trace the history of ceramics.
The **Musée Municipal de
l'Evêché** houses some 500
Limousin enamels, as well as
works by Impressionist painters such as Renoir, who was
born in the city. This area
was a centre of Resistance
operations in World War II;
the **Musée de la Résistance et**
de la Déportation has a
collection of exhibits relating
to Resistance acitivities.

🏛 **Musée National
Adrien-Dubouché**
Pl Winston Churchill. **Tel** *05 55 33
08 50.* ⏰ *Wed–Mon (phone to
check).* ⏺ *1 Jan, 1 May, 25 Dec.*
🖼 🔲
www.musee-adriendebouche.fr

🏛 **Musée Municipal de
l'Evêché, Musée de l'Email**
Pl de la Cathédrale. **Tel** *05 55 45 98
10.* ⏰ *Wed–Mon (phone to check).*

🏛 **Musée de la Résistance et
de la Déportation**
Rue de la Règle, Jardin de L'Evêché.
Tel *05 55 45 98 23.*

Environs
Resistance activity in the
Limousin led to severe repri-
sals. On 10 June 1944 at the
village of **Oradour-sur-Glane**,
25 km (16 miles) NW of
Limoges, SS troops burned
alive the entire population. The
ruins have been kept as a
shrine, and a new village built
nearby. The lively town of St-
Junien close by has been a
glove-making town since the
Middle Ages, and it still
supplies today's designers
with luxury leather items.

Aubusson ❷

Creuse. 🏛 *5,000.* 🚍 ℹ *rue Vieille
(05 55 66 32 12).* 🚏 *Sat.* **www**.ot-
aubusson.fr

Aubusson owes its renown to
the exceptionally pure waters
of the Creuse, perfect for
making the delicately coloured dyes used for tapestries
and rugs. Tapestry production
was at its zenith in the 16th
and 17th centuries, but by the
end of the 18th century the
Revolution and patterned
wallpaper had swept away the
clientele.

In the 1940s, Aubusson was
revived, largely due to the
artist Jean Lurçat, who persuaded other modern artists
to design for tapestry. The
**Musée Départemental de la
Tapisserie** displays a
permanent collection of these
modern works. All 30 workshops welcome visitors – at
the **Manufacture St Jean** you
can watch tapestries and
custom-made carpets being
made by hand and restored.

🏛 **Musée Départemental de
la Tapisserie**
Av des Lissiers. **Tel** *05 55 83 08 30.*
⏰ *Wed–Mon (Tue pm Jul–Aug).* 🖼
🔲

🏛 **Manufacture St Jean**
3 rue St Jean. **Tel** *05 55 66 10 08.*
⏰ *Mon–Fri.* 🖼 🖼

Environs
A single street of 15th-century
houses and a Roman bridge
comprise **Moûtier-d'Ahun,**

**Tapestry restoration at the
Manufacture St Jean in Aubusson**

Romanesque church at Moûtier-d'Ahun near Aubusson

tucked into the lush Creuse valley. Vestiges of a Benedictine abbey can still be detected in the half-Roman-esque, half-Gothic church with its elaborate stone portal. The choir has wooden stalls, for which it is worth paying a visit to the church. They are masterpieces of late 17th-century carving with fantastical and intricately worked motifs of flora and fauna representing the many different facets of Good and Evil in figurative form. Today there is a garden where the nave once was.

Montluçon ❸

Allier. 👥 45,000. 🚆 🚌 🛈 5 pl Piquand (04 70 05 11 44). 🛍 Tue–Sun.

Montluçon is the economic centre of the region, a small town with a medieval core. At its heart there is a Bourbon château, now the **Musée des Musiques Populaires**, housing a collection of *vielles* (hurdy-gurdies). Upstairs is a display of traditional instruments – bagpipes, oboes – and some regional faïence. The 12th-century **Eglise de St-Pierre** is a surprise, with giant stone columns and a huge barrel-vaulted ceiling.

🏛 Musée des Musiques Populaires
Château des Ducs de Bourbon. **Tel** 04 70 08 73 50. ◯ 10am–6pm Wed–Mon. ● some public hols. 🖾

Moulins ❹

Allier. 👥 23,000. 🚆 🚌 🛈 rue François Péron (04 70 44 14 14). 🛍 Tue & Fri. **www**.pays-bourbon.com

Capital of the Bourbonnais and seat of the Bourbon Dukes since the 10th century, Moulins flourished during the early Renaissance. Moulins' most celebrated sight is the Flamboyant Gothic **Cathédrale Notre-Dame**, where members of the Bourbon court appear amid the saints in the 15th- and 16th-century stained-glass windows. The treasury contains a luminous 15th-century Virgin and Child triptych by the "Master of Moulins". Benefactors Pierre II, Duke of Bourbon, and his wife Anne de Beaujeu, bedecked in embroidery and jewels, are shown being introduced to a less richly dressed Madonna.

The tower keep and the single remaining wing of the Bourbon **Vieux Château** house a superb collection of sculpture, painting and decorative art from the 12th to the 16th centuries. Housed in the former cavalry barracks is a magnificent collection of 10,000 theatrical costumes.

🔒 Cathédrale Notre-Dame
Pl de la Déportation. **Tel** 04 70 20 89 65. **Treasury** ◯ Mon–Sat. 🖾 ♿

Stained-glass windows at the Cathédrale Notre-Dame in Moulins

Château de Lapalisse ❺

Allier. **Tel** 04 70 99 36 67.
☐ Apr–Oct: daily. 🖼 🎫

In the early 16th century, the Marshal of France, Jacques II de Chabannes, hired Florentine architects to reconstruct the feudal château-fort at Lapalisse, creating a refined Renaissance castle, which has been inhabited ever since by his descendants. The *salon doré* (gilded room) has a beamed ceiling panelled in gold, and two huge 15th-century Flemish tapestries showing the Crusader Knight Godefroy de Bouillon and Greek hero Hector, two of the nine classic braves of chivalric legend.

Environs

From Lapalisse, the D480 leads up through the beautiful Besbre valley past a handful of other small, well-preserved châteaux, including **Château de Thoury**.

♣ **Château de Thoury**
Dompierre. **Tel** 04 70 42 00 41.
Courtyard and exterior ☐ Apr–May: Sat, Sun & public hols; Jun–Nov: daily.

Gilded ceiling, Château de Lapalisse

Vichy ❻

Allier. 🏠 27,000. 🚉 🚌 ℹ 19 rue du Parc (04 70 98 71 94). 🛒 Wed.
www.vichytourisme.com

This small city on the river Allier has long been known for its hot and cold springs, and reputed cures for rheumatism, arthritis and digestive complaints. The letter-writer Madame de Sévigné and the daughters of Louis XV visited in the late 17th and 18th centuries – the former compared the showers to "a rehearsal for Purgatory". The

Interior of the original Thermal Establishment building in Vichy

visits of Napoleon III in the 1860s put Vichy on the map and made taking the waters fashionable. The small town was spruced up and became a favourite among the French nobility and the world's wealthy middle classes. These days, the grand old Thermal Establishment, built in 1900, has been turned into shopping galleries. The modern baths are state-of-the-art and strictly

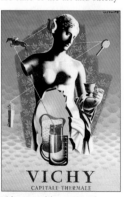

Vichy poster (about 1930–50) by Badia-Vilato

for medical purposes. A doctor's prescription and a reservation 30 days in advance are required for all treatments.

Vichy's fortunes changed for the better once again in the 1960s with the damming of the Allier, creating a huge lake in the middle of town, which rapidly became a thriving centre for watersports and international events. For a small fee, you can have a taste of sports from aikido to waterskiing or learn canoeing on the 3-km (2-mile) long artificial river.

The focal point of life in Vichy is the **Parc des Sources** in the centre of town, with its turn-of-the-century bandstand (afternoon concerts in season), Belle Epoque glass-roofed shopping galleries, and the Grand Casino and Opera House. Here there is gambling every afternoon and musical performances in the evenings, and an atmosphere of gaiety pervades. Also open to the public are the beautiful bronze taps of the **Source**

Célestin, in a riverside park containing vestiges of a convent bearing the same name. Only by making an effort to imagine the city in grainy black-and-white newsreel style is there the slightest reminder of the wartime Vichy government which was based in the town from 1940–44 *(see p65)*.

♣ Source Célestin
Bd du Président Kennedy. ☐ *daily.* ⬤ *Dec–Jan.* ♿

Thiers ❼

Puy de Dôme. 🏠 *13,500.* 🚉 🚌
ℹ Pl de Pirou (04 73 80 65 65).
🔺 *Thu & Sat.* **www**.ville-thiers.fr

According to the writer La Bruyère, Thiers "seems painted on the slope of the hill", hanging dramatically as it does on a ravine over a sharp bend in the river Durolle. The city has been renowned for cutlery since the Middle Ages, when legend has it that Crusaders brought back techniques of metalwork from the Middle East. With grindstones powered by dozens of waterfalls on the opposite bank of the river, Thiers produced everything from table knives to guillotine blades, and cutlery remains its major industry today, much of it on display in the Cutlery Museum, the **Musée de la Coutellerie**.

The Old Town is filled with mysterious quarters like "the Corner of Chance" and "Hell's Hollow", honeycombed with tortuous streets and well-restored 14th–17th-century houses. Many have elaborately carved wooden façades, like the Maison du Pirou in place

PILGRIMAGES AND OSTENSIONS

Parishes in the Auvergne and the Limousin are renowned for honouring their saints in outdoor processions. Ascension Day sees the Virgin of Orcival carried above the village by night, accompanied by gypsies and their children for baptism. Every seven years a score of villages in the Limousin hold *Ostensions*, when the saints' relics are paraded through the streets into the surrounding woods. The *Ostension* season begins the Sunday after Easter and runs until June. The next event in the seven-year cycle will be held in 2009.

The Virgin of Orcival, carried in procession above the village (1903)

Pirou. The view to the west from the rampart terrace, towards Monts Dômes and Monts Dore, is particularly splendid at sunset.

🏛 Musée de la Coutellerie
58 rue de la Coutellerie. **Tel** 04 73 80 58 86. ☐ *Jul & Aug: daily; Oct–Jun: Tue–Sun.* ⬤ *Jan–mid-Feb, 1 May, 1 Nov, 25 Dec & Jan.* 📷♿
www.musee-coutellerie-thiers.com

Issoire ❽

Puy de Dôme. 🏠 *15,000.* 🚉 🚌
ℹ pl Charles de Gaulle (04 73 89 15 90). 🔺 *Sat.* **www**.sejours-issoire.com

Most of old Issoire was destroyed in the 16th-century Wars of Religion. The present-day town has been an important industrial centre since the end of World War II.

Not only does Issoire have a thriving aeronautical tradition, it is also a mecca for glider pilots who come from miles around to take advantage of the strong local air currents.

Issoire's colourful 12th-century abbey church of **St-Austremoine** is one of the great Romanesque churches of the region. The capitals depict scenes from the *Life of Christ* (one of the Apostles at the Last Supper has fallen asleep at table), and imaginary demons and beasts. The 15th-century fresco of the *Last Judgment* shows Bosch-like figures of sinners being cast into the mouth of a dragon or carted off to hell. The nearby Tour de l'Horloge has scenes of Renaissance history.

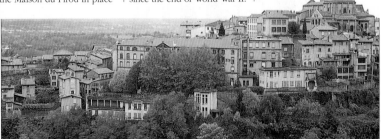

Thiers from the south, spreading over the slopes above the river Durolle

St-Nectaire 🟑

Puy de Dôme. 🏔 *750*. 🚉 ℹ *Les Grands Thermes (04 73 88 50 86).* 🗓 *Jul–Aug: Sun am.*
www.ville-saint-nectaire.fr

The Auvergne is noted for Romanesque churches. The **Eglise St-Nectaire** in the upper village of St-Nectaire-le Haut, with its soaring, elegant proportions, is one of the most beautiful. The 103 stone capitals, 22 of them poly-chrome, are vividly carved, and the treasury includes a gold bust of St Baudime and a wooden Notre-Dame-du-Mont-Cornadore, both marvels of 12th-century work-manship. The lower village, St-Nectaire-le-Bas, has more than 40 hot and cold springs.

Environs

The 12th-century citadel of **Château de Murol**, partially in ruins, offers costumed guides demonstrating medieval life and knightly pursuits. It is wonderful for children.

🏰 Château de Murol
Murol. **Tel** 04 73 26 02 00. 🔲 Apr–Oct: daily; Nov–Mar: Sat, Sun & public & school hols. 🎧 🎥 📷
www.chateaudumurol.fr

Fontaine d'Amboise (1515) in Clermont-Ferrand

Clermont-Ferrand 🔟

Puy de Dôme. 🏔 *141,000*. ✈ 🚉 🚉 ℹ *pl de la Victoire (04 73 98 65 00).* 🗓 *Mon–Sat.*
www.ot-clermont-ferrand.fr

Clermont-Ferrand began as two distinct – and rival – cities, united only in 1630. Clermont is a lively commercial centre and student town, with thriving cafés and restaurants.

It was a Celtic settlement before the Roman era, had a cathedral as early as the 5th century, and by 1095 was significant enough for the pope to announce the First Crusade there. The Counts of Auvergne, challenging the episcopal power of Clermont, made their base in what is now old Montferrand, a short drive from Clermont city centre. Built on a bastide pattern, it is a time warp of quiet streets and Renaissance houses.

Clermont's more ancient origins are well illustrated at the **Musée Bargoin** with its remarkable collections of locally found Roman domestic artifacts (closed Mondays).

Place St-Pierre is Clermont's principal marketplace, with a daily food market – especially good on Saturdays. Nearby, the pedestrianized rue du Port leads steeply downhill from the **Fontaine d'Amboise** (1515) to the **Basilique Notre-Dame-du-Port**. This is one of the most important Roman-esque churches in the region. The stone interior is beauti-fully proportioned, with a magnificent raised choir and vivid carved capitals – look for Charity battling Avarice, in the form of two knights with chain mail and pikes.

The contrast with the black lava **Cathédrale de Notre-Dame-de-l'Assomption** is startling, from austere 12th-century Romanesque to high-flying 13th-century Gothic.

Raised choir in the Basilique Notre-Dame-du-Port

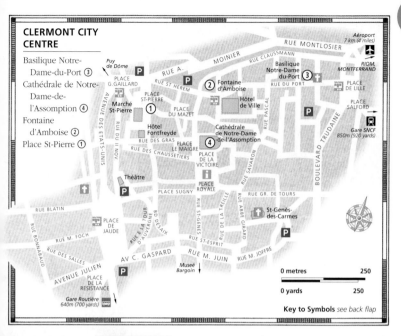

CLERMONT CITY CENTRE

Basilique Notre-Dame-du-Port ③

Cathédrale de Notre-Dame-de-l'Assomption ④

Fontaine d'Amboise ②

Place St-Pierre ①

The graceful lines of the interior are due to the strong local stone used for construction, allowing pillars to be thinner and the whole structure lighter. The dark volcanic rock provides a foil for the jewel-like 12th–15th-century stained-glass windows, which are believed to be from the same workshop as Sainte-Chapelle's in Paris (*see p84*).

The old section of Montferrand thrived from the 13th to the 17th centuries, and many fine houses – known as *hôtels particuliers* – built by prosperous merchants have survived. Some of the best of

Michelin man, c.1910

these, with Italianate loggias, mullioned windows and intriguing courtyards, line ancient **rue Kléber**. Between Clermont and old Montferrand lies a third mini-city, the headquarters and factories of the Michelin rubber-and-tyre company, founded here in 1830, which dominates the town.

Environs

Once the rival of Clermont-Ferrand for supremacy in Auvergne, **Riom** is a sombre provincial town of black stone houses and lava fountains. The 14th-century château of Duke Jean de Berry was razed in the 19th century to build the Palais de Justice; all that remains is the delicate Sainte-Chapelle with its lovely 15th-century stained-glass windows.

Riom's greatest treasure is a graceful Madonna holding an infant with a small bird in his hand. The statue is housed in the Eglise de Notre-Dame-du-Marthuret, originally built in the 14th century, but much rearranged since then.

Choir inside the Cathédrale de Notre-Dame-de-l'Assomption

Orcival ⑪

Puy de Dôme. 🏠 *300.*
ℹ *04 73 65 89 77.*

Crammed with hotels and crowded in summer, Orcival is nevertheless well worth visiting for its Romanesque church, the **Basilique d'Orcival**, which many would say is the best in the region. Completed at the beginning of the 12th century, and typically Auvergne Romanesque in style, the apse is multi-tiered and the side walls are supported by powerful buttresses and strong arches. Inside, the ornate silver and vermilion *Virgin and Child* (in the formal, forward-facing position known as "in majesty") is enigmatic in its rigid, square chair. With an interior lit by 14 windows and a spacious crypt, the proportions of the building itself are the most graceful aspect.

Virgin and Child in the Basilique d'Orcival

Aerial view of Puy de Dôme in the Monts Dômes range

Monts Dômes ⓬

Puy de Dôme. 🚠 🚍 🔲 *Clermont-Ferrand.* 🚩 *Foot of Puy de Dôme (04 73 62 21 45: Apr–mid-Nov). Montlosier (04 73 65 64 00).* **www**.parc-volcans-auvergne.com

The youngest range of the Auvergne volcanoes at 4,000 years old, the Monts Dômes, or Chaîne des Puys, encompasses 112 extinct volcanoes aligned over a 30-km (19-mile) stretch just west of Clermont-Ferrand. At the centre, the **Puy de Dôme** towers above a high plateau. A concentric road off the N922 spirals up the peak at a steady 12 per cent gradient, while the steeper, original switchback Roman path is still used by hikers.

At the summit, half an hour further, are the vestiges of the Roman temple of Mercury and a meteorological/telecommunications tower. On a rare clear day, the view across the volcano will take away whatever breath you have left.

The controversial new **Parc**

The volcanic Roche Tuilière below Col de Guéry in the Monts Dore

Européen du Volcanisme, Vulcania, uses the latest technology to simulate volcanic activity in its 2ha (5acre) underground circuit.

In the southwest corner of the Monts Dômes region is the **Château de Cordès**, a small, privately owned 15th-century manor house with formal gardens designed by Le Nôtre *(see p179)*.

♣ **Vulcania**
D941B, Saint-Ours-les-Roches.
Tel *04 73 19 70 00.* ◯ *Apr–Aug: daily; Mar & Sep–Oct: Wed–Sun.* 🅿
🅰 🍽 🔲 ◻ *Documentation centre* www.vulcania.com

♣ **Château de Cordès**
Orcival. **Tel** *04 73 65 81 34.*
◯ *Easter–Oct: daily (phone in advance for visits out of season).* 🔳 🅿

Monts Dore ⓭

Puy de Dôme. 🚠 *Clermont-Ferrand.*
🚍 🔲 *Le Mont-Dore.* 🚩 *Montlosier, Aydat (04 73 65 64 00).*

Three giant volcanoes – the Puy de Sancy, the Banne d'Ordanche and the Puy de l'Aiguiller – and their secondary cones make up the Monts Dore: dark green, heavily wooded mountains laced with rivers and lakes and dotted with summer and winter resorts for skiing, hiking, paragliding, canoeing and sailing.

The 1,886-m (6,185-ft) **Puy de Sancy** is the highest point in Central France. It can be reached by taking a shuttle from the town of Le Mont-Dore to the cable car which goes up to the peak, followed by a long hike across open terrain. From Le Mont-Dore, there is an

exhilarating scenic drive on the D36 which leads to the **Couze-Chambon valley**, a beautiful stretch of high moorland threaded with waterfalls.

The area has two popular spa towns, **La Bourboule**, for children's ailments, with its casino, and Le Mont-Dore, with its grandiose turn-of-the-century **Etablissement Thermal**.

Below the Col de Guéry on the D983, the eroded volcanic **Roche Sanadoire** and **Roche Tuilière** stand up like two gigantic gateposts. From their peaks are far-reaching views over the wooded Cirque de Chausse and beyond.

Church at La Bourboule in the Monts Dore

Uzerche ⓮

Corrèze. 🏚 *3,000.* 🚍 🔲 🚩 *pl de la Libération (05 55 73 15 71).*
🛒 *20th of each month.*

Uzerche is an impressive sight: grey slate roofs, turrets and belltowers rising from a hill above the Vézère river. This prosperous town never capitulated during the conflicts of the Middle Ages, and earlier withstood a seven-year siege by Moorish forces in 732: the townspeople sent a feast out to their enemy – in fact, the last of their supplies. The Moors, thinking such lavish offerings meant the city had stores to spare, gave up.

The Romanesque **Église St-Pierre** crests the hill above the town. Beyond Uzerche, the Vézère cuts through the green gorges of the Saillant.

CANTAL CHEESE

Transhumance is still practised in the Auvergne, with the local Salers cattle kept in barns in the valleys during winter and led up to mountain pastures for the summer. The robust grasses and flowers – gentian, myrtle, anemone – on which the cows graze produce a flavoursome milk that is the basis for the region's great cheese, Cantal. Curds were once turned and pressed through cheesecloth by hand, but now modern methods prevail. Cantal is the key ingredient in *aligot* – the potato-and-cheese purée flavoured with garlic that is one of the region's most famous dishes.

Salers cattle enjoying rich pastures

Turenne ⑮

Corrèze. 🏠 750. 🚃 🚌
🛈 pl de Belvédère (05 55 24 08 80).

Turenne is one of the most appealing medieval towns in the Corrèze. Crescent-shaped and clustered on the cliffside, the town was the last independent feudal fiefdom in France, under the absolute rule of the La Tour d'Auvergne family until 1738. Henri de la Tour d'Auvergne, their most illustrious member, was a marshal of France under Louis XIV, and one of the greatest soldiers of modern times.

Now the sole remains of the **Château de Turenne** are the 13th-century Clock Tower and 11th-century Tower of Caesar, from which there is a quite stunning 360-degree view of the Cantal mountains across to the Dordogne

valley. Not far away is the 16th-century collegiate church and the **Chapelle des Capucins** dating from the 18th century.

🏰 **Château de Turenne**
Tel 05 55 85 90 66. ☐ Apr–Oct: daily; Nov–Mar: Sun pm. 🌐
www.chateau-turenne.com

Collonges-la-Rouge ⑯

Corrèze. 🏠 400. 🚃 Brive, then bus to Collonges. 🛈 av de l'Auvitrie (05 55 25 32 25)

There's something a little unsettling about Collonges' unique carmine sandstone architecture, quite beautiful in individual houses, though the overall effect is both austere and fairytale-like.

Founded in the 8th century, Collonges came under the rule

of Turenne, whose burghers built the sturdy turreted houses in the surrounding vineyards. Look out for the communal bread oven in the marketplace, and the 11th-century church, later fortified with a tower keep. The church's unusual carved white limestone tympanum shows a man driving a bear, and other lively figures.

Salers ⑰

Cantal. 🏠 400. 🚌 summer only.
🛈 pl Tyssandier d'Escous (04 71 40 70 68). 🏪 Wed.

A solid, handsome town of grey lava houses and 15th-century ramparts, Salers sits atop a steep escarpment at the edge of the Cantal mountains. It is one of few virtually intact Renaissance villages in the region. The church has an admirable polychrome *mise au tombeau* (entombment), dated 1495, and five elaborate 17th-century Aubusson tapestries.

From the fountain, streets lead up to the cliff edge, and allow views of the surrounding valleys, with the ever-present sound of cowbells in the distance. The town is very crowded in summer, but it makes a good starting point for excursions to the Puy Mary (*see p364*), the huge barrage at Bort-les-Orgues, the nearby Château de Val and the Cère valley to the south.

Medieval Château de Val at Bort-les-Orgues near Salers

Puy Mary peak in the volcanic Monts du Cantal

Monts du Cantal ⑱

Cantal. ⊠ *Aurillac.* 🚌 🚉 *Lioran.*
🛈 *Aurillac (04 71 48 46 58).*

The Cantal mountains were originally one enormous volcano – the oldest and the largest in Europe, dating from the Tertiary period. The highest peaks, the **Plomb du Cantal** at 1,855 m (6,086 ft) and the **Puy Mary** at 1,787 m (5,863 ft), are surrounded by crests and deep river valleys. Driving the narrow roads is a thrill, compounded by the views at every hairpin turn. Between peaks and gorges, rich mountain pastures provide summer grazing for red-gold Salers cows (*see p363*). From the **Pas de Peyrol**, the highest road pass in the country at 1,589 m (5,191 ft), it's about a 25-minute journey on foot to the summit of the Puy Mary.

Environs

One of the finest of the Auvergne châteaux, **Château d'Anjony** was built by Louis II d'Anjony, a supporter of Joan of Arc (*see pp300–1*). Highlights are the 16th-century frescoes: in the chapel, scenes from the Life and Passion of Christ, and upstairs in the *Salle des Preux* (Knights' Room), a dazzling series of the nine heroes of chivalry. To the south lies the small town of **Aurillac**, a good base for exploring the Cantal region.

♖ **Château d'Anjony**
Tournemire. *Tel 04 71 47 61 67.*
◯ *Jul–Aug: daily; mid-Feb–mid-Nov: daily pms.* 📷 🎫 *obligatory.*

La Chaise-Dieu ⑲

Haute-Loire. 👥 *700.* 🚌 🛈 *pl de la Mairie (04 71 00 01 16).* 🛒 *Thu.*
www.tourisme.fr/lachaisedieu

Sombre and massive, midway between Romanesque and Gothic, the 14th-century abbey church of **St-Robert** is the prime reason to visit the small village of La Chaise-Dieu. The building is an amalgam of styles; the choir, however, is sensational: 144 oak stalls carved with figures of Vice and Virtue. Above them, entirely covering the walls, are some of the loveliest tapestries in France. Made in Brussels and Arras in the early 16th century and depicting scenes from the Old and New Testaments, they are rich in colour and detail.

Statue of Notre-Dame-de-France at Le Puy

On the outer walls of the choir the 15th-century wall painting of the *Danse Macabre* shows Death in the form of skeletons leading rich and poor alike to their inevitable end. Beyond the cloister is the Echo room, in which two people whispering in opposite corners can hear one another perfectly. A Baroque Music Festival from mid-August to September makes the abbey crowded.

Le Puy-en-Velay ⑳

Haute-Loire. 👥 *20,500.* ⊠ 🚌 🚉
🛈 *2 pl de Clauzel (04 71 09 38 41).*
🛒 *Sat.* 🎪 *Sep.*
www.ot-lepuyenvelay.fr

Located in the bowl of a volcanic cone, the town of Le Puy teeters on a series of rock outcrops and giant basalt pillars. The town has three peaks, each topped with a landmark church or statue. Seen from afar, this is one of the most impressive sights in France.

Now a commercial and tourist-oriented town, Le Puy's star attraction is its medieval **Holy City**. This became a pilgrimage centre after the Bishop of Le Puy, Gotescalk, made one of the first pilgrimages to Santiago de Compostela in 962, and built the **Chapelle St-Michel d'Aiguilhe** on his return.

Detail of *Danse Macabre* at St-Robert, in La Chaise-Dieu

THE AUVERGNE'S BLACK MADONNAS

The cult of the Virgin Mary has always been strong in the Auvergne and this is reflected in the concentration of her statues in the region. Carved in dark walnut or cedar, now blackened with age, the Madonnas are believed to originate from the Byzantine influence of the Crusaders. Perhaps the most famous Madonna is the one in Le-Puy-en-Velay, a 17th-century copy of one which belonged to Louis IX in the Middle Ages.

Louis IX's Black Virgin

Pilgrims from eastern France and Germany assembled at the **Cathédrale de Notre-Dame** with its famous Black Madonna and "fever stone" – a Druid ceremonial stone with healing powers embedded in one of its walls – before setting off for Compostela.

Built on an early pagan site, the Cathédrale de Notre-Dame is a huge Romanesque structure. Multiform arches, carved palm and leaf designs and a chequerboard façade show the influences of Moorish Spain, and indicate the considerable cultural exchange that took place with southern France in the 11th and 12th centuries. In the transept are Romanesque frescoes, notably an 11th–12th-century St Michael; in the sacristy, the treasury includes the Bible of Theodolphus, a handwritten document from the era of Charlemagne. The cathedral is the centre of the Holy City complex that dominates the upper town, encompassing a baptistry, cloister, Prior's house and Penitents' chapel.

The colossal red statue of **Notre-Dame-de-France**, on the pinnacle of the Rocher Corneille, was erected in 1860, cast from 213 cannons captured at Sebastopol during the Crimean War. The statue is reached by a steep pathway, and can be climbed by an iron ladder on the inside.

The Chapelle St-Michel, like the cathedral, shows Moorish influences in the trefoil decoration and coloured mosaics on the rounded arch over the main entrance. It seems to grow out of a giant finger of lava rock and is reached by a steep climb. The church is thought to be located on the site of a Roman temple to Mercury, and its centre dates from the 10th century, although most of the building was constructed a century later. The floor has been constructed to follow the contours of the rock in places,

and the interior is ornamented with faded 10th-century murals and 20th-century stained-glass.

In the lower city, narrow streets of 15th- and 16th-century houses lead to the Vinay Garden and the **Musée Crozatier**, which has a collection of hand-made lace from the 16th century to the present. The museum also has a surprisingly good collection of medieval *objets d'art* and 15th-century paintings, with works attributed to de Heem and Salomon Ruysdael.

In mid-September, Le Puy transforms itself into masked and costumed Renaissance carnival for the Bird King Festival, an ancient tradition celebrating the skill of the city's best archers *(see p38)* .

Chapelle St-Michel d'Aiguilhe
Aiguilhe. *Tel* 04 71 09 50 03.
Feb–mid-Nov: daily; Christmas: pms only. 1 Jan, 25 Dec.

Notre-Dame-de-France
Rocher Corneille. *Tel* 04 71 05 45 52. daily.

Musée Crozatier
Jardin Henri Vinay. *Tel* 04 71 06 62 40.
Wed–Mon (summer: daily).
Oct– Apr: Sun am; 1 Jan, 1 Nov, Dec.

Chapelle St-Michel d'Aiguilhe, standing on a finger of lava rock

Ruins of the Castle of Calmont d'Olt at Espalion in the Lot Valley

Vallée du Lot ㉑

Aveyron. ✈ Aurillac, Rodez. ▯ Rodez, Séverac-le-Château. ▯ Espalion, Rodez. ℹ Espalion (05 65 44 10 63). www.valleedulot.com

From Mende and the old river port of La Canourgue all the way to Conques, the river Lot (or Olt in old usage) courses through its fertile valley past orchards, vineyards and pine forests. **St Côme d'Olt**, near the Aubrac mountains, is an unspoiled, fortified village whose 15th-century church is surrounded by Medieval and Renaissance houses. At **Espalion**, the pastel stone houses and a turreted 16th-century castle are reflected in the river, which runs beneath a 13th-century arched stone bridge. The town has one of the best markets in the region on Friday mornings. Just outside town is the 11th-century Perse Church, whose carved capitals portray battling knights and imaginary birds sipping from a chalice.

Estaing was once the fiefdom of one of the greatest families of the Rouergue, dating back to the 13th-century. The village nestles beneath its massive château (now a convent) on the river bank. The road passes through the Lot Gorge on the way to **Entraygues** ("between waters") where the old quarter and 13th-century Gothic bridge are worth a visit. Beyond Entraygues the river widens to join the Garonne.

Conques ㉒

See pp368–9.

Rodez ㉓

Aveyron. 🏠 26,000. ✈ ▯ ▯ ℹ pl Foch (05 65 75 76 77). 🛒 Wed, Fri (eve) & Sat. www.ot-rodez.fr

Like many medieval French cities, Rodez was politically divided: the shop-lined **place du Bourg** on one side of town and **place de la Cité**, near the cathedral, on the other, reflect

Entombment in Rodez Cathedral

conflicting secular and ecclesiastical interests. Rodez's commercial centre, the largest in the region, is probably the main attraction now, though the 13th-century huge pink stone **Cathédrale Notre-Dame** is worth a look, with its fortress-like west façade, and its magnificent, ornate belltower. The 15th-century choir stalls show a superb panoply of creatures, including a winged lion and one naughty fellow exposing his derrière.

Environs
Southeast (45kms/28 miles) lies Saint Léons, birthplace of Jean-Henri Fabre, the famous entymologist. Here is **Micropolis**, part interactive museum, part theme park, dedicated to the glory of insects (closed Nov–Feb). Go to see the breathtaking film of the same name, if nothing else.

ROBERT LOUIS STEVENSON

Robert Louis Stevenson (1850–94), best known for his novels *Treasure Island, Kidnapped* and *Dr Jekyll and Mr Hyde,* was also an accomplished travel writer. In 1878, he set off across the remote Cévennes mountain range with only a small donkey, Modestine, for company. His classic account of this eventful journey, *Travels with a Donkey in the Cévennes,* was published in the following year.

Robert Louis Stevenson

Dramatic scenery in Corniche des Cévennes national park

Corniche des Cévennes ㉔

Lozère, Gard. 🚉 Nîmes. 🚌 Alès.
🚌 St-Jean-du-Gard.
ℹ️ St-Jean-du-Gard (04 66 85 32 11).
www.cevennes-parcnational.fr

The dramatic Corniche road from Florac on the Tarn to St-Jean-du-Gard was cut in the early 18th century by the army of Louis XIV in pursuit of the Camisards, Protestant rebels who had no uniforms but fought in their ordinary shirts (*camiso* in the *langue d'oc*). The route of the D983 makes a spectacular drive. Fascination with the history of the Camisards was one of the reasons that Robert Louis Stevenson undertook his fabled trek in the Cévennes with Modestine, recounted in his *Travels with a Donkey*.

At St-Laurent-de-Trèves, where fossil remains suggest dinosaurs once roamed, there is a view of the Grands Causses and the peaks of Lozère and Aigoual. The Corniche ends in St-Jean-du-Gard, where the **Musée des Vallées Cévenoles**, depicting peasant life, is located in a former 17th-century inn.

🏛 Musée des Vallées Cévenoles
95 grand' rue, St-Jean-du-Gard.
Tel 04 66 85 10 48. ⬜ Jul–Aug: 10am–7pm daily; Apr–Jun, Sep–Oct: 10am–noon, 2–7pm daily; Nov–Mar Tue, Thu, Sun pm. ⬤ 1 Jan, 25 Dec.
📷 www.museedescevennes.com

Grands Causses ㉕

Aveyron. ✈️ Rodez-Marcillac. 🚉
🚌 Millau. ℹ️ Millau (05 65 60 02 42).
🗓 Wed & Fri. **www**.ot-milau.fr

The Causses are vast, arid limestone plateaux, alternating with surprisingly green, fertile canyon valleys. The only sign of life at times is a bird of prey wheeling in the sky, or an isolated stone farm or shepherd's hut. The whole area makes for some desolate hiking for those who like solitude.

The four Grands Causses – Sauveterre, Méjean, Noir and Larzac – stretch out east of the city of Millau, from Mende in the north to the valley of the Vis river in the south.

Among the sights in the Causses are the *chaos* – bizarre rock formations reputed to resemble ruined cities, and named accordingly: there's the chaos of **Montpellier-le-Vieux, Nîmes-le-Vieux** and **Roquesaltes. Aven Armand** and the **Dargilan Grotto** are vast and deep natural underground grottoes with equally astonishing formations.

A good place to head for in the windy reaches of the Larzac Causse is the strange, rough-hewn stone village of **La Couvertoirade**, a fully-enclosed citadel of the Knights Templar in the 12th century. The unpaved streets and medieval houses are an austere reminder of the dark side of the Middle Ages. Entrance to the village is free, with a fee for the tour of the ramparts.

The Causse du Larzac's best-known village is probably **Roquefort-sur-Soulzon**, a small grey town terraced on the side of a crumbled limestone outcrop. It has one main street and one major product, Roquefort cheese. This is made from unpasteurized sheep's milk, seeded with a distinctive blue mould grown on loaves of bread, and aged in the warren of damp caves above the town.

View over Méjean, one of the four plateaux of the Grands Causses

Conques ㉒

The village of Conques clusters around the splendid Abbaye de Ste-Foy, hemmed into a rugged site against the hillside. Sainte Foy was a young girl who became an early Christian martyr; her relics were first kept at a rival monastery in Agen. In the 9th century a monk from Conques stole the relics, thereby attracting pilgrims to this remote spot and firmly establishing Conques as a halt on the route to Santiago de Compostela *(see pp400–1)*.

12th-century reliquary

The treasury holds the most important collection of medieval and Renaissance gold work in western Europe. Some of it was made in the abbey's own workshops as early as the 9th century. The Romanesque abbey church has beautiful stained-glass windows by Pierre Soulages (1994), and its tympanum is a triumph of medieval sculpture.

View of the church from the village

The broad transepts were able to accommodate crowds of pilgrims.

Nave Interior
Pure and elegantly austere, the Romanesque interior dates from 1050–1135. The short nave soars to a height of 22 m (72 ft), with three tiers of arches topped by 250 decorative carved capitals.

Tympanum
This sculpture from the early 12th century depicts the Last Judgment, *with the Devil in Hell (shown) in the lower part of the sculpture and Christ in Heaven in the tympanum's central position.*

CONQUES' TREASURES

The treasures date from the 9th to the 19th century, and are prized for both their beauty and their rarity. The gold-plated wood and silver reliquary of Ste Foy is studded with gems, rock crystal and even an *intaglio* of Roman Emperor Caracalla. The body is 9th century, but the face may be older, possibly 5th century. Other magnificent pieces include an "A"-shaped reliquary said to be a gift from Charlemagne; the small but exquisite Pépin's shrine from AD 1000; and a late 16th-century processional cross.

The precious reliquary of Ste-Foy

Romanesque Chapels
The east end is three-tiered, topped by the blind arcades of the choir and a central bell-tower. Three chapels surround the eastern apse, built to accommodate extra altars for the celebration of mass.

Treasury
The precious contents of the treasury were hidden by the townspeople to prevent their destruction during the French Revolution. Perhaps surprisingly, all were returned.

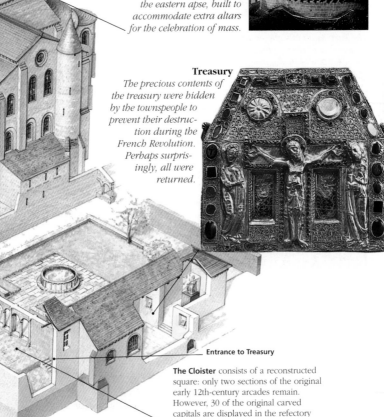

Entrance to Treasury

The Cloister consists of a reconstructed square: only two sections of the original early 12th-century arcades remain. However, 30 of the original carved capitals are displayed in the refectory and in the Musée Fau.

Gorges du Tarn ㉖

Near the beginning of its journey to meet the river Garonne, the Tarn flows through some of Europe's most spectacular gorges. For millions of years, the Tarn and its tributary the Jonte have eaten their way down through the limestone plateaux of the Cévennes, creating a sinuous forked canyon some 25 km (15 miles) long and nearly 400 m (1,300 ft) deep. The gorges are flanked by rocky bluffs and scaled by roads with dizzying bends and panoramic views, which are incredibly popular in the high season. The surrounding plateaux, or *causses*, are eerily different, forming an open, austere landscape, dry in summer and snow-clad in winter, where wandering sheep and isolated farms are sometimes the only signs of life.

Point Sublime
From 800 m (2,600 ft) up, there are stunning views of a major bend in the Tarn gorge, with the Causse Méjean visible in the distance.

Outdoor Activities
The Tarn and Jonte gorges are popular for canoeing and river-rafting. Although relatively placid in summer, melting snow can make the rivers hazardous in spring.

Pas de Souci
Just upriver from Les Vignes, Pas de Souci flanks a narrow point in the gorge as the Tarn makes its way northwards.

Chaos de Montpellier-le-Vieux
Situated on the flank of the Causse Noir off the D110 is a remarkable geological site – bizarre rock formations created by limestone erosion.

La Malène
An old crossing-point between the Causse de Sauveterre and the Causse Méjean, this village, with its 16th-century fortified manor, is a good starting point for boat trips.

VISITORS' CHECKLIST

Lozère. ✈ *Rodez-Marcillac.* 🚊 *Mende, Banassac, Séverac-le-Château.* 🚌 *Milau.* ℹ *Le Rozier (summer: 05 65 62 60 89). St-Enimie (04 66 48 53 44).* **www**.office dutourisme-gorgesdutarne.com

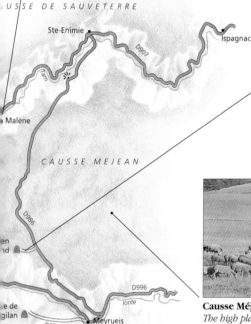

Aven Armand Caves
On the Causse Méjean, many stalactites in the caves are tinted by minerals that are deposited by the slowly trickling water.

Causse Méjean
The high plateaux or causses are a botanist's paradise in spring and summer, with over 900 species of wild flowers, including orchids.

THE WILD CEVENNES

One of the least populated parts of France, this area is well known for its wild flowers and birds of prey, and griffon vultures were once common here. These giant but harmless scavengers nearly died out in the 20th century through being hunted, but now a reintroduction programme has led to growing numbers breeding in the Gorges de la Jonte.

Yellow wort

Kidney vetch

Green-winged orchid

Wild flowers *found in this thinly populated area include unusual alpine plants.*

The griffon vulture, *which now breeds in the region, has a wingspan of over 2.5 m (8 ft).*

THE RHÔNE VALLEY AND FRENCH ALPS

LOIRE · RHÔNE · AIN · ISÈZÈRE · DRÔME
ARDÈCHE · HAUTE-SAVOIE · SAVOIE · HAUTES-ALPES

Its two most important geographical features, the Alps and the river Rhône, give this region both its name and its dramatic character. The east is dominated by majestic snowcapped peaks, while the Rhône provides a vital conduit between north and south.

The Romans recognized this strategic route when they founded Lyon over 2,000 years ago. Today Lyon, with its great museums and fine Renaissance buildings, is the second city of France. It is one of the country's most vital commercial and cultural centres as well as the undisputed capital of French gastronomy. To the north lie the flat marshlands of the Dombes and the rich agricultural Bresse plain. Here, too, are the famous Beaujolais vineyards which, along with the Rhône vineyards, make the region such an important wine producer.

The French Alps are among the most popular year-round resort areas in the world, with internationally renowned ski stations such as Chamonix, Mégève and Courchevel, and historic cities like Chambéry, capital of Savoy before it joined France. Elegant spa towns line the shores of Lac Léman (Lake Geneva). Grenoble, a bustling university city and high-tech centre, is flanked by two of the most spectacular nature reserves in France, the Chartreuse and the Vercors.

To the south, orchards and fields of sunflowers give way to brilliant rows of lavender interspersed with vineyards and olive groves. Châteaux and ancient towns dot the landscape. Mountains and pretty, old-fashioned spa towns characterize the rugged Ardèche, and the deeply scoured gorges along the river Ardèche offer some of the wildest scenery in France.

The restored Ferme de la Forêt at St-Trivier-de-Courtes, north of Bourg-en-Bresse

◁ Annecy's medieval quarter

Exploring the Rhône Valley and French Alps

Lyon is the region's largest city, famed for its historic buildings and gastronomic tradition. Wine lovers can choose between the vineyards of the Beaujolais, Rhône Valley and Drôme region to the south. To the west, the Ardèche offers rugged wilderness, canoeing and climbing. Spa devotees from around the world flock to Évian-les-Bains and Aix-les-Bains, while the Alps are a favourite destination for sports enthusiasts *(see pp322–3)*.

SIGHTS AT A GLANCE

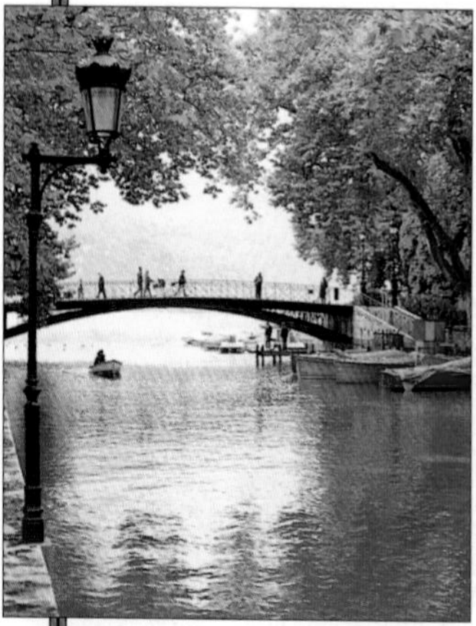

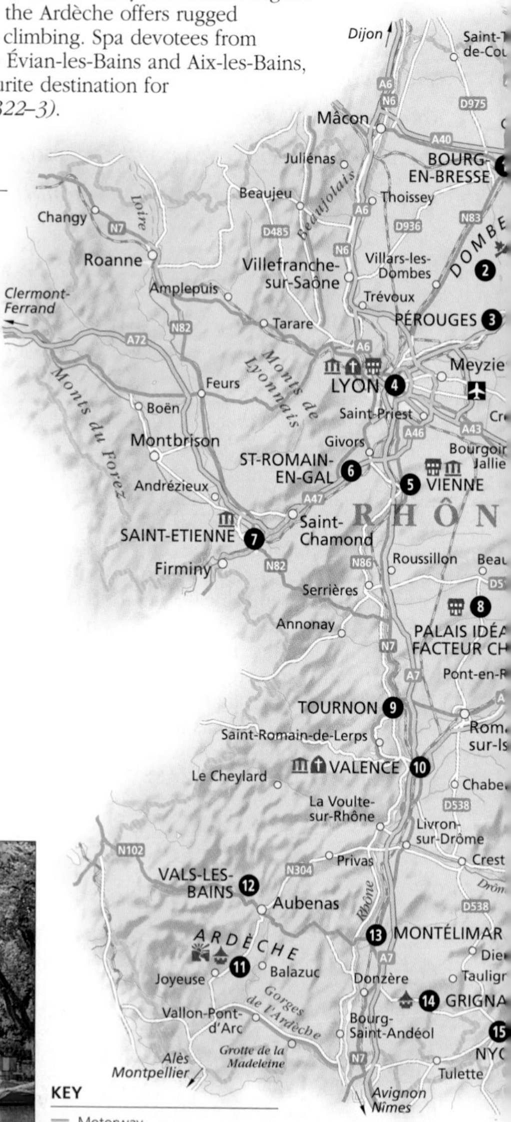

KEY

- Motorway
- Motorway under construction
- Major road
- Secondary road
- Minor road
- Scenic route
- Main railway
- Minor railway
- International border
- Regional border
- Summit

The Pont des Amours in Annecy

For additional map symbols *see back flap*

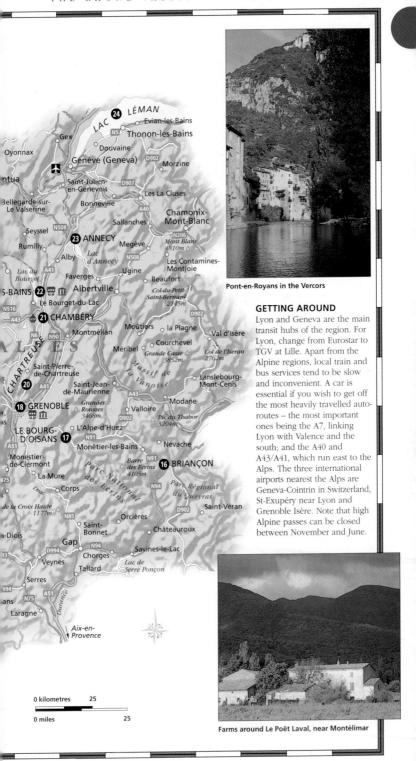

Pont-en-Royans in the Vercors

GETTING AROUND

Lyon and Geneva are the main transit hubs of the region. For Lyon, change from Eurostar to TGV at Lille. Apart from the Alpine regions, local train and bus services tend to be slow and inconvenient. A car is essential if you wish to get off the most heavily travelled auto-routes – the most important ones being the A7, linking Lyon with Valence and the south; and the A40 and A43/A41, which run east to the Alps. The three international airports nearest the Alps are Geneva-Cointrin in Switzerland, St-Exupéry near Lyon and Grenoble Isère. Note that high Alpine passes can be closed between November and June.

Farms around Le Poët Laval, near Montélimar

0 kilometres   25

0 miles   25

Bourg-en-Bresse ❶

Ain. 🏠 43,000. 🚊 🚌 🛈 Centre Culturel Albert Camus, 6 av Alsace-Lorraine (04 74 22 49 40). 🗓 Wed, Sat. www.bourg-en-bresse.org

Bourg-en-Bresse is a busy market town, with some beautifully restored half-timbered buildings. It is best known for its tasty *poulet de Bresse* (chickens raised in the flat agricultural region of Bresse and designated *appellation contrôlée, see p319*); and its abbey church of **Brou** on the southeast edge of town.

The latter, no longer a place of worship, has become one of the most visited sites in France. Flamboyant Gothic in style, it was built between 1505 and 1536 by Margaret of Austria after the death of her husband Philibert, Duke of Savoy, in 1504.

The couple's finely sculpted Carrara marble tombs can be seen in the choir, along with the tomb of Margaret of Bourbon, Philibert's mother, who died in 1483. Notice also the beautifully carved choir stalls, stained-glass windows, and rood screen with its elegant basket-handle arching.

The adjacent cloisters house a small museum with a good collection of 16th- and 17th-century Dutch and Flemish masters, as well as contemporary works by local artists.

Environs
About 24 km (15 miles) north of Bourg-en-Bresse at St-Trivier-de-Courtes, the restored **Ferme-Musée de la Forêt** offers a look at farm life in the region in the 17th century. The ancient house has what is known locally as a Saracen chimney, with a brick hood in the centre of the room, similar to constructions in Sicily and Portugal, and a collection of antique farm implements.

Bresse chickens

🏛 **Ferme-Musée de la Forêt**
Tel 04 74 30 71 89. 🗓 Jul–Sep: daily; Apr–Jun & Oct: w/e & public hols. 📷 ♿

Tomb of Margaret of Austria in the abbey church of Brou at Bourg-en-Bresse

The Dombes ❷

Ain. ✈ Lyon. 🚊 Lyon, Villars les Dombes, Bourg-en-Bresse. 🚌 Villars-les-Dombes (from Bourg-en-Bresse). 🛈 3 pl de Hôtel de Ville, Villars-les-Dombes (04 74 98 06 29).

This flat, glacier-gouged plateau south of Bourg-en-Bresse is dotted with small hills, ponds and marshes, making it popular with anglers and bird-watchers.

In the middle of the area at **Villars-les-Dombes** is an ornithological park, the **Parc des Oiseaux**. Over 400 species of native and exotic birds live here, including tufted herons, vultures, pink flamingoes, emus and ostriches.

🦅 **Parc des Oiseaux**
Route Nationale 83, Villars-Dombes. **Tel** 04 74 98 05 54. 🗓 daily. ● Dec–Feb. 📷 ♿

Pérouges ❸

Ain. 🏠 900. 🚊 Meximieux-Pérouges. 🚌 🛈 04 74 61 01 14. www.perouges.org

Originally the home of immigrants from Perugia, Pérouges is a fortified hilltop village of medieval houses and cobblestone streets. In the 13th century it was a centre of linen-weaving, but with the mechanization of the industry in the 19th century, the local population fell from 1,500 to 90.

Restoration of its historic buildings and a new influx of craftsmen have breathed new life into Pérouges. Not surprisingly, the village has often been used as the setting for historical dramas such as *The Three Musketeers* and *Monsieur Vincent*. The village's main square, place de la Halle, is shaded by a huge lime tree planted in 1792 to honour the Revolution.

A Tour of Beaujolais

Beaujolais is an ideal area for wine tasting, offering delicious, affordable wine and glorious countryside. The south of the region produces most of the Beaujolais Nouveau, released fresh from the cellars on the third Thursday of November each year. In the north are the ten superior quality *cru* wines – St-Amour, Juliénas, Moulin-à-Vent, Chénas, Fleurie, Chiroubles,

Côte de Brouilly

Morgon, Brouilly, Côte de Brouilly and Regnié – most of which can be visited in a day's drive. The distinctive *maisons du pays* have living quarters built over the wine cellar. Almost every village has its *cave* (wine cellar), offering tastings and a glimpse of the wine culture that dominates local life.

Juliénas ①
Famous for *coq au vin*, this village stores and sells wine in its church, château, and the Maison de la Dime, a 16th-century tithe house.

Moulin-à-Vent ②
This 17th-century windmill has lovely views of the Saône valley. Tastings of the oldest *cru* in the region are held in the *caves* next door.

Vineyard of Gamay grapes

Chiroubles ⑦
A bust in the village square honours Victor Pulliat, who saved the vines from the phylloxera blight in the 1880s by using American vine stocks.

Fleurie ③
The chapel of the Madonna (1875) stands guard over the vineyards, and village restaurants serve local *andouillettes au Fleurie*.

Villié-Morgon ④
Wine-tasting is in the cellars of the 18th-century château in the village centre. The Château de Corcelles nearby has a Renaissance courtyard.

Beaujeu ⑥
Once the ancient capital of the region, Beaujeu offers tastings in its 17th-century hospices. This Renaissance wooden building houses a shop, information centre and museum.

Brouilly ⑤
The hill, with its tiny 19th-century chapel of Notre-Dame du Raisin, offers fine views and an annual Beaujolais wine festival.

KEY

▬▬▬	Tour route
	Other roads
✷	Viewpoint

0 kilometres 2
0 miles 1

MACON →
Chénas
Romanèche-Thorins
D26
D32
D18
D26
D68
D9
D68
D266
D68
D37
Régnié-Durette
Cercié
VILLEFRANCHE-SUR-SAONE

Street-by-Street: Lyon ❹

On the west bank of the river Saône, the restored old
quarter of Vieux Lyon is an atmospheric warren of
cobbled streets, *traboules* (covered passageways),
Renaissance palaces, first-class restaurants, lively
bouchons (bistros) and bohemian shops. It is also
the site of the Roman city of Lugdunum, the
commercial and military capital of Gaul
founded by Julius Caesar in 44 BC.
Vestiges of this prosperous city can be
seen in the superb Gallo-Roman
museum at the top of Fourvière hill.
Two excavated Roman theatres still stage
performances from opera to rock concerts.
At the foot of the hill is the finest collection
of Renaissance mansions in France – a
testimony to the enormous wealth brought to
the city by banking, printing and the silk trade.

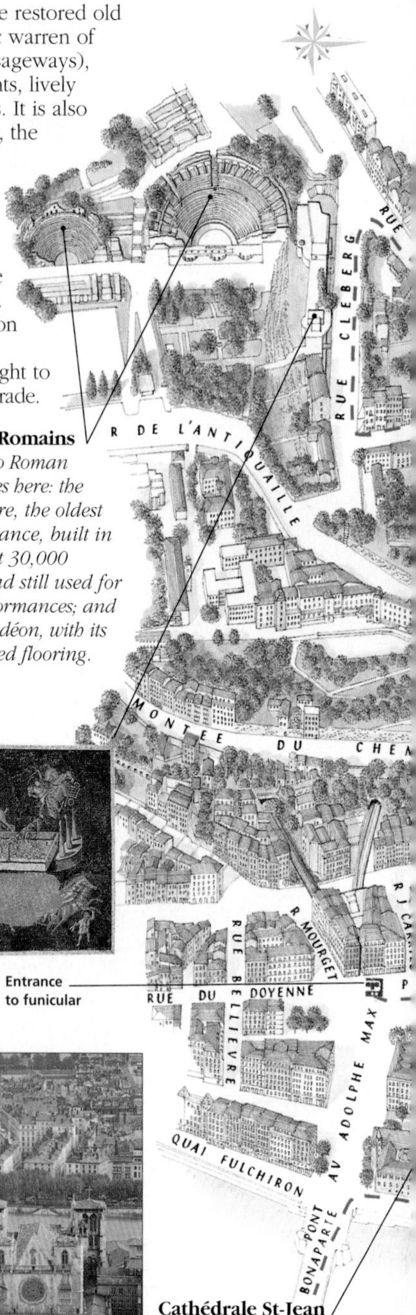

★ Théâtres Romains
*There are two Roman
amphitheatres here: the
Grand Théâtre, the oldest
theatre in France, built in
15 BC to seat 30,000
spectators and still used for
modern performances; and
the smaller Odéon, with its
geometric tiled flooring.*

★ Musée de la Civilisation Gallo-Romaine
*This underground museum
contains a rich collection of
statues, mosaics, coins and
inscriptions evoking Lyon's
Roman past.*

Entrance
to funicular

STAR SIGHTS

* ★ Théâtres Romains

* ★ Musée de la
  Civilisation
  Gallo-Romaine

* ★ Basilique Notre-Dame
  de Fourvière

Cathédrale St-Jean
*Begun in the late 12th century
cathedral has a 14th-century ast
nomical clock that shows relig
feast days till the year 2019.*

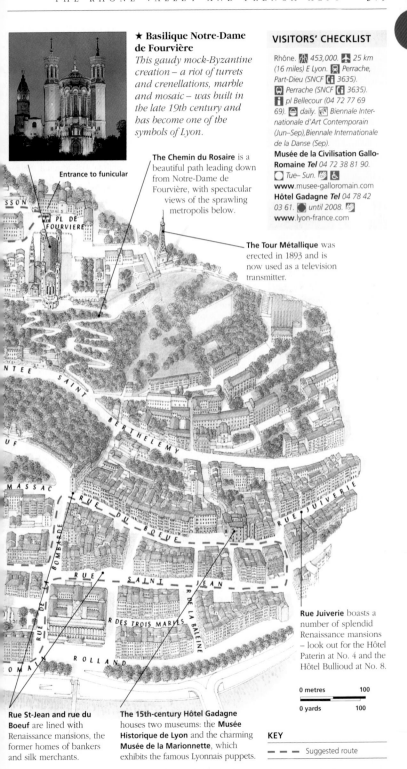

★ **Basilique Notre-Dame de Fourvière**
This gaudy mock-Byzantine creation – a riot of turrets and crenellations, marble and mosaic – was built in the late 19th century and has become one of the symbols of Lyon.

Entrance to funicular

The Chemin du Rosaire is a beautiful path leading down from Notre-Dame de Fourvière, with spectacular views of the sprawling metropolis below.

The Tour Métallique was erected in 1893 and is now used as a television transmitter.

Rue Juiverie boasts a number of splendid Renaissance mansions – look out for the Hôtel Paterin at No. 4 and the Hôtel Bullioud at No. 8.

Rue St-Jean and rue du Boeuf are lined with Renaissance mansions, the former homes of bankers and silk merchants.

The 15th-century Hôtel Gadagne houses two museums: the **Musée Historique de Lyon** and the charming **Musée de la Marionnette**, which exhibits the famous Lyonnais puppets.

VISITORS' CHECKLIST

Rhône. 453,000. 25 km (16 miles) E Lyon. Perrache, Part-Dieu (SNCF 3635). Perrache (SNCF 3635). pl Bellecour (04 72 77 69 69). daily. Biennale International d'Art Contemporain (Jun–Sep), Biennale Internationale de la Danse (Sep).
Musée de la Civilisation Gallo-Romaine *Tel* 04 72 38 81 90. Tue–Sun. www.musee-galloromain.com
Hôtel Gadagne *Tel* 04 78 42 03 61. until 2008. www.lyon-france.com

0 metres	100
0 yards	100

KEY

– – – Suggested route

Exploring Lyon

France's second city, dramatically sited on the banks of the Rhône and Saône rivers, has been a vital gateway between the north and south since ancient times. On arriving you immediately feel a *brin du sud*, or touch of the south. The crowds are not as quick-stepping as they are in Paris, and the sun is often shining here when it's rainy and cold in the north. Despite its importance as a banking, textile and pharmaceutical centre, most of the French immediately associate Lyon with their palates. The city is packed with restaurants, ranging from simple *bouchons* (bistros) to some of the most opulent tables in France.

The rue St-Jean in Vieux Lyon

The Presqu'île

The heart of Lyon is the Presqu'île, the narrow peninsula of land between the Saône and Rhône rivers, just north of their confluence. A pedestrianized shopping street, the rue de la République, links the twin poles of civic life: the vast **place Bellecour**, with its equestrian statue of Louis XIV in the middle, and the **place des Terreaux**. The latter is overlooked by Lyon's ornate 17th-century Hôtel de Ville (town hall) and the Palais St-Pierre, a former Benedictine convent and now the home of the **Musée des Beaux Arts**. In the middle of the square is a monumental 19th-century fountain by Bartholdi, sculptor of the Statue of Liberty.

Behind the town hall, architect Jean Nouvel's futuristic **Opéra de Lyon** – a black barrel vault of steel and glass encased in a Neo-Classical shell – was remodelled to a controversial design in 1993.

A few blocks to the south, the **Musée de l'Imprimerie** illustrates Lyon's contribution to the early days of printing in the late 15th century.

Two other museums worth visiting in the Presqu'île are the **Musée des Tissus**, which houses an extraordinary collection of silks and tapestries dating from early Christian times to the present day, and the **Musée des Arts Décoratifs**, which displays a range of tapestries, furniture, porcelain and *objets d'art*.

Nearby, the **Abbaye St-Martin d'Ainay** is an impressively restored Carolingian church dating from 1107.

LYON CITY CENTRE

Abbaye St-Martin d'Ainay ⑬
Amphithéâtre des Trois Gaules ①
Basilique Notre-Dame
    de Fourvière ⑨
Cathédrale St-Jean ⑫
Eglise St-Polycarpe ②
Hôtel Gadagne ⑦
Hôtel de Ville ④
Musée de la Civilisation
    Gallo-Romaine ⑩
Musée de l'Imprimerie
    et de la Banque ⑥
Musée des Arts Décoratifs ⑭
Musée des Beaux Arts ⑤
Musée Historique des
    Tissus ⑮
Opéra de Lyon ③
Théâtres Romains ⑪
Tour Métallique ⑧

| 0 metres | 250 |
| 0 yards | 250 |

KEY

▢ Street-by-Street map
pp378–9

Key to Symbols *see back flap*

Food market on quai St-Antoine

Musée des Beaux Arts

Lyon's Musée des Beaux Arts showcases the country's largest and probably most important collection of art after the Louvre. The museum is housed in the 17th-century Palais St-Pierre, a former Benedictine convent for the daughters of the nobility. The Musée d'Art Contemporain, formerly located in the Palais St-Pierre, is now at 81 quai Charles de Gaulle, north of the Parc Tête d'Or. Housed in a building designed by Renzo Piano, it specializes in works dating from after the mid-1900s.

La Croix-Rousse

This area north of Presqu'île became the centre of the city's silk-weaving industry in the 15th century. It is traced with covered passages known as *traboules*, used by weavers to transport their finished fabrics. To get a sense of them, enter at No. 6 place des Terreaux and continue along till you reach the **Eglise St-Polycarpe**. From here, it is a short walk to the ruins of the **Amphithéâtre des Trois Gaules**, built in AD 19, and the **Maison des Canuts**, with its traditional silk loom.

La Part-Dieu

This modern business area on the east bank of the Rhône has a TGV station, a huge shopping complex and the **Auditorium Maurice-Ravel** for important cultural events.

🏛 **Musée de l'Imprimerie**
13 rue de la Poulaillerie.
Tel 04 78 37 65 98.
⬜ Wed–Sun. ⬤ public hols. 🖼 🎫

🏛 **Musée des Tissus**
34 rue de la Charité. **Tel** 04 78 38 42 00. ⬜ Tue–Sun. ⬤ public hols. 🖼

🏛 **Musée Arts Décoratifs**
30 rue de la Charité. **Tel** 04 78 38 42 00. ⬜ Tue–Sun. ⬤ public hols. 🖼

🏛 **Maison des Canuts**
10–12 rue d'Ivry. **Tel** 04 78 28 62 04. ⬜ Mon–Sat. ⬤ public hols. 🖼 🎫

Environs

Bourgoin-Jallieu, southeast of Lyon, still prints silk for today's fashion houses, and has an excellent renovated **Musée du Textile**.

ANTIQUITIES

Included in this wide-ranging collection on the first floor are Egyptian archaeological finds, Etruscan statuettes and 4,000-year-old Cypriot ceramics. Temporary exhibits, with a separate entrance on 16 rue Edouard Herriott, are also on the ground and first floors.

SCULPTURE AND OBJETS D'ART

Occupying the old chapel on the ground floor, the sculpture department includes works from the French Romanesque period and Italian Renaissance, as well as late 19th- and early 20th-century pieces.

Represented are Rodin and Bourdelle (whose statues also appear in the courtyard), Maillol, Despiau and Pompon among others. The huge *objets d'art* collection, on the first floor, comprises medieval ivories, bronzes and ceramics, coins, medals, weapons, jewellery, furniture and tapestries.

Odalisque (1841) by James Pradier

PAINTINGS AND DRAWINGS

The museum's superb collection of paintings occupies the first and second floors. It covers all periods and includes works by Spanish and Dutch masters, the French schools of the 17th, 18th and 19th centuries, Impressionist

Fleurs des Champs (1845) by Louis Janmot of the Lyon School

and modern paintings, as well as works by the Lyon School, whose exquisite flower paintings were used as sources of inspiration by the designers of silk fabrics through the ages. On the first floor, the Cabinet d'Arts Graphiques has over 4,000 drawings and etchings by such artists as Delacroix, Poussin, Géricault, Degas and Rodin (by appointment only).

🏛 **Musée des Beaux Arts**
Palais St-Pierre, 20 pl des Terreaux.
Tel 04 72 10 17 40. ⬜ Wed–Mon.
⬤ public hols. 🖼 🎫 ♿

La Méduse (1923) by Alexeï von Jawlensky

Châtiment de Lycurgue in the Musée Archéologique, St-Romain-en-Gal

Vienne ❺

Isère. 🏠 *30,000.* 🚊 🚌 ℹ️ *cours Brillier (04 74 53 80 30).* 🕑 *Sat.* 🎷 *International Jazz Festival (end Jun–mid-Jul).* **www**.vienne-tourisme.com

No other city in the Rhône Valley offers such a concentration of architectural history as Vienne. Located in a natural basin of land between the river and the hills, this site was recognized for both its strategic and aesthetic advantages by the Romans, who vastly expanded an existing village when they invaded the area in the 1st century BC.

The centre of the Roman town was the **Temple d'Auguste et Livie** (10 BC) on place du Palais, a handsome structure supported by

Vienne's Temple d'Auguste et Livie (1st century BC)

Corinthian columns. Not far away off place de Miremont are the remains of the **Jardin Archéologique de Cybèle**, a temple dedicated to the goddess Cybèle, whose worship involved orgiastic rites.

The **Théâtre Romain**, at the foot of Mont Pipet off rue du Cirque, was one of the largest amphitheatres in Roman France, capable of seating over 13,000 spectators. It was restored in 1938, and is now used for a variety of events, including an international jazz festival. From the very top seats the view of the town and river is spectacular.

Other interesting Roman vestiges include a fragment of Roman road in the public gardens, and on the southern edge of town, the **Pyramide du Cirque**, a curious structure about 20 m (65 feet) high that was once the centrepiece of the chariot racetrack. The **Musée des Beaux Arts et d'Archéologie** also has a good collection of Gallo-Roman artifacts, as well as 18th-century French faïence.

The **Cathédrale de St-Maurice** is the city's most important medieval monument. It was built between the 12th and 16th century and represents an unusual hybrid of Romanesque and Gothic styles. The interior has three aisles but no transept, and contains many fine Romanesque sculptures. Two

of Vienne's earliest Christian churches are the 12th-century **Eglise St-André-le-Bas**, with richly carved capitals in its nave and cloister, and the **Eglise St-Pierre**, parts of which date from the 5th and 6th centuries. The latter houses the **Musée Lapidaire**, a museum of stone-carving with a collection of bas-reliefs and statues from Gallo-Roman buildings.

🏛 **Musée des Beaux Arts et d'Archéologie**
Pl de Miremont. **Tel** *04 74 85 50 42.* 🕑 *Apr–Oct: Tue–Sun; Nov–Mar: Tue–Fri & Sat–Sun pms.* 🔴 *1 Jan, 1 May, 1 & 11 Nov, 25 Dec.* 🏛

🏛 **Musée Lapidaire**
Pl St-Pierre. **Tel** *04 74 85 20 35.* 🕑 *Tue–Sun.* 🔴 *Nov–Mar: Sat & Sun am, 1 Jan, 1 May, 1 & 11 Nov, 25 Dec.* 🏛 ♿ 🏛 🏛

Vienne's Cathédrale de St-Maurice

St-Romain-en-Gal ❻

Rhône. 🏠 *1,300.* 🚊 *Vienne.* ℹ️ *Vienne (04 74 53 80 30).*

In 1967, building work in this commercial town directly across the Rhône from Vienne revealed extensive remains of a significant Roman community dating from 100 BC to AD 300. It comprises the remnants of villas, public baths, shops and warehouses. Of particular interest is the House of the Ocean Gods, with a magnificent mosaic floor depicting the bearded Neptune and other ocean images.

Much of what has been unearthed during the ongoing excavations is housed in the

Musée Archéologique
adjoining the ruins. The impressive collection includes household objects, murals and mosaics. The star exhibit is the *Châtiment de Lycurgue*, a mosaic discovered in 1907.

🏛 **Musée Archéologique**
Tel 04 74 53 74 01. ◯ Tue–Sun. ●
some publ hols. 🎫 🔒 ♿ restr. 🔲
📱 www.musee-gallo-romain.com

St-Étienne ❼

Loire. 🏘 180,000. ✈ 🚉 🚌
ℹ️ *16 av de la Libération (08 92 70 05 42).* 🏪 *daily.* www.tourisme-st-etienne.com

The dour industrial renown brought to this city by coal-mining and armaments is slowly being shaken off, with urban redevelopment well underway and a spanking new tramway. The downtown area around place des Peuple is lively. Nearby, Jean-Michel Wilmotte has overhauled the **Musée d'Art et d'Industrie**, which covers St-Étienne's in-dustrial background, including the development of the revo-lutionary Jacquard loom, and world-class collections of, amongst other things, cycles and ribbon-making machines.

To the north of the city, the **Musée d'Art Moderne** has a collection of 20th-century art including works by Andy Warhol and Frank Stella.

Detail of the bizarre Palais Idéal du Facteur Cheval at Hauterives

🏛 **Musée d'Art et d'Industrie**
2 pl Louis Comte. **Tel** *04 77 49 73 00.* ◯ Wed–Mon. ● some public hols. 🎫 ♿ 🔲

🏛 **Musée d'Art Moderne**
La Terrasse. **Tel** *04 77 79 52 52.* ◯ Wed–Mon. ● some public hols. 🎫 ♿

Palais Idéal du Facteur Cheval ❽

Hauterives, Drôme. 🚌 🚉 *Romans-sur-Isère* **Tel** *04 75 68 81 19.* ◯ daily. ● *1, 15–31 Jan, 25 Dec.* 🎫 📷 🔒 ♿ www.facteurcheval.com

At Hauterives, 25 km (15 miles) north of Roman-sur-Isère on the D538, is one of the greatest follies of France, an eccentric "palace" constructed of stones and evoking Egyptian, Roman, Aztec and Siamese styles of architecture. It was built by a local postman, Ferdinand Cheval, who collected the stones during his daily rounds. His neighbours thought him mad, but the project attracted the admiring attention of Picasso, the surrealist André Breton and other artists.

The interior of the palace is inscribed with numerous mottos and exhortations by Cheval, the most poignant of which refers to his assiduous efforts to realize his lifelong fantasy: "1879–1912: 10,000 days, 93,000 hours, 33 years of toil".

THE RHÔNE'S BRIDGES

The Rhône has played a crucial role in French history, transporting armies and commercial traffic between the north and south. It has always been dangerous, a challenge to boatmen and builders for centuries. In 1825 the brilliant engineer, Marc Seguin, built the first suspen-sion bridge using steel wire cables. This was followed by another 20 along the length of the Rhône, forever trans-forming communications between east and west.

Suspension bridge over the Rhône at Tournon-sur-Rhône

The town of Tournon-sur-Rhône

Tournon-sur-Rhône **9**

Ardèche. ⚐ 10,000. 🚉 ℹ️ *Hôtel de la Tourette (04 75 08 10 23).* 🐓 *Wed & Sat.* **www**.ville-tournon.com

Situated at the foot of impressive granite hills, Tournon is a lovely town with gracious tree-lined promenades and an imposing 11th–16th-century **château**. The latter houses a museum of local history, and has fine views of the town and river from its terraces.

The adjacent **Collégiale St-Julien**, with its square bell-tower and elaborate façade, is an interesting example of the Italian influence on architecture in the region during the 14th century. Inside is a powerful *Résurrection*, painted in 1576 by Capassin, a pupil of Raphael.

On quai Charles de Gaulle, the **Lycée Gabriel-Fauré** is the oldest secondary school in France, dating from 1536. Directly across the Rhône from Tournon, the village of **Tain l'Hermitage** is famous for its steep-climbing vineyards which produce both red and white Hermitage, the finest of all Rhône wines.

Environs
From Tournon's main square, the place Jean Jaurès, a narrow, twisting road signposted the **Route Panoramique** leads up the villages of Plats and St-Romain-de-Lerps to St-Péray. This route offers breathtaking views at every turn, and, at St-Romain, you are rewarded with a superb panorama extending over 13 *départements*.

Valence **10**

Drôme. ⚐ 67,000. 🚉 🚌 ℹ️ *11 bd Bancel (08 92 70 70 99).* 🐓 *Thu & Sat.* 🎵 *Summer Music (Jul).* **www**.valence-tourisme.com

Valence is a large, thriving market town set on the east bank of the Rhône and looking across to the cliffs of the Ardèche. Its principal sight is the Romanesque **Cathédrale St-Apollinaire** on place des Clercs, founded in 1095 and rebuilt in the 17th century.

Alongside the cathedral in the former bishop's palace, the small **Musée des Beaux Arts** contains a collection of late 18th-century chalk drawings of Rome by Hubert Robert.

A short walk from here are two Renaissance mansions. The **Maison des Têtes** at No. 57 Grande Rue was built in 1532 and is embellished with the sculpted heads of ancient Greeks including Aristotle, Homer and Hippocrates. On rue Pérollerie, the **Maison Dupré-Latour** has a finely sculptured porch and staircase.

The **Parc Jouvet**, south of avenue Gambetta, offers 6 hectares (14 acres) of pools and gardens, with fine views across the river to the ruined **Château de Crussol**.

🏛 **Musée des Beaux Arts**
4 pl des Ormeaux. *Tel 04 75 79 20 80.* ◐ *until 2011.* 📷

The limestone Pont d'Arc

The Ardèche **11**

Ardèche. ✈️ *Avignon.* 🚉 *Montélimar* 🚌 *Montélimar, Vallon Pont d'Arc.* ℹ️ *Vallon Pont d'Arc (04 75 88 04 01).* **www**.vallon-pont-darc.com

Over the course of thousands of years, wind and water have endowed this south-central region of France

CÔTES DU RHÔNE
Rising in the Swiss Alps and travelling south to the Mediterranean, the mighty Rhône is the common thread that links the many vineyards of the Rhône Valley. A hierarchy of *appellations* divides into three levels of quality: at the base, the regional Côtes du Rhône provides the bulk of the Rhône's wines; next, Côtes du Rhône-Villages comprises a plethora of picturesque villages; and, at the top, there are 13 individual *appellations*. The most famous are the steep slopes of Hermitage and Côte Rôtie in the northern Rhône, and historic Châteauneuf-du-Pape *(see p503)* in the south. The lion's share of production is of red wine, which, based on the syrah grape, is often spicy, full-bodied and robust.

Harvest in a Côtes du Rhône vineyard

with such a wild and rugged landscape that it is often more reminiscent of the American southwest than the verdure commonly associated with the French countryside. This visible drama is repeated underground as well, since the Ardèche is honeycombed with enormous stalagmite- and stalactite-ornamented caves. The most impressive are the **Aven d'Orgnac** (*aven* meaning pothole) to the south of Vallon-Pont-d'Arc, and the **Grotte de la Madeleine**, reached via a signposted path from the D290.

For those who prefer to stay above ground, the most arresting natural scenery in the region is the **Gorges de l'Ardèche**, best seen from the D290, a two-lane road with frequent viewpoints that parallels the recessed river for 32 km (20 miles). Nearly at the head of the gorge, heading west, is the **Pont d'Arc**, a natural limestone "bridge" spanning the river, created by erosion and the elements.

Canoeing and white-water rafting are the two most popular sports here. All the equipment necessary can be rented locally; operators at Vallon-Pont-d'Arc (among many other places) rent out two-person canoes and organize return transport from St-Martin d'Ardèche, 32 km (20 miles) downstream. Note that the river Ardèche is one of France's fastest flowing rivers – it is safest in May and June; by autumn its waters can be

The village of Vogüé on the banks of the river Ardèche

unpredictable and dangerous, especially for beginners.

The softer side of the region is found in its ancient and picturesque villages, gracious spa towns, vineyards and plantations of Spanish chestnuts (from which the delectable *marron glacé* is produced).

Some 13 km (8 miles) south of Aubenas, the 12th-century village of **Balazuc** is typical of the region, its stone houses built on a clifftop overlooking a secluded gorge of the river Ardèche. There are fine views as you approach on the D294.

Neighbouring **Vogüé** is nestled between the river Ardèche and a limestone cliff. A tiny but atmospheric village, its most commanding sight is the 12th-century **Château de Vogüé**, once the seat of the barons of Languedoc. Rebuilt in the 17th century, the building houses a museum featuring exhibitions about the region.

♠ Château de Vogüé
Tel 04 75 37 01 95. ◯ *Easter–Jun: Thu–Sun pms; Jul–mid-Sep: daily; mid-Sep–Nov: w/e pms.* 🖼 📷
www.chateaudevogue.net

The Gorges de l'Ardèche, between Vallon-Pont-d'Arc and Pont St-Esprit

Vals-les-Bains ⑫

Ardèche. 🏠 *3,700.* 🚉 *Montélimar.* 🛈 *rue Jean Jaurès (04 75 37 49 27).* 🗓 *Thu & Sun (& Tue in summer).*

This small spa town retains a hint of its past elegance. It is situated in the valley of the Volane, where there are at least 150 springs, of which all but two are cold. The water, which contains bicarbonate of soda and other minerals, is said to help with digestive problems, rheumatism and diabetes.

Discovered around 1600, Vals-les-Bains is one of the few spas in southern France to have been overlooked by the Romans. The town reached the height of its popularity in the late 19th century, and most of its parks and architecture retain something of the Belle Epoque. Vals is a convenient first stop for an exploration of the Ardèche, with plenty of hotels and restaurants.

Environs
About 8 km (5 miles) east of Vals is the superb Romanesque church of **St-Julien du Serre**.

A farm near Le Poët Laval, east of Montélimar

Montélimar ®

Drôme. 🏠 33,000. 🚊 🚌
ℹ️ allées Provençales (04 75 01 00
20). 🏪 Wed–Sat. www.montelimar-
tourisme.com

Whether you choose to make
a detour to Montélimar will
largely depend on how sweet
a tooth you might have. The
main curiosity of this market
town is its medieval centre,
chock-full of shops selling
almond-studded nougat. This
splendid confection has been
made here since the start of
the 17th century, when the
almond tree was first introduced into France from Asia.

The **Château des Adhémar**,
a mélange of 12th-, 14th- and
16th-century architecture,
surveys the town from a tall
hill to the east.

♣ Château des Adhémar
Tel 04 75 00 62 30. ⬜ Apr–Oct:
daily; Nov–Mar: Wed–Mon. ⬤ 1
Jan, 25 Dec. 🎫 ♿

Environs
The countryside east of
Montélimar is full of picturesque medieval villages and
scenic routes. **La Bégude-de-
Mazenc** is a thriving little holiday centre, with its fortified
Old Town perched on a hilltop.
Further east is **Le Poët Laval**, a
tiny medieval village of honey-
coloured stone buildings set in
the Alpine foothills. **Dieulefit**,
the capital of this beautiful
region, has several small hotels
and restaurants, as well as
facilities for tennis, swimming
and fishing. To the south, the
fortified village of **Taulignan**
is known for its truffles.

Grignan ®

Drôme. 🏠 1,360. 🚊 ℹ️ pl du Jeu
de Ballon (04 75 46 56 75). 🏪 Tue.
www.tourisme-paysdegrignan.com

Attractively situated on a
rocky hill surrounded by fields
of lavender, this charming little
village owes its fame to
Madame de Sévigné (see p91),
who wrote many of her celebrated letters while staying at
the **Château de Grignan**.

Built during the 15th and
16th centuries, the château is
one of the finest Renaissance
structures in this part of France.
Its interior contains a good
collection of Louis XII furniture and Aubusson tapestries.

From the château's terrace,
a panoramic view extends as
far as the Vivarais mountains
in the Ardèche. Directly below
the terrace, the **Eglise de St-
Saveur** was built in the 1530s,
and contains the tomb of
Madame de Sévigné, who died
here in 1696 at the age of 69.

♣ Château de Grignan
Tel 04 75 91 83 50. ⬜ Apr–Oct:
daily; Nov–Mar: Wed–Mon.
⬤ 1 Jan, 25 Dec. 🎫 📷 obligatory

Nyons ®

Drôme. 🏠 7,000. 🚌 ℹ️ pl de la
Libération (04 75 26 10 35). 🏪 Thu.
www.paysdenyons.com

Nyons is synonymous with
olives in France, since the
region is a major centre of
olive production. All manner of
olive products can be bought
here at the colourful Thursday
morning market, from soap to
tapenade, the olive paste so
popular in the south.

The **Quartier des Forts** is
Nyons' oldest quarter, a warren
of narrow streets and stepped
alleyways, the most rewarding
of which is the covered rue
des Grands Forts. Spanning the
river Aygues is a graceful 13th-
century bridge; on its town side
are several old mills turned
into shops where you can see
the enormous presses once
used to extract olive oil. The
Musée de l'Olivier further
explains the cultivation of the
olive tree and the myriad local
uses found for its fruit.

There is a fine view of the
area from the belvedere overlooking the town. Sheltered as
it is by mountains, Nyons enjoys an almost exotic climate,
with all the trees and plants of
the Riviera to be found here.

🏛 Musée de l'Olivier
Av des Tilleuls. **Tel** 04 75 26 12
12. ⬜ daily. 🎫 📷 ♿

Environs
From Nyons, the D94 leads
west to **Suze-la-Rousse**, a
pleasant wine-producing village which, during the Middle
Ages, was the most important
town in the area. Today, it is
best known for its "university
of wine", one of the most respected centres of oenology in

The hilltop town of Grignan and its Renaissance château

Olive groves just outside Nyons

the world. It is housed in the 14th-century **Château de Suze-la-Rousse**, the hunting lodge of the princes of Orange. The interior courtyard is a masterpiece of Renaissance architecture and some rooms preserve original paint and stuccowork.

♠ Château de Suze-la-Rousse
Tel 04 75 04 81 44. ◯ Apr–Oct: daily; Nov–Mar: Wed–Mon. ● 1 Jan, 25 Dec. 🦽 🖼 🗖

Playing *boules* in Nyons

Briançon **16**

Hautes Alpes. 🏙 12,000. 🚉 🚌
🛈 1 pl du Temple. (04 92 21 08 50).
🛒 Wed. 🎵 *Classical Music (Aug), Crafts (Jul)*. **www**.briancon.com

Briançon – the highest town in Europe at 1,320 m (4,330 ft) – has been an important stronghold since pre-Roman times, guarding as it does the road to the Col de Montgen-

èvre, one of the oldest and most important passes into Italy. At the beginning of the 18th century, the town was fortified with ramparts and gates – still splendidly intact – by Louis XIV's military architect, Vauban. If driving, park at the Champs de Mars, and enter the pedestrianized Old Town via the **Porte de Pignerol**. This leads to the **grande rue**, a steep, narrow street with a stream running down the middle, bordered by lovely period houses. The nearby **Eglise de Notre-Dame** dates from 1718, and was also built by Vauban with an eye to defence. To visit Vauban's **citadel**, stop by the tourist office, which organizes guided tours.

Briançon is a major sports centre, with skiing in winter; rafting, cycling and parapente in summer (*see pp660–61*).

Environs
Just west of Briançon, the **Parc National des Ecrins** is the largest of the French national parks, offering lofty peaks and glaciers, and a magnificent variety of Alpine flowers.

The **Parc Régional du Queyras** is reached from Briançon over the rugged Col de l'Izoard. A wall of 3,000-m (9,850-ft) peaks separates this wild and beautiful national park from neighbouring Italy.

Le Bourg d'Oisans **17**

Isère. 🏙 3,000. 🚌 to Grenoble.
🚌 to Le Bourg d'Oisans. 🛈 quai
Girard (04 76 80 03 25). 🛒 Sat.

Le Bourg d'Oisans is an ideal base from which to explore the Romanche valley. The area provides numerous opportunities for outdoor sports such as cycling, rock-climbing and skiing, in the nearby resort of **L'Alpe d'Huez**.

Silver and other minerals have been mined here since the Middle Ages, and today the town has a scientific reputation as a centre for geology and mineralogy. Its **Musée des Minéraux et de la Faune des Alpes** is renowned for its collection of crystals and precious stones.

🏛 Musée des Minéraux et de la Faune des Alpes
Pl de l'Eglise. *Tel* 04 76 80 27 54.
◯ 2–6pm daily (Jul–Aug: 11am–7pm). ● Nov, 25 Dec, 1 Jan. 🦽

LIFE ON HIGH
The Alpine ibex is one of the rarest inhabitants of the French Alps, living high above the tree line for all but the coldest part of the year. Until the creation of the Parc National de la Vanoise (*see p323*), this sure-footed climber had become almost extinct in France, but after rigorous conservation there are now over 500. Both males and females have horns; in the oldest males they can be almost 1 m (3 ft) long.

An ibex in the Parc National de la Vanoise

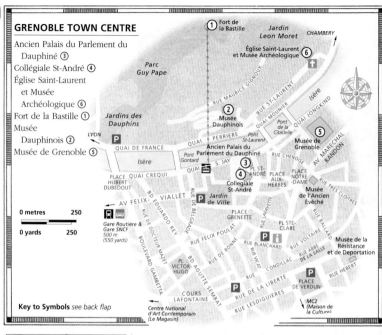

GRENOBLE TOWN CENTRE

Ancien Palais du Parlement du
Dauphiné ③
Collégiale St-André ④
Église Saint-Laurent
et Musée
Archéologique ⑥
Fort de la Bastille ①
Musée
Dauphinois ②
Musée de Grenoble ⑤

0 metres   250

0 yards   250

Key to Symbols see back flap

Grenoble's imposing former
town hall

Grenoble ⑱

Isère. 🏛 165,000. 🚆 🚌 ✈
ℹ 14 rue de la République
(04 76 42 41 41). 🗓 Tue–Sun.
www.grenoble-isere.info

Ancient capital of the
Dauphiné region and site of
the 1968 Winter Olympics,
Grenoble is a thriving city,
home to the science-oriented
University of Grenoble, and a
centre of chemical and electronics industries and nuclear
research. It is attractively situated at the confluence of the
Drac and Isère rivers, with the
Vercors and Chartreuse
massifs to the west and north.

A cable car starting at quai
Stéphane-Jay whisks you up
to the 19th-century **Fort de**
la Bastille, where you are
rewarded with superb views of
the city and surrounding mountains. From here, paths lead
down through the Parc Guy
Pape and Jardin des Dauphins
to the **Musée Dauphinois**, a
regional museum in a 17th-
century convent devoted to
local history, arts and crafts.
Nearby, **Église Saint-Laurent et**
Musée Archéologique exhibits
decorative and religious art as
well as Gallo-Roman and
medieval artifacts.

On the left bank of the Isère,
the focus of life is the pedestrian area around the lively
place Grenette. Nearby, the
place St-André is the heart of
the medieval city, overlooked
by Grenoble's oldest buildings
including the 13th-century
Collégiale St-André and the
16th-century **Ancien Palais du**
Parlement du Dauphiné.

The **Musée de Grenoble**
exhibits art from every period,
including works by Chagall,
Picasso and Matisse. The
Musée de l'Ancien Evêché
recounts the history of Isère,
and includes a visit to the 4th-
century baptistry. On rue
Hébert, the **Musée de la Résis-**
tance et de la Déportation has
documents relating to the
French Resistance. Temporary
displays of contemporary art
can be seen at **Le Magasin**
(Centre National d'Art
Contemporain), a renovated
warehouse on the cours
Berriat. In the Quartier Mal-
herbe, **MC2** (Maison de la
Culture) hosts everything from
concerts and dance to theatre.

🏛 **Musée Dauphinois**
30 rue Maurice Gignoux. **Tel** 04 76
85 19 01. 🗓 Wed–Mon. ⬤ 1 Jan,
1 May, 25 Dec. ♿

🏛 **Église Saint-Laurent et**
Musée Archéologique
Pl St-Laurent. **Tel** 04 76 44 78 68.
🗓 Tue–Sun.

Grenoble's gondola cable car

For hotels and restaurants in this region see pp577–80 and pp632–4

🏛 **Musée de Grenoble**
5 pl de Lavalette. **Tel** 04 76 63 44
44. ◯ Wed–Mon. ● 1 Jan, 1 May,
25 Dec. 🖼 ♿ 🗐 🗂 🗓

🏛 **Musée de l'Ancien Evêché**
2 rue Très Cloîtres. **Tel** 04 76 03 15
25. ◯ daily. ● Tue am. ♿

🏛 **Musée de la Résistance et
de la Déportation**
14 rue Hébert. **Tel** 04 76 42 38 53.
◯ daily. ● 1 Jan, 1 May, 25
Dec. 🖼 ♿

🏛 **Le Magasin (CNAC)**
155 cours Berriat. **Tel** 04 76 21 95
84. ◯ Tue–Sun pms only (during
exhibs). ♿

🏛 **MC2**
4 rue Paul Claudel. **Tel** 04 76 00 79
79. ◯ varies – phone to check. 🖼
♿ www.mc2grenoble.fr

The Vercors ⑲

Isère & Drôme. ✈ Grenoble. 🚆
Romans-sur-Isère, St-Marcellin, Grenoble. 🚌 Pont-en-Royans, Romans-
sur-Isère. 🛈 Pont-en-Royans (04 76
36 09 10). www.parc-du-vercors.fr

To the south and west of
Grenoble, the Vercors is one
of the most magnificent
regional parks in France – a
wilderness of pine forests,
mountains, waterfalls, caves
and deep, narrow gorges.
The D531 out of Grenoble
passes through **Villard-de-
Lans** – a good base for excursions – and continues west to
the dark **Gorges de la
Bournes**. About 8 km (5 miles)
further west, the hamlet of
Pont-en-Royans is sited on a
limestone gorge, its stone
houses built into the rocks
overlooking the river Bourne.
South of Pont-en-Royans
along the D76, the **Route de
Combe-Laval** snakes along a
sheer cliff above the roaring
river. The **Grands Goulets**, 6.5
km (4 miles) to the east, is a
spectacularly deep, narrow
gorge overlooked by sheer
cliffs that virtually shut out
the sky above. The best-
known mountain in the park
is the **Mont Aiguille**, a soaring
outcrop of 2,086 m (6,844 ft).
The Vercors was a key base
for the French Resistance
during World War II. In July
1944 the Germans launched
an aerial attack on the region,
flattening several of its villages.
There are Resistance museums
at Vassieux and Grenoble.

Cows grazing in the Chartreuse

The Chartreuse ⑳

Isère & Savoie. ✈ Grenoble,
Chambéry. 🚆 Grenoble, Voiron.
🚌 St-Pierre-de-Chartreuse. 🛈 St-
Pierre-de-Chartreuse (04 76 88 62 08).

From Grenoble, the D512
leads north towards
Chambéry into the Chartreuse,
a majestic region of mountains
and forests where hydroelec-
tricity was invented in the late
19th century. The **Monastère
de la Grande Chartreuse** is
the main local landmark, situated just west of St-Pierre-de-
Chartreuse off the D520-B.

Founded by St Bruno in
1084, the monastery owes its
fame to the sticky green and
yellow Chartreuse liqueurs first
produced by the monks in
1605. The recipe, based on
a secret herbal elixir of 130
ingredients, is now produced
in the nearby town of Voiron.

The monastery itself is
inhabited by about 40 monks
who live in silence and seclusion. It is not open to visitors,
but there is a museum at the
entrance, the **Musée de la
Correrie**, which faithfully
depicts the daily routine of
the Carthusian monks.

🏛 **Musée de la Correrie**
St-Pierre-de-Chartreuse. **Tel** 04 76
88 60 45. ◯ Apr–Oct: daily. 🖼

A farm in the pine-clad mountains of the Chartreuse

Chambéry ㉑

Savoie. 👥 61,000. 🚆 🚌 🚏
ℹ️ 24 bd de la Colonne (04 79 33 42
47). 🛒 Tue, Sat. **www**.chambery-
tourisme.com

Once the capital of Savoy,
this dignified city has aristocratic airs and a distinctly
Italianate feel. Its best-loved
monument is the splendidly
extravagant **Fontaine des
Eléphants** on rue de Boigne.
It was erected in 1838 to
honour the Comte de Boigne,
a native son who left to his
home town some of the
fortune he amassed in India.

The **Château des Ducs de
Savoie**, at the opposite end of
rue de Boigne, was built in the
14th century and is now mostly
occupied by the Préfecture.
Only parts of the building can
be visited, such as the late
Gothic Ste-Chapelle.

On the southeast edge of
town is the 17th-century
country house, **Les
Charmettes**, where
the philosopher
Rousseau lived with
his mistress Madame
de Warens. It is
worth a visit for its
gardens and museum
of memorabilia.

♣ **Les Charmettes**
892 chemin des
Charmettes. **Tel** 04 79 33
39 44. ⬜ Wed–Mon.
⬤ public hols. 🔊

The Lac du Bourget at Aix-les-Bains

Aix-les-Bains ㉒

Savoie. 👥 26,000. 🚆 🚌
ℹ️ pl Maurice Mollard (04 79 88 68
00). 🛒 Wed & Sat am. 🎵 Rock
Music (Jul).

The great Romantic poet
Lamartine rhapsodized over
the beauty of Lac du Bourget,
site of the gracious spa
town of Aix-les-Bains.
The heart of the town
is the 19th-century
Thermes Nationaux,
thermal baths which
were first enjoyed by
the Romans over 2,000
years ago – in the
basement the remains
of the original Roman
baths can still be
seen. Today, this huge
establishment receives
more *curistes* than any

Roman statue in
the Temple of Diana

other spa in France. Opposite
the baths, the 2nd-century AD
Temple of Diana contains a
collection of Gallo-Roman artifacts. The nearby **Musée Faure**
has some stunning Impressionist paintings by Degas and
Sisley, Rodin sculptures and
Lamartine memorabilia.

♨ **Thermes Nationaux**
Pl Maurice Mollard. **Tel** 04 79 35 38
50. ⬜ May–Oct: Tue & Sat;
Nov–Apr: Wed. 🎫 obligatory. ⬤
mid-Dec–Jan, 1 May, 14 Jul, 15
Aug. 📷 📷 **www**.thermaix.com

🏛 **Musée Faure**
Villa des Chimères, 10 b des Côtes.
Tel 04 79 61 06 57. ⬜ Wed–Mon
(mid-Nov–Feb: Wed–Sun). ⬤ 18
Dec–2 Jan, public hols. 📷 ♿

Environs
Boats leave from Aix's Grand
Port and sail across Lac du
Bourget to the **Abbaye
d'Hautecombe**, a Benedictine
abbey containing the mausoleum of the Savoyard dynasty.

The small town of **Le
Revard**, just east of Aix on the
D913, has spectacular views
of the lake and Mont Blanc.

Annecy ㉓

Haute Savoie. 👥 51,000. ✈️ 🚌
🚆 ℹ️ 1 rue Jean Jaurès (04 50 45
00 33). 🛒 Tue, Fri–Sun. **www**.lac-
annecy.com 🎆 Fête du Lac (firework
display; 1st Sat Aug).

Annecy is one of the most
charming towns in the Alps,
set at the northern tip of Lac

Annecy's 12th-century Palais de l'Isle, with the Thiou canal in the foreground

For hotels and restaurants in this region see pp577–80 and pp632–4

Cycling along the shores of Lac Léman (Lake Geneva)

d'Annecy and surrounded by snow-capped mountains. Its small medieval quarter is laced with canals, flower-covered bridges and arcaded streets. Strolling around is the main attraction here, though there are a couple of specific sights worth having a look at more closely: the formidable **Palais de l'Isle**, a 12th-century prison in the middle of the Thiou canal; and the turreted **Château d'Annecy**, set high on a hill above the town with impressive views of Vieil Annecy and the crystal-clear lake beyond.

The best spot for swimming and watersports is at the eastern end of the avenue d'Albigny near the Imperial Palace hotel, while boat trips leave from quai Napoléon III.

Environs

One of the best ways to enjoy the area's spectacular scenery is to take a boat from Annecy to **Talloires**, a tiny lakeside village celebrated for its hotels and restaurants. Facing Talloires across the lake is the 15th-century **Château de Duingt** (not open to visitors).

On the west bank of the lake, the Semnoz mountain and its summit, the **Crêt de Châtillon**, offer superb views of Mont Blanc and the Alps (see pp322–3).

Lac Léman ㉔

Haute Savoie & Switzerland. ✈ Geneva. 🚇 🚌 Geneva, Thonon-les-Bains, Évian-les-Bains. 🛈 Thonon-les-Bains (04 50 71 55 55).

The stirring scenery and gentle climate of the French shore of Lake Geneva (Lac Léman to the French) has made it a popular and fashionable resort area since the first spa buildings were erected at Évian-les-Bains in 1839.

Yvoire is a fine place to begin a visit to the area. This medieval walled fishing port is guarded by a massive 14th-century castle, and its tightly packed houses are bedecked with colourful flower boxes.

Further east along Lac Léman is **Thonon-les-Bains**, a prosperous, well-manicured little spa town perched on a cliff overlooking the lake. A funicular takes you down to Rives, the small harbour at the foot of the cliffs, where sailboats can be rented and excursion boats to the Swiss cities of Geneva and Lausanne call in. Just outside the town is the 15th-century **Château de Ripaille**, made famous by its one-time resident, Duke Amadeus VIII, who later became antipope (Felix V).

Though it has been modernized and acquired an international reputation for its eponymous spring water, **Évian-les-Bains** still exudes a polite *vie en rose* charm. The tree-lined lakefront promenade teems with leisurely strollers, while more energetic types can avail themselves of all kinds of sporting facilities including tennis, golf, riding, sailing and skiing in the winter. State-of-the-art spa treatments are available, and the exotic domed casino is busy at night, offering blackjack, roulette and baccarat among other games.

From Évian there are daily ferries across Lake Geneva to Lausanne in Switzerland, as well as coach excursions into the surrounding mountains.

Hôtel Royal in Évian-les-Bains (see p578)

SOUTHWEST FRANCE

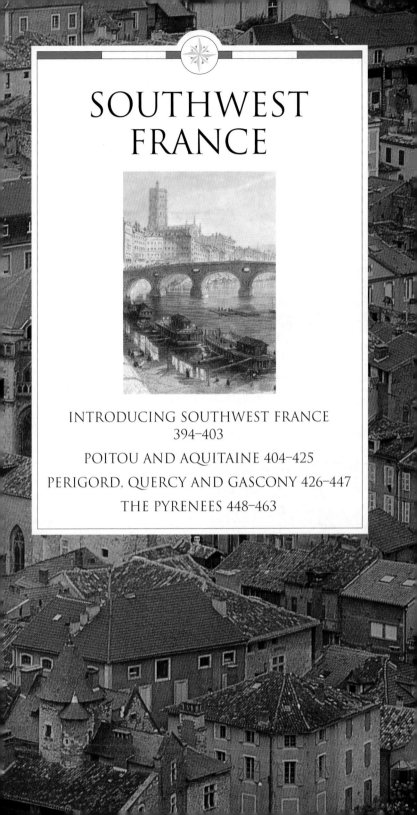

INTRODUCING SOUTHWEST FRANCE
394–403

POITOU AND AQUITAINE 404–425

PERIGORD, QUERCY AND GASCONY 426–447

THE PYRENEES 448–463

Introducing Southwest France

The southwest is farming France, a green and peaceful land nurturing crops from sunflowers to *foie gras*. Other key country products include Landes forest timber, Bordeaux wines and Cognac. Major modern industries, including aerospace, are focused on the two chief cities, Bordeaux and Toulouse. Visitors are mainly drawn to the wide Atlantic beaches, the ski slopes of the Pyrenees and the rural calm of the Dordogne. The major sights of this favoured region are shown here and include some of France's most celebrated Romanesque buildings.

La Rochelle

Roman Ruins, Saintes

La Rochelle's harbour *is today a haven for pleasure yachts as well as an important commercial port (see p416). Tour de la Chaîne and Tour St-Nicolas protect the entrance of the old port. The town's historic centre is filled with cobbled streets lined by merchants' houses.*

Grand Théâtre, Bo

Bordeaux *is a town of grand buildings and monuments, including its theatre. The Monument aux Girondins, with its magnificent bronze statues and fountains, stands at the 18th-century Esplanade des Quinconces (see pp420–22).*

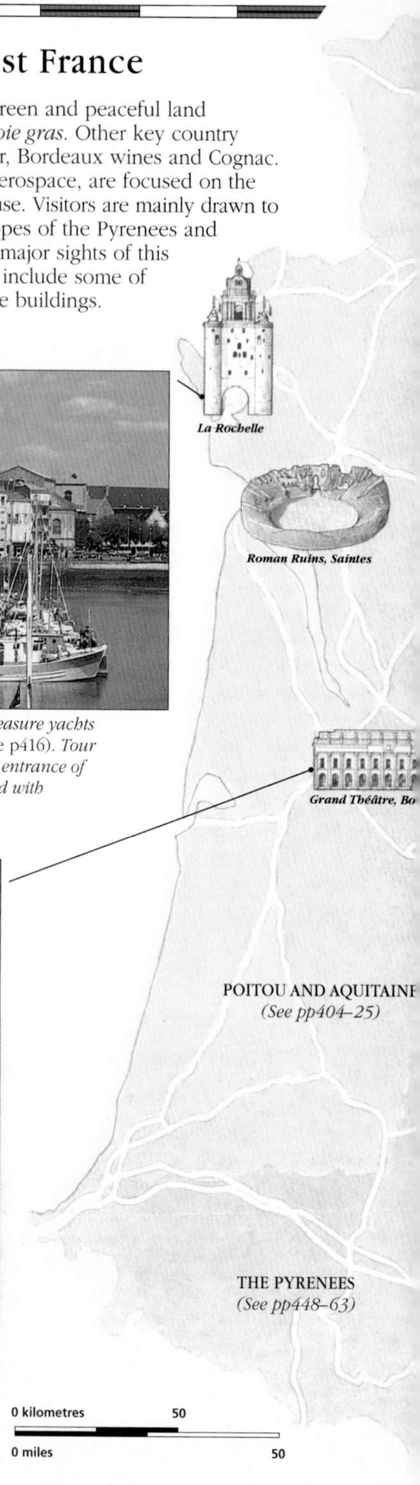

POITOU AND AQUITAINE
(See pp404–25)

THE PYRENEES
(See pp448–63)

| 0 kilometres | 50 |
| 0 miles | 50 |

*e-Dame-la-
de, Poitiers*

Notre-Dame-la-Grande *is the
queen among Poitiers' churches
(see pp412–13) It has fine
stained-glass windows and
a splendid Romanesque
façade, richly decorated
in the Poitevin style.*

**PERIGORD, QUERCY
AND GASCONY**
(See pp426–47)

Rocamadour *is both a place of
pilgrimage and a tourist sight, its
chapels and shrines clinging to
the edge of the rocky hillside
(see pp436–7). Among its many
venerated features is the statue
of the Black Virgin and Child.*

Lascaux

Rocamadour

Moissac

St-Sernin, Toulouse

Albi Cathedral

Moissac Abbey *is the pre-
eminent medieval monastery in
southwest France (see pp442–3).
Its tympanum, representing the
Apocalypse, and the cloister
capitals are outstanding examples
of Romanesque sculpture.*

Cirque de Gavarnie

The Flavours of Southwest France

"Great cooking and great wines make a paradise on earth," said Henri IV of his own region, Gascony. The southwest does indeed fulfil the requirements of the most demanding gourmet. The Atlantic coast supplies fine seafood; Bordeaux produces some of France's best wines to complement its rich cooking; geese and ducks provide the fat that is key to local cuisine; and regional produce includes delicacies such as *foie gras*, truffles and wild mushrooms. The Pyrenees offer beef and lamb grazed on mountain pastures, cheese and *charcuterie*, and the Basque country adds the spicy notes of red peppers and fine chocolate.

Espelette peppers

Walnuts, one of the southwest's most famous products

POITOU AND AQUITAINE

The coast is famous for its seafood, and is the most important oyster-producing region of France – the oysters of Marennes-Oleron are of especially high quality. The species of blue algae on which they feed give them a distinctive green colouring. Oysters are usually served simply with lemon or shallot

vinegar, but in Bordeaux they like to eat them with little sausages. Mussels are also raised here, and the sea yields a variety of fish. Eels, lamprey and sturgeon are caught in the Gironde estuary.

Poitou-Charentes is one of France's main goat-rearing areas, producing cheeses such as *chabichou de Poitou*, a small, soft, cylindrical cheese of distinct flavour.

PERIGORD, QUERCY AND GASCONY

High-quality ducks, geese and poultry form the basis of the cuisine of this region, and their fat is a key ingredient of many dishes from simple *pommes sarladaises* (potatoes cooked in goose fat) to *confit*, where entire duck legs are preserved in their own fat. The ultimate

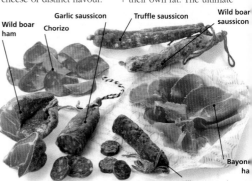
Garlic saussicon   Truffle saussicon   Wild boar saussicon
Wild boar ham   Chorizo
Bayonne ham
Bilberry saussicon
Selection of traditional southwestern *charcuterie*

REGIONAL DISHES AND SPECIALITIES

Duck is one of the essential ingredients of southwestern cooking, and is served in a variety of ways. The *magret* is the breast – the best of all coming from a duck that has been bred for *foie gras*. Usually served pink *(rose)*, it may be served with a variety of sauces but is most perfectly complemented by the smoky flavour of local cèpe mushrooms in season. Duck **Pink garlic**   *confit* is usually made with the legs, but gizzards are also preserved in this way. *Foie gras* is the most expensive (and controversial) product, resulting from the process of *gavage*, when the duck or goose is force-fed maize to enlarge and enrich its liver. *Foie gras* can be eaten freshly cooked, served with sauce or fruit, or preserved and served with toast or brioche, ideally accompanied by a sweet white wine such as Sauternes.

Omelette aux truffes *For this luxurious omelette the filling is local black truffles, with more sliced over the top.*

Fattened Toulouse geese, the source of *foie gras*

southwestern dish has to be *cassoulet*, a stew of duck or goose, sausages, pork and white beans topped with a crust of breadcrumbs; it arouses fierce competition among the dedicated chefs of the region.

Luxury ingredients enhance these basics: walnut oil is added to salads, and slivers of expensive truffles perfume sauces or omelettes. Wild mushrooms are eagerly sought in season, and are most delicious cooked simply with garlic, shallots and parsley. The region is one of the main producers of garlic, which appears studded into meat or served as whole baked heads. The finest fruits include *reines-claudes* (green-gages) and the celebrated plums of Agen, which are dried as prunes or added to dishes of rabbit or hare.

THE PYRENEES

From the mountains pastures come beef and lamb of high quality, including Barèges mutton, as well as river trout, and an array of excellent *charcuterie*. Strong cheeses

Fishermen opening oysters at a local maritime festival

of goat's or ewe's milk are sometimes served with jam made from the black cherries of Itxassou. One of the most popular dishes is *garbure*, a hearty stew of cabbage, bacon and confit of duck or goose.

Basque cuisine has its own distinct identity, with the red Espelette pepper adding a touch of spice to chorizo, *piperade* or chipirones (baby squid cooked in their own ink). Succulent Bayonne ham is made from pigs that forage for acorns and chestnuts. Bayonne was also home to the first chocolatiers in France, 17th-century Jewish refugees from the Inquisition, and the town still makes top-quality dark, bitter chocolate.

ON THE MENU

Cagouilles à la charentaise Snails with sausage meat, herbs and wine.

Entrecôte à la bordelaise Steak in sauce of red wine, shallots and bone marrow.

Farçi poitevin Cabbage stuffed with bacon, pork and sorrel.

Gasconnade Leg of lamb with garlic and anchovy.

Mouclade Mussels in curry sauce, from the spice port of La Rochelle.

Salade landaise Salad of *foie gras*, gizzards and *confit*.

Ttoro Basque mixed fish and shellfish stew with potatoes, tomatoes and onions.

Cassoulet *This is a stew of white beans cooked with a variety of sausages and cuts of meat, such as pork or duck.*

Piperade *Eggs are added to a stew of peppers, onions, tomatoes and garlic, with Bayonne ham laid on top.*

Croustade *Thin pastry is layered with melted butter, and apples, perfumed with Armagnac and vanilla.*

France's Wine Regions: Bordeaux

Barrel-making

Bordeaux is the world's largest fine wine region, and, for red wines, certainly the most familiar outside France. Following Henry II's marriage to Eleanor of Aquitaine, three centuries of courtly commerce with England ensured that claret was served at the finest foreign tables. In the 19th century, canny merchants capitalized on this fame and brought fantastic financial prosperity to the region, and with it, the famous 1855 Classification of the Médoc, a league table of châteaux that is still very much in force today.

LOCATOR MAP

⬜ Bordeaux wine region

Picking red Merlot grapes at Château Palmer

Cos d'Estournel, *like all the châteaux included in the 1855 league of crus classés ("classed growths"), proudly proclaims the fact on its label.*

Lac

WINE REGIONS

The great wine-producing areas of Bordeaux straddle two great rivers; the land between the rivers ("Entre-Deux-Mers") produces lesser, mainly white wines. The rivers, and the river port of Bordeaux itself, have been crucial to the trade in Bordeaux wines; some of the prettiest châteaux line the river banks, enabling easy transportation.

KEY FACTS ABOUT BORDEAUX WINES

Location and Climate
Climatic conditions may vary not only from one year to another, but also within the region itself. The soils tend to be gravelly in the Médoc and Graves, and clayey on the right bank.

Grape Varieties
The five main red grape varieties are **Cabernet Franc**, **Cabernet Sauvignon**, **Merlot, Petit Verdot** and **Malbec**. Cabernet Sauvignon is the dominant grape on the west side of the Gironde, Merlot to the east. Most Bordeaux reds are, however, a blend of grapes. **Sauvignon Blanc** and **Sémillon** are grown and often blended for both dry and sweet whites.

Good Producers
(reds) Latour, Margaux, Haut-Brion, Cos d'Estournel, Léoville Las Cases, Léoville Barton, Lascombes, Pichon Longueville, Pichon Lalande, Lynch-Bages, Palmer, Rausan-Ségla, Duhart Milon, d'Angludet, Leoville Poyferré, Branaire Ducru, Ducru Beaucaillou, Malescot St-Exupéry, Cantemerle, Phélan-Segur, Chasse-Spleen, Poujeaux, Domaine de Chevalier, Pape Clément, Cheval Blanc, Canon, Pavie, l'Angelus, Troplong Mondot, La Conseillante, Lafleur, Trotanoy.

Good Vintages
(reds) 2005, 2003, 2000, 1998, 1996.

Haut-Brion, *in the top division of Bordeaux's Classification, was and still is the single Graves château in this league of Médoc properties.*

Arcach

Cap
Ferret

Lac de
et de Sa

The famous legend *that guarantees château-bottling originated in Bordeaux, as a check to unscrupulous merchants.*

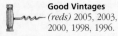

One of many wine-producing properties in the St-Emilion district

Entre-Deux-Mers, largely undistinguished, has some good producers.

St-Emilion *has its own crus classés league: Cheval Blanc shares top ranking.*

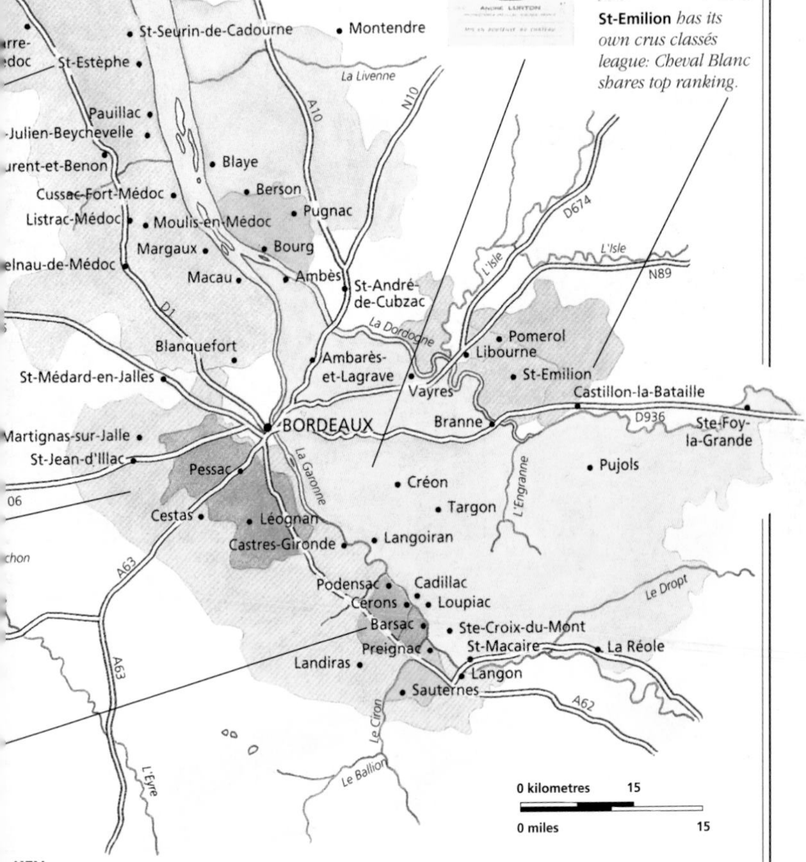

St-Christoly-Médoc

St-Seurin-de-Cadourne · Montendre

arre-
doc   St-Estèphe

La Livenne

Pauillac

-Julien-Beychevelle

urent-et-Benon   Blaye

Cussac-Fort-Médoc   Berson

Listrac-Médoc   Moulis-en-Médoc   Pugnac

Margaux   Bourg

elnau-de-Médoc   Macau   Ambès

St-André-
de-Cubzac

Blanquefort

St-Médard-en-Jalles   Ambarès-
et-Lagrave   Pomerol

Libourne

Vayres   St-Emilion

Martignas-sur-Jalle   Branne   Castillon-la-Bataille

St-Jean-d'Illac   Ste-Foy-
la-Grande

BORDEAUX

06   Pessac   Créon   Pujols

Cestas   Targon

chon   Léognan

Castres-Gironde   Langoiran

Podensac   Cadillac

Cérons   Loupiac

Barsac   Ste-Croix-du-Mont

Preignac   St-Macaire   La Réole

Landiras   Langon

Sauternes

Gironde

La Garonne

La Dordogne

L'Isle

L'Engranne

Le Dropt

Le Ciron

Le Baillon

L'Eyre

| 0 kilometres | 15 |
| 0 miles | 15 |

KEY

Médoc	Graves	Sauternes
Blaye	Pessac-Léognan	Libournais District
Bourg	Cérons	Pomerol
Entre-Deux-Mers	Barsac	St-Emilion

The Road to Compostela

Scallop symbol

Throughout the Middle Ages millions of Christians visited Santiago de Compostela in Spain to pay homage at the shrine of St James (Santiago). They travelled across France staying in monasteries or simple shelters and would return with a scallop shell, the symbol of St James, as a souvenir. Most pilgrims went in hope of redemption and were often on the road for years. In 1140, a monk called Picaud wrote one of the world's first travel guides about the pilgrimage. Today, travellers can follow the same routes, passing through ancient towns and villages with their magnificent shrines and churches.

Foreign pilgrims joined at ports such as St Malo.

The original cathedral *of Santiago de Compostela was built in 813 by Alfonso II over the tomb of St James. In 1075 construction started on the grandiose Romanesque church seen today which has, among other later additions, a resplendent 17th–18th-century Baroque façade.*

The routes converged on Santiago de Compostela.

Most pilgrims crossed the Pyrenees at Roncesvalles.

James the Greater, *an apostle, came to Spain to spread the Gospel, according to legend. On his return to Judaea, he was martyred by Herod. His remains were taken to Spain by boat and lay hidden for 800 years.*

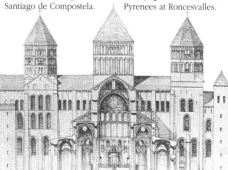

The powerful Cluny monastery *in Burgundy (see pp48–9), and its affiliated monasteries, played an important role in promoting the pilgrimage. They built shelters and set up churches and shrines housing precious relics, to encourage the pilgrims on their way.*

THE PILGRIMS' WAY

Paris, Vézelay *(see pp336–7)*, Le Puy *(see p364)* and Arles are the rallying points for the four "official" routes across France. They cross the Pyrenees at Roncesvalles and Somport, and merge at Puente la Reina to form one route, culminating at the shrine on the Galician coast.

WHAT TO SEE TODAY

Huge Romanesque churches, including Ste-Madeleine at Vézelay *(see p336)*, Ste-Foy at Conques *(pp368–9)* and St-Sernin at Toulouse *(p447)*, along with many small chapels, were built to accommodate large numbers of pilgrims.

Basilique Ste-Madeleine, Vézelay

Conques purloined relics to boost its prestige.

Le Puy was a main rallying point for pilgrims.

The first recorded pilgrim *was the bishop of Le Puy in 951. But pilgrims have probably been coming to Santiago since 814, soon after the saint's tomb was found.*

The reliquary *of Ste-Foy, at Conques, is in one of many elaborate shrines on the way which drew crowds of pilgrims. A saint's relics were thought to have miraculous powers.*

The name *Santiago de Compostela is believed to originate from the Latin* Campus stellae *(field of stars). Legend has it that strange stars were seen hovering over a field in 814 and on 25 July, now the feast of Santiago, the saint's remains were found. Subsequent evidence showed that St James's remains were never in Compostela after all.*

Caves of the Southwest

Southwest France is well-known for its spectacular rock formations, created by the slow accumulation of dissolved mineral deposits. Caves and rock shelters exist throughout limestone country in France. But in the foothills of the Pyrenees and the Dordogne they also have something else to offer the visitor: a collection of extraordinary rock paintings, some dating back to the last Ice Age. These art forms were created when prehistoric peoples evolved and began engraving, painting and carving. This unique artistic tradition lasted for more than 25,000 years, reaching its zenith around 17,000 years ago. Some very fine examples of cave painting are still visible today.

Ancient cave paintings at Lascaux

CAVES OF THE DORDOGNE

There are many different cave systems to visit in or near the Dordogne valley. The entire Périgord region contains one of the densest concentrations of prehistoric sites anywhere in the world. In an uncertain climate, its rivers flanked by caves and rock shelters proved very attractive to prehistoric man.

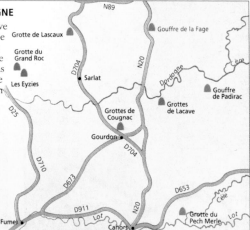

0 kilometres   20
0 miles   20

CAVE FORMATION

Limestone is laid down in layers containing fissures that allow water to penetrate beneath the surface. Over thousands of years, the water slowly dissolves the rock, first forming potholes and then larger caverns. Stalactites develop where water drips from the cave roof; stalagmites grow upwards from the floor.

Grotte du Grand Roc in the Vézère valley, Périgord

Fissure   Limestone layers

Impermeable rock

1 Water percolates through fissures, slowly dissolving the surrounding rock.

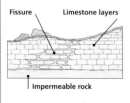

Pothole

Fallen rocks   Chamber

2 The water produces potholes and loosens surrounding rocks, which gradually fall away.

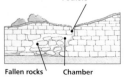

Cavern formed by rockfall

Stalactites   Stalagmites

3 Dripping water containing dissolved limestone forms stalactites and stalagmites.

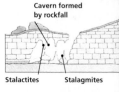

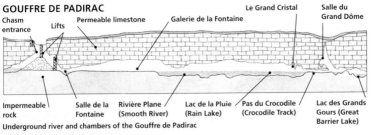

GOUFFRE DE PADIRAC

Chasm entrance — Lifts — Permeable limestone — Galerie de la Fontaine — Le Grand Cristal — Salle du Grand Dôme

Impermeable rock — Salle de la Fontaine — Rivière Plane (Smooth River) — Lac de la Pluie (Rain Lake) — Pas du Crocodile (Crocodile Track) — Lac des Grands Gours (Great Barrier Lake)

Underground river and chambers of the Gouffre de Padirac

Prehistoric caves at Les Eyzies

THE STORY OF CAVE ART

The first prehistoric cave paintings in Europe were discovered in northwest Spain in 1879. Since then, over 200 decorated caves and rock shelters have been found in Spain and France, mainly in the Dordogne region. A wide range of clues, from stone lamps to miraculously preserved footprints, has helped prehistorians to work out the techniques the cave artists used. But their motives are still not clear. Nearly all the paintings are of animals, with few humans, and many of them are in inaccessible underground chambers. The paintings undoubtedly had a symbolic or magical significance; a new theory suggests they were the work of shamans.

VISITING THE CAVES

Cougnac contains chasms ("gouffres") and galleries and its prehistoric paintings include human figures. Around **Les Eyzies** (*see pp434–5*) are the major caves of **La Mouthe**, **Les Combarelles**, and **Font de Gaume**, which have some beautiful prehistoric paintings, drawings and engravings, as does **Rouffignac** in its extensive network of caves. **Grand Roc** has chambers containing a profusion of stalactites and stalagmites. For more unusual rock formations, the chasm at **La Fage**, northeast of Les Eyzies, leads to chambers and galleries with some magnificent examples.

On the south bank of the Dordogne, an underground river and lake with extraordinary rock formations can be seen at **Lacave**. The gigantic chasm and caverns at **Padirac** (*p438*) are even more spectacular. The caves at **Lascaux** with the finest prehistoric paintings have been closed but the exceptional replica at **Lascaux II** (*p434*) is well worth seeing. Further south, **Pech-Merle's** caverns (*p438*) have impressive rock formations.

The techniques used by Ice Age artists, who worked by lamplight, included cutting outlines into soft rock, using natural contours as part of the design. Black lines and shading were produced by charcoal, while colour washes were applied with mineral pigments such as kaolin and haematite. Hand silhouettes were made by sucking up diluted pigment and blowing it through a plant stem to form a fine spray. When the hand was removed from the rock, its eerie shape was left behind.

Decorated stone lamp discovered in Lascaux cave

Kaolin

Charcoal

Haematite

The Great Bull from the Hall of Bulls frieze at Lascaux

POITOU AND AQUITAINE

DEUX-SÈVRES · VIENNE · CHARENTE-MARITIME
CHARENTE · GIRONDE · LANDES

This vast area of southwest France spans a quarter of the country's windswept Atlantic coastline, a great expanse of fine sandy beaches. The region stretches from the marshes of the Marais Poitevin to the great pine forests of the Landes. Central to it is the celebrated wine region of Bordeaux and its great châteaux.

The turbulent history of Poitou and Aquitaine, fought over for centuries, has left a rich architectural and cultural heritage. The great arch and amphitheatre at Saintes bear witness to Roman influence in the area. In the Middle Ages, the pilgrimage route to Santiago de Compostela *(see pp400–1)* created an impressive legacy of Romanesque churches, such as those at Poitiers and Parthenay, as well as tiny chapels and glowing frescoes. The Hundred Years' War *(see pp52–3)* caused great upheaval but also resulted in the construction of mighty defence keeps by the English Plantagenet kings. As a result of the Wars of Religion *(see pp54–5)*, many towns, churches and châteaux were destroyed and had to be rebuilt.

Present-day Poitiers is a big, thriving commercial centre. To the west are the historic ports of La Rochelle and Rochefort. Further south, the wine-producing district of Bordeaux combines with Cognac, famous for its brandy, to supply an important part of the region's income. The city of Bordeaux is as prosperous today as in Roman times, combining a lively cultural scene with elegant 18th-century architecture. Its wines complement the region's cuisine: lampreys, mussels and oysters from the coast; and salty lamb and goat's cheeses from the inland pastures.

Shuttered houses in St-Martin-de-Ré, on Ile de Ré, off the coast of La Rochelle

◁ The seaside resort of Arcachon by the sandy dunes of the Bassin d'Arcachon

Exploring Poitou and Aquitaine

Blessed with a seemingly endless Atlantic coastline, abundant navigable waterways, excellent ports and the finest wine and brandy in the world, the region is ideal for a relaxing holiday. Today most summer visitors head straight for the beaches with their thundering waves, but there is also a lush countryside inland with a lot to offer. Fine medieval architecture can be seen along the pilgrim's route to Santiago de Compostela *(see pp400–1)*, and châteaux of all shapes and sizes characterize the wine districts around Bordeaux. The only modern city of major importance in the region, Bordeaux is worth a visit for its elegant 18th-century architecture as well as for its rich cultural life. The vast man-made forest of Les Landes also adds to this greatly undervalued corner of France.

Beachlife in Bassin d'Arcachon on the Côte d'Argent

GETTING AROUND

The region's main motorway is the A10 connecting Paris and Poitiers with Bordeaux and points east, such as Toulouse, west to Rochefort and south to Bayonne and Spain. This road carries most of the area's heavy traffic, relieving the excellent smaller roads. Bordeaux can be reached by TGV direct from Lille (Eurostar interchange), and the Paris–Poitiers–Angoulême–Bordeaux TGV line has halved rail travel times (Paris–Bordeaux 3¼ hr). Bordeaux, Poitiers and La Rochelle have international airports (direct flights to UK), and Bordeaux also has coach services to most European capitals. Poitiers has buses to nearby towns.

For additional map symbols *see back flap*

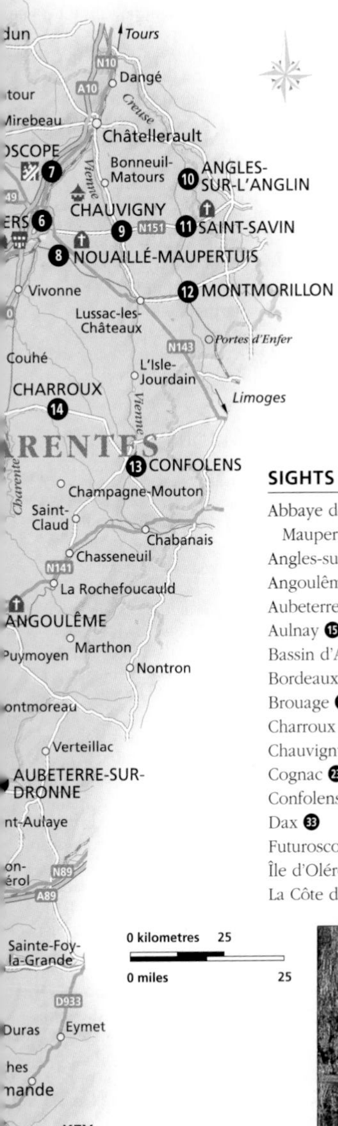

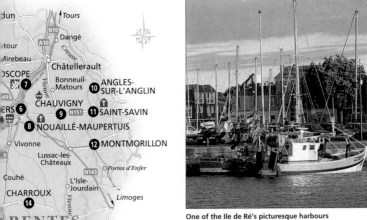

One of the Ile de Ré's picturesque harbours

dun · Tours
tour · Dangé
Mirebeau
OSCOPE **7** · Châtellerault
· Bonneuil-Matours **10** · ANGLES-SUR-L'ANGLIN
ERS **6** · CHAUVIGNY **9** · SAINT-SAVIN **11**
8 NOUAILLÉ-MAUPERTUIS
Vivonne · **12** MONTMORILLON
Lussac-les-Châteaux
Portes d'Enfer
Couhé · L'Isle-Jourdain · Limoges
CHARROUX **14**
ARENTES
13 CONFOLENS
Champagne-Mouton
Saint-Claud · Chabanais
Chasseneuil
La Rochefoucauld
ANGOULÊME
Puymoyen · Marthon · Nontron
ontmoreau · Verteillac
AUBETERRE-SUR-DRONNE
nt-Aulaye
on-érol
Sainte-Foy-la-Grande
Duras · Eymet
hes
mande

SIGHTS AT A GLANCE

0 kilometres 25

0 miles 25

KEY

 Motorway

Major road

Secondary road

Minor road

Scenic route

Main railway

Minor railway

Regional border

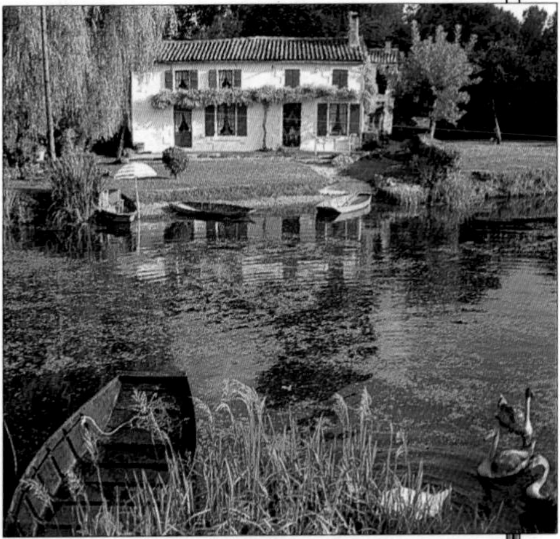

Boats moored at Coulon in the Marais Poitevin

Rose window of St-Médard, Thouars

Thouars ❶

Deux-Sèvres. 🏠 12,000. 🚘 🚌
🛈 3 bis bd Pierre Curie (05 49 66 17
65). 🛍 Tue & Fri. **www**.pays-
thouarsais.com

Thouars, on a rocky outcrop
surrounded by the river
Thouet, is on the border between Anjou and Poitou. There
are as many roofs of northern
slate as of southern red tiles.

In the centre lies **Eglise St-
Médard**. Its Romanesque
façade is a perfect example of
the Poitevin style that is typical
of the region *(see p412)*, although a splendid Gothic rose
window has been added. Lined
with half-timbered medieval
houses, the rue du Château
leads up to the 17th-century
château which dominates the
town. It now houses a *lycée*
and is open to the public
during the summer.

East of Thouars lies the
moated **Château d'Oiron**,
which now hosts contemporary
art exhibitions. A masterpiece
of Renaissance architecture, it
was largely built from 1518–49.

🏰 **Château d'Oiron**
79100 Oiron. **Tel** 05 49 96 51 25.
⬜ daily. ⬛ some public hols. 🎫

Parthenay ❷

Deux-Sèvres. 🏠 10,500. 🚘 🚌
🛈 8 rue de la Vau-St-Jacques (05 49
64 24 24). 🛍 Wed. **www**.cc-
parthenay.fr

Parthenay is a classic, sleepy
provincial town, except on
Wednesday mornings, when
France's second biggest livestock market is held here. In
the Middle Ages, the town was
an important halt on the route
to Santiago de Compostela
(see pp400–1) and it is easy to
imagine the processions of
pilgrims in the medieval
quarter. Steep and cobbled,
rue de la Vau-St-Jacques
winds up to the 13th-century
ramparts, leading on from the
fortified Porte St-Jacques
which guards a 13th-century
bridge over the river Thouet.

West of Parthenay, the 12th-
century church of **St-Pierre de
Parthenay-le-Vieux** has a
splendid Poitevin façade,
featuring Samson and the Lion
and a cavalier with a falcon.

Marais Poitevin ❸

Charente-Maritime, Deux-Sèvres,
Vendée. ✈ La Rochelle. 🚘 Niort.
🚌 Coulon, Arçais, Marans. 🛈 2 rue
de l'Eglise, Coulon (05 49 35 15 20).
www.parc-marais-poitevin.fr

The Poitevin marshes, which
have been slowly drained
with canals, dykes and sluices
for a thousand years, cover
about 80,000 hectares (197,000
acres) between Niort and the
sea. The area is now a regional
park, divided into two parts.
To the north and south of the
Sèvre estuary is the Marais
Désséché (dry marsh), where
cereal and other crops are
grown. The huge swathe of
the Marais Mouillé (wet marsh)
is upstream towards Niort.

The wet marshes, known
as the Venise Verte (Green
Venice), are the most interesting. They are crisscrossed by
a labyrinth of weed-choked
canals, adorned by waterlilies,
and irises, shaded by poplars
and beeches, and support a
rich variety of birds and other
wildlife. The *maraîchins* who
live here stoutly maintain that
much of the huge, water-
logged forest is unexplored.
The picturesque whitewashed
villages hereabouts are all
built on higher ground, and
the customary means of transport is a flat-bottomed boat,
known as a *platte*.

Coulon, St-Hilaire-la-Palud,
La Garette and Arçais, as well
as Damvix and Maillezais in
the Vendée, are all convenient
starting points for boat trips
around the marshes. Boats

Medieval houses lining the cobbled rue de la Vau-St-Jacques in Parthenay

Flat-bottomed boats moored at Coulon in the Marais Poitevin

can be rented with or without a guide. Make sure you bring plenty of insect repellent.

Coulon is the largest and best equipped village, and a popular base for visiting the area. In the aquarium here lurks the ugliest freshwater fish in captivity in France, the *silure* or sheat-fish. From here there are also river cruises departing along the main channel of the Sèvre.

The Plantagenet donjon in Niort, now housing a local museum

Niort **4**

Deux-Sèvres. 59,000.
16 rue du Petit St-Jean (05 49 24 18 79). Thu & Sat.
www.niortourisme.com

Once a medieval port by the green waters of the Sèvre, Niort is now a prosperous industrial town specializing in machine tools, electronics, chemicals and insurance.

Its closeness to the marshes is evident in local specialities – eels, snails and angelica. This herb has been cultivated in the wetlands for centuries and is used for anything from liqueur to ice cream.

The town's immediate attraction is the huge 12th-century donjon overlooking the Vieux Pont. Built by Henry II and Richard the Lion-Heart, it played an important role during the Hundred Years' War and was later used as a prison. One prisoner was the father of Madame de Maintenon *(see p56)*, who

spent her childhood in Niort. The donjon is now a museum of local arts and crafts, and archaeology. The **Musée d'Agesci** in avenue de Limoges exhibits ceramics, sculpture and paintings from the 16th to 20th centuries.

Environs
Halfway to Poitiers is the small town of **St-Maixent-L'Ecole**. A marvel of light and space, its abbey church is a Flamboyant Gothic reconstruction by François Le Duc (1670) of a building destroyed during the Wars of Religion. Further west, the **Tumulus de Bougon** consists of five tumuli (burial mounds), the oldest dating from 4500 BC.

Melle **5**

Deux-Sèvres. 4,400. rue E Traver (05 49 29 15 10). Fri.

A Roman silver mine was the origin of Melle, which in the 9th century had the only mint in Aquitaine. Later its fame derived from the *baudet du Poitou*, an especially sturdy mule bred in the area. Now Melle is better known for its churches, of which the finest is **St-Hilaire**. Built in a delightful riverside setting, it has a 12th-century Poitevin façade with an equestrian statue of the Emperor Constantine above the north door.

Environs
To the northwest, the abbey in **Celles-sur-Belle** has a great Moorish doorway which contrasts strongly with the rest of the church, a 17th-century restoration in Gothic style.

Equestrian statue of Constantine on the façade of St-Hilaire, Melle

Canal in the Venise Verte region of the Marais Poitevin ▷

Poitiers

Three of the greatest battles in French history were fought around Poitiers, the most famous in 732 when Charles Martel halted the Arab invasion. After two periods of English rule *(see p51)* the town thrived during the reign of Jean de Berry (1369–1416), the great sponsor of the arts. Its university, founded in 1431, made Poitiers a major intellectual centre and saw Rabelais among its students. The Wars of Religion left Poitiers in chaos and not until the late 19th century did any major development take place. Today, however, the town is a modern and dynamic regional capital with a rich architectural heritage in its historic centre.

Fresco in Eglise
St-Hilaire-le-Grand

🔒 Notre-Dame-la-Grande

Despite its name, Notre-Dame-la-Grande is not a large church. One of Poitiers' great pilgrim churches, it is most celebrated as a masterpiece of lively 12th-century Poitevin sculpture, notably its richly detailed façade. In the choir is a Roman-esque fresco of Christ and the Virgin. Most of the chapels were added in the Renaissance.

🏛 Palais de Justice

Pl Alphonse Lepetit. *Tel 05 49 50 22 00.* ⬜ *Mon–Fri.*
Behind the bland Renaissance façade is the 12th-century great hall of the palace of the Angevin kings, Henry II and Richard the Lion-Heart. This is thought to be the scene of Joan of Arc's examination by a council of theologians in 1429.

🔒 Cathédrale St-Pierre

The 13th-century carved choir stalls in St-Pierre are by far the oldest in France. Note the huge 12th-century east window showing the Crucifixion. The

Pillars with colourful geometrical patterns in Notre-Dame-la-Grande

NOTRE-DAME-LA-GRANDE

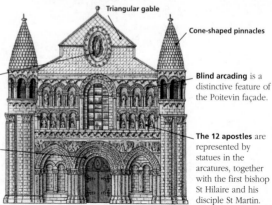

Triangular gable

Cone-shaped pinnacles

Christ in Majesty is shown in the centre of the gable, surrounded by symbols of the evangelists.

Blind arcading is a distinctive feature of the Poitevin façade.

The 12 apostles are represented by statues in the arcatures, together with the first bishop St Hilaire and his disciple St Martin.

The portals on the Poitevin façade are deep and richly sculpted, often showing a pronounced Moorish influence.

tiny figures of the cathedral's patrons (Henry II and Eleanor of Aquitaine) are crouched at the foot of the window. Its organ (1787–91), made by François-Henri Cliquot, is one of the most prestigious and beautiful in Europe.

🏛 Espace Mendès France

1 pl de la Cathédrale. *Tel 05 49 50 33 08.* ◯ *Tue–Sun.* 🖾
This museum contains a state-of-the-art planetarium, complete with laser shows to help explain the mysteries of the universe, plus regular events and exhibitions.

🔒 Eglise St-Hilaire-le-Grand

Fires and reconstructions have made St-Hilaire a mosaic of different styles. With its origins in the 6th century, the church still displays an 11th-century belltower and a 12th-century nave.

🔒 Baptistère St-Jean

Rue Jean Jaurès. ◯ *Jul–Aug: daily; Sep–Jun: Wed–Mon.* 🖾
The polygonal 4th-century Baptistère St-Jean is one of the oldest Christian buildings in France. Many of the earliest converts were baptized here. Now a museum, it contains Romanesque frescoes of Christ and Emperor Constantine, and some Merovingian sarcophagi.

🏛 Musée Sainte-Croix

3 bis rue Jean Jaurès. *Tel 05 49 41 07 53.* ◯ *Jun–Sep: Mon pm–Sun; Oct– May: Tue–Fri all day, Sat–Mon pms only.* 🔴 *some public hols.* 🖾
Musée Sainte-Croix exhibits prehistoric, Gallo-Roman and medieval archaeology, and a wide range of paintings and 19th-century sculpture. Five bronzes by Camille Claudel are on show, including *La Valse*. There is also a large collection of contemporary art.

🏛 Médiathèque François Mitterrand

4 rue de l'Université. *Tel 05 49 52 31 51.* ◯ *Tue–Sat.* 🔴 *public hols.*
This modern building, in the historic quarter, is home to the **Maison du Moyen Age**, which displays a collection of medieval manuscripts, maps and engravings.

VISITORS' CHECKLIST

Vienne. 🏠 *87,000.* ✈ *5 km (3 miles) W Poitiers.* 🚉 🚌 ℹ *45 pl Charles de Gaulle (05 49 41 21 24).* 🚌 *Sat, Tue & Thu.* 🎵 *Concerts Allumés (end Sep– beg Oct).* www.ot-poitiers.fr

One of Futuroscope's most popular attractions: the large-screen cinema

Futuroscope ❼

Jaunay-Clan. 🚉 *Tel 05 49 49 30 80.* ◯ *daily.* 🔴 *Jan.* 🖾 🍴 🛁
www.futuroscope.com

Futuroscope is a fantastic theme park 7 km (4.5 miles) north of Poitiers, exploring visual technology in a futuristic environment. Attractions evolve yearly and include simulators, 3D and 360° screens and the "magic carpet" cinema, with one of its screens on the floor, creating the sensation of "flying". The cinema has the biggest screen in Europe.

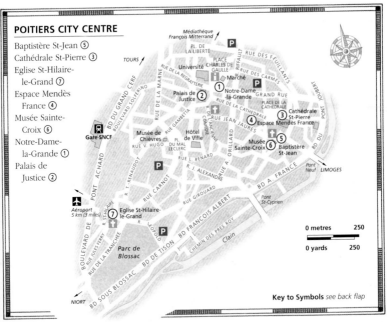

POITIERS CITY CENTRE

0 metres 250
0 yards 250

Key to Symbols *see back flap*

The castle ruins of Angles-sur-l'Anglin with the old watermill in the foreground

Abbaye de Nouaillé-Maupertuis ⑧

Nouaillé-Maupertuis. **Tel** *05 49 55 35 69.* **Church** ◯ *9am–6pm.* ⚫ *restricted.* 📷 *summer only.*

On the banks of the river Miosson lies the Abbaye de Nouaillé-Maupertuis. First mentioned in 780, the abbey became independent in 808 and followed the Benedictine rule. Apart from the beauty of the site, it is also worth visiting the church, built in the 11th–12th centuries and reconstructed several times. Behind the altar is the 10th-century sarcophagus of St-Junien, with three great heraldic eagles carved on the front.

More interesting is the nearby battlefield, scene of the great English victory at Poitiers by the Black Prince in 1356. The view has altered little in 600 years. Drive down the small road to La Cardinerie (to the right off the D142), which leads to the river crossing at Gué de l'Omme, the epicentre of the battle. There is a monument halfway up the hill where the heaviest fighting took place and where the French king Jean le Bon was isolated and captured. He had put up a heroic single-handed resistance with nothing but his battle-axe, and his small son Philippe to tell him where the next English knight was coming from.

Chauvigny ⑨

Vienne. 🏠 *7,300.* 🚌 ℹ *5 rue St-Pierre (05 49 46 39 01).* ⚫ *Sat.* **www**.chauvigny.cg86.fr

Chauvigny, on its steep promontory overlooking the broad river Vienne, displays the ruins of no fewer than four fortified medieval castles. Stone from the local quarry was so plentiful that nobody ever bothered to demolish earlier castles for building material.

Nevertheless, the best thing in this town is the 11th–12th-century **Eglise St-Pierre**, whose decorated capitals are a real treasure – particularly those in the choir. The carvings represent biblical scenes along with monsters,

Monster capitals in Eglise St-Pierre in Chauvigny

sphinxes and sirens. Look for the one which says *Gofridus me fecit* (Gofridus made me), with wonderfully natural scenes of the Epiphany.

Environs
Nearby is the lovely **Château de Touffou**, a Renaissance dream on the banks of the Vienne, with terraces and hanging gardens. Just north of it is the sleepy village of **Bonneuil-Matours**, with fine choir stalls in its Romanesque church.

⛪ **Château de Touffou**
Bonnes. **Tel** *05 49 56 08 48.* ◯ *mid-Jun– mid-Sep: daily; mid-Sep– mid-Jun: for groups only by appt.* 📷

Angles-sur-l'Anglin ⑩

Vienne. 🏠 *430.* ℹ *in the church (05 49 48 86 87).* ⚫ *Sat & Sun.* **www**.anglessuranglin.com

The village of Angles lies in an extremely beautiful riverside setting, dominated by its castle ruins. Adding to the charm is an old watermill by the slow-running river Anglin, graced by waterlilies and swaying reeds. Try to avoid visiting in summer, as the narrow streets become too crowded for comfort.

Angles is also famous for its tradition of fine needlework, the *jours d'Angles*, which is determinedly maintained by the local women today (their workshops can be visited).

St-Savin ⓫

Vienne. 🏠 *1,100.* 🚌
🛈 *20 pl de la Libération (05 49 48 11 00).* 🗓 *Fri.*

The glory of St-Savin is its 11th-century abbey church with its slender Gothic spire and huge nave.

The abbey had enormous influence until the Hundred Years' War, when it was burnt down. It was later pillaged several times during the Wars of Religion. Despite restoration work by monks in the 17th century and again in the 19th century, the church appears quite untouched.

Its interior contains the most magnificent series of 12th-century Romanesque frescoes in Europe. These wallpaintings were among the very first in France to be classified as a *Monument Historique* in 1836. Some of the frescoes were restored in 1967–74 and have been protected by UNESCO since 1983. A full-scale replica of the St-Savin murals can be seen at the Palais de Chaillot in Paris *(see pp110–11).* The abbey-museum explains the historical context and techniques of these murals.

Belltower of St-Savin

Montmorillon ⓬

Vienne. 🏠 *7,600.* 🚌 🛈 *2 pl du Maréchal Leclerc (05 49 91 11 96).* 🗓 *Wed & Sat.*

Montmorillon, built on both banks of the calm river Gartempe, has its origins in the 11th century. Like most towns in the region it had a difficult time during the Hundred Years' War and the Wars of Religion. Some buildings survived, such as **Eglise Notre-Dame**, which has beautiful frescoes in its 12th-century crypt (contact tourist office for key). They include scenes from the life of St Catherine of Alexandria.

Environs
Half an hour's walk from the Pont de Chez Ragon, south of Montmorillon, is the **Portes d'Enfer**, a dramatically shaped rock above the sudden rapids of the Gartempe.

Confolens ⓭

Charente. 🏠 *3,000.* 🚌 🛈 *rue Henri Desaphie (05 45 84 22 22).* 🗓 *Wed & Sat.*

On the border with Limousin, Confolens was once an important frontier town with several churches, but now suffers from rural exodus. Efforts to prevent the town's isolation include the annual international folklore festival. Every August the town is transformed into a tumultuous mix of music, costumes and crafts from all over the world.

Of historical interest is the medieval bridge across the Vienne, heavily restored in the early 18th century.

Charroux ⓮

Vienne. 🏠 *1,500.* 🛈 *2 route de Chatain (05 49 87 60 12).* 🗓 *Thu.*

The 8th-century **Abbaye St-Sauveur** in Charroux was once one of the richest abbeys in the region. Today it has become no more than a ruin open to the sky (phone 05 49 87 62 43 to arrange a visit).

Its chief contribution to history was made in the 10th century, when the Council of Charroux declared the "Truce of God", the earliest-known attempt to regulate war in the manner of the Geneva convention. Rules included: "Christian soldiers may not plunder churches, strike priests or steal peasants' livestock while campaigning."

The huge tower marking the centre of the church, and some superb sculpture from the original abbey portal in the small museum here, give an idea of its original splendour.

ST-SAVIN WALL PAINTINGS

The frescoes of St-Savin represent Old Testament history from the Creation to the Ten Commandments. The sequence starts to the left of the entrance with the Creation of the stars and of Eve. It continues with scenes from Noah's Ark to the Tower of Babel, the story of Joseph and the parting of the Red Sea. It is believed that all the frescoes were created by the same group of artists, due to the similarity in style. Their harmonious colours – red and yellow ochre, green, black and white – have been softened by time.

Noah's Ark, from a 12th-century wall painting in St-Savin

Aulnay ⑮

Charente-Maritime. 🏠 1,400. ℹ️
290 av de l'Eglise (05 46 33 14 44).
Thu & Sun. **www**.aulnay.info

Perhaps the most unusual fact
about the lovely 12th-century
Eglise St-Pierre at Aulnay is
that it was all built at once;
there is no ill-fitting apse or
transept added to an original
nave. Surrounded by nothing
but cypresses, it has remained
the same since the time of the
great pilgrimages.

The church is covered in
glorious sculpture, particularly
the outside of the south
transept. It is a rare example
of a complete Romanesque
façade, with rank on rank of
raucous monsters and graceful
human figures. Look for the
donkey with a harp. Inside
the church there is a pillar
decorated with elephants,
inscribed "Here be Elephants".

Façade of Eglise St-Pierre at Aulnay

La Rochelle ⑯

Charente-Maritime. 🏠 80,000. ✈️
🚉 🚌 ℹ️ quai Georges Simenon, Le
Gabut. 🅿️ daily. **www**.larochelle-
tourisme.com

La Rochelle, a commercial
centre and busy port since
the 11th century, has suffered
much from a distressing ten-
dency to back the wrong side
– the English and the Calvin-
ists, for example. This led to
the ruthless siege of the city
by Cardinal Richelieu in 1628,
during which 23,000 people
starved to death. The walls

Tour St-Nicolas in La Rochelle

were destroyed and the city's
privileges withdrawn. The
glory of La Rochelle is the old
harbour surrounded by stately
buildings. The harbour is now
the biggest yachting centre on
France's Atlantic coast. On
either side of its entrance are
Tour de la Chaîne and **Tour St-
Nicolas**. A huge chain used to
be strung between them to
ward off attack from the sea.

La Rochelle is easy to
explore on foot, though its
cobbled streets and arcades
can be congested in high
summer. To get an overview,
climb the 15th-century **Tour
de la Lanterne**. Its inner walls
were covered in graffiti by
prisoners, mostly mariners, in
the 17th–19th centuries. Ships
are the most common motif.

The study of the 18th-century
scientist Clément Lafaille is
preserved in the renovated
Muséum d'Histoire Naturelle,
complete with shell collection
and display cabinets. There are
also stuffed animals and
African masks. The town's
relation to the New World is
treated in the **Musée du Nouveau Monde**. Emigration,
commerce and the slave trade
are explained through old
maps, paintings and artifacts.

The richly decorated 16th-
century courtyard façade of
the **Hôtel de Ville** is worth a
visit, as is the delightful
collection of perfume bottles
in the **Musée du Flacon à
Parfum** in the parfumerie at
No. 33 rue du Temple.

Next to the Vieux Port is the
huge **Aquarium**. Transparent
tunnels lead through tanks
with different marine biotopes,
including sharks and turtles.

🗼 **Tour de la Lanterne**
Le Port. **Tel** 05 46 4156 04. ⏰
mid-May–mid-Sep: daily; mid-
Sep–mid-May: Tue–Sun. 🔴 1 Jan, 1
May, 1 & 11 Nov, 25 Dec. 🎫

🏛️ **Muséum d'Histoire
Naturelle**
28 rue Albert Premier. **Tel** 05 46 41
18 25. ⏰ phone to check. 🎫 ♿

🏛️ **Musée du Nouveau
Monde**
10 rue Fleuriau. **Tel** 05 46 41 46 50.
⏰ Wed–Mon. 🔴 Sat am & Sun
am, 1 Jan, 1 May, 14 Jul, 1 & 11 Nov,
25 Dec. 🎫

🐟 **Aquarium**
Bassin des Grands Yachts. **Tel** 05 46
34 00 00. ⏰ daily. 🎫 ♿ 🛍️ 📷
www.aquarium-larochelle.com

Environs
Ile de Ré, also known as the
white island, is a long stretch
of chalky cliffs and dunes,
with a rich birdlife. Since 1988
it has been connected to the
mainland by a 3-km (2-mile)
long bridge. Head for **Ars-en-
Ré**, in the middle, or **St-
Martin-de-Ré**, the island's
main town. There are plenty of
seafood restaurants serving
locally grown oysters.

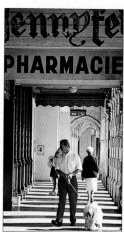
Arcade in rue du Palais, La Rochelle

Rochefort ⑰

Charente-Maritime. 🏠 27,000. 🚉
🚌 ℹ️ av Sadi-Carnot (05 46 99 08
60). 🅿️ Tue, Thu & Sat.
www.ville-rochefort.fr

The historic rival of La
Rochelle, Rochefort was
purpose-built by Colbert (see

Phare des Baleines on the eastern point of the Ile de Ré, opposite La Rochelle

pp56–7) in the 17th century to be the greatest shipyard in France, producing over 300 sailing vessels per year.

This maritime heritage can be traced in the **Corderie Royale** from 1670. Beautifully restored, the building houses an exhibition on ropemaking. The **Musée de la Marine** displays models of the ships built in the arsenal. The reconstruction of the frigate *Hermione* can be seen nearby.

Rochefort is also famous as the birthplace of the flamboyant writer Pierre Loti (1850–1923). The author's extravagant **Maison de Pierre Loti** is filled with lush souvenirs in an oriental decor.

The **Musée d'Art et d'Histoire** has an interesting ethnographic collection and a relief map of the old shipyard.

La Corderie Royale
Centre International de la Mer, rue Audebert. *Tel 05 46 87 01 90.*
daily. 1 Jan, 25 Dec.

Musée de la Marine
Pl de la Galissonnière. *Tel 05 46 99 86 57.* daily. 1 May, mid-Dec–Jan.

Maison de Pierre Loti
141 rue Pierre Loti. *Tel 05 46 99 16 88.* Wed– Mon. Jan, 1 & 11 Nov, 25 Dec. only.

Musée d'Art et d'Histoire
63 av Charles de Gaulle. *Tel 05 46 82 67 80.* Tue–Sun. 1 Jan, 2 wks Nov, 25 Dec. only.

Environs

Ile d'Aix is served by a ferry from Fouras on the mainland. Napoleon was briefly kept here before being exiled to St Helena. There are Napoleonic mementos in the **Musée Napoléonien**. The camel he rode in the Egyptian campaign is in the **Musée Africain**.

Musée Napoléonien
30 rue Napoléon. *Tel 05 46 84 66 40.* Wed–Mon. 1 May.

Musée Africain
Rue Napoléon. *Tel 05 46 84 66 40.* Wed–Mon. 1 May.

Napoleon, who was detained at Ile d'Aix in 1814

Île d'Oléron ⑱

Charente-Maritime. La Rochelle. Rochefort, La Rochelle, Saintes then bus. from La Rochelle (in summer). Bourcefranc (05 46 85 65 23).

Accessible from the mainland by bridge, Oleron is the second largest French island after Corsica, and a very popular holiday resort. Its south coast, the **Côte Sauvage**, is all dunes and pine forest, with excellent beaches at Vert Bois and Grande Plage, near the fishing port of La Cotinière. The north is used for farming and fishing.

The train from **St-Trojan** makes an interesting excursion through dunes and woodlands to the Pointe de Maumusson (Easter–Oct).

Brouage ⑲

Charente-Maritime. 580. 2 rue de Québec, Hiers-Brouage (05 46 85 19 16).

Cardinal Richelieu's fortress at Brouage, his base during the Siege of La Rochelle (1627–8), once overlooked a thriving harbour, but its wealth and population declined in the 18th century as the ocean receded. In 1659, Marie Mancini was sent into exile here by her uncle, Cardinal Mazarin, who did not approve of her liaison with Louis XIV. The king never forgot the beautiful Marie. Even on his way back from his wedding, he stayed alone at Brouage in the room once occupied by his first great love. Today the **ramparts** form a peaceful backdrop for the villagers working in the mussel beds below.

Environs

There are two reasons to go to **Marennes**, southwest of Brouage: the famous green-tinged oysters and the view from the steeple of Eglise St-Pierre-de-Sales. Nearby is the 18th-century **Château de la Gataudière** with an exhibition of horsedrawn vehicles.

One of Royan's five popular beaches

Royan ⓴

Charente-Maritime. 🚶 17,500. 🚌
🚆 ⛴ to Verdon only. 🚌 Rond-
Point de la Poste (05 46 05 04 71). ⛴
Tue–Sun. www.royan-tourisme.com

Badly damaged by Allied
carpet-bombing at the end of
World War II, Royan is now
thoroughly modern and
completely different in tone
from the rest of the towns
on this weather-beaten coast.
With five beaches of fine
sand, here called *conches*, it
becomes a heavily populated
resort in the summer months.

Built between 1955 and
1958, **Eglise Notre-Dame** is a
remarkable early example of
reinforced concrete architecture. Its interior is flooded
with colour and light by the
stained-glass windows.

A change from all the
modern architecture is offered
by the outstanding Renaissance
Phare de Cordouan. Various
lighthouses have been erected
on the site since the 11th
century. The present one was
finished in 1611, with a chapel

inside. The construction was
later reinforced and 30 m
(130 ft) added to its height.
Since 1789 the only thing that
has changed is the lighting
method. Boat trips in summer
include Phare de Cordouan
and leave from Royan harbour.

Talmont-sur-Gironde ㉑

Charente-Maritime. 🚶 83.
🚌 rue de l'Église (05 46 90 16 25).

The tiny Romanesque **Eglise
Ste-Radegonde** is perched on
a spit of land overlooking the
Gironde. Built in 1094, the
church's apse was designed to
resemble the prow of a ship –
which is apt, since the nave
has already fallen into the
sea. A 15th-century façade
closes off what's left. Inside
are richly decorated capitals,
including a tableau of St
George and the Dragon.

Talmont is a jewel of a
village, packed full of little
white houses and colourful
hollyhocks in summer.

Saintes ㉒

Charente-Maritime. 🚶 26,000. 🚆
🚌 🚌 Villa Musso, 62 cours National
(05 46 74 23 82). ⛴ Tue–Sun.
www.ot-saintes.fr

Capital of the Saintonge
region, Saintes has an extra-
ordinarily rich architectural
heritage. For centuries it
boasted the only bridge over
the lower Charente, well used
by pilgrims on their way to
Santiago de Compostela.
The Roman bridge no longer
exists but you can still admire
the magnificent **Arch of
Germanicus** (AD 19) which
used to mark its entrance.

On the same side of the
river is the beautiful **Abbaye
aux Dames**. Consecrated in
1047, it was modernized in
the 12th century. During the
17th–18th centuries noble
ladies were educated here.
Look for the decorated portal
and the vigorous 12th-century
head of Christ in the apse.

On the left bank is the 1st-
century Roman **amphitheatre**.
Further away lies the rather
unknown gem, **Eglise St-
Eutrope**. In the 15th century,
this church had the misfortune
to effect a miraculous cure of
the dropsy on Louis XI. In a
paroxysm of gratitude, he did
his best to wreck it with ill-
considered Gothic additions.
Luckily, its rare Romanesque
capitals have survived.

Arch of Germanicus in Saintes

Cognac ㉓

Charente. 🚶 20,000. 🚆 🚌 🚌 16
rue du 14 Juillet (05 45 82 10 71). ⛴
Tue–Sun. www.tourism-cognac.com

Wherever you spot the black
lichen stains from alcohol
evaporation on the exterior of
the buildings in this port, you

Necropolis in the monolithic Eglise St-Jean in Aubeterre-sur-Dronne

may be sure that you are looking at a storehouse of cognac.

All the great cognac houses do tours – a good one is chez **Cognac Otard**, situated in the 15th–16th-century château where François I was born. The distillery was established in 1795 by a Scot named Otard, who ruthlessly demolished an old chapel in the process. Luckily much of the Renaissance architecture was saved and can be seen during the tour, which includes a cognac-tasting.

Cognac in traditional snifter

The basic material for cognac is local white wine low in alcohol, which is then distilled. The resultant pale spirit is aged in oak barrels for 4–40 years before being bottled. The skill lies in the blending – therefore the only guide to quality is the name and the duration of ageing.

⊞ Cognac Otard
Château de Cognac, 127 bd Denfert-Rochereau. *Tel* 05 45 36 88 86.
◯ Apr–Oct: daily; Nov–Dec: Mon–Fri.
● 1 May & public hols in winter. 🎫
● obligatory.

Angoulême ❷❹

Charente. 👥 46,000. ▨ ▨ ▮ pl des Halles (05 45 95 16 84). ▨ daily.
www.angouleme-tourisme.com

The celebrated 12th-century **Cathédrale St-Pierre**, which dominates this thriving industrial centre, is the fourth to be built on the site. One of its most interesting features is the Romanesque frieze on the façade, wonderfully rich in detail. Some exaggerated restoration work was carried out by the 19th-century architect Abadie. In his eagerness to wipe out all details added after the 12th century, he destroyed a 6th-century crypt. Unfortunately he was also let loose on the old château, transforming it into a Neo-Gothic **Hôtel de Ville** (town hall).

However, the 15th-century tower where Marguerite d'Angoulême was born in 1492 still stands. A statue of her can be seen in the garden. Sister of François I, she spoke six languages, had an important role in foreign politics and wrote a popular work, *Heptaméron*. The ramparts offer a long bracing walk with views over the Charente Valley. A vintage car race takes place along the ramparts in mid-September. The **Centre National de la Bande Dessinée et de l'Image** has a reference collection of French print and film cartoons dating back to 1946.

🏛 Centre National de la Bande Dessinée et de l'Image
121 rue de Bordeaux. *Tel* 05 45 38 65 65. ◯ Tue–Sun (w/e pms only).
● Jan, public hols. 🎫 🛢 ▣ ⬜
Cinema www.cnbdi.fr

Environs
Angoulême used to be famous for its papermills. The **Moulin du Verger** at Puymoyen has a museum and still produces paper in the traditional 18th-century manner.

▥ Moulin du Verger
Tel 05 45 61 10 38. ◯ daily.

Aubeterre-sur-Dronne ❷❺

Charente. 👥 390. ▨ ▮ pl du Château (05 45 98 57 18). ▨ Thu, Sun

The chief ornament of this pretty white village is the staggering monolithic **Eglise St-Jean**. Dug out of the white chalky cliff that gave the village its name (Alba Terra – White Earth), some parts of it date back to the 6th century. Between the Revolution and 1860, it served as the village's cemetery. It contains an early Christian baptismal font and an octagonal reliquary.

The Romanesque Eglise St-Jacques at the top of the village has a fine sculpted façade.

Detail from the Romanesque façade of Cathédrale St-Pierre in Angoulême

Street-by-Street: Bordeaux ㉖

Built on a curve of the river Garonne,
Bordeaux has been a major port since pre-
Roman times and for centuries a focus and
crossroads of European trade. Today
Bordeaux shows little visible evidence of
the Romans, Franks, English or the Wars
of Religion that have marked its past. This
forward-looking town, the fifth largest in
France, is an industrial and maritime sprawl
surrounding a noble 18th-century centre.

Along the waterfront of this wealthy wine
metropolis is a long sweep of elegant
Classical façades, first built to mask the
medieval slums behind. Adding to the
magnificence are the Esplanade des
Quinconces, the Grand Théâtre
and the place de la Bourse.

Eglise Notre-Dame, built 1684–1707

★ Grand Théâtre
*Built in 1773–80, the theatre
is a masterpiece of the
Classical style, crowned by
9 statues of the muses.*

STAR SIGHTS

- ★ Grand Théâtre
- ★ Esplanade des Quinconces
- ★ Place de la Bourse

KEY

– – – Suggested route

```
0 metres        100
0 yards         100
```

The quais, lined with graceful
façades, make a beautiful
walk along the Garonne.

★ Place de la Bourse
*This elegant and harmonious
square is flanked by two
majestic 18th-century
buildings, Palais de la Bourse
and Hôtel des Douanes.*

★ **Esplanade des Quinconces**
Replacing the 15th-century Château de Trompette, this vast space of tree-lined esplanades with statues and fountains was created in 1827–58.

VISITORS' CHECKLIST

Gironde. 🏙 220,000. ✈ 10 km (6 miles) W Bordeaux. 🚉 Gare St-Jean, rue Charles Domerq. 🚌 Allée de Chartres. 🛈 12 cours du 30 Juillet (05 56 00 66 00). 🛒 daily. 🎷 L'Eté Girondin (jazz; Jul–Aug); Fête du Vin Nouveau (Oct). **www**.bordeaux-tourisme.com

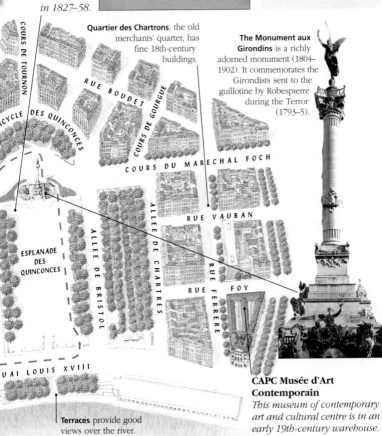

Quartier des Chartrons, the old merchants' quarter, has fine 18th-century buildings.

The Monument aux Girondins is a richly adorned monument (1804–1902). It commemorates the Girondists sent to the guillotine by Robespierre during the Terror (1793–5).

COURS DE TOURNON
RUE BOUDET
COURS DE GOURGUE
BICYCLE DES QUINCONCES
COURS DU MARECHAL FOCH
ALLEE DE CHARTRES
RUE VAUBAN
ALLEE DE BRISTOL
ESPLANADE DES QUINCONCES
RUE FERRERE
RUE FOY
QUAI LOUIS XVIII

Terraces provide good views over the river.

CAPC Musée d'Art Contemporain
This museum of contemporary art and cultural centre is in an early 19th-century warehouse.

Loading wine barrels in 19th-century Bordeaux

THE BORDEAUX WINE TRADE

After Marseille, Bordeaux is the oldest trading port in France. From Roman times the export of wine was the basis for a modest prosperity, but under English rule (1154–1453, *see pp50–53*), the merchants began making immense fortunes from their monopoly of wine sales to England. After the discovery of the New World, Bordeaux took advantage of its Atlantic position to diversify and extend its wine market. Today the Bordeaux region produces over 44 million cases of wine per year.

GRAND THEÂTRE DE BORDEAUX

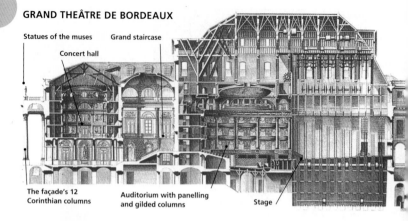

Statues of the muses   Grand staircase

Concert hall

The façade's 12
Corinthian columns

Auditorium with panelling
and gilded columns

Stage

Exploring Bordeaux
Much of central Bordeaux is grand streets and 18th-century mansions. A triangle made by cours Clemenceau, cours de l'Intendance and allées de Tourny has chic boutiques and cafés. Cathédrale St-André is another focal point, with good museums nearby. Both the *quais* and the Chartrons district around the Jardin Public are being renovated and are well worth exploring.

🏛 Grand Théâtre
Place de la Comédie. *Tel 05 56 00 85 95.*
Built by the architect Victor Louis, the 18th-century Grand Théâtre is one of the finest Classical constructions of its type in France. The auditorium is renowned for its extraordinary acoustics. The spectacular main staircase was later imitated by Garnier for the Paris Opéra (*see p97*).

🔒 Eglise St-Seurin
This church is somewhat chaotic with a patchwork of styles ranging from the 11th to the 18th century. Most interesting are the 6th-century Gallo-Roman sarcophagi in the crypt, and a fine 14th-century bishop's throne.

🔒 Basilique St-Michel
It took 200 years to build the massive Basilique St-Michel, begun in 1350. Recently restored, this triple-naved edifice has a remarkable statue of St Ursula with her flock of penitents. Its freestanding belfry, built in 1472–92, is the tallest in southern France (114 m).

🏛 Musée des Beaux-Arts
20 cours d'Albret. *Tel 05 56 10 20 56.*
◯ *Wed–Mon.* ● *public hols.*
Housed in two wings of the Hôtel de Ville, the excellent collection of paintings here ranges from the Renaissance to our time. Masterpieces include works by Titian, Veronese, Rubens, Delacroix, Corot, Renoir, Matisse and Boudin.

🏛 Musée des Arts Décoratifs
39 rue Bouffard. *Tel 05 56 00 72 50.*
◯ *Wed–Mon.* ● *public hols.*
If you're interested in elegant furnishings and fine porcelain, stop off at this exceptional collection, housed in the suitably refined 18th-century Hôtel de Lalande.

🏛 Musée d'Aquitaine
20 cours Pasteur. *Tel 05 56 01 51 00.*
◯ *Tue–Sun.* ● *public hols.*
This important museum traces life in the region from prehistoric times to the present, through artifacts, furniture and viticulture tools. Among its

**Calm street in Bordeaux by the
Porte de la Grosse Cloche**

more spectacular exhibits are the Tayac treasure from the 2nd century BC, and the Garonne treasure, a hoard of over 4,000 Roman coins.

🔒 Cathédrale St-André
The nave of this gigantic church was begun in the 11th century and modified 200 years later. The Gothic choir and transepts were added in the 14th and 15th centuries. The excellent medieval sculptures on the Porte Royale include scenes from the Last Judgement.

🏛 CAPC Musée d'Art Contemporain
Entrepôt Lainé, 7 rue Ferrère.
Tel 05 56 00 81 50. ◯ *Tue–Sun.*
● *public hols.*
This superbly converted 19th-century warehouse merits a visit, whatever you make of its high-profile temporary exhibitions and permanent collection of contemporary art.

St-Émilion ㉗

Gironde. 🏠 2,450. 🚊 🚌 🛈 pl des Créneaux (05 57 55 28 28). 🛒 Sun.
www.saint-emilion-tourisme.com

This charming village in the middle of the red wine district to which it gives its name, dates back to an 8th-century hermit, Émilion, who dug out a cave for himself in the rock. A monastery followed, and by the Middle Ages St-Émilion had become a small town. Today medieval houses still line the narrow streets, and parts of the 12th-century ramparts remain. The interior of the church dug out of the chalky cliff by followers of Saint Émilion after his death is somewhat ruined by concrete columns put up to prevent its collapse.

Famous châteaux in the district include the elegant **Figeac, Cheval Blanc** and **Ausone,** all of them St-Émilion Premiers Grands Crus Classés.

Vineyard close to Margaux in the Médoc region west of Bordeaux

Pauillac ㉘

Gironde. 🚹 5,700. 🚌 🚆 🚉 *La Verrerie (05 56 59 03 08).* 🚩 *Sat.* **www.**pauillac-medoc.com

One of the most famous areas in the Médoc wine region (*see pp398–9*) is the commune of Pauillac. Three of its châteaux are Médoc Premiers Grands Crus Classés.

The **Château Mouton-Rothschild** uses leading artists to create its wine labels and has a small museum of paintings on wine themes from all over the world. The **Château Lafite-Rothschild** is of medieval origin and the **Château Latour** is recognizable by its distinctive stone turret. They can be visited by appointment

(contact the tourist office). The town of Pauillac is situated on the west bank of the Gironde. In the 19th century it was the bustling arrival point for transatlantic steamships, but now the sleepy port is mostly used by pleasure boats. There are picturesque river views from the quais and plenty of cafés serving the local wine.

BORDEAUX WINE CHÂTEAUX

The château is at the heart of the quality system in Bordeaux, the world's largest fine wine region. A château includes a vineyard and a building which can range from the most basic to the grandest, historic as well as modern. But the château is also the symbol of a tradition and the philosophy that a wine's quality and character spring from the soil. Some châteaux welcome visitors for wine tasting as well as buying. The Maison du Vin and the tourist office in Bordeaux (*see p421*) offer information and tours.

Latour *in Pauillac is famous for its powerful wines and the medieval stone turret that appears on its label.*

Cheval Blanc, *a great château in the St-Émilion area, boasts a rich, spicy Premier Grand Cru.*

Margaux, *built in 1802, produces a classic Margaux Premier Cru of the same elegant proportions as its Palladian façade.*

Palmer, *dating from 1856, is Neo-Renaissance in style and produces a very fine Margaux Troisième Cru.*

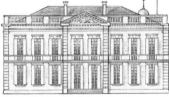

Gruaud-Larose *is a cream-coloured château with a Classical façade, distinguished by its full-bodied St-Julien Deuxième Cru Classé.*

Vieux Château Certan *is Belgian-owned and one of the great historic properties of Pomerol. Its wines are consistently in the first rank in the district, challenged only by Pétrus.*

The immense Dune du Pilat, stretching almost 3 km (2 miles) south of the inlet to Bassin d'Arcachon

La Côte d'Argent 29

Gironde, Landes. 🚊 Bordeaux, Biarritz.
🚌 Soulac-sur-Mer, Arcachon, Labenne,
Dax. 🚌 Lacanau, Arcachon, Mimizan.
ℹ️ Lacanau (05 56 03 21 01),
Mimizan-Plage (05 58 09 11 20),
Capbreton (05 58 72 12 11).

The long stretch of coast between Pointe de Grave on the Gironde estuary and Bayonne *(see p452)* is called La Côte d'Argent – the Silver Coast. It is virtually one vast beach of shifting sand dunes. Treeplanting has now slowed down their progress.

The coast is dotted with seaside resorts like **Soulac-sur-Mer** in the north, followed by the big **Lacanau-Océan** and **Mimizan-Plage**. Down in the south is **Hossegor** with its salty lake, and **Capbreton**. Modern holiday resorts have been integrated with the old.

Inland are lakes popular for fishing and boating. They are connected to each other and the ocean by lively water currents, such as the **Courant d'Huchet** from Etang de Léon. Boat trips are available.

Bassin d'Arcachon 30

Gironde. 👥 11,500. ⛴ to Cap Ferret.
🚉 🚌 ℹ️ espl Georges Pompidou
(05 57 52 97 97). 🛒 Wed, Sat–Sun.
www.arcachon.com

In the middle of the Côte d'Argent the straight coastline suddenly forms a lagoon. Famous for its natural beauty, fine beaches and oysters, the Bassin d'Arcachon is a protected area, perfect for holidaymakers, sailing enthusiasts and oyster-eaters.

The basin is dotted with smaller amorphous resorts, beaches and fishing/oyster villages, all worth exploring.

Cap Ferret, the northern headland that protects the basin from stiff Atlantic winds, is a preserve of the wealthy, whose luxurious villas stand among the pines. Look for the small road under the trees from Lège, which leads to the wild, magnificent beach of Grand-Crohot.

Between Cap Ferret and Arcachon, near Gujan-Mestras, the **Parc Ornithologique du Teich** provides care and shelter for damaged birds and endangered species. For the bird watcher, there are two fascinating walks, each carefully marked: an introductory one, and another of greater length. Both provide concealed observation points from which people can watch the wild fowl without disturbing them.

Arcachon was created as a seaside resort in 1845. Its popularity grew and in the late 19th and early 20th centuries the elegant villas in Ville d'Hiver were built. The livelier Ville d'Eté, facing the lagoon, has a casino and sports facilities.

The immense **Dune du Pilat** is the largest sand dune in Europe. It is nearly 3 km (2 miles) long, 104 m (340 ft) high and 500 m (1,625 ft) wide. Aside from the view, the dune is a great vantage point in autumn for viewing flocks of migratory birds as they pass overhead on their way to the sanctuary at Le Teich.

🦅 Parc Ornithologique du Teich

Le Teich. **Tel** 05 56 22 80 46. ⬜ daily. 🏷 ♿ 🚻 🍴 **www**.parc-ornithologique-du-teich.com

Parc Ornithologique du Teich, a bird sanctuary in Bassin d'Arcachon

LANDES FOREST

The vast, totally artificial 19th-century forest of Les Landes was an ambitious project to make use of an area of sand and marshes. Pines and grasses were planted to anchor the coastal dunes, and inland dunes were stabilized with a mixture of pines, reeds and broom. In 1855 the land was drained, and is now covered with pine groves and undergrowth, preserving a delicate ecological balance.

Pine trees in the Landes forest

Les Landes **③**

Gironde, Landes. ✈ *Bordeaux, Biarritz.* 🚆 *Morcenx, Dax, Mont-de-Marsan.* 🚌 *Mont-de-Marsan.* 🛈 *Mont-de-Marsan (05 58 05 87 37).*

Almost entirely covered by an immense pine forest, the Landes area extends over the two *départements* of Gironde and Landes. The soil here is uniformly sandy. Until a century ago the whole region became a swamp in winter, because of a layer of tufa (porous rock) just under the surface which retained water from the brackish lakes. Any settlement or agriculture close to the sea was impossible due to the constantly shifting dunes. Furthermore, the mouth of the Adour river kept moving from Capbreton to Vieux-Boucau and back, a distance of 32 km (20 miles).

The Adour was fixed near Bayonne by a canal in the 16th century. This was the start of the slow conquest of the Landes. The planting of pine trees ultimately wiped out the migrant shepherds and their flocks. Today the inner Landes is still very under-populated,

but wealthy from its pinewood and pine derivatives. The coastal strip has a large influx of holidaymakers.

In 1970, part of the forest was made into a nature park. Here, a small steam train takes visitors to **Marqueze**, where a typical 19th-century *airial* (clearing) has been restored. It commemorates the vanished world of Les Landes before the draining of the marshes, when shepherds still used stilts to get about. There are traditional *auberges landaises*, wooden houses with sloping roofs, as well as henhouses built on stilts because of the foxes. In **Luxey** a museum recalls old techniques of tapping and distillation of resin.

Levignacq, near the coast, is a perfect Landais village with a remarkable 14th-century fortified church full of charming naive frescoes.

Mont-de-Marsan **③**

Landes. 🏠 *32,000.* 🚆 🚌 🛈 *6 pl du Général Leclerc (05 58 05 87 37).* 🛒 *Tue & Sat.* **www**.mont-de-marsan.org

A bullfighting mecca, Mont-de-Marsan attracts all the great bullfighters of France and Spain during the summer season. A less bloodthirsty local variant of the sport, very popular here, is the *course landaise*, in which the object is to vault over the horns and back of a charging cow.

The administrative capital of the Landes is also known for its hippodrome and the production of poultry and *foie gras*.

Sculpture from the first half of the 20th century can be seen at **Musée Despiau-Wlérick**.

Dax **③**

Landes. 🏠 *20,000.* 🚆 🚌 🛈 *cours Foch (05 58 56 86 86).* 🛒 *Sat, Sun am.*

The thermal spa of Dax is second only to Aix-les-Bains (*see p390*) in importance. Its hot springs, with a constant temperature of 64° C (147° F) and tonic mud from the Adour, have been soothing aches and pains and promoting tranquillity since the time of Emperor Augustus.

Apart from the 13th-century doorway of the otherwise 17th-century **Cathédrale Notre-Dame**, there isn't much of architectural interest in this warm, peaceful town. But the promenade along the river Adour is charming and the bullring is world-renowned.

La Force (1937) by Raoul Lamourdieu, in the bullfighting capital of Mont-de-Marsan

PERIGORD, QUERCY AND GASCONY

DORDOGNE · LOT · TARN · HAUTE GARONNE
LOT-ET-GARONNE · TARN-ET-GARONNE · GERS

*S*outhwest France is an archaeologist's heaven, for the region has been continuously inhabited by mankind for tens of thousands of years, longer than any other area in Europe. The landscape of these historic regions seems to have an ancient familiarity, derived from centuries of people living in harmony with the land.

The great cave sites around Les Eyzies and Lascaux harbour the earliest evidence we possess of primitive art. The castles, bastides *(see p445)* and churches that grace the countryside from Périgueux to the Pyrenees, from the Bay of Biscay to Toulouse and beyond to the Mediterranean, belong to a far more recent past. From the coming of Christianity until the late 18th century, this lovely region was the battlefield for a string of conflicts. The English fought and lost the Hundred Years' War for Aquitaine (1345–1453); this was followed by intermittent Wars of Religion, in which Catholics fought Huguenots (French Protestants) in a series of massacres and guerilla wars *(see pp52–3)*.

Today nothing is left of these old struggles but crumbling ramparts, keeps and bastides, which are part of the region's cultural and artistic heritage, attracting thousands of visitors every year. Yet it is as well to remember that all the great sights here, from the abbey church at Moissac, whose 12th-century portal is a masterpiece of Romanesque art, to the awesome clifftop site of Rocamadour, have suffered at one time or another from the attacks of marauding soldiers.

This region may seem incomparably rich in all the ingredients for a good holiday – uncluttered landscapes, empty roads, clean rivers and good regional cuisine – but the economy is fragile. Over the last century, the southwest has suffered a decline in the old peasant way of life, resulting in a population migration from the countryside to the towns.

Périgord geese, reared for the area's celebrated *foie gras*

◁ La Roque-Gageac in the Dordogne Valley

Exploring Périgord, Quercy and Gascony

The market towns of Périgueux, Cahors and Albi make good bases for exploring the region, and are quieter alternatives to Toulouse – the only major urban centre. Elsewhere, the green hills and sleepy villages of Gascony and Périgord (also known as the Dordogne) are mainly for those who appreciate the slow pace of life in the countryside. But if you want more than peace and good food, this region offers some of France's finest medieval architecture, and Europe's most important prehistoric caves, notably Lascaux.

The medieval hilltop town of Cordes

GETTING AROUND

The west–east Autoroute des Deux Mers (A62-A61) is the main road through the region, linking Bordeaux, the Atlantic coast and the Mediterranean. The new A20 from Limoges provides alternative access to the Dordogne and Quercy. Buses and mainline railways, including a Bordeaux–Marseille TGV, pass along the same two axes. They meet at Toulouse, where an international airport has daily flights to and from most European destinations.

KEY

═══	Motorway
═══	Major road
━━━	Secondary road
═══	Minor road
━━━	Scenic route
┅┅┅	Main railway
───	Minor railway
━━━	Regional border

SIGHTS AT A GLANCE

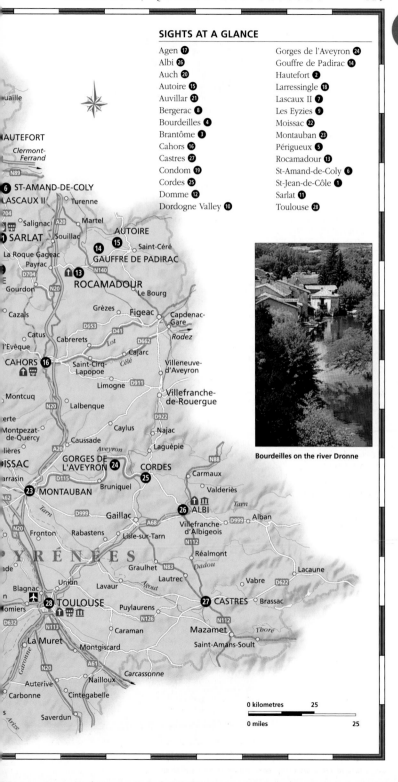

Bourdeilles on the river Dronne

0 kilometres   25

0 miles   25

St-Jean-de-Côle ●

Dordogne. 🚶 350. 🛈 pl du
Château (05 53 62 14 15).
🎏 Floralies (Apr–May).

St-Jean-de-Côle's medieval,
humpbacked bridge gives the
best view of this lovely
Dordogne village set in hilly
countryside. Stone and half-
timbered houses, roofed with
the distinctive red-brown tiles
of the region, cram the
narrow streets around the
main square. Here stand a
covered market place, château
and 12th-century church.

The cupola of the church
used to be the largest in the
region – too large, it seems,
for it fell down twice in the
18th and 19th centuries. The
second time it happened
the builders gave up, and
there has been a plank ceiling
ever since.

**Main square in the lovely village of
St-Jean-de-Côle**

Hautefort ●

Tel 05 53 50 51 23. **Château** ☐ Apr–
Oct: daily (Mar & Nov: Sat, Sun &
hols, pms only). ● Dec–Feb. 🎫 📷
oblig. ⚓ gr fl & gdn only.

Hautefort clings to the
sides of a steep hill topped
by a massive 17th-century
château, one of the finest in
southwest France. Partially
fortified, built as a pleasure
palace in honour of King
Louis XIII's secret love, the
Marquis de Hautefort's
beautiful sister Marie, the castle
is surrounded by French gardens on terraces with superb
views of the rolling green
country of northeast Périgord.
In the village, the hospice, of
a similar date, has a fascinating museum of early medical
and dental implements.

Brantôme Abbey, with belfry

Brantôme ●

Dordogne. 🚶 2,100. ☐ 🛈 bd
Charlemagne (05 53 05 80 52). 🛒 Fri.
www.ville-brantome.fr

Surrounded on all sides by
the river Dronne, Brantôme is
sometimes called the Venice
of the Périgord Vert. Its
medieval abbey and 11th-
century belfry (reputedly the
oldest still standing in
France), together with the
verdant rockface behind,
provide a dramatic backdrop
for this picturesque town.

Pierre de Bourdeille, the poet
(1540–1614), was appointed
abbot here in his youth. His
lovers allegedly included Mary,
Queen of Scots. After a crip-
pling fall, Bourdeille retired
here in 1569 to write his racy
memoirs. It is possible to wander the stone staircases and
cloisters, and through the main
courtyard to the intriguing
troglodyte dwellings in the
cliff behind. In one is a huge
crucifixion scene cut into the
stone during the 16th century.
Just 12 km (7 miles) northeast,
near Villars, lies the fine
Renaissance **Château de
Puyguilhem** and **Grotte de
Villars**. Discovered in 1953,
these caves are extensive and
on several different levels.
Apart from spectacular rock
formations, there are some
marvellous 1,700-year-old
cave paintings.

⚓ **Château de Puyguilhem**
Villars. **Tel** 05 53 54 82 18. ☐
Jul–Aug; daily; Sep–Jun: Sun–Tue &
Thu. ● 1 Jan, 25 Dec. 🎫 ⚓

💥 **Grotte de Villars**
Cluzeau, Brantôme. **Tel** 05 53 54 82
36. ☐ Apr–Oct: daily. 🎫 📷 oblig.

Bourdeilles ●

Dordogne. 🚶 800. 🛈 Place Tilleuls
(05 53 03 42 96).

This small town has everything – a narrow Gothic
bridge with cutwater piers
spanning the Dronne, a mill
upstream and a medieval
château. The 16th-century
additions to the castle were
designed in a hurry by the
châtelaine Jacquette de Mont-
bron, when expecting Queen
Catherine de' Medici to visit.
When the royal visit was called
off, so were the building
works. The highlight of the
château is the gilded first-floor
salon, decorated in the 1560s
by Ambroise le Noble, of the
Fontainebleau School.

⚓ **Château de Bourdeilles**
Tel 05 53 03 73 36. ☐ Apr–Oct:
Wed–Sun (Jul & Aug: daily); phone to
check in other months. ● Jan. 🎫 📷

The impressive Château de Bourdeilles towering above the town

Cathédrale St-Front in Périgueux, restored in the 19th century

Périgueux ❺

Dordogne. 🏠 35,000. ✈ 🚉 🚌
🛈 26 pl Francheville (05 53 53 10 63). 🛒 daily.
www.tourisme-perigueux.fr

The ancient and truly gastronomic city of Périgueux, like its neighbours Bergerac and Riberac, should be visited on market day, when stalls in the lively squares in the medieval part of town offer the pick of local specialities, including truffles (Nov–Mar), *charcuterie* and the succulent pies called *pâtés de Périgueux*.

Périgueux, now the busy regional capital, has long been the crossroads of Périgord. The earliest part remaining today is the quarter known as **La Cité**, once the important Gallo-Roman settlement of Vesunna. La Domus de Vesonne, a Gallo-Roman museum, has just opened on site. From Roman times to the Middle Ages, this

was the focus of Périgueux. Most of the fabric of Vesunna was pulled down in the 3rd century, but some vestiges of a temple, a huge arena and a sumptuous villa remain. The **Eglise St-Etienne** nearby dates back to the 12th century.

Walking up the hill from La Cité to the city's dazzling white cathedral you pass through bustling streets and squares, each with its market activity. This is the medieval quarter of **Le Puy St-Front**, which began to flourish as pilgrims on their way to Santiago de Compostela (see p400) visited the cathedral. As they brought prestige and wealth to the quarter, it gradually eclipsed La Cité.

At the top stands the imposing **Cathédrale St-Front**, the largest in southwestern France. The Romanesque construction was heavily

19th-century stained glass in Cathédrale St-Front

restored in the 19th century, when architect Paul Abadie added the fanciful domes and cones. He later used St-Front as inspiration for the Sacré-Coeur in Paris (see p134).

Other gems of medieval and Renaissance architecture include **Maison Estignard**, at No. 3 rue Limogeanne, with its unusual corkscrew staircase, and houses along rue Aubergerie and rue de la Constitution.

Also in the cathedral quarter is the **Musée d'Art et d'Archéologie du Périgord**, one of the most comprehensive prehistory museums in France, with remnants of burials dating back 70,000 years. Beautiful Roman glass, mosaics, earthenware and other artifacts from Vesunna are in the Gallo-Roman museum.

🏛 **Musée d'Art et d'Archéologie du Périgord**
22 cours Tourny. *Tel* 05 53 06 40 70.
◯ Wed–Mon. ● public hols. 🖼

St-Amand-de-Coly ❻

Dordogne. *Tel* La Mairie (05 53 51 47 85). ◯ daily.

This abbey church is an outstanding example of fortress architecture, built in the 12th–13th centuries by Augustinian monks to protect their monastery. There are two lines of defence: a high stone rampart and, behind it, the arched tower of the church itself. The tower looks more like a castle keep, and was once pierced by a score of arrow slits.

Inside, the church is beautifully simple, with pure lines, a flat ribbed vault, 12th-century cupola, a soaring nave and a stone floor sloping upwards to the altar. Yet even this interior was arranged for defence, with a gallery from which enemies within the building could be attacked.

St-Amand was heavily damaged during the Hundred Years' War. Later, in 1575, it survived a siege by 2,000 Huguenot cavalry and a six-day bombardment by cannon. Religious life here finally came to an end after the Revolution.

Sarlat ⓫

Sculptures of geese in Sarlat

Sarlat-la-Caneda possesses the highest concentration of medieval, Renaissance and 17th-century façades of any town in France. Its prosperity was a reflection of the privileged status it was granted in return for loyalty to the French crown during the Hundred Years' War. Behind the nondescript rue de la République are narrow lanes and archways, and ancient, ochre-coloured stone town houses rich in ornamental detail. Protected by law since 1962, Sarlat's buildings now form an open-air museum. The town is also famous for one of the best markets in France.

Rue des Consuls contains 15th-, 16th- and 17th-century mansions, built for the town's middle-class merchants, magistrates and church officials.

Rue Jean-Jacques Rousseau was the main street until rue de la République (known as "La Traverse") was built in the 19th century.

Place de la Liberté
The Renaissance heart of Sarlat is now lined with luxury shops and cafés.

Town walls

Walnuts, a key Périgord crop

SARLAT MARKET

Every Wednesday, the great Sarlat food market is held in place de la Liberté, and every Saturday there is a full-scale fair which attracts locals from all around. Sarlat lies at the heart of the nation's *foie gras* and walnut trades. These typical Périgord products absorb much of the town's attention and supply a good proportion of its revenue, as they did during Sarlat's heyday in the 13th and 14th centuries. Other local specialities are black truffles dug up in the woods in January, and wild mushrooms. Seek out, too, the cheeses of every shape, age and hue, and the huge range of pork delicacies available, which may be potted, fresh, smoked, dried, salted, fried, baked or boiled.

Bulbs of pink garlic

KEY

– – – Suggested route

| 0 metres | 50 |
| 0 yards | 50 |

Rue de la Salamandre
This lane was named after the salamander emblem of King François I, seen on many of the town's 16th-century houses.

VISITORS' CHECKLIST

Dordogne. 🏠 *11,000.*
🚉 av de la Gare.
ℹ️ rue Tourny (05 53 31 45 45).
🛒 Wed & Sat.
🎭 Theatre (Jul–Aug); Film (Nov).
www.ot-sarlat-perigord.fr

Lanterne des Morts (Lantern of the Dead)
The conical tower in the cemetery was built to commemorate St Bernard's sermons in Sarlat in August 1147.

Cathédrale St-Sacerdos
Built largely in the 16th and 17th centuries, the cathedral is remarkable for its magnificent 18th-century organ.

The Chapelle des Pénitents Bleus, built in pure Romanesque style, is the last vestige of the 12th-century abbey.

The former Bishop's Palace, with remains of a 16th-century loggia and a Renaissance interior, is now a tourist office which puts on excellent summer exhibitions.

Cour des Fontaines
A pure spring here attracted the monks who founded Sarlat's first abbey in the 9th century.

Painting of a bull from the original cave at Lascaux

Lascaux II ❼

Montignac. **Tel** 05 53 51 95 03.
🕐 Feb–Dec daily, times vary – phone
to check. 🔴 Jan, 25 Dec. 🎟 ✔
www.perigord.tm.fr

Lascaux is the most famous
of the prehistoric sites
clustered around the junction
of the rivers Vézère and Beune
(see pp402–3). Four boys
came across the caves and
their astonishing palaeolithic
paintings in 1940, and the
importance of their discovery
was swiftly recognized.

Lascaux has been closed to
the public since 1963 because
of deterioration, but an exact
copy has been created a few
minutes' walk down the hillside, using the same materials.
The replica is beautiful and
should not be spurned: high-
antlered elk, bison, bulls and
plump horses cover the walls,
moving in herds or files,
surrounded by arrows and
geometric symbols thought to
have had ritual significance.

Bergerac ❽

Dordogne. 👥 28,000. ✈ 🚊 🚌
ℹ 97 rue Neuve d'Argenson (05 53
57 03 11). 🔵 Wed & Sat.
www.bergerac-tourisme.com

This small port, a tobacco
farming and commercial
centre, spreads itself over
both sides of the Dordogne.
Chief attractions are its extraordinary **Musée du Tabac**
(tobacco museum), and its
food and wine which are
invariably excellent. Bergerac's
most celebrated wine is Monbazillac, a sweet white wine,
often drunk on ceremonial
occasions. On show in the
small, lively museum are
some Native American pipes.

🏛 Musée du Tabac
Maison Peyrarède, pl du Feu.
Tel 05 53 63 04 13. 🕐 Tue–Sun.
🔵 Sun ams (mid-Nov–mid-Mar:
Sat & Sun), public hols. 🎟 ♿

Les Eyzies ❾

Dordogne. 👥 900. 🚊 ℹ 19 av
de la Préhistoire (05 53 06 97 05). 🔵
Mon (Apr–Oct). **www**.leseyzies.com

Four major prehistoric sites
and a group of smaller caves
cluster around the unassuming village of Les Eyzies.
Head first for the **Musée
National de Préhistoire**, in a
new building at the foot of a
16th-century castle over-
looking the village. The
timelines and other exhibits
are useful for putting the vast
warren of prehistoric painting
and sculpture into context.

The **Grotte de Font de
Gaume** is the logical first stop
after the museum at Les
Eyzies. This cave, discovered
in 1901, contains probably
the finest ensemble of prehistoric paintings still open to
the public in France.

Close by is the **Grotte des
Combarelles**, with engravings
of bison, reindeer, magic
symbols and human figures.

Les Eyzies, a centre for the area's concentration of prehistoric caves

Further on, you reach the rock shelter of **Abri du Cap Blanc**, discovered in 1909, with a rare, life-size frieze of horses and bison sculpted in the rock.

On the other side of Les Eyzies is the cave system at **Rouffignac**, a favourite place for excursions since the 15th century. There are 8 km (5 miles) of caves here, 2.5 km (1.5 miles) of which are served by electric train. The paintings include drawings of mammoths, and a frieze of two bison challenging each other to combat.

Tickets for all the caves sell out fast, especially in summer, so arrive early. Some must be booked two weeks ahead.

Musée National de Préhistoire

🏛 Musée National de Préhistoire
Tel 05 53 06 45 65. ◯ Jul & Aug: daily; Sep–Jun: Wed–Mon. ● 25 Dec, 1 Jan. 🖼 🚫 🅿 🔄

🏚 Grotte de Font de Gaume
Tel 05 53 06 86 00. ◯ by appt; book 1 month ahead. ● some public hols.

🏚 Grotte des Combarelles
Tel 05 53 06 86 00. ◯ Sun–Fri by appt (book fortnight ahead). ● some public hols. 🖼

🏚 Abri du Cap Blanc
Marquay, Les Eyzies. **Tel** 05 53 06 86 00. ◯ Apr–Oct: Sun–Fri (phone at all other times to arrange group visits). 🖼 🔄

🏚 Grotte de Rouffignac
Tel 05 53 05 41 71. ◯ Apr–Oct: daily. 🖼 🔄

Dordogne Valley ❿

Dordogne. ✈ Bergerac. 🚆 Bergerac, Le Buisson de Cadouin. 🚌 Beynac. 🛈 Le Buisson de Cadouin (05 53 22 06 09)

Probably no river in France crosses so varied a landscape

View of Domme from the medieval gateway of Porte de la Combe

and such different geological formations as the Dordogne. Starting in deep granite gorges in the Massif Central, it continues through fertile lowlands, then enters the limestone Causse country around Souillac. By the time the Dordogne has wound down to the Garonne, it is almost 3 km (2 miles) wide.

Don't be put off by the valley's touristy image. It is a beautiful area for wandering. Several villages make good stopping-off points, such as Limeuil, Beynac and La Roque-Gageac from where *gabarres* (river boats) ferry visitors (Easter–Oct).

Perched high above the river, southwest of Sarlat, is the 17th-century **Château de Marqueyssac**. Its topiary park offers panoramic views from Domme to Beynac, and of the Château de Castelnaud on the opposite river bank.

Sarlat ⓫

See pp432–3.

Domme ⓬

Dordogne. 🏘 1,030.
🛈 pl de la Halle (05 53 31 71 00).
🛒 Thu. www.ot-domme.com

Henry Miller wrote: "Just to glimpse the black, mysterious river at Domme from the beautiful bluff…is something to be grateful for all one's life." Domme itself is a neat bastide *(see p445)* of golden stone, with medieval gateways still standing. People come here to admire the view, which takes in the Dordogne valley from Beynac in the west to Montfort in the east, and wander the maze of old streets inside the walls. There is also a large cavern under the 17th-century covered market where the inhabitants hid at perilous moments during the Hundred Years' War and the 16th-century Wars of Religion. Despite a seemingly impregnable position, 30 intrepid Huguenots managed to capture Domme by scaling the cliffs under cover of night and opening the gates.

A *cingle* (loop) of the river Dordogne, seen from the town of Domme

Rocamadour ⑬

Rocamadour became one of the most famous centres of pilgrimage following a spate of miracles heralded, it is claimed, by the bell above the Black Virgin and Child in the Chapel of Notre-Dame. This was followed by the discovery in 1166 of an ancient grave and sepulchre containing an undecayed body, said to be that of the early Christian hermit St Amadour. Although the town suffered with the decline of pilgrimages in the 17th and 18th centuries, it was heavily restored in the 19th century. Still a holy shrine, as well as a popular tourist destination, Rocamadour's site on a rocky plateau above the Alzou valley is phenomenal. The best views are to be had from the hamlet of L'Hospitalet.

Black Virgin and Child

The Château stands on the site of a fort which protected the sanctuary from the west.

St Michael's Chapel contains well-preserved 12th-century frescoes.

General View
Rocamadour is at its most breathtaking in the sunlight of early morning: the cluster of medieval houses, towers and battlements seems to sprout from the base of the cliff.

The Tomb of St Amadour once held the body of the hermit called *roc amator* (lover of rock), from whom the town took its name.

Grand Stairway
Pilgrims would climb this broad flight of steps on their knees as they said their rosaries. The stairway leads to a square on the next level, around which the main pilgrim chapels are grouped.

The Chapel of St John the Baptist faces the fine Gothic portal of the Basilica of St-Sauveur.

The Basilica of St-Sauveur, a late 12th-century sanctuary, backs on to the bare rock face.

St Anne's Chapel dates from the 13th century, and contains a 17th-century gilded altar screen.

Ramparts

Cross of Jerusalem

VISITORS' CHECKLIST

Lot. 630. 5 km (3 miles) SW Rocamadour. Maison du Tourisme (05 65 33 22 00).
Chapel of Notre-Dame
Jun–Sep: 8am–9pm; Oct–May: 8:30am–6:30pm.
www.rocamadour.com

Stations of the Cross
Pilgrims encounter the Cross of Jerusalem and 14 stations marking Jesus's journey to the Cross on their way up the hillside to the château.

Chapel of St Blaise (13th century)

Rocamadour Town
Now a pedestrian precinct, its main street is lined with souvenir shops to tempt the throngs of pilgrims.

Chapel of Notre-Dame (Miracles)
St Amadour's body was found in the cliff, near the Black Virgin Chapel. A statue of the Black Virgin, the supreme object of veneration, stands on the altar.

Gouffre de Padirac 🄯

Lot. *Tel 05 65 33 64 56.*
⬭ *Apr–mid-Oct: daily.*

Formed by the collapse of a
cave, this huge crater measures 35 m (115 ft) wide and
103 m (337 ft) deep. The
underground river and stunning succession of galleries
(see p403) were discovered in
1889. The immense chamber
known as the Salle du Grand
Dôme dwarfs the tallest of
cathedrals. Take a jacket, as
the cave is a constant 13° C.

Autoire 🄯

Lot. 🚶 *250.*

This is one of the loveliest
places in Quercy, the fertile
area east of Périgord. There
are no grand monuments or
dramatic history, just a beautifully unspoiled site at the
mouth of the Autoire gorge.
The **Château de Limarque** on
the main square, and the
Château de Busqueille overlooking it, are both built in
characteristic Quercy style,
with turrets and small towers.
Elsewhere, elaborate, raised
dovecotes typical of the region
stand in the middle of fields
or are attached to houses.
   Outside Autoire, past a 30-m
(100-ft) waterfall, a path climbs
to a rock amphitheatre giving
panoramic views of the region.

**The picturesque village of Autoire,
seen from across the gorge**

Cahors 🄯

Lot. 🚶 *21,500.* 🚉 🚌
ℹ *pl François Mitterrand (05 65 53
20 65).* 🛒 *Wed & Sat am.*
www.mairie-cahors.fr

The chief town of rural
Quercy, 2,000-year-old
Cahors is encircled by the
natural defences of the river
Lot. This small commercial
centre is famous for truffles, a
Saturday morning market, and
the dark, heady Cahors wine
which was produced as far
back as Roman times. Cahors'
main street is boulevard
Gambetta, a typical southern
thoroughfare lined with plane
trees, cafés and shops. This
street, like many others in
France, was named after Léon
Gambetta (1838–82), who
was born in Cahors and led
France to recovery after the
war with Prussia in 1870.
   Cathédrale de St-Etienne,
entrenched behind the narrow
streets of Cahors' Old Town,

A Tour of Two Rivers

Flanked by beautiful limestone cliffs, the
beautiful Lot and Célé valleys feature ancient
medieval villages and castles, narrow gorges and
rushing waterfalls along lazy stretches of river. An
unhurried tour of both valleys, around 160 km (100
miles), is best spread over two days, to savour the
gastronomic delights as well as the superb views. A
relaxing way to enjoy the beautiful scenery of the
Lot valley is by train (all-day or half-day trips with
Quercyrail) from Cahors to Cajarc. The slow,
winding road from Cahors, well-known for the
14th-century Pont Valentré, meanders beside the
wide river Lot. This is the home of truffles, *confit*
(conserve) of duck and goose, delicious goat's
cheese and the deeply coloured Cahors wine.

Grotte de Pech-Merle ①
This 25,000-year-old prehistoric site
outside Cabrerets has huge chambers
painted with mammoths, horses,
bison and human figures.

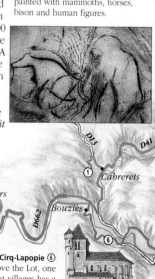

CAHORS

Vers

Cabrerets ①

Bouzies

St-Cirq-Lapopie ⑥
Perched high above the Lot, one
of France's prettiest villages has a
15th-century church and timber-
framed houses built into the cliffs.

dates back to 1119. It has some fine medieval details: don't miss the lively figures of the Romanesque north door and tympanum, which depict the Ascension, or the huge cupola above the nave (said to be the largest in France). They are covered in 14th-century frescoes depicting the stoning of St Stephen (St-Étienne). The Renaissance cloisters are decorated with some intricate, though damaged, carvings.

Also worth seeking out in the cathedral quarter is the ornate 16th-century **Maison de Roaldès**, its north façade decorated with tree, sun and rose of Quercy motifs. It was here that Henri of Navarre (who later became King Henri IV) stayed for one night in 1580 after besieging and capturing Cahors.

The town's landmark monument is the **Pont Valentré**, a fortified bridge with seven pointed arches and

The fortified Pont Valentré spanning the river Lot at Cahors

three towers that spans the river. It was built between 1308 and 1360, and has withstood many attacks since then. A breathtaking sight, it is claimed that the bridge is one of the most photographed monuments in the whole of France.

An alternative way to enjoy the scenery is to take a leisurely 90-minute boat trip through the lock from a wharf near the bridge (Apr–Oct).

Environs
Situated about 60 km (37 miles) to the west of Cahors in Fumel is the **Château de Bonaguil**, a superb example of military architecture dating from the Middle Ages.

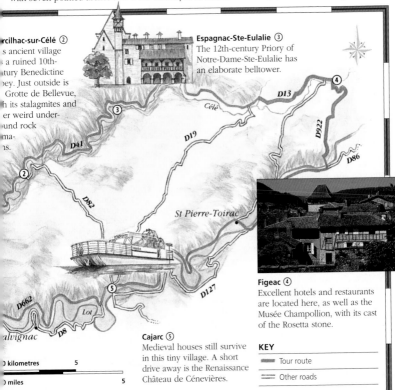

rcilhac-sur-Célé ②
s ancient village a ruined 10th-tury Benedictine bey. Just outside is Grotte de Bellevue, h its stalagmites and er weird underound rock rma-s.

Espagnac-Ste-Eulalie ③
The 12th-century Priory of Notre-Dame-Ste-Eulalie has an elaborate belltower.

St Pierre-Toirac

Figeac ④
Excellent hotels and restaurants are located here, as well as the Musée Champollion, with its cast of the Rosetta stone.

Cajarc ⑤
Medieval houses still survive in this tiny village. A short drive away is the Renaissance Château de Cénevières.

KEY

▬▬▬ Tour route

═══ Other roads

) kilometres   5

) miles   5

Orchards and vineyards outside Agen

Agen ⑰

Lot-et-Garonne. 🏘 *32,200.* ✈ 🚃
🚌 ℹ *107 bd Carnot (05 53 47 36
09).* 🛍 *Tue–Sun.* **www.ot-agen.org**

In a nationwide poll, the
inhabitants of Agen – an
attractive, unhurried provincial
capital on the Garonne – were
shown to be easily the most
contented people in France.
The town is the mecca of
French rugby (its team has
won three championship titles
in recent years), and the prune
production centre of France.

   The town has treasures in
addition to happy citizens and
succulent plums. The **Musée
Municipal des Beaux-Arts**
contains paintings by Goya,
including his *Ascent in a Hot-
Air Balloon,* Sisley's *September
Morning,* Corot's landscape
L'étang de Ville d'Avray and
works by Picabia. Undisputed
jewel of the collection is the
Vénus du Mas, a beautifully

proportioned marble statue
dating from the 1st century BC,
discovered nearby in 1876.

   Around the town, vast orchards of regimented plum
trees are a prominent feature
of the landscape. Crusaders
returning from the Middle East
brought the fruit to France in
the 11th century, and monks in
the Lot valley nearby were
the first to dry plums for
prunes in commercial quantities. Agen's factories now produce approximately 35,500
tonnes of prunes each year.

🏛 Musée Municipal des Beaux-Arts
Pl du Docteur Esquirol. **Tel** *05 53 69
47 23.* ⏰ *Wed–Mon.* ● *1 Jan, 1
May, 1 Nov, 25 Dec.* 📷

Environs
The fortified village of Moirax
has a 12th-century Roman-
esque church of great beauty
and symmetry, formerly part
of a Cluniac priory. Two of

the appealingly sculpted
capitals depict biblical accounts
of Daniel in the lions' den,
and Original Sin.

Larressingle ⑱

Gers. 🏘 *150.* 🚌 *to Condom.*
ℹ *Condom (05 62 28 00 80).*

With its ramparts, ruined
donjon (defence tower) and
fortress gate, Larressingle is a
tiny fortified village in the
middle of the Gascon countryside. It dates from the 13th
century, and is one of the last
remaining Gascon villages
with its walls still intact. The
state of preservation is unique,
and gives an idea of what life
must have been like for the
small, embattled local communities who had to live for
decades under conditions of
perpetual warfare.

Condom ⑲

Gers. 🏘 *8,000.* 🚌 ℹ *pl Bos-
suet (05 62 28 00 80).* 🛍 *Wed, Sat
am, Sun am.*

Long a centre for the
Armagnac trade, Condom is a
market town built around the
late-Gothic **Cathédrale St-
Pierre**. In 1569 during
the Wars of Religion, the
Huguenot (French Protestant)
army threatened to demolish
the cathedral, but Condom's
citizens averted this by paying
a huge ransom.

   The river Baïse skirts the
town centre. Notable among
Condom's fine 17th–18th-
century mansions is the **Hôtel
de Cugnac** on rue Jean-Jaurès,
with its ancient *chai* (wine
and spirit storehouse) and
distillery. On the other side of
the town centre, the **Musée
de l'Armagnac** is the place to
find out, finally, what the
difference between the
brandy of Armagnac and
   Cognac really is.

🏛 Musée de l'Armagnac
2 rue Jules Ferry. **Tel** *05 62
28 47 17.* ⏰ *Apr–Oct:
Wed–Mon; Nov–Mar:
Wed–Sun pms.* ● *Jan, public
hols.* 📷 ♿ *gr.fl.*

ARMAGNAC

Armagnac is one of the world's most expensive brandies. It is also one of the leading
products of southwest France: approximately
6 million bottles are produced annually, 45
per cent of which are exported to 132
countries. The vineyards of Armagnac
roughly straddle the border between the
Gers and the Lot-et-Garonne regions
and the Landes. Similar in style to
Cognac, its more famous neighbour,
Armagnac's single distillation leaves
more individual flavours in the spirit.
The majority of small, independent
producers offer direct sale to the
public: look out for the battered,
often half-hidden farm signs
advertising *Vente Directe.*

A Tenarèze Armagnac

D'ARTAGNAN

Gascons call their domain the "Pays d'Artagnan" after Alexandre Dumas' rollicking hero from *The Three Musketeers* (1844). The character of d'Artagnan was based on Charles de Batz, a typical Gascon whose chivalry, passion and impetuousness made him ideal as a musketeer, or royal bodyguard. De Batz's life was as fast and furious as that of the fictional hero, and he performed a feat of courtliness by arresting Louis XIV's most formidable minister without causing the slightest offence. The French have other opinions on the Gascon nature too: a *promesse de Gascon*, for example, means an empty promise.

Statue of Dumas' musketeer d'Artagnan in Auch

windows show a mix of prophets, patriarchs and apostles, with 360 individually characterized figures and exceptional colours. Three depict the key biblical events of Creation, the Crucifixion and the Resurrection.

Auch went through an urbanization programme in the 18th century, when the allées d'Etigny, flanked by the grand Hôtel de Ville and Palais de Justice, were built. Some fine houses from this period line the pedestrianized rue Dessoles. Auch's restaurants are known for their hearty dishes, including *foie gras de canard* (fattened duck liver).

Auch ⓴

Gers. 🚆 25,000. 🚉 🚌 🚻 1 rue Dessoles (05 62 05 22 89). 🔄 Thu & Sat. **www**.auch-tourisme.com

The ancient capital of the Gers department, Auch (pronounced "Ohsh") has long been a sleepy place which comes alive on market days. The new town by the station is not a place which encourages you to linger. Head instead for the Old Town on the outcrop

Medallion from Cathédrale Ste-Marie

overlooking the river Gers. If you climb the 234 stone steps from the river, you arrive directly in front of the recently restored late-Gothic **Cathédrale Ste-Marie**, begun in 1489. The furnishings of the cathedral are remarkable: highlights are the carved wooden choir stalls depicting more than 1,500 biblical, historical and mythological characters, and the equally magnificent 15th-century stained glass, attributed to Arnaud de Moles. The

Auvillar ⓶

Tarn-et-Garonne. 🚆 1,000. 🚻 pl de la Halle (05 63 39 89 82).

A perfect complement to the high emotion of Moissac *(see pp442–3)*, Auvillar is one of the loveliest hilltop villages in France. It has a triangular marketplace lined with half-timbered arcades at its centre, and extensive views from the promenade overlooking the river Garonne. There are picnic spots along this panoramic path plus an orientation map. This includes all but the chimneys visible in the distance, belonging to the nuclear plant at Golfech.

Sunflowers, a popular crop in southwest France grown for their seeds and oil

Moissac 🅲

The village of Moissac nestles among vineyards of sweet Chasselas grapes, with the abbey of St-Pierre its undisputed highlight. Founded in the 7th century by a Benedictine monk, the abbey was subsequently ransacked by Arabs, Normans and Hungarians. In 1047, Moissac abbey was united with the rich foundation at Cluny and prospered under the direction of Abbot **Abbot Durand** Durand de Bredon. By the 12th century it had become the pre-eminent monastery in southwest France. The south portal created during this period is a masterpiece of Romanesque sculpture.

Abbey of St-Pierre
The church's exterior belongs to two periods: one part, in stone, is Romanesque, the other, in brick, is Gothic.

Christ in Majesty
The figure of Christ sits in judgment at the centre of the scene. He holds the Book of Life in His left hand and raises His right in benediction.

Tympanum
The lower register of the balanced, compact tympanum shows the expressive "24 Elders with crowns of gold" from St John's vision.

★ South Portal
The carved south portal (1100–1130) is a masterful translation into stone of St John's dramatic vision of the Apocalypse (Book of Revelation, Chapters 4 and 5). The Evangelists Matthew, Mark, Luke and John appear as "four beasts full of eyes". Moorish details on the door jambs reflect the contemporary cultural exchange between France and Spain.

VISITORS' CHECKLIST

Tarn-et-Garonne. 13,000.
6 pl Durand de
Bredon (05 63 04 01 85). Sat,
Sun ams. Abbey Tel 05 63 04
66 84. 10am–6pm daily
(9am–7pm summer). for
cloisters. 6.30pm Mon–Fri,
7pm Sat, 10.30am Sun.

★ Cloister
The late 11th-century cloister is lined with alternate double and single columns in white, pink, green and grey marble. In all, there are 76 richly decorated arches.

FLOORPLAN: CHURCH AND CLOISTER

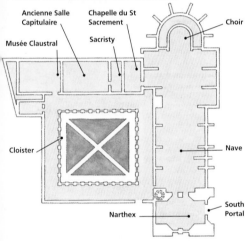

Ancienne Salle Capitulaire
Chapelle du St Sacrement
Musée Claustral
Sacristy
Choir
Cloister
Nave
Narthex
South Portal

Cloister Capitals
Flowers, beasts and scenes from both the Old and New Testaments are featured in these superbly sculptured 11th-century Romanesque capitals.

STAR FEATURES
★ South Portal
★ Cloister

Montauban ㉓

Tarn-et-Garonne. 55,000.
4 rue du Collège (05 63
63 60 60). Sat, Wed.
www.montauban-tourisme.com

Montauban deserves more attention than it usually gets, as Toulouse's little pink-brick sister and the capital of the 17th-century "Protestant Republic" of southern France. The painter Ingres was born here in 1780, and the town's great treasure is the **Musée Ingres**, a 17th-century palace with an exceptional bequest of paintings and 4,000 drawings, plus works by Van Dyck, Tintoretto, Courbet and sculptor Emile Bourdelle, an associate of Rodin, also from here.

Above all, Montauban is a civilized shopping centre, with a double-arcaded main square (place Nationale) built in the 17th and 18th centuries. A few streets away lies the stark white **Cathédrale Notre-Dame**, built on the orders of Louis XIV in 1692, in the backlash against Protestant heresy.

🏛 Musée Ingres
Palais Episcopal, 13 rue de l'Hôtel de Ville. *Tel* 05 63 22 12 91. Tue–Sun (Jul–Aug: daily). 1 Jan, 14 Jul, 1 Nov, 11 Nov, 25 Dec.

Gorges de l'Aveyron ㉔

Tarn-et-Garonne. Toulouse.
Montauban, Lexos. Montauban.
Montauban (05 63 63 60 60).

At the Gorges de l'Aveyron, the sweltering plains of Montauban change abruptly to cool, chestnut-wooded hills. Here the villages are of a different stamp from those of Périgord and Quercy, displaying an obsession with defence.

The château at Bruniquel, founded in the 6th century, is built over the lip of a precipice, reached by a steep walk through the village. Further along the D115, the village of Penne's position on the tip of a giant rock fang is even more extreme. The gorge narrows and darkens; from St-Antonin-Noble-Val, clamped to its rock face, the valley turns towards Cordes.

Cordes ㉕

Tarn. 👥 1,050. 🚉 🚌 ℹ️ pl Jean
Ranelcals (05 63 56 00 52). 🛍️ Sat.
www.cordes-sur-ciel.org

Sometimes known as Cordes-
sur-Ciel, this is a fitting
description as the town seems
suspended against the skyline. During the 13th-century
Cathar wars the entire town
was excommunicated. Devastating epidemics of plague
later sent it into decline, and
the town was in an advanced
state of decay at the beginning of the 20th century.

Restoration work under the
care of the artist Yves Brayer
began in the 1940s. The ramparts and many of the gates
which the town's founder,
Albigensian Count Raymond
VII of Toulouse, built in 1222
have been well preserved.
Also intact are Gothic houses
like the 14th-century **Maison
du Grand Fauconnier**, with
falcons carved on its façade,
and the **Maison du Grand
Veneur** (Great Huntsman's
House) which line the unbe-
lievably steep cobbled streets.

Today, Cordes on its hilltop
still exudes a sense of loss. The
town of which Albert Camus
once wrote "Everything is
beautiful there, even regret",
is now completely dependent
on tourism. "Medieval" crafts
aimed at visitors abound, but
nothing remains of the exuberant weaving, *pastel* (blue
pigment) and leather industries
which paid for so many of
Cordes' ancient buildings. The
Jardin du Paradis offers a
corner of beauty and hope.

Cathédrale Ste-Cécile perched above the town of Albi

Albi ㉖

Tarn. 👥 50,000. 🚉 🚌
ℹ️ pl Ste-Cécile (05 63 49 48 80).
🛍️ Sat. www.albi-tourisme.fr

Like many another large town
in this region, Albi is not only
red, but also red hot, and
definitely not for afternoon
visits. You need to get up in
the cool early morning to
walk the streets around the
market and the cathedral.

Then make for the **Musée
Henri de Toulouse-Lautrec** in
the Palais de la Berbie ahead
of the crowds. The museum
contains the most complete
permanent collection of the
artist's work in existence,
including paintings, drawings
and his famous posters for
the Moulin-Rouge. There are
also canvases by Matisse,
Dufy and Yves Brayer. After a
stroll around the beautiful
terraced gardens, head for the
vast red-brick **Cathédrale Ste-
Cécile**, built in the aftermath of
the Albigensian crusade in
1265. It was intended as a
reminder to potential heretics
that the Church meant business. From a distance, its

semi-circular towers and
narrow windows give it the
appearance more of a fortress
than a place of worship. Every
feature, from the huge belltower to the apocalyptic fresco
of the *Last Judgement*, is on a
giant scale, built deliberately
to dwarf the average person.
The effect is breathtaking.

🏛 **Musée Toulouse-Lautrec**
Palais de la Berbie.
Tel 05 63 49 48 70.
◻ Apr–Sep: daily; Oct–Mar: Wed–
Mon (museum under renovation so
some sections may be closed).
🔲 1 Jan, 1 May, 1 Nov, 25 Dec. 🏷
🔲 🏠 www.musee-toulouse-
lautrec.com

Castres ㉗

Tarn. 👥 45,500. ✈️ 🚉 🚌
ℹ️ 3 rue Milhau-Ducommun (05 63
62 63 62). 🛍️ Tue–Sat.
www.tourisme-castres.com

Castres has been a centre for
the cloth industry since the
14th century. Today it is also
the headquarters of one of
France's biggest pharma-
ceutical companies. In the
large collection of Spanish art
in the **Musée Goya**, the artist
himself is well represented by
a large, misty council scene
and by a series of powerful
prints, *Los Caprichos*. Outside,
the formal gardens between
the town hall and the river
Agout were designed in the
17th century by Le Nôtre
(*see p179*), the landscape
architect of Vaux-le-Vicomte
and Versailles.

🏛 **Musée Goya**
Hôtel de Ville. **Tel** 05 63 71 59 30 or
05 63 71 59 27. ◻ Jul–Aug: daily;
Sep–Jun: Tue–Sun. 🔲 1 Jan, 1 May,
1 Nov, 25 Dec. 🏷

TOULOUSE-LAUTREC

Comte Henri de Toulouse–
Lautrec was born in Albi
in 1864. Crippled at 15 as
a result of two falls, he
moved to Paris in 1882,
recording the life of the
city's cabarets, brothels,
racecourses and circuses.
A dedicated craftsman, his
bold, vivid posters did
much to establish litho-
graphy as a major art form.
Alcoholism and syphilis
led to his early death at
the age of 36.

Lautrec's *La Modiste* (1900)

Bastide Towns

Bastide towns were hurriedly built in the 13th century by both the English and the French, to encourage settlement of empty areas before the Hundred Years' War. They are the medieval equivalent of "new towns", with their planned grid of streets and fortified perimeters. Over 300 bastide towns and villages still survive between Périgord and the Pyrenees.

A broad arcaded marketplace *is the central feature of most bastides. Montauban's arcades still shelter a variety of shops.*

Lauzerte, *founded in 1241 by the Count of Toulouse, is a typical bastide town of grey stone houses. The town, long an English outpost, is perched for security on the brow of a hill.*

The church could be used as a keep when the bastide's outer fortifications had been breached.

The central square is surrounded by a grid of interconnecting streets and alleys. This differs markedly from the usual jumble of medieval houses and lanes.

Stone houses protected the perimeter.

MONFLANQUIN

This military bastide town was built by the French in 1256 on a strategic north–south route. It changed hands several times during the Hundred Years' War.

Today, the bastides *form a convenient network of market towns, known as the* route des bastides. *The best time to visit them is on market day, when the central squares are crammed with stalls.*

Porte de la Jane *in Cordes is a typical bastide feature. These narrow gateways were easily barred by portcullises.*

Toulouse ⓘⓝⓕⓞ

Toulouse, the most important town in southwest France, is the country's fourth largest metropolis, and a major industrial and university city. The area is also famous for its aerospace industry (Concorde, Airbus, the Ariane space rocket all originated here), as shown by the new Cité de l'Espace just outside the city.

Best seen on foot, Toulouse has fine regional cuisine, two striking cathedrals, lively street life and a rose-brick Old Town which, as the French say, is "pink at dawn, red at noon and mauve at dusk".

The river Garonne, crossed by the Pont Neuf

Houseboats at their moorings on the Canal du Midi

Exploring Toulouse

This warm southern city has steadily expanded, crescent-like, from its original Roman site on the Garonne. First it was a flourishing Visigoth city, then a Renaissance town of towered brick palaces built with the wealth generated by the *pastel* (blue pigment) and grain trades. The grandest of these palaces still survive in the Old Town, centred around Place du Capitole and the huge 18th-century **Hôtel de Ville**. Here, and in place St-Georges and rue Alsace-Lorraine, is the main concentration of shops, bars and cafés. The city's large student population keeps prices down in the numerous cafés, oyster bars and bookstores, and in the fleamarket, held on Sundays in place St-Sernin.

A ring of 18th- and 19th-century boulevards encircles the city, surrounded in turn by a tangle of autoroutes. The left bank of the Garonne is under development (St-Cyprien) and

is linked by Toulouse's new driverless metro. The former abattoir has been superbly converted into a centre for modern and contemporary art, **Les Abattoirs** (Tue–Sun), the highlight of which is Picasso's theatre backdrop *Minotaur disguised as Harlequin*.

ⓘ Les Jacobins

This church was begun in 1229 and completed over the next two centuries. It was the first Dominican convent, founded to combat dissent. The Jacobins' convent became the founding institution of Toulouse University. Its church, a Gothic masterpiece, features a soaring, 22-branched palm tree vault in the apse. The delicate Gothic Chapelle St-Antonin (1337) contains frescoes of the Apocalypse dating from 1341.

ⓜ Musée des Augustins

21 rue de Metz. **Tel** 05 61 22 21 82. ⚪ *daily.* ⚫ *1 Jan, 1 May, 25 Dec.* 🄳 ♿ 🄲 www.augustins.org

Palm vaulting in the apse of Les Jacobins

Toulouse became a centre of Romanesque art owing to its position on the route to Santiago de Compostela (see p400). The museum has sculpture from the period and 12th-century Romanesque capitals, as well as cloisters from a 14th-century Augustinian priory. There are also 16th–19th-century French, Italian and Flemish paintings here, including work by Ingres, Delacroix, Constant and Laurens.

Façade of Musée des Augustins

🏛 Fondation Bemberg

Hôtel d'Assézat, 7 pl d'Assézat. *Tel* 05 61 12 06 89. ◯ *Tue–Sun.* ⬤ *1 Jan, 25 Dec.* 🏛 ♿ 📷

This 16th-century palace houses the collection of local art lover Georges Bemberg, and covers Renaissance paintings, *objets d'art* and bronzes, as well as 19th–20th-century French paintings.

| 0 metres | 250 |
| 0 yards | 250 |

Key to Symbols see back flap

⛪ Basilique de St-Sernin

Pl St-Sernin. *Tel* 05 61 21 80 45. ◯ *daily.*

This is the largest Romanesque basilica in Europe, built in the 11th–12th centuries to accommodate pilgrims. Highlights are the octagonal brick belfry, with rows of decorative brick arches topped by pepperpot turrets and a spire. Beautiful 11th-century marble bas-reliefs of Christ and the symbols of the Evangelists by Bernard Gilduin are in the ambulatory.

🏛 Cité de l'Espace

Av Jean Gonord. *Tel* 08 20 37 72 23. ◯ *daily.* ⬤ *Jan.* 🏛 ♿ 🍴 📷 🎬 www.cite-espace.com

Southeast of Toulouse, this vast "space park" includes a planetarium, interactive exhibits related to the exploration of space, the Terradome "film-experience" on the history of the earth, and a lifesize replica of the Ariane 5 rocket, where visitors can learn how, in theory at least, to launch rockets and satellites.

The tiered, 12th-century tower of Basilique de St-Sernin

SIGHTS AT A GLANCE

THE PYRENEES

PYRÉNÉES-ATLANTIQUES · HAUTES-PYRÉNÉES
ARIÈGE · HAUTE-GARONNE

The mountains dominate life in the French Pyrenees. A region in many ways more Spanish than French, over centuries its remote terrain and tenacious people have given heretics a hiding place and refugees an escape route. Today it is the last remaining wilderness in southern Europe and a habitat for rare animal species.

Heading east from the Atlantic coast, the hills are wonderfully lush after the plains of Aquitaine. The deeper the Pyrenees are penetrated, the steeper the valley sides and the more gigantic the snow-clad peaks become. This is magnificent, empty, dangerous country, to be approached with caution and respect. In summer the region offers over 1,600 km (1,000 miles) of walking trails, as well as camping, fishing and climbing. In winter there is both cross-country and downhill skiing at the busy resorts along the border, much livelier than their Spanish counterparts.

Historically, the Pyrenees are known as the birthplace of Henri IV, who put an end to the Wars of Religion in 1593 and united France, though the region has been characterized more often by independent fiefdoms. The region's oldest inhabitants, the Basque people *(see p455)* have maintained their own language and culture, and their resorts of Bayonne, Biarritz and St-Jean-de-Luz reflect this, looking to the sea and to summer visitors for their livelihood.

Inland, Pau, Tarbes and Foix rely on tourism and medium-scale industry, while Lourdes receives four million pilgrims every year. For the rest, life has been regulated by agriculture, though economic constraints today are causing an exodus from the land.

Countryside around St-Lizier, in the heart of the Pyrenean countryside

◁ Barèges, a ski resort and spa town in the Hautes-Pyrénées

Exploring the Pyrenees

The towering Pyrenees cut across southwest France from the Mediterranean to the Atlantic coast, encompassing the craggy citadel of Montségur, the pilgrimage centre of Lourdes, Pau in the hilly Béarn country, and the Basque port of Bayonne. This formidable range, an unspoiled paradise for walkers, fishermen and skiers, is as lush on its French side as it is arid in Spain, and contains the wild and beautiful Parc National des Pyrénées. Throughout the region, visitors can expect cool temperatures and grandiose scenery. Lovers of art and architecture will be richly rewarded by St-Bertrand-de-Comminges and St-Jean-de-Luz, among the region's important sights.

Marzipan sweets, a speciality of southwest France

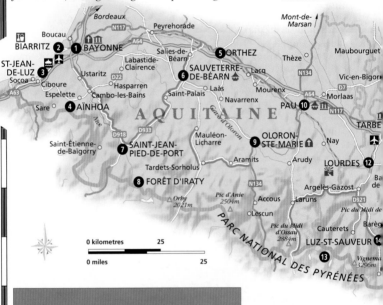

The galleried church in the Basque village of Espelette

GETTING AROUND

Access to the Basque coast in the western Pyrenees is via the A63 from Bordeaux. The length of the Pyrenees, including the mountain valleys, is served by the A64 which now runs all the way from Bayonne to Toulouse, via Orthez, Pau, Tarbes and St-Gaudens. Once you are high up, expect narrow, twisting roads and slow driving. The scenic but demanding D918/118 corniche road crosses 18 high passes between the Atlantic and the Mediterranean.

There are airports at Biarritz, Pau and Lourdes. These three towns, together with Orthez and Tarbes, are on the rail route which loops south between Bordeaux and Toulouse.

SIGHTS AT A GLANCE

Wild pottock ponies on moorland in the Forêt d'Iraty

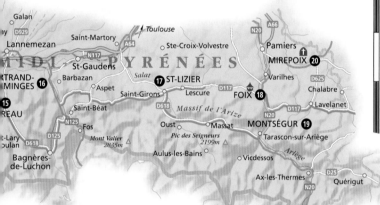

St-Jean-de-Luz seen from Ciboure, across the Nivelle estuary

KEY

- ═ Motorway
- ═ Major road
- ═ Secondary road
- ═ Minor road
- ═ Scenic route
- ═ Main railway
- ─ Minor railway
- ▬ International border
- ─ Regional border
- △ Summit

Bayonne ❶

Pyrénées-Atlantiques. 🏠 42,000.
🚉 🚌 ℹ️ pl des Basques (05 59 46
01 46). 🛒 Mon–Sat (am only).
www.bayonne-tourisme.com

Bayonne, capital of the
French Basque country, lies
between two rivers – the
turbulent Nive which arrives
straight from the mountains,
and the wide, languid Adour.
An important town since
Roman times because of its
command of one of the few
easily passable roads to
Spain, Bayonne prospered as
a free port under English rule
from 1154 to 1451. Since then
it has successfully withstood
14 sieges, including a particularly bloody one directed by
Wellington in 1813.

Grand Bayonne, the district
around the cathedral, can be
easily explored on foot. The
13th-century **Cathédrale Ste-
Marie** was begun under
English rule and is northern
Gothic in style. Look for the
handsome cloister and the
15th-century knocker on the
north door – if a fugitive
could put a hand to this, he
was entitled to sanctuary. The
pedestrianized streets around
form a lively shopping area,
especially the arcaded rue du
Port Neuf, with cafés serving
hot chocolate, a Bayonne
speciality. (Fine-quality choc-
olate-making was introduced
by the Jews who fled Spain at
the end of the 15th century,
and it has remained a spec-

Lighthouse at Biarritz

iality of the town.) Bayonne is
also famous for its ham.

Petit Bayonne lies on the
opposite side of the quay-
lined river Nive. The **Musée
Basque** gives an excellent
introduction to the customs
and traditions of the Basque
nation, with reconstructed
house interiors and exhibits
on seafaring. Nearby, the
Musée Bonnat has a superb
art gallery. The first floor here
is a must for art lovers, with
sketches by Leonardo, Van
Dyck, Rubens and Rembrandt
and paintings by Goya, Corot,
Ingres and Constable.

🏛 **Musée Basque**
37 quai des Corsaires. **Tel** 05 59 46
61 90. 🕐 Tue–Sun. 🔴 public hols.
🖼 👨‍🦽 ℹ️ www.musee-basque.com

🏛 **Musée Bonnat**
5 rue Jacques Lafitte. **Tel** 05 59 59
08 52. 🕐 Jul–Sep: daily; Oct–Jun:
Wed–Mon. 🔴 public hols.
🖼 👨‍🦽 www.musee-bonnat.com

Biarritz ❷

Pyrénées-Atlantiques. 🏠 30,000.
✈️ 🚉 🚌 ℹ️ Javalquinto, square
d'Ixelles (05 59 22 37 10). 🛒 daily.
www.ville-biarritz.fr

Biarritz, west of Bayonne,
has a grandiose centre, but has
been developed along the
coast by residential suburbs.
The resort began as a whaling
port but was transformed into
a playground for the European
rich in the 19th century. Its
popularity was assured when
Empress Eugénie discovered
its mild winter climate during
the reign of her husband,
Napoleon III. The town has

three good beaches, with the
best surfing in Europe, two
casinos, and one of the last
great luxury hotels in Europe,
the Palais (see p586), formerly
the residence of Eugénie.

In the port des Pêcheurs, the
Musée de la Mer aquarium is
home to specimens of some
of the marine life found in the
Bay of Biscay. Below it, a narrow causeway leads across to
the Rocher de la Vierge, offering far-reaching views along
the whole of the Basque coast.
The Musée du Chocolat is fine
compensation for a rainy day.

🏛 **Musée de la Mer**
Esplanade du Rocher-de-la-Vierge, 14
plateau de l'Atalaye. **Tel** 05 59 22 33
44. 🕐 Apr–Oct: daily; Nov–Mar: Tue–
Sun. 🔴 2nd–3rd wk Jan, 1 Jan, 25
Dec. 🖼 👨‍🦽 ℹ️ 🖥
www.museedelamer.com

Altar in Eglise St-Jean-Baptiste

St-Jean-de-Luz ❸

Pyrénées-Atlantiques. 🏠 13,000.
✈️ Biarritz. 🚉 🚌 ℹ️ pl Maréchal
Foch (05 59 26 03 16). 🛒 Tue & Fri.
www.saint-jean-de-luz.com

St-Jean is a sleepy fishing
village out of season and
a scorching tourist town in
August, with shops to rival
the chic rue du Faubourg St-
Honoré in Paris. In the 11th
century whale carcasses were
towed here to feed the whole
village. The natural harbour
protects the shoreline,
making it one of the few
beaches safe for swimming
along this stretch of coast.

One of the most important
historical events in St-Jean was
the wedding of Louis XIV
and the Infanta Maria Teresa

**Grand Bayonne, clustered around
the twin-spired cathedral**

For hotels and restaurants in this region see pp585–8 and pp640–3

St-Jean-de-Luz, a fishing village that explodes into life in summer

of Spain in 1660, a union that had the effect of sealing the long-awaited alliance between France and Spain, only to embroil the two countries ultimately in the War of the Spanish Succession. This wedding took place at the **Eglise St-Jean-Baptiste**, still the biggest and best of the great Basque churches, a triple-galleried marvel with a glittering 17th-century altarpiece and an atmosphere of gaiety and fervour. The gate through which the Sun King led his bride was immediately walled up by masons: a plaque now marks the place. The **Maison Louis XIV**, with its contemporary furnishings, is where the king stayed in 1660, and is worth a look.

The port is busy in the summer, while the restaurants behind the covered markets serve sizzling bowls full of *chipirons* – squid cooked in their own ink – a local speciality. Place St-Louis is a delightful place to sit and watch the world go by.

🏛 **Maison Louis XIV**
Place Louis XIV. **Tel** 05 59 26 01 56.
◯ Jun–Sep: daily. 📷

Environs
On the other side of the river Nivelle, Ciboure was the birthplace of composer Maurice Ravel. It is characterized by 18th-century merchants' houses, steep narrow streets

and seafood restaurants. A two-hour coastal walk leads to the neighbouring village of **Socoa**, where the lighthouse on the clifftop offers a fine view of the coast all the way to Biarritz.

Basque men in traditional berets

Aïnhoa ➍

Pyrénées-Atlantiques. 🏠 610. 🚌
ℹ La Mairie (05 59 29 92 60).

A tiny township on the road to the Spanish border, Aïnhoa was founded in the 12th century as a waystation on the road to Santiago de

Compostela *(see pp400–1)*. The main street of 17th-century whitewashed Basque houses and a galleried church from the same period survive.

Environs
There is a similar church in the village of Espelette nearby. Typically Basque in style, the galleries boosted the seating capacity and had the added effect of separating the men from the women and children in the main part of the church. Espelette is the trading centre for *pottocks*, an ancient local breed of pony, auctioned here at the end of January. It is also the shrine of the local crop, the red pimento pepper, especially in October when a pepper festival is held here.

At the foot of the St-Ignace pass lies the pretty mountain village of **Sare**. From here you can reach the summit of la Rhune by cog railway. This provides the best vantage point in the entire Pays Basque. The descent on foot is worthwhile.

Basque farmhouse near Espelette

Sauveterre-de-Béarn and the remains of the fortified bridge over the Gave d'Oloron, the Pont de la Légende

Orthez ❺

Pyrénées-Atlantiques. 🏠 11,000. 🚉
🚌 ℹ Maison Jeanne d'Albret, rue
Bourg Vieux (05 59 38 32 84). 🛒
Tue; Nov–Mar: foie gras market Sat.

Orthez is an important Béarn
market town, its 13th–14th-
century fortified bridge a vital
river crossing point over the
Gave de Pau in the Middle
Ages. It has a spectacular
Saturday morning market held
from November to February,
selling *foie gras*, smoked and
air-cured Bayonne hams, and
all kinds of poultry and fresh
produce. Fine buildings line
the rue Bourg Vieux,
especially the house of
Jeanne d'Albret, mother of
Henry IV, on the corner of
rue Roarie. Jeanne's
enthusiasm for the Protestant
faith alienated both her own
subjects and Charles X, and
ultimately caused the Béarn
region to be drawn into the
Wars of Religion (1562–93).

Sauveterre-de-Béarn ❻

Pyrénées-Atlantiques. 🏠 1,400.
🚌 ℹ pl Royale (05 59 38 32 86).
🛒 Sat.

An attractive market town,
Sauveterre is well worth an
overnight stay. It has
breathtaking views southward

over the Gave d'Oloron, the
graceful single arch of the
river's fortified bridge, and the
16th-century **Château de Nays**.
Fishermen gather here for the
annual world salmon-fishing
championships, in the fast-
flowing Oloron (April to July).

Be sure, also, to visit the
Château de Laàs, 9 km (5.5
miles) along the D27 from
Sauveterre, which has an
excellent collection of 18th-
century decorative art and
furniture – notably the bed
Napoleon slept in on the
night after his defeat at
Waterloo. There is also a
pretty park with a maze.

♠ Château de Laàs
Tel 05 59 38 91 53. ◯ Apr–Oct: Wed–
Mon (Apr: pm only; Jul–Aug: daily). 📷

**The Château de Nays at Sauveterre
in the Béarn region**

St-Jean-Pied-de-Port ❼

Pyrénées-Atlantiques. 🏠 1,400. 🚉
🚌 ℹ 14 pl du Général de Gaulle
(05 59 37 03 57, 08 10 75 36 71). 🛒
Mon. **www.**pyrenees-basques.com

The old capital of Basse-
Navarre lies at the foot of the
Roncesvalles Pass. Here the
Basques crushed the rear-
guard of Charlemagne's army
in 778 and killed its commander, Roland, later glorified
in the *Chanson de Roland*.

Throughout the Middle Ages
this red sandstone fortress-
town was famous as the last
rallying point before entering
Spain on the pilgrim road to
Santiago de Compostela (*see
pp400–1*). As soon as a group
of pilgrims was spotted, the
townsfolk would ring the
church bells to show them the
way, and the pilgrims would
sing in response.

Visitors and pilgrims in all
seasons still provide St-Jean
with its income. They enter
the narrow streets of the upper
town on foot from the Porte
d'Espagne, and pass cafés,
hotels and restaurants on the
way up. The ramparts are
worth the steep climb, as is the
citadel with panoramic views.

On Mondays the town hosts
a craft market, Basque *pelote*
matches and, in summer,
shows with bulls.

Forêt d'Iraty ❽

Pyrénées-Aquitaine. 🚌 St-Jean-Pied-de-Port 🚏 ℹ️ St-Jean-Pied-de-Port (05 59 37 03 57), Larrau (05 59 28 51 29).

A wild plateau of beech woods and moorland, the Forêt d'Iraty is famous for its cross-country skiing and walking. Here the ancient breed of Basque ponies, the *pottocks*, run half-wild. These creatures have not changed at all since the prehistoric inhabitants of the region traced their silhouettes on the walls of local caves.

The tourist office at St-Jean-Pied-de-Port publishes maps of local walks. The best begins at the Chalet Pedro car park, south of the lake on the Iraty plateau, and takes you along the GR10 to 3,000-year-old standing stones on the western side of the Sommet d'Occabé.

Oloron-Ste-Marie ❾

Pyrénées-Atlantiques. 👥 11,400. 🚌 🚏 ℹ️ allée du Compte de Tréville (05 59 39 98 00). 🛒 Fri. www.tourisme-oloron.com

Oloron, a small town at the junction of the Aspe and the Ossau valleys, has grown from a Celtiberian settlement. There are huge agricultural fairs here in May and September, and the town is famed for producing the

Cathédrale Ste-Marie

famous classic French berets. The town's great glory is the doorway of the Romanesque **Cathédrale Ste-Marie**, with its biblical and Pyrenean scenes. Spain lies just on the other side of the Somport pass at the head of the mountainous Aspe valley, and the influence of Spanish stonemasons is evident in Oloron's **Eglise Sainte-Croix** with its Moorish-style vaulting. These are Oloron's only sights, leaving time to head up the Aspe valley to try one of the area's famous ewe's cheeses, or mixed cow and goat's cheeses.

A side road leads to Lescun, huddled around its church, beyond which is a spectacular range of saw-toothed peaks topped by the **Pic d'Anie** at 2,504 m (8,215 ft), one of the most beautiful spots in the Pyrenees. Sadly, at nearby Somport a controversial highway and tunnel project was permitted, despite its posing a threat to the traditional mountain agricultural economy, and the last habitat of the Pyrenean brown bear.

High moorland above the Forêt d'Iraty, long denuded of timber for use by the French and Spanish navies

Gobelin tapestry in the Château de Pau

Pau ⑩

Pyrénées-Atlantiques. 🏠 87,000. ✈
🚃 🚌 🛈 pl Royale (05 59 27 27
08). 🛍 Mon–Sat. **www**.pau.fr

A lively university town, with
elegant Belle Epoque
architecture and shady parks,
Pau is the capital of the Béarn
region, and the most interesting big town in the central
Pyrenees. The weather in
autumn and winter is mild,
so this has been a favourite
resort of affluent foreigners,
especially the English, since
the early 19th century.

Pau is chiefly famous as the
birthplace of King Henry IV.
His mother, Jeanne d'Albret,
travelled for 19 days by carriage from Picardy, in the
eighth month of her preg-
nancy, just to have her baby
here. She sang during her
labour, convinced that if she
did so, Henry would grow up
as tough and resilient as she
was. As soon as the infant was
born, his lips were smeared
with garlic and local Jurançon
wine, in keeping with the
traditional custom.

The town's principal sight is
the **Château de Pau**, first remodelled in the 14th century
for the ruler of Béarn, Gaston
Phoebus (see p463). It was
heavily restored 400 years
later. Marguerite d'Angoulême,
sister of the King of France,
resided here in the late 16th
century, and transformed the
town into a centre for the arts
and free thinking.

◁ Foothills of the Pyrenees

The château's 16th-century
Gobelin tapestries, made by
Flemish weavers working in
Paris, are fabulous. (The
Maison Carré in Nay – 18 km
towards Lourdes – exhibits the
former Musée Béarnais' important collection of artifacts
retracing the history, traditions
and culture of the Béarn.)

Outside, the boulevard des
Pyrénées affords both glorious
views of the gardens below
and a glimpse of the highest
Pyrenean peaks, often snow-
capped year round. Continue
from here to the eclectic **Musée
des Beaux-Arts**, where there
is a splendid Degas, the
Cotton Exchange, New Orleans;
Rubens' Last Judgment, and a
work by El Greco.

⛪ **Château de Pau**
Rue du Château. **Tel** 05 59 82 38 02.
☐ daily. ● 1 Jan, 1 May, 25 Dec.
🎫 📷 🛈 **www**.musee-chateau-
pau.fr

Château de Pau, birthplace of Henry IV in 1553

🏛 **Musée des Beaux-Arts**
Rue Mathieu Lalanne. **Tel** 05 59 27
33 02. ☐ Wed–Mon. ● some
public hols. 🎫 ♿ restricted.

Tarbes ⑪

Hautes-Pyrénées. 🏠 48,000. ✈
🚃 🚌 🛈 3 cours Gambetta
(05 62 51 30 31). 🛍 Thu.

Tarbes is the most prosperous
town in the Bigorre region, a
centre for chemical and
engineering industries with
good shops and a major agricultural market. The **Jardin
Massey** in the middle of town
was designed at the turn of
the 19th century and is one of
the loveliest parks in the
southwest. It has many rare
plants, including the North
American sassafras. Its museum
has a collection of 16th–20th-
century European art.

The **Maison du Cheval** and
the Haras National (National
Stud), with its thoroughbred
stallions, should not be missed.

🏛 **La Maison du Cheval**
Chemin du Mauhourat. **Tel** 05 62 56 30
80. ☐ Mon–Fri pms. ● public hols.
🎫 📷

Lourdes ⑫

Hautes-Pyrénées. 🏠 15,000. 🚃 🚌
🚌 Easter–mid-Oct. 🛈 pl Peyramale
(05 62 42 77 40). 🛍 Wed–Sun.
www.lourdes-infotourisme.com

Lourdes, one of the great
modern shrines of Europe,
owes its celebrity to visions of
the Virgin experienced by 14-
year-old Bernadette Soubirous
in 1858. Four million people

annually visit **Grotte Massabielle**, the cave where the visions occurred, and the room on rue des Petits-Fossés where Bernadette's family lived, in search of miracle cures. The **Musée de Lourdes** gives information about Bernadette's life and the shrine.

Visit the **Grottes de Bétharram** for underground rides by boat and train, or the **Musée Pyrénéen**, about the pioneers who opened up these ranges.

🏛 Musée de Lourdes
Parking de l'Egalité. *Tel* 05 62 94 28 00. ◯ Apr–Oct: daily; Nov–Mar: Mon–Fri. 🚫 ♿

🌿 Grottes de Bétharram
St-Pé-de-Bigorre. *Tel* 05 62 41 80 04. ◯ Feb–late Mar: Mon–Fri pms; late Mar–late Oct: daily. 🚫 ♿

Spectacular limestone formations at the Grottes de Bétharram

Pilgrims participating in open-air mass at Lourdes

🏛 Musée Pyrénéen
Château Fort, rue du Fort. *Tel* 05 62 42 37 37. ◯ daily. ● public

Parc National des Pyrénées ⑬

See pp460–61.

Luz-St-Sauveur ⑭

Hautes-Pyrénées. 🏠 1,200. 🚉 to Lourdes. 🚌 🛈 pl du 8 mai (05 62 92 30 30). 🛒 Mon am. **www**.luz.org

Luz-St-Sauveur is an attractive spa town, with an unusual church built in the 14th century by the Hospitaliers de Saint Jean de Jérusalem (later the Knights of Malta), an order established to protect pilgrims. The church is fortified with gun slits that look out over the town and valley, and provided protection for pilgrims on the way to Santiago de Compostela.

Environs
The elegant spa town of **Cauterets** makes a good base for climbing, skiing and walking in the rugged mountains of the Bigorre region.

Gavarnie is a former waystation on the Santiago de Compostela pilgrim route. A good track, accessible on foot or by donkey, leads from the village to the spectacular natural rock amphitheatre known as the **Cirque de Gavarnie**. Here the longest waterfall in Europe, at 240 m (787 ft), cascades off the mountain into space, encircled by eleven 3,000-m (9,800-ft) peaks.

Tourists can now share much of the **Observatoire Pic du Midi de Bigorre** with scientists. Access is by cablecar from La Mongie to Le Taoulet and then up to the summit. Alternatively there are a number of walks up to the Pic (4 hours minimum).

The French are justly proud of the Observatory, which has supplied the clearest images of Venus and other planets in the solar system so far obtained from the Earth's surface. The 1-m (3.2-ft) telescope mapped out the moon for NASA's Apollo missions.

🏛 Observatoire Pic du Midi de Bigorre
Tel 08 25 00 28 77. ◯ daily (unless weather forbids). ● Nov. 🚫 🖥 🍴

THE MIRACLE OF LOURDES

In 1858 a young girl named Bernadette Soubirous experienced 18 visions of the Virgin at the Grotte Massabielle near the town. Despite being told to keep away from the cave by her mother – and the local magistrate – she was guided to a spring with miraculous healing powers. The church endorsed the miracles in the 1860s, and since then, many people claim to have been cured by the holy water. A huge Religious City of shrines, churches and hospices has since grown up around the spring, with a dynamic tourist industry to match.

Bernadette's vision

Parc National des Pyrénées ⑬

Pyrenean ibex

The Pyrenees National Park, designated in 1967, extends 100 km (62 miles) along the French and Spanish frontier. It boasts some of the most spectacular scenery in Europe, ranging from meadows glimmering with butterflies to high peaks, snow-capped even in summer. Variations in altitude and climate make the park rich in flora and fauna. One of the most enjoyable ways to see it is on foot: within the park are 350 km (217 miles) of well-marked footpaths.

Vallée d'Aspe
Jagged peaks tower above the Vallé d'Aspe and the Cirque de Lescun. This area is now threatened by a ne motorway (see p455).

Col du Somport, the Somport pass (1,632 m/5,354 ft), is a rugged route into Spain, snow-bound December–April.

Pic d'Anie
The limestone-flanked 2,504-m (8,215-ft) Pic d'Anie overlooks rich upland pastures watered by melting snow. In spring, the ground is ablaze with Pyrenean varieties of gentian and columbine, found nowhere else.

Pic du Midi d'Ossau
A tough trail leads fro the Bious-Artigues lak the base of the Pic du Midi d'Ossau and encircles the formidal tooth-shaped summit (2,884 m/9,462 ft).

PYRENEAN WILDLIFE

The Pyrenees are home to a rich variety of wild creatures, many of them unique to the range. The ibex, a member of the antelope family, is still numerous in the valleys of Ossau and Cauterets. Birds of prey include the Egyptian, griffon and bearded vultures. Ground predators range from the rare Pyrenean lynx, to civet, pine marten and stoat. The desman, a tiny aquatic mammal related to the mole, is found in many of the mountain streams.

Pyrenean fritillary *flowers through late spring and early summer in mountain pastures.*

The Turk's Cap Lily *flowers June–August on rocky slopes up to 2,200 m (7,218 ft).*

èche de Roland
famous breach in the sheer
t of the Cirque de Gavarnie
ns a gateway between France
d Spain.

TIPS FOR WALKERS

The park is crossed by a network of numbered trails. Each is well signposted and shows the length of time needed. Mountain huts offer a meal and a bed for the night. For maps and information visit the Park Office at Cauterets (05 62 92 50 50) or at Luz-St-Sauveur (05 62 92 38 38), both open year-round, or visit www.parc-pyrenees.com.

Walking the trail in high summer

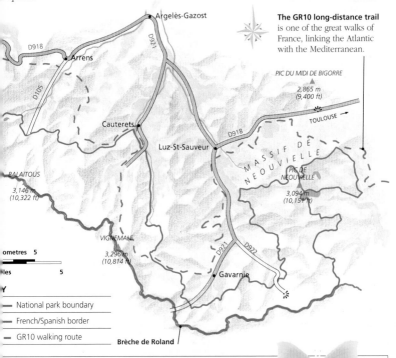

The GR10 long-distance trail is one of the great walks of France, linking the Atlantic with the Mediterranean.

Argelès-Gazost

D918
Arrens

D921

D105

PIC DU MIDI DE BIGORRE
2,865 m
(9,400 ft)

TOULOUSE

Cauterets

Luz-St-Sauveur

D918

M A S S I F   D E
N E O U V I E L L E

PIC DE
NEOUVIELLE
3,094 m
(10,151 ft)

BALAITOUS
3,146 m
(10,322 ft)

VIGNEMALE
3,296 m
(10,814 ft)

D921   D922

ometres 5

iles   5

Gavarnie

Y

— National park boundary

— French/Spanish border

— GR10 walking route

Brèche de Roland

Egyptian vulture *is seen*
over the Pyrenees, especially
rocky cliff faces.

Pyrenean bears *are close to*
extinction but a few still live in
the Ossau and Aspe valleys.

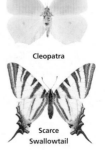

Cleopatra

Scarce
Swallowtail

These butterflies *are among*
several colourful species found
at high altitudes.

Arreau ⑮

Hautes-Pyrénées. 🏠 865. 🚌
🛈 Château des Nestes (05 62 98 63
15). 🛒 Thu. www.vallee-aure.com

Arreau stands at the junction
of the rivers Aure and
Louron. A small, bustling
half-timbered town with good
shops and restaurants, this is
the place to buy the basics
(maps, walking boots, spiked
walking sticks) for hiking or
fishing in the mountains.

Environs
St-Lary Soulan is a ski resort
up the valley, a base for
exploring the entire Massif
du Néouvielle in summer; the
roads leading from the town
will get you up to very high
altitudes by car before you
need to walk. Head for the
village of Fabian and the
smattering of lakes above it,
where the GR10 (see p461)
and other well-marked trails
criss-cross the peaks. Here
you may see golden eagles
or an enormous lammergeier
soaring over the snow fields.

St-Bertrand-de-Comminges ⑯

Haute-Garonne. 🏠 300. 🚌
Montrejeau, then taxi. 🚌
🛈 Les Olivetains, parvis de la
Cathédrale (05 61 95 44 44).

The pretty hilltop town
of St-Bertrand is the most
remarkable artistic and historic site in the Central
Pyrenees and the venue for
an acclaimed music festival
in summer (see p37). Some of

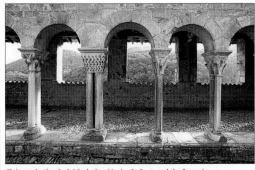

Cloisters in the Cathédrale Ste-Marie, St-Bertrand-de-Comminges

the best sculpture in the region
adorns the portal of the
Cathédrale Ste-Marie. The
adjoining Romanesque and
Gothic cloisters contain sarcophagi, carved capitals and
statues of the four Evangelists.

St-Bertrand's origins lie on
the plain below, in the city
founded by the great Roman
statesman Pompey in 72 BC.
At that time it consisted of
two thermal baths, a theatre,
a temple, a market and a
Christian basilica. All were
destroyed by Gontran, the
grandson of Clovis (see p212)
in 585, and six centuries were
to pass before the Bishop of
Comminges, Bertrand de l'Isle,
saw the site as a potential
location for a new cathedral
and monastery. The town,
which was relatively unimpor-
tant in political terms, became
re-established as a major
religious centre.

Inside the cathedral, look out
for the 66 magnificent carved
choirstalls and the 16th-century
organ case. The tomb of
Bertrand de l'Isle is situated at
the far end of the choir, with

an altar beside it; the beautiful
marble tomb in the Virgin's
chapel just off the nave is that
of Hugues de Châtillon, a
bishop who provided funds
for the completion of the
cathedral in the 14th century.

🛈 **Cathédrale Ste-Marie**
Tel 05 61 89 04 91. 🕐 daily.
🔵 Sun am 🎟️ 📷

Fresco in the Cathédrale St-Lizier

St-Lizier ⑰

Ariège. 🏠 1,900. 🚌 🛈 pl de
l'Eglise (05 61 96 77 77).

St-Lizier is located in the
Ariège, a region famous for its
steep-sided valleys and wild
mountain scenery. The village
dates back to Roman times,
and by the Middle Ages was
an important religious centre,
only to be superseded in the
12th century by St-Girons nearby. St-Lizier has the distinction
of possessing two cathedrals;
the finer is the 12th–14th-
century **Cathédrale St-Lizier** in
the lower town. It boasts
Romanesque frescoes and a
cloister with carved columns,

The imposing 12th-century Cathédrale Ste-Marie above St-Bertrand

For hotels and restaurants in this region see pp585–8 and pp640–3

Avignon, *enclosed by massive ramparts, became papal territory when popes decamped from Rome* (see p503) *in the 14th century, taking up residence in the Palais des Papes which towers over the town. In the summer the town is the scene of the popular Avignon Festival.*

s des Papes, Avignon

PROVENCE AND THE COTE D'AZUR
(See pp498–531)

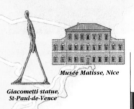

*Giacometti statue,
St-Paul-de-Vence*

Musée Matisse, Nice

argue

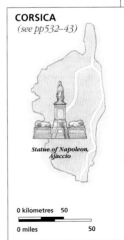

CORSICA
(see pp532–43)

*Statue of Napoleon,
Ajaccio*

0 kilometres	50
0 miles	50

The Côte d'Azur *has attracted sunworshippers and celebrities since the 1920s* (see pp474–5). *The coast also offers some prize collections of 20th-century art* (pp472–3) *and yearly events such as the Cannes Film Festival and Antibes Jazz Festival.*

The Flavours of the South of France

Mediterranean France has a fresh, sunny cuisine, with ripe and flavourful fruit and vegetables, fresh fish and seafood, and lean meat from mountain pastures. Good dishes are enhanced by key ingredients: olive oil, garlic and aromatic herbs. Markets are a colourful feast of seasonal produce all year round. Whether you opt for a picnic choice of local hams, sausage, bread and cheese to eat on the beach, share a simple lunch of tomato salad and grilled fish or lamb in a village bistro, or indulge in the sophisticated cuisine of one of France's top chefs, you can be sure of food that is not only authentic and delicious, but healthy too.

Local olives and olive oil

Preserving anchovies in seasoned olive oil in Languedoc-Roussillon

LANGUEDOC-ROUSSILLON

There is a robust Catalan flavour to the food of this region bordering Spain. Spices and almonds add an exotic touch to the fruit and vegetables produced in abundance on the Roussillon plain, and the grass-fed beef and lamb of the Mediterranean Pyrenees. Fish is

plentiful: Sète is the largest fishing port on the French Mediterranean, huge oyster and mussel beds thrive in the saltwater lagoons of the coast and the little fishing port of Collioure is famous for its anchovies. Local dishes include *brandade de morue*, a speciality of Nîmes, squid stuffed with anchovies and snails with garlic and ham. Roussillon is famous for its peaches and apricots, and the cherries of Ceret are

always the first to be harvested in France. Goat's milk is the main source of cheese, with round, orange-rinded Pélardon the most common.

PROVENCE

This is the land of the olive and of rich green olive oil. These are evident in a wide range of dishes, such as *aioli*, a rich mayonnaise of olive oil and garlic, served with vegetables or fish;

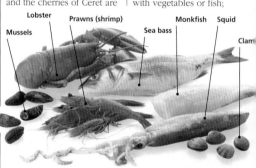

Lobster   Prawns (shrimp)   Monkfish   Squid

Mussels   Sea bass   Clam

Selection of Mediterranean seafood available in the south of France

REGIONAL DISHES AND SPECIALITIES

The *cuisine du soleil*, "cuisine of the sun", has produced several classic dishes. *Bouillabaisse* is the most famous. The ingredients of this fish stew vary from place to place, though Marseille claims the original recipe. A variety of local seafood (always including *rascasse*, or scorpion fish) is cooked in stock with tomatoes and saffron. The fish liquor is traditionally served first, with croûtons spread with *rouille*, a spicy mayonnaise, and the fish served afterwards. Once a fishermen's supper, it is now a luxury item you may need to order 24 hours in advance. A simpler version is *bourride*, a garlicky fish soup. Rich red wine stews, known as *daubes*, are another speciality, usually made with beef, but sometimes tuna or calamari. Other classics include *ratatouille* and *salade niçoise*.

Fresh figs

Artichauts à la barigoule
Small violet artichokes are stuffed with bacon and vegetables, cooked in wine.

Dried spices and herbs on sale at the market in Nice

tapenade, a purée of olives, anchovies and capers; and *pissaladière*, a type of pizza made with onions, olives and anchovies, with a distinct Italian accent. Vegetables play a leading role: courgettes (zucchini) or tomatoes stuffed in the Niçois style with meat, rice and herbs; baby artichokes sautéed with bacon; or aromatic *pistou*, a bean and vegetable soup laced with a sauce of basil and garlic. Mediterranean fish is highly prized, and is often best appreciated simply grilled. Meat includes game and rabbit, Sisteron lamb, grazed on high mountain pastures, and the bull's meat stew of the Camargue, served with nutty local red rice. There is also ripe fruit aplenty, from juicy figs to fragrant Cavaillon melons to the vivid lemons of Menton.

CORSICA

The cuisine of Corsica is a robust version of the Mediterranean diet. Chestnuts were once the staple food of the island, and the flour is still widely used. There is a

Ripe chestnuts on the tree in a Corsican forest

huge variety of *charcuterie*, including flavoursome hams and sausages, smoked, cured or air-dried in the traditional way. Wild boar is a delicacy, stewed with chestnuts in red wine. Roast goat *(cabri roti)* is served as a festive meal, spiked with garlic and rosemary. Game, from rabbit to pigeon and partridge, is also very popular. On the coast there is locally caught fish and seafood, including monkfish, squid, sea urchins and sardines, the latter most delicious stuffed with herbs and Brocciu, a ricotta-style soft cheese. Local honey is redolent of mountain herbs, and jams are made from a huge variety of ingredients.

ON THE MENU

Beignets des fleurs de courgette Courgette (zucchini) flower fritters.

Estoficada Salt cod stewed with tomatoes, potatoes, garlic and olives.

Fougasse Flat olive oil bread often studded with olives.

Ratatouille Stew of aubergine (eggplant), tomatoes, courgettes (zucchini) and peppers.

Salade Niçoise Lettuce with hard-boiled egg, olives, green beans, tomatoes and anchovies.

Socca Chickpea (garbanzo) pancakes, a speciality of Nice.

Tourte des blettes Pie of chard, raisins and pine kernels.

Brandade de morue *Dried salted cod is cooked in water, then beaten with olive oil and milk to make a purée.*

Bœuf en daube *Beef is marinated in red wine, onions and garlic, then stewed with orange peel and tomato.*

Crème catalane *Originating in Spain, this dessert is an eggy custard topped with a flambéed sugar crust.*

France's Wine Regions: the South

A massive arc stretching from Banyuls, in the extreme southern corner of France, to Nice, close to the Italian border, encompasses the Mediterranean vineyards of Languedoc-Roussillon and Provence. This was for a century an area of mass-produced wine, and much is still of *vin de table* quality. Today, however, the more dynamic producers are applying new technology to traditional and classic grape varieties to revive southern France's nobler heritage of generous, warm, aromatic wines, redolent of sun-baked stone, the scent of wild herbs, and the shimmering waters of the Mediterranean.

Cellar sign, Banyuls

LOCATOR MAP

☐ *Languedoc-Roussillon & Provence*

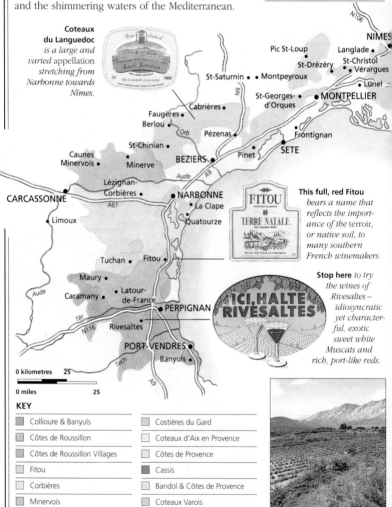

Coteaux du Languedoc *is a large and varied appellation stretching from Narbonne towards Nîmes.*

This full, red Fitou *bears a name that reflects the importance of the terroir, or native soil, to many southern French winemakers.*

Stop here *to try the wines of Rivesaltes – idiosyncratic yet characterful, exotic sweet white Muscats and rich, port-like reds.*

0 kilometres 25
0 miles 25

KEY

☐ Collioure & Banyuls
☐ Côtes de Roussillon
☐ Côtes de Roussillon Villages
☐ Fitou
☐ Corbières
☐ Minervois
☐ Coteaux du Languedoc
☐ Costières du Gard
☐ Coteaux d'Aix en Provence
☐ Côtes de Provence
☐ Cassis
☐ Bandol & Côtes de Provence
☐ Coteaux Varois
☐ Bellet

Rugged valley slopes in Corbières

Hand-picking grapes for Côtes de Provence red wine

WINE REGIONS

Both in the Provence wine region, east of Aix and Marseille, and in the larger Languedoc-Roussillon area to the west, new quality wine *appellations* such as Cabardès (north of Carcassonne), are joining the more familiar names.

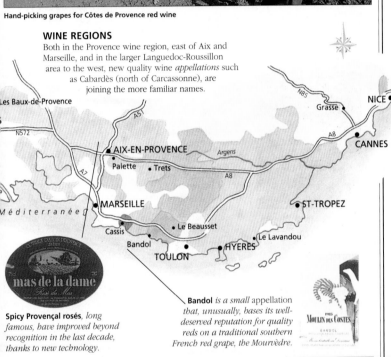

Les Baux-de-Provence

NICE

Grasse

CANNES

AIX-EN-PROVENCE

Palette • Trets

Argens

ST-TROPEZ

Méditerranée

MARSEILLE

Cassis

• Le Beausset

Bandol

Le Lavandou

HYÈRES

TOULON

Spicy Provençal rosés, *long famous, have improved beyond recognition in the last decade, thanks to new technology.*

Bandol *is a small appellation that, unusually, bases its well-deserved reputation for quality reds on a traditional southern French grape, the Mourvèdre.*

KEY FACTS ABOUT WINES OF THE SOUTH

Location and Climate
A warm and sunny climate helps to create generously alcoholic wines. The flat coastal plains support acres of vines, but generally the best sites are on the schist and limestone hillsides.

Grape Varieties
Mass-production grapes such as **Aramon** are giving way to quality varieties such as **Syrah**, **Mourvèdre** and **Grenache**. **Cabernet Sauvignon, Merlot** and **Syrah**, and the whites **Chardonnay, Sauvignon Blanc** and **Viognier**, are increasingly used for *vins de pays*. Rich, sweet whites are made from the aromatic, honeyed **Muscat** grape.

Good Producers
Corbières & Minervois: La Voulte Gasparets, Saint Auriol, Lastours, Villerambert-Julien.
Faugères: Château des Estanilles, Château de la Liquière.
St Chinian: Château Cazal-Viel, Domaine Navarre, Cave de Roquebrun.
Coteaux du Languedoc and vins de pays: Mas Jullien, Château de Capitoul, Domaine de la Garance, Mas de Daumas Gassac, Pech-Celeyran. *Roussillon*: Domaine Gauby, Domaine Sarda Malet. *Provence*: Domaine Tempier, Château Pibarnon, Domaine de Trévallon, Mas de la Dame, Domaine Richeaume, La Courtade, Château Simone, Château Pradeaux, Château de Bellet.

Artists and Writers in the South of France

Artists and writers have helped create our image of the South of France – the poet Stephen Liégeard even gave the Côte d'Azur its name in 1887. Many writers, French and foreign, found a haven in the warmth of the south. From Cézanne to Van Gogh, Monet to Picasso, artists have been inspired by the special light and brilliant colours of this seductive region. Today it is rich in art museums, some devoted to single artists like Matisse, Picasso and Chagall, others with varied collections such as those in Céret, Nîmes, Montpellier, St-Tropez, St-Paul-de-Vence and Nice *(see pp482–527)*.

Monet's palette

Picasso and Françoise Gilot on the Golfe Juan, 1948

Paul Cézanne's studio in Aix-en-Provence *(see p511)*

FESTIVE LIGHT

The Impressionists were fascinated by the effects of light, and Monet was entranced by "the glaring festive light" of the south which made colours so intense he said no one would believe they were real if painted accurately. In 1883 Renoir came with him to the south, returning often to paint his voluptuous nudes in the filtered golden light. Bonnard too settled here, painting endless views of the red tiled roofs and palm trees.

Post-Impressionists Van Gogh and Gauguin arrived in 1888, attracted by the region's rich colours. Cézanne, who was born in Aix in 1839, analysed and painted the structure of nature, above all the landscape of Provence and his beloved Mont-Ste-Victoire. Pointillist Paul Signac came to St-Tropez to paint sea and sky in a rainbow palette of dots.

THE WILD BEASTS

The Fauves, dubbed "Wild Beasts" for their unnaturally bright and wild colours, led one of the first 20th-century avant-garde movements, founded by Matisse in Collioure in 1905 *(see p29)*. Other Fauves included Derain, Vlaminck, Marquet, Van Dongen and Dufy. Matisse visited Corsica in 1898, and then St-Tropez, and was inspired by the sensuality of Provence to paint the celebrated *Luxe, Calme et Volupté*. Eventually he settled in Nice, where he painted his great series of Odalisques. He wrote, "What made me stay are the great coloured reflections of January, the luminosity of daylight." The exquisite blue-and-white chapel he designed in Vence is one of the most moving of his later works *(see p523)*.

Vincent Van Gogh's *Sunflowers* (1888)

PICASSO COUNTRY

The South of France is, without question, Picasso country. His nymphs and sea urchins, his monumental women running on the beach, his shapes and colours, ceramics and sculpture are all derived from the hard shadows and bright colours of the south.

Pablo Picasso was born in Malaga in Spain in 1881, but he spent much of his life on the French Mediterranean, developing Cubism with Braque in Céret in 1911, and arriving in Juan-les-Pins in 1920. He was in Antibes when war broke out in 1939, where he painted *Night Fishing at Antibes*, a luminous nocturnal seascape. He returned in 1946 and was given the Grimaldi Palace to use as a studio. It is now a Picasso Museum *(see p521)*. He also worked in Vallauris, producing ceramics and sculptures *(see p522)*.

Deux Femmes Courant sur la Plage (1933) by Pablo Picasso

LOST CAVIAR DAYS

Just as F Scott Fitzgerald wrote the Jazz Age into existence, he created the glittering image of life on the Riviera with *Tender is the Night*. He and Zelda arrived in 1924 attracted, like many expatriate writers, by the warm climate and the cheap, easy living. "One could get away with more on the summer Riviera, and whatever happened seemed to have something to do with art," he wrote. They passed their villa on to another American, Ernest Hemingway. Many other writers flocked there including Katherine Mansfield, DH Lawrence, Aldous Huxley, Friedrich Nietzsche, Lawrence Durrell and Graham Greene. Some, like Somerset Maugham, led a glamorous lifestyle surrounded by exotic guests. Colette was an early visitor to St-Tropez, and in 1954, Françoise Sagan captured the youthful hedonism of the time in her novel, *Bonjour Tristesse*.

Scott and Zelda Fitzgerald with daughter

NEW REALISM

In the 1950s Nice produced its own school of artists, the *Nouveaux Réalistes*, including Yves Klein, Arman, Martial Raysse, Tinguely, César, Niki de Saint Phalle and Daniel Spoerri *(see pp526–7)*. They explored the possibilities of everyday objects – Arman sliced violins, packaged and displayed trash; Tinguely exploded TV sets and cars. They had a light-hearted approach, "We live in a land of vacations, which gives us the spirit of nonsense," said Klein. He painted solid blue canvases of his personal colour, International Klein Blue, taking the inspiration of the Mediterranean to its limit.

PROVENÇAL WRITERS

The regions of Provence and Languedoc have always had a distinct literary identity, ever since the troubadours in the 12th–13th centuries composed their love poetry in the *langue d'oc* Provençal, a Latin-based language. In the last century, many regional writers have been inspired by the landscape and local traditions. They were influenced by the 19th-century Felibrige movement to revive the language, led by Nobel prize-winning poet Frédéric Mistral. Some, like Daudet and film-maker turned writer Marcel Pagnol, celebrate the Provençal character; others, such as Jean Giono, explore the connection between nature and humanity.

Frédéric Mistral in the *Petit Journal*

Beaches in the South of France

The glamorous Mediterranean coast is France's foremost holiday playground. To the east lie the Riviera's big, traditional resorts such as Menton, Nice, Cannes and Monte-Carlo. To the west are smaller resorts in coves and bays like St-Tropez and Cassis. Further on is the Camargue reserve at the mouth of the Rhône. West of the Rhône, making a majestic curve reaching almost to the Spanish border, is the long, sandy shore of Languedoc-Roussillon, where a string of purpose-built resorts range from modernistic beach cities to replicas of fishing villages.

The Carlton Hotel logo

The beaches are sandy west of Antibes; eastwards, they are naturally shingly, so any sand is imported. Anti-pollution drives mean that most beaches are now clean, except in a few spots west of Marseille and around Nice. Beaches around towns often charge fees but are usually well equipped.

A rail poster by Domergue advertising the Côte d'Azur

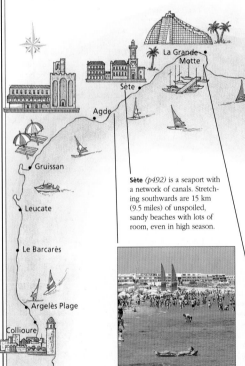

La Grande Motte

Sète

Agde

Gruissan

Leucate

Le Barcarès

Argelès Plage

Collioure

Stes-Maries-de-la-Mer

Ma

MEDITERRANEE

0 kilometres 25

0 miles 25

Sète *(p492)* is a seaport with a network of canals. Stretching southwards are 15 km (9.5 miles) of unspoiled, sandy beaches with lots of room, even in high season.

Stes-Maries-de-la-Mer *(p510)*, set among the sand dunes of the Camargue, offers white sandy beaches and a naturist beach 6 km (4 miles) to the east. Horse-riding is available.

Cap d'Agde (p487) *is a vast modern resort with long, golden sandy beaches and sports facilities of all kinds. It has Europe's largest naturist resort, accommodating 20,000 visitors.*

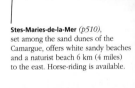

La Grande-Motte (p495) *is a huge purpose-built beach resort with excellent sports facilities, famous for its bizarre ziggurat architecture.*

In Victorian times *the Côte d'Azur, or Riviera, was the fashionable holiday venue of Europe's royalty and rich. They came to gamble and escape northern winters. Summer bathing did not come into vogue until the 1920s. Today the Riviera is busy all year round with the glamorous beaches and nightlife still a major attraction.*

Menton *(p529)* has a warm climate in winter, giving beach weather all year. Its sheltered, shingly beaches are backed by beautiful villas.

Cannes *(p520)* takes great pride in its golden beaches, keeping them scrupulously clean: most are private with entrance fees.

Cassis *(p513) is a charming fishing village with a popular casino, white cliffs and some lovely hidden creeks nearby.*

St-Tropez *(p516) is flanked by golden beaches mostly occupied by stylish "clubs" offering amenities at a price.*

Nice *(p526), has a visually dramatic waterfront with a wide, handsome promenade, but the beach itself is stony and has a busy highway alongside.*

Cap Ferrat *(p528) is a wooded peninsula which has a 10-km (6-mile) craggy cliff walk offering glimpses of grand villas and private beaches.*

LANGUEDOC-ROUSSILLON

AUDE · GARD · HÉRAULT · PYRÉNÉES-ORIENTALES

The two distinct provinces of Languedoc and Roussillon stretch from the foothills of the Pyrenees on the Spanish border to the mouth of the Rhône. The flat beaches and lagoons of the coast form a purpose-built sunbelt accommodating millions of holidaymakers every year. In between is a dry, sunburned land producing half of France's table wine and the season's first peaches and cherries.

Beyond such sensuous pleasures are many layers of history, not least the unification of the two provinces. The formerly independent Languedoc once spoke Occitan, the tongue of the troubadours, and still cherishes its separate identity. Roussillon was a Spanish possession until the treaty of the Pyrenees in 1659. Its Catalan heritage is displayed everywhere from the road signs to the Sardana dance, and the flavour of Spain is evident in the popularity of bullfights, paella, and gaudily painted façades.

This stretch of coastline was the first place in Gaul to be settled by the Romans, their enduring legacy evident in the great amphitheatre at Nîmes and the magnificent engineering of the Pont du Gard. The abbeys of St-Martin-du-Canigou, St-Michel-de-Cuxa and St-Guilhem-le-Désert are superb examples of early Romanesque architecture, unaffected by Northern Gothic. The great craggy Cathar castles and the perfectly restored medieval Cité of Carcassonne bear witness to the bloody battles of the Middle Ages.

In parts, the region remains wild and untamed: from the high plateaux of the Cerdagne, to the wild hills of the Corbières or the remote uplands of Haut Languedoc. But it also has the most youthful and progressive cities in France: Montpellier, the ancient university city and capital of the region, and Nîmes with its exuberant *feria* and bullfights. The whole area is typified by an insouciant mixture of ancient and modern, from Roman temples and postmodern architecture in its cities to solar power and ancient abbeys in the mountains.

A sunny stretch of coastline at Cap d'Agde

◁ The abbey of Saint-Martin-du-Canigou perched on Mount Canigou

Exploring Languedoc-Roussillon

Languedoc-Roussillon combines miles of gentle coastline with a rugged hinterland. Its clean, sandy beaches are perfect for family holidays, with resorts ranging from traditional fishing villages to new purpose-built resorts. Inland is quieter, with acres of vineyards in the Corbières and Minervois and mountain walks in the Haut Languedoc and Cerdagne. A rich architectural heritage ranges from Roman to Romanesque, contrasting with the modern, vibrant atmosphere of the main cities.

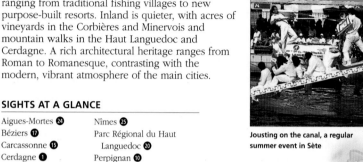

Jousting on the canal, a regular summer event in Sète

SIGHTS AT A GLANCE

Aigues-Mortes ㉔
Béziers ⑰
Carcassonne ⑮
Cerdagne ①
Céret ⑥
Collioure ⑧
Corbières ⑫
Côte Vermeille ⑦
Elne ⑨
Golfe du Lion ⑭
La Grande-Motte ㉓
Minerve ⑯
Montpellier ㉒
Narbonne ⑬

Nîmes ㉕
Parc Régional du Haut Languedoc ⑳
Perpignan ⑩
Pézenas ⑲
Pont du Gard ㉖
Prieuré de Serrabone ⑤
St-Guilhem-le-Désert ㉑
St-Martin-du-Canigou ④
St-Michel-de-Cuxa ③
Salses ⑪
Sète ⑱
Villefranche-de-Conflent ②

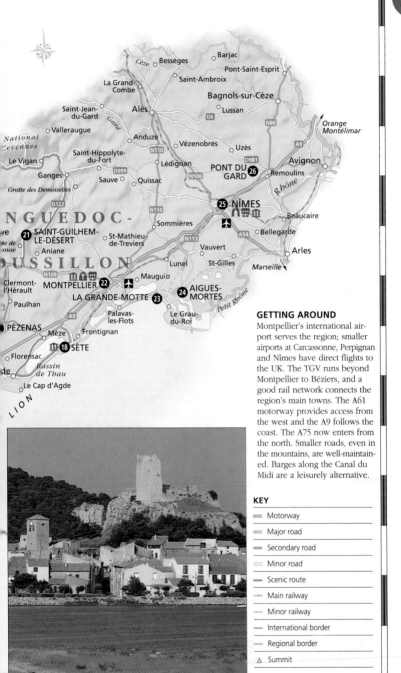

Barjac
Bessèges
Pont-Saint-Esprit
Cèze
Saint-Ambroix
La Grand-Combe
Bagnols-sur-Cèze
Saint-Jean-du-Gard
Alès
Lussan
D6
N86
Orange
Montélimar
National
Cévennes
Vallerauge
Anduze
Gard
Vézenobres
Uzès
A9
Le Vigan
Saint-Hippolyte-du-Fort
N110
Avignon
Ganges
Lédignan
D981
PONT DU GARD **26**
Rémoulins
Sauve
Quissac
N106
Rhône
Grotte des Demoiselles
D122
NÎMES **25**
D999
N110
Sommières
Beaucaire
SAINT-GUILHEM-LE-DÉSERT **21**
St-Mathieu-de-Treviers
Bellegarde
Aniane
N113
A54
Arles
Vauvert
Lunel
St-Gilles
Marseille
OUSSILLON
N109
Mauguio
Clermont-l'Hérault
MONTPELLIER **22**
AIGUES-MORTES **24**
Paulhan
LA GRANDE-MOTTE **23**
A9
Palavas-les-Flots
Le Grau-du-Roi
Petit Rhône
PÉZENAS
Mèze
Frontignan
Florensac
18 SÈTE
Bassin
de Thau
Le Cap d'Agde
LION

GETTING AROUND

Montpellier's international airport serves the region; smaller airports at Carcassonne, Perpignan and Nîmes have direct flights to the UK. The TGV runs beyond Montpellier to Béziers, and a good rail network connects the region's main towns. The A61 motorway provides access from the west and the A9 follows the coast. The A75 now enters from the north. Smaller roads, even in the mountains, are well-maintained. Barges along the Canal du Midi are a leisurely alternative.

KEY

Motorway	
Major road	
Secondary road	
Minor road	
Scenic route	
Main railway	
Minor railway	
International border	
Regional border	
△ Summit	

0 kilometres   25

0 miles   25

The ruined Barbarossa tower at Gruissan on the Golfe du Lion

Cerdagne ❶

Pyrénées-Orientales. *Perpignan.*
Mont Louis, Bourg Madame.
Mont Louis (04 68 04 21 97).
www.mont-louis.net

The remote Cerdagne, an independent state in the Middle Ages, is today divided between Spain and France. Its high plateaux offer skiing and walking among clear mountain lakes and pine and chestnut forests. The Little Yellow Train is an excellent way to sample it in a day. Stops include **Mont Louis**, a town fortified by Vauban, Louis XIV's military architect, which still accommodates French troops; the huge ski resort of **Font-Romeu; Latour-de-Carol** and the tiny village of **Yravals** below it. Nearby **Odeillo** is the site of a huge solar furnace, 45 m (150 ft) tall and 50 m (165 ft) wide. Established in 1969, its giant curved mirrors create a remarkable sight in the valley.

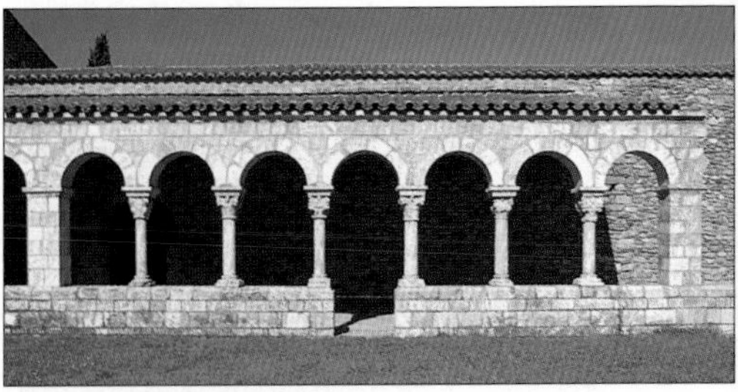

Abbey cloisters of St-Michel-de-Cuxa

Villefranche-de-Conflent ❷

Pyrénées-Orientales. 330.
32 bis rue St-Jacques (04 68 96 22 96).

In medieval times Villefranche's position at the narrowest point of the Têt valley made it an eminently defensible fortress against Moorish invasion. Today, fragments of 11th-century walls remain, along with massive ramparts, gates and Fort Liberia high above the gorge, all built by Vauban in the 17th century. The 12th-century **Eglise de St-Jacques** has fine carved capitals from the workshops of St-Michel-de-Cuxa, and Catalan painted wooden statues, including a 14th-century *Virgin and Child*. The 13th-century oak door is embellished with intricate local wrought ironwork, a craft which still features on many of the shop signs in town. From the streets of locally quarried pink marble you can make the climb up to the **Grottes des Canalettes**, a superb underground setting for concerts. The Little Yellow Train will take you to the magnificent mountain plain of the Cerdagne (phone 04 68 96 63 63 to book).

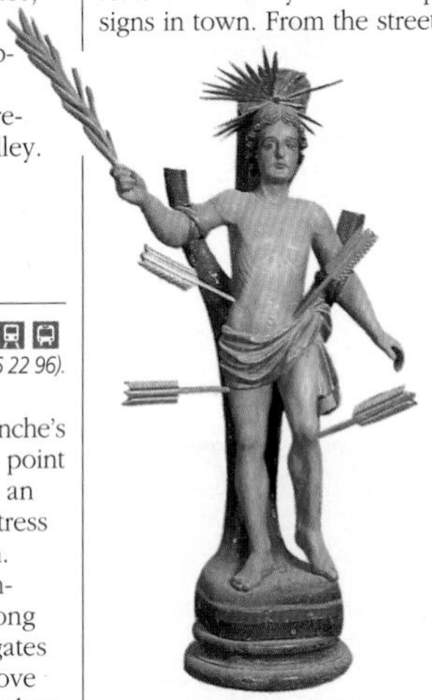

Statue in St-Jacques, Villefranche

THE LITTLE YELLOW TRAIN

Arrive early for the best seats in the carriages of *Le Petit Train Jaune* which winds its way on narrow-gauge tracks through gorges and across towering viaducts up into the Cerdagne, stopping at small mountain stations along the way. Built in 1910 to improve access to the mountains, it now operates mainly for tourists, beginning at Villefranche-de-Conflent and terminating at Latour-de-Carol.

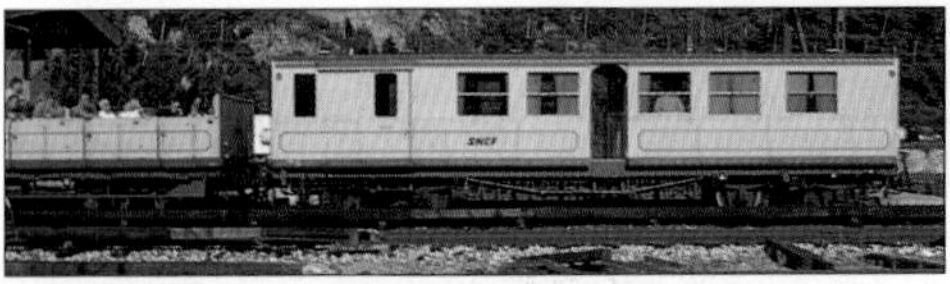

The Little Yellow Train, with open carriages for summer visitors

St-Michel-de-Cuxa ❸

Prades, Pyrénées-Orientales. ***Tel*** *04 68 96 15 35.* *daily.* *Sun am, religious hols.*

Prades, a small, pink marble town in the Têt valley, is typical of the local style. The **Eglise St-Pierre** has a southern Gothic wrought iron belfry and a Baroque Catalan interior. But the town is distinguished by the beautiful pre-Romanesque abbey of St-Michel-de-Cuxa which lies 3 km (2 miles) further up the valley, and by the legacy of the Spanish cellist Pablo Casals. Casals spent many years here in exile from Franco's Spain; every August the abbey provides the setting for the Prades music festival held in his memory.

An early example of monastic architecture, St-Michel-de-Cuxa abbey was founded by Benedictine monks in 878 and rapidly became renowned throughout France and Spain. Distinctive keyhole arches showing Moorish influence pierce the massive walls of the abbey church, which was consecrated in 974. The mottled pink marble cloisters, with their superbly carved capitals, were added later, in the 12th century.

After the Revolution the building was abandoned, and

its famous carvings looted. From 1913, George Grey Bernard, a visiting American artist, began to discover some of the capitals incorporated in local buildings. He sold the carvings to the Metropolitan Museum of Art in New York in 1925, where they formed the basis of the Cloisters Museum – a faithful re-creation of a Romanesque abbey in the unlikely setting of Manhattan.

St-Martin-du-Canigou ❹

Casteil. *Tel* 04 68 05 50 03.
⭕ (guided tours only: tour lasts one hour; times vary with seasons) Easter–Sep: daily; Oct–Easter: Tue–Sun. 📷

Saint-Martin-du-Canigou is situated in a spectacularly remote site a third of the way up Pic du Canigou, on a jagged spur of rock approached only by jeep or a 40-minute climb on foot from Casteil or by hiring a jeep from Vernet-les-Bains. The abbey was built between 1001 and 1026, and financed by Guifred, Count of Cerdagne, who abandoned his family and entered the monastery in 1035. He was buried there 14 years later in a tomb he carved from the rock himself, which can still be seen. The church is early

Nun at St-Martin

Serrabone priory's chapel tribune, with columns of local marble

Romanesque, based on a simple basilican plan. Two churches are built, quite literally one on top of the other, making the lower church the crypt for the upper building.

The abbey complex is best viewed from above by continuing up the path. From there, its irregular design clinging to the rock is framed by the dramatic mountain setting – the ensemble a tribute to the ingenuity and vitality of its early builders.

Prieuré de Serrabone ❺

Boule d'Amont. *Tel* 04 68 84 09 30.
⭕ daily. ● 1 Jan, 1 May, 1 Nov, 25 Dec. 📷

Perched high up on the northern flanks of Pic du Canigou, the sacred mountain of the Catalans, is the priory of Serrabone. A final lap of hairpin bends on the approach road (the D618) reveals the simple square tower and round apse of this remote Romanesque abbey, surrounded by a botanical garden of local herbs and woodland plants clinging to the mountain side.

Inside the cool, austere 12th-century building is a surprisingly elaborate chapel tribune, its columns and arches glowing from the local red-veined marble, carved by the anonymous Master of Cuxa, whose work appears throughout the region. Note the strange beasts and verdant flora featured in the capital carvings, especially the rose of Roussillon.

The 11th-century cloister of St-Martin-du-Canigou

Céret ❻

Pyrénées-Orientales. 🏠 *8,000*. 🚌
ℹ️ *av Clémenceau (04 68 87 00 53).*
🏛️ *Sat, Tue eve Jul–Aug.* 🎭 *Fête des
Cerises (May/Jun).* **www**.ot-ceret.fr

Céret is a cherry town,
surrounded by a cloud of
pink blossom in the early
spring, and producing the
very first fruits of the year.
The tiled and painted façades
and loggias of the buildings
have a Spanish feel and the
town was popular with
Picasso, Braque and Matisse.
Today Céret is distinguished
by the **Musée d'Art Moderne**,
its sophisticated modern
architecture housing a
remarkable collection which
includes Catalan artists Tapiès
and Capdeville, 50 works
donated by Picasso, including
a series of bowls painted with
bullfighting scenes, and
works by Matisse, Chagall,
Juan Gris and Salvador Dalí.

The town's Catalan heritage
is evident in regular bullfights
held in the arena, and in its
Sardana dance festivals in July.

🏛️ **Musée d'Art Moderne**
8 bd Maréchal Joffre. **Tel** *04 68 87 27
76.* ⏰ *May–Sep: daily; Oct–Apr: Wed–
Mon.* ⬤ *1 Jan, 1 May, 1 Nov, 25 Dec.*
📷 ♿ **www**.musee-ceret.com

Environs
From Céret the D115 follows
the Tech valley to the spa

Statue by Aristide Maillol, Banyuls

town of **Amélie-les-Bains**,
where fragments of Roman
baths have been discovered.
Beyond, in **Arles-sur-Tech**, the
Eglise de Ste-Marie contains
12th-century frescoes, and a
sarcophagus be-
side the church
door which, ac-
cording to local
legend, produces
drops of unac-
countably pure
water every year.

Catalan flag

Côte Vermeille ❼

Pyrénées-Orientales. 🚊 *Perpignan.*
🚌 *Collioure, Cerbère.* 🚌 *Collioure,
Banyuls-sur-Mer.* ℹ️ *Collioure (04 68
82 15 47), Cerbère (04 68 88 42 36).*
www.collioure.com

Here the Pyrenees meet the
Mediterranean, the coast
road twisting and turning
around secluded pebbly coves

and rocky outcrops. The
vermeille (vermilion-tinted)
rock of the headlands gives
this stretch of coast, the loveliest in the region, its name.

The Côte Vermeille extends
all the way to the Costa Brava
in northern Spain. With its
Catalan character, it is as redolent of Spain as of France.
Argelès-Plage has three
sandy beaches and a palm-
fringed promenade, and is
the largest camping centre in
Europe. The small resort of
Cerbère is the last French
town before the border, flying
the red and gold Catalan flag
to signal its true allegiance.
All along the coast, terraced
vineyards cling to the rocky
hillsides, producing
strong, sweet wines
like Banyuls and
Muscat. The difficult
terrain makes harvest-
ing a laborious
process. Vines were
first cultivated here by
Greek settlers in the 7th
century BC, and Banyuls itself
has wine cellars dating back
to the Middle Ages.

Banyuls is also famous as
the birthplace of Aristide
Maillol, the 19th-century
sculptor, whose work can be
seen all over the region. **Port
Vendres**, with fortifications
built by the indefatigable
Vauban (architect to Louis XIV)
is a fishing port, renowned for
its anchovies and sardines.

The spectacular Côte Vermeille, seen from the coast road south of Banyuls

Collioure harbour, with one of its beaches and the Eglise Notre-Dame-des-Anges

Collioure ❽

Pyrénées-Orientales. 🏠 *3,000.*
🚉 🚌 ℹ️ *pl du 18 juin (04 68 82 15 47).* 🌂 *Wed & Sun.* **www**.collioure.com

The colours of Collioure first attracted Matisse here in 1905: brightly stuccoed houses sheltered by cypresses and gaily painted fishing boats, all bathed in the famous luminous light, and washed by a gentle sea. Other artists including André Derain worked here under Matisse's influence and were dubbed *fauves* (wild beasts) for their wild experiments with colour. Art galleries and souvenir shops now fill the cobbled streets, but this small fishing port has changed surprisingly little since then, with anchovies still its main business. Three salting houses are evidence of this tradition.

Three sheltered beaches, both pebble and sand, nestle round the harbour, dominated by the bulk of the **Château Royal**, which forms part of the harbour wall. It was first built by the Knights Templar in the 13th century, and Collioure became the main port of entry for Perpignan, remaining under the rule of Spanish Aragon until France took over in 1659. The outer fortifications were reinforced ten years later by Vauban, who demolished much of the

original town in the process. Today the château can be toured, or visited for its exhibitions of modern art.

The **Eglise Notre-Dame-des-Anges** on Collioure's quayside was rebuilt in the 17th century to replace the church which was destroyed by Vauban. A former lighthouse was incorporated as a belltower. Inside the church are no fewer than five Baroque altarpieces by Joseph Sunyer and other Catalan masters of the genre.

Be warned that Collioure is extremely popular in July and August, with visitors cramming the tiny streets. Long queues of traffic are possible, too, though the building of another route, the D86, has helped to ease congestion.

⛴ **Château Royal**
Tel *04 68 82 06 43.* 🕐 *daily.*
🔴 *1 Jan, 1 May & 25 Dec.* 🎫

Elne ❾

Pyrénées-Orientales. 🏠 *6,500.* 🚉 🚌
ℹ️ *pl Sant-Jordi (04 68 22 05 07).*
🌂 *Mon, Wed, Fri.* **www**.ot-elne.fr

The ancient town of Elne accommodated Hannibal and his elephants in 218 BC on his epic journey to Rome, and was one of the most important towns in Roussillon until the 16th century. Today it is famed for the 11th-century **Cathédrale de Ste-Eulalie et Ste-Julie**, with its superb cloister. Milky blue-veined marble has been carved into exquisite capitals, embellished with a riot of flowers, figures and arabesques. The side nearest the cathedral dates from the 1100s; the remaining three are 13th–14th-century. From the front of the cathedral are views of the vines and orchards of the surrounding plain.

Carved capital at Elne, showing "The Dream of the Magi"

A wide, sandy beach near Perpignan, almost purpose-built for family holidays

Perpignan ❿

Pyrénées-Orientales. 🏠 108,000. ✈ 🚉 🚌 ℹ *Palais des Congrès (04 68 66 30 30).* 🛒 *daily.*
www.perpignantourisme.com

Catalan Perpignan has a distinctly southern feel, with palm trees lining the Têt river promenade, house and shop façades painted vibrant turquoise and pink, and the streets of the Arab quarter selling aromatic spices, couscous and paella.

Today Perpignan is the vibrant capital of Roussillon, and has an important position on the developing Mediterranean sunbelt. But it reached its zenith in the 13th and 14th centuries under the kings of Majorca and the kings of Aragón, who controlled great swathes of northern Spain and southern France. Their vast **Palais des Rois de Majorque** still straddles a sub-

stantial area in the southern part of the city.

Perpignan's strong Catalan identity is evident during the twice-weekly summer celebrations when the Sardana is danced in the place de la Loge. It is a key Catalan symbol. Arms raised, concentric circles of dancers keep step to the accompaniment of a Catalan woodwind band.

One of Perpignan's finest buildings, the **Loge de Mer**, lies at the head of the square. Built in 1397 to house the Maritime Exchange, only the eastern section retains the original Gothic design. The rest of the building was rebuilt in Renaissance style in 1540 with sumptuous carved wooden ceilings and sculpted window frames. While visitors

Devout Christ in St-Jean

are sometimes offended by the sight of a fast-food restaurant inside, the result is that the Loge de Mer has avoided becoming a hushed museum piece. Instead, it remains the centre of Perpignan life – elegant cafés cluster round it, producing a constant buzz of activity.

Next door is the **Hôtel de Ville** with its pebble stone façade and wrought iron gates. Inside, parts of the arcaded courtyard date back to 1315; at the centre is Aristide Maillol's allegorical sculpture, *The Mediterranean* (1950).

To the east is the labyrinthine cathedral quarter of St-Jean, made up of small streets and squares containing some fine 14th- and 15th-century buildings.

🔒 Cathédrale St-Jean
Pl de Gambetta. 🔘 *daily.*
Topped by a wrought iron belfry, this cathedral was begun in 1324 and was finally ready for use in 1509. It is constructed almost entirely from river pebbles layered with red brick, a style common throughout the region due to the scarcity of other building materials.

Inside the gloomy interior the nave is flanked by gilded altarpieces and painted wooden statues, with a massive pre-Romanesque marble font. A cloistered cemetery adjoins the church and the Chapel of

THE ANNUAL PROCESSION DE LA SANCH

There is a very Catalan atmosphere in Perpignan during the annual Good Friday procession of the Confraternity of La Sanch (Brotherhood of the Holy Blood). Originally dedicated to the comfort of condemned prisoners in the 15th century, members of the brotherhood still wear macabre red or black robes as they carry sacred relics and the crucifix from the Chapel of the Devout Christ to the cathedral.

the Devout Christ with its precious, poignantly realistic medieval wooden Crucifixion. The cathedral replaced the 11th-century church of St-Jean-le-Vieux, whose superb Romanesque doorway can be glimpsed through the gates to the left of the main entrance.

⚜ Palais des Rois de Majorque
2 rue des Archers. *Tel* 04 68 34 48 29. ◯ daily. ● 1 Jan, 1 May, 1 Nov, 25 Dec. 🖼
Access to the vast 13th-century fortified palace of the Kings of Majorca is as circuitous today as it was intended to be for invading soldiers. Flights of steps zigzag within the sheer red-brick ramparts, begun in the 15th century and added to successively over the next two centuries. Eventually, the elegant gardens and substantial castle within are revealed, entered by way of the Tour de l'Hommage, from the top of which is a panoramic view of city, mountains and sea.

The palace itself is built around a central arcaded courtyard, flanked on one side by the Salle de Majorque, a great hall with a triple fireplace and giant Gothic arched windows. Adjacent, two royal chapels built one above the other show southern Gothic style at its best: pointed arches, patterned frescoes and elaborate tilework demonstrating a distinct Moorish influence. The fine rose marble doorway of the upper King's Chapel is a typical example of the Roussillon Romanesque style,

Courtyard in the Hôtel de Ville

although the sculpted capitals are Gothic. Today the great courtyard is sometimes used for concerts.

🏛 Musée d'Arts et de Traditions Populaires du Roussillon
Le Castillet. *Tel* 04 68 35 42 05. ◯ Wed–Mon. ● 1 Jan, 1 May, 1 Nov. 🖼
The red-brick tower and pink belfry of the Castillet, built as the town gate in 1368, was at one time a prison and is all that remains of the town walls. It now houses a collection of Catalan craft objects, agricultural implements, kitchen furniture, looms, and terracotta pots for storing water and oil. It also holds art exhibitions.

🏛 Musée Rigaud
16 rue de l'Ange. *Tel* 04 68 35 43 40. ◯ Wed–Mon. ● public hols. 🖼 &
This magnificent 18th-century mansion has an eclectic art collection dominated by the work of Hyacinthe Rigaud (1659–1743), who was born in Perpignan and was court painter to Louis XIV and Louis XV. The first floor has a room of

portraits, including works by David, Greuze and Ingres; the Dufy, Picasso and Maillol room; and the Primitifs Catalan, 14th–16th-century Catalan and Spanish paintings, among them the *Retable de la Trinité* (1489) by the Master of Canapost.

The museum also represents the 20th century: Alechinsky, Appel and others from the late 1940s European Cobra movement; the Catalan artist Pierre Daura; and modern Roussillon painters like Brune, Terrus and Violet.

Fort tower and ramparts, Salses

Salses ⓫

Pyrénées-Orientales. 🏠 2,500. 🚉 🛈 pl de la République (04 68 38 66 13). 🔄 Wed.

Looking like a giant sand-castle against the ochre earth of the Corbières vineyards, the **Fort de Salses** stands at the old frontier of Spain and France. It guards the narrow defile between the mountains and the Mediterranean lagoons, and was built by King Ferdinand of Aragon between 1497 and 1506 to defend Spain's possession of Roussillon. Its massive walls and rounded towers are a classic example of Spanish military architecture, designed to deflect the new threat posed by gunpowder.

Inside were underground stabling for 300 horses and a subterranean passageway around the inner courtyard.

There is a wonderful view from the keep over the lagoons and surrounding coastline.

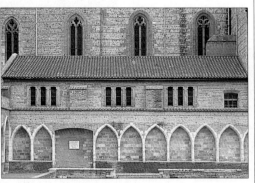
The pebble and red-brick Cathédrale de St-Jean in Perpignan

Vineyards covering the hilly terrain of the Corbières

Corbières ⑫

Aude. ✈ Perpignan. ■ Narbonne,
Carcassonne, Lézignan-Corbières.
■ Narbonne, Carcassonne,
Lézignan-Corbières. ⓘ Lézignan-
Corbières (04 68 27 05 42).
www.lezignan-corbieres.fr/tourisme

Still one of the wildest parts
of France with few roads, let
alone villages, the Corbières
is best known for its wine
and the great craggy hulks of
the Cathar castles (see p491).
Much of the land is untamed
garrigue (scrubland) fragrant
with honeysuckle and broom;
south-facing slopes have been
cleared and planted with vines.
   To the south are the spectacular medieval castles of
Peyrepertuse and **Quéribus**,
the latter one of the last Cathar
strongholds. **Villerouge-
Termenes** celebrates its
turbulent past with an annual
medieval banquet. To the
west is the barren, uninhabited
Razès area in the upper Aude
valley. Its best-kept secret is
the village of **Alet-les-Bains**,
with beautifully preserved
half-timbered houses and the
remains of a Benedictine
abbey, battle-scarred from the
Wars of Religion.

Narbonne ⑬

Aude. ♟ 48,000. ■ ■ ⓘ pl
Roger Salengro (04 68 65 15 60).
🖘 Thu & Sun.
www.mairie-narbonne.fr

Narbonne is a medium-
sized, cheerful town profiting
from the booming wine
region that surrounds it. The
town is bisected by the tree-
shaded Canal de la Robine; to
the north is the restored
medieval quarter with many
elegant shops and good restaurants. Located here is one
of Narbonne's most intriguing
tourist attractions, the
Horreum. This underground
warren of granaries and grain
chutes dates from the 1st
century BC, when Narbonne
was a major port and capital
of the largest Roman province
in Gaul.
   The town prospered through
the Middle Ages until the 15th
century when the harbour
silted up and the course of
the river Aude altered, taking
Narbonne's fortunes with it.
By then, an important bishopric had been established and
an ambitious cathedral project,
modelled on the great Gothic
cathedrals of the North, was

underway. However, the full
grandiose design was abandoned and just the chancel,
begun in 1272, became the
**Cathédrale St-Just et St-
Pasteur** we see today.
   It is still enormous, enhanced by 14th-century
sculptures, fine stained-glass
windows and an 18th-century
carved organ. Aubusson and
Gobelin tapestries adorn the
walls, and the Chapel of the
Anonciade houses a treasury
of manuscripts, jewelled
reliquaries and tapestries.
   The unfinished transept
now forms a courtyard, and
between the cathedral and
the **Palais des Archevêques**
(Archbishops' Palace), lie
cloisters with four galleries of
14th-century vaulting.
   This huge palace and cathedral complex dominates the
centre of Narbonne. Between
the Palais des Archevêques'
massive 14th-century towers
is the town hall, with a 19th-
century Neo-Gothic façade by
Viollet-le-Duc (see p200), the
architect who so determinedly

The vaulted chancel of Cathédrale
St-Just et St-Pasteur in Narbonne

CANAL DU MIDI

From Sète to Toulouse the 240-km (149-mile)
Canal du Midi winds its way between plane
trees, vineyards and sleepy villages. The complex system of locks, aqueducts and bridges is
a remarkable feat of engineering, built by the
Béziers salt-tax baron Paul Riquet. Completed
in 1681, it encouraged Languedoc trade and
established a vital link, via the Garonne river,
between the Atlantic and the Mediterranean.
Today it is plied by holiday barges (04 67 22 81 00).

Tranquil waterway of the Canal du Midi

For hotels and restaurants in this region see pp588–90 and pp643–6

The Cistercian Abbaye de Fontfroide (1093), southwest of Narbonne

restored medieval France. The palace itself is divided into the Palais Vieux (Old Palace) and the Palais Neuf (New Palace). Narbonne's most important museums are in the Palais Neuf, on the left as you enter through the low medieval arches of the passage de l'Ancre. The **Musée d'Archéologie et de Préhistoire** collection includes fragments of Narbonne's Roman heritage, from milestones and parts of the original walls to an assemblage of domestic objects, coins, tools and glassware. The **Chapelle la Madeleine** is decorated with a 14th-century wall painting and houses a collection of Greek vases, sarcophagi and mosaics.

In the archbishops' former apartments is the **Musée d'Art et d'Histoire**, which is as interesting for its luxurious furnishings and richly decorated ceilings as for its art collection. This includes some fine paintings by Canaletto, Brueghel, Boucher and Veronese as well as a large selection of local earthenware.

South of the Canal de la Robine are a number of fine mansions, including the Renaissance **Maison des Trois Nourrices** on the corner of rue des Trois-Nourrices and rue Edgard-Quinet. Nearby is the **Musée Lapidaire**, with architectural fragments from Gallo-Roman Narbonne, and the 13th-century Gothic **Basilique St-Paul-Serge**. The present building retains the crypt and some sarcophagi of an earlier church on this site.

Horreum
Rue Rouget-de-l'Isle. *Tel 04 68 90 30 54.* ☐ *Apr–Sep: daily; Oct–Mar: Tue–Sun.* ● *1 Jan, 1 May, 1 & 11 Nov, 25 Dec.* 🔲

Musée d'Archéologie et de Préhistoire/Musée d'Art et d'Histoire
Palais des Archevêques. *Tel 04 68 90 30 54.* ☐ *Apr–Oct: daily; Nov–Mar: Tue–Sun.* ● *1 Jan, 1 May, 1 & 11Nov, 25 Dec.* 🔲

Musee Lapidaire
Eglise Notre-Dame de Lamourguié. *Tel 04 68 90 30 54.* ☐ *Apr–Sep: daily; Oct–Mar: Tue–Sun.* ● *1 Jan, 1 May, 1 Nov, 11 Nov, 25 Dec.* 🔲 ♿

Environs
Southwest (13 km/8 miles), the Cistercian **Abbaye de Fontfroide** has an elegant cloister. The abbey is tucked away in a quiet valley, surrounded by cypress trees.

Golfe du Lion ⓮

Aude, Hérault. 🚶 🚌 🚗 *Montpellier.* 🚆 *Sète.* 🅸 *La Grande Motte (04 67 56 42 00).* **www**.ot-lagrandemotte.fr

Languedoc-Roussillon's shoreline (100 km/65 miles) forms an almost unbroken sweep of sandy beach. Only at its southern limits does it break into the rocky inlets of the Côte Vermeille. Purpose-built resorts created since the 1960s emphasize eco-friendly, low-rise family accommodation, some in local styles, others with imaginative architecture.

La Grande Motte marina has distinctive ziggurat-style buildings *(see p495)*. **Cap d'Agde** has Europe's largest naturist quarter. Inland **Agde**, founded by ancient Greek traders, is built of black basalt and has a fortified cathedral. **Port Leucate** and **Port Bacarès** are ideal for watersports. An older town is **Sète** *(see p492)*. A feature of the flat Languedoc coast is its étangs – large shallow lagoons. Those nearest the Camargue are the haunt of thousands of wading birds.

A wide, sandy beach on the Cap d'Agde

Carcassonne ⑮

The citadel of Carcassonne is a perfectly restored medieval town, and protected by UNESCO. It crowns a steep bank above the river Aude, a fairy-tale sight of turrets and ramparts overlooking the Basse Ville below. The strategic position of the citadel between the Atlantic and the Mediterranean and on the corridor between the Iberian peninsula and the rest of Europe led to its original settlement, consolidated by the Romans in the 2nd century BC. It became a key element in medieval military conflicts. At its zenith in the 12th century, it was ruled by the Trencavels who built the château and cathedral. Military advances and the Treaty of the Pyrenees in 1659, which relocated the French–Spanish border, hastened its decline. The attentions of architectural historian Viollet-le-Duc *(see p200)* led to its restoration in the 19th century.

The Restored Citadel
Restoration of La Cité has always been controversial. Critics complain it looks to new, favouring a more romantic ruin.

★ **Le Château**
A fortress within a fortress, the château has a moat, five towers and defensive wooden galleries on the walls.

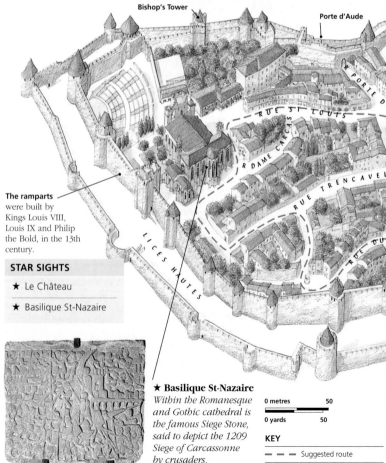

Bishop's Tower

Porte d'Aude

RUE ST LOUIS

R PORTE D'A

R DAME CARCAS

RUE TRENCAVEL

RUE DU

LICES HAUTES

The ramparts
were built by Kings Louis VIII, Louis IX and Philip the Bold, in the 13th century.

STAR SIGHTS

★ Le Château

★ Basilique St-Nazaire

★ **Basilique St-Nazaire**
Within the Romanesque and Gothic cathedral is the famous Siege Stone, said to depict the 1209 Siege of Carcassonne by crusaders.

| 0 metres | 50 |
| 0 yards | 50 |

KEY

– – – Suggested route

RELIGIOUS PERSECUTION

Carcassonne's strategic position meant it was often at the centre of religious conflict. The Cathars (*see p491*) were given sanctuary here in 1209 by Raymond-Roger Trencavel when besieged by Simon de Montfort in his crusade against heresy. In the 14th century the Inquisition continued to root out the Cathars. This painting depicts intended victims in the Inquisition Tower.

Les Emmurés de Carcassonne, JP Laurens

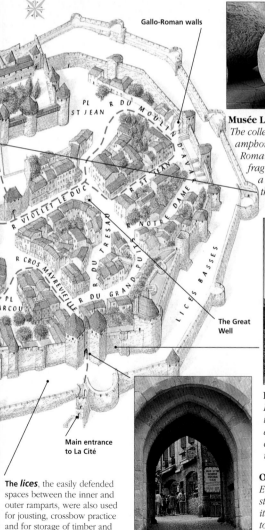

Gallo-Roman walls

Musée Lapidaire

The collection includes Roman amphorae and terracotta, Romanesque murals and fragments from the cathedral, a set of Gothic windows and these medieval stone missiles.

The Great Well

Porte Narbonnaise

Flanked by two sandstone towers, built in 1280, the defences included two portcullises, two iron doors, a moat and a drawbridge.

Main entrance to La Cité

The *lices*, the easily defended spaces between the inner and outer ramparts, were also used for jousting, crossbow practice and for storage of timber and other materials.

Old City Entrance

Entering La Cité is still a step back in time, although it is one of France's top tourist destinations, filled with souvenir shops.

Béziers with its medieval cathedral, seen from Pont Vieux in the southwest

Minerve ⓰

Hérault. 👥 100. 🚉 rue des Martyrs (04 68 91 81 43). www.minerve-tourisme.com

In the parched, arid hills of the Minervois, surrounded by vines and not much else, Minerve appears defiant on its rocky outcrop at the confluence of the rivers Cesse and Briant. It is defended by what the Minervois call the "Candela" (Candle), an octagonal tower which is all that remains of the medieval château. In 1210, the small town resisted the vengeful Simon de Montfort, scourge of the Cathars, in a siege lasting seven weeks. This culminated in the execution of 140 Cathars, who were burned at the stake.

Today visitors enter Minerve by a high bridge spanning the gorge. Turn right and follow the route of the Cathars past the Romanesque arch of the Porte des Templiers to the 12th-century **Eglise St-Etienne**. Outside the church is a crudely carved dove, symbol of the Cathars, and within is a 5th-century white marble altar table, one of the oldest artifacts in the region.

A rocky path follows the riverbed below the town, where the water has cut out caves and two bridges – the Grand Pont and the Petit Pont – from the soft limestone.

Béziers ⓱

Hérault. 👥 70,000. ✈ 🚉 🚌 🛈 29 av Saint Saëns (04 67 76 84 00). 🗓 Fri. www.beziers-tourisme.com

Famous for its bullfights and rugby, and the wine of the surrounding region, Béziers has several other points of interest. The town seems turned in on itself, its roads leading up to the massive 14th-century **Cathédrale St-Nazaire**, with its fine sculpture, stained glass and frescoes. In 1209, several thousand citizens were massacred in the crusade against the Cathars. The papal legate's troops were ordered not to discriminate between Catholics and Cathars, but to "Kill them all. God will recognize his own!"

Statue of the engineer Paul Riquet in the allées Paul Riquet, Béziers

The **Musée du Biterrois** holds exhibitions on local history, wine and the Canal du Midi, engineered in the late 17th century by Paul Riquet, Béziers' most famous son (see p486). His statue presides over the Allées Paul Riquet, the broad esplanade at the foot of the hill. This is lined by two double rows of plane trees and large canopied restaurants, a civilized focus to this otherwise business-like town.

🏛 **Musée du Biterrois**
Caserne St-Jacques. **Tel** 04 67 36 81 60. 🔵 Tue–Sun. ⬤ 1 Jan, Easter, 1 May, 25 Dec. 🎫 🔣

Environs
Overlooking the Béziers plain and the mountains to the north is Oppidum d'Ensérune, a superb Roman site, with substantial foundations. The **Musée de l'Oppidum d'Ensérune** has a good archaeological collection, from Celtic, Greek, and Roman vases to jewellery, funeral fragments and weapons.

The **Château de Raissac** (between Béziers and Lignan) houses an unusual 19th-century faïence museum and modern workshop in its stables (Tue–Sat).

🏛 **Musée de l'Oppidum d'Ensérune**
Nissan lez Ensérune. **Tel** 04 67 37 01 23. 🔵 daily; Sep–Apr: Tue–Sun. ⬤ public hols. 🎫 🔣 limited.

The Cathars

The Cathars (from Greek *katharos*, meaning pure) were a 13th-century Christian sect critical of corruption in the established church. Cathar dissent flourished in independent Languedoc as an expression of separatism, but the rebellion was rapidly exploited for political purposes. Peter II of Aragon was keen to annex Languedoc, and Philippe II of France joined forces with the pope to crush the Cathar heretics in a crusade led by Simon de Montfort in 1209. This heralded the start of over a century of ruthless killing and torture.

CATHAR CASTLES
The Cathars took refuge in the defensive castles of the Corbières and Ariège. Peyrepertuse is one of the most remote, difficult to get to even today: a long, narrow stone citadel hacked from a high, craggy peak over 609 m (2,000 ft) high.

Cathars *(also known as Albigensians) believed in the duality of good and evil. They considered the material world entirely evil. To be truly pure they had to renounce the world, and be non-violent, vegetarian and sexually abstinent.*

The crusade *against the Cathars was vicious. Heretics' land was promised to the crusaders by the pope, who assured forgiveness in advance of their crimes. In 1209, 20,000 citizens were massacred in Béziers and, the following year, 140 were burned to death in Minerve. In 1244, 225 Cathars died defending one of their last fortresses at Montségur.*

CATHAR COUNTRY
Castles and towns with a Cathar association, some of them spectacular sites, are concentrated in Languedoc-Roussillon, the centre of Catharism in the Middle Ages.

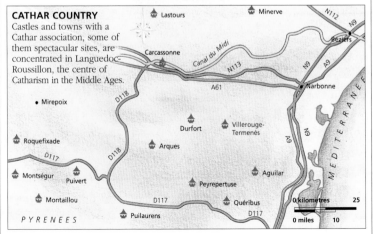

Lastours
Minerve
N112
N9
Carcassonne
Canal du Midi
Béziers
N113
N9
A9
A61
Narbonne
Mirepoix
D118
Durfort
Villerouge-Termenès
A9
N9
Roquefixade
D118
Arques
D117
D118
Montségur
Puivert
Peyrepertuse
Aguilar
Montaillou
D117
Quéribus
D117
PYRENEES
Puilaurens

MEDITERRANEE

0 kilometres   25
0 miles   10

The impressive Grand Hôtel *(see p590)* on quai de la Résistance, Sète

Sète ⓲

Hérault. 🏠 *40,400.* 🚉 🚌 ⛴
ℹ️ *60 grand' rue Mario Roustan
(04 67 74 71 71)* 🛒 *Wed & Fri.*
www.ot-sete.fr

Sète is a major fishing and
industrial port. It has a
gutsier, more raffish air than
much of the leisure-oriented
Mediterranean, with its shops

Cimetière Marin in Sète, burial
place of the poet Paul Valéry

selling ships' lamps and
propellers, and its quayside
restaurants full of hungry
sailors demolishing vast
platters of mussels, oysters
and sea snails straight off the
boat. Most of Sète's restaurants can be found in a stroll
along the Grand Canal, with
its Italianate houses painted
in pastel colours and with
wrought iron balconies overlooking Sète's network of
canals and bridges. Boisterous
water jousting tournaments,
dating back to 1666, form part
of the patron saint's festival in
August *(see p37).*

The **Musée International
des Arts Modestes** displays
everyday objects (including
some by well-known contemporary designers) in amusing
new contexts, within a renovated canalside warehouse.

Above the town is the
Cimetière Marin, where Sète's
most famous son, poet Paul
Valéry (1871–1945), is buried.
There is a small museum and
breathtaking views of the
coast and the mountains.

🏛 **Musée International des
Arts Modestes**
23 quai du Maréchal de Lattre de
Tassigny. *Tel 04 67 18 64 00.*
🕐 *Tue–Sun.* 🔴 *public hols.* 🈳 ♿
www.miam.org

Pézenas ⓳

Hérault. 🏠 *8,000.* 🚉 ℹ️ *pl
Gambetta (04 67 98 36 40).* 🛒 *Sat.*
www.pezenas-tourisme.fr

Pezenas is a compact and
charming little town easily
appreciated in a gentle stroll of
its main sights, and abounding
in revealing small details, frag-
mentary evidence of its past
brilliance as the seat of local
government in the 16th–17th
centuries. Then the town also
played artistic host to many
glittering troupes of musicians
and actors, including Molière.

Best of all are the glimpses
of fine houses through courtyard doorways, such as the
Hôtel des Barons de Lacoste,
at 8 rue François-Oustrin, with
its beautiful stone staircase,
and the **Maison des Pauvres** at
12 rue Alfred Sabatier, with its
three galleries and staircase.

Look out for the medieval
shop window on rue Triperie-
Vieille, and just within the
14th-century **Porte Faugères**
(Faugères Gate) the narrow
streets of the Jewish ghetto,
which has a chilling feeling
of enclosure. Shops selling
antiques, second-hand goods
and books abound. All
around the town, vines stretch
as far as the eye can see.

The stone foyer of the Hôtel des
Barons de Lacoste in Pézenas

Parc Régional du Haut Languedoc ⓴

Hérault, Tarn. ✕ *Béziers.*
🚋 *Béziers, Bédarieux.* 🚌 *St-Pons-de-Thomières, Mazamet, Lamalou-les-Bains* ℹ️ *St-Pons-de-Thomières (04 67 97 38 22).*
www.parc-haut-languedoc.fr

The high limestone plateaux and wooded slopes of upper Languedoc are a world away from the coast. From the Montagne Noire, a mountainous region between Béziers and Castres, up into the Cévennes is a landscape of remote sheep farms, eroded rock formations and deep river gorges. Much of this area has been designated the Parc Régional du Haut Languedoc, the second largest of the French national parks after Ecrins.

St-Pons-de-Thomières is the entrance, with access to forest and mountain trails for walking and riding, plus a wildlife research centre, where one can glimpse the mouflons (wild mountain sheep), eagles and wild boar which were once a common sight in the region.

If you take the D908 from St-Pons through the park you pass the village of **Olargues** with its 12th-century bridge over the river Jaur. **Lamalou-les-Bains**, on the park's eastern edge, is a small spa town with a restored Belle Epoque spa building and theatre, and a soporifically slow pace.

Outside the park boundaries to the northeast there are spectacular natural phenomena. At the **Cirque de Navacelles**, the river Vis has joined up with itself cutting out an entire island. On it sits the peaceful village of Navacelles, visible from the road higher up. The **Grotte des Demoiselles** is one of the most magnificent in an area full of caves, where you walk through a calcified world. A funicular train takes visitors from the foot of the mountain to the top.

The **Grotte de Clamouse** is also an extraordinary experience, the reflections from underground rivers and pools flickering on the cavern roofs, with stalagmites resembling dripping candles.

🏛 **Grotte des Demoiselles**
St-Bauzille-de-Putois. **Tel** 04 67 73 70 02. ⬜ *daily.* ⬛ *1 Jan, 25 Dec.* 📷
www.demoiselles.com

🏛 **Grotte de Clamouse**
Rte de St-Guilhem-le-Désert, St-Jean-de-Fos. **Tel** 04 67 57 71 05. ⬜ *Feb–Oct: daily; Nov–Jan: Sun–Fri.* 📷
www.clamouse.com

Apse of St-Guilhem-le-Désert

St-Guilhem-le-Désert ⓴

Hérault. 🏠 *250.* 🚌 ℹ️ *Maison Communale (04 67 57 44 33).* **www**.st-guilhem-le-desert.com

Tucked away in the Celette mountains, St-Guilhem-le-Désert is no longer as remote as when Guillaume of Aquitaine retired here as a hermit in the 9th century. After a lifetime as a soldier, Guillaume received a fragment of the True Cross from Emperor Charlemagne and established a monastery in this ravine above the river Hérault.

Vestiges of the first 10th-century church have been discovered but most of the building is a superb example of 11th–12th-century Romanesque architecture. Its lovely apsidal chapels dominate the heights of the village, behind which the carved doorway opens on to a central square.

Within the church is a sombre barrel-vaulted central aisle leading to the sunlit central apse. Only two galleries of the cloisters remain: the rest are in New York, along with carvings from St-Michel-de-Cuxa (*see p481*).

Extraordinary limestone formations at the Grotte de Clamouse

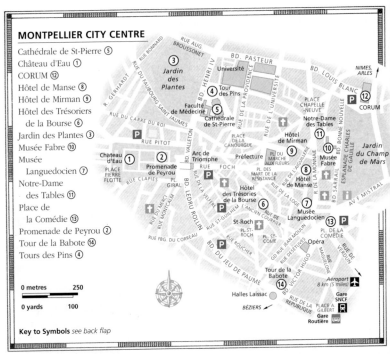

MONTPELLIER CITY CENTRE

0 metres　　250
0 yards　　100

Key to Symbols *see back flap*

Open-air café in the place de la Comédie, Montpellier

Montpellier ㉒

Hérault. 250,000.
30 allée Jean de Lattré de Tassigny
(04 67 60 60 60). daily. *Festival
International Montpellier Danse
(Jun–Jul).* www.ot-montpellier.fr

Montpellier is one of the
liveliest and most forward-
looking cities in the south, with
a quarter of its population
under 25. Sometimes on a
summer evening in university
term time it resembles more a
rock festival than the capital
of Languedoc-Roussillon.

Centre of the action is the
egg-shaped **place de la
Comédie**, known as "l'Oeuf"
("the egg"), with its 19th-cen-
tury opera house fronted by
the Fontaine des Trois Graces
and surrounded by buzzing
cafés. An esplanade of plane
trees and fountains leads to the
CORUM, an opera and conference centre typical of the
city's brave new architectural
projects. The best of these is
Ricardo Bofill's Postmodern
housing complex known as
Antigone, which is modelled
on St Peter's in Rome.

Montpellier was founded
relatively late for this region
of ancient Roman towns, developing in the 10th century
as a result of the spice trade
with the Middle East. The city's
medical school was founded
in 1220, partly as a result of
this cross-fertilization of
knowledge between the two
cultures, and remains one of
the most respected in France.

Most of Montpellier was
ravaged by the Wars of Religion in the 16th century. Only
the **Tour de la Babote** and the
Tours des Pins remain of the
12th-century fortifications.
There are few fine churches,

the exceptions being the
Cathédrale de St-Pierre and
the 18th-century **Notre-Dame
des Tables**.

Reconstruction in the 17th
century saw the building of
elegant mansions with courtyards, stone staircases and
balconies. Examples open to
the public include **Hôtel de
Manse** on rue Embouque-
d'Or, **Hôtel de Mirman** near
place des Martyrs de la
Resistance and **Hôtel des
Trésoriers de la Bourse**. The
Hôtel des Lunaret houses the
Musée Languedocien which
exhibits Romanesque and
prehistoric artifacts.

Another 17th-century building houses the renovated
Musée Fabre with a collection

PONT DU GARD　← To Uzès

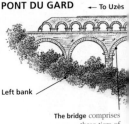

Left bank

The bridge comprises
three tiers of
continuous arches.

of mainly French paintings. Highlights include Courbet's famous *Bonjour M. Courbet*, Berthe Morisot's *L'Eté*, Robert Delaunay's *Nature Morte Portugaise*, and some evocative paintings of the region by Raoul Dufy and François Desnoyer.

A good place to view the city's position between mountains and sea is from the **Promenade de Peyrou**, a grand 18th-century square dominated by the **Château d'Eau** and the aqueduct which used to serve the city. North of here is the **Jardin des Plantes**, France's oldest botanical gardens (1593).

🏛 **Musée Languedocien**
7 rue Jacques Coeur. *Tel* 04 67 52 93 03. ◻ Mon–Sat. ● public hols. 🈂

🏛 **Musée Fabre**
39 bd Bonne Nouvelle. *Tel* 04 67 14 83 00. ◻ Tue–Sun. 🈂 ▮ ▯ ◍

Château d'Eau, Montpellier

La Grande-Motte ㉓

Hérault. 🉐 6,600. 🚊 ▮ av Jean-Bene (04 67 56 42 00). 🅰 Sun (& Thu: mid-Jun–mid-Sep).

The bizarre white ziggurats of this modern marina exemplify the development of the Languedoc-Roussillon coast. One of a number of new

La Grande-Motte

cities on the lagoons south of Montpellier, there are marinas and facilities for every kind of sport from tennis and golf to watersports, all flanked by golden beaches and pine forests. To the east are Le Grau-du-Roi, once a tiny fishing village, and Port-Camargue, with its big marina.

Aigues-Mortes ㉔

Gard. 🉐 6,200. 🚊 🚍 ▮ pl St Louis (04 66 53 73 00). 🅰 Wed & Sun. **www**.ot-aiguesmortes.fr

The best approach to this perfectly preserved walled town is across the salt marshes of the Petite Camargue. Now marooned 5 km (3 miles) from the sea, the imposing defences of this once important port have become a tourist experience, worth visiting more for the effect of the ensemble than the tacky shops within. Aigues-Mortes ("Place of Dead Waters") was established by Louis XI in the 13th century to consolidate his power on the Mediterranean, and built according to a strict

grid pattern. By climbing up the **Tour de Constance** you can walk out onto the rectangular walls, which afford a superb view over the Camargue.

Environs
To the northeast is **St-Gilles-du-Gard**, also once an important medieval port. Today it is worth a detour to see the superbly sculpted 12th-century façade of its abbey church. This was originally established by the monks of Cluny abbey as a shrine to St Gilles, and a resting place on the famous pilgrimage route to Santiago de Compostela *(see pp400–1)*.

Nîmes ㉕

See pp496–7.

Pont du Gard ㉖

Gard. ▮ 08 20 90 33 30. 🚍 from Nîmes. **www**.pontdugard.fr

No amount of fame can diminish the first sight of the 2,000-year-old Pont du Gard. The Romans considered it the best testimony to the greatness of their Empire, and at 49 m (160 ft) it was the highest bridge they ever built.

It is made from blocks of stone, hauled into place by slaves using an ingenious system of pulleys. The huge build-up of calcium in the water channels suggests the aqueduct was in continuous use for 400–500 years, carrying water to Nîmes along a 50-km (31-mile) route from the springs at **Uzès**. This charming town has an arcaded marketplace and several fine medieval towers.

Water channel →

To Nîmes →

Right bank

Roman inscriptions include a damaged phallus carving as a good luck symbol.

Some stones weighed up to six tonnes.

Nîmes ㉕

Listed number one on the tourist map of Nîmes is the bus stop designed by Philippe Starck, who is also credited with reworking the city's pedestrian zone. Such innovations are part of the city's current design renaissance. Architectural projects range from imaginative housing to a glittering new arts complex, under the guidance of a dynamic mayor. An important crossroads in the ancient world, Nîmes is equally well known for its Roman antiquities such as the amphitheatre, the best preserved of its kind. The city is also famous for its festivals and bullfights (*feria*). These are good times to see the rest of Nîmes with its museums, archaeological collections and Old Town of narrow streets and intimate squares.

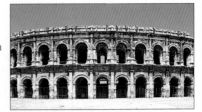

Arches of the Roman amphitheatre

0 metres
0 yards
① Tour Magne
② Mont Cavalier
Temple de Diane
③ Jardin de la Fontaine
ALÈS
RUE DE LA TOUR MAGNE
RUE ROUGET
RUE DES BÉNÉDICTINS
RUE PASTEUR
RUE TRAJAN
QUAI DE LA FONTAINE
QUAI DE LA FONTAINE
RUE BOISSIER
RUE GRETRY
P
RUE DES CHASSAINTES
P
PLACE J. GUESTE
RUE FERNAND PELLOUTIER
RUE MARESCHAL
BOULEVARD JEAN-JAURES
BOULEVARD JEAN-JAURES
RUE EMILE JAMAIS
RUE DELON SOUBEYRAN
RUE BEC DE L
RUE DE L'HOTEL
RUE RENAN
RUE LOU

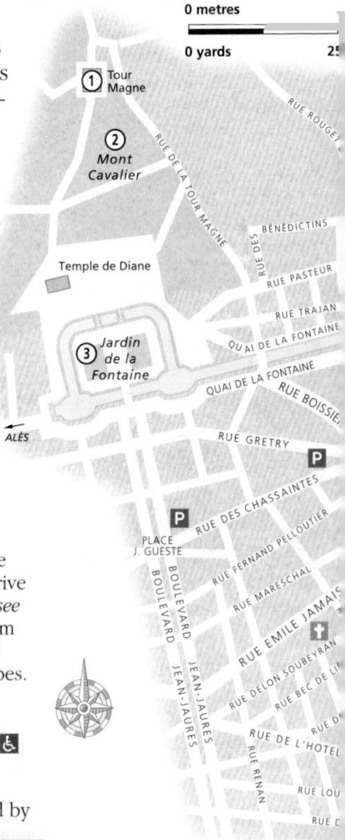

Historic Nîmes
Nîmes has had a turbulent history, suffering particularly during the 16th-century Wars of Religion when the Romanesque **Cathédrale Notre-Dame et St-Castor** was badly damaged. During the 17th and 18th centuries the town prospered from textile manufacturing, one of the most enduring products being denim or "de Nîmes". Many of the fine houses of this period have been restored and elegant examples can be seen on rue de l'Aspic, rue des Marchands and rue du Chapitre in the Old Town. Just outside the town centre is the futuristic apartment building, **Nemausus I**.

The Roman gate, the **Porte Auguste**, built 20 years before the temple of **Maison Carrée**, was once part of one of the longest city walls in Gaul. Of the original arches still standing, two (large) were for carts and chariots and two (smaller) ones for pedestrians. The other major Roman remnant is the **Castellum**, where water used to arrive from the Pont du Gard *(see p495)*. From the Castellum it was distributed around the city through thick pipes.

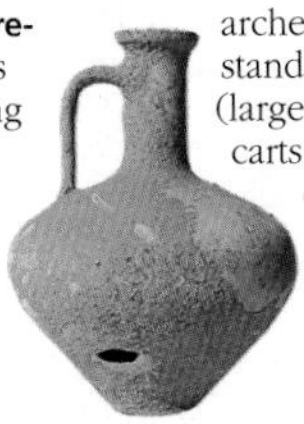

Jug from Musée Archéologique

Jardin de la Fontaine
Quai de la Fontaine. ◯ *daily.* ♿
When the Romans arrived in Nîmes, they found a town established by

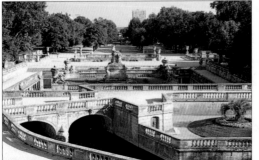

Jardin de la Fontaine, with a view over the city

SIGHTS AT A GLANCE

Carré d'Art/Musée d'Art Contemporain ⑥
Castellum ④
Cathédrale Notre-Dame et St-Castor ⑧
Jardin de la Fontaine ③
Les Arènes ⑩
Maison Carrée ⑤
Mont Cavalier ②
Musée Archéologique ⑨
Musée des Beaux Arts ⑪
Porte Auguste ⑦
Tour Magne ①

the Gauls, centred on the source of a spring. They named the town Nemausus, after their river god. In the 18th century, formal gardens were constructed, and a network of limpid pools and cool stone terraces remains. High above the garden on Mont Cavalier is the octagonal Tour Magne, once a key part of the Roman walls, offering a great view of the city.

Arms of the city in a sculpture by Martial Raysse

venue for concerts, sporting events and bullfights.

🏛 Maison Carrée
Pl de la Maison Carrée. **Tel** 04 66 21 82 56. ◯ daily. ● pub hols.
Square House is a very prosaic name for this elegant Roman temple, the pride of Nîmes. Built around AD 2, it is one of the best preserved in the world, with finely fluted Corinthian columns and a sculpted frieze.

🏛 Musée des Beaux Arts
Rue Cité Foulc. **Tel** 04 66 67 38 21. ◯ Tue–Sun. ● 1 Jan, 1 May, 1 Nov, 25 Dec. &
This fine arts museum houses an eclectic collection of Dutch, French, Italian and Flemish works, notably Jacopo Bassano's *Susanna and the Elders*, and the *Mystic Marriage of St Catherine* by Michele Giambono. The Gallo-Roman mosaic of *The Marriage of Admetus*, discovered in 1882, is on the main floor.

🏛 Musée Archéologique
Musée d'Histoire Naturelle, 13 bis bd Amiral Courbet. **Tel** 04 66 76 73 45. ◯ Tue–Sun. ● 1 Jan, 1 May, 1 Nov, 25 Dec. &
The museum's collection of Roman statues, ceramics, glass, coins and mosaics is housed in Nîmes' natural history museum. The exhibits include important Iron Age menhir statues.

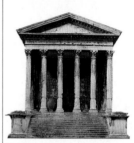

The Maison Carrée

🏛 Carré d'Art/ Musée d'Art Contemporain
Pl de la Maison Carrée. **Tel** 04 66 76 35 35. ◯ Tue–Sun. ● 1 Jan, 1 May, 1 Nov, 25 Dec. & &
Nîmes' arts complex, by the British architect Sir Norman Foster, opened in 1993. Five floors of this glass and steel temple, which was built in tribute to the Maison Carrée opposite, lie underground. The complex has a library, a roof-terrace restaurant around a huge glass atrium, and the Musée d'Art Contemporain. Works cover the main European art movements from the 1960s on, and include works by Raysse, Boltanski and Lavier for France.

🏛 Les Arènes
Bd des Arènes. **Tel** 04 66 21 82 56. ◯ daily. ● public holidays and performance days. & &
All roads lead to the amphitheatre, Les Arènes. Built at the end of the 1st century AD, the design of the oval arena and tiers of stone seats accommodated huge crowds of up to 20,000 spectators. Today it is in use again, a perfect

Bullfight at Les Arènes in Nîmes

Key to Symbols *see back flap*

PROVENCE AND THE COTE D'AZUR

BOUCHES-DU-RHÔNE · VAUCLUSE · VAR
ALPES-DE-HAUTE-PROVENCE · ALPES-MARITIMES

rom its herb-scented hills to its yacht-filled harbours, no other region of France fires the imagination as strongly as Provence. The vivid landscape and luminous light have inspired artists and writers from Van Gogh to Picasso, Scott Fitzgerald to Pagnol.

The borders of Provence are defined by nature: to the west, the Rhône; south, the Mediterranean; and north, where the olive trees end. To the east are the Alps and a border which has shifted over the centuries between France and Italy. Within is a contrasting terrain of plummeting gorges, Camargue saltflats, lavender fields and sun-drenched beaches.

Past visitors have left their mark. In Orange and Arles, the buildings of Roman *Provincia* are still in use. Fortified villages like Èze were built to withstand the Saracen pirates who plagued the coast in the 6th century.

In the 19th century, rich Europeans sought winter warmth on the Riviera; by the 1920s, high society was in residence all year, and their elegant villas remain. The warm sunlight nurtures intense flavours and colours. Peppers, garlic and olives transform a netful of Mediterranean fish into that vibrant epitome of Provençal cuisine, *bouillabaisse*.

The image of Provence bathed in sunshine is marred only when the bitter Mistral wind scours the land. It has shaped a people as hardy as the olive tree, yet quick to embrace life to the full the moment the sun returns.

Cap Martin, seen from the village of Roquebrune

◁ Lavender fields near the Gorges du Verdon

Exploring Provence

This sun-drenched southeastern region is France's most popular holiday destination. Sunworshippers cram the beaches in the summer months, and entertainment includes opera, dance and jazz festivals, bullfights, casinos and *boules* games. Inland is a paradise for walkers and nature lovers, with remote mountain plateaus, perched villages and dramatic river gorges.

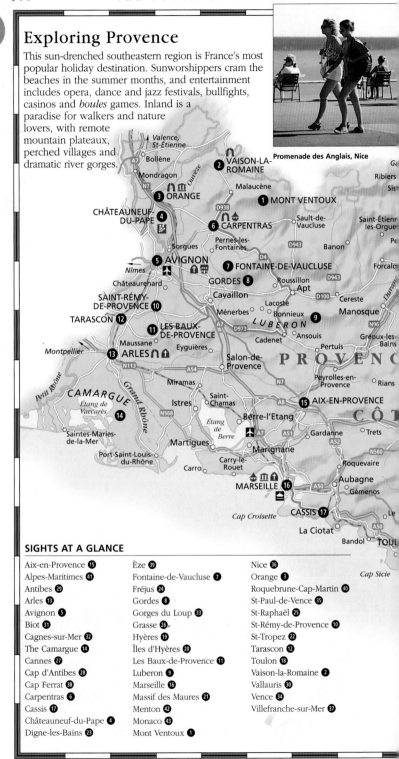

Promenade des Anglais, Nice

Valence, St-Étienne

Bollène

Mondragon

VAISON-LA-ROMAINE **2**

Malaucène

ORANGE **3**

MONT VENTOUX **1**

CHÂTEAUNEUF-DU-PAPE **4**

CARPENTRAS **6**

Sault-de-Vauclouse

Saint-Étienne-les-Orgue

Pernes-les-Fontaines

Banon

Sorgues

Nîmes

AVIGNON **5**

FONTAINE-DE-VAUCLUSE **7**

Forcalo

Châteaurenard

GORDES **8**

Roussillon

Apt

Cavaillon

Cereste

SAINT-RÉMY-DE-PROVENCE **10**

Lacoste

Ménerbes

Bonnieux

LUBERON

Manosque

TARASCON **12**

LES BAUX-DE-PROVENCE **11**

9

Maussane

Ansouis

Gréoux-les-Bains

Montpellier

ARLES **13**

Eyguières

Cadenet

Pertuis

Salon-de-Provence

PROVENC

Miramas

Peyrolles-en-Provence

Rians

CAMARGUE

Istres

Saint-Chamas

AIX-EN-PROVENCE **15**

Étang de Vaccarès

14

Berre-l'Etang

CÔT

Saintes-Maries-de-la-Mer

Étang de Berre

Gardanne

Trets

Port-Saint-Louis-du-Rhône

Martigues

Marignane

Roquevaire

Carro

Carry-le-Rouet

MARSEILLE **16**

Aubagne

Gémenos

Cap Croisette

CASSIS **17**

La Ciotat

Le

Bandol

TOUL

Cap Sicie

SIGHTS AT A GLANCE

Aix-en-Provence **15**

Alpes-Maritimes **41**

Antibes **29**

Arles **13**

Avignon **5**

Biot **31**

Cagnes-sur-Mer **32**

The Camargue **14**

Cannes **27**

Cap d'Antibes **28**

Cap Ferrat **38**

Carpentras **6**

Cassis **17**

Châteauneuf-du-Pape **4**

Digne-les-Bains **23**

Èze **39**

Fontaine-de-Vaucluse **7**

Fréjus **24**

Gordes **8**

Gorges du Loup **33**

Grasse **26**

Hyères **19**

Îles d'Hyères **20**

Les Baux-de-Provence **11**

Luberon **9**

Marseille **16**

Massif des Maures **21**

Menton **42**

Monaco **43**

Mont Ventoux **1**

Nice **36**

Orange **3**

Roquebrune-Cap-Martin **40**

St-Paul-de-Vence **35**

St-Raphaël **25**

St-Rémy-de-Provence **10**

St-Tropez **22**

Tarascon **12**

Toulon **18**

Vaison-la-Romaine **2**

Vallauris **30**

Vence **34**

Villefranche-sur-Mer **37**

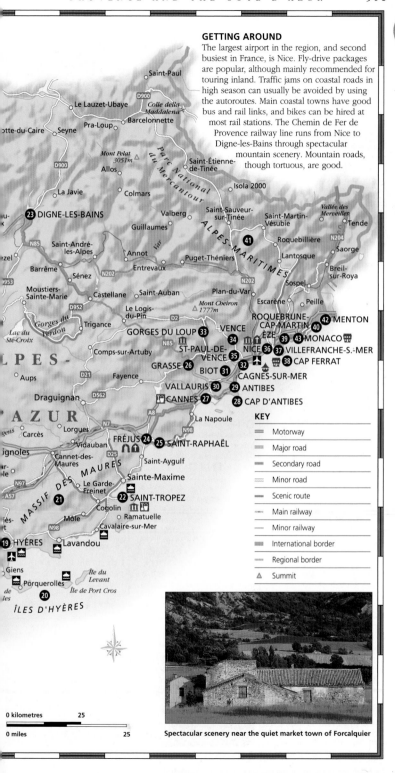

GETTING AROUND

The largest airport in the region, and second busiest in France, is Nice. Fly-drive packages are popular, although mainly recommended for touring inland. Traffic jams on coastal roads in high season can usually be avoided by using the autoroutes. Main coastal towns have good bus and rail links, and bikes can be hired at most rail stations. The Chemin de Fer de Provence railway line runs from Nice to Digne-les-Bains through spectacular mountain scenery. Mountain roads, though tortuous, are good.

Saint-Paul

Le Lauzet-Ubaye

Colle della Maddalena

Barcelonnette

Pra-Loup

otte-du-Caire   Seyne

Parc National du Mercantour

Mont Pelat 3051m

Saint-Étienne-de-Tinée

Allos

La Javie   Colmars

Isola 2000

23 DIGNE-LES-BAINS

Valberg   Saint-Sauveur-sur-Tinée

Saint-Martin-Vésubie

Vallée des Merveilles

Guillaumes

ALPES-MARITIMES

Tende

Saint-André-les-Alpes

N85

41

Roquebillière

N204

Saorge

Annot   Puget-Théniers

Lantosque

Barrême

Sénez

N202

Entrevaux

Breil-sur-Roya

Moustiers-Sainte-Marie

Castellane   Saint-Auban

Plan-du-Var

Sospel

D952

Le Logis-du-Pin

Mont Cheiron △ 1777m

Escarène   Peille

Gorges du Verdon

Lac du Ste-Croix

Trigance   D2

ROQUEBRUNE-CAP-MARTIN

42 MENTON

VENCE

ÈZE   **39**   **40**

GORGES DU LOUP 33

34

43 MONACO

Comps-sur-Artuby

N85

ST-PAUL-DE-VENCE

35

NICE **36**   **37 VILLEFRANCHE-S.-MER**

L P E S -

Aups   D21

Fayence

GRASSE 26

BIOT 31

32

38 CAP FERRAT

Draguignan   D562

VALLAURIS 30

CAGNES-SUR-MER

29 ANTIBES

A Z U R

N7

A8

La Napoule

28 CAP D'ANTIBES

gens   Lorgues

N98

KEY

Carcès

FRÉJUS **24**   **25 SAINT-RAPHAËL**

ignoles

Vidauban

D25

Saint-Aygulf

Cannet-des-Maures

N97

Le Garde-Freinet

Sainte-Maxime

21

Môle

22 SAINT-TROPEZ

Cogolin   Ramatuelle

N98

Cavalaire-sur-Mer

19 HYÈRES   Lavandou

Giens

Porquerolles

Île du Levant

20

Île de Port Cros

ÎLES D'HYÈRES

▬	Motorway
▬	Major road
▬	Secondary road
═	Minor road
▬	Scenic route
⌁	Main railway
---	Minor railway
▬	International border
▬	Regional border
△	Summit

0 kilometres   25

0 miles   25

Spectacular scenery near the quiet market town of Forcalquier

Mont Ventoux ❶

Vaucluse. ✈ Avignon. 🚌 Orange.
🚌 Bedoin. 🛈 Chalet d'Acceuil du
Mont Ventoux.

The name means "Windy
Mountain" in Provençal. A
variety of flora and fauna may
be found on the lower slopes
but only moss survives at the
peak, where the temperature
can drop to –27°C (–17° F).
The bare white scree at the
summit makes it look snow-
capped even during summer.

Ventoux is the mountain on
which the legendary British
cyclist Tommy Simpson died
during 1967's Tour de France.
Today, a road leads to the
radio beacon pinnacle, but the
trip should not be attempted
in bad weather. At other times,
spectacular views from the top
make the effort worthwhile.

**Roman mosaic from the Villa du
Paon in Vaison-la-Romaine**

Vaison-la-
Romaine ❷

Vaucluse. 🏠 6,100. 🚌
🛈 pl du Chanoine Sautel (04 90 36
02 11). 🛒 Tue.
www.vaison-la-romaine.com

This site has been settled
since the Bronze Age, but its
name stems from five
centuries as a Roman town.

Although the upper town,
dominated by the ruins of a
12th-century castle, has some
charming narrow streets, stone
houses and fountains, Vaison's
main attractions lie on the
opposite side of the river.

The **Roman City** is split into
two districts: Puymin and La
Villasse. At Puymin, an
opulent mansion, the Villa du
Paon, and a Roman theatre
have been uncovered.

In 1992, the river Ouvèze
burst its banks, taking many

lives in Vaison and the nearby
area. Damage to some ruins,
such as the Roman bridge,
has since been repaired.
Also at Vaison is the fine
Romanesque **Cathédrale
Notre-Dame-de-Nazareth**,
with medieval cloisters.

🔛 Roman City
Fouilles de Puymin & Musée Théo
Desplans, pl du Chanoine Sautel.
Tel 04 90 36 0211. ⭕ daily. ⬤ 1
Jan, 25 Dec. 🎟 ✔ ♿ restr. 🅿

Orange ❸

Vaucluse. 🏠 30,000. 🚌 🚉 🛈 5 cours
Aristide Briand (04 90 34 70 88). 🛒 Thu.
www.otorange.fr

Orange is a thriving regional
centre. The fields, orchards and
great vineyards of the Côtes
du Rhône make it an
important marketplace for
produce such as grapes, olives,
honey and truffles. Visitors
should explore the area around
the 17th-century Hôtel de Ville,
where attractive streets open
on to quiet, shady squares.
Orange has two of the greatest
Roman monuments in Europe.

🔛 Roman Theatre
Rue Madeleine-Roch, pl de Frères-
Mounet. ***Tel*** 04 90 51 17 60. ⭕ daily.
🎟 ✔ entrance also valid for Musée
d'Orange. ♿ 🅿 🔲
Dating from the 1st-century
AD reign of Augustus, the
well-preserved theatre has
perfect acoustics. It is still
used for theatre performances
and concerts. The back wall
rises to a height of 36 m (120 ft)
and is 103 m (338 ft) wide. In
2006 an immense glass roof,
built high above the theatre
so as not to affect the acoustics, replaced the original roof,
which was destroyed in a fire.

**Statue of Augustus Caesar in the
Roman Theatre at Orange**

🔛 Triumphal Arch
Av de l'Arc de Triomphe.
The triple-arched monument
was built about AD 20. It is
elaborately decorated with
battle scenes, military trophies
and inscriptions to the glory
of Tiberius.

🏛 Musée d'Orange
Rue Madeleine-Roch. ***Tel*** 04 90 51
17 60. ⭕ daily. 🎟
Relics here reflect the history
of Orange, including 400
marble fragments, the earliest
of which dates to the reign of
the Emperor Vespasian in the
1st century BC.

Châteauneuf-du-
Pape ❹

Vaucluse. 🏠 2,100. 🚌 Sorgues, then
taxi. 🛈 pl du Portail (04 90 83 71
08). 🛒 Fri. **www**.chateauneuf.com

Here, in the 14th century, the
popes of Avignon chose to
build a new castle (*château
neuf*) and plant the vineyards
from which one of the finest

View across the vineyards of Châteauneuf-du-Pape

wines of the Côtes du Rhône is produced. Now almost every doorway in this attractive little town seems to open into a *vigneron's* cellar.

After the Wars of Religion *(see pp54–55)*, all that remained of the papal fortress were a few fragments of walls and tower, but the ruins look spectacular and offer magnificent views across to Avignon and the Vaucluse uplands beyond.

Wine festivals punctuate the year, including the Fête de la Véraison in August *(see p38)*, when the grapes start to ripen, and the Ban des Vendages in September, when the grapes are ready to be harvested.

Avignon 5

Vaucluse. 88,312. ⊠ ⊞ 🖾 🛈 41 cours Jean Jaurès (04 32 74 32 74). 🚐 Tue–Sun. 🎭 Festival d'Avignon (3 wks Jul) www.ot-avignon.fr

Massive ramparts enclose one of the most fascinating towns in southern France. The **Palais des Papes** *(see pp504-5)* dominates, but the town contains other riches. To the north of the Palais is the 13th-century **Musée du Petit Palais**, once the Archbishop of Avignon's residence. It has received such guests as Cesare Borgia and Louis XIV. Now a museum, it displays Romanesque and Gothic sculpture and medieval paintings, with works by Botticelli and Carpaccio.

Rue Joseph-Vernet and rue du Roi-René are lined with splendid 17th- and 18th-century houses. There are also fine churches, such as the **Cathédrale de Notre-Dame-des-Doms**, and the 14th-century **Eglise St-Didier**. The **Musée Lapidaire** contains statues, mosaics and carvings from pre-Roman Provence. The **Musée Calvet** features a superb array of exhibits, such as wrought-iron works and Roman finds. It also gives an overview of French art during the past 500 years, with works by Rodin, Utrillo and Dufy.

Two major modern and contemporary art collections, the **Musée Angladon** and the **Collection Lambert**, have

Pont St-Bénézet and the Palais des Papes in Avignon

recently been added to the city's cultural repertoire. The former has works by Van Gogh, Cézanne and Modigliani, while the latter features minimalist and conceptual art.

The place de l'Horloge is the centre of Avignon's social life, with pavement cafés and a merry-go-round from 1900. One of the prettiest streets is the rue des Teinturiers. Until the 19th century, brightly pat-

Open-air performance at the Avignon Festival

terned calico called *indiennes* was printed here – inspiration for today's Provençal patterns. Avignon's renowned 12th-century bridge, the **Pont St-Bénézet**, was largely destroyed by floods in 1668. People danced on an island below the bridge but over the years, as the famous song testifies, *sous* has become *sur*.

Avignon hosts France's largest festival, which includes ballet, drama and classical concerts. The "Off" festival features 600 companies from all areas of show business.

🏛 **Musée du Petit Palais**
Pl du Palais. **Tel** 04 90 86 44 58. ◯ Wed–Mon. ● 1 Jan, 1 May, 14 Jul, 1 Nov, 25 Dec. 🖾 🛈 🗹

🏛 **Musée Lapidaire**
27 rue de la République. **Tel** 04 90 86 33 84. ◯ Wed–Mon. ● 1 Jan, 1 May, 25 Dec. 🖾 🛦 restricted

🏛 **Musée Calvet**
65 rue Joseph Vernet. **Tel** 04 90 86 33 84. ◯ Wed–Mon. ● 1 Jan, 1 May, 25 Dec. 🛦 restricted. 🖾 🗹

Palais des Papes

Pope Clement VI (1342–52)

Confronted with factional strife in Rome and encouraged by the scheming of Philippe IV of France, Pope Clement V moved the papal court to Avignon in 1309. Here it remained until 1377, during which time his successors transformed the modest episcopal building into the present magnificent palace. Its heavy fortification was vital to defend against rogue bands of mercenaries. Today it is empty of the luxurious trappings of 14th-century court life, as virtually all the furnishings and works of art were destroyed or looted in the course of the centuries.

Benedict XII's cloister incorporates the guest and staff wings, and the Benedictine chapel.

Trouillas tower

Belltower

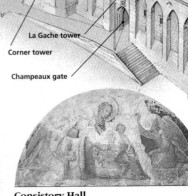

Military Architecture
The palace and its ten towers were designed as an impregnable fortress. It eventually covered an area of 15,000 sq m (148,000 sq ft).

La Gache tower

Corner tower

Champeaux gate

THE AVIGNON POPES

Seven "official" popes reigned in Avignon until 1376. They were followed by two "anti-popes", the last of whom, Benedict XIII, fled in 1403. Popes or anti-popes, few were known for their sanctity. Clement V died eating powdered emeralds, prescribed as an indigestion cure; Clement VI (1342–52) thought that the best way to honour God was through luxury. Petrarch was shocked by "the filth of the universe" at court. In 1367, Urban V tried to return the Curia (papal court) to Rome, a move that became permanent in 1377.

Benedict XII (1334–42)

Consistory Hall
Simone Martini's frescoes (1340) were taken from the cathedral to replace works destroyed by fire in the papal reception hall in 1413.

Papal Power

More like a war-lord's citadel than a papal palace, the building's heavy fortification reflects the insecure climate of 14th-century religious life.

VISITORS' CHECKLIST

Pl du Palais, Avignon. *Tel* 04 90 27 50 00. ◯ Nov–mid-Mar: 9.30am–5.45pm; mid-Mar–Oct: 9am–7pm (Jul–Sep: 9am–8pm). Last adm: 1 hr before closing.
🖼️📷📶♿
www.palais-des-papes.com

★ Grand Tinel

A series of fine 17th- and 19th-century Gobelin tapestries now hang in the vast banqueting hall, where cardinals gathered to elect a new pope.

Angels' tower

★ Stag Room

Fourteenth-century hunting frescoes and ceramic tiles make Clement VI's study the palace's most lovely room.

Pope's chamber

Great courtyard

BUILDING THE PALACE

The palace comprises Pope Benedict XII's simple Palais Vieux (1334–42) and Clement VI's flamboyant Palais Neuf (1342–52). Ten towers, some of which are more than 50 m (164 ft) high, are set in the walls to protect its four wings.

The Great Chapel is 20 m (66 ft) high and covers an area of 780 sq m (8,400 sq ft).

The Great Audience Hall is divided into two naves by five columns with bestiary sculpture on their capitals.

STAR FEATURES

★ Grand Tinel

★ Stag Room

KEY

☐ By Benedict XII (1334–42)

☐ By Clement VI (1342–52)

Carpentras ⑥

Vaucluse. 🚶 29,000. 🚌 🛈 Hôtel Dieu, pl A. Briand (04 90 63 00 78). 🌐 Fri.

In 1320, Carpentras became capital of the papal county of Venaissin, and remained so until 1791. Modern boulevards trace the former ramparts, with only one original gate, the Porte d'Orange, surviving.

In the Middle Ages the town was home to a large Jewish community; today, that community is small. The 1367 **Synagogue** is the oldest in France. The Sanctuary has been restored but the baths and bakery are unchanged.

While not openly persecuted under papal rule, many Jews changed faith, entering **Cathédrale St-Siffrein** by the Porte Juive (Jews' Door).

The Law Courts were built in 1640 as the episcopal palace. The Criminal Court has 17th-century carved tablets of the local towns. In the pharmacy of the Hôtel-Dieu, the 18th-century cupboards are painted with quaint figures of monkey "doctors". More regional art and history is on show at the **Musée Sobirats**.

🔯 Synagogue
Pl de la Mairie. **Tel** 04 90 63 39 97. ⬜ Mon–Fri. ⬤ Jewish feast days.

🏛 Musée Sobirats
Rue du Collège. **Tel** 04 90 63 04 92. ⬜ Wed–Mon. ⬤ publ hols. 🎟

Riverfront and watermill at Fontaine-de-Vaucluse

Fontaine-de-Vaucluse ⑦

Vaucluse. 🚶 600. 🚌 🛈 chemin du Gouffre (04 90 20 32 22).

The main attraction here is the source of the river Sorgue. It is the most powerful spring in France, gushing at up to 90,000 litres (19,800 gallons) per second from an underground river at the foot of a cliff. It powers the Moulin à Papier Vallis Clausa (papermill), which produces handmade paper using the same methods as in the 15th century, and now sells maps, prints and lampshades. There are also several museums. One is devoted to the poet Petrarch, who lived and wrote here, and another to the French Resistance of World War II.

Gordes ⑧

Vaucluse. 🚶 2,000. 🚌 pl du Château (04 90 72 02 75). 🌐 Tue. **www**.gordes-village.com

Perched villages abound in Provence but Gordes is said to attract the most visitors. Dominated by a 16th-century château, the town forms such a harmonious whole that it might have been designed by an architect. The arcaded medieval lanes add to the attractive hilltop position.

Just south lies the **Village des Bories**, a bizarre, primitive habitat. Bories are tiny beehive-shaped huts built of overlapping dry stones. The construction techniques are thought to date back to Neolithic times. This group was inhabited from the 16th to the early 20th century.

The **Abbaye de Sénanque**, to the north, is a fine Romanesque Cistercian monastery.

🏰 Château de Gordes
Tel 04 90 72 02 75. ⬜ daily. ⬤ 1 Jan, 25 Dec. 🎟

🏠 Village des Bories
Rte de Cavaillon. **Tel** 04 90 72 03 48. ⬜ daily. ⬤ 1 Jan, 25 Dec. 🎟 **www**.gordes-village-des-bories.com

Luberon ⑨

Vaucluse. ✈ Avignon. 🚆 Cavaillon, Avignon. 🚌 Apt. 🛈 Cavaillon (04 90 71 32 01). **www**.cavaillon-luberon.com

A huge limestone range, the Montagne du Luberon is one of the most appealing areas of Provence. Rising to 1,125 m (3,690 ft), it combines wild

Perched village of Gordes

For hotels and restaurants in this region see pp590–4 and pp646–50

areas with picturesque villages. Almost the entire area is designated a regional nature park. Within it are more than 1,000 plant species and cedar and oak forests. The wildlife is varied, with eagles, vultures, snakes, beavers, wild boar and the largest European lizards. The park headquarters are in **Apt**, the capital of the Luberon.

Once notorious as the haunt of highwaymen, the Luberon hills now hide sumptuous holiday homes. The major village is **Bonnieux**, with its 12th-century church and 13th-century walls. Also popular are **Roussillon**, with red ochre buildings, **Lacoste**, the site of the ruins of the Marquis de Sade's castle, and **Ansouis**, with its 14th-century Eglise St-Martin and 17th-century castle. **Ménerbes** drew to it the writer Peter Mayle, whose tales of life here brought this quiet region a worldwide audience.

Herb stall at St-Rémy-de-Provence

St-Rémy-de-Provence ❿

Bouches-du-Rhône. *11,000.* *pl Jean Jaurès (04 90 92 05 22).* *Wed, Sat.* **www**.saintremy-de-provence.com

For centuries St-Rémy, with its boulevards, fountains and narrow streets, had two claims to fame. One was that Vincent Van Gogh spent a year here, in 1889–90, at the St-Paul-de-Mausole hospital. *Wheat Field with Cypress* and *Ravine* are among the 150 works he produced here. St-Rémy-de-Provence was also the birthplace in 1503 of Nostradamus, known for his prophecies. But, in 1921, St-Rémy found new fame when archaeologists unearthed the fascinating Roman ruins at **Glanum**. Little remains of the ancient city, sacked in AD 480 by the Goths, but the site impresses. Around the ruins of a Roman arch are foundations and a vast mausoleum, decorated with scenes such as the death of Adonis.

Glanum
Tel *04 90 92 23 79.* *Apr–Aug: daily; Sep–Mar: Tue–Sun.* *1 Jan, 1 May, 1 & 11 Nov, 25 Dec.*

Les Baux-de-Provence ⓫

Bouches-du-Rhône. *460.* *Arles.* *La Maison du Roy (04 90 54 34 39).* **www**.lesbauxdeprovence.com

One of the strangest places in Provence, the deserted citadel of Les Baux stands like a natural extension of a huge rocky plateau. The ruined castle and old houses overlook the Val d'Enfer (Infernal Valley), with its weird rocks, once the haunt of witches and goblins according to legend.

In the Middle Ages Les Baux was home to powerful feudal lords, who claimed descent from the Magus Balthazar. It was the most famous of the Provençal Cours d'Amour, at which troubadours sang the praises of high-born ladies. The ideal of everlasting but unrequited courtly love contrasts with the war-like nature of the citadel's lords.

The glory of Les Baux ended in 1632. It had become a Protestant stronghold and Louis XIII ordered its destruction.

Deserted medieval citadel of Les Baux-de-Provence

The living village below has a pleasant little square, the 12th-century **Eglise St-Vincent** and the **Chapelle des Pénitents Blancs** next door, decorated by local artist Yves Brayer, whose work can be seen in the **Musée Yves Brayer**.

In 1821 bauxite was discovered (and named) here. The disused quarries now form the backdrop for spectacular audio-visual displays, known as the **Cathédrale d'Images**.

To the southwest are the ruins of the **Abbaye de Montmajour**. Its has a 12th-century Romanesque church, noted for its circular crypt.

Parading the Tarasque, 1850

Tarascon ⓬

Bouches-du-Rhône. *13,000.* *16 bd Itam (04 90 91 03 52).* *Tue & Fri.* **www**.tarascon.org

According to legend, the town takes its name from the Tarasque, a monster, half-animal and half-fish, which terrorized the countryside. It was tamed by Sainte Marthe, who is buried in the church here. An effigy of the Tarasque is still paraded through the streets each June *(see p37)*.

The striking 15th-century **Château du Roi René** on the banks of the Rhône is one of the finest examples of Gothic military architecture in Provence. Its sombre exterior gives no hint of the beauties within: the Flemish-Gothic courtyard; the spiral staircase; and painted ceilings of the banqueting hall.

Opposite is Beaucaire, a ruined castle and gardens.

Château du Roi René
Bd du Roi René. ***Tel*** *04 90 91 01 93.* *Apr–Aug: daily; Sep–Mar: Tue–Sun.* *some public hols.*

Arles ⑬

Few other towns in Provence combine all the region's charms so well as Arles. Its position on the Rhône makes it a natural, historic gateway to the Camargue *(see pp510–11)*. Its Roman remains, such as the arena and Constantine's baths, are complemented by the ochre walls and Roman-tiled roofs of later buildings. A bastion of Provençal tradition and culture, its museums are among the best in the region.

Emperor Constantine

Van Gogh spent time here in 1888–9, but Arles is no longer the industrial town he painted. Visitors are now its main business, and entertainment ranges from the Arles Festival to bullfights.

Palais Constantine was once a grand imperial palace. Now only its vast Roman baths remain, dating from the 4th century AD. They are remarkably well-preserved and give an idea of the luxury that bathers enjoyed.

Musée Réattu

This museum, in the old Commandery of the Knights of Malta, houses witty Picasso sketches, paintings by the local artist Jacques Réattu (1760–1833) and sculptures by Ossip Zadkine, including La Grande Odalisque (1932), above.

Museon Arlaten

In 1904 the poet Frédéric Mistral used his Nobel Prize money to establish this museum devoted to his beloved native Provence. Parts of the collection are arranged in room settings, and even the museum attendants wear traditional Arles costume.

Espace Van Gogh, in a former hospital where the artist was treated in 1889, is a cultural centre devoted to his life and work.

★ Eglise St-Trophime

This church combines a noble 12th-century Romanesque exterior with superb Romanesque and Gothic cloisters. The ornate main portal is carved with saints and apostles.

Tourist information

| 0 metres | 100 |
| 0 yards | 100 |

For hotels and restaurants in this region see pp590–4 and pp646–50

Les Alyscamps by Paul Gauguin

LES ALYSCAMPS

A tree-lined avenue of broken medieval tombs is the focal point of these "Elysian Fields" to the southeast of Arles. It became Christian in the 4th century and was a prestigious burial ground until the 12th century. Some sarcophagi were sold to museums; others have been neglected. Mentioned in Dante's *Inferno*, painted by Van Gogh and Gauguin, it is a place for thought and inspiration.

VISITORS' CHECKLIST

Bouches-du-Rhône. 52,600.
25 km (15 miles) NW Arles.
av Paulin Talabot. bd des Lices (04 90 18 41 20). Wed, Sat. Arles Festival (Jul); Prémice du Riz (Sep). **Musée Réattu**
Tue–Sun. **Museon Arlaten**
Jul–Sep: daily; Oct– Jun: Tue–Sun. **Both** public hols.
www.arlestourisme.com

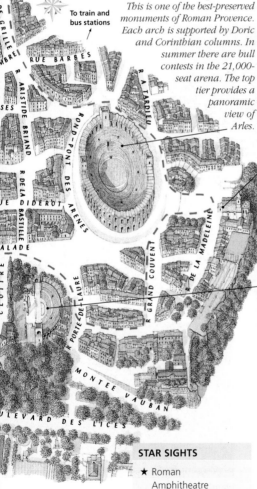

To train and bus stations

★ Roman Amphitheatre
This is one of the best-preserved monuments of Roman Provence. Each arch is supported by Doric and Corinthian columns. In summer there are bull contests in the 21,000-seat arena. The top tier provides a panoramic view of Arles.

Notre-Dame-de-la-Major
is the church in which the *gardians* (cowboys) of the Camargue celebrate the feast day of their patron saint, St George. Although the building dates from the 12th to 17th centuries, a Roman temple existed on this spot hundreds of years earlier.

STAR SIGHTS

★ Roman Amphitheatre

★ Roman Theatre

★ Eglise St-Trophime

KEY

– – – Suggested route

★ Roman Theatre
Once a fortress, its stones were later used for other buildings. Today, the theatre stages the Arles Festival. Its remaining columns are called the "two widows".

The Camargue 🄮

Camargue
gardian

The Rhône delta was responsible for the formation of more than 112,000 ha (280,000 acres) of wetlands, pastures, dunes and salt flats that make up the Camargue, but human efforts are needed to preserve it. The region now maintains a fragile ecological balance, in which a unique collection of flora flourishes, including tamarisk and narcissi, and fauna such as egrets and ibises. The pastures provide grazing for sheep, cattle and small white Arab-type horses, ridden by the *gardians* or cowboys, a hardy community who traditionally lived in thatched huts *(cabanes)* and still play their part in keeping Camargue traditions alive.

Sunset over the Camargue

Black Bulls
In a Provençal bull contest (known as a course*), the animals are not killed. Instead, red rosettes are plucked from between their horns with a small book.*

0 kilometres   5

0 miles   5

N572

D570

Mas du
Pont de

D37

Méjanes •   P

PLAINE
DE LA
CAMARGUE

Le Petit Rhône

Etang de Va

D570

PARC REGIONAL DE CA

P

PETITE CAMARGUE

Centre de
Ginès

Stes-Maries-de-la-Mer

MEDITERRANEE

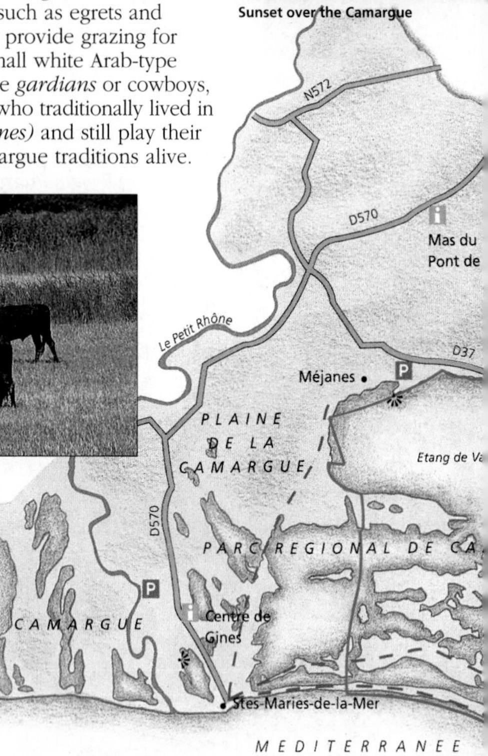

Les Stes-Maries-de-la-Mer
The May gypsy pilgrimage to this fortified church marks the legendary arrival by boat in AD 18 of Mary Magdalene, St Martha and the sister of the Virgin Mary. Statues in the church depict the event.

Flamingoes
These striking birds are always associated with the Camargue, but the region supports many other breeds, including herons, kingfishers, owls and birds of prey. The area around Ginès is the best place to see them.

For hotels and restaurants in this region see pp590–4 and pp646–50

KEY

— Nature reserve boundary

– – Walking routes

– – Walking and cycling routes

VISITORS' CHECKLIST

Bouches-du-Rhône. ✈ Mont-
pellier-Méditerranée, 90 km (56
miles) east. 🚉 🚌 av Paulin
Talabot, Arles. ℹ 5 av Van
Gogh, Saintes-Maries-de-la-Mer.
Tel 04 90 97 82 55.
🎎 Les Pèlerinages (end May,
end Oct).
Musée Baroncelli, rue Victor
Hugo, Saintes-Maries-de-la-Mer.
Tel 04 90 97 87 60. ☐ Aug–
mid-Nov: times vary, phone to
check. ● mid-Nov–Jul. 🈲
www.saintesmaries.com

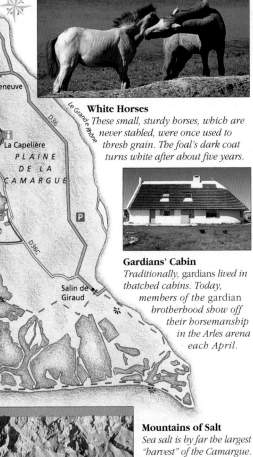

White Horses
*These small, sturdy horses, which are
never stabled, were once used to
thresh grain. The foal's dark coat
turns white after about five years.*

Gardians' Cabin
*Traditionally, gardians lived in
thatched cabins. Today,
members of the gardian
brotherhood show off
their horsemanship
in the Arles arena
each April.*

Mountains of Salt
*Sea salt is by far the largest
"harvest" of the Camargue.
Throughout the summer,
vast brine pans evaporate
and the crystals are heaped
into shimmering camelles
up to 8 m (26 ft) high.*

Aix-en-Provence ⑮

Bouches du Rhône. 🏠 126,000.
🚉 🚌 ℹ 2 place du Général-de-
Gaulle (04 42 16 11 61). ● daily.
www.aixenprovencetourism.com

Founded by the Romans in
103 BC, Aix was frequently
attacked, first by the Visigoths
in AD 477, later by Lombards,
Franks and Saracens. Despite
this, the city prospered. By the
end of the 12th century it was
capital of Provence. A centre
of art and learning, it reached
its peak in the 15th century
during the reign of "Good
King" René. He is shown in
Nicolas Froment's *Triptych of
the Burning Bush* in the 13th-
century Gothic **Cathédrale de
St-Sauveur**, also noted for its
16th-century walnut doors,
Merovingian baptistry and
Romanesque cloisters.

Aix is still a centre of art
and learning, and its many
museums include the **Musée
Granet** of fine arts and archaeology, and the **Musée des
Tapisseries** (tapestries), in the
Palais de l'Archevêché.

Aix has been called "the
city of a thousand fountains".
Three of the best are situated
on cours Mirabeau. On one
side are 17th- and 18th-cen-
tury buildings with wrought-
iron balconies; on the other
are cafés – so much a part of
the city's social life. The Old
Town centres on place de
l'Hôtel de Ville, with its colourful flower market. In the
northwest of town is the **Pavillon de Vendôme**, housing
furniture and works of art by
Van Loo. Aix's most famous
son is Paul Cézanne. The
Atelier Cézanne is kept as it
was when he died in 1906.
Montagne Ste-Victoire,
inspiration for many of his
paintings, is 15 km (9 miles)
east of Aix.

🏛 **Musée Granet**
Pl St-Jean de Malte. **Tel** 04 42 52 88
32. ☐ Tue–Sat. **www.**agglo-
paysdaix.fr 🈲 ℹ
🏛 **Musée des Tapisseries**
28 pl des Martyrs de la Résistance.
Tel 04 42 23 09 91. ☐ Wed–Mon.
● some public hols. 🈲
🏠 **Atelier Cézanne**
9 av Paul Cézanne. **Tel** 04 42 21 06
53. ☐ daily. ● some public hols. 🈲
ℹ **www.**atelier-cezanne.com

Old harbour of Marseille, looking towards the quai de Rive Neuve

Marseille ⑯

Bouches-du-Rhône. 🏠 *900,000.*
✈ 🚉 🚌 ⛴ 🛈 *4 La Canebière
(04 91 13 89 00).* 🗓 *daily.*
www.marseille-tourisme.com

A Greek settlement, founded
in the 7th century BC, then
called Massilia, Marseille was
seized by the Romans in 49
BC. It became the "Gateway
to the West" for most Oriental
trade. France's largest port and
second-largest city has close
links with the Middle East
and North Africa. It is exotic
and lively, with an outdated
reputation for drug trafficking.

In Marseille, narrow stepped
streets, quiet squares and fine
18th-century façades contrast
with the bustle of boulevard
Canebière and the Cité
Radieuse, Le Corbusier's post-
war radical housing complex.

The old harbour now only
handles small boats, but its
daily fish market is renowned.

Marseille has many
excellent museums. Those in
the old harbour area include
the **Musée des Docks
Romains**, the **Musée d'Histoire de Marseille**, the **Musée
du Vieux Marseille**, and the
upbeat **Musée de la Mode**.

In the shopping area to the
south is the **Musée Cantini**,
housing the 20th-century art

collection of sculptor Jules
Cantini. It includes Surrealist,
Cubist and Fauve paintings.

Right the other side of the
city, in one of the finest
houses in Marseille, is the
Musée Grobet-Labadié, with
its fine furniture, tapestries,
17th–19th century paintings
and rare musical instruments.

🏛 Musée des Beaux-Arts
Palais Longchamp, pl Henri Dunan.
Tel *04 91 145930* 🗓 *Tue–Sun.* ⬤
until 2008/9. 🖼 🚻
This museum is housed in the
handsome 19th-century Palais
Longchamp. Works include
Michel Serre's graphic views
of Marseille's plague of 1721,
Pierre Puget's town plans for
the city and murals depicting
it in Greek and Roman times.

⚓ Château d'If
Tel *04 91 59 02 30.* 🗓 *Apr–Aug:
daily; Sep–Mar: Tue–Sun.* 🖼 🚻

The Château d'If (Castle of
Yew) stands on a tiny island 2
km (1 mile) southwest of the
port. A formidable fortress, it
was built in 1529 to house
artillery, but never put to
military use and later became
a prison. Alexandre Dumas'
fictional "Count of Monte
Cristo" was supposed to have
been imprisoned here, and
visitors can see a special cell,
complete with escape hole.
Most real-life inmates were
either common criminals or
political prisoners.

🔒 Notre-Dame-de-la-Garde
Built between 1853 and 1864,
this Neo-Byzantine basilica
dominates the city. Its belfry,
46 m (151 ft) high, is capped
by a huge gilded statue of the
Virgin. The lavishly decorated
interior has coloured marble
and mosaic facings.

🔒 Abbaye de St-Victor
Similar to a fortress in
appearance, the abbey was
rebuilt in the 11th century
after destruction by the
Saracens. In the French
Revolution, the rebels used
it as a barracks and prison.

There is an intriguing crypt
in the abbey's church, with
an original catacomb chapel
and a number of pagan and
Christian sarcophagi.

On 2 February each year, St-
Victor becomes a place of
pilgrimage. Boat-shaped cakes
are sold to commemorate the
legendary arrival of St Mary
Magdalene, Lazarus and St
Martha nearly 2,000 years ago.

🔒 Cathédrale de la Major
Built in Neo-Byzantine style,
this is the largest 19th-century
church in France, 141 m (463
ft) long and 70 m (230 ft) high.
In the crypt are the tombs of
the bishops of Marseille. By it

Le Corbusier's innovative Cité Radieuse in Marseille

Fish market at Marseille

is the small and beautiful Ancienne Cathédrale de la Major.

🕀 Vieille Charité
Rue de la Charité. *Tel 04 91 14 58 80.*
◯ *Tue–Sun.* ◉ *public hols.* 🈺 ♿
In 1640, the construction of a shelter "for the poor and beggars" of Marseille was begun by royal decree. 100 years later, Pierre Puget's hospital and domed church were opened. Now, the restored building houses the Musée d'Archéologie Egyptienne, with its fine collection of Egyptian artifacts; the Musée des Arts Africains is on the second floor.

Cassis ⑰

Bouches-du-Rhône. 🏘 *8,000.* 🚉 🚌
🈺 *quai Moulins, Le Port (08 92 25 98 92).* 🔄 *Wed & Fri.* **www**.ot-cassis.fr

Many of the villages along this coast have been built up, to the point where they have all but lost their original charm, but Cassis is still much the same little fishing port that attracted artists such as Dufy, Signac and Derain. This is a place in which to relax at a waterside café, watching the fishermen or street performers, while enjoying a plate of seafood and a bottle of the local dry white wine for which Cassis is famous.

From Marseille to Cassis the coastline forms narrow inlets, the **Calanques**, their jagged white cliffs (some as much as 400 m/1,312 ft high) reflected in dazzling turquoise water. Wildlife abounds here, with countless seabirds, foxes, stone martens, bats, large snakes and lizards. The flora is no less impressive, with more than 900 plant species, of which 50 are classified as rare. The En-Vau and Sormiou Calanques are especially lovely.

Toulon ⑱

Var. 🏘 *170,000.* ✈ 🚉 🚌 ⛴
🈺 *334 av de la République (04 94 18 53 00).* 🔄 *Tue–Sun.*
www.toulontourisme.com

In 1793 this naval base was captured by an Anglo-Spanish fleet, but was retaken by the young Napoleon Bonaparte. The **Musée National de la Marine** is a focus for history. The **Musée d'Art de Toulon**, housed in an Italian Renaissance building, has a collection of works representing Fauvism, Minimalism and Realism. The tower of the former town hall is all that remains of pre-war Quai Cronstadt (rebuilt and renamed Quai Stalingrad). The war-damaged Old Town has a few original buildings, and the fish market is worth a visit.

🏛 Musée National de la Marine
Pl Monsenergue. *Tel 04 94 02 02 01.*
◯ *Wed–Mon.* ◉ *mid-Dec–Jan.* 🈺
♿ *restr.* 🛈**www**.musee-marine.fr

🏛 Musée d'Art de Toulon
113 bd Maréchal Leclerc. *Tel 04 94 36 8100.* ◯ *Tue–Sun.* ◉ *mid-Dec–Jan.* 🈺

Paul Signac's *Cap Canaille*, painted at Cassis in 1889

Tour of the Gorges du Verdon

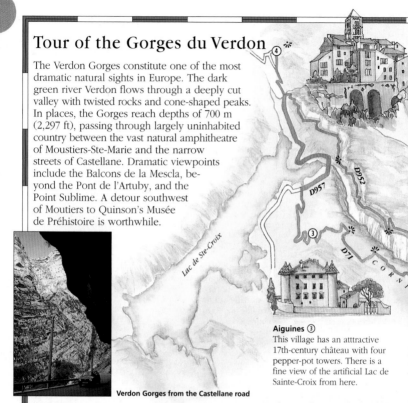

The Verdon Gorges constitute one of the most dramatic natural sights in Europe. The dark green river Verdon flows through a deeply cut valley with twisted rocks and cone-shaped peaks. In places, the Gorges reach depths of 700 m (2,297 ft), passing through largely uninhabited country between the vast natural amphitheatre of Moustiers-Ste-Marie and the narrow streets of Castellane. Dramatic viewpoints include the Balcons de la Mescla, beyond the Pont de l'Artuby, and the Point Sublime. A detour southwest of Moutiers to Quinson's Musée de Préhistoire is worthwhile.

Aiguines ③
This village has an atttractive 17th-century château with four pepper-pot towers. There is a fine view of the artificial Lac de Sainte-Croix from here.

Verdon Gorges from the Castellane road

Hyères ⑲

Var. 🏠 *54,000.* ✈ 🚉 🚌 ⛴
ℹ️ *Av Ambroise Thomas (04 94 01 84 50).* **www**.hyeres-tourisme.com
📅 *Tue, Sat & 3rd Thu of month.*

Towards the end of the 18th century, Hyères became one of the first health resorts of the Côte d'Azur. Among its subsequent visitors were Queen Victoria and writers Robert Louis Stevenson and Edith Wharton.

The main sights are found in the medieval streets of the Vieille Ville, which lead past the spacious, flagstoned place Massillon to a ruined castle and views over the coast.

Modern Hyères is imbued with a lingering Belle Epoque charm which has become popular with experimental film-makers. It continues to attract a health-conscious crowd and is a major centre for aquatic sports.

Fishing off Porquerolles, the largest of the Iles d'Hyères

For hotels and restaurants in this region see pp590–4 and pp646–50

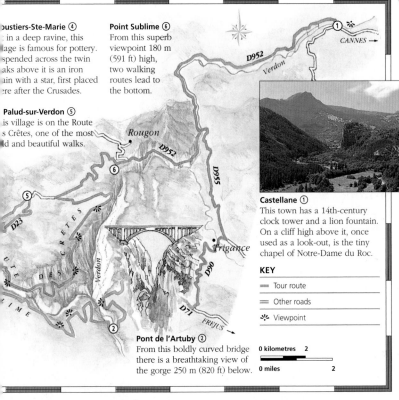

oustiers-Ste-Marie ④
: in a deep ravine, this
lage is famous for pottery.
spended across the twin
aks above it is an iron
ain with a star, first placed
re after the Crusades.

Point Sublime ⑥
From this superb
viewpoint 180 m
(591 ft) high,
two walking
routes lead to
the bottom.

Palud-sur-Verdon ⑤
is village is on the Route
s Crêtes, one of the most
ld and beautiful walks.

Rougon

Trigance

Castellane ①
This town has a 14th-century
clock tower and a lion fountain.
On a cliff high above it, once
used as a look-out, is the tiny
chapel of Notre-Dame du Roc.

KEY

▭	Tour route
▭	Other roads
✳	Viewpoint

Pont de l'Artuby ②
From this boldly curved bridge
there is a breathtaking view of
the gorge 250 m (820 ft) below.

0 kilometres 2

0 miles 2

Îles d'Hyères ⑳

Var. ✈ Toulon-Hyères. 🚉 🚌 🛥
Hyères. 🛈 Hyères (04 94 018450).
www.hyeres-tourisme.com

Locally known as the Îles
d'Or, after the gold colour of
their cliffs, this glamorous trio
of islands can be reached by
boat from Hyères, Le
Lavandou and, in summer,
Cavalaire and Port-de-Miramar.
   Porquerolles, the largest of
the three, measures 7 km (4.5
miles) by 3 km (2 miles). It is
covered in rich vegetation,
much of which, for instance
the Mexican bellombra tree,
was introduced from a variety
of exotic foreign climes.
   The island's main town,
also known as Porquerolles,
looks more like a north
African colonial settlement
than a Provençal village. It
was established in 1820 as a
retirement town for Napoleon's
most honoured troops. All the

island's beaches lie along the
northern coastline. The best,
the long, sandy Plage Notre-
Dame, one of the finest
beaches in Provence, sits in a
sheltered bay about an hour's
walk from Porquerolles.
   A stroll around lush, hilly
Port-Cros, covering just 2.5 sq
km (1 sq mile), takes the best
part of a day. It rises to
195 m (640 ft), the highest
point on any of the islands.
   Port-Cros has been a national park since 1963. A unique
reserve of flora and fauna, its
waters are also protected.
There is even a 300-m (984-ft)
scenic swimming route. You
can buy a waterproof guide
to the underwater wildlife.
   The wild, virtually treeless
Île du Levant is reached by
boat from Port-Cros. Its main
draw is the oldest naturist
resort in France, Héliopolis,
founded in 1931. The eastern
half of the island, controlled
by the French navy, is permanently closed to the public.

Massif des Maures ㉑

Var. ✈ Toulon-Hyères. 🚉 Hyères,
Toulon or Fréjus. 🚌 Bormes-les-
Mimosas. 🛥 Toulon. 🛈 1 pl
Gambetta, Bormes-les-Mimosas (04
94 01 38 38).

The dense wilderness of pine,
oak and sweet chestnut
covering the Maures mountain
range probably gave rise to
its name, meaning dark or
gloomy. It extends nearly
65 km (40 miles) between
Hyères and Fréjus.
   The D558 north of Cogolin
offers a route to the heart of
the Maures. Along the way is
La Garde-Freinet, well-known
for its bottle cork industry.
   Northwest of Cannet-des-
Maures lies the Abbaye de
Thoronet. With the abbeys at
Sénanque, in Vaucluse, and
Silvacane, in the Bouches-du-
Rhône, it is known as one of
the "Three Sisters" of Provence.

Harbourside at St-Tropez

St-Tropez ㉒

Var. 🏛 6,000. 🚌 🈯 quai Jean
Jaurès (04 94 97 45 21). 🅿 Tue & Sat.
www.ot-saint-tropez.com

The geography of St-Tropez
kept it untouched by the
earliest development of the
Côte d'Azur. Tucked away at
the tip of a peninsula, it is the
only north-facing town on the
coast and so did not appeal
to those seeking a warm and
sheltered winter resort. In
1892 the painter Paul Signac
was among the first outsiders
to respond to its unspoiled
charm, encouraging friends,
such as the painters Matisse
and Bonnard, to join him. In
the 1920s the Parisian writer
Colette also made her home
here. St-Tropez also began to
attract star-spotters, hoping
for a glimpse of celebrities
such as the Prince of Wales.

During World War II the
beaches around St-Tropez
were the scene of Allied
landings, and part of the
town was heavily bombed.
Then, in the 1950s, young
Parisians began to arrive, and
the Bardot-Vadim film helped
to create the reputation of
modern St-Tropez as a
playground for gilded youth.
The wild public behaviour
and turbulent love affairs of
Roger Vadim, Brigitte Bardot,
Sacha Distel and others left
fiction far behind. Mass
tourism followed, with visitors
once again more interested in
spotting a celebrity than in
visiting the **Musée Naval** in the
16th-century citadel above the
town, or the **Musée de
l'Annonciade** with its

outstanding collection of
works by Signac, Derain,
Rouault, Bonnard and others.
Bardot had a villa at La
Madrague, but tourists invaded
her privacy, so she left.

Today, there are far more
luxury yachts than fishing
boats moored in St-Tropez
harbour. Its cafés make ideal
bases for people- and yacht-
watching. Another centre of
the action is place des Lices,
both for the Harley-Davidson
set and the morning market.

The best beaches are to be
found just outside the town,
including the golden curve of
Pampelonne, jammed with
beach clubs and fashionable
restaurants. This is the beach
on which to see and be seen.
St-Tropez has no train station,
so driving and parking can be
a nightmare in summer.

It is said that St-Tropez
takes its name from a Roman
soldier martyred as a Christian
by the Emperor Nero. Each
year in May a *bravade* in his

honour takes place when an
effigy of the saint is carried
through the town to the accompaniment of musket fire.

Nearby are two small towns
of differing character but equal
charm. **Port-Grimaud** was only
built in 1966 but the sensitive
use of traditional architecture
makes it seem older. Most of
its "streets" are canals and
many homes have their own
mooring. Up in the hills, the
winding streets of **Ramatuelle**
have been restored to bijou
perfection by the largely
celebrity population.

🏛 **Musée Naval**
Montée de la Citadelle. *Tel* 04 94
97 59 43. ⬤ for renovation until
2008. 📷

🏛 **Musée de l'Annonciade**
Pl Grammont. *Tel* 04 84 17 84 10.
◯ Dec–Oct: Wed–Mon. ⬤ 1 Jan,
Ascension, 1 May, Nov, 25 Dec.
📷 🈯 📷

Stylish solution to the traffic
problems in St-Tropez

BRIGITTE BARDOT

In 1956, Brigitte Bardot's film,
And God Created Woman,
was shot in St-Tropez by her
new husband, Roger Vadim.
By settling in St Tropez, "BB"
the sex-goddess changed the
fortunes of the sleepy little
fishing village and ultimately
the Côte d'Azur, making it
the centre of her hedonistic
lifestyle. In 1974, on her
40th birthday, she celebrated
her retirement from films at
Club 55 on Pampelonne
Beach, and now devotes her
time to her animal sanctuary.

Brigitte Bardot in 1956

Digne-les-Bains ㉓

Alpes-de-Haute-Provence. 🏛
17,000. 🚉 🚌 🛈 *Rond-Point du 11
Novembre 1918 (04 92 36 62 62).* 🛒
Wed, Sat. **www.**ot-dignelesbains.fr

This charming spa town in
the foothills of the Alps
features in Victor Hugo's *Les
Misérables*. A trip on the *Train
des Pignes* from Nice offers
superb views. Apart from the
spa, Digne also offers a lavender festival *(see p38)* and
the **Musée Alexandra David-
Néel**, a Himalayan centre.

🏛 **Musée Alexandra David-
Néel**
27 ave du Maréchal Juin. *Tel 04 92
31 32 38.* ⭘ *daily.* ♿ *restricted.* 🔲
🎥 www.alexandra-david-neel.org

Fréjus ㉔

Var. 🏛 53,000. 🚉 🚌 🛈 *325 rue
Jean Jaurès (04 94 51 83 83).* 🛒
🛒 *Tue, Wed, Fri & Sat.* **www.**frejus.fr

The modern town of Fréjus is
dwarfed in importance by two
impressive historic sites. The
remains of the Roman port of
Amphithéâtre (founded by
Julius Caesar in 49 BC) may
not be as complete as those at
Orange or Arles but they are
of exceptional variety. A great
amphitheatre, fragments of an
aqueduct, a theatre and part of
a rampart gateway remain.
The sea has receded over the
centuries and there are few
traces of the original harbour.

The cathedral on place
Formigé marks the entrance
to the **Cité Episcopale**. The
fortified enclave includes the
5th-century baptistry, one of
the oldest in France, and the
cathedral cloister, its coffered
medieval roof decorated with
scenes from the Apocalypse.

In 1959 Fréjus was hit by a
wall of water as the Malpasset
Barrage burst. To the north the
ruined dam can still be seen.

🏛 **Amphithéâtre**
Rue Henri Vadon. *Tel 04 94 51 34 31.*
⭘ *Tue–Sun.* ● *1 Jan, 1 May, 25
Dec.* ♿ 🎥

🏛 **Cité Episcopale**
58 rue de Fleury. *Tel 04 94 51 26
30.* ⭘ *Apr–Aug: daily.* ● *1 Jan, 1
May, 1 & 11 Nov, 25 Dec.* 🎥
cloisters. 🎥

THE CREATION OF A PERFUME

The best perfumes begin as a formula of essential
oils extracted from natural sources. The blend of
aromas is created by a perfumer called a "nose" because of his or her exceptional sense of smell. A
perfume may use as many as 300 essences, all
painstakingly extracted from plants by various
methods: steam distillation, extraction by
volatile solvents and *enfluerage a froid* (for
costly or potent essences). With this process,
pungent blossoms are placed onto layers of fats
for several days until the fats are saturated.

Lavender water

The oils are then
"washed" out
with alcohol, and
when this evaporates,
it leaves the "pure"
perfume essence behind.

Grasse flowers

St-Raphaël ㉕

Var. 🏛 40,000. 🚉 🚌 🛈 *rue
Waldeck Rousseau (04 94 19 52 52).*
www.saint-raphael.com

Delightfully situated, St-
Raphaël is a charming, old-
style Côte d'Azur resort with
Art Nouveau architecture and
a palm-fronded promenade.
Aside from its beaches,
it offers a marina, a casino,
Roman ruins, a 12th-century
church and a museum with
treasures from a Roman wreck
found by Jacques Cousteau.

It was here that Napoleon
Bonaparte landed in 1799 on
his return from Egypt.

Grasse ㉖

Alpes-Maritimes. 🏛 45,000. 🚌
🛈 *Palais des Congrès, 2 cours
Honoré Cresp (04 93 36 66 66).*
🛒 *Tue–Sun.*
www.grasse-riviera.com

Cradled by hills,
with views out to
sea, Grasse is
surrounded by
fields of lavender,
mimosa, jasmine and
roses. Grasse has
been the centre of
the world's perfume
industry since the
16th century, when
Catherine de'
Médici set the
fashion for
scented leather
gloves. At that
time, Grasse

---

was also known as the centre
for leather tanning. The
tanneries have gone, but the
perfume houses founded in
the 18th and 19th centuries
are still in business, although
today Grasse perfumes are
made from imported flowers
or chemicals. Fragonard and
Molinard have museums, but
the best place to learn is at
the **Musée Internationale de
la Parfumerie**, which has a
garden of fragrant plants.

Grasse was the birthplace
of Jean-Honoré Fragonard,
the artist. The **Villa-Musée
Fragonard** is decorated with
murals by his son. Fragonard's
only religious work is in the
**Cathédrale de Notre-Dame-
du-Puy** in the Old Town, with
three paintings by Rubens.
The place aux Aires and the
place du Cours typify Grasse's
charm, surrounded by streets
with Renaissance staircases
and balconies.

🏛 **Musée International
de la Parfumerie**
8 pl du Cours. *Tel 04 93 36 80
20.* ● *until 2008/2009.*
🎥 ♿ 🔲

🏛 **Villa-Musée
Fragonard**
23 bd Fragonard.
Tel 04 93 36 01 61.
⭘ *daily.*
● *public hols.*
🎥 🔲
www.museedegrasse.
com

**Statue honouring
Jean-Honoré
Fragonard in Grasse**

Lavender fields near Puimoisson, Alpes-de-Haute-Provence ▷

High summer on the beach at Cannes, overlooked by the Carlton Hotel

Cannes ㉗

Alpes-Maritimes. ▨ 70,000. ☒ ☒
☒ ℹ *Palais des Festivals, 1 La
Croisette (04 92 99 84 22).* ☒ *Tue–
Sun.* **www**.cannes.fr

Just as Grasse is synonymous
with the perfume industry,
the first thing that most people
associate with Cannes is its
many festivals, especially the
International Film Festival.
There is much more to the

city than these glittering events.
It was Lord Brougham, the
British Lord Chancellor, who
put Cannes on the map,
although Prosper Mérimée,
Inspector of Historic Monuments, allegedly visited Cannes
two months before him. Lord
Brougham stopped here in
1834, unable to reach Nice
due to a cholera outbreak
there. Struck by the beauty
and mild climate of what was
then just a small fishing port,

he built a villa here. Other
foreigners followed and Cannes
became established as a top
Mediterranean resort.

The Old Town which Lord
Brougham knew is centred in
the Le Suquet district, on the
slopes of Mont Chevalier. Part
of the old city wall can still be
seen on place de la Castre,
which is dominated by the
Notre-Dame de l'Espérance,
built in the 16th and 17th centuries in the Provençal Gothic
style. An 11th-century watch
tower is another attractive
feature of the quarter, and the
castle keep houses the **Musée
de la Castre**, the eclectic finds
of a 19th-century Dutch
explorer, Baron Lycklama.

The famed **boulevard de la
Croisette** is lined with gardens
and palm trees. One side is
occupied by luxury boutiques
and hotels such as the
Carlton, built in Belle Epoque
style, whose twin cupolas
were modelled on the breasts
of La Belle Otero, a famous
member of the 19th-century
demi-monde. Opposite are
some of the finest sandy
beaches on this coast. The
glamour of the Croisette, once
one of the world's grandest
thoroughfares, seems faded in
the noise and fumes of summer.

🏛 Îles de Lérins

☒ *depart from: Gare Maritime, Vieux
Port.* ℹ *Horizon (04 92 98 71 36 for
Île Ste-Marguerite), Planaria (04 92
98 71 38 for Île St-Honorat).*
Just off the coast from Cannes
are the Îles de Lérins. The fort
on **Île Sainte-Marguerite** is
where the mysterious Man in
the Iron Mask was imprisoned
in the late 17th century. A

CANNES FILM FESTIVAL

The first Cannes Film Festival took place in 1946 and,
for almost 20 years, it remained a small and exclusive
affair, attended by the artists and celebrities who lived
or were staying on the coast. The arrival of the "starlet",
especially Brigitte Bardot, in the mid-1950s marked the
change from artistic event to media circus, but Cannes
remains the international marketplace for film-makers
and distributors, with the *Palme d'Or* award conferring
high status on its winner. The annual film festival is
held in the huge Palais des Festivals, opened in 1982.
It has three auditoriums, two exhibition halls,
conference rooms, a casino, night-club and restaurant.

Gérard Depardieu and family arriving at the festival

For hotels and restaurants in this region see pp590–4 and pp646–50

popular theory is that his face had to be hidden because he resembled someone very important indeed – possibly even Louis XIV. Visitors can see the tiny cell that held him for over ten years.

Ile Saint-Honorat has an 11th-century tower in which the resident monks took refuge during raids by the Saracens. There are also five ancient chapels. Both islands offer peaceful woodland walks, fine views and quiet coves for swimming.

Beside the Boulevard de la Croisette

Cap d'Antibes ㉘

Alpes-Maritimes. ✈ Nice. 🚃 🚌 Antibes. 🚌 Nice. 🛈 Antibes (04 97 23 11 11).

With its sumptuous villas in their lush grounds, this rocky, wooded peninsula, known as "the Cap" to its regular visitors, has been a symbol of luxury life on the Riviera since it was frequented by Scott Fitzgerald and the rich American set in the 1920s. One of the wealthiest of all, magnate Frank Jay Gould, invested in the resort of Juan-les-Pins and it became the focus of high life on the Cap. Today, memories of the Jazz Age live on at the Jazz Festival, when international stars perform under the pines (see p37).

At the highest point of the peninsula, the sailors' chapel of **La Garoupe** has a collection of votive offerings and a 14th-century Russian icon. Nearby is the **Jardin Thuret**, created in 1856 to acclimatize

tropical plants. Much of the exotic flora of the region began its naturalization here.

🌺 **Jardin Thuret**
62 bd du Cap. **Tel** 04 97 21 25 03.
⬜ Mon–Fri. ⬤ public hols.

Antibes ㉙

Alpes-Maritimes. 🏠 70,000. 🚃 🚌 🛥 🛈 11 pl du Général de Gaulle (04 97 23 11 11). 🛍 Tue–Sun.
www.antibesjuanlespins.com

The lively town of Antibes was founded by the Greeks as Antipolis and settled by the Romans. In the 14th century, Savoy's possession of the town was contended by France until it fell to them in 1481, after which **Fort Carré** was built and the port, now a centre of Mediterranean yachting, was remodelled by Vauban.

The Château Grimaldi, formerly a residence of Monaco's ruling family, was built in the 12th century. It now houses the **Musée Picasso**. In 1946 the artist used part of the castle as a studio and, in gratitude, donated all 150 works completed during his

The Goat (1946) by Pablo Picasso

stay, including *The Goat*. Most are inspired by his love of the sea, including *La Joie de Vivre*.

The pottery in the **Musée d'Histoire et d'Archéologie** includes objects salvaged from shipwrecks from the Middle Ages to the 18th century.

🏛 **Musée Picasso**
Château Grimaldi. **Tel** 04 92 90 54 20. ⬤ until 2008. 📷 ♿ 📱

🏛 **Musée d'Histoire et d'Archéologie**
1 Bastion St-André. **Tel** 04 93 34 00 39. ⬜ Tue–Sun. ⬤ public hols. 📷
♿ 📱

Sailing boats in the harbour at Antibes

Vallauris

Alpes-Maritimes. 🏛 24,000. 🚌 🚕
🅘 square 8 mai 1945 (04 93 63
82 58). **www**.vallauris-golfe-juan.fr
📅 Tue–Sun.

Vallauris owes its fame to the influence of Pablo Picasso, who rescued the town's pottery industry. In 1951, the village authorities commissioned Picasso to paint a mural in the deconsecrated chapel next to the castle, and his *War and Peace* (1952) is the chief exhibit of the **Musée National Picasso**. In the main square is a bronze statue, *Man with a Sheep*, donated by Picasso.

🏛 Musée National Picasso
Place de la Libération. **Tel** 04 93 64
71 83. ☐ Wed–Mon. ● 1 Jan, 1
May, 1 Nov, 11 Nov, 25 Dec. 📷 ♿
ground floor only. 📷
www.musee-picasso.vallauris.fr

Biot ③

Alpes-Maritimes. 🏛 8,200. 🚌 🚕 🅘
46 rue St-Sebastien (04 93 65 78 00).
📅 Tue, Fri. **www**.biot.fr

A typical little hill village, Biot has retained its charm and has always attracted artists and artisans. The best known is Fernand Léger who made his first ceramics here in 1949. Examples of these and other works by him are shown in the **Musée Fernand Léger** outside town. Its external wall boasts a huge mosaic by the artist.
　The town is also famous for its bubble-flecked glassware. The craft of the glassblowers can be seen (and purchased) at the **Verrerie de Biot**.

🏛 Musée Fernand Léger
255 chemin du Val-de-Pome. **Tel** 04
92 91 50 30. ☐ Wed–Mon. ● 1
Jan, 1 May, 25 Dec. 📷 ♿ 📷 📷

🏛 La Verrerie de Biot
5 chemin des Combes. **Tel** 04 93 65
03 00. ☐ daily. ● 25 Dec. ♿

Renoir's studio at the Musée Renoir, Les Collettes in Cagnes-sur-Mer

Cagnes-sur-Mer ③

Alpes-Maritimes. 🏛 45,000. 🚌 🚕
🅘 6 bd Maréchal Juin (04 93 20 61
64). 📅 Tue–Sun. **www**.cagnes-
tourisme.com

Cagnes-sur-Mer is divided into three districts. The oldest and most interesting is Haut-de-Cagnes, with its steep streets, covered passageways and ancient buildings, including a number of Renaissance arcaded houses. The other districts are Cagnes-Ville, the modern town where hotels and shops are concentrated, and Cros-de-Cagnes, a seaside fishing resort and yachting harbour. The **Château Grimaldi** in Haut-de-Cagnes was built in the 14th century and reworked in the 17th by Henri Grimaldi. Behind the fortress walls is a shady court-yard with a 200-year-old pepper tree. The surrounding marble columns conceal a museum devoted to the olive tree and a small collection of modern Mediterranean art. There is also a group of paintings bequeathed by *chanteuse* Suzy Solidor. The 40 works, all portraits of her, are by artists such as Marie Laurencin and Cocteau. On the ceiling of the banqueting hall is a vast illusionistic fresco of the *Fall of Phaeton* attributed to Carlone in the 1620s.
　The last 12 years of Pierre Auguste Renoir's life were spent in Cagnes, at the **Musée Renoir, Les Collettes**. The house has been kept almost exactly as it was when he

Exterior of the Musée Fernand Léger in Biot, with a mural by the artist

died in 1919 and contains ten of his paintings. It is set in an olive grove, along with his great bronze *Venus Victrix*.

⚜ Château Grimaldi
Tel 04 92 02 47 30. ◯ *Dec–mid-Nov: Wed–Mon.* ● *mid-Nov–2 Dec, 1 Jan, 1 May, 25 Dec.* ▨

🏛 Musée Renoir, Les Collettes
Tel 04 93 20 61 07. ◯ *Wed–Mon.* ● *1–22 Nov.* ▨ 🚻

La Ferme des Collettes (1915) by Renoir, in Cagnes-sur-Mer

Gorges du Loup ③

Alpes-Maritimes. ⟁ *Nice.* ▢ *Cagnes-sur-Mer.* ▢ *Grasse.* ⟁ *Nice.* ⓘ *Tourrettes-sur-Loup (04 93 24 18 93).* www.tourrettessurloup.com

The river Loup rises in the Pre-Alps behind Grasse and cuts a deep path down to the Mediterranean. Along its route are dramatic cascades and spectacular views. The superb countryside is crowned by the perched villages for which the region is famous.

Gourdon owes much of its appeal to its ancient houses, grouped round a 12th-century **Château** built on the site of a Saracen stronghold and perched dizzyingly on the cliffside. Its terraced gardens were laid out by Le Nôtre *(see p179)*. The museum houses a collection of naive art including a work by Henri Rousseau.

Tourrettes-sur-Loup is a fortified village in which the ramparts are formed by the outer houses. It is surrounded by fields of violets, for which it is famous, grown for use in perfume and candied sweets.

⚜ Château de Gourdon
Tel 04 93 09 68 02. ◯ *Jun–Sep: daily; Oct–May: Wed–Mon pm.* ▨ www.chateau-gourdon.com

Vence ㉞

Alpes-Maritimes. 👥 *17,000.* ▣ ⓘ *pl du Grand Jardin (04 93 58 06 38).* ⌂ *Tue & Fri.* www.ville-vence.fr

Vence's gentle climate has always been its main attraction; today it is surrounded by holiday villas. It was an important religious centre in the Middle Ages. The **Cathédrale** was restored by Vence's most famous bishop, Antoine Godeau. A 5th-century Roman sarcophagus serves as its altar and there are Carolingian wall carvings. Note, too, the 15th-century carved choir stalls and Godeau's tomb.

Just within the ramparts of the Old Town, which retains its 13th–14th-century town gates, is place du Peyra, once a Roman forum. Its urn-shaped fountain, built in 1822, still provides fresh water. On the edge of town, the **Chapelle du Rosaire** was built from 1947–51 and decorated by Henri Matisse,

Domed roof in Vence

in gratitude to the nuns who nursed him during an illness. On its white walls, biblical scenes are reduced to simple black lines tinted by splashes of light from the blue and yellow stained-glass windows.

ⓘ Chapelle du Rosaire
Av Henri Matisse. *Tel 04 93 58 03 26.* ◯ *Mon–Thu (Mon–Sat school hols).* ● *mid-Nov– mid-Dec, and public hols.* ▨

Market day in the Old Town of Vence

Street-by-Street: St-Paul-de-Vence ㉟

Restaurant sign, St-Paul-de-Vence

One of the most famous and visited hill villages of the Nice hinterland, St-Paul-de-Vence was once a French frontier post facing Savoy. Its 16th-century ramparts offer views over a landscape of cypress trees, and red-roofed villas with palm trees and swimming pools. The village has been heavily restored but its winding streets and medieval buildings are authentic. It has proved a magnet for artists, both established and aspiring, throughout the 20th century. Today galleries and studios dominate the village.

View of St-Paul-de-Vence
The local landscape is a favourite subject for artists. Neo-Impressionist Paul Signac (1863–1935) painted this view of St-Paul.

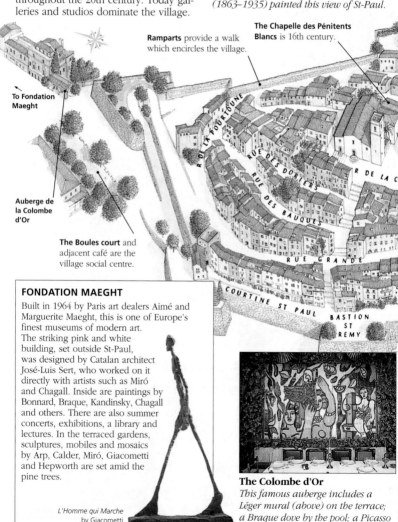

Ramparts provide a walk which encircles the village.

The Chapelle des Pénitents **Blancs** is 16th century.

To Fondation Maeght

R DE LA FOURTOUNE

RUE DES DORIERS

R DE LA C

RUE DES BAUQUES

RUE GRANDE

COURTINE ST PAUL

BASTION ST REMY

Auberge de la Colombe d'Or

The Boules court and adjacent café are the village social centre.

FONDATION MAEGHT

Built in 1964 by Paris art dealers Aimé and Marguerite Maeght, this is one of Europe's finest museums of modern art. The striking pink and white building, set outside St-Paul, was designed by Catalan architect José-Luis Sert, who worked on it directly with artists such as Miró and Chagall. Inside are paintings by Bonnard, Braque, Kandinsky, Chagall and others. There are also summer concerts, exhibitions, a library and lectures. In the terraced gardens, sculptures, mobiles and mosaics by Arp, Calder, Miró, Giacometti and Hepworth are set amid the pine trees.

L'Homme qui Marche
by Giacometti

The Colombe d'Or
This famous auberge includes a Léger mural (above) on the terrace; a Braque dove by the pool; a Picasso and a Matisse in the dining room.

The **Musée d'Histoire de Saint-Paul** has local waxwork scenes from the town's past.

Le Donjon, a grim medieval building, was used as a prison until the 19th century.

Eglise Collégiale
Begun in the 12th century, the church's treasures include a painting of St Catherine, attributed to Tintoretto.

VISITORS' CHECKLIST

Alpes-Maritimes. 2,900.
12 pl du Grand Jardin, Vence
(04 93 58 37 60). 2 rue grande
(04 93 32 81 63). **Fondation
Maeght** daily. Library,
lectures, concerts. www.saint-
pauldevence.com

Grand Fountain
This charming cobble-stoned place has a pretty urn-shaped fountain.

Rue Grande
The doors of the 16th- and 17th-century houses bear coats of arms.

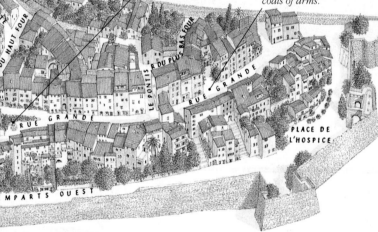

CELEBRITY VILLAGE

The Colombe d'Or (Golden Dove) auberge *(see p574)* was popular with many of the artists and writers who flocked to the Riviera in the 1920s. Early patrons included Picasso, Soutine, Modigliani, Signac, Colette and Cocteau. They often paid for their rooms and meals with paintings, resulting in the priceless collection that can be seen by diners today. The rich and famous have continued to come to St-Paul: Zelda and F Scott Fitzgerald had a dramatic fight over Isadora Duncan at dinner here one night, and Yves Montand married Simone Signoret on the terrace. A photo display of celebrity visitors in St-Paul museum features Sartre and de Beauvoir, Greta Garbo, Sophia Loren, Burt Lancaster and Catherine Deneuve.

Artist Marc Chagall (1887–1985), who moved to St-Paul-de-Vence in 1950

Nice ㊱

The largest resort on the Mediterranean coast and the fifth biggest city in France, with its second busiest airport, Nice was founded by the Greeks and colonized by the Romans. Its temperate winter climate and verdant subtropical vegetation have long attracted visitors. Until World War II it was favoured by aristocrats, including Tsar Nicholas I's widow who visited in 1856 and Queen Victoria who stayed in 1895. This glittering past has contributed to Nice becoming capital of the Côte d'Azur, and today it is also a centre for business conferences and package holidays. Nice has worthy museums, good beaches and an atmospheric street life. Best of all is Carnival: 18 days of celebrations finishing on Shrove Tuesday in a fireworks display and the Battle of the Flowers (see p39).

Yachts at anchor in Nice harbour

Nice's Old Quarter

Exploring Nice

The promenade des Anglais, running right along the seafront, was built in the 1830s with funds raised by the English colony. Today it is an eight-lane, 8-km (5-mile) highway, with galleries, shops and grand hotels like the **Negresco**, reflecting Nice's prosperity.

Nice also has a dark side, recorded in 1982 by English author, Graham Greene. He wrote a controversial attack on Jacques Médecin, the city's right-wing mayor, who fled to South America to avoid standing trial in France.

Nice was Italian until 1860, and the pastel façades and balconies of the Old Town have a distinctly Italianate feel. It lies at the foot of a hill still known as the Château for the castle which once stood there. The district is largely restored and its tall, narrow buildings house artists and galleries, boutiques and restaurants. The daily flower market in the cours Saleya should not be missed.

The **Cimiez** district, on the hills overlooking the town, is the fashionable quarter of Nice. The old monastery of Notre-Dame-de-Cimiez is well worth a visit. Lower down the Cimiez hillside are Les Arènes, remains of an extensive Roman settlement with vestiges of the great baths and an amphitheatre. Artifacts from the excavations are on show at the archaeological museum, next to the Musée Matisse. At the foot of the Cimiez hill is the **Musée Chagall**.

🏛 Musée Matisse

164 av des Arènes de Cimiez.
Tel 04 93 81 08 08. ◯ Wed–Mon.
● some public hols. 🖼 🔊 🚻
Inspired by the Mediterranean light, Matisse spent many years in Nice. The museum, housed in and below the 17th-century Arena Villa, displays drawings, paintings, bronzes, fabrics and artifacts. Highlights include *Still Life With Pomegranates* and his last completed work, *Flowers and Fruits.*

🏛 Palais Lascaris

15 rue Droite. **Tel** 04 93 62 72 40.
◯ Wed–Mon. ● some public hols.
This stuccoed 17th-century palace is decorated with ornate woodwork, Flemish tapestries and illusionistic ceilings thought to be by Carlone. Its small but delightful collection includes a reconstruction of an 18th-century apothecary's shop.

🏛 Musée d'Art Moderne et d'Art Contemporain

Promenade des Arts. **Tel** 04 97 13 42 01. ◯ Tue–Sun. ● 1 Jan, Easter, 1 May, 25 Dec. 🖼 🔊 🚻
www.mamac-nice.org
The museum occupies a strikingly original complex of four marble-faced towers linked by glass passageways. The collection is particularly strong in Neo-Realism and Pop Art, with works by Andy Warhol, Jean Tinguely and Niki de Saint-Phalle. Also well-represented are such Ecole de Nice artists as César, Arman and Yves Klein.

Blue Nude IV (1952) by Henri Matisse

An azure view – relaxing on the promenade des Anglais

VISITORS' CHECKLIST

Alpes-Maritimes. 🏘 349,000.
✈ 7 km (4.5 miles) SW. 🚆 av
Thiers (36 35). 🚌 5 bd Jean
Jaurès (04 93 85 61 81). ⚓ quai
du Commerce (08 92 70 74 07).
🛈 5 prom des Anglais (04 92 14
48 00). 🗓 Tue–Sun. 🎭 Carnival.
www.nicetourism.com

🔒 Cathédrale Ste-Réparate

This 17th-century Baroque building is surmounted by a handsome tiled dome. Its interior is lavishly decorated with plasterwork, marble and original panelling.

🏛 Musée Chagall

36 av du Docteur Ménard. **Tel** 04 93 53 87 20. ☐ Wed–Mon. ⚫ 1 Jan, 1 May, 25 Dec. 🖼 ♿ 🏷
This is the largest collection of works by Marc Chagall, with paintings, drawings, sculpture, stained glass and mosaics. Best of all are the 17 canvases of the artist's *Biblical Message*.

🏛 Musée des Beaux-Arts

33 av des Baumettes. **Tel** 04 92 15 28 28. ☐ Tue–Sun. ⚫ 1 Jan, Easter, 1 May, 25 Dec. 🖼 ♿ restr.
The 19th-century home of a Ukrainian princess displays works sent to Nice by Napoleon III after Italy ceded the city to France in 1860, as well as paintings by Impressionists and Post-Impressionists, such as Renoir, Monet and Dufy.

🏛 Palais Masséna

65 rue de France. **Tel** 04 93 88 11 34. ⚫ until 2008/2009. 🖼 ♿ 🏷
This 19th-century Italianate villa exhibits religious works, paintings by Niçois primitives, white-glazed faïence and Josephine's gold cloak.

🔒 Cathédrale Orthodoxe Russe St-Nicolas

Completed in 1912, the cathedral was built in memory of a young Tsarevitch who died of consumption here in 1865. The exterior is of pink brick and grey marble with elaborate mosaics. The interior is resplendent with icons and fine woodwork.

🏛 Musée des Arts Asiatiques

405 prom des Anglais. **Tel** 04 92 29 37 00. ☐ Wed–Mon. ⚫ 1 Jan, 1 May, 25 Dec. 🖼 ♿ 🏷
Exhibits of ancient and contemporary art from across Asia, in Kenzo Tange's uncluttered white marble and glass setting.

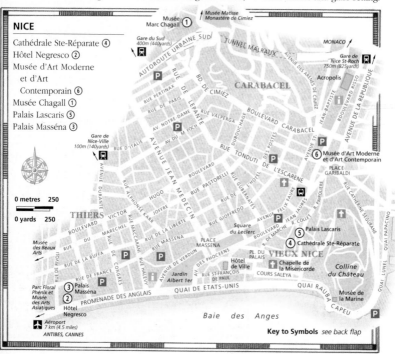

NICE

Cathédrale Ste-Réparate ④
Hôtel Negresco ②
Musée d'Art Moderne et d'Art Contemporain ⑥
Musée Chagall ①
Palais Lascaris ⑤
Palais Masséna ③

0 metres 250
0 yards 250

Key to Symbols *see back flap*

Chapelle de St-Pierre, Villefranche

Villefranche-sur-Mer ③⑦

Alpes-Maritimes. 🏛 6,649. 🚉
🚌 ℹ *Jardin François Binon (04 93 01 73 68).* 🏪 *Sat & Sun.*
www.villefranche-sur-mer.com

One of the most perfectly situated towns on the coast, Villefranche lies at the foot of hills forming a sheltered amphitheatre. The town over-looks a beautiful natural har-bour which is deep enough to be a naval port of call.

The bright and animated waterfront is lined by Italian-ate façades, with cafés and bars from which to watch the fishermen. Here, too, is the medieval **Chapelle de St-Pierre**, which, after years of service storing fishing nets, was restored in 1957 and decora-ted by Jean Cocteau. His fres-coes depict non-religious images and the life of St Peter.

Also worth a visit is the 16th-century **Citadelle St-Elme**, incorporating the town hall and two art galleries.

Behind the harbour, the streets are narrow, winding, and often stepped. Walking through them, you get the odd glimpse of the harbour. The vaulted 13th-century rue Obscure has always provided shelter from bombardment, right up to World War II.

🔷 **Chapelle de St-Pierre**
Quai Amiral Courbet. ***Tel*** *04 93 76 90 70.* ◯ *mid-Dec–mid-Nov: Tue–Sun.* ⬤ *25 Dec.* 🔲 ♿

Cap Ferrat ③⑧

Alpes-Maritimes. ✈ *Nice.* 🚊 *Nice.*
🚌 *Beaulieu-sur-Mer.* 🚌 ℹ *St-Jean-Cap-Ferrat (04 93 76 08 90).*
www.ville-saint-jean-cap-ferrat.fr

The peninsula of Cap Ferrat boasts some of the most sumptuous villas found on the Riviera. From 1926 until the author's death, the best-known was Somerset Maugham's Villa Mauresque, where he received celebrities from Noël Coward to Winston Churchill.

High walls shield most of the exclusive villas, but poss-ibly the best one is open to the public. The **Villa Ephrussi de Rothschild** is a terracotta and marble mansion set in themed gardens on the crest of the cape. It belonged to the Baroness Ephrussi de Rothschild, who bequeathed it to the Institut de France in 1934. It is furnished as she left it, with her collections of

priceless porcelain, items that belonged to Marie Antoinette and a unique collection of drawings by Fragonard.

The town of **Beaulieu** lies where the cape joins the main-land. A pleasant marina with an exceptionally mild climate and very fine hotels, it is the site of another unique house, the extraordinary **Villa Kerylos**. Built between 1902 and 1908 for archaeologist Theodore Reinach in imitation of an ancient Greek residence, it contains lovingly reproduced mosaics, frescoes and furniture.

🏛 **Villa Ephrussi de Rothschild**
Cap Ferrat. ***Tel*** *04 93 01 33 09.*
◯ *Feb–Oct: daily; Nov–Jan: Mon–Fri pms, w/e & sch & publ hols: daily.* 🔲 ♿ 🔲 🔲 🔲
www.culturespaces.com

🏛 **Villa Kerylos**
Imp Gustave Eiffel, Beaulieu. ***Tel*** *04 93 01 01 44.* ◯ *as above.* 🔲 ♿ 🔲
www.villa-kerylos.com

Greek-style Villa Kerylos at Beaulieu on Cap Ferrat

Louis XV salon at the Villa Ephrussi de Rothschild, Cap Ferrat

Eze ㊴

Alpes-Maritimes. 🚶 3,100. 🚉 🚌
🛈 pl Général de Gaulle (04 93 41 26
00). **www**.eze-riviera.com

For many, Eze is the ultimate
perched village, balancing on
a rocky pinnacle high above
the Mediterranean. Every
summer, thousands of visitors
stream through the 14th-
century fortified gate and
throng the narrow streets. The
flower-decked buildings are
almost all shops, galleries and
craft workshops. At the top of
the village, the château is
surrounded by the lush tropical
plants of the **Jardin Exotique**.
The view from here is superb.

Further along the Upper
Corniche is the Roman Alpine
Trophy **La Turbie** (see pp46
–7). This vast 6 BC structure
dominates the surrounding
village, with magnificent views
towards Monaco and Italy.

🌸 **Jardin Exotique**
Rue du Château. **Tel** 04 93 41 10
30. ◻ daily. ◼ 1 Jan, 25 Dec. 🈺

🏛 **La Turbie**
◻ Apr–mid-Sep: daily; mid-Sep–Mar:
Tue–Sun. ◼ public hols. 🈺 📷 🛈

Roquebrune-Cap-Martin ㊵

Alpes-Maritimes. 🚃 Nice. 🚉 🚌
🛈 218 av Aristide Briand (04 93 35
62 87). ◼ Wed. **www**.roquebrune-
cap-martin.com

The medieval village of
Roquebrune overlooks the
wooded cape where the villas
of the rich and famous still
abound. Visitors here have

included Coco Chanel and
Greta Garbo. The cape has
not always been kind – poet
WB Yeats died here in 1939
and architect Le Corbusier was
drowned off the coast in 1965.

In 1467 Roquebrune believed
that by performing scenes
from the Passion it escaped
the plague, and every August
it continues this tradition.

View from Roquebrune

Alpes-Maritimes ㊶

Alpes-Maritimes. 🚃 Nice. 🚉 Nice.
🚉 Peille. 🚌 Nice. 🛈 La Mairie, Peille
(04 93 91 71 71). **www**.peille.fr

In the hinterland of the Côte
d'Azur, it is still possible to
find quiet, unspoiled villages
off the tourist track. The tiny
twin villages of **Peille** and
Peillon are typical. Both have
changed little since the Middle
Ages, perched on outcrops
over the Paillon river, their
streets a mass of steps and
arches. Peille, the more remote, even has its own dialect.
The Alpes-Maritimes countryside is also unspoiled, its

craggy gorges, tumbling rivers
and windswept plateaux just a
few hours from the coast. Of
note are the ancient rock carvings of the **Vallée des Merveilles** and rare wildlife in the
Parc National du Mercantour.

Menton ㊷

Alpes-Maritimes. 🚶 30,000. 🚉 🚌
🛈 Palais de l'Europe, 8 av Boyer (04
92 41 76 76). ◼ daily.
www.menton.fr

Menton's beaches, with the
Alps and the golden buildings
and Belle Epoque villas of the
Old Town as a backdrop,
would be enough to lure most
visitors. In the 19th century,
Queen Victoria and famous
writers and poets often
holidayed here. Tropical gardens and citrus fruits thrive in
the town's perfect climate,
mild even in February for the
lemon festival (see p39).

The **Basilica St-Michel** is a
superb example of Baroque
architecture in yellow and
pink stone. The square before
it is paved with a mosaic of the
Grimaldi coat of arms.
The **Salle des Mariages** in the
Hôtel de Ville was decorated
in 1957 by Jean Cocteau. Drawings, paintings, ceramics
and stage designs by the
renowned artist are displayed
in the **Musée Jean Cocteau**,
housed in a 17th-century fort.
Inside the Palais Carnolès, the
Musée des Beaux-Arts features
works from the Middle Ages
to the 20th century.

🎭 **Salle des Mariages**
Hôtel de Ville. **Tel** 04 92 10 50 00.
◻ Mon–Fri. ◼ public hols. 🈺

🏛 **Musée Jean Cocteau**
Vieux Port. **Tel** 04 93 57 72 30. ◻
Wed–Mon. ◼ public hols. 🈺

🏛 **Musée des Beaux-Arts**
3 av de la Madone. **Tel** 04 93 35 49
71. ◻ Wed–Mon. ◼ public hols.

**Mosaic at the Musée Jean Cocteau
in Menton**

Monaco

Travellers to Monaco by car would do well to take the Moyenne Corniche, one of the most beautiful highways in the world, with incomparable views of the Mediterranean coastline. Arriving among the skyscrapers of Monaco today, it is hard to envisage the turbulence of its history. At first a Greek settlement, later taken by the Romans, it was bought from the Genoese in 1297 by the Grimaldis who, in spite of bitter family feuds and at least one political assassination, still rule as the world's oldest ruling dynasty. Monaco covers 1.9 sq km (0.74 sq miles) and, although its size has increased by one-third in the form of landfills, it still occupies an area smaller than that of New York's Central Park.

Aerial view of Monaco

Grand Casino

Exploring Monaco

Monaco owes its renown principally to its Grand Casino. Source of countless legends, it was instituted in 1878 by Charles III to save himself from bankruptcy. The first casino was opened in 1865 on a barren promontory (later named Monte-Carlo in his honour) across the harbour from ancient Monaco-Ville. So successful was Charles's money-making venture that, by 1870, he was able to abolish taxation for his people. Today, Monaco is a tax haven for thousands, and its residents have the highest per capita income in the world.

Visitors come from all over the world for the Grand Prix de Monaco in May and the Monte-Carlo Rally in January (*see p39*). Many of the greatest singers perform in the opera season. There is a fireworks festival (July–August), and an international circus festival at the end of January as well as world-class ballet and concerts. Facilities exist for every sort of leisure activity, and there is much else to enjoy without breaking the bank, including **Fort Antoine** and the neo-Romanesque **Cathédrale**.

🎰 Grand Casino

Place du Casino. **Tel** 00 377 92 16 20 20. ○ daily, from noon. &
www.montecarloresort.com
Designed in 1878 by Charles Garnier, architect of the Paris Opéra (*see p97*), and set in formal gardens, the Casino gives a splendid view over Monaco. The lavish interior is still decorated in Belle Epoque style, recalling an era when this was the rendezvous of Russian Grand Dukes. Anyone can play the odds on the one-armed bandits of the Salon Blanc or the roulette wheels of the Salons Européens. Even the most exclusive of the gaming rooms can be visited at a price, but their tables are for the big spenders only.

♣ Palais Princier

Place du Palais. **Tel** 00 377 93 25 18 31. ○ Apr–Nov: daily.
Monaco-Ville, the seat of government, is the site of the 13th-century Palais Princier. The interior, with its priceless furniture and carpets and its

Skyscrapers and apartment blocks of modern Monte-Carlo

MONACO'S ROYAL FAMILY

Prince Albert II officially assumed the Monaco throne in July 2005, three months after his father died, aged 81, ending a reign of over 55 years. Prince Rainier III was an effective ruler, descended from a Grimaldi who entered the Monaco fortress in 1297. His wife, former film star Grace Kelly, died tragically in 1982. Prince Albert and his sisters, Caroline and Stephanie, remain a focus of media attention.

Prince Rainier III, Princess Grace and Princess Caroline

VISITORS' CHECKLIST

Monaco. 🏙 *35,000.* ✈ *7 km (4.5 miles) SW Nice.* 🚉 *av Prince Pierre (SNCF: 36 35).* 🚌 *2a bd des Moulins (00 377 92 16 61 16).* 🛒 *daily.* 🎪 *Festival du Cirque (Jan–Feb); International Fireworks Festival (Jul–Aug); Fête Nationale Monégasque (19 Nov).* **www**.monaco-congres.com

magnificent frescoes, is only open to the public in the summer. The changing of the guard is at 11:55am.

🏛 Musée des Souvenirs Napoléoniens et Archives Historiques du Palais

Pl du Palais. *Tel 00 377 93 25 18 31.* 🛒 *Apr–Dec: daily; Jan–Mar: Tue–Sun.* 🔴 *1 Jan, 1 May, Grand Prix, 25 Dec.* 🔲

A genealogical tree on the wall traces the family links between the Grimaldis and Bonapartes. Also on show are Napoleon's

Guard outside the Palais Princier

personal effects and clothing, and numerous portraits.

🐟 Musée Océanographique

Av Saint-Martin. *Tel 00 377 93 15 36 00.* 🛒 *daily.* 🔲 🔲 🔲 🔲

This museum was founded in 1910 by Prince Albert I, using his casino profits. Its aquarium, fed with sea water, holds rare species of marine plants and animals. The museum houses an important scientific collection, diving equipment and model ships. Marine explorer Jacques

Cousteau established his research centre here.

🌿 Jardin Exotique

62 bd du Jardin Exotique. *Tel 00 377 93 15 29 80.* 🛒 *daily.* 🔴 *19 Nov, 25 Dec.* 🔲 🔲 *restr.* 🔲 🔲

These gardens are considered to be the finest in Europe, with a huge range of tropical and subtropical plants. In the park, a museum of anthropology offers evidence that bears, mammoths and hippopotami once lived on the coast here.

🏛 Musée des Automates et Poupées d'Autrefois

17 av Princesse Grace. *Tel 00 377 93 30 91 26.* 🛒 *daily.* 🔴 *1 Jan, 1 May, Grand Prix, 19 Nov, 25 Dec.* 🔲 🔲

This museum houses over 400 dolls from the 18th and 19th centuries. The delightful automata are set in motion several times each day.

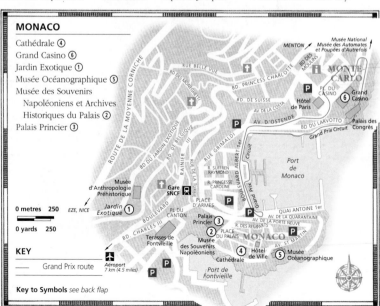

MONACO

0 metres   250

0 yards   250

KEY

—— Grand Prix route

Aéroport
7 km (4.5 miles)

Key to Symbols *see back flap*

CORSICA

HAUTE-CORSE · CORSE-DU-SUD

Corsica, where the people speak their own language, has all the attributes of a mini-continent. There are tropical palm trees, vineyards, olive and orange groves, forests of chestnut and indigenous pine, alpine lakes and cool mountain torrents filled with trout. Most distinctive of all is the parched maquis (scrub), heavy with the scent of myrtle, which Napoleon swore he could smell from Elba.

The fourth largest island in the Mediterranean after Sicily, Sardinia and Cyprus, Corsica has been a problem and a bafflement to mainland France ever since 1769, when it was "sold" to Louis XV by the Genoese for 40 million francs. Before that, following years of struggle, the Corsican people had enjoyed 14 years of independence under the revered leadership of Pasquale Paoli. They understandably felt cheated by the deal with the French, and have resented them ever since. To holiday-makers visiting the island – in July and August tourists outnumber the inhabitants six to one – the Corsican–French relationship may be a matter of indifference. However, there is a strong (and sometimes quite violent) separatist movement, which does deter some tourists. As a result, Corsica's wild beauty has been preserved to an extent not seen in the rest of the Mediterranean.

For 200 years, from the 11th to the 13th century, Corsica was a colony of the old Tuscan republic of Pisa, whose builders founded beautifully proportioned Romanesque churches. These buildings are, along with the megalithic stone warriors in Filitosa, the noblest monuments to be seen here. For the rest, the birthplace of Napoleon is a place of wild seacoasts and mountain peaks, one of the last unspoiled corners of the Mediterranean: poor, depopulated, beautiful, old-fashioned and doggedly aloof.

The village of Oletta in the Nebbio region around St-Florent

◁ A fisherman with feline friends in Bastia

Exploring Corsica

Corsica's main appeal is its scenery: a wildly beautiful landscape of mountains, forests, myrtle-scented maquis and countless miles of sandy beaches. Late spring (when the wild flowers are in bloom) and early autumn are the best times to visit – the temperature is moderate and there aren't too many visitors. The island is renowned for its superb hiking trails, some of which become cross-country skiing trails during the winter. Downhill skiing is also possible in February and March.

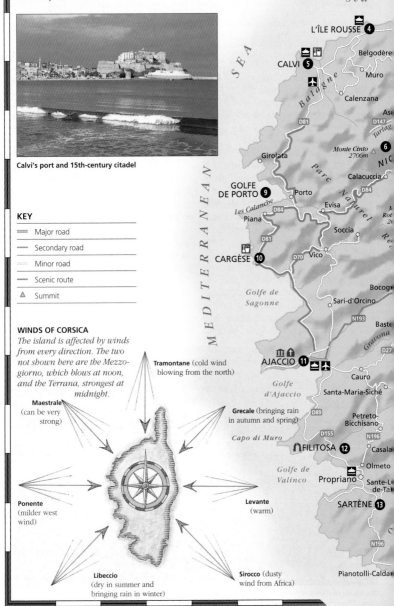

Calvi's port and 15th-century citadel

KEY

▬▬	Major road
▬	Secondary road
⋯⋯	Minor road
▬	Scenic route
▲	Summit

WINDS OF CORSICA

The island is affected by winds from every direction. The two not shown here are the Mezzo-giorno, which blows at noon, and the Terrana, strongest at midnight.

Maestrale (can be very strong)

Tramontane (cold wind blowing from the north)

Grecale (bringing rain in autumn and spring)

Ponente (milder west wind)

Levante (warm)

Libeccio (dry in summer and bringing rain in winter)

Sirocco (dusty wind from Africa)

Ligurian Sea

L'ÎLE ROUSSE ④

Belgodère

CALVI ⑤

Muro

Calenzana

Balagne

Ase

D147

Tartag

Monte Cinto 2706m ⑥

NIC

D81

Calacuccia

Parc

D84

GOLFE DE PORTO ⑨

Porto

Girolata

Evisa

Les Calanche

Piana

D84

Soccia

Naturel

Vico

SOCCIA

M Rot 20

D81

CARGÈSE ⑩

D70

Golfe de Sagonne

Reg

Sari-d'Orcino

Bocog

N193

Baste

Gravona

AJACCIO ⑪

D27

Cauro

Golfe d'Ajaccio

Santa-Maria-Siché

D89

Petreto-Bicchisano

Capo di Muro

N196

D155

FILITOSA ⑫

Casala

Golfe de Valinco

Olmeto

Propriano

Sante-L de-Ta

SARTÈNE ⑬

N196

Pianotolli-Calda

Map Labels

CAP CORSE **1**
Rogliano
Centuri-Port
Macinaggio
Pino
Luri
olfe de
-Florent
Canari
Monte Stello
△ 1307m
Nonza
Erbalunga
des
tes
Lavasina
Patrimoniog
FLORENT 3
Oletta
ietro-
Tenda
Casatorra
Murato
Borgo
Golo
Casamozza
te-Nuovo
Ponte-Leccia
Vescovato
Morosaglia
Francardo
Piedicroce
CASTAGNICCIA 8
Figareto
Moriani-Plage
Cervione
CORTE
Prunete
Phare-d'Alistro
Venaco
Bravone
Vezzani
Tavignano
Vivario
avona
Aléria
Ghisonaccia
15
Mignataja
Travo
te Incudine
2136m
Solenzara
Zonza
Conca
Lecci
Porto-Vecchio
ari
BONIFACIO
BASTIA 2
ORIENTALE
CÔTE

SIGHTS AT A GLANCE

Ajaccio **11**
Bastia **2**
Bonifacio **14**
Calvi **5**
Cap Corse **1**
Cargèse **10**
The Castagniccia **8**
Corte **7**
Côte Orientale **15**
Filitosa **12**
Golfe de Porto **9**
L'Île Rousse **4**
The Niolo **6**
St-Florent **3**
Sartène **13**

The Calanche cliffs in the Golfe de Porto

GETTING AROUND

Car ferries (which should be booked well in advance) depart from Marseille, Nice and Toulon, arriving at Bastia, L'Île Rousse, Calvi, Ajaccio, Propriano and Porto-Vecchio. There are also ferries from Sardinia to Bonifacio, and from Genoa, Livorno and La Spezia to Bastia. Small airports are at Ajaccio, Bastia, Calvi and Figari. Corsica's roads are narrow, twisting and often tortuously slow, though breathtaking views reward the effort. A car is a must for exploring the island, as public transport is limited. Carry spare petrol – filling stations are few and far between.

```
0 kilometres        20
0 miles          10
```

Corte's Old Town, with its citadel high up on a rocky outcrop

Cap Corse ❶

Haute-Corse. 🚆 *Bastia*. 🚌 *Bastia, Macinaggio, Rogliano*. 🚢 *Bastia*.
ℹ️ *pl St-Nicolas, Bastia (04 95 54 20 40)*. www.corsica.net

Cap Corse is the northern tip of Corsica, 40 km (25 miles) in length but seldom more than 12 km (7.5 miles) wide, pointing like an accusatory finger towards Genoa.

There are two roads out of Bastia to the cape: the D81 leading west across the mountains and joining up with the D80 after the wine village of Patrimonio; and the D80 travelling north along the eastern shore to **Erbalunga** and **Macinaggio**. The road is narrow and twisting, a taste of what awaits you in Corsica.

From the coastal village of **Lavasina**, the D54 leads left off the D80 to Pozzo; from here it is a 5-hour round trip on foot to the 1,307-m (4,300-ft) summit of **Monte Stello**, the highest peak on the cape. The 360-degree view from the top takes in St-Florent to the west, the massif of central Corsica to the south and the Italian island of Elba to the east.

Further up the coast, the restored **Tour de Losse** is one of many 16th-century Genoese towers along the coast – part of an elaborate system which enabled all Corsican towns to be warned within two hours of impending barbarian raids.

The charming 18th-century fishing port of **Centuri**, near the tip of the peninsula on the west coast, is an ideal spot for a delicious seafood feast. **Pino**, a pretty little village

The village of Erbalunga on the east coast of Cap Corse

straggling down the green mountainside further to the south, has no hotel, only a lovely little church dedicated to the Virgin, full of model ships placed there by mariners grateful for her protection.

On the way south along the vertiginous lower corniche, be sure to turn left up the hill to **Canari**. One of the larger villages in this area, Canari has a jewel of a 12th-century Pisan church, Santa Maria Assunta, a magnificent view across the sea, and a thoroughly convivial hotel-restaurant. All the by-roads in this thickly wooded area seem to lead somewhere interesting. There are literally dozens of picturesque hamlets in the vicinity, and it should be borne in mind that from this point onwards the landscape becomes steadily less attractive as the road winds on past the old asbestos workings and beaches of black sand below **Nonza**.

Bastia ❷

Haute-Corse. 🏘️ *39,000*. 🚆 🚌
🚢 ℹ️ *pl St-Nicolas (04 95 54 20 40)*. 🛒 *Tue–Sun*.
www.bastia-tourisme.com

A thriving port and the administrative capital of Upper Corsica, Bastia is utterly different in style from its sedate west coast rival, Ajaccio. The Genoese citadel and colourful 19th-century Italianate buildings around the old port are for many people their first taste of the authentic Mediterranean – as it was half a century ago, and as it stubbornly remains in our imagination.

The centre of Bastia's life is the **place St-Nicolas**, facing the wharf where ferries from the mainland and Italy arrive. Heading south along the waterfront you come to the **place de l'Hôtel de Ville**, site of a daily food market. Bordering the square are the early 17th-century **Chapelle de l'Immaculée Conception**, with its ornate 18th-century interior, and the mid-17th-century **Eglise de St-Jean-Baptiste**, whose façade dominates the Vieux Port.

From here it is a short walk up to the 16th-century **citadel**, where there are two more churches worth seeing: the Rococo **Chapelle Sainte-Croix**, with its striking *Black Christ*, fished out of the sea by Bastiais fishermen in 1428; and the 15th-century **Sainte-Marie**, which has a *Virgin* made of a tonne of solid silver.

Bastia's Vieux Port seen from the Jetée du Dragon

For hotels and restaurants in this region see pp594–5 and pp650–1

St-Florent ❸

Haute-Corse. 🏛 *1,500.* 🔲 🄸
*Bâtiment Administratif (04 95 37
06 04).* 🄴 *1st Wed of month.*

St-Florent is almost a
Corsican St-Tropez – chic,
affluent, and packed with
yachts from all over the
Mediterranean. Its citadel,
which houses photography
exhibitions, dates from 1439,
and is a fine example of
Genoese military architecture.
The town itself is pleasant to
wander around; its main
attraction, the 12th-century
Pisan **Cathédrale de Santa
Maria Assunta**, lies just inland
on the road to Poggio-d'Oletta.

Environs
A leisurely 4-hour circuit by car
of the **Nebbio** region, which
extends in an amphitheatre
around St-Florent, might take
in the following: **Santo Pietro
di Tenda; Murato**, famous for
its magnificent **Eglise de San
Michele de Murato**, a 12th-
century Pisan Romanesque
construction built of white and
green stone; the **San Stefano**
pass, with the sea on either
side; **Oletta**, which produces a
special blue cheese made from
ewes' milk; the **Teghime** pass;
and finally the wine village of
Patrimonio, where there is
a strange, big-eared menhir
dating from 900–800 BC.

Along the coast to the west
of St-Florent lies the barren, uninhabited **Désert des Agriates**.
If you can face the 10-km
(6-mile) haul to the sea – on
foot, by bike or by motorbike
– the Saleccia beach is the
most beautiful on the island.

San Michele de Murato

L'Île Rousse ❹

Haute-Corse. 🏛 *2,850.* 🔲 🄰 🄴
🄸 *pl Paoli (04 95 60 04 35).*
🄴 *daily.* **www.ot-ile-rousse.fr**

Founded in 1758 by
Pasquale Paoli, leader of
independent Corsica, L'Île
Rousse is today a major
holiday resort and ferry
terminal. The centre of
town is the plane-shaded
place Paoli, dominated
by a marble statue of
Corsica's national hero.
On the north side of the
square is the covered
market, with the Old
Town just beyond.

In the summer months
L'Île Rousse becomes
hideously overcrowded,
its beaches a mass of
sun-starved bodies. It is
worth travelling 10 km
(6 miles) up the coast to
Lozari, which offers a magnificent, virtually unspoiled
stretch of sand.

Environs
One very pleasant way to
discover the **Balagne** region is
to take the tram-train from
L'Île Rousse to Calvi and
back. This odd little service
runs all year (more frequent
in summer), roughly keeping
to the coastline and stopping
at Algajola, Lumio and various
villages along the way.

Calvi ❺

Haute-Corse. 🏛 *5,280.* 🔲 🄰 🄴
🄸 *Port de Plaisance (04 95 65 16 67).*
🄴 *daily.* **www.balagne-corsica.com**

Calvi, where Nelson lost his
eye in an "explosion of
stones" in 1794, is today half
military town, half cheap holiday resort. Its 15th-century
citadel is garrisoned by a
crack French regiment of the
foreign legion; while beyond
the ferry port is a seedy,
apparently endless camp-
site and trailer park.

The town makes a
half-hearted case for
being the birthplace of
Christopher Columbus,
but there is no real evi-
dence to support this.
A much better claim to
fame is the food, which is
very good and reasonably
priced by Corsican stan-
dards. There is also a very
respectable jazz festival
at Calvi towards the
end of June.

Outside town, the
19th-century **Chapelle
de Notre-Dame de la Serra** is
gloriously sited on a hilltop
commanding extensive views
in all directions.

French foreign
legionnaire

The Chapelle de Notre-Dame de la Serra, 6 km (3.5 miles) southwest of Calvi

Corte's 15th-century citadel seen at dawn

The Niolo ❻

Haute-Corse. 🚉 *Corte.* ℹ️ *Calacuccia (04 95 48 05 22).*

The Niolo, west of Corte, extends westward to the Vergio pass and the upper Golo basin, and to the east as far as the Scala di Santa Regina. It includes Corsica's highest mountain, the 2,700-m (8,859-ft) **Monte Cinto**, and its biggest river, the **Golo**, which meets the sea south of Bastia.

Alone of the various regions of Corsica, the Niolo persists in the cultivation of livestock as its economic mainstay.

The main town, **Calacuccia**, is suitable for excursions to Monte Cinto. The nearby ski resort of **Haut Asco** is best reached by the D147 from **Asco**, but enthusiasts can walk from Calacuccia (8–9 hours). To the south is the huge forest of **Valdu Niello**.

Corte ❼

Haute-Corse. 🏛️ *6,700.* 🚉 🚌 ℹ️ *La Citadelle (04 95 46 26 70).* 🛒 *Fri.* **www**.corte-tourisme.com

In the geographical centre of Corsica, Corte was the chosen capital of the independence leader Pasqual Paoli from 1755–69, and today is the seat of the island's university. In the Old Town is the 15th-

century citadel, housing the **Museu di a Corsica**. Its exhibits relate to traditional Corsican life and anthropology.

Corte is the best base for exploring nearby mountain areas, especially as it stands exactly halfway along the GR20, the legendary 220-km (137-mile) trail from Calenzana to Conca.

🏛️ Museu di a Corsica
La Citadelle. **Tel** *04 95 45 25 45.* ⏰ *Apr–Jun & Oct: Tue–Sun; Jul–Sep: daily; Nov–Mar: Tue–Sat.* ⚫ *public hols.* 🎫♿🚻📷

Environs
Don't miss the wildly beautiful **Gorges de la Restonica**, about 12 km (7.5 miles) out of town via the D623. Above these gorges adventurous walkers may wish to make the well-marked climb to the snow-fed **Lac de Melo** (allow 60–90 minutes); or the **Lac de Capitello**, 30 minutes further on, where the snow stays as late as early June. The path – in winter a cross-country ski trail – follows the river.

South of Corte, the **Forêt de Vizzavona** features beech and pine woodland crisscrossed by trout-filled streams and walking trails (notably the GR20). It is a perfect refuge from the summer heat and is also an excuse to take the small-gauge train up from Ajaccio or Bastia, which stops at Vizzavona.

The Castagniccia ❽

Haute-Corse. 🛫 *Bastia.* 🚉 *Corte, Ponte Leccia.* 🚌 *Piedicroce, La Porta, Valle-d'Alesani.* ℹ️ *Piedicroce (04 95 35 82 54).* **www**.castagniccia.net

East of Corte is the hilly, chestnut-covered region of Castagniccia (literally "small chestnut grove"), which most Corsicans agree is the very heart and kernel of the island. It was here that independence leader Pasquale Paoli was born in 1725, and that the revolts against Genoa and later France began in earnest in 1729. Alas, many of the villages in this beautiful, remote area are nearly empty, their inhabitants having joined the 800,000 or so Corsicans (almost three times the present population) who live and work in mainland France or Italy. It seems hard to believe that in the 17th century, when the great chestnut forests introduced here by the Genoese were at the height of their production, this was the most prosperous and populated region in Corsica.

The D71 from Ponte Leccia (north of Corte) to the east coast winds through the centre of the Castagniccia region, and to see it at a leisurely pace will take the best part of a day. Arm yourself with a picnic before you start, as there is little to be had in the way of supplies en route.

◁ **Limestone cliffs of Bonifacio** *(see p543)*

Golfe de Porto ❾

Corse-du-Sud. 🛫 🚉 🚢 *Ajaccio.*
🚌 *Porto.* ℹ️ *Porto (04 95 26 10 55).* www.porto-tourisme.com

Porto is sited at the head of the Golfe de Porto, one of the most beautiful bays in the Mediterranean, which for the sake of its fauna and flora has been included in UNESCO's list of the world's common cultural heritage sites. The town has a magnificent Genoese watchtower – the perfect spot for admiring the sunset – and regular boat excursions (Apr–Oct) to the Calanche, Scandola and Girolata.

The **Calanche** begin 2 km (1.2 miles) out of Porto, on the road to Piana. These 300-m (1,000-ft) red granite cliffs plunge sheer to the sea, and are quite simply breathtaking. They are accessible only by boat or on foot: well-defined trails start from the Tête du Chien and the Pont de Mezanu, while boat tickets are available at Porto's Hôtel Le Cyrnée.

East of Porto are the Gorges de la Spelunca, accessed by a mule route punctuated by Genoese bridges.

Just south of Porto along a spectacular corniche drive passing under granite archways, lies the pretty village of **Piana**, a good base for visiting this whole area, with information on recommended walks. One particularly worthwhile destination is the cove at **Ficajola** just below Piana – a truly delightful beach.

Porto's marina and Genoese watchtower

Environs

The road over the mountains from Porto to Calvi offers no more than a taste of this grandiose corner of Corsica – you have to take to the sea to view it properly (ferries from Porto and Galéria). **Girolata**, a tiny hamlet north of Porto, can be reached only by sea or via a mule track (4 hours round trip on foot) from a clearly marked point 23 km (14 miles) north of Porto on the D81.

At the mouth of the Golfe de Girolata, the **Réserve Naturelle de Scandola**, instituted in 1975, is the first land-and-sea reserve in France, covering over 1,000 hectares (2,500 acres) of sea, and a similar area of cliffs, caves and maquis. Marine life is abundant in these clear, protected waters; the birds include ospreys, puffins and falcons.

CORSICAN FLOWERS

For lovers of wild flowers, Corsica is a Mediterranean jewel. Much of the island is covered with maquis, a tangle of aromatic shrubs and low trees which flowers from late winter onwards. Among its dense variety are the showy rockroses, which shower the ground with short-lived pink or white petals, and brilliant yellow broom. Grassy and rocky slopes are good places to spot the widespread tassel hyacinth and the Illyrian sea lily which grows only in Corsica and Sardinia.

Rock-rose

The town of Piana with the Calanche in the background

Spanish broom

Illyrian sea lily

Tassel hyacinth

For hotels and restaurants in this region see pp594–5 and pp650–1

Cargèse's Greek rite church

Cargèse ⑩

Corse-du-Sud. ⋈ 1,000. 🚌 ⓘ *rue du Docteur Dragacci (04 95 26 41 31).* www.cargese.net

Cargèse overlooks the sea from a promontory between the bays of Sagone and Pero. It is a small town with an odd history: many of the people who live here are the descendants of 17th-century Greek refugees from Turkish rule, given asylum in Corsica.

A few Cargèsiens still speak Greek, and their icon-filled Eastern (Greek) rite church faces its Catholic counterpart in an attitude that must once have seemed confrontational. Nowadays the old rivalries have vanished, and the Ortho-dox priest and Catholic *curé* often stand in for one another.

There are many splendid beaches in the vicinity, notably at **Pero** and **Chiuni** just to the north, and at **Ménasina** and **Stagnoli** to the south.

Ajaccio ⑪

Corse-du-Sud. 🏠 60,000. ✈ 🚌 🚉 ⓘ *3 bd du Roi Jérôme (04 95 51 53 03).* 🛒 *Tue–Sun.* www.ajaccio-tourisme.com

Ajaccio, a noisy, busy town by Corsican standards, was the birthplace of Napoleon Bonaparte in 1769. Napoleon never returned to Corsica after crowning himself emperor of the French in 1804, but the town – modern capital of nationalist Corsica – celebrates his birthday every 15 August.

The 16th-century **Cathédrale Notre-Dame de la Miséricorde**, where Napoleon was baptized in 1771, houses Delacroix's painting *Vierge du Sacré-Coeur*.

A few streets away, the **Maison Bonaparte**, where Napoleon was born and spent his childhood, contains family portraits, period furniture and assorted memorabilia.

Much more interesting is the superb collection of artworks assembled on the coat-tails of Napoleon by his unscrupulous uncle, Cardinal Fesch, who merrily looted churches, pal-aces and museums during the Italian campaign and brought the swag home to Ajaccio. Housed in the 19th-century Palais Fesch, the **Musée Palais Fesch** contains the finest collection of Italian primitive art in France after the Louvre. Among its masterpieces are works by Bellini, Botticelli, Titian and Veronese, Bernini and Poussin. Next to the Palais Fesch stands the **Chapelle Impériale**, built in 1855 by Napoleon III to accommodate the tombs of the Bonapartes.

From here, walk back along the quay to the Jetée de la Citadelle, which offers superb views of the town, the marina and the Golfe d'Ajaccio. The adjacent 16th-century **citadel** is occupied by the army.

🏛 **Maison Bonaparte**
Rue St-Charles. *Tel 04 95 21 43 89.* 🛒 *Mon pm–Sun.*

🏛 **Musée Palais Fesch**
50 rue Cardinal Fesch. *Tel 04 95 21 48 17.* 🛒 *Apr–Jun, Sep: Tue–Sun; Jul–Aug: daily; Oct–Mar: Tue–Sat.* 🛒 *public hols.* 🎫 ♿ www.musee-fesch.com

Environs

From the Quai de la Citadelle there are daily excursions to the **Îles Sanguinaires** at the mouth of the Golfe d'Ajaccio.

At Vero, 21 km (13 miles) northeast on the N193, is an unusual park, **A Cupulatta**, with over 150 species of tortoises and turtles (Apr–Oct).

A statue-menhir at Filitosa

Filitosa ⑫

Centre Préhistorique de Filitosa, Corse-du-Sud. *Tel 04 95 74 00 91.* 🛒 *Apr–Oct: daily.* 🎫 ♿ *mus. only.*

The 4,000-year-old, life-size stone warriors of Filitosa are the most spectacular relics of megalithic man in Corsica. Discovered in 1946, these phallus-like granite menhirs represent an interesting pro-gression from mere silhouettes to more detailed sculpture, etched with human features and even weapons.

The five most recent and most sophisticated figures (about 1500 BC) stand around a thousand-year-old olive

Statue of Napoleon by Laboureur in place Maréchal Foch, Ajaccio

For hotels and restaurants in this region see pp594–5 and pp650–1

The fortified Old Town of Bonifacio, with the harbour in the foreground

tree, in the field below a tumulus. Other finds, which include a heavily armed warrior with shield, helmet and sword, can be seen in the site's archaeological museum.

Sartène ⑬

Corse-du-Sud. 🏠 *3,600.* 🖼 🛈 *cours Soeur Amélie (04 95 77 15 40).* 🏠 *summer: daily; winter: Sat.*

Sartene is a medieval fortified town of narrow cobbled streets and grey granite houses rising above the Rizzanese valley. Founded by the Genoese in the early 16th century, it has survived attacks by Barbary pirates and centuries of bloody feuding among the town's leading families.

Despite all this, Sartène has a reputation for deep piety, reinforced each year by the oldest and most intense Christian ceremony in Corsica, the Good Friday Catenacciu (literally, the "chained one"). A red-hooded penitent, barefoot and in chains, drags a wooden cross through the Old Town in a re-enactment of Christ's ascent to Golgotha.

Environs

In the centre of town in Sartène's former prison, the **Musée de la Préhistoire Corse** has a fascinating collection of artifacts from the Neolithic period, the Bronze Age and Iron Age.

🏛 **Musée de la Préhistoire Corse**
Rue Croce. **Tel** *04 95 77 01 49.* 🔵 *for renovation until 2008; phone to check.* 🈂

Bonifacio ⑭

Corse-du-Sud. 🏠 *2,700.* 🖼 🛈 🛈 *rue Fred Scamaroni (04 95 73 11 88).* 🏠 *Wed.* **www**.bonifacio.fr

Bonifacio is the southernmost town in Corsica, dramatically sited on a limestone and granite cliff peninsula with stunning views *(see pp538–9)*. Its handsome harbour at the foot of the cliffs is the focus of life: cafés, restaurants and boutiques abound and boats depart regularly for neighbouring Sardinia and the uninhabited island of Lavezzi.

From the harbour, steps lead up to Bonifacio's fortified Old Town. The citadel, which was built by the conquering Genoese at the end of the 12th century, has long been the town's main defensive post, and from 1963–83 was the headquarters of the French foreign legion. From here, wander down to the tip of the promontory to see the three old windmills and the ruins of a Franciscan monastery.

Côte Orientale ⑮

Haute-Corse & Corse-du-Sud. 🚶 *Bastia.* 🛈 *Aléria, Salenzara, Porto-Vecchio.* 🚢 *Bastia, Porto-Vecchio.* 🛈 *Aléria (04 95 57 01 51), Porto-Vecchio (04 95 70 09 58).*

The flat, rather dreary alluvial plain stretching from Bastia to Solenzara has been rich farmland since 1945, the year it was finally drained and rid of malaria. More recently, holiday resorts and even high-rise hotels have mushroomed along the coast, cashing in on its long, sandy beaches.

The best sight in **Mariana**, which is otherwise uncomfortably close to the Bastia-Poretta airport, is the early 12th-century cathedral of Mariana known as **La Canonica**. A short distance away is the slightly older **Eglise de San Perteo**, surrounded by meadows.

About halfway down the coast, the port of **Aléria**, originally a Greek colony and the base for Rome's conquest of Corsica in 259 BC, is interesting for its rich archaeological heritage. Just outside town, a museum housed in the 16th-century Fort de Matra chronicles daily life in Roman Aléria.

Towards the southern tip of the island, the fortified town of **Porto-Vecchio**, built by Corsica's Genoese conquerors, is now an extremely popular seaside resort. The setting is perfect for the conventional seaside holiday, with umbrella pines, cork oak forests and glorious white sandy beaches within easy reach of the town, especially at **Palombaggia** and **Pinarello**.

The Golfe de Porto-Vecchio

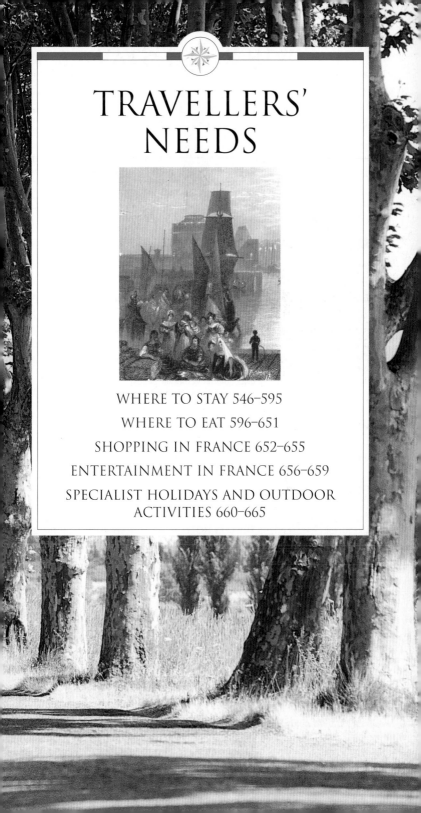

TRAVELLERS' NEEDS

WHERE TO STAY

Many of France's 22,000 registered hotels are charming, idiosyncratic and good value. On these four pages, the types of hotel on offer are summarized and tips provided on what to expect from French hotels. The hotel listings pages *(see pp550–95)* describe some of the best hotels around the country in every price category and style, from slick, modern chain hotels to small, classic, family-run establishments. Also included are *chambres d'hôte* (a sort of French bed and breakfast), which range from simple farms to grandiose châteaux, as well as the best hostels. France is one of the most popular countries in the world for self-catering holidays and information is given on renting a rural home or *gîte*, and how to get the most out of a camping holiday.

The Hôtel Euzkadi at Espelette in the Pyrenees *(see p586)*

THE CLASSIC FAMILY HOTEL

If you're touring on a budget, the small, family-run, family-orientated hotel lurking in virtually every village and town is for you. It's likely to be the focal point of the village, with the bar and dining-room (if the food is up to standard) full of locals. The atmosphere is entirely informal, with children, cats and dogs happily at home. In the hotel's dozen or so bedrooms, old-fashioned charm will make up for a lack of sprightliness and, perhaps, the mere trickle of hot water from the shower.

The annual *Logis de France* guide details over 4,000 of these family-run, mainly one- and two-star hotel-restaurants. They tend to be located in small towns or rural locations; there are none in Paris. Most are no more than roadside inns, but off the beaten track you will discover many converted farmhouses and inexpensive seaside hotels. While the *Logis* is a useful reference source, the quality of places listed can be uneven.

THE CHATEAU HOTEL

Many of France's châteaux and mansions have been converted into luxury hotels. They include everything from Renaissance piles with sweeping lawns to medieval castles with battlements and keeps. Grand hotels can be found all over France, with rich pickings in the Loire, the Savoie, the Haute-Savoie and the Rhône delta. The properties included in the **Relais et Châteaux** brochure are recommended.

Typically, rooms are beautifully designed and the food is *haute cuisine*. Bedrooms range from grand suites to more simple abodes, often in converted farm-buildings, making it possible, if you're willing to forgo four-poster beds and antiques, to live in luxury without breaking the bank.

THE CITY HOTEL

Every big city has a clutch of hotels close to the train station or port. They range from cheap accommodation to a grand hotel or two. The most famous city hotels are the palace hotels in Paris and the Riviera resorts such as Nice and Cannes. Note that many city hotels do not have a restaurant or a salon and it is always worth checking the quality of the bedroom before you book it.

THE MODERN CHAIN HOTEL

Outlets of modern hotel chains are useful for inexpensive pitstops if you're travelling through France. Many are situated on the outskirts of towns by motorways or main roads. The cheapest are the one-star, no-frills **Formule 1** motels, offering bedrooms with a double and single bed and no en suite facilities.

Two-star chains include **Ibis/Campanile, Hotels Première Classe** and **Etap**. Three-star chains include **Novotel** and **Mercure**; both offer en suite accommodation and usually allow one child to stay with no charge, provided the

Le Négresco in Nice on the Côte d'Azur *(see p593)*

The Meurice hotel in the Tuileries Quarter of Paris *(see p555)*

whole family sleeps in one room (Novotel has free accommodation for two under-16s).

THE RESTAURANT-WITH-ROOMS

Throughout France, many upmarket restaurants also offer accommodation. Usually, the bedrooms match the restaurant's smartness and are priced accordingly. Sometimes, though, gourmet restaurants have simple bedrooms hidden away upstairs – great finds for those who like to splash out on food while saving on lodging. Refer to the restaurant listings on pages 600–51.

MEALS AND FACILITIES

In high season, many resort hotels insist on half board or *demi-pension* (a per person rate for the room, dinner and breakfast). There is also full board or *pension*, which covers lunch too. While it is cheaper to opt for inclusive rates, meals come from set or limited-choice menus, which often omit the more interesting dishes.

Many smaller family-run hotels do not provide meals on Sunday evenings and often stop serving dinner as early as 9pm on other days.

Rooms usually have double beds; twin or single beds must be requested when booking. All mid-range hotels have a choice of bathroom facilities. A short walk down the corridor to a separate bathroom can reduce the room rate considerably. A bathroom with a bath *(un bain)* is usually more expensive than one with a shower *(une douche)*; *un cabinet de toilette* has a basin and bidet, without a bath, shower or a WC. If you do not have *pension* or *demi-pension* accommodation, breakfast is often charged as an extra. Go instead to the local café, as it tends to be cheaper and more filling.

Hôtel de l'Abbayce at Talloires in the French Alps *(see p579)*

GRADINGS

French hotels are graded from nought stars to four stars (plus "four star luxury"). Stars indicate precisely the hotel's facilities. Hotels with two or more stars must have a lift where appropriate, a phone in every bedroom and at least 40 per cent of their bedrooms en suite. Three-star hotels must offer breakfast in the bedroom and have 80 per cent en suite rooms. Only four-star hotels must have room service and all of their rooms en suite.

PRICES

Rates, inclusive of tax and service, are quoted per room (apart from *pension* and *demi-pension* arrangements). There is usually a small supplement for a third person in a room for two, and little reduction for single travellers.

As a rule, the higher the star rating the more you pay. Rates for a double room start from about 25€ per night for a one-star hotel and go up to 80€ or more for a four-star hotel. Costs also vary geographically with remote rural areas like Brittany being the cheapest. For equivalent accommodation in fashionable areas like the Dordogne and Provence expect to pay 20 per cent more, and a further 20 per cent again for Paris and the Côte d'Azur. Prices vary seasonally too, with coastal and alpine areas putting up their tariffs by up to 50 per cent in peak periods.

BOOKING

Always book well in advance for Paris, and for hotels in popular tourist areas in July and August.

In resort areas, most hotels shut down from October to March, so phone ahead when travelling out of season to make sure the place is open.

Reservations can normally be held with a credit card at all but the humblest hotels. If you want to make a booking while you are in France, there are tourist offices in all main cities which provide a hotel reservation service up to eight days in advance.

The dining room of the Grand Hôtel, Sète (see p590)

BED AND BREAKFAST

French bed and breakfasts, called *chambres d'hôte*, come in all shapes and sizes, from tiny cottages to elaborate châteaux full of family portraits and antiques, plus some *fermes-auberges (see p597)*. In all cases you will stay in a private home, and should not expect hotel services or amenities. Many offer dinner – *table d'hôte* – on request, where you usually dine *en famille*. Over 25,000 rural *chambres d'hôte* are registered and inspected by **Gîtes de France**. Look out for the yellow and green *chambres d'hôte* signs on the roadside.

The Gîtes de France logo

Roadside signs also lead to many B&Bs that are not registered. Information on these is available from local tourist offices.

SELF-CATERING

The fabled *gîte* is a rural holiday home often converted from a farmhouse or its outbuildings. A *gîte* holiday is a popular and relatively cheap way to see France, particularly out of season, but you must book many months in advance for the best *gîtes*.

Gîtes de France registers some 42,500 *gîtes*, all inspected and graded to indicate the level of facilities. You can book from a selection of 2,500 in the company's main brochure (available from the London office), or direct. Each of its 95 regional offices produces a booklet with all the *gîtes* in its *département*, which comes with a booking form. These are also available through the head office in Paris, **Maison des Gîtes de France**, which itself publishes a series of listings catering for those with more specialised requirements. These include *gîtes* for skiing, *gîtes* with horses, rural *gîtes* and serious luxury *gîtes*.

France has plenty of other kinds of self-catering accommodation: expensive south-coast villas; ski resort chalets; city and coastal apartments. The *Allo Vacances* brochure, available through the **French Government Tourist Office**, gives the addresses of estate agents handling holiday lets.

CAMPING

Eleven thousand official sites are spread around France's diverse countryside. The **Fédération Française de Camping et de Caravaning (FFCC)** publishes a comprehensive list, updated every year. Gîtes de France's *Camping à la Ferme* guide covers some simpler sites on farm land.

Campsites are graded from one to four stars. Three- and four-star sites are usually impressively spacious with plenty of amenities and electricity connections for a percentage of tents and caravans. One- and two-star sites always have toilets, a public phone and running water (though in one-star sites sometimes only cold water). What they lack in facilities they often make up for in peacefulness and rural charm.

Note, some sites only accept visitors with a **camping carnet**. *Carnets* are available from the AA, RAC and the clubs listed on the facing page.

HOSTELS

Hostels are a money-saving option for single travellers, though cheap hotels are often no more expensive for those travelling with a partner.

The IYHF's Hostelling guide details the **FUAJ**'s (Fédération Unie des Auberges de Jeunesse) 220 hostels around France, open to all ages and offering dormitory accommodation. If you are not a member of the **YHA** (Youth Hostel Association) in your home

A Bordeaux camp site in high season

country, you have to pay a small surcharge each time you stay in a French youth hostel. **UCRIF** (Union des Centres de Rencontres Internationales de France) has 50 centres with a cultural bent scattered around France. All have single, shared and dormitory accommodation and a restaurant.

In summer, you can stay in university rooms. Contact **CROUS** (Centre Régional des Oeuvres Universitaires et Scolaires) for details. *Gîtes d'étape* are usually large farmhouses with dormitories close to walking, cycling and horse-riding routes. Gîtes de France's *Gîtes d'Etape et de Séjour* guide details 1,600 sites.

DISABLED TRAVELLERS

A number of associations publish information on accommodation throughout France with wheelchair access: the **Association des Paralysés de France (APF)**, the **Groupement pour l'Insertion des Personnes Handicapées Physiques (GIHP)**, and Gîtes de

The Carlton Intercontinental in Cannes (see p592)

France's guide *Accessibles*. APF have their own travel company, APF Evasion, to help organise a holiday, as do **Voyages Asah**, which has a fleet of specially adapted vehicles. **Les Compagnons du Voyage** (part of SNCF/ RATP), can organise transport, escorted or not, on all public transport networks throughout France (see Directory below for details).

FURTHER INFORMATION

The invaluable *Traveller in France Reference Guide*, listing hotel chains, reservation agencies and companies for every type of package holiday, is published by the French Government Tourist Office. It also distributes *Logis de France* guides, and all the booklets for château-hotels and château-B&Bs. However, it only distributes the *Relais et Châteaux* guide over the counter.

The first port of call for all non-hotel accommodation in the French countryside should be Gîtes de France, including for B&B (brochures available from their Paris shop).

When in France, local tourist offices are the best source of information for B&Bs and self-catering accommodation.

Loisirs Accueil are special booking agencies which deal with queries for hotels, campsites, *gîtes* and B&Bs in their area. A list of all 53 offices in France is available from the UK French Tourist Office.

DIRECTORY

CHAIN HOTELS

Campanile
Tel 08 25 00 30 03 France
www.campanile.fr

Etap
Tel 08 92 68 08 91 France
www.etaphotel.com

Formule 1
Tel 08 92 685 685 France
www.hotelformule1.com

Hotel Première Classe
Tel 08 25 00 30 03 France

Ibis
Tel 0870 609 0963 UK.
Tel 0892 686 686 France.
www.ibishotel.com

Novotel
Tel 0870 609 0961 UK.
Tel 0825 884 444 France.
www.novotel.com

Relais et Châteaux
Tel 0870 242 0052 UK.
Tel 0825 32 32 32 France.
www.relaischateaux.com

SELF-CATERING & B&B

Gîtes de France
59 St-Lazare, 75009 Paris.
Tel 01 49 70 75 75 or 08 91 16 22 22 (last-minute bookings).
www.gites-de-france.fr
Brochures can be obtained from Maison de la France, London.
www.franceguide.com

CAMPING

Fédération Française de Camping et de Caravaning (FFCC)
78 rue de Rivoli, 75004 Paris. *Tel 01 42 72 84 08.*
Fax 01 42 72 70 21.
www.ffcc.fr

HOSTELS

CROUS
39 av G-Bernanos, 75231 Paris Cedex 05.
Tel 01 40 51 37 84.
www.crous-paris.fr

FUAJ (Féderation Unie des Auberges de Jeunesse)
27 rue Pajol, 75018 Paris.
Tel 01 44 89 87 27.
www.fuaj.fr

UCRIF
27 rue de Turbigo, 75002 Paris. *Tel 01 40 26 57 64.*

YHA (Youth Hostel Association)
Trevelyan House, Matlock Derbyshire DE4 3YH.
Tel 0870 870 8868.
www.yha.org.uk

American Youth Hostel Association
8401 Colesville Road, Suite 60, Silver Spring, MD 20910. *Tel (301) 495 1240.* www.hiusa.org

DISABLED TRAVELLERS

APF
17 bd August Blanqui, 5013 Paris. *Tel 01 40 78 69 00.*
Fax 01 45 89 40 57.
www.apf.asso.fr

GIHP
10 rue Georges de Porto-Riche, 75014 Paris.
Tel 01 43 95 66 36.
Fax 01 45 40 40 26.
www.gihpnational.org

Les Compagnons du Voyage
163 bis, av de Clichy 75017 Paris
Tel 01 53 11 11 12.
www.compagnons.com

Voyages Asah
4 rue Charcot, 75013 Paris
Tel 01 42 03 61 67.
www.asah75.org

FURTHER INFORMATION

Maison de la France Office
178 Piccadilly, London W1V 0AL.
Tel 090 6824 41 23 (within UK only).
www.franceguide.com

Choosing a Hotel

Hotels have been selected across a wide price range for facilities, good value, and location. All rooms have private bath, TV, air conditioning, and are wheelchair accessible unless otherwise indicated. Most have Internet access, and in some cases, fitness facilities may be offsite. The hotels are listed by area. For map references, *see pp154-169.*

PRICE CATEGORIES
The following price ranges are for a standard double room and taxes per night during the high season. Breakfast is not included, unless specified:
€ under 80 euros
€€ 80–130 euros
€€€ 130–180 euros
€€€€ 180–250 euros
€€€€€ over 250 euros

PARIS

BEAUBOURG AND LES HALLES Hôtel Roubaix   €€
6 rue Greneta, 75003 **Tel** *01 42 72 89 91* **Fax** *01 42 72 58 79* **Rooms** *53*   **Map** *9 B1*

In an area with few good places to stay, Hôtel Roubaix is a pleasantly old-fashioned and inexpensive choice. The owners are exceptionally friendly and the rooms are clean, if a little shabby. The hotel is popular with repeat guests, so be sure to book a room in advance. **www.hotel-de-roubaix.com**

CHAILLOT QUARTER Hameau de Passy   €€€
48 rue de Passy, 75016 **Tel** *01 42 88 47 55* **Fax** *01 42 30 83 72* **Rooms** *32*   **Map** *5 B3*

In the heart of the residential quarter of Passy, a stone's throw from the Eiffel Tower and the Trocadero, Hameau de Passy lies in a private lane, which is an oasis of green. Guest rooms overlook the garden. Breakfast can be served in your room, upon request. **www.hameaudepassy.com**

CHAILLOT QUARTER Hôtel du Bois   €€€
11 rue du Dôme, 75016 **Tel** *01 45 00 31 96* **Fax** *01 45 00 90 05* **Rooms** *41*   **Map** *2 D5*

Two minutes from the Arc de Triomphe and the Champs Elysées, Hôtel du Bois is ideal for haute-couture boutique lovers. Behind a typically Parisian façade is an interior exuding British charm – Georgian furniture in the lounge, thick patterned carpets and fine prints in the guest rooms. **www.hoteldubois.com**

CHAILLOT QUARTER Concorde La Fayette   €€€€€
3 pl du Général Koenig, 75017 **Tel** *01 40 68 50 68* **Fax** *01 40 68 50 43* **Rooms** *1000*   **Map** *1 C2*

The formulaic Concorde La Fayette with its fascinating tower (one of the few in Paris) is thoroughly high-tech. Its facilities include a fitness club, a bar on the 33rd floor, restaurants and a shopping gallery. The guest rooms afford truly splendid views over Paris and the Bois de Boulogne. **www.concorde-lafayette.com**

CHAILLOT QUARTER Costes K   €€€€€
81 av Kléber, 75016 **Tel** *01 44 05 75 75* **Fax** *01 44 05 74 74* **Rooms** *83*   **Map** *2 D5*

Not to be confused with the more expensive Hôtel Costes, this hotel is located just steps from the Eiffel Tower. It was designed and decorated by Spanish architect Ricardo Bofill, who used sycamore, stucco, marble and stainless steel to create a feel of luxury. Cool Asian-style guest rooms. **www.hotelcostesk.com**

CHAILLOT QUARTER Hôtel Keppler   €€€€€
12 rue Keppler, 75016 **Tel** *01 47 20 65 05* **Fax** *01 47 23 02 23* **Rooms** *49*   **Map** *2 E5*

After extensive renovations the Keppler is a chic and refined 4-star hotel. High ceilings throughout add to the sense of space. New facilities such as plasma screens, satellite TV and allergy-free pillows are welcome innovations. **www.hotel-keppler-paris.federal-hotel.com**

CHAILLOT QUARTER Raphaël   €€€€€
17 av Kléber, 75016 **Tel** *01 53 64 32 00* **Fax** *01 53 64 32 01* **Rooms** *85*   **Map** *2 D4*

This hotel is the epitome of discreet elegance, where film stars come to be sheltered from the paparazzi. The decor is opulent, and the roof terrace bar is the loveliest in Paris, popular with the jet set. There are amazing views of the city especially at night when the monuments are illuminated. **www.raphael-hotel.com**

CHAMPS-ELYSEES Atala   €€€
10 rue Chateaubriand, 75008 **Tel** *01 45 62 01 62* **Fax** *01 42 25 66 38* **Rooms** *50*   **Map** *2 E4*

Situated in a quiet street near the Champs-Elysées, the Atala's rooms overlook a tranquil garden with tall trees. The guest rooms are functional rather than charming. Book a room on the eighth floor for a spectacular view of the Eiffel Tower. **www.hotelatala.com**

CHAMPS-ELYSEES Résidence Lord Byron   €€€€
5 rue Chateaubriand, 75008 **Tel** *01 43 59 89 98* **Fax** *01 42 89 46 04* **Rooms** *31*   **Map** *2 E4*

Close to the Etoile, the Résidence Lord Byron is a small, discreet hotel with a courtyard garden for breakfast. Its bright guest rooms are quiet but small; if you want more space, ask for a salon room or a ground-floor room. **www.escapade-paris.com**

Key to Symbols *see back cover flap*

CHAMPS-ELYSEES Claridge-Bellman   €€€€€

37 rue François 1er, 75008 **Tel** *01 47 23 54 42* **Fax** *01 47 23 08 84* **Rooms** *42*   *Map 2 F5*

The Claridge-Bellman is a miniature version of the old Claridge Hotel and is managed by its former directors. The hotel has a truly traditional feel. It is quiet, sober and efficiently run, and is furnished throughout with tapestries and antiques. **www.hotel-claridge-bellman.com**

CHAMPS-ELYSEES Four Seasons George V   €€€€€

31 av George V, 75008 **Tel** *01 49 52 70 00* **Fax** *01 49 52 71 10* **Rooms** *246*   *Map 2 E5*

This legendary hotel, dotted with salons, old furniture and art, lost a little of its charm when it was renovated. But it gained a stunning restaurant, Le Cinq, which boasts the world's top sommelier and an award-winning chef. There is also a great spa. Sheer opulence. **www.fourseasons.com/paris**

CHAMPS-ELYSEES Hotel Chambiges   €€€€€

8 rue Chambiges, 75008 **Tel** *01 44 31 83 83* **Fax** *01 40 70 95 51* **Rooms** *34*   *Map 6 F1*

An elegant, cosy hotel on a quiet street just 5 minutes from the Champs-Elysées. Warm colours and a classically Parisian atmosphere suffuse the whole place. In warm weather, enjoy breakfast on the flowery patio. **www.hotelchambiges.com**

CHAMPS-ELYSEES Hôtel Vernet   €€€€€

26 rue Vernet, 75008 **Tel** *01 44 31 98 00* **Fax** *01 44 31 85 69* **Rooms** *51*   *Map 2 E4*

Gustave Eiffel (architect of the Eiffel Tower) created the dazzling glass roof of the dining room here. The impressive lobby has Persian rugs, precious woods, antiques and parquet flooring. The rooms are large and quiet. Guests have free use of the Royal Monceau's fitness club and spa. **www.hotelvernet.com**

CHAMPS-ELYSEES Le Bristol   €€€€€

112 rue du Faubourg-St-Honoré, 75008 **Tel** *01 53 43 43 00* **Fax** *01 53 43 43 01* **Rooms** *180*   *Map 3 A4*

One of Paris's finest hotels, the Bristol's large rooms are sumptuously decorated with antiques and magnificent marble bathrooms. The period dining room, with its Flemish tapestries and glittering crystal chandeliers, has been given rave reviews. There is a wonderful swimming pool. **www.hotel-bristol.com**

CHAMPS-ELYSEES Plaza Athénée   €€€€€

25 av Montaigne, 75008 **Tel** *01 53 67 66 65* **Fax** *01 53 67 66 66* **Rooms** *188*   *Map 6 F1*

The last word in luxury, the legendary Plaza Athénée is popular with honeymooners, aristocracy and haute couture shoppers. The restaurant by Alain Ducasse is wonderfully romantic, while Le Bar du Plaza is now the hottest address in Paris for cocktails. **www.plaza-athenee-paris.com**

CHAMPS-ELYSEES San Régis   €€€€€

12 rue Jean-Goujon, 75008 **Tel** *01 44 95 16 16* **Fax** *01 45 61 05 48* **Rooms** *44*   *Map 7 A1*

Since it opened in 1923 the opulent San Régis has been popular with the jet set, who are drawn to its quiet, central location. A particularly welcoming, intimate luxury hotel, it is full of antiques and overstuffed sofas. Some rooms have wonderful balcony views over the rooftops. **www.hotel-sanregis.fr**

INVALIDES AND EIFFEL TOWER QUARTER Grand Hôtel Levêque   €€

29 rue Cler, 75007 **Tel** *01 47 05 49 15* **Fax** *01 45 50 49 36* **Rooms** *50*   *Map 6 F3*

The Levêque lies between the Eiffel Tower and the Invalides on a pedestrianized street with a quaint fruit-and-vegetable market. The great location isn't the only attraction – guest rooms are well kept and the hotel also provides Internet access. **www.hotel-leveque.com**

INVALIDES AND EIFFEL TOWER QUARTER Hôtel de Varenne   €€€

44 rue de Bourgogne, 75007 **Tel** *01 45 51 45 55* **Fax** *01 45 51 86 63* **Rooms** *24*   *Map 7 B2*

Hidden beyond the hotel's severe façade is a narrow courtyard garden where guests breakfast in the summer. The bedrooms, recently refurbished in elegant Louis XVI or Empire style, are impeccable. The hotel is popular with French government officials. **www.hoteldevarenne.com**

INVALIDES AND EIFFEL TOWER QUARTER Hôtel Bourgogne et Montana   €€€€

3 rue de Bourgogne, 75007 **Tel** *01 45 51 20 22* **Fax** *01 45 56 11 98* **Rooms** *32*   *Map 7 B2*

Situated in front of the Assemblée Nationale, this hotel has an air of sobriety. Its features include a mahogany bar, an old-fashioned elevator and a circular hall with pink marble columns. The guest rooms were recently refurbished in an aristocratic style. Extremely stylish. **www.paris-hotel-montana.com**

INVALIDES AND EIFFEL TOWER QUARTER Hôtel de Suède St-Germain   €€€€

31 rue Vaneau, 75007 **Tel** *01 47 05 00 08* **Fax** *01 47 05 69 27* **Rooms** *40*   *Map 7 B4*

Located near the Orsay and Rodin museums, Hôtel de Suède St-Germain offers elegant rooms, decorated in late 18th-century style with pale colours. Guests receive an exceptionally warm welcome. The deluxe rooms offer a view over the park. A lovely little garden to breakfast in completes the picture. **www.hoteldesuede.com**

INVALIDES AND EIFFEL TOWER QUARTER Duc de St-Simon   €€€€€

14 rue de St-Simon, 75007 **Tel** *01 44 39 20 20* **Fax** *01 45 48 68 25* **Rooms** *34*   *Map 7 C3*

The Hôtel Duc de St-Simon is justifiably one of the most sought-after hotels on the south side of the Seine. A charming 18th-century mansion furnished with antiques, it lives up to its aristocratic pretensions. **www.hotelducdesaintsimon.com**

LATIN QUARTER Hôtel Esmeralda   €

4 rue St-Julien-le-Pauvre, 75005 **Tel** *01 43 54 19 20* **Fax** *01 40 51 00 68* **Rooms** *19*   **Map** *9 A4*

The much-loved bohemian Hôtel Esmeralda lies in the heart of the Latin Quarter. With old stone walls and beamed ceilings, its charm has seduced the likes of Terence Stamp and Serge Gainsbourg. The best rooms overlook Notre-Dame cathedral. Breakfast is not provided here.

LATIN QUARTER Hôtel des Grandes Ecoles   🔲🅿   €€

75 rue Cardinal Lemoine, 75005 **Tel** *01 43 26 79 23* **Fax** *01 43 25 28 15* **Rooms** *51*   **Map** *9 B5*

This hotel is a cluster of three small houses around a beautiful garden, where you can breakfast in good weather. The rooms are all comfortable and furnished with traditional 18th-century-style floral wallpaper; some open on to the courtyard. Internet access is available. **www.hotel-grandes-ecoles.com**

LATIN QUARTER Hôtel des Grands Degrès de Notre Dame   🍴   €€

10 rue des Grands Degrès, 75005 **Tel** *01 55 42 88 88* **Fax** *01 40 46 95 34* **Rooms** *10*   **Map** *9 B4*

An exceptionally friendly place to stay. The staff are genuinely welcoming and the wood-panelling and oak beams around the building make it even more special. Lovely, clean bedrooms with Internet access available. The Bar Restaurant and Tea Room serves great food at a low price. **www.lesdegreshotel.com**

LATIN QUARTER Hôtel de Notre-Dame   🔲📧   €€€

19 rue Maître Albert, 75006 **Tel** *01 43 26 79 00* **Fax** *01 46 33 50 11* **Rooms** *34*   **Map** *9 B5*

The picturesque Hôtel de Notre-Dame overlooks Notre-Dame cathedral and the Seine on one side, and the Panthéon on the other. The furnishings are functional, but some rooms have beams or an old stone wall. The main appeal here is the location. The hotel has its own sauna and Wi-Fi access. **www.hotel-paris-notredame.com**

LATIN QUARTER Hôtel des Grands Hommes   🔲♿📧   €€€

17 pl du Panthéon, 75005 **Tel** *01 46 34 19 60* **Fax** *01 43 26 67 32* **Rooms** *31*   **Map** *13 A1*

Teachers at the Sorbonne frequent this quiet family hotel close to the Jardin du Luxembourg. It boasts a great view of the Panthéon from the attic rooms on the upper floor. The guest rooms are comfortable. Wi-Fi service is available. **www.hoteldesgrandshommes.com**

LATIN QUARTER Hôtel du Panthéon   🔲♿📧   €€€

19 pl du Panthéon, 75005 **Tel** *01 43 54 32 95* **Fax** *01 43 26 64 65* **Rooms** *36*   **Map** *13 A1*

This hotel is managed by the same family as the Hôtel des Grands Hommes: the welcome is equally warm and the decor similarly Classical. Extra romance and luxury can be found in room 33 with its divine four-poster bed. Wi-Fi available in the reception room only. **www.hoteldupantheon.com**

LUXEMBOURG QUARTER Hôtel du Globe   €€

15 rue des Quatre-Vents, 75006 **Tel** *01 43 26 35 50* **Fax** *01 46 33 62 69* **Rooms** *14*   **Map** *8 F4*

Occupying a 17th-century building by the Jardin du Luxembourg, the popular Hôtel du Globe provides excellent accommodation. The recently renovated guest rooms are decorated with antique furniture and colourful fabrics. Breakfast is brought to your room. Reserve in advance. **www.globe-paris-hotel.com**

LUXEMBOURG QUARTER Hôtel Récamier   🔲   €€

3 bis pl St-Sulpice, 75006 **Tel** *01 43 26 04 89* **Fax** *01 46 33 27 73* **Rooms** *30*   **Map** *8 E4*

Situated on the place St-Sulpice, the mid-sized Hôtel Récamier is a family hotel that exudes an air of old-fashioned charm. The Récamier is a favourite spot with both writers and Left Bank tourists. The guest rooms overlooking the square have lovely views.

LUXEMBOURG QUARTER Aviatic   🔲🅿📧   €€€

105 rue de Vaugirard, 75006 **Tel** *01 53 63 25 50* **Fax** *01 53 63 25 55* **Rooms** *43*   **Map** *8 E5*

True to its Parisian past and long-standing family hotel tradition, the much-loved Aviatic combines bohemian style with modern comforts. The rooms are individually decorated with charming pieces found at local flea markets and warm, bright textiles. Parking is available for an additional fee. **www.aviatic.fr**

MONTMARTRE Regyn's Montmartre   €

18 pl des Abbesses, 75018 **Tel** *01 42 54 45 21* **Fax** *01 42 23 76 69* **Rooms** *22*   **Map** *4 E1*

Near Sacré-Cœur, this is an impeccably kept budget hotel. The top-floor guest rooms have views of the Eiffel Tower. Around the corner is Tabac des Deux Moulins at 15 rue le Pic, where Amélie worked in the film *Amélie*. **www.regynsmontmartre.com**

MONTMARTRE Terrass Hôtel   🔲🍴📧   €€€€€

12-14 rue Joseph-de-Maistre, 75018 **Tel** *01 44 92 34 14* **Fax** *01 42 52 29 11* **Rooms** *100*   **Map** *4 E1*

Montmartre's most luxurious hotel, the rooms here are comfortably, if unremarkably, furnished. A few rooms retain the original Art-Deco woodwork. The big draw is the rooftop restaurant, where in the summer fashionable Parisians take in a world-class view. **www.terrass-hotel.com**

MONTPARNASSE Hôtel Apollon Montparnasse   🔲🅿📧   €€

91 rue Ouest, 75014 **Tel** *01 43 95 62 00* **Fax** *01 43 95 62 10* **Rooms** *33*   **Map** *11 C3*

Close to the Parc des Expositions of the Porte de Versailles, the Apollon Montparnasse is decorated with Grecian statues and fine furnishings. The guest rooms are simple, but well equipped. Parking is available for an additional fee. The hotel also provides Wi-Fi facilities. **www.apollon-montparnasse.com**

MONTPARNASSE Hôtel Delambre Montparnasse

35 rue Delambre, 75014 **Tel** *01 43 20 66 31* **Fax** *01 45 38 91 76* **Rooms** *30* **Map** *12 D2*

Located a few steps from Montparnasse cemetery, and close to the Jardin de Luxembourg and the Latin Quarter, this hotel mixes modern and classical styles. Guest rooms are simply furnished, with all modern conveniences. **www.hoteldelambre.com**

MONTPARNASSE Hôtel Le Sainte Beuve

9 rue Ste Beuve, 75006 **Tel** *01 45 48 20 07* **Fax** *01 45 48 67 52* **Rooms** *22* **Map** *12 D1*

The Ste-Beuve is a small, carefully restored hotel for aesthetes and habitués of the Rive Gauche galleries. There is a fireplace in the hall, the rooms are pleasantly decorated in pastel shades and several classic, contemporary paintings add to the atmosphere. **www.paris-hotel-charme.com**

MONTPARNASSE Villa des Artistes

9 rue de la Grande Chaumière, 75006 **Tel** *01 43 26 60 86* **Fax** *01 43 54 73 70* **Rooms** *59* **Map** *12 D2*

The Villa des Artistes aims to recreate Montparnasse's artistic heyday when Modigliani, Beckett and Fitzgerald were all visitors here. The guest rooms are clean, but the main draw is the large patio garden and fountain, where you can breakfast in peace. **www.villa-artistes.com**

MONTPARNASSE Le Saint-Grégoire

43 rue de l'Abbé Grégoire, 75006 **Tel** *01 45 48 23 23* **Fax** *01 45 48 33 95* **Rooms** *20* **Map** *7 C5*

Le Saint-Grégoire is a fashionable townhouse hotel with immaculately decorated guest rooms with 19th-century furnishings. Book a room with a delightful private terrace. At the centre of the drawing room is a charming fireplace. Parking is available for an additional fee. **www.lesaintgregoire.com**

OPERA QUARTER Ambassador

16 bd Haussmann, 75009 **Tel** *01 44 83 40 40* **Fax** *01 42 46 19 84* **Rooms** *300* **Map** *4 E4*

One of Paris's best Art Deco hotels, the Ambassador has been restored to its former glory with plush carpeting and antique furniture. The ground floor has pink marble columns, Baccarat crystal chandeliers and Aubusson tapestries. The restaurant, 16 Haussmann, is popular with Parisian gourmets. **www.hotelambassador-paris.com**

OPERA QUARTER Edouard VII Hotel

39 av de l'Opéra, 75002 **Tel** *01 42 61 56 90* **Fax** *01 42 61 47 73* **Rooms** *69* **Map** *4 E5*

The only hotel on the impressive Avenue de l'Opéra, the Edouard VII is centrally located between the Louvre and the Opéra Garnier, which makes it perfect for sightseeing. Request a room at the front for a breathtaking view over the Opéra House. Inventive cooking by chef Gilles Choukroun in the hotel restaurant. **www.edouard7hotel.com**

OPERA QUARTER Le Grand Hôtel Intercontinental

2 rue Scribe, 75009 **Tel** *01 40 07 32 32* **Fax** *01 40 07 30 30* **Rooms** *478* **Map** *4 D5*

Directly next to the Opéra Garnier, this hotel is a sumptuous example of good taste. The rooms all have pictures with a musical theme reflecting the hotel's location. The opulent restaurant, the Café de La Paix, is renowned in the Opéra Quarter. **www.paris.intercontinental.com**

ST-GERMAIN-DES-PRES Grand Hôtel des Balcons

3 rue Casimir Delavigne, 75006 **Tel** *01 46 34 78 50* **Fax** *01 46 34 06 27* **Rooms** *50* **Map** *8 F5*

Embellished with Art Nouveau features, this hotel has a beautiful hall with stained-glass windows and striking 19th-century-style lamps and wood panelling. Most guest rooms, quiet and well-decorated, enjoy a balcony. High-speed Internet access with Wi-Fi is available. **www.balcons.com**

ST-GERMAIN-DES-PRES Hôtel de Lille

40 rue de Lille, 75007 **Tel** *01 42 61 29 09* **Fax** *01 42 61 53 97* **Rooms** *20* **Map** *8 D2*

The jewel-like Hôtel de Lille is situated near the Orsay and Louvre museums in the heart of Faubourg St-Germain. The modern, standard guest rooms are small and the bar is minute. There is a charming lounge in the arched basement, where breakfast is served. **www.hotel-paris-Lille.com**

ST-GERMAIN-DES-PRES Hôtel du Quai Voltaire

19 quai Voltaire, 75007 **Tel** *01 42 61 50 91* **Fax** *01 42 61 62 26* **Rooms** *33* **Map** *8 D2*

Overlooking the river, this hotel was once the favourite of Blondin, Baudelaire and Pissarro, and has featured in several films. It is best to avoid the rooms facing the quay, as they suffer from traffic noise. Higher floors are quieter, though, and the views are superb. **www.quaivoltaire.fr**

ST-GERMAIN-DES-PRES Hôtel des Marronniers

21 rue Jacob, 75006 **Tel** *01 43 25 30 60* **Fax** *01 40 46 83 56* **Rooms** *37* **Map** *8 E3*

Situated between a courtyard and a garden, this hotel provides perfect tranquillity. The cosy, renovated rooms are decorated with country fabrics. Those on the fourth floor garden side provide memorable views over the Parisian rooftops and the St-Germain-des-Prés church steeple. **www.paris-hotel-marronniers.com**

ST-GERMAIN-DES-PRES Hôtel des Sts-Pères

65 rue des Sts-Pères, 75006 **Tel** *01 45 44 50 00* **Fax** *01 45 44 90 83* **Rooms** *39* **Map** *8 E3*

Situated in one of the old aristocratic mansions of St-Germain-des-Prés, this hotel has quiet, large rooms – the best has an outstanding fresco. The lounge bar is popular with authors from the nearby publishing houses. **www.esprit-de-france.com**

ST-GERMAIN-DES-PRES Hôtel d'Angleterre

€€€€
44 rue Jacob, 75006 **Tel** *01 42 60 34 72* **Fax** *01 42 60 16 93* **Rooms** *27*   **Map** *8 E3*

Once the British Embassy, the Hôtel d'Angleterre has retained many of the original features, including the fine old staircase, the exquisite garden and the salon mantelpiece. The guest rooms are individually decorated; many have exposed beams and wonderful four-poster beds. **www.hotel-dangleterre.com**

ST-GERMAIN-DES-PRES Hôtel de l'Abbaye St-Germain

€€€€
10 rue Cassette, 75006 **Tel** *01 45 44 38 11* **Fax** *01 45 48 07 86* **Rooms** *44*   **Map** *8 D5*

A 17th-century abbey, just steps from the Jardin du Luxembourg, this charming hotel has a history as a preferred hideout for artists and writers. Its finely furnished guest rooms and apartments have been tastefully done up and provided with modern facilities. **www.hotel-abbaye.com**

ST-GERMAIN-DES-PRES L'Hôtel

€€€€€
13 rue des Beaux-Arts, 75006 **Tel** *01 44 41 99 00* **Fax** *01 43 25 64 81* **Rooms** *20*   **Map** *8 E3*

A riot of exuberance and opulence, this Jacques Garcia-designed hotel is gloriously decadent. Each room is unique; the Oscar Wilde suite, where the Irish author died and which boasts period furnishings, is the most famous. There's also a beautiful spa. **www.l-hotel.com**

ST-GERMAIN-DES-PRES Lutétia

€€€€€
45 bd Raspail, 75006 **Tel** *01 49 54 46 46* **Fax** *01 49 54 46 00* **Rooms** *230*   **Map** *8 D4*

The Lutétia is a mainstay of glamour on the south side of the river. The building's style is partly Art Nouveau and partly Art Deco, and has been restored throughout. Publishers and chic shoppers are regular customers in the restaurant. The location is convenient. **www.lutetia-paris.com**

ST-GERMAIN-DES-PRES Relais Christine

€€€€€
3 rue Christine, 75006 **Tel** *01 40 51 60 80* **Fax** *01 40 51 60 81* **Rooms** *51*   **Map** *8 F4*

Always full, the Relais Christine is the epitome of the *hôtel de charme*. Part of a cloister from a 16th-century abbey, the hotel is a romantic, peaceful haven. The guest rooms, especially the deluxe rooms, are bright and spacious. Wi-Fi facilities are available. Reserve in advance. **www.relais-christine.com**

THE MARAIS Hôtel Caron de Beaumarchais

€€
12 rue Vieille du Temple, 75004 **Tel** *01 42 78 14 15* **Fax** *01 40 29 06 82* **Rooms** *19*   **Map** *9 C3*

Pretty 18th-century-style fabrics and crystal chandeliers adorn this elegant boutique hotel. The rooms are cosy, yet not too small, with wooden beams and oodles of character. There are also 21st-century touches, such as internet access and air conditioning. **www.carondebeaumarchais.com**

THE MARAIS Hôtel de la Bretonnerie

€€
22 rue Ste-Croix de la Bretonnerie, 75004 **Tel** *01 48 87 77 63* **Fax** *01 42 77 26 78* **Rooms** *29*   **Map** *9 C3*

Carved stone walls and an arched dining room in the basement are some of the charming features of Hôtel de la Bretonnerie, housed in a 17th-century mansion. Its spacious rooms, with beams and antique furniture, are each decorated differently. Service is warm and friendly. **www.bretonnerie.com**

THE MARAIS Hôtel du Septième Art

€€
20 rue St-Paul, 75004 **Tel** *01 44 54 85 00* **Fax** *01 42 77 69 10* **Rooms** *23*   **Map** *10 D4*

A film buff's dream, this charming hotel is stuffed full with movie mementoes. The rooms are clean and all have a cinematic touch, from advertising posters to mini-statuettes of Marilyn Monroe. An ideal place to retire after a long day of sightseeing. There's also a tea room. Friendly staff. **www.paris-hotel-7art.com**

THE MARAIS Hôtel des Deux-Iles

€€€
59 rue St-Louis-en-l'Ile, 75004 **Tel** *01 43 26 13 35* **Fax** *01 43 29 60 25* **Rooms** *17*   **Map** *9 C4*

It's a privilege to be able to stay on the Ile St-Louis, and this converted 17th-century mansion offers an affordable way to do so. Here the atmosphere is peaceful, the small bedrooms are attractive and the lounge has a real fire. **www.deuxiles-paris-hotel.com**

THE MARAIS St-Paul-le-Marais

€€€
8 rue de Sévigné, 75004 **Tel** *01 48 04 97 27* **Fax** *01 48 87 37 04* **Rooms** *28*   **Map** *10 D3*

Close to the historic place des Vosges, this hotel has wooden beams and old stone, with simple and modern furniture. Request a room facing the courtyard to avoid the noise of traffic coming from the rue de Sévigné. **www.hotelsaintpaullemarais.com**

THE MARAIS Hôtel du Bourg Tibourg

€€€
19 rue du Bourg-Tibourg, 75004 **Tel** *01 42 78 47 39* **Fax** *01 40 29 07 00* **Rooms** *30*   **Map** *9 C3*

This stylish spot was decorated by top interior designer Jacques Garcia and is extremely popular with fashionable visitors to Paris. The rooms are opulent and all bathrooms are fully clad in black marble. The beautiful interior courtyard is a pleasant feature. **www.hotelbourgtibourg.com**

THE MARAIS Pavillon de la Reine

€€€€€
28 pl des Vosges, 75003 **Tel** *01 40 29 19 19* **Fax** *01 40 29 19 20* **Rooms** *56*   **Map** *10 D3*

Set back from the marvellous place des Vosges, the Pavillon de la Reine is the best hotel in the Marais. Incredibly romantic, the hotel has a peaceful courtyard and sumptuous guest rooms, furnished with excellent reproduction antiques. **www.pavillon-de-la-reine.com**

Key to Price Guide *see p550* **Key to Symbols** *see back cover flap*

TUILERIES QUARTER Hôtel Sainte Honoré €

85 rue St-Honoré, 75001 **Tel** *01 42 36 20 38* **Fax** *01 42 21 44 08* **Rooms** *29*   **Map** *8 F2*

Close to Concorde, the Tuileries, the Louvre and the Palais-Royal, the Sainte Honoré has an attractive green façade and an excellent location. The rooms, recently renovated and equipped with all modern amenities, are extremely well kept. Very good value. **www.parishotel.com**

TUILERIES QUARTER Brighton €€€

218 rue de Rivoli, 75001 **Tel** *01 47 03 61 61* **Fax** *01 42 60 41 78* **Rooms** *65*   **Map** *8 D1*

A real insiders' location, the Brighton provides a much-sought-after Rivoli address without the sky-high prices. The guest rooms have beautiful, high ceilings and large windows that look out either over the Jardin des Tuileries or over the courtyard. **www.esprit-de-france.com**

TUILERIES QUARTER Hôtel de Crillon €€€€€

10 pl de la Concorde, 75008 **Tel** *01 44 71 15 00* **Fax** *01 44 71 15 02* **Rooms** *147*   **Map** *7 C1*

With its magnificent location on the glittering place de la Concorde, the Crillon offers unsurpassed elegance. The hotel has a fine Royal Suite and terrace, a sublime dining room and a fashionable bar designed by French fashion designer, Sonia Rykiel. **www.crillon.com**

TUILERIES QUARTER Hôtel du Louvre €€€€€

Pl André Malraux, 75001 **Tel** *01 44 58 37 44* **Fax** *01 44 58 38 01* **Rooms** *177*   **Map** *8 E1*

This, the first luxury hotel in France, was built in 1855 by order of Napoleon III. The lavish rooms have spectacular views: the Pissarro Suite is where the artist painted his view of the place du Théâtre Français. From room 551 you can admire the opera house from your bath! **www.hoteldulouvre.com**

TUILERIES QUARTER Meurice €€€€€

228 rue de Rivoli, 75001 **Tel** *01 44 58 10 10* **Fax** *01 44 58 10 15* **Rooms** *125*   **Map** *8 D1*

The Meurice is a perfect example of successful restoration, with excellent replicas of the original plasterwork and furnishings. The staff here are unfailingly helpful and the hotel offers personalized shopping and art-buying tours. The hotel's spa is first rate. **www.meuricehotel.com**

TUILERIES QUARTER Regina €€€€€

2 pl des Pyramides, 75001 **Tel** *01 42 60 31 10* **Fax** *01 40 15 95 16* **Rooms** *120*   **Map** *8 E1*

Surprisingly, the Regina is unknown to most tourists, even though it is popular with the media. The lounge is famous for its stunning Art Nouveau wooden decorations, and many films have been shot here. Some of the rooms have superb views. **www.regina-hotel.com**

TUILERIES QUARTER Ritz €€€€€

15 pl Vendôme, 75001 **Tel** *01 43 16 30 70* **Fax** *01 43 16 45 38* **Rooms** *162*   **Map** *4 D5*

A legendary address, the Ritz still lives up to its reputation, combining elegance and decadence. The Louis XVI furniture and chandeliers are all original, and the floral arrangements are works of art. The Hemingway Bar is home to the glitterati. **www.ritzparis.com**

ILE DE FRANCE

BARBIZON Hostellerie La Dague €

5 grande rue, 77630 **Tel** *01 60 66 40 49* **Fax** *01 60 69 24 59* **Rooms** *25*

Located in an artists' village in the heart of the forest, this rustic ivy-clad manor house has a romantic setting. It is popular with Parisians, so book early. The bright rooms have pretty floral furnishings; there is also a modern annex. The traditional French restaurant is charming. **www.ladague.com**

ENGHIEN-LES-BAINS Grand Hôtel Barrière €€€€

85 rue Général de Gaulle, 95880 **Tel** *01 39 34 10 00* **Fax** *01 39 34 10 01* **Rooms** *50*

In the heart of this bustling spa town overlooking a lake, the Grand Hôtel lives up to its name. The interior was recently re-styled by Jacques Garcia. The rooms are luxurious, some in Louis XV style. The hotel has a traditional gourmet restaurant, and a casino. **www.lucienbarriere.com**

FONTAINEBLEAU Grand Hôtel de l'Aigle Noir €€€€

27 pl de Napoléon Bonaparte, 77300 **Tel** *01 60 74 60 00* **Fax** *01 60 74 60 01* **Rooms** *18*

This prestigious mansion overlooks Fontainebleau château and its vast park. The elegant rooms are decorated in styles ranging from Louis XIII to Napoléon III. The conciergerie can organize a host of activities in the area and the bar serves snacks all day. **www.hotelaiglenoir.com**

MAFFLIERS Château de Maffliers €€

Allée des Marronniers, 95560 **Tel** *01 34 08 35 35* **Fax** *01 34 08 35 00* **Rooms** *99*

This 19th-century château lies in the heart of the L'Isle d'Adam forest, surrounded by a huge private park. The contemporary guest rooms have all modern conveniences. Some non-smoking and wheelchair-accessible rooms. Bikes available to explore the forest. **www.accor-hotels.com**

POIGNY-EN-FORET Le Château de Poigny   🅿️   €

2 rue de l'Eglise, 78125 **Tel** *01 34 84 73 42* **Fax** *01 34 84 74 38* **Rooms** *7*

Near Rambouillet, this is a charming rustic hotel with a peaceful atmosphere. Each guest room is individually decorated with period furniture, some with four-poster beds. Tennis court and bikes are available. There are three restaurants in the nearby village.

ROISSY-CHARLES-DE-GAULLE Novotel Roissy Charles-de-Gaulle   🄵🅿️🍽🚹🗒   €€€

Charles de Gaulle airport, 95705 **Tel** *01 49 19 27 27* **Fax** *01 49 19 27 99* **Rooms** *200*

Facing the airport runways, this chain hotel is convenient for stop-overs. The guest rooms have double-glazing to minimize noise, and come equipped with modern amenities. Service is professional and efficient. There is also a traditional restaurant. **www.accorhotels.com**

ST-GERMAIN-EN-LAYE Pavillon Henri IV   🄵🅿️🍽🚹   €€€

19-21 rue Thiers, 78100 **Tel** *01 39 10 15 15* **Fax** *01 39 73 93 73* **Rooms** *42*

This sumptuous hotel is housed in a historic lodge built by Henri IV. It was here in 1638 that Louis XIV was born, and later where Dumas wrote *The Three Musketeers*. There is a wonderful panorama of Paris, and a gourmet restaurant. The rooms are stylish. **www.pavillonhenri4.fr**

ST-SYMPHORIEN LE CHATEAU Château d'Esclimont   🄵🅿️🍽🏊🚹🗒🗒   €€€€

28700 **Tel** *02 37 31 15 15* **Fax** *02 37 31 57 91* **Rooms** *53*

This magnificent 16th-century fairytale château has a private forest, tennis courts, a golf course and a fitness circuit. This turreted building offers meticulously kept, comfortable rooms. The gourmet restaurant provides impeccable service. Dogs are welcome. **www.esclimont.com**

VERSAILLES Hôtel de Clagny   €

6 impasse de Clagny, 78000 **Tel** *01 39 50 18 09* **Fax** *01 39 50 85 17* **Rooms** *21*

The welcome in this quiet hotel near the train station is genuinely friendly. The rooms are simply furnished and clean, but unremarkable. There are numerous restaurants in the vicinity, and the owners of the Hôtel de Clagny are only too pleased to offer guidance.

VERSAILLES Trianon Palace   🄵🅿️🍽🏊🚹🗒🗒   €€€€€

1 bd de la Reine, 78000 **Tel** *01 30 84 50 00* **Fax** *01 30 84 50 01* **Rooms** *192*

This is undoubtedly the most splendid hotel in the region. Built in Regency style, the hotel offers gorgeous, luxury guest rooms. The gourmet restaurant is the jewel in the crown. There is even a hammam (Turkish bath) for guests. **www.western.com**

LE NORD & PICARDY

AMIENS Hôtel de Normandie   🅿️   €

1bis rue Lamartine, 80000 **Tel** *03 22 91 74 99* **Fax** *03 22 92 06 56* **Rooms** *28*

This pleasant hotel with a red brick and stucco façade stands in a quiet street near the cathedral and railway station. The rooms are spacious, with modern furnishings. The hotel has an arrangement with Le T'Chiot Zinc, an inexpensive traditional restaurant where meals can be taken. Parking is extra. **www.hotelnormandie-80.com**

AMIENS Victor Hugo   €

2 rue de l'Oratoire, 80000 **Tel** *03 22 91 57 91* **Fax** *03 22 92 74 02* **Rooms** *10*

This friendly family hotel near the famous Gothic cathedral has a stone Bible carved into the façade. An old wooden staircase leads to the guest rooms. It makes an ideal base for exploring the city and is within easy walking distance of shops, restaurants and bars.

ARMBOUTS-CAPEL Hôtel du Lac   🅿️🍽   €

2 bordure du Lac, 59380 **Tel** *03 28 60 70 60* **Fax** *03 2861 06 39* **Rooms** *66*

This modern hotel stands on the banks of lake Armbouts, on the outskirts of Dunkirk. Non-smoking rooms are available, and some rooms have a lake view. The dining room opens onto a terrace, overlooking the garden and the Flemish countryside. **www.hoteldulacdk.com**

BERCK-SUR-MER Hôtel Neptune   🄵🅿️🍽🚹   €

Esplanade Parmentier, 62600 **Tel** *03 21 09 21 21* **Fax** *03 21 09 29 29* **Rooms** *63*

This excellent, ultra modern hotel is right on the seafront. The guest rooms are airy, many with a view. The rooms are fully adapted for disabled guests. The restaurant, with its impressive view, serves traditional local food, including seafood and steak. **www.hotel-cote-opale.com**

BOULOGNE-SUR-MER Hôtel Hamiot   🄵🅿️🍽   €€

1 rue Faidherbe, 62200 **Tel** *03 21 31 44 20* **Fax** *03 21 83 71 56* **Rooms** *12*

This lively portside hotel-restaurant has refurbished but somewhat old-fashioned rooms with plain walls, coloured bedspreads and dark furniture. The soundproofing is good. The Grand Restaurant has an excellent menu and a view; the less expensive Brasserie has a busy terrace. **www.hotelhamiot.com**

CALAIS Kyriad
Digue G Berthe, 62100 **Tel** *03 21 34 64 64* **Fax** *03 21 34 35 39* **Rooms** *44*

Right on the beach, behind lines of old-fashioned bathing huts, is this modern hotel-restaurant. The guest rooms accommodate up to three people, and are wheelchair-accessible. The restaurant has a changing menu. **www.hotel-plage-calais.com**

CAMBRAI Château de la Motte Fénélon
Square Château, 59400 **Tel** *03 27 83 61 38* **Fax** *03 27 83 71 61* **Rooms** *40*

Set in its own gardens, this 1850s château is handsomely decorated with grand guest rooms in the main building, and more modest rooms in the annexes. There is also a tennis court. The restaurant serves excellent traditional cuisine in a brick-vaulted cellar.

CHANTILLY-GOUVIEUX Château de la Tour
Chemin de la Chaussée, 60270 **Tel** *03 44 62 38 38* **Fax** *03 44 57 31 97* **Rooms** *41*

Just 20 minutes from Charles de Gaulle airport, this imposing *fin-de-siècle* residence and its matching extension is a haven of luxury set in 12 acres of grounds. The dining room has beautiful wood flooring. There is a pleasant terrace, and facilities for disabled guests. **www.lechateaudelatour.fr**

FERE-EN-TARDENOIS Château de Fère
Route de Fismes, 02130 **Tel** *03 23 82 21 13* **Fax** *03 23 82 37 81* **Rooms** *19 (plus 7 suites)*

In the background of this 16th-century hotel, set in vast grounds, are the ruins of the medieval castle of Anne de Montmorency. Each guest room here is unique, and the two dining rooms are splendid – with an amazing wine cellar. There are full facilities for disabled visitors. **www.chateauxhotels.com/fere**

GOSNAY La Chartreuse du Val de Saint Esprit
1 rue de Fouquières, 62199 **Tel** *03 21 62 80 00* **Fax** *03 21 62 42 50* **Rooms** *63*

On the outskirts of Béthune, this hotel is housed in an elegant château dating from 1764. Spacious guest rooms overlook the tree-filled park. There are three restaurants: the Chartreuse for the gourmet, Robert II for traditional cuisine and Le Vasco for trendier guests. **www.lachartreuse.com**

LAON-VILLE HAUTE Hôtel La Bannière de France
11 rue Franklin Roosevelt, 02000 **Tel** *03 23 23 21 44* **Fax** *03 23 23 31 56* **Rooms** *18*

Housed in a coaching inn dating from 1685, this hotel provides a good base for exploring the ancient city of Laon. The excellent guest rooms have recently been refurbished. The dining room combines classic cuisine with old-world charm. **www.hoteldelabannieredefrance.com**

LE TOUQUET Hôtel Blue Cottage
41 rue Jean Monnet, 62520 **Tel** *03 21 05 15 33* **Fax** *03 21 05 41 60* **Rooms** *25*

This contemporary hotel stands in the centre of town, near the beach. It is close to the covered market and the lively rue St Jean. The rooms are spacious and modern; non-smoking rooms are also available. The restaurant rotates its menu daily, with a buffet in the evenings. **www.blue-cottage.com**

LE TOUQUET Novotel
Front de mer, 62520 **Tel** *03 21 09 85 30* **Fax** *03 21 09 85 40* **Rooms** *149*

The perfect place for a body overhaul, this hotel stands next to the beach and near a thalassotherapy centre. Its amenities include a covered swimming pool and a fitness centre, and the guest rooms have been recently refurbished. The restaurant specializes in seafood. **www.accorhotels.com**

LILLE Des Tours
27 rue des Tours, 59000 **Tel** *03 59 57 47 00* **Fax** *03 59 57 47 99* **Rooms** *64*

Right in the centre of old Lille, this hotel is ideally situated for visiting the tourist attractions, and even has garage parking (extra charge). The public rooms are decorated with bright contemporary paintings, and the guest rooms are modern and attractive. Just outside is a range of restaurants. **www.hotel-des-tours.com**

LILLE Alliance Couvent des Minimes
17 quai du Wault, 59000 **Tel** *03 20 30 62 62* **Fax** *03 20 42 94 25* **Rooms** *80*

This converted 17th-century convent combines ancient and modern elements. Traditional Flemish brick arches surround the dining room with its sensational roof, while the guest rooms have benefited from the best of modern design. Disabled guests are fully catered to. **www.alliance-lille.com**

LONGPONT Hôtel de l'Abbaye
8 rue des Tourelles, 02600 **Tel** *03 23 96 02 44* **Fax** *03 23 96 02 44* **Rooms** *11*

Located between Soissons and Villers-Cotterets, this hotel is named after the nearby 12th-century abbey, and is nearly as old. The guest rooms are old-fashioned and comfortable. The popular restaurant serves *cuisine du terroir*, grillades and game in winter.

LUMBRES Moulin de Mombreux
Route de Beyenghem, 62380 **Tel** *03 21 39 62 44* **Fax** *03 21 93 61 34* **Rooms** *24*

This romantic 18th-century mill, hidden in its own grounds on the banks of the river Bléquin, works its charm on all who visit. Guests fall asleep to the sound of a waterfall. The restaurant is furnished with antiques and fine exposed beams. **www.moulindemombreux.com**

MAUBEUGE Hôtel Shakespeare

3 rue du Commerce, 59600 **Tel** *03 27 65 14 14* **Fax** *03 27 64 04 66* **Rooms** *35*

This is a functional and efficiently run hotel with friendly staff where you can stay without breaking the bank. It has an old-style frontage with a covered terrace for the bistro restaurant, which features a selection of grilled food. **www.grandhotelmaubeuge.fr**

MONTREUIL Le Darnetal

Pl Poissonerie, 62170 **Tel** *03 21 06 04 87* **Fax** *03 21 86 64 67* **Rooms** *4*

A small hotel in the upper town of Montreuil, the rooms here are old-fashioned. The auberge is decorated with a host of pictures, knick knacks and copper ornaments. It also has a popular traditional restaurant with excellent oysters in champagne; book ahead. **www.darnetal-montreuil.com**

MONTREUIL Château de Montreuil

4 chaussée des Capucins, 62170 **Tel** *03 21 81 53 04* **Fax** *03 21 81 36 43* **Rooms** *18*

The only relais château in Nord Pas de Calais, this elegant manor house is located inside the ramparts of the Montreuil that was once on the sea, before the sea retreated. There are lovely gardens, and a fine restaurant with an excellent wine list. **www.chateaudemontreuil.com**

PERONNE Hostellerie des Remparts

23 rue Beaubois, 80200 **Tel** *03 22 84 0 22* **Fax** *03 22 84 31 96* **Rooms** *16*

A classic Logis de France, set in the ramparts of this historic town that hosts a fine museum on World War I – the Historial. British servicemen are remembered here. The hotel itself is splendidly old-fashioned with comfortable rooms and a good traditional restaurant. **www.logis-de-france.fr**

REUILLY-SAUVIGNY L'Auberge le Relais

2 rue de Paris, 02850 **Tel** *03 23 70 35 36* **Fax** *03 23 70 35 36* **Rooms** *7*

A good base for visiting the champagne cellars just over the border, as well as in Epernay and Reims, this hotel-restaurant has pretty, brightly coloured rooms and a pleasant conservatory overlooking a lovely garden. There is also a gourmet restaurant. **www.relaisreuilly.com**

SARS-POTERIE Hôtel du Marquais

65 rue Général de Gaulle, 59216 **Tel** *03 27 61 62 72* **Fax** *03 27 57 47 35* **Rooms** *11*

Originally part of a series of farm buildings, this is now a friendly, family-run hotel. The modern colour scheme complements the antique furniture and photographs. On sunny days, breakfast is served in the garden. There is also a private tennis court. **www.hoteldumarquais.com**

ST OMER Hôtel St-Louis

25 rue d'Arras, 62500 **Tel** *03 21 38 35 21* **Fax** *03 21 38 57 26* **Rooms** *30*

At this stone-built former coaching inn you can see the arches where horses and carriages were led through to the stables. The hotel, which is well placed to visit St Omer, has disabled access, and the rooms in the annex have been recently refurbished. There is also a brasserie. **www.hotel-saintlouis.com**

ST QUENTIN Grand Hôtel

6 rue Dachery, 02100 **Tel** *03 23 62 69 77* **Fax** *03 23 62 53 52* **Rooms** *24*

Located between the train station and the centre of St Quentin, the Grand Hôtel is a good base from which to explore the World War I battlefields and nearby British and American cemeteries. The guest rooms are well designed and tastefully decorated.

VERVINS La Tour du Roy

45 rue du Général Leclerc, 02140 **Tel** *03 23 98 00 11* **Fax** *03 23 98 00 72* **Rooms** *22*

Steeped in history, this prestigious 17th-century château with its three towers was the site of German army headquarters in 1870, 1914 and 1940. General de Gaulle stayed here in 1956. The château has stately bedrooms, and a fine restaurant. **www.latourduroy.com**

WIMEREUX Hôtel du Centre

78 rue Carnot, 62930 **Tel** *03 21 32 41 08* **Fax** *03 21 33 82 48* **Rooms** *25*

This hotel is in a distinguished old building in the main street of this seaside resort between Boulogne and Calais. The comfortable guest rooms have been updated, while the restaurant retains all the period charm of the original building. **www.hotelducentre-wimereux.com**

CHAMPAGNE

ANDELOT Le Cantarel

Pl Cantarel, 52700 **Tel** *03 25 01 31 13* **Fax** *03 25 03 15 41* **Rooms** *8*

Rural tranquillity is available here at an affordable price. This classic small hotel is well placed to explore southern Champagne, Langres and Colombey-les-Deux-Eglises. Or just ramble in the 240,000 hectares of forest in the area. The Cantarel has a good restaurant and pizzeria. **www.lecantarel.com**

Key to Price Guide *see p550* **Key to Symbols** *see back cover flap*

BAZEILLES L'Auberge du Port
Route de Remilly, 08140 **Tel** *03 24 27 13 89* **Fax** *03 24 29 35 58* **Rooms** *20*

This quiet country hotel just outside the historic city of Sedan has pleasing flower-filled gardens by the river Meuse, a theme reflected by the flowery fabrics in the newly renovated guest rooms. The restaurant overlooks the river and surrounding countryside and there is a lovely veranda. Closed 2–22 August. **www.auberge-du-port.fr**

CHALONS-EN-CHAMPAGNE Hôtel du Pot d'Etain
18 pl de la République, 51000 **Tel** *03 26 68 09 09* **Fax** *03 26 68 58 18* **Rooms** *29*

Right in the centre of Châlons-en-Champagne in the heart of the champagne vineyards, this hotel is housed in an attractive building dating from the 15th century. The pleasant bedrooms are furnished with antiques. Enjoy homemade pastries and croissants for breakfast. **www.hotel-lepotdetain.com**

CHAMPILLON Royal Champagne
Bellevue, 51160 **Tel** *03 26 52 87 11* **Fax** *03 26 52 89 69* **Rooms** *25*

The ideal retreat for Champagne enthusiasts, this former coaching inn is now a relais château with a first-class reputation as a hotel and restaurant. The elegant bedrooms offer superb views over the vineyards and the Valley of the Marne. The wine list is outstanding. **www.royalchampagne.com**

CHARLEVILLE-MEZIERES Hôtel de Paris
24 av Georges Corneau, 08000 **Tel** *03 24 33 34 38* **Fax** *03 24 59 11 21* **Rooms** *27*

Le Paris is just 5 minutes from the centre of the capital of the French Ardennes and its fine main square – the place Ducale. Fronted by a bourgeois residence, the hotel occupies three separate buildings. The modern rooms have been insulated for sound. Nearby are restaurants. **www.hoteldeparis08.fr**

COURCELLES-SUR-VESLE Château de Courcelles
8 rue du Château, 02220 **Tel** *03 23 74 13 53* **Fax** *03 23 74 06 41* **Rooms** *18*

A very special hotel, this perfect Louis XIV château was built in the 1690s. The buildings have been splendidly restored, with a fine restaurant, a special wine list, 20 hectares of parkland, good sports facilities and disabled access. The trees still display shrapnel from WWI. **www.chateau-de-courcelles.fr**

EPERNAY Hôtel de la Cloche
3 pl Mendès-France, 51200 **Tel** *03 26 55 15 15* **Fax** *03 26 55 64 88* **Rooms** *19*

The best value inexpensive hotel in Epernay, the Hôtel de la Cloche is just a few metres from the church of Notre Dame and a short walk to the avenue de Champagne, where the famous names have their establishments. Guest rooms are bright with modern furnishings.

EPERNAY Micheline & Jean-Marie Tarlant
Oeuilly Route Nationale 3, 51480 **Tel** *03 26 58 30 60* **Fax** *03 26 58 37 31* **Rooms** *4*

This special *chambre d'hôte* is in a converted wine-grower's cottage on a Champagne estate, which has been tended by the Tarlant family since 1687. The cheerful, renovated rooms are situated above the cellars, with fine views. A kitchen is available and restaurants are 5 km (3 miles) away. **www.tarlant.com**

ETOGES Château d'Etoges
4 rue Richebourg, 51270 **Tel** *03 26 59 30 08* **Fax** *03 26 59 35 57* **Rooms** *20*

Now a grand private hotel (*chambre d'hôte*), the original medieval fortress was converted to a fairytale castle in the 17th century. The building is protected by the *monuments historiques*. There is an excellent restaurant, and guests may use a boat on the moat. **www.etoges.com**

FAGNON Abbaye de Sept Fontaines
Fagnon, 08090 **Tel** *03 24 37 38 24* **Fax** *03 24 37 58 75* **Rooms** *23*

Originally a 12th-century monastery, rebuilt in 1693, this château hotel has the distinction of having hosted Marshal Foch, Emperor William II of Germany and General de Gaulle. There is a huge lawn and a childrens' play area, a nine-hole golf course, a restaurant and a quiet terrace. **www.abbayeseptfontaines.fr**

GIVET Les Reflets Jaunes
2 rue Général de Gaulle, 08600 **Tel** *03 24 42 85 85* **Fax** *03 24 42 85 86* **Rooms** *17*

Recently refurbished with disabled access, Les Reflets Jaune stands in the centre of this frontier town near Belgium. The city was fortified by Vauban and was the birthplace of Etienne Méhul, composer of the revolutionary song *Le Chant du Départ*. Restaurants are nearby. **www.les-reflets-jaunes.com**

HAYBES SUR MEUSE l'Ermitage Moulin Labotte
52 rue Edmond Dromart, 08170 **Tel** *03 24 41 13 44* **Fax** *03 24 40 46 72* **Rooms** *10*

In the heart of the Ardennes forest, this mill dating from the end of the 18th century houses a hotel and restaurant. The great cogs from the mill still adorn the dining room. Comfortable guest rooms are furnished in traditional style. The restaurant serves local cuisine. **www.moulin-labotte.com**

LANGRES Grand Hôtel de l'Europe
23 rue Diderot, 52200 **Tel** *03 25 87 10 88* **Fax** *03 25 87 60 65* **Rooms** *26*

An old coaching inn on the main street of this attractive town, the Grand Hôtel de l'Europe has recently refurbished guest rooms, which are quieter at the back. The restaurant serves typical country food. Langres was the birthplace of Diderot, editor of the famous encyclopedia. **www.relais-sud-champagne.com**

MAGNANT Le Val Moret   P ⑪ ⚞ ⅋   €

10110 **Tel** *03 25 29 85 12* **Fax** *03 25 29 70 81* **Rooms** *42*

This pretty, flower bedecked modern motel on the A5 from Troyes to Dijon is ideally placed to explore the Champagne route in Aube and Nigloland entertainment park for children. There is secure parking. The restaurant is good, with a recognized chef and quality wine list. **www.le-val-moret.com**

MESNIL-ST-PERE Auberge du Lac - Au Vieux Pressoir   P ⑪ ▤ ⅋   €€

5 rue du 28 Août 1944, 10140 **Tel** *03 25 41 27 16* **Fax** *03 25 41 57 59* **Rooms** *21*

A typical half-timbered Champagne house in a village on the edge of the Lac d'Orient, Europe's biggest manmade lake, this hotel provides fantastic bird-watching opportunities, especially in April and September. The hotel is accessible for disabled guests, with a good restaurant. **www.auberge-du-lac.fr**

MOUSSEY Domaine de la Creuse   P   €€

10800 **Tel** *03 25 41 74 01* **Fax** *03 25 73 13 87* **Rooms** *5*

Stunning rural *chambre d'hôte* in a beautifully modernized 18th-century farm, typical of this part of the Aube-en-Champagne. It is a 10-minute drive from the Michelin-starred restaurant, La Parentale. The combination is hard to beat as a base to explore this attractive area. **www.domainedelacreuse.com**

REIMS Grand Hôtel de l'Univers   ⎘ P ⑪ ⅋   €

41 bd Foch, 51100 **Tel** *03 26 88 68 08* **Fax** *03 26 40 95 61* **Rooms** *42*

On a tree-lined boulevard, this Art Deco hotel provides a haven from the bustle of the city. Rooms are cosy if a little chintzy, with matching bedspreads and curtains, but there is wireless Internet access. The refurbished restaurant serves excellent meals; try the pan-fried scallops with citrus. **www.hotel-univers-reims.com**

REIMS Hôtel Crystal   ⎘ P   €

86 place Drouet d'Erlon, 51100 **Tel** *03 26 88 44 44* **Fax** *03 26 47 49 28* **Rooms** *31*

This 1920s hotel in the busiest part of Reims is surprisingly quiet, with pleasantly decorated rooms. The lobby and elevator retain their Art Deco style, and there is a garden, where breakfast is served in summer. The nearby place Drouet Derlon has a choice of restaurants. **www.hotel-crystal.fr**

REIMS Château Les Crayères   ⎘ P ⑪ ⚞ ▤ ⅋   €€€€€

64 bd Henry Vasnier, 51100 **Tel** *03 26 82 80 80* **Fax** *03 26 82 65 52* **Rooms** *20*

Superbly aristocratic château with every luxury set in an English-style park next to the Roman *crayères* – the wine cellars of the Champagne houses which have been cut into the chalk. There is a superb restaurant, one of the best in France. **www.lescrayeres.com**

SEDAN Le Château Fort   ⎘ P ⑪   €€

Port des Princes, 08200 **Tel** *03 24 26 11 00* **Fax** *03 24 27 19 00* **Rooms** *53*

For years no one knew what to do with Europe's largest fortress. Now it hosts an exciting new hotel, under the banner of France Patrimoine, restored to the highest standards of the *monuments historiques*. Some rooms have disabled access, and there is a good restaurant. **www.hotelfp-sedan.com**

SEPT SAULX le Cheval Blanc   P ⑪   €€

2 rue Moulin, 51400 **Tel** *03 26 03 90 27* **Fax** *03 26 03 97 09* **Rooms** *24*

Between Reims and Chalons en Champagne in the middle of prestigious vineyards, this excellent hotel is attractively furnished. The rooms open on to the delightful gardens on the river Vesle. The beautifully presented restaurant has a terrace with flowers. Hotel is closed Feb, & Tue from Oct-Apr. **www.chevalblanc-sept-saulx.com**

ST-DIZIER Le Gambetta   ⎘ P ⑪ ⅋   €

62 rue Gambetta, 52100 **Tel** *03 25 56 52 10* **Fax** *03 25 56 39 47* **Rooms** *63*

This modern hotel in the centre of St-Dizier offers great value for money. Disabled guests are catered for. Breakfast is served as a buffet. Many guests are drawn to the bird-watching opportunities at the nearby Lac du Der-Chantecoq. **www.citotel.com**

TROYES Champs des Oiseaux   P   €€

20 rue Linard Gonthier, 10000 **Tel** *03 25 80 58 50* **Fax** *03 25 80 98 34* **Rooms** *12*

The finest hotel in Troyes, this is located by the cathedral in the town centre. The sheer charm of the restored 15th- and 16th-century buildings as well as top service never fail to impress. The planted courtyards and brick half-timbered walls make for a memorable stay. Snacks are served. **www.champdesoiseaux.com**

TROYES La Maison de Rhodes   P ⅋   €€€

18 rue Linard Gonthier, 10000 **Tel** *03 25 43 11 11* **Fax** *03 25 43 10 43* **Rooms** *11*

A sister hotel to the Champ des Oiseaux, this is almost as grand, with stunningly restored 16th-century architecture, including brick and timber galleries and stairways. Though a newer hotel, it is just as popular. The hotel has disabled access, and a restaurant for guests who book a table. **www.maisonderhodes.com**

VIGNORY Le Relais Verdoyant   P ⑪ ⚞   €

Quartier de la Gare, 52320 **Tel** *03 25 02 44 49* **Fax** *03 25 01 96 89* **Rooms** *7*

Just outside the village of Vignory, this converted farm in a peaceful hamlet makes for a relaxing stay. It is a few kilometres from Colombey les Deux Eglises, where the great cross of Lorraine marks the resting place of Général de Gaulle. Excellent, reasonably priced restaurant. **www.le-relais-verdoyant.com**

Key to Price Guide *see p550* **Key to Symbols** *see back cover flap*

WILLIERS Chez Odette   P �11   €€€

Rue Principale, 08110 **Tel** *03 24 55 49 55* **Fax** *03 24 55 49 59* **Rooms** *6*

Right by the Belgian border, this recently opened hotel is an exercise in contrasts – on the outside it looks like a country family hotel and bistro, but inside it is startlingly elegant, with ultra modern decor and furnishings. There is a gastronomic restaurant, a bistro and a bar. **www.chez-odette.com**

ALSACE & LORRAINE

COLMAR Hostellerie Le Marechal   ⊞ � �11 ▤   €€

4 pl Six Montagnes Noires, 68000 **Tel** *03 89 41 60 32* **Fax** *03 89 24 59 40* **Rooms** *30*

This luxurious 16th- and 17th-century house, by the river Lauch in the old part of the city, is home to the Hostellerie Le Marechal. Some of the guest rooms have four-poster beds and views of the canal. The candlelit restaurant, A L'Echevin, faces the canal. **www.le-marechal.com**

COLMAR Hôtel St Martin   ♣ ▤   €€

38 grand' rue, 68000 **Tel** *03 89 24 11 51* **Fax** *03 89 23 47 78* **Rooms** *40*

Near the Schwendi fountain in the middle of Alsace's most picturesque town, this hotel comprises three houses dating from the 14th and 17th centuries and an inner courtyard with a Renaissance stair turret. There are a number of good restaurants on the doorstep. **www.hotel-saint-martin.com**

DIEVE Hostellerie du Château des Monthairons   ♣ P �11 ♣   €€

Monthairons, 55320 **Tel** *03 29 87 78 55* **Fax** *03 29 87 73 49* **Rooms** *25*

This grand 19th-century château is in its own walled grounds, south of Verdun. Its features include two chapels, a heronry and a private beach on the Meuse. First-floor rooms are furnished with antiques; the others are modern. The restaurant has a terrace overlooking the countryside. **www.chateaudesmonthairons.com**

DRACHENBRONN Auberge du Moulin des 7 Fontaines   P �11   €

1 sept Fontaines, 67160 **Tel** *03 88 94 50 90* **Fax** *03 88 94 54 57* **Rooms** *12*

Hidden in the forest, this auberge is run by the Finck family in typical rural Alsace style. The old-style bedrooms are situated in the converted 18th-century mill. There are exceptional-value meals on the terrace in summer. It is a great favourite with hikers. **www.auberge7fontaines.com**

EGUISHEIM Hostellerie du Pape   ♣ �11   €€

10 grand rue, 68420 **Tel** *03 89 41 41 21* **Fax** *03 89 41 41 31* **Rooms** *33*

This hotel is a former *maison de vigneron*, a wine-grower's house with vine-covered balconies. It is named in honour of Pope Leon IX, who was born in the village in 1002. His statue is nearby. The restaurant serves traditional local dishes. **www.hostellerie-pape.com**

EPINAL Hôtel Le Manoir   ♣ P �11 ♣ ▤ ♿   €€

5 av Provence, 88000 **Tel** *03 29 29 55 55* **Fax** *03 29 29 55 56* **Rooms** *12*

Built in 1876, this fine old house is equipped with modern conveniences, including high-speed Internet access, games console and access for disabled visitors. The guest rooms are a good size, some with jacuzzis. Spa treatments available. The top-class restaurant has a good wine list. **www.manoir-hotel.com**

GERARDMER Le Manoir au Lac   P �11 ≋ ♣ ▤   €€€

Route d'Epinal, 88400 **Tel** *03 29 27 10 20* **Fax** *03 29 27 10 27* **Rooms** *14*

This small hotel occupies a lakeside house dating from the 1830s. It was once a favourite of French literary icon, Guy de Maupassant. The rooms are in a separate chalet. Everything centres on the lake, with swimming and water sports. The restaurant has a terrace. **www.manoir-au-lac.com**

KAYSERSBERG Hôtel Constantin   ♣ P   €

10 rue Père Kohlman, 68240 **Tel** *03 89 47 19 90* **Fax** *03 89 47 37 82* **Rooms** *20*

A beautifully restored 17th-century house in the centre of the old town conceals a hotel that has been modernized to create stylish rooms. Breakfast is served in the conservatory; other meals are available next door at the Relais du Château, owned by the same family. **www.hotel-constantin.com**

LA PETITE PIERRE Aux Trois Roses   ♣ P �11 ≋ ♣ ♥   €

19 rue Principale, 67290 **Tel** *03 88 89 89 00* **Fax** *03 88 70 41 28* **Rooms** *40*

This hotel is in an 18th-century house in the middle of this attractive hilltop village. Some of the pleasant rooms have balconies, and there is a guest lounge with an open fire. Excellent value for money. The dining room serves traditional Vosgian dishes. The village is home to the Maison du Parc. **www.aux-trois-roses.com**

LAPOUTROIE Les Alisiers   P �11   €€

5 rue du Faudé, 68650 **Tel** *03 89 47 52 82* **Fax** *03 89 47 22 38* **Rooms** *16*

This attractive hotel has grown out of a pretty converted farm dating from 1819. The refurbished guest rooms are decorated in country style. The terrace has fabulous views of the hills and valleys. From the dining room you can enjoy the excellent food and the view at the same time. **www.alisiers.com**

LUNEVILLE Château d'Adoménil
       P   11 ≋ 大 目   €€€

54300 Tel 03 83 74 04 81 Fax 03 83 74 21 78 Rooms 14

This imposing Relais Château in an extensive park on the river Meurthe is not far from the 18th-century splendours of Nancy. The guest rooms are splendidly bourgeois in the château itself or Provençal in theme in the beautiful outbuildings. The restaurant is a gourmet rendezvous. **www.adomenil.com**

METZ Grand Hôtel de Metz
       🔲 P   €

3 rue des Clercs, 57000 Tel 03 87 36 16 33 Fax 03 87 74 17 04 Rooms 62

A stylish hotel on a pedestrianized street in the centre of this fine, underrated city, with French and Prussian architecture. The hotel is an interesting combination of Baroque entrance hall and rustic rooms, near the cathedral and the covered market. Good restaurants are nearby. **www.hotel-metz.com**

MOLSHEIM Hôtel Bugatti
       🔲 P   €

Rue de la Commanderie, 67120 Tel 03 88 49 89 00 Fax 03 88 38 36 00 Rooms 48

A practical, modern hotel with good rooms opposite the famous Bugatti factory where the legendary racing cars are built. Some old models are on display at the museum in the town centre. Guests have access to the pool and fitness centre at the Hotel Diana, a short distance away. **www.hotel-le-bugatti.com**

NANCY Hôtel Albert Ier Astoria
       🔲 P 目   €

3 rue Armée Patton, 54000 Tel 03 83 40 31 24 Fax 03 83 28 47 78 Rooms 83

Right next to the main railway station, the rooms in this hotel are modern, overlooking a leafy courtyard. There is no restaurant, but meals can be taken in the *restaurant partenaire* the Bistro du Boucher, which serves simple local dishes. **www.albert1-astoria-astoria.com**

NANCY Grand Hôtel de la Reine
       🔲 P 11 目   €€€

2 pl Stanislas, 54000 Tel 03 83 35 03 01 Fax 03 83 32 86 04 Rooms 42

Experience the Ancien Régime in Europe's finest Neo-Classical square – the stunningly restored place Stanislas. The hotel occupies the house originally built in 1752 for the steward to Stanislas, Duke of Lorraine, the last king of Poland. A host of famous visitors includes Tsar Alexander I of Russia. **www.hoteldelareine.com**

OBERNAI Hôtel Restaurant des Vosges
       🔲 11   €

5 pl de la Gare, 67210 Tel 03 88 95 53 78 Fax 03 88 49 92 65 Rooms 20

A cheerful and welcoming small hotel by the train station, this is a mixture of old and modern buildings with a pleasant, traditional atmosphere. The rooms are exceptionally well kept. The restaurant is a cross between traditional Alsace and bistro style. **www.hotel-obernai.com**

REMIREMONT Hôtel du Cheval de Bronze
       大   €

59 rue Charles de Gaulle, 88200 Tel 03 29 62 52 24 Fax 03 29 62 34 90 Rooms 35

A former coaching inn, set behind the 17th-century arcades of this attractive town in the foothills of the Vosges, this simple provincial hotel is ideal for visiting the Vosges mountains. The Ballon d'Alsace is an easy drive, as is the World War I mountain battlefield Hartmannswillerkopf. No restaurant, but the owner will make recommendations.

SAVERNE Chez Jean
       🔲 P 11   €

3 rue Gare, 67700 Tel 03 88 91 10 19 Fax 03 88 91 27 45 Rooms 25

A four-storey traditional Alsace house in the centre of town, this was once a convent. The rooms are tastefully decorated in local style. There are good views of the surrounding hills. There is a sauna for guests' use. The Winstubs' Rosestiebele restaurant is on the ground floor. **www.chez-jean.com**

SELESTAT Auberge des Alliés
       11   €

39 rue des Chevaliers, 67600 Tel 03 88 92 09 34 Fax 03 88 92 12 88 Rooms 17

Set in the old town, part of this hotel-restaurant occupies a house dating from 1537. The city contained one of the finest schools in Europe; its unique library holds the *Cosmographiae Introductio*, with the first reference to America in print. Rooms are small and simple, with old-fashioned decor. **www.auberge-des-allies.com**

SELESTAT Hostellerie Abbaye de la Pommeraie
       🔲 P 11 目   €€€

8 av Maréchal Foch, 67600 Tel 03 88 92 07 84 Fax 03 88 92 08 71 Rooms 13

In the old city of Selestat, famous for its centuries-old library, this fine 17th-century building was once part of the medieval Baumgarten Abbey. The guest rooms are everything you would expect of a Relais Château, and there are two very good restaurants. **www.pommeraie.fr**

STRASBOURG Au Cerf d'Or
       🔲 11 ≋ 大 目   €

6 pl de l'Hôpital, 67000 Tel 03 88 36 20 05 Fax 03 88 36 68 67 Rooms 43

An inexpensive base for visiting the sights of old Strasbourg, this old-style half-timbered Alsace hotel has refurbished rooms throughout. The main hotel has more charming rooms, but the annex has a small pool and a sauna. There are several restaurants on the nearby waterfront. **www.cerf-dor.com**

STRASBOURG Relais Mercure
       🔲 P 目   €€

3 rue du Maire Kuss, 67000 Tel 03 88 32 80 80 Fax 03 88 23 05 39 Rooms 52

Part of the Mercure chain, this hotel in an older building retains some of its individuality. It has been extensively refurbished with bay windows and an attractive breakfast terrace. It is conveniently located between the train station and La Petite France, though not in the best area. **www.accor-hotels.com**

Key to Price Guide *see p550* **Key to Symbols** *see back cover flap*

NORMANDY

ALENÇON Hôtel le Chapeau Rouge ▢▤ €

3 bd Duchamp, 61000 **Tel** *02 33 26 20 23* **Fax** *02 33 26 54 05* **Rooms** *14*

This modern, serviceable hotel was built in the 1960s. Just 10 minutes' walk from the town centre at a busy crossroads, the rooms have double-glazing to muffle the traffic noise. The decor is stylish and classic, and the rooms are well equipped. There is a relaxed atmosphere. **www.lechapeaurouge.fr**

ARROMANCHES-LES-BAINS Hôtel de la Marine ▨▢▥▦ €

Quai du Canada, 14117 **Tel** *02 31 22 34 19* **Fax** *02 31 22 98 80* **Rooms** *28*

A comfortable, no-frills hotel especially suitable for families, La Marine is situated in the town centre. Most of the well-maintained rooms look out over the Channel and the port. There is a panoramic restaurant which has a wonderfully fresh daily menu. **www.hotel-de-la-marine.fr**

AUDRIEU Château d'Audrieu ▢▥▧▦ €€€

Le Château, 14250 **Tel** *02 31 80 21 52* **Fax** *02 31 80 24 73* **Rooms** *29*

This 18th-century château was transformed into a luxurious hotel in 1976. A short distance from Bayeux, it has an immense park, providing wonderful views. The stunning guest rooms are elegantly furnished with period pieces. There is an excellent gourmet restaurant. **www.chateaudaudrieu.com**

BAGNOLES DE L'ORNE Bois Joli ▥▦ €€

12 av Philippe du Rozier, 61140 **Tel** *02 33 37 92 77* **Fax** *02 33 37 07 56* **Rooms** *20*

This fine 19th-century hotel has pleasant, bright sunny guest rooms with classic, Regency-style furnishings. The building is surrounded by grassy grounds. Nearby are thermal spas, a lake, golf course and a casino. The restaurant serves traditional Normandy cuisine. **www.hotelboisjoli.com**

BENOUVILLE Le Manoir Hastings et la Pommeraie ▢▥▦ €€

18 av de la Côte de Nacre, 14970 **Tel** *02 31 44 62 43* **Fax** *02 31 44 76 18* **Rooms** *16*

Located near the village church in a former 17th-century priory, the original building has pretty rooms and a restaurant. The rooms in the recent addition are more comfortable but less characterful. The restaurant terrace overlooks the garden. **www.manoirhastings.com**

CABOURG Hôtel du Parc ▢▦ €

31–33 av du Général Leclerc, 14390 **Tel** *02 31 91 00 82* **Fax** *02 31 91 00 18* **Rooms** *17*

This hotel consists of two century-old buildings in the heart of the city, not far from the beach. The rooms are simply furnished and in bright tones, and there is soundproofing. Reserve a room at the rear for a more peaceful night's sleep. There is free parking for guests. **www.hotelduparc-cabourg.com**

CAEN Best Western Le Dauphin ▨▢▥▦▩▣ €€

29 rue Gémare, 14000 **Tel** *02 31 86 22 26* **Fax** *02 31 86 35 14* **Rooms** *37*

In a quiet but central location, this old priory has been tastefully renovated, retaining original features such as the arched windows and stone walls. The rooms are comfortable; non-smoking and family rooms are available. There is a breakfast buffet, and a gourmet restaurant. **www.le-dauphin-normandie.com**

CAEN Hôtel Mercure Porte de Plaisance ▨▢▥▦▤ €€€

1 rue Courtonne, 14000 **Tel** *02 31 47 24 24* **Fax** *02 31 47 43 88* **Rooms** *129*

An atmosphere of quiet elegance pervades, with every attention paid to the guests' comfort. The rooms of this chain hotel, centrally located opposite the harbour, are cosy and tastefully furnished. Disabled guests are catered for, and there is parking for an additional charge. **www.accorhotels.com**

CEAUX Le Relais du Mont ▢▥▦ €

La Buvette, 50220 **Tel** *02 33 70 92 55* **Fax** *02 33 70 94 57* **Rooms** *28*

South of Avranches, this hotel faces west and enjoys splendid sunsets over the bay of Mont-St-Michel. A recently built hotel with decent-sized, well-maintained rooms. There are good facilities, family rooms and an excellent restaurant. **www.hotel-mont-saint-michel.com**

CHERBOURG L'Ambassadeur ▨▢▦ €

22 quai de Caligny, 50100 **Tel** *02 33 43 10 00* **Fax** *02 33 43 10 01* **Rooms** *40*

Perfectly situated for a peaceful night, lulled to sleep by the sound of the sea. The rooms at this city centre hotel are simply furnished but comfortable, and most overlook the port. Nearby is a wide choice of restaurants and the casino. Excellent breakfasts. **www.ambassadeurhotel.com**

DEAUVILLE Hôtel Normandy Barrière ▨▢▥▧▦▩ €€€€€

38 rue J Mermoz, 14800 **Tel** *02 31 98 66 22* **Fax** *02 31 98 66 23* **Rooms** *271*

Deauville's landmark, this Anglo-Normandy manor house is a luxury hotel with beautiful, spacious rooms and fitness facilities. The large Belle Epoque dining room serves classic, traditional Normandy fare. Although it has been modernized, the hotel retains its 1920s charm. **www.lucienbarriere.com**

ETRETAT DOMAINE ST CLAIR Le Donjon
`P` `ᴿ` `ⵓ`   €€

Chemin de St Clair, 76790 **Tel** *02 35 27 08 23* **Fax** *02 35 29 92 24* **Rooms** *21*

Stunningly situated with panoramic views of the village and cliffs of Etretat, this 19th-century Anglo-Norman château has comfortable rooms, some with private spa baths. The rooms are individually decorated with four-poster beds and period furniture. **www.hoteletretat.com**

EVREUX Hôtel de Paris
€

32 rue Harpe, 27000 **Tel** *02 32 39 12 97* **Rooms** *6*

Situated in a quiet location near the cathedral and city centre, Le Paris has clean, simple rooms with private bathrooms and no television. Continental breakfast is served in the bar, which is open in the early evening for a pre-dinner drink. There are restaurants nearby.

FECAMP Vent d'Ouest
€

3 av Gambetta, 76400 **Tel** *02 35 28 04 04* **Fax** *02 35 28 75 96* **Rooms** *15*

A friendly welcome awaits guests here in the centre of Fécamp, a busy fishing port and the only major town along the Côte d'Albâtre. Apart from the Palais Benedictine, there is not much to see. The unpretentious hotel has gaily painted, well-equipped rooms and a pretty breakfast room. **www.hotelventdouest.tm.fr**

FONTENAI-SUR-ORNE Le Faisan Doré
`P` `ᴿ` `ⵓ`   €

Rte Paris, 61200 **Tel** *02 33 67 18 11* **Fax** *02 33 35 82 15* **Rooms** *14*

A decent-sized hotel in the Suisse Normande region, close to Argentan. Newly renovated, the quieter rooms overlook the pretty garden. There is a well-stocked bar with over 140 different wines. Meals can be taken in the brightly decorated restaurant, or outside in summer. **www.lefaisandore.com**

GRAND CHAMP MAISY Hôtel Duguesclin
`P` `ᴿ`   €

4 quai Henri Crampon, 14450 **Tel** *02 31 22 64 22* **Fax** *02 31 22 34 79* **Rooms** *25*

This friendly modern hotel is located on the seafront promenade. The rooms are comfortably furnished and well maintained. The excellent restaurant specializes in seafood. Parking is available. This fishing port is a good base for visiting the D-Day landing beaches at Pointe du Hoc. **www.hotel-restaurant-leduguesclin.com**

GRANVILLE Hôtel Michelet
`P`   €

5 rue Jules Michelet, 50400 **Tel** *02 33 50 06 55* **Fax** *02 33 50 12 25* **Rooms** *19*

The hotel is close to the shops, restaurants and the casino in this charming historic port. An attractive Colonial-style building, tastefully renovated, with simply furnished, well-kept rooms, some with a view. Convenient for the beach and thalasso centre. Free parking. **www.hotel-michelet-granville.com**

HONFLEUR La Ferme Siméon
`P` `ᴿ` `≋` `ⵓ` `ᵀ`   €€€€€

Rue Adolphe Marais, 14600 **Tel** *02 31 81 78 00* **Fax** *02 31 89 48 48* **Rooms** *34*

Ancient farmhouse mansion that was the haunt of the Impressionist artists from the Honfleur school. Now a luxury hotel, restaurant and spa centre. Beautifully converted guest rooms; spacious and charmingly furnished. The oak-beamed restaurant serves excellent food. **www.fermesaintsimeon.fr**

ISIGNY-SUR-MER Hôtel de France
`P` `ᴿ` `ⵓ`   €

13 rue Emile-Demagny, 14230 **Tel** *02 31 22 00 33* **Fax** *02 31 22 79 19* **Rooms** *18*

A friendly and comfortable small hotel on one of the main streets in this picturesque town. Isigny is famous for dairy products: butter, cheese, crème fraîche. The 100-year-old building, set around a courtyard, has simple, well-kept rooms. The restaurant favours local produce. **www.hotel-France-isigny.com**

L'AIGLE Hôtel du Dauphin
`ᴿ` `ⵓ`   €€

Pl de la Halle, 61300 **Tel** *02 33 84 18 00* **Fax** *02 33 34 09 28* **Rooms** *30*

A fine stone-built inn, established in 1618. The original stables were razed during the bombardment of L'Aigle in 1944. Now the hotel, which has been in the same family for 60 years, has a restaurant, a brasserie and a shop. The rooms are functional, and there is a comfy lounge. **www.hoteldudauphin.free.fr**

LE PETIT ANDELY La Chaîne d'Or
`P` `ᴿ` `ⵓ`   €

27 rue Grande, 27700 **Tel** *02 32 54 00 31* **Fax** *02 32 54 05 58* **Rooms** *11*

This 18th-century staging post was once a toll house for crossing the Seine. It is now a refined, elegant hotel. The guest rooms are well maintained, comfortable and decorated in pastel colours. Most have a view of the Seine. Good, innovative restaurant. **www.hotel-lachainedor.com**

LISIEUX Grand Hôtel de l'Espérance
`⌨` `P` `ᴿ` `ⵓ`   €

16 bd Ste-Anne, 14100 **Tel** *02 31 62 17 53* **Fax** *02 31 62 34 00* **Rooms** *100*

A large efficiently run hotel in the heart of Lisieux has spacious, smartly furnished rooms; some non-smoking. There are also rooms for disabled guests. The facilities include a gift shop, foreign exchange, room service and lounge bar. The restaurant serves traditional Normandy fare. **www.lisieux-hotel.com**

MACE Hôtel Île de Sées
`P` `ᴿ` `ⵓ`   €

Vandel, 61500 **Tel** *02 33 27 98 65* **Fax** *02 33 28 41 22* **Rooms** *16*

A rural hotel surrounded by a large park set in the heart of Normandy studfarm country. This traditional half-timbered former dairy is a friendly hotel with pleasant, cosy rooms in soft pastel tones. An ideal place to unwind and relax. Delicious food served in the comfortable restaurant. **www.ile-sees.fr**

Key to Price Guide *see p550* **Key to Symbols** *see back cover flap*

MESNIL-VAL Hostellerie de la Vieille Ferme 🅿 🍴 🏃 €

23 rue de la Mer, 76910 **Tel** *02 35 86 72 18* **Fax** *02 35 86 12 67* **Rooms** *33*

An 18th-century farmhouse with several attractively converted outbuildings make up this Anglo-Norman hotel complex set in its own park near the beach. The guest rooms are romantically old-fashioned, wiith oak beams and great views. Rustic-style seafood restaurant. **www.hotel-france.com**

MONT ST MICHEL Auberge St Pierre 🍴 €€

Grande rue, 50170 **Tel** *02 33 60 14 03* **Fax** *02 33 48 59 82* **Rooms** *21*

On the main road of Mont-St-Michel that leads to the abbey, this 15th-century half-timbered building sheltered by ramparts now houses a hotel with comfortable, simple rooms. It is calm at night, but be prepared for lots of bustle early in the morning. The restaurant is good. **www.auberge-saint-pierre.fr**

MORTAGNE AU PERCHE Le Tribunal 🏃 €

4 pl Palais, 61400 **Tel** *02 33 25 04 77* **Fax** *02 33 83 60 83* **Rooms** *21*

Some rooms in this pretty hotel date back to the 13th century. It is a well-kept establishment with plush guest rooms and great baths. A stay here gives an experience of pleasant simplicity. The restaurant serves local dishes, on an outside terrace in summer. **http://perso.wanadoo.fr/hotel.du.tribunal.61.normandie**

MORTAIN Hôtel de la Poste 🅿 🍴 🏃 €

1 pl des Arcades, 50140 **Tel** *02 33 59 00 05* **Fax** *02 33 69 53 89* **Rooms** *27*

On the spectacular Cherbourg peninsula, this attractive 19th-century house overlooks the lovely river in Mortain. A pleasant family-run hotel with comfortable, quiet rooms and good service. Fine restaurant with an excellent wine list. Disabled facilities and a private garage. **www.hoteldelaposte.fr**

PONT AUDEMER Belle-Île-sur-Risle 🅿 🍴 ≋ 🏃 🔽 €€€

112 route de Rouen, 27500 **Tel** *02 32 56 96 22* **Fax** *02 32 42 88 96* **Rooms** *20*

Set on an island in its own large garden of ancient trees and roses, the hotel has a fitness centre, sauna, and two pools (outdoor and indoor). The recently renovated rooms are comfortable and elegant, ideal for a relaxing stay. Superb cuisine in the 19th-century rotunda. **www.bellile.com**

PONT DE L'ARCHE Hôtel de la Tour 🅿 €

41 quai Foch, 27340 **Tel** *02 35 23 00 99* **Fax** *02 35 23 46 22* **Rooms** *18*

This attractive 18th-century Norman house sits at the river's edge, backing on to the village's ramparts. The interior reveals typical Normandy architecture with timber and brick walls. The good-sized rooms are individually decorated. Patio garden. Restaurants nearby. **www.hoteldelatour.org**

ROUEN Hôtel Notre-Dame 🅿 €

4 rue de la Savonnerie, 76000 **Tel** *02 35 71 87 73* **Fax** *02 35 89 31 52* **Rooms** *28*

This was the home of Bishop Cauchon, Joan of Arc's accuser, until his death in 1442. This hotel located between the cathedral and the Seine has spacious rooms decorated in contemporary colours. The staff are friendly. Good buffet breakfast. Choice of restaurants nearby. **www.hotel-notre-dame.fr**

ROUEN Le Vieux Carré €

34 rue Ganterie, 76000 **Tel** *02 35 71 67 70* **Fax** *02 35 71 19 17* **Rooms** *13*

City-centre hotel near the Musée des Beaux Arts and a short walk from the cathedral. This charming timbered 18th-century building hides prettily decorated, intimate guest rooms. Cosy atmosphere and attentive service. There is a shaded cobbled courtyard and tearoom. **www.vieux-carre.fr**

SAINT-LO Hôtel Mercure 🈵 🅿 🍴 🏃 €

5-7 av de Briovère, 50000 **Tel** *02 33 05 08 63* **Fax** *02 33 05 15 15* **Rooms** *67*

Opposite the town's ramparts, this modern hotel has comfortable and well-proportioned guest rooms; newly renovated, attractive, quiet. The restaurant "Le Tocqueville" is in a large room with lovely views of the Vire river. Regional specialities. Cosy bar. **www.mercure.com**

ST-PATERNE Château de St-Paterne 🅿 🍴 ≋ 🏃 €€€

Le Château, 72610 **Tel** *02 33 27 54 71* **Fax** *02 33 29 16 71* **Rooms** *8*

Henry IV's 15th-century love-nest is set in a private park just on the outskirts of Alençon. This is not so much a hotel as a family château, where a fixed menu is served *en famille* to guests in the candlelit dining room. Magnificent rooms with stately furnishings. **www.chateau-saintpaterne.com**

ST-VAAST-LA-HOUGUE Hôtel de France 🅿 🍴 🏃 €

20 rue de Maréchal Foch, 50550 **Tel** *02 33 54 42 26* **Fax** *02 33 43 46 79* **Rooms** *34*

A lovely country house hotel near the fishing harbour of St-Vaast, renowned for its oysters. Country-style cosy rooms, most overlooking the exotic garden. The restaurant "Des Fuchsias" is set in a conservatory and serves delicious warm oyster dishes. Good buffet breakfast, too. **www.france-fuchsias.com**

SAINT-VALERY-EN-CAUX Les Hêtres 🅿 🍴 €€

Rue des Fleurs, 76460 **Tel** *02 35 57 09 30* **Fax** *02 35 57 09 31* **Rooms** *4*

A typical Norman-style timbered 1627 house set in the Caux countryside between Fécamp and Dieppe. Guest rooms are luxurious, spacious and individually decorated with modern furnishings. First-floor rooms have views of the garden. Innovative cuisine in the restaurant. **www.leshetres.com**

VERNON Hôtel d'Evreux ⬛🟦🟫 €

11 pl d'Evreux, 27200 **Tel** *02 32 21 16 12* **Fax** *02 32 21 32 73* **Rooms** *12*

This typical Norman building in the centre of Vernon, behind magnificent lime trees, is a former coaching inn now fully renovated with bright sunny rooms and old-fashioned furniture. The restaurant, with its giant fireplace, serves innovative traditional fare. Parking is available. **www.hoteldevreux.fr**

BRITTANY

AUDIERNE Le Goyen 🟦🟫 €

Pl Jean-Simon, 29770 **Tel** *02 98 70 08 88* **Fax** *02 98 70 18 77* **Rooms** *26*

Most of the bedrooms in this restored old building overlook the fishing port that supplies the hotel's superb restaurant. The old-fashioned decor is cosy, with frilly floral hangings and well-worn armchairs. The rooms, however, are comfortable and well equipped. Pay parking opposite. **www.le-goyen.com**

BENODET Armoric 🟦⬛🟦🟫 €

3 rue Penfoul, 29950 **Tel** *02 98 57 04 03* **Fax** *02 98 57 21 28* **Rooms** *30*

This classic hotel is set in private gardens close to the harbour, beach and casino. The rooms are elegantly furnished and spacious. A copious buffet is served at breakfast; at other times the restaurant serves succulent local seafood. **www.armoric-benodet.com**

BREST Hôtel de la Corniche ⬛🟦🟫 €

1 rue Amiral-Nicol, 29200 **Tel** *02 98 45 12 42* **Fax** *02 98 49 01 53* **Rooms** *16*

This modern hotel, built of local stone in the Breton style, is on the west side of the city near the naval base. It is conveniently located for walks along the scenic coastline. The rooms are simply furnished. The hotel restaurant offers a set evening menu four nights per week; reservations required. **www.hotel-la-corniche.com**

CARNAC Lann Roz ⬛🟦🟫 €

36 av de la Poste, 56340 **Tel** *02 97 52 10 48* **Fax** *02 97 52 24 36* **Rooms** *13*

A friendly hotel with a pretty garden ten minutes' walk from the beach. The rooms are fresh and bright, decorated in pale blues and pinks. The typical Breton dining room with oak beams and open fireplaces serves local specialities. There is a terrace and garden. **www.lannroz.com**

CHATEAUBOURG Pen'Roc 🟦⬛🟦🟫🟦 €€

La Penière en St Didier, 35221 **Tel** *02 99 00 33 02* **Fax** *02 99 62 30 89* **Rooms** *29*

A short drive from Rennes, this family hotel is located in the Vitré countryside. Originally an old Breton farmhouse, the rooms are modern and there are excellent facilities, including sauna, *hammam* (Turkish bath) and jacuzzi. Regional dishes served in the restaurant. **www.penroc.fr**

DINAN Moulin de la Fontaine des Eaux ⬛ €

Vallée de la Fontaine des Eaux, 22100 **Tel** *02 96 87 92 09* **Fax** *02 96 87 92 09* **Rooms** *5*

Set in a wooded valley 5 minutes from the port of Dinan, this converted 18th-century watermill overlooks its own lake and grounds. This is a *chambre d'hôte* only; there is no restaurant, but breakfast is provided. Simply furnished rooms, with disabled access. Private parking. **www.dinanbandb.com**

DINARD Hôtel Printania 🟦🟫 €

5 av Georges V, 35801 **Tel** *02 99 46 13 07* **Fax** *02 99 46 28 32* **Rooms** *57*

This friendly family-run hotel is decorated in typical Breton style with ornate box beds, Quimper faience and carved wooden furniture. Located near the beach, there are fine sea views. The restaurant specializes in seafood and fish, served by staff in traditional costume. **www.printaniahotel.com**

DOL DE BRETAGNE Domaine des Ormes 🟦⬛🟦🟦🟫🟦 €

35120 **Tel** *02 99 73 53 00* **Fax** *02 99 73 53 55* **Rooms** *45*

This is part of a privately owned holiday resort with an 18-hole golf course, aquaparc, horse-riding school and adventure park. The guest rooms are charming – there are even 18 cosy tree-houses with rooms, accessible by rope ladder! The restaurant serves classic French food. **www.lesormes.com**

FOUESNANT Mona Lisa à Cap Coz 🟦⬛🟫 €

Plage de Cap Coz, 29170 **Tel** *02 98 51 18 10* **Fax** *02 98 56 03 40* **Rooms** *51*

Only minutes from Concarneau, this seafront hotel has direct access to the beach. The rooms are bright and cheerful, decorated in a nautical style with polished wood. Most have balconies with a sea view, and there are some family rooms. **www.monalisahotels.com**

ILE DE GROIX Hôtel de la Marine 🟦🟫 €€

7 rue du Général de Gaulle, 56590 **Tel** *02 97 86 80 05* **Fax** *02 97 86 56 37* **Rooms** *22*

Expect a warm welcome at this hotel in the middle of the beautiful island of Groix. This relaxing hideaway has charming guest rooms, which overlook either the sea or the garden terrace. At the restaurant, great care is taken in the preparation of fine fish dishes. **www.hoteldelamarine.com**

Key to Price Guide *see p550* **Key to Symbols** *see back cover flap*

LE CONQUET La Pointe Ste Barbe 🗖 🅿 🍴 🏃 €€

Pointe Ste Barbe, 29217 **Tel** *02 98 89 00 26* **Fax** *02 98 89 14 81* **Rooms** *49*

Near Brest at the northwest tip of Brittany, this hotel overlooks the port. The modern rooms are large and comfortable, some with an ocean view. There is direct access to the beach and cruises to Ouessant island. Parking available. The restaurant specializes in fish and seafood. **www.hotelpointesaintebarbe.com**

LOCQUIREC Le Grand Hôtel des Bains 🗖 🅿 🍴 🏊 🍴 €€€€

15 rue de L'Eglise, 29241 **Tel** *02 98 67 41 02* **Fax** *02 98 67 44 60* **Rooms** *36*

Convenient for visiting the Armorique Regional Park, this Belle Epoque spa hotel has gardens that lead to a sandy beach. Rooms have stylish contemporary furnishings, most with balconies. Beauty and health treatments are available. Restaurant open evenings only. The chef uses fresh, local produce. **www.grand-hotel-des-bains.com**

MORLAIX Hôtel de l'Europe 🗖 🍴 €

1 rue d'Aiguillon, 29600 **Tel** *02 98 62 11 99* **Fax** *02 98 88 83 38* **Rooms** *60*

This Second Empire hotel, located in the city centre, has an elegant and richly decorated interior. The guest rooms are well equipped and soundproofed. Each room is different, from traditional to modern. Service is attentive. Buffet breakfast. The brasserie is good value. **www.hotel-europe-com.fr**

PAIMPOL Repaire de Kerroc'h 🗖 🅿 🍴 €

29 quai Morand, 22500 **Tel** *02 96 20 50 13* **Fax** *02 96 22 07 46* **Rooms** *13*

This former 18th-century home of a wealthy pirate, near the port, has pleasant rooms, some with views. The guest rooms are cosy, many with parquet flooring. Drinks can be taken around a roaring fire in winter, or on the pretty terrace in summer. Fish specialities in the restaurant.

PENESTIN SUR MER Hôtel Loscolo 🅿 🍴 €€

La Pointe de Loscolo, 56760 **Tel** *02 99 90 31 90* **Fax** *02 99 90 32 14* **Rooms** *12*

A traditional building with slate roof, on a cape with magnificent sea views to both sides and good walking nearby. The rooms are comfortable; some have a private terrace. The breakfast is copious; half-board rates are good value. The restaurant serves rich cuisine. **www.hotelloscolo.com**

PLEVEN Manoir du Vaumadeuc 🅿 🏃 €€€

Le Vaumadeuc, 22130 **Tel** *02 96 84 46 17* **Fax** *02 96 84 40 16* **Rooms** *13*

This grand old manor house nestles in the Fôret de la Hunaudaye. The building dates from the 15th century, and inside the magnificent granite staircase leads you to the first-floor guest rooms. The wooded park around it has a beautiful rose garden and lake. Heliport and parking. **www.vaumadeuc.com**

QUIBERON Hôtel Bellevue 🅿 🍴 🏊 🏃 €€€

Rue de Tiviec, 56173 **Tel** *02 97 50 16 28* **Fax** *02 97 30 44 34* **Rooms** *38*

Located near the seafront, casino and thalassotherapy centre, this modern hotel forms an L-shape around the heated swimming pool. The guest rooms are comfortable; the restaurant is airy and bright. Poolside buffet breakfast or Continental breakfast in your room. Demi-*pension* only. Private parking. **www.bellevuequiberon.com**

QUIMPER Hôtel Gradlon 🅿 🏃 €€

30 rue de Brest, 29000 **Tel** *02 98 95 04 39* **Fax** *02 98 95 61 25* **Rooms** *20*

Just two minutes' walk from the historic city centre, this hotel has charming, peaceful rooms – a few overlooking the enclosed flower garden and fountain. Some disabled access. Continental breakfast is served on the pretty veranda. Cosy salon bar with open fire. **www.hotel-gradlon.com**

RENNES Le Coq-Gadby 🗖 🅿 🍴 🏃 €€€

156 rue d'Antrain, 35700 **Tel** *02 99 38 05 55* **Fax** *02 99 38 53 40* **Rooms** *11*

An elegant 17th-century building just 5 minutes' drive from the city centre. Calm and intimate with classic period furnishings, polished parquet floors and ornate mirrors. The guest rooms "Olympe", "Louis XV", "Louis XVI" and "Anglaise" are vast and elegant. Spa and sauna next door to hotel. **www.lecoq-gadby.fr**

ROSCOFF Hôtel Bellevue 🏃 €

Bd Ste Barbe, 29681 **Tel** *02 98 61 23 38* **Fax** *02 98 61 11 80* **Rooms** *18*

This old Breton house, just a few minutes from the ferry terminal, enjoys fine views of the sea and old port. The guest rooms are a little cramped, but bright and quiet. At the back of the building is a pleasant patio garden where Continental breakfast is served on warm days.

ST MALO Hôtel Elizabeth 🅿 🏃 €€€

2 rue des Cordiers, 35400 **Tel** *02 99 56 24 98* **Fax** *02 99 56 39 24* **Rooms** *17*

This hotel is located within the ramparts of the old town, just 2 minutes' drive from the ferry terminal. The building has a 16th-century stone façade. The interior is classic in style, if a little sombre. Rooms are comfortable and well equipped. Friendly owners, and private garage. **www.st-malo-hotel-elizabeth.com**

ST THEGONNEC Ars Presbital Coz 🅿 🍴 €

18 rue de Gividic, 29410 **Tel** *02 98 79 45 62* **Fax** *02 98 79 48 47* **Rooms** *6*

Rustic, comfortable bed and breakfast. This 18th-century building, once a presbytery, has six spacious guest rooms. No television. Breakfast can be taken outside on the terrace. Mme Prigent, the owner, will prepare a three-course dinner if you reserve before midday. Large garden with parking.

VANNES Hôtel La Marébaudière
🔲 P 🔧   €€

4 rue Aristide Briand, 56000 **Tel** *02 97 47 34 29* **Fax** *02 97 54 14 11* **Rooms** *41*

A stylish hotel conveniently situated a short walk from the beautifully preserved old walled town. Quiet bedrooms overlook the garden. Buffet breakfast served in the dining room, or Continental breakfast brought to you by room service. Private parking. Wide choice of restaurants nearby. **www.marebaudiere.com**

THE LOIRE VALLEY

AMBOISE Le Choiseul
P 🍴 ≋ 🔧 ▤   €€€

36 quai Charles-Guinot, 37400 **Tel** *02 47 30 45 45* **Fax** *02 47 30 46 10* **Rooms** *32*

An ivy-covered 18th-century manor house set in elegant grounds, with views of the Loire. The comfortably sized guest rooms are tastefully decorated. The airy restaurant serves sophisticated cuisine. There are pretty flower-filled walks and tennis courts. **www.le-choiseul.com**

ANGERS Hôtel Mail
P   €

8 rue des Ursules, 49100 **Tel** *02 41 25 05 25* **Fax** *02 41 86 91 20* **Rooms** *26*

A charming hotel in a quiet corner of the city centre, this 17th-century building was once part of a convent. The bedrooms are tastefully decorated. A particularly good breakfast is served in the dining room. There is also a shaded courtyard with tables. Friendly owners. **www.hotel-du-mail.com**

ANGERS Hôtel Anjou
🔲 P 🍴 🔧 ▤   €€

1 bd de Maréchal Foch, 49100 **Tel** *02 41 21 12 11* **Fax** *02 41 87 22 21* **Rooms** *53*

The interior of this city-centre hotel has eclectic decoration, with Art Deco mosaics, 17th- and 18th-century fixtures, ornate ceilings and stained-glass windows. The rooms are spacious and elegantly furnished. 'Le Salamandre' restaurant is recommended. Parking available. **www.hotelanjou.fr**

AZAY LE RIDEAU La Petite Loge
P 🔧   €

15 route de Tours, 37190 **Tel** *02 47 45 26 05* **Rooms** *5*

Not your typical hotel, this is a house on a small side street that offers accommodation. There are five rooms, each with its own entrance and bathroom. Breakfast is served in the dining room, and guests have use of a kitchen and outdoor barbecue area.

AZAY LE RIDEAU Manoir de la Rémonière
P ≋ 🔧   €€

La Chapelle St Blaise, 37190 **Tel** *02 47 45 24 88* **Fax** *02 47 45 45 69* **Rooms** *9*

This 15th-century manor house in romantic grounds faces the château at Azay le Rideau. The guest rooms are spacious; some traditional, others modern. The interior has been beautifully restored. Outdoor activities include hot-air ballooning, archery and fishing. Perfect for children. **www.manoirdelaremoniere.com**

BEAUGENCY Hôtel de la Sologne
P 🔧   €

6 pl St Firmin, 45190 **Tel** *02 38 44 50 27* **Fax** *02 38 44 90 19* **Rooms** *16*

This typical Sologne stone building on the main square overlooks the ruined castle keep of St Firmin. The bedrooms are small, but cosy and bright, simply furnished. There is a pretty flower-decked patio where breakfast can be taken. Private parking available. **www.hoteldelasologne.com**

BOURGES Le Bourbon
🔲 P 🍴 🔧 ▤   €€€

Bd République, 18000 **Tel** *02 48 70 70 00* **Fax** *02 48 70 21 22* **Rooms** *60*

An ancient 17th-century abbey building in the centre of Bourges now houses this comfortable hotel. The bright spacious rooms are furnished in a modern, elegant style. Impressive salon bar and gastronomic restaurant in the former chapel St Ambroix. Parking available. **www.hoteldebourbon.fr**

CHAMPIGNE Château des Briottières
P 🍴 ≋ 🔧   €€€€

Rte Marigné, 49330 **Tel** *02 41 42 00 02* **Fax** *02 41 42 01 55* **Rooms** *10*

Family-run 18th-century château set in the 50-hectare park à l'Anglaise. The rooms have luxurious furnishings with canopied beds and rich fabrics. There is also a charming cottage with double rooms for families. Romantic dinners as well as cooking classes are on offer; reservations required. **www.briottieres.com**

CHARTRES Le Grand Monarque
P 🍴 🔲   €€

22 place des Epars, 28005 **Tel** *02 37 18 15 15* **Fax** *02 37 36 34 18* **Rooms** *50*

This converted 16th-century staging post, with massively thick stone walls, has been managed by the same family since the 1960s; part of the Best Western network. The rooms are simple. There is a pleasant bistro, and a gastronomic restaurant, "Le Georges". **www.bw-grand-monarque.com**

CHÊNEHUTTE-LES-TUFFEAUX Le Prieuré
P 🍴 ≋ 🔧   €€€€

Le Prieuré, 49350 **Tel** *02 41 67 90 14* **Fax** *02 41 67 92 24* **Rooms** *36*

This former priory, dating from the 12th century, has magnificent views over the Loire. The bedrooms have a romantic, refined decor, two with fireplaces. The elegant restaurant serves gourmet cuisine with the best regional produce, like pike-perch with red Champigny wine sauce. **www.prieure.com**

Key to Price Guide *see p550* **Key to Symbols** *see back cover flap*

CHENONCEAUX Hostel du Roy
P ⛏ ☂ €

9 rue du Dr Bretonneau, 37150 **Tel** *02 47 23 90 17* **Fax** *02 47 23 89 81* **Rooms** *32*

A sprawling hotel-restaurant, with a 16th-century fireplace and a dining room hung with hunting trophies. The well-equipped rooms are simple and appealing, and the atmosphere relaxing. There is a garden and pretty terrace. The restaurant serves classic dishes, including game in season. **www.hostelduroy.com**

CHENONCEAUX Hôtel du Bon Laboureur
P ⛏ ≋ ☂ ▤ €€

6 rue de Dr Bretonneau, 37150 **Tel** *02 47 23 90 02* **Fax** *02 47 23 82 01* **Rooms** *25*

Near the famous château, this inn is set in its own park. The bedrooms are located in the collection of 18th-century stone dwellings. They are small but well equipped and have designer bathrooms. Some are suitable for disabled guests. The oak-beamed restaurant is good. **www.bonlaboureur.com**

CHINON Hostellerie Gargantua
P ⛏ €

73 rue Voltaire, 37500 **Tel** *02 47 93 04 71* **Fax** *02 47 93 08 02* **Rooms** *8*

This hotel, in the ancient Palais du Boulliage with its pointed roof and turret, is a local landmark. The guest rooms are comfortable, if cramped. Each has a theme, from Jeanne d'Arc and Richelieu to the Empire period. Pleasant dining room and terrace. Modern and classic cuisine. **www.hotel-gargantua.com**

CHINON Hôtel Diderot
€

4 rue Buffon, 37500 **Tel** *02 47 93 18 87* **Fax** *02 47 93 37 10* **Rooms** *27*

The palm and olive trees that grow around the 18th-century building testify to the mild climate. This elegant creeper-clad hotel is found on a quiet street near Chinon city centre. The rooms are calm, simple and well-maintained. Breakfast served in a rustic dining room. Free municipal parking nearby. **www.hoteldiderot.com**

CHINON Château de Marçay
⬚ P ⛏ ≋ ☂ ▤ €€€€

Le Château, 37500 **Tel** *02 47 93 03 47* **Fax** *02 47 93 45 33* **Rooms** *34*

Elegant hotel in this restored 15th-century fortified château. Enjoy the lovely views over the surrounding parkland and vineyards from the well-appointed bedrooms. Refined and aristocratic atmosphere, impeccable service and cuisine. **www.chateaudemarcay.com**

CHOUZE SUR LOIRE Château des Réaux
P ☂ €€€

Le Port-Boulet, 37140 **Tel** *02 47 95 14 40* **Fax** *02 47 95 18 34* **Rooms** *10*

A lovingly restored brick and stone Renaissance château with fairy-tale turrets. The comfortable guest rooms are old-fashioned, with floral hangings and wallpaper. The owners are friendly and enjoy showing visitors around the property. Stroll and admire the park, or play tennis.

COUR-CHEVERNY Hôtels des Trois Marchands
P ⛏ €

Pl de l'Eglise, 41700 **Tel** *02 54 79 96 44* **Fax** *02 54 79 25 60* **Rooms** *24*

Just a kilometer (0.6 mile) from the château, this ancient coaching inn with a garden has been in the same family since 1865. The bedrooms are comfortably furnished in a rustic style. Take breakfast in one of the three Louis XIII dining rooms. Excellent restaurant. Parking available. **www.hoteldes3marchands.com**

FONTEVRAUD-L'ABBAYE Le Prieuré St-Lazare
⬚ P ⛏ ☂ €€

38 rte St Jean de l'Habit, 49590 **Tel** *02 41 51 73 16* **Fax** *02 41 51 75 50* **Rooms** *52*

The surroundings of this hotel, housed in the former St Lazare priory within the famous royal abbey complex, are stunning. The rooms are elegantly decorated in a modern, contemporary style. The restaurant, in the ancient cloister, is a gourmet's delight. ● mid-Nov–Mar. **www.hotelfp-fontevraud.com**

GENNES Aux Naulets d'Anjou
P ⛏ ≋ ☂ €

18 rue Croix de la Mission, 49350 **Tel** *02 41 51 81 88* **Fax** *02 41 38 00 78* **Rooms** *19*

At the edge of the village in private grounds, this hotel is quiet and comfortable. The warm welcome compensates for the lack of architectural interest. The rooms are simple and bright. The restaurant serves traditional cuisine with no frills. Reading room and lounge. **www.hotel-lesnauletsdanjou.com**

GIEN La Poularde
⛏ €

13 quai de Nice, 45500 **Tel** *02 38 67 36 05* **Fax** *02 38 38 18 78* **Rooms** *9*

On the banks of the river Loire, just steps away from the Musée de la Faïencerie, this hotel is functional and somewhat lacking in charm. The 19th-century bourgeois house has pleasant rooms simply furnished with Louis-Philippe furniture. The restaurant serves excellent food.

LA CHARTRE SUR LE LOIR Hôtel de France
P ⛏ ≋ ☂ €

20 pl de la République, 72340 **Tel** *02 43 44 40 16* **Fax** *02 43 79 62 20* **Rooms** *24*

This ivy-clad hotel in the city centre has a delightful garden bordering the river. Good value standard-sized bedrooms. Simply furnished, but comfortable. The bar and the brasserie are basic, but the dining room is pleasant. Generous portions of good food. Pretty garden terrace. ● Jan–mid-Mar.

LE CROISIC Fort de l'Océan
P ⛏ ≋ ☂ ▤ €€€€

Pointe du Croisic, 44490 **Tel** *02 40 15 77 77* **Fax** *02 40 15 77 80* **Rooms** *9*

A Vauban construction, 17th-century ramparts enclose this former fortress facing the sea. Nothing remains of the harsh military lifestyle. Comfort is key, and the guest rooms are stylish and comfortable, some equipped for disabled visitors. The restaurant serves wonderful seafood. **www.hotelfortocean.com**

LE MANS Ibis Centre

Quai Ledru-Rollin, 72000 **Tel** *02 43 23 18 23* **Fax** *02 43 24 00 72* **Rooms** *85*

This standard Ibis hotel is pleasantly situated overlooking the river Sarthe and the old quarter. This is the best budget hotel in Le Mans, with simple, well-equipped rooms (some with disabled access) and a good buffet breakfast. Parking is available. The restaurant serves dinner. **www.ibishotel.com**

LOCHES Hôtel de France

6 rue Picois, 37600 **Tel** *02 47 59 00 32* **Fax** *02 47 59 28 66* **Rooms** *19*

In an elegant former staging post built of local tuffeau stone with a traditional slate roof, this hotel is situated near the historic medieval gate. The rooms are simply furnished, comfortable and well maintained. Restaurant serves good regional dishes such as home-smoked salmon.

LUYNES Domaine de Beauvois

Route de Cléré-les-Pins, 37230 **Tel** *02 47 55 50 11* **Fax** *02 47 55 59 62* **Rooms** *36*

This Renaissance manor house built around a 15th-century tower overlooks its own lake. The park is so vast that the pathways are signposted. Rooms are large and comfortable, with luxurious marble bathrooms. Enjoy a candlelit dinner in the acclaimed restaurant. **www.grandesetapes.fr**

MONTBAZON Château d'Artigny

Route de Monts, 37250 **Tel** *02 47 34 30 30* **Fax** *02 47 34 30 39* **Rooms** *65*

This 20th-century château has grounds overlooking the River Indre. The grandiose classical exterior is matched by a formal Empire-style interior. The Baroque-style guest rooms are sumptuous. The splendid rotunda restaurant serves gourmet regional specialities. Superb wine list. **www.grandesetapes.fr**

MONTLOUIS SUR LOIRE Château de la Bourdaisière

25 rue de la Bourdaisière, 37270 **Tel** *02 47 45 16 31* **Fax** *02 47 45 09 11* **Rooms** *20*

A magnificent château refurbished as luxury accommodation. Gabrielle d'Estrées, mistress of Henri IV, was born here in 1565. Some of the elegant, luxurious guest rooms have period furniture. The pavilion in the grounds houses six bedrooms. The gardens are open to the public. **www.chateaulabourdaisiere.com**

MONTREUIL-BELLAY Relais du Bellay

96 rue Nationale, 49260 **Tel** *02 41 53 10 10* **Fax** *02 41 52 45 17* **Rooms** *42*

The 17th-century main building and stylishly furnished annex house the guest rooms. All are calm and quiet, some with disabled access. Heated pool, sauna, Turkish bath, jacuzzi and gym available. The Splendid hotel, which shares the hotel grounds, has a restaurant. **www.splendid-hotel.fr**

MUIDES SUR LOIRE Château de Colliers

41500 **Tel** *02 54 87 50 75* **Fax** *02 54 87 03 64* **Rooms** *5*

This château, a short drive east of Blois in the woods, is both rustic and grand. In the 18th century it belonged to a governor of Louisiana. There is a delightfully romantic room, at the top of the building, with Empire period furniture and a roof terrace. Dinner is by reservation only. **www.bienvenuauchateau.com**

NANTES Amiral

26 bis rue Scribe, 44000 **Tel** *02 40 69 20 21* **Fax** *02 40 73 98 13* **Rooms** *49*

Cinemas, theatre, restaurants and Passage Pommeraye are on the doorstep of this city centre hotel. The soundproofing in the bedrooms is good. The façade is modern and bright, and the guest rooms are fully equipped and comfortable. Continental breakfast. **www.hotel-nantes.fr**

NANTES Hôtel La Pérouse

3 allée Duquesne, 44000 **Tel** *02 40 89 75 00* **Fax** *02 40 89 76 00* **Rooms** *46*

Named after a French navigator, this chic hotel with its zen atmosphere opened in 1993. The rooms have glossy wooden flooring and crisp contempory furniture. Reasonably quiet. The breakfast buffet is good. Free access to nearby gym for guests. **www.hotel-laperouse.fr**

NANTES Jules Verne

3 rue de Couëdic, 44000 **Tel** *02 40 35 74 50* **Fax** *02 40 20 09 35* **Rooms** *65*

Part of the Best Western group, this modern hotel is functional rather than attractive. It stands in a busy pedestrian square in the city centre, well placed for visiting the sights. Reasonably sized comfortable rooms with satellite TV, some with disabled access. Good buffet breakfast. Parking for a fee.

NEURY EN CHAMPAGNE Château de la Renaudière

72240 **Tel** *02 43 20 71 09* **Fax** *02 43 20 75 56* **Rooms** *3*

A gracious château owned by the Marquis de Mascureau, set among rolling meadows between Le Mans and Laval. All the guest rooms have private bathrooms, and are tastefully furnished with period furniture. The charming owners enjoy introducing visitors to the region.

NOIRMOUTIER EN L'ILE Hotel Fleur de Sel

Rue des Saulniers, 85330 **Tel** *02 51 39 09 07* **Fax** *02 51 39 09 76* **Rooms** *35*

This hotel stands in the heart of a vast landscaped Mediterranean-style garden with a swimming pool. Some guest rooms are decorated with English-style pine and face the pool; others have a marine theme and private terrace. The chef serves the best cuisine in the Vendée. **www.fleurdesel.fr**

Key to Price Guide *see p550* **Key to Symbols** *see back cover flap*

ONZAIN Domaine des Hauts de Loire ⊞⊞≋★⋔⊟ €€€€
Route d'Herbault, 41150 **Tel** *02 54 20 72 57* **Fax** *02 54 20 77 32* **Rooms** *32*

This former hunting lodge with large grounds retains its grandeur, with richly furnished, bright, comfortable guest rooms. This is an unashamedly expensive place to relax. The chef prepares cutting-edge and classic food, served with superb local wines. There is a tennis court. **www.domainehautsdeloire.com**

ORLEANS Jackotel ⊞⊞ €
18 Cloître St-Aignan, 45000 **Tel** *02 38 54 48 48* **Fax** *02 38 77 17 59* **Rooms** *61*

This small hotel stands in the medieval centre of Orléans, near the cathedral, surrounded by a good choice of restaurants. A former cloister, its charming inner courtyard leads you to the place St-Aignan just in front of the church. Very comfortable rooms, although dated. Parking too. **www.jackotel.com**

ROCHECORBON Domaine des Hautes Roches ⊞⊞⊞≋★ €€€€
86 quai de la Loire, 37210 **Tel** *02 47 52 88 88* **Fax** *02 47 52 81 30* **Rooms** *15*

Surrounded by Vouvray vineyards, near Tours, this was once a monks' residence. Fully restored, it has all modern comforts. The underground rooms, hewn into the tuffeau chalk in this 'troglodyte' hotel, are spacious and characterful. Dine in the château, or on the terrace. **www.leshautesroches.com**

ROMORANTIN-LANTHENAY Grand Hôtel du Lion d'Or ⊞⊞⊞⊟ €€€€
69 rue Georges Clémenceau, 41200 **Tel** *02 54 94 15 15* **Fax** *02 54 88 24 87* **Rooms** *16*

This former Renaissance mansion house is now a gastronomic halt in an historic town. From the outside the building is unimpressive, but the interior has instant charm. The luxury bedrooms lead off from a cobbled courtyard. The decor is authentic Napoléon III. Formal gardens. **www.hotel-liondor.fr**

SALBRIS Le Parc ⊞⊞★ €€
8 av d'Orléans, 41300 **Tel** *02 54 97 18 53* **Fax** *02 54 97 24 34* **Rooms** *23*

Large beautiful house set in its own park with 100-year-old trees. Classic or modern, the bedrooms are comfortable and calm. Features include high ceilings, fireplaces and period furniture. Some rooms have private balconies that overlook the magnificent grounds. **www.leparcsalbris.com**

SAUMUR La Croix de la Voulte ⊞≋ €
Route de Boumois, 49400 **Tel** *02 41 38 46 66* **Fax** *02 41 38 46 66* **Rooms** *4*

This manor house, outside Saumur, dates from the 15th century. Built at a crossroads or *croix*, it was the turning point for the royal huntsmen. The bedrooms are all different, two with original Louis XIV fireplaces, and classic furnishings. Breakfast served at poolside in fine weather. **www.lacroixdelavoulte.com**

SAUMUR Hôtel Anne d'Anjou ⊞⊞★ €€
32-34 quai Mayaud, 49400 **Tel** *02 41 67 30 30* **Fax** *02 41 67 51 00* **Rooms** *45*

The decor in this elegant mansion, sitting between the river Loire and the château, is sophisticated and romantic. This fine building with its impressive façade, grand staircase and painted ceiling has guest rooms decorated in Empire or contemporary style. Breakfast in the courtyard. **www.hotel-anneanjou.com**

SILLE-LE-GUILLAUME Relais des Etangs de Guibert ⊞⊞ €
Neufchâtel-en-Saosnois, 72600 **Tel** *02 43 97 15 38* **Fax** *02 43 33 22 99* **Rooms** *15*

North of Le Mans, this beautiful stone-built country house is situated at the edge of the forest in a charming and romantic setting, with a turret overlooking the flower-filled grounds and lake. Individually decorated rooms in warm tones, some with original beamed ceilings. Friendly.

SOUVIGNY-EN-SOLOGNE Ferme des Foucault ⊞ €
Ménestreau-en-Villette, 45240 **Tel** *02 38 76 94 41* **Fax** *02 38 76 94 41* **Rooms** *3*

Deep in the forest in the Sologne countryside is this attractive redbrick and timber farmhouse. The immense bedrooms are cosy, with superb bathrooms. One even has a fireplace. The other rooms are decorated with paintings by the owner's daughter. Friendly, relaxed atmosphere. **www.ferme-des-foucault.com**

ST LAURENT NOUAN Hôtel Le Verger ⊞★ €
14 rue du Port-Pichard, 41220 **Tel** *02 54 87 22 22* **Fax** *02 54 87 22 82* **Rooms** *14*

Ideally placed for visiting the famous Loire châteaux, and only 8 km (5 miles) from Chambord, this 19th-century bourgeois house has an interior courtyard and fountain. The rooms are well maintained, spacious and calm. The wooded park ensures a peaceful stay. **www.hotel-le-verger.com**

ST NAZAIRE Au Bon Acceuil ⊞★ €€
39 rue Marceau, 44600 **Tel** *02 40 22 07 05* **Fax** *02 40 19 01 58* **Rooms** *17*

This enchanting hotel in a peaceful corner of the city centre had the fortune to escape the destruction of World War II. The guest rooms are simple, modern and functional. The dining room is a little gloomy, but serves good seafood. Friendly and welcoming atmosphere. **www.au-bon-accueil44.com**

ST PATRICE Château de Rochecotte ⊞⊞⊞≋★ €€€€
St Patrice, Langeais, 37130 **Tel** *02 47 96 16 16* **Fax** *02 47 96 90 59* **Rooms** *35*

Situated a short way from Langeais, Prince Talleyrand's château was completely renovated and opened as an elegant hotel in 1986. It is set in a charming, tranquil 19-acre park and woodland. The guest rooms are large, each with a view. The interior is decorated sumptuously. **www.chateau-de-rochecotte.fr**

TOURS Hôtel de l'Univers
🔲🅿️🍴🗄 €€€€€

5 bd Heurteloup, 37000 **Tel** *02 47 05 37 12* **Fax** *02 47 61 51 80* **Rooms** *85*

Statesmen and royals have stayed at this luxurious hotel. A picture gallery depicts the famous guests since 1846. Elegant architecture, right in the city centre, with large prettily furnished bedrooms. The restaurant serves classic gourmet cuisine. Private garage. **www.hotel-univers.fr**

VITRY-AUX-LOGES Château de Plessis-Beauregard
🅿️⛲🎣 €€

Le Plessis, 45530 **Tel** *02 38 59 47 24* **Fax** *02 38 59 47 48* **Rooms** *3*

Located beside the Fôret d'Orléans, this turreted, brick château has light, airy rooms. The guest rooms, authentically furnished in the Empire style, overlook the flower-filled gardens. Chat with your hosts at breakfast, or in the evening around the fireplace. Bikes available. **www.chateaux-france.com/plessisbeauregard/**

VOUVRAY Château de Jallanges
🅿️🍴⛲🎣 €€€

9 Jallange, Vernou sur Brenne, 37210 **Tel** *02 47 52 06 66* **Fax** *02 47 52 11 18* **Rooms** *7*

An imposing Renaissance brick château, and now a family home, the comfortable guest rooms are furnished with style. Guests are taken on a guided tour from the private chapel to the top of the turrets from where there is a superb view. A good base for exploring Touraine. **www.jallanges.com**

BURGUNDY & FRANCHE-COMTE

ARBOIS Jean-Paul Jeanet
🔲🅿️🍴 €€

9 rue de l'Hôtel de Ville, 39600 **Tel** *03 84 66 05 67* **Fax** *03 84 66 24 20* **Rooms** *19*

In the centre of this picturesque town, Jeanet offers modern good amenities and comfort. This ancient convent houses this tastefully decorated, elegant hotel. Well-proportioned bedrooms, charming garden and attentive staff. The restaurant cuisine is impressive. **www.jeanpauljeunet.com**

ARC-ET-SENANS La Saline Royale
🅿️ €

Arc-et-Senans **Tel** *03 81 57 43 21* **Rooms** *31*

To stay in this World Heritage site and architectural museum is a unique experience combining comfortable, high-class dormitory accommodation with Louis XVI magnificence. The breathtaking salt works, an 18th-century masterpiece by Nicolas Ledoux, takes in guests but you must book well in advance. **www.salineroyale.com**

ARNAY-LE-DUC Chez Camille
🅿️🍴 €€

1 pl Edouard-Herriot, 21230 **Tel** *03 80 90 01 38* **Fax** *03 80 90 04 64* **Rooms** *13*

The former holiday residence of a Marechal de France, this attractive hotel offers spacious, comfortable rooms with double-glazing, a warm welcome and a peaceful atmosphere. Glass-covered interior courtyard and a modern dining room serving delicious food. **www.chez-camille.fr**

AUTUN Hôtel de la Tête Noire
🔲🅿️🍴🗄 €

3 rue Arquebuse, 71400 **Tel** *03 85 86 59 99* **Fax** *03 85 86 33 90* **Rooms** *31*

A simple, well-kept hotel. The modern, spacious, bright bedrooms are decorated in a rustic style with painted wooden furniture. Good sound-proofing. The restaurant serves classic dishes using local products. Professional, attentive service. **www.hoteltetenoire.fr**

AUXERRE Hôtel Normandie
🔲🅿️📺🗄 €

41 bd Vauban, 89000 **Tel** *03 86 52 57 80* **Fax** *03 86 51 54 33* **Rooms** *47*

Attractive ivy-clad 19th-century country house close to the centre of town. Charming, with modern amenities, the bedrooms are stylish and comfortable. The quietest rooms are found in the new wing. Cosy lounge bar and large outside terrace. Sauna available. Attentive service. **www.hotelnormandie.fr**

AVALLON Le Relais Fleuri
🅿️🍴⛲🎣📺🗄 €

La Cerce, 89200 **Tel** *03 86 34 02 85* **Fax** *03 86 34 09 98* **Rooms** *48*

Situated 6 km (4 miles) from the centre of this fortified town, this ancient staging post stands in its own grounds. The spacious, modern and comfortable bedrooms are found in the annexes, and open out on to either the garden or the pool. Good value traditional cuisine. **www.relais-fleuri.com**

BEAUNE Le Home
🅿️ €

138 route Dijon, 21200 **Tel** *03 80 22 16 43* **Fax** *03 80 24 90 74* **Rooms** *20*

Just outside town, set back from the main road, is this homely hotel in a charming garden. A former Burgundy farmhouse that Mme Jacquet and her daughter Mathilde have decorated in English style. Cosy, relaxing sitting rooms and comfortable bedrooms. Excellent wine cellar. **www.lehome.fr**

BEAUNE Hôtel Le Cep
🔲🅿️🗄 €€€

27 rue Maufoux, 21200 **Tel** *03 80 22 35 48* **Fax** *03 80 22 76 80* **Rooms** *62*

In the heart of the Old Town is this elegant hotel, renovated in a Renaissance style. Legend has it that Louis XIV preferred to stay here rather than at the hospice. The rooms, some with Baroque decor, are ornately furnished with antiques. Each is named after local wine. **www.hotel-cep-beaune.com**

Key to Price Guide *see p550* **Key to Symbols** *see back cover flap*

BELFORT Grand Hôtel du Tonneau d'Or

€€

1 rue Reiset, 90000 **Tel** *03 84 58 57 56* **Fax** *03 84 58 57 50* **Rooms** *52*

Centrally located near citadel, this hotel has majestic Haussmann architecture, with intricate wrought-iron work on the balconies. Inside, the reception area is equally impressive. The bedrooms are modern; some are non-smoking. Good food at the Art Deco-style brasserie. **www.tonneaudor.fr**

BOUILLAND Le Vieux Moulin

€€

Le Village, 21420 **Tel** *03 80 21 51 16* **Fax** *03 80 21 59 90* **Rooms** *26*

A recently renovated watermill set in the Rhône valley in this spectacular Burgundy village. Modern, comfortable rooms with simple, stylish furnishings. Views of either the river or the surrounding countryside. Sauna, jacuzzi and fitness centre. Renowned contemporary restaurant. **www.le-moulin-de-bouilland.com**

CHABLIS Hostellerie des Clos

€

Rue Jules-Rathier, 89800 **Tel** *03 86 42 10 63* **Fax** *03 86 42 17 11* **Rooms** *36*

The owner has renovated a medieval convent in the middle of this famed wine village. A charming atmosphere with bright, comfortable, modern rooms. One of the best restaurants in the region (Michelin-starred), with a wine list to match. Terrace overlooks a delightful garden and vineyards. **www.hostellerie-des-clos.fr**

CHAILLY-SUR-ARMANÇON Château de Chailly

€€€€€

Rue Dessous, 21320 **Tel** *03 80 90 30 30* **Fax** *03 80 90 30 00* **Rooms** *45*

One façade of this beautifully restored château is ornately Renaissance, while another recalls the building's medieval heritage. Luxury accommodation with spacious, meticulously maintained rooms. Facilities include a golf course, tennis, jacuzzi, Turkish bath and four eateries. **www.chailly.com**

CHATEAU CHINON Hôtel du Vieux Morvan

€

8 pl Gudin, 58120 **Tel** *03 86 85 05 01* **Fax** *03 86 85 02 78* **Rooms** *24*

It was here that François Mitterand learned that he had become President – for years he visited this hotel. The manageress has since retired, but the hotel retains its rustic old-world charm. Comfortable rooms and attentive service. The restaurant has a panoramic view. **www.auvieuxmorvan.com**

CLUNY Hostellerie de Bourgogne

€€

Pl de l'Abbaye, 71250 **Tel** *03 85 59 00 58* **Fax** *03 85 59 03 73* **Rooms** *16*

This old-fashioned stone-built auberge stands next to the magnificent Cluny abbey. The guest rooms have views of either the abbey or the garden. One is named Lamartine after the poet, who was a regular visitor. The restaurant serves excellent food and local Mâcon wines. **www.hotel-cluny.com**

DIJON Hostellerie le Sauvage

€

64 rue Monge, 21000 **Tel** *03 80 41 31 21* **Fax** *03 80 42 06 07* **Rooms** *22*

This attractive half-timbered hotel was a staging post in the 15th century. Located in the city centre near the historic sites, it can be noisy – the quietest rooms overlook a lovely interior cobbled courtyard, where meals can be taken in fine weather. Excellent service. Good breakfast. **www.hotellesauvage.com**

DIJON Le Jacquemart

€

32 rue Verrerie, 21000 **Tel** *03 80 60 09 60* **Fax** *03 80 60 09 69* **Rooms** *31*

In the heart of the city, near the Palais des Ducs, the Musée des Beaux Arts, and the lucky owl. An attractive 18th-century bourgeois house with decent-sized rooms and antique-style furniture. The decor is sombre, but characterful. Quiet and comfortable. Continental breakfast. **www.hotel-lejacquemart.fr**

DOLE la Chaumière

€

346 av du Maréchal-Juin, 39100 **Tel** *03 84 70 72 40* **Fax** *03 84 79 25 60* **Rooms** *19*

This ancient farmhouse, outside the city centre of the charming former capital of Comté, has authentic furniture that matches the ambience. Elegant and comfortable, well-maintained and soundproofed rooms ensure a tranquil night. Excellent restaurant with creative cuisine. **www.chateauxhotels.com**

FONTETTE Hôtel Crispol

€

St-Père-sous-Vézelay, 89450 **Tel** *03 86 33 26 25* **Fax** *03 86 33 33 10* **Rooms** *12*

The famous Vézelay hillside makes a magnificent backdrop to this well-planned modern hotel. Contemporary guest rooms are hung with paintings done by the owner-artist. Chic and luxurious atmosphere. The elegant restaurant with a panoramic view serves imaginative cooking. **www.crispol.com**

GEVREY-CHAMBERTIN Hôtel les Grands Crus

€€

Route des Grands Crus, 21220 **Tel** *03 80 34 34 15* **Fax** *03 80 51 89 07* **Rooms** *24*

A light, airy hotel with wonderful views over the grands crus vineyards. Located in the heart of the Côte de Nuits, this country house built in a typical Burgundian style has traditionally furnished rooms that overlook the garden. The comfy lounge centres around an open fireplace. **www.hoteldesgrandscrus.com**

JOIGNY Hôtel Rive Gauche

€

Chemin du Port au Bois, 89300 **Tel** *03 86 91 46 66* **Fax** *03 86 91 46 93* **Rooms** *42*

This modern hotel stands on the left bank of the river Yonne, with a view of the medieval town of Joigny opposite. The recently redecorated rooms are well equipped. The pleasantly situated dining room with a terrace faces the river and grounds. Efficient, professional service. **www.hotel-le-rive-gauche.fr**

LEVERNOIS Le Parc
Levernois, 212000 **Tel** *03 80 24 63 00* **Fax** *03 80 24 21 19* **Rooms** *17*   P   €

This hotel comprises two old vine-covered country houses set behind a wonderful wrought-iron gate. Centred around a large courtyard, and surrounded by parkland, this hotel provides a relaxing retreat. Old-fashioned style with quaint rooms. Pleasant lounge and dining room. **www.hotelleparc.fr**

LIGNY-LE-CHATEL Relais St-Vincent
14 Grand Rue, 89144 **Tel** *03 86 47 53 38* **Fax** *03 86 47 54 16* **Rooms** *15*   P ⏏ ⛷   €

Situated in the Yonne, not far from Auxerre, this 17th-century half-timbered house was once home to the bailiff of Ligny. Perfectly preserved charm with oak beams, the rooms are well equipped with modern comforts. The restaurant serves regional specialities.

MACON Hôtel Bellevue
416 quai Lamartine, 71000 **Tel** *03 85 21 04 04* **Fax** *03 85 21 04 02* **Rooms** *24*   P ⛷ ▤   €€

A 17th-century building with rooms overlooking the Saône river. Elegance pervades, with an impressive spiral staircase leading to the comfortable bedrooms. Richly furnished, well-maintained and very professional hotel. Board games are available for children. **www.ila-chateau.com/bellevue**

MAILLY LE CHATEAU Le Castel
13 rue Golf, 89660 **Tel** *03 86 81 43 06* **Fax** *03 86 81 49 26* **Rooms** *5*   P ⏏   €

In this fortified village, Le Castel offers comfortable, tranquil rooms. It is situated near the church in an attractive garden, from where you can see the Morvan hill. The rooms in this 18th-century manor house are furnished traditionally. Its *table d'hôte* serves Burgundy and French cuisine. **www.lecastelmailly.com**

MALBUISSON Hôtel Le Lac
31 Grand Rue, 25160 **Tel** *03 81 69 34 80* **Fax** *03 81 69 35 44* **Rooms** *54*   P ⏏ ⛷   €

Perched above the lake of St-Point in the Jura mountains, this imposing, elegant 1930s building has prettily decorated rooms, some with a lake view. The atmosphere is comfortable and pleasant, although service is abrupt – but that's normal for the region. Great buffet breakfast. **www.lelac-hotel.com**

NANTOUX Domaine de la Combotte
2 La Combotte, 21190 **Tel** *03 80 26 02 66* **Fax** *03 80 26 07 84* **Rooms** *6*   P ⛷ ⏏   €€

Near Beaune, this family-run wine estate offers *chambres d'hôte*. Large comfortable rooms, one with wheelchair access and one family room. Well-equipped, with modern decor. The owners delight in sharing their passion for wine and truffles. **www.lacombotte.com**

NUITS-ST-GEORGES Hôtel la Gentilhommière
13 vallée de la Serrée, 21700 **Tel** *03 80 61 12 06* **Fax** *03 80 61 30 33* **Rooms** *31*   P ⏏ ⛷ ▤ ▤   €€

This former 16th-century hunting lodge with its typical Burgundy tiled roof is now a beautiful hotel and renowned restaurant. The bedrooms are classically furnished, and the suites are decorated in styles from colonial to zen. Well-mastered cuisine. Terrace overlooks the river. **www.lagentilhommiere.fr**

POLIGNY Hostellerie des Monts de Vaux
Monts Vaux, 39800 **Tel** *03 84 37 12 50* **Fax** *03 84 37 09 07* **Rooms** *10*   P ⏏ ▤   €€€

Run by the Carrion family since 1967, this hotel occupies an elegant coaching inn on the outskirts of Poligny, in lovely gardens. The rooms are decorated in a bourgeois style with antique furniture. Refined atmosphere. Good Jura cuisine and wine in the restaurant. **www.hostellerie.com**

PORT-LESNEY Château de Germigney
Le Parc, 39600 **Tel** *03 84 73 85 85* **Fax** *03 84 73 88 88* **Rooms** *20*   P ⏏ ⛷ ▤   €€€€

This hotel is located just 6 km (4 miles) from Arc-et-Senans in its own grounds bordering the Loue river. This exquisite château has tastefully decorated rooms with modern facilities. Smaller, less expensive rooms are in the annex. Exceptional restaurant and natural water pool. Relaxed and unstuffy service. **www.chateaudegermigney.com**

PULIGNY-MONTRACHET Le Montrachet
Pl des Marroniers, 21190 **Tel** *03 80 21 30 06* **Fax** *03 80 21 39 06* **Rooms** *30*   P ⏏   €€

A quiet resting spot in the heart of Burgundy wine country. This elegant country house with converted coach house provides comfortable lodgings in a chic rustic environment. The gastronomic restaurant overlooks the tree-lined square of this wine village. Excellent wine list. **www.le-montrachet.com**

SAULIEU Le Relais Bernard Loiseau
2 rue d'Argentine, 21210 **Tel** *03 80 90 53 53* **Fax** *03 80 64 08 92* **Rooms** *33*   P ⏏ ⛷ ▤ ▤   €€€€€

A renowned hotel and acclaimed restaurant established by the late Bernard Loiseau. Modern comfort and traditional Burgundy furnishings – wooden panelled walls, red floor tiles. The refined rooms have either a fireplace, or balcony overlooking the gardens à l'Anglaise. Fine service. **www.bernard-loiseau.com**

SENS Hôtel Paris et de la Poste
97 rue de la République, 89100 **Tel** *03 86 65 17 43* **Fax** *03 86 64 48 45* **Rooms** *30*   P ⏏ ▤   €

In the heart of Sens near the cathedral St-Etienne, this traditional hotel has well-maintained rooms with rustic or modern decor. All rooms are spacious and comfortable, and some open on to an interior courtyard. Relaxed atmosphere. Regional dishes in the traditional restaurant. **www.hotel-paris-poste.com**

Key to Price Guide *see p550* **Key to Symbols** *see back cover flap*

ST-GERVAIS-EN-VALLIERE Moulin d'Hauterive ⊞⊞⊞⊞⊞ €

Hameau de Chaublanc, 71350 **Tel** *03 85 91 55 56* **Fax** *03 85 91 89 65* **Rooms** *20*

Not far from Beaune, in a secluded setting on the bank of the Dheune river, this converted watermill was built in the 12th century by the monks of Citeaux abbey. Each room is unique, tastefully furnished with antiques. The owner-chef serves inventive home-cooking. **www.moulinhauterive.com**

TOURNUS Château de Beaufer ⊞⊞ €€€

Route d'Ozenay, 71700 **Tel** *03 85 51 18 24* **Fax** *03 85 51 25 04* **Rooms** *6*

Choose between a room in the ivy-clad 18th-century turreted château or one in the annex. The bedrooms are classically furnished with ornately decorated bathrooms. Attractive grounds, and horseriding is available. Dinner can be arranged, *table d'hôte*, by reservation.

VEZELAY L'Espérance ⊞⊞⊞⊞⊞ €€€€

St-Père-sous-Vézelay, 89450 **Tel** *03 86 33 39 10* **Fax** *03 86 33 26 15* **Rooms** *30*

The guest rooms here are in three buildings: the main building has classic furnishings, Moulin has rustic charm, and Pré des Marguerites is contemporary, with terraces overlooking the garden. Wonderful restaurant, excellent but expensive wines, and impeccable service. **www.marc-meneau-esperance.com**

VONNAS Georges Blanc ⊞⊞⊞⊞⊞ €€€

Pl Marché, 01540 **Tel** *04 74 50 90 90* **Fax** *04 74 50 08 80* **Rooms** *48*

Sumptuous hotel-restaurant in an ancient timbered and brick mansion, surrounded by a garden. The luxurious rooms were decorated by Pierre Chaduc. The atmosphere sways between refinement and opulence; the decor mixes Louis XIII and rustic styles. Most bathrooms have jacuzzis. Spa with sauna. **www.georgesblanc.com**

THE MASSIF CENTRAL

AUBUSSON Hôtel de France ⊞⊞⊞ €€

6 rue des Déportés, 23200 **Tel** *05 55 66 10 22* **Fax** *05 55 66 88 64* **Rooms** *22*

In the centre of Aubusson, a town famous for its tapestries, is this smart inexpensive hotel in an elegant 18th-century mansion. Guest rooms have tapestries and pretty fabrics that complement the antique furniture. Facilities include an interior courtyard, bar and private garage. **www.laubussonlefrance.com**

BEAULIEU-SUR-DORDOGNE Les Charmilles ⊞ €

20, bd Saint Rodolphe de Turenne, 19120 **Tel** *05 55 91 29 29* **Fax** *05 55 91 29 30* **Rooms** *8*

This cheerful little hotel makes a perfect base for exploring the upper Dordogne valley. It's in a lovely, quiet spot near Beaulieu's Romanesque church, surrounded by greenery. Flower-filled terrace, sparkling rooms (named after local strawberries) and a decent restaurant. **www.auberge-charmilles.fr**

BEAUZAC L'Air du Temps ⊞⊞ €

Confolent, 43590 **Tel** *04 71 61 49 05* **Fax** *04 71 61 50 91* **Rooms** *8*

Mid-way between St-Etienne and Le-Puy-en-Velay lies this popular restaurant-with-rooms. The restaurant is the star attraction here, but the guest rooms are bright and fresh. The hotel is just east of Beauzac at the gateway to the Loire gorges.

BELCASTEL Du Vieux Pont ⊞⊞⊞ €€

Le Bourg, 12390 **Tel** *05 65 64 52 29* **Fax** *05 65 64 44 32* **Rooms** *7*

Being lulled to sleep by the murmuring of the river is just one of the attractions of this unpretentious hotel. Rooms are spacious, light and airy, and all have river views. Across the medieval cobbled bridge, the same family also run an imaginative but affordable restaurant. **www.hotelbelcastel.com**

BRIVE-LA-GAILLARDE La Truffe Noire ⊞⊞⊞⊞ €€

22 bd Anatole-France, 19100 **Tel** *05 55 92 45 00* **Fax** *05 55 92 45 13* **Rooms** *27*

Brive's grandest hotel has been welcoming guests since 1893. Despite its city-centre location, public areas retain the air of a hunting lodge, with baronial chimneys and oak panelling. Guest rooms are colourful with huge beds. Classic French fare in the restaurant. Parking available. **www.la-truffe-noire.com**

CALVINET Hôtel Beauséjour ⊞⊞⊞ €

Rte de Maurs, 15340 **Tel** *04 71 49 91 68* **Fax** *04 71 49 98 63* **Rooms** *10*

In a small village renowned for its traditional architecture, this restaurant-with-rooms occupies a restored farmhouse. Inside, however, the decor is resolutely modern, with uncluttered, pine-floored rooms and swish bathrooms. The restaurant serves equally distinctive cuisine. **www.cantal-restaurant-puech.com**

CHAMALIERES Hôtel Radio ⊞⊞⊞⊞ €€

43 av Pierre et Marie Curie, 63400 **Tel** *04 73 30 87 83* **Fax** *04 73 36 42 44* **Rooms** *25*

Built in the 1930s, this Art Deco hotel on a hill overlooking Clermont-Ferrand retains its original mosaics, mirrors and decorative ironwork, alongside radio memorabilia. Spacious rooms have period furnishings, some with balconies. First-class restaurant and attentive service. **www.hotel-radio.fr**

CLERMONT-FERRAND Le Petit Bonneval P ⅋ €

Av de la République, Pérignat-Lès-Sarliève 63170 **Tel** *04 73 79 11 11* **Fax** *04 73 79 19 98* **Rooms** *6*

A short distance southeast of Clermont, this is a traditional hotel with comfortable and recently renovated bedrooms. The decor is fresh, with cool tones, classic furnishings and well-equipped bathrooms. The restaurant serves gourmet Auvergne cuisine in the cosy dining room or on the shady terrace in summer.

COCURES La Lozerette P ⅋ €

Le Village, 48400 **Tel** *04 66 45 06 04* **Fax** *04 66 45 12 93* **Rooms** *21*

A country inn near Florac that's been in the same family for three generations, here you will find hospitality and hearty regional cuisine. The modernized guestrooms are big and airy. There's also a shady garden. Good base for National Parc des Cévennes and Stevenson trail. **www.lalozerette.com**

LAGUIOLE Relais de Laguiole P ⅋ €

Espace Les Cayres, 12210 **Tel** *05 65 54 19 66* **Fax** *05 65 54 19 49* **Rooms** *30*

Modern hotel with bright and breezy guest rooms, some with balcony or separate salon. Facilities include a heated indoor pool, spa and solarium, while children will enjoy the play area and big garden. The restaurant dishes up tasty local fare – don't miss the *aligot*. **www.relais-laguiole.com**

LIMOGES Hôtel de la Paix P €

25 pl Jourdan, 87000 **Tel** *05 55 34 36 00* **Fax** *05 55 32 37 06* **Rooms** *31*

Among the best-value accommodation in Limoges is this nicely old-fashioned hotel near the centre. It is well maintained and offers a good choice of rooms. Some have balconies and generous bathrooms. Old phonographs and mechanical musical instruments fill the lobby.

LIMOGES Hôtel Jeanne d'Arc P €

17 av du Général-de-Gaulle, 87000 **Tel** *05 55 77 67 77* **Fax** *05 55 79 86 75* **Rooms** *50*

A surprisingly atmospheric hotel near Limoges train station and within walking distance of the centre. The building has been tastefully renovated without losing its 19th-century feel. The rooms are stylish and equipped with all the three-star comforts you'd expect. **www.hoteljeannedarc-limoges.fr**

MILLAU Château de Creissels P ⅋ €

Rte de St-Afrique, 12100 **Tel** *05 65 60 16 59* **Fax** *05 65 61 24 63* **Rooms** *30*

A short distance from Millau is this 12th-century château with stunning views over the Tarn valley and the Millau viaduct. Rooms in the 1970s extension are comfortable and quiet, with balconies overlooking the gardens. Enjoy local dishes in the stone-vaulted restaurant. **www.chateau-de-creissels.com**

MOULINS Hôtel de Paris P €

21 rue de Paris, 03000 **Tel** *04 70 44 00 58* **Fax** *04 70 34 05 39* **Rooms** *27*

A convenient stopover at the gateway to the Massif Central, Moulin's top address lies in the historic centre close to the cathedral. Rooms are plush, if sometimes on the small side. The hotel has an up-and-coming restaurant, elegant bar and a garden. The service can't be faulted. **www.hoteldeparis-moulins.com**

MUR-DE-BARREZ Auberge du Barrez P ⅋ €

Av du Carladez, 12600 **Tel** *05 65 66 00 76* **Fax** *05 65 66 07 98* **Rooms** *18*

A welcoming, modern hotel in the heart of hiking country. Unfussy, slightly retro furnishings in the guest rooms, which are light and spacious; some open directly on to the garden. After a day in the hills, Christian Gaudel's award-winning cooking is a bonus. **www.aubergedubarrez.com**

PAILHEROLS Auberge des Montagnes P ⅋ €

Le Bourg, 15800 **Tel** *04 71 47 57 01* **Fax** *04 71 49 63 83* **Rooms** *23*

On the flanks of the Monts du Cantal, it's worth seeking out this cosy mountain auberge. In winter there are log fires; in summer head for the large garden with a children's play area. The restaurant attracts locals from miles around with its good-value country cooking. **www.auberge-des-montagnes.com**

PONTGIBAUD Hôtel Saluces P €

Rue de la Martille, 15140 **Tel** *04 71 40 70 82* **Fax** *04 71 40 71 74* **Rooms** *8*

Located in the centre of this beautiful Renaissance town, this 15th–16th-century house looks like a small château. It is family-run and offers a warm welcome. The rooms are large, attractively decorated, and each has its own bath/shower. There is a bar and afternoon teas are served in the salon. **www.hotel-salers.fr**

SALERS Le Bailliage P ⅋ €€

Rue Notre-Dame, 15410 **Tel** *04 71 40 71 95* **Fax** *04 71 40 74 90* **Rooms** *26*

Recently upgraded to three stars, the Bailliage is one of the nicest places to stay in this attractive mountain town. Cheaper rooms occupy a separate annex, but all are comfortable and some positively jolly. There's a garden and a restaurant in which to sample Salers cheese. **www.salers-hotel-bailliage.com**

ST GERVAIS D'AUVERGNE Castel-Hôtel 1904 P ⅋ €

Rue de Castel, 63390 **Tel** *04 73 85 70 42* **Fax** *04 73 85 84 39* **Rooms** *17*

Rooms are surprisingly affordable in this turreted château where period furniture, oak beams and highly polished floors ensure a homely atmosphere. Guest rooms are set round an attractive courtyard. There are two good restaurants: one rustic, the other grand. **www.castel-hotel-1904.com**

Key to Price Guide *see p550* **Key to Symbols** *see back cover flap*

ST JEAN DU BREUL Hôtel du Midi Papillon
P ⑪ 🏊 **€**

Le Bourg, 12230 **Tel** *05 65 62 26 04* **Fax** *05 65 62 12 97* **Rooms** *18*

A peaceful, friendly hotel overlooking a flower-filled garden and the river Dourbie. Ask for a room overlooking the river. The hotel has a garden and heated pool as well as a restaurant dishing up excellent home cooking. Book well ahead. Closed mid-November to Easter. **www.hotel-midi-papillon.com**

ST-BONNET-LE-FROID Le Clos des Cimes
P ⑪ 🗐 **€€€**

Le Bourg, 43290 **Tel** *04 71 59 93 72* **Fax** *04 71 59 93 40* **Rooms** *12*

Gourmet pilgrims compete for rooms at this fabulous auberge deep in the countryside. The prize is a luxurious room with original artworks and stunning views over the valley. The Marcon family run the place with tremendous attention to detail. Prepare to be pampered. Cooking lessons available. Closed Jan–Easter. **www.regismarcon.fr**

ST-NECTAIRE Mercure St-Nectaire
🔲 P ⑪ 🏊 📺 **€€**

Les Bains Romains, 63710 **Tel** *04 73 88 57 00* **Fax** *04 73 88 57 02* **Rooms** *71*

This upmarket chain hotel in a park in the spa town of St-Nectaire wins plenty of accolades for its gourmet restaurant. Guest rooms are equipped to three-star standards; all rooms are non-smoking. Facilities include a bar serving lighter meals, two pools, a sauna and parking. **www.accor.com**

TENCE Hostellerie Placide
P ⑪ **€€**

1 route d'Annonay, 43190 **Tel** *04 71 59 82 76* **Fax** *04 71 65 44 46* **Rooms** *12*

A vine-covered village auberge that's been in the Placide family for four generations. The Belle-Epoque decor is bright and cheery, the rooms impeccable – all are non-smoking. After a regal dinner, relax in leather armchairs over a brandy, or stroll in the garden. Closed January to March. **www.hostellerie-placide.fr**

VICHY Le Pavillon d'Enghien
🔲 ⑪ 🏊 **€**

32 rue Callou, 03200 **Tel** *04 70 98 33 30* **Fax** *04 70 31 67 82* **Rooms** *22*

A small hotel opposite the Callou baths. Inside you'll find a warm welcome and a touch of Vichy's pre-war spa atmosphere. Spacious rooms mostly overlook the interior garden. Personal service and a good restaurant. **www.pavillondenghien.com**

VICHY Aletti Palace Hotel
🔲 ⑪ 🏊 🗐 **€€**

3 pl Joseph-Aletti, 03200 **Tel** *04 70 30 20 20* **Fax** *04 70 98 13 82* **Rooms** *129*

Vichy's top hotel oozes Belle-Epoque grandeur from its stately reception hall to the crystal chandeliers. Guest rooms have been modernized but are tranquil and well proportioned. Fine restaurant and a terraced pool. In World War II, the Aletti was home to Vichy's Minister of War. **www.aletti.fr**

VILLEFORT Hôtel Balme
P ⑪ **€**

Pl du Portalet, 48800 **Tel** *04 66 46 80 14* **Fax** *04 66 46 85 26* **Rooms** *16*

Tucked away in a small town on the edge of the Cévennes national park is this handsome 1930s hotel. After dining in the elegant, empire-style restaurant – a difficult choice between local classics and oriental flavours – retire to one of the modest but comfortable guest rooms. **www.hotelbalme.free.fr**

VITRAC Auberge de la Tomette
P ⑪ 🏊 🎋 📺 **€€**

Le Bourg, 15220 **Tel** *04 71 64 70 94* **Fax** *04 71 64 77 11* **Rooms** *15*

A lovely country retreat set in huge gardens with a games area for children. Recent enhancements include a heated pool, sauna and *hammam*. The rooms are restful and spacious; six designed for families. Equal thought and attention goes into the cooking. **www.auberge-la-tomette.com**

YSSINGEAUX Le Bourbon
P ⑪ **€**

5 pl de la Victoire, 43200 **Tel** *04 71 59 06 54* **Fax** *04 71 59 00 70* **Rooms** *11*

The Perrier family have gone in for bold, modern colours in this well-run hotel between St-Etienne and Le-Puy. Rooms are well-equipped, while the restaurant showcases produce from nearby farms. The day starts with a hearty breakfast featuring local honey and chestnut spreads. **www.le-bourbon.com**

THE RHONE VALLEY & FRENCH ALPS

AIX-LES-BAINS Hôtel le Manoir
P ⑪ 🏊 🎋 **€€**

37 rue Georges 1er, 73105 **Tel** *04 79 61 44 00* **Fax** *04 79 35 67 67* **Rooms** *73*

A charming old hotel in the converted outbuildings of Palace Splendide-Royal, within walking distance of both thermal baths. The bedrooms are cosily furnished, some with balconies overlooking the grounds. Romantic setting for dining on classic dishes. Sauna and *hammam*. **www.hotel-lemanoir.com**

ANNECY Hôtel de l'Abbaye
P **€€**

15 chemin de l'Abbaye, 74940 **Tel** *04 50 23 61 08* **Fax** *04 50 23 61 71* **Rooms** *18*

A hotel, full of character, occupying a 15th-century abbey set in its own gardens. A stone archway leads to a cobbled courtyard surrounded by a wooden gallery with access to the bedrooms. Charming rooms, some with jacuzzi. Quiet, comfortable atmosphere. Buffet breakfast. **www.hotelabbaye-annecy.com**

BAGNOLS Château de Bagnols
Le Bourg, 69620 **Tel** *04 74 71 40 00* **Fax** *04 74 71 40 49* **Rooms** *21*

In 1987 Lady Hamlyn restored this château north of Lyon, surrounded by Beaujolais vineyards, and created a luxury hotel. The 13th-century building has turrets, moat and drawbridge. The rooms are richly decorated in velvet, silk and antiques. Michelin-starred restaurant. **www.bagnols.com**

BOURG-EN-BRESSE Hôtel du Prieuré
49-51 bd de Brou, 01000 **Tel** *04 74 22 44 60* **Fax** *04 74 22 71 07* **Rooms** *14*

A charming contemporary building surrounded by gardens and enclosed within a 16th-century stone wall, only a minute's walk from the Eglise de Brou. Well-proportioned, sunny bedrooms are furnished in Louis XV, Louis XVI or Bressan style; most have a view of the grounds.

BRIANÇON Hôtel Cristol
6 route d'Italie, 05100 **Tel** *04 92 20 20 11* **Fax** *04 92 21 02 58* **Rooms** *24*

Well-kept, traditional hotel. The recently redecorated rooms are modern, airy and bright; some have balconies with a view of the Vauban fortifications. Friendly service, and children are well catered for here. Charming dining room serves interesting themed menus.

CHAMBERY Hôtel des Princes
4 rue de Boigne, 73000 **Tel** *04 79 33 45 36* **Fax** *04 79 70 31 47* **Rooms** *45*

Situated in the grandest section of the Old Town, near La Fontaine des Elephants, this charmingly old-fashioned hotel has quiet, comfortable rooms, though not very spacious. The service is welcoming and friendly. There are several restaurants nearby to choose from. **www.hoteldesprinces.eu**

CHAMONIX MONT BLANC Le Hameau Albert 1er
119 impasse du Montenvers, 74402 **Tel** *04 50 53 05 09* **Fax** *04 50 55 95 48* **Rooms** *36*

Part of a hotel complex including the traditional hotel Albert 1er, the authentic and unusual Chalet Soli and the chic La Ferme. The large chalet-hotel has stunning views of Mont Blanc. The well-proportioned rooms have elegant designer furniture. Two good restaurants, one with a Michelin star. Sauna. **www.hameaualbert.fr**

CHONAS L'AMBALLAN Domaine de Clairefontaine
Chemin des Fontanettes, 38121 **Tel** *04 74 58 81 52* **Fax** *04 74 58 80 93* **Rooms** *28*

Set in a magnificent park in a small village south of Vienne, among 300-year-old trees, this former manor house has impeccably furnished rooms. The recently built annex has more modern rooms with balconies. The restaurant has a good reputation but can be inconsistent. **www.domaine-de-clairefontaine.fr**

CORDON Le Cordonant
Les Darbaillets, 74700 **Tel** *04 50 58 34 56* **Fax** *04 50 47 95 57* **Rooms** *15*

A friendly family-run hotel at this ski resort west of Chamonix, the trim, well-kept chalet has a garden. The rooms are comfortable, with pretty rustic furniture. The best rooms have great views of Mont Blanc. The restaurant serves hearty alpine cuisine. Good value.

DIVONNE-LES-BAINS Château de Divonne
115 rue des Bains, 01220 **Tel** *04 50 20 00 32* **Fax** *04 50 20 03 73* **Rooms** *34*

From this charming 19th-century mansion set in a large park, not far from Geneva, there are panoramic views of Mont Blanc and Lake Geneva. Inside is a monumental staircase. The rooms are richly furnished. Tennis courts on site, and golf course nearby. Classic cuisine. **www.chateau-divonne.com**

EVIAN-LES-BAINS Hôtel de la Verniaz et ses Chalets
Av d'Abondance, Neuvecelle-Eglise, 74500 **Tel** *04 50 75 04 90* **Fax** *04 50 70 78 92* **Rooms** *37*

Set on a hill above Evian, this former 17th-century Savoyard farm is now a glamorous establishment consisting of an elegant villa and five chalets, each with a private garden. The hotel offers elegant, smartly furnished rooms. The young chef creates refined dishes. **www.verniaz.com**

EVIAN-LES-BAINS Hôtel Royal
Rive Sud du Lac de Genève, 74500 **Tel** *04 50 26 85 00* **Fax** *04 50 75 61 00* **Rooms** *153*

An imposing hotel situated on the water's edge by Lake Geneva. Four restaurants, jogging trails, spa treatments, a private garden and a children's club are all on offer. Rooms and suites are tastefully decorated and most have impressive views over the lake. **www.royalparcevian.com**

GRENOBLE Splendid Hôtel
22 rue Thiers, 38000 **Tel** *04 76 46 33 12* **Fax** *04 76 46 35 24* **Rooms** *45*

Smart centrally located hotel in a quiet location, with a walled garden. The guest rooms range from classical to modern, with gaily painted frescoes. Efficient service and amenities. Continental and *à la carte* breakfast served in the dining room, or garden terrace. **www.splendid-hotel.com**

LA CHAPELLE-EN-VERCORS Hôtel Bellier
Av Goulets, 26420 **Tel** *04 75 48 20 03* **Fax** *04 75 48 25 31* **Rooms** *12*

In the Vercors massif region southwest of Grenoble, this well-kept chalet hotel stands on a rocky outcrop overlooking the countryside. Family run and friendly, with spacious guest rooms. Dining room has rustic Savoyard furniture. Closed November to Easter. **www.hotel-bellier.com**

Key to Price Guide *see p550* **Key to Symbols** *see back cover flap*

LE POET LAVAL Les Hospitaliers
P ¶ ≋ €€

Vieux Village, 26160 **Tel** 04 75 46 22 32 **Fax** 04 75 46 49 99 **Rooms** 20

A beautifully restored hotel in the centre of a tiny hilltop medieval village east of Montélimar. The elegantly furnished bedrooms, in the old stone buildings, are spacious and quiet. The restaurant offers first-class service, excellent cuisine and a wide range of good Rhône valley wines. **www.hotel-les-hospitaliers.com**

LYON Hôtel des Artistes
⊠ 目 €€

8 rue Gaspard-André, 69002 **Tel** 04 78 42 04 88 **Fax** 04 78 42 93 76 **Rooms** 45

Close to the place Bellecour, the Saône River and next door to the Theâtre des Célestins, this delightful hotel is a favourite haunt of actors. Pleasant, bright, airy rooms. Breakfast is served in an attractive room that is decorated with a Jean Cocteau-style fresco. **www.hoteldesartistes.fr**

LYON Hôtel Carlton
⊠ 目 €€€

4 rue Jussieu, 69002 **Tel** 04 78 42 56 51 **Fax** 04 78 42 10 71 **Rooms** 83

In the heart of the Presqu'île near the Rhône, this recently renovated classic hotel retains traces of its elegant Belle Epoque days. The bedrooms are elegant, furnished in an Art Deco, 1920s or English style. Non-smoking rooms available. Buffet breakfast. Efficient service. **www.accor.com**

LYON Cour des Loges
⊠ P ¶ ≋ 目 €€€€€

6 rue du Bœuf, 69005 **Tel** 04 72 77 44 44 **Fax** 04 72 40 93 61 **Rooms** 62

This luxury hotel occupies four renovated Renaissance mansions around a central galleried courtyard in Vieux Lyon. The reception area has a stunning glass roof. The elegant rooms blend Renaissance and contemporary decor. The restaurant serves classic cuisine. **www.courdesloges.com**

MALATAVERNE Domaine du Colombier
P ¶ ≋ 目 €€

Route de Donzère, 26780 **Tel** 04 75 90 86 86 **Fax** 04 75 90 79 40 **Rooms** 25

Occupying a 14th-century manor house south of Montélimar, this hotel set in pretty grounds was once a stop-over for pilgrims. The bedrooms are bright and stylish, some with a balcony or terrace overlooking the garden. The dining room opens out on to a patio. **www.domaine-colombier.com**

MANIGOD Hôtel-Chalets de la Croix-Fry
P ¶ ≋ 大 €€€

Route du Col de la Croix-Fry, 74230 **Tel** 04 50 44 90 16 **Fax** 04 50 44 94 87 **Rooms** 10

High on a mountain pass east of Annecy, this delightful chalet-style hotel combines Alpine rustic with comfort in a friendly atmosphere. The wooden interior is charming, decorated with Savoyard furniture. The guest rooms are cosy. Closed May and October–November. **www.hotelchaletcroixfry.com**

MEGEVE Le Fer à Cheval
⊠ P ¶ ≋ ▼ €€€€€

36 route du Crêt-d'Arbois, 74120 **Tel** 04 50 21 30 39 **Fax** 04 50 93 07 60 **Rooms** 49

A charming, intimate hotel, this was originally a group of four chalets built by the village blacksmith in 1938. Authentic Savoyard interior with rustic furniture. Candlelit dinner served around a stone fireplace in winter. Closed mid-April–mid-June and mid-September–mid-January. **www.feracheval-megeve.com**

MORZINE Hôtel les Prodains
P ¶ ≋ 大 €

Village des Prodains, 74110 **Tel** 04 50 79 25 26 **Fax** 04 50 75 76 17 **Rooms** 15

At the foot of the slopes in this Haute Savoie village, this chalet-style hotel has reasonably sized, comfortable bedrooms with quaint Alpine furnishings. In summer walks and picnics are arranged; in winter ski directly from hotel. Sauna and solarium. Decent restaurant. Half board. **www.hotellesprodains.com**

PEROUGES Ostellerie du Vieux Pérouges
P ¶ €€€

Pl du Tilleuil, 01800 **Tel** 04 74 61 00 88 **Fax** 04 74 34 77 90 **Rooms** 28

This historic inn is a filmmaker's dream, converted from 13th-century buildings and set in a medieval hilltop village. The four ancient houses are clustered around the main square. The decor is different in each house. Ultra-classic cuisine serving regional dishes with precision.

ROMANS SUR ISERE Hôtel l'Orée du Parc
P ≋ 大 目 €€

6 av Gambetta, 26100 **Tel** 04 75 70 26 12 **Fax** 04 75 05 08 23 **Rooms** 10

After visiting the Palais Idéal du Facteur Cheval, head 25 km (16 miles) south to Romans, and relax in this charming hotel. A tastefully renovated 20th-century manor house in its own park, all the rooms are non-smoking and filled with modern, elegant furnishings. **www.hotel-oreeparc.com**

ST ETIENNE Hôtel Albatros
⊠ P ¶ ≋ €€

67 rue St Simon, 42000 **Tel** 04 77 41 41 00 **Fax** 04 77 38 28 16 **Rooms** 47

A newer hotel, conveniently located at the edge of the city centre, on a hill opposite the city's golf course. Modern, comfortable pretty guest rooms have cane furniture and floral fabrics. There is also a salon, a bar and a bright restaurant serving classic French cuisine. **www.hotel-albatros.fr**

TALLOIRES Hôtel l'Abbaye
P ¶ 大 €€€

Chemin des Moines, 74290 **Tel** 04 50 60 77 33 **Fax** 04 50 60 78 81 **Rooms** 32

This elegant hotel occupying a former 17th-century Benedictine abbey is beautifully situated on the shores of Lac d'Annecy. Cézanne used to be a regular guest. The large rooms have wonderfully decorated period ceilings and antique furniture. Attractive garden and good restaurant. **www.abbaye-talloires.com**

TALLOIRES Hôtel Le Cottage Fernand Bise

Au Bord du Lac, 74290 **Tel** *04 50 60 71 10* **Fax** *04 50 60 77 51* **Rooms** *35*

Very large for a "cottage", this hotel occupying a spectacular lakeside setting is made up of three Alpine chalets. The guest rooms have views of the lake or the mountains. Lovely gardens and swimming pool, perfect for relaxing. Good food served in the tasteful dining room or on the patio. **www.cottagebise.com**

TOURNON-SUR RHONE La Chaumière

Quai Farconnet, 07300 **Tel** *04 75 08 07 78* **Fax** *04 75 07 79 34* **Rooms** *10*

Old-fashioned charm prevails in this Provençal-style 18th-century auberge facing a lovely square near the Rhône riverbank. Traditional rooms are comfortable and clean with exposed oak beams. The restaurant is excellent and has a sunny terrace. Garage parking.

VAL D'ISERE Christiania

Chef Lieu, 73152 **Tel** *04 79 06 08 25* **Fax** *04 79 41 11 10* **Rooms** *69*

Splendid modern chalet with a magnificent view of the ski slopes at this popular resort for the rich and famous. Luxurious fully equipped rooms, all with balconies, are decorated in an elegant Alpine theme. Pamper yourself in the health and fitness centre. Superb buffet breakfast. **www.hotel-christiania.com**

VALLON PONT D'ARC Le Clos des Bruyères

Route des Gorges, 07150 **Tel** *04 75 37 18 85* **Fax** *04 75 37 14 89* **Rooms** *32*

Situated in the Gorges d'Ardèche, this modern hotel, built in a Provençal style, has bedrooms that open on to the pool via a balcony or terrace. Family rooms are available. Hire a canoe or quad and take a picnic to explore the river and countryside. Nautical-themed restaurant. **www.closdesbruyeres.net**

POITOU & AQUITAINE

ANGOULEME Hôtel du Palais

4 pl Francis-Louvel, 16000 **Tel** *05 45 92 54 11* **Fax** *05 45 92 01 83* **Rooms** *49*

On a shady square in the centre of Angoulême, near the cathedral, stands this welcoming hotel. Wrought-iron work and rich red fabrics lend a certain grandeur. Guest rooms have old-style charm, some renovated with big balconies. Garage parking, and plenty of restaurants in the vicinity. **www.hotel-angouleme.fr**

ARCACHON Hôtel Le Dauphin

7 av Gounod, 33120 **Tel** *05 56 83 02 89* **Fax** *05 56 54 84 90* **Rooms** *50*

This well-run hotel dating from the late 19th century is instantly recognizable from its red-and-white brickwork. It's located a few blocks back from the sea in a quiet residential district. Spick-and-span rooms have simple pine furnishings and white walls. **www.dauphin-arcachon.com**

BORDEAUX La Maison du Lierre

57 rue Huguerie, 33000 **Tel** *05 56 51 92 71* **Fax** *05 56 79 15 16* **Rooms** *12*

Close to Bordeaux's chic Golden Triangle, this small hotel – its homely atmosphere more like a *chambre d'hôte* - has been renovated with flair. Rooms are stylish. Generous homemade breakfasts may be served in the interior courtyard. It is wise to book ahead. **www.maisondulierre.com**

BORDEAUX Best Western Bayonne Etche-Ona

4 rue Martignac, 33000 **Tel** *05 56 48 00 88* **Fax** *05 56 48 41 60* **Rooms** *63*

This is two hotels in one: the contemporary Bayonne and (just round the corner) the more atmospheric Etche-Ona with its Basque-inspired decor. Both occupy elegant 18th-century mansions in the heart of the Golden Triangle and offer comfortable rooms and top-notch service. **www.bordeaux-hotel.com**

CAP-FERRET La Maison du Bassin

5 rue des Pionniers, 33950 **Tel** *05 56 60 60 63* **Fax** *05 56 03 71 47* **Rooms** *7 (plus 4 annex rooms)*

Ultra-chic and highly sought-after address at the end of the Cap-Ferret peninsula. A colonial ambience is achieved with highly polished wood, cane chairs and arty knick-knacks. Try one of the tasty tropical rums as an aperitif, before dining on the tropical veranda. Reservations by phone only. **www.lamasiondubassin.com**

CELLES-SUR-BELLE Hostellerie de l'Abbaye

1 pl des Epoux-Laurant, 79370 **Tel** *05 49 32 93 32* **Fax** *05 49 79 72 65* **Rooms** *20*

If you are looking for accommodation near Poitiers, this lovely, tranquil hotel in a former abbey is hard to beat. The building has been lovingly converted to combine rustic charm with modern refinements – at reasonable prices. The food is excellent and the service impeccable. **www.hotel-restaurant-abbaye.com**

CIERZAC Le Moulin de Cierzac

Route de Cognac, 17520 **Tel** *05 45 83 01 32* **Fax** *05 45 83 03 59* **Rooms** *7*

A short drive south of Cognac, this hotel-restaurant in a 17th-century mansion set in extensive grounds. Pleasant rooms contain exposed beams; some have river views. The restaurant serves local specialities. Afterwards, choose your *digestif* from a vast array of cognacs. **www.moulindecierzac.com**

Key to Price Guide *see p550* **Key to Symbols** *see back cover flap*

CLAM Le Vieux Logis

P ⊓ ≋ | €

3 rue 8 mai 1945, 17500 **Tel** *05 46 70 20 13* **Fax** *05 46 70 20 64* **Rooms** *10*

Modest but welcoming, this little restaurant-with-rooms is a short drive north of Jonzac. The accommodation is in wooden chalets, each with a terrace opening onto the garden. They are simple but well maintained. The restaurant is well known locally for its good-value home cooking. **www.vieuxlogis.com**

COGNAC Les Pigeons Blancs

P ⊓ 杰 | €€

110 rue Jules-Brisson, 16100 **Tel** *05 45 82 16 36* **Fax** *05 45 82 29 29* **Rooms** *6*

In the heart of the cognac vineyards, this 17th-century auberge offers a warm welcome and a handful of unfussy but immaculate rooms decked out with period furniture. Two are non-smoking. Other facilities include an excellent restaurant and a garden. Baby-sitting available.

COULON Le Central

P ⊓ 目 | €

4 rue d'Autremont, 79510 **Tel** *05 49 35 90 20* **Fax** *05 49 35 81 07* **Rooms** *13*

Situated in the mysterious fens of the Marais Poitevin, this traditional village hotel has been in the same family for three generations. The guest rooms are nothing fancy, but bright and clean. Downstairs is a deservedly popular restaurant. You'll need to book well ahead. Disabled access. **www.hotel-lecentral-coulon.com**

EUGENIE-LES-BAINS La Maison Rose

P ⊓ ≋ ▼ | €€€

334 rue René Vielle, 40320 **Tel** *05 58 05 06 07* **Fax** *05 58 51 10 10* **Rooms** *31*

The illustrious chef Michel Guérard draws worshippers to Eugénie, a thermal spa dating back to the 18th century. This, the most modest of his three hotels, feels like a country house, from the rose-filled garden to the pretty guest rooms – not lavish but absolutely immaculate. **www.michelguerard.com**

GRENADE-SUR-L'ADOUR Pain Adour et Fantaisie

⊓ 杰 目 | €€

14-16 pl des Tilleuls, 40270 **Tel** *05 58 45 18 80* **Fax** *05 58 45 16 57* **Rooms** *11*

This elegant hotel overlooking Grenade's arcaded central square on one side, and the river on the other, is home to one of the region's best restaurants. In keeping with the hotel's 17th-century architecture, antiques, oak panelling and parquet predominate. Spacious rooms. **www.chateauxhotelsfrance.com/fantaisie**

HOSSEGOR Les Hortensias du Lac

P ≋ | €€€

1578 av du Tour du Lac, 40150 **Tel** *05 58 43 99 00* **Fax** *05 58 43 42 81* **Rooms** *16*

This hotel, set in pine forests not far from the ocean and overlooking Hossegor lake, provides a peaceful retreat. Guest rooms in the 1930s villa are tranquil, with their neutral tones offset against dark wood, all with a terrace or balcony. Splendid champagne buffet breakfast. **www.hortensias-du-lac.com**

LA ROCHELLE Les Brises

⊞ P | €€

Chemin de la Digue-Richelieu, 17000 **Tel** *05 46 43 89 37* **Fax** *05 46 43 27 97* **Rooms** *48*

A comfortable and popular hotel within walking distance of the vieux port and the bustling city centre. It's worth paying extra for a seafront room. Not only are they more spacious, but they also benefit from balconies with wonderful views out to sea and the offshore islands. **www.hotellesbrises.com**

LE BOIS-PLAGE-EN-RE Hôtel L'Océan

P ⊓ ≋ | €€

172 rue St-Martin, 17580 **Tel** *05 46 09 23 07* **Fax** *05 46 09 05 40* **Rooms** *29*

There's a real seaside feel to this hotel on the southern coast of the Île de Ré. Potted palms, giant parasols and sun-bleached wooden decking outside; inside, pretty pastels and marine motifs for the rooms. Not surprisingly, ultra-fresh fish dominates the restaurant menu. **www.re-hotel-ocean.com**

MAGESCQ Relais de la Poste

P ⊓ ≋ 杰 ▼ 目 | €€€€

24, av de Maremne, 40140 **Tel** *05 58 47 70 25* **Fax** *05 58 47 76 17* **Rooms** *16*

This small and wonderfully relaxed hotel set in a 19th-century coaching inn has a garden and nicely landscaped pools. It combines comfort, celebrated cuisine, fine wines and family tradition. You're not far from the sea here, with Bayonne and Biarritz within easy striking distance. **www.relaisposte.com**

MARGAUX Le Pavillon de Margaux

P ⊓ ≋ | €€

3 rue Georges-Mandel, 33460 **Tel** *05 57 88 77 54* **Fax** *05 57 88 77 73* **Rooms** *14*

In the centre of Margaux village, this handsome hotel provides a comfortable base for exploring the Médoc vineyards. Guest rooms, which are "sponsored" by local wine châteaux, are individually styled. Some have antiques and four-posters, others rattan and floral fabrics. **www.pavillondemargaux.com**

MIMIZAN-PLAGE L'Atlantique

P ⊓ | €

38 av de la Côte-d'Argent, 40200 **Tel** *05 58 09 09 42* **Fax** *05 58 82 42 63* **Rooms** *32*

Surfers and sun-worshippers alike will love this low-key hotel caught between the Côte d'Argent's glorious beaches and the Landes forest. It's a friendly place, with renovated guest rooms. Half-board is obligatory in July and August. Still, you'll eat well on fresh fish. **www.hotelatlantique-landes.com**

MONTBRON Hostellerie Château Ste-Catherine

P ⊓ ≋ 杰 | €

Route de Marthon, 16220 **Tel** *05 45 23 60 03* **Fax** *05 45 70 72 00* **Rooms** *18*

Napoléon's wife, Joséphine de Beauharnais, lived in this distinguished 17th-century château set in a park. Its stately interior is on a monumental scale with a sweeping staircase, elegant mirrored and chandeliered salons, and huge, high-ceilinged rooms. **www.chateausaintecatherine.fr**

NIEUIL Château de Nieuil `P 🍴 ☕ 🔥 ▤` €€

16270 **Tel** *05 45 71 36 38* **Fax** *05 45 71 46 45* **Rooms** *14*

King François I hunted in the extensive park surrounding this superb Renaissance château with its pepper-pot towers and sweeping staircase. A quiet night is assured in the elegant, comfortable rooms. The stables now house an excellent restaurant. **www.chateaunieuilhotel.com**

PARTHENAY Hôtel du Nord `P 🍴` €

86 av du Général de Gaulle, 79200 **Tel** *05 49 94 29 11* **Fax** *05 49 64 11 72* **Rooms** *10*

The best option in Parthenay, an attractive medieval town famous for its livestock market, is this modest hotel opposite the train station. Businesslike guest rooms offer en-suite bathrooms, television and telephone. The restaurant serves French classics and regional fare. **www.hotelnordparthenay.fr**

ROYAN Les Bleuets `P ▤` €

21 façade de Foncillon, 17200 **Tel** *05 46 38 51 79* **Fax** *05 46 23 82 00* **Rooms** *16*

Immaculate little hotel with a nautical theme, from the hull-shaped reception desk to rooms decorated with marine motifs. The more expensive rooms have balconies and sea views; the rest overlook a small garden. The hotel is 2 minutes from the ferry port. **www.hotel-les-bleuets.com**

SABRES Auberge des Pins `P 🍴 🔥` €€

Route de la Piscine, 40630 **Tel** *05 58 08 30 00* **Fax** *05 58 07 56 74* **Rooms** *25*

From the moment you enter this attractive farmhouse, deep in the forests of the Landes Regional Park, you know you're in for a treat. This is country living at its best: old-style hospitality, homely rooms, open fires in winter and quiet corners to curl up in with a book. Fine restaurant. **www.aubergedespins.fr**

SOUSTONS Hôtel du Lac `P 🍴` €

63 av Galleben, 40140 **Tel** *05 58 41 18 80* **Fax** *05 58 41 29 84* **Rooms** *7*

A refurbished and unpretentious restaurant-with-rooms facing Soustons lake and a short drive from the ocean. It's worth paying a little extra for a balcony room on the front to benefit from the expansive views. The restaurant is well-loved locally for its seafood and typical landaise dishes. **www.hoteldulac-batby.com**

ST-EMILION Au Logis des Remparts `P ☕ ▤` €€

18 rue Guadet, 33330 **Tel** *05 57 24 70 43* **Fax** *05 57 74 47 44* **Rooms** *17*

Outside peak season, when prices drop, this modest hotel provides a comfortable overnight stop. Its main draws are the sizeable terraced garden and swimming pool. The rooms lack character, but those on the back benefit from views over the vineyards. **www.saint-emilion.org**

ST-EMILION Hostellerie de Plaisance `📶 P 🍴 ▤` €€€€€

Pl du Clocher, 33330 **Tel** *05 57 55 07 55* **Fax** *05 57 74 41 11* **Rooms** *17 (plus 4 suites)*

Upscale hotel in an exceptional location overlooking St-Emilion and its famous vineyards. Luxurious rooms boast the full range of amenities, including magnificent bathrooms. Some have private terraces. The service is top-notch and the restaurant one of the region's best. **www.hostelleriedeplaisance.com**

ST-GROUX Les Trois Saules `P 🍴 🔥` €

Le Bourg, 16230 **Tel** *05 45 20 31 40* **Fax** *05 45 22 73 81* **Rooms** *10*

In the countryside just north of Angoulême and within easy access of the N10, this simple hotel makes a convenient stop. It occupies an attractive lakeside building surrounded by gardens with a play area for children. The rooms are tidy if basic, but the restaurant compensates.

ST-TROJANS-DES-BAINS Le Homard Bleu `P 🍴` €

10 bd de la Plage, 17370 **Tel** *05 46 76 00 22* **Fax** *05 46 76 14 95* **Rooms** *20*

This unassuming hotel lies on the Île d'Oléron's southeast tip. Simple, fresh rooms have sea-view balconies and themed blue-and-white decor, or green tones and views of pine woods and mimosa to the back. Restaurant serves fresh seafood, including lobster *(homard)*. **www.homardbleu.fr**

TRIZAY Les Jardins du Lac `P 🍴 ☕ 🔥` €€

Lac du Bois Fleuri, 17250 **Tel** *05 46 82 03 56* **Fax** *05 46 82 03 55* **Rooms** *8*

A well-run hotel midway between Rochefort and Saintes. The modern buildings are surrounded by landscaped gardens with a trout lake and woodland. Airy and well-maintained rooms all offer lake views. Meals are served outside in fine weather. A lovely, relaxing place to stay. **www.jardins-du-lac.com**

PERIGORD, QUERCY & GASCONY

AGEN Hôtel Château des Jacobins `P ▤` €€

1 pl des Jacobins, 47000 **Tel** *05 53 47 03 31* **Fax** *05 53 47 02 80* **Rooms** *15*

Built in the early 19th century, this small, ivy-clad château with a walled garden is an oasis of calm in the city centre. The rooms are elegantly decorated with period furniture and chandeliers. There's secure parking and you'll find plenty of fine restaurants within easy walking distance. **www.chateau-des-jacobins.com**

Key to Price Guide *see p550* **Key to Symbols** *see back cover flap*

ALBI Le Vieil Alby   P ⅰ   €

23-25 rue Toulouse-Lautrec, 81000 **Tel** *05 63 54 14 69* **Fax** *05 63 54 96 75* **Rooms** *9*

A warm welcome and excellent value are guaranteed at this traditional, family-run hotel in the heart of Albi's historic centre. Though nothing fancy, the rooms are spacious, comfortable and well maintained. All are non-smoking. Reserve well in advance. Garage parking available.

BEYNAC Hôtel du Chateau   ⅰ ≋   €

La Balme, 24220 **Tel** *05 53 29 19 20* **Fax** *05 53 28 55 56* **Rooms** *15*

Attractive rooms, a good restaurant and friendly service make this small hotel the best accommodation option in this picturesque village on the Dordogne. Front rooms overlook the river, though traffic might disturb light sleepers (despite double-glazing). Free Internet connection. **www.hotelduchateau-dordogne.com**

BRANTOME Hôtel Chabrol   ⅰ   €

57 rue Gambetta, 24310 **Tel** *05 53 05 70 15* **Fax** *05 53 05 71 85* **Rooms** *18*

A nicely old-fashioned hotel ideally situated in the centre of Brantôme yet still benefitting from a riverside location. The prettily decorated rooms, all light, calm and airy, represent good value for money. Those on the front look across the river to the medieval abbey. **www.lesfrerescharbonnel.com**

BRANTOME Le Moulin de l'Abbaye   P ⅰ ⚥ ≣   €€€€

1 route de Bourdeilles, 24310 **Tel** *05 53 05 80 22* **Fax** *05 53 05 75 27* **Rooms** *19*

Treat yourself to a night of luxury in this romantic, creeper-covered mill on the River Dronne. Rooms are in the mill and in two handsome old houses nearby, but all share the same fresh yet sophisticated decor. Terraced waterside gardens proivde the perfect breakfast spot. **www.moulin-abbaye.com**

CAHORS Le Grand Hôtel Terminus   🅿 ⅰ ≣   €

5 av Charles de Freycinet, 46000 **Tel** *05 65 53 32 00* **Fax** *05 65 53 32 26* **Rooms** *22*

Cahors' top hotel occupies a grand mansion 2 minutes from the train station. Inside, you'll find 1920s-style decor, including stained-glass windows, and a reassuring air of efficiency. Rooms have less character, though most have generous bathrooms. Restaurant has a vast wine cellar. **www.balandre.com**

CALES Le Petit Relais   P ⅰ ≋   €

Pl du Village, 46350 **Tel** *05 65 37 96 09* **Fax** *05 65 37 95 93* **Rooms** *13*

A quiet village inn of the old style, with cosy rooms and abundant *bonhomie*. There's also a good traditional restaurant, where meals are served on a flowery terrace in fine weather, and a large garden at the back. The hotel makes a handy base for exploring nearby Rocamadour, and runs hunting excursions. **www.le-petit-relais.fr**

CASTILLONNES Hôtel Restaurant Les Remparts   ⅰ

26 rue de la Paix, 47330 **Tel** *05 53 49 55 85* **Fax** *05 53 49 55 89* **Rooms** *9*

An attractive hotel set back from the road in the middle of Castillonnès, a medieval bastide. Through an arched entrance way, the 15th-century building has been tastefully renovated to provide spacious, soothing rooms. Popular regional cuisine restaurant with a romantic setting.

CHAMPAGNAC-DE-BELAIR Le Moulin du Roc   P ⅰ ≋ ⚥ ≣   €€€

Av Eugène le Roy, 24530 **Tel** *05 53 02 86 00* **Fax** *05 53 54 21 31* **Rooms** *13*

In a magical setting on the river Dronne, just outside Brantôme, is this luxury hotel hidden under swathes of greenery in a converted 17th-century watermill. In addition to the sumptuous, individually styled rooms, there is a superb restaurant, an indoor pool and tennis court. **www.moulinduroc.com**

CHANCELADE Château des Reynats   🅿 P ⅰ ≋   €€€

Av des Reynats, 24650 **Tel** *05 53 03 53 59* **Fax** *05 53 0344 84* **Rooms** *37*

Just west of Périgueux, this charming 19th-century château makes for an agreeable night's stay. Standard rooms in the "Orangerie" annex are bright and breezy, but for real atmosphere upgrade to the château rooms. There's a top-notch resturant, too, and spacious grounds. **www.chateau-hotel-perigord.com**

COLY Manoir d'Hautegente   P ⅰ ≋ ≣   €€

Haute Gente, 24120 **Tel** *05 53 51 68 03* **Fax** *05 53 50 38 52* **Rooms** *15*

Not far from Sarlat and the Lascaux caves is this picturesque manor house, once the mill and forge of an abbey. It is now a family-run, friendly hotel with log fires, private fishing and well-tended riverside gardens. Half-board mandatory in high-season; the food is excellent. **www.manoir-hautegente.com**

CONDOM Le Logis des Cordeliers   P ≋   €

Rue de la Paix, 32100 **Tel** *05 62 28 03 68* **Fax** *05 62 68 29 03* **Rooms** *21*

Modern hotel offering modest but well priced rooms in the centre of Condom. Picture windows lend space and light and many rooms have balconies overlooking the pool. There is no in-house restaurant, but you can eat in the highly rated Table des Cordeliers next door. **www.logisdescordeliers.com**

CORDES SUR CIEL Le Grand Ecuyer   P ⅰ ≣   €€

Grand Rue Raymond VII, 81170 **Tel** *05 63 53 79 50* **Fax** *05 63 53 79 51* **Rooms** *13*

This former hunting lodge of the Counts of Toulouse has long been popular with notables such as de Gaulle and François Mitterand. Gothic touches abound, from the sculpted façade to stone flags, huge fireplaces, antique furniture and plush upholstery. Renowned restaurant. **www.thuries.fr/gastronomie/lge_hotel.php**

DOMME L'Esplanade   P ⑪ 🗏   €€
Rue du Pont Carrel, 24250 **Tel** *05 53 28 31 41* **Fax** *05 53 28 49 92* **Rooms** *25*

Perched on the edge of a cliff, the best rooms in this elegant hotel offer panoramic views of the Dordogne valley. Some have canopied four-poster beds to match the refined, opulent decor. Less dramatic but very comfortable rooms are among the streets of the medieval bastide. Closed mid-Nov–Mar.

DURAS Hostellerie des Ducs   P ⑪ ≅ 🗏   €
Bd Jean-Brisseau, 47120 **Tel** *05 53 83 74 58* **Fax** *05 53 83 75 03* **Rooms** *16*   **Map**

Situated in the picturesque Côte-de-Duras wine region between the Dordogne and Garonne rivers is this low-key, family-run hostelry overlooking a 14th-century fortress. The flower-filled gardens of the former convent complement the peaceful rooms. Excellent regional cuisine. **www.hostellerieducs-duras.com**

FIGEAC Hôtel des Bains   P 🗏   €
1 rue du Griffoul, 46100 **Tel** *05 65 34 10 89* **Fax** *05 65 14 00 45* **Rooms** *19*   **Map**

A simple, welcoming and well-tended hotel immediately across the river Célé from Figeac's glorious medieval centre. The renovated rooms, some with balconies, offer excellent value. Breakfast and drinks are served on the terrace in fine weather. Plenty of restaurants in the vicinity. **www.hoteldesbains.fr**

LA COQUILLE Hôtel des Voyageurs   P ⑪ ≅ 🛝   €
12 rue de la République, 24450 **Tel** *05 53 52 80 13* **Fax** *05 53 62 18 29* **Rooms** *8*

A small, villlage hotel conveniently placed midway between Périgueux and Limoges. It offers well-priced, comfortable rooms. There's also a garden with pool and a children's play area. The restaurant serves tasty regional fare inside or on the terrace in summer. **www.hotelvoyageurs.fr**

LACAVE Le Pont de l'Ouysse   P ⑪ ≅ 🗏   €€€
Le Pont de l'Ouysse, 46200 **Tel** *05 65 37 87 04* **Fax** *05 65 32 77 41* **Rooms** *12*

There's a Provençal air to this chic restaurant-with-rooms in riverside gardens not far from Rocamadour. Inside, cool creams blend with ochre hues, and rooms are fabulously quiet. In their fourth generation, the Chambon family have created a real hideaway. Inventive cuisine. **www.lepontdelouysse.fr**

LECTOURE Hôtel de Bastard   P ⑪ ≅   €
Rue Lagrange, 32700 **Tel** *05 62 68 82 44* **Fax** *05 62 68 76 81* **Rooms** *29*

Despite its name, this elegant hotel is one of the best in the Gers. Antique furnishings are coupled with modern comforts in an 18th-century townhouse. Facilities include a small garden, sun deck and swimming pool. Refined regional cuisine makes the restaurant perennially popular. **www.hotel-de-bastard.com**

LES EYZIES-DE-TAYAC Le Moulin de la Beune   P ⑪   €
2 rue du Moulin-Bas, 24620 **Tel** *05 53 06 94 33* **Fax** *05 53 06 98 06* **Rooms** *20*

Shady gardens beside the river Beune provide a haven of peace tucked off Les-Eyzies' busy main road. The rooms, in a converted mill building, are simple and fresh, with crisp white cottons and large windows ensuring plenty of light. There's also an excellent restaurant. **www.moulindelabeune.com**

MARTEL Relais Ste-Anne   P ≅ 🗏   €€
Rue du Pourtanel, 46600 **Tel** *05 65 37 40 56* **Fax** *05 65 37 42 82* **Rooms** *16*

Behind the discrete entrance hides a lovely old building, once a girls' boarding school complete with chapel, in spacious grounds. Everything is designed for a relaxing stay, from the beautifully appointed rooms – some with private terrace – to the heated pool. Hearty breakfasts. **www.relais-sainte-anne.com**

MERCUES Château de Mercuès   🖻 P ⑪ ≅ 🛝 🆈   €€€€€
46090 **Tel** *05 65 20 00 01* **Fax** *05 65 20 05 72* **Rooms** *30*

Dominating the Lot valley is this turreted 13th-century château where the bishops of nearby Cahors once lived. It is now a luxury hotel offering rooms on a suitably grand scale, gourmet dining among chandeliers or in the courtyard, tennis courts and extensive parkland. **www.chateaudemercues.com**

MOISSAC Le Moulin de Moissac   🖻 P ⑪ 🗏   €
Esplanade du Moulin, 82200 **Tel** *05 63 32 88 88* **Fax** *05 63 32 02 08* **Rooms** *30*

Though not the most attractive building, this hotel in a former mill more than compensates with its quiet, riverside location, efficient service and well-equipped rooms. All come with DVD/CD player, wifi Internet and coffee machine. Central Moissac is a stroll away. **www.lemoulindemoissac.com**

NONTRON Le Grand Hôtel Pélisson   🖻 P ⑪ ≅   €
3 pl Alfred Agard, 24300 **Tel** *05 53 56 11 22* **Fax** *05 53 56 59 94* **Rooms** *23*

This well-run provincial hotel has been in the same family for 50 years. A friendly and unassuming place with guest rooms overlooking the market square or the pretty garden at the back. The restaurant serves good fare, either in the oak-beamed dining room or outside.

PERIGUEUX Hôtel Régina   🖻 P 🗏   €
14 rue Denis Papin, 24000 **Tel** *05 53 08 40 44* **Fax** *05 53 54 72 44* **Rooms** *41*

This hotel opposite the train station is one of the better accommodation options in Périgueux, the 'capital' of the Dordogne. The rooms are bright and airy, if lacking in character. Those at the front have double glazing. A 10-minute walk to the centre with its choice of restaurants. **www.perigueux.comfort-hotel.fr**

Key to Price Guide *see p550* **Key to Symbols** *see back cover flap*

PUY-L'EVEQUE Hôtel Bellevue 🖼️ P ⓝ 🔲 €

Pl de la Truffière, 46700 **Tel** *05 65 36 06 60* **Fax** *05 65 36 06 61* **Rooms** *11*

A modern hotel perched above the honey-coloured houses of Puy-l'Evêque to the west of Cahors. All rooms have panoramic views of the Lot valley and its neatly tended vineyards. The decor is contemporary. The restaurant has a reputation for adventurous, cosmopolitan cuisine. **www.lothotel-bellevue.com**

REVEL Hôtel du Midi P ⓝ €

34 bd Gambetta, 31250 **Tel** *05 61 83 50 50* **Fax** *05 61 83 34 74* **Rooms** *17*

This lovely auberge has been welcoming visitors to Revel, a 14th-century bastide and thriving market town, for more than 200 years. It is still a traditional country inn, with pleasant rooms, a garden and excellent home cooking. A good base for exploring the Montagne Noire. **www.hotelrestaurantdumidi.com**

RIBERAC Hôtel de France ⓝ €

3 rue Marc-Dufraisse, 24600 **Tel** *05 53 90 00 61* **Fax** *05 53 91 06 05* **Rooms** *12*

Book ahead for a room in this charming hotel tucked down a side street off Ribérac's market square. Imaginative décor and use of colour make even the smallest rooms bright and cheerful. The same artistic touches are apparent in the restaurant and in the small flower-filled garden. **www.hoteldefranceriberac.com**

ROCAMADOUR Domaine de la Rhue P 🏊 €€

46500 **Tel** *05 65 33 71 50* **Fax** *05 65 33 72 48* **Rooms** *14*

A short drive from Rocamadour is this peaceful hotel in beautifully converted 19th-century stables. Exposed beams and stonework give the spacious rooms an upscale rustic charm. Some come with a terrace, others with a kitchenette. The nearest restaurants are in Rocamadour. **www.domainedelarhue.com**

SARLAT-LA-CANEDA Hôtel des Récollets P €

4 rue Jean-Jacques Rousseau, 24200 **Tel** *05 53 31 36 00* **Fax** *05 53 30 32 62* **Rooms** *18*

Though nothing fancy, this small hotel in the heart of medieval Sarlat is a reliable option for a quiet stay. Guest rooms are modern, but traces of the building's 17th-century origins can be found in the bare stone walls and the interior courtyard – once a cloister – where breakfast is served. **www.hotel-recollets-sarlat.com**

ST-CIRQ-LAPOPIE Hôtel de la Pélissaria P 🏊 €€

Le Bourg, 46330 **Tel** *05 65 31 25 14* **Fax** *05 65 30 25 52* **Rooms** *10*

An intimate hotel in a medieval clifftop village above the Lot river. The 16th-century house features tiled or polished wood floors, exposed stone walls and oak beams aplenty. The most appealing rooms occupy separate buildings in the gardens. Most rooms have lovely views. **http://perso.wanadoo.fr/hoteldelapelissaria**

TAMNIES Hôtel Laborderie P ⓝ 🏊 ✠ €

Le Bourg, 24620 **Tel** *05 53 29 68 59* **Fax** *05 53 29 65 31* **Rooms** *39*

Between Sarlat and Les-Eyzies lies this modern, family-run hotel. It has expanded over the years from the original auberge to offer a wide choice of rooms in three new annexes overlooking the pool. Children will also appreciate the large, grassy park. The restaurant is good, too. **www.hotel-laborderie.com**

TOULOUSE Hôtel Albert 1er 🖼️ 🔲 €

8 rue Rivals, 31000 **Tel** *05 61 21 17 91* **Fax** *05 61 21 09 64* **Rooms** *50*

A good-value and well-run hotel tucked down a side street near the central place du Capitole. The foyer's potted palms and Toulousain brick set the tone. The rooms are cheerful and of a decent size, with modern bathrooms. There's a small lounge and a breakfast room. **www.hotel-albert1.com**

TOULOUSE Hôtel des Beaux Arts P 🖼️ ⓝ 🔲 €€

1 pl du Pont Neuf, 31000 **Tel** *05 34 45 42 42* **Fax** *05 34 45 42 43* **Rooms** *19*

Behind a beautiful Belle Epoque façade, beside the Pont Neuf, lies a chic hotel with modern comforts. The less expensive rooms are on the small side – better to upgrade for river views and more space. For a special occasion, opt for room 42 with its own tiny terrace among the roof tiles. **www.hoteldesbeauxarts.com**

VITRAC Hôtel La Treille P ⓝ €

Le Port, 24200 **Tel** *05 53 28 33 19* **Fax** *05 53 30 38 54* **Rooms** *8*

Conveniently located just 7 km (4 miles) south of Sarlat you'll find this small, welcoming hotel on the banks of the Dordogne. The stylish rooms make for a pleasant stay at reasonable prices. The hotel also has a fine restaurant – meals are served in a pretty room swathed in greenery. **www.latreille-perigord.com**

THE PYRENEES

AINHOA Ithurria P ⓝ 🏊 🔲 €€

Pl du Fronton, 64250 **Tel** *05 59 29 92 11* **Fax** *05 59 29 81 28* **Rooms** *27*

This pretty 17th-century Basque inn was a stop on the pilgrimage route to Compostela. Opposite is the village's *pelota* court. Rooms are comfortable and prettily decorated, and the cosy dining room has an open fireplace, oak beams, and a menu with local specialities. **www.ithurria.com**

ANGLET Château de Brindos

P ⅋ ♨ ⚐ 🗐   €€€€€

1 allée du Château, 64600 **Tel** *05 59 23 89 80* **Fax** *05 59 23 89 81* **Rooms** *34*

Set in extensive, wooded grounds, this luxurious country house hotel offers gracious living beside a peaceful lake. Modern facilities include a weight room, sauna and *hammam*, with the beach and a golf course a short drive away. Enjoy breakfast on the jetty over the lake. **www.chateaudebrindos.com**

ARGELES-GAZOST Hôtel les Cimes

P ⅋ ♨ ⚐   €

1 pl d'Ourout, 65400 **Tel** *05 62 97 00 10* **Fax** *05 62 97 10 19* **Rooms** *25*

Rooms in this unassuming modern hotel, dating from the 1950s, are comfortable, if unexciting. Some have balconies overlooking the tranquil gardens, and a few are studios with kitchenettes. There is a games area for children. The hotel also has a sauna. **www.hotel-lescimes.com**

ARGELES GAZOST Hôtel le Miramont

P ⅋ 🗐   €€

44 av des Pyrénées, 65400 **Tel** *05 62 97 01 26* **Fax** *05 62 97 56 67* **Rooms** *27*

This stylish hotel harking back to the 1930s is set amid manicured gardens in an attractive spa town. Eight rooms, furnished with antiques, are in a separate villa in the gardens, sharing the facilities of the main wing. Chef Pierre Pucheu serves Atlantic-Pyrenees delicacies. **www.hotelmiramont.com**

ARREAU Hôtel d'Angleterre

P ⅋ ♨ ⚐   €

Rte Luchon, 65240 **Tel** *05 62 98 63 30* **Fax** *05 62 98 69 66* **Rooms** *20*

This 17th-century inn, set in a pretty village of slate-roofed houses in the foothills of the Pyrenees, offers a good restaurant, plainly furnished but comfortable rooms, a garden, swimming pool, terrace and children's games area. A great base for exploring the stunning countryside. **www.hotel-angleterre-arreau.com**

AUDRESSEIN L'Auberge d'Audressein

P ⅋   €

Village Le Bourg, 09800 **Tel** *05 61 96 11 80* **Fax** *05 61 96 82 96* **Rooms** *9*

A tiny inn hidden in the forested Vallee de la Bellongue, L'Auberge d'Audressein offers the simple life in some of the prettiest scenery in the western Pyrenees. The pleasant restaurant, with wonderful views from its veranda, serves outstanding regional cuisine. **www.auberge-audressein.com**

AURIGNAC Le Cerf Blanc

P ⅋   €

Rue St-Michel, 31420 **Tel** *05 61 98 95 76* **Fax** *05 61 98 76 80* **Rooms** *9*

Le Cerf Blanc is really a restaurant with rooms rather than a full-service hotel. This modest country house has grand views and simple, cosy, small rooms. The excellent restaurant is regarded as one of the best in the region, with fish and game dominating the menu. You can eat from the *menu du jour* at the bar, or more elaborately on the terrace.

BARBAZON Hostellerie de l'Aristou

P ⅋   €

Rte de Sauveterre, 31510 **Tel** *05 61 88 30 67* **Fax** *05 61 95 55 66* **Rooms** *7*

L'Aristou is a 19th-century farmhouse which has been converted into a rustic inn, and the bedrooms are decorated and furnished in keeping with its history. Outdoor tables with stunning mountain views are among the attractions of this non-smoking hostelry in the hills.

BIARRITZ Inter Hotel Windsor

P ⅋   €€

Grande Plage, 64200 **Tel** *05 59 24 08 52* **Fax** *05 59 24 98 90* **Rooms** *48*

Standing above the Grande Plage of lively Biarritz, this comfortable townhouse property has spacious rooms (with fine views from those facing the sea) and easy access to the beach and seafront public swimming pool. The restaurant serves good seafood and local dishes. **www.hotelwindsorbiarritz.com**

BIARRITZ Hôtel du Palais

P ⅋ ♨ ⚐ ⚐ 🗐   €€€€€

1 av de l'Impératrice, 64200 **Tel** *05 59 41 64 00* **Fax** *05 59 41 67 99* **Rooms** *132*

The grande dame of Biarritz's hotel scene, with an ambience harking back to the resort's Belle Epoque heyday. A magnificent heated seawater pool, direct beach access, a putting green, a playground and kids' pool complement the lovely rooms and outstanding restaurants. **www.hotel-du-palais.com**

ESPELETTE Hôtel Euskadi

P ⅋ ♨ ⚐   €

285 rte Karrika Nagusia, 64250 **Tel** *05 59 93 91 88* **Fax** *05 59 93 90 19* **Rooms** *32*

Set in quiet countryside not far from the Atlantic beaches, this small and friendly family-run hotel has a pretty terrace, well-appointed rooms, a large swimming pool, tennis courts and secure parking. Owners Michèle and André Darriadou's restaurant serves Basque-influenced dishes. **www.hotel-restaurant-euskadi.com**

EUGENIE LES BAINS Les Prés d'Eugénie

P ⅋ ♨ ⚐ 🗐   €€€€€

334 rue René Vielle, 40320 **Tel** *05 58 05 06 07* **Fax** *05 58 51 10 10* **Rooms** *35*

Michel Guérard's highly acclaimed hotel has six gorgeous suites in addition to its simple but luxurious bedrooms. The 19th-century manor is famed for its *cuisine minceur* restaurants which offer residents the option of losing weight while revelling in some of France's finest cooking. **www.michelguerard.com**

FOIX Hôtel Lons

⅋   €

6 pl G-Dutilh, 09000 **Tel** *05 34 09 28 00* **Fax** *05 61 02 68 18* **Rooms** *38*

Overlooking the river, this no-nonsense former coaching inn has big, old-fashioned bedrooms – with a choice of WC or bath – at an affordable price. The restaurant is also uncompromisingly old-fashioned, with a menu that emphasizes hefty local dishes. **www.hotel-lons-foix.com**

Key to Price Guide *see p550* **Key to Symbols** *see back cover flap*

FOIX Le Poulsieu

Le Poulsieu, 09000 **Tel** *05 61 02 77 72* **Fax** *05 61 02 77 72* **Rooms** *5*

A fabulous place for a relaxing family holiday, with games for children, a pretty garden, open-air dining on the veranda and a shared kitchen for guests who like to cater for themselves. For those who don't, the Dutch owners will cook dinner on request. Tranquil rural surroundings. **www.ariege.com/le-poulsieu**

LOURDES Grand Hôtel de la Grotte

66 rue de la Grotte, 65100 **Tel** *05 62 94 58 87* **Fax** *05 62 93 20 50* **Rooms** *76*

One of the grandest hotels in the historic pilgrimage town of Lourdes, close to the famous grotto and fortress, with large rooms furnished opulently in Louis XVI style – some with views of the cathedral. The restaurants offer a choice of buffet or brasserie dining. **www.hoteldelagrotte.com**

LUZ ST SAUVEUR Hôtel le Montaigu

9 route Vizos, 65120 **Tel** *05 62 92 81 71* **Fax** *05 62 92 94 11* **Rooms** *35*

Overlooked by the ruins of a medieval castle, Le Montaigu offers modern facilities in scenic surroundings. The bedrooms lack character, but the view from the balcony rooms compensates for the bland décor. Pleasant restaurant with a bar that opens onto the gardens. **www.hotelmontaigu.com**

MIREPOIX La Maison des Consuls

6 pl Maréchal Leclerc, 09500 **Tel** *05 61 68 81 81* **Fax** *05 61 68 81 15* **Rooms** *8*

Housed in a charming 14th-century building that was once the district's courtroom, this hotel is located on a renowned medieval square in the heart of this picturesque little town. The rooms are filled with an eclectic array of antiques. The café-bar serves breakfast and snacks. **www.maisondesconsuls.com**

MIREPOIX Relais Royal

8 rue Maréchal Clauzel, 09500 **Tel** *05 61 60 19 19* **Fax** *05 61 60 14 15* **Rooms** *8*

This 18th-century building was once the mayor's residence, and today it blends grand tradition with modern facilities. The rooms are huge, and reached by an imposing staircase. Staying here feels like being a guest at an aristocratic house-party. Small restaurant with modern fare. **www.relaisroyal.com**

OLORON STE MARIE Hôtel Alysson

Bd Pyrénées, 64400 **Tel** *05 59 39 70 70* **Fax** *05 59 39 24 47* **Rooms** *32*

In a pleasant small town poised between the lowlands and the Pyrenees, this hotel has small, well-designed modern rooms, excellent cooking, and an attractive open-air terrace-bar. Lots of pale wood panelling. The enormous restaurant opens onto the attractive gardens. **www.alysson-hotel.fr**

ORTHEZ Reine Jeanne

44 rue Bourg Vieux, 64300 **Tel** *05 59 67 00 76* **Fax** *05 59 69 09 63* **Rooms** *30*

Occupying an 18th-century building in this historic Béarnaise town straddling the Gave de Pau river, this pleasant hotel has small guest rooms around a sheltered courtyard, as well as a modern wing with larger rooms. Country-style restaurant with traditional cooking. **www.reine-jeanne.fr**

PAU Hôtel Continental

2 rue Maréchal Foch, 64000 **Tel** *05 59 27 69 31* **Fax** *05 59 27 99 84* **Rooms** *75*

This comfortable hotel in the centre of historic Pau has huge old-fashioned bedrooms, just a couple of minutes' walk from the castle and a choice of restaurants. Opened in 1912, the Continental has old-world charm but with up-to-date facilities. Nearby parking. **www.bestwestern-continental.com**

PAU Hôtel du Parc Beaumont

1 av Edouard VII, 64000 **Tel** *05 59 11 84 00* **Fax** *05 59 11 85 00* **Rooms** *72*

This luxurious modern hotel, part of the Concorde group, stands in beautiful grounds next to Pau's casino and palm-lined boulevard with great views of the Pyrenees. Rooms are lavishly furnished, and there is a heated pool, whirlpool, sauna and *hammam* (Turkish bath). **www.hotel-parc-beaumont.com**

SARE Hôtel Arraya

Pl du Village, 64310 **Tel** *05 59 54 20 46* **Fax** *05 59 54 27 04* **Rooms** *24*

Modern facilities blend with old-world character at this half-timbered hotel on the pilgrimage route to Compostela. Whitewashed stone walls are half-covered in foliage, bedrooms are rustic, decorated in Basque colours, and the restaurant serves regional specialities. Closed Nov–March. **www.arraya.com**

SAUVETERRE DE BEARN La Maison de Navarre

Quartier St Marc, 64390 **Tel** *05 59 38 55 28* **Fax** *05 59 38 55 71* **Rooms** *7*

This pink mansion house in a beautiful medieval village has bright, airy guest rooms. Comfortable, good value for money, and child-friendly. The family donkey, Zebulon, lives in the garden, and the beaches of the Atlantic coast are not too far away. Excellent restaurant. **www.lamaisondenavarre.com**

ST-BERTRAND DE COMMINGES Hôtel Comminges

Pl Cathedrale, 31510 **Tel** *05 61 88 31 43* **Fax** *05 61 94 98 22* **Rooms** *14*

This tiny, charming hotel stands in the centre of one of France's prettiest villages, in the shadow of the beautiful cathedral. The hotel was once a convent, and its large guest rooms and public areas are full of antiques. Delightful, shaded breakfast terrace. Restaurants nearby.

ST-ETIENNE DE BAÏGORRY Hôtel Arcé   🅿️ 🍴 ⛆ 📺   €€

Rte Col d'Ispeguy, 64430 **Tel** *05 59 37 40 14* **Fax** *05 59 37 40 27* **Rooms** *20*

This welcoming Basque inn is set in the Aldudes valley, in the foothills of the Pyrenees, ideal for exploring the Basque country. The pool is on the opposite bank of the river, along with a tennis court. Pleasant restaurant terrace. Renovated guest rooms. Closed mid-November to mid-March. **www.hotel-arce.com**

ST GIRONS Hôtel Eychenne   🅿️ 🍴 ⛆   €€

8 av Paul Laffont, 09200 **Tel** *05 61 04 04 50* **Fax** *05 61 96 07 20* **Rooms** *45*

The former coaching inn has been run by the same family for seven generations, and the light, airy bedrooms and gracious public areas are filled with antiques and heirlooms. The facilities are modern, however, and there is a pretty garden where you can lunch in the open air. **www.ariege.com/hotel-eychenne/**

ST JEAN-DE-LUZ La Devinière   🅿️   €€€

5 rue Loquin, 64500 **Tel** *05 59 26 05 51* **Fax** *05 59 51 26 38* **Rooms** *10*

The bedrooms in this charming 18th-century building are all different, prettily decorated and furnished with antiques, artworks and rare books. There is a cosy lounge-library with an open fireplace and a grand piano, and a breakfast-tea room. Tiny garden. No restaurant. **www.hotel-la-deviniere.com**

ST JEAN-PIED-DE-PORT Hôtel les Pyrénées   🅿️ 🍴 ⛆ 🏋️ 📺 🍴   €€€

19 pl du Général-de-Gaulle, 64220 **Tel** *05 59 37 01 01* **Fax** *05 59 37 18 97* **Rooms** *20*

This 18th-century coaching inn stands at the French end of the Roncevaux pass, where the pilgrims' route to Santiago de Compostela crosses the Pyrenees. Immaculate rooms, health club with heated outdoor pool, and a restaurant offering both gastronomic and budget menus. **www.hotel-les-pyrenees.com**

LANGUEDOC-ROUSSILLON

AIGUES-MORTES Hôtel des Croisades   🅿️ 🍴 🍴   €

2 rue du Port, 30220 **Tel** *04 66 53 67 85* **Fax** *04 66 53 72 95* **Rooms** *15*

Just outside the ramparts, beside the canal, this appealing hotel has a pretty garden, modern and well-equipped rooms, and helpful staff. The sights of historic Aigues Mortes are a short walk away, and the wetlands and beaches of the Camargue are nearby. Parking for a fee. **www.lescroisades.fr**

AIGUES-MORTES Hôtel St Louis   🅿️ 🍴   €€

10 rue Amiral Courbet, 30220 **Tel** *04 66 53 72 68* **Fax** *04 66 53 75 92* **Rooms** *22*

Spacious rooms with modern comforts and a location next to the famous Constant Tower make this friendly hotel in an 18th-century building one of the better places to stay in Aigues-Mortes. Good restaurant, pretty patio, and garage parking available for a fee. **www.lesaintlouis.fr**

BARJAC Hôtel Le Mas du Terme   🅿️ 🍴 ⛆ 🏋️ 🍴   €

Route de Bagnoles sur Ceze, 30430 **Tel** *04 66 24 56 31* **Fax** *04 66 24 58 54* **Rooms** *23*

Set among its own vineyards and lavender fields, this sturdy old stone farmhouse-hotel in the heart of the Ardèche has plenty of character, lovely surroundings, charming bedrooms and public areas, and a fine restaurant. Activities for children include riding, ping-pong and *boules*. **www.masduterme.com**

BEZIERS Hôtel le Champ-de-Mars   🅿️   €

17 rue de Metz, 34500 **Tel** *04 67 28 35 53* **Fax** *04 67 28 61 42* **Rooms** *10*

This family-run establishment offers comfortable, good-sized bedrooms. Located in a quiet side street, it is close to the sights, restaurants and cafés of historic Béziers. Baskets filled with geraniums adorn the front, while most rooms overlook the small, flower-filled back garden. **www.hotel-champdemars.com**

BOUZIGUES La Côte Bleue   🅿️ 🍴 ⛆   €

Av Louis Tudesq, 34140 **Tel** *04 67 78 31 42* **Fax** *04 67 78 35 49* **Rooms** *32*

This modern hotel close to the charming fishing village of Meze, on the inner shore of the calm Thau lagoon, has somewhat bland rooms but fantastic sea views from the balconies. Its highly regarded restaurant specializes in plump, tasty oysters, shellfish and crustaceans.

CARCASSONNE Hôtel du Soleil Le Terminus   🖥️ 🅿️ 🍴 ⛆ 🏋️   €

2 av Maréchal Joffre, 11000 **Tel** *04 92 80 74 00* **Fax** *04 68 80 74 01* **Rooms** *110*

Built in 1913, this once-grand hotel retains traces of its heyday, including a vast, marble-floored lobby and staircase. It is located across from the train station, close to the canal basin and a 2-minute walk from the market square in the heart of Carcassonne's modern quarter. **www.vacances-soleil.fr**

CARCASSONNE Hôtel de la Cité   🖥️ 🍴 ⛆ 🍴   €€€€€

Pl August-Pierre Pont, 11000 **Tel** *04 68 71 98 71* **Fax** *04 68 71 50 15* **Rooms** *53*

The finest hotel in the Languedoc-Roussillon region, with immaculate service, opulent rooms, a glorious pool, formal gardens, superb restaurants and an unbeatable location within Carcassonne's medieval town, La Cité. Golf, canoeing and white-water rafting are available nearby. **www.hoteldelacite.com**

Key to Price Guide *see p550* **Key to Symbols** *see back cover flap*

CARCASSONNE-LA-CITE Des Trois Couronnes ▢🅿🍴♨🗖 €€

2 rue Trois Couronnes, 11000 **Tel** *04 68 25 36 10* **Fax** *04 68 25 92 92* **Rooms** *68*

This business-like hotel looks across the river Aude towards the battlements of medieval Carcassonne, and its fourth-floor restaurant has unbeatable views of the floodlit ramparts at night. Very good value, with much better facilities than most local hotels in its price bracket. **www.hotel-destroiscouronnes.com**

CASTILLON DU GARD Le Vieux Castillon ▢🅿🍴♨🗖🗖 €€€€

Rue Turion Sabatier, 30210 **Tel** *04 66 37 61 61* **Fax** *04 66 22 73 73* **Rooms** *33*

Restored buildings in a medieval village have been converted into a stylish, discreet and prestigious hotel with fine facilities and wonderful food. Le Vieux Castillon is part of the prestigious Relais et Châteaux consortium, living up to demanding standards. Book well in advance. **www.vieuxcastillon.com**

CERET Hôtel-restaurant Vidal 🅿🍴 €

4 pl Soutine, 66400 **Tel** *04 68 87 00 85* **Fax** *04 68 87 62 33* **Rooms** *18*

This small hotel in the centre of Céret, housed in an 18th-century building which was once a bishop's mansion, is a real find. The rooms are a decent size, there is a friendly café-bar on the ground floor, and a formal restaurant serving set menus and *à la carte* Catalan dishes. **www.hotelvidalceret.com**

CERET La Terrasse au Soleil 🅿🍴♨🗖🗖🗖 €€€

1500 route de Fontfrede, 66400 **Tel** *04 68 87 01 94* **Fax** *04 68 87 39 24* **Rooms** *34*

This hotel is perched on the slopes above the village of Céret (where Picasso lived and worked) and has great views of Mt Canigou and the Pyrenees. The restaurant is renowned for its regional cuisine. This is a great place for an active family, with pretty rooms and good facilities. **www.terrasse-au-soleil.com**

COLLIOURE Relais des Trois Mas 🅿🍴♨🗖 €€€€

Route de Port-Vendres, 66190 **Tel** *04 68 82 05 07* **Fax** *04 68 82 38 08* **Rooms** *23*

This lovely hotel comprises several restored old buildings in pine-shaded gardens, with superb views of the Côte du Vermeille and the port and town of Collioure. Most rooms have terraces or verandas, and all have sea views. La Balette restaurant has a fine traditional menu. **www.relaisdestroismas.com**

LEZIGNAN-CORBIERES Mas du Gaujac 🅿🍴🗖 €

Rue Gustave Eiffel, 11200 **Tel** *04 68 58 16 90* **Fax** *04 68 58 16 91* **Rooms** *21*

Lezignan is a sleepy town perfectly placed for exploring the vineyards, mountains and Cathar castles of the Corbières region. Mas de Gaujac is an attractive new hotel built in traditional style in the centre of town, with comfortable rooms and simple, traditional food in the restaurant. **www.logis-de-france.fr**

MINERVE Relais Chantovent 🍴 €

17 grande rue, 34210 **Tel** *04 68 91 14 18* **Fax** *04 68 91 81 99* **Rooms** *10*

Accommodation is at a premium in the fortified village of Minerve, so the Relais Chantovent is a worthwhile discovery. The buildings have been painstakingly restored and the bedrooms are simple – only one has en-suite bathroom. The terrace restaurant has views over the gorge.

MOLITG-LES-BAINS Grand Hôtel Thermale ▢🅿🍴♨🗖🗖 €€

Molitg-les-bains, 66500 **Tel** *04 68 05 00 50* **Fax** *04 68 05 02 91* **Rooms** *114*

This spacious, lakeside spa hotel in the mountains is spacious and peaceful. Amenities include two pools, games area for children, tennis courts, boulodrome and shops. A range of health treatments is on offer, along with local activities such as hiking, cycling and angling. **www.chainethermale.fr**

MONTPELLIER Hôtel du Palais ▢🗖 €

3 rue Palais des Guilhem, 34000 **Tel** *04 67 60 47 38* **Fax** *04 67 60 40 23* **Rooms** *26*

The Hôtel du Palais is in an attractive, century-old building in the heart of the old quarter of Montpellier. Bedrooms are on the small side, but with welcoming personal touches such as fresh flowers. A good choice for a budget short break. Plenty of restaurants nearby. **www.hoteldupalais-montpellier.fr**

MONTPELLIER Hôtel Ulysse 🅿 €

338 ave St Maur, 34000 **Tel** *04 67 02 02 30* **Fax** *04 67 02 16 50* **Rooms** *23*

This quirky hotel with its emphasis on wrought-iron furniture has an Art Deco feel. Located in a quiet residential district, there is has no restaurant (except for breakfast) but the pick of Montpellier's fine eating establishments are not far away. Secure parking available. **www.hotel-ulysse.com**

MONTPELLIER Hôtel Guilhem ▢🅿🗖🗖 €€

18 rue JJ Rousseau, 34000 **Tel** *04 67 52 90 90* **Fax** *04 67 60 67 67* **Rooms** *35*

A comfortable hotel with well-equipped bedrooms. Located in the centre of Montpellier, there are views of the cathedral and university buildings, and rear rooms have views of a pretty hidden garden. Good places to eat in the area, with beaches and the Camargue nearby. **www.leguilhem.com**

NARBONNE Grand Hôtel du Languedoc ▢🅿🍴🗖 €

22 bd Gambetta, 11100 **Tel** *04 68 65 14 74* **Fax** *04 68 65 81 48* **Rooms** *40*

This stylish hotel in a 19th-century building is a short walk from Narbonne's cathedral, city-centre shopping, markets and museums. The popular restaurant retains traces of its Belle Epoque elegance. Spacious rooms with high ceilings, air-conditioning and soundproofing. **www.hoteldulanguedoc.com**

NIMES L'Orangérie

🅿️ 🍴 ♨️ 🛁 📺 🖥️ ♿ €€

755 rue Tour de l'Evèque, 30000 **Tel** *04 66 84 50 57* **Fax** *04 66 29 44 55* **Rooms** *37*

Part of the Best Western group, this hotel combines a great location in a wooded park outside the centre of Nîmes with a super array of facilities, including an outdoor pool, gym, solarium, steam room, hot tub, and children's play area. The restaurant serves traditional cuisine. **www.orangerie.fr**

NIMES New Hôtel la Baume

🛏️ 🖥️ €€€

21 rue Nationale, 30000 **Tel** *04 66 76 28 42* **Fax** *04 66 76 28 45* **Rooms** *34*

Housed in an elegant 17th-century townhouse, la Baume is one of the most pleasant places to stay in Nîmes. A short step from the sights, it blends old-world charm with modern facilities. Some rooms are even listed as historic monuments. No restaurant, but a welcoming café-bar. **www.new-hotel.com**

PERPIGNAN Hôtel de la Loge

🖥️ €

1 rue des Fabriques d'en Nabot, 66000 **Tel** *04 68 34 41 02* **Fax** *04 68 34 25 13* **Rooms** *22*

This affordable hotel in the heart of Perpignan's medieval quarter is housed within the walls of a 16th-century Catalan mansion with a mosaic forecourt and fountain. Its comfortable rooms all have en-suite facilities. Unassuming and cosy, ideal for a short break. **www.hoteldelaloge.fr**

PERPIGNAN Park Hôtel

🛏️ 🅿️ 🍴 🖥️ 🛁 ♿ €€

18 bd J. Bourrat, 66000 **Tel** *04 68 35 14 14* **Fax** *04 68 35 48 18* **Rooms** *69*

Part of the Best Western group, this modern hotel only 5 minutes from the historic centre of Perpignan has a degree of charm, with attractively decorated rooms, helpful staff, and up-to-date facilities. The menu at the Chapon Fin restaurant surpasses its bland exterior. **www.parkhotel-fr.com**

QUILLAN Hôtel Cartier

🛏️ 🅿️ 🍴 €

31 bd Charles de Gaulle, 11500 **Tel** *04 68 20 05 14* **Fax** *04 68 20 22 57* **Rooms** *28*

The family-run Hôtel Cartier is housed in a 1950s Art Deco building in the centre of Quillan. The clean, comfortable rooms are simple, almost Spartan, with neutral colours. The restaurant is similarly unassuming, but friendly, affordable and as popular with locals as it is with visitors. **www.hotelcartier.com**

SETE Grand Hôtel

🛏️ 🅿️ 🍴 🖥️ €€

17 quai de Tassigny, 34200 **Tel** *04 67 74 71 77* **Fax** *04 67 74 29 27* **Rooms** *43*

Set beside Sète's famous canal, this 19th-century building exudes faded grandeur, and its conservatory-restaurant is one of the finest in Sète. Rooms are freshly decorated and well-equipped – the best have balconies overlooking the canal. Service is extremely professional. **www.legrandhotelsete.com**

SOMMIERES Auberge du Pont-Romain

🛏️ 🅿️ 🍴 ♨️ ♿ €€

2 rue Emile-Jamais, 30250 **Tel** *04 66 80 00 58* **Fax** *04 66 80 31 52* **Rooms** *19*

This sturdy, stone-built 19th-century building was a wool factory until the Michel family converted it into a welcoming auberge. The rooms are charmingly individual, and there is a peaceful, shaded garden. Chef Bernard Michel and pâtissier Frédéric Michel serve fine regional cooking. **www.aubergedupontromain.com**

ST CYPRIEN-PLAGE Le Mas d'Huston

🛏️ 🅿️ 🍴 ♨️ 📺 🖥️ 🛁 ♿ €€€€

Golf St Cyprien, 66750 **Tel** *04 68 37 63 63* **Fax** *04 68 37 6 464* **Rooms** *50*

Set in 200 hectares of parkland, Le Mas d'Huston has 9- and 18-hole golf courses on its doorstep, and the sea is just a short distance away. All rooms are air-conditioned and have a terrace or balcony, mini-bar, safe and satellite TV. Restaurants are mainly buffet-style. **www.golf-st-cyprien.com**

UZES Le Mas d'Oléandre

🅿️ ♨️ 🛁 €€

Saint-Médiers, 30700 **Tel** *04 66 22 63 43* **Fax** *04 66 03 14 06* **Rooms** *6*

Outside the lovely village of Uzès, this hotel is housed in a lovingly restored array of farm buildings. There is a large garden with shady nooks and a pool with a panoramic view of the countryside. Restaurants nearby, and lavish *table d'hôte* meals on request. **www.masoleandre.com**

VILLENEUVE-LES-BEZIERS Anges-Gardiens

€

7 rue de la Fontaine, 34420 **Tel** *04 67 39 87 15* **Fax** *04 67 32 00 95* **Rooms** *4*

Beautifully restored period bed and breakfast in historic Béziers near the Mediterranean beaches – and only a minute's stroll from the Canal du Midi. This friendly establishment is good for solo travellers. Rooms are simple but with period touches. Evening meals available. **www.aux-anges-gardiens.com**

PROVENCE AND THE COTE D'AZUR

AIX EN PROVENCE Hôtel des Augustins

🖥️ 🛏️ €€€

3 rue Masse, 13100 **Tel** *04 42 27 28 59* **Fax** *04 42 26 74 87* **Rooms** *29*

In a converted 12th century convent, with the reception housed in a 15th-century chapel, the Hôtel des Augustins offers a haven of peace in the heart of bustling Aix. The rooms are large and comfortable in traditional Provençal style. No restaurant, but places to eat nearby. **www.hotel-augustins.com**

Key to Price Guide *see p550* **Key to Symbols** *see back cover flap*

AIX EN PROVENCE Hôtel St Christophe

2 av Victor Hugo, 13100 **Tel** *04 42 26 01 24* **Fax** *04 42 38 53 17* **Rooms** *60*

This superb townhouse hotel has bedrooms with all modern facilities – book in advance to secure a room with a tiny balcony. Decorated in Art Deco style, the ground floor is a bustling old-fashioned brasserie of the best kind, with tables indoors and out. Very central location. **www.hotel-saintchristophe.com**

ANTIBES L'Auberge Provençale

61 pl Nationale, 06600 **Tel** *04 93 34 13 24* **Fax** *04 93 34 89 88* **Rooms** *16*

A large, welcoming townhouse under the spreading plane trees of Antibes' bustling main square. The spacious, comfortable, clean rooms are furnished simply with rustic Provençal furniture and canopied beds. Old-fashioned atmosphere in one of the Riviera's trendiest spots. **www.aubergeprovencale.com**

ANTIBES Mas Djoliba

29 av Provence, 06600 **Tel** *04 93 34 02 48* **Fax** *04 93 34 05 81* **Rooms** *13*

Mas Djoliba is a big, old-fashioned farmhouse set among lots of greenery, with palm trees surrounding the pool terrace. Convenient for old Antibes and the beaches nearby, it is perfect for a romantic weekend or a longer stay. Closed end October–early February. **www.hotel-djoliba.com**

ARLES Hôtel Calendal

5 rue Porte de Laure, 13200 **Tel** *04 90 96 11 89* **Fax** *04 90 96 05 84* **Rooms** *38*

This relaxing hotel in the historic centre of Arles, near the Roman arena, has charmingly decorated and air-conditioned rooms, a few with balconies overlooking the arena or the Roman theatre. Breakfast is served in the garden, which is shaded by palm trees. **www.lecalendal.com**

ARLES Hôtel d'Arlatan

26 rue du Sauvage, 13200 **Tel** *04 90 93 56 66* **Fax** *04 90 49 68 45* **Rooms** *47*

The former 15th-century town residence of the Comtes d'Arlatan, this is one of the most beautiful historic hotels in the region. The rooms are furnished with antiques. Glass panels in the salon floor reveal 4th-century Roman foundations. Walled garden and stone terrace. **www.hotel-arlatan.fr**

ARLES Hôtel Nord-Pinus

Pl Forum, 13200 **Tel** *04 90 93 44 44* **Fax** *04 90 93 34 00* **Rooms** *26*

A unique hotel overlooking the central square where Van Gogh painted the Café de Nuit, the Nord Pinus is an Arles landmark. Its guests have included Mistral, Picasso and Cocteau. Classified as a national monument, its modernized rooms are comfortable. Respected restaurant. **www.nord-pinus.com**

BEAULIEU SUR MER Le Select Hôtel

1 pl Charles de Gaulle, 06310 **Tel** *04 93 01 05 42* **Fax** *04 93 01 34 30* **Rooms** *19*

A small, simple and affordable option for Riviera travellers on a budget, the Select Hôtel is close to the train station (it can be a little noisy) and offers small, simple rooms and a pension atmosphere. Ask for a room overlooking the square (the site of Beaulieu's daily market).

BEAULIEU SUR MER La Réserve de Beaulieu

5 bd du Général Leclerc, 06310 **Tel** *04 93 01 00 01* **Fax** *04 93 01 28 99* **Rooms** *37*

A luxury hotel right on the seafront, in the heart of Beaulieu near the sailing harbour. The elegant rooms are decorated in warm pastel tones, and there is a magnificent pool next to the sea. The gastronomic restaurant has 2 Michelin stars. **www.reservebeaulieu.com**

BIOT Hôtel des Arcades

16 pl des Arcades, 6410 **Tel** *04 93 65 01 04* **Fax** *04 93 65 01 05* **Rooms** *12*

This 15th-century inn is a quirky haven of tranquillity. The rooms are small (even poky) but undeniably atmospheric. Top-floor rooms have terraces with views to the sea. The bar serves as breakfast room and restaurant, which you share with the local bohemian set and their dogs.

BORMES LES MIMOSAS Le Bellevue

14 pl Gambetta, 83230 **Tel** *04 94 71 15 15* **Fax** *04 94 05 96 04* **Rooms** *10*

This is a simple, family-run hotel. Rooms are unfussy and scrupulously clean – some have views over the terracotta roofs of Bormes les Mimosas to the beaches of the Mediterranean. Friendly, efficient service. The small restaurant serves tasty, unpretentious food. **www.bellevuebormes.fr.st**

CANNES Hôtel Molière

5-7 rue Molière, 06400 **Tel** *04 93 38 16 16* **Fax** *04 93 68 29 57* **Rooms** *24*

This 19th-century building is very close to la Croisette, Cannes' sea-front esplanade, with bright and comfortable rooms and balconies overlooking an attractive garden where breakfast is served. Good value and very much in demand – book well in advance. **www.hotel-moliere.com**

CANNES Hôtel Splendid

4 rue Felix Faure, 06400 **Tel** *04 97 06 22 22* **Fax** *04 93 99 55 02* **Rooms** *62*

This white wedding-cake of a hotel with its Belle Epoque frontage right in the centre of Cannes has fantastic views of the yacht harbour from the rooftop restaurant, and some sea-facing rooms have great balconies. Very good service, and a warm, friendly atmosphere. **www.splendid-hotel-cannes.fr**

CANNES Carlton Inter-Continental

58 la Croisette, 06400 **Tel** *04 93 06 40 06* **Fax** *04 93 06 40 25* **Rooms** *338*

The grandest of the grand, this is where the stars come to stay. During the film festival, there is a long waiting list for reservations. Art Deco surroundings, with discreetly luxurious facilities in the rooms and public areas, and a private beach with loungers and parasols. **www.intercontinental.com/cannes**

CANNES Eden Hôtel

133 rue d'Antibes, 06400 **Tel** *04 93 68 78 00* **Fax** *04 93 68 78 01* **Rooms** *116*

This new boutique hotel is bright, colourful and trendy, with a hint of 1960s retro complementing the modern feel. Close to the town's fashionable shopping streets, its facilities are being enhanced with the addition of a heated pool, whirlpool, massage room and fitness centre. **www.eden-hotel-cannes.com**

CAP D'ANTIBES La Garoupe et Gardiole

60–74 chemin de la Garoupe, 06160 **Tel** *04 93 93 33 33* **Fax** *04 92 67 61 87* **Rooms** *37*

Pines and cypresses surround the pink 1920s buildings of this delightful (and delightfully affordable, by Cap d'Antibes standards) hotel. Tiled floors, beamed ceilings and whitewashed walls perpetuate the rural image. Bedrooms are light and airy. Shady terrace and pretty pool. **www.hotel-lagaroupe-gardiole.com**

CAP D'ANTIBES Hôtel du Cap (Eden Roc)

Bd Kennedy, 61060 **Tel** *04 93 61 39 01* **Fax** *04 93 67 76 04* **Rooms** *120*

Built in 1870, this is the ultimate Antibes palace, and a hideaway for the rich and famous. Most accommodation is in luxury suites or apartments. Seaside cabanas are available and there is a huge heated seawater pool. Superb food, obsequious service and state-of-the-art facilities. **www.hotel-du-cap-eden-roc.com**

CASSIS Les Jardins de Cassis

Rue Favier, 13260 **Tel** *04 42 01 84 45* **Fax** *04 42 01 32 38* **Rooms** *36*

The most pleasant place to stay in the picturesque port of Cassis, this hotel with good facilities is much in demand, so book early. The guest rooms, in a cluster of buildings painted in pastel shades, are small but well planned. The pool is in a garden of lemon trees and bougainvillea. **www.hotel-lesjardinsde-cassis.com**

CASTELLANE Nouvel Hôtel du Commerce

Pl Centrale, 04120 **Tel** *04 92 83 61 00* **Fax** *04 92 83 72 82* **Rooms** *35*

This hotel, in the picturesque small town of Castellane, makes a good base for exploring the surrounding area. The pretty, well equipped and immaculate rooms overlook the market square or the crag that surmounts Castellane. The dining room veranda is a lovely, airy spot. **www.hotel-fradet.com**

EZE Château Eza

Rue de la Pise, 06360 **Tel** *04 93 41 12 24* **Fax** *04 93 41 16 64* **Rooms** *10*

This remarkable building is a collection of medieval houses perched at the summit of Eze's "eagle's nest". Once home to Prince William of Sweden, it has been converted into a tiny jewel of a luxury hotel with elegant rooms and utterly breathtaking views from its terraces. **www.chateaueza.com**

FONTVIEILLE La Régalido

Rue F. Mistral, 13990 **Tel** *04 90 54 60 22* **Fax** *04 90 54 64 29* **Rooms** *15*

La Régalido is a pleasant converted olive oil mill in the centre of sleepy Fontvieille. This is the area's most luxurious and welcoming hotel, with tastefully decorated and inviting rooms and a delightful flower garden with palms and fig trees. The restaurant serves top Provençal cuisine. **www.laregalido.com**

JUAN LES PINS Eden Hôtel

16 av Gallet, 06160 **Tel** *04 93 61 05 20* **Fax** *04 93 92 05 31* **Rooms** *17*

It is hard to find a better budget option than the Eden in Juan-les-Pins. Dating from the 1930s, it has a certain faded charm, with unpretentious rooms (some with sea views) and a location close to the beach. Service is friendly. Breakfast is served on a pleasant terrace. No restaurant.

JUAN LES PINS Hôtel des Mimosas

Rue Pauline, 06160 **Tel** *04 93 61 04 16* **Fax** *04 93 92 06 46* **Rooms** *40*

Palm trees surround this gracious hotel, built at the turn of the 19th century and offering character and style at a reasonable rate. The hotel is beautifully presented, with comfortable, cool, simply furnished rooms. Request a quieter room overlooking the swimming pool. **www.hotelmimosas.com**

LES ARCS SUR ARGENS Logis du Guetteur

Pl du Château, 83460 **Tel** *04 94 99 51 10* **Fax** *04 94 99 51 29* **Rooms** *13*

Within the tower of an 11th-century castle – a prominent landmark overlooking the small village – this cosy hotel is a fine place to stay in summer or winter, almost equidistant between Mediterranean beaches and Alpine ski slopes. Views from the ramparts are epic. **www.logisduguetteur.com**

LES BAUX DE PROVENCE L'Hostellerie de la Reine Jeanne

Grande rue, 13520 **Tel** *04 90 54 32 06* **Fax** *04 90 54 32 33* **Rooms** *10*

This old house in the centre of one of Provence's most charming – and most-visited – villages has a dozen rooms, each different and attractively decorated and simply furnished. Not ideal for small children, and parking nearby is always a challenge. **www.la-reinejeanne.com**

Key to Price Guide *see p550* **Key to Symbols** *see back cover flap*

LES BAUX DE PROVENCE Auberge de la Benvengudo

P 🍴 ≋ ⚹ 📺 🖳 €€€

Vallon de l'Arcoule, 13520 **Tel** *04 90 54 32 54* **Fax** *04 90 54 42 58* **Rooms** *23*

With comfortable, lavishly decorated bedrooms, a large garden and tennis court, this attractive country house near the hilltop village of Les Baux is one of the most charming places to stay on the fringes of the Bouches du Rhône. It is a good base for exploring the region. **www.benvengudo.com**

MARSEILLE Le Ruhl

P 🍴 ⚹ 🖳 €€€

269 corniche Kennedy, 13007 **Tel** *04 91 52 01 77* **Fax** *04 91 52 49 82* **Rooms** *14*

The Ruhl is better known as a highly rated seafood restaurant than as a hotel, but its rooms are comfortable enough. Those in front – with large terraces and the best views across the bay to the island fortress of Chateau d'If – suffer from traffic noise.

MENTON Hôtel Aiglon

P 🍴 ⚹ 🛁 ≋ 🖳 €€

7 av de la Madone, 06500 **Tel** *04 93 57 55 55* **Fax** *04 93 35 92 39* **Rooms** *28*

Not far from the seafront, the Aiglon offers every comfort, including a heated swimming pool and a luxuriant garden. Housed in a charming 19th-century townhouse, it is nicely decorated and has a good restaurant with tables on a terrace shaded by palms. **www.hotelaiglon.net**

MOUSTIERS STE MARIE La Bastide de Moustiers

P 🍴 ⚹ ≋ 🖳 ♿ €€€€€

Chemin de Quinson, 04360 **Tel** *04 92 70 47 47* **Fax** *04 92 70 47 48* **Rooms** *12*

Outside one the region's prettiest villages, La Bastide de Moustiers is housed in a 17th-century building, but contains the latest facilities. Surrounded by a gorgeous garden, the hotel has sweeping views of the surrounding mountains and a good restaurant. Room with disabled access. **www.bastide-moustiers.com**

NICE La Belle Meunière

P ⚹ €

21 av Durante, 06000 **Tel** *04 93 88 66 15* **Fax** *04 93 82 51 76* **Rooms** *17*

This is a simple and unpretentious hotel with clean, comfortable and relatively quiet rooms, but few other facilities. The location is convenient, there is parking (extremely useful in Nice), and this is one of the few area budget hotels offering this level of comfort.

NICE Hôtel Windsor

🍴 ≋ ⚹ 📺 🖳 €€

11 rue Dalpozzo, 06000 **Tel** *04 93 88 59 35* **Fax** *04 93 88 94 57* **Rooms** *57*

The Hôtel Windsor provides a wide array of services and facilities, including a pool in an exotic palm garden, a children's play area, and a health and beauty centre offering massage and a sauna. Some rooms are individually decorated by local artists. Snack bar and restaurant. **www.hotelwindsornice.com**

NICE La Pérouse

P 🍴 ≋ 📺 🖳 €€€€

11 quai Rauba-Capeu, 06300 **Tel** *04 93 63 34 63* **Fax** *04 93 62 59 41* **Rooms** *58*

La Pérouse has the best view in Nice. At the eastern end of the Baie des Anges, it perches on a clifftop site between the Promenade des Anglais and the port. Sea-facing rooms have small terraces. Very peaceful. In summer the restaurant has tables beneath lemon trees. **www.hotel-la-perouse.com**

NICE Le Negresco

P 🍴 🛁 ⚹ 📺 🖳 €€€€€

37 promenade des Anglais, 06000 **Tel** *04 93 16 64 00* **Fax** *04 93 88 35 68* **Rooms** *121*

The Negresco is the grande dame of Riviera hotels and has been a landmark on the promenade des Anglais since it opened in 1913, with a seemingly endless list of rich and famous guests. Superbly decorated and furnished with works of art, flawless service and modern facilities. **www.hotel-negresco-nice.com**

SEILLANS Hôtel des Deux Rocs

P 🍴 ⚹ €€€

Place Font d'Amont, 83440 **Tel** *04 94 76 87 32* **Fax** *04 94 76 88 68* **Rooms** *14*

This 18th-century Provençal mansion on the village square has a strong family atmosphere, decorated with antiques and traditional fabrics. Rooms at the front are the biggest and brightest. Mediterranean cuisine is served beside the square's fountain in summer. **www.hoteldeuxrocs.com**

ST JEAN CAP FERRAT Clair Logis

P ⚹ ♿ €€€

12 av Prince Rainier de Monaco, 06230 **Tel** *04 93 76 11 85* **Fax** *04 93 76 51 82* **Rooms** *18*

This old-fashioned villa set in a large, lush garden has attracted a list of famous guests including General de Gaulle. The rooms are comfortable in a slightly old-fashioned way, with smaller, more modern rooms in the annex. There is no pool, but the beach is not far away. **www.hotel-clair-logis.fr**

ST JEAN CAP FERRAT La Voile d'Or

P 🍴 🛁 ≋ ⚹ 📺 🖳 €€€€€

Port de St-Jean, 06230 **Tel** *04 93 01 13 13* **Fax** *04 93 76 11 17* **Rooms** *45*

Not quite the most expensive hotel in St-Jean but not far off, La Voile d'Or is worth every cent – service is superb and the rooms are immaculate. Two pools, views of the yacht harbour and the coast, and beach pavilions. Excellent restaurant in classic French culinary tradition. **www.lavoiledor.fr**

ST PAUL DE VENCE Hostellerie des Remparts

🍴 ⚹ €€

72 rue grande, 06570 **Tel** *04 93 32 09 88* **Fax** *04 93 32 06 91* **Rooms** *9*

In the heart of this picturesque village, the Hostellerie des Remparts offers modern comforts in a medieval setting. Its rooms are furnished with antiques, and have marvellous views. There is a small garden terrace. The village is car-free and parking is some distance away. **www.hotel-les-remparts.net**

ST PAUL DE VENCE La Colombe d'Or
🅿🍴🏊🎿🏃🛗 €€€€€

Pl de Gaulle, 06570 **Tel** *04 93 32 80 02* **Fax** *04 93 32 77 78* **Rooms** *26*

The most luxurious place to stay in St Paul, this former farmhouse in a fabulous setting once hosted Impressionist painters, and originals by Picasso and Matisse grace its walls. The guest list is still impressive, and early reservations are necessary. The restaurant is highly rated. **www.la-colombe-dor.com**

ST TROPEZ Lou Cagnard
🅿🛗🏃 €€

Av Paul Roussel, 83990 **Tel** *04 94 97 04 24* **Fax** *04 94 97 09 44* **Rooms** *19*

Occupying an old town house, this small hotel is only a minute's walk away from St Tropez's lively square, the place des Lices. Request a room overlooking the small garden with its shady mulberry trees; there is no air conditioning, and rooms in the front are noisy with open windows. **www.hotel-lou-cagnard.com**

ST TROPEZ Hôtel Le Mouillage
🅿🏊🛗 €€€€

Port du Pilon, 83990 **Tel** *04 94 97 53 19* **Fax** *04 94 97 50 31* **Rooms** *12*

This tiny hotel is a real find, with bedrooms that contrast traditional Provençal fabrics and paintwork with an eclectic array of furnishings from North Africa, India and Bali. Excellent service. A romantic hideaway for a weekend or a week. Parking is available. **www.hotelmouillage.fr**

ST TROPEZ La Ponche
🅿🍴🏃🛗 €€€€€

Port des Pêcheurs, 83990 **Tel** *04 94 97 02 53* **Fax** *04 94 97 78 61* **Rooms** *18*

For those looking for a boutique hideaway in St Tropez, this cluster of one-time fishermen's cottages may fit the bill. The bedrooms are large and artfully chic, and include two family-size rooms. Among the famous guests have been Pablo Picasso and 1950s film star Romy Schneider. **www.laponche.com**

VENCE Mas de Vence
🅿🍴🌊🏊🎿🛗♿ €€

539 av Hugues, 06140 **Tel** *04 93 58 06 16* **Fax** *04 93 24 04 21* **Rooms** *40*

This modern establishment may not appeal to those looking for somewhere quaint, but its architecture and colours are in keeping with Provençal tradition and it has excellent facilities including air-conditioned, insulated rooms, a small garden, and a terrace restaurant. **www.azurline.com**

VILLEFRANCHE-SUR-MER Hôtel Versailles
🅿🍴🌊🏊🛗 €€

7 bd Princesse Grace, 06230 **Tel** *04 93 76 52 52* **Fax** *04 93 01 97 48* **Rooms** *46*

This modern hotel has enough facilities for a longer stay, including a swimming pool, a restaurant specializing in Provençal cuisine, a large terrace and bedrooms with great views. Perhaps its only (slight) drawback is its location on a busy thoroughfare. Secure parking. **www.hotelversailles.com**

VILLEFRANCHE-SUR-MER Hôtel Welcome
🅿🌊🛗 €€€€

3 quai Amiral Courbet, 06230 **Tel** *04 93 76 27 62* **Fax** *04 93 76 27 66* **Rooms** *36*

This ochre-painted hotel has a period charm and attractive views of the sea and the port of Villefranche. Most rooms have balconies or terraces – ask for one overlooking the bay. Close to the beach. Artist Jean Cocteau stayed here after the death of his partner in the 1920s. **www.welcomehotel.com**

CORSICA

AJACCIO Hôtel Fesch
🌊🏃🛗 €€

7 rue Cardinal Fesch, 20000 **Tel** *04 95 51 62 62* **Fax** *04 95 21 83 36* **Rooms** *77*

This long-established hotel is situated in a pedestrian street in the centre of town. Open year round, it provides a good base for visiting local historic sites. Napoleon Bonaparte's house and the Fesch museum are a 5-minute walk away. The rooms are large with solid furnishings. Closed mid-Dec–mid Jan. **www.hotel-fesch.com**

AJACCIO Hôtel Kallisté
🅿🛗 €€

51 cours Napoléon, 20000 **Tel** *04 95 51 34 45* **Fax** *04 95 21 79 00* **Rooms** *48*

Right in the middle of the busy Cours Napoléon, the rooms are surprisingly quiet in this well-run, clean hotel. Wrought-iron banisters and exposed stone walls add a rustic touch to the building, which dates back to 1864. Just a few minutes' walk to the train and bus stations. **www.hotel-kalliste-ajaccio.com**

BASTIA Hôtel Posta Vecchia
🌊🏃🛗 €€

Quai des Martyrs de la Libération, 20200 **Tel** *04 95 32 32 38* **Fax** *04 95 32 14 05* **Rooms** *49*

Conveniently situated in the heart of the city, this busy hotel is next to the bustling, colourful, old port with its lively restaurants. Ask for a room in the front so that you can watch the evening promenade along the tree-lined quay. Public parking in front. **www.hotel-postavecchia.com**

BASTIA Hôtel Pietracap
🅿🏊🏃🛗 €€€

Route San Martino, San Martino di Lota, 20200 **Tel** *04 95 31 64 63* **Fax** *04 95 31 39 00* **Rooms** *39*

Supremely comfortable hotel in a beautiful setting along the coast road from Bastia. A large park with 100-year-old olive trees separates the hotel from the sea. Large outdoor swimming pool. Private car park. Closed Dec–Apr. **www.hotel-pietracap.com**

Key to Price Guide *see p550* **Key to Symbols** *see back cover flap*

BONIFACIO Hôtel le Royal

8 rue Fred Scamaroni, 20169 **Tel** *04 95 73 00 51* **Fax** *04 95 73 04 68* **Rooms** *14*

Busy hotel in the old town with views over the cliffs and sea. Freshly painted, pastel-coloured rooms. The cathedral is a few minutes' walk away, and steps lead down to the lively quayside. The little tourist train stops just outside. The restaurant serves mainly local dishes.

BONIFACIO Hôtel Santa Teresa

Quartier Saint-François, 20169 **Tel** *04 95 73 11 32* **Fax** *04 95 73 15 99* **Rooms** *48*

Spectacularly situated, at the top of the cliffs, this imposing hotel was originally a police garrison, built in 1897. Several of the elegant rooms have balconies from which you can enjoy the magnificent sea views reaching to Sardinia. Private parking. Closed mid-Oct–Apr. www.hotel-santateresa.com

CALVI Hôtel Balanea

6 rue Clémenceau, 20260 **Tel** *04 95 65 94 94* **Fax** *04 95 65 29 71* **Rooms** *38*

Comfortable hotel in the town centre on the quayside, with an uninterrupted view across the bay to the mountains. Rooms are spacious and well decorated, with large bathrooms. At night, join the cosmopolitan crowd at one of the many port restaurants. Closed Jan. www.hotel-balanea.com

CALVI Hostellerie l'Abbaye

Route Santore, 20260 **Tel** *04 95 65 04 27* **Fax** *04 95 65 30 23* **Rooms** *43*

This pretty ivy-covered hotel was built on the walls of a 16th-century abbey. Ideally positioned on a slight incline, just above the port, it is set back from the road and is surrounded by an immaculate garden. A 5-minute walk takes you to the town centre. Closed in winter. www.hostellerie-abbaye.com

CORTE Hôtel de la Paix

9 av Général de Gaulle, 20250 **Tel** *04 95 46 06 72* **Fax** *04 95 46 23 84* **Rooms** *64*

Pleasant family hotel, built in 1932, on a quiet square in the town centre. The interior has been renovated, with parquet floors throughout. Some rooms have terraces; those at the back have views over the gardens and mountains. Parking nearby. Closed for 10 days at Christmas.

ÎLE ROUSSE Hôtel Santa Maria

Route du Port, 20220 **Tel** *04 95 63 05 05* **Fax** *04 95 60 32 48* **Rooms** *56*

Superbly situated on the road to the islet of Île Rousse, this charming hotel has its own little beach and is just a short walk to the main square, with its shops and restaurants. All rooms have a terrace with sea views. Restaurant serves lunch in July and August. www.hotelsantamaria.com

PIANA Les Roches Rouges

Route Porto, 20115 **Tel** *04 95 27 81 81* **Fax** *04 95 27 81 76* **Rooms** *30*

Built in 1912, this splendid hotel retains all the charm of that era. Large, simply furnished rooms look out onto the bay of Porto, nominated by UNESCO as one of the world's five most beautiful bays. Excellent dining room with terrace and garden. Closed Nov–Mar. www.lesrochesrouges.com

PORTO Le Maquis

Porto, 20150 **Tel** *04 95 26 12 19* **Fax** *04 95 26 12 77* **Rooms** *6*

Quiet family-run hotel on the outskirts of town, on the coast road to Calvi. Surprisingly sophisticated menu in the charming restaurant. Dramatic views over the mountains. Comfortable rooms, pretty garden, and parking available. Closed Dec–Jan.

PORTO-VECCHIO Chez Franca

Route de Bonifacio, 20137 **Tel** *04 95 70 15 56* **Fax** *04 95 72 18 41* **Rooms** *14*

This modern hotel is conveniently situated between the town and the port. A lot of care has gone into the renovation of the rooms. The superb beaches of Guilia and Palombaggia are a few kilometres away. Good base for excursions to Zonza and Bavella. Closed Dec. www.francahotel.com

SARTENE Hôtel St Damianu

Quartier San Damien, 20100 **Tel** *04 95 70 55 41* **Fax** *04 95 70 55 78* **Rooms** *28*

A cracker of a new hotel. Large airy rooms have terraces with fabulous views of the gulf of Valinco or the mountains. Facilities include a huge swimming pool surrounded with teak decking, a garden, *hammam*, disabled access, secure parking, and an excellent dining room. Closed Nov–Apr. www.sandamianu.fr

ST FLORENT Hôtel Maxime

Route La Cathédrale, 20217 **Tel** *04 95 37 05 30* **Fax** *04 95 37 13 07* **Rooms** *19*

Set back from the street on the way to the 12th-century cathedral of Santa Maria Assunta, this modern hotel is an oasis of calm only a 1-minute walk from the hurly-burly of the fashionable port. Pleasant, airy rooms with sea views from the top floor.

VIZZAVONA Hôtel du Monte D'Oro

Col de Vizzavona RN 193, 20219 **Tel** *04 95 47 21 06* **Fax** *04 95 47 22 05* **Rooms** *30*

You'll feel as though you are in an Agatha Christie novel the moment you walk into this charming hotel, built in 1880 and set in the forest on the road between Ajaccio and Bastia. Wood-panelled corridors, large living room and elegant dining room serving organic food. A *gite* is also available for rent. Closed Nov–Apr. www.monte-oro.com

WHERE TO EAT

The French consider eating well an essential part of their national birthright. There are few other places where people are as passionately knowledgeable about their cuisine and their wine. Restaurant reviews, as well as cooking and food shows on television, are avidly followed and the general quality of both fresh food and restaurant offerings is vastly better in France than it is in most other European countries.

This introduction to the restaurant listings, which are arranged by region and town *(see pp600–51)*, looks at the different types of restaurant in France and gives practical tips on eating out, reading menus, ordering and service – everything you need to know to enjoy your meal. At the front of the book is a guide to a typical menu and an introduction to French wine *(see pp24–7)*. The main food and wine features are at the beginning of each of the five regional sections.

FRENCH EATING HABITS

The traditional large meal at noon survives mainly in rural regions. In cities, lunch is increasingly likely to consist of a sandwich, salad or a steak in a café, while dinner is the main meal of the day. Usually, lunch is from noon to 2pm and dinner is from 8 to 10pm, with last orders taken 30 minutes before closing time.

Some family-owned places are closed at weekends, so it may be difficult to find a meal anywhere outside your hotel on Sundays, except in large cities. Off the beaten track and in resort towns, restaurants and hotels are often closed out of season, so it is advisable to ring ahead.

Over the past few decades, French eating habits have changed dramatically. The growing popularity of the cuisine of former French colonies means that North African and Vietnamese places are now easy to find, as are Chinese restaurants. Burger and Tex-Mex joints are also popular with young people. As city-dwellers and suburbanites in France have become almost as health-conscious as other Europeans, there has been an explosion of "light" foods; and the rise of the *hypermarchés* (hypermarkets) has resulted in less fresh produce on the menu as more frozen and prepared food is eaten.

REGIONAL COOKING

One of the great pleasures of travelling in France is sampling the country's regional

Typical elegant terrace restaurant in Provence

cuisine. In every *département* of France, menus will nearly always include local specialities, which reflect predominant local products and agriculture. A good way to divide France gastronomically is the butter/olive oil divide. In the north, butter is generally used in cooking; in the south, olive oil; and in the southwest, goose and duck fat predominate.

Each region takes great pride in its own cuisine. Nationally, the best-known dishes come from four regions: Alsace, a province with close German ties; the southwest, where *cassoulet*, a rich stew of white beans, tomatoes, sausage and duck is a well-loved dish; the Alps, which gave *fondue* to the nation; and Provence, famed for *bouillabaisse*, a rich fish soup from Marseille.

The gastronomic capital of France is, however, considered to be Lyon, which boasts a significant proportion of France's best restaurants and many superb no-nonsense bistros known as *bouchons*.

La Cigale, a Belle Epoque brasserie in Nantes *(see p623)*

RESTAURANTS

Encompassing the whole alphabet of French cuisine, restaurants in France range from tiny whitewashed places with rush-bottomed chairs to stately, wood-panelled château dining rooms and the top kitchens of famous chefs. Many hotels have fine restaurants open to non-residents, a selection of which can be found in the hotel listings (see pp550–95).

Prices for restaurants of the same rating are more or less consistent throughout France except in large cities, where they can be more expensive. The quality of the food and service, though, is the most significant price factor and you can easily spend over 150€ per head to eat at one of the top establishments.

There are several different kinds of French cuisine that you may come across. *Haute cuisine* is the traditional cooking method, where the flavour of the food is enhanced with rich sauces. *Nouvelle cuisine* challenged this method, especially for the diet-conscious, in using light rather than creamy sauces which bring out the texture and colour of the ingredients. *Cuisine bourgeoise* is French home cooking. *Cuisine des Provinces* uses high-quality ingredients to prepare traditional rural dishes. *Jeune Cuisine Française* is the latest trend, where young chefs have rebelled against Michelin traditions to create their own cooking style.

BISTROS

When the French go out to eat, they are most likely to visit the broadest class of restaurant, the bistro. Bistros vary enormously – some urban bistros are formally decorated, while those in smaller cities and in the country tend to be more casual. Generally they offer a good, moderately

The restaurant L'Excelsior at Nancy in Lorraine (see p614)

priced meal from a traditional menu of an *entrée* or *hors d'oeuvre* (starter), *plats mijotés* (simmered dishes) and *grillades* (grilled fish and meats), followed by cheese and dessert.

BRASSERIES

Brasseries have their origin in Alsace and were originally attached to breweries; the name brasserie actually means brewery. Usually found in larger cities, they are big, bustling places, many with fresh shellfish stands outside. They serve beer on tap as well as a *vin de la maison* (house wine) and a variety of regional wines. Menus include simple fish and grilled meat dishes along with Alsatian specialities like *choucroute garnie* (sauerkraut with sausage and pork). Prices are very much on a par with those you would pay at bistros. Like cafés, brasseries are usually open from morning until night and serve food all day long.

Camembert

FERME-AUBERGES

In the country you may eat at a simple "farm inn", where good, inexpensive meals, often made with fresh farm produce, are taken with your host's family as part of your room and board. For more details on *ferme-auberges*, see under Bed and Breakfast on page 548.

CAFES

Cafés represent the soul of France. Every place but the tiniest hamlet can be counted on to have a café, open as a rule from early in the morning until 10pm or so. They serve drinks, coffee, tea, simple meals and snacks such as salads, omelettes and sandwiches throughout the day, and usually provide a cheaper breakfast than most hotels.

As well as serving refreshments, cafés are a good source of information and provide the traveller with endless opportunities to observe the French at their most relaxed.

In villages, almost the entire population might drift in and out of the single café during the course of a day, while large cities have cafés that cater for a specific clientele, such as workers or students. Paris's most famous cafés were traditional meeting places for intellectuals and artists to exchange ideas (see p152).

Auberge du XII Siècle at Saché in the Loire Valley (see p624)

Tables outside a café in the Old Town of Nice on the Côte d'Azur

BISTRO ANNEXES

Over the past few years, baby-bistros or bistro annexes have appeared in larger cities, especially Paris and Lyon, as a new category of restaurant. They are lower-priced sister eateries of the famous – and much more expensive – restaurants run by well-known chefs. Many of them offer *prix-fixe* (fixed-price) menus and the chance to sample the cooking of a celebrated kitchen in relaxed surroundings.

FAST FOOD

If you want to avoid the American fast food chains, wine bars and *salons du thé* are also good value for light meals. Cafeterias, found in some shopping centres, serve tasty food at reasonable prices.

RESERVATIONS

In cities and larger towns it is always best to make a reservation, especially from May to September. This rarely applies to cafés or in the country, where you can walk into most places without a reservation. However, if you are travelling in remote rural and resort areas off season, it is worth checking first that the restaurant is open all year.

If you have a reservation and your plans change, then you should call and cancel. Smaller restaurants, in particular, must fill all their tables to make a profit, and "no-shows" threaten their livelihood.

READING THE MENU AND ORDERING

When the menu is presented, you'll usually be asked if you'd like an aperitif. Since many French people do not drink spirits before a meal, this could be Kir (white wine mixed with a dash of black-currant liqueur), vermouth, light port (drunk in France as a cocktail) or a soft drink.

Opening the menu, *les entrées* or *hors d'oeuvre* are starters. *Les plats* are the main courses, and most restaurants will offer a *plat du jour*, or daily special; these are often seasonal or local dishes of particular interest. A selection of dishes from a classic French menu is given on pages 24–5.

Cheese is served as a separate course between the main course and dessert. Coffee is served black, unless you specify *"crème"*. Alternatively, you can ask for a *tisane*, or herbal tea.

WINE

As restaurants put a large mark-up on wine, it is better to further your connoisseurship with bottles purchased in shops, rather than when dining out. Local wine, however, is often served in carafes. Ordering a *demi* (50 cl) or *quart* (25 cl) carafe is a cheap way to try out a region's wines.

French law divides the country's wines into four classes, in ascending order of quality: Vin de Table, Vin de Pays, Vin Délimité de Qualité Supérieure (VDQS) and Appellation d'Origine Contrôlée (AOC).

The Vin de Table wines are rarely found in restaurants, but in choosing a regional wine (Vins de Pays upwards), refer to the wine features in the regional sections of this book. For an introduction to French wine, see pages 26–7.

When in doubt, order the house wine. Few restaurants will risk their reputation on an inferior house wine, and they often provide value for money.

WATER

Tap water is supplied on request free of charge, and is perfectly safe to drink. The French also pride themselves on their wide range of mineral waters. Favourite mealtime brands include Evian and the slightly fizzy Badoit.

Le Moulin de Mougins *(see p650)*

HOW TO PAY

Visa/Carte Bleue (V) is the most widely accepted credit card in France. Mastercard/Access (MC) is also commonly accepted, while American Express (AE) and Diners Club (DC) tend to be accepted only in upmarket establishments. However, you should always carry plenty of

La Tour d'Argent in the Latin Quarter of Paris *(see p603)*

cash, especially when touring the countryside, as many smaller restaurants still do not take any credit cards. If in doubt, ask when you make a reservation.

SERVICE AND TIPPING

The pace of a French meal is generally leisurely. People think nothing of spending 4 hours at the table, so if you are pressed for time, go to a café or brasserie. A service charge of 12.5 to 15 per cent is almost always included in the price of your meal, but most French people leave a few euro cents behind in a café, and an additional 5 per cent or so of the total bill in other restaurants. In the grander restaurants, which pride themselves on their service, an additional tip of 5 to 10 per cent is correct.

Thirty euro cents is sufficient for toilet attendants, and 50 or 70 euro cents an item is appropriate for the cloakroom attendant.

DRESS CODE

Even when dressed casually, the French are generally well turned out; visitors should aim for the same level of presentable comfort. Running shoes, shorts, beach clothes or active sportswear are unacceptable everywhere except cafés or beachside places.

The restaurant listings indicate which restaurants require men to wear a jacket and tie *(see pp600-51)*.

CHILDREN

French children are introduced early to restaurants and as a rule are well-behaved. Consequently, children are well-received almost everywhere in France. However, few restaurants provide special facilities like high-chairs or baby seats, as children are expected to behave sensibly, and there is often not much room for push-chairs.

PETS

Dogs are usually accepted at all but the most elegant restaurants. As the French are great

The Eychenne hotel-restaurant at St-Girons in the Pyrenees *(see p588)*

dog lovers, do not be surprised to see your neighbour's lapdog sitting on the next door *banquette*.

SMOKING

Despite all attempts to circumvent the no-smoking laws, especially in restaurants and cafés, the French have had to bow to the inevitable and should now adhere to government regulations about smoking in public.

Therefore, in line with other European countries, since 2007 smoking has been banned in all public places throughout France.

An elegant dining room in a hotel in Evian-les-Bains

WHEELCHAIR ACCESS

Though the restaurants of newer hotels usually provide wheelchair access, it is often restricted elsewhere. A word when you are booking your table should ensure that you are given a conveniently located table and assistance, if needed, when you arrive.

The listings show restaurants with wheelchair access.

Refer also to page 549 of this book, which gives the names and addresses of some organizations which provide advice to disabled travellers in France.

VEGETARIAN FOOD

France remains difficult for vegetarians, although some progress has been made in recent years. In most non-vegetarian restaurants the main courses are firmly orientated towards meat and fish. However, you can often fare well by ordering from the *entrées* and should never be timid about asking for a dish to be served without its meat content. Provided you make your request in advance, most smart restaurants will prepare a special vegetarian dish.

Only larger cities and university towns are likely to have fully fledged vegetarian restaurants. Otherwise cafés, pizzerias, crêperies and oriental restaurants are good places to find vegetarian meals.

PICNICS

Picnicking is the best way to enjoy the wonderful fresh produce, local bread, cheeses and *charcuterie* from the markets and enticing shops to be found all over France. For more details see pages 652–5.

Picnics are also a good way to eat cheaply and enjoy the French countryside. Picnicking areas along major roads are well marked and furnished with tables and chairs, but country lanes are better still.

Choosing a Restaurant

The restaurants in this guide have been selected across a wide range of price categories for their good value, exceptional food and interesting location. This chart lists the restaurants by region, in chapter order. Map references for Paris restaurants correspond with the Paris Street Finder, *see pp154–69*.

PRICE CATEGORIES
The following price ranges are for a three-course meal for one, including a half-bottle of house wine, tax and service:

€ under 30 euros
€€ 30–45 euros
€€€ 45–60 euros
€€€€ 60–90 euros
€€€€€ over 90 euros

PARIS

BASTILLE China Club
€€

50 rue de Charenton, 75012 **Tel** *01 43 43 82 02* **Map** *10 F5*

This Chinese restaurant is revolutionary in an extremely glamorous way. China Club has Colonial chic decor as well as superior Asian cuisine. The house specialities include delicious five-spice crispy pigeon and fresh sautéed sole with ginger-plum sauce. Jazz and world music concerts are regular fixtures.

BASTILLE Boca Chica
€€€

58 rue de Charonne, 75011 **Tel** *01 43 57 93 13* **Map** *10 F4*

Boca Chica boasts funky decor, trendy tunes and Spanish fare. Tapas, paella, grilled sardines, pork ribs and *gâteau basque* are all on the menu. On Mondays, there's a clairvoyance night here with a fortune teller who reads Tarot cards, while salsa is featured every Wednesday night.

BASTILLE Blue Elephant
€€€€

43 rue de la Roquette, 75011 **Tel** *01 47 00 42 00* **Map** *10 F3*

An island of refinement in the trendy Bastille area, with a tropical decor of lush plants, gurgling fountains and Thai woodwork. Superbly presented Thai cuisine: *som tam* (green papaya, dried shrimp and lime salad) and cashew chicken served in a fresh pineapple. Sunday brunch.

BEAUBOURG AND LES HALLES Aux Tonneaux des Halles
€

28 rue Montorgueil, 75001 **Tel** *01 42 33 36 19* **Map** *9 A1*

A genuine Parisian bistro, Aux Tonneaux des Halles is one of the last surviving bistros of its kind, with its real zinc bar, smoky interior and one of the tiniest kitchens in Paris. Service is not particularly quick, but when the food is this good, who cares! The wine list offers good value.

BEAUBOURG AND LES HALLES La Victoire Suprême du Coeur
€

41 rue des Bourdonnais, 75001 **Tel** *01 40 41 93 95* **Map** *9 A2*

Comforting vegetarian fare served in a bright blue-and-white dining room. Mushrooms are a speciality here, as in mushroom pâté or roast mushrooms with blackberry sauce. Desserts include a famous berry crumble. No alcohol served except cider; try the biodynamic carrot juice.

BEAUBOURG AND LES HALLES Le Louchebem
€

31 rue Berger, 75001 **Tel** *01 42 33 12 99* **Map** *8 F2*

A former butcher's shop ("louchebem" means butcher in old French slang), meat is what this no-nonsense eatery is all about, with portions designed more for rugby players than ballet dancers. *L'assiette du rôtisseur* (three-meat roast platter, each with its own sauce) is a classic, and the *aiguillette à la ficelle* (beef stew) is prepared traditionally.

BEAUBOURG AND LES HALLES Café Beaubourg
€€

43 rue Saint-Merri, 75004 **Tel** *01 48 87 63 96* **Map** *9 B2*

With views of the animated piazza of the Beaubourg museum, Café Beaubourg has elegant and contemporary decor. Simple and reliable, if slightly overpriced, fare is guaranteed – a variety of tartares, grilled meats and fish. The menu even offers a light and tasty Thai salad.

BEAUBOURG AND LES HALLES Saudade
€€

34 rue des Bourdonnais, 75001 **Tel** *01 42 36 03 65* **Map** *9 A2*

Probably Paris's finest Portuguese restaurant, with all the tiles you expect to see along the Tajus, not the Seine. The staple salt cod is prepared in fritters, with tomato and onion or potatoes and eggs, or try the roast suckling pig or *cozido* (Portuguese stew). Good selection of wine and port.

BEAUBOURG AND LES HALLES Au Pied du Cochon
€€€

6 rue Coquillière, 75004 **Tel** *01 40 13 77 00* **Map** *8 F1*

This colourfully restored brasserie was once popular with high society, who came to observe the workers in the old market and to savour the onion soup. Although touristy, this huge place is fun, and its menu has something for everyone (including excellent shellfish). Still one of the best places after a night out.

Key to Symbols *see back cover flap*

BEAUBOURG AND LES HALLES Georges
19 rue Beaubourg, 75004 **Tel** *01 44 78 47 99*

€€€€

Map 9 B2

On the top floor of the Pompidou Centre, the Georges offers stunning views. Light and inspired cuisine, such as cherry tomato and goat's cheese cake, *sole meunière*, lamb with chutney and macaroons. Roasted scallops with lemon butter is a hit. Minimalist decor, with lots of steel and aluminium.

CHAILLOT AND PORTE MAILLOT Chez Géraud
31 rue Vital, 75016 **Tel** *01 45 20 33 00*

€€

Map 5 B3

Géraud Rongier, the jovial owner, is a scrupulous observer of *cuisine du marché*, using what's fresh at the market each day to create dishes like shoulder of lamb cooked on a spit, *sabodet* sausage in red wine sauce, skate with mustard or roast pigeon with port sauce. The mural was specially created for the restaurant.

CHAILLOT AND PORTE MAILLOT Oum El Banine
16 bis rue Dufrenoy, 75016 **Tel** *01 45 04 91 22*

€€

Map 5 A1

The owner of this small, Moroccan restaurant in the chic residential quarter learned her art from her mother. Good *harira* (a thick, spicy soup), flavourful tagines, *pastilla* (a savoury puff-pastry tart) and *brik* (stuffed pastry triangle). *Couscous* served with five choices of *ragoût*.

CHAILLOT AND PORTE MAILLOT La Plage
Port Javel, 75015 **Tel** *01 40 59 41 00*

€€€

Map 5 B5

A spectacular site facing the Statue of Liberty on the Ile aux Cignes, the French and Mediterranean cuisine here is as good as the view. The huge terrace is the place to be seen at lunchtime, as well as an idyllic spot for a summer candlelit dinner. The decor is an attractive mix of wood and pastel tones. Service can be slow.

CHAILLOT AND PORTE MAILLOT La Butte Chaillot
110 bis av Kléber, 75016 **Tel** *01 47 27 88 88*

€€€€

Map 2 D5

This is the boutique restaurant of the renowned, not to say deified, chef Guy Savoy. The bistro cuisine includes snail salad, oysters with a cream mousse, roast breast of veal with rosemary and apple tart. The clientele are smartly attired, so make sure you dress up.

CHAILLOT AND PORTE MAILLOT Zebra Square
3 pl Clément Ader, 75016 **Tel** *01 44 14 91 91*

€€€€

Map 5 B4

Part of the Hotel Square complex, a modern building with stylish, minimalist decor spiced up by splashes of zebra prints. Equally modern fare: crab cakes, aubergine (eggplant) *carpaccio* and salmon tartare. Brunch on Sundays. A hit with the fashion and media crowd.

CHAILLOT AND PORTE MAILLOT Le Relais du Parc
55–57 av Raymond Poincaré, 75016 **Tel** *01 47 27 59 59*

€€€€€

Map 5 C1

In this historic townhouse, Alain Ducasse and Joel Robuchon create France's great "classic" dishes. Each culinary region is featured, and dishes include *turbot de Bretagne*, *chevreuil d'Alsace* (venison) and *fois gras de canard des Landes*. Enviable wine list highlights the Bordeaux region. Michelin starred.

CHAMPS-ELYSEES Le Stübli
11 rue Poncelet, 75017 **Tel** *01 42 27 81 86*

€

Map 2 E3

A little corner of Germany with a patisserie, deli and tearoom. For lunch, try one of the classics, such as sauerkraut. The apple *strudel*, *linzertorte* and authentic Viennese hot chocolate make for a fine afternoon tea. Lunch is served on the terrace. German beer and wine are available.

CHAMPS-ELYSEES L'Ascot
66 rue Pierre Charron, 75008 **Tel** *01 43 59 28 15*

€€

Map 2 F5

The present restaurant is an offshoot of the original Sébillon, based in the bourgeois suburb of Neuilly since 1913. The menu specializes in meat, and puddings are traditional French. Inside, the decor is stately, with red banquettes and lots of dark wood.

CHAMPS-ELYSEES Le Bœuf sur le Toit
34 rue du Colisée, 75008 **Tel** *01 53 93 65 55*

€€

Map 3 A4

Highly inspired by the 1930s *Les Années Folles*, this building was formerly a cabaret venue (The Ox on the Roof). Exemplifying the classic Paris Art Deco brasserie, its changing menu can include *sole meunière*, snails, *foie gras* and *crème brûlée*. The speciality is *crêpes suzette*.

CHAMPS-ELYSEES La Fermette Marbeuf 1900
5 rue Marbeuf, 75008 **Tel** *01 53 23 08 00*

€€€

Map 2 F5

Fabulous Belle Epoque mosaics, tiles and ironwork were discovered beneath the formica walls of this Champs Elysées bistro. La Fermette Marbeuf also serves good brasserie-style food, including a commendable set menu with a wide range of *appellations contrôlées* wines.

CHAMPS-ELYSEES Verre Bouteille
85 av des Ternes, 75017 **Tel** *01 45 74 01 02*

€€€

Map 1 C2

Verre Bouteille proves that simple is tasty. The house speciality is skewered steak with *dauphinois* potatoes, but the goat's cheese ravioli, *foie gras* and chocolate cake are also superb. If you're on a budget bear in mind that lunch is much cheaper than dinner here.

CHAMPS-ELYSEES Guy Savoy   📧🔲🍷   €€€€

18 rue Troyon, 75017 Tel 01 43 80 40 61   **Map 2 D3**

A handsome dining room and professional service further complement the remarkable cuisine of Guy Savoy. The three Michelin-starred menu includes oysters in aspic, Bresse chicken with a sherry vinegar glaze, poached or grilled pigeon with lentils, and an extraordinary dessert list.

CHAMPS-ELYSEES Sens   🅿📧   €€€€

23 rue Ponthieu, 75008 Tel 01 42 25 95 00   **Map 3 A5**

This new concept restaurant, clad in soft greys and silvers, makes clever use of lighting to create the urban-chic feel that attracts the trendy crowd. Plastic, trunk-like pillars prop up the mezzanine, and young chef Christophe Fluck serves interesting Mediterranean-influenced dishes.

CHAMPS-ELYSEES Pavillon Ledoyen   🅿🚹📧🔲🍷   €€€€€

1 av Dutuit, 75008 Tel 01 53 05 10 01   **Map 7 B1**

The cuisine at Pavillon Ledoyen is refined with turbot fillet and mashed potatoes with truffle butter and *Mille-feuilles de Krampouz croustillante avec crème de citron* (lemon cream slice). Ask for a table in the dining room – a re-creation of a 1950s grill room – or one on the terrace.

ILE DE LA CITE AND ILE SAINT-LOUIS Au Rendez-Vous des Camionneurs   🚹📷   €

72 quai des Orfèvres, 75001 Tel 01 43 54 88 74   **Map 8 F3**

This restaurant situated on the picturesque Ile de la Cité can satisfy even the biggest appetite. Veal stew in white sauce is the house speciality, along with *foie gras* terrine and puff pastry filled with tomato, basil and mozzarella. Extra charges apply during the evening.

ILE DE LA CITE AND ILE SAINT-LOUIS La Rose de France   🚹📷   €€

24 pl Dauphine, 75001 Tel 01 43 54 10 12   **Map 8 F3**

Majestic setting overlooking a 17th-century square. Updated French classics, with specialities like the John Dory with rhubarb, ginger and Basmati rice. More traditional is the duck fillet in *ratatouille*. A *cuisine du marché* restaurant, La Rose uses the freshest produce from the day's market.

INVALIDES AND EIFFEL TOWER QUARTER L'Oeillade   🚹🍷   €€

10 rue de St-Simon, 75007 Tel 01 42 22 01 60   **Map 7 C3**

A welcoming restaurant featuring deep-fried smelt, *pipérade* (stewed sweet peppers, tomatoes and garlic) with poached egg, *sole meunière*, cod *brandade* (salt cod and garlic purée), roast lamb with cumin and *île flottante* (whipped egg whites in vanilla custard). Varied wine list and price range.

INVALIDES AND EIFFEL TOWER QUARTER La Villa Corse   🚹📧📷🍷   €€

164 bd de Grenelle, 75015 Tel 01 53 86 70 81   **Map 6 E5**

In a pleasant neighbourhood, La Villa Corse is one of the city's best restaurants for fresh and strongly flavoured Corsican-Mediterranean cuisine. The menu features wild boar stew, olive veal, Brocciu cheese and chestnut bread – a speciality from the city of Bonifacio. Good choice of Corsican wines.

INVALIDES AND EIFFEL TOWER QUARTER Le Troquet   🅿🚹📷   €€

21 rue François Bonvin, 75015 Tel 01 45 66 89 00

This is a jewel in an unlikely residential street with a view of the Eiffel Tower. Locals soak up the friendly atmosphere and devour Basque chef Christian Etchebest's fabulous cooking. Expect unusual dishes such as smoked eel tart with avocado purée and apples.

INVALIDES AND EIFFEL TOWER QUARTER L'Arpège   🚹📧🍷   €€€€

84 rue de Varenne, 75007 Tel 01 47 05 09 06   **Map 7 B3**

Alain Passard's three-star restaurant near the Musée Rodin is one of the most highly regarded in Paris. It has striking pale-wood decor and sprightly young service as well as excellent food. The lobster and turnip vinaigrette and duck Louise Passard are classics. Don't miss the apple tart.

INVALIDES AND EIFFEL TOWER QUARTER Le Jules Verne   🅿🚹📧📷🔲🍷   €€€€€

2nd platform, Eiffel Tower, 75007 Tel 01 45 55 61 44   **Map 6 D3**

This is no tourist trap: reservations at the Jules Verne on the second platform of the Eiffel Tower are among the hardest to obtain in Paris. The sleek, all-black decor suits the monument perfectly and the pretty, flavourful cuisine is very good, indeed.

JARDIN DES PLANTES QUARTER Marty Restaurant   🅿🚹♿📷   €€

20 av des Gobelins, 75005 Tel 01 43 31 39 51   **Map 13 B3**

The Marty was established by E Marty in 1913 and is still family-run. The interior is authentic Art Deco in style, but the cuisine steals the show. The menu features hearty fare, such as roast duck or rabbit casserole, and seasonal dishes, such as gazpacho. Excellent *crème brûlée*.

LATIN QUARTER Le Grenier de Notre Dame   🅿🚹♿📷🍷   €

18 rue de la Bûcherie, 75005 Tel 01 43 29 98 29   **Map 9 A4**

Le Grenier de Notre Dame opened in the 1970s and still exudes its original hippie atmosphere. Mostly organic ingredients go into the filling meals such as fish gratin, vegetarian casserole or vegetarian escalope in breadcrumbs. Good choice of reasonably priced wines, including Château Chaurignac Bordeaux.

LATIN QUARTER Le Balzar
49 rue des Ecoles, 75005 **Tel** *01 43 54 13 67*   **Map** *9 A5*

There's a fair choice of brasserie food here but the main attraction is the Left Bank ambience. Traditionally dressed waiters weave their way among the hustle and bustle, providing express service, with archetypal brasserie decor to match: there are large mirrors and comfortable leather seats.

LATIN QUARTER Le Petit Pontoise
9 rue Pontoise, 75005 **Tel** *01 43 29 25 20*   **Map** *9 B5*

This is a popular neighbourhood venue, where herbs and spices are used inventively. A perfect menu will probably be composed of a *Risoto à la Truffe*, followed by a duck *parmentier* and stir-fried *foie gras* and, finally, a hot vanilla *soufflé*. Reservations recommended.

LATIN QUARTER La Tour d'Argent
15–17 quai de la Tournelle, 75005 **Tel** *01 43 54 23 31*   **Map** *9 B5*

Established in 1582, originally in a stone tower, the Tour appears to be eternal. The young chefs hired by patrician owner Claude Terrail have rejuvenated the classic menu at this luxurious panoramic restaurant, with one of the finest wine cellars. The ground-floor bar is also a gastronomic museum. The lunch menu is cheaper than dinner.

LATIN QUARTER La Truffière
14 rue Blainville, 75005 **Tel** *01 46 33 29 82*   **Map** *13 A1*

This classic Latin Quarter address is best in winter, when you can warm up under a medieval vaulted ceiling in front of a roaring fire. The *prix-fixe* lunch menu is by far the best value for money, but if truffles are your favourite there are plenty of dishes to splash out on.

LATIN QUARTER L'Atelier Maître Albert
1 rue Maître Albert, 75005 **Tel** *01 56 81 30 01*   **Map** *9 B5*

Dishes from the rôtisserie are this restaurant's speciality. Traditional fare such as veal kidneys and mouthwatering chocolate cake are the chief attractions. Other specialities include veal, mixed salad *du moment* and chicken livers. The antique fireplace is a nice touch. This is another Guy Savoy restaurant.

MONTMARTRE Amour
8 rue de Navarin, 75009 **Tel** *01 48 78 31 80*   **Map** *4 F2*

Food at this low-key but trendy bistro, with vintage decor below Montmartre in the fashionable 9th *arrondissement*, is a cross between all things French and Anglo Saxon. Think fish and chips, burgers and *crème brulée*. In summer request a table in the pretty courtyard.

MONTMARTRE Au Grain de Folie
24 rue la Vieuville, 75018 **Tel** *01 42 58 15 57*   **Map** *4 F1*

Paris has few vegetarian restaurants, and this one has a truly cosy feel. The main courses consist of salads with interesting combinations of vegetables and grains (most of which are organic). Au Grain de Folie's apple crumble is highly recommended, so be sure to leave room.

MONTMARTRE La Famille
41 rue des Trois Frères, 75009 **Tel** *01 42 52 11 12*   **Map** *4 F1*

The contemporary French cuisine at La Famille is as delicious as it is avant-garde. Don't be surprised if your meal is presented with a smiley face drawn in the sauce! The marinated salmon in a thyme and rosemary crust is excellent. The decor borders on minimalist.

MONTMARTRE Le Wepler
14 pl de Clichy, 75018 **Tel** *01 45 22 53 24*   **Map** *6 D1*

Established in 1892, this retro-style brasserie is open until late into the night. Good for afternoon tea, early evening cocktails and pre- or post-show suppers. Le Wepler serves appetizing large shellfish platters as well as sauerkraut, *andouillette* (sausage) and *confit de canard*.

MONTMARTRE Beauvilliers
52 rue Lamarck, 75018 **Tel** *01 42 54 54 42*

Montmartre's best restaurant and one of the most festive in Paris, this is where effusive chef Edouard Carlier delves into old cookbooks to create favourites such as *escabèche* of red mullet (specially marinated), veal *rognonnade* (loin of veal with kidney) and a very lemony lemon tart.

MONTPARNASSE La Régalade
49 av Jean Moulin, 75014 **Tel** *01 45 45 68 58*   **Map** *11 C5*

Gourmet fare for a bargain at this traditional bistro. Try the duck *foie gras* casserole or pan-fried cod with leek vinaigrette for a main course, and the chef's speciality Grand Marnier soufflé for dessert. The seasonal menu is based on a *cuisine du marché*. Reservations essential.

MONTPARNASSE Port Manech
52 rue du Montparnasse, 75014 **Tel** *01 43 21 96 98*   **Map** *12 D2*

Port Manech is just like a little piece of Brittany right here in Paris. Try the tasty pancakes such as Provençal (mushrooms and snail butter), washed down perfectly with a cup of cider. There is a large choice of flambéed pancake varieties for dessert.

MONTPARNASSE Daléa
📋🔲 €€

13 bd Edgar-Quinet, 75014 **Tel** *01 40 47 02 43* **Map** *12 D2*

This casual-chic bar cum restaurant, with its mahogany panelling, rose petal-encrusted lights and "easy listening" music is a fashionable address for Parisians south of the Saint-Germain-des-Prés quarter. Cuisine is French with a twist, including smoked salmon with goat's cheese, steak *tartare* and apricots with pistachio caramel.

MONTPARNASSE La Cagouille
🔲🔲 €€

10–12 pl Constantin Brancusi, 75014 **Tel** *01 43 22 09 01* **Map** *11 C3*

This large venue, on the stark new place Brancusi in the rebuilt Montparnasse district, is one of Paris's best fish restaurants. Fish is served simply with few sauces or adornments. Unusual seasonal delicacies might include black bay scallops and *vendangeurs* (tiny red mullet).

MONTPARNASSE La Coupole
📋🔲 €€

102 bd du Montparnasse, 75014 **Tel** *01 43 20 14 20* **Map** *12 D2*

This famous brasserie has been popular with the fashionistas, artists and thinkers since its creation in 1927. Under the same ownership as Brasserie Flo, it has a similar menu: shellfish, smoked salmon and good desserts. Lamb curry is a speciality. Open from breakfast until 2am.

MONTPARNASSE Contre-Allée
📋♿🔲🔲 €€€

83 av Denfert-Rochereau, 75014 **Tel** *01 43 54 99 86* **Map** *12 E3*

Sylvain Pineau (former chef at the Crillon) conjures up mouth-watering dishes such as lamb steak in a herb crust with potatoes sautéed in goose fat, scallops and parsley butter. The decor is minimalist, with lots of dark wood, and the service is friendly.

OPERA QUARTER Chartier
🔲♿ €

7 rue du Faubourg Montmartre, 75009 **Tel** *01 47 70 86 29* **Map** *4 F4*

Despite its impressive 1900s decor, Chartier caters to people on a budget, mostly students and tourists, though some of the old *habitués* still come back for the basic cuisine (hard-boiled eggs with mayonnaise, house pâté, roast chicken and pepper steak). Expect no-frills service; the waiters are very busy.

OPERA QUARTER Angl'Opéra at Hôtel Edouard VII
🔲📋🔲🔲 €€

39 av de l'Opéra, 75002 **Tel** *01 42 61 86 25* **Map** *4 E5*

Chef Gilles Choukroun's chic yet unpretentious venue has a smart dining area and relaxing bar. The food is as unusual as it is delicious, with dishes such as *foie gras crème brûlée* or confit of beef with sea snails. The wine list is equally eclectic, and the service is excellent. Closed at weekends.

OPERA QUARTER La Vaudeville
🔲🔲🔲 €€

29 rue Vivienne, 75002 **Tel** *01 40 20 04 62* **Map** *4 F5*

This is one of seven brasseries owned by Paris's reigning brasserie king, Jean-Paul Bucher. Good shellfish, Bucher's famous smoked salmon, many fish dishes as well as classic brasserie standbys like pig's trotters and *andouillette* (tripe sausage). Quick, friendly service and a noisy ambience make it fun.

OPERA QUARTER Willi's Wine Bar
🔲🔲 €€

13 rue des Petits-Champs, 75001 **Tel** *01 42 61 05 09* **Map** *8 F1*

Original wine posters cover the walls of this wine bar, and over 250 vintages are kept in the cellar. The menu includes onion tart with a salad topped with pine nuts, beef *fricassée* with braised chicory (endive) and rosemary sauce, and bitter chocolate terrine.

OPERA QUARTER Le Grand Colbert
🔲 €€€

2–4 rue Vivienne, 75002 **Tel** *01 42 86 87 88* **Map** *4 F5*

Situated in the restored Galérie Colbert owned by the Bibliothèque Nationale, this must be one of the prettiest brasseries in Paris. The menu offers classic fare – herring fillets with potatoes or cream, snails, onion soup, whiting Colbert (in breadcrumbs) and grilled meats.

OPERA QUARTER Café Drouant
🔲🔲📋♿🔲🔲🔲 €€€€

18 rue Gaillon, 75002 **Tel** *01 42 65 15 16* **Map** *4 E5*

Founded in the 19th century, this is one of Paris's most historic restaurants. The café, not to be confused with the more expensive restaurant, is a fashionable spot serving excellent food until late. The dinner menu is extremely good value. Look up at the famous shellfish-motif ceiling.

OPERA QUARTER La Fontaine Gaillon
🔲🔲📋🔲🔲 €€€€

1 rue de la Michodière, 75002 **Tel** *01 47 42 63 22* **Map** *4 E5*

Housed in a 17th-century mansion, Fontaine Gaillon is partly owned by legendary film actor Gérard Depardieu. The menu showcases sautéed John Dory, Merlan Colbert with sorrel purée, *confit de canard* and lamb chops. The interiors are comfortable, and there is a good wine list.

SAINT-GERMAIN-DES-PRES Chez les Filles
€

64 rue du Cherche Midi, 75006 **Tel** *01 45 48 61 54* **Map** *7 C5*

Moroccan sisters run this charming little tearoom, with exotic afternoon tea breaks. Tagines, salads and *couscous* are on the lunch menu, and a Berber brunch is served on Sundays. The interior features wrought-iron work and kilims bearing Moroccan accents.

Key to Price Guide *see p600* **Key to Symbols** *see back cover flap*

SAINT-GERMAIN-DES-PRES Polidor 🖼🚻♿ €

41 rue Monsieur le Prince, 75006 **Tel** *01 43 26 95 34* **Map** 8 F5

Once frequented by Verlaine and Rimbaud, this is bohemian Paris incarnate. The place has kept its reputation by sticking to traditional cuisine at rock-bottom prices. Grilled steak, *daube de bœuf*, Marengo veal (slow cooked with tomatoes) and various dessert tarts feature on the menu.

SAINT-GERMAIN-DES-PRES Brasserie Lipp 🚻📧♿🍴🍷🎵 €€

151 bd St Germain, 75006 **Tel** *01 45 48 53 91* **Map** 8 E4

This is the brasserie that everyone loves to hate, yet its clientele, which includes entertainers and politicians, keeps returning for the good food. The dishes include herring in cream and a huge *millefeuille* (custard cream) pastry. Ask to be seated downstairs with the "in" crowd; upstairs is referred to as "Siberia".

SAINT-GERMAIN-DES-PRES Coffee Parisien 🚻♿ €€

4 rue Princesse, 75006 **Tel** *01 43 54 18 18* **Map** 8 E4

With wooden panelling, punctuated with pictures of American presidents, this is one of the best places for brunch. American classics dominate the menu, including one of the best burgers in Paris (with bacon and cheese), eggs Benedict and all sorts of pancakes and sundaes.

SAINT-GERMAIN-DES-PRES Yugaraj 🚻📧🎵 €€

14 rue Dauphine, 75006 **Tel** *01 43 26 44 91* **Map** 8 F3

Yugaraj is still considered by many to be the best Indian restaurant in Paris. The chef, proud of his high-quality products, emphasizes dishes from his native northern India, and key spices are brought in directly from the subcontinent. The wine list is surprisingly good, too.

SAINT-GERMAIN-DES-PRES Barroco 🚻📧 €€€

23 rue Mazarine, 75006 **Tel** *01 43 26 40 24* **Map** 8 F3

Serving Brazilian cuisine: *feijoada* (black bean casserole), *churrasco* (grilled meat) and Portuguese-style cod. The chic and cosy interior is complete with a library. Entertaining Brazilian musical groups perform at the Barroco several nights a week.

SAINT-GERMAIN-DES-PRES Procope 🎵 €€€

13 rue de l'Ancienne Comédie, 75006 **Tel** *01 40 46 79 00* **Map** 8 F4

Opened in 1686, Paris's oldest café welcomed literary and political figures such as Voltaire and Diderot. Nowadays, it's still a hub for the intelligentsia, who sit alongside those curious about this historical place. *Coq au vin* (chicken cooked in wine) is the speciality. Shellfish platters, too.

SAINT-GERMAIN-DES-PRES Jacques Cagna 🅿🚻📧♿🎵 €€€€€

14 rue des Grands Augustins, 75006 **Tel** *01 43 26 49 39* **Map** 8 F4

This elegant 17th-century townhouse showcases chef-owner Jacques Cagna's trinkets and excellent classic-cum-modern cuisine. Try the red mullet salad with *foie gras*, pigeon *confit* with turnips, and a classic Paris-Brest (choux pastry filled with praline cream). Admirable wine list.

THE MARAIS Aux Vins de Pyrénées 🚻♿🍴🎵 €

25 rue Beautreillis, 75004 **Tel** *01 42 72 64 94* **Map** 9 C3

A very old bistro with a friendly and typically Parisian atmosphere. The day's menu, written on a blackboard, typically features grilled meats. Excellent choice of wines by the glass (particularly good value Bordeaux and lesser-known wines from Southwest France). Extra charges for a menu à la carte.

THE MARAIS Le Baracane €

38 rue des Tournelles, 75004 **Tel** *01 42 71 43 33* **Map** 10 E3

A tiny restaurant with good-quality food at reasonable prices. The fixed-price menu is particularly good value. Southwestern cuisine includes delicious rabbit *confit*, braised oxtail, pears poached in Madeira and Cassis (blackcurrant liqueur), and superb homemade chestnut bread.

THE MARAIS Chez Jenny 🚻📧♿🍴 €€

39 bd du Temple, 75003 **Tel** *01 44 54 39 00* **Map** 10 D1

This huge brasserie on the place de la République, with waitresses in traditional dress, has been a bastion of Alsatian cooking since it was founded over 60 years ago. The *choucroute* (sauerkraut) *spéciale Jenny* makes a hearty meal, followed by a sorbet and a fruit liqueur.

THE MARAIS Le Bar à Huîtres 🅿🚻📧♿🍴 €€

33 bd Beaumarchais, 75003 **Tel** *01 48 87 98 92* **Map** 10 E3

Oysters predominate in Paris's three Bars à Huîtres (the other two are in Montparnasse and St-Germain-des-Prés). You can compose your own seafood platter to start, followed by a choice of fish or meat dishes. Convenient for the Place de la Bastille and the Marais.

THE MARAIS Le Colimaçon 🚻📧🎵 €€

44 rue Vieille du Temple, 75004 **Tel** *01 48 87 12 01* **Map** 9 C3

Le Colimaçon (snail) refers to the restaurant's centrepiece: a corkscrew staircase. A listed building dating from 1732, it has period wooden beams in the ceiling. Snails are also on the menu, along with frogs' legs in parsley and tomato sauce and *gigot de sept heures* (sautéed lamb chops).

THE MARAIS Trésor
5–7 rue du Trésor, 75004 **Tel** *01 42 71 35 17*
€€   **Map** *9 C3*

The decor of the tiny and trendy Trésor is defined by a contemporary elegance, with a touch of kitsch. Lasagne, grilled steak in wine sauce, and tiramisu show the blending of French and Italian cooking. Wide selection of wines, whiskeys and cocktails. Service is not always with a smile but the dining room opens onto a pleasant terrace.

THE MARAIS Auberge Nicolas Flamel
51 rue de Montmorency, 75003 **Tel** *01 42 71 77 78*
€€€   **Map** *9 B1*

Located in Paris's oldest house (1407) and named after the famous alchemist who lived here, this restaurant's specialities include *Tatin de foie gras poellé* (pan-fried foie gras) and *Gala au pain d'épices*. The *tour de force* here is *gigot de sept heures* (lamb, slow roasted for 7 hours), from a medieval recipe. Comprehensive wine list.

THE MARAIS L'Ambroisie
9 pl des Vosges, 75004 **Tel** *01 42 78 51 45*
€€€€€   **Map** *10 D3*

In a former jewellery shop restored by Chef Bernard Pacaud, this is one of only seven Michelin three-star restaurants in Paris. The cuisine includes a mousse of sweet red peppers, truffle *feuilleté* (layered pastry) and langoustines. Reservations accepted one month in advance.

TUILERIES QUARTER Café Marly
93 rue de Rivoli, 75001 **Tel** *01 49 26 06 60*
€€   **Map** *8 E2*

In a wing of the Louvre, this is a handy restaurant when feet ache and bellies rumble after trekking round the galleries. You'll find everything from salads and burgers to traditional and contemporary French cuisine. It's also in a top spot for a coffee on the terrace overlooking the Louvre's main thoroughfare.

TUILERIES QUARTER Barlotti
35 pl du Marché St-Honoré, 75001 **Tel** *01 44 86 97 97*
€€€€   **Map** *8 D1*

From the creators of super-trendy Buddha Bar and Barrio Latino comes this flashy, Italy-themed restaurant with its impressive atrium. Aubergine (eggplant) pasta, prawn risotto and cod satisfy the most delicate palates. Great Sunday brunch, and less expensive lunches.

TUILERIES QUARTER Le Grand Véfour
17 rue de Beaujolais, 75001 **Tel** *01 42 96 56 27*
€€€€€   **Map** *12 F1*

This 18th-century restaurant is considered by many to be Paris's most attractive. The chef Guy Martin effortlessly maintains his third Michelin star with dishes such as scallops with Beaufort cheese, cabbage ravioli with a truffle cream and endive *galette* (pancake).

ILE DE FRANCE

BARBIZON L'Angélus
31 rue grande, 77630 **Tel** *01 60 66 40 30*
€€€

Though on a main street, L'Angélus has rustic auberge-like atmosphere. Named after Millet's work of art painted at Barbizon, this well-presented restaurant serves traditional cuisine. The soups are excellent, especially on cold nights in the dining room complete with fireplace. Terrace dining in fine weather.

BARBIZON Hôtellerie du Bas-bréau
20 rue grande, 77630 **Tel** *01 60 66 40 05*
€€€€

Author Robert Louis Stevenson has been among the celebrated guests at this hotel-restaurant with its classic menu and enormous wine list. Much-praised cooking, including St-Pierre with a parmesan crust, succulent roast lamb with courgettes with a chestnut stuffing, and Grand Marnier soufflé.

DAMPIERRE Auberge Saint-Pierre
1 rue de Chevreuse, 78720 **Tel** *01 30 52 53 53*
€€€

This half-timbered inn facing the grand château de Dampierre has a rustic, convivial dining room. The gourmet menu has fine dishes such as tartare of potatoes with *foie gras*, salad of baby scallops with white radish, stuffed quail with lentils and chicken leg with *foie gras* stuffing.

DAMPIERRE Les Ecuries du Château
Château de Dampierre, 78720 **Tel** *01 30 52 52 99*
€€€

An exceptional, sophisticated setting in the former stables and saddle room of the château, Les Ecuries offers a traditional menu with classic meat and fish dishes, such as shredded duck with apples and pan-fried *noisette* of *lapin*. Classic wine list. The gardens provide a fitting backdrop.

FONTAINEBLEAU Le Caveau des Ducs
24 rue de Ferrare, 77300 **Tel** *01 64 22 05 05*
€€€

Near the château de Fontainebleau, this restaurant has a carved staircase leading to the magnificent 17th-century cellars that house the dining room, decorated with tapestries and chandeliers. Classic cuisine, such as snails in puff pastry. Good lunch menu of main course salad and a glass of wine.

Key to Price Guide *see p600* **Key to Symbols** *see back cover flap*

MAISONS-LAFFITTE La Vieille Fontaine 　　　　€€€
8 av Grétry, 78600 **Tel** *01 39 62 01 78*

An elegant setting inside a beautiful white mansion near the Maisons-Laffitte Park. Seasonal menus offer gastronomic cuisine in an unpretentious manner. Delicious, well-presented dishes like a pastilla of duck with honey, served with a celery charlotte or pumpkin shortbread. Reasonably priced wine.

NEUILLY-SUR-SEINE Le Bistro d'à Côté 　　　　€€
4 av Boutard, 92200 **Tel** *01 47 45 34 55*

Authentic Parisian bistro decorated with a collection of antique coffee grinders. Adored by locals, traditional dishes are served, such as rabbit and pistachio pâté, or braised lamb with olives. The small pots of chocolate cream are a must for dessert. Good value lunch menu.

PROVINS Aux Vieux Ramparts 　　　　€€€
3 rue Couverte, 77160 **Tel** *01 64 08 94 00*

In the medieval part of town, this timbered building boasts two restaurants and a hotel. The Petite Ecu offers traditional fare, while the Aux Vieux Ramparts is a gastronomic restaurant serving creative fare such as prawns with aubergine caviar, carpaccio of monk fish and chocolate tart.

RAMBOUILLET Le Cheval Rouge 　　　　€
78 rue du Général de Gaulle, 78120 **Tel** *01 30 88 80 61*

A small restaurant near the château with a good-humoured chef who presents specialities such as terrine of red onions, steak seasoned with five peppers, confit of pheasant with chicory and stuffed quail *à la champenoise*. Great midday buffet. Some tables are in the conservatory.

RUEIL-MALMAISON Relais de St-Cucufa 　　　　€€€
114 rue Générale-de-Miribel, 92500 **Tel** *01 47 49 79 05*

Combining Breton and Italian flair, the chefs present a traditional menu that includes morille soup with poached egg; lobster, grapefruit and avocado salad; platter of grilled shellfish; fillet of beef and roast lamb. Enjoy lunch in the attractive garden or dinner in front of the fire. Classic wine selection.

ST-GERMAIN-EN-LAYE Ermitage des Loges 　　　　€€€
11 av des Loges, 78100 **Tel** *01 39 21 50 90*

In an elegant setting near the château, this restaurant is frequented by locals. The young chef enlivens classic dishes, such as salmon and sole with saffron, duck fillet with red cabbage prepared with honey, curried polenta, and pistachio and cherry bread pudding.

ST-OUEN Le Soleil 　　　　€€€
109 av Michelet, 93400 **Tel** *01 40 10 08 08*

Steps away from the St-Ouen flea market and a short drive from the Stade de France, this charming bistro has a vibrant interior. The menu includes gazpacho with prawns, spicy duck with black rice or a more classic choice such as a Charolais entrecôte. Good, slightly expensive wine. Book ahead.

VERSAILLES Le Valmont 　　　　€€€
20 rue au Pain, 78000 **Tel** *01 39 51 39 00*

Refined cuisine at this bistro tucked behind the market hall. Chef Philippe Mathieu presents an ambitious menu with dishes such as *mille feuille* of haddock and celery, St-Pierre with pleurote mushrooms and chocolate dessert with Kirsch-infused cherries. Good wines by the glass.

VERSAILLES Restaurant Chez Lazare 　　　　€€
18 rue de Satory, 78000 **Tel** *01 39 50 41 45*

When you have tired of traditional French cuisine, try this fun South American restaurant for a well-prepared affordable meal. Seated underneath tiers of copper pots, diners relax and tuck into good old-fashioned grilled fish and steak. Pleasant, friendly service.

VERSAILLES La Terrasse 　　　　€€€
11 rue St-Honoré, 78000 **Tel** *01 39 50 76 00*

A fun restaurant specializing in southwestern cuisine. On a warm day the large, shaded terrace is a godsend. The decor inside is bright and kitsch. Try one of their *assiettes gourmandes*, a huge plate filled with delights such as duck, *foie gras*, prawns, truffles and sautéed potatoes.

LE NORD & PICARDY

AIRE-SUR-LA-LYS Hostellerie des Trois Mousquetaires 　　　　€€
Château de la Redoute, rte de Béthune, 62120 **Tel** *03 21 39 01 11*

Rural peace and the charm of a 19th-century mansion in its own grounds with a lake. Unusually, the kitchens are visible, and serve imaginative classic cuisine. The varied menu includes regional dishes. A popular destination with visitors from the UK; book ahead.

AMIENS Bistro des Chefs

12 rue Flatters, 80000 **Tel** *03 22 92 75 46* **Fax** *03 22 92 83 68*

A lively bistro in the centre of Amiens near the famous cathedral – which was built to house the supposed head of John the Baptist, and described by John Ruskin as the most perfect creation in mediaeval Christianity. Local specialities and traditional dishes include tripe and *blanquette de veau*.

AMIENS L'Aubergade

78 route Nationale, 80480 **Tel** *03 22 89 51 41* **Fax** *03 22 95 44 05*

Mediterranean-looking restaurant run by Eric Boutte, a young chef who won his first star and is making a name for himself. After working in top Paris restaurants, he returned to Amiens with a vision for his restaurant. His favourite ingredient is duck. Other dishes include pan-fried scallops with *foie gras* and lime soufflé with prunes.

ARRAS La Rapière

44 grand place, 62000 **Tel** *03 21 55 09 92*

Set in the heart of the finest city of French Flanders, on the Grand Place – one of a series of squares built during the Middle Ages when Arras was a great commercial centre. La Rapière offers unpretentious, good-value food. Try the *carbonade flamande* – Flemish stew – and the various offerings on the regional menu.

ARRAS La Faisanderie

45 grand place, 62000 **Tel** *03 21 48 20 76*

Also on the magnificent Grand Place, with its spectacular scrolled gable façades, this restaurant is housed in a 17th-century building with a splendid brick vaulted dining room. The cuisine is dictated by what the chef finds at the market. The best of several restaurants on the square, by far.

BERGUES Le Bruegel

1 rue du Marché aux Fromages, 59380 **Tel** *03 28 68 19 19* **Fax** *03 28 68 67 12*

Bergues is just outside Dunkirk and is a pleasant surprise. This is a very popular restaurant for families, with long tables and waiters in medieval dress. The picturesque building by the canal dates from 1597, when Spain ruled Flanders. Pork cheeks and lentils and other Flemish dishes with beer are the order of the day.

BOULOGNE-SUR-MER La Matelote

80 bd Ste Beuve, 62200 **Tel** *03 21 30 17 97* **Fax** *03 21 83 29 24*

One of the rising gastronomic stars, this is a top-notch seafood restaurant on the seafront, opposite the National Marine centre. The interior is smart, with sea-going ornaments and a red-and-gold Louis XVI motif. Try the warm lobster with artichoke hearts and basil or monkfish in parmesan.

CALAIS Histoire Ancienne

20 rue Royale, 62100 **Tel** *03 21 34 11 20* **Fax** *03 21 96 19 58*

This is a modernized restaurant that has managed to preserve its image as an old-fashioned bistro, with a zinc counter and the old-style bench seating. It is located opposite the Parc Richelieu. The well prepared menu is split between grilled meats and traditional local dishes.

CALAIS Le Channel

3 bd de la Résistance, 62100 **Tel** *03 21 34 42 30* **Fax** *03 21 97 42 43*

A good fish restaurant right next to the harbour, the yacht club and the Bassin du Paradis, with a fine view of the boats coming and going. The restaurant is bright and nicely decorated with painted woodwork. It has a wine list to be proud of. An ideal spot to wait for the ferry.

CAMBRAI L'Escargot

10 rue Général de Gaulle, 59400 **Tel** *03 27 8124 54* **Fax** *03 27 83 95 21*

An unsophisticated but agreeable establishment in the centre of town. Traditional dishes served by pleasant staff feature local ingredients – including 60 different regional cheeses. Try the snails with melted *tomme de Cambrai* or *andouillette de Cambrai* with mustard sauce.

CASSEL Estaminet T'Kasteel Hof

Rue St-Nicolas, 59670 **Tel** *03 28 40 59 29*

There are sweeping views of the flat countryside from this Flemish-style *estaminet* (no-frills café) which serves local dishes, often with local cheeses, accompanied by beer. It was at Cassel that the "Grand Old Duke of York", son of George III, marched his 10,000 men up to the top of the hill (as popularized in a song).

COMPIEGNE Bistro des Arts

35 cours Guynemer, 60200 **Tel** *03 44 20 10 10* **Fax** *03 44 20 61 01*

A lively bistro serving sophisticated, good-value fare. Located in the centre of town, with an artistic atmosphere. Chairs and red leather benches, but no tablecloths. Each day's menu is put up on the slate according to the market. The cuisine is traditional French, and usually includes a meat and a fish dish.

COMPIEGNE Alain Blot

2 rue Maréchal Foch, Rethondes, 60153 **Tel** *03 44 85 60 24* **Fax** *03 44 85 92 35*

The proprietor's motto is that seafood should be "a simple expression of the sea". This starred restaurant, with a delightful dining room and veranda opening onto an immaculate garden, is known for its range of classic dishes, such as grilled bass with caramelized red onion. Book ahead.

Key to Price Guide *see p600* **Key to Symbols** *see back cover flap*

DOUAI La Terrasse
36 terrasse St-Pierre, 59500 **Tel** *03 27 88 70 04* **Fax** *03 27 88 36 05*

An excellent hotel and restaurant in a lane next to the Collégiale St Pierre, with an extensive wine list of over 1,000 references. The opulent restaurant is decorated with paintings. Try the chef's inspiration – smoked salmon stuffed with asparagus and grilled scallops with black pudding.

DUNKIRK Estaminet Flamand
6 rue des Fusiliers-Marins, 59140 **Tel** *03 28 66 98 35*

Having suffered from many wars, Dunkirk is not a scenic tourist destination. It has, however, retained its culinary traditions, exemplified here in this pleasant *estaminet* (simple café). Delicious and authentic Flemish cuisine including marrow bones, *Maroilles* cheese, beer tart and sugar tart.

DUNKIRK L'Estouffade
2 quai de la Citadelle, 80000 **Tel** *03 28 63 92 78* **Fax** *03 28 63 92 78*

A small, popular restaurant specializing in seafood, with views of the port. In summer there is a quiet terrace onto the quay that runs alongside the commercial basin. Turbot is a speciality here. Desserts include chocolate and fruit specialities.

DURY LES AMIENS La Bonne Auberge
63 route Nationale, Dury, 80480 **Tel** *03 22 95 03 33*

This bright and fresh-looking restaurant is much decorated with flowers in the summer. The modestly priced menu varies daily, according to the offerings at the market and the inspiration of the chef. Fish dishes are a regular feature of La Bonne Auberge.

LILLE Au Barbue d'Anvers
1 bis, rue Saint-Etienne, 59000 **Tel** *03 20 55 11 68*

This new *estaminet lillois*, just off the Grand Place, is always full, thanks to first-class service, bright modern decor and excellent regional dishes. Try *Waterzoi* – poached chicken and braised rabbit cooked together. There is a fine selection of 30 local beers and a good wine list.

LILLE Au bout des doigts
5 rue St-Joseph, 59000 **Tel** *03 20 74 55 95*

A new concept for the French in dining out, meals at this restaurant comprise a selection of 8–10 small dishes. There are no knives and you can eat with your fingers. The cooking is based on mixing flavours, and the wine is drawn from all over the world. The decor is contemporary.

LILLE Le Compostelle
4 rue Saint-Etienne, 59800 **Tel** *03 28 38 08 30* **Fax** *03 28 38 08 39*

Just off the Grand Place is this former 16th-century hostel on the route to the shrine of St-Jacques de Compostelle (Santiago de Compostela) in northwest Spain. Today the hostel combines old-fashioned charm with contemporary decor. The chef provides a nice blend of regional and traditional cuisine.

MONTREUIL-SUR-MER Auberge de la Grenouillère
Rue de la Grenouillère, La Madeleine-sous-Montreuil **Tel** *03 21 06 07 22* **Fax** *03 21 86 36 36*

Three kilometres from Montreuil, this Picardy farm on the banks of the Canche is furnished traditionally with copper, antique sideboards and wall paintings of frogs enjoying a good meal. The modern menu is backed up by a good wine list. Tasty crayfish and frogs' legs.

POIX DE PICARDIE L'Auberge de la Forge
14 rue du 49ème Régiment BCA, Caulières, 80290 **Tel** *03 22 38 00 91* **Fax** *03 22 38 08 48*

A former staging post on the way from Amiens to Neufchatel, this half-timbered Picardy inn serves old-fashioned hearty fare. The restaurant is smart and attractive. The chef's speciality is duck, in various forms. The *endives gratinées*, ham with *Maroilles* cheese, and endives and scallops are also good.

RECQUES-SUR-HEM Château de Cocove
Av de Cocove **Tel** *03 21 82 68 29* **Fax** *03 21 82 72 59*

This fine 18th-century château, halfway between Calais and St-Omer, is a real rural retreat. Napoleon had parties here while waiting to invade England. The restaurant is in the beautifully restored old stone stables. Trays of shellfish can be specially prepared if ordered in advance.

ROYE La Flamiche
20 pl de l'Hôtel de Ville, 80700 **Tel** *03 22 87 00 56* **Fax** *03 22 78 46 77*

Known as a prestige gastronomic restaurant throughout the area, Madame Klopp has run this impeccable establishment for many years. Try the pan-fried scallops, the tajine of Somme eels or local *flamiche* with leeks. The dining room is filled with an exhibition of sculpture and paintings.

SANGATTE Les Dunes
Route Nationale 48, Blériot Plage, 62231 **Tel** *03 21 34 54 30* **Fax** *03 21 97 17 43*

This hotel and restaurant is located on Blériot Plage where, in 1909, an intrepid Frenchman set out on his successful attempt to be the first man to cross the Channel in powered flight. Today this is very handy for the Channel Tunnel. Great seafood: try the cassoulet of mussels.

SARS-POTERIES L'Auberge Fleurie
P 🏃 🍴 €€€

67 rue Général de Gaulle, 59216 **Tel** *03 27 61 62 48* **Fax** *03 27 61 56 66*

This grand farmhouse with pretty gardens has been converted into a restaurant serving classic French cooking at its best. The pike-perch on a bed of cabbage and bacon is good, as is the shellfish. In winter, venison, wild boar and partridge feature regularly on the menu.

STEENVOORDE Auprès de mon Arbre
🏃 🍴 €€

932 rte d'Ecke, 59114 **Tel** *03 28 49 79 49*

In this town, famous for its carnival giants which parade each year through the centre, and for its church steeple with its high belfry, this restaurant is well regarded. The owner was the chef at a well-known Lille restaurant before settling here in the late 1990s. Classic French as well as traditional Flemish cuisine.

ST-QUENTIN Le Pot d'Etain
P 🏃 ♿ 🍴 €

Route Nationale 29, Holnon, 2760 **Tel** *03 23 09 34 35* **Fax** *03 23 09 34 39*

An unpretentious but dynamic hotel and restaurant ruled over with a rod of iron by Madame Moulin. The huge hacienda-style dining room has a pleasant terrace for summer dining. Shellfish are the speciality, especially lobster grilled with scallops and taragon.

WIMEREUX Hôtel Atlantique
P 🏃 🍴 €€€€

Digue de mer, 1st floor, 62930 **Tel** *03 21 32 41 01* **Fax** *03 21 87 46 17*

Right on the promenade, with a great view of the sea, as you would expect. The chef Alain Delpierre comes as something of a surprise in this old-fashioned setting. Red mullet in a salad with balsamic vinegar is one speciality. There are also 18 refurbished guest rooms – ask for one facing the Channel.

CHAMPAGNE

AIX-EN-OTHE Auberge de la Scierie
P 🏃 ♿ 🍴 🍷 €€

La Vove, 10160 **Tel** *03 25 46 71 26.* **Fax** *03 25 46 65 69*

Auberge de la Scierie is run by a Franco-Australian-British couple, who worked together at the Savoy in London, and together speak five languages. They specialize in shellfish with a distinctly Oriental flavour. This auberge, set in 8 acres of grounds, also has guest rooms, and cookery courses are offered.

AMBONNAY Auberge Saint-Vincent
🏃 📋 ♿ €€€

1 rue St Vincent, 51150 **Tel** *03 26 57 01 98* **Fax** *03 26 57 81 48*

This attractive 17th-century auberge, in a village on the edge of the beautiful Parc Régional de la Montagne de Champagne et de Reims, has a chimney decorated with antique kitchen implements. Modern local dishes are served here, and guest rooms are available.

ARSONVAL Hostellerie de la Chaumière
P 🏃 ♿ 🍴 €€€

Arsonval, 10200 **Tel** *03 25 27 91 02* **Fax** *03 25 27 90 26*

For many years now this hospitable Anglo-French couple have been welcoming guests to their restaurant and hotel overlooking the Aube. It is close to the route de Champagne. Dishes include home-made *foie gras*, and some of the best kidneys and bacon in France. Rustic dining room, with wooden beams.

AUBRIVES Debette
P 🏃 ♿ €€

2 pl Louis Debette, 08320 **Tel** *03 24 41 64 72* **Fax** *03 24 41 10 31*

Typical Ardennais establishment serving excellent traditional local food in a rustic setting – including home-grown fruit and vegetables. This is a modestly priced restaurant (rooms are also available in the hotel). The chef makes his own *terrine de sanglier* - wild boar and *terrine de foie gras*.

BAR-SUR-AUBE Le Cellier aux Moines
🏃 €

Rue Général Vouillemont, 10200 **Tel** *03 25 27 08 01* **Fax** *03 25 01 56 22*

As the name implies, this huge 12th-century cellar in the centre of this pleasant old town (once the main route to Switzerland) has been converted into a restaurant with a vineyard theme. The staff wear *vignerons'* outfits for groups. Try the *andouillette* (tripe sausage) with excellent local Chaource cheese.

CHALONS-EN-CHAMPAGNE Au Carillon Gourmand
🏃 📋 🍴 €

15 bis pl Monseigneur Tissier, 51000 **Tel** *03 26 64 45 07* **Fax** *03 26 21 06 09*

In the centre of the old town in the Notre-Dame-de-Vaux quarter, this welcoming restaurant has a pleasant covered terrace that opens onto the street. The *plat du jour* (dish of the day) is chosen according to what is best at the market. Try carpaccio of salmon or spiced duck pâté.

CHALONS-EN-CHAMPAGNE Les Ardennes
🏃 🍴 €€

34 pl de la République, 51000 **Tel** *03 26 68 21 42* **Fax** *03 26 21 34 55*

The dining room in this 17th-century house is sectioned off with old beams and has a big open fire. Local meat dishes like *boudin blanc* predominate. Seafood is popular in summer, with oysters when in season. There is also a wide selection of tempting desserts.

Key to Price Guide *see p600* **Key to Symbols** *see back cover flap*

CHAUMONT St-Louis · P · · €

11 rue Saint-Louis, 52000 **Tel** *03 25 01 26 87*

Simple but cheerful establishment that serves pancakes with different fillings. It is located in the the old quarter of this once important town, and makes a good place to break the journey north-south. Spot the grand entrances to the old town houses and the outside staircases.

COMBEAUFONTAINE Le Balcon · P · · €€€

1 pl 15 Juin 1940, 70120 **Tel** *03 84 92 11 13* **Fax** *03 84 92 15 89*

This good old-fashioned provincial restaurant, half an hour from Langres, deserves recognition. Try the chef's recommendation – the *menu gourmand* – and you will come away more than satisfied in body and wallet. The brasserie offers good weekday lunches. Rooms are also available.

EPERNAY La Table Kobus · · €

3 rue Dr Rousseau, 51200 **Tel** *03 26 51 53 53* **Fax** *03 26 58 42 68*

An original brasserie near the centre of this town that is all about champagne. Uniquely, you can bring your own bottle of champagne to drink with your meal. The menu is classic French cuisine. The home-made terrine of *foie gras fait maison* is particularly recommended.

FOUCHERES Auberge de la Seine · P · · €€

1 faubourg de Bourgogne, 10260 **Tel** *03 25 40 71 11* **Fax** *03 25 40 84 09*

A picturebook posting inn halfway between the Côte des Bar and the Champagne vineyards. The restaurant in Louis XIII-style opens onto a pretty riverside terrace. The chef, who has run the kitchens of other starred restaurants in the area, specializes in lobster.

JOINVILLE Le Soleil d'Or · P · · €€

9 rue Capucins, 52300 **Tel** *03 25 94 15 66* **Fax** *03 25 94 39 02*

This 17th-century house, with elegant guest rooms and a restaurant, was the home of the Guise family. The dining room is decorated with statues from a 14th-century convent, and there is an agreeable covered terrace. An original menu that changes every day.

LANGRES La Pignata · · €

59 rue Diderot, 52200 **Tel** *03 25 87 63 70*

Italian restaurant serving pizzas and other tasty dishes, such as veal with Milanese sauce or seafood tagliatelle, with house wine. It is located in the centre of this historic fortress town. Wander the old cramped streets and try to spot the first barracks allocated to the Foreign Legion, in 1832.

LANGRES Le Lion d'Or · P · · €€

Route de Vesoul, 52200 **Tel** *03 25 87 03 30* **Fax** *03 25 87 60 67*

Besides the restaurant, on offer here are modern rooms, an African bar and a garden terrace. The dining room overlooks lac Liez – suitable for sailing, swimming and fishing. A walk round the part-Roman, part-medieval ramparts of this hilltop city is a must. Dishes, such as pan-fried *foie gras* and veal *fricassée* will not disappoint.

LE MESNIL-SUR-OGER Le Mesnil · · €€€

2 rue Pasteur, 51190 **Tel** *03 26 57 95 57* **Fax** *03 26 57 78 57*

In a pretty wine-growing village in the heart of the Champagne vineyards, is this gourmet restaurant, set in an attractive old house. The restaurant owner is happy to show clients round his fine wine cellars. The village is the home of the museum of the vine and wine in the Maison Launois.

L'EPINE Aux Armes de Champagne · P · · €€€€

31 av de Luxembourg, 51460 **Tel** *03 26 69 30 30* **Fax** *03 26 69 30 26*

A top-class establishment, with a restaurant and hotel rooms, next to the basilique Notre Dame. Classic French cuisine is prepared with vegetables from the restaurant's garden, such as asparagus with truffle sauce and flakes of *foie gras* or lobster with apricots. Good vegetarian selection.

NOGENT-SUR-SEINE Au Beau Rivage · P · · €€

20 rue Villiers-aux-Choux, 10400 **Tel** *03 25 39 84 22* **Fax** *03 25 39 18 32*

This riverside hotel and restaurant comes highly recommended, particularly since the bedrooms have been refurbished. An attractive terrace looks out from the dining room onto the Seine. French traditional *cuisine gastronomique*, with *foie gras* and rabbit on a menu that will make your mouth water.

REIMS La Brasserie Boulingrin · · €

48 rue Mars, 51100 **Tel** *03 26 40 96 22* **Fax** *03 26 40 03 92*

This famous Reims brasserie and a regular meeting place for locals has kept its Art Deco mosaics of jolly grape harvesters *vendangeurs en Champagne*. Good value and a lively place to dine, near the covered market. Oysters and *steak tartare* are specialities. There is also a large selection of champagnes.

REIMS Château les Crayères · · €€€€€

64 bd Vasnier, 51100 **Tel** *03 26 82 80 80* **Fax** *03 26 82 65 52*

In the former home of the Pommery Champagne family, this gourmet retreat allows visitors to relax in sumptuous guest rooms and savour superb cuisine. The dining room is grand, with huge windows and tapestries. Try the lobster, veal and ham spaghetti, or almond biscuit with lemon and raspberry cream.

REIMS L'Assiette Champenoise   🅿 🏃 📋 ♿ 🚗 🍴 🍷   €€€€€

40 av Paul Vaillant-Couturier, Tinqueux, 51430 **Tel** *03 26 84 64 64* **Fax** *03 26 04 15 69*

A rising gastronomic star which is relatively inexpensive. Lobster dishes are a speciality, and pigeon and lamb are other favourites. Housed in an elegant *maison de maitre*, the restaurant now has two rosettes, and the hotel has been extended and modernized. Attractions include a beautiful flower garden and a pleasing terrace.

SIGNY LE PETIT Au Lion d'Or   🅿 🏃 ♿   €€€

Pl de l'Eglise, 08380 **Tel** *03 24 53 51 76* **Fax** *03 24 53 36 96*

On the circuit of fortified churches, this restaurant and hotel is housed behind an 18th-century red-brick façade. The non-smoking Louis XIII restaurant serves a delicious *foie gras* with a wild rose jam. Skilfully prepared fish is another speciality of this well-run dining establishment.

ST DIZIER La Gentilhommière   🏃 ♿ 🚗 🍷   €€

29 rue Jean Jaurès, 52100 **Tel** *03 25 56 32 97* **Fax** *03 25 06 32 66*

The best restaurant in town, it is easily recognised by the two life-sized figures in front, dressed in the style of the *bourgeois gentilhomme*. Refined cuisine, including sweetbreads flambéed in fine brandy, braised shin of beef and *daurade royale* with asparagus, and Provençal cakes.

ST IMOGES La Maison du Vigneron   🅿 🏃 ♿ 🚗 🍷   €€€

Route Nationale 51, 51160 **Tel** *03 26 52 88 00* **Fax** *03 26 52 86 03*

Between Reims and Epernay, in a village in the heart of the Parc Régionale de la Montagne Noire et de Reims, is this good restaurant and Champagne house. Excellent regional dishes imaginatively prepared and, if you wish, accompanied by the owner's Champagne vintages.

STE MENEHOULD Le Cheval Rouge   🏃 ♿ 🚗 🍷   €

1 rue Chanzy, 51800 **Tel** *03 26 60 81 04* **Fax** *03 26 60 93 11*

Two places to eat in one establishment: the restaurant, with its distinctive fireplace, or in the much cheaper brasserie, which specializes in pigs' trotters. Monsieur Fourreau, the owner of the establishment, sends pigs' trotters all over Europe.

TROYES Au Jardin Gourmand   🏃 🚗   €

31 rue Paillot de Montabert, 10000 **Tel** *03 25 73 36 13* **Fax** *03 25 73 36 13*

In the heart of the old town, with its forest of half-timbered houses, this charming restaurant quietly pleases all who come here. The speciality is the local delicacy, *andouillette* (tripe sausage). Pleasant small panelled dining room and delightful terrace for eating out in summer. Try the lavender ice cream.

TROYES les Crieurs de Vin   🏃 🍷   €

4 pl Jean Jaurès, 10000 **Tel** *03 25 40 01 01*

An inexpensive wine bar with an agreeably raffish air run by two wine fanatics. In the front they sell wine to take away, and in the back they sell it to accompany their bistro-style menu. Lots of exposed beams and bare wooden tables. The traditional French menu is on a blackboard.

TROYES Le Céladon   🏃   €€€

31 rue de la Cité, 10000 **Tel** *03 25 80 58 23*

An excellent restaurant in attractive premises, Xavier Delavenne's first-class reputation was established in the South West, where he cooked in prestigious restaurants. He aims to do for himself what he has done for others – take his restaurant to the top. Traditional French cuisine with very select ingredients.

VILLEMOYENNE Parentele   🅿 🏃 📋 ♿ 🚗 🍷   €€€€

32 rue Marcelin Lévêque, 10260 **Tel** *03 25 43 68 68* **Fax** *03 25 43 68 69*

This restaurant is making a name for itself with crayfish cooked in coconut cream and ravioli *au foie gras*. In a short time the local boys, who came home to the premises where their grandparents ran a café, have won their first rosette. Experts say the Champagne wine list is perfect.

ALSACE & LORRAINE

BAERENTHAL L'Arnsbourg   🅿 🏃 📋 🍴 🍷   €€€€€

18 untermuhlthal, 57230 **Tel** *03 87 06 50 85* **Fax** *03 87 06 57 67*

One of only 26 three-rosette restaurants in France, hidden in a pretty glade in the forest of the northern Vosges. Brother and sister team Jean-Georges and Cathy Klein conjure up light imaginative dishes, such as *grillade de foie gras* of duck with crystalized lemon, accompanied by great wines. Sensible prices, all things considered.

BITCHE Le Strasbourg   🅿 🏃 📋 🚗   €€

24 rue Col. Teyssier, 57230 **Tel** *03 87 96 00 44* **Fax** *03 87 96 11 57*

Excellent hotel restaurant in the shadow of Vauban's fascinating citadelle, which contains a memorial to the American infantry that liberated the town. Le Strasbourg has a big traditional dining room, with a beautiful white moulded fireplace. The cuisine here is traditional, with *foie gras* and a range of fish dishes.

Key to Price Guide *see p600* **Key to Symbols** *see back cover flap*

COLMAR Le Caveau de St Pierre

24 rue de la Herse, 68000 **Tel** 03 89 41 99 33

Built in 1568 into the medieval fortifications, this restaurant stands in the Little Venice quarter, reached by a boardwalk along the canal. Warm traditional decor with painted beams. Specialities include fillet of beef cooked in a sauce of local Munster cheese, fish dishes and *choucroute* (pickled cabbage served with sausage and bacon).

COLMAR La Maison des Têtes

19 rue des Têtes, 68000 **Tel** 03 89 24 43 43 **Fax** 03 89 24 58 34

A fine Renaissance house built in 1609 is the setting of this traditional old town restaurant with attractive wood-panelled dining room. The *foie gras* in apple marmalade or pan-fried with a dash of the finest Marc de Gewurztraminer is recommended. There is also an attractive inner terrace.

ILLHAEUSERN L'Auberge de l'Ill

2 rue de Collonges, 68970 **Tel** O3 89 71 89 00 **Fax** 03 89 71 82 83

The Mecca of Alsacien cuisine, and still a Haeberlin family affair, this restaurant has held three rosettes for 38 years! Set on the banks of the river Ill in the heart of the village, with gardens and storks nesting. Lobster "Prince Vladimir", salmon souflé, terrine of goose *foie gras* with truffles.

KAYSERSBERG Restaurant Saint Alexis

Restaurant Saint Alexis, 68240 **Tel** 03 89 73 90 38

Hidden in the hills above the vineyards of Kaysersberg and Riquewihr, this old farm, set in cherry orchards by a chapel dating in part from the 5th century, houses a popular restaurant. Every menu starts with soup, followed by meat pie or stewed cockerel or game and omelette. Book ahead.

KAYSERSBERG Au Lion d'Or

66 rue Général de Gaulle, 68240 **Tel** 03 89 47 11 16 **Fax** 03 89 47 19 02

Right in the old town, a lot of history surrounds this excellent, unpretentious institution, built in 1521 and run by the same family since 1724. A carved lion's head decorates the door into the restaurant. The characterful dining room has a big open fire in winter. Traditional dishes include wild game, *foie gras* and sauerkraut.

LEMBACH Ferme Gimbelhof

Route Forestière, 67510 **Tel** 03 88 94 43 58

Upgraded Alsacien farm lost in the hills right on the German frontier, 10 km (6 miles) north of Lembach and only an hour from Strasbourg. Across the valley is the magnificent ruined château de Fleckenstein. Excellent local dishes. This very professional and modestly priced establishment is well supported by both Germans and locals.

LES THONS Le Couvent des Cordeliers

Les Thons, 88410 **Tel** 03 29 07 90 84

A fine ramshackle collection of 15th-century monastery buildings north of Renaissance Châtillon-sur-Saône is home to this unusual restaurant. The owner roasts slices of gammon over an open fire. Very popular; book ahead and ask to be seated downstairs, *"en bas"*. There is a free museum.

MARLENHEIM Le Cerf

30 rue Général de Gaulle, 67520 **Tel** 03 88 87 73 73 **Fax** 03 88 87 68 08

At the northern end of the Route des Vins, this old coaching inn, owned by the same family since 1930, serves modernized traditional Alsace dishes. It has a reputation for serving a good square meal, even second helpings. *Choucroute* with suckling pig and pan-fried *foie gras*. Rooms available.

METZ Le Bistrot des Sommeliers

10 rue Pasteur, 57000 **Tel** 03 87 63 40 20 **Fax** 03 87 63 54 46

A gastronomic experience wrapped up in brasserie clothing. The chef was formerly second in one of France's top restaurants. The wine list is outstanding, with 400 different labels covering the whole country. Excellent bistro-style food, with a mostly business clientele. Crayfish *vol au vent* is a speciality.

METZ Restaurant des Roches

29 rue Roches, 57000 **Tel** 03 87 74 06 51 **Fax** 03 87 75 40 04

Set on the ground floor of an 18th-century building opposite France's oldest theatre, this restaurant specializes in fish – bass, daurade and turbot – and shellfish. You can pick your own live lobster from the glass tank. In summer there is a terrace for dining alongside the Moselle.

MOOSLARGUE A l'Ange

14 rue Principale, 68580 **Tel** 03 89 25 64 34

A good-value family restaurant deceptively lost in the Sundgau countryside, but only half an hour from Basle, and frequented by Swiss customers. The local delicacy – fillets of carp coated with sesame seed and chips with tartar sauce – forms part of the wider menu.

NANCY L'Excelsior

50 rue Henri Poincaré, 54000 **Tel** 03 83 35 24 57

This classic Nancy brasserie with Belle Epoque decor and stained-glass windows is a famous rendezvous. Excellent service, and you can even reserve your table over the Internet if you are clever enough. L'Excelsior serves refined dishes with *foie gras* and *choucroute garnie*.

OBERNAI La Cloche

P 🏃 ▤ 🖼　　　€

90 rue Général Gouraud, 67210 **Tel** *03 88 49 90 43*

In a 14th-century house with original panelling and windows, is this tavern-style restaurant. Located in the heart of the old town, it offers traditional Alsace cuisine with Munster cheese in the sauces. Always two different fish on the menu, and *tarte flambée* in the evenings. Excellent service.

RIEDISHEIM Restaurant de la Poste

P 🏃 🍴 🖳　　€€€€

7 rue Général de Gaulle, Riedisheim, 68400 **Tel** *03 89 44 07 71* **Fax** *03 89 64 32 79*

A coaching inn since 1850, six generations of the Kieny family have maintained this restaurant with its elegant dining rooms. You will find traditional Alsace cooking with suckling pig a speciality, according to the season. They are also great experts in cooking with chocolate.

RIQUEWIHR Le Sarment d'Or

P 🏃　　　€€€

4 rue du Cerf, 68340 **Tel** *03 89 86 02 86* **Fax** *03 89 47 99 23*

In a beautiful 16th-century house, tucked away in a quiet Renaissance street of this wonderfully preserved village, this restaurant's beamed dining room is elegantly decorated. The cooking combines invention and tradition. Warm *kugelhopf* cake for breakfast from the family shop just nearby. Rooms available.

SARREGUEMINES Le Casino des Sommeliers

P 🏃 🖼　　　€

4 rue Col. Cazals, 57200 **Tel** *03 87 02 90 41* **Fax** *03 87 02 90 28*

In an Art Deco room dating from 1830, this restaurant offers first-class bistro-style cuisine. Try pigs' trotters stuffed with sweetbreads in a cream of mushroom sauce. Le Casino des Sommeliers has a pleasant terrace overlooking the park of the Casino des Faïenceries and the river Sarre.

SAVERNE Taverne Katz

P 🏃 🖼　　　€€

80 grand rue, 67700 **Tel** *03 88 71 16 56*

In the centre of the town opposite the huge château, this taverne was built in 1605 and is still beautifully preserved inside and out with a traditonal flowered terrace and polished wood in the dining room. The food is French with a regional slant, and includes duck with *foie gras* and medallions of rabbit.

STRASBOURG Pâtisserie Winter

🏃　　　€

25 rue du 22 Novembre, 67000 **Tel** *03 88 32 85 40* **Fax** *03 88 32 85 40*

This is a good place for the ordinary visitor to Strasbourg, who does not have the expense account of a Member of the European Parliament. Simple meals at reasonable prices at this location in the city centre. Good salads and *pâtisseries* with beer or wine.

STRASBOURG Au Crocodile

P 🏃 ▤ 🍴 🖳　　€€€€€

10 rue Outre, 67000 **Tel** *03 88 32 13 02* **Fax** *03 88 75 72 01*

One of the finest restaurants in France's other capital. Splendid polished woodwork, elegant decor and the famous crocodile brought back from a campaign in Egypt by an Alsatian Captain in the French army. Super service and light original cusine. A truly great wine list that covers the world.

VERDUN Hostellerie le Coq Hardi

P 🏃 ♿ 🖳　　€€€€

Av de la Victoire, 55100 **Tel** *03 29 86 36 36* **Fax** *03 29 86 09 21*

This traditional, classic French provincial hotel and restaurant has good food, a great wine list and an elegant dining room. Try the langoustine lasagne and snails. The bistro option provides cheaper, quick meals, such as steak and chips. There is a pleasant summer terrace.

WINDSTEIN Auberge de la Faveur

P 🏃 🖼　　　€

33 rue des Châteaux, 67110 **Tel** *03 88 09 24 41*

An exceptional little hotel-restaurant between two ruined medieval castles in the regional park, run by two sculptors. On the D53 between Jaegerthal and Dambach turn up the valley of the Windstein and keep going until you get to the top. The rooms are basic but the food is good and there are great views. Closed Dec–Jan.

WISSEMBOURG Daniel Rebert

🏃 ▤ 🖼　　　€

7 pl du Marché aux Choux, 67100 **Tel** *03 88 94 01 66* **Fax** *03 88 54 38 78*

Daniel Rebert is one of the best chocolatiers and pâtissiers in France. In the shadow of his luxury production of cakes and chocolates there is a discrete *salon de thé*, serving light lunches. Afterwards, you can choose the cakes and chocolates from the dizzying display to take home.

NORMANDY

ACQUIGNY Hostellerie d'Acquigny

🏃　　　€€€

1 rue d'Evreux, 27400 **Tel** *02 32 50 20 05*

This former coaching inn houses a charming restaurant. The regulars appreciate the inexpensive set menus, but it is worth choosing *à la carte*: tatin andouillette with Livarot cheese, cod with chorizo, and fillet of pork accompanied by an apple gelée. Animated service.

Key to Price Guide *see p600* **Key to Symbols** *see back cover flap*

ALENÇON Au Petit Vatel

72 pl du Commandant-Desmeulles, 61000 **Tel** *02 33 26 23 78* **Fax** *02 33 82 64 57*

The neon sign detracts from this attractive stone building on the small square in the town centre. Here, traditional cuisine benefits from local produce. Good, simple cooking includes salad of Camembert fritters, Norman chicken legs, and ice-cream *mille feuille* served with apples and calvados.

AUMALE La Villa des Houx

6 av Général de Gaulle, 76390 **Tel** *02 35 93 93 30* **Fax** *02 35 93 03 94*

A former *gendarmerie* (police station), this is an ideal place to stop along the route from Rouen to Amiens. The menu offers the refined taste of real Normandy cuisine. In the rustic dining room try the apricot *foie gras* for starters, followed by boned quail cooked in a salt crust and Calvados soufflé.

BAYEUX La Table du Terroir

42 rue St Jean, 14400 **Tel** *02 31 92 05 53* **Fax** *02 31 92 05 53*

In summer, dining on the terrace is a treat; in winter the rustic dining-room is welcoming, with large convivial wooden tables and old hewn stone walls. La Table du Terroir specializes in meat dishes, home-made pâtés and terrines. The desserts are delicious, too.

BRIQUEVILLE-SUR-MER L'Auberge de la Maison Blanche

D20, 50290 **Tel** *02 33 61 65 62*

The coastal location of this restaurant, north of Granville, dictates the menu of fresh fish and shellfish – the local sea whelks are the speciality. Surprising but delicious combinations are prepared by the excellent chef, such as skate with Camembert cheese. Local lamb is a speciality.

CARTERET Marine

11 rue de Paris, 50270 **Tel** *02 33 53 83 31* **Fax** *02 33 53 39 60*

At this restaurant, near the port, chef Laurent Cesne prepares inventive dishes such as the salmon *mille-feuille*, plaice with honey and thyme, pigs' trotters and cèpe mushrooms and duck breast with cumin. Modern, comfortable dining room; precise and attentive service. Wine list matches food.

CHERBOURG Le Faitout

25 rue Tour-Carrée, 50100 **Tel** *02 33 04 25 04* **Fax** *02 33 04 60 36*

A bastion of tradition, Le Faitout is located in an old quarter of the city. This animated bistro-style restaurant serves family-style dishes *par excellence*. Sample the veal kidneys in mustard and cream sauce, Barfleur mussels, grilled sardines and a wonderfully crispy confit of duck.

COSQUEVILLE Au Bouquet de Cosqueville

Hameau Remond, 50330 **Tel** *02 33 54 32 81* **Fax** *02 33 54 63 38*

Good portions of fresh seafood, such as lobster cooked in cider, local fish and shellfish, served at this elegantly rustic restaurant in an ivy-clad house in the village centre. Freshest local produce chosen with care. Tasty crêpes and *crème brulée* for dessert. Impressive wine list.

COURSEILLES SUR MER Paris

Pl 6-Juin, 14470 **Tel** *02 31 37 45 07* **Fax** *02 31 37 51 63*

A good-value-for-money restaurant in this relaxed seaside resort, north of Caen, on the Côte Nacre. Friendly service in the simply furnished dining room, where simple seafood and meat dishes are prepared with care. The terrace and veranda outside are protected from the gusty sea breezes.

DEAUVILLE Le Spinnaker

52 rue Mirabeau, 14800 **Tel** *02 31 88 24 40* **Fax** *02 31 88 43 58*

After a stroll along the seafront promenade, make your way to one of Normandy's finest fish restaurants. An attractive modern dining room specializes in fish and seafood, and also grilled meat dishes. Delicious baked lobster in cider vinegar, or turbot with shallots. Friendly, attentive service.

DIEPPE Bistrot de Pollet

23 rue Tête de Bœuf, 76200 **Tel** *02 35 84 68 57*

Small, friendly bistro-style restaurant with chef's daily suggestions, depending on the catch of the day, in the old fishing quarter of the port. Simple unfussy fish dishes: haddock salad, grilled sardines, poached sole and bass. Limited selection of wines. Packed with locals and regulars; book ahead.

DOMFRONT Auberge Grand Gousier

1 pl Liberté, 61700 **Tel** *02 33 38 97 17* **Fax** *02 33 30 89 25*

Domfront escaped destruction during the bombardments of 1944, and this family-run auberge is testimony to this, standing in the medieval town centre with its authentic fireplace. The speciality is stuffed seafood and gratin of cockles. The portions are generous and the welcome genuine.

DOZULE Le Pavé d'Auge

Les Halles, Beuvron en Auge, 14430 **Tel** *02 31 79 26 71* **Fax** *02 31 39 04 45*

The talented chef serves food made from locally sourced produce. The dining room, in the renovated ancient village market hall, has lots of charm. The menus focus on fish, with a small choice of meat and poulty. Choose from Isigny oysters or grilled langoustines, and then braised hake or *rascasse*.

FALAISE l'Attache   P ⃗   €€€
Route de Caen, 14700 **Tel** *02 31 90 05 38* **Fax** *02 31 90 57 19*

Reservations recommended for this restaurant in the heart of Calvados. A beautifully renovated former staging post, with the dining room decorated in relaxing tones. The classic repertoire has an added dimension – the chef uses long-forgotten plants and aromatic herbs to flavour his cuisine. Impeccable service.

FOURGE Moulin de Fourges   P ⃗ 🏠 ♥   €€€€
38 rue du Moulin, 27630 **Tel** *02 32 52 12 12* **Fax** *02 32 52 92 56*

A beautiful riverside watermill that would no doubt have pleased Monet, who lived at nearby Giverny. Local produce innovatively used to achieve astonishing results, such as the duo of *foie gras*, one cooked in port, the other marinated in lavender. Pleasant dining area, and decent wines.

GISORS Le Cappeville   ⃗ ♥   €€€
17 rue Cappeville, 27410 **Tel** *02 32 55 11 08* **Fax** *02 32 55 93 92*

Rustic restaurant in the oldest part of town, serving traditional Normandy cuisine. The chef Pierre Potel shows his skill in creating tasty dishes using local produce. Try the succulent lamb braised in cider, and calvados-flavoured soufflé. La Cappeville has a friendly, relaxed atmosphere.

GRANVILLE La Citadelle   P ⃗ 🗐 ♿ 🏠   €€
34 rue du Port, 50406 **Tel** *02 33 50 34 10* **Fax** *02 33 50 15 36*

Overlooking the bay of St-Michel, the reliable cooking and the view over the fishing port from the terrace is enough to draw anyone over the bridge. Elegant, modern dining room serves generous portions. The freshest seafood platter in town, the biggest portion of sole, and Norman scallops.

HONFLEUR La Terrace et l'Assiette   🏠 ♥   €€€
8 pl Saint-Catherine, 14600 **Tel** *02 31 89 31 33* **Fax** *02 31 89 90 17*

Attractive traditional timber and brick building with a terrace opposite the church. Wonderfully fresh seafood dishes, lobster omelette, sole and turbot. Simplicity is the key, using the best produce. Savour the mackerel terrine and the *noble dorade grise* (sea bream). Good white wine selection.

HONFLEUR La Ferme St Siméon   ♿ 🏠 ♥ ♥   €€€€€
Rue A.Marais, 14600 **Tel** *02 31 81 78 00* **Fax** *02 31 89 48 48*

Simply the best place to eat in this pretty fishing port. The experienced chef produces dishes with a touch of personality, such as langoustine with a shellfish gelée served with creamed cauliflower, which has a perfect balance of textures. Elegant dining room with a beamed ceiling. Great wine list.

LA FERRIERE AUX ETANGS Auberge de la Mine   ⃗ ♿   €€
Le Gué-Plat, 61450 **Tel** *02 33 66 91 10* **Fax** *02 33 96 73 90*

At this former mine-workers' cantine traditional Norman dishes are produced with originality, such as large crab ravioli with frothy sauce, and roast pollack with herbs. Also, old favourites like a potato *galette* with Livarot cheese. Excellent cheese board and desserts.

LA FERTE MACE Auberge de Clouet   ⃗ 🏠 ♥   €€€
Clouet, 61600 **Tel** *02 33 37 18 22* **Fax** *02 33 38 28 52*

Centrally located restaurant in this delightful, historic market town in the Cotentin region. After exploring the sites, a meal of local specialities awaits you, either in the rustic dining room, or outside on the floral terrace. Classic Normandy fare, such as duck breast and Camembert salad, and seafood. Convivial atmosphere.

LE BEC HELLOUIN Restaurant de la Tour   ⃗ 🏠   €
Pl Guillaume Le Conquérant, 27800 **Tel** *02 32 44 86 15*

Just a short walk from the ancient abbey in this charming village. This pretty timbered building serves traditional Norman cuisine. Sample duck, the speciality, in all guises: *foie gras* starter, and sautéed duck breast or confit of duck. Attractive terrace for summer dining. Book ahead.

LES ANDELYS La Chaine d'Or   P ⃗ ♿ 🏠 ♥   €€€€
27 rue Grande, 27700 **Tel** *02 32 54 00 31* **Fax** *02 32 54 05 68*

Book a table in this restaurant to taste such delicacies as oysters in Champagne sauce, cream of scallop soup, turbot with lobster coulis, grilled langoustines, or roast farm chicken *à la vanille*. Romantic setting on the banks of the Seine in an 18th-century auberge. Rooms available.

LYONS LA FORET Restaurant de la Halle   ⃗ ♿ 🏠   €€
Pl Benserade, 27480 **Tel** *02 32 49 49 92*

An attractive, traditional Norman village surrounded by the largest beech forest in Europe merits this good local restaurant, located opposite the ancient market hall. Simple, straightforward, delicious cuisine, especially the lamb cooked with rosemary. Starchy service.

MERVILLE-FRANCEVILLE Chez Marion   P ⃗   €€€
La pl de la Plage, 14810 **Tel** *02 31 24 23 39* **Fax** *02 31 24 88 75*

This lovely restaurant with a friendly welcome specializes in seafood. The owner, Marion's great-grandson, prepares classic fish and shellfish dishes to perfection. There is a pick-your-own lobster tank in the attractive dining area. There are also rooms available at Chez Marion.

Key to Price Guide *see p600* **Key to Symbols** *see back cover flap*

MONT-ST-MICHEL Auberge St Pierre

Grande rue, 50170 **Tel** *02 33 60 14 03* **Fax** *02 33 48 59 82*

Lamb grazed on the surrounding salt marshes, known as *agneau pré salé*, features on the menu in this charming timbered 15th-century building. Seafood is also a house speciality. Try the favourites such as crab or salmon. Fresh local produce is used in the preparation of traditional dishes.

MONT-ST-MICHEL La Mère Poulard

Grande rue, 50170 **Tel** *02 33 89 68 68*

A deluxe brasserie on the famous Mont St-Michel, where visitors come from all over the world to sample the famous omelette Mère Poulard, cooked in a long-handled pan over a fire. Also delicious are the *pré-salé* lamb (lamb fed on the surrounding salt marshes), and spit-roasted pig.

PONT L'EVEQUE Auberge de l'Aigle d'Or

68 rue de Vaucelles, 14130 **Tel** *02 31 65 05 25* **Fax** *02 31 65 12 03*

A well-maintained 16th-century coaching inn with a pretty courtyard provides an attractive setting for a good-value meal of *escargots Pays d'Auge*, and free-range chicken cooked in a cider sauce. The menu changes seasonally and ensures the best local produce. Attentive service.

PONT L'EVEQUE Le Dauphin

Le Breuil en Auge, 14130 **Tel** *02 31 65 08 11* **Fax** *02 31 65 12 08*

A reservation is essential for this sought-after restaurant. The owners spare no effort, and take great pride in the cuisine. Chef Régis Lecomte uses local produce with flair. Sample Isigny oysters, a terrine of guinea fowl with *foie gras*, and rabbit cooked with chervil and vermouth. Good wine selection.

PONT SAINT-PIERRE Hostellerie La Bonne Marmite

10 rue René Raban 27300 **Tel** *02 32 49 70 24* **Fax** *02 32 48 12 41*

A top Logis de France not too far from Rouen in an old coaching inn. The dining room is as elegant as the building, with a *caisson* ceiling. Try the *foie gras de canard à l'ancienne* and the lobster ravioli. This is Norman cooking at its best. The wine cellar boasts some fine old Bordeaux.

PUTANGES PONT ECREPIN Hôtel du Lion Verd

Pl de l'Hôtel de Ville, 61210 **Tel** *02 33 35 01 86* **Fax** *02 33 39 53 32*

This welcoming hotel-restaurant sits on the riverside of the Orme. The menu offers local Normandy produce with pride and a refreshing approach. The result is wonderful: beef with Camembert cream, Auge Valley *cochon de lait* (suckling pig). Good home-made desserts.

ROUEN Le 37

37 rue St-Etienne-des-Tonneliers, 76000 **Tel** *02 35 70 56 65*

Attractive city-centre bistro, chic and zen, presents a cuisine that is a touch more modern than its celebrated parent, Gill. Enjoy savoury dishes such as sweet and sour pork, cod with onion confit and sweet potato, and for dessert a caramel tart. Reservations recommended.

ROUEN La Couronne

31 pl Vieux Marché, 76000 **Tel** *02 35 71 40 90* **Fax** *02 35 71 05 78*

In the oldest auberge in France, dating from 1345, the experienced, talented chef ensures that you pass a memorable moment with classic gourmet dishes such as *foie gras* with chestnuts, veal with fried beetroot and duck *à la Rouennaise*. Great Normandy cheeses.

ROUEN Restaurant Gill

8-9 quai de la Bourse, 76000 **Tel** *02 35 71 16 14* **Fax** *02 35 71 96 91*

A highly recommended restaurant on the Seine quays. For nearly 20 years chef Gilles Tournadre has been creating sophisticated dishes in this elegant dining room. Specialities include crayfish salad, Pigeon *à la rouennaise* and fillet of bass with asparagus. Remarkable wine list.

SEES Le Gourmand Candide

14 pl du Général de Gaulle, 61500 **Tel** *02 33 27 91 28*

This friendly establishment serves fine Normandy cuisine. Unpretentious, well-cooked food is perfected by the chef. Specialities include duck breast and confit, and *andouille* (tripe sausage) with apple and *pommeau*. Classic and consistent, at reasonable prices.

ST GERMAIN DE TALLEVENDE Auberge St Germain

Pl de l'Eglise, 14500 **Tel** *02 31 68 24 13* **Fax** *02 31 68 89 57*

Next to the church in a village in the heart of the Calvados countryside, this old granite-built auberge has a cosy, intimate dining room with low oak-beamed ceilings and a fireplace. This is an ideal place for families, with good regional home cooking that caters for all tastes. Friendly service.

STE CECILE Le Manoir de l'Acherie

Acherie, 50800 **Tel** *02 33 51 13 87* **Fax** *02 33 51 33 69*

In this old-fashioned manor house, with rooms in a converted chapel, the produce of Normandy features highly, such as cream, apples, calvados and cider. Expect to find ham and lamb either braised in calvados, or served in a cider-flavoured sauce. Even the apple tart is flambéed in this apple brandy. Good cheeseboard.

TROUVILLE SUR MER Régence P & €€
132 bd Fernand Moureaux, 14360 **Tel** *02 31 88 10 71* **Fax** *02 31 88 10 71*

Beautiful interior with mirrors and 19th-century woodpanelling decorated by hungry Impressionist painters. The charming service and refined ambience lend to the feeling of elegance and good value. Not far from the shore, the seafood and shellfish are the house specialities. Well-presented dishes.

VEULES LES ROSES Les Galets P & & €€€
3 rue Victor Hugo, 76980 **Tel** *02 35 97 61 33* **Fax** *02 35 57 06 23*

Traditional brick-built restaurant close to the pebbly beach, which is typical of the Côte d'Albâtre. Comfortable dining area inside, and lovely terrace outside. If you want to have a meal by the sea, this is just the place, but book ahead. Classic dishes prepared with care, and vegetarian dishes are cooked to order.

VILLERS BOCAGE Les Trois Rois P & €€€
2 pl Jeanne d'Arc, 14310 **Tel** *02 31 77 00 32* **Fax** *02 31 77 93 25*

In a vast square surrounded by a garden and vegetable patch, this restaurant flaunts all the characteristics of a traditional Norman restaurant. Spacious, elegant dining area serving generous portions of well-prepared local dishes, such as tripe and fresh fish dishes. Efficient service.

BRITTANY

AUDIERNE Le Goyen P & & & & €€€
Pl Jean-Simon, 29770 **Tel** *02 98 70 08 88* **Fax** *02 98 70 18 77*

Classic seafood cuisine is served at this hotel-restaurant facing the sea. Deliciously fresh oysters and seafood platters are a good choice. The menu also includes roasted monkfish on a bed of spinach with a vermouth sauce, or panfried *coquille St-Jacques* (scallops) accompanied by asparagus.

AURAY L'Eglantine & & €€
17 pl St Saveur, St Goustan, 56400 **Tel** *02 97 56 46 55*

Right on the port of St Goustan with a stunning view of the old clipper. Delicious sole and turbot is simply prepared. Sea bass and monkfish medallions are accompanied by elaborate sauces. The seafood platters are exquisite. Other dishes include pigeon and succulent steak.

BELLE ILE EN MER La Désirade & & & €€€
Le Petit Cosquet, 56360 **Tel** *02 97 31 35 26*

This family hotel and restaurant is in an attractive, traditional Brittany farmhouse only a few minutes from the beach. The chef specializes in fresh ingredients, with fish and seafood to the fore. Picnics can be ordered for a day's outing on the shore of this wonderful island.

BREST La Fleur de Sel & €€€
15 bis rue de Lyon, 29200 **Tel** *02 98 44 38 65* **Fax** *02 98 44 38 53*

A modern bright city centre restaurant, with simple, comfortable furnishings. The dishes are prepared with precision. Try the artichokes with mussels, and the *riz au lait* (rice pudding with almond millk). Good value for money, especially the *fomule* at midday. Service is a little stuffy.

BREST Océania & ▤ & & & €€€€
82 rue de Siam, 29200 **Tel** *02 98 80 66 66* **Fax** *02 98 80 65 60*

Possibly Brest's most elegant restaurant, styled as a cruise ship on the ground floor of the hotel of the same name. The wine list is extensive, with scores of vintages and a good range of champagnes. Beautifully presented dishes, such as monkfish with artichoke *ragoût*, and rabbit confit with shallots.

CARANTEC Restaurant Patrick Jeffroy P & & & & €€€€€
20 rue Kélénn, 29660 **Tel** *02 98 67 00 47* **Fax** *02 98 67 08 25*

A magnificent view over Kélénn beach from the restaurant in this fabulous 1930s manor house hotel. Shellfish in abundance. Classic and modern cuisine combine to perfection. Warm oysters with balsamic sauce; langoustines in cider; spicy scallops and crab. Extensive choice of Loire valley wines.

CARNAC La Bavolette & & €€
9 allée du Parc, 56340 **Tel** *02 97 52 19 69*

One of the classier eating places at the popular seaside resort of Carnac-Plage. Fish *brochettes* and sardine terrine are among the favourites. La Bavolette's specialities include fish soup served with a rich garlicy *aioli* and croutons, and flambéed langoustines.

CESSON-SEVIGNE La Hublais P & & & €
28 rue de Rennes, 35510 **Tel** *02 99 83 11 06* **Fax** *02 29 45 65 82*

Just five minutes' drive from Rennes, this former inn has been revived by a new owner and has been updated with a bright, contemporary interior. The restaurant is now predominantly a crêperie, also serving a selection of grills and salads as well as galettes.

Key to Price Guide *see p600* **Key to Symbols** *see back cover flap*

CONCARNEAU Le Petit Chaperon Rouge 🏃🔲 €

7 pl Duguesclin, 29900 **Tel** *02 98 60 53 32*

Following the 'Little Red Riding Hood' theme with its wicker baskets and red tablecloths, this crêperie near the harbour has a delicious choice of savoury and sweet fillings, such as La Blandette (goat's cheese, spinach, ham and cream) and Mère Grande (banana and honey flambéed with rum).

DINAN La Mère Pourcel 🔲📖 €€€€

3 pl des Merciers, 22100 **Tel** *02 96 39 03 80* **Fax** *02 96 39 49 91*

This restaurant in a stunning timbered Gothic building is a Dinan landmark, serving generous portions of seasonal gourmet cuisine. Locally reared lamb is on offer, along with more innovative dishes such as cod with truffles. Good selection of wines. The tables are on the cobbled street.

GUIMILIAU Ar Chupen 🏃♿🔲 €

43 rue de Calvaire, 29400 **Tel** *02 98 68 73 63*

After admiring the richly decorated church, step down the road to this restaurant in a renovated Breton farmhouse. Traditional lacy galettes, made with sarrazin flour, and crêpes are prepared to order. The choice of fillings seems endless. Good place for children, and vegetarians. Friendly staff.

HEDE L'Hostellerie du Vieux Moulin 🅿🏃🔲 €€

Ancienne route de St Malo, 35630 **Tel** *02 99 45 45 70* **Fax** *02 99 45 44 86*

Built in the 19th century as part of a complex to supply water power, the restaurant overlooks the Hédé castle, with the ruins of the old watermill in the grounds. Good-value lunchtime menus, including pan-fried scallops, lightly grilled langoustines, and succulent duck. Rooms available.

LE CONQUET Le Relais de Vieux Port 🏃♿🔲 €

1 quai Drellach, 29217 **Tel** *02 98 89 15 91*

You can almost dangle your feet in the water as you sit to choose the fillings for your crêpe. Seafood is the house speciality. Try a crêpe filled with fresh scallops or prawns accompanied by a green salad. Leave room for dessert, especially the Bonne Maman with caramelized apples and whipped cream.

LORIENT Le Neptune 🏃 €€

15 av de la Perrière, 56100 **Tel** *02 97 37 04 56* **Fax** *02 97 87 07 54*

The haul at the nearby fishing port of Keroman determines the dish of the day at this restaurant. Modern interior, with some tables in a pretty conservatory at the rear of the dining room. The menu includes flambéed lobster, and fricassée of monkfish. Generous portions and friendly service.

MORLAIX Le Sterne 🏃 €€

Quai de Léon, Port de Plaisance, 29600 **Tel** *02 98 15 12 12*

Located on a barge moored to the harbour quay, the seafood dishes at this restaurant are stunning, with an original twist. Try the sea bass cooked in Breton cider, or the delicately flavoured langoustine *ragoût*. Fresh oysters and mussels also feature on the menu. Reserve ahead.

PAIMPOL L'Islandais 🏃🔲 €

19 quai Morand, 22500 **Tel** *02 96 20 93 80* **Fax** *02 96 20 72 68*

A popular crêperie overlooking the lively Paimpol harbour. The chef presents a good selection of traditional Breton galettes, always a favourite with children and a good option for vegetarians. Shellfish is abundant, with fresh oysters, mussels, lobsters and langoustines. Expect to pay more for seafood.

PERROS-GUIREC Le Gulf Stream 🅿🏃🔲 €€

26 rue des Sept-Iles 22700 **Tel** *02 96 23 21 86* **Fax** *02 96 49 06 61*

An excellent and reasonably priced hotel-restaurant with a warm, family feel. There are fine views of the coast from the dining room. As well as the expected fish and other seafood, the restaurant serves traditional French food according to the season. There is also a good wine list.

PLOUBALAY Crêperie le Château d'Oh 🅿🏃 €

15 route Dinard, 22650 **Tel** *02 96 27 36 98*

This is a simple *crêperie* that doubles as a *grillade*, with a view to die for. Located at the top of a water tower, views stretch to Mont-St-Michel, Dinan and St Jacut. Huge selection of *gallettes* – pancakes with savoury fillings, such as scallops flambéed in Calvados, and plenty of hearty steaks.

QUIBERON Le Relax 🅿🏃♿🔲📖 €

27 bd Castéro, 56170 **Tel** *02 97 50 12 84*

With lovely sea views and a pretty garden, this restaurant is guaranteed to make you relax. A wide selection of superbly cooked seasonal fish, as well as mussels, langoustines, crabs and oysters. Tasty seafood sauerkraut. Good wine cellar and a sommelier who knows his stuff, but is not stuffy.

QUIMPER L'Ambroisie 🏃 €€€

49 rue Elie Fréron, 29000 **Tel** *02 98 95 00 02*

Located just at the end of one of the tiny streets in the centre of Quimper, a short walk from the cathedral. Good simple cuisine using quality produce. Try the langoustines with a cappuccino of fresh green peas, the delicious turbot with shallots, and strawberries and verbena ice cream.

RENNES Le Bocal P'Ty

6 rue d'Argentre, 35000 **Tel** 02 99 78 34 10

Reservations recommended at this busy restaurant. Bottling jars filled with glass beads and shells line the interior. Traditional dishes include *andouillette* (tripe sausage) with apple sauce, or try a speciality, such as sautéed pork in Carambar (a French caramel sweet). Good choice for children and vegetarians.

RENNES Le Corsaire

52 rue d'Antrain, 35700 **Tel** 02 99 36 33 69 **Fax** 02 99 36 33 69

Classic and upmarket, with a deservedly good local reputation. An interesting menu offers turbot with fennel and orange, crab on a bed of seaweed, and abalone (type of mollusc). The set menu offers a more traditional choice with lamb and garlic, and braised oxtail. Stylish mirrored dining room.

ROSCOFF Le Surcouf

14 rue Amiral Révellière, 29680 **Tel** 02 98 69 71 89 **Fax** 02 98 69 71 89

Near the church, this brasserie-style restaurant serves regional cuisine. The fixed-price menus have a wide choice of local coastal produce. Start with a plate of mussels, sea snails, whelks and a half-dozen oysters. For the main course, choose a lobster from the tank, or the delicious seafood casserole.

ROSCOFF Le Temps de Vivre

17-19 pl Lacaze-Douthiers, 29680 **Tel** 02 98 61 27 28 **Fax** 02 98 61 19 46

The acclaimed chef Jean-Yves Crenn does wonderful things with vegetables in this restaurant facing the sea. Seafood is the speciality: lobster on a *gelée* of tomatoes, langoustines with carrots, St-Pierre with a cauliflower cream sauce. Good selection of wines. Friendly staff.

ST-BRIEUC Amadeus

22 rue de Gouët, 22000 **Tel** 02 96 33 92 44 **Fax** 02 96 33 92 44

In one of this historic town's oldest buildings, this elegant gourmet restaurant specializes in fish – truffle-topped sea bass, tuna *ratatouille* and fillet of sole are all outstanding. The wide range of tempting desserts includes Amaretto chocolate cake, and Breton butter biscuits with fruit.

ST-BRIEUC Restaurant Aux Pesked

59 rue de Légué, 22000 **Tel** 02 96 33 34 65

A gourmet city-centre restaurant a short walk from the cathedral. Elegant decor, and a lovely view of the Légué valley from the terrace. Remarkable, creative cuisine, mainly fish-based. Specialities include monkfish with liquorice marinade served with aubergine and apricot, and caramel soufflé.

ST-MALO Restaurant L'Epicerie

18 rue de la Herse, 35400 **Tel** 02 23 18 34 55

Within the ramparts, near to the Grande Porte, this bistro-style restaurant serves locally sourced produce and fish from Erquy port. The kitchen and the dining room are almost one. The menu depends on the season and the pick of the market, and so changes daily.

ST-MALO Le Chalut

8 rue de la Corne de Cerf, 35400 **Tel** 02 99 56 71 58 **Fax** 02 99 56 71 58

One of St Malo's best restaurants, the chef excels in fish dishes and well-chosen produce simply prepared. Monkfish and artichokes with sherry butter, and St-Pierre and white asparagus with langoustine sauce are examples of the delicious dishes on offer. Good selection of cheese, too.

VANNES Table des Gourmets

6 rue Alexandre-le-Pontois, 56000 **Tel** 02 97 47 52 44

Tasty meals at reasonable prices served in this restaurant opposite the ramparts. The chef uses regional ingredients with originality. Try the sautéed lobster with girolle mushrooms, or the *croustillant* of pigeon with perfumed rice. The wine list includes organic producers.

VITRE La Taverne de l'Ecu

12 rue Baudairie, 35500 **Tel** 02 99 75 11 09 **Fax** 02 99 75 82 97

This half-timbered Renaissance house provides an historic ambience for a meal in one of two dining rooms. Menu changes seasonally. Try the wild boar with spicy apple chutney, roast leg of rabbit or one of the good fish dishes. Home-made bread accompanies your meal. Vegetarian choices are available.

THE LOIRE VALLEY

AMBOISE Le Choiseul

36 quai C.Guinot, 37400 **Tel** 02 47 30 45 45 **Fax** 02 47 30 46 10

Elegant 18th-century hotel with a pretty garden and views of the Loire from the airy dining room. The sophisticated menu changes seasonally; in spring a meal might include asparagus, in summer roast pike-perch with crab *béarnaise* sauce, or quail's eggs served with sage *tempura*. Good Touraine wines and many other regional wines.

Key to Price Guide see p600 **Key to Symbols** see back cover flap

ANGERS La Ferme 🏃♿🚬 €

2 pl Freppel, 49000 **Tel** *02 41 87 09 90*

A hectic restaurant, near the cathedral, which spills out onto the shady terrace in summer. Souvenirs of bygone farming days hang on the walls of the rustic dining room. Copious portions of traditional, homely dishes like *poule au pot* (pot-boiled chicken with vegetables), *coq au vin* and *cassoulet*. For dessert, giant profiteroles.

ANGERS Le Lucullus 🏃 €€

5 rue Hoche, 49000 **Tel** *02 41 87 00 44* **Fax** *02 41 87 00 44*

This pretty restaurant carved into the tuffeau rock has two lovely vaulted dining rooms. Classic dishes and regional specialities served with an added touch from the chef. Try the tasty sautéed scallops with saffron-flavoured sauce, the crayfish brochettes and the classic fillet of beef with morille mushrooms.

BEAUGENCY Le P'tit Bateau 🏃♿🚬 €€

54 rue du Pont, 45190 **Tel** *02 38 44 56 38* **Fax** *02 38 46 44 37*

Near the château, the P'tit Bateau is the most appealing restaurant in town. Popular with locals, it offers traditional cuisine in a rustic dining room with exposed beams and open fireplace. Fresh fish, game in season and wild mushrooms feature on the menu. There is a courtyard terrace for sunny days.

BLOIS L'Orangerie du Château 🅿🏃♿🚬🍷 €€€

1 av Jean Laigret, 41000 **Tel** *02 54 78 05 36* **Fax** *02 54 78 22 78*

Housed in the 15th-century château's former winter garden, the fine setting is matched by the food and wine here. The menu features regional favourites with a traditional approach, such as roast saddle of lamb served with a goat's cheese polenta, and ravioli of langoustine. A dependable wine list with good Touraine producers.

BLOIS Au Rendez-vous des Pêcheurs 🏃🍽🚬🍷 €€€€

27 rue du Foix, 41000 **Tel** *02 54 74 67 48*

Well known regionally, this restaurant is famed for its menu focusing on seafood and fish creations like Loire pike-perch with leek salad, stuffed courgette flowers and roast sea bass. There is also Sologne game, in season, and a good selection of wines from Cheverny and Montlouis. Book ahead.

BOUCHEMAINE La Terrasse 🏃 €€

4 pl Rouzebouc, 49080 **Tel** *02 41 77 11 96* **Fax** *02 41 77 25 71*

Located in a hamlet on the confluence of the rivers Loire and Maine, this restaurant has a panoramic view. Menu features freshly caught eels, pike-perch, salmon and other freshwater fish. Classic dishes are excellently prepared, such as *sandre au beurre blanc* (pike-perch in butter). Ironically, there is no terrace.

BOURGES La Courcillière 🏃🚬 €€

Rue de Babylone, 18000 **Tel** *02 48 24 41 91*

By the marshes overlooking the river Yèvre, it's worth the 20-minute walk from the city centre for freshwater fish and local cooking – classic dishes such as pike-perch fillet, eel in red wine or delicious salmon. Traditional dining area with modern bright decor, and delightful terrace. Attentive service.

BOURGES Le Jacques Cœur 🚬 €€€

3 pl Jacques Cœur, 18000 **Tel** *02 48 26 53 01* **Fax** *02 48 26 58 05*

Facing the Palais Jacques Cœur, in front of the church, the typical Berry cuisine in this restaurant is excellent. There are flavourful fish dishes, such as monkfish in a rich tomato sauce, classic *coq au vin*, and chocolate profiteroles. The small, intimate dining areas are decorated in period style.

BOURGUEIL Le Moulin Bleu 🏃🚬🍷 €€€

7 rue du Moulin-Bleu, 37140 **Tel** *02 47 97 73 13* **Fax** *02 47 97 79 66*

The house at the foot of this pretty blue mill has two vaulted dining rooms serving traditional dishes in a friendly atmosphere. The cuisine remains faithful to the region, with Touraine-reared veal served with a Vouvray butter sauce. Good Bourgueil producers on the wine list. In the off-season only open Friday and Saturday evenings.

BRACIEUX Le Relais de Bracieux 🅿🏃♿🚬🍴🍷 €€€€

1 av de Chambord, 41250 **Tel** *02 54 46 41 22* **Fax** *02 54 46 03 69*

After visiting nearby Chambord and the Cheverny vineyards, take a break at this gourmet restaurant in a former coaching inn. Enthusiastic chef Bernard Robin uses the best products to create excellent dishes, such as truffle-flavoured roast Touraine chicken, with puréed potato seasoned with *demi-sel* butter.

CHARTRES Le Grand Monarque 🏃🍽♿🚬🍷 €€€€

22 pl des Epars, 28000 **Tel** *02 37 18 15 15* **Fax** *02 37 36 34 18*

Within this magnificent 17th-century staging post are both a gourmet 'le Georges' restaurant, and a brasserie serving traditional food. The cuisine is ambitious and flavourful, with dishes such as red mullet and Loire eel in vinaigrette, and bass cooked in a clay crust. Excellent desserts. First-rate wine cellar.

CHENONCEAU Auberge de Bon Laboureur 🏃🍽♿🚬 €€€€

6 rue de Docteur Bretonneau, 37150 **Tel** *02 47 23 90 02* **Fax** *02 47 23 82 01*

Refined classic cuisine is served in this former coaching inn just a few minutes from the château. The produce is seasonal and vegetables come from their own vegetable patch. A typical menu could include langoustine *bisque*, bass with green and white asparagus, and shortbread biscuit topped with lemon and citrus-flavoured cream.

CHINON Les Années 30   🏃♿🖼   €€€
78 rue Haute St-Maurice, 37500 **Tel** *02 47 93 37 18* **Fax** *02 47 93 33 72*

This elegant little eatery on the way up to the château has a chef who has brought back the spark to this menu. Stéphane Charles presents dishes such as a tartare of oysters with a seaweed tempura, and roast pike-perch served with a risotto flavoured with ginger and citrus fruit. Good local wines.

CLISSON La Bonne Auberge   🏃   €€€€
1 rue Olivier de Clisson, 44190 **Tel** *02 40 54 01 90* **Fax** *02 40 54 08 48*

A comfortable auberge in the city centre with three attractive dining rooms, one set in a conservatory with garden views. The specialities here include lobster gratin, *paupiettes* of sea bass, scallops with truffles and pigeon breast in red Chinon sauce. The desserts are delicate, and the selection of Muscadets is good.

CONTRES La Botte d'Asperges   🏃▤♿🍷   €€
52 rue Pierre-Henri Mauger, 41700 **Tel** *02 54 79 50 49* **Fax** *02 54 79 08 74*

Locally grown asparagus features prominently on the menu, in season. Behind the rustic atmosphere is an inspirational chef who prepares such delights as squid stuffed with ratatouille and pan-fried langoustines with cardamom. Small, well-chosen wine list. You can also take food away.

DOUE-LA-FONTAINE Auberge de la Bienvenue   🅿🏃🖼   €€
104 route de Cholet, 49700 **Tel** *02 41 59 22 44* **Fax** *02 41 59 93 49*

A pretty inn situated in this town of roses. The menu offers elaborate, savoury preparations using welcome favourites, such as langoustines in saffron sauce, or calf's liver in port and pepper sauce. Other dishes include local products such as pike-perch, crayfish, lamb and wild mushrooms.

FONTEVRAUD-L'ABBAYE La Licorne   🏃♿🖼🍷   €€€€
Allée Sainte-Catherine, 49590 **Tel** *02 41 51 72 49* **Fax** *02 41 51 70 40*

Next to the splendid abbey, this popular restaurant has a pretty courtyard terrace and elegant dining room. The menu includes creations such as prawns and basil ravioli in morel sauce and, for dessert, strawberries flavoured with roses. Good Saumur wines. Book ahead.

GENNES Auberge du Moulin de Sarré   🍽🅿🏃♿🖼   €
Route de Louerre, 49350 **Tel** *02 41 51 81 32*

After taking a tour of the 16th-century watermill (the only working one in the region), try either the menu of *fouées* (warm bread puffs, made from flour ground at the mill) with fillings such as goat's cheese or *rillettes* (duck pâté), or the fresh trout menu (fished on the spot). Reservations are required.

GIEN Restaurant la Poularde   🏃▤♿   €€€
13 quai de Nice, 45500 **Tel** *02 38 67 36 05* **Fax** *02 38 38 18 78*

A classic restaurant on the banks of the Loire, serving traditional cuisine in an elegantly furnished dining room, with Gien tableware. The menu includes succulent crispy langoustines, and local pike-perch cooked in Chinon wine with mushrooms. Game appears on the menu in season.

LAMOTTE BEUVRON Hôtel Tatin   🏃▤🖼🍷   €€
5 av de Vierzon, 41600 **Tel** *02 54 88 00 03* **Fax** *02 54 88 96 73*

This elegant hotel-restaurant serves traditional fare made with fresh local produce. The menu includes *foie gras*, salad of home-made pâté and warm goat's cheese, pike-perch, pigeon, steak and the famous *tarte Tatin*. There is a good selection of quality Sancerre and Cheverny wines.

LE MANS Le Nez Rouge   🏃🖼   €€
107 grande rue, 72000 **Tel** *02 43 24 27 26*

A charming timbered restaurant in the medieval part of Le Mans. The young chef has trained in some of the best restaurants in France. His dishes are based on the freshest produce, such as lobster and veal sweetbreads. The dining room is cosy and intimate, and there is a terrrace across the road. Book ahead.

LE MANS Le Beaulieu   🏃▤🖼🍷   €€€€
24 rue des Ponts-Neufs, 72000 **Tel** *02 43 87 78 37* **Fax** *02 43 87 78 27*

Gastronomic cuisine is offered in this elegant restaurant in a 15th-century house in the Old Town. The appetizing dishes use the most noble produce, such as veal sweetbreads with truffles, langoustines, lobster and caviar, *foie gras* and potatoes with truffles, and beef with truffles. Worth a treat.

LES SABLES D'OLONNE Fleurs des Mers   🏃   €
5 quai Guiné, 85100 **Tel** *02 51 95 18 10* **Fax** *02 51 33 40 61*

At this restaurant at the port there are two comfortable dining areas from where you can watch the boats coming and going. The menu is based around the catch of the day, with simple classic fish dishes and fresh shellfish. Efficient service. Fleurs des Mers tends to fill up in summer, so book ahead.

MALICORNE-SUR-SARTHE La Petite Auberge   🏃🖼   €€€
5 pl du Guesclin, 72270 **Tel** *02 43 94 80 52* **Fax** *02 43 94 31 37*

In summer dine on the riverside terrace and watch the boats go by; in winter take refuge around the magnificent medieval fireplace. Enjoy classic cuisine with an innovative twist, such as delicious gratin of scallops with smoked salmon or perfectly cooked steak with a red Bourgueil wine sauce.

Key to Price Guide *see p600* **Key to Symbols** *see back cover flap*

MONTBAZON La Chancelière Jeu de Cartes 🏃📋♿🏠🍷 €€€

1 pl des Marronniers, 37250 **Tel** *02 47 26 00 67* **Fax** *02 47 73 14 82*

Modern, sophisticated cuisine prepared with precision. This restaurant proposes savoury but uncomplicated dishes such as a *tagine* of monkfish, or stir-fried chicken and giant prawns with lemongrass. Well-selected wine list with good Vouvray and Bourgeuil producers.

MONTOIRE-SUR-LE-LOIR Le Cheval Rouge 🅿🏃♿🏠 €€

Pl Foch, 41800 **Tel** *02 54 85 07 05* **Fax** *02 54 85 17 42*

After visiting the chapel and prior's lodging where Ronsard (16th-century French poet) spent his last years, stop off and dine on classic cuisine in this ancient staging post. Enjoy well-prepared regional dishes in the attractive dining room or outside on the shady terrace with its 100-year-old plane tree.

MONTSOREAU Diane de Méridor 🏃 €€

12 quai Philippe de Commines, 49730 **Tel** *02 41 51 71 76* **Fax** *02 41 51 17 17*

While dining you have a view of the château which was the film-setting for the interpretation of la Dame de Montsoreau by Alexandre Dumas. Carved out of tuffeau rock, in this town perched above the Loire, this restaurant is rustic with exposed beams and an open fireplace. It specializes in freshwater fish dishes cooked to perfection.

NANTES Le Pressoir 🍷 €€

11 quai de Turenne, 44000 **Tel** *02 40 35 31 10*

More than a simple bistro, this restaurant is a newcomer on the quays. The young chef presents interesting dishes such as *carpaccio of grison* (cured beef), roast bass, bass with leeks cooked in a truffle-flavoured juice, and steak with morille mushrooms. The wine list is extensive, many by the glass. Book ahead.

NANTES La Cigale 🏃🏠🍷 €€

4 pl Graslin, 44000 **Tel** *02 51 84 94 94* **Fax** *02 51 84 94 95*

This ornate Belle Epoque brasserie dates from 1895 when it was frequented by celebrated writers and Nantes elite. The quality of the cuisine matches the exceptional interior. Oysters, *carpaccio* of salmon and beef *à la plancha* (cooked on a hot plate). Open all day. Extensive wine list.

NANTES Les Temps Changent ♿🏠🍷 €€€

1 pl Aristide-Briand, 44000 **Tel** *02 51 72 18 01*

Excellent chef with a vision of modern cuisine. This welcoming venue provides quality French dishes that combine classic produce and inventive cooking. Menu includes *foie gras à la plancha* with baby vegetables and hot and cold red mullet with mini-fennel and tapenade. Interesting wines.

NANTES L'Atlantide 📋♿🍴🍷 €€€€

16 quai Ernest-Renaud, 44000 **Tel** *02 40 73 23 23* **Fax** *02 40 73 76 46*

Simply the best place in town to eat, with a dining room on the fourth floor that offers a superb view. Exotic innovative cuisine is served up by this well-travelled chef, including spider crab with avocado and tomatoes accompanied by a light mango sauce. Remarkable wine list.

ONZAIN Domaine des Hauts de Loire 🅿📋♿🏠🍴🍷 €€€€€

Route de Herbault, 41150 **Tel** *02 54 20 72 57* **Fax** *02 54 20 72 57*

Gastronomic cuisine is served in this former hunting lodge, set within its own park. Superb dishes are presented by chef Rémy Giraud, such as caviar with new potatoes from Noirmoutier, braised beef in Montlouis wine, pike-perch with girolle mushrooms and rhubarb *mille feuille*. Classic wine list.

ORLEANS La Chancellerie 🏃♿🏠🍷 €€€

27 pl du Martroi, 45000 **Tel** *02 38 53 57 54*

This lively brasserie-restaurant is located on the town's main square. Built by order of the Duke of Orléans in 1754, it was used to keep the carriages, and later became the omnibus station. The interior has high ceilings, a marble bar, leather banquettes and brass trimmings. Staple fare enlivened by good wines. Snacks and salads are also available.

ORLEANS La Petite Marmite 📋 €€

178 rue de Bourgogne, 45000 **Tel** *02 38 54 23 83* **Fax** *02 38 54 41 81*

Le Petite Marmite has a quaint dining area with exposed beams, old prints and pictures on the walls, and an extensive menu of traditional, unfussy cuisine. Choose from *coq au vin*, snails, *andouillette* (tripe sausage), confit of duck, and game in season. Book ahead.

ORLEANS Les Antiquaires 🅿🏃📋🏠🍷 €€€€

2 rue Au lin, 45000 **Tel** *02 38 53 52 35* **Fax** *02 38 62 06 95*

Popular with locals for its inventive cuisine, the well-known chef Philippe Bardau prepares contemporary dishes such as pan-fried asparagus with a morel sauce, and roast pigeon with a smoked aubergine mousse. The dining room is decorated in warm tones. Great selection of local wines.

ROCHECORBON Les Hautes Roches 🅿♿🏠🍴🍷 €€€€€

86 quai Loire, 37210 **Tel** *02 47 52 88 88* **Fax** *02 47 52 81 30*

The dining room in this château is decorated in contemporary tones and serves meticulously prepared classic cuisine. The chef prepares irresistible dishes, such as a terrine of lapin, Racan pigeon with lemon confit, and Grand Marnier soufflé. The cellar has wonderful wines from the best local producers.

ROMORANTIN-LANTHENAY Le Lion d'Or `P ▤ & 🖩 🍴 ⏰` €€€€€
69 rue Georges-Clemenceau, 41200 **Tel** *02 54 94 15 15* **Fax** *02 54 88 24 87*

This hotel-restaurant is set in a beautiful Renaissance manor house. Classic cuisine is prepared by a talented chef. Service is precise and professional. Subtle, elegant dishes using the best local produce, game in autumn, vegetables and fish in season. Good selection of wines from all regions.

SACHE Auberge du XII siècle `🚻 & 🖩 ⏰` €€€€
1 rue du Château, 37190 **Tel** *02 47 26 88 77* **Fax** *02 47 26 88 21*

In an historic building, a stone's throw from the Balzac museum, the dining room has a rustic atmosphere with exposed beams. There is a good choice of fixed-price menus with classic dishes, such as roast langoustines, poached turbot with oysters and chocolate fondant.

SALBRIS Domaine de Valaudran `P 🚻 & 🖩` €€€
Rue de Romorantin, 41300 **Tel** *02 54 97 20 00* **Fax** *02 54 97 12 22*

Reputed to be the best place in Sologne to hunt, the restaurant in an 18th-century country house benefits from superb game in season, such as pigeon breast with cauliflower and cocoa-flavoured sauce. Other fine dishes include *tartare* of bass with oysters and caviar, or pan-fried duck liver with Puy lentils.

SANCERRE Auberge la Pomme d'Or `🚻 &` €€
Pl de la Mairie, 18300 **Tel** *02 48 54 13 30* **Fax** *02 48 54 19 22*

This small restaurant in a former coaching inn serves classic dishes. The savoury cuisine uses seasonal produce from the region. Enjoy the simplicity of the Chavignol goat's cheese, pike-perch, Sologne pigeon in honey or shredded duck with raspberry vinegar complemented by a glass of Sancerre.

SAUMUR Auberge St Pierre `🚻 🖩` €€
6 pl St Pierre, 49400 **Tel** *02 41 51 26 25* **Fax** *02 41 59 89 28*

On a square near the château in a former 15th-century monastery, this convivial restaurant serves regional specialities prepared with care. Dishes include pike-perch fillet and chicken cooked in Loire wine. Accompany a regional cheese with a glass of fruity red wine, such as St Nicolas de Bourgueil.

SOUVIGNY-EN-SOLOGNE Auberge de la Grange aux Oies `🚻 & 🖩` €€
2 rue Gâtinais, 41600 **Tel** *02 54 88 40 08* **Fax** *02 54 88 91 06*

Located in the centre of this charming village, opposite the 12th-century church, in a picturesque timbered building. The restaurant serves classic cuisine with an uplifting modern touch, using local Sologne produce. Tasty, succulent dishes are prepared, such as free-range chicken with a cognac-flavoured stuffing.

ST-OUEN LES VIGNES L'Aubinière `🚻 ▤ & 🖩 ⏰` €€€€
29 rue Jules Gautier, 37530 **Tel** *02 47 30 15 29* **Fax** *02 47 30 02 44*

North of Amboise, this small rustic restaurant opens onto a pretty garden that leads down to the river. Enjoy the creations of chef Jacques Arrayet, who serves outstanding dishes including roast langoustine with green pea sorbet, and a caramel of beetroot served with a succulent stuffed leg of guinea fowl.

THOUARCE Le Relais de Bonnezeaux `P 🚻 ▤` €€
Route Angers, 49380 **Tel** *02 41 54 08 33* **Fax** *02 41 54 00 63*

This large, pleasant dining room is located in a converted railway station overlooking the vineyards – this is sweet wine country. Imaginative cuisine with regional produce in dishes such as pigeon with an Anjou sauce and the speciality eel braised in Bonnezeaux.

TOURS L'Atelier Gourmand `& 🖩 ⏰` €
37 rue Etienne Marcel, 37000 **Tel** *02 47 38 59 87* **Fax** *02 47 37 66 12*

A charming small restaurant in a 15th-century building in the old part of Tours. Fabrice Bironneau presents a competitively priced, interesting menu. Fresh dishes include succulent rabbit terrine accompanied by red fruits, ragoût of lamb and a fondant of chocolate. Warm, homely ambience.

TOURS L'Arche de Meslay `P 🚻 & 🖩 ⏰` €€
14 rue Ailes in Parçay Meslay, 37210 **Tel** *02 47 29 00 07* **Fax** *02 47 29 04 04*

Worth the 9-km (6-mile) detour from the city centre, this refined, contemporary restaurant has a sunny terrace and a kitchen in full view. Watch the chef prepare a delicious lobster with chipped vegetables, *bouillabaisse tourangelle* (regional fish stew) or tuna tataki with a sesame seed crust.

TOURS L'Odéon `🚻 ⏰` €€€
10 pl de la Gare, 37000 **Tel** *02 47 20 12 65*

Just a short walk from Tours' station, this Art Deco-style restaurant provides quality French regional dishes such as smoked salmon, duck with roasted apples and cider sauce, and delicious dark chocolate profiteroles. The wine list is extensive.

TOURS Jean Bardet `P 🚻 ▤ 🍴 ⏰` €€€€€
57 rue Groison, 37000 **Tel** *02 47 41 41 11* **Fax** *02 47 51 68 72*

In a Napoléon III mansion house with an opulent dining room, this gastronomic temple of the Loire serves inspired dishes, including lightly smoked Racan pigeon with liquorice-flavoured sauce, and pineapple glazed with dark rum accompanied by gingerbread ice-cream. Jean Bardet has a great wine list.

Key to Price Guide *see p600* **Key to Symbols** *see back cover flap*

VEIGNE Moulin Fleuri
`P` `🚶` `🖼` €€

Route de Ripault, 37250 **Tel** *02 47 26 01 12* **Fax** *02 47 34 04 71*

In an ancient watermill on the banks of the Indre river, classic cuisine is presented by chef Alain Chaplin in a menu that focuses on local ingredients like Racan pigeon, *rillettes de Tours*, *andouillette* (tripe sausage), pike-perch and Richelieu truffles. There is also a decent children's menu.

VENDOME La Vallée
`P` `🚶` `♿` `🖼` `🍷` €€

34 rue Barré-de-St-Venant, 41100 **Tel** *02 54 77 29 93*

This restaurant serves well-prepared traditional dishes by chef Marc Georget, who is respectful of the quality of the produce. Offerings include Loire valley asparagus in season, fish from Brittany and well-sourced veal. Classic, rustic dining room. Good regional wines too.

VIGNOUX SUR BARANGEON Le Prieuré
`P` `🚶` `♿` `🖼` €€€

2 route de St Laurent, 18500 **Tel** *02 48 51 58 80* **Fax** *02 48 54 56 01*

Near to Vierzon, this lovely hotel-restaurant was built in 1862 to serve as the village presbytery. High-quality gourmet cuisine is served in the elegant dining room or on the covered terrace by the pool. Expect to find dishes such as roast pike-perch with Berry lentils and *foie gras*.

VILLANDRY Domaine de la Giraudière
`P` `🚶` `♿` `🖼` €€

Route de Druye, 37510 **Tel** *02 47 50 08 60* **Fax** *02 47 50 06 60*

There are three dining rooms with original features in this 17th-century farmhouse near the château. It is a working farm of mainly goats, which is reflected in the menu – goat's cheese marinated in herbs, goat's cheese *quenelles* (dumplings), kid goat. Home-produced pâtés, charcuterie and tarts.

VOUVRAY La Cave Martin
`🚶` `🖼` `🍷` €

66 vallée Coquette, 37210 **Tel** *02 47 52 62 18*

In this wine village, this restaurant carved into the tuffeau rock has a rustic menu with *andouillettes* (tripe sausages), duck breast and confit, and a decent choice of salads. Start with a glass of local fizzy wine, and finish with an unctuous sweet Vouvray with dessert. Book ahead.

BURGUNDY & FRANCHE-COMTE

ARBOIS La Balance Mets et Vins
`♿` `🖼` `🍷` €€€

47 rue de Courcelles, 39600 **Tel** *03 84 37 45 00* **Fax** *03 84 66 14 55*

The owner's concept is to match good food and wine in this establishment, funded by six vignerons and other local people. Modern and bright dining room offers local gastronomic dishes and Jura wines from local producers. Pass a pleasant moment finding the right match for your dish.

AUXERRE Le Jardin Gourmand
`P` `🚶` `♿` `🖼` €€€

56 bd Vauban, 89000 **Tel** *03 86 51 53 52* **Fax** *03 86 52 33 82*

Adventurous and inventive dishes are on offer at this attractive dining room in a former wine-grower's house. Try the fillet of beef cooked with liquorice, or wild boar with cloves. The menu changes with the season, and with the chef's vegetable garden. Wonderful cheeses. Pleasant patio. Book ahead.

BEAUNE La Ciboulette
`🚶` `▤` `♿` `🍷` €

69 rue Lorraine, 21200 **Tel** *03 80 24 70 72* **Fax** *03 80 22 79 71*

A delightful little bistro frequented by locals; always a good sign. The basic decor is in contrast with the high standard of cooking. Hearty dishes, such as steak with pungent Epoisses cheese. The best value in town. Local wine merchants come here to choose from the excellent wine list.

BEAUNE La Bouzerotte
`🚶` `🖼` €€

Bouze les Beaune, 21200 **Tel** *03 80 26 01 37* **Fax** *03 80 26 09 37*

In winter, a roaring fire makes this the cosiest place in Burgundy. In summer, enjoy watching Burgundian life pass by on the terrace. Hearty dishes, made using regional produce, are cooked to order. Rustic setting and friendly village atmosphere. The wine list is rather basic.

BEAUNE La Buissonnière
`P` `🚶` `🖼` `🍷` €€

Ladoix Serrigny, 21550 **Tel** *03 80 26 43 58*

Intimate and welcoming restaurant with tables in either the contemporary glass-covered area or the former cellar around the old wine press. Feast on generous portions of seasonal Burgundy cooking. Located in a vineyard, the wine list is exceptional. Menus are chosen to match the wines.

BEAUNE Ma Cuisine
`▤` `🍷` €€

Passage St-Hélène, 21200 **Tel** *03 80 22 30 22* **Fax** *03 80 24 99 79*

Pierre Escoffier is a wine connoisseur who decided to open this restaurant to share his passion with his customers. First choose your bottle, then something simple but good to eat from a choice of snails, *jambon persillé* (roasted ham with parsley), roast pigeon, or entrecôte steak with mushroom sauce.

BEAUNE Hostellerie de Levernois

€€€€

Route de Cobertault, Levernois, 21200 **Tel** *03 80 24 73 58* **Fax** *03 80 22 78 00*

This beautiful old mansion with formal gardens occupies an idyllic country setting. The classic restaurant serves up "serious" cuisine, such as snails with garlic, lightly smoked pigeon and *foie gras* with caramelized turnips in blackcurrant sauce, or salmon smoked over vine cuttings. Vast wine list. Faultless service.

BELFORT Le Pot au Feu

€€

27 bis grand' rue, 90000 **Tel** *03 84 28 57 84* **Fax** *03 84 58 17 65*

This bustling restaurant in a 17th-century vaulted cellar serves homely dishes alongside modern, innovative cuisine. Opt for the *pot au feu*, which is a braised beef and vegetable stew, or pan-fried veal kidneys with morille mushrooms, or salmon sushi with wasabi and horseradish sauce.

BESANÇON L'O à la Bouche

€

9 rue du Lycée, 25000 **Tel** *03 81 82 09 08* **Fax** *03 81 82 16 38*

The chef Eric Aucant has trained in some of the best restaurants in France. This cosy contemporary restaurant in a stone cellar offers lovely cuisine – fine, serious and consistent. Try the delicious pike-perch mousse wrapped in cabbage or potato *mille feuille* served with local Morteau sausage.

CHAGNY Château de Bellecroix

€€€

Route Nationale 6, 71150 **Tel** *03 85 87 13 86* **Fax** *03 85 91 28 62*

This delightful turreted château, close to Beaune and Cluny, was once the property of the Order of the Knights of Malta and boasts an impressive Neo-Gothic dining room. The menu focuses on French dishes using local produce in classics such as snails, braised veal and *Bresse poulet*. Good regional wine list.

CHAGNY Lameloise

€€€€€

36 pl d'Armes, 71150 **Tel** *03 85 87 65 65* **Fax** *03 85 87 03 57*

Family owned for more than a century, Lameloise is known for its reassuring classic French dishes. Well-mastered Burgundian cooking: braised oxtail with truffle purée, ravioli of snails with garlic stock, vanilla macaroon with pistachio cream. Pure, powerful flavours done to perfection.

CHAINTRE La Table de Chaintré

€€€

Le Bourg, 71570 **Tel** *03 85 32 90 95* **Fax** *03 83 32 91 04*

Not far from Mâcon, this well-established restaurant comes highly recommended, with a menu that changes weekly. Try the *menu découverte* with four small main dishes, cheese and dessert, or order *à la carte* favourites or more elaborate dishes like frothy white truffle soup with asparagus. Great desserts.

CHALON-SUR-SAONE L'Air du Temps

€

7 rue de Strasbourg, 71100 **Tel** *03 85 93 39 01* **Fax** *03 85 93 39 01*

Plainly furnished restaurant, with flavours and colours that explode on the palate. The regional menu changes every 15 days and uses seasonal ingredients. The chef simplifies classic dishes, and delicacies include *escargots* and roasted veal fillet. Friendly service.

CHASSAGNE-MONTRACHET Le Chassagne

€€€

4 impasse Chenevottes, 21180 **Tel** *03 80 21 94 94* **Fax** *03 80 21 97 77*

Definitely the right place to enjoy a glass of Chassagne at the Chassagne restaurant. Try the deliciously fresh crayfish served with sesame oil and shards of parmesan, accompanied by the local Chardonnay, or the veal and truffle purée with a good red Pinot. The quality outweighs the price.

CHATEAUNEUF La Fontaine

€€€

Chateauneuf, 71740 **Tel** *03 85 26 26 87* **Fax** *03 85 26 26 87*

Situated at the edge of the village in a former workshop for cloth weaving, the interior of this restaurant is decorated in a retro style with an extravagant pink and pistachio mosaic and a lovely fountain. The menu offers innovative interpretations of traditional dishes. Good-value fixed-price menus.

COURLANS Auberge de Chavannes

€€€

1890 av Chalon, 39570 **Tel** *03 84 47 05 52* **Fax** *03 84 43 26 53*

This delightful bourgeois auberge is situated in the Jura near to Lons-le-Saunier, taking advantage of its location at the confluence of two regions – Bresse for poultry and Jura for wines. The specialities include rolled Bresse chicken breast and scallops seasoned with cooked oranges, honey, vinegar and curry.

DIJON Le Bistrot des Halles

€

10 rue Bannelier, 21000 **Tel** *03 80 49 94 15*

At lunchtime this 1900s-style bistro is roaring. Located next to the market, it attracts food merchants and local business people with its meat pie, *jambon persillé* and *bœuf bourguignon*. Well-known Dijon chef Jean-Pierre Billoux, who has an up-market restaurant in Dijon centre, oversees this bistro.

DIJON Le Chabrot

€€

36 rue Monge, 21000 **Tel** *03 80 30 69 61* **Fax** *03 80 50 02 35*

The cosy interior, chatty owner and regional specialities make this restaurant popular. Le Chabrot presents traditional dishes with an innovative twist, such as the *pain d'épices* (gingerbread) ice cream. There is a good selection of Burgundy wines, some sold by the glass.

Key to Price Guide *see p600* **Key to Symbols** *see back cover flap*

DIJON Le Pré aux Clercs · 🚹🚲🍷 €€€
13 pl de la Libération, 21000 Tel 03 80 38 05 05 Fax 03 80 38 16 16

Run by Jean-Pierre Billoux, one of the most renowned chefs in Dijon. Traditional rustic ingredients with a novel modern twist result in unique dishes, such as caramelized lamb. The fixed-price menus offer classic dishes, such as a *foie gras* terrine. Charming dining area and good choice of Burgundy wines.

DIJON Philippe le Bon · 🅿🚹🚲🍷 €€€
18 rue Ste-Anne, 21000 Tel 03 80 30 73 52 Fax 03 80 30 95 51

This hotel-restaurant named after a Valais duke offers superb cuisine. The well-presented dishes are either served in the elegant medieval dining room or in the pretty garden. There is a *menu terroir*, with local dishes using locally sourced ingredients, such as ox cheek cooked in a Burgundy wine sauce.

DOLE La Chaumière · 🅿🚹🚲 €€€€
346 mal-Juin, 39100 Tel 03 84 70 72 40 Fax 03 84 79 25 60

You need an open mind and a curious nature to enjoy the cuisine at this delightful, elegant restaurant. There are creative, unusual dishes such as monkfish with black olive oil, cucumber in yogurt with mustard leaves, Brie stuffed with herbs and pistachio, and upside-down raspberry tart. Take the plunge. Rooms available.

FONTANGY Ferme auberge de la Morvandelle · 🅿🚹♿ €
Précy-sous-Thil, 21390 Tel 03 80 84 33 32

This is a working farm, open to guests only at the weekend. The dining area is in a converted barn, providing an authentic countryside experience. The farm supplies many of the ingredients for its home-made dishes such as chicken liver salad, roast guinea fowl and fruit tarts. Book ahead.

GEVREY-CHAMBERTIN Le Bon Bistrot · 🚹🚲🍷 €
Rue de Chambertin, 21220 Tel 03 80 34 33 20

Traditional Burgundian fare at this friendly bistro. No fixed price menus; simply make your own choice from six starters and seven main courses. Favourites include snails in garlic butter, *jambon persillé* (roasted ham in parsley), *coq au vin* (chicken cooked in wine) and *andouillette* (tripe sausages). Well-chosen regional wines.

GEVREY-CHAMBERTIN Chez Guy · 📋🚲🍷 €
3 pl de la Mairie, 21220 Tel 03 80 58 51 51 Fax 03 80 58 50 39

A pleasant little restaurant with a charming dining room with exposed oak beams, and a terrace for fine days. Simple local cuisine such as *coq au vin*, and hearty *joue de bœuf*; both cooked slowly in red wine. A good selection of wines fairly priced. Good service.

LA CROIX BLANCHE Le Relais Mâconnais · 🅿🚹♿🚲🍷 €€€€
Berze la Ville, 71960 Tel 03 85 36 65 47

Near Mâcon, in southern Burgundy, this restaurant has been in the same family for three generations. Elegant dining room, pretty flower-filled terrace and adept cooking. Burgundy beef in a red Mâcon wine sauce and sliced duck liver glazed with strawberry vinegar are typical dishes. Good Mâcon wines.

MEURSAULT Relais de la Diligence · 🅿🚹🚲🍷 €
23 rue de la Gare, 21190 Tel 03 80 21 21 32 Fax 03 80 21 64 69

In a drab location by an old railway station, this building has an imposing stone façade. This Relais bulges with locals on a Sunday lunchtime. Inside are three bright, comfortable dining areas, two overlooking the vineyards. Large quantities of traditional Burgundy fare, such as a superb *boeuf bourguignon*.

NEVERS Jean-Michel Couron · 📋🍷 €€
21 rue St-Etienne, 58000 Tel 03 86 61 19 28 Fax 03 86 36 02 96

Intimate, elegant restaurant, attentive service and remarkable cuisine. Well-mastered dishes using the best produce to create perfectly balanced flavours in dishes such as *foie gras* with a honey and lavender sauce, and apple compôte flavoured with cumin. Good wines by the glass.

NITRY Auberge de la Beursaudière · 🅿🚹📋🚲🍷 €€
Chemin de Ronde, 89310 Tel 03 86 33 69 69 Fax 03 86 33 69 60

A typical Morvan welcome awaits here, where the staff wear peasant costume. The portions are generous. The menu includes *andouillette de Clamecy* (tripe sausage), veal hock, *corniotte Morvandelle* (cheese filled pastry), *côte de bœuf* and *tournedos* (thick medallion of beef). Rooms available.

PIERRE PERTHUIS Les Deux Ponts · 🅿🚹♿🚲 €€€
Pierre Perthuis, 89450 Tel 03 86 32 31 31 Fax 03 86 32 35 80

This roadside hotel-restaurant is located on the Compostela route where medieval pilgrims rested their weary feet. The authentic inn serves a varied menu using the freshest local ingredients in the original dining room. There are outside tables on the pretty flower-filled terrace. Pleasant service.

PORT LESNEY Le Bistro Pontarlier · 🚹♿🚲🍷 €€€
Port Lesney, 39600 Tel 03 84 73 85 85 Fax 03 84 73 88 88

One of the best-value restaurants in the region, this bistro is well established in the old school house of a pretty wine-growing village in the Arbois area. It is associated with the luxury hotel, Château de Germigny, in the same village, with the same chefs and cuisine – but simpler and less expensive. Excellent bistro atmosphere.

POUILLY-SUR-LOIRE Le Relais Fleuri Coq Hardi   目🏃♿🏧🖥   €€

45 av de la Tuilerie, 58150 **Tel** *03 86 39 12 99* **Fax** *03 86 39 14 15*

Set in a large park with river views of the Loire, the Relais Fleuri has a warm and welcoming rustic interior. The restaurant offers a large variety of fresh fish dishes, including turbot with blue poppies. Owners and staff offer friendly service.

PULIGNY-MONTRACHET La Table d'Olivier Leflaive   目🏃♿🏧🖥   €€€

Pl du Monument, 21190 **Tel** *03 80 21 37 65* **Fax** *03 80 21 33 94*

Located in a famous wine village, this rustic restaurant is named after its founder, who makes all the wines himself. The restaurant specializes in wine-tasting lunches in which cold meats, Bresse chicken and Burgundy cheeses are offered alongside wines to taste, such as St-Aubin, Bourgogne Blanc and Puligny-Montrachet. Reservations required.

QUARRE LES TOMBES Auberge de l'Atre   P🏃♿🏧   €€€

Les Lavaults, 89630 **Tel** *03 86 32 20 79* **Fax** *03 86 32 28 25*

The decorative interior of this restaurant in the Morvan region contrasts with the rustic simplicity of the building. The dining room has an authentic hearth, or *âtre*, and there is an attractive terrace. There are classic dishes, such as cocktail of forest mushrooms and soufflé flavoured with *marc de bourgogne*.

SAULIEU Hôtel de la Poste   P🏃目♿🖥   €€

1 rue Grillot, 21210 **Tel** *03 80 64 05 67* **Fax** *03 80 64 10 82*

This is a former 17th-century coaching inn with well-preserved charm. The Belle Epoque dining room serves classic dishes with a modern touch. Sample the *foie gras* with salad and fried gizzards, snails in red wine and garlic, and Charolais beef in truffle juice. The wine list focuses on Burgundy producers.

SAULIEU Le Relais Bernard Loiseau   🏃目♿🍴🖥   €€€€€

2 rue d'Argentine, 21210 **Tel** *03 80 90 53 53* **Fax** *03 80 64 08 92*

This restaurant remains one of France's best. The new chef Patrick Bertron has successfully taken on the challenge, motivated by Mme Loiseau. There well-mastered imaginative interpretations of traditional dishes such as pike-perch with a shallot fondue. Delicious desserts. Extensive wine list.

SEMUR EN AUXOIS Les Minimes   P♿   €

39 rue de Vaux, 21140 **Tel** *03 80 97 26 86*

Plain no-frills cooking in a dining room to match. The bistro-style interior serves traditional, regional cuisine at a reasonable price. From the cheeseboard choose the pungent Epoisses, made in the village just down the road, accompanied by a glass of local wine. The welcome is particularly friendly.

SENS Le Cos des Jacobins   目🏃♿   €€

49 grande rue, 89100 **Tel** *03 86 95 29 70* **Fax** *03 86 64 22 96*

Installed in the former concierge of the Banque de France, this classy restaurant serves traditional French cuisine. The soups are excellent, ranging from the hearty to the voluptuous. The yellow painted walls and black leather chairs lend a refined air to this better than average reastaurant.

SENS La Madeleine   P目🖥   €€€€

1 rue Alsace-Lorraine, 89100 **Tel** *03 86 65 09 31* **Fax** *03 86 95 37 41*

With the two Michelin star rating, here you will find elegant, refined cuisine with great attention to the ingredients. Seasonal menus offer specialities such as *foie gras* with cassis, sea bass and a gorgeously gooey chocolate mousse with raspberry sauce. Good Chablis and Irancy wines. Book ahead.

ST LAURENT SUR SAONE Le St Laurent   🏃♿🏧   €€

1 quai Bouchacourt, 01750 **Tel** *03 85 39 29 19* **Fax** *03 85 38 29 77*

George Blanc's chic bistro overlooking Mâcon and Saône is filled with 1900s kitsch. Abstract paintings, old photos and moleskin seating set the scene for adventurous versions of local specialities. Try the snail ravioli, local Bresse chicken in a cream sauce with morille mushrooms or strawberry shortbread. Mâcon and Beaujolais wines.

ST PERE SOUS VEZELAY L'Espérance   P目♿🏧🍴🖥   €€€€€

St Père sous Vézelay, 89450 **Tel** *03 86 33 39 10* **Fax** *03 86 33 26 15*

L'Espérance serves perhaps the greatest food in Burgundy, in an elegant dining room that opens out onto a terrace with superb views. Marc Meneau, one of France's finest chefs, presents modern classics, such as lobster with macaroni and seafood sauce, sardine with Aquitaine caviar, and tender succulent Quercy lamb. Classic wine list.

TONNERRE Le Saint Père   P🏃🏧   €€€

2 rue Georges Pompidou, 89700 **Tel** *03 86 55 12 84*

Regarded locally as one of the best-value restaurants in the area. The chef specializes in traditional Burgundy dishes using the excellent local cheese, l'Epoisses. From the restaurant you can see the fine Hôtel-Dieu, with its hospital museum founded in the 13th century.

TOURNUS Le Restaurant Greuze   P🏃目♿🍴🖥   €€€€€

1 rue A Thibaudet, 71700 **Tel** *03 85 51 09 11* **Fax** *03 85 51 75 42*

Ultra-classic cuisine and decor, the restaurant itself is a monument to a bygone era. Here's the place to enjoy some of the best classic cooking in France, such as roast potatoes with frogs' legs cooked in a garlic and parsley sauce, or rack of roast pork with sage sauce and mashed potatoes. Good Mâcon and Beaujolais wines.

Key to Price Guide *see p600* **Key to Symbols** *see back cover flap*

VERDUN-SUR-LE-DOUBS L'Hostellerie Bourguignonne
2 av Pdt-Borgeot, 71350 **Tel** *03 85 91 51 45* **Fax** *03 85 91 53 81*

On the riverbank, in the heart of the countryside, this rustic establishment serves unpretentious, straightforward cooking with local ingredients. They do a very good local Charolais beef fillet, and hot lemon and raspberry gratin for dessert. Excellent wine list.

VILLARS FONTAINE Auberge du Coteau
Villars Fontaine, 21700 **Tel** *03 80 61 10 50* **Fax** *03 80 61 30 32*

Take the D35 and head west from Nuit St-Georges to find, sitting among the hillside vineyards, this cosy country inn that serves hearty Burgundy fare. A good choice is the *fondue bourguignonne*, accompanied by a glass of the local Hautes-Côtes de Nuits wine. Relaxed atmosphere and a large terrace.

VILLENEUVE SUR YONNE Auberge La Lucarne aux Chouettes
7 quai Bretoche, 89500 **Tel** *03 86 87 18 26* **Fax** *03 86 87 22 63*

Renovated by actress Leslie Caron, this 17th-century inn has a lovely setting by the river Yonne. Dining outside on the terrace is delightful in summer. The dining room is cosy with exposed beams. The menu presents traditional dishes, such as snails and wild mushroom salad.

VILLERS-LE-LAC Le France
8 pl Cupillard, 25130 **Tel** *03 81 68 00 06* **Fax** *03 81 68 09 22*

The cuisine here is fine and inventive, full of contrasts but still simple. The chef has his own herb garden outside, and an expansive selection of spices collected during his travels. The dining room is airy and bright. Try the Jura snails in an absinthe infusion, or rabbit with honey and ginger. Refreshing sorbets.

VONNAS Georges Blanc
Pl Marché, 01540 **Tel** *04 74 50 90 90* **Fax** *04 74 50 08 80*

A popular shrine of cooking with smooth service in a dining room crammed with antiques. The ambience wavers between the refined and the rustic. Inventive cuisine is prepared by M Blanc and his two sons, including frogs' legs served with a spicy butter and turbot accompanied by assorted shellfish. Excellent wines.

THE MASSIF CENTRAL

ALLEYRAS Le Haut Allier
Pont d'Alleyras, 43580 **Tel** *04 71 57 57 63* **Fax** *04 71 57 57 99*

This hotel-restaurant nestled in the Allier gorge is well worth seeking out for its warm welcome and inventive cuisine. Local produce features in traditional dishes such as saddle of lamb, or combines with more exotic flavours in prawns marinated Thai-style. The set menus represent excellent value.

AUMONT-AUBRAC Restaurant Prouhèze
2 rte du Languedoc, 48130 **Tel** *04 66 42 80 07* **Fax** *04 66 42 87 78*

The award-winning chef uses only the freshest ingredients to create elegant and unusual flavours. Menu highlights include scallop and *foie gras* parcels served with figs and apples and pan-fried fillet of Aubrac beef with morille mushrooms. The sister restaurant, Le Compostelle, serves less expensive country fare.

AURILLAC La Terroir du Cantal
Place des Docks, 15000 **Tel** *04 71 64 31 26*

Cheese fans will love this farmhouse-style restaurant run by local producers, Fromageries Morin. On the menu are hearty mountain dishes, such as *pounti* – a coarse-cut terrine of minced beef, vegetables and prunes served in thick slices, stuffed cabbage and Cantal cheese melted over crusty bread.

AURILLAC La Reine Margot
19 rue Guy de Veyre, 15000 **Tel** *04 71 48 26 46* **Fax** *04 71 48 26 46*

Warm, earthy tones, murals and highly polished wood create a 1950s ambience. Here you can tuck into rustic dishes of the Auvergne, with high-quality ham, pork, beef and local tripe, though there's also a good choice of fish. You can round things off with an apple tart and caramel coulis. Generous portions.

BEAUZAC L'Air du Temps
Confolent, 43590 **Tel** *04 71 61 49 05* **Fax** *04 71 61 50 91*

Just outside Beauzac, this hotel-restaurant rustles up well-priced local cuisine. Menus change with the seasons, but regularly feature green lentils from Puy-en-Velay, Grazac snails and a tasty verveine liqueur. The decor is bright and breezy, with big picture windows and a covered veranda.

BLESLE La Bougnate
Pl de Vallat, 43450 **Tel** *04 71 76 29 30* **Fax** *04 71 76 29 39*

At this hotel-restaurant in an 18th-century auberge, you'll be greeted by a roaring log fire in winter. In summer, tables spill onto the terrace. Plenty of choice on the three set menus. Meat eaters will be tempted by the succulent Salers beef. To finish the meal, try the local cheeses or home-made desserts. Rooms are also available.

BOUSSAC Le Relais Creusois

40 Maison Dieu, rte de la Châtre, 23600 **Tel** *05 55 65 02 20* **Fax** *05 55 65 13 60*

Do not be put off by the incongruous exterior or the downbeat decor – this is award-winning cuisine. The chef seeks inspiration from far and wide to deliver original dishes, such as as veal with carrots caramelized with Muscat. Some tables afford views over the beautiful Petite Creuse valley. Phone to make sure it is open. Closed Jan–mid-Mar.

CALVINET Hôtel Beauséjour

Rte de Maurs, 15340 **Tel** *04 71 49 91 68* **Fax** *04 71 49 98 63*

Stylish hotel-restaurant with warm Mediterranean colours, exposed brick and picture windows. Equal care goes into the preparation of the seasonal menu with locally sourced ingredients, such as chestnuts, Cantal cheeses, wild mushrooms and green lentils in combination with local pork and other meats.

CLERMONT-FERRAND Le Comptoir des Saveurs

6 pl Saint-Pierre, 63000 **Tel** *04 73 37 10 31*

Located in the centre of town next to the St-Pierre market, Le Comptoir's *cuisine nouvelle* is creative and follows season. Menus change daily, depending on what is available at local markets. Small servings are available for those who want to try more than one dish. Gastronomic cooking in a modern, relaxed atmosphere.

CLERMONT-FERRAND Restaurant Anglard

17 rue Lamartine, 63000 **Tel** *04 73 93 52 25* **Fax** *04 73 93 29 25*

In one of Clermont's top restaurants, Gérard Anglard presents classic dishes, such as roast pigeon with raspberry sauce, and a superb warm apple tart. Alternatively, you can see what is in store on the daily *menu du marché*. The fresh, modern decor will not distract from what is on your plate.

CLERMONT-FERRAND Brasserie Danièle Bath

Pl Saint-Pierre, 63000 **Tel** *04 73 31 23 22* **Fax** *04 73 31 08 33*

The chef at this popular "gastro-brasserie" right on the market square alternates between rustic and refined with great panache. The bistro ambience is unusually relaxed for this level of dining, and it's not expensive, if you stick to the set menus. Lots of interesting young wines.

FLORAC La Source du Pêcher

Rue Remuret, 48400 **Tel** *04 66 45 03 01* **Fax** *04 66 45 28 82*

Charming little restaurant in a converted mill where you can watch the fish jumping while you eat. Regional produce takes pride of place – duck with bilberries, local lamb, Lozère trout and chestnut-flower honey, depending on the season. Excellent choice of Languedoc wines. Closed from November to Easter.

LAGUIOLE Michel Bras

Route de l'Aubrac, 12210 **Tel** *05 65 51 18 20* **Fax** *05 65 48 47 02*

A wall of glass overlooks the Aubrac countryside from this 3-star hilltop restaurant. Michel and Sebastien Bras are renowned for their cutting-edge cuisine. The mouthwatering *biscuit tiède de chocolat coulant* topped with iced double-cream is out of this world. Closed Nov–Easter.

LE PUY-EN-VELAY Lapierre

6 rue des Capucins, 43000 **Tel** *04 71 09 08 44*

For more than 30 years those in the know have been beating a path to Estelle Thivilliers' delightful little restaurant. The draw is her simple and flavoursome country cooking, to which she brings a distinctly feminine touch – the savoury mousses never fail to hit the spot. Good choice of local wines.

LE PUY-EN-VELAY Tournayre

12 rue Chênebouterie, 43000 **Tel** *04 71 09 58 94* **Fax** *04 71 02 68 38*

In the heart of the medieval quarter, a 16th-century chapel complete with vaulted roof and exposed stone walls makes an impressive setting. Feast on top-quality local beef or wonderfully prepared fish dishes before tucking into the groaning cheeseboard. There is a good range of fixed-price menus.

LIMOGES Chez François

Pl de la Motte, 87000 **Tel** *05 55 32 32 79* **Fax** *05 55 32 87 39*

Unbeatable value and a convivial atmosphere at this restaurant inside Limoges' covered market hall. It is only open at lunchtime. Be sure to get here early for a place at the communal tables – or prepare to queue. The food is nothing fancy, but well cooked and tasty. The single, three-course menu changes daily.

LIMOGES L'Amphitryon

26 rue de la Boucherie, 87000 **Tel** *05 55 33 36 39* **Fax** *05 55 32 98 50*

Chic contemporary dining space in the heart of old Limoges. The food is sophisticated and the flavours delicate, in keeping with the Limoges porcelain on which it is served. A regular favourite is the fillet of Limousin beef, while desserts centre around seasonal fruits.

MILLAU Auberge de la Borie Blanque

La Borie Blanque, rte de St-Germain, 12100 **Tel** *05 65 60 85 88*

Locals and tourists rub shoulders at this low-key eatery run by a friendly mother-and-daughter team. Favourites include herb-crusted roast lamb, old-fashioned beef stew and omelette cooked Aveyron-style with potatoes and slices of dried sausage. The menu represents incredible value. Closed 2 weeks Feb.

Key to Price Guide *see p600* **Key to Symbols** *see back cover flap*

MONTLUCON Le Grenier à Sel

`P ⌘ ▤ ⅙ 🛏 🍴` `€€€`

10 rue Ste-Anne, 03100 **Tel** *04 70 05 53 79* **Fax** *04 70 05 87 91*

This ivy-covered 16th-century mansion has huge fireplaces and an elegant dining room decked out in restful pastel tones. In fine weather, meals may be served on the enchanting terrace. Try *foie gras* or lobster quenelle with shellfish coulis. Good-value set menus.

MOUDEYRES Le Pré Bossu

`P 🛏 🍴 🍷` `€€€`

Le Bourg, 43150 **Tel** *04 71 05 10 70* **Fax** *04 71 05 10 21*

Restaurant-with-rooms that's well worth seeking out for the peaceful location and expertly executed cuisine. Many of the herbs and vegetables – including old-fashioned varieties – come from the garden. There is even a vegetarian menu – a rare treat in this corner of France. Dinner only. Closed November to Easter.

MOULINS Restaurant des Cours

`⌘ ▤ 🍷` `€€€`

36-38 cours Jean-Jaurès, 03000 **Tel** *04 70 44 25 66* **Fax** *04 70 20 58 45*

In the capital of the Bourbon region is this upmarket yet refreshingly unstuffy restaurant. House specials focus around regional produce, notably Bourbonnais lamb and Charolais beef, though the fish dishes are equally tempting. Inventive desserts include warm chocolate cake with grated coconut.

MURAT Le Jarrousset

`P ⌘ ⅙ 🛏 🍴` `€€€`

Route de Clermont-Ferrand, 15300 **Tel** *04 71 20 10 69* **Fax** *04 71 20 15 26*

Surrounded by attractive gardens, just east of Murat, is this discreet restaurant. The chef seeks inspiration from top-quality ingredients, most of them sourced locally. The gastronomic menu changes every season, allowing for lots of creativity.

RODEZ Le Kiosque

`⌘ ⅙ 🛏` `€€`

Av Victor-Hugo, 12000 **Tel** *05 65 68 56 21* **Fax** *05 65 68 47 88*

Near the music kiosk in the middle of the public gardens, the terrace of this airy 1930s-style eatery provides the perfect spot to kick back and watch the world go by. As for the food, the star attraction is the rainbow array of seafood. Also generous salads and meat dishes.

RODEZ Le Saint-Amans

`⌘ ▤ 🍴` `€€`

12 rue de la Madeleine, 12000 **Tel** *05 65 68 03 18*

Le Saint-Amans is a long-established restaurant near St-Amans cathedral. This is traditional cooking with sophistication – *aligot* (potato mashed with fresh cheese) with roquefort sauce, and lamb sweetbreads perfumed with orange and served with an onion confit. The intimate dining room will appeal to romantics.

SARPOIL La Bergerie de Sarpoil

`P ⌘ ▤ 🛏 🍴` `€€`

63490 **Tel** *04 73 71 02 54* **Fax** *04 73 71 02 54*

A short drive from Issoire, one of the region's best-loved restaurants occupies a 16th-century coaching inn. Even the cheapest menus offer excellent dishes like terrine of rainbow trout with smoked salmon and leeks, and slow-cooked pork. In winter there is a roaring fire; in summer tables are set up on the shady terrace.

ST-BONNET-LE-FROID Auberge des Cimes

`P ⌘ ▤ ⅙ 🍴 🍷` `€€€€€`

Le Bourg, 43290 **Tel** *04 71 59 93 72* **Fax** *04 71 59 93 40*

The restaurant at the Clos des Cimes hotel recently won its third Michelin star. Depending on the season, you'll feast on lobster, roast lamb, lobster with a sweet-sour sauce, or fragrant mushrooms. Dessert might be a *brochette* of banana with caramelized cherries. Closed January to mid March.

ST-JULIEN-CHAPTEUIL Vidal

`P ⌘ ⅙ 🛏 🍴` `€€€`

Pl du Marché, 43260 **Tel** *04 71 08 70 50* **Fax** *04 71 08 40 14*

In a sleepy village surrounded by mountain peaks, the Vidal family run a convivial restaurant decorated with murals depicting local scenery. With dishes such as the *foie gras* trilogy, it would appear that, at the Vidal, three is the magic number! Closed mid-Jan–Feb.

UZERCHE Restaurant Jean Teyssier

`P ⌘ ▤` `€€`

Rue du Pont-Turgot, 19140 **Tel** *05 55 73 10 05* **Fax** *05 55 98 43 31*

A taste of the Mediterranean has come to the Corrèze with dishes such as giant prawn risotto, Limousin beef polenta, or lobster salad with citrus fruits and vanilla-enhanced vinaigrette. Wonderful panoramic restaurant with views of the Vezère. Closed mid-Feb–mid-Mar.

VICHY Brasserie du Casino

`⅙ 🛏 🍴` `€`

4 rue du Casino, 03200 **Tel** *04 70 98 23 06* **Fax** *04 70 98 53 17*

A veritable institution on the Vichy restaurant scene, across the road from the Grand Casino. Dine in stylish Art Deco surroundings – all wood and mirrors and big bench-seats – on upscale brasserie fare. *Foie gras* served warm with a pear chutney and raspberry charlotte are among the classics on offer.

VICHY La Table d'Antoine

`⌘ ▤ ⅙ 🛏 🍴 🍷` `€€€`

8 rue Burnol, 03200 **Tel** *04 70 98 99 71* **Fax** *04 70 98 99 71*

Considering this is one of Vichy's most sought-after addresses, prices remain remarkably affordable. Menus are varied and change constantly, but always feature a fine selection of fish, most of them line-caught, as well as succulent meat dishes. Quantities are generous and the service irreproachable.

THE RHONE VALLEY AND FRENCH ALPS

AIX LES BAINS Brasserie de la Poste €
32 av Victoria, 73100 **Tel** *04 79 35 00 65*

Lively brasserie, ideal for people-watching and an apéritif. Traditional unfussy dishes served in a friendly, efficient manner in a gaily decorated dining area. For a hearty meal, opt for the stewed beef and cheese fondue. Or for a lighter option, try one of a selection of ten different salads. Reasonably priced.

ANNECY La Rotunde €€€€
3 bd de la Corniche, 74000 **Tel** *04 50 51 43 84* **Fax** *04 50 45 56 49*

The panoramic dining room at the hotel les Trésoms has a magnificent view. Savoury dishes and local delicacies are given an innovative touch. The menus change regularly and always include seasonal ingredients with a mixture of flavours and textures.

BOURG EN BRESSE Chez Blanc €€
19 pl Bernard, 01000 **Tel** *04 74 45 29 11* **Fax** *04 74 24 73 69*

Lively city-centre brasserie appealing to locals and tourists. The chef learned his craft from renowned chef, Georges Blanc. The dishes tend towards local products from Bresse and Dombes such as sauteed frogs' legs, Bresse chicken roast or with a cream sauce, blue Bresse cheese and to finish a lime-flavoured crumble.

CHAMBERY La Chaumière €€
14 rue Denfert Rochereau, 73000 **Tel** *04 79 33 16 26* **Fax** *04 79 33 16 26*

A cosy rustic restaurant situated in the Vieille Ville, near the theatre. The interior is modestly decorated and simply furnished, but the warm and friendly welcome compensates. There is a sunny terrace that borders the roadside. Good quality traditional dishes. Fish, duck and *foie gras* are bargains.

CHAMBERY L'Essentiel €€€€
183 pl de la Gare, 73000 **Tel** *04 79 96 97 27* **Fax** *04 79 96 17 78*

Passionate cuisine from this young chef, who is always exploring new ideas. At its best the food is expressive; lamb accompanied by aubergine and ricotta cannelloni and a *compôte* of red peppers is delicious. The desserts are wonderful. There is an interesting wine list, especially Rhônes.

CHAMONIX La Calèche €
18 rue Paccard, 74400 **Tel** *04 50 55 94 68* **Fax** *04 50 55 87 13*

Typical Savoyard fare served in this three-storey building crammed with antiques. *Tartiflette, fondue* and *raclette* for cheese lovers. Alternatively a delicious dish of beef braised in local wine. Entertainment on Tuesday evenings with folk music, dancing, and films of the region.

CHAMONIX L'Impossible €
9 chemin du Cry, Route des Pélerins, 74400 **Tel** *04 50 53 20 36* **Fax** *04 50 53 58 91*

A former farmhouse in the Savoyard mountains, there is a strong emphasis here on cheese dishes: *fondue, gratins* and *tartiflette* (a baked dish with potato, cheese and ham). Traditional meat dishes simply prepared. Plain *entrecôte* and *tournedos* steak can be grilled over the open fire.

CHAMONIX Le Hameau Albert 1er €€€
119 impasse Montenvers, 74402 **Tel** *04 50 53 05 09* **Fax** *04 50 55 95 48*

Luxury Savoyard hotel-restaurant in the mountains, with a view of Italy. The superb cooking of Pierre Carrier tempts the palate. The vegetable patch next door provides him with inspiration for Piemonte risotto, or fish accompanied by a gratin of chard. Good cheeseboard.

COLLONGES AU MONT D'OR Paul Bocuse €€€€€
40 quai de la Plage, 69660 **Tel** *04 72 42 90 90* **Fax** *04 72 27 85 87*

Paul Bocuse has become an institution for French cooking, and is simply irreplaceable. Try delicacies such as black truffle soup with pastry, or the cooked-to-perfection turbot with its *beurre blanc* sauce, or the legendary gratin of lobster. The wines are also superb. Reserve a table well in advance.

CONDRIEU La Reclusière €€
14 route Nationale, 69420 **Tel** *04 74 56 67 27* **Fax** *04 74 56 80 05*

After a morning's tasting in one of the most prestigious wine regions of France, stop at this elegant manor house. There are two dining rooms, both bright and contemporary. The cuisine is exemplary, classic produce with a modern fresh touch. Wonderful wine list; a different glass proposed with each course.

COURCHEVEL Le Chabichou €€€€
Quartier des Chenus, 73120 **Tel** *04 79 08 00 55* **Fax** *04 79 08 33 58*

Reserve a table by the huge windows to enjoy views of the mountains. With two Michelin stars, Le Chabichou offers exotic and creative cuisine at one of the most popular restaurants in this extensive resort. Refined ambience and old-school favourites, such as *bouillabaisse* and crayfish ravioli.

Key to Price Guide *see p600* **Key to Symbols** *see back cover flap*

EVIAN LES BAINS Chez Tante Marie

€€

Route de Bernex, 74500 **Tel** *04 50 73 60 35* **Fax** *04 50 73 61 73*

Elegant chalet perched above the lake, with pretty flower-filled window boxes. The Alpine setting matches the chef's cuisine to perfection. Good choice of menus offering fish, meat and poultry dishes. Try the home-smoked *charcuterie*, an authentic *tartiflette* or prawns flambéed in whisky.

GRENOBLE La Cour de Miracles

€€

7 bis pl Paul Vallier, 38000 **Tel** *04 38 37 00 10* **Fax** *04 76 24 42 34*

This lively restaurant, opposite Parc Paul Mistral, was created by circus owner Thierry Chiaberto, and Jean Bourbon. The dining room offers an international menu for a broad mix of diners. There is a circus show on Wednesdays, and a magic show on Tuesday evenings and Saturday mornings.

GRENOBLE Le Chasse-Spleen

€€

6 pl Lavalette, 38000 **Tel** *04 38 37 03 52* **Fax** *04 76 63 01 58*

Well situated in central Grenoble, Le Chasse-Spleen is known for the quality of its cooking. Dishes are inventive, such as the *parmentier* of minced oxtail with *foie gras* speciality and the regional dessert baba with Chartreuse. Inside, walnut-drying racks hang from the ceiling, and Baudelaire's poems decorate the walls.

GRENOBLE A Ma Table

€€€

92 cours Jean-Jaurès, 38000 **Tel** *04 76 96 77 04* **Fax** *04 76 96 77 04*

There are regular changes to the menu, depending on seasonal local produce, at this small prettily decorated restaurant. Well-mastered cuisine shows in dishes such as fillet of beef in red wine, and desserts like the melt-in-your-mouth chocolate *ganache*. Book ahead.

GRENOBLE Auberge Napoléon

€€€€

7 rue de Montorge, 38000 **Tel** *04 76 87 53 64* **Fax** *04 76 87 80 76*

In memory of the emperor himself, this elegant Empire-style dining room with ornate ceilings and large flower vases serves a consistently good menu that changes every season. Elegant and inventive cooking, and a selection of specially prepared home-made chocolates. The wine list is carefully chosen, and the service is relaxed.

LAMASTRE Restaurant Barattéro

€€€€

Pl Seignobos, 07270 **Tel** *04 75 06 41 50* **Fax** *04 75 06 49 75*

This is an elegant restaurant with an attractive garden, at the Hotel Midi in the lovely Ardèche town of Lamastre. Classic cuisine such as pan-fried *foie gras* salad, crayfish with a richly flavoured sauce and Ardèche chestnut soufflé. The wine list focuses on St-Joseph and St-Péray.

LE GRAND BORNAND La Ferme de Lormay

€€€

Lormay, 74450 **Tel** *04 50 02 24 29*

Chez Albert, as it's known to the regulars, is a delightful authentic Alpine chalet. The delicious Savoyarde cuisine served here includes vegetable soup with smoked ham, and chicken with crayfish. Locally produced cheeses are accompanied by a glass of Mondeuse.

LYON Chez Carlo

€

22 rue du Palais Grillet, 69002 **Tel** *04 78 42 05 79* **Fax** *04 78 37 36 62*

The best pizza in town is found at Chez Carlo. Located in a backstreet not far from the place de Bellecour, this rustic Italian restaurant has three dining rooms serving good antipasti, veal escalope, osso bucco and a selection of pasta dishes. Good Italian wines. Reservations are required.

LYON Le Mercière

€€

56 rue Mercière, 69002 **Tel** *04 78 37 67 35* **Fax** *04 72 42 28 34*

Chic, lively Lyonnais brasserie with its own *traboule* (medieval passageway) crossing the dining room. Frequented by both tourists and locals, the menu includes regional specialities such as ravioli served in a truffle stock, Bobosse *andouillette* (tripe sausage) and a mouthwatering chocolate mousse. Good Rhône wines.

LYON Brasserie Georges

€€

30 cour Verdun, 69002 **Tel** *04 72 56 54 54* **Fax** *04 78 42 51 65*

Huge, bustling city-centre bistro with fast service and a splendid Art Deco interior. The extensive menu includes a choice of Lyonnais specialities such as *andouillette* (tripe sausage) and Dauphinoise potatoes, but also a variety of seafood dishes, sauerkraut and omelette. Good choice for children and vegetarians.

LYON Brasserie de l'Est

€€€

Gare des Brotteaux, 69006 **Tel** *04 37 24 25 26* **Fax** *04 37 25 25 25*

Bocuse has opened his third Lyon brasserie in the ancient railway station building at Brotteaux. The kitchen is on full view to diners. Enjoy perfectly accomplished brasserie-style dishes while watching the toy train circling around. There is a lively, bustling atmosphere here.

LYON Léon de Lyon

€€€€€

1 rue Pléney, 69001 **Tel** *04 72 10 11 12* **Fax** *04 72 10 11 13*

The expert chef and owner serves classic produce with a modern twist in the heart of the city. Intimate dining area. Seasonal menus offering artichoke and *foie gras*, carp with Nantua sauce, roast venison, wild strawberry tart and stewed rhubarb.

MEGEVE Le Sauvageonne Chez Nano 　　　　　　　🅿🚶♿🎴　　€€

Hameau du Leutaz, 74120 **Tel** *04 50 91 90 81* **Fax** *04 50 58 75 44*

Set in an ancient farmhouse, this good-value restaurant is frequented by tourists and trendy locals. The freshest produce is used. Professional, well-mastered cuisine with wonderfully simple yet tasty dishes. Succulent fish and tender meat. Nano Fanara takes a regular turn to welcome diners.

MEGEVE Le Vieux Megève 　　　　　　　　　🚶　　€€€

58 pl de la Résistance, 74120 **Tel** *04 50 21 16 44* **Fax** *04 50 93 06 69*

This authentic 1880s chalet has original features in the dining room: a large fireplace, polished wood panelling and traditional tablecloths. The regional specialities touch on all the basics, such as the hearty fondue Savoyard and filling cheese *raclette* with locally smoked ham. Try bilberry tart for dessert.

MORZINE La Chamade 　　　　　　　　　🚶♿🎴　　€€€

Morzine, 74110 **Tel** *04 50 79 13 91* **Fax** *04 50 79 27 48*

Traditional Alpine family-run restaurant with a wide menu. Pizzas cooked in wood-fired ovens, cheese platters, and regional fare such as piglet and *charcuterie* (cold meats). Good selection of starters including warm Reblochon salad, marinated salmon and duck breast salad, and chocolate paradise for dessert.

ROANNE La Troisgros 　　　　　　🅿🚶📋♿🍽♟　€€€€€

Pl Jean Troisgros, 42300 **Tel** *04 77 71 66 97* **Fax** *04 77 70 39 77*

La Troisgros is one of the most prestigious restaurants in France, with elegant contemporary decor. Sit in the dining room with its pure lines and zen atmosphere and feast on delights such as crayfish with smoked anchovies and orange zest, or lamb cutlets with citrus-curry crust. There is also a specialized food library.

ST ETIENNE Nouvelle 　　　　　　　　　🚶📋♿　　€€€€

30 rue St Jean, 42000 **Tel** *04 77 32 32 60* **Fax** *04 77 41 77 00*

Elegant setting and attentive staff as well as culinary treats make this a very popular restaurant. The cuisine uses rustic ingredients and adds a modern "trendy" touch. Venison takes on another dimension when accompanied by chicory braised with cocoa beans. Frequented by the St-Etienne bourgeoisie.

ST-AGREVE Domaine de Rilhac 　　　　　　🅿🚶♿　　€€€€

Rilhac, 07320 **Tel** *04 75 30 20 20* **Fax** *04 75 30 20 00*

Located in a peaceful corner of the Ardèche, in this recently renovated farmhouse, chef Ludovic Sinz creates classic dishes with an innovative approach. On the menu there is a choice of beef carpaccio in red wine, tartare of trout with lentils and walnut oil and, to finish, nougat ice cream with chestnuts.

ST-MARTIN-DE-BELLEVILLE La Bouitte 　　　　🅿🚶🎴　　€€€€

St Marcel, 73440 **Tel** *04 79 08 96 77* **Fax** *04 79 08 96 03*

In a charming Alpine chalet, this restaurant serves inventive dishes using regional Alpine herbs. Tantalizing starter of potato soup with truffle slices and pigeon cooked with care. There is also a very good selection of cheese and desserts.

TALLOIRES La Villa des Fleurs 　　　　　　🅿🚶🎴　　€€

Route du Port, 74290 **Tel** *04 50 60 71 14* **Fax** *04 50 60 74 06*

The cuisine at this charming stone-built house set in its own grounds focuses on fish caught in Lake d'Annecy, a stone's throw away. Try the succulent local féra fish, or the poached trout. Traditional regional dishes are also served. Dine outside with a view of the lake in fine weather. Pleasant service. Rooms available.

THONON LES BAINS Le Comte Rouge 　　　　　　　　♿　　€

10 bd du Canal, Place des Arts, 74200 **Tel** *04 50 71 06 04* **Fax** *04 50 81 93 49*

A centrally-located hotel-restaurant, not far from the railway station, with an old-fashioned rustic charm. The restaurant serves dishes prepared with local produce, and specializes in fish. Try the filets de féra (locally caught lake fish), or the crayfish gratin. Attentive service, and reasonably priced menu.

TOURNON Le Tournesol 　　　　　　　　　🚶🎴♟　　€€

44 av Maréchal Foch, 07300 **Tel** *04 75 07 08 26* **Fax** *04 75 07 08 26*

Smart restaurant near the riverside with a panoramic view of the Hermitage vineyards. The interior is smart and contemporary, and the young chef shows his originality in dishes such as *foie gras* with fig chutney, or bass fillet pan-fried with almond oil. Home-made desserts. Well-chosen wines.

VALENCE Restaurant Pic 　　　　　🅿🚶📋♿🎴♟♟　€€€€€

285 av Victor Hugo, 26000 **Tel** *04 75 44 15 32* **Fax** *04 75 40 96 03*

Refined restaurant with inspirational cuisine. Poached sole seasoned with Tellicherry pepper served with fennel flavoured with saffron and Drôme pigeon in a nut crust have enhanced the reputation of this constantly evolving, non-conventional establishment. Great Rhône wines.

VIENNE Les Saveurs du Marché 　　　　　　🚶📋♿♟　　€€

34 cours du Verdun, 38200 **Tel** *04 74 31 65 65* **Fax** *04 74 31 65 65*

Friendly restaurant just a few minutes from the city centre offering traditional French cuisine at reasonable prices, especially the midday menu. Evening meals are more elaborate. The menu changes with the seasons and in summer has a Mediterranean feel. Over 150 quality wines.

Key to Price Guide *see p600* **Key to Symbols** *see back cover flap*

POITOU & AQUITAINE

ANGOULEME Le Terminus
€€

3 pl de la Gare, 16000 **Tel** *05 45 95 27 13* **Fax** *05 45 94 04 09*

Chic, modern restaurant where good food, prompt service and well-priced menus make up for the location on a busy main road. Ultra-fresh seafood takes pride of place, with particular mention of the mixed fish grill and Spanish *fricassée* of monkfish. Leave room for one of the wicked desserts.

ARCACHON Chez Yvette
€€

59 bd du Général Leclerc, 33120 **Tel** *05 56 83 05 11* **Fax** *05 56 22 51 62*

Seafood doesn't come much fresher than at this venerable Arcachon restaurant run by former oyster farmers. Success stories include lamprey *à la bordelaise* (eel-like fish cooked in wine) and roast turbot, but it is hard to resist the spectacular seafood platters. It's wise to book ahead.

ARCINS Le Lion d'Or
€€

11 route de Pauillac, 33460 **Tel** *05 56 58 96 79*

A small and welcoming village auberge in the heart of the Médoc vineyards north of Margaux. Loved by locals who appreciate the traditional seasonal cooking. Local Pauillac lamb is a springtime favourite, while in autumn the accent is on game. No fixed menus, but prices remain reasonable.

BORDEAUX Bistrot d'Edouard
€

16 pl du Parlement, 33000 **Tel** *05 56 81 48 87* **Fax** *05 56 48 51 74*

On one of Bordeaux's prettiest squares, this fuss-free bistro offers a broad range of inexpensive fixed-price menus. Don't expect gourmet dining, but the food is reliable, covering everything from salads, omelettes, vegetarian dishes and fish to regional specialities. Outside dining in summer.

BORDEAUX Le Café du Musée
€

Musée d'Art Contemporain, 7 rue Ferrère, 33000 **Tel** *05 56 44 71 61* **Fax** *05 57 95 81 70*

Splendid lunch spot on top of the contemporary art museum. Modern decor complements stylish dishes ranging from *foie gras* and oysters to duck spring rolls and sashimi. The Sunday buffet is a must on the Bordeaux scene. Also serves coffee, desserts and light meals until 6pm.

BORDEAUX La Tupina
€€€

6 rue Porte de la Monnaie, 33800 **Tel** *05 56 91 56 37* **Fax** *05 56 31 92 11*

The heart of La Tupina is the open fire over which succulent meats are grilled and in winter a cauldron of soup bubbles away. This is an excellent place to try bordelais specialities such as lamprey in wine, grilled shad or baby eels cooked in olive oil with garlic and hot pepper. Simple, old-fashioned desserts.

BRESSUIRE Le Bouchon
€

9 rue Ernest Pérochon, 79300 **Tel** *05 49 74 66 34* **Fax** *05 49 81 28 03*

In the midst of the deeply agricultural Bocage region, discover this family-run inn. Here, in a delightfully relaxed atmosphere, you can feast on honest country dishes such as chicken-liver terrine, *andouillette* (tripe sausage) and a heart-warming beef stew, all prepared with passion. Good-value local wines.

CELLES-SUR-BELLE Hostellerie de l'Abbaye
€€

1 pl des Epoux-Laurant, 79370 **Tel** *05 49 32 93 32* **Fax** *05 49 79 72 65*

Hotel-restaurant in a charming medieval village. The setting, in particular the beautifully tended courtyard garden, is especially alluring. From the open kitchens come elegant dishes such as *filet mignon*, or try the roast lamb with courgette and Parmesan gâteau. Friendly, discreet service.

COGNAC Les Pigeons Blancs
€€€

110 rue Jules-Brisson, 16100 **Tel** *05 45 82 16 36* **Fax** *05 45 82 29 29*

Owned by the same family since the 17th century, this former post house is renowned for its excellent service, wine and food. The popular daily menu really does change every day. Veal sweetbreads with an aged red Pineau sauce and a glass of VSOP cognac is a sure-fire winner. Fabulous dessert trolley.

COULON Le Central
€€

4 rue d'Autremont, 79510 **Tel** *05 49 35 90 20* **Fax** *05 49 35 81 07*

A deservedly popular hotel-restaurant in the Marais. Indulge yourself with original dishes such as snail crumble or eel gratin. More traditional fare includes *foie gras* and lamb with lashings of herbs and garlic – an absolute classic. Portions are generous. Book ahead. Closed Feb.

EUGENIE-LES-BAINS La Ferme aux Grives
€€€

111 rue Thermes, 40320 **Tel** *05 58 05 05 06* **Fax** *05 58 51 10 10*

The more "rustic" of Michel Guérard's much acclaimed restaurants still serves sublime food. Normally heavy southwestern dishes are reinvented for a modern palate, from the home-smoked salmon with herring "caviar" to the crispy gaufre with Chantilly cream and stewed cherries.

GRENADE-SUR-L'ADOUR Pain Adour et Fantaisie

P ⚑ ♿ 🏧 ⛱ 🍴 €€€

14-16 pl des Tilleuls, 40270 **Tel** *05 58 45 18 80* **Fax** *05 58 45 16 57*

Elegant, Michelin-starred restaurant run by a former pupil of Michel Guérard. Trademark dishes include duck *foie gras* flavoured with local *jurançon* wine and juniper. Fish and seafood changes with the seasons. Good-value lunch menu, and a romantic riverside terrace for summer dining.

JARNAC Restaurant du Château

P ⚑ 🍴 ♿ 🍴 €€€

15 pl du Château, 16200 **Tel** *05 45 81 07 17* **Fax** *05 45 35 35 71*

This restaurant near Château Courvoisier is renowned throughout the Cognac region for producing quality regional cuisine. Highlights are the roasted vegetable terrine with seafood vinaigrette, spicy monkfish with a *confit* of tomatoes, and a refreshing Cognac-laced soufflé for dessert and a Cognac digestif to round things off.

LA ROCHELLE Le Boute en Train

⚑ ♿ 🏧 €

7 rue des Bonnes Femmes, 17000 **Tel** *05 46 41 73 74* **Fax** *05 46 45 90 76*

You are assured a warm welcome at this lively French bistro where all the fresh foodstuffs come from the nearby market. This means a great choice of daily dishes and a menu which changes with the seasons. Fortunately, the chocolate mousse is a standard. Book ahead.

LA ROCHELLE Le Comptoir des Voyages

🍴 🏧 🍴 €€

22 rue St-Jean du Perot, 17000 **Tel** *05 46 50 62 60* **Fax** *05 46 41 90 80*

A new addition to the Coutanceau stable, this time with a colonial theme – potted palms, rattan chairs and flavours from around the world. From the single menu you might start with a fragrant pork samoussa, followed by prawns with spicy bamboo and end up with a spicy nougat ice cream. Simply sublime.

LANGON Claude Darozze

P ⚑ ♿ 🏧 🍴 €€€€

95 cours du Général-Leclerc, 33210 **Tel** *05 56 63 00 48* **Fax** *05 56 63 41 15*

Inside this unassuming hotel-restaurant you'll find wonderfully over-the-top decor and some of the region's best food and wine. Depending on the season, you might be regaled with a carpaccio *de thon rouge* (red tuna) with goat's cheese croûtons followed by oysters and a stunning Grand Marnier soufflé, light as air.

MIMIZAN Hôtel Atlantique

⚑ €€

38 av de la Côte d'Argent, 40200 **Tel** *05 58 09 09 42* **Fax** *05 58 82 42 63*

Very popular, modestly priced restaurant in a hotel on the seafront at the north end of the beach. Seafood is a speciality, with good *soupe de poisson* as well as regional gastronomic favourites such as *magret de canard, confit de canard* and wild boar with prunes.

MONT-DE-MARSAN Didier Garbage

P ⚑ 🍴 ♿ 🏧 🍴 €€€

RN 134, Uchacq-et-Parentis, 40090 **Tel** *05 58 75 33 66* **Fax** *05 58 75 22 77*

One of France's up-and-coming chefs turns out authentic landaise cuisine in his convivial, slightly rustic restaurant outside Mont-de-Marsan. Look forward to lamprey, elvers (freshwater eels) and expertly crafted fish dishes, in addition to meats and luscious deserts. There's also a bistro for casual dining.

MONTMORILLON Le Lucullus

⚑ 🍴 ♿ €

4 bd de Strasbourg, 86500 **Tel** *05 49 84 09 09* **Fax** *05 49 84 58 68*

A traditional country auberge where the food takes precedence. The set menus change frequently and present plenty of choice, including a vegetarian option. Sample sweetbreads with local honey, or roast lobster with *foie gras*. The attached brasserie offers cheaper, less formal dining.

NIORT La Table des Saveurs

⚑ 🍴 ♿ €€

9 rue Thiers, 79000 **Tel** *05 49 77 44 35* **Fax** *05 49 16 06 29*

Despite its town-centre location and classy cuisine, this popular restaurant offers excellent value for money. Even the cheapest menu includes three courses. This is regional cooking, which means plenty of fish dishes, such as a *fricassée* of sole and Dublin Bay prawns doused in local Pineau liqueur.

PAULLIAC Château Cordeillan-Bages

P ⚑ 🍴 ♿ 🏧 🍴 €€€€€

61 rue Vignerons, 33250 **Tel** *05 56 59 24 24* **Fax** *05 56 59 01 89*

Very much an up-and-coming restaurant in the heart of Bordeaux's vineyards – its third Michelin star is close. The Pauillac lamb is a signature dish, representing traditional cuisine; the molecular cuisine proposes dishes such as virtual sausage with lentils. Well worth a splurge.

POITIERS Le Poitevin

⚑ 🍴 ♿ €

76 rue Carnot, 86000 **Tel** *05 49 88 35 04* **Fax** *05 49 52 88 05*

The exterior is nothing to shout about, but inside you'll find a warren of rooms with exposed beams and an open fire. Rustic surroundings which chime perfectly with the top-notch Poitou cuisine. Typical dishes feature snails, eels and mussels – *mouclade* comprises mussels in a creamy curry sauce.

POITIERS Maxime

⚑ 🍴 🍴 €€€

4 rue St Nicolas, 86000 **Tel** *05 49 41 09 55* **Fax** *05 49 41 09 55*

Poitier's most sophisticated restaurant is far from stuffy. Nor will eating here break the bank. Highlights include lobster salad with Aquitaine caviar and sole and smoked *foie gras* served with a trilogy of chipped vegetables. Desserts are equally delicious. Closed mid-Jul–mid-Aug.

Key to Price Guide *see p600* **Key to Symbols** *see back cover flap*

ROCHEFORT La Belle Poule 🚶🚲 €€

Route de Royan, 17300 **Tel** *05 46 99 71 87* **Fax** *05 46 83 99 77*

A modern building made more agreeable thanks to a massive fireplace and lots of greenery. The chef uses herbs and spices to splendid effect in his regionally inspired dishes. Favourites include fricassée of monkfish with baby onions, an aromatic leg of lamb and stewed oxtail with Jerusalem artichokes.

ROYAN La Jabotière 🚶♿🚲🍷 €€€

Esplanade de Pontaillac, 17200 **Tel** *05 46 39 91 29* **Fax** *05 46 38 39 93*

Modern cuisine in a renovated beachfront restaurant. Sample scallops with herb cannelloni and a turmeric vinaigrette, or duck fillet stuffed with walnuts, finishing with an apple and apricot soufflé. In summer, the terrace is packed with customers enjoying the excellent lunch deals.

SABRES Auberge des Pins 🅿🚶♿🚲🍷 €€

Route de la Piscine, 40630 **Tel** *05 58 08 30 00* **Fax** *05 58 07 56 74*

Gorgeous landaise farmhouse run by an adorable family. The oak-lined dining room provides the perfect setting for typical landaise cuisine, ranging from flavourful asparagus and fresh fish to duck in all its guises. Best of all, though, is the boned pigeon stuffed with *foie gras*. Good selection of local wines and armagnac.

SAINTES Relais du Bois St-Georges 🅿🚶▤♿🚲🍷 €€€€€

Rue de Royan, 17100 **Tel** *05 46 93 50 99* **Fax** *05 46 93 34 93*

Two first-class restaurants, part of a hotel on the outskirts of Saintes in big, beautiful grounds with lawns, a tennis court, an indoor pool, a lake, a croquet lawn and piano bar. The gastronomic restaurant serves excellent seafood. The bistro, La Table du Bois, is much cheaper, serving good local dishes.

ST-CLEMENTS-DES-BALEINES - ILE DE RE Le Chat Botté 🅿🚶♿🚲 €€€

20 rue de la Mairie, 17590 **Tel** *05 46 29 42 09* **Fax** *05 46 29 29 77*

This stylish restaurant is renowned on the Ile de Ré for the quality of its seafood. Among chef Daniel Massé's signature dishes you'll find warm oysters served with Pineau liqueur sauce and flaky seabass in a pastry shell. The flavours are allowed to speak for themselves. On fine days tables are set up in the gardens.

ST-EMILION L'Envers du Décor 🚶♿🚲🍷 €

11 rue du Clocher, 33330 **Tel** *05 57 74 48 31* **Fax** *05 57 24 68 90*

Local vignerons rub shoulders with tourists in this delightful little bistro-cum-wine bar. The menu runs the gamut from omelettes and salads to more elaborate regional dishes, or you can choose from daily specials on the chalkboard. Winner of the award for the best wine list in France in its class.

ST-MARTIN-DE-RE La Baleine Bleue 🚶♿🚲🍷 €€€

Ilot du Port, 17410 **Tel** *05 46 09 03 30* **Fax** *05 56 09 30 86*

The fish couldn't be much fresher at this celebrated portside restaurant. Menus change daily depending on the catch, but typical offerings are scallop carpaccio, home-smoked salmon and cod with aubergines. For dessert, try the prunes cooked in spiced red wine with caramelized walnut ice cream.

PERIGORD, QUERCY & GASCONY

AGEN Mariottat 🅿🚶▤♿🚲🍷 €€

25 rue Louis-Vivent, 47000 **Tel** *05 53 77 99 77* **Fax** *05 53 77 99 79*

It comes as a surprise to find this elegant restaurant tucked down a very ordinary backstreet, but inside the 19th-century mansion, with its chandeliers and high ceilings, you're in for a treat. Duck reigns supreme – *assiette tout canard* is the signature dish, alongside succulent Agen prunes and summer fruits.

ALBI Le Jardin des Quatre Saisons 🅿🚶▤♿🚲🍷🍷 €€

19 bd de Strasbourg, 81000 **Tel** *05 63 60 77 76* **Fax** *05 63 60 77 76*

A gourmet restaurant that won't break the bank, here there are just three menus, each with a wide selection of dishes. Here at Le Jardin des Quatre the cooking is very much seasonal, but among the regular favourites you'll find *foie gras* in various guises, seafood *pot au feu* and roast pigeon.

ALBI Le Vieil Alby 🚶🚲 €

23-25 rue Toulouse-Lautrec, 81000 **Tel** *05 63 38 28 23*

This welcoming and well-priced hotel-restaurant is a good place to try typical local dishes, such as a raddish and pork liver salad, followed by *cassoulet* or perhaps tripe cooked Albi-style. All desserts are homemade. In warm weather, dine in the lovely interior courtyard with its retractable roof.

AUCH Le Daroles 🚶🚲 €

4 pl Libération, 32000 **Tel** *05 62 05 00 51* **Fax** *05 62 05 00 51*

In the centre of the upper town, near the cathedral, Le Daroles is a bright and breezy brasserie, all dark wood, mirrors and burnished brasswork. Don't expect any culinary fireworks, but the food is tasty and provides something for everyone, from steak *tartare* to large salads.

BERGERAC La Cocotte des Halles 🏃🖼 €

Pl du Marché-Couverte, 24100 **Tel** *05 53 24 10 00* **Fax** *05 53 24 10 00*

Red-and-white cheque cloths set the tone in this popular little restaurant in the market hall. Choose from daily specials featured on the chalkboard. Typical dishes include duck *confit* with *pommes sarladaises* (potatoes fried with parsley and garlic). A lovely spot for a light lunch.

BRANTOME Les Frères Charbonnel 🅿🏃♿🖼🍽 €€€

57 rue Gambetta, 24310 **Tel** *05 53 05 70 15* **Fax** *05 53 05 71 85*

The restaurant of the Hôtel Chabrol has a well deserved reputation for its upscale regional cuisine and excellent service. Black périgord truffles add style to omelettes and to the house special, pike-perch *vol-au-vent*. These can be enjoyed in the dining room, or on the riverside terrrace. Closed Feb.

BRANTOME Le Moulin de l'Abbaye 🅿🏃🖼🍽🍷 €€€€

1 route de Bourdeilles, 24310 **Tel** *05 53 05 80 22* **Fax** *05 53 05 75 27*

Dine in luxury on innovative dishes such as duck *foie gras* poached in walnut liqueur, or grilled pigeon flavoured with almond oil and Jamaican pepper. Luscious desserts might include a gratin of strawberries with white chocolate. A magical setting and impeccable service. Closed Nov–Apr.

BUZET-SUR-BAISE Le Vigneron 🅿🏃🍽♿🖼 €

Bd de la République, 47160 **Tel** *05 53 84 73 46* **Fax** *05 53 84 75 04*

A village restaurant with old-fashioned cooking. Most people opt for the excellent-value four-course *menu du jour* (not served on Sundays), which includes *hors-d'oeuvre* buffet and impossibly wicked dessert trolley – the gâteau of layered crêpes and cream coated in meringue is not to be missed. Closed Feb–mid-Mar.

CAHORS Le Lamparo 🏃🍽♿🖼 €

76 rue Georges-Clémenceau, 46000 **Tel** *05 65 35 25 93* **Fax** *05 65 23 83 45*

Bustling first-floor restaurant opposite the market hall, with a large terrace for fine-weather dining. The menu ranges from pasta and wood-fired pizza to copious salads, grills and local fare, with a few fish dishes for good measure. It's nothing fancy, but reliable with generous portions.

CAHORS Le Balandre 🅿🏃🍽🍽🍷 €€€

5 av Charles-de-Freycinet, 46000 **Tel** *05 65 53 32 00* **Fax** *05 65 53 32 26*

For fine dining in Cahors, head for the restaurant in the Hôtel Terminus, where 1930s decor complements refined Quercy cuisine. Rustic dishes, such as roast Quercy lamb laced with juniper juice, are given a modern twist. Or try egg poached with *foie gras* and truffle sauce. Cahors wines feature strongly.

CHAMPAGNAC-DE-BELAIR Le Moulin du Roc 🏃🖼🍽🍷 €€€

Champagnac-de-Belair, 24530 **Tel** *05 53 02 86 00* **Fax** *05 53 54 21 31*

A romantic waterside setting plus top-notch cuisine at affordable prices make this gourmet restaurant stand out. The lunch menu (not served on Sundays) offers particularly good value. Scallops with Espelette pepper and green-apple *feuilleté* glazed with cognac are just two of the treats in store.

DOMME L'Esplanade 🏃🍽🖼🍽🍷 €€€

Le Bourg, 24250 **Tel** *05 53 28 31 41* **Fax** *05 53 28 49 92*

Welcoming and efficient service, well-presented dishes and an unbeatable panorama of the Dordogne valley keep customers coming back to this hotel restaurant. Ask for a window or terrace table. Signature dishes include lamb with *foie gras* and truffles, and the delectable chocolate trilogy.

FIGEAC La Cuisine du Marché 🏃🍽🖼🍽 €€

15 rue Clermont, 46100 **Tel** *05 65 50 18 55* **Fax** *05 65 50 18 55*

In a former wine cellar in the heart of Figeac's medieval core, this attractive restaurant takes pride in using only the freshest ingredients. Star billing goes to its wide range of fish dishes, though you'll also find plenty of local classics, all prepared in the open kitchen. The set menus represent good value.

FRANCESCAS Le Relais de la Hire 🏃🖼🍽🍷 €€€

11 rue Porte-Neuve, 47600 **Tel** *05 53 65 41 59* **Fax** *05 53 65 86 42*

The chef of this upmarket village restaurant near Nérac makes full use of his herb garden and edible flowers to create dishes that are a feast for all the senses. Try the temping artichoke soufflé with *foie gras* or zander stuffed with crayfish, followed by desserts that look almost too good to eat.

GAILLAC Les Sarments 🏃♿ €€

27 rue Cabrol, 81600 **Tel** *05 63 57 62 61* **Fax** *05 63 57 62 61*

The brick arches and exposed beams of this 14th-century wine vault in the heart of old Gaillac provide a striking setting for the beautifully presented food that tends towards the traditional, but with imaginative touches. Particularly fine desserts. Good opportunity to sample Gaillac wines at reasonable prices.

LACAVE Le Pont de l'Ouysse 🏃🍽♿🖼🍽🍷 €€€€

Le Pont de l'Ouysse, 46200 **Tel** *05 65 37 87 04* **Fax** *05 65 32 77 41*

A chic restaurant-with-rooms not far from Rocamadour. It's in a lovely riverside setting, sheltered under an imposing cliff. Inventive variations on local dishes include truffle ravioli and fig baked in walnut liqueur with an almond glaze. There are good-value lunch menus, but it is magical dining under the trees at night.

Key to Price Guide *see p600* **Key to Symbols** *see back cover flap*

LES EYZIES-DE-TAYAC Le Vieux Moulin

P ♿ 🖼 🛏 🍷 €€€

2 rue du Moulin-Bas, 24620 **Tel** *05 53 06 94 33* **Fax** *05 53 06 98 06*

Dine on well-priced regional cuisine in a 17th-century mill, with its rustic interior, or beside the river in peaceful, flower-filled gardens. Among the simple but beautifully prepared dishes, choose from *escalope* of foie gras with truffle sauce or truffle risotto, with pigeon casserole to follow. Closed Nov–Apr.

MANCIET La Bonne Auberge

P ♿ 🖼 🛏 🍷 €€

Pl du Pesquerot, 32370 **Tel** *05 62 08 50 04* **Fax** *05 62 08 58 84*

The same family has been running this small hotel-restaurant for 40 years, and it shows in the quality of the creative southwestern cuisine. The platter of local specialities is a great introduction to Gascon fare, and the snail *cassoulet* is very good. Fabulous armagnac list – some over 100 years old.

MARMANDE Le Moulin d'Ané

P ♿ ♿ 🖼 🍷 €€

Virazeil, 47200 **Tel** *05 53 20 18 25* **Fax** *05 53 89 67 99*

Consistently excellent seasonal cuisine in this restored 18th-century watermill near Marmande. Typical southwestern dishes include succulent blonde d'Aquitaine beef, tender fillets of duck breast, and apple tart laced with armagnac. Be sure to try the exceptionally plump and juicy Marmande tomatoes.

MONBAZILLAC La Tour des Vents

P ♿ 🖼 €€

Moulin de Malfourat, 24240 **Tel** *05 53 58 30 10* **Fax** *05 53 58 89 55*

Book a window or terrace table to enjoy the wonderful views over the Dordogne valley to Bergerac. Good-value menus offer local specialities, including *foie gras* and duck, but also fish and seafood. There is even a vegetarian option. Treat yourself to a glass of sweet Monbazillac with *foie gras* or dessert.

MONPAZIER La Bastide

P ♿ ♿ €

52 rue St-Jacques, 24540 **Tel** *05 53 22 60 59* **Fax** *05 53 22 09 20*

Real, old-school French cookery at its best. Gleaming tableware and starched cloths announce that you're in for a treat. Crusty walnut bread, *foie gras*, sweetbreads and truffles, rounded off with a lip-smacking sorbet – it's all ultra-fresh and skilfully prepared. Prices are very reasonable. Closed Feb.

MONTAUBAN Le Couvert des Drapiers

♿ 🖼 €

27 pl Nationale, 82000 **Tel** *05 63 92 91 03* **Fax** *05 63 91 18 29*

A great spot for a light lunch or a relaxed evening meal under the arcades of Montauban's dramatic central square. The food is eclectic, with a range of salads, well-priced daily specials such as beef-and-lamb skewers or veal cutlets, followed by an eye-catching dessert buffet. The *tarte tatin* is a winner. The *menu du jour* is good value.

MONTREAL-DU-GERS Chez Simone

♿ 🖼 🍷 €€

3 rue Aurensan, 32250 **Tel** *05 62 29 44 40* **Fax** *05 62 29 49 94*

Much admired by people in the know, due to the chef's creative use of top-quality local produce and generous helpings. House specials include *foie gras* of duck and goose served *nature*, allowing the flavours to speak for themselves. Good local wines and fine armagnacs.

PERIGUEUX Le Clos Saint-Front

♿ 🔳 🖼 🍷 €

5 rue de la Vertu, 24000 **Tel** *05 53 46 78 58* **Fax** *05 53 46 78 20*

Reservations are recommended at this restaurant near Périgueux's prehistory museum, with its inventive, inexpensive cuisine and peaceful courtyard garden. According to the season, you could opt for lamb flavoured with spices and rosemary, or sole served with an onion, thyme and lemon compote.

PERIGUEUX L'Essentiel

♿ 🖼 🍷 €€

8 rue de la Clarté, 24000 **Tel** *05 53 35 15 15* **Fax** *05 53 35 15 15*

Another city-centre restaurant where it's wise to reserve. The dining room's sunny southern colours complement southwestern dishes perfectly, such as salt cod with braised fennel flavoured with liquorice. There's also a pretty, pocket-sized garden.

PUJAUDRAN Le Puits St-Jacques

P ♿ 🔳 🖼 🛏 🍷 €€€€

Pl de la Mairie, 32600 **Tel** *05 62 07 41 11* **Fax** *05 62 07 44 09*

Michelin-starred restaurant where you can feast on a *tatin* of foie gras and cherries, or Aveyron lamb married with fennel, lemon and wine sauce. Neither pretentious nor too pricey, if you opt for a set menu. Rustic chic ambience, with lots of red Toulousain brick work and a pleasant patio.

PUJOLS Auberge Lou Calel

P ♿ 🖼 🍷 €€

Le Bourg, 47300 **Tel** *05 53 70 46 14* **Fax** *05 53 70 49 79*

The sister-restaurant to Pujol's famous La Toque Blanche offers less exalted but nevertheless fine dining at an affordable price. To kick off the meal, try the apple and *foie gras tatin* drizzled with a honey vinaigrette. On fine days tables spill onto the terrace with views over the Lot valley.

PUYMIROL Les Loges de l'Aubergade

P ♿ 🔳 ♿ 🖼 🛏 🍷 €€€€

52 rue Royale, 47270 **Tel** *05 53 95 31 46* **Fax** *05 53 95 33 80*

One of the southwest's great restaurants is set in a beautiful medieval lodge on a hilltop. Here Michel Trama creates sublime dishes such as *foie gras* pan fried and served with caramelized carrots. Equally theatrical setting with Baroque drapes and exposed stone, and a gorgeous Italianate courtyard.

REVEL Hôtel du Midi   🅿🚻♨ €€
34 bd Gambetta, 31250 **Tel** *05 61 83 50 50* **Fax** *05 61 83 34 74*

Hotel restaurant that's well known in the area for its faithful renditions of local classics. A perennial favourite is *cassoulet* – the hearty stew of potted duck, toulouse sausages and tarbais haricot beans. Bring a big appetite. The particularly good-value set lunch fills up the restaurant on weekdays.

RIBERAC Le Chevillard   🚻♿♨ €
Gayet, rte de Bordeaux, 24600 **Tel** *05 53 91 20 88*

For that quintessential French experience, try this friendly auberge in a lovely old farmhouse west of Ribérac. Famous for its groaning buffets (*hors-d' œuvre*, seafood and dessert), it also offers a good range of meat and fish dishes. Prices are reasonable; the lunch menu represents exceptional value.

ROCAMADOUR Jehan de Valon   🚻📋♨🍽 €€€
Cité Médiévale, 46500 **Tel** *05 65 33 63 08* **Fax** *05 65 33 65 23*

Elegant restaurant perched on the edge of a gorge in the middle of medieval Rocamadour. Consistently well-prepared and presented dishes showcase local delicacies: smoked duck, succulent Quercy lamb and Rocamadour's very own goats' cheese served with a crunchy walnut salad. Closed mid-Nov–mid-Feb.

SARLAT Le Régent   🚻♨ €
6 pl de la Liberté, 24200 **Tel** *05 53 31 06 36* **Fax** *05 53 59 03 91*

Watch the world go by from the pavement terrace of this popular brasserie on Sarlat's main square. The food is nothing fancy, but reliable and not expensive, considering the location. The menu covers everything from salads to regional cuisine. From November to Easter open for lunch only.

SORGES Auberge de la Truffe   🅿🚻📋♨ €€€
Le Bourg, 24420 **Tel** *05 53 05 02 05* **Fax** *05 53 05 39 27*

Sorges is the self-proclaimed truffle "capital" of France, and this auberge is the perfect place to sample Périgord's "black diamond". The top-price menu features truffles with every course. Less expensive fare is on offer, too, and the set menus start at a reasonable price. Truffle-hunting weekends are offered.

ST-MEDARD Le Gindreau   🅿🚻📋♨🍽 €€€€
Le Bourg, 46150 **Tel** *05 65 36 22 27* **Fax** *05 65 36 24 54*

In a hamlet northwest of Cahors, Alexis Pélissou has created one of the region's finest restaurants. Using top-quality local produce, he reinvents traditional standards for modern tastes. Meals are served in the former schoolhouse or on the terrace shaded by chestnut trees. Big choice of local wines.

TOULOUSE Brasserie Flo Les Beaux Arts   🚻📋♨ €€
1 quai de la Daurade, 31000 **Tel** *05 61 21 12 12* **Fax** *05 61 21 14 80*

An authentic and bustling brasserie serving a broad range of dishes, from salads and seafood to southwestern favourites. To start, you could opt for a flavoursome dish of scallops baked with chanterelle mushrooms, followed by a seafood *pot-au-feu*, and prune-and-armagnac ice cream. The menu changes regularly.

TOULOUSE Les Jardins de l'Opéra (Dominique Toulousy)   🚻📋🍽 €€€€
1 pl du Capitole, 31000 **Tel** *05 61 23 07 76* **Fax** *05 61 23 63 00*

Gourmet dining at its most refined in the restaurant of the Grand Hôtel de l'Opéra. Hushed tones and widely spaced tables create a suitably reverent atmosphere for dishes such as whole lobster garnished with a seaweed crust, or figs cooked in Banyuls wine and filled with vanilla ice cream. Impeccable service.

TURSAC La Source   🚻♨ €
Le Bourg, 24620 **Tel** *05 53 06 98 00* **Fax** *05 53 35 13 61*

If you're looking for somewhere to eat while exploring the Vézère valley, try this friendly little village restaurant. Simple, tasty dishes include wild mushroom soup and walnut pie. There's a vegetarian menu, using produce fresh from the garden, and some international options, for a change. Closed Jan–Mar.

VAREN Le Moulin de Varen   🅿🚻📋♿ €€
Le Bourg, 82330 **Tel** *05 63 65 45 10* **Fax** *05 63 65 45 12*

A converted mill in the Aveyron gorges, near the lovely town of St-Antonin-de-Noble-Val. There's no carte, but plenty of choice on the set menus, all of which offer excellent value for money. The food is beautifully presented and the atmosphere relaxed. Closed mid-Nov–Feb.

THE PYRENEES

AX LES THERMES L'Orry le Saquet   🚻♨ €€
Route Nationale 20, 09110 **Tel** *05 61 64 31 30* **Fax** *05 61 64 00 31*

This small, friendly hilltop hotel-restaurant has a high reputation. The menu and carte are varied, with imaginative, richly flavoured dishes that change seasonally – snail *tatin* with spicy tomato sauce, rock lobster and squid served with coconut milk.

BAGNERES DE LUCHON Les Caprices d'Etigny
P ☆ 🗐 ⅃ 🍴 ▮   €

30 bis allées d'Etigny, 31110 **Tel** *05 61 94 31 05*

Fine mountain views from the tables in the conservatory-style dining room. The menu stresses local lamb and beef grilled over a wood fire, and trout from the nearby Lac d'Oo presented in a number of different styles. The good wine list emphasizes the finer wines of southwestern France.

BAGNERRES DE BIGORRE L'Auberge Gourmande
P ☆   €€

4 pl du 14 Juillet, 65200 **Tel** *05 62 95 52 01*

This Pyrenean spa town has one of the region's better markets with fresh produce – which finds its way to the kitchen of this welcoming restaurant in Gerdes, outside Bagnerres de Bigorre. The menu emphasizes dishes such as stuffed pork chop, rabbit in sage, and *ragoût* of *escargots*.

BAREGES Auberge du Lienz (Chez Louisette)
☆ ⅃   €€

Route Lienz, 65120 **Tel** *05 62 67 17* **Fax** *05 62 92 65 15*

A good choice for an *après-ski* meal, at the foot of the local pistes, with stunning views of the Pic du Midi de Bigorre. Menu mainstays include mutton stewed in Madeira wine, trout, and sumptuous soufflés. The *pièce de résistance* is the ham *garbure* – a hefty dish of ham, bacon and cabbage.

BAYONNE Le Bayonnais
☆ 🗐 ⅃ 🍴 ▮   €

24 rue Marengo, 64100 **Tel** *05 59 25 61 19* **Fax** *05 59 59 00 64*

With a handful of tables on the terrace and more inside, this small restaurant has a well-deserved reputation for imaginative dishes, such as baby lamb, sole with lentils, chestnut soup with *foie gras*, and pastilla with figs. Well-chosen wine list emphasizes regional wines and major names from elsewhere in France.

BAYONNE Auberge du Cheval Blanc
P ☆ 🗐 ⅃   €€€

68 rue Bourgneuf, 64100 **Tel** *05 59 59 01 33* **Fax** *05 59 59 52 25*

Stray from the set menu to eat *à la carte* at this well-regarded hotel in the riverside Petit Bayonne quarter. The menu changes with the seasons, with local dishes, such as *xamano* (ham and mashed potatoes), fine Atlantic seafood, interesting soups and casseroles, and delicious desserts. Respectable wine list. Closed Feb.

BIARRITZ Le Clos Basque
☆ 🍴   €

12 rue L. Barthou, 64200 **Tel** *05 59 24 24 96* **Fax** *05 59 22 34 46*

Regional specialities are the order of the day at this small, cheerful tavern, with its Spanish-style whitewashed wall, coloured tiles and summer terrace. Book ahead as the place fills up quickly with local diners as well as visitors, especially in high season and at weekends.

BIARRITZ Chez Albert
P ☆ 🍴   €€

Port des Pêcheurs, 64200 **Tel** *05 59 24 43 84* **Fax** *05 59 24 20 13*

From the terrace there are superb views of Biarritz's picturesque fishing harbour and surrounding cliffs and beaches, making this fine seafood restaurant popular. Arrive early for the best tables. Piled platters of seafood, freshly caught lobster, sole, sea bream, tuna and sardines are among the treats here.

BIARRITZ Le Sissinou
☆ 🗐 ▮   €€€

5 av Maréchal Foch, 64200 **Tel** *05 59 22 51 50* **Fax** *05 59 22 50 58*

Managed by chef Michel Cassou-Debat – a veteran of some of France's top establishments – Sissinou is one of Biarritz's most talked-about restaurants. Elegant in a minimalist way. Wonderful food such as tuna carpaccio and a fricassée of veal sweetbreads served with carrots flavoured with balsamic vinegar and desserts that invite indulgence.

BIELLE L'Ayguelade
P ☆ 🗐 ☆ 🍴 ⅃   €€

Bielle, 64260 **Tel** *05 59 82 60 06* **Fax** *05 59 82 60 06*

Family-run establishment serving gastronomic cuisine in a convivial atmosphere. Try the traditional *garbure*, fillet of Blonde Aquitaine (beef) with morille mushrooms, and Jurançon-imbued mousse glacé. Good selection of wines from the southwest and stunning views of the Falaise des Vautours from the terrace. Closed Jan.

FOIX Le Sainte Marthe
P ☆ 🍴   €€

21 rue N. Peyrevidal, 09000 **Tel** *05 61 02 87 87* **Fax** *05 61 05 19 00*

A gourmet paradise that lives up to its reputation, Le Sainte Marthe pays fine attention to detail in providing some of the best traditional dishes of the region. This is old-fashioned French regional cuisine at its best, a decent wine list, a friendly welcome, and a great location beneath the medieval castle. Closed Jan.

LARRAU Etchemaïté
P ☆ 🍴 ▮   €€

Larrau, 64560 **Tel** *05 59 28 61 45* **Fax** *05 59 28 72 71*

This family-run mountain inn and restaurant has a spectacular location and a cosy dining room with open fireplace and great views. Favourites are lamb and duck dishes garnished with apples, *cèpes*, or *foie gras* and there is usually a good choice of Atlantic seafood, too. Varied wine list.

LONS Le Fer à Cheval
P ☆ 🍴 ▮   €€€

1 av Martyrs du Pont Long, 64000 **Tel** *05 59 32 17 40* **Fax** *05 59 72 97 53*

A former coaching inn in Lons on the outskirts of Pau, the cuisine here centres on local produce, traditionally prepared. Choose from pork, duck and *foie gras*, Pyrenean mountain lamb, Atlantic oysters and fish, a tempting dessert trolley and a fine cheeseboard. Pleasant shaded terrace.

MIREPOIX Les Remparts
6 cours Louis Pons Tande, 09500 **Tel** *05 61 68 12 15*

The speciality of the house is trout cooked in Hypocras, the sweet dessert wine of the region. The restaurant has two dining rooms: one in a cosily converted cellar, the other with a wide wood-beamed ceiling and colourful paintwork. Robust classic dishes of the region. Children's menu is available.

MONTSEGUR Costes
Le Village, 09300 **Tel** *05 61 01 10 24* **Fax** *05 61 03 06 28*

This simple café-restaurant is part of a family-run hotel beneath the crag that is home to Montségur's ruined castle. An array of tasty local dishes, mostly prepared on the open wood fire – game, duck, wild mushrooms, pork and, of course, *cassoulet*. Just the thing after the steep clamber to the castle. Phone to check if open in winter period.

ORTHEZ Au Temps de la Reine Jeanne
44 rue Bourg-Vieux, 64300 **Tel** *05 59 67 00 76* **Fax** *05 59 69 09 63*

This rustic eating-place is attached to a comfortable country inn. The menu is equally rustic, with plenty of local dishes, including offal and rich meaty dishes. Liver, black pudding, suckling pig, *foie gras*, *cassoulet* and monkfish all make an appearance. Good value.

PAMIERS Le Roi Gourmand
21 rue Pierre Sémard, 09100 **Tel** *05 61 60 12 12* **Fax** *05 61 60 61 02*

This medium-sized, simply decorated restaurant-hotel in the heart of Pamiers offers surprisingly innovative dishes such as warm *foie gras* infused with sweet Hypocras dessert wine, local lamb, trout, a range of other novel dishes, and a splendid assortment of desserts and pungent mountain cheeses.

PAU Chez Pierre
16 rue Louis Barthou, 64000 **Tel** *05 59 27 76 86* **Fax** *05 59 27 08 14*

Chez Pierre exudes 19th-century elegance and prides itself on the old-fashioned, club-like atmosphere that harks back to Pau's heyday as a British expatriate's hideaway. Classic French regional cooking along with some surprises, such as cod with espelette peppers, and an extensive wine list.

PAU La Planche de Bœuf
30 rue Pasteur, 64000 **Tel** *05 59 27 62 60* **Fax** *05 59 27 62 60*

La Planche de Bœuf is popular with local diners, especially in winter, and you will need to roll up early to get a table next to the open fire. The menu is meaty, with tasty beef from the farms of the surrounding Béarn and lamb from the Pyrenees, accompanied by a good wine list emphasizing the southwest.

ST BERTRAND DE COMMINGES Le Lugdunum
Valcabrère, 31510 **Tel** *05 61 94 52 05* **Fax** *05 61 94 52 06*

Fried snails in cumin sauce, stuffed dates, spiced wine – this restaurant takes its inspiration from Roman times. Owner Hélène Pedrazzini points out the Romans loved this region for its wines, and is happy to explain the menu to visitors. There are more familiar dishes, too. Quirky, friendly and highly recommended.

ST GAUDENS La Connivence
Rte de Sauveterre, Valentine, 31800 **Tel** *05 61 95 29 31* **Fax** *05 61 88 36 42*

The outdoor terrace with its fine views is one of the main attractions of La Connivence. The bill of fare is traditional, as is the atmosphere, but helpings are generous and the wine list, though limited, is well chosen. Service is prompt and friendly. An unpretentious spot for lunch or dinner. Closed for lunch on Saturday and Sunday dinner.

ST JEAN-DE-LUZ Restaurant Petit Grill Basque
2 rue St-Jacques, 64500 **Tel** *05 59 26 80 76* **Fax** *05 59 26 80 76*

One of the most affordable eating places in normally pricy St-Jean-de-Luz, with the accent on simple, good Basque home cooking using fresh local ingredients. The fish soup is excellent, as are the grilled squid and the peppers stuffed with cod, and many other Basque dishes. Well-priced and unassuming wine list.

ST JEAN-DE-LUZ Restaurant Txalupa
Pl Corsaires, 64500 **Tel** *05 59 51 23 34*

Txalupa is a favourite local restaurant. Expect the best catches of the Atlantic coast prepared in dishes such as king prawns in a hot vinegar dressing, sardines in tomato salsa, oysters and lots of other shellfish, tuna, cod and monkfish. Extensive wine list, and imaginative desserts. Book ahead.

ST LARY SOULAN La Grange
13 rte Autun, 65170 **Tel** *05 62 40 07 14*

This old-fashioned farm building at St-Lary-Soulan in the high Pyrenees is a delightful place to stop for lunch. A well-appointed and attractively decorated restaurant, it exudes rustic charm. The traditional bill of fare includes robust meaty main dishes, with game, beef and lamb grilled over a wood fire.

ST SULPICE-SUR-LEZE La Commanderie
Pl de l'Hôtel de Ville, 31410 **Tel** *05 61 97 33 61* **Fax** *05 61 97 32 60*

In a fortified *bastide* village famous for its medieval architecture, La Commanderie has fans all over the world for its innovative cooking. Chef Jean Pierre Crouzet creates dishes such as vegetable ragoût with morille mushrooms and ewe's cheese and roast pigeon with garlic and juniper. Lovely, spacious dining room. Closed Jan–mid-Feb.

Key to Price Guide *see p600* **Key to Symbols** *see back cover flap*

TARBES L'Ambroisie

P 🔥 📋 📶 🍷   €€€

48 rue Abbé Torné, 65000 **Tel** *05 62 93 09 34* **Fax** *05 62 93 09 24*

The top restaurant in Tarbes attracts plaudits for dishes ranging from roast pigeon to *foie gras* in peach compote. Housed in a 19th-century church building, the restaurant offers a changing menu, brisk service, and food worth lingering over. Wine list features the finer Madiran domains. Book ahead.

TARBES L'Aragon

P 🔥 📋 📶   €€€

2 route de Lourdes, Juillan, 65000 **Tel** *05 62 32 07 07* **Fax** *05 62 32 92 50*

One of the great restaurants in Tarbes, but at an affordable price. More elaborate meals are available from the gastronomic menu, but you can dine equally well from the inexpensive set bistro menu. Recently renovated, l'Aragon offers a choice of dining areas. It is located in Juillan, on the outskirts of Tarbes. Rooms are available.

LANGUEDOC-ROUSSILLON

AIGUES-MORTES Les Enganettes

🔥 📋 📶   €

12 rue Morceau, 30220 **Tel** *04 66 53 69 11*

With tables outside, on the pavement and in a more secluded inner courtyard, Les Enganettes serves an imaginative array of Mediterranean, Camarguais, Spanish, Italian and Moroccan-influenced dishes. There are frequent musical evenings with live piano music and the set menus and *à la carte* dishes are very good value.

AIGUES-MORTES Le Café des Bouzigues

🔥 📋 📶   €€

7 rue Pasteur, 30220 **Tel** *04 66 53 93 95*

It is usually easy to find a table in this large traditional bistro. The menu is strongly Mediterranean, with plenty of regional seafood, Provençal dishes and reasonably priced wines from Provence and Languedoc. Lamb with thyme and garlic and peach salad are among the outstanding dishes.

ANDUZE Auberge des Trois Barbus

P 🔥 📋 📶   €€

Rte de Mialet, Generagargues, 20140 **Tel** *0466 617212*

Deep in the Cevennes above the Camisards valley, with spectacular views, this rustic hotel-restaurant has the added attraction of a pool that diners may use for an after-lunch dip. Traditional Cevennes and Languedoc dishes as well as more adventurous offerings. Delicious *foie gras* and truffles. Closed Feb–mid-Mar.

ARGELES SUR MER L'Amadeus

P 🔥 📋 📶   €

Av Platanes, 66700 **Tel** *04 68 81 09 05* **Fax** *04 68 81 12 10*

L'Amadeus is well regarded for its Catalan dishes and local produce, which ranges from generous platters of seafood, including marinated Collioure anchovies and Bouzigues oysters, to *bouillabaisse* (fish stew) and its Catalan version, *zarzuela* – a hearty seafood and lobster stew. Closed Jan–May.

ARLES SUR TECH Les Glycines

P 🔥 ♿ 📶   €

Rue du Jeu de Paume, 66150 **Tel** *04 68 39 10 09* **Fax** *04 68 39 83 02*

Arles sur Tech is a place that beckons you to pause for a while, and this hotel-restaurant is an excellent place for a lunch stop. It is very good value for money, with a lovely wisteria-covered patio and a menu that emphasizes regional cuisine and local produce, with plenty of ham, pork and sausage dishes.

BEZIERS Octopus

🔥 📋 🍷   €€€

12 rue Boiledieu, 34500 **Tel** *04 67 49 90 00* **Fax** *04 67 28 06 73*

Béziers has no shortage of quality places to eat, but Octopus stands out from the crowd. With fresh, chic decor, this restaurant feels very welcoming. The modern menu is balanced by a well-chosen list of wines from the Languedoc-Roussillon vineyards.

BEZIERS L' Ambassade

🔥 📋 🍷   €€€€

22 bd Verdun, 34500 **Tel** *0467 76 06 24* **Fax** *04 67 76 74 05*

The outstanding wine list makes this one of the region's favourite restaurants, with an attractive Scandinavian-style interior. Chef Patrick Olry's cooking is equally outstanding, with a seasonally changing menu that combines old and new influences and a truly mouth-watering choice of desserts and cheeses.

CAP D'AGDE Le Brasero

🔥 📋 📶   €

Port Richelieu, rue Richelieu, 34300 **Tel** *04 67 26 24 75* **Fax** *04 67 26 24 75*

Overlooking the port with its yachts and fishing boats, Le Brasero has a well-earned reputation for good-value seafood. Its seafood platters are generous and varied, and other marine delights include grilled fish of all kinds, fresh anchovies, squid, tuna and swordfish. Grilled meat dishes also available. Book ahead.

CARCASSONNE L'Ecurie

P 🔥 📶   €

43 boulevard Barbes, 11000 **Tel** *04 68 72 04 04* **Fax** *04 68 25 31 90*

Housed in 18th-century stable buildings, "The Stables" is worth a visit just to sit in these elegant old-fashioned surroundings. A favourite with local people, its restaurant tends towards meat dishes, traditionally presented. There is a pretty inner courtyard with tables in the shade or in the sun.

CARCASSONNE Chez Fred

31 bd Omer Sarraut, 11000 **Tel** *04 68 72 02 23* **Fax** *04 68 71 52 64*

This friendly, unpretentious bistro is close to the station and the canal harbour, with tables in two cosy dining rooms and on a shaded terrace. The menu is full of regional specialities – *cassoulet* is predictably presented, but there are also seafood dishes, trout, *crêpes*, and a variety of meat grills.

CARCASSONNE Le Languedoc

32 allée d'Iéna, 11000 **Tel** *04 68 25 22 17* **Fax** *04 68 25 04 14*

This restaurant appeals to people who like their surroundings and cuisine to be traditionally French, even a little staid. The menu features all the regional classics, and Le Languedoc is one of the best places for *cassoulet* – the hearty bean and sausage casserole that is the Languedoc's most typical dish.

CASTELNAUDARY Au Petit Gazouillis

5 rue de l'Arcade, 11400 **Tel** *04 68 23 08 18*

This is an absolutely typical, no-nonsense local bistro with a limited menu of traditional regional dishes, including what may be the best *cassoulet* in the world. Beloved by Castelnaudary locals, it also serves great duck, and has a very reasonable assortment of regional wines. Unpretentious almost to a fault.

CASTELNAUDARY Grand Hotel Fourcade

14 rue des Carmes, 11400 **Tel** *04 68 23 02 08* **Fax** *04 68 94 10 67*

Cassoulet is the *tour de force* at this restaurant in a cosy small hotel near the Canal du Midi at Castenaudary – which claims to be the capital of cassoulet. A former Carmelite convent, the restaurant is decorated in old-fashioned style, with a pink and ochre-yellow colour scheme appropriate to the region.

CASTELNOU L'Hostal

Carrer de la Pator, 66300 **Tel** *04 68 53 32 08*

Simply presented local dishes feature in this country-style tavern, housed in an old building in one of the most attractive Catalan villages in the region. Book ahead for weekends, when the restaurant rapidly fills with locals who flock in for the traditional Catalan feast of grilled meat and snails.

COLLIOURE La Frégate

24 bd Camille Peletan, 66190 **Tel** *04 68 82 06 05* **Fax** *04 68 82 55 00*

La Frégate's two dining rooms are adorned with colourful Hispanic tiles and solid oak and leather tables and chairs, lending an air of dignified comfort. This is not a shorts-and-sandals place, even if you dine on the terrace, where each table has its own awning. Catalan-style seafood dishes are the order of the day.

COLLIOURE La Balette

114 route de Port-Vendres, 66190 **Tel** *04 68 82 05 07* **Fax** *04 68 82 38 08*

Specialities at this cheerful restaurant, part of the Relais des Trois Mas *(see Where to Stay p689)*, include soused Collioure anchovies marinaded in Banjul wine vinegar, grilled or pan-fried red mullet, clam *ratatouille*, and lobster *fricasee*. Set above the picturesque bay of Collioures. Book ahead in summer.

CUCUGNAN Auberge du Vigneron

2 rue Achille Mir, 11350 **Tel** *04 68 45 03 00* **Fax** *04 68 45 03 08*

The dining room is in the cool wine cellar of a charming inn in the heart of an attractive Corbières village. The menu is Catalan-influenced, with fresh seafood and duck prepared in a variety of ways, even with figs or peaches. The wine list is unpretentious, with a good choice of the muscular reds of the Corbières domains.

MINERVE Relais Chantovent

17 grand rue, 34210 **Tel** *04 68 91 14 18* **Fax** *04 68 91 81 99*

The hotel-restaurant in picturesque Minerve *(see Where to Stay p689)* has a light, airy dining room and a terrace with breathtaking views across the Gorges du Brian, which made this village a formidable fortress in the Middle Ages. Well-prepared regional dishes – *cassoulet*, *magret de canard*, *foie gras*, trout. Closed mid-Nov–mid-Mar.

MONTPELLIER Petit Jardin

20 rue Jean-Jacques Rousseau, 34000 **Tel** *04 67 60 78 78* **Fax** *04 67 66 16 79*

The menu is locally-inspired in this pretty restaurant in Montpellier's historic quarter. The 'Little Garden' is tucked away from the street, and diners may eat indoors, looking out at its greenery, or in the garden among the flowers, fruit trees and potted herbs. Dishes include fish soup and lamb with garlic and rosemary.

MONTPELLIER Anis at Canisses

47 av Toulouse, 34000 **Tel** *04 67 42 54 48* **Fax** *04 67 56 39 17*

The avenue Toulouse is one of Montpellier's liveliest thoroughfares, but this charming little eating place with its courtyard under the leaves of a spreading apricot tree lets the world go by. Its take on the traditions of Languedoc and Catalan cooking is well worth trying. Ideal for couples.

MONTPELLIER La Réserve Rimbaud

820 av de St-Maur, 34000 **Tel** *04 67 72 52 53*

Sophisticated dining at this excellent restaurant attached to a four-star hotel on the banks of the Lez, with lovely terrace tables under the trees, and river views. Attractive surroundings, fine wine list and a bill of fare that includes dishes such as grilled clams, monkfish with herbs, olives and *aioli*.

Key to Price Guide *see p600* **Key to Symbols** *see back cover flap*

MONTPELLIER Jardin des Sens · 🅿🎎📋🈯🖾🍷 · €€€€€
11 av St Lazare, 34000 **Tel** *04 99 58 38 38* **Fax** *04 99 58 38 39*

Probably the best restaurant in town. Continuously innovative, with regional specialities given a new twist, such as turbot with pumpkin ravioli with a light cèpe sauce, and some delicious juxtapositions such as veal sweetbreads and prawns. The wine list features finer wines of the Corbières slopes and the domains of the Languedoc.

NARBONNE Le Petit Comptoir · 🎎 · €
4 bd du Maréchal Joffre, 11100 **Tel** *04 68 42 30 35* **Fax** *04 68 41 52 71*

Looks like a typical little Narbonnais café-bar – but tucked away at the back is an elegant small restaurant with attentive waiters and a menu that picks the best of local market produce. Tasty dishes such as anchovy-filled monkish steak and tomato and mackerel quiche. A real find. Book ahead.

NARBONNE Brasserie Co · 🎎🖾 · €€
1 bd Dr Ferroul, 11100 **Tel** *04 68 32 55 25* **Fax** *04 68 32 57 74*

An up-to-the-minute brasserie-restaurant that is popular with younger local visitors. Brasserie Co's design and furnishings are sleek and modern, and so is the drinks list, with a choice of cocktails and wines. The menu is up-to-date too, with more than a hint of nouvelle cuisine and international fusion.

NARBONNE Le Table de St-Crescent · 🅿🖾 · €€
Domaine St-Crescent, 68 ave Général Leclerc, 11100 **Tel** *04 68 41 37 37* **Fax** *04 68 41 01 22*

An address to impress, with a superb, seasonally influenced menu that combines the best produce of the Mediterranean with that of the Languedoc hinterland, with wines to match. Oyster ravioli, truffles, *confit* of honeyed aubergine, cold gazpacho with wild berries and more. Perfect for a special evening.

NIMES Nicolas · 🎎 · €
1 rue Poise, 30000 **Tel** *04 66 67 50 47* **Fax** *04 66 76 06 33*

A traditional establishment in the heart of old Nîmes, Nicolas is usually packed with local diners tucking into monkfish *bourride* (a *bouillabaisse*-like stew), anchovies Provençale and similar regional delights. Closed Mon, Sat lunch, Sun dinner.

NIMES Aux Plaisirs des Halles · 🎎📋🖾🍷 · €€€
4 rue Littré, 30000 **Tel** *04 66 36 01 02* **Fax** *04 66 36 08 00*

With a particularly good regional wine list from the Languedoc, Corbières, Minervois, Provence and Hérault, Aux Plaisirs des Halles is decorated with clean, modern lines. French cuisine with a provençal influence by chef Sébastien Granier. Closed Sun, Mon; two weeks Oct–Nov; two weeks Feb.

NIMES Le Bouchon et L'Assiette · 🎎📋🍷 · €€€
5 bis rue Sauve, 30000 **Tel** *04 66 62 02 93* **Fax** *04 66 36 08 00*

One of the more upmarket restaurants in Nîmes, housed in a lovely old building next to the Fontaine gardens. The creative menu includes lightly grilled skate with rocket and capers, and the wine list is decent. Closed Tue, Wed; mid-Jul–mid-Aug.

NIMES Lisita · 🎎📋🖾🍷 · €€€€
2 bd des Arènes, 30000 **Tel** *04 66 67 29 15* **Fax** *04 66 67 25 32*

Lisita is not to be missed. This is one of the most popular restaurants in Nîmes, serving cutting-edge food and an outstanding wine list. The surroundings are attractive too, with modern design set off by old stone walls in two rooms, plus an attractive terrace. Closed Sun, Mon.

OLARGUES Domaine de Rieumégé · 🅿🎎🖾 · €€
Route de St Pons, 34390 **Tel** *04 67 97 73 99* **Fax** *04 67 97 78 52*

This former farm has been converted into an upmarket guesthouse and a wonderful place to eat, set in the beautiful wooded hills of the Parc Natural du Haut Languedoc, 3 km (2 miles) from the attractive village of Olargues. Foie gras terrine, fig purée and chicken with freshwater crayfish are among the highlights.

PERPIGNAN Les Antiquaires · 🎎📋 · €€
Pl Desprès, 66000 **Tel** *04 68 34 06 58* **Fax** *04 68 35 04 47*

Dining here is a little like being seated in a museum, surrounded by antique furniture and works of art. A loyal local following, which appreciates the cosy atmosphere and traditional approach to classic French cooking, with a strong local slant. Closed Sun dinner, Mon; first three weeks Jul.

PERPIGNAN Le Chapon Fin · 🎎📋♿ · €€€
18 bd Jean Bourrat, 66000 **Tel** *04 68 35 14 14* **Fax** *04 68 35 48 18*

Formal dress is not *de rigueur*, but you may want to look smart for a meal at this gourmet restaurant in one of Perpignan's better hotels. Fine regional produce, Catalan cuisine, very attractive decoration and a pleasant bar. Closed Sun; last two weeks Aug.

PERPIGNAN Le Mas Vermeil · 🅿🎎📋🖾 · €€€
Traverse de Cabestany, 66000 **Tel** *04 68 66 95 96* **Fax** *04 68 66 89 13*

One address, two options: the posher restaurant, with outdoor tables beside a fountain pool, or the more affordable brasserie, with a simpler bill of fare and a generous buffet lunch on Tuesdays and Saturdays. Both serve rich, hearty Catalan-style dishes. Closed Sun dinner, Mon.

PEZENAS Aprés le Déluge
5 av Maréchal Plantavit, 34120 **Tel** *04 67 98 10 77*

Lively little restaurant in a 14th-century building, with tables in several small rooms or on the terraces. Dishes include duck breast with exotic fruit, cuttlefish in garlic butter and *crème brulée* with lavender. Weekly jazz piano concerts. Closed Jul–Aug: dinner; Jan–Mar: Mon–Thu .

PORT-VENDRES La Cote Vermeille
Quai Fanal, 66660 **Tel** *04 68 82 05 71* **Fax** *04 68 82 05 71*

This super seafood restaurant has a great quayside location with views of the fishing harbour and coastline. Fishing nets, lobster pots and stuffed fish adorn the walls, and fresh fish, shellfish, squid and lobster adorn the menus. Closed Mon, Sun.

SAILLAGOUSE L'Atalaya
Rte Départementale 33, Llo, 66800 **Tel** *04 68 04 70 04* **Fax** *04 68 04 01 29*

The cuisine at this pretty inn perched above an attractive village 5 minutes from the Spanish border is classic French, with regional produce. L'Atalaya is located at the tiny hamlet of Llo and has fine views of the surrounding countryside. Closed Mon–Fri lunch.

SETE La Palangrotte
Quai de la Marine, 34200 **Tel** *04 67 74 80 35* **Fax** *04 67 74 97 20*

In Sète there is nowhere more pleasant to sample the famous oysters and other shellfish of the Etang de Thau lagoon than this cheerful marine-themed restaurant. Some of the best seafood on the coast, better for lunch than dinner. Closed Mon, Sun dinner (except Jul, Aug).

ST MARTIN DE LONDRES Les Muscardins
19 route Cevennes, 34380 **Tel** *04 67 55 75 90* **Fax** *04 67 55 70 28*

Surprising to find such a sophisticated dining experience in a little country town, but Les Muscardins is worth a special expedition for grilled scallops with asparagus, tomato *tartare* and fried dates, lobster salad in truffle butter, and lamb roasted in oriental spices. The surroundings are elegant.

ST PONS DE THOMIERES Les Bergeries de Ponderach
Route Narbonne, 34220 **Tel** *04 67 97 02 57* **Fax** *04 67 97 29 75*

Specialities in the restaurant of this pretty 17th-century country inn include red mullet, *confit de canard*, spiced crayfish salad and wild mushrooms. Original art work adorns the walls inside (there is also a small gallery); outside there are tables in a flower-filled courtyard, shaded by trees. Closed Nov–Mar.

VILLEFRANCHE DE CONFLENT Auberge St-Paul
7 pl Eglise, 66500 **Tel** *04 68 96 30 95* **Fax** *04 68 96 05 60 30*

Originally a 13th-century chapel, this village restaurant has an attractive terrace and a charming, rustic dining room. The menu is cosmopolitan, with fresh local produce and a sophisticated wine list, with fine Bordeaux and Roussillon vintages. Closed Sun dinner, Mon, Tue; Jan; a week mid–Jun.

PROVENCE AND THE COTE D'AZUR

AIX EN PROVENCE Brasserie Léopold
2 av Victor Hugo, 13090 **Tel** *04 42 26 01 24* **Fax** *04 42 38 53 17*

Classic French brasserie with dozens of tables and bustling waiters, on the ground floor of the comfortable Hôtel Saint-Christophe in the centre of Aix. A great place for a full-scale meal, a snack or just a drink at any time of day or year. Strong on regional cuisine and traditional brasserie fare.

AIX EN PROVENCE Relais Sainte Victoire
Av Stephen Gauthier, Beaurecueil, 13100 **Tel** *04 42 66 94 98* **Fax** *04 42 66 85 96*

Book ahead for a table on the terrace of this delightful country inn at Beaurecueil, at the foot of Mont Sainte-Victoire. Excellent views. The food combines fresh Provençal produce with a modern approach – honey-glazed lamb and grilled sardines with sun-dried tomatoes. Closed Sun dinner, Mon, Fri lunch.

AIX-EN-PROVENCE L'Aixquis
22 rue Victor Leydet, 13100 **Tel** *04 42 27 76 16* **Fax** *04 42 93 10 61*

An up-to-date array of dishes and a good wine list have made this one of Aix's most popular eating places. L'Aixquis is located in a narrow lane in central Aix. Chef Benoît Strohm is known for excellent Provençal cooking, such as rabbit marinated in herbs. Closed Sun, Mon lunch.

AIX-EN-PROVENCE Le Clos de la Violette
10 av Violette, 13100 **Tel** *04 42 23 30 71* **Fax** *04 42 21 93 03*

This is an elegant address in a chic mansion standing in its own gardens: tranquil, intimate and perfect for a romantic evening. People do dress up a little to eat here. The wine list is extensive (and very strong on local and Provençal wines) and the menu is Provençal with a modern edge. Closed Sun, Mon.

Key to Price Guide *see p600* **Key to Symbols** *see back cover flap*

AIX EN PROVENCE Mas d'Entremont
P 🏠 🖼 🍷   €€€€€

Quartier des Platrières, 13090 **Tel** *04 42 17 42 42* **Fax** *04 42 21 15 83*

The food is imaginative, the list of Provençal wines is good if not outstanding, and the setting in a lush park above Aix at Célony is delightful. Plenty of regional meat and fish. In summer, dine on a lovely terrace overlooking the gardens, with fine views. The dining room has huge picture windows overlooking the surrounding park.

ARLES Bistrot Le 16
📋 ♿ 🖼   €

16 rue du Dr Fanton, 13200 **Tel** *04 90 93 77 36*

Offering a good range of salads, this bouchon-style restaurant offers good value for money, and its changing menus use lots of locally grown produce. There's been a recent change of ownership but it still fills up quickly, so come early for lunch or dinner. Closed Sun.

ARLES La Gueule du Loup
📋 🍷   €€

39 rue des Arènes, 13200 **Tel** *04 90 96 96 69* **Fax** *04 90 96 96 69*

La Gueule du Loup ("the Wolf's Maw") is more welcoming than its ferocious name implies, with a menu that changes virtually daily and serves up exquisite Provençal cuisine in charmingly rustic surroundings. Prompt service and a good choice of wines. Not cutting-edge cuisine, but good at what it does. Closed Sun, Mon lunch.

ARLES Lou Marques
🏠 📋 🖼 🍷   €€€

Bd Lices, 13200 **Tel** *04 90 52 52 52* **Fax** *04 90 52 52 53*

Lou Marques – the restaurant of the venerable Hôtel Jules César – is one of the best places to eat in Arles, with a central location, pleasant terrace with tables under white umbrellas, and a bill of fare that concentrates on classic Provençal dishes. Dignified surroundings. Closed Nov–Apr; Sat, Sun.

AVIGNON La Fourchette
🏠 📋 ♿ 🍷   €€

17 rue Racine, 84000 **Tel** *04 90 85 20 93* **Fax** *04 90 85 57 60*

Much loved locally, La Fourchette is a quirky little place with walls adorned by antique forks and festival posters. The menu is traditional Provençal, with a modern take on dishes such as duck breast in garlic and vegetable crêpes. Excellent choice of cheeses. Closed Sat, Sun. Reservations required.

AVIGNON Le Petit Bedon
🏠 ♿ 🖼 🍷   €€

70 rue Joseph-Vernet, 84000 **Tel** *04 90 82 33 98* **Fax** *04 90 85 58 64*

Le Petit Bedon, just inside the walls of Avignon's old quarter, has a good reputation for tasty dishes such as poached vegetables with tapenade and *pistou*, *bourride de loup* (monkfish stew), and courgette puree with garlic. Amiable atmosphere. Provençal wines. Closed Sun, Mon.

AVIGNON Hiély-Lucullus
🏠 📋 🍷   €€€

5 rue de la République, 84000 **Tel** *04 90 86 17 07* **Fax** *04 90 86 32 38*

Old-fashioned, bourgeois provincial restaurant with a long history of catering to the gourmands of Avignon. Decorated in Belle Epoque style, the restaurant has a menu concentrating on the classics, such as *foie gras flan* with morels. On the first floor of a medieval building.

AVIGNON Christian Etienne
🏠 📋 🖼 🍷   €€€€

10 rue Mons, 84000 **Tel** *04 90 86 16 50* **Fax** *04 90 86 67 09*

The wine list is strong on Provençal and Rhône Valley vintages, the location in the medieval heart of Avignon near the Papal Palace is hard to beat, and the food is equally unbeatable in this highly regarded restaurant, with menus that emphasize imaginatively treated local produce. Closed Sun, Mon (except in Jul).

AVIGNON La Mirande
🏠 📋 🖼 🍷 ♿   €€€€€

4 pl de la Mirande, 84000 **Tel** *04 90 14 20 20* **Fax** *04 90 86 26 85*

One of the most delicious places to eat in Avignon, with tables outside beneath olive trees and the floodlit walls of the Palais des Papes or indoors in a grand dining room in what was once a cardinal's palace. Extensive, dazzling menu and wine list. Friendly service. Book ahead. Closed Tue, Wed.

BIOT Les Terraillers
P 🏠 📋 🖼 🍷   €€€€

11 route Chemin Neuf, 06410 **Tel** *04 93 65 01 59* **Fax** *04 93 65 13 78*

Sophisticated restaurant serving dishes that are rich in every sense of the word, flavoured with truffles and the herbs of surrounding hills. The *foie gras escalope* is not to be missed, and the lamb is a culinary triumph. The wine list highlights some of the better *vins de pays* of Provence. Closed Wed, Thu.

BONNIEUX La Bastide de Capelongue
🏠 📋 ♿ 🖼 🍷   €€€€€

84160 **Tel** *04 90 68 06 69* **Fax** *04 90 68 31 76*

Two Michelin stars keep this fine restaurant ahead of the local competition. Reservations essential – especially during the Cannes Film Festival, when it is packed with stars. The menu celebrates the produce and flavours of the Luberon hills and the Mediterranean coast such as truffles *en-croûte* and roasted venison.

CAGNES Fleur de Sel
📋 🍷   €

85 Montée de la Bourgade, 06800 **Tel** *04 93 20 33 33* **Fax** *04 93 20 33 33*

Delightful small restaurant serving unpretentious cooking at affordable prices – especially the set menus. Attractively rustic surroundings – the restaurant is in the heart of the village of Haut de Cagnes, next to the medieval church. Adequate choice of inexpensive wines. Closed Wed, Thu lunch.

CAGNES Le Cagnard

45 rue Sous Barri, Haut de Cagnes, 06800 **Tel** *04 93 20 73 21* **Fax** *04 93 22 06 39*

The outstanding Cagnard has an epicurean menu with truffles, pigeon, langoustine and more, elegantly served in the surroundings of a 14th-century mansion, accompanied by some of the best wines of Provence and the Gard region. Part of the Relais et Châteaux group. Closed Mon lunch, Tue lunch, Thu lunch.

CANNES Le Comptoir des Vins

13 bd de la République, 06400 **Tel** *04 93 68 13 26* **Fax** *04 93 68 52 51*

This wine-cellar restaurant does things a little differently – you choose your wine first, then decide what to eat with it. The wine list is extensive, the food hearty and simple. Surprisingly, this is more of a lunchtime place than a night spot. Closed Mon–Wed dinner, Sun.

CANNES La Cave

9 bd del la République, 06400 **Tel** *04 93 99 79 87*

La Cave has been running for around two decades and is popular with both locals and tourists. Its large choice of traditional, Provençal dishes is made from fresh, locally sourced ingredients. The wine list has over 350 references, including an excellent selection from local producers. Closed Sat lunch, Sun.

CANNES 38 The Restaurant

38 rue des Serbes, 06400 **Tel** *04 92 99 79 60* **Fax** *04 923 99 26 10*

It is difficult to eat more lavishly than in the posh surroundings of the Royal Gray, where diners can expect some of the finest cooking in Cannes – but at a surprisingly affordable price, and with courteous service. The accent is on Provençal flavours and Mediterranean seafood. Extensive wine list.

CANNES La Palme d'Or

73 la Croisette, 06400 **Tel** *04 92 98 74 14* **Fax** *04 93 39 03 38*

Children are not actually barred from this restaurant of the stars, nor is it essential to wear a tie – but diners who are not dressed to impress may feel self-conscious here. The food is imaginative and superb, with an impressive, costly wine list. Reservations required. Closed Sun, Mon.

CARPENTRAS Chez Serge

90 rue Cottier, 84200 **Tel** *04 90 63 21 24* **Fax** *04 90 11 70 68*

Chez Serge is a surprising discovery in sleepy Carpentras – a mix of old and new that is reflected in its style and in its menus. There's inventive, refined international cooking and the owners work with many local wine producers to put on evening wine tastings. Fresh fish is cooked in imaginative ways and wild mushrooms feature often on the menu.

CARRY-LE-ROUET L'Escale

Promenade du Port, 13620 **Tel** *04 42 45 00 47* **Fax** *04 42 44 52 03*

Wonderfully inventive fish dishes such as sautéed sea urchin with apples are the keynotes of this delightful restaurant with tables on a terrace overlooking the small port of Carry. There are fantastic views along the Mediterranean coast, and in cooler weather the indoor dining room is cosy. Book ahead for weekends.

CASTELLANE Auberge du Teillon

Route Napoléon - la Garde, 04120 **Tel** *04 92 83 60 88*

Pleasant country inn 6 km (4 miles) from the busy tourist hot-spot of Castellane. The bill of fare is unpretentious and changes according to the seasons, emphasizing traditional Provençal dishes, simply prepared including home-smoked salmon. Rooms available. Closed Nov–Mar; Sun dinner, Mon.

CAVAILLON Restaurant Prévôt

353 av de Verdun, 84300 **Tel** *04 90 71 32 43* **Fax** *04 90 71 97 05*

A gastronomic treat in the heart of the pretty market town of Cavaillon, where chef Jean-Jacques Prévôt is mad about melons – his restaurant has them as a decorative motif and there is even a set menu dedicated to the gourd family. Melon and scallops are recommended. Good portfolio of wines. Closed Sun, Mon.

CHATEAU-ARNOUX La Bonne Etape

Chemin du Lac, 04160 **Tel** *04 92 64 00 09* **Fax** *04 92 64 37 36*

This charming inn, located in a nondescript market town, has an outstanding array of dishes and emphasizes fresh local produce, especially lamb. The wine list is lengthy, featuring vintages from almost every French region. The dining room is decorated with paintings and tapestries.

CHATEAUNEUF DU PAPE La Mère Germaine

3 rue Commandant Lemaitre, 84230 **Tel** *04 90 83 54 37* **Fax** *04 90 83 50 27*

Surrounded by vineyards, this restaurant has an outstanding list of local and regional wines. The cooking is classic Provençal, servings are generous and La Mère Germaine offers good value and friendly service. Go for lunch to enjoy the view.

COLLOBRIERES La Petite Fontaine

1 pl de la Republique, 83610 **Tel** *04 94 48 00 12* **Fax** *04 94 48 03 03*

This simple restaurant is in the centre of Collobrières, a sleepy hill village in the heart of the Massif des Moaures. Specialities include chicken and garlic *fricassée*, rabbit with fresh herbs and duck with wild mushrooms, complemented by wines from the local wine co-operative. Closed Sun dinner, Mon.

Key to Price Guide *see p600* **Key to Symbols** *see back cover flap*

DIGNE-LES-BAINS Le Grand Paris 🏃♿🖼🍷 €€€
19 bd Thiers, 04000 **Tel** *04 92 30 58 00* **Fax** *04 92 32 32 82*

This rather grand hotel-restaurant has an air of bourgeois respectability that may be a little off-putting to some – for a more relaxed atmosphere, sit outside on the terrace. Classic food, such as *brandade* (mashed potatoes) with peppers, lamb *mignonette*, and pigeon. Good choice of Rhône and Provençal wines.

EZE Troubadour 🍷 €€€€
4 rue du Brec, 06360 **Tel** *04 93 41 19 03*

Pleasant, traditional restaurant in the centre of Eze's labyrinth of stone buildings that can only be reached on foot. The Troubadour has three small dining rooms, tucked inside medieval walls and offering a respite from the summer sun. Set menus and à la carte options feature classic Provençal cooking. Closed Sun, Mon.

FAYENCE Le Castellaras 🏃🖼🍷 €€€
Route de Seillans, 83440 **Tel** *04 94 76 13 80* **Fax** *04 94 84 17 50*

Le Castellaras serves dishes that balance tradition with innovation: lamb fillet with tarragon sauce; scampi marinated in olive oil, lemon and tarragon; polenta in truffle oil. The wine list draws mainly from the Côtes de Provence vineyards. Closed Mon, Tue (except Jul–Aug). Book ahead.

FAYENCE Le Moulin de la Camandoule 🏃🗎🖼 €€€
Chemin de Notre Dame des Cyprès, 83440 **Tel** *04 94 76 00 84* **Fax** *04 94 76 10 40*

In an ancient olive mill, this hotel-restaurant benefits from a peaceful and idyllic setting. Chef Phillipe Choissy offers several menus and à la carte dishes of high quality; the flavours are Provençal and the ingredients all fresh and seasonal. Lunch is often served on the terrace. Closed Wed, Thu.

FONTVIEILLE Le Régalido 🏃🗎🖼 €€€€
1 rue Frédéric Mistral, 13990 **Tel** *04 90 54 60 22* **Fax** *04 90 54 64 29*

This attractive restaurant is attached to a charming hotel (*see Where to Stay p692*) with a pretty terrace and elegant dining room. The menu embraces Mediterranean and Provençal influences and classic recipes, and leans heavily on regional produce. Regional wine list. Closed lunch (except Sun).

GIGONDAS Les Florets 🏃🖼🍷 €€
Route des Dentelles, 84190 **Tel** *04 90 65 85 01* **Fax** *04 90 65 83 80*

The terrace of this hotel-restaurant has fine views of the Dentelles de Montmirail. Well-presented regional cooking is complemented by the fine wines of the Gigondas region. The restaurant is popular, so arrive early or book ahead. Closed Wed.

GRASSE Bastide St Antoine 🅿🏃🗎🖼🍷♿ €€€€€
48 av H. Dunant, 06130 **Tel** *04 93 70 94 94* **Fax** *04 93 70 94 95*

Jacques Chibois's superb restaurant is attached to his delightful boutique-hotel in Grasse's quartier St-Antoine, with a menu that will excite gourmets and lovers of inventive French cuisine – duckling, truffles, and an inventive approach to vegetables. There is also an excellent, mainly Provençal wine list.

JUAN LES PINS Les Pêcheurs 🏃🗎♿🍷🍷 €€€€
10 bd Maréchal Juin, Cap d'Antibes, 06160 **Tel** *04 92 93 13 30* **Fax** *04 92 93 15 04*

The Hotel Juana has recently exchanged its celebrated rooftop restaurant for this luxurious restaurant on the beach with high-tech touches and a vast terrace. Chef Francis Chauveau's cuisine is delicious and creative. Indulge in the grilled sea bass with lemons and marinated vegetables. Closed Tues, Wed (except Jul–Aug).

LA CADIERE D'AZUR Hostellerie Bérard 🏃🗎🖼🍷 €€€
Av Gabriel Peri, 83740 **Tel** *04 94 90 11 43* **Fax** *04 94 90 01 94*

This renowned hotel-restaurant in the converted buildings of an 11th-century convent has a fine view over the Bandol vineyards. Owner and chef Rene Bérard does marvellous things with fish and shellfish, including a sublime mussel soup flavoured with saffron. Local Bandol wines. Closed Mon lunch, Sat lunch.

MARSEILLE Chez Madie (Les Galinettes) 🏃🗎🖼🍷 €
138 quai du Port, 13000 **Tel** *04 91 90 40 87*

A Marseillais institution for generations (it is now in the hands of the granddaughter of the eponymous founder). Legendary *bouillabaisse*, *bourride* and other fish dishes are complemented by tripe and pigs' trotters. Definitely not for vegetarians, nor for picky children.

MARSEILLE Les Arcenaulx 🗎♿🖼🍷 €€
25 cours d'Estienne d'Orves, 13000 **Tel** *04 91 59 80 40*

In the former warehouse district north of the Vieux Port, Les Arcenaulx occupies the former premises of a 17th-century publisher. A great place to start or end an evening's bar-hopping around the neighbouring streets. Favourite Provençal dishes include rabbit and sardine and ginger *pâté*. Closed Sun.

MARSEILLE Restaurant Michel 🏃🗎♿🖼🍷 €€€€
6 rue des Catalans, 13000 **Tel** *04 91 52 64 22* **Fax** *04 91 59 23 05*

Bouillabaisse is the speciality of the house at this fine, busy brasserie. Other fish dishes include *bourride*, sardines, and the always reliable catch of the day, fresh and simply grilled. Popular with locals – get there early to be sure of a table. Wine list includes names from Bandol and Cassis.

MENTON A'Braïjade Meridionale   🏃🍴♿   €€

66 rue Longue, 06500 **Tel** *04 93 35 65 65* **Fax** *04 93 35 65 65*

In one of the narrow alleys of the old quarter of Menton, A Braijade Meridonale has a near-obsession with lemon-flavoured dishes with a hint of North Africa – lemon-marinated brochettes, lemons stuffed with tuna, eggs, olives, capers and *aioli*, lemon-grilled chicken and lamb paprika are among the offerings.

MONACO Zebra Square   P🏃🍴🍷♿   €€€€

10 av Princesse Grace, 98000 **Tel** *00 377 99 99 25 50* **Fax** *00 377 99 99 25 60*

This trendy restaurant is an offshoot of one of Paris's smartest hotel-restaurants and lives up to its name with zebra stripes everywhere. The menu is multi-cultural and features good grills, seafood and fusion recipes. Great location, with terrace tables right on the sea. The best choice in Monaco for lunch or dinner.

MOUGINS Le Moulin de Mougins   🏃♿🍷   €€€€€

Notre-Dame-de-Vie, route départementale 3, 06250 **Tel** *04 93 75 78 24* **Fax** *04 93 90 18 55*

Alain Llorca's 2-Michelin-star restaurant is the place for a special treat, with superb, imaginative cuisine that leans towards seafood prepared in new ways. The wines include some of the very best of Provence. The garden terrace is adorned by modern sculptures. Closed Mon. Reservations are essential.

MOUSTIERS La Treille Muscate   🍷   €

Pl de l'Eglise, 04360 **Tel** *04 92 74 64 31* **Fax** *04 92 74 63 75*

Excellent food such as *pistou* of vegetables in this lovely little Provençal bistro, with a great location on the main square of one of the region's prettiest villages. Good value, with a choice of set menus and a decent wine list, La Treille Muscate is especially pleasant for a relaxed al fresco lunch. Closed Wed.

NICE Le Boccaccio   🍷   €€€

7 rue Massena, 06000 **Tel** *04 93 87 71 76* **Fax** *04 93 82 09 06*

One of the best places for seafood in Nice, the central Boccaccio is on a bustling car-free street. The interior design is imaginative, with stained-glass windows and tables spread over several floors, and the bill of fare features the best fish dishes – fresh, simply prepared and with attentive service.

ST TROPEZ Le Café   🏃🍴   €€€€

Pl Lices, 83900 **Tel** *04 94 97 44 69*

A typical "Zinc" bar in a great central position of St-Tropez, serving delicious fish soup, prawns in pastis sauce, and home-made *foie gras*. On market days the terrace is swamped with locals, before the *pétanque* (French bowls) players take control of the square.

VENCE Table d'Amis Jacques Maximin   P🏃🍴🍷   €€€€€

689 chemin de la Gaude, 6140 **Tel** *04 93 58 90 75* **Fax** *04 93 58 22 86*

Specialities at this tremendous gastronomic restaurant include roast rabbit *parmentier*, roast monkfish, and an ever-changing array of innovative dishes inspired from the seas and slopes of Provence. The surroundings are lush and the dining room is graced by works of art. Reservations essential.

VILLEFRANCHE-SUR-MER L'Oursin Bleu   🏃🍴♿🍷   €€€

11 quai Courbet, 06230 **Tel** *04 93 01 90 12* **Fax** *04 93 01 80 45*

A bubbling aquarium in the foyer hints that this cheerful little eating place puts the accent on fresh fish. The location is delightful, on the quayside, with tables under umbrellas on the terrace and a dining room decorated with seafaring memorabilia. The ideal place for a long, lazy, summer lunch. Closed Tue; Jan.

CORSICA

AJACCIO Pampasgiolu   🍷   €€

15 rue de la Porta, 20000 **Tel** *04 95 50 71 52.*

Book ahead at this popular eating place in the old city, with its attractive, rustic dining rooms and small terrace. Try the *spuntini* (snack) platters of fish or meat local specialities or go for the veal with olives. Good desserts including chestnut fondant. Closed Sun, Mon lunch.

AJACCIO Palm Beach   P🏃   €€€

Route des Sanguinaires, 20000 **Tel** *04 95 52 01 03*

Excellent restaurant in a beach setting on the road to the Sanguinaires islands. Elegant dining room and terrace with magnificent view over the bay. The English chef offers impeccably cooked dishes such as line-caught sea bass in salt, saddle of lamb in a herb crust or fillet of beef with wild garlic. Sumptuous desserts.

BASTIA Au Café des Intimes   🏃   €€

9 pl Hôtel de Ville, 20200 **Tel** *04 95 31 87 23*

Specializing in Middle-Eastern food, this animated restaurant in the bustling marketplace serves fresh fish in tagines and couscous. If you are very hungry, try the "Royal" couscous, a feast of chicken, lamb, spicy meatballs and vegetables. Desserts include iced cream caramel with hot chocolate sauce.

Key to Price Guide *see p600* **Key to Symbols** *see back cover flap*

BASTIA Le Caveau de Marin

Quai des Martyrs de la Libération, 20200 **Tel** *04 95 31 62 31*

Situated on the esplanade in proximity to the old port, this superior restaurant offers regional specialities and fresh seafood. Choose from pasta with *boutargue* (silver mullet roe), grilled meats and piles of langoustines fished from the nearby lagoons. Small quiet terrace and a rather elegant dining room. Closed Jan.

BONIFACIO La Caravelle

37 quai Camparetti, 20169 **Tel** *04 95 73 00 03*

The most elegant place to eat on the bustling quayside. Spanking fresh seafood is served in dishes such as lobster risotto, seafood platter and langoustine in basil butter. Cheese is served with walnuts and dried pears, and desserts include old favourites like crêpes suzettes. Smart attire. Reservations recommended.

CALVI L'Abri Côtier

Rue Joffre, 20260 **Tel** *04 95 65 12 76*

Panoramic views from the huge windows in this portside restaurant with a cosmopolitan menu of sushi with ginger, carpaccio of fish, breast of duck, sea bass with citrus fruit or grilled Corsican veal, all beautifully presented. Finish your meal with spiced bananas or chestnut macaroon with ice cream. Closed mid-Nov–mid-March.

CALVI Le Bout du Monde

Plage du Calvi, 20260 **Tel** *04 95 65 15 41*

Excellent food at this friendly but classy beach spot. You'll be spoiled for choice between seafood platters, langoustine ravioli, scallops in orange butter, grilled rib of beef or huge salads, followed by caramelized apple tart or chestnut cream. Closed Feb, lunchtime in winter.

CORTE U Museu

13 Quart Quatre Fountains, 20250 **Tel** *04 95 61 08 36*

At the foot of the citadelle in the old town, this large restaurant has several dining rooms, including a tree-shaded terrace. There is a wide choice of dishes ranging from pizzas, pastas and salads to traditional Corsican dishes of white beans and lamb, *brocciu*-stuffed lasagne (stuffed with a Corsican cheese) and grilled meats with herbs.

ILE ROUSSE A Siesta

Promenade à Marinella, 20220 **Tel** *04 95 60 28 74* **Fax** *04 95 60 27 03*

Fresh seafood is the pride of this trendy beach restaurant. On hot nights they'll move the tables directly onto the beach so you can dine under the stars on spidercrabs, lobsters or *bouillabaisse*. Other choices include seafood ravioli and carpaccio of fish. Excellent desserts and wine list. Closed Nov–Mar.

PORTO Mini-Golfe

Porto Marina, 20150 **Tel** *04 95 26 17 55*

Leave the main complex of restaurants and shops and cross over the Japanese-style wooden bridge to reach this eucalyptus-shaded beach hideaway. A wide choice of grilled meats, fish salads and pastas, with an accent of oriental spices from the Antillaise chef. Closed Oct–Apr.

PORTO VECCHIO Le Tourisme

Cours Napoléon, 20137 **Tel** *04 95 70 06 45*

Popular establishment in the upper town, facing the church. This friendly place, decorated in a brasserie style, serves Provençal and Corsican specialities. Large choice of fish and meat dishes, featuring Corsican veal and game in season. Owner will order lobster for you with 24 hours' notice. Closed Sun lunch.

PORTO VECCHIO Le Bistro

4 quai Paoli, 20137 **Tel** *04 95 70 22 96*

Lively eating spot situated in the yachting harbour in the lower town. Pretty dining room and large terrace. Fresh seafood with a choice of red mullet with anchovies and tomatoes, sea bream or grilled spiny lobster. Excellent *tartare* of beef or civet of wild boar, in season. There's a new tapas bar and a good choice of *crêpes suzettes*. Closed Feb.

PROPRIANO Le Cabanon

Av Napoléon, 20110 **Tel** *04 95 76 06 76*

Brochettes of tiger prawns and scallops are among the most popular dishes at this charming quayside restaurant. Start with fish soup or aubergine (eggplant) caviar and follow with grilled red mullet or sea bream in white wine sauce. Or try the oysters from the east coast lagoons. Excellent cheeses.

SARTENE Auberge Santa Barbara

Alzone (3 km [2miles] out of Sartène on the road to Propriano), 20100 **Tel** *04 95 77 09 06* **Fax** *04 95 77 09 09*

Outdoor eatery in lovely gardens, owned by Corsica's foremost female chef, Gisèle Lovichi. Choose between homemade charcuterie or country soup with its vegetable salad, and stuffed leg of lamb or saddle of lamb with herb crust. Finish with *fiadone*, a dessert made with Corsican cheese, lemons and eggs. Closed mid-Oct–Feb.

ST-FLORENCE La Rascasse

Rue Strada Nova, 20217 **Tel** *04 95 37 06 99*

Inventive cooking in this smart fish restaurant in a prime position on the port. Ensconce yourself on the terrace and study the yachts as you wait for your order of fish soup, seafood risotto, or grilled squid. Try the classic *bouillabaisse* or a grilled lobster, and leave room for one of the sublime desserts.

Shopping in France

Shopping in France is a delight. Whether you go to the hypermarkets and department stores, or seek out the small specialist stores and markets, you will be tempted by stylish French presentation and the quality of goods on offer. Renowned for its food and wine, France also offers world-famous fashion, perfume, pottery, porcelain and crystal. This section provides guidelines on opening hours, and the range of goods stocked by the different types of stores. There are also details of quintessentially French products which are worth hunting down and a size conversion chart to aid clothes shopping.

Olive Oil from Baux

Fresh nectarines and melons on sale at a market stall

OPENING HOURS

Food shops open anywhere between 7–8am and close around noon for lunch. In the north, the lunch break generally lasts for 2 hours; in the south, it is 3–4 hours (except in resorts, where it is shorter). After lunch, most food shops re-open until 7pm or later.

Bakeries open early and close early, although many stay open until 1pm or later, to catch the late baguette buyers and to serve a range of lunchtime snacks.

Supermarkets, department stores and most hypermarkets remain open all day, with no lunchtime closure.

General opening hours for non-food shops are 9am–6pm Monday through Saturday, often with a break for lunch. Many of these shops are closed on Monday mornings, and the smaller shops may stay closed all day. In the tourist regions, however, shops usually open every day in high season.

Sunday is by far the quietest shopping day, although most food shops (and newsagents) are open in the morning. Virtually every shop in France is closed on Sunday afternoon.

HYPERMARKETS AND DEPARTMENT STORES

Hypermarkets (*hypermarchés* or *grandes surfaces*) can be found on the outskirts of every sizeable town: look for signs indicating *centre commercial*. Much bigger than supermarkets, they sell mainly groceries, but their other lines include clothing, home accessories and electronic equipment. They also sell discount petrol (gasoline). **Carrefour**, **Casino**, **Auchan**, **Leclerc** and **Intermarché** are the biggest.

Department stores (*grands magasins*), such as **Monoprix** and **Franprix** are usually found in town centres. The more upmarket **Printemps** and **Galeries Lafayette** also have out-of-town locations.

A local bakery, which often sells pastries as well as bread

SPECIALIST SHOPS

One of the pleasures of shopping in France is that specialist food shops continue to flourish, despite the influx of supermarkets and hypermarkets. The *boulangerie* (bakery) is frequently combined with a *pâtisserie* selling cakes and pastries. The *traiteur* sells prepared foods. *Fromagers* (cheese shops) and other shops specializing in dairy products *(produits laitiers)* may be combined, but the *boucherie* (butcher) and *charcuterie* (pork butcher-delicatessen) are often separate shops. For general groceries go to an *épicerie* or *alimentation*, but don't confuse this with an *épicerie fine* – a delicatessen.

Cleaning and household products are available from a *droguerie*, while hardware is bought from a *quincaillerie*. The term *papeterie* (stationer) covers both the expensive, specialist retailers and their hypermarket equivalents.

MARKETS

This guide lists the market day for every town featured in the Area by Area section. To find out where the market is, ask a passerby for *le marché*. Markets are held in the morning and usually finish promptly at noon. Look for local producers, including those with only one or two special items to sell, as their goods are often more reasonably priced and of better quality than stalls with multiple items. By law, price tags include the origin of all produce: *pays* means local. Chickens from Bresse are marketed wearing a red, white and blue badge with the name of the producer. If you are visiting markets over several weeks, look for items just coming into season, such as fresh walnuts, the first wild asparagus, early artichokes or wild strawberries. At the market, you can also buy spices and herbs, some offbeat peculiarities (such as decorative cabbages), shoes and clothing.

The year is full of seasonal regional markets in France, specializing in such things as truffles, hams, garlic, *foie gras* and livestock. *Foires artisanales* may be held at the same time as the seasonal markets, selling local produce and crafts.

REGIONAL PRODUCE

French regional specialities are available outside their area of origin, but it is more interesting to buy them locally as their creation and flavour reflect the traditions, tastes and climate of the region.

Provence, in the south, prides itself on the quality of its olive oil, the best of which is made from the first cold pressing, lovingly decanted every day for a week. If you cannot get to a niche olive oil producer in Provence, head to **Oliviers et Co** which has branches throughout the country, and sells an excellent selection of oils. Be sure to indulge in a tasting session to sample the flavours. In the temperate north, the delicious Camembert cheese is the product of fresh Norman milk that has been cured for at least three weeks.

Popular drinks are also associated with particular regions. Pastis, made from aniseed, is popular in the south. Calvados, made in Normandy from apples, is popular in the north. Crème

Sausages and cheeses, regional specialities on offer in a Lyon market

de Fruit de Dijon, the secret ingredient to many a good cocktail or dessert, comes in many flavours (from peach to wild strawberry) in addition to the well-known black-currant – **Crème de Cassis**. Visit local producers to buy good versions of this thick, alcoholic syrup.

To a large extent, location determines the quality of regional produce. For example, the culinary tradition of Lyon *(see pp380–1)*, France's premier gastronomic city, stems from the proximity of Charolais cattle, Bresse chickens and pork, wild game from La Dombes, and the finest Rhône Valley wines.

Alongside sachets of dried herbs from Provence and plaited strings of garlic and onions, be sure to buy the seasoning loved by all self-respecting francophile cooks – salt from the Ile de Ré *(see p416)* or Guerande. If you happen to be visiting the area, check out the salt flats and pick up the crumbly coarse grains at a local market. The Fleur de Sel is a delicate flaky variety and the Sel Marin is a grey, coarser type of salt.

BEAUTY PRODUCTS

French women are renowned for their beauty, and there is a plethora of good beauty products in France. The major French labels, such as **Chanel** and **Guerlain**, are available overseas, but die-

hard cosmetics fans should scour the local beauty counters to find special products that are only on sale in France.

While in Paris, beauty junkies must visit the Chanel store on the rue Cambon and the Guerlain store on the Champs Elysées to buy scent that is only available in those particlaur stores. Throughout the rest of the country, supermarket brands such as Evian, Eau Thermale d'Avene and Barbara Gould are huge hits with magazine beauty editors. In particular, the cold cream by Eau Thermale d'Avene, the foaming cleanser by Barbara Gould and Evian's facial toning gel can be found in many a fashionista's make-up bag. Similarly many a groomed Parisian swears by Nuxe's cult body oil *Huile Prodigeuse*, Caudalie's *Vinotherapary Cabernet* body scrub (with grape extracts) and Elancyl's anti-cellulite toning cream.

Oenobiol tanning supplement capsules and Phytomer's hair care range are considered absolutely necessary by St-Tropez beach lovers looking to lessen sun damage to hair and skin.

A more traditional approach to French grooming can be found by buying *savon de marseilles* – good-quality traditional soap made with plenty of oil.

True scent aficionados should head for Grasse *(see p517)*, the perfume capital of the world. Be sure to visit the three largest scent factories, **Fragonard**, **Molinard** and **Galimard**, all of which have scent available for purchase.

Pastis 51, drunk in the south

Provençal dried herbs for culinary use and for making teas

ACCESSORIES

French fashion is rightfully famous, but aside from the main couture labels and stores (see pp142–4), the best way to get the French look is to accessorize à la Français. In keeping with the French tradition of specialist local trades, there are certain regions that excel in producing accessories.

For a start, a hand-made umbrella from Aurillac (see p364) is guaranteed to chase away rainy-day blues in style. The best-known umbrella manufacturers are **L'Ondée au Parapluie d'Aurillac**, **Piganiol** and **Delos**, who will customize one for you with a photograph of whomever you choose to chase away the storms.

Beautiful hands are easily available courtesy of the glove trade in Millau. Visit **L'Atelier Gantier** (the Glove Workshop) to pick up a stunning pair of expertly hand-stiched leather gloves in one of a seemingly endless array of colours.

More casual chic can be found with brightly coloured wicker baskets from local markets and hardware stores. These quickly turn a casual ensemble into boho-chic outfit. Beachside boutiques are great places for picking up stylish sarongs, beads and bracelets for any trip to la plage (the beach). **K Jacques** sandals from St-Tropez have long been must-have items among the fashion set.

When it is time to hit the slopes rather than the beach, French skiwear labels such as Rossignol can be a good buy, but only at the end of the season. At the height of piste time, ski resort shops are expensive. Once the snow starts to melt, however, ex-rental gear including skis and boots can be picked up relatively cheaply, while ski jackets, hats and après ski wear tends to be gloriously cut-price.

HOUSEHOLD GOODS

If you are in the market for housewares, the best stores are **Ikea**, **Cèdre Rouge** and **Habitat**. **Truffaut** sells garden furniture, and **Leroy Merlin** is the hypermarket of the DIY, home improvement world.

It is surprisingly rare to see the whole range of kitchen goods in a specialist shop. Instead, try the kitchen section of department stores. General hardware shops stock cast-iron cooking equipment. White china is sold in specialist shops.

Travelling through Normandy provides the perfect excuse for sampling many wonderful products, not least the crème de chantilly, but for tableware fans or lingerie lovers, the lace industry here is also guaranteed to please. While the **Alençon** lace is extremely expensive and mainly finds its way onto couture sold in top Parisian stores, hitting the shops in Argentan, Chantilly (see pp204–5) and Bayeux (see pp252–3) is likely to yield exquisite yet affordable pieces. It is worth hunting around for lace pieces which can be used to liven up an outfit: lace has made a fashion comeback in recent times and a customized delicate flower on a bag or blouse is à la mode.

Lace curtains are easy to come by, as are lovely table-cloths. The easiest way to be sure not to miss anything, is to take "the lace road" and tour the lace museums and boutiques of Alençon, Argentan, Caen (see pp253–4), Courseulles, Villedieu-les-Poêles and La Perrière.

With a beautiful tablecloth in place, you can proceed to pick up stunning crystal from which to sniff, swirl and sip great French wine. The most famous French crystal maker, **Baccarat**, has a museum where you can take in some of their amazing creations and a store where you can buy a little Baccarat bauble to take home with you. A cheaper French crystal maker which is still elegant for every-day wear is **Crystal d'Arques**. You can tour the small museum in the factory and buy stemware at discount prices in the factory store.

Pottery is available at reasonable prices, especially near centres of production, such as Quimper (see p274) in Brittany, Aubagne near Marseille and Vallauris (see p522) near Grasse.

Porcelain from Limoges (see p356) sets off any meal beautifully: a dinner set from the **Royal Limoges** factory store can be a great investment.

Similarly, stunning **Aubusson** tapestries are seriously expensive and unlikely to be an impulse holiday purchase. However, interior design fanatics could do worse than plan their tapestry or rug purchase

SIZE CHART

Women's dresses, coats and skirts

French	36	38	40	42	44	46	48
British	8	10	12	14	16	18	20
American	4	6	8	10	12	14	16

Women's shoes

French	36	37	38	39	40	41
British	3	4	5	6	7	8
American	5	6	7	8	9	10

Men's suits

French	44	46	48	50	52	54	56	58
British	34	36	38	40	42	44	46	48
American	34	36	38	40	42	44	46	48

Men's shirts

French	36	38	39	41	42	43	44	45
British	14	15	15½	16	16½	17	17½	18
American	14	15	15½	16	16½	17	17½	18

Men's shoes

French	39	40	41	42	43	44	45	46
British	6	7	7½	8	9	10	11	12
American	7	7½	8	8½	9½	10½	11	11½

around a trip to the home of weaving in Aubusson *(see pp356–7).*

Finishing touches are fun to shop for and can certainly be more frivolous. Be sure to visit the local markets for gingham cotton napkins, linen cleaning cloths and seafood accoutrements (such as lobster crackers and oyster forks). In Provence be sure to stock up on cheap, brightly coloured cookware – tagines, terracotta bowls and painted plates are all in abundance.

WINE

To buy wine straight from the vineyards and wine co-operatives, follow the tasting *(dégustation)* signs to vineyards *(domaines).* You may be expected to buy at least one bottle, except where a small fee is charged for wine-tasting. Wine co-operatives make and sell the wine of small producers. Here you can buy wine in 5- and 10-litre containers *(en tonneau)*, as well as in bottles. Wine sold *en tonneau* is duty-free, and customers receive a permit *(laissez-passer)* indicating destination. Bottled wine sold by co-ops is not duty-free. **Nicolas** is France's main wine off-licence, with many branches.

FACTORY OUTLETS

The French sales system is very rigid *(see p140)* but true bargain hunters know that factory shops have some items on sale all year round. The biggest factory outlets in France can be found in and around Troyes in outlet malls called **Marques Avenue** (Brands Avenue), **Marques City** (Brands City) and **McArthur Glenn**, a large American outlet. They sell everything from Yves Saint Laurent suits to Black and Decker drills, Cristofle silverware and Bonpoint babygros. As different an experience as you can get from browsing around French markets and local specialist stores, what factory outlets lack in charm they make up for in bargains. If a whole new wardrobe is in order, it is definitely worth a trip.

DIRECTORY

HYPERMARKETS AND DEPARTMENT STORES

For details of addresses, visit the following websites

Auchan
www.auchan.fr

Carrefour
www.carrefour.fr

Casino
www.supercasino.fr

Franprix
www.franprix.fr

Galeries Lafayette
www.galerieslafayette.com

Intermarché
www.intermarche.com

Leclerc
www.e-leclerc.com

Monoprix
www.monoprix.fr

Printemps
www.printemps.com

REGIONAL PRODUCE

Crème de Cassis
Gabriel Boudier
14 rue de Cluj
21007 Dijon
Tel 03 80 74 33 33

Oliviers et Co
For details of addresses,
visit www.oliviers-co.com

BEAUTY PRODUCTS

Chanel
29 rue Cambon 75008
Paris
Tel 01 42 86 28 00

Fragonard
20 bd Fragonard 06130
Grasse
Tel 04 93 36 44 65
www.fragonard.com

Galimard
73 route de Cannes
06130 Grasse
Tel 04 93 09 20 00
www.galimard.com

Guerlain
68 av des Champs
Elysées, 75008 Paris
Tel 01 45 62 52 57
www.guerlain.fr

Molinard
60 bd Victor Hugo 06130
Grasse
Tel 04 93 36 01 62
www.molinard.com

ACCESSORIES

L'Atelier Gantier
21 rue Droite
12100 Millau
Tel 05 65 60 81 50

Delos
14 rue Rocher
15000 Aurillac
Tel 04 71 48 86 85
www.delos-france.com

K Jacques
25 rue Allard
83990 St Tropez
Tel 04 94 97 41 50
www.lestropeziennes.com

L'Ondée au Parapluie d'Aurillac
27 rue Victor Hugo
15000 Aurillac
Tel 04 71 48 29 53

Piganiol
9 rue Ampère
15000 Aurillac
Tel 04 71 63 42 60

HOUSEHOLD GOODS

Alençon Lace Museum
Cour carrée de la Dentelle
61000 Alençon
Tel 02 33 32 40 07

Aubusson
Manufacture Saint-Jean
3 rue Saint-Jean
23200 Aubusson
Tel 05 55 66 10 08

Baccarat
20 rue des Cristalleries
54120 Baccarat
Tel 03 83 76 60 06
www.baccarat.com

Cèdre Rouge
www.lecedrerouge.com

Cristal d'Arques
Zone industrielle, 62510
Arques *Tel 03 21 95 46 47*

Habitat
www.habitat.net

Ikea
www.ikea.com

Leroy Merlin
www.leroymerlin.fr

Royal Limoges
28 rue Donzelot
Accès par le quai du Port
du Naveix
87000 Limoges
Tel 05 55 33 27 30
www.royal-limoges.fr

Truffaut
www.truffaut.com

WINE

Nicolas
www.nicolas.com

FACTORY OUTLETS

Marques Avenue
Av de la Maille, 10800
Saint Julien les Villas
Tel 03 25 82 80 80
www.marquesavenue.com

Marques City
35 rue Danton
10150 Pont Sainte
Marie
Tel 03 25 46 37 48

McArthur Glenn
ZI des magasin d'usines du
Nord 10150
Pont Sainte Marie
Tel 03 25 70 47 10

Entertainment in France

Paris is one of the world's great entertainment cities, but France's reputation as a centre of excellence in the arts extends well beyond the capital. Whether you prefer to attend theatre or catch a film, listen to jazz or techno, or watch modern dance, the country has a wide array of choices. The regional chapters in this guide will give you an insight into local gems, while these pages provide an overview of entertainment trends and events. Major festivals, such as Avignon and Cannes, occupy an important place in French hearts, so book well ahead if you plan to attend. For small festivals and local happenings, tourist office websites have up-to-the-minute listings.

The spectacular setting of Avignon Theatre at night

THEATRE

Going to the theatre in France can be as formal or intimate as you choose. A trip to a major theatre can involve dressing up, making special *souper* (late dinner) reservations at a nearby restaurant specializing in theatre-goers, and quaffing exorbitantly priced champagne during the interval. On the other hand, a trip to a small-scale theatre can be about casual dress, cheap tickets and becoming totally absorbed in the show because of the intimacy and immediacy of the venue.

Recent years have seen major French movie stars head back to the stage, such as Gérard Depardieu and Fanny Ardant in *The Beast in the Jungle*, reflecting the popularity of the theatre. Whatever the genre, the French love an evening *au*

théâtre, be it a French farce, which shows no sign of fading in popularity, or a festival of street theatre.

France's biggest theatre festival is at **Avignon** *(see p503)* which is held during three weeks in July and is mainly open-air. It also includes ballets, drama and classical concerts.

Circus is also dear to the French. In small towns, summertime is often heralded by the circus loudhailer strapped to the top of a car cruising the streets and inviting adults and children alike to flock to the big top.

Large-scale *spectacles* or shows are another popular form of theatre, be they massive musicals or *son et lumières* performances. Marionettes are also given due respect in France, where puppet shows go beyond traditional Punch and Judy territory.

FILM

La Septième Art, as the French refer to film, reveals the respect with which the genre is held. From the Lumière brothers and their innovative technology to contemporary critical smashes, such as *The Chorus* and *Amélie Poulain* to the *Nouvelle Vague*, France's influence on film is undeniable. The French are supportive of local, independent cinemas, and small towns are often fiercely protective of their screening centre. So when visiting the cinema, try to avoid the behemoths of UGC and Gaumont and instead head to a tiny *salle de cinéma*. If your

language skills won't stretch to seeing a French film while in France, be sure to catch the VO *(Version Originale)* of any other language films, which will be screened in the film's original language. VF *(Version Française)* denotes a dubbed screening in French. As any expatriate in France knows, hearing a strange French voice coming out of a Hollywood A-lister's mouth is likely to dull any enjoyment of a major blockbuster movie.

Another thing to bear in mind is the French attitude to snacking. Essentially it is only acceptable for children, and even then only at a designated time after school. While French cinemas do have concession stands selling popcorn and sweets, it is only the foreigners who can be heard munching throughout the tense parts of the film. On the other hand, some French cinemas have bars and restaurants attached, so that film goers can dissect the movie over a meal. Many cinemas run mini directors' festivals with several films shown back to back, attracting serious film buffs and those curious to learn more.

As the fame of **Cannes** *(see p520)* reflects, film festivals are taken seriously by the French. Cannes itself is a maelstrom of media hype, old-school glamour and shiny new cash. It is an amazing experience if you can get tickets to any of the films or parties, but these are notoriously difficult to get as they are by invitation only.

Poster promoting La Rochelle international film festival

Red carpet and razzamatazz at the Cannes film festival

An easier way to experience the fabulous side of film is to attend the lower-key American film festival in **Deauville** *(see p255)*. This event is seen as a major launching pad for US independent films looking for European release, and attracts big stars and cult directors alike. The competition section of the festival has ten films in the running each year. The chic town of Deauville is small and accessible and, while the chance of bumping into a huge star is slim, it feels possible.

The film festival in **La Rochelle** *(see p416)*, the second largest in France, does not attract big actors, but film fans will not be disappointed with the large selection of movies on offer.

A truly great way to catch a film in France is at an open-air festival. There are many such events throughout the country; check local listings so as not to miss out. And if you are lucky enough to be in Arles *(see pp508–9)*, an epic experience can be had at their annual showing of historical Roman block-busters, screened against the backdrop of a magnificent Roman amphitheatre. Contact **Théâtre Antique** for details.

DANCE

Dancing is a way of life in France. From formal lessons to spontaneous outbreaks of grooving in the village square, moving to music is central to all types of celebration. Most foreigners' first experience with French dancers occurs in a nightclub and is, more often than not, accompanied by an expression of surprise. In even the most upscale nightclub, it is not unusual to see trendy twentysomethings jiving away to *le rock*, a formal form of rock and roll dancing. French teens are taught *le rock* before being unleashed on the party scene, and a basic understanding of its signature twirls and twists is considered vital to being a good dancer.

The love affair with formal dance sessions starts young, but lasts until late in life: tea dances are a major fixture of most older people's social calendars. Community centres, sports halls, restaurants and chic nightclubs often host *thé dansants* (tea dances), normally in the late afternoon or early evening.

Another way to experience French dance culture is to head to a *guingette*, a moored party boat with a convivial, old-fashioned atmosphere. People here dance the *quadrille* or the *musette* to accordion music, spinning around on the banks of the river. While the guingettes were traditionally clustered around the Marne river, they have now spread throughout France and are definitely worth seeking out if your travels take you close to a major tributary.

In general, lots of dancing takes place near to water in France. Those looking to get into the groove in the south should take their dancing shoes to the quays in Bordeaux and Marseille.

Of course, once a year, on 13 and 14 July, a most unusual impromptu dancing venue springs up around the country with the *Bals des Pompiers*. The "Firemen's Balls" are a national institution when the French of all ages head down to their local fire station to celebrate Bastille day by dancing to everything from Piaf to hip hop until the early hours of the morning.

If you would prefer to watch rather than participate, there are several major dance festivals that celebrate the dance traditions of different regions. The **Gannat festival** held in the Auvergne *(see p353)* is a fine example of a regional dance extravaganza, as is the **Festival Interceltique de Lorient** *(see p270)* which celebrates Celtic music and dance. The main international dance festivals are held in **Montpellier** *(see pp494–5)* and **Lyon** *(see pp378–81)*. These provide a wonderful opportunity to enjoy major contemporary dance talent from around the world.

Wonderful costumes and choreography at the Montpellier dance festival

MUSIC

The French music scene is about far more than Johnny Hallyday, although it must be said that the ageing rocker still manages to sell stacks of records, concert tickets and gossip magazines. It should also be pointed out that he is actually Belgian, but the French have taken him to their hearts anyway. Neither is the scene just about Bob Sinclair, Daft Punk, Air and "Le French Touch". However, the fact that both dance music and rock happily coexist in the French charts reflects a truism of the music scene over here, which is that there is space for all kinds of tunes. *Chanson* has made a huge comeback over recent years as the success of the movement's poster boy Benjamin Biolay reveals. The new French *chanson* scene is dominated by Biolay, although other well-known artists in this genre include Vincent Delerm and Benabar.

Female crooners are also all the rage; listen to Lara Fabian or reality TV pop star Chimène Badi for confirmation of this.

The other recent musical phenomenon in France came off the back of a hit film *The Chorus* (*Les Choristes*, 2004) which has seen impressive soundtrack sales, and one can at least speculate on the impact it might have had on attendance at evensong.

The event which best symbolizes this musical cornucopia is the Fête de la Musique. Every year on 21 June, France resonates to the sound of this national music festival. Amateur and professional musicians alike set up their stages throughout villages and towns and peform. The best way to enjoy this is to walk around and try and take in as many different "concerts" as possible, but be aware that for some wannabe rock stars this is their only chance to shine, regardless of whether or not they can sing. Musical quality aside, what is most impressive about the Fête de la Musique is the sheer

number of genres that one can hear in a few streets. Ranging from full orchestras to one-man rap artists, you can expect to hear everything from accordion music to panpipes, *chanson*, hip hop and electro.

If you prefer your festivals a little more specialized, visit one of the events focusing on the very best of everything from chamber music to jazz. The July **Festival of Francofolies** in La Rochelle (*see p416*) brings together French music enthusiasts from around the world just as **Jazz in Antibes** draws top performers to this chic seaside town (*see p521*). The **Chorégies d'Orange**, France's oldest opera festival, takes place throughout July and August in the well-preserved Roman amphitheatre, which retains perfect acoustics. The organ festival in **Aubusson** (*see pp356–7*) focuses around the amazing organ in the Sainte Croix church and **La Roque d'Anthéron** looks set to continue to pull in piano-loving crowds. The **Colmar international festival** (*see p227*) is a major draw for classical music buffs, and the **Aix festival** (*see p511*) is a must for any serious fan, while the **Montpellier** (*see pp494–5*) **and Radio France** event appeals to music lovers throughout the world.

CLUBS

Cool clubs and artful partying most definitely exist outside the capital city, despite what Parisians may believe. There are, of course, bars, clubs and discos throughout the country, and night owls looking to dance are unlikely to be disappointed by the range of options on offer. Small local venues can be great fun, and community events such as open-air parties and festivals are almost always worth a look-in.

In general, nightclubs open late and even in small towns, don't really get going till after midnight. The French are more likely to nurse a few drinks rather than dash around buying multiple

rounds, and shots are almost unheard of over here. It is considered uncouth to drink wine outside of mealtimes, although champagne is always a good thing! The prevailing custom is to club together with friends and buy a bottle of spirits between you. The nightclub will present you with plenty of mixers and – the big benefit of going for this option – you will usually get a table all to yourselves. Tables are generally reserved for those in possession of a full bottle of spirits; a single gin and tonic does not warrant a seat. As extravagant as this may seem, it is generally cheaper than buying individual drinks for four or more people.

In terms of dress code, trainers are almost always forbidden, and the smarter the better could be seen as the rule. In house or hip-hop clubs strict dress codes tend to be relaxed. However, in more traditional *boites de nuit* (night clubs) getting glammed-up is the way to go. Clubs with difficult door policies can often be out-foxed by late diners. If you are worried about getting in, call ahead and make a dinner reservation. Alternatively flaunt designer labels at the doormen.

To experience one of France's most glamorous clubs head to **Les Planches** – an uber-chic spot outside Deauville (*see p255*). Aside from its swimming pool in which starlets frolick at 3am, vintage cars tear around town rounding up party goers with a generally hedonistic atmosphere, Les Planches offers a friendly, fun vibe.

Up in the mountains **Dicks Tea Bar** in Val d'Isère, Meribel and Chamonix (*see p322*) is an upscale chain of chic, jumping Alpine party places.

The Cote d'Azur (*see pp499–531*) is, of course, renowned for its hedonistic nightlife. **Les Caves du Roy** in the Hotel Byblos and **Nikki Beach** in St Tropez (*see p516*) are perfect for the jet set, while **Jimmy'z** in Monaco (*see pp530–1*) is the place to hang out with highrollers.

SPECTATOR SPORTS

Sporting enthusiasts are spoiled for choice in France, with opportunities to indulge in spectator sport throughout the country. If you don't want to wait to see the *grande finale* of the **Tour de France** in Paris, why not see it start in Brittany *(see pp268–85)*. Alternatively, taking in the spectacle from a tiny village en route is a great experience (drivers beware: the Tour takes precedence and the traffic will be stopped for a very, very long time).

If football is more your thing, then head to the Olympic stadia to catch huge teams, such as **Lyon** and **Marseille**, in action.

Surfing fans should make for Biarritz *(see p452)*, Lacanau *(see p424)* and Hossegor *(see p424)* to watch the tournaments there, while ski aficionados might want to watch the European Cup in Les Trois Vallées *(see p322)*.

Golfers flock to the **PGA Open** held outside Paris and to the **LPGA in Evian**, which is the world's second most valuable tournament after the US Open.

Riders will be drawn to one of France's national studs at the **Haras National de Pompadour** for dressage, show-jumping and other competitions throughout the year. Similarly, equine enthusiasts should not miss out on exciting horse racing at the renowned **Chantilly Racecourse**.

The **Le Mans** 24-hour car race is an institution, as is the famous **Grand Prix** in Monaco *(see pp530–1)*. The **French Grand Prix** at Magny Cours, south of Nevers *(see pp339–40)* is also well worth a visit.

No visitor to France in the summer should miss out on one of the greatest spectator sports of them all: head to the village square and take in a game of *petanque* (also known as *boules*).

DIRECTORY

Specialist Holidays and Outdoor Activities

France offers an amazing variety of leisure and sport activities, making it a wonderful choice for a specialist holiday. The French take great pride in the *art de vivre*, which entails not only eating and drinking well, but also pursuing special interests and hobbies. For the best in entertainment and spectator sports, festivals and annual events, see *France through the Year* on pages 36–9. Information on leisure and sporting activities in a particular region is available from the tourist offices listed for each town in this guide. The suggestions below cover the most popular, and also the more unusual, pursuits.

Students honing their culinary skills on a Hostellerie Bérard cookery course

SPECIALIST HOLIDAYS

French government tourist offices *(see p669)* have an extensive range of information on travel companies that offer special interest holidays, and can send you a copy of *The Traveller in France Reference Guide*.

If you want to improve your French, many language courses are available. These are very often combined with other activities, such as cooking or painting. For more information, request *Cours de français pour étudiants étrangers* (French courses for foreign students) from the **French Institute** in London.

Young people can enjoy a French-speaking holiday by working part time on the restoration of historic sites with **Union REMPART** (*Union pour la Réhabilitation et Entretien des Monuments et du Patrimoine Artistique*).

A tantalizing array of gastronomic courses is on offer, to introduce you to classical French cuisine or the cooking of a particular region, for example the **Hostellerie Bérard**. For experienced cooks, more advanced courses are available. Wine-appreciation courses are always popular.

There are numerous art and crafts courses throughout the country, catering to everyone from the absolute beginner to the most accomplished artist.

Nature lovers can enjoy the national parks *(parcs nationaux)* and join organized bird-watching and botanical trips in many areas, including the Camargue, the Cévennes and Corsica.

Le Guide des Jardins en France, published by Actes

Painting the picturesque French landscape

Sud, is a useful reference guide when visiting France's many beautiful gardens.

GOLF

There are golf courses all over France, especially along the north and south coasts and in Aquitaine. Players have to reach a minimum standard and obtain a licence in order to play, so be sure to take your handicap certificate with you. Top courses offer weekend or longer tutored breaks geared to all levels of experience. The **Fédération Française de Golf** will provide a list of all the courses throughout France.

Specialist golf packages, including deluxe hotel accommodation, can be ideal for serious golfers and their non-golfing partners alike. The spectacular Hotel Royal and its renowned **Evian Masters** golf course is a very exclusive, pampering option. The 18-hole course is guaranteed to appeal to fans. There is also a spa and five swimming pools, perfect for lazing. The climbing wall, squash and tennis courts will appeal to more active visitors.

In the south, the **Radisson SAS Biarritz** teams up with the **American Golf School** to offer a team of golf pros who are adept at coaching children, beginners and also experts. Their summer schools and master classes are highly sought after.

The **Hotel des Mougins**, with a lovely address on the "avenue du Golf", is situated near to ten prestigious golf courses, including the Golf Country Club Cannes, the Royal Mougins Golf Club and the Golf d'Opio-Valbonne. The hotel can arrange rounds at the different clubs, and offers packages which include extras, such as lunch in the clubhouse.

The **Golf Hotel Grenoble Charmeil** can organize green fees for three courses, including the Grenoble International course. In Brittany, the **Golf Hotel du Prieure** has a 19th-century manor house interior and an impressive 27-hole golf course, surrounded by the Mesnil forest.

TENNIS

Tennis is a very popular sport in France, and courts for hourly hire can be found in almost every town. It is a good idea to bring your own equipment with you, as hire facilities may not be available.

HIKING

In France, more than 60,000 km (38,000 miles) of long-distance tracks, known as *Grandes Randonnées* (GR), are clearly marked. There are also 80,000 km (50,000 miles) of the shorter *Petites Randonnées* (PR).

The routes vary in difficulty and include long pilgrim routes, alpine crossings and tracks through national parks. Some *Grandes* and *Petites Randonnées* are open for mountain biking as well as horse riding.

Topo Guides, published by **Féderation Française de la Randonnée Pédestre**, describe the tracks, providing details of transport, places for overnight stops and food shops. A series geared specifically toward families is *Promenades et Randonnées*.

CYCLING

For advice on cycling in France, contact the British **CTC** (Cyclists' Touring Club) or the **Fédération Française de Cyclisme**.

Mountain biking - a great way to explore

Escaping into the forest at Fontainebleau (see pp180–1)

Serious cyclists could live their dream by joining up for a Tour de France stage vacation with the **Velo Echappe** *Etape du Tour* team. The company organizes two types of adventure – a fully guided programme or a self-guided option. They handle all the registration forms and paperwork for participants, and on the guided option they will put you up in a hotel a block away from the end of the stage. Preparation for this kind of adventure doesn't just involve getting into training; applications to the tour company must be received by the end March every year to have a chance to ride along with the Tour de France professionals.

At the other end of the scale, people who enjoy a gentle bike ride could opt for a wine cycling tour through the vineyards of France. Freewheeling down the Route des Grands Crus in Burgundy may be more than enough holiday exercise for some. **Duvine Adventures** organize tours that take in famed vineyards such as La Tache, Romanée-Conti and Nuit-St-Georges. The riding includes flat spells and hills, and the rest and relaxation involves excellent lunches.

Local tourist offices provide details about riding facilities in their area. *Gîtes de France (see p549)* offer dormitory accommodation in the vicinity of well-known tracks.

HORSE RIDING

There are many reputable companies that offer riding breaks from one-hour treks to long weekends or holidays of a week or more. The best way to choose is to decide which type of countryside you would prefer to see from the saddle. If the Mont St Michel (*see pp256–61*) and the beaches of Brittany appeal, then **A La Carte Sportive** offer stables with horses trained in trekking, for beginners and intermediates. For more experienced riders, riding a Camargue mount through the countryside of Provence (*see pp510–11*) is a wonderful treat. **Ride in France** organizes rides through beautiful scenery, vineyards and picturesque villages,

Hiking along the Gorges du Verdon in Provence (see pp514–15)

allowing riders to experience the flora and fauna of the area. Horse lovers with a taste for the historical, or those hankering after a little luxury, could do worse than to sign up for a break with the **Cheval et Chateaux** company which organizes horse-riding tours around chateaux in the Loire. Not only do riders get to take in the majesty of the chateaux of the region, the overnight accommodation also comes courtesy of a castle. It makes an ideal way to play lord or lady of the manor while indulging in a passion for trekking.

MOUNTAIN SPORTS

The French mountains, especially the Alps and the Pyrenees, provide a wide range of sporting opportunities. In addition to winter downhill skiing and *ski de fond* (cross-country), the mountains are enjoyed in the summer by rock-climbers and mountaineers, and by those skiers who can't wait for winter and so indulge in some of Europe's best glacier skiing.

Climbers should contact the **Féderation Française de la Montagne et de l'Escalade** for more information on the best climbing locations and other useful tips.

Winter sports fans should join the serious skiers and snowboarders who head to the French hills in droves every season. The mountains here have terrain to satisfy all levels of expertise from toddlers in the kids' club through to death-defying off-piste athletes, adrenalin junkie snowboarders, kite-surfers and middle-of-the-road snow fans who are happiest cruising blue runs and eating in slope-side restaurants.

SKIING

Undoubtedly, France has some of the best ski resorts anywhere in the world. The sheer scale of some of the larger areas can be quite daunting if you're on a week-long trip – especially to those who insist on covering all the trails on the map. The Trois Vallées ski area (*see p322*), for example, is made up of three valleys which include the resorts of Courchevel, Méribel, Val Thorens and Les Ménuires. Added together, they comprise a staggering 600 km (375 miles) worth of pistes.

The Trois Vallées is an excellent example of how French ski resorts differ wildly in style. Super-chic stations such as Courchevel and Meribel draw skiers from around the world, often dressed in cutting-edge ski fashion and using the latest high-tech equipment. In these resorts the hotels – especially those dubbed to be "in", such as the **Hotel Byblos des Neiges** in Courchevel – are expensive, and eating and drinking in the "see and be seen spots" here puts a significant dent in the most generous of holiday budgets. On the other hand, resorts which are considered less glamorous, such as Vals Thorens and Les Menuires, can be enjoyed without designer labels and huge credit card limits.

The main consideration when choosing a resort should be the percentage of terrain to suit your ability. For example, a beginner might be miserable in a resort aimed at experts and offering only a few green runs. Similarly, a confident intermediate looking to improve will be frustrated by a ski area full of easy cruising slopes.

It is also important to think about whether or not it matters to you if the village is picturesque. Die-hard ski fans can overlook ugly concrete architecture in towns such as Flaine, while those looking for the bigger picture would be best off heading to somewhere pretty, such as La Clusaz or Megève (*see p322*).

The proximity of accommodation to piste is also very important; most people find it is worth paying a premium for accommodation near the slopes, rather than having to stagger back in heavy boots carrying your skis after a long day's schussing.

Aside from obvious concerns such as nightlife, children's crèches and the efficiency of lift networks, it can also be useful to look at historic snow reports for the last few years for the time you are planning your trip. The weather can be unpredictable though so be sure to also check the resorts' snow-making capabilities. Armed with these details you should be in a good position to pick the right resort for you but remember, while the Alps get most of the attention, the Pyrenees can offer some seriously good skiing, too.

AERONAUTICAL SPORTS

Learning to fly in France can be relatively inexpensive. Information on the different flying schools is available from the **Fédération Nationale Aéronautique**. There are also plenty of opportunities to learn the exhilarating skills of gliding, paragliding and hang gliding. For more information, contact the **Fédération Française de Vol Libre**.

If piloting a plane is a little too much, you can opt for ballooning instead. France has an illustrious ballooning history, being the birthplace of the Montgolfier brothers who pioneered the art in 1783. **Aeroparis** provide a tethered taste of adventure in Paris with a trip into the air in the **Parc André-Citroën**, but floating unfettered over the countryside can be arranged by several companies around the country. **France Balloons** can organize trips over Fontainebleau (*see pp180–1*) outside Paris or over the Burgundian vineyards. Alternatively, they offer the opportunity to apppreciate the spectacular chateaux of the Loire from a balloon. In Provence **Hot Air Balloon Provence** can float you over the picturesque villages, cornfields and vines of the Lubéron (*see pp506–7*).

WATER SPORTS

Whitewater rafting, kayaking and canoeing all take place on many French rivers, especially in the Massif Central. More information on these sports and the best places to take part can be obtained from the **Fédération Française de Canoë-Kayak**.

The Atlantic coast around Biarritz (*see p452*) offers some of the best surfing and windsurfing in Europe. Excellent windsurfing can also be found in Brittany, with **Wissant** in particular being a big draw. A charming small fishing village, Wissant is considered a decent stop on any windsurf trip.

Surfers who prefer to do it without the sail head to **Hossegor** outside Biarritz (*see* *p452*) for fantastic waves. The surfing here is world-class and perhaps not ideal for beginners, but the after-surf scene is great fun for anyone who is more interested in lying on the beach or paddling at the shore than carving up the water.

Similarly the town of **Lacanau** (*see p424*) plays host to international surf competitions, drawing wave fans from all over the world.

Sailing and waterskiing are also very popular in France. Contact the **Fédération Française de Voile** for more details. Training schools and equipment hire are found at places along the coast and on lakes.

If cruising on a boat is your kind of thing, there are many outlets that can help. One of the swankier options is to take a **Sunsail** bareboat tour around the Côte d'Azur, although this option is only available to those who have reached a certain level of boatmanship. The company also offers a range of skippered tours around the beautiful coastline.

Swimming facilities throughout the country are generally good, although beaches in the South of France can become very crowded in high season (*see pp474–5*).

HUNTING & FISHING

Although hunting is a popular sport in France, a *permis de chasse* is required, for which there is a fee. You will need a copy of your own national hunting licence and to pass an exam in French, which makes it difficult for visitors. There are regional variations on the season, depending on the type of hunting. Since the hunting ban came into force in England, many French hunts have found English hunters a welcome boost to their numbers.

All kinds of fishing, for both fresh and seawater fish, are available, depending on the individual area. Local fishing shops sell the *carte de pêche*, which gives details of regulations.

NATURISM

There are nearly 90 naturism centres in France. These are mostly located in the south and southwest of the country, as well as in Corsica. Information in English can be obtained from French Government Tourist Offices (*see p669*), or from the **Fédération Française de Naturisme**.

PUBLIC EVENTS

To join the French as they enjoy their spare time, look out for local football and rugby matches, cycling races or other sporting events suited to spectators.

Special seasonal markets and local *fêtes* often combine antiques fairs and *boules* tournaments with rock and pop concerts, making an enjoyable day out.

SPA HOLIDAYS

France is renowned for its sea-water based thalasso-therapy spa techniques, with many centres, salons and hotels offering "thalasso" treatments. The seaside towns and resorts seem to be the most logical place to head for ocean-based treatments, and not surprisingly there are some excellent spots dotted around the coastline.

Chic seaside town Deauville (*see p255*) plays host to upscale spa seekers in the **Algotherm Thalassotherapy Spa**. Similarly the **Sofitel Thalassa** in Quiberon (*see p278*) offers top-class water therapy. More water therapy can be found near the springs at Vichy (*see pp358–9*) at the **Sofitel Les Celestins** spa and at the **Royal Parc Evian** (*see p391*).

Wine in France is considered to be almost as important as water, so it is not surprising that a spa specialising in "vinotherapy" or wine therapy has hordes of loyal fans. Head to **Les Sources de Caudalie** spa among the vines near Bordeaux and indulge in a vinosource grape facial and cabernet scrub.

If big name treatments are your thing, you should head to **Le Mas Candille** which

hosts the first Shiseido spa in continental Europe. The products used are as exceptional as one would expect from such a swanky brand, and the techniques are Oriental-based.

Finally, if a thoroughly indulgent approach to a spa session is your idea of holiday heaven, then splurge at the new **Four Seasons Terre Blanche** in Provence. The half-day retreat of total indulgence involves a salt and oil scrub, an aromatherapy massage, an acupressure facial and an oriental head massage. If you want to go *à la carte*, you can choose from a wide range of delights, such as an eye-lifting facial, a body-toning massage or an Oshadi clay wrap.

If you can't escape from the city, the **Caudalie** spa at the Hotel Meurice and the **Four Seasons** spa at the George V can provide the ultimate escape and spa break right in the centre of Paris.

YOGA

The beautiful countryside in France provides the perfect backdrop for a restorative yoga retreat holiday. **La Buissiere** in the Lot valley (*see p366*) offers relaxing and fun hatha yoga holidays in a holistic setting. Hiking, massage and relaxing by the pool all form part of the philosophy here so it's the ideal place for a relaxed and wholesome week.

Another excellent option is a break at the **Domaine de la Grausse** in the foothills of the Pyrenees, where walking and visiting local waterfalls, chateaux, medieval villages and even taking in some cave paintings are all on the agenda. Those with any energy left over can take advantage of options to go mountain biking, riding, playing golf and fishing.

Beginners and experienced yoga fans alike are welcome at the **Durga Sadhini Centre**, which specializes in hatha and also astanga yoga. Both individual retreats and group holidays can be arranged at the centre.

GOURMET

For gourmets looking to learn how to recreate some of the stunning meals enjoyed in French restaurants, or wine buffs seeking to increase their knowledge and cellar at the same time, there are many excellent options. The sheer number of cookery classes available throughout the country may seem over-whelming, so the first step in choosing an activity holiday of this kind is to consider your initial skill level and what you wish to achieve from the break. From die-hard kitchen disasters to budding restaurateurs, there is a gourmet break in France which will suit.

Two options for beginner chefs are the "cookery holiday" from **Cook in France** which emphasizes fun rather than serious hard work in the kitchen and Rosa Jackson's cooking school, **Les Petits Farcis**, in Nice (*see pp526–7*) where she guides food-lovers around the town's glorious fresh produce stalls explaining how to spot the best melon, or how to cook the intimidating artichoke. The Cook in France team offers many specialized

courses (such as matching wine to food) alongside their standard culinary classes while Rosa Jackson's cooking school offers the opportunity to rustle up a menu depending on what looks great in the market that particular day.

Budding culinary stars might want to head to Provence to learn from the master's pupils with the lessons at **La Bastide de Moustiers**, Alain Ducasse's provencal inn in Moustiers-Sainte-Marie (*see pp514–15*). The lessons take place in the hotel's kitchen with Michelin-starred chef Vincent Maillard and his team, all of whom are former Ducasse pupils. The lessons focus on Provençal cooking with an emphasis on local produce from the garden and village markets.

Oenophiles, on the other hand, might like to join with the **French Wine Explorers** who offer tours around vineyards. Alternatively, arranging wine classes via the French tourist office can be an excellent idea. **Wine Travel Guides** has an informative website for independent travellers, listing vineyards that are recommended by regional wine experts.

ARTS AND CRAFTS

France is a top choice for creative people looking to get away from it all and to express themselves in beautiful surroundings. Whether your preferred method of expression is scribbling in a notebook by yourself on the banks of a river, or perfecting your pastel technique in an art master class, there is an outlet for you somewhere in France.

Mas Saurine offers residential and non-residential painting holidays in the Pyrenees, 30 minutes from Perpignan. Small group classes, geared to different levels of ability, are taught in an old stone barn by exhibiting artists.

Courses in crafts, such as glass painting and scrapbook making, are on offer at **La Croix Rompue**, a delightful farmhouse in Normandy. The classes are small and the setting very relaxing.

Those with a passion for seeing life through a lens are well catered for with photography courses in **Les Vignes** in Noailles, just an hour's drive from Toulouse. Here, photography courses suitable for all ages and abilities are offered.

DIRECTORY

SPECIALIST HOLIDAYS

French Institute
17 Queensberry Place,
London SW7 2DT
United Kingdom
Tel 020 7073 1350.
www.institut-
français.org.uk

Union REMPART
1 rue des Guillemites,
75004 Paris.
Tel 01 42 71 96 55.
www.rempart.com

GOLF

Radisson SAS Biarritz and Ameri-can Golf School
1 Carrefour Hélianthe
64200 Biarritz
Tel 05 59 01 13 13 www.
biarritz.radissonsas.com

Fédération Française de Golf
68 rue Anatole France,
92300 Levallois Perret.
Tel 01 41 49 77 00.
www.ffgolf.org

Golf Hotel Grenoble Charmeil
38210 Saint Quentin sur Isère
Tel 04 76 93 67 28 www.
golfhotelgrenoble.com

Golf Hotel du Prieure
Domaine de St-Yvieux
35540 Le Tronchet
Tel 02 99 58 96 69
www.saintmalogolf.com

Hotel des Mougins
205 av du Golf 06250
Mougins
Tel 04 92 92 17 07
www.hotel-de-
mougins.com

Hotel Royal and Evian Masters
South Shore Lake Geneva
74500 Evian
Tel 04 50 26 85 00
www.evianroyalresort.
com

HIKING

Fédération Française de Randonnée Pédestre
14 rue Riquet, 75019 Paris.
Tel 01 44 89 93 93.
www.ffrandonnee.fr

CYCLING

CTC
Parklands, Railton Rd,
Guildford, Surrey GU2
9JX United Kingdom.
Tel 0870 873 0060.
www.ctc.org.uk

Duvine Adventures
www.duvine.com

Fédération Française de Cyclisme
5 rue de Rome, 93561
Rosny-sous-Bois.
Tel 01 49 35 69 00.
www.ffc.fr

Velo Echappe
www.veloechappe.
com

HORSE RIDING

A La Carte Sportive
www.carte-sportive.com
Tel 02 33 48 52 36

Cheval et Châteaux
www.cheval-et-
chateaux.com

Ride in France
www.rideinfrance.com

DIRECTORY

MOUNTAIN SPORTS

Fédération Française de la Montagne et de l'Escalade
8–10 quai de la Marne, 75019 Paris.
Tel 01 40 18 75 50.
www.ffme.fr

SKIING

For information on the different resorts, visit the following websites:

www.Flaine.com
www.laclusaz.com
www.megeve.com
www.les3vallees.com
www.courcheval.com
www.meribel.net
www.valthorens.com
www.lesmenuires.com

Hotel Byblos des Neiges
B.P. 98
73122 Courchevel
Tel 04 79 00 98 00
www.byblos.com

AERONAUTICAL SPORTS

Aeroparis
Parc André-Citroën
75015 Paris
Tel 01 44 26 20 00
www.aeroparis.com

France Balloons
Tel 08 10 60 01 53
www.franceballoons.com

Fédération Française de Vol Libre
4 rue de Suisse,
06000 Nice.
Tel 04 97 03 82 82.
www.ffvl.fr

Fédération Nationale Aéronautique
155 av Wagram,
75017 Paris.
Tel 01 44 29 92 00.
www.fna.asso.fr

Hot Air Balloon Provence
www.montgolfiere-provence.com

WATER SPORTS

Fédération Française de Canoë-Kayak
87 quai de la Marne,
94340 Joinville-le-Pont.
Tel 01 45 11 08 50.
www.ffck.org

Fédération Française de Voile
17 rue Henri Bocquillon,
75015 Paris.
Tel 01 40 60 37 00.
www.ffvoile.org

Hossegor Tourist Office
Pl des Halles – B.P. 6
40150 Hossegor.
Tel 05 58 41 79 00
www.hossegor.fr

Lacanau Tourist Office
Pl de l'Europe
33680 Lacanau.
Tel 05 56 03 21 01
www.lacanau.com

Sunsail
www.sunsail.com

Wissant Tourist Office
Pl de la Mairie
62179 Wissant.
Tel 03 21 82 48 00
www.ville-wissant.fr

NATURISM

Fédération Française de Naturisme
www.ffn-naturisme.com

SPA HOLIDAYS

Algotherm
10 rue Alexander Fleming
14200 Herouville-Saint-Clair
Tel 02 31 06 16 26
www.algotherm.fr

Four Seasons Provence
Domaine de Terre Blanche
83440 Tourrettes
Var
Tel 04 94 39 90 00
www.fourseasons.com

Hotel Four Seasons George V
31 av George V 75008
Paris
Tel 01 49 52 70 00
www.fourseasons.com

Hotel Meurice
228 rue de Rivoli
75001 Paris
Tel 01 44 58 10 10
www.meuricehotel.com

Le Mas Candille
Bd Clément Rebuffel
06250
Tel 04 92 28 43 43
www.lemascandille.com

Royal Parc Evian
Rive Sud du Lac de Génève
74501 Evian-les-Bains
Tel 04 50 26 85 00
www.evianroyalresort.com

Sofitel Les Celestins Vichy
111 bd des Etats-Unis
03200 Vichy
Tel 04 70 30 82 00
www.sofitel.com

Sofitel Thalassa Quiberon
Pointe de Goulvars
BP 10802 Quiberon Cedex
56178 Quiberon
Tel 02 97 50 20 00
www.sofitel.com

Les Sources de Caudalie
Chemin de Smith Haut Lafitte
33650 Bordeaux–Martillac
Tel 05 57 83 83 83
www.sources–caudalie.com

YOGA

La Buissière Yoga Retreat Centre
46700 Duravel
Tel 05 65 36 43 51
www.yogafrance.com

Domaine de la Grausse
09420 Clermont la Grausse, Ariège
Tel 05 61 66 30 53
www.yoga-in-france.com

Durga Sadhini Centre
46800 St Matre
Lot
Tel 05 65 21 76 20
www.nawajyoti.com

GOURMET

La Bastide de Moustiers
Chemin de Quinson
04360 Moustiers-Sainte-Marie
Tel 04 92 70 47 47
www.bastide-moustiers.com

Cook in France
Tel 05 53 30 24 05
www.cookinfrance.com

French Wine Explorers
www.wine-tours-france.com

Hostellerie Bérard
83740 La Cadière d'Azur
Tel 04 94 90 11 43
www.hotel-berard.com

Les Petits Farcis
7 rue du Jésus
06300 Nice
Tel 06 81 67 41 22
www.petitsfarcis.com

Wine Travel Guides
www.winetravelguides.com

ARTS AND CRAFTS

La Croix Rompue
Besneville Briquebec
Tel 02 33 93 58 74

Mas Saurine
Comi de l'Estrada 66320
Joch
Tel 04 68 05 85 66
www.mas-saurine.net

Les Vignes
Le Bourg
81170 Noailles
Tel 05 63 40 59 22
www.photohols.com

SURVIVAL
GUIDE

PRACTICAL INFORMATION

France is justifiably proud of its many attractions, for which it has excellent tourist information facilities. Both in France and abroad, French Government Tourist Offices are an invaluable source of reference for practical aspects of your stay. Most towns and large villages in France have a tourist information office; the rele-

Tourist information logo

vant address and telephone number is provided for each town and area listed in this guide. Domestic tourism in France creates peak holiday migration periods, especially between 14 July and 31 August. Consequently, the hotel and restaurant trades are seasonal. A little forward planning will allow you to avoid the pitfalls of seasonal closure.

MANNERS

The French have rituals of politeness which are easy to pick up. In shops be ready to say *Bonjour Monsieur/Madame* before asking for what you want, then *merci* when you receive your change, and *Merci, au revoir Monsieur/Madame* when you get your purchases and leave.

Shake hands when introduced to someone, or any time when a hand is proffered. In small communities, locals may greet you with a *Bonjour Monsieur/Madame* in the street even if they have never seen you before. For other useful expressions, refer to the phrase book *(pp719–20)*.

VISAS

Currently there are no visa requirements for EU nationals or visitors from the United States, Canada, Australia or New Zealand who plan to stay in France for under three months. For trips over three months, visas should be obtained prior to departure from your local French consulate. Visitors from most other countries require a tourist visa. Anyone planning to study or work in France should apply to their local French consulate several months in advance about visa requirements.

TAX-FREE GOODS AND CUSTOMS INFORMATION

Visitors resident outside the EU can reclaim the sales tax TVA, or VAT, on French goods if more than 175€ is spent in one shop in one day. Get a *détaxe* receipt and take the

goods (unopened) out of the country within three months. The form should be presented to customs when leaving the country. The reimbursement will be sent on to you.

Exceptions for *détaxe* rebate are food and drink, medicines, tobacco, cars and motorbikes, though tax can be reimbursed for bicycles. More information and advice is available from the **Centre de Renseignements des Douanes.**

Sign for tourist office in smaller towns and villages

TOURIST INFORMATION

All major cities and large towns have *offices de tourisme*. Small towns and even villages have *syndicats d'initiative*. Both can provide town plans, advice on accommodation, and information on regional recreational and cultural activities.

You can also get information before you leave for France from **French Government Tourist Offices (FGTO)** (or Maisons de la France as they are officially known), or by

phoning or writing to local tourist offices (see headings for each town in this guide) or to the appropriate Regional Tourist Board *(Comité Régional de Tourisme)* – ask the FGTO for the address.

ADMISSION CHARGES

Most museums and monuments in France charge an entrance fee, usually from 2€ to 7.5€. This may be reduced or waived on Sundays. Discounts are usually available to students, under 7s, under 18s, under 26s (carrying valid identification) and over 60s.

OPENING HOURS

This guide lists which days of the week sights are open. Generally, hours are from 10am–noon and 2–5pm with one late evening per week. Most sights close on major public holidays. National museums and sights are normally closed on Tuesdays, with a few exceptions which close on Mondays. Municipal museums normally close on Mondays. Churches open every day but shut at lunchtime. Opening hours for private museums may not comply with standard opening times.

See page 652 for details on opening hours for shops; page 672 for banks; and pages 596–7 for restaurants.

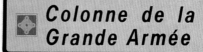

Sign to monument of cultural importance

◁ Menton, Côte d'Azur with backdrop of the Alps

Visitors taking the weight off weary feet

FACILITIES FOR THE DISABLED

When parking, the international orange card scheme applies. In general, however, France is not yet very wheelchair friendly. While most larger museums and major sites, as well as restaurants, now provide at least partial wheelchair access, the very nature of many of the chateaux and fortified monuments implies inaccessibility. Various organisations (with websites) have more or less complete information: the **GIHP** (Groupement pour l'Insertion des Personnes Handicapées Physiques), and the **Association des Paralysés de France,** whose travel branch, APF Evasion, runs specialist holidays, as do Voyages Asah (see p549). The **CIDJ** (Centre d'Information et de Documentation Jeunesse) has information for young disabled travellers.

FRENCH TIME

France is one hour ahead of Greenwich Mean Time (GMT) in both winter and summer. The French use the 24-hour clock eg 7pm = 19:00.

Queuing for the Eiffel Tower

STUDENT INFORMATION

Students with valid identity cards (the ISIC or International Student Identity Card) benefit from many discounts. **CIDJ** offices provide a comprehensive service for students.

ELECTRICAL ADAPTORS

The voltage in France is 220 volts. Plugs have two round pins, or three round pins for applications which need to be earthed. Some hotels offer built-in adaptors for shavers only.

Standard French two-pin plug for electrical appliances

CONVERSION CHART

Imperial to metric
1 inch = 2.54 centimetres
1 foot = 30 centimetres
1 mile = 1.6 kilometres
1 ounce = 28 grams
1 pound = 454 grams
1 pint = 0.6 litre
1 gallon = 4.6 litres

Metric to imperial
1 millimetre = 0.04 inch
1 centimetre = 0.4 inch
1 metre = 3 feet 3 inches
1 kilometre = 0.6 mile
1 gram = 0.04 ounce
1 kilogram = 2.2 pounds
1 litre = 1.8 pints

DIRECTORY

EMBASSIES

Australia
4 rue Jean Rey, 75015 Paris.
Map 6 D3. **Tel** 01 40 59 33 00.
www.austgov.fr

United Kingdom
35 rue du Faubourg St-Honoré
Paris 75008. **Map** 3 C5.
Tel 01 44 51 31 00.
www.amb-grandebretagne.fr
Consular offices: Bordeaux, Lille,
Lyon, Marseille.

United States
2 av Gabriel, 75008 Paris.
Map 3 A5. **Tel** 01 43 12 22 22.
www.amb-usa.fr.

FRENCH GOVERNMENT TOURIST OFFICES

Australia
French Tourist Bureau, Level 13,
25 Bligh St, Sydney NSW 2000.
Tel (2) 9231 52 44.

United States
French Government Tourist
Office, 444 Madison Avenue,
New York, NY 10022.
Tel (1) 514 288 1904.

UK
French Government Tourist Office
(Maison de la France),
178 Piccadilly, London W1V 0AL.
Tel 0906 8244 123 within UK.
www.franceguide.com

USEFUL ADDRESSES

Centre de Renseignements des Douanes
84 rue d'Hauteville, 75010 Paris.
Map 14 F3. **Tel** 08 20 02 44 44.
Fax 01 53 24 68 30.
◻ 9am–5pm Mon–Fri.
www.douane.gouv.fr

CIDJ www.cidj.com
101 quai Branly, 75015 Paris.
Map 6 E2. **Tel** 08 25 09 06 30.
◻ 10am–6pm Mon, Wed, Fri, 1–
6pm Thu, 9:30–1pm Sat.

GIHP
10 rue Georges de Porto-Riche,
75014 Paris. **Tel** 01 43 95 66 36.
www.gihpnational.org

Paris Convention and Visitors Bureau Headquarters
25 rue des Pyramides, 75001 Paris.
Map 8 E1. **Tel** 08 92 68 30 00.
◻ 10am–7pm Mon–Sat, 11am–
7pm Sun & public hols. ● 1
May, 1 Nov. **www**.parisinfo.com

Personal Security and Health

On the whole, France is a safe place for visitors: take normal precautions, such as sensible care of your possessions at all times, and avoid unfamiliar or unfrequented residential urban areas after dark. If you fall ill during your stay, pharmacies generally offer good advice. Consulates and consular departments at your embassy are a good source of help and advice in an emergency *(see p669)*. For serious medical problems, this section gives the numbers of the emergency services.

French pharmacy sign

PERSONAL SECURITY

Violent crime is not a major problem in France. Take the usual precautions you would at home. Avoid risky city neighbourhoods. If you are involved in an argument or car accident avoid confrontation. In potentially difficult situations you should stay calm and speak French if you can; this may defuse the situation.

LEGAL ASSISTANCE

Nearly all travel insurance policies cover legal costs up to a certain level, as do comprehensive motor policies, in the event of any legal action or advice being needed, for example after an accident. If you do not have this cover, telephone your nearest consulate or, as a last resort, telephone the local *Ordre des Avocats* (lawyers' association) for the name of a good local lawyer.

INTERPRETERS

Translation and interpretation is offered by professional translators. Contact the **Société Française des Traducteurs** *(see below)*.

PERSONAL PROPERTY

Make sure you insure your possessions before arrival. Beware of pickpockets, especially on the Paris metro during the busy rush hour (particularly just as the carriage doors are closing). Keep all valuables securely concealed and, if carrying a handbag or case, never let it out of your sight. You should also keep an especially close eye on your mobile phone and camera. Only take as much cash as you think you will need. Traveller's cheques are the safest method of carrying large sums of money.

Telephone or visit the police to report crimes which take place in towns, missing persons or stolen property, robbery or assault. The *commissariat de police* is the headquarters. In small towns and villages, go to the *mairie* (town hall), which will only be open during office hours. If your passport is lost or stolen, call your consulate *(see p669)*.

If you are involved in a traffic accident outside a town you may be asked to accompany the other driver to the nearest *gendarmerie*. The *gendarmerie nationale* is a military organization which deals with all crimes outside urban areas. Making a statement (a *PV* or *procès-verbal*) can be a lengthy process. Take

your identity papers (and your vehicle papers, if relevant) with you when you go to make a statement.

MEDICAL TREATMENT

All European Union nationals are entitled to French social security coverage. However, treatment must be paid for and hospital rates vary widely. Reimbursements may be obtained if you have acquired a European Health Insurance Card before you travel, but the process for claims can be long and complicated.

All travellers should consider purchasing travel insurance. Non-EU nationals are obliged to carry medical insurance, taken out before they arrive.

In the case of a medical emergency call **SAMU** (*Service d'Aide Médicale Urgence*). However, it is often faster to call **Sapeurs Pompiers** (the fire service), who offer a first aid and ambulance service. This is particularly true in rural areas where the local fire-station is likely to be much

Gendarme

Fireman

DIRECTORY

EMERGENCY NUMBERS

Ambulance (SAMU)

Tel 15 or 18 (Sapeurs Pompiers).

Fire (Sapeurs Pompiers)

Tel 18 or 112.

Police and Gendarmerie

Tel 17.

INTERPRETERS

Société Française des Traducteurs

www.sft.fr

closer than the ambulance service based in town. The paramedics are called *secouristes*.

Casualty departments (*service des urgences*) in public hospitals can deal with most medical problems. Your consulate should be able to recommend an English-speaking doctor in the area.

PHARMACIES

In France, pharmacists can diagnose health problems and suggest appropriate treatments. They are also trained to identify mushrooms: take any you are unsure about to them to eliminate danger.

Pharmacies have a green cross outside. A card in the window will give details of the nearest *pharmacie de garde* for Sunday openings and night openings.

Police car

Fire engine

Ambulance

Fire hazard poster

IN THE OPEN AIR

Forest fires are a major risk in many parts of France. High winds can mean fires spread rapidly in winter as well as summer. Keep well away from an area where there is a fire, as its direction can change quickly. Make sure you do not start a fire with campfires or a cigarette butt.

When walking in the mountains or sailing, notify your route to the relevant authority and observe local regulations posted in the area.

During the hunting season (Sep–Feb and especially Sundays) dress in visible colours when out walking. Avoid areas where hunters are staked out in hides or beating through the undergrowth *(see p661)*.

PUBLIC TOILETS IN FRANCE

Modern pay toilets are now found in many towns. Do not let children under ten use the toilets on their own as the automatic cleaning function can be dangerous. The best policy is to use toilets in cafés or restaurants where you are a customer, or go to a department store. It is customary to leave a tip in a basket (the baskets are clearly visible) for the lavatory attendant. Toilet facilities are provided on the *autoroute* at drive-in rest areas every 20 km (12 miles), as well as at the major service areas.

1 Put the amount indicated in the slot.

2 Press the button to open sliding door. **3** The light indicates vacant or engaged.

Banking and Local Currency

You may bring any amount of currency into France, but anything over 7,500€ (cash and cheques) must be declared on arrival. The same applies when you leave. Traveller's cheques are the safest way to carry money abroad, but credit cards, which can be used to withdraw local currency, are by far the most convenient. Bureaux de change are located at airports, large railway stations, and in some hotels and shops, but banks usually offer the best rates of exchange.

Credit card cash dispenser

USING BANKS

Most French banks have a bureau de change, but rates can vary. Most banks also now have ATMs (automatic teller machines) outside (or in an indoor area open 24 hr/day), which accept credit cards in the **Visa/Carte Bleue** or **Mastercard** groups and debit cards (Switch, Maestro, Cirrus), enabling you to withdraw money in local currency directly from your own bank account. Bear in mind that ATMs may run out of notes before the end of the weekend.

If there is no ATM, you can withdraw up to 300€ per day on Visa at the foreign counter of a bank showing the Visa sign. The bank may need to obtain telephone authorization for such withdrawals first.

BANKING HOURS

As a general rule, banks in northern France are open Mon–Fri approximately 9am–4:30 or 5:15pm. However, some are open only till noon, and many will close at noon on the working day before a holiday. In southern France, banks are normally open Tue–Sat, approximately 8am–12 noon and from 1:30–4:30pm. Around a public holiday, they are usually closed from Friday noon to Tuesday morning.

BUREAUX DE CHANGE

Outside Paris, independent bureaux de change are rare except in major railway stations and areas with a high density of tourists. Privately owned bureaux de change can have variable rates: check commission and minimum charges first.

CARDS AND CHEQUES

Travellers' cheques can be obtained from **American Express, Travelex** or your bank. If you know that you will spend most of them, it is best to have them issued in Euros. American Express cheques are widely accepted in France. If cheques are exchanged at an Amex office no commission is charged. In the case of theft, cheques are replaced at once.

Because of the high commissions charged, many French businesses do not accept the American Express credit card. The most commonly used credit card is Carte Bleue/Visa. Eurocard/Mastercard is also widely accepted.

Credit cards issued in France are now "smart cards", which means they have a *puce* (a microchip capable of storing data instead of a magnetic strip on the back). Many retailers have machines designed to read both smart cards and magnetic strips. You will usually be asked to tap in your PIN code *(code confidentiel)* and press the green key *(validez)* on a small keypad by the cash desk. Some non-French cards cannot be read in the smart card slot. Persuade the cashier to swipe the card through the magnetic reader *(bande magnétique)*.

Machine to read credit cards

CONVERSION CHART

The following chart is a rough guide to equivalent currency values, rounded up or down for ease of use.

Euros	Francs
1	6.5
5	33
10	65
20	130
25	165
50	330
75	495
100	650
150	980

DIRECTORY

FOREIGN BANKS

American Express
11 rue Scribe, 75009 Paris.
Map 4 D5.
Tel 01 47 14 50 00.

Barclays
24 bis av de l'Opéra, 75001 Paris.
Map 4 E5.
Tel 01 44 86 00 00.

HSBC
22 pl de la Madeleine, 75008 Paris.
Map 3 C5.
Tel 01 44 71 10 00.

LOST CARDS AND TRAVELLER'S CHEQUES

American Express
Tel 01 47 77 72 00 (cards).
Tel 08 00 90 86 00 (cheques).

Mastercard
Tel 0800 90 13 87.

Travelex/Mastercard Services
Tel 0800 908 330 (toll free).

Visa/Carte Bleue
Tel 08 92 70 57 05.

THE EURO

The Euro (€), the single European currency, is now operational in 13 of the 27 member states of the EU. Austria, Belgium, Finland, France, Germany, Greece, Ireland, Italy, Luxembourg, Netherlands, Portugal, Slovenia and Spain all chose to join the new currency; other member states including Denmark, the UK and Sweden chose to stay out for now. France's Overseas Departments (Réunion etc) also all now use the euro. Euro notes are identical throughout all 13 countries, bearing architectural drawings of fictitious monuments. The coins, however, have one side identical (the value side), and one side unique to each country. Both notes and coins are valid and interchangeable within each of the 13 countries.

Bank Notes
Euro bank notes have seven denominations. The 5€ note (grey in colour) is the smallest, followed by the 10€ note (pink), 20€ note (blue), 50€ note (orange), 100€ note (green), 200€ note (yellow) and 500€ note (purple). All notes show the stars of the European Union.

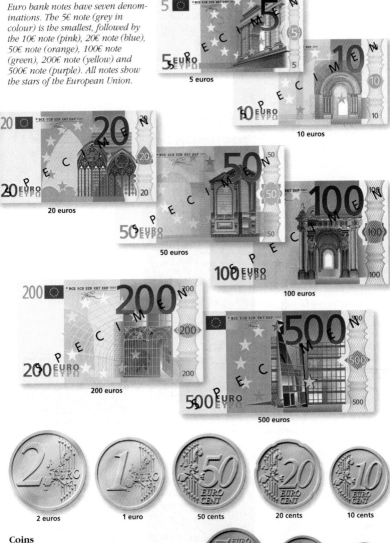

5 euros

10 euros

20 euros

50 euros

100 euros

200 euros

500 euros

2 euros   1 euro   50 cents   20 cents   10 cents

Coins
The euro has eight coin denominations: 1 euro and 2 euros; 50 cents, 20 cents, 10 cents, 5 cents, 2 cents and 1 cent. The 2- and 1-euro coins are both silver and gold in colour. The 50-, 20- and 10-cent coins are gold. The 5-, 2- and 1-cent coins are bronze.

5 cents   2 cents   1 cent

Communications

French telecommunications are sophisticated and efficient. They are run by France Télécom; the postal service is *La Poste*. Public telephones are located in most public places. To use them, you usually need a phonecard *(télécarte)*.

Post offices *(bureaux des postes)* are identified by the blue-on-yellow La Poste sign. La Poste used to be called the PTT, so road signs often still indicate PTT.

Foreign language newspapers are available in most large towns. Some TV channels and radio stations broadcast foreign-language programmes.

Sign for public telephone

TELEPHONING IN FRANCE

To use a payphone *(cabine téléphonique)*, you need a phone card *(télécarte)*. Sold in tabacs, post offices and some newsagents, these are available in 50 or 120 telephone units, and are simple to use. Remember to buy a new card *before* the old one runs out! For local calls, a unit lasts up to 6 minutes. Many phones now also accept credit cards (with a PIN number).

Few payphones take coins. Cheap rates operate from 7pm to 8am Monday to Friday, as well as all day Saturday and Sunday and on public holidays. In cafés, payphones are token-operated and are reserved for the use of patrons. Some post offices have telephone booths *(cabines)* where you can telephone first and pay after the call. This is cheaper than making long-distance calls from hotels, which can add hefty surcharges.

The Minitel electronic directory, still very popular despite the internet, can also be used free in post offices.

Home Direct calling service, or *pays directe*, lets you book the call through an operator in your country, and pay by credit card or by reversing the charges. Sometimes you can also call a third country.

All French telephone numbers have ten digits. The first two digits indicate the region: 01 indicates Paris and the Ile de France; 02, the northwest; 03, the northeast; 04, the southeast (including Corsica); and 05, the southwest. Do not dial the initial zero when phoning from abroad.

USING A PHONECARD TELEPHONE

1 Lift receiver and wait for a dialling tone.

2 Insert the télécarte, arrow side up, in the direction that the arrow is pointing.

3 The display will show how many units are stored on the card and then tell you to dial.

4 Key in the number and wait to be connected.

5 If you want to make another call, do not replace the receiver; simply press the green follow-on call button.

6 When you have finished the call, replace the receiver. The card will emerge from the slot. Remove it.

7 If card runs out in mid-call, it will re-emerge; remove it and insert another.

French phonecard

HOW TO KEY INTO MINITEL

Minitel provides a variety of services through a screen and keyboard connected to the telephone line. To use Minitel, press the telephone symbol and enter the Minitel number and code. For directory information, press the telephone symbol and key in 3611. When beeping starts, press Connexion/Fin. Specify the service or name of supplier required. Enter town or area. Press Envoi to search. To disconnect, press Veille or Connexion/Fin. Charges vary and are displayed on the screen.

TV AND RADIO

All TV channels in France show commercials. The major nationwide TV channels are *TF1* and *France 2*, both offering a lightweight mass-audience mix of soaps, game shows, discussion and movies. *France 3*, with wildlife, documentaries, debate, arts programmes and classic films, is regional television, locally made and presented in every part of France, though national and international issues are also covered. *France 5* and the Franco-German high-culture *ARTE*, specialising in arts, classical music and films, share a channel (and show relatively few commercials). *M6* shows magazine programmes on topical issues, money, etc, as well as devoting a lot of time to pop music. *Canal Plus* (or *Canal +*) is the popular "extra channel" available to subscribers only, though a few programmes are shown uncoded. Most hotels subscribe, allowing guests to enjoy the channel's diverse mix of music, sport exclusives, family programmes screened early in the day, and adult movies (including porn) in the late evening.

Other popular subscription cable and satellite channels in France (collectively known as *TPS*, or *télévision par satellite*) include English-language *MTV, CNN, Sky* and *BBC World*, as well as several in French and other languages. English-language films on French television are generally subtitled at first (look out for the letters "*VO*" – *Version Originale*); dubbed versions appear later ("*VF*" – *Version Française*).

UK radio stations can be picked up in France, including *Radio 4* during the day (648 AM or 198 long wave). On the same wavelength, *BBC World Service* broadcasts through the night, with news in English every hour. *Voice of America* can be found at 90.5, 98.8 and 102.4 FM. *Radio France International* (738 AM) gives daily news in English from 3–4pm. French radio stations favour phone-ins and French pop music, or, on more highbrow stations, lengthy intellectual discussions – for fluent French speakers.

MOBILE PHONES

Most new mobile phones brought from another European or Mediterranean country can be used in France exactly as at home. However, US-based mobiles need to be "triple band" to be used in France. Mobile phones are also readily available for hire in France if required. Remember that making and receiving international mobile calls can be very expensive.

INTERNET ACCESS

After a slow start, the number of French language sites grew rapidly and the Internet is now widely accessible everywhere in France, including in many hotels and in Internet cafés. The French modem socket is incompatible with US and UK plugs. Although adaptors are available, it is cheaper to buy a French modem lead.

Foreign newspapers sold in France

NEWSPAPERS AND MAGAZINES

Buy your newspapers and magazines at a newsagent (*maison de la presse*) or a news-stand (*kiosque*). Every region of France is served by major local newspapers, which are much more popular than Paris-based national ones. The main national dailies are – from right to left on the political spectrum – weighty, intelligent *Le Figaro*, tabloid *France Soir*, quirky *Le Monde* (comes out in the afternoon), *Libération* on the intellectual left and the Communist paper *L'Humanité*.

In resorts and large cities, many British newspapers are available on the day of publication. Some are European editions, like *Financial Times Europe* and *The Guardian Europe*. Other papers may arrive a day or two late, as do Sunday newspapers. English-language international papers and magazines include *The Weekly Telegraph, Guardian International, USA Today, The Economist, Newsweek* and *The International Herald Tribune*.

USEFUL FRENCH DIALLING CODES

- **Directory enquiries** dial 118 712.
- **International directory enquiries**, for all countries, dial 32 12.
- **International telegrams** dial 0800 33 44 11. For telegrams in France, dial 36 55.
- **Home Direct** (reverse charge), dial 0800 99, then the country code (preceded by 00).
- To ring **France** dial: from the UK and US: 00 33; from Australia: 00 11 33. Omit the first 0 of the French area code.
- To make direct international calls, dial 00, wait for the tone, then dial the country code, area code (omit the initial zero) and the number.
- The middle pages of the telephone directory give the cost of calls per minute for each country and list their country codes, Home direct codes etc.
- The country codes for the following are: **Australia**: 61; **Canada and USA**: 1; **Eire**: 353; **New Zealand**: 64; **UK**: 44.
- **Low-rate period** (for most places): 7pm–8am Mon–Fri, all day Sat, Sun and public hols. **In the case of emergencies**, dial 17.

LA POSTE

Road sign giving directions to the post office

USING LA POSTE

The postal service in France is fast and usually reliable, although the service has declined over the last few years. However, it is not cheap, especially when sending a parcel abroad, as all sea-mail services have now been discontinued.

At La Poste, postage stamps *(timbres)* are sold singly or in carnets of seven or ten. Common postage stamps are also sold at tabacs. You can also buy phonecards *(télécartes)*, cash or send international money orders *(mandats)*, and call abroad.

Post offices also provide, for a small collection fee, a mail holding service *(poste restante)* so you can receive mail care of post offices in France. As an address, the sender should write the recipient's surname in block capitals before the first name, followed by "Poste Restante", then the postcode and name of the town it is to be sent to. Unless specified otherwise, mail will go to that town's main post office. When sending a letter poste restante it is wise to underline the surname, as French officials may otherwise assume the first name is the family name.

Post offices usually open from 9am–5pm Mon–Fri, often with a break for lunch, and 9am–noon on Saturdays. Post

offices in large towns and all cities can get extremely busy (queues are long and tempers are short) when they first open in the mornings, so do try to drop in at some other time of the day.

SENDING A LETTER

Letters are posted in yellow mail boxes which often have separate slots for the town you are in, the *département* and other destinations *(autres destinations)*.

There are eight different price zones for international mail. EU countries are the cheapest, Australasia the most expensive. You can also buy aerograms, which cost the same for all countries.

A postman *(un facteur)*

POSTCODES

All French addresses have five-digit postcodes. The first two digits represent the *département (see opposite)*. If they are followed by 000, this indicates the main town in that *département*, so, for example, Bordeaux is 33000. France's largest cities, Paris, Lyon and Marseille, are divided into *arrondissements*, which are shown in the last two digits of the postcode.

A distinctive yellow French mail box

Carnet of ten stamps

The town hall in Compiègne

LOCAL GOVERNMENT IN FRANCE

A complex jigsaw, France's local government operates in a three-tier system – *région*, *département* and *commune*. The country used to comprise separate semi-autonomous provinces or duchies, like Provence and the smaller Anjou. During the Revolution, these were replaced by a standard-sized network of 96 *départements*. These are administrative units mostly named after rivers, for example Haute-Loire, each ruled by a *préfet* appointed in Paris.

The system had its strengths, but was too state-controlled for a modern democracy. Now some of the prefect's power has gone to the *département*'s elected council. For some functions the *départements* have been grouped into 22 *régions*, each with an elected assembly. Several, like Brittany and Alsace, roughly correspond to the old provinces; others are hybrids, like Centre and Rhône-Alpes.

At a lower level, France remains split up into around 35,000 *communes* (parishes or boroughs), ranging from big cities like Paris or Lyon to tiny villages. Each *commune* has its elected mayor, a figure of great local influence, ruling from the *mairie* (town hall). This system is cumbersome, yet village communes refuse to merge, so great is the pull of local pride.

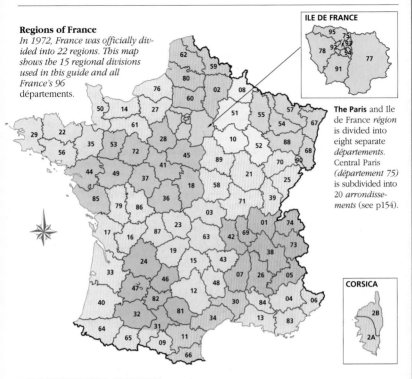

Regions of France
In 1972, France was officially divided into 22 regions. This map shows the 15 regional divisions used in this guide and all France's 96 départements.

ILE DE FRANCE

The Paris and Ile de France *région* is divided into eight separate *départements.* Central Paris *(département 75)* is subdivided into 20 *arrondissements* (see p154).

CORSICA

THE DEPARTEMENTS OF FRANCE

PARIS AND ILE DE FRANCE

75 Paris
77 Seine-et-Marne
78 Yvelines
91 Essonne
92 Hauts-de-Seine
93 Seine-St-Denis
94 Val-de-Marne
95 Val-d'Oise

NORTHEAST FRANCE

Le Nord and Picardy
02 Aisne
59 Nord
60 Oise
62 Pas-de-Calais
80 Somme

Champagne
08 Ardennes
10 Aube
51 Marne
52 Haute-Marne

Alsace and Lorraine
54 Meurthe-et-Moselle
55 Meuse
57 Moselle
67 Bas-Rhin
68 Haut-Rhin
88 Vosges

WESTERN FRANCE

Normandy
14 Calvados
27 Eure
50 Manche
61 Orne
76 Seine-Maritime

Brittany
22 Côtes d'Armor
29 Finistère

35 Ille-et-Vilaine
56 Morbihan

The Loire Valley
18 Cher
28 Eure-et-Loir
36 Indre
37 Indre-et-Loire
41 Loir-et-Cher
44 Loire-Atlantique
45 Loiret
49 Maine-et-Loire
53 Mayenne
72 Sarthe
85 Vendee

CENTRAL FRANCE

Burgundy and Franche-Comté
21 Côte d'Or
25 Doubs
39 Jura
58 Nièvre
70 Haute-Saône
71 Saône-et-Loire
89 Yonne
90 Territoire de Belfort

The Massif Central
03 Allier
12 Aveyron
15 Cantal
19 Corrèze
23 Creuse
43 Haute-Loire
48 Lozère
63 Puy-de-Dôme
87 Haute-Vienne

Rhône Valley and French Alps
01 Ain
05 Hautes Alpes
07 Ardèche
26 Drôme
38 Isère
42 Loire

69 Rhône
73 Savoie
74 Haute-Savoie

SOUTHWEST FRANCE

Poitou and Aquitaine
16 Charente
17 Charente-Maritime
33 Gironde
40 Landes
79 Deux-Sèvres
86 Vienne

Périgord, Quercy and Gascony
24 Dordogne
32 Gers
46 Lot
47 Lot-et-Garonne
81 Tarn
82 Tarn-et-Garonne

The Pyrenees
09 Ariège
31 Haute-Garonne
64 Pyrénées-Atlantiques
65 Hautes-Pyrénées

THE SOUTH OF FRANCE

Languedoc-Roussillon
11 Aude
30 Gard
34 Hérault
66 Pyrénées-Orientales

Provence and the Côte d'Azur
04 Alpes-de-Haute-Provence
06 Alpes-Maritimes
13 Bouches-du-Rhône
83 Var
84 Vaucluse

Corsica
2A Corse-du-Sud
2B Haute-Corse

TRAVEL INFORMATION

France enjoys sophisticated air, road and rail travel. Direct flights from the Americas, Africa, Asia and Europe serve Paris and regional airports. Paris is the hub of Europe's high-speed rail network, with Eurostar to London, Thalys to Brussels and TGV to Geneva. There's a vast internal rail network too. Motorways cross into all surrounding countries, including, via Eurotunnel, the UK. France is also served by frequent Channel and Mediterranean ferries.

ARRIVING BY AIR

France is served by nearly all international airlines. Some airports near the border, such as Geneva, Basle and Luxembourg, can also be used for destinations in France.

Airlines with regular flights from the UK to France include **British Airways, British Midland, Ryanair, EasyJet** and **Air France**. From the US there are flights direct to Paris from about 20 cities, mainly on **American, Delta, United, Northwest, Continental, Alitalia** and **Air France**. From Canada, **Air France** and **Air Canada** fly direct to Paris.

Qantas provides connecting flights from Australia and New Zealand.

AIR FARES

No-frills budget airlines like Ryanair and EasyJet provide affordable flights, some several times daily, from

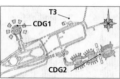

CDG Airport *Terminals CDG1, CDG2 and T3 are linked by shuttle buses. Departures are on the lower level and arrivals on the upper level in CDG1.*

CDG1 is used for international flights, except those of Air France.

Taxis (Door 20, Arrivals)

Car-hire agencies (Door 28, Arrivals)

Roissybus (Door 30, Arrivals)

PARIS ROISSY-CHARLES-DE-GAULLE (CDG)

There are two main terminals, CDG1 and CDG2. T3 is for charter flights. Taxis to central Paris cost 36€–45€.

Air France buses go to Porte Maillot and Charles de Gaulle-Etoile. The journey takes about 40 minutes. Air France buses also go to Montparnasse TGV train station. The journey takes around 50 minutes. RATP buses (Roissybus) leave every 20 minutes for L'Opéra.

The journey takes about 50 minutes, depending on traffic conditions, and costs about 8€.

All the major car hire companies can be found at the airport. A limousine service is also available, but this must be reserved in advance, and costs 120€–160€ to Paris.

A fast and cheap way to the centre is by train. With a station in CDG2, and linked to CDG1 by a free shuttle, the RER reaches Châtelet-les-Halles, in the heart of Paris, in less than 40 minutes and the Gare du Nord in 35 minutes.

CDG2 also has its own TGV station, with direct lines to Lille (1 hr), Bordeaux (4 hrs), and Lyon (2 hrs), and connections to much of the TGV network.

CDG2E is the airport's latest extension, opposite CDG2F, and has now re-opened.

Airport Information
Tel 3950 (CDG). **www**.adp.fr

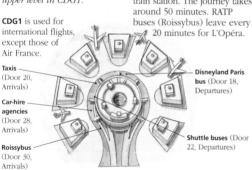

Disneyland Paris bus (Door 18, Departures)

Shuttle buses (Door 22, Departures)

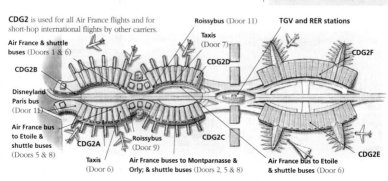

CDG2 is used for all Air France flights and for short-hop international flights by other carriers.

Air France & shuttle buses (Doors 1 & 6)

CDG2B

Disneyland Paris bus (Door 11)

Air France bus to Etoile & shuttle buses (Doors 5 & 8)

CDG2A

Taxis (Door 6)

Roissybus (Door 9)

Air France buses to Montparnasse & Orly; & shuttle buses (Doors 2, 5 & 8)

CDG2C

Roissybus (Door 11)

Taxis (Door 7)

CDG2D

TGV and RER stations

CDG2F

CDG2E

Air France bus to Etoile & shuttle buses (Door 6)

London and regional UK and Irish airports to a variety of French destinations. Many fly to small local airports such as Carcassonne, Perpignan, Nîmes and Bergerac. Low-season promotional fares can be at literally giveaway prices.

Classic full-service major airlines (American Airlines, Delta, British Airways, Air France, British Midland) also offer frequent flights to Paris and Nice, and some other cities. Their fares are highest in school holidays and half terms, especially in summer, though APEX ("Advance Purchase") fares give substantial savings. Note that APEX fares are ideal for a vacation, as they require you to pre-book outward and return flights that cannot be changed or cancelled.

Getting to or from France on the national carrier, Air France

FLIGHT TIMES

Flight times to Paris from various cities are: London: 1 hour; Dublin: 90 minutes; Montreal: 7½ hours; New York: 8 hours; Los Angeles: 12 hours; Sydney: 23 hours.

INTERNATIONAL AIRPORTS

Main airports in France serving international and domestic flights are listed overleaf, along with transport details. Below are details of Paris's two main airports.

Orly Airport
The two terminals, Orly Sud and Orly Ouest, are linked by a mini-métro (Orlyval), but they are within walking distance of one another.

Orly Ouest is largely used for domestic flights.

Air France buses (Arrival Level, Door D)
Orlyrail (Arrival Level, Door G)
Jetbus (Arrival Level, Door C)
Orlyval (Departure Level, Hall 2, Door W)
Taxis (Arrival Level, Doors H & I)
Orlybus (Arrival Level, Door J)

Orly Sud handles a wider range of services, including the majority of international and charter flights.

Taxis (Doors L & M)
Air France buses (Door J, Hall A)
Orlybus (Door H, Hall A)
Jetbus (Door H, Hall A)
Orlyval (Door K)
Orlyrail (Door J, Hall A)

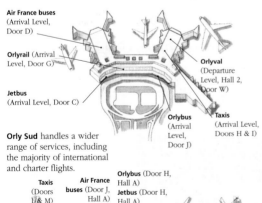

ORLY AIRPORT (ORY)

There are two terminals: Orly Sud and Orly Ouest. Taxis take 25–45 minutes to the city centre, depending on the traffic, and cost about 25€.

Air France buses leave the airport every 12–20 minutes and take around 30 minutes to central Paris (stops at Les Invalides and Montparnasse).

The RATP Orlybus leaves every 20 minutes and takes about 25 minutes to reach the Denfert-Rochereau metro.

The Jetbus service connects Orly to Villejuif-Louis Aragon metro, and departs from the airport every 15–20 minutes.

Shuttle buses link the airport with RER line C at Pont de Rungis, from where trains leave every 15 minutes for Gare d'Austerlitz (25 minute journey). An automatic train, Orlyval, links the airport with RER line B at Antony, from where trains depart every 4–8 minutes for Châtelet in central Paris (35 minute journey).

Car rental companies at the airport include Avis, Budget, Europcar, Hertz and National Citer. A chauffeur-driven limousine to central Paris costs around 80€.

Airport Information
3950 (Orly). **www.**adp.fr

FRANCE BY AIR

The main domestic airline is **Air France**. Unless you are eligible for discounted air fares (which are usually based on various complicated combinations of age and frequency of travel), it may be cheaper and faster, for some routes at least, to travel on the high-speed railways (*see p683*).

CHANNEL FERRIES

In addition to the Eurotunnel vehicle-carrying rail shuttles through the Channel Tunnel (*see p682*), there are several ship or catamaran crossings between the UK and Continental ports.

P&O Ferries runs services between Dover and Calais, with frequent crossings especially in high season (crossing time is approximately 1½ hours). The Channel Island specialists, **Condor Ferries**, have a fast ferry from Poole to St Malo (crossing time approximately 4½ hrs), which operates from the end of May to early October only. It also operates a ferry from Weymouth to St Malo, via Jersey or Guernsey.

Brittany Ferries runs a 9-hour service from Portsmouth to St-Malo, a 6-hour service from Portsmouth to Caen, a 3-hour service from Portsmouth to Cherbourg, and a 6-hour service from Plymouth to Roscoff. From Poole to Cherbourg, Brittany have a conven-

tional ship (with a crossing time of approximately 4¼ hours), and a fast ferry, the Condor Vitesse (crossing time approximately 2¼ hours). They also have a service to Santander in Spain, and sail from Cork in Eire to Roscoff.

Freight carrier **Norfolkline** also takes cars on its 2-hour Dover to Dunkerque crossing, while **P&O North Sea Ferries** sail from Hull to Zeebrugge in Belgium, which has good road links to the whole of north-east France. **Transmanche Ferries** has crossings from Newhaven to Dieppe (with a crossing time of about 3¾ hrs).

THE CHANNEL TUNNEL

The Channel Tunnel is a 52-km (31-mile) rail tunnel which runs beneath the English Channel – 39 km (23 miles) of it under the water, in the earth beneath the bottom of the sea. Its English terminal is at Folkestone in Kent, and the French terminal at Sangatte, 3 km (2 miles) from Calais. The terminal leads directly onto motorway – the M20 in England, the A16 in France.

EURO TUNNEL

Eurotunnel logo

There are two ways to use the Channel Tunnel. For vehicles and their passengers, **Eurotunnel** rail shuttles carry vehicles (passengers remain with their cars) on specially constructed trains between Folkestone and Calais (35 minutes). Eurotunnel trains depart every 15–60 minutes according to demand.

Alternatively, rail passengers without vehicles can board

AIRPORT
Bâle-Mulhouse
Bastia-Poretta
Bordeaux-Mérignac
Lille-Lesquin
Lyon-St-Exupéry
Marseille-Provence
Montpellier-Méditerranée
Nantes Atlantique
Nice-Côte d'Azur
Strasbourg
Toulouse-Blagnac

Eurostar trains at London or Ashford and disembark at Calais-Fréthun, Lille or Paris. On the French side of the Channel, Eurostar cruises at 300 km/hr (186 mph). The journey from London to Paris takes 2 hours 35 minutes, or, to Lille, 2 hours. There are up to 24 departures daily from London to Paris. There are also weekly Eurostar services direct to Disneyland Resort (daily during school holidays), and in winter there are two trains weekly from London direct to the ski resorts of the French Alps. Pre-booking is advised, and often entails much lower advance-purchase fares.

OTHER CROSSINGS

Car ferries sail to Corsica from Marseille, Nice and Toulon all year round. The ferries are run by **SNCM Ferryterranée**, **CTN** and **Corsica Ferries**. In the high season, SNCM sail weekly to Sardinia from Toulon and Marseille. SNCM and CTN also go to Tunis, Oran, Skikda and Bejaia from Marseille.

Corsica Ferries, Corsica Marittima and **CMN** connect Corsica to Italy, with crossings from Bastia, Calvi, Ajaccio, L'Ile Rousse, Porto-Vecchio and Propriano to Genoa, Livorno, Elba and Sardinia (mainly in summer).

Compagnie Marocaine de Navigation (Comanov) has a luxury two-night car ferry service between Sète and Tangier.

Plying the Mediterranean with SNCM Ferryterranée

INFORMATION	DISTANCE FROM CITY	TAXI TO CITY	BUS DETAILS
03 89 90 31 11	25 km (16 miles)	40€–45€	Mulhouse centre 30 mins
04 95 54 54 54	20 km (13 miles)	32€–42€	City centre 25 mins
05 56 34 50 50	12 km (8 miles)	23€–30€	Gare St-Jean 30–45 mins
08 91 67 32 10	10 km (5 miles)	18€–23€	Lille SNCF 30 mins
08 26 80 08 26	25 km (16 miles)	38€–45€	Perrache SNCF 40 mins
04 42 14 14 14	25 km (16 miles)	35€–45€	St-Charles SNCF 25 mins
04 67 20 85 85	7 km (4 miles)	15€–18€	City centre 20 mins
02 40 84 80 00	12 km (8 miles)	18€–23€	City centre 20 mins
0820 423 333	6 km (4 miles)	23€–30€	Gare Routière 20 mins
03 88 64 67 67	15 km (9 miles)	23€–30€	City centre 30 mins
08 25 38 00 00	9 km (5 miles)	23€–30€	Gare Routière Marengo 30 mins

DIRECTORY

AIRLINES

Air France
Tel 0820 820 820.
www.airfrance.fr.

American Airlines
Tel 0810 872 872.
www.aa.com

British Airways
Tel 0825 825 400.
Tel 0845 773 3377 in UK.
www.ba.com

British Midland
Tel 0870 60 70 555 in UK.
www.flybmi.com

Delta Airlines
Tel 08 11 64 00 05.
www.delta.com.

EasyJet
Tel 0870 600 0000 in UK.
Tel 08 99 70 00 41.
www.easyjet.com

Qantas
Tel 0820 820 500.
Tel 020-8846 0466 in UK
www.qantas.com

Ryanair
Tel 08 92 23 23 75
(France), 0906 270 5656 (UK).
www.ryanair.com

FERRY SERVICES

Brittany Ferries
Tel 08 25 82 88 28.
Tel 08709 076 103 (UK).
www.brittany-ferries.com

Compagnie Marocaine de Navigation
Tel 04 67 46 68 00.

Condor Ferries
Tel 08 25 13 51 35
(France), 0870 243 5140
(UK).
www.condorferries.com

Corsica Ferries
Tel 08 25 09 50 95.
www.corsicaferries.com

Norfolkline
Tel 03 28 28 95 50
(France).
Tel 0870 870 1020 (UK)
www.norfolkline-ferries.com

P&O
Tel 08 25 12 01 56.
Tel 08705 980 333 in UK.
www.poferries.com

SNCM
Ferryterranée,
Corsica Marittima
CTN & CMN
Tel 3260 (special no. 24-hrs for all ports).
www.sncm.fr

Transmanche Ferries
Tel 0800 917 12 01 in UK.
Tel 08 00 65 01 00 in France.
www.transmanche ferries.com

TRAVEL AGENCIES

Aix-en-Provence
Usit Connections,
7 cours Sextius,
13100 Aix-en-Provence.
Tel 04 42 93 48 48.

Bordeaux
Usit Connections,
284 rue St-Cathérine,
33000 Bordeaux.
Tel 05 56 33 89 90.

Lyon
Forum Voyages, 10 rue
Président Carnot, 69002
Lyon. *Tel 04 72 40 20 98.*

Nice
Valadou Protour,
12 av Félix Faure, 06000
Nice. *Tel 04 93 13 16 16.*

Paris
Directours,
90 av des Champs-
Elysées, 75008 Paris.
Tel 01 45 62 62 62.
www.directours.com
Nouvelles Frontières,
12 rue Auber, 75009 Paris.
Tel 08 25 00 08 25.
www.nouvelles-frontieres.fr

O.T.U.
119 rue St-Martin, 75004
Paris.
Tel 01 40 29 12 22.
Usit Connect Odysia,
85 bd St-Michel, 75005
Paris. *Tel 08 25 08 25 25.*
www.odysia.fr

Usit Connections,
31bis rue Linné
75005 Paris.
Tel 01 44 08 71 20.

Toulouse
Usit Connections,
5 rue des Lois,
31000 Toulouse.
Tel 05 61 11 52 42.

London
Student Travel Centre,
24 Rupert Street,
London W1D 6DQ,
Tel 020 7434 1306.
Trailfinders,
194 Kensington High St,
London W8 6BD.
Tel 020 7938 3939.
www.trailfinders.com

CHANNEL TUNNEL

Eurostar
Tel 0123 361 7575 and
08705 186 186 in UK.
www.eurostar.com

Eurotunnel
Tel 0810 63 03 04.
Tel 08705 35 35 35 in UK.
www.eurotunnel.com

Travelling by Train

SNCF logo

The French state railway, Société Nationale des Chemins de Fer (**SNCF**), runs Europe's most comprehensive national rail network. Its services include high-speed long-distance TGVs and mainline expresses, over-night sleepers, Motorail, and rural lines that reach every corner of the country. Lines closed for economic reasons are replaced by SNCF's modern buses, free to rail pass holders. Travel off the main lines can be slow, though – some cross-country journeys are quicker via Paris.

ARRIVING IN FRANCE

For travellers arriving from Britain, **Eurostar** gives access to the whole French rail network. At Lille, two hours from London, passengers can catch TGVs bypassing Paris and continuing southeast to Lyon, the Rhone valley and the Mediterranean, or southwest to Brittany, the Loire Valley and SW France. Under three hours from London St Pancras, Eurostar reaches Gare du Nord, as do express **Thalys** trains serving Brussels, Amsterdam and Cologne.

From the capital's six train stations, trains fan out to about 6,000 destinations throughout France. Non-TGV trains depart from Gare de l'Est (east), Gare St-Lazare (north) and Gare d'Austerlitz (southeast). The main TGV stations are Gare du Nord, Gare Montparnasse, which serves Brittany, west and southwest France, and Gare de Lyon, for Burgundy, Lyon and the Rhône, Marseille and the Mediterranean.

Travelling by train and car through France with Motorail

TRAVELLING AROUND FRANCE BY TRAIN

France has always been known for the punctuality of its trains, and also for a positive attitude to investment in the state-owned rail system. It is easy and enjoyable to travel in France by train. TGVs running on new High Speed Lines are the pride of the SNCF (the national railway company), with journey times such as Lille-Lyon or Paris-Marseille in just 3 hrs. Note that in some towns, the new TGV station is separate from the main station, and can be out of the town centre. Apart from TGVs, frequent, fast and comfortable main-line express trains provide a comprehensive city-to-city service, while the rural lines provide connections to smaller towns and villages, sometimes on rather older, slower rolling stock.

Rail traveller with luggage trolley

Symbol for Paris suburban trains

Some of these train journeys, for example in mountain regions, are a worthwhile experience in their own right. SNCF is also the largest bus operator in France, filling in the gaps where railway lines have been closed. There are also very good local and suburban train services in the largest cities, and the excellent RER (*Reseau Express Régional*) train network in the Paris area. When purchasing a rail ticket – whether in France or

abroad – it is also possible to pre-book a car (*Train + Auto*), bike (*Train + Vélo*) or hotel (*Train + Hôtel*) to await you at your destination.

Sleeper trains are a convenient way to travel long distances at night with accommodation in first or second class *couchette* (bunk bed) compartments. Motorists can travel overnight with their cars on **Motorail**, in France called TAC (*Train-Auto-Couchette*) or TAA (*Train-Auto-Accompagné*) from Paris Bercy. Motorail trains run (May–mid-October) direct from Calais to the Dordogne, Toulouse, Narbonne, Avignon or Nice. As well as enjoying a less stressful journey, Motorail customers may also book Channel crossings at lower fares. Another way to avoid a long drive is to send your car by **AutoTrain** from Paris (Bercy); driver/passengers travel separately by train.

Not all trains have restaurant cars or bars, even on long journeys. TGV trains have bars with light meals, but reservations must be made in advance for the at-seat meal service available in first class.

Information on these services is available from **Rail Europe** in London and New York, or the SNCF in France, as well as from their respective websites *(see p685)*. Leaflets are available at most French stations.

FARES AND PASSES

There is a basic fare for each rail journey, but numerous discounts are available on French trains. These reduced fares and travel passes are for certain categories of passengers. Substantial fare discounts of 25–50% are offered to over 60s (*Découverte Senior*), under 26s (*Découverte 12–25*), up to four adults travelling with a child under 12 (*Découverte Enfant Plus*), or anyone booking between two weeks and two months in advance (*Prem's*).

Rail **passes** give even larger fare reductions. Strictly for non-residents, the **France Railpass** can only be bought outside France. It gives unlimited travel for 3 to 7 days. If you are planning to travel in other countries too, choose **Eurodomino** passes for individual countries, allowing travel between 3 and 8 days, or **InterRail**, which gives 12, 22 or 30 days' travel for under 26s (or, for a higher price, over 26s) in different zones of Europe.

Discounts and passes are not valid on certain dates and times. The SNCF *Calendrier Voyageurs* (Travellers' Calendar), available at all stations, shows blue and white periods. Almost all fare reductions are valid only in blue periods. The white period is normally only Monday 5–10am, and Friday and Sunday 3–8pm.

The TGV, with its distinctive-looking "nose"

TGV RAIL SERVICE

Trains à Grande Vitesse, or high-speed trains, travel at speeds up to 300 km/h (186 mph). There are four routes: TGV Nord from Paris Gare du Nord, TGV Atlantique from Paris Gare Montparnasse, TGV Sud-Est from Paris Gare de Lyon and TGV Est from Paris Gare de l'Est.

KEY

- Nord
- Atlantique
- Sud-Est
- Est

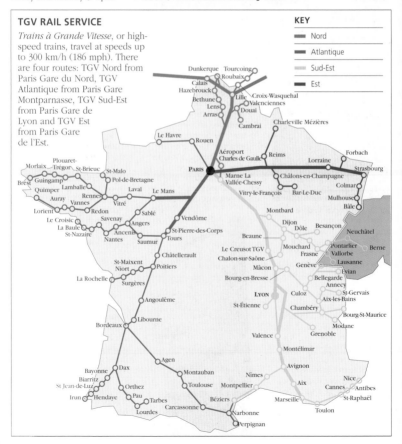

PRIVATE RAILWAYS

Privately run railways are numerous but mostly serve as tourist attractions rather than transport options. However, **Chemins de Fer de Provence** runs the Train des Pignes over the 150-km (90-mile) spectacular route from Nice to Digne. In Corsica, **Chemins de Fer de Corse** operates two routes, Bastia–Calvi and Calvi–Ajaccio.

BOOKING WITHIN FRANCE

Automatic ticket and reservation machines *(billetterie automatique)* are found at main stations. They take credit cards or coins. You can also check train times

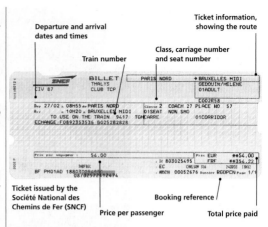

Departure and arrival dates and times

Train number

Class, carriage number and seat number

Ticket information, showing the route

Ticket issued by the Société National des Chemins de Fer (SNCF)

Price per passenger

Booking reference

Total price paid

An automatic ticket machine

and fares and make reservations by phoning **SNCF** or via their website *(see p685)*. Tickets may be purchased by credit card, then collected at the station or sent free to your home address if you book enough in advance.

Reservations are compulsory for travel by TGV, for all trains on public holidays, and for a *couchette* or *siège inclinable* (reclinable seat) and must be made at least 5 minutes before departure. Both reservations and tickets must be validated in a *composteur* machine *(right)* before boarding the train – failure to do so can incur an on-the-spot fine.

BOOKING OUTSIDE FRANCE

Tickets and passes for rail travel (including Motorail) in France can be booked and paid for in advance direct from **SNCF**. Book online on their website (allow 7 days for ticket delivery), or by phone on 36 35 (this is a special SNCF recorded information line). You can pay for your tickets by credit card. Online booking is also possible on the **Eurostar** website.

Foreign rail travel agents like **Rail Europe** can take bookings by post, by phone, online, or in person at their London shop. Rail Europe bookings must be made between 14 and 60 days in advance, and a small charge is made for credit card bookings. Note that

reservations made in another country may be difficult or impossible to change in France; any alterations to your booking should be made by the original issuing company.

TIMETABLES

French railway timetables change twice a year in May and September.

Stations sell the SNCF's Ville-à-Ville timetable which details all mainline routes nationwide. SNCF also sell regional timetables.

Free leaflets give information on travelling with children, reduced fares, train travel for the disabled and the TGV network *(see pp682–3)*. Some regions, such as Provence-Alpes-Côte d'Azur, have a regional TER (Transports Express Régionaux) timetable which includes coach travel.

Bear in mind that trains in France (unlike rail services in other countries) are punctual. Your train will almost certainly leave on time!

Composteur Machine
Yellow composteur *machines are located in station halls and at the head of each platform. Insert tickets and reservations separately, printed side up, in the machine. The* composteur *will punch your ticket and print the time and date on the back. A penalty may be imposed by the inspector on the train if you fail to do this.*

ARRIVING BY COACH

The modern coaches operated by **Eurolines** travel to 270 destinations in Europe, including many in France.

There are three departures daily (five in summer) to Paris from Victoria Coach Station in London, dropping off at Bagnolet in eastern Paris. The trip takes about 9 hours and tickets may be purchased from the booking office at Victoria. Eurolines have one-way tickets, returns and round trips throughout Europe.

TRAVELLING AROUND FRANCE BY COACH

Long-distance coaches generally only operate where trains don't offer a good service (eg Geneva to Nice). SNCF (the state railway) operates coaches and issues regional TER (*Transports Express Régionaux*) combined bus and train timetables and tickets.

Eurolines offer a wider range of destinations than most. They also offer excursions and arrange accommodation.

Local buses run from a town's *Gare Routière* (which is often at the Gare SNCF). Timetables are geared to carry students and people going to work, so the morning departure time from a village may be very early.

TAXIS

In the provinces prices vary from one region to another. All taxis must carry meters (*compteurs*). The pick-up charge should be about 2€ plus 0.5€ or more per km. You may be able to agree a price for a long journey. Look for a *station de taxi* outside airports or railway stations or in the centre of town. As hailing a taxi is only common practice in France's large cities, you have to book a taxi by telephone in rural areas.

CYCLE TRAVEL

Although cycling is popular in France, few long-distance trains carry bicycles. TER (ie regional) trains generally do carry bikes. They are indicated on the timetable by a bicycle symbol. In most instances, however, a bicycle has to be sent as a separate package. The drawback is that you may have to wait up to four days for delivery.

Alternatively, you can hire a bicycle. Through the SNCF, you can reserve a rental bike at a number of stations when you buy your ticket (*see Train + Vélo p682*). Cycle shops in many towns have touring cycles or mountain bikes for hire, and may also hire mopeds and light motorcycles.

Rural France is ideal for cycling due to its large network of uncrowded roads. There are, however, few cycle lanes in towns. For more details on waymarked cycle routes, see page 661.

Paris is also excellent for cycling, being reasonably flat and manageably small with many back streets where traffic is restricted, and about 150 km (103 miles) of cycle lanes (*pistes cyclables*). A free map, *Paris à Vélo*, is available in metro, RER and bus stations.

HITCH-HIKING

It is not easy to get around France by hitch-hiking. You must look clean and "normal" to have any chance of a lift, especially since it is car rather than truck drivers who will be your best bet. The safest and easiest way to hitch-hike long-distance is through **Allostop,** who have branches in many major towns and will arrange lifts for a reasonable rate.

DIRECTORY

INFORMATION AND RESERVATIONS

SNCF France

Tel 36 35.

www.voyages-sncf.com

Eurostar London St-Pancras International

Tel 0123 3617 575 and

08705 186 186 (UK).

www.eurostar.com

Rail Europe

178 Piccadilly,

London W1 0BA

Tel 0870 8371 371 (UK).

www.raileurope.co.uk

Rail Europe Group

Westchester One,

44 South Broadway,

White Plains, New York,

NY 10601

Tel 888 438 7245

(freephone in US).

www.raileurope.com

PRIVATE RAILWAYS

Chemins de Fer de Provence

Tel 04 97 03 80 80.

www.trainprovence.com

Chemins de Fer de Corse

Ajaccio

Tel 04 95 23 11 03.

Bastia

Tel 04 95 32 80 61.

Calvi

Tel 04 95 65 00 61.

EUROLINES

London

Tel 0870 580 8080.

www.eurolines.co.uk

Victoria Coach Station

164 Buckingham Palace Road, London

SW1 W9TP.

Tel 020 7730 3466.

EUROLINES COACH STATIONS IN FRANCE

Paris

28 av du Général de Gaulle, 93170, Bagnollet.

Tel 08 92 89 90 91.

www.eurolines.fr

Bordeaux

32 rue Charles Domercq.

Tel 05 56 92 50 42.

Lyon

Gare de Perrache.

Tel 04 72 56 95 30.

Marseille

Place Victor Hugo.

Tel 04 91 50 57 55.

Nice

5 bd Jean Jaurès.

Tel 04 93 80 42 20.

Strasbourg

Pl d'Austerlitz.

Tel 03 90 22 14 60.

Toulouse

68–70 bd Pierre Sémard.

Tel 05 61 26 40 04.

HITCH-HIKING

Allostop

30 rue Pierre Sémard,

Paris 75009.

Tel 08 25 80 36 66.

www.allostop.net

On the Road

The classic Citroën 2 CV

France has one of the densest road networks in Europe, with modern motorways which allow quick and easy access to all parts of the country. However, you can save money on tolls and explore France in a more leisurely way by using some of the other high-quality roads which dissect the country. This section outlines both alternatives and gives instructions on how to use the motorway toll booths and French parking meters *(horodateurs)*, as well as some of the rules governing driving in France. There are also tips on where to buy petrol, how to get weather and traffic forecasts, where to hire a car and how to get the best road maps.

Motorway and main road signs

GETTING TO FRANCE BY CAR

There is a good choice of car-ferry operators from the UK *(see p680)*. You can profit from discount fares for short breaks, a flat rate for a car with up to five passengers, or by buying tickets for the crossing in conjunction with Motorail *(see pp682 and 685)*.

You can also take the car on the Eurotunnel shuttle *(p680)* through the Channel Tunnel.

WHAT TO TAKE

Many motor insurers now offer a green card, which gives full cover abroad, as a free extension with fully comprehensive policies. The AA, RAC and Europ Assistance have special policies providing a rescue and recovery service.

It is compulsory to take the original registration document for the car, a current insurance certificate, or green card, and a valid driving licence. You should also carry a passport or National ID card. A sticker showing the country of registration must be displayed near the rear number plate. The headlights of right-hand drive cars must be adjusted for left-hand driving or have deflector kits fitted (available at most ports). You must also carry spare headlight bulbs and a red warning triangle if your car does not have hazard warning lights. When driving in ski resorts in winter, snow chains *(chaînes)* are essential.

BUYING PETROL IN FRANCE

Diesel fuel *(gazole* or *gas-oil)* is comparatively cheap in France and is sold everywhere. Leaded petrol *(super)* and unleaded petrol *(sans plomb)* are more expensive, and leaded is now sometimes hard to find. Rural stations may close on Sundays. Large supermarkets and hypermarkets sell all of them at a discount. A map *(la carte de l'essence moins chère)*, available from French Government Tourist Offices *(see p669)*, shows the location of stations close to motorway exits. Filling up the tank is known as *faire le plein*.

Some of the most widely available car hire firms in France

RULES OF THE ROAD

Unless road signs indicate otherwise, *priorité à droite* means that you must give way to any vehicle joining the road from the right, except on roundabouts or from private property. Most major roads outside built-up areas have the right of way indicated by *passage protégé* signs. Contrary to convention in the UK, flashing headlights in France means the driver is claiming the right of way.

Other French motoring rules include the compulsory wearing of seat belts, the use of booster seats for all children under 10, and the obligation to carry a valid driving licence or identification papers at all times. For further details consult the RAC website *(see p689)*.

40 km/h (25 mph) speed limit

SPEED LIMITS AND FINES

Speed limits in France are as follows:
• On autoroutes:130 km/h (80 mph); 110 km/h (70 mph) when it rains.
• On dual carriageways: 110 km/h (70 mph); 90–100 km/h (55–60 mph) when it rains.
• On other roads: 90 km/h (55 mph); 80 km/h (50 mph) when it rains.
• In towns: 50 km/h (30 mph). This applies anywhere in a village, hamlet or city, unless marked otherwise. In some places it may be lower. Normal limits may not be shown.

On the spot fines of around £100 are summarily levied for not stopping at a Stop sign, for overtaking where forbidden, or other driving offences. Drunk-driving can lead to confiscation of the vehicle or even imprisonment.

**Sign indicating
one-way system**

**No entry for any
vehicles**

*Passage protégé ends,
priorité à droite starts*

MOTORWAYS

Most motorways in France have a toll system *(autoroutes à péage)*, and vary considerably in price. City bypasses are usually free. Some longer sections of motorway may also be free, eg on the A26 and A75. Tolls can be paid with either credit cards or cash. Where only small sums are involved, you throw coins into a large receptacle and the change is given automatically.

Much of the *autoroute* network has been built in the last 25 years. It includes good rest areas and picnic spots 10–20 km (6–12 miles) apart, petrol stations at every 40 km (25 miles), and emergency phones every 2 km (1¼ miles). Service areas include shops, takeaway food and restaurants, fax and telephone facilities.

OTHER ROADS

In France the RN *(route nationale)* and D *(départementale)* roads are a good alternative to motorways. *Bis/Bison futée* signs are posted for alternative routes which avoid heavy traffic.

Sunday is usually a good day to travel as there are very few trucks on the road. Try to avoid travelling at the French holiday rush periods known as *grands départs*. The worst times are weekends in mid-July, and at the beginning and end of August when holidays begin and end.

If you are by-passing rather than driving into Paris, it is more advisable to take the motorways on either side of the city, avoiding the busy *boulevard périphérique* which encircles central Paris.

ROAD CONDITIONS AND WEATHER FORECASTS

Local radio stations report on road conditions – look out for motorway signs listing their frequencies. CRICR (Centre Régional d'Information et de Coordination Routières) lines give general information on regional road conditions. The CNIR (Centre National d'Information Routière) line covers the whole of France.

The RAC sell a tailor-made route-planning information service, giving scenic options and road conditions.

To get weather forecasts in English for the English Channel and throughout France ring **The Met Office** or **Holiday Weatherline**.

**Sign for Channel Tunnel
terminal**

USING THE AUTOROUTE TOLL

When you join an autoroute, collect a ticket from the machine. This identifies your starting point on the autoroute. You do not pay until you reach an exit toll. You are charged according to the distance travelled and the type of vehicle used.

Motorway Sign
These signs indicate the name and distance to the next toll booth. They are usually blue and white; some show the tariff rates for cars, motorbikes, trucks and caravans.

Toll Booth with Attendant
When you hand in your ticket at a manned toll booth, the attendant will tell you the cost of your journey on the autoroute and the price will be displayed. You can pay with coins, notes, credit cards or with a cheque in Euros. A receipt is issued on request.

Automatic Machine
On reaching the exit toll, insert your ticket into the machine and the price of your journey is displayed in Euros. You can pay either with coins or by credit card. The machine will give change and can issue a receipt.

USING AN HORODATEUR MACHINE

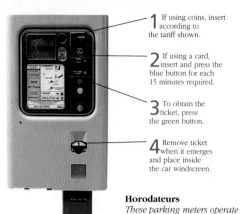

1 If using coins, insert according to the tariff shown.

2 If using a card, insert and press the blue button for each 15 minutes required.

3 To obtain the ticket, press the green button.

4 Remove ticket when it emerges and place inside the car windscreen.

Horodateurs
These parking meters operate from 9am–7pm Mon–Fri. Unless otherwise indicated, parking is free Sat–Sun, public holidays and in August.

PARKING

Parking regulations vary from town to town. Most operate pay-and-display systems *(horodateurs)*. Some machines accept a parking payment card, which can be bought at tobacconists. Provincial towns often offer free parking from noon to 1:30pm. Parking is normally limited to 2 hours. In small towns, parking is confined to one side of the street only, alternating at different times of the month. Signs indicate where parking is allowed.

In larger cities, especially Paris, finding a parking space can be a problem. Due to the competition for spaces, cars are frequently "bumped" to create more room.

If you are in an area where parking discs are in use, the local tourist office will supply you with one. Temporary parking discs are sometimes sold at *tabacs*.

CAR HIRE

All the main international car-hire companies operate in France. It is worth ringing around before you leave for France as there are many special offers for rentals booked and prepaid in the UK or USA.

One smaller company offers very competitive rates – **Autos Abroad**. They are brokers who use cars owned by other car hire companies, like **Budget** and **Citer**. You may find that hiring a car from this company works out at half the price of the standard rental.

For car hire booked in combination with flights, your travel agent can usually organize a good deal. SNCF (the French state railway) offers combined train and car-hire fares *(see p682)*, with convenient collection points at 200 stations in France. Phone **Rail Europe** for information *(see directory opposite)*.

For non-EU residents planning to drive in France for a minimum of three weeks, the best option is the short-term tax-free purchase-and-buy-back service (sometimes called TT leasing) offered by **Citroën**, **Peugeot** and **Renault**.

For the ultimate convenience in luxury travel, information on chauffeur-driven car hire can be obtained from the **Automobile Club de l'Ile de France**.

MAPS

In this guide, each chapter begins with a map of the region showing all the sights and giving useful tips on getting around. If you wish to avoid using motorways, the *Bison Futé* map of France recommends alternative routes. It is available from French Government Tourist Offices *(see p669)*.

For driving shorter distances and for cycling, it is very pleasant to use the smaller D *(département)* roads marked in yellow or white on **Michelin** maps, and often quite empty of traffic. The red Michelin maps of France (scale 1:1,000,000) are useful for planning a trip. The excellent Michelin atlas of France has generously overlapping maps at a scale of 1:200,000, and is by far the most comprehensive and legible atlas for driving currently available. At the same scale, a series of

Mountain cyclists in the Alps

regional maps with yellow covers is sold in different sheet sizes. Maps showing the whole country are also available (red covers). Larger scale maps (green covers) are currently only available for the south of France and the area surrounding Paris. A series called *Alentours de,* also at 1:100,000 scale, focus on the areas round Bordeaux, Nancy, Nantes, Poitiers, Rouen and Strasbourg.

IGN (Institut Géographique National) is the equivalent of the British Ordnance Survey. The whole of France is available in sheets at 1:250,000, 1:100,000, 1:50,000 and 1:25,000. **Espace IGN**, just off the Champs-Elysées in Paris, is a haven for map lovers. The **Roger Lascelles Touring Map,**

at 1:1,000,000, is recommended, as are their Red Cover Maps at 1:250,000. Refer to page 628 for walking and cycling maps.

In France, all newsagents and petrol stations stock the more commonly used maps. In the UK, **Stanfords** is perhaps the best place to look for anything out of the ordinary – apart from its original London shop, it now has shops in Bristol and Manchester (*see below*). Waterstone's bookshops also have a good selection.

The town maps included in this guide locate all the important sights. You can usually get town plans free from tourist offices, although

A selection of French road maps

for large towns you might need the more detailed maps published by Michelin or Blay (available from Roger Lascelles in the UK).

DIRECTORY

CAR HIRE

ADA
Tel 0825 169 169.
Tel 01 44 24 55 56 (Paris).
Tel 02 98 43 42 90 (Brest).
Tel 02 98 60 59 59 (Concarneau)
www.ada.fr

Autos Abroad
Tel 0870 066 7788 (UK).

Avis
Tel 0820 05 05 05.
www.avis.fr

Budget
Tel 0870 1539 170 (UK).
Tel 0825 00 35 64.
www.budget.com

Citer
Tel 01 44 38 61 61.
www.citer.fr

Europcar
Tel 0845 758 5375 (UK).
Tel 0825358 358.
www.europcar.com

Hertz
Tel 0870 850 2677 (UK).
Tel 01 39 38 38 38 (France).
www.hertz.fr

Rent a Car
Tel 08 91 70 02 00.
www.rentacar.fr

Sixt-Eurorent
Tel 08 20 00 74 98.
www.sixt.com

Rail Europe
Tel 08705 371 371 (UK).
www.raileurope.co.uk

TT LEASING

Citroën
25 rue de Constantinople 75008 Paris.
Map 3B2.
Tel 01 44 70 60 60.

Peugeot Sodexa
115 av de l'Arche, 92400 Courbevoie.
Tel 01 49 04 81 81 (Paris).
Fax 01 47894940.

Renault Rent
Renault Ventes Spéciales Exportation, 186 av Jean-Jaurès, 75019 Paris.
Tel 08 10 40 50 60.
Fax 01 40 40 34 20 (Paris).
www.renault-rent.com

WEATHER FORECASTS

Holiday Weatherline
Tel 0870 600 4242 (from UK only) France forecasts.

The Met Office
Tel 0870 900 0100 (within UK).
Tel +44 (0) 1392 885 680 (from abroad).
www.met-office.gov.uk
www.meteo.fr

ROAD CONDITIONS

RAC
Great Park Road, Bradley Stoke, Bristol BS32 4QN.
Tel 08705 722 722.
www.rac.co.uk

CNIR
Tel 08 26 0220 22.
Autoroutes Information
Tel 08 92 68 10 77.
www.autoroutes.fr

Bison Futé
Tel 08 26 02 20 22.
www.bisonfute.equipement.gouv.fr

MAPS

AA
30–31 Haymarket London SW1X 4EU.
Tel 08706 000 371.
www.theaa.co.uk

Institut Géographique National
107 rue la Boétie 75008 Paris. **Map** 2 F5.
Tel 08 20 20 73 74.
www.ign.fr

Michelin
Espace Opéra, 32 av de l'Opéra, 75002 Paris. **Map** 4E5. **Tel** 01 42 68 05 20.
www.viamichelin.com

Roger Lascelles
Steam Mill Rd, Manningtree, Essex CO11 2QT.
Tel 01255 870 595 (UK).
www.rogerlascellesmaps.co.uk

Stanfords
12–14 Long Acre, London WC2E 9LP.
Tel 020 7836 1321.
Fax 020 632 8928.

39 Spring Gardens, Manchester M2 2BG.
Tel 0161 831 0250.
Fax 0161 831 0257.

29 Corn Street, Bristol BS11HT.
Tel 01179 299 966.
www.stanfords.co.uk

General Index

Acknowledgments

Dorling Kindersley would like to thank the following people whose contributions and assistance have made the preparation of this book possible.

Main Contributors
John Ardagh, Rosemary Bailey, Judith Fayard, Lisa Gerard-Sharp, Robert Harneis, Alister Kershaw, Alec Lobrano, Anthony Roberts, Alan Tillier, Nigel Tisdall.

Contributors and Consultants
John Ardagh is a writer and broadcaster, and author of many books on France, among them *France Today* and *Writers' France*.

Rosemary Bailey has written and edited several guides to regional France, including *Burgundy*, the *Loire Valley* and the *Côte d'Azur*.

Alexandra Boyle is a writer and editor who has worked in publishing in England and France for 20 years.

Elsie Burch Donald, editor and writer, is the author of *The French Farmhouse*.

David Burnie B.Sc. has written over 30 books on natural sciences, including *How Nature Works*.

Judith Fayard, an American based in Paris, was Paris bureau chief for *Life* magazine for 10 years, and is now European editor of *Town & Country*. She contributes to various publications, including the *Wall Street Journal*.

Lisa Gerard-Sharp is a writer and broadcaster and author of several regional guides to France and Italy.

Robert Harneis is editorial correspondent for the English language newspaper *French News*.

Colin Jones is Professor of History at Exeter University. His books include *The Longman Companion to the French Revolution* and *The Cambridge Illustrated History of France*.

Alister Kershaw is an Australian writer and broadcaster who has lived in the Loire Valley for 30 years.

Alec Lobrano is an American writer, based in Paris. He is the European editor of *Departures* magazine and contributes to *International Herald Tribune, Los Angeles Times* and *The Independent*.

Anthony Roberts is a writer and translator who has lived in Gascony for 15 years, contributing to various publications including *The Times, World of Interiors* and *Architectural Digest*.

Anthony Rose is the wine correspondent of *The Independent* and co-author of *The Grapevine*.

Jane Sigal is the author of two books on French food, *Normandy Gastronomique* and *Backroom Bistros, Farmhouse Fare*.

Alan Tillier is the main contributor to the *Eyewitness Guide to Paris*. He has lived in Paris for more than 20 years as correspondent for various journals, including the *International Herald Tribune, Newsweek* and *The Times*.

Nigel Tisdall is a travel writer and author of guides to Brittany and Normandy.

Patricia Wells is food critic of the *International Herald Tribune* and author of the *Food Lovers' Guide to Paris* and the *Food Lovers' Guide to France*.

Additional Contributors
Nathalie Boyer, Caroline Bugler, Ann Cremin, Jan Dodd, Bill Echikson, Robin Gauldie, Adrian Gilbert, Peter Graham, Marion Kaplan, Jim Keeble, Alexandra Kennedy, Rolli Lucarotti, Fred Mawer, Lyn Parry, Andrew Sanger, Katherine Spenley, Clive Unger-Hamilton, Roger Williams.

Additional Photography
Jo Craig, Andy Crawford, Michael Crockett, Mike Dunning, Philip Enticknap, Steve Gorton, Alison Harris, John Heseltine, Roger Hilton, Andrew Holligan, Oliver Knight, Eric Meacher, Neil Mersh, Roger Moss, Robert O'Dea, Ian O'Leary, Tony Souter, Alan Williams, Peter Wilson.

Additional Illustrations
Dinwiddie Maclaren, John Fox, Nick Gibbard, Paul Guest, Stephen Gyapay, Kevin Jones Associates, Chris Orr, Robbie Polley, Sue Sharples.

Additional Cartography
Colourmap Scanning Limited; Contour Publishing; Cosmographics; European Map Graphics; Meteo-France. Street Finder maps: ERAMaptec Ltd (Dublin), adapted with permission from original survey and mapping by Shobunsha (Japan).

Cartographic Research
Jennifer Skelley, Rachel Hawtin (Lovell Johns); James Mills-Hicks, Peter Winfield, Claudine Zarte (Dorling Kindersley Cartography).

Design and Editorial Assistance
Peter Adams, Azeem Alam, Elizabeth Ayre, Laetitia Benloulou, Steve Bere, Sonal Bhatt, Uma Bhattacharya, Hilary Bird, Anna Brooke, Arwen Burnett, Cate Craker, Maggie Crowley, Lisa Davidson, Helen Foulkes, Fay Franklin, Tom Fraser, Catherine Gauthier, Eric Gibory, Emily Green, Vinod Harish, Elaine Harries, Victoria Heyworth-Dunne, Paul Hines, Nicholas Inman, Sarah Jackson-Lambert, Nancy Jones, Delphine Lawrance, Siri Lowe, Francesca Machiavelli, Lesley McCave, Ella Milroy, Malcolm Parchment, Lyn Parry, Helen Partington, Shirin Patel, Alice Peebles, Alice Pennington-Mellor, Marianne Petrou, Pollyanna Poulter, Pete Quinlan, Salim Qurashi, Marisa Renzullo, Philippa Richmond, Baishakhee Sengupta, Shailesh Sharma, Kunal Singh, Shruti Singhi, Andrew Szudek, Helen Townsend, Dora Whitaker, Fiona Wild, Nicholas Wood, Irina Zarb.

Special Assistance
Mme Jassinger, French Embassy Press Department;

Peter Mills, Christine Lagardère, French Railways Ltd.

Photographic Reference
Altitude, Paris; Sea and See, Paris; Editions Combier, Maçon; Thomas d'Hoste, Paris.

Photography Permissions
Dorling Kindersley would like to thank the following for their assistance and kind permission to photograph at their establishments: The Caisse Nationale des Monuments Historiques et des Sites; M. A. Leonetti, the Abbey of Mont St-Michel; Chartres Cathedral; M. Voisin, Château de Chenonceau; M. P Mistral, Cité de Carcassonne, M. D. Vingtain, Palais des Papes, Avignon; Château de Fontainebleau; Amiens Cathedral; Conques Abbey; Fontenay Abbey; Moissac Abbey; Vézelay Abbey; Reims Cathedral and all the other churches, museums, hotels, restaurants, shops, galleries and sights too numerous to thank individually.

Picture Credits
t = top; tl = top left; tc = top centre; tr = top right; cla = centre left above; ca = centre above; cra = centre right above; cl = centre left; c = centre; cr = centre right; clb = centre left below; cb = centre below; crb = centre right below; bl = bottom left; b = bottom; bc = bottom centre; br = bottom right; (d) = detail.

Works of art have been reproduced with the permission of the following copyright holders; ©ADAGP, Paris and DACS, London 2006: 29c, 29crb, 30bl, 63tl, 64–65, 65tl (d), 90t, 93cra, 93cb, 93bl, 93br, 99t, 213b, 351t, 335br, 482t, 508ca, 522b, 524bc, 524br, 529br; ©ARS, NY and DACS, London 2006: 92c; ©DACS, London 2006: 93t, 381br, 422t; © Succession H. Matisse/DACS, London 2006:29bl, 92bl, 526br; © Succession Picasso/DACS, London 2006: 88cl, 90b, 473t, 521t.

Photos achieved with the assistance of the EPPV and the CSI: 136–7; Photo of Euro Disneyland Park and the Euro Disneyland Paris ® 178cr; The characters, architectural works and trademarks are the property of The Walt Disney Company. All rights reserved; Courtesy of the Maison Victor Hugo, Ville de Paris: 91t; Musée National des Châteaux de Malmaison et Bois-Preau: 173b; Musée de Montmartre, Paris: 133t; Musée National de la Legion d'Honneur: 60t; © Sundancer: 142bl.

The publisher would like to thank the following individuals, companies and picture libraries for permission to reproduce their photographs: AIR FRANCE/D TOULORGE: 679t; ALAMY IMAGES: Glenn Harper 96tl, Michael Juno 239c; ALPINE GARDEN SOCIETY/CHRISTOPHER GREY-WILSON: 460bl, 460br; AGENCE PHOTO AQUITAINE: D. Lelann 421tl; ANCIENT ART AND ARCHITECTURE COLLECTION: 47 crb, 50c, 50cb, 52br, 57bl, 252–3b, 335bl, 382t, 434t, 438b; PHOTO AKG, BERLIN: 45cra, 46bl, 58bc, 55crb, 402t, 403b; ARCHIVES PHOTOGRAPHIQUES, PARIS/DACS: 422t; by kind permission of www.ARTINSWFRANCE. COM: 660b; ATELIER BRANCUSI/CENTRE GEORGES POMPIDOU, PARIS: Bernard Prerost 93br; ATELIER DU REGARD/A ALLEMAND: 442cl, 442cr, 442b.

HOSTELLERIE BERARD: 660cl; BIBLIOTHÈQUE NATIONALE, DIJON: 49cb; F. BLACKBURN: 461bl; GERARD BOULLAY/PHOTOLA: 87bl, 87cra; BRIDGEMAN ART LIBRARY: Albright Knox Art Gallery, Buffalo, New York 275br; Anthony Crane Collection 211br; Bibliothèque Nationale, Paris 50cr–51cl, 52t, 53cr, 69bl; British Library, London 52bl, 68br, 292c, 293br, 293tl; Bonhams, London 59tc, 62tl; Château de Versailles, France 69tr; Christies, London 29c, 513b; Giraudon 28tr, 28tl, 56cr–57cl, 57tl, 59tl, 69bc, 181b, 334c, 343c, 365t; Guildhall Library, Corporation of London 417b; Hermitage, St Petersburg 29bl; Index 472b; Kress Collection, Washington DC 293bl; Lauros-Giraudon 46t, 69br; Musée des Beaux Arts, Quimper 243c; Musée Condé, Chantilly 50tl, 57tr, 68bl, 69tc, 69tcl, 69cb, 204t, 293c; Musée d'Orsay, Paris 28cb; Musée du Quai Branly, Paris 112cb; Paul Bremen Collection 255t; Sotheby's New York 55t; V&A Museum, London 338b; Walters Art Gallery, Baltimore, Maryland 356t; JOHN BRUNTON: 514b; MICHAEL BUSSELLE: 182–3.

CAMPAGNE, CAMPAGNE: 350t; C. Guy 325t; Lara 191cr; B. Lichtstein 217b, 324cl; Pyszel 190bl; CNMHS, PARIS/DACS: Longchamps Delehaye 213tl; CASTELET/GROTTE DE CLAMOUSE: 493b; COLLECTION CDT GARD: 325bl; CDT LOT: 439b; CEPHAS: Stuart Boreham 260–1; Hervé Champollion 322tr, 334t, 350b; Mick Rock 38c, 398tl, 398cl, 471t, 518–9; JEAN LOUP CHARMET: 47b, 50br, 52clb, 58t, 62cl, 62clb, 63tl, 63tc, 64bl, 64br, 65crb, 214b, 243b, 265br, 269b, 274t, 281b, 300br, 343br, 358b, 359t, 361c, 401cr, 401br, 421b, 475t, 507t, CITÉ DES SCIENCES ET L'INDUSTRIE: Michel Lamoureux 136ca, 137br, 137c; Pascal Prieur 136tr; Michel Viard 136cb; BRUCE COLEMAN: Udo Hirsch 371br; Flip de Nooyer 387br; Hans Reinhard 323tl, 323tr; PHOTOS EDITIONS COMBIER, MÂCON: 203t; CORBIS: Gary Braasch 469c; Michael Busselle 13cl; Ray Juno 10cl; Reuters 657tl; JOE CORNISH: 116, 234–5, 370br, 448.

DANSMUSEET, STOCKHOLM/PETER STENWALL: 64cr–65cb; DOHERTY: 245tc; E. Donard; 35tr, 35c, 35cl, 35bc; EDITIONS D'ART DANIEL DERVEAUX: 400cr–401cl; PHOTO DASPET, AVIGNON: 504bl.

ET ARCHIVE: 300bl; Cathedral Treasury, Aachen 4t; 48cl; Musée Carnavalet, Paris 61tl; Museum of Fine Arts, Lausanne 55br; Musée d'Orsay, Paris 61cra; Musée de Versailles 56b; 299bl; National Gallery, Scotland 58br; Victoria and Albert Museum, London 53tl; 343bl; EUROPEAN COMMISSION: 672; MARY EVANS PICTURE LIBRARY: 9c, 46br, 50bl, 51c, 53b, 54tl, 56cla, 58c, 62b, 63cr, 63br, 65br, 113cl, 177b, 183c, 191t, 197b, 235c, 279t, 291b, 293tr, 301bl, 315c, 366b, 393c, 455t, 465c, 473b, 508tl, 545c, 667c; Explorer 31b, 54clb.

FESTIVAL D'AVIGNON: Marc Chaumeil 656cl; FESTIVAL INTERNATIONAL DU FILM DE LA ROCHELLE: 656br; PHOTO FLANDRE, AMIENS: 193b; FRANCE TÉLÉCOM: 674cr; M REYNARD 674B; FRENCH RAILWAYS/SNCF: 682bl, 683t.

GIRAUDON, PARIS: 8–9, 15t, 29cra, 29br, 46ca, 48tl; 48clb, 49tl, 50cl, 52cr–53cl, 56tl, 56clb, 58cl, 60cl, 60cr–61cl, 333br, 347br, 369b, 491cb MS Nero EII pt.2 fol. 20V0; Lauros-Giraudon 44tl, 44bc, 45t,

45crb, 45cb, 45br, 47tc, 49tr, 51crb, 55cr, 60clb, 60br, 351b, 491cl; Musée d'Art Moderne, Paris 29tr; Musée de Beaux Arts, Quimper 28cl; TELARCI 49cr; RONALD GRANT ARCHIVE: 21b, 66clb; LA HALLE SAINT PIERRE: *Untitled* Stavroula Feleggakis 133br; SONIA HALLIDAY PHOTOGRAPHS: Laura Lushington 309tr; ROBERT HARDING PICTURE LIBRARY: 30bl, 37tr, 39tr, 39cl, 43b, 112br, 240tl, 243tr, 322bl, 322br, 323br, 349t, 400cla, 437cr, 461tr, 489b, C. Bowman 452t; Explorer, Paris 39cr, 67br, 101br, 179b, 362t, 371tr, 460cb, 461tl, 484b, 497br, 660b, 669b, 688b; R. Francis 86clb, 676c; D.Hughes 392–3; W.Rawlings 49br, 67tl, 237tl, 256b; A.Wolfitt 26tr, 170, 548b; JOHN HESELTINE: 139c; Honfleur, Musée BOUDIN: 262b; DAVID HUGHES: 2–3, 367t, 367b; THE HULTON DEUTSCH COLLECTION: 191br, 301br, 473c, 516b; FJ Mortimer 190tl.

THE IMAGE BANK: Peter Miller 372; IMAGES: 323c, 460cl, 460tr; JACANA: F Gohier 460tl; JM Labat 461bc; TREVOR JONES: 204b.

MAGNUM PHOTOS LTD: Bruno Barbey 20b, 31tr, 36bl; R Capa 472tr; P Halsman 525b; THE MANSELL COLLECTION: 31tl, 282t, 295b, 459b, 504tl; MILEPOST 961/2: Bob Walkley 683t; JOHN MILLER: 224b, 336tr, 407b; MONTPELLIER DANSE FESTIVAL: 657br; MUSÉE DE L'ANNONCIADE, ST-TROPEZ: 524tr; MUSÉE D'ART MODERNE ET CONTEMPORAIN DE STRASBOURG: Edith Rodeghiero 231t; MUSÉE DES BEAUX ARTS, CARCASSONNE: 489tl; MUSÉE DES BEAUX ARTS, DIJON: 343tl; MUSÉE DES BEAUX ARTS DE LYON: 381tl, 381bl, 381br; MUSÉE DE LA CIVILISATION GALLO-ROMAINE, LYON: 47cr, 378cl; MUSÉE DEPARTMENTAL BRETON, QUIMPER: 274bl; MUSÉE FLAUBERT, ROUEN: 265bl; MUSEUM NATIONAL D'HISTOIRE NATURELLE, PARIS: 138c; COURTESY OF THE MUSÉE MATISSE, NICE: 526b; MUSÉE NATIONAL D'ART MODERNE, PARIS: 92clb, 93t, 93cr, 93cb, 335br; Succession Henri Matisse 92bl; MUSÉE RÉATTU, ARLES: M Lacanaud 508ca; CLICHÉ MUSÉE DE SENS/J.P. ELIE: 330tl; MUSÉE TOULOUSE-LAUTREC, ALBI: 444b.

SERVICE NATIONAL DES TIMBRES POSTE ET DE LA PHILATÉLIE: designed by Eve Luquet 676bl; NETWORK PHOTOGRAPHERS: Barry Lewis 338t; Rapho/Mark Buscail 661tl; Rapho/De Sazo 661tr; PICTURES COLOUR LIBRARY: 402b, 426, 544, 666–7; MICHEL LE POER TRENCH: 30br; CENTRE GEORGES POMPIDOU: Bernard Prerost 93b; POPPERFOTO: 251c; PYRENEES MAGAZINE/DR: 400bl. REDFERNS: William Gottlieb: 64clb; RETROGRAPH ARCHIVE: M. Breese 474tl, 474tr; RÉUNION DES MUSÉES NATIONAUX: Musée des Antiquités Nationales 403c; Musée Guimet 111t; Musée du Louvre 57ca, 101bl, 102t, 102bl, 102br, 103tl, 103c, 103b; Musée Picasso 88cl, 90b, 473t; Musée de Versailles 179t; RF REYNOLDS: 245bc.

REX FEATURES: Sipa 22t; ROCAMADOUR: 437t; ROGER-VIOLLET: 113tc; FOUNDATION ROYAUMONT: J Johnson 172t; RÉUNION DES MUSÉES NATIONAUX: *Le Duo* (1937) by Georges Braque, Collections du Centre Pompidou, Musée Nationaux d'Art Moderne, 93ra.

SIPA PRESS: 132bl; PHOTO SNCM/SOUTHERN FERRIES: 680b; SNCF – SERVICE PRESSE VOYAGES FRANCE EUROPE: 664bc; SPECTRUM COLOUR LIBRARY: P Thompson 249el; FRANK SPOONER PICTURES: Bolcina 37b; Uzan 66br; Simon 67ca; Gamma Press 39b, 67crb; JEAN MARIE STEINLEN: 404; TONY STONE IMAGES: 322c, 326; SYGMA: 531t; C de Bare 36t; Walter Carone 150t; P Forestier 314–5; Frederic de la Fosse 520b; D Goldberg 21c; L'Illustration 108tl; T Prat 436c; L de Raemy 67bl.

EDITIONS TALLANDIER: 42, 44cb, 47tl, 48br, 48br–49bl, 51t, 51b, 52cl, 53tr, 54br, 58clb, 58bl, 58cr–59cl, 59crb, 59bl, 61tr, 61crb, 61br, 63bl, 63bc, 64cla, 64crb, 65tc, 65tr; TOURIST OFFICE SEMUR-EN-AUXOIS: 335t; COLLECTION L. TREILLARD: © Man Ray Trust/ ADAGP, Paris and DACS, London 2006 65tll(d).

JEAN VERTUT: 44br–45bl; VISUAL ARTS LIBRARY: 28b; VIEW PICTURES: Paul Rafferty 135b.

WORLD PICTURES: 323bl.

ZEFA: 178c, 351t; O. ZIMMERMAN/MUSÉE D'UNTERLINDEN 6800 COLMAR: 227t.

Front Endpaper: All special photography except THE IMAGE BANK rcb; PICTURES COLOUR LIBRARY lcr; JEAN MARIE STEINLEIN lcl; TONY STONE IMAGES rca.

Back Endpaper: All special photography except JOE CORNISH lbl.

Jacket
Front - DK IMAGES: Max Alexander bl; GETTY IMAGES: Image Bank/Peter Adams main image. Back - CEPHAS PICTURE LIBRARY: Stuart Boreham tl; CORBIS: Sygma/P. Forestier cla; DK IMAGES: Max Alexander clb; Kim Sayer bl. Spine - DK IMAGES: b; GETTY IMAGES: Image Bank/Peter Adams t.

All other images © Dorling Kindersley. For more information see www.DKimages.com

---